Women in Congress
1917–2006

PREPARED UNDER THE DIRECTION OF

The Committee on House Administration of the
U.S. House of Representatives

VERNON J. EHLERS, CHAIRMAN

JUANITA MILLENDER-MCDONALD, RANKING MEMBER

BY THE

Office of History and Preservation,
Office of the Clerk,
U.S. House of Representatives

U.S. GOVERNMENT PRINTING OFFICE, WASHINGTON, D.C., 2006

107th Congress
H. Con. Res. 66
House Document 108-223
U.S. Government Printing Office
Washington, D.C.: 2006

Library of Congress Cataloging-in-Publication Data

Women in Congress, 1917–2006 / prepared under the direction of the
    Committee on House Administration of the U.S. House of
    Representatives, by the Office of History and Preservation, Office
    of the Clerk, U.S. House of Representatives.
        p. cm. — (House document ; 108–223)
    "An updated version of House document 101–238, entitled
Women in Congress, 1917–1990"—Introd.
    "Matthew A. Wasniewski, editor-in-chief"—T.p. verso.
    Includes bibliographical references and index.
    1. United States. Congress—Biography. 2. Women legislators
—United States—Biography.   I. Wasniewski, Matthew A. (Matthew
Andrew), 1969– . II. United States. Congress. House. Committee
on House Administration. III. United States. Congress. House.
Office of History and Preservation. IV. Women in Congress, 1917–1990.
JK1030.W66 2006
328.73092'2—dc22
    [B]   2006030660

For sale by the Superintendent of Documents, U.S. Government Printing Office
Internet: bookstore.gpo.gov Phone: toll free (866) 512-1800; DC area (202) 512-1800
Fax: (202) 512-2250 Mail: Stop IDCC, Washington, DC 20402-0001
ISBN 0-16-076753-9

HOUSE CONCURRENT RESOLUTION NO. 66

ONE HUNDRED SEVENTH CONGRESS, FIRST SESSION

SUBMITTED BY THE HON. MARCY KAPTUR

Resolved by the House of Representatives (the Senate concurring),

SECTION 1. PRINTING OF REVISED VERSION OF "WOMEN IN CONGRESS, 1917–1990." An updated version of House Document 101–238, entitled "Women in Congress, 1917–1990" (as revised by the Library of Congress), shall be printed as a House document by the Public Printer, with illustrations and suitable binding, under the direction of the Committee on House Administration of the House of Representatives.

SECTION 2. NUMBER OF COPIES. In addition to the usual number, there shall be printed 30,700 copies of the document referred to in section 1, of which—(1) 25,000 shall be for the use of the Committee on House Administration of the House of Representatives; and (2) 5,700 shall be for the use of the Committee on Rules and Administration of the Senate.

Approved by the House April 4, 2001
Approved by the Senate April 24, 2001

COMPILED AND EDITED UNDER THE DIRECTION
OF THE
COMMITTEE ON HOUSE ADMINISTRATION OF THE
U.S. HOUSE OF REPRESENTATIVES
VERNON J. EHLERS OF MICHIGAN, CHAIRMAN
JUANITA MILLENDER-MCDONALD OF CALIFORNIA, RANKING MEMBER

ROBERT W. NEY of Ohio
JOHN L. MICA of Florida
JOHN T. DOOLITTLE of California
THOMAS M. REYNOLDS of New York
CANDICE MILLER of Michigan

ROBERT A. BRADY of Pennsylvania
ZOE LOFGREN of California

KAREN L. HAAS, CLERK OF THE U.S. HOUSE OF REPRESENTATIVES

OFFICE OF HISTORY AND PRESERVATION
OFFICE OF THE CLERK OF THE HOUSE
MATTHEW A. WASNIEWSKI, *Editor in Chief*
KATHLEEN JOHNSON, *Writer and Researcher*
ERIN M. LLOYD, *Writer and Researcher*
LAURA K. TURNER, *Writer and Researcher*

Contents

WOMEN IN CONGRESS

An Introduction

Like all history, the story of women in Congress is defined by change over time: From a complete lack of representation in Congress before 1917, women have advanced to party leadership at the start of the 21st century. At times during the roughly 90 years women have served in Congress, change has been almost imperceptible, as exemplified by the subtle shift in women's committee assignments after World War II. At other times, change has been bold and dramatic, as evidenced by the 1992 "Year of the Woman" elections. Several questions, important not only to women's history in Congress but also to the development of Congress itself, have recurred throughout the process of researching and writing this book. How have women Members of Congress reacted to the political culture and traditions of Capitol Hill? Have women changed the way Congress conducts its business, or have they modified their behavior to conform with the institution? Have the experiences of the women Senators differed from those of women Representatives and, if so, what might account for these differences? What kinds of experiences do Congresswomen have in common, despite the differences in their legislative styles and political ideologies?

LEGISLATIVE STYLES

For decades, observers of Congress have studied the influence of the "insider" and "outsider" legislative roles.[1] The insider influences colleagues by earning their trust and respect through one-on-one contact and personal persuasion by being accessible, performing favors, and ceaselessly networking. The outsider route accrues power by appealing to external sources like the media and public opinion and most often favors "a more ideological, issue-oriented" approach than that of the insider.[2] Many women Members have followed one of two approaches: 1) assimilating into the institution and minimizing gender differences by de-emphasizing "women's issues" or 2) stressing their role as partisan spokespersons or advocates for feminism and "women's issues." The latter style often involved "surrogate" representation, meaning a Congresswoman spoke for a cross section of American women beyond the borders of her district or state.[3] These contrasting legislative styles have contributed to a constant tension among women Members about the best way to promote women's political participation.

This book portrays four successive generations of Congresswomen whose legislative role evolved over time, because of changed perceptions about gender roles and because of the new opportunities that resulted. The first two generations of women in Congress (1917–1934 and 1935–1954) tried to integrate themselves as knowledgeable, "professional" insiders.[4] Chiefly, they aimed to fit as seamlessly as possible into the institution. Mary T. Norton of New Jersey, Edith Nourse Rogers of Massachusetts, and Frances Bolton of Ohio practiced this approach, achieving considerable success as respected and, at times, influential insiders. Even during these first generations, however, there were exceptions to the rule, particularly in the careers of Clare Boothe Luce of Connecticut and Helen Gahagan Douglas of California. Both Luce and Douglas used the celebrity they had achieved before they came to Congress to act as national spokeswomen for their respective parties and legislative interests: Luce was a critic of the Franklin D. Roosevelt administration's policies during wartime, and Douglas was an advocate for postwar liberal causes like civil rights.

By the third generation of women in Congress

Jeannette Rankin of Montana, a suffragist and peace activist, and the first woman to serve in Congress, delivers her first full speech on the House Floor on August 7, 1917. Rankin addressed the need for federal intervention in copper mining during a period of unrest between labor unions and mining companies.

(1955–1976), the trend for Congresswomen to work inside the institution was still prevalent. Among the more successful Congresswomen in this regard were Julia Hansen of Washington, who became the first woman to chair an Appropriations subcommittee and headed an influential internal reforms committee in the 1970s, and Leonor Sullivan of Missouri, a widow who succeeded her late husband, became the dean of House women, a committee chair, and a leading opponent of efforts to create a Congresswomen's caucus.

Yet, changes were afoot because of an influx of Congresswomen who pushed an increasingly feminist agenda. Martha Griffiths of Michigan, first elected in 1954, was a transitional figure. Griffiths was one of the first truly career-oriented Congresswomen, having been a state legislator and judge in Michigan before she was elected to the House. A forceful advocate for the causes she championed, particularly the sexual discrimination clause in Title VII of the 1964 Civil Rights Act and the Equal Rights Amendment of 1972, Griffiths attracted media publicity for these issues. Griffiths was also the first woman to secure a seat on the influential Ways and Means Committee.

Later Congresswomen in the third generation and fourth generation (1977–2006) for example, Bella Abzug of New York, Shirley Chisholm of New York, and Patricia Schroeder of Colorado, firmly embraced a style of advocacy that tended more toward the outsider approach. Serving as partisan advocates for women and for special causes like reproductive rights, antiwar and arms reduction agendas, and government transparency, these Members often took their cases to the court of public opinion rather than working to shape legislation behind the scenes. Though successful at publicizing key issues, the outsider approach had its drawbacks. For many women Members, it complicated the process of crafting legislation and moving it through to completion by undermining their ability to rally colleagues to their cause through more subtle tactics. An illustrative example (again, one of the earliest) is that of Helen Douglas, who had little patience for adapting to the institutional traditions on Capitol Hill and even less of an inclination to master legislative processes. "Helen could not have gotten a bill passed making

> *Women Members of the 1920s were a curiosity both for their male colleagues and the national press, which devoted considerable attention to their arrival.*

December 25th a holiday," recalled Ed Lybeck, her campaign manager. But, Lybeck noted, because Congresswoman Douglas used her celebrity to bring public attention to key liberal issues, "she was a light in the window for liberals at a time when things were very dark."[5]

Time will tell how women in the fourth generation and subsequent generations respond to these legislative roles, but their increasing numbers, their ability to drive a legislative agenda via their successful caucus, and their increased power on committees and in leadership positions suggest that women Members are in a better position than ever to navigate an "insider" route to influence. Their choice to pursue an insider or outsider strategy, however, will be affected by their legislative agendas as much as by their personal styles. An insider strategy, for example, is often the most effective for routine legislative issues, such as modifying the tax code or securing appropriations for a district project, whereas an outsider strategy that mobilizes the media, interest groups, and public opinion is often preferable when a Member seeks to introduce a new idea or an issue that is strongly resisted in Congress.

What the insider–outsider divide also suggests, if tangentially, is that for most of the history of women in Congress, women Members have not had a single-track legislative agenda. In fact, for most of the time they have been in Congress, women have purposefully eschewed (or been unable to sustain) a narrow focus on women's issues. The ability to publicize and legislate on women's issues was a relatively late (third generation) development—signaled by the creation of the Women's Caucus in 1977—and it met with considerable resistance even among women Members. The success of the Women's Caucus as a bipartisan mechanism for pushing health, education, and economic legislation important to women occurred at a time when women Members had attained committee assignments across a spectrum of jurisdictions and legislative interests. Thus, along with their new ability to promote legislation important to American women, female Members of Congress also had unprecedented ability to legislate on virtually every facet of American life, including international relations, military affairs, commerce and industry, technology, and education.

Political scientists have often sought to determine the effects on Congress of legislative norms, the unwritten but widely accepted rules according to which Members conduct business. Which informal "folkways," such as apprenticeship and issue specialization, existed? How did Members who resisted these traditions fare in relation to those who accepted them? Did these norms change over time, especially during the influx of new membership, as with the "Watergate Babies" in 1975 or the "Republican Revolutionaries" in 1995? And, more generally, has the institution of Congress been changed by individuals, or has individuals' integration into the institution changed them?[6] These questions are open to considerable debate.

Most early women in Congress clearly and purposefully adapted to the institution. Many latter women Members chose instead to challenge institutional norms or to embrace their role as surrogate advocates for all women. Between Jeannette Rankin's election in 1916 and the "Year of the Woman" in 1992, a revolution occurred in terms of Congresswomen's collective work, educational experience, political status, economic clout, and independence from traditional familial roles. Experience engendered confidence. Millicent Fenwick of New Jersey described her initial foray into politics as following "the typical female pattern. I always wanted things in the most foolish, over-modest, hesitant way." Her work as a state legislator and official changed her approach. "I finally learned that when a man wants more he says, 'Listen, George, I want a bit of

the action,'" Fenwick observed. "Well, [women have] been taught: 'You have to wait to be invited to dance.'"[7] Women's attainment of rough equality with male colleagues in these areas enabled them to adapt to and navigate the institution of Congress. In this sense, it is impossible to separate the history of women in Congress from larger social and historical movements that shaped the course of U.S. history.

Irwin Gertzog has noted the development of three distinct legislative roles of women in Congress. Gertzog characterizes the "gentlewoman amateur" in the period roughly between 1917 and World War II as a woman whose route to political office depended more on her matrimonial connections than on her political savvy or qualifications. Early southern widows best exemplified this role. The "neutral professional" in the 1940s and 1950s had some precongressional political experience and a measure of legislative success but purposefully avoided women's issues. This legislative role was exemplified by Representatives Norton, Chase Woodhouse of Connecticut, Cecil Harden of Indiana, and Margaret Chase Smith of Maine, who later became a Senator. The modern "feminist colleague," from the 1960s onward, insisted on equality with male colleagues, gained important committee assignments and leadership roles, and developed an agenda on women's issues. Women like Representatives Griffiths and Patsy Mink of Hawaii, and other House Members who eventually moved on to the Senate, such as Barbara Mikulski of Maryland and Barbara Boxer of California, possessed these traits.[8]

These patterns are readily apparent among the generations of women Members featured in this book. For the pioneer generation of Congresswomen, who came into office between 1917 and 1934, a marital or other familial connection was the most common route to political office. A large percentage of them were widows who succeeded their late husbands, and most lacked experience in elective office. Only one, Kathryn O'Loughlin McCarthy of Kansas, had experience as a state legislator. McCarthy was also the only first-generation woman in Congress who was trained as a lawyer. Women Members of the 1920s were viewed as a curiosity by their male colleagues and the national press, which devoted considerable attention to their arrival in Washington. Most Congresswomen, however, were never really given the chance to integrate into the institution. Unable to serve on

Above: *Jeannette Rankin (right) on April 2, 1917, with Carrie Chapman Catt, president of the National American Woman Suffrage Association, at the group's headquarters in Washington, D.C. Later that historic day, Rankin was officially sworn into the 65th Congress.*

IMAGE COURTESY OF THE MONTANA HISTORICAL SOCIETY, HELENA

Above right: *A Jeannette Rankin campaign button.*

IMAGE COURTESY OF THE COLLECTION OF JOSEPH SHOEMAKER

powerful committees, they were relegated to panels tending to the routine upkeep of federal agencies or of Congress itself. Most women served on committees with oversight of issues considered as belonging to the women's sphere, such as education, nursing, and veterans' affairs. However, there were notable exceptions, such as Florence Kahn of California, who served on the Appropriations Committee; Mary Norton, who served on the Labor Committee; and Ruth Hanna McCormick, who served on the Naval Affairs Committee.

The second generation of women in Congress—elected from 1935 through 1954—served a long institutional apprenticeship. Once the initial interest in their participation in Congress subsided, women Members slowly made inroads. More of them had precongressional careers and experience in elective office, qualifying them for better committee assignments and more areas of legislative expertise. Powerful male colleagues offered a measure of support, particularly Speakers Sam Rayburn of Texas and Joe Martin of Massachusetts, who promoted women to key committee assignments. For the first time, women were assigned to prominent committees, such as Agriculture, Judiciary, and Armed Services in the House. In the Senate, Margaret Chase Smith won a position on the influential Armed Services Committee. Under the tutelage of senior Congresswomen, the second generation preferred to integrate into the institution and work its way up through the ranks by gaining seniority. Some were selected to leadership positions in the official organizations of Democrats and Republicans in both chambers; Representative Leonor Sullivan served as Secretary of the House Democratic Caucus in the 1950s and 1960s, and Margaret Chase Smith chaired the Senate Republican Conference from 1967 to 1973.

The third generation in Congress, first elected between 1955 and 1976, proved to be an important transition. Although the number of women in Congress had not significantly increased, women had achieved a modest share of influence both in terms of appointments to powerful committees, such as Ways and Means and Appropriations in the House, and in terms of initial strides toward breaking into leadership. More important, the years from the early 1960s to the mid-1970s marked a major sexual revolution in American society, as women demanded economic, political, and social equality with men. A new wave of feminists in Congress sought economic and constitutional equality through such legislative undertakings as the sex clause in Title VII of the 1964 Civil Rights Act and the

Rebecca Latimer Felton of Georgia (seated) is greeted by prominent political women in Washington, D.C. Felton, the first woman to serve in the U.S. Senate, was appointed for a day in November 1922.
IMAGE COURTESY OF THE LIBRARY OF CONGRESS

Equal Rights Amendment. These efforts were supported by women in Congress with near unanimity. For the first time in half a century, the number of women Members who came to Congress with experience in elective office exceeded the number who came to Congress by way of a marital or familial connection.

The fourth generation of women in Congress—those elected after 1977—enjoyed unprecedented growth and influence. More than half the women who have served in Congress were elected during this period. Women Members organized a special caucus solely devoted to developing legislation on women's issues and to educating the public and Congress about them. The numbers of women in Congress soared, essentially doubling in the 1992 elections, and continued to climb steadily into the early 21st century. In January 1977, 18 women served in the House; none served in the Senate. Early in the 109th Congress in 2005, there were 70 women serving in the House and 14 serving in the Senate. As the numbers of women Members increased, they became able to attain assignments on more-influential committees. Especially in the House, where incumbents have a long-standing advantage in re-election campaigns, women Members who were elected and decided to stay were better able to acquire more seniority and to chair or become Ranking Members on more committees and, particularly, subcommittees. They also began a rapid ascent into the ranks of congressional leadership in both parties and in both chambers.

Congresswomen's experiences have varied, depending on the peculiarities of the chamber in which they served.9

In addition to differences in membership and parliamentary procedure, opportunities to serve on committees, election requirements, and the availability of mentors and leadership patrons have affected women's congressional careers. The size of the House (435 Members) meant there were more (and larger) committees women could choose from to develop legislative expertise. In the Senate, the 100 Members had more committee assignments than their House counterparts, so women were more likely to receive at least one prominent assignment. This was true of the four women between 1930 and 1980 who served more than an abbreviated term (Hattie Caraway of Arkansas, on Commerce; Margaret Chase Smith, on Armed Services and Appropriations; Maurine Neuberger of Oregon, on Agriculture; and Nancy L. Kassebaum of Kansas, on Foreign Relations). Compared with their House colleagues, however, Senators tend to be generalists, rather than specialists.[10]

Moreover, the constitutional requirement that House Members be elected has benefited women by providing more opportunities. Particularly in the case of sudden deaths of sitting Representatives, special elections have proven disruptive because (depending on state law) they must occur on relatively short notice. Local party leaders have sometimes chosen widows because of their experience as political advisers to or surrogates for their husbands. Just as often, party leaders have nominated widows because their names made them electable and because their choice forestalled or prevented intraparty skirmishes. Conversely, interim Senators may be appointed by state governors, offering in many cases an opportunity for party continuity and a longer window before the election of a successor to a full, six-year term. Thus, in the Senate, choosing a widow was less desirable, except as a means of postponing a choice between competing factions (as with Dixie Bibb Graves of Alabama) or of boosting a governor's political fortunes with a bloc of voters (as with Rebecca Felton of Georgia). A number of early women Senators were appointees, but women in the House, including many who served long terms, clearly benefited more from special elections.

Finally, women in the House had more female predecessors and colleagues and, consequently, more mentors. Before 1992, 116 women had served in House history and only 18 had served in Senate history (11 of the latter served just long enough to finish the remainder of their predecessors' term). As recently as the first session of the 95th Congress (1977), there were no women serving in the Senate; women in the Senate were a novelty until the 1990s. For much of the 20th century, only one or two women served simultaneously in the upper chamber— islands in a sea of male colleagues. There was virtually no female support. By contrast, from 1951 on, a minimum of 10 women served in the House—enough to provide, if not an issues caucus, then at least a network for advice and a forum for exchange and camaraderie. Moreover, long-serving deans in this group, among them Mary Norton, Frances Bolton, and Leonor Sullivan, tried to set an example for the junior Members. In addition, key leadership figures in both parties in the House displayed on a number of occasions a willingness to promote women to middle- and, at times, top-tier committee posts.

SHARED EXPERIENCES OF WOMEN IN CONGRESS

Though each generation of women in Congress had distinctive traits, experiences shared by women Members united them across the decades. One enduring pattern, called the "widow's mandate," the "widow's succession," or the "matrimonial connection," has been an important route for women to attain congressional office—especially the women in the first three generations.[11] Between 1917 and 1976, 95 women served in the House and the Senate; a third (34) were widows who were elected or appointed to succeed their late husbands. At present, 46 widows (a fifth of the women who have served in Congress) have directly succeeded their husbands. When familial connections are considered (wives who succeeded living husbands or husbands who were nonincumbent candidates, wives appointed by husbands, or daughters of Members), the percentages are even more startling. Up to 1976, 46 percent of all women Members had benefited from a familial connection. By 2005, a familial connection was still prominent in the careers of more than a quarter (27 percent) of all women Members.

Yet, these statistics suggest that the incidence of the widow's mandate, while still high, has recently declined. Among the third and fourth generations, ever-greater numbers of Congresswomen have drawn on experience in elective office rather than on experience supporting or advising a male family member in political office. Moreover, the influence of the widow's mandate, real and perceived, has been magnified by several factors. First, an unusually high number of women who received party nominations to run for their husband's former seat won their general elections. From 1923 through 2005, 38 out of an estimated 46 House widows who were nominated to run for their husband's seat won their elections.[12] That number is far higher than the number of women elected to the House who were neither incumbents nor widows. Through the 1992 election, for example, just 14 percent of these women won their elections.[13]

A chief commonality among widows in Congress has been the brevity of their service; half of the 46 congressional widows served one term or less. This trend was particularly prevalent among widows from the South (14 served one term or less) who were nominated by their parties to serve as temporary placeholders until a sustainable male successor could be chosen. There have been, of course, notable exceptions; it is these widows who readily adapted to the institution because of extensive experience with their husbands, and subsequently distinguished themselves, who created in the public mind an enduring image of the prototypical widow successor. For instance, the longest-serving woman in congressional history, Edith Nourse Rogers (1925–1960), was a widow, and several other widows exercised considerable influence in Congress for many years, in some cases more than their husbands, for example, Florence Prag Kahn (1925–1937),

Frances Bolton (1940–1969), Margaret Chase Smith (1940–1973), and Lindy Boggs of Louisiana (1973–1991). As a group, widows have tended to receive more press attention because of the tragic or unlikely circumstances of their entry into political office, thus reinforcing public perceptions about the power of the widow's mandate.[14]

Familial duties and social expectations concerning a woman's role in the family contributed to another shared experience among women in Congress. Congresswomen from the pioneer generation onward have striven to balance the demands of their private family life, and public perceptions about women's responsibility to fulfill those demands, with those of their public career. This added responsibility has not been incumbent on their male colleagues. The third and fourth generations of women to enter Congress, especially, were confronted with this challenge, since more of them entered political office with young children.

Motherhood was a two-edged sword, providing Congresswomen with unique burdens as well as with legislative insights. Representative Emily Douglas of Illinois understood well how family responsibilities could affect women's participation in politics. Douglas was elected to

Florence Kahn of California (facing camera) and Edith Nourse Rogers of Massachusetts in early 1927, using Congress's first cloakroom for women Members. A House Page (far left) delivers a book to Kahn. IMAGE COURTESY OF THE LIBRARY OF CONGRESS

the House in 1944 as the mother of an 11-year-old daughter while her husband, Paul, who later became a U.S. Senator, was overseas in the military. "What everybody needs to make a good race is a good wife," Congresswoman Douglas observed. "Now that's where a woman is handicapped. When a man goes into politics and wins his wife is happy and proud to pull up stakes, corral her children, and move to the designated center of government. But a woman's position is different, in that her husband often has a business, she has her home to maintain, and her children are established in school."[15] Yet, Congresswomen also understood that motherhood and familial duties provided them with a unique perspective on legislation (e.g., personal knowledge of the cost of groceries and household products) that was not always prioritized by Congressmen. "I am sure I became a finer Congresswoman for being a mother," Chase Woodhouse of Connecticut said. "It gave me a better understanding of people's problems. Yes, there were conflicts. Yes, I was thought of as a peculiar creature. But the kids were my motivation. . . . They become in the end the reason for striving."[16] Both Congresswoman Douglas's and Congresswoman Woodhouse's sentiments are echoed throughout this book.

In addition to their familial responsibilities, Congresswomen were challenged by widespread and enduring social expectations about the "natural" or "proper" role for women—as wives, mothers, and caregivers. The power of the traditional conception of a woman's role is aptly illustrated by the career of Representative Coya Knutson of Minnesota. Elected to Congress in 1954, Knutson emerged as a promising advocate for education reform and agricultural issues. Her career was destroyed in 1958, however, when her abusive and jealous husband falsely accused her of abandoning the family. In 1950s America, that accusation was especially powerful. Most women Members of Congress were not confronted with such direct attacks, but many, especially those who were young or single, faced subtle discrimination on the campaign trail by male political opponents who stressed their roles as fathers and family men. Women faced doubters even within their own ranks. Shortly after Patricia Schroeder's 1972 election to the House, one of her feminist women colleagues asked how she planned to raise her toddlers and simultaneously advance in her congressional career.

Finally, women in Congress have shared the experience of being a minority, whether they were "insiders" or "outsiders," whether they were one-term congressional widows or accomplished committee chairs, and whether or not they had familial duties in addition to their professional responsibilities. While the number of women in Congress has varied, women have always been in the minority. Women in Congress have not marched unobstructed toward equality; like all women in American society, Congresswomen have faced barriers and challenges to their overall advancement.

As many women Members have observed, Congress has been exceptionally resistant to changes in gender roles taking place in American society. Again, each generation of Congresswomen faced different hurdles. Early women in Congress lacked basic necessities. For instance, it was not until the 1960s that women Members secured nearby bathroom facilities and a lounge near the House Floor; women in the Senate did not have such facilities until the mid-1990s. Congresswomen had limited access to congressional gym and exercise facilities built for men, into the 1990s. Women chipped away at the reluctance of committee chairs and congressional leadership to assign them to key committees, breaking down many of those barriers in the 1950s and 1960s in the House and in the 1980s and 1990s in the Senate. But even as women gained legislative expertise and seniority, their participation in congressional leadership lagged for several decades. Then, with women's entry into top party positions in the early 21st century, that barrier, too, seemed broken. Women now participate in unprecedented ways at every level of Congress. Nevertheless, history suggests new challenges lie ahead.

The Historiography of *Women in Congress*

The history of this record of women in Congress is nearly three decades old and spans a period of remarkable political achievements by women. The present volume originated with the first edition of *Women in Congress* (H. Con. Res. 664, Report No. 94-1732, 94th Congress, 29 September 1976), compiled and published at the time of the U.S. Bicentennial. Proposed by Congresswoman Lindy Boggs, who chaired the Joint Committee on Arrangements for the Commemoration of the Bicentennial, the booklet profiled 95 women who had served in Congress (85 Representatives and 11 Senators; Margaret Chase Smith served in both chambers). The author, Susan J. Tolchin, was then the director of the Washington Institute for Women in Politics at Mount Vernon College. Each

Member was profiled in a 200- to 400-word biography, and basic information appeared in a header for each entry. The entries were arranged alphabetically in two sections, one for former Members and the other for current Members. A thumbnail picture accompanied each profile.

Of the Members, the author wrote in a brief introduction, "Few patterns emerged from this group: these women reflected the societies and the era in which they lived; they were a microcosm of prevailing ideologies and political styles."[17] Written against the backdrop of the women's rights movement and a surge of female participation in local government, the first edition of *Women in Congress* anticipated a not-too-distant day when women would "move toward equal representation within government." Tolchin wrote, "Local and state offices act as the seedbed for higher office; we now find many more women running for Congress and the State House as a result of these great strides toward increased representation at lower levels."[18] Though women would play a greater role in government, their ascent through the political ranks no doubt occurred more slowly than Tolchin and many other observers envisioned.

The second edition of *Women in Congress* (H. Con Res. 167, H. Doc. No. 101-238, 101/2) was authorized by the House and the Senate in 1989. By that point, 129 women had served in Congress—115 Representatives and 16 Senators (Barbara Mikulski and Margaret Chase Smith had served in both chambers). Again, Congresswoman Boggs was an important influence behind the project, introducing the printing resolution as chair of the Commission on the Bicentenary of the U.S. House of Representatives. Of the profiled Members, Boggs wrote, "The story of their lives illustrates an important dimension of the struggle for full participation by all citizens in the political process of our national government. Their congressional service was a prominent legacy of the long campaign for woman's suffrage and for the acceptance of women in political institutions so long the exclusive domain of men. . . . Although most have supported some form of women's rights, what unites their careers is not a uniform political stance but rather a common experience with the movement to open political office to women and offer them an equal voice in the federal government."[19]

Compiled by the Office of the Historian of the U.S. House of Representatives (which was created in 1983 in preparation for the House Bicentennial), the second edition of *Women in Congress* had a format similar to that of the first edition. Published for the first time as a hardbound book, the volume contained Member profiles that were slightly longer than those in the first edition (250 to 700 words), with basic biographical information incorporated into the narrative. In this edition, the profiles of former and current Members were merged into one section, which again was arranged alphabetically. Larger pictures accompanied the individual profiles.

THE PRESENT EDITION

In early 2001, Representative Marcy Kaptur of Ohio introduced House Concurrent Resolution 66 for the printing of a revised edition of the book. The resolution, which passed the House on April 4, 2001, and was agreed to by the Senate on April 24, 2001, authorized the Library of Congress to compile "an updated version" of *Women in Congress, 1917–1990*. In late 2001, the Library of Congress transferred the project to the Office of the Clerk of the U.S. House of Representatives. In July 2002, the Office of History and Preservation (OHP) was created under the Clerk, and OHP staff began working on the publication soon afterward.

In scope, structure, and concept, the third edition of *Women in Congress* differs substantially from its predecessors. In 1992, the year after the previous edition was published, 28 women were elected to Congress—more than the total number of women who were elected or appointed to Congress in any previous decade. From 1991 to 2005, nearly 100 women were elected to Congress—roughly 40 percent of all the women who have served in the history of the institution.[20] Also, congressional women became more diverse in the latter part of the 20th century. Patsy Mink, elected in 1964, was the first non-Caucasian woman elected to Congress and one of just three Asian-American Congresswomen. Only five African-American women had served in Congress before 1990; New York Representative Shirley Chisholm was the first in 1969. Between 1990 and 2004, 19 black women were elected to Congress, including Carol Moseley-Braun, the first African-American woman elected to the U.S. Senate. The first Hispanic-American woman elected to Congress, in 1989, was Florida Representative Ileana Ros-Lehtinen. Seven more Hispanic-American women were elected in the next 15 years. The current volume of *Women in Congress* profiles the 229 women who have served in Congress (145 former Members and 84 incumbents).

The structure of this edition reflects the dramatic growth, changing characteristics, and increased influence

Ruth Hanna McCormick of Illinois, daughter of U.S. Senator Marcus Hanna of Ohio and wife of Senator Medill McCormick of Illinois, won election to the House of Representatives in 1928. Congresswoman McCormick drew on her experience as a suffrage lobbyist and National Republican Party official. This picture was taken in 1914, a year after McCormick and other activists completed a successful campaign in which the Illinois state legislature granted women the right to vote.

IMAGE COURTESY OF THE LIBRARY OF CONGRESS

of women Members. Unlike its predecessors, this volume is organized chronologically, to represent more accurately the effects of historical trends on women's entry into Congress. The individual profiles have been expanded, with more emphasis on congressional service. Contextual essays analyze political and institutional developments affecting women's participation in Congress. Appendices include women's committee assignments, leadership positions, and familial connections in Congress. An index is provided for easy reference. Photographs of each Member are included in the book. Like the first edition of *Women in Congress*, this edition contains separate sections for former and current Members.

Part I contains expanded profiles of former Members (averaging 1,500 words), with an emphasis on congressional service. The profiles of a few outstanding House and Senate careers exceed 2,000 words, and the profiles of widows who served brief terms—and for whom the record is fragmentary at best—range from 550 to 750 words. Each profile consists of a brief section on the Member's precon-

gressional career, followed where possible by a detailed analysis of the subject's first campaign for congressional office; subsequent re-election efforts; information about committee assignments, leadership, and major legislative initiatives; and a brief summary of the Member's postcongressional career.

The profiles of former Members are arranged chronologically, rather than alphabetically, allowing a fuller perspective of the era in which a Member served. Accordingly, this section is divided into four periods, with an introductory essay about the institutional developments, legislative agendas, and social changes that shaped each generation of Congresswomen.

The four successive generations of women in Congress are grouped into the following sections.

- *"I'm No Lady, I'm a Member of Congress":*
  Women Pioneers on Capitol Hill, 1917–1934
  (contextual essay and 20 Member profiles)

- *Onto the National Stage: Congresswomen in an*
  Age of Crises, 1935–1954
  (contextual essay and 36 Member profiles)

- *A Changing of the Guard: Traditionalists, Feminists,*
  and the New Face of Women in Congress, 1955–1976
  (contextual essay and 39 Member profiles)

- *Assembling, Amplifying, and Ascending: Recent Trends*
  Among Women in Congress, 1977–2006
  (contextual essay and 50 Member profiles)

Part II of *Women in Congress* contains biographical profiles of current Members, with information on precongressional careers, first House or Senate campaigns, committee and leadership positions, and legislative achievements. Because these Members' careers are still in progress, however, definitive accounts must await a later date. Accordingly, the profiles in Part II differ in tone and style from those for former Members, and they are about half as long (750 words). Moreover, the profiles of current Members are arranged alphabetically, rather than chronologically. This section includes profiles of the 75 women who have served in two or more Congresses. The nine freshman Members elected to the 109th Congress, who are embarking on their congressional careers, are covered separately in a résumé format in the book's first appendix.

Bibliographic information for the profiles of current

and former Members is provided in a separate section, and where applicable, information about the location of Members' manuscript collections is included at the end of their individual profiles. Manuscript information has been drawn from House and Senate records used to compile and maintain the online *Biographical Directory of the U.S. Congress* at http://bioguide.congress.gov. The editors have referenced, where applicable, Members' major manuscript collections and other repositories with significant holdings, i.e., the transcript of an oral history or extended correspondence. This information is intended to be a resource for the general reader and a starting point for the scholarly researcher.

The literature on women's history, which has grown into one of the most dynamic fields in the historical profession, has largely been created since the 1970s.[21] The

First Lady Eleanor Roosevelt (left) and Representative Clare Boothe Luce of Connecticut were leading women within their respective political parties. Roosevelt promoted the political careers of women in government, including Congress, during her husband Franklin's four terms as U.S. President. Luce, a national celebrity before winning election to the House in 1942, was a prominent critic of the Roosevelt administration's wartime policies.

IMAGE COURTESY OF THE NATIONAL ARCHIVES AND RECORDS ADMINISTRATION

editors consulted several useful general texts on women's history, including Rosalind Rosenberg, *Divided Lives: American Women in the Twentieth Century* (New York: Hill and Wang, 1992); William Chafe, *The Paradox of Change: American Women in the Twentieth Century* (New York: Oxford University Press, 1991); Sarah Evans, *Born for Liberty: A History of Women in America* (New York: Free Press, 1989); Nancy Cott, *The Grounding of Modern Feminism* (New Haven, CT: Yale University Press, 1987); and Nancy Woloch, *Women and the American Experience, 2nd edition* (New York: McGraw-Hill, 1994).

Though the field has flourished in recent years, it still is marked by significant historiographical gaps, including the underrepresentation of congressional women in the secondary literature. A few of the most famous women in Congress—Margaret Chase Smith, Clare Boothe Luce, Coya Knutson, and Ruth Hanna McCormick—have been the subjects of thorough biographical treatments. Most others have not, including prominent legislative figures such as Mary Norton, Edith Nourse Rogers, Florence Kahn, Katharine St. George, Martha Griffiths, Julia Butler Hansen, Edith Green, Leonor Sullivan, Patsy Mink, and Nancy Kassebaum. One aim of these profiles is to generate interest in future studies of these Congresswomen and in studies of other, lesser-known but significant individuals, including Alice Robertson, Ruth Pratt, Kathryn O'Loughlin McCarthy, Marguerite Stitt Church, Vera Buchanan, and Florence Dwyer.

Several sources were indispensable in the compilation of this book. Any inquiry into a Member's congressional career should begin with the *Biographical Directory of the United States Congress*, http://bioguide.congress.gov. Maintained by the House Office of History and Preservation and the Senate Historical Office, this publication is easily searchable and contains basic biographical information about Members, pertinent bibliographic references, and information about manuscript collections. It is updated daily with the latest available information.

In the early phase of research, the editors also consulted standard reference sources such as the *American National Biography*, the *Dictionary of American Biography*, and *Current Biography*. Various editions of the *Almanac of American Politics* (Washington, D.C.: National Journal, Inc.) and *Politics in America* (Washington, D.C.: Congressional Quarterly Press) also were starting points in the research on many former and current women Members in the post-1977 period. For biographical sketches of women in Congress from 1917 to 1973, the editors used Hope

Chamberlin's *A Minority of Members: Women in the U.S. Congress* (New York: Praeger, 1973). However, this book lacks footnotes. Karen Foerstel's *Biographical Dictionary of Congressional Women* (Westport, CT: Greenwood Press, 1999), though spare, includes endnotes and contains information through the 1998 elections. Marcy Kaptur's *Women of Congress: A Twentieth-Century Odyssey* (Washington, D.C.: Congressional Quarterly Press, 1996) is a useful study with extended profiles of roughly a dozen prominent House and Senate women. An invaluable study of changing patterns among Congresswomen is Irwin Gertzog's *Congressional Women: Their Recruitment, Integration, and Behavior* (Westport, CT: Praeger, 1995).

Since this edition of *Women in Congress* was revised and updated extensively, much of the information was researched using primary sources, particularly, published official congressional records and scholarly compilations of congressional statistics.

Congressional election results for the biennial elections from 1920 forward are available in the Clerk's "Congressional Elections," published by the Government Printing Office (GPO) or in PDF format at http://clerk.house.gov/members/electionInfo/elections.html. Michael J. Dubin et al., *United States Congressional Elections, 1788–1997* (Jefferson, NC: McFarland and Company, Publishing, Inc., 1998) contains results for both general and special elections. For information on district boundaries and reapportionment, the editors relied on Kenneth C. Martis, *The Historical Atlas of Political Parties in the United States Congress, 1789–1989* (New York: Macmillan Publishing Company, 1989).

Committee assignments and information about jurisdiction may be found in two indispensable scholarly compilations: David T. Canon, Garrison Nelson, and Charles Stewart III, *Committees in the U.S. Congress, 1789–1946*, 4 volumes (Washington, D.C.: Congressional Quarterly Press, 2002) and Garrison Nelson, *Committees in the U.S. Congress, 1947–1992*, 2 volumes (Washington, D.C.: Congressional Quarterly Press, 1994). In addition, the editors consulted the *Congressional Directory*, a GPO publication that dates back into the 19th century. The directory is available at GPO from the 104th Congress forward. See http://www.gpoaccess.gov/cdirectory/index.html.

Legislation, floor debates, roll call votes, bills, resolutions, and public laws back to the 1980s may be searched on the Library of Congress's THOMAS Web site at http://thomas.loc.gov. A useful print resource that discusses major acts of Congress is Steven V. Stathis's

A campaign poster for Bella Abzug of New York. Abzug, who served three terms from 1971 to 1977, was one of the institution's most colorful individuals.

IMAGE COURTESY OF THE LIBRARY OF CONGRESS

Landmark Legislation, 1774–2002: Major U.S. Acts and Treaties (Washington, D.C.: Congressional Quarterly Press, 2002). Floor debates about legislation can be found in the *Congressional Record* (1873 to the present), which is available at the THOMAS Web site from 1989 to the present; an index of the *Record* from 1983 to the present is available at http://www.gpoaccess.gov/cri/index.html. The editors also consulted the official proceedings in the *House Journal* and the *Senate Journal*. For House roll call votes back to the second session of the 101st Congress, visit the House Clerk's Web site at http://clerk.house.gov/legisAct/votes.html.

For print copies of the *Congressional Directory*, the *Congressional Record*, the *House Journal*, or the *Senate Journal*, consult your nearest federal depository library. A GPO locator for federal depository libraries may be accessed at

Technology now permits research that even a decade ago would have been impossible. Using an online database, the editors were able to review key historical newspapers for the entire period of this book, including the *New York Times*, the *Washington Post*, the *Los Angeles Times*, the *Christian Science Monitor*, and the *Wall Street Journal*. News accounts and feature stories, particularly on the first generation of women in Congress, have done much to fill in the details about some of the more obscure women Members. Many of these newspaper citations appear in the notes.

Significant photo research was carried out for this edition of *Women in Congress*. Previous editions included only a head-and-shoulders image of each Member. Individual picture credits were not indicated in the 1976 edition, though a photo acknowledgment page was included at the end of the book. In the 1991 edition, a photo credit was included with each picture, but many images were credited to Members' offices that no longer exist or to the collection of the House Historian whose office closed in the mid-1990s.

In the current edition of *Women in Congress*, the editors strove to provide accurate information for all images that are accessible from public, private, and commercial repositories (with the expectation that researchers and the general public might wish to acquire photo reproductions). Among the major photo collections that were used for this project were the Prints and Photographs Division of the Library of Congress (Washington, D.C.), the Still Pictures Branch of the National Archives and Records Administration (College Park, MD), the *Washington Star* Collection of the Martin Luther King, Jr., Memorial Library's Washingtonian Division (Washington, D.C.), and the photo archives of the Associated Press. The editors also referenced a half-dozen Members' manuscript collections to locate images for publication in the book. For a small number of Member images, the Office of History and Preservation in the U.S. House of Representatives is cited. In addition, feature images illustrating legislative issues accompany the contextual essays. The images of the current Members were provided by their offices, which should serve as the point of contact for persons seeking an official image.

Finally, the new edition of *Women in Congress* includes historical tables and appendices for reference by specialists and the general reader. Nine appendices contain (a) brief profiles of the freshman Members of the 109th Congress; (b) a list of women Members by Congress from the 65th Congress (1917–1919) to the 109th Congress (2005–2007); (c) a historical list of states and territories represented by women; (d) a list of House and Senate committees on which women have served; (e) a list of women who have chaired full committees; (f) a list of women who have chaired subcommittees; (g) a list of women who have served in party leadership; (h) a list of women of color in Congress; and (i) a list of the familial connections (marital, paternal, filial, etc.) of women Members. Research notes are included at the end of the individual profiles, the introduction, and the contextual essays, and a comprehensive index appears at the end of this book.

ACKNOWLEDGMENTS

Colleagues in the history and archival fields offered valuable assistance throughout the production of this publication. A photo of Jeannette Rankin's first official floor speech was made available by the National Archives and Records Administration, with the help of Richard Hunt and Jessie Kratz from the Center for Legislative Archives. Peggy Appleman of the Washingtoniana Division of the Martin Luther King, Jr., Memorial Library provided cheerful and timely assistance locating images in files of the now-defunct *Washington Star* newspaper. The following institutions and repositories also helped secure images of women Members: Department of Energy, National Nuclear Security Administration; Franklin D. Roosevelt Presidential Library; Tennessee State Library & Archives; Ellis County (KS) Historical Society; Georgia State University Library; Special Collections & Archives, Auburn University; South Dakota State Archives; Louisiana State University Library; Oregon Historical Society; Library of Congress Prints and Photographs Division; National Archives and Records Administration Still Pictures Branch; the Lyndon Baines Johnson Presidential Library; the United States Postal Service; Texas Southern University, Barbara Jordan Archives; and the U.S. Senate Historical Office.

The *Women in Congress* project team also acknowledges the courteous and professional staffs of the U.S. House of Representatives Library; the Office of Publication Services (OPS) in the Office of the Clerk, especially OPS Chief Janice Wallace-Hamid and editors Marcie Kanakis and Chiedu Ozuzu; the U.S. Senate Library; the Office of the U.S. Senate Curator; and the Manuscript Division at the Library of Congress. Special thanks are extended to the following colleagues, who work daily in the thickets of congressional history and who graciously took time from their busy schedules to review the manuscript for this book and provide valuable comments: Richard Baker, Donald A. Ritchie, and Betty Koed of the Senate Historical Office and Donald R. Kennon of the U.S. Capitol Historical Society.

Finally, the project team thanks the supportive and collegial staff of the Office of History and Preservation. This publication would not have been possible without the conceptual framework developed by former OHP Chief Kenneth Kato. Early on, Ken saw the potential for expanding upon earlier editions of *Women in Congress.* His help as a writer and editor, insights as a political scientist, and constant encouragement sustained the project. The project team also thanks OHP colleagues Farar Elliott, House Curator and Chief of OHP; Robin Reeder, House Archivist; Andrew Dodge; Karen McKinstry; Felicia Wivchar; Catherine Wallace; Joe Wallace; and Toni Coverton.

Matthew Wasniewski
Editor and OHP Publications Manager

Kathleen Johnson, Erin M. Lloyd, Laura K. Turner
Writers and Researchers

NOTES

1   See, for example, Nelson W. Polsby's article "Two Strategies of Influence: Choosing a Majority Leader, 1962," reprinted in Robert L. Peabody and Nelson W. Polsby, eds., *New Perspectives on the House of Representatives,* 4th edition (Baltimore: The Johns Hopkins University Press, 1992): 260–290.

2   Peabody and Polsby, *New Perspectives on the House of Representatives:* 282.

3   See, for example, Jane Mansbridge, "The Many Faces of Representation," Working Paper, 1998, John F. Kennedy School of Government, Harvard University; and Jane Mansbridge, "Should Blacks Represent Blacks and Women Represent Women? A Contingent 'Yes,'" *Journal of Politics* 61 (1999): 628–657.

4   Irwin Gertzog, *Congressional Women: Their Recruitment, Integration, and Behavior,* 2nd edition (Westport, CT: Praeger, 1995): 254–257.

5   Ingrid Winther Scobie, *Center Stage: Helen Gahagan Douglas—A Life* (New York: Oxford, 1992): xv–xvi. See also Richard Fenno, *Home Style: House Members in Their Districts* (Boston: Little, Brown, 1978). Elsewhere Fenno has written, "Dramatic analogies are appropriate to politics because politicians, like actors, perform before audiences and are legitimized by their audiences"; see his "U.S. House Members and Their Constituencies: An Exploration," *American Political Science Review* 71, part 2 (September 1977): 898. See also Ralph Huitt and Robert L. Peabody, *Congress: Two Decades of Analysis* (New York: Harper and Row, Publishers, 1969): 170.

6   For studies that have addressed aspects of the question of institutional

versus individual change, see Donald R. Matthews's, *U.S. Senators and Their World* (Chapel Hill: University of North Carolina Press, 1960), especially the chapter "Folkways of the U.S. Senate." See also Morris Fiorina, *Congress: Keystone of the Washington Establishment,* 2nd edition (New Haven, CT: Yale University Press, 1989) and Ross K. Baker, *House and Senate,* 3rd edition (New York: W.W. Norton & Company, 2001). On the issue of changing norms and traditions, see Herbert F. Weisberg, Eric S. Heberlig, and Lisa M. Campoli, *Classics in Congressional Politics* (New York: Longman, 1999): especially 192–200; and Glenn R. Parker, *Studies of Congress* (Washington, D.C.: Congressional Quarterly Press, 1985): 75–80.

7   Judy Bacharach, "Millicent Fenwick," 23 February 1975, *Washington Post:* 137.

8   Gertzog, *Congressional Women:* 243–264, especially 251.

9   For a standard reference source on the differences between the structure and operations of the U.S. House of Representatives and the U.S. Senate, see the aforementioned study by Baker, *House and Senate.*

10 Baker, *House and Senate:* 55, 68–70.

11 Irwin Gertzog is a leading analyst of the "matrimonial connection." See his discussion in Gertzog, *Congressional Women:* 17–36. See also his early analysis, Irwin Gertzog, "Changing Patterns of Female Recruitment to the U.S. House of Representatives," *Legislative Studies Quarterly* IV (no. 3, August 1979): 429–445.

12 Gertzog, *Congressional Women:* 34; Office of History and Preservation statistics 1995–2005. See Appendix I: "Marriage/Familial Connections of Women Representatives and Senators in Congress."

13 Gertzog, *Congressional Women:* 20–21.

14 Perceptions generated by media coverage of a widow Member's exceptional circumstances or achievements often masked the rather one-sided statistical realities. Most widows of Congressmen never even received their husbands' party nomination. For instance, in the House from 1916 to April 15, 2005, 422 Representatives died in office. All but Edith Nourse Rogers, Vera Daerr Buchanan, and Patsy T. Mink were male. Many were bachelors or widowers, but about 300 had wives who could have been tapped to replace them. Yet, roughly only one in six of these widows was nominated to succeed her husband. See Gertzog, *Congressional Women:* 19. Statistics through the 102nd Congress (1991–1993) are Gertzog's. An additional 18 individuals died in office from the 103rd through the 108th Congresses (1993 to January 1, 2005).

15 Martha Rhyne, "The Douglas Duo Raps Feminine Refusal to Accept Political Role," 25 February 1945, *Washington Post:* S1.

16 "A Pioneering Feminist Savors Grandmother Role," 10 May 1981, *New York Times.*

17 Susan Tolchin, *Women in Congress, 1917–1976* (Washington, D.C.: Government Printing Office, 1976): iii.

18 Tolchin, *Women in Congress, 1917–1976:* iii.

19 Office of the Historian, U.S. House of Representatives, *Women in Congress, 1917–1990* (Washington, D.C.: Government Printing Office, 1991): v.

20 Mildred Amer, "Women in the United States Congress, 1917–2004," CRS (1 July 2004).

21 See, for example, Linda Gordon's historiographical essay "U.S. Women's History" in *The New American History,* ed. Eric Foner (Philadelphia: Temple University Press, 1997).

VISUAL STATISTICS I

This section includes visual representations of various statistical breakdowns of women in Congress.

Additional sections of statistics represented visually appear after each contextual essay.

Number of Women in Congress[1]
65TH–109TH CONGRESSES (1917–2007)

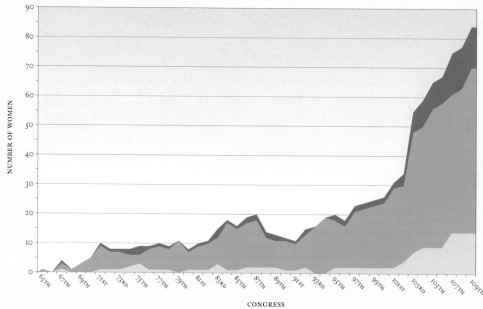

CONGRESS

Women as a Percentage of Congress[2]
65TH–109TH CONGRESSES (1917–2007)

Despite an exponential increase throughout the 1990s in the number of women in Congress, women have not exceeded 15.5 percent of the total congressional membership.

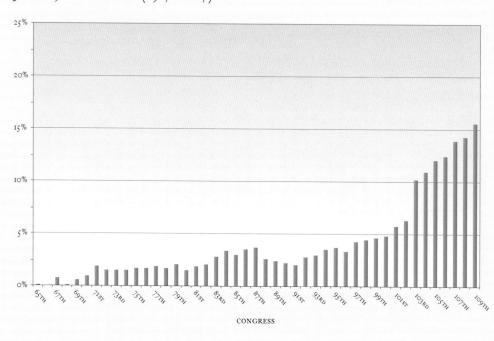

CONGRESS

---

1. Source: Appendix B: Women Representatives and Senators by Congress (1917–2006).

2. Sources: Appendix B: Women Representatives and Senators by Congress (1917–2006); Office of the Clerk, U.S. House of Representatives; U.S. Senate Historical Office.

Widow's Mandate[3]

65TH–109TH CONGRESSES (1917–2007)

SENATE WIDOWS HOUSE WIDOWS
OTHER WOMEN IN CONGRESS

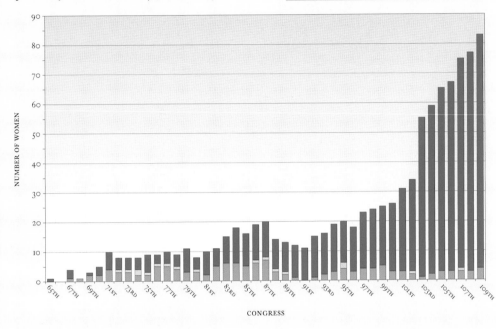

A Congress-by-Congress overview comparing the incidence of women succeeding their late husbands in the House and Senate, with the incidence of women being elected or appointed without a marital connection.

Widows in Congress[4]

AS A PERCENTAGE OF ALL WOMEN WHO SERVED IN CONGRESS

A series of graphs depicting the declining, but still common, occurrence of women succeeding their late husbands in Congress.

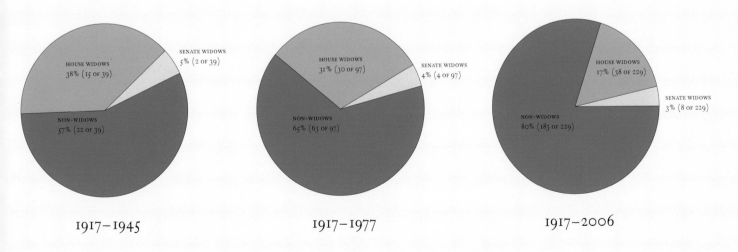

1917–1945   1917–1977   1917–2006

---

3. Source: Appendix I: Marriage/Familial Connections of Women Representatives and Senators in Congress.

4. Source: Appendix I: Marriage/Familial Connections of Women Representatives and Senators in Congress.

★ PART ONE ★

Former Women Members

"I'm No Lady, I'm a Member of Congress"

WOMEN PIONEERS ON CAPITOL HILL, 1917–1934

GREAT TRIUMPHS AND HISTORIC FIRSTS highlight women's initial foray into national political office. Four years after Jeannette Rankin was elected to the House of Representatives in 1916, women won the right to vote nationally, with the ratification of the 19th Amendment in 1920. Rebecca Felton of Georgia became the first woman to serve in the U.S. Senate in 1922. That same year, Alice Robertson of Oklahoma became the first woman to preside over the House of Representatives. In 1923, Representative Mae Ella Nolan of California became the first woman to chair a congressional committee. Two other women followed her lead, including Mary Norton of New Jersey, the first woman elected from the East Coast, who would chair four House committees during her quarter-century career. In 1932, Hattie Caraway became the first woman elected to the Senate. Several other women attained prominent committee positions, including Representative Florence Prag Kahn of California, the first woman to serve on the powerful Appropriations Committee.

Nevertheless, women were still a distinct minority of the 435 House Members; at their peak during this period, nine served in the 71st Congress (1929–1931). They lacked the power to focus congressional attention on the issues that were important to them.

Jeannette Rankin of Montana, a suffragist and peace activist, was the first woman to serve in Congress. PAINTING BY SHARON SPRUNG, 2004, COLLECTION OF THE U.S. HOUSE OF REPRESENTATIVES

The official program for the March 3, 1913, National American Woman Suffrage Association's procession in Washington, D.C. The cover features a woman seated on a horse and blowing a long horn, from which is draped a "votes for women" banner. The U.S. Capitol is in background.

IMAGE COURTESY OF THE LIBRARY OF CONGRESS

Alice Paul (second from left), chairwoman of the militant National Woman's Party, and officers of the group in front of their Washington headquarters, circa 1920s. They are holding a banner emblazoned with a quote from suffragist Susan B. Anthony: "No self-respecting woman should wish or work for the success of a party that ignores her sex."

IMAGE COURTESY OF THE LIBRARY OF CONGRESS

Without seniority, and facing institutional prejudices, the early Congresswomen viewed leadership positions as an elusive quest. These adversities raise several questions: What routes did these pioneer women take to be elected to Congress? How did they relate to the women's rights movement in America? Once they arrived in Congress, what agendas did they pursue? What were their legislative interests and committee assignments? What changes did they effect on Capitol Hill? And finally, were they able, or even inclined, to craft a unique identity for themselves?

THE WOMEN'S RIGHTS MOVEMENT, 1848–1920

The beginning of the fight for women's suffrage in the United States, which predates Jeannette Rankin's entry into Congress by nearly 70 years, grew out of a larger women's rights movement. That reform effort evolved during the 19th century, initially emphasizing a broad spectrum of goals before focusing solely on securing the franchise for women. Women's suffrage leaders, moreover, often disagreed about the tactics for and the emphasis (federal versus state) of their reform efforts. Ultimately, the suffrage movement provided political training for some of the early women pioneers in Congress, but its internal divisions foreshadowed the persistent disagreements among women in Congress and among women's rights activists after the passage of the 19th Amendment.

The first gathering devoted to women's rights in the United States was held July 19–20, 1848, in Seneca Falls, New York. The principal organizers of the Seneca Falls Convention were Elizabeth Cady Stanton, a mother of four from upstate New York, and the Quaker abolitionist Lucretia Mott.[1] About 100 people attended the convention; two-thirds were women. Stanton drafted a "Declaration of Sentiments, Grievances, and Resolutions," that echoed the preamble of the Declaration of Independence: "We hold these truths to be self-evident: that all men and women

are created equal." Among the 13 resolutions set forth in Stanton's "Declaration" was the goal of achieving the "sacred right of franchise."[2]

The sometimes-fractious suffrage movement that grew out of the Seneca Falls meeting proceeded in successive waves. Initially, women reformers addressed social and institutional barriers that limited women's rights; including family responsibilities, a lack of educational and economic opportunities, and the absence of a voice in political debates. Stanton and Susan B. Anthony, a Massachusetts teacher, met in 1850 and forged a lifetime alliance as women's rights activists. For much of the 1850s they agitated against the denial of basic economic freedoms to women. Later, they unsuccessfully lobbied Congress to include women in the provisions of the 14th and 15th Amendments (extending citizenship rights and granting voting rights to freedmen, respectively).

In the wake of the Civil War, however, reformers sought to avoid marginalization as "social issues" zealots by focusing their message exclusively on the right to vote.[3] In 1869 two distinct factions of the suffrage movement emerged. Stanton and Anthony created the National Woman Suffrage Association (NWSA), which directed its efforts toward changing federal law and opposed the 15th Amendment because it excluded women. Lucy Stone, a one time Massachusetts antislavery advocate and a prominent lobbyist for women's rights, formed the American Woman Suffrage Association (AWSA).[4] Leaders of the AWSA rejected the NWSA's agenda as being racially divisive and organized with the aim to continue a national reform effort at the state level. Although California Senator Aaron Sargent introduced in Congress a women's suffrage amendment in 1878, the overall campaign stalled. Eventually, the NWSA also shifted its efforts to the individual states where reformers hoped to start a ripple effect to win voting rights at the federal level.

During the 1880s, the two wings of the women's rights movement struggled to maintain momentum. The AWSA was better funded and the larger of the two groups, but it had only a regional reach. The NWSA, which was based in New York, relied on its statewide network but also drew recruits from around the nation, largely on the basis of the extensive speaking circuit of Stanton and Anthony. Neither group attracted broad support from women, or persuaded male politicians or voters to adopt its cause. Susan B. Anthony and Ida H. Harper cowrote, "In the indifference, the inertia, the apathy of women, lies the greatest obstacle to their enfranchisement." Historian Nancy Woloch described early suffragists' efforts as "a crusade in political education by women and for women, and for most of its existence, a crusade in search of a constituency."[5]

The turning point came in the late 1880s and early 1890s, when the nation experienced a surge of volunteerism among middle-class women—activists in progressive causes, members of women's clubs and professional societies, temperance advocates, and participants in local civic and charity organizations. The determination of these women to expand their sphere of activities further outside the home helped legitimate the suffrage movement and provided new momentum for the NWSA and the AWSA. By 1890, seeking to capitalize on their newfound "constituency," the two groups united to form the National American Woman Suffrage Association (NAWSA).[6] Led initially by Stanton and then by Anthony, the NAWSA began to draw on the support of women activists in organizations as diverse as the Women's Trade Union League, the Woman's Christian Temperance Union (WCTU), and the National Consumer's League.

Suffragists parade in New York City in 1916 with a banner that reads "President Wilson favors votes for women." Woodrow Wilson, a reluctant convert to the cause, eventually supported the 19th Amendment which passed the House in 1918 and was ratified by the states in 1920.

IMAGE COURTESY OF THE LIBRARY OF CONGRESS

Rebecca Latimer Felton of Georgia, the first woman to serve in the U.S. Senate, poses at her desk in the Senate Office Building. Felton's appointment to an unexpired term in 1922 lasted a day.

IMAGE COURTESY OF THE LIBRARY OF CONGRESS

Sculptor Adelaide Johnson's Portrait Monument to Lucretia Mott, Elizabeth Cady Stanton, and Susan B. Anthony, honors three of the suffrage movement's leaders. Unveiled in 1921, the monument is featured prominently in the Rotunda of the U.S. Capitol.

For the next two decades, the NAWSA worked as a nonpartisan organization focused on gaining the vote in states, though managerial problems and a lack of coordination initially limited its success. The first state to grant women complete voting rights was Wyoming in 1869. Three other western states—Colorado (1893), Utah (1896), and Idaho (1896)—followed shortly after NAWSA was founded. But prior to 1910, only these four states allowed women to vote. Between 1910 and 1914, the NAWSA intensified its lobbying efforts and additional states extended the franchise to women: Washington, California, Arizona, Kansas, and Oregon. In Illinois, future Congresswoman Ruth Hanna McCormick helped lead the fight for suffrage as a lobbyist in Springfield, when the state legislature granted women the right to vote in 1913; this marked the first such victory for women in a state east of the Mississippi River. A year later, Montana granted women the right to vote, thanks in part to the efforts of another future Congresswoman, Jeannette Rankin.

Despite the new momentum, however, some reformers were impatient with the pace of change. In 1913, Alice Paul, a young Quaker activist who had experience in the English suffrage movement, formed the rival Congressional Union (later named the National Woman's Party).[7] Paul's group freely adopted the more militant tactics of its English counterparts, picketing and conducting mass rallies and marches to raise public awareness and support. Embracing a more confrontational style, Paul drew a younger generation of women to her movement, helped resuscitate the push for a federal equal rights amendment, and relentlessly attacked the Democratic administration of President Woodrow Wilson for obstructing the extension of the vote to women.

In 1915, Carrie Chapman Catt, a veteran suffragist since the mid-1880s and a former president of the NAWSA, again secured the organization's top leadership post. Catt proved an adept administrator and organizer, whose "Winning Plan" strategy called for disciplined and relentless efforts to achieve state referenda on the vote, especially in non-Western states.[8] Key victories—the first in the South and East—followed in 1917 when Arkansas and New York granted partial and full voting rights, respectively. Beginning in 1917, President Wilson (a convert to the suffrage cause) urged Congress to pass a voting rights amendment. Another crowning achievement also occurred that year when Montana's Jeannette Rankin (elected two years after her state enfranchised women) was sworn into the 65th Congress on April 2, as the first woman to serve in the national legislature.

Catt's steady strategy of securing voting rights state by state and Paul's vocal and partisan protest campaign coincided with the Wilson administration's decision to intervene in the First World War—a development that provided powerful rhetoric for and a measure of expediency for granting the vote.[9] The NAWSA publicly embraced the war cause, despite the fact that many women suffragists, including Rankin, were pacifists. Suffrage leaders suggested that the effort to "make the world safe for democracy" ought to begin at home, by extending the franchise. Moreover, they insisted, the failure to extend the vote to women might impede their participation in the war effort just when they were most needed to play a greater role as workers and volunteers outside the home. Responding to these overtures, the House of Representatives initially passed a voting rights amendment on January 10, 1918, but the Senate did not follow suit before the end of the 65th Congress. It was not until after the war, however,

Women crowd a voting poll in New York City during elections in 1922. After passage of the 19th Amendment two years earlier, the major political parties scrambled to register women. But a potent voting bloc of women voters, which some observers predicted, never materialized.

IMAGE COURTESY OF THE LIBRARY OF CONGRESS

that the measure finally cleared Congress with the House again voting its approval by a wide margin on May 21, 1919, and the Senate concurring on June 14, 1919. A year later, on August 26, 1920, the 19th Amendment, providing full voting rights for women nationally, was ratified when Tennessee became the 36th state to approve it.

Continued Challenges

But achieving the right to vote, while ending one phase of the women's rights movement, set the stage for the equally arduous process of securing women a measure of power in local and national political office. Scholars have debated whether the women's movement underwent fundamental change or sustained continuity in the years before and after 1920.[10] However, most agree that Rankin and those who followed her into Congress during the 1920s faced a Herculean task in consolidating their power and in sustaining legislation that was important to women. Several factors contributed to these conditions.

The Progressive Era, in which several waves of activists, moving from the local to national level, pursued democratic reforms within political, social, and cultural contexts, had helped sustain the women's rights movement. But the Progressive Era waned after the U.S. entered World War I. With its passing, the public enthusiasm for further efforts decreased, contributing to women's difficulty in the early 1920s to use their new political gain as an instrument for social change.

Just when women gained the vote, voter participation declined nationally. Fewer men and women were attuned to national political issues which, increasingly, were defined by special-interest groups and lobbies.

As Carrie Chapman Catt pointed out, in winning the vote reformers lost the single unifying cause that appealed to a broad constituency of women. The amalgam of the other reform causes tended to splinter the women's rights movement, because smaller communities of women were investing their energies across a larger field of competing programs.

American-born Nancy Langhorne Astor (Lady Astor), left, and Alice Robertson make an appearance at the National Press Club in Washington, D.C., in 1922. In 1919, Lady Astor became the first woman to serve as a Member of the British Parliament. Robertson, elected from an Oklahoma district to the U.S. House in 1920, was the second woman to serve in Congress.

IMAGE COURTESY OF THE LIBRARY OF CONGRESS

Cartoons from the early 20th century illustrate contrasting views on women's roles in American society. Above, a cartoon published in 1920, shortly after passage of the 19th Amendment, is titled "The Sky Is Now Her Limit." It depicts a woman carrying buckets on a yoke, looking up a ladder with rungs that ascend from "Slavery" and "House Drudgery" to "Highest Elective Offices" including Congress and the presidency. Below, a cartoon published in 1912 suggests an opposite outcome for women who leave the home and familial duties for careers and a greater role in public life.

IMAGES COURTESY OF THE LIBRARY OF CONGRESS

Women, contrary to the expectations of many on both sides of the suffrage debate, did not vote as a single, unified bloc. They split over party affiliation, key issues, and the vagaries of parochial politics. They also voted in far lower percentages than predicted. Finally, to the consternation of feminist reformers, they did not vote independently; instead, their voting preferences tended to mirror those of the men in their families.

Complicating these factors was the overarching reality that the political culture would take decades to adjust to the enfranchisement of women. The expectation was that women would be loyal followers under the banner of one or the other major party, with men charting the course. Emily N. Blair, a Missouri suffragist and the vice president of the Democratic National Committee (beginning in 1924) observed: "Women were welcome to come in as workers but not as co-makers of the world. For all their numbers, they seldom rose to positions of responsibility or power. The few who did fitted into the system as they found it. All standards, all methods, all values, continued to be set by men."[11] Carrie Chapman Catt made a similar assessment, noting that there was, at least in one sense, continuity between the suffrage struggle and the 1920s: women's marginalization. She noted that "the unwillingness to give women even a small share of the political positions which would enable them to score advantage to their ideals," was a condition all too familiar for "any old time suffragist."[12]

In Congress, particularly, the pioneer Congresswomen, with several notable exceptions, were far outside the party power structure. Not only did they face institutional prejudices, but many of them (nearly three-quarters of the first generation) were dependent on their husbands or their fathers for their positions. Moreover, these first women in Congress would not agree among themselves which form the political participation of American women should take: as public officeholders or as participants in nonpartisan reform groups?

Nevertheless, fortified by the constitutional victory of suffrage reformers in 1920, the handful of new women in Congress embarked on what would become a century-long odyssey to broaden women's role in government, so that in Catt's words, they might "score advantage to their ideals." The profiles in this book about these pioneer women Members and their successors relate the story of that odyssey during the course of the 20th century and into the 21st century.

EARLY CONGRESSWOMEN'S BACKGROUNDS

A majority of the early congressional women were born in the 1880s and 1890s and came of age during the Progressive Era. Culturally, the first generation of women in Congress had several commonalities. They were all white; the first non-Caucasian woman would not be elected until nearly half a century after Jeannette Rankin entered Congress. Most were raised Protestant, although there were several notable exceptions: including the first Catholic and the first Jewish women in Congress (Mae Nolan and Florence Kahn, respectively), who represented neighboring districts in San Francisco. Moreover, these women pioneers were exceedingly well-educated, partly because many came from well-to-do families that could afford private schooling and postsecondary education. Many were sent to elite finishing schools. More than half (13) attended university or college and several others graduated from trade schools. Before coming to Congress, many participated as volunteers and organizers in civic organizations and the social welfare endeavors typical of Progressive Era reformers. These activities included suffrage and electoral reform, missionary and education work, public health, nursing, veterans' affairs issues, legal aid, and childcare. Rankin, at age 36, was the youngest woman elected to Congress during this pioneer generation. Two other women, Mae Nolan of California and Katherine Langley of Kentucky, were in their late 30s as well. At the opposite end of the spectrum was 87-year-old Senator Rebecca Felton. The median age of the women elected to Congress through the mid-1930s was 50. (By contrast, the median age of the men entering Congress during the same period was about 46.)[13]

Few women could draw on previous electoral experience. Mary Norton (a New Jersey County freeholder), Ruth Baker Pratt (a New York City alderman), and Kathryn O'Loughlin McCarthy (a Kansas State representative), were the only women in this era who had held public office before they came to Congress. Several other women had prominent careers as lobbyists, activists, or party officials. Rankin was widely known as an advocate for suffrage reform and Edith Nourse Rogers was a national spokesperson for World War I veterans before she came to Congress. Perhaps the most qualified candidate was Ruth Hanna McCormick, a suffrage lobbyist and GOP official and the daughter of former Ohio Senator and Republican kingmaker Mark Hanna. In 1918, McCormick was appointed head of the newly created Republican Women's National Executive Committee (RWNEC). Initially she assured GOP men that women "do not want jobs, but want good men in office. They have come into politics with their knitting to stay." Subsequently McCormick worked to remove male oversight by the Republican National Executive Committee (RNEC) and secured the power for the RWNEC to make its own appointments. In 1919 she admonished male RNEC colleagues, saying "I marvel at the apprehension of some of you regarding our citizenship. . . . This is our country no less than yours, gentlemen."[14] However, extensive precongressional experience in politics or public affairs was the exception rather than the rule among this group of pioneers.

THE WIDOW AND FAMILIAL CONNECTIONS

More often than not, the pioneer women in Congress gained experience in public affairs as political confidantes and campaign surrogates for the Congressmen to whom they were married or otherwise related. Ironically, it was personal tragedy rather than a shared interest in reform that provided political entrée for most early women in Congress. Beginning with Representative Mae Nolan in 1923, eight of the women who followed Rankin into Congress between 1917 and 1934 were widows who succeeded their late husbands. None had held political office. Several, however, were among their husbands' most trusted political advisors, particularly Edith Nourse Rogers and Florence Prag Kahn.

So prevalent was the practice of wives succeeding husbands in this and later generations that the term "widow's mandate," or "widow's succession" was coined to explain it.[15] The prevailing expectation was that the women would serve briefly and provide a seamless transition by carrying forward the legislative business and district interests of their deceased husbands. Local party officials, especially in the one-party South, recruited widow candidates for reasons of political expediency: to

Left to right: Alice Robertson of Oklahoma, Mae Ella Nolan of California, and Winnifred Mason Huck of Illinois pose on the House entrance steps of the U.S. Capitol, February 15, 1923.

Winnifred Mason Huck of Illinois practices her golf game at the Potomac Park Links in Washington, D.C., in November 1922 with the Washington Monument in the background. Golf was an increasingly popular sport—driven partly by the success of its first bona fide U.S. superstar, Bobby Jones. Huck and later women in Congress took up the sport, in part, to interact with male colleagues who often used the links as an informal forum for transacting legislative business.

In this January 1926 photo, Congresswomen Florence Kahn of California (left) and Mary Norton of New Jersey flank Representative John P. Hill of Maryland. The three Members sought to modify the Volstead Act which enforced the 18th Amendment (ratified in 1919) that prohibited the manufacture, sale, and transportation of alcohol inside the United States, as well as its importation into the country. Prohibition ended with the repeal of the 18th Amendment in late 1933.

IMAGE COURTESY OF THE LIBRARY OF CONGRESS

hold the seat while awaiting a male successor or to avoid a protracted intraparty fight for an open seat. Media stereotypes reinforced this limited role. Marking the retirement of congressional widow Effiegene Wingo of Arkansas, the *New York Sun* reflected on the phenomenon of widow's succession. "Some of the women who have inherited a seat in Congress have demonstrated their individual ability," the *Sun* observed, "but of most of them it can be said that they submitted with dignity and good taste to a false code of chivalry, served unostentatiously and departed the Capitol quietly, wondering what the men who invented the term-by-inheritance thought they were doing."[16]

While most widows left Capitol Hill after filling out a brief, unexpired term, some, like Rogers, whose 35 years in the House make her the longest-serving congressional woman, enjoyed public careers that far eclipsed those of their male predecessors. Hattie Wyatt Caraway of Arkansas, too, rejected the convention that widows were mere placeholders. As the second woman appointed to the Senate and later elected to fill out the remaining 10 months of her husband's term, Caraway shocked the Arkansas political establishment in May 1932 when she announced her candidacy for a full term. "The time has passed when a woman should be placed in a position and kept there only while someone else is being groomed for the job," she told reporters en route to an election victory and a 12-year Senate career.[17]

Another dimension to this phenomenon, may be described more properly as the familial connection. Four women from this era drew upon the experience of fathers who were established politicians (Winnifred Huck, Ruth Bryan Owen, McCormick, and McCarthy). Huck directly succeeded her late father with no experience in elective politics. In still another twist on the familial connection, Katherine Langley won a special election to succeed her husband, Kentucky Representative John Wesley Langley, after he was convicted and sent to prison for violating Prohibition. All told, 14 of these 20 pioneers drew upon precongressional experience as the wives or daughters of officeholders.

MEDIA CURIOSITIES

By virtue of their gender, the earliest women in Congress were media celebrities: chronicled, quoted, and scrutinized. Perhaps none received more attention than Rankin, whose 1916 election catapulted her into the national spotlight. Manufacturing companies sought her endorsement; cranks sent offers of marriage. She received an unusually large amount of visitors and mail—by one account, 300 letters daily.[18] These demands required her to hire three secretaries to join her in her one-room office.[19] Rankin agreed to write a monthly column for Chicago's *Sunday Herald*, and she signed a lucrative contract ($500 per lecture) with a New York speakers bureau. "To be suddenly thrown into so much limelight was a great shock," Rankin recalled. "It was very hard for me to understand, to realize that it made a difference what I did and didn't do from then on."[20]

An eager press corps soon pegged Alice Mary Robertson of Oklahoma, the second woman in Congress, as a font of colorful quotes. Shortly before assuming office in 1921, Robertson told a reporter that she intended to be a model House freshman: fastidious and silent. "I would rather be like a humble little light that shines a long distance across the prairies than a brilliant sky rocket that flashes in midair for a few seconds and then falls to the earth with a dull thud," Robertson said. "If people think that I am going to do something sensational they are mistaken. I am a conservative. The platform upon which I was elected is: 'I am a Christian. I am an American. I am a Republican.'" But her propensity to speak her mind made "Miss Alice" the object of intense press coverage. The matronly Congresswoman later declared that Members who wasted taxpayers' money with verbose speeches and parliamentary stalling tactics ought to be "spanked good and plenty."[21]

Other women were thrust into the spotlight as the offspring of prominent political families. The *New York Times* and the *Washington Post* ran lengthy feature stories on two famous daughters whose fathers were avowed political enemies: Ruth Bryan Owen (a daughter of Democratic giant William Jennings Bryan) and Ruth McCormick (the daughter of Mark Hanna). During her 1928 campaign, McCormick became the first woman featured on the cover of *Time* magazine.[22] Before an adoring press gallery, Owen and McCormick entered the House arm in arm on April 15, 1929, the first day of the 71st Congress (1929–1931), and were sworn in as new Representatives.[23]

Those uncomfortable with Washington social circles or reticent about the media glare received less charitable press coverage, which often focused on a Member's mannerisms, attire, and physical attributes rather than on substantive legislative issues. Katherine Langley was singled out for her flamboyance. "She offends the squeamish by her unstinted display of gypsy colors on the floor and the conspicuousness with which she dresses her bushy blue-black hair," wrote one reporter.[24] Representative Mae Nolan complained that she was regularly misquoted and misrepresented. The press took unmerciful delight in noting that she had taken up golf in her quest for a slimmer figure. Gradually, Congresswoman Nolan withdrew from the spotlight, eventually shunning floor speeches, lobbyists, and especially, journalists. When she retired after a brief House career, the *Washington Post* declared "in Congress 2 years, she did no 'talking.'"[25]

LEGISLATIVE INTERESTS AND ACHIEVEMENTS

The majority of the early women Members legislated in areas deemed by their society to be gender-appropriate; women were viewed as caregivers, educators, and consumers. The pioneer women in Congress were scattered across more than 30 committees, most of which ranked as lower-tier panels. Not surprisingly, the largest number of House women (five) served on the Committee on Woman Suffrage before it was disbanded in December 1927. Other assignments given to women Members included seats on committees like Education (four); World War Veterans' Legislation (four); Civil Service (four); Public Buildings and Grounds (four); and Indian Affairs (three).

There were exceptions to this trend. Several women obtained posts on upper-tier committees like Appropriations (Kahn), Naval Affairs (McCormick), Banking and Currency (Pratt), Irrigation and Reclamation (Greenway), and Foreign Affairs (Owen, Rogers, and Wingo).[26] Two women, Mae Ella Nolan and Mary Norton, chaired House committees during this period—Expenditures in the Post Office and District of Columbia, respectively. In the Senate, Hattie Caraway served on two important panels, Agriculture and Forestry and Commerce (eventually rising to second-ranking majority Member on the latter). From the 73rd Congress (1933–1935) through the 78th Congress (1943–1945), Caraway also chaired the

Margaret Speaks, daughter of Representative John C. Speaks of Ohio, sells peanuts to Representative Edith N. Rogers of Massachusetts and Massachusetts Senator Frederick H. Gillett (former Speaker of the House) at the 1926 baseball game between congressional Democrats and Republicans.

IMAGE COURTESY OF THE LIBRARY OF CONGRESS

Kathryn O'Loughlin McCarthy of Kansas and her husband, Daniel McCarthy, wed shortly after Kathryn was sworn into Congress in early 1933. She met Daniel, a newly elected Kansas state senator, on the campaign trail in 1932. He had initially opposed women holding public office. "I want it understood that I am not out of politics," Congresswoman McCarthy declared on her wedding day. "I consider marriage an asset and not a liability in the political field."

IMAGE COURTESY OF THE ELLIS COUNTY (KS) HISTORICAL SOCIETY

"There are hundreds of men to care for the nation's tariff and foreign policy and irrigation projects. But there isn't a single woman to look after the nation's greatest asset: its children."

—JEANNETTE RANKIN

Enrolled Bills Committee, a minor panel that ensured that the text of bills passed by the House and Senate was identical and was delivered to the White House for the President's signature.

From their earliest days in Congress, women's legislative interests were not monolithic. Members' agendas derived from unique political beliefs, personal ideologies, and constituencies, all of which shaped the contours of their legislative efforts. From her Appropriations seat, Florence Kahn won funding for two major Bay Area projects—the Golden Gate Bridge and the Bay Bridge and helped build up local military installations. Edith Rogers, as chair of the hospitals subcommittee of the World War Veterans' Legislation Committee, procured millions in funding for a national network of veterans' hospitals. Ruth Owen authored legislation to combat the fruit fly, which threatened agricultural interests in her Florida district. From her seat on the Foreign Relations Committee, Owen promoted American participation in international conferences; at the outset of the Great Depression, she advocated the creation of a Cabinet-level department to oversee the health and welfare of families and children—a "Department of Home and Child." Even Rankin, while focusing in her first term on woman suffrage, tended to the needs of miners in her district from her seat on Public Lands.

Congressional women did not vote as a bloc or always agree on the viability of legislation and programs that directly affected their gender as illustrated by the stark differences between the first and second women in Congress (Rankin and Robertson). Rankin, former secretary of the NAWSA, focused on issues affecting women and children. "There are hundreds of men to care for the nation's tariff and foreign policy and irrigation projects," she told voters on the campaign trail. "But there isn't a single woman to look after the nation's greatest asset: its children."[27] Once in the House, she worked to pass a constitutional amendment for the vote in Congress and also sponsored a bill to create an education program on women's health. That legislation came before the House several years later as part of the Sheppard–Towner Maternal and Infancy Act, which allocated $1.25 million annually in federal money for prenatal, maternal, and infant health care education through public health nurses supervised by the Children's Bureau. This marked one of the earliest efforts in U.S. history to secure federal funding social welfare.[28]

Robertson was the only woman in Congress when the Sheppard–Towner legislation was introduced in May 1921. A disciple of limited federal government, she refused to endorse it. She was also an avowed foe of the powerful lobbying groups that backed the measure, namely the League of Women Voters (the NAWSA's incarnation after 1920) and the National Woman's Party (NWP). Congresswoman Robertson denounced the bill as an intrusion into women's private lives. Nevertheless, Sheppard–Towner was signed into law on November 23, 1921, demonstrating the lobbying power and public relations savvy of women's groups while highlighting the glaring lack of women's power within Congress. "If Members could have voted in the cloakroom it would have been killed," recalled a male Representative.[29]

In fact, the legislation that most affected women in the 1920s was won primarily by the organized lobbying of voluntary associations when very few women were in Congress. The Cable Act of 1922 granted married women U.S. citizenship independent of their husband's status, and provided citizenship protection for women who married aliens or who gained U.S. citizenship by marrying an American citizen. The Lehlbach Act of 1923 improved the merit system of the civil service, making it easier for women to secure federal jobs. After intense lobbying by women's groups, Congress passed the Child Labor Amendment to the Constitution on June 2, 1924, which sought to achieve national uniformity for child labor standards. This amendment would have given Congress the power "to limit, regulate, and prohibit the labor of persons under 18 years of age," had it been subsequently ratified by the states. Finally, in 1923, the NWP pushed for and won the introduction of the Equal Rights Amendment on the 75th Anniversary of the Seneca Falls (NY) Convention of women reformers. The measure was reintroduced scores of times in subsequent Congresses but it languished in committee for nearly 50 years. In the interwar years, no woman Member publicly aligned herself with it both because it was perceived as a threat to existing labor protections for women and because of mistrust of the NWP and its militant tactics.[30]

Several major public policy issues recur in these profiles. One was the debate about Prohibition, the federal ban on alcohol. Congress passed the 18th Amendment in December 1917, prohibiting the manufacture, sale, or transportation of intoxicating liquor within or into the United States. The states ratified the amendment in January 1919. The passage of the Volstead Act later that October over a presidential veto provided the mechanism that enforced the amendment. Lauded by "dry" temperance advocates and derided by "wet" opponents, Prohibition proved a divisive and ultimately unsuccessful attempt to regulate morality through federal legislation. It was eventually repealed in 1933 by the 21st Amendment.

For the women in Congress during this initial period, Prohibition was a significant issue. Women had played a prominent role as temperance reformers and agitators, since the early part of the 19th century. Among the best-known was the leader of the WCTU, Frances Willard, who wielded tremendous influence in the late 1800s as a key congressional lobbyist for Prohibition.[31] None of the early women in Congress were as strident. Most addressed Prohibition in one of two arenas, either on the campaign trail or in legislative initiatives. They were evenly divided over the issue. Among its supporters were Rogers, Owen, Oldfield, and

The women of the 71st Congress (1929–1931) pose on the Capitol steps. From left to right they are: (front row) Pearl Oldfield of Arkansas, Edith Nourse Rogers of Massachusetts, Ruth Baker Pratt of New York, and Ruth Hanna McCormick of Illinois; (back row) Ruth Bryan Owen of Florida, Mary Norton of New Jersey, and Florence Kahn of California.

IMAGE COURTESY OF THE LIBRARY OF CONGRESS

New Yorkers queue up in a bread line near the intersection of Sixth Avenue and 42nd Street in New York City in 1932 during the depths of the Great Depression. One in four American workers were unemployed as a result of the prolonged economic crisis.

IMAGE COURTESY OF THE FDR LIBRARY/NATION-

AL ARCHIVES AND RECORDS ADMINISTRATION

McCormick. Rogers's "dry" position was an important factor in her initial special election. Owen's Florida constituents turned her out of office in 1932 when she was reluctant to support legislation repealing Prohibition. Opposition to Prohibition became politically more expedient in the early 1930s, when the focus on the debate shifted from morality to economics. Mary Norton offered the first bill to repeal Prohibition laws. Congresswomen Pratt, Jenckes, and McCarthy also supported efforts to repeal the Volstead Act, arguing that this action might help revive the flagging economy. Jenckes and McCarthy, who hailed from agricultural districts, argued that renewed production of grain-based spirits would benefit farmers.

Another issue that affected women Members during this era was the decade-long argument concerning the payment of a bonus to World War I veterans. The American Legion lobbied Congress shortly after the First World War to fund a bonus for servicemen to compensate them for the wages they lost when they left higher-paying civilian jobs to serve in uniform. Congress approved a bonus in 1922, but the bill was vetoed by President Warren Harding. In May 1924, over the veto of President Calvin Coolidge, Congress passed the Soldiers Bonus Act, which provided veterans a bonus of $1.25 for each day of overseas duty and $1 for each day of domestic service—payable in 1945.

Veterans could borrow up to 25 percent of their total bonus amount from a fund created by the bill.[32] By the early 1930s, with the country mired in a devastating depression, veterans organized a march on Washington, D.C., to demand immediate payment of the bonus. The Bonus March on the capital in 1932 involved thousands of protesters and their families who set up camp in the Anacostia Flats, a short distance from the U.S. Capitol. In June 1932, the House approved the bonus bill but the Senate rejected it. Protesters who remained afterward were forcibly ejected by army troops, who used tanks and tear gas to disperse them.

Care for the welfare of servicemen was another arena in which women were widely recognized as experts, because of the development of a large female nursing corps in the years during and after the Civil War.[33] Women Members used that authority to weigh in on both sides of this debate. Congresswoman Robertson, an ally of servicemen during World War I, voted against the first Bonus Bill in 1922, angering so many constituents that they turned her out of office the following year. Congresswoman Nolan was an early advocate of a bonus and challenged the Coolidge administration to make it a higher priority than tax cuts for the wealthy. Willa Eslick of Tennessee was watching from the House Gallery in June 1932 when her husband, Edward, collapsed and died of a heart attack in an impassioned speech supporting the Bonus Bill. At the urging of local servicemen, Eslick ran for her late husband's seat and won election to a brief term, which she dedicated to his legislative

30 ★ WOMEN IN CONGRESS

agenda. Isabella Greenway of Arizona, long a patron of veterans, helped renew the debate for a bonus payment after she was elected to Congress in 1933. Greenway was an ally of Franklin and Eleanor Roosevelt, but her relations with the administration eventually cooled when the President's Economy Act of 1933 called for cuts to servicemen's pensions and denied a proposed $2 billion bonus.

The debates over Prohibition and the soldiers' bonus ultimately culminated with the onset of yet another challenge confronting women in Congress during this period, the Great Depression. The stock market crash in October 1929, preceded by years of rampant stock speculation and ineffectual federal regulatory policies spread economic ruin throughout the country. Investors' mounting losses, sharply lower consumer spending, plummeting agricultural prices, and widespread runs on banks sent the economy into a three-year skid. By the winter of 1932–1933, more than 5,500 banks had been shut down, nearly one in four Americans was unemployed, and the gross national product had declined by nearly a third.[34]

The Great Depression decisively influenced the careers of congressional women. For Republicans, it proved disastrous. In 1930, Ruth McCormick's bid for the U.S. Senate was undercut by growing disillusionment with the Herbert Hoover administration's policies for economic recovery. Two years later, Ruth Pratt fell victim to a similar trend when she lost her Manhattan House seat. A trio of Democratic Arkansas widows—Oldfield, Wingo, and Caraway—focused on relief for their agricultural constituencies through a variety of federal measures. Democrats Kathryn O'Loughlin McCarthy and Virginia Jenckes were elected from traditionally Republican districts in 1932 by agricultural constituencies desperate for federal relief. Isabella Greenway of Arizona campaigned partly on her cachet as a friend of the Roosevelt family and partly on her ability to translate that influence into public works jobs for Arizonans. But even for Democratic supporters of the New Deal there were perils and disagreements. Kansas farmers revolted against the Agricultural Adjustment Act, a cornerstone of the early New Deal, and voted McCarthy out of office after only one term. While Congresswomen Jenckes and Greenway supported emergency government programs to prime the economic pump, they were much more skeptical about later New Deal programs that sought to establish a social welfare system including unemployment insurance and old-age pensions.

Crafting an Identity

The passage of the 19th Amendment in 1920 marked a great divide in the women's rights movement in America. A central "paradox of change" for newly enfranchised women was embedded in the suffrage movement itself. Some reformers had sought to liberate women by making them politically equal to men, whereas others fought for the vote believing that women's interests were inherently different from men's, requiring special advocacy that could not be co-opted by existing institutions.[35] This central question, in one form or another, remained unresolved through much of the 20th century and has persisted throughout the history of women in Congress. Did women's historical underrepresentation give these pioneer Congresswomen the responsibility to advocate for all women, even for those beyond the prescribed borders of their districts or states, or could they best promote women's political advancement by eschewing a narrow set of "women's issues"?

Congresswomen in this era favored the latter choice and tended to limit their support to legislation that addressed issues affecting women within the context of their traditional roles as wives, mothers, and dependents.[36] Ruth Baker Pratt of New York refused to champion women's special interests in Congress and, on one occasion, proclaimed that "sex had no place whatever in politics."[37] Nevertheless, she used her profile to urge women to participate in local politics. Pearl Oldfield, the widow of a powerful Arkansas Congressman, agreed with Pratt's assessment. After serving two years in the House, she retired, telling the *New York Times*, "No one should seek or expect public office simply because of her sex, but she has an equal right to appeal to the voters for support on the basis of her comparative ability to render public service."[38] The press reinforced these views. The *Washington Post* celebrated Ruth McCormick's 1930 Senate bid because the Congresswoman "made a straightforward fight for the nomination without appealing for support on the ground that women are entitled to representation. If she wins, it will be on her own merit. If she should lose, she would nevertheless be credited with the most remarkable campaign ever conducted by a woman."[39]

Mary Norton, adept at navigating toward power within the institution, captured that spirit most succinctly when she rebuffed a male colleague who deferred to her as a "lady" during a debate. "I'm no lady, I'm a Member of Congress," Norton replied, "and I'll proceed on that basis." Her remark encapsulated the belief shared by most of her female contemporaries on the Hill—Democrat and Republican—that the surest way for women to attain power and influence in Congress was to work within the prescribed system to mitigate gender differences. That belief would be subsequently reevaluated and challenged.

NOTES

1   Standard biographies of these two women include Lois W. Banner, *Elizabeth Cady Stanton: A Radical for Women's Rights* (Boston: Little, Brown, and Company, 1980); and Margaret Hope Bacon, *Valiant Friend: The Life of Lucretia Mott* (New York: Walker Publishing, 1980).

2   For more on the convention at Seneca Falls, its participants, and the larger movement it spawned, see Ellen DuBois, *Feminism and Suffrage: The Emergence of an Independent Women's Movement in the U.S., 1848-1869* (Ithaca, NY: Cornell University Press, 1978). For an overview of the period from the Civil War through 1920, see Nancy Woloch, *Women and the American Experience,* 2nd ed. (New York: McGraw-Hill, Inc., 1994): especially 326–363.

3   See, for example, DuBois, *Feminism and Suffrage:* 21–52; Woloch, *Women and the American Experience:* 327.

4   For more on Lucy Stone, see Andrea Moore Kerr, *Lucy Stone: Speaking Out for Equality* (New Brunswick, NJ: Rutgers University Press, 1992).

5   Woloch, *Women and the American Experience:* quotes from 328; see also 329–336.

6   Woloch, *Women and the American Experience:* 334–335.

7   For more on Alice Paul and the National Woman's Party, see Inez Haynes Gillmore, *Up Hill with Banners Flying* (Penobscott, ME: Traversity Press, 1964).

8   For a biography of Catt, see Robert Booth Fowler, *Carrie Catt: Feminist Politician* (Boston: Northeastern University Press, 1986).

9   Woloch, *Women and the American Experience:* 353.

10 Historians debate this point vigorously. William L. O'Neill, in his *Feminism in America: A History* 2nd revised ed. (New Brunswick, NJ: Rutgers University Press, 1989), argues that feminists themselves were responsible for the failure to mobilize women voters in the 1920s. O'Neill believes that the decision taken in the 19th century to focus on the vote to the exclusion of other "social" issues ultimately undermined feminist reform efforts 1) prolonging the suffrage struggle and 2) depriving the movement of cohesiveness after the ratification of the 19th Amendment in 1920. Nancy Cott, in *The Grounding of Modern Feminism* (New Haven, CT: Yale University Press, 1988), challenged O'Neill's assertions about the shortcomings of the feminist movement, insisting in part that though the movement struggled in the arena of electoral politics after 1920, it flourished among a host of new volunteer and civic women's

organizations. In this regard, Cott sees more continuity between the pre- and post-1920 eras than does either O'Neill or William Chafe, in *The Paradox of Change: American Women in the 20th Century* (New York: Oxford University Press, 1991). Both O'Neill and Chafe stress discontinuity, particularly Chafe, who suggests that women "were caught in a no-win situation" because a shift away from mass political participation had devalued the importance of the ballot. "It appears that the entire political culture was shifting, and even though supposed progress had been made in democratizing the electoral process during the 1910s through direct election of senators, the initiative, referendum and reform, direct primaries, and woman suffrage, the actual value of casting votes at the ballot box had diminished substantially." See Chafe's discussion, *The Paradox of Change*: 31.

11 Quoted in Woloch, *Women and the American Experience*: 357.

12 Quoted in Melanie Gustafson, *Women and the Republican Party, 1854–1924* (Urbana: University of Illinois Press, 2003): 194.

13 Allan G. Borgue, Jerome M. Clubb, Carroll R. McKibbin, and Santa A. Traugott, "Members of the House of Representatives and the Processes of Modernization, 1789–1960," *Journal of American History*, 63 (September 1976): 275–302; figures on 291. Roughly 30 percent of men, however, were elected in their 30s.

14 Gustafson, *Women and the Republican Party, 1854–1924*: 179–180; see also Kristie Miller, *Ruth Hanna McCormick: A Life in Politics, 1880–1944* (Albuquerque: University of New Mexico Press, 1994).

15 The importance of the widow's mandate is discussed in the introduction to this book. For a full treatment of this phenomenon, see Irwin N. Gertzog, *Congressional Women: Their Recruitment, Integration, and Behavior* (Westport, CT: Praeger, 1995): 17–36.

16 "Pro and Con," 18 June 1932, *Washington Post*: 6.

17 Susan M. Hartmann, "Caraway, Hattie Ophelia," *American National Biography* Vol. 4 (New York: Oxford University Press, 1999): 369–370.

18 Norma Smith, *Jeannette Rankin: America's Conscience* (Helena: Montana Historical Society, 2002): 115.

19 Smith, *Jeannette Rankin*: 115. The House Office Building had been opened in 1908 and was meant to accommodate all House Members and committees. By and large, each Member was assigned a one-room office.

20 Quoted in Smith, *Jeannette Rankin*: 104; see also, Hannah Josephson, *Jeannette Rankin, First Lady In Congress—A Biography* (Indianapolis, IN: Bobbs-Merrill, 1974): 57. A highly unusual feature of the lecture contract was that if she voted against a war resolution, the contract could be terminated. Josephson, *Jeannette Rankin*: 62–63; 67.

21 "'Miss Alice' To Be Meek in Congress," 26 February 1921, *Washington Post*: 10; "Spankings to Silence Talkative In House Advocated by Miss Alice," 5 March 1923, *Washington Post*: 4.

22 Miller, *Ruth Hanna McCormick: A Life in Politics*: 193. McCormick appeared in the 23 April 1928 edition, weeks after her Illinois primary victory. Senator Margaret Chase Smith appeared on a *Time* cover in 1959, marking the 40th anniversary of the suffrage amendment .

23 Winifred Mallon, "Another Hanna Looks to the Senate," 9 June 1929, *New York Times*: SM4.

24 Hope Chamberlin, *A Minority of Members: Women in the U.S. Congress* (New York: Praeger, 1973): 64.

25 Constance Drexel, "Mrs. Nolan No 'Crusader'; Mrs. Barrett Gains Note," 24 February 1924, *Washington Post*: ES 3; "In Congress 2 Years, She Did No 'Talking,'" 5 March 1925, *Washington Post*: 9.

26 For committee attractiveness during this period, see Charles Stewart III, "Committee Hierarchies in the Modernizing House, 1875–1947," *American Journal of Political Science* 36 (No. 4, November 1992): 835–856.

27 Smith, *Jeannette Rankin*: 102.

28 Theda Skocpol, *Protecting Soldiers and Mothers: The Political Origins of Social Policy in the United States* (Cambridge, MA: The Belknap Press of Harvard University Press, 1992): especially 494–522.

29 Quoted in Chafe, *The Paradox of Change*. 27.

30 Gertzog, *Congressional Women*: 148–152.

31 For more on temperance and Prohibition, see Ruth Bordin's *Woman and Temperance: The Quest for Power and Liberty, 1873–1900* (New Brunswick, NJ: Rutgers University Press, 1990) and Thomas R. Pegram, *Battling Demon Rum: The Struggle for a Dry America, 1800–1933* (Chicago: Ivan R. Dee Publishers, 1998).

32 Steven Stathis, *Landmark Legislation, 1774–2002* (Washington, D.C.: Congressional Quarterly Press, 2003): 185–186.

33 See, for example, Susan M. Reverby, *Ordered to Care: The Dilemma of American Nursing, 1850–1945* (New York: Cambridge University Press, 1987).

34 For a thorough treatment of the Great Depression era, see David M. Kennedy, *Freedom From Fear* (New York: Oxford, 2004).

35 Chafe, *The Paradox of Change*: 23.

36 Gertzog, *Congressional Women*: 148.

37 Chamberlin, *A Minority of Members*: 78.

38 "Mrs. Oldfield Decries Feminist in Politics," 19 February 1931, *New York Times*: 3.

39 "Ruth McCormick," 10 April 1930, *Washington Post*: 6.

VISUAL STATISTICS 11

Congressional Service[1]

This timeline depicts the span of congressional service for women first sworn-in between 1917 and 1934.

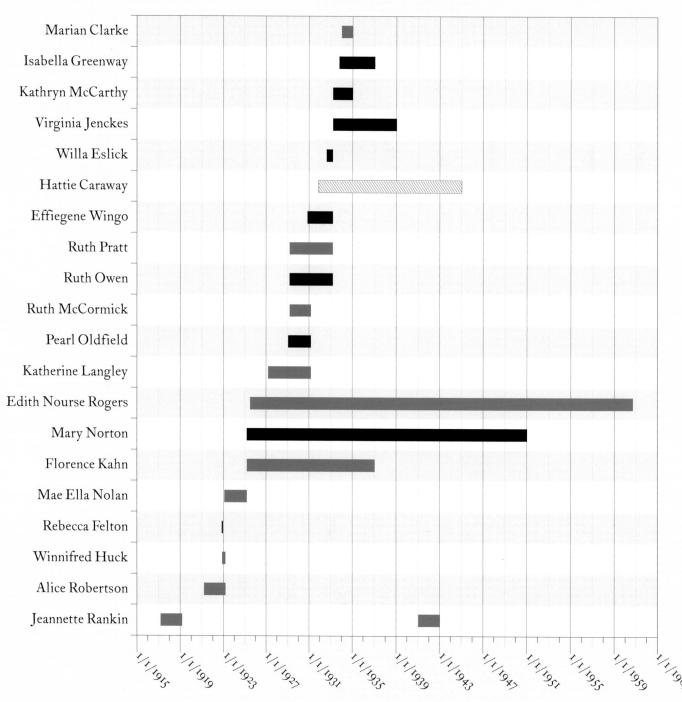

1. Source: *Biographical Directory of the United States Congress, 1774–2005* (Washington D.C.: Government Printing Office, 2005); also available at http://bioguide.congress.gov.

House and Senate Party Affiliation[2]

65TH–73RD CONGRESSES
(1917–1935)

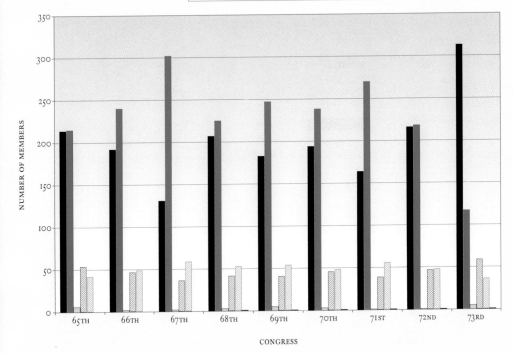

This chart depicts the party affiliation of all Members of Congress from 1917 to 1935. The following chart depicts a party breakdown only for women Members during this time period.

Party Affiliation: Women in Congress

65TH–73RD CONGRESSES (1917–1935)

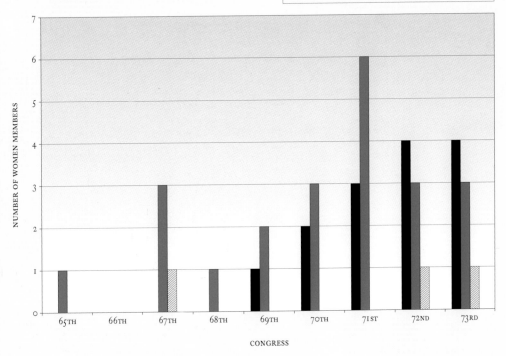

2. House numbers do not include Delegates or Resident Commissioners. Sources: Office of the Clerk, U.S. House of Representatives; U.S. Senate Historical Office.

Jeannette Rankin
1880–1973

UNITED STATES REPRESENTATIVE ★ REPUBLICAN FROM MONTANA
1917–1919, 1941–1943

Jeannette Rankin's life was filled with extraordinary achievements: she was the first woman elected to Congress, one of the few suffragists elected to Congress, and the only Member of Congress to vote against U.S. participation in both World War I and World War II. "I may be the first woman member of Congress," she observed upon her election in 1916. "But I won't be the last."[1]

Jeannette Rankin, the eldest daughter of a rancher and a schoolteacher, was born near Missoula, Montana, on June 11, 1880. She graduated from Montana State University (now the University of Montana) in 1902 and attended the New York School of Philanthropy (later the Columbia University School of Social Work). After a brief period as a social worker in Spokane, Washington, Rankin entered the University of Washington in Seattle. It was there that she joined the woman suffrage movement, a campaign that achieved its goal in Washington State in 1910. Rankin became a professional lobbyist for the National American Woman Suffrage Association (NAWSA). Her speaking and organizing efforts helped Montana women gain the vote in 1914.

When Rankin decided in 1916 to run for a House seat from Montana, she had two key advantages: her reputation as a suffragist and her politically well-connected brother, Wellington, who financed her campaign. Some national woman suffrage leaders feared she would lose and hurt the cause. The novelty of a woman running for Congress, however, helped Rankin secure a GOP nomination for one of Montana's two At-Large House seats on August 29, 1916.[2] Rankin ran as a progressive, pledging to work for a constitutional woman suffrage amendment and emphasizing social welfare issues. Long a committed pacifist, she did not shy away from letting voters know how she felt about possible U.S. participation in the European war that had been raging for two years: "If they are going to have war, they ought to take the old men and leave the young to propagate the race."[3] Rankin came in second, winning one of Montana's seats. She trailed the frontrunner, Democratic Representative John M. Evans, by 7,600 votes, but she topped the next candidate—another Democrat—by 6,000 votes. Rankin ran a nonpartisan campaign in a Democratic state during a period of national hostility toward parties in general. And this was the first opportunity for Montana women to vote in a federal election. "I am deeply conscious of the responsibility resting upon me," read her public victory statement.[4]

Rankin's service began dramatically when Congress was called into an extraordinary April session after Germany declared unrestricted submarine warfare on all Atlantic shipping. On April 2, 1917, she arrived at the Capitol to be sworn in along with the other Members of the 65th Congress (1917–1919).[5] Escorted by her Montana colleague, Rankin looked like "a mature bride rather than a strong-minded female," an observer wrote, ".... When her name was called the House cheered and rose, so that she had to rise and bow twice, which she did with entire self-possession."[6]

That evening, Congress met in Joint Session to hear President Woodrow Wilson ask to "make the world safe for democracy" by declaring war on Germany. The House debated the war resolution on April 5th. Given Rankin's strong pacifist views, she was inclined against war. Colleagues in the suffrage movement urged caution, fearing that a vote against war would tarnish the entire cause. Rankin sat out the debate over war, a decision she later regretted.[7] She inadvertently violated House rules by making a brief speech when casting her vote. "I want to stand by my country, but I cannot vote for war," she told the House. "I vote no."[8] The final vote was 374 for the war resolution and 50 against. The Helena *Independent* likened her to "a dagger in the hands of the German propagandists, a dupe of the Kaiser, a member of the Hun army in the United States, and a crying schoolgirl"—even though Montana mail to Rankin's office ran against U.S. intervention.[9] NAWSA distanced the suffrage movement from Rankin: "Miss Rankin was not voting for the suffragists of the nation—she represents Montana."[10] Others, such as Representative Fiorello LaGuardia of New York, were quick to defend her.[11]

As the first woman Member, Rankin was on the front-lines of the national suffrage fight. During the fall of 1917 she advocated the creation of a Committee on Woman Suffrage, and when it was created she was appointed to it.[12] When the special committee reported out a constitutional amendment on woman suffrage in January 1918, Rankin opened the very first House Floor debate on this subject.[13] "How shall we answer the challenge, gentlemen?" she asked. "How shall we explain to them the meaning of democracy if the same Congress that voted to make the world safe for democracy refuses to give this small measure of democracy to the women of our country?"[14] The resolution narrowly passed the House amid the cheers of women in the galleries, but it died in the Senate.[15]

Rankin did not ignore her Montana constituency in the midst of this activity. She was assigned to the Committee on Public Lands, which was concerned with western issues. When a mine disaster in Butte resulted in a massive protest strike by miners over their working conditions, violence soon broke out. Responding to pleas from more-moderate miner unions, Rankin unsuccessfully sought help from the Wilson administration through legislation and through her personal intervention in the crisis. These efforts failed as the mining companies refused to meet with either her or the miners.[16] Rankin expected the mining interests to extract a cost for her support of the striking miners. "They own the State," she noted. "They own the

Government. They own the press."[17]

Prior to the 1918 election, the Montana state legislature passed legislation replacing the state's two At-Large seats with two separate districts, and Rankin found herself in the overwhelmingly Democratic western district.[18] Faced with the possibility of running against an incumbent or running in a district controlled by the other party, she decided to run for the U.S. Senate. Rankin ran on the slogan "Win the War First," promising to support the Wilson administration "to more efficiently prosecute the war."[19] In a three-way contest, Rankin came in second in the Republican senatorial primary, less than 2,000 votes behind the winner.[20]

Charges that Republicans were bribing her to withdraw compelled her to undertake what she knew was an impossible task—running in the general election on a third-party ticket. "Bribes are not offered in such a way that you can prove them, and in order to prove that I didn't accept a bribe I had to run," she would later recall.[21] The incumbent, Democratic Senator Thomas Walsh, did not underestimate Rankin: "If Miss R. had any party to back her she would be dangerous."[22] In the end, Rankin finished third, winning a fifth of the total votes cast, while Walsh won re-election with a plurality. Ironically, the Republican candidate for Rankin's House district narrowly won.[23]

Afterwards, Rankin divided her time between pacifism and social welfare. She attended the Women's International Conference for Permanent Peace in Switzerland in 1919 and joined the Women's International League for Peace and Freedom. In 1928, she founded the Georgia Peace Society after purchasing a farm in that state. Rankin became the leading lobbyist and speaker for the National Council for the Prevention of War from 1929 to 1939. She also remained active in advocating social welfare programs. During the early 1920s she was a field secretary for the National Consumers' League. Rankin's activities largely consisted of lobbying Congress to pass social welfare legislation, such as the Sheppard–Towner bill and a constitutional amendment banning child labor.

It was the looming war crisis in 1940 that brought Rankin back to Congress. She returned to Montana with her eye on the western House district held by first-term Republican Representative Jacob Thorkelson—an outspoken anti-Semite.[24] Rankin drew on her status as the first woman elected to Congress to speak throughout the district to high school students on the issue of war and peace. When the Republican primary results were in, Rankin defeated three candidates, including the incumbent.[25] In the general election, she faced Jerry J. O'Connell, who had been ousted by Thorkelson from Congress in the previous election. Rankin went into the race confident that

out. In this raging debate, Rankin had taken an arms-length attitude towards the leading isolationist group, the America First Committee. Largely made up of opponents to the New Deal policies of Franklin Roosevelt, Rankin found herself out of sympathy with much of their domestic agenda.[30]

Nevertheless, Rankin made her pacifist views known early in the session. During deliberations over the Lend-Lease Bill to supply the Allied war effort, she offered an unsuccessful amendment in February 1941 requiring

"How shall we answer the challenge, gentlemen? How shall we explain to them the meaning of democracy if the same Congress that voted to make the world safe for democracy refuses to give this small measure of democracy to the women of our country?"

—JEANNETTE RANKIN, FIRST HOUSE FLOOR DEBATE ON WOMAN SUFFRAGE, JANUARY 1918

the mining industry no longer carried the hefty political influence she faced earlier.[26] Eminent Progressives endorsed her: Senator Robert M. LaFollette, Jr., of Wisconsin and Mayor Fiorello LaGuardia of New York City.[27] On election day Rankin won re-election to the House with 54 percent of the votes cast for a second term—just less than a quarter of a century after she was elected to her first term.[28] "No one will pay any attention to me this time," the victor predicted. "There is nothing unusual about a woman being elected."[29]

As it had 24 years earlier, the threat of war dominated the start of Rankin's new term. She gained appointments to the Committee on Public Lands and the Committee on Insular Affairs, two lower-tier committees that, nevertheless, proved useful to her western constituency. By the time of Rankin's election, the war in Europe was in full force and a debate about U.S. involvement had broken

specific congressional approval for sending U.S. troops abroad. "If Britain needs our material today," she asked, "will she later need our men?"[31] In May she introduced a resolution condemning any effort "to send the armed forces of the United States to fight in any place outside the Western Hemisphere or insular possessions of the United States."[32] She repeated her request the following month to no avail. That Rankin's stance was not an unusual one was demonstrated by the close margin granting President Franklin Roosevelt's request to allow American merchant ships to be armed in the fall of 1941.[33]

Rankin was en route to Detroit on a speaking engagement when she heard of the attack on Pearl Harbor by the Japanese. She returned to Washington the next morning, determined to oppose U.S. participation in the war.[34] Immediately after President Roosevelt addressed a Joint Session of Congress, the House and Senate met to deliberate on a declaration of war. Rankin repeatedly tried to gain recognition once the first reading of the war resolution was completed in the House. In the brief debate on the resolution, Speaker Sam Rayburn of Texas refused to recognize her and declared her out of order. Other Members called for her to sit down. Others approached her on the House Floor, trying to convince her to either vote for the war or abstain.[35] When the roll call vote was taken, Rankin voted "No" amid what the Associated Press described as "a chorus of hisses and boos."[36] Rankin went on to announce, "As a woman I can't go to war, and I refuse to send anyone else."[37] The war resolution passed the House 388–1.

Condemnation of her stand was immediate and intense, forcing Rankin briefly to huddle in a phone booth before receiving a police escort to her office.[38] "I voted my convictions and redeemed my campaign pledges," she told her constituents.[39] "Montana is 100 percent against you," wired her brother Wellington.[40] In private, she told friends "I have nothing left but my integrity."[41] The vote essentially made the rest of Rankin's term irrelevant. Having made her point, she only voted "present" when the House declared war on Germany and Italy.[42] She found that her colleagues and the press simply ignored her. She chose not to run for re-election in 1942, and her district replaced the isolationist Republican with an internationalist Democrat who had served in three branches of the military, Mike Mansfield.

Rankin continued to divide her time between Montana and Georgia in the years after she left Congress. India became one of her favorite excursions; she was drawn by the nonviolent protest tactics of Mohandas K. Gandhi. During the Vietnam War, she led the Jeannette Rankin Brigade, numbering 5,000, in a protest march on Washington in January 1968 that culminated in the presentation of a peace petition to House Speaker John McCormack of Massachusetts. Her 90th birthday in 1970 was celebrated in the Rayburn House Office Building with a reception and dinner. At the time of her death, on May 18, 1973, in Carmel, California, Rankin was considering another run for a House seat to protest the Vietnam War.

FOR FURTHER READING

Biographical Directory of the United States Congress, "Jeannette Rankin," http://bioguide.congress.gov

Board, John C. "Jeannette Rankin: The Lady From Montana." *Montana* 17 (July 1967): 2–17.

Josephson, Hannah. *Jeannette Rankin, First Lady in Congress: A Biography* (Indianapolis: Bobbs-Merrill, 1974).

Smith, Norma. *Jeannette Rankin: America's Conscience* (Helena: Montana Historical Society Press, 2002).

MANUSCRIPT COLLECTIONS

Montana Historical Society (Helena, MT). *Papers:* 1917–1963, 5.5 linear feet. Papers consist primarily of correspondence reflecting concerns of Jeannette Rankin's constituents. Also included in the papers are subject files documenting appointments to military academies, invitations, and requests for government brochures. There is also some personal correspondence, financial records, news clippings, maps, and photographs. A finding aid is available in the repository.

Radcliffe Institute for Advanced Study, Harvard University (Cambridge, MA), Schlesinger Library, http://www.radcliffe.edu/schles. *Papers:* 1879–1976, 5.5 feet. Includes correspondence, card files, financial papers, articles, speeches, pamphlets, leaflets, scrapbooks, clippings, photographs, tapes, and a film depicting aspects of her life. Best documented is her vote against World War II and the consequent public reaction, though both terms in Congress are covered. Other correspondence reflects her involvement in the suffrage movement, Vietnam War protest, election reform, and the women's movement, with information on the Women's International League for Peace and Freedom and the Jeannette Rankin Brigade. News clippings make up over one half of the collection.

Some family correspondence with Jeannette Rankin's sisters is included. An unpublished finding aid is available in the repository and on microfilm.

University of California (Berkeley, CA), The Bancroft Library. *Oral History:* 1972, 293 pages. A transcript of the original interview with Jeannette Rankin by Malca Chall from June through August 1972. The interview was conducted as part of the University of California–Berkeley's Suffragists Oral History Project. In the interview, Jeannette Rankin discusses her role in national politics during World War I and World War II, the women's rights movement, and pacifism. Additional materials include photographs, copies of news clippings, magazine articles, and her writings.

NOTES

1 Cited in Winifred Mallon, "An Impression of Jeannette Rankin," *The Suffragist* (March 31, 1917).

2 Norma Smith, *Jeannette Rankin: America's Conscience* (Helena: Montana Historical Society Press, 2002): 99.

3 Smith, *Jeannette Rankin*: 101.

4 Ibid., 104.

5 Hannah Josephson, *Jeannette Rankin, First Lady in Congress: A Biography* (Indianapolis, IN: Bobbs–Merrill, 1974): 68–70.

6 *Washington Wife: Journal of Ellen Maury Slayden from 1897–1919* (New York: Harper & Row, 1962, 1963): 299.

7 In December 1917 during the debate over war with Austria–Hungary, Rankin did speak, though she voted in favor of the resolution. At that time, she said, "I still believe that war is a stupid and futile way of attempting to settle international disputes. I believe that war can be avoided and will be avoided when the people, the men and women in America, as well as in Germany, have the controlling voice in their government." See, Josephson, *Jeannette Rankin*: 84; Smith, *Jeannette Rankin*: 114.

8 Josephson, *Jeannette Rankin*: 76; Smith, *Jeannette Rankin*: 112; and Nancy Unger, "RANKIN, Jeannette Pickering," *American National Biography* (*ANB*) 18 (New York: Oxford University Press, 1999): 142.

9 Josephson, *Jeannette Rankin*: 77; see page 75 for public opinion mail.

10 Smith, *Jeannette Rankin*: 113.

11 Josephson, *Jeannette Rankin*: 66.

12 When the committee was established, there was a move to make Rankin the chair, despite her belonging to the minority party. See, Josephson, *Jeannette Rankin*: 93–94.

13 Smith, *Jeannette Rankin*: 123.

14 Josephson, *Jeannette Rankin*: 97–98.

15 Ibid., 99; Smith, *Jeannette Rankin*: 125–126.

16 Josephson, *Jeannette Rankin*: 88–92; Smith, *Jeannette Rankin*: 127–133.

17 Smith, *Jeannette Rankin*: 131.

18 Josephson, *Jeannette Rankin*: 102–103; Smith, *Jeannette Rankin*: 133–134.

19 Smith, *Jeannette Rankin*: 135.

20 Oscar Lanstrum received 18,805 votes and Rankin 17,091 out of 46,027 cast. See, Smith, *Jeannette Rankin*: 137.

21 Josephson, *Jeannette Rankin*: 104. See also, Smith, *Jeannette Rankin*: 137–138.

22 Smith, *Jeannette Rankin*: 140.

23 Michael J. Dubin et al., *U.S. Congressional Elections: 1788–1997* (Jefferson, NC: McFarland & Company, Inc., Publishers, 1998): 424; 428.

24 Smith, *America's Conscience*: 172–173. For a contemporary press account of Thorkelson's reputation see, "Democracy's Mental Dissolution Pictured as Nazi Goal in U.S.," 20 July 1940, *Christian Science Monitor*: 15.

25 Smith, *Jeannette Rankin*: 172–175; Josephson, *Jeannette Rankin*: 153–155.

26 Josephson, *Jeannette Rankin*: 156.

27 Smith, *Jeannette Rankin*: 176.

28 "*Election Statistics, 1920 to Present*," Office of the Clerk, http://clerk.house.gov/members/electionInfo

29 Smith, *Jeannette Rankin*: 177.

30 Josephson, *Jeannette Rankin*: 157; Smith, *Jeannette Rankin*: 180.

31 Smith, *Jeannette Rankin*: 180–181; Josephson, *Jeannette Rankin*: 158.

32 Josephson, *Jeannette Rankin*: 158–159.

33 Robert Dallek, *Franklin D. Roosevelt and American Foreign Policy, 1932–1945* (New York: Oxford University Press, 1995): 290–292.

34 Josephson, *Jeannette Rankin*: 160–161; Smith, *Jeannette Rankin*: 183.

35 Josephson, *Jeannette Rankin*: 161–162. The Mutual Radio Network, which had broadcast the president's address, continued broadcasting in the House Chamber. As a result, portions of the House debate went out live over the radio until House officials realized what was happening during the roll call. As part of a National Public Radio feature, Walter Cronkite reports on this broadcast focusing on the war of wills between Speaker Rayburn and Rankin. "The Lone War Dissenter: Walter Cronkite Remembers Pearl Harbor, Jeanette Rankin," *NPR's All Things Considered* http://www.npr.org/programs/atc/features/2001/dec/cronkite/011207.cronkite.html (accessed August 10, 2004; site now discontinued).

36 Josephson, *Jeannette Rankin*: 162.

37 Unger, "Rankin, Jeannette Pickering," *ANB*: 142.

38 Josephson, *Jeannette Rankin*: 162; Smith, *Jeannette Rankin*: 183.

39 Smith, *Jeannette Rankin*: 184.

40 Ibid.

41 Ibid.

42 Josephson, *Jeannette Rankin*: 163–164; Smith, *Jeannette Rankin*: 186.

Alice Mary Robertson
1854–1931

UNITED STATES REPRESENTATIVE ★ REPUBLICAN FROM OKLAHOMA
1921–1923

Alice Robertson, the next woman to follow Jeannette Rankin into Congress, was her predecessor's polar opposite. Colorful, quotable, conservative, and hostile to the women's suffrage movement and its many leaders, Robertson's single term in the House hinged on her rejection of a significant piece of legislation—a proposed World War I Veterans Bonus Bill.

Alice Mary Robertson was born on January 2, 1854, in the Tullahassee Mission in the Creek Nation Indian Territory, now in Oklahoma. Her parents, William Schenck Robertson and Ann Eliza Worcester Robertson, were missionary school teachers committed to assisting displaced Cherokee. After attending Elmira College in New York from 1873 to 1874, Robertson took a job as the first female clerk at the Indian Office at the Department of the Interior in Washington, D.C. Making a brief stop in Pennsylvania in 1879 to work at the Carlisle Indian School, Robertson returned to Oklahoma. In 1885, she founded the Minerva Home—a boarding school to train Native-American girls in domestic skills. This institution later became Henry Kendall College (the present-day University of Tulsa).[1]

Robertson's missionary work put her within a network of progressive reformers and opened the door to a career in politics. In 1891, she earned the admiration of rising GOP politician Theodore Roosevelt, who later described her as "one of the great women of America." In 1905 then-President Roosevelt appointed Robertson the postmistress of Muskogee, Oklahoma, where she served until 1913. In addition to her patronage job, Robertson operated a 50-acre dairy farm with an on-site café, which she named "Sawokla," based on an Indian word meaning "gathering place." Both the farm and the café became a social magnet,

drawing politicians, former students, journalists, and local folk. During World War I, she endeared herself to many servicemen by distributing food to soldiers in transit through the local train station. In 1916, the GOP nominated her to run for county superintendent of public instruction, but Robertson lost.[2]

Robertson ran as a Republican for an eastern Oklahoma congressional seat in 1920, challenging a three-term Democratic incumbent, William Wirt Hastings. Trained as a lawyer, Hastings was a formidable opponent who had long ties to the Cherokee Nation; however, Robertson believed she could best represent the interests of her prospective constituents. "There are already more lawyers and bankers in Congress than are needed," Robertson said. "The farmers need a farmer, I am a farmer. The women need a woman to look after their new responsibilities. The soldier boys need a proven friend. I promise few speeches, but faithful work. You can judge my past performances." Robertson campaigned actively only in the confines of the Sawokla Café, where she sidled up to tables of voters and talked politics over a bowl of soup. Lacking coverage from local newspapers, she bought space in the classifieds to reach voters. In a year in which the GOP did well nationally at the polls, Robertson was part of a Republican groundswell in Oklahoma that unseated three Democratic incumbents and made the state's House delegation majority Republican. With support from farmers and veterans, she narrowly defeated Hastings, by 228 votes out of nearly 50,000 cast.[3]

In the 67th Congress (1921–1923), Robertson was rewarded for her lifelong work on Native-American welfare with a seat on the Committee on Indian Affairs. She also received assignments on the Committee on

Expenditures in the Interior Department and, as the only woman in Congress, on the Committee on Woman Suffrage.

During Representative Robertson's term in Congress, her work on the Committee on Indian Affairs proved frustrating. Bills and committee reports introduced by Robertson remained unconsidered, and on her final day in office, Robertson scolded her colleagues for their lack of attention to the obligations she felt they owed to Native Americans.[4] "I have kept watch through the years of the tribesmen with whom I took the peace obligation so long ago—an obligation never broken," she said, "I protest against such action as . . . would take in depriving thousands of helpless Indian people of the strong defense they can receive through the Interior Department."[5]

Considering Robertson's tepid support for the vote, her assignment to the Committee on Woman Suffrage insulted many reformers. Robertson once remarked that exchanging the privileges associated with Victorian-era womanhood for the political rights enjoyed by men was like, "bartering the birthright for a mess of pottage." She was an avowed critic of women's groups, including the League of Women Voters, "or any other organization that will be used as a club against men." Robertson repeatedly tangled with prominent national women's groups leaders and discouraged participation in nonaligned, nonpartisan groups. "There is an unfortunate tendency on the part of women just now, having hardly found themselves in politics, to criticize faults rather than to encourage virtues," Robertson lectured. "They call themselves non-partisan and stand on the side as harsh critics instead of going right in at the very source of government in their own immediate communities to build up what is best." Robertson advised women to gain valuable experience in local office and state legislatures before seeking candidacy to national office. Women "have gone into politics the wrong way, beginning at the top instead of the bottom," she once observed. "You wouldn't think of jumping into a big Packard car and trying to run it until you had learned how. When a woman shows she is fitted for office, she will receive the call to office just as a man does."[6]

Robertson opposed one of the first major pieces of

legislation that affected women—the Sheppard–Towner Maternity and Infancy Act of 1921, which provided for educating the public about pregnancy and other prenatal and infant issues. Despite intense lobbying from women's groups and a strong measure of support in her district, she testified against the "better baby" measure in committee and voted against it on the House Floor. As the only witness to oppose the bill in its entirety, Robertson told the House Interstate Commerce Committee that it was "dangerous class legislation, separating women from the men." Robertson believed the bill would create a federal bureau that would intrude on family life. She also preferred the money be spent on material support, worrying that instructional programs might foster "an autocratic, undefined, practically uncontrolled yet Federally authorized center of propaganda."[7]

The traditionally minded 67-year-old matron posed little threat to the folkways of the male-dominated House. One newspaper reporter described her in the vein of a former House Speaker: "built on the same architectural lines as the late Champ Clark and moving with the same deliberate tread . . . her costume was always black and of cut behind the prevailing mode." Robertson quickly gained the respect of her male colleagues because of her steadfast determination to shun feminist overtures. "I came to Congress to represent my district," she declared, "not women." On June 20, 1921, during a roll call vote on funding for a United States delegation to the centennial celebrations of Peru's independence, Robertson became the first woman to preside over a session of the House of Representatives.[8]

Robertson soon alienated a core group of constituents—World War I veterans—when she opposed a measure that would have allowed them to receive an early payment on their military service pensions. President Warren Harding vetoed the "Soldiers Bonus Bill" in 1922, but it passed over the veto of President Calvin Coolidge in 1924.[9] Robertson suggested that such government doles would only increase public dependency on an ever-growing bureaucracy. She faced withering attacks from veterans' groups inside and outside her district, including

WOMEN "HAVE GONE INTO
POLITICS THE WRONG WAY,
BEGINNING AT THE TOP INSTEAD OF
THE BOTTOM. YOU WOULDN'T THINK
OF JUMPING INTO A BIG PACKARD
CAR AND TRYING TO RUN IT UNTIL
YOU HAD LEARNED HOW. WHEN A
WOMAN SHOWS SHE IS FITTED
FOR OFFICE, SHE WILL RECEIVE THE
CALL TO OFFICE JUST AS
A MAN DOES."

—ALICE ROBERTSON
WASHINGTON POST
MARCH 4, 1923

the Women's Auxiliary of the American Legion, which judged her "unworthy of American womanhood."[10]

Congresswoman Robertson's other legislative work accorded with her district. She secured authorization for the construction of a veterans' hospital in Muskogee to assist the more than 91,000 Oklahomans who served in World War I.[11] Robertson also won approval for an amendment that increased the subsistence rate and rent money for army and navy nurses. She supported higher tariff rates and stricter immigration quotas—positions which Oklahomans broadly approved. Like many midwestern politicians, Robertson also opposed the entry of the United States into the League of Nations. She challenged Representative Meyer London of New York when he urged the release of labor leader Eugene V. Debs from prison.

But when staking out her interest in a second term, Robertson admitted that she had not been able to steer enough money into her beleaguered district to overcome her unpopular votes. "I haven't been able to get any 'pie,' speaking in the language of the restaurant, and there are a lot of Republicans down in Oklahoma who are mighty hungry," she told a reporter. She formally declared her candidacy for a second term and won the GOP primary but faced her nemesis, William Hastings, in the 1922 general election. Statewide, Democrats surged back into office, claiming seven of Oklahoma's eight House seats. Hastings prevailed, with 58 percent of the vote to Robertson's 42 percent, and went on to serve an additional six terms in the House.[12]

Robertson spent the last decade of her life trying, with little success, to fit back into life in Muskogee. In April 1923, a month after she left the House, President Harding appointed her as a welfare worker in the Muskogee Veterans' Hospital. With memories of her Bonus Bill vote fresh in the minds of local servicemen, she was eventually ousted from the hospital position. In 1925 a fire destroyed her Sawokla home and the café, which prompted Robertson to tell a local reporter that she was certain "some of her enemies had set it." Robertson spent her last years supported by generous friends and family and died in relative obscurity on July 1, 1931, at the Muskogee Veterans' Hospital.[13]

FOR FURTHER READING

Biographical Directory of the United States Congress, "Alice Mary Robertson," http://bioguide.congress.gov

James, Louise B. "Alice Mary Robertson—Anti-Feminist Congresswoman." *Chronicles of Oklahoma* 55 (Winter 1977–1978): 454–62.

Morris, Cheryl. "Alice M. Robertson: Friend or Foe of the American Soldier." *Journal of the West* 12 (April 1973): 307–16.

Spaulding, Joe Powell. "The Life of Mary Alice Robertson." Ph.D. Dissertation, University of Oklahoma, 1959.

Stanley, Ruth M. "Alice M. Robertson, Oklahoma's First Congresswoman." *Chronicles of Oklahoma* 45 (Autumn 1967): 259–89.

MANUSCRIPT COLLECTIONS

University of Oklahoma (Norman, OK), Western History Collections.

University of Tulsa (Tulsa, OK), Department of Special Collections, McFarlin Library. *Papers:* 1820–1931, approximately 25 feet. Personal and business papers, correspondence, photographs, a large collection of newspaper clippings, memorabilia, and writings. A finding aid is available in the repository and online: http://www.lib.utulsa.edu/speccoll/roberamo.htm.

NOTES

1 Alice Robertson's maternal father, Samuel A. Worcester, argued before the U.S. Supreme Court on behalf of the political autonomy of the Cherokee Nation in the 1832 legal case *Worcester v. Georgia*; "Woman Congress Member Likes D.C.," 9 November 1920, *Washington Post*: 1.

2 Hope Chamberlin, *A Minority of Members: Women in the U.S. Congress* (New York: Praeger, 1973): 39; for the section on her relationship with Theodore Roosevelt, see also Nancy Shoemaker, "Robertson, Alice Mary," *American National Biography* 18 (New York: Oxford, 1999): 621–622.

3 Chamberlin, *A Minority of Members*: 39; "Miss Robertson of Oklahoma," 13 November 1920, *New York Times*: 10.

4 Robertson introduced two bills and two committee reports appropriating funds and granting relief to Native American Tribes (HR 8273, HR 10495, H. Rep. 11140, H. Rep. 1452), none of which were ever considered (see the *Congressional Record*, House, 67th Congress).

5 *Congressional Record*, House, 67th Cong., 4th sess. (3 March 1923): 5679.

6 Cited in Susan Tolchin, *Women in Congress* (Washington, D.C.: Government Printing Office, 1976); and in Chamberlin's *A Minority of Members*: 39; "Against League of Women," 10 February 1921, *Washington Post*: 6; "Robertson Says Women Must Take Election Risk," 16 March 1922, *Washington Post*: 5; Mayme Ober Peak, "'Miss Alice' Is Content After One Term to Retire to Her Sawokla Farm in Oklahoma," 4 March 1923, *Washington Post*: 75. Robertson's remark about the Packard car was not aimed at any particular woman suffrage leader, Rankin included.

7 Chamberlin, *A Minority of Members*: 41; Constance Drexel, "Miss Alice Fights 'Better–Baby' Bill," 24 July 1921, *Washington Post*: 6.

8 Peak, "'Miss Alice' Is Content After One Term to Retire to Her Sawokla Farm in Oklahoma"; "Woman Presides at House Session; First in History," 21 June 1921, *Washington Post*: 1; "Woman Presides in Congress; Precedent Broken Amid Cheers," 21 June 1921, *New York Times*: 1; Shoemaker, "Robertson, Mary Alice," *ANB*.

9 Stephen W. Stathis, *Landmark Legislation: 1774-2002* (Washington, D.C.: Congressional Quarterly Press, 2003): 185.

10 Chamberlin, *A Minority of Members*: 42; Tolchin, *Women in Congress*: 71.

11 Chamberlin, *A Minority of Members*: 41; Arrell Morgan Gibson, *The History of Oklahoma* (University of Oklahoma Press: 1972): 140.

12 "Can't Get Any 'Pie,' But Won't Give Up," 5 December 1921, *New York Times*: 1; "Miss Robertson Opens Reelection Campaign," 5 July 1922, *Washington Post*: 10.

13 "Muskogee County, Oklahoma: Turning Back the Clock," (Muskogee, OK: Muskogee Publishing Co., 1985) http://www.rootsweb.com/~okmuskog/peopleplaces/turnback11.html (accessed 1 August 2003).

Winnifred S. Huck
1882–1936

UNITED STATES REPRESENTATIVE ★ REPUBLICAN FROM ILLINOIS
1922–1923

Winnifred S. Huck, the third woman elected to Congress, spent her short House career carrying on the legacy of her father, William E. Mason, as an ardent and articulate pacifist. As the first wife and mother elected to Congress, she vowed to look after the needs of married women and families and to promote world peace.

Winnifred Sprague Mason was born in Chicago, Illinois, on September 14, 1882. She was the daughter of William, an attorney and a former schoolteacher, and Edith Julia White Mason. Winnifred's father served as a Republican in the U.S. House of Representatives from 1887 until 1891 and in the U.S. Senate from 1897 to 1903. He returned to the House in 1917 to fill an Illinois At-Large seat. During his congressional career, Mason consistently championed labor rights, took a strong antitrust position, and was an avowed pacifist. He was one of the first American politicians to advocate an independent Cuba following the Spanish-American War and to recognize an autonomous Irish Republic. Colleagues and the press denounced the pacifist Mason when he opposed American intervention in World War I, a conflict he shunned as a "dollar war." Winnifred Huck attended public schools in Chicago until her father's first election to the House took the family to Washington, D.C. She graduated from Washington's Central High School. In 1904, she married her high school sweetheart, Robert W. Huck. The couple raised four children: Wallace, Edith, Donald, and Robert, Jr. Robert Huck, Sr., a civil engineer, became a steel company executive, moving the family to Colorado. Later he worked as a construction engineer for the deep waterways commission, relocating the family to Chicago, where Winnifred Huck became active in her hometown community.[1]

When Representative William Mason died in office on June 16, 1921, Winnifred Huck announced that she would be a candidate in the April 22nd primary to fill her father's At-Large seat for the remainder of his term in the 67th Congress (1921–1923) and would also run for a full term in the 68th Congress (1923–1925). On her prospects, Huck commented, "I have come into the political world like a clap of thunder out of a clear sky," but also cited a longtime interest in politics due to her father's influence. Without spending any money on her campaign, and lacking the endorsement of the Illinois Republican Women's Club, Huck narrowly won the nomination. In the primary for the full term, however, she lost the nomination to Henry R. Rathbone, who was later the runner-up in the general election to fellow Republican Richard Yates.[2]

In the special election on November 7, 1922, Huck defeated Democrat Allen D. Albert, amassing more than 850,000 votes and 53 percent of the total turnout. In declaring victory, Huck said "I am going to take my four children to Washington and get busy. I am for world peace, but against entangling alliances and I want to see the soldiers get a bonus." When Huck arrived in Washington, state officials in Illinois had not provided her with credentials. She was concerned that she would not be able to take her seat, later writing, "A Congressman-elect might forget to wear his shoes on the day of his inauguration, but he would never forget to bring his credentials." Illinois Representative James Mann vouched for her election, and the House unanimously agreed to swear Huck into the 67th Congress on November 20, 1922. She was the first woman to represent Illinois.[3]

During her brief fourteen-week tenure, she served on the Committee on Expenditures in the Department of Commerce, the Committee on Reform in the Civil Service, and the Committee on Woman Suffrage. She also was a member of the "Progressive Bloc," a group of like-minded Senators and Representatives who gathered in informal committees to discuss the legislative agenda. Huck focused her energies on continuing her father's legislative goals, including support for restrictions on child labor and separate citizenship rights for married women. Winnifred Huck most vocally carried on William Mason's legacy, however, as a pacifist with the goal of creating lasting peace following the end of World War I.[4]

Huck disdained the custom which required new Members of Congress to remain silent and proceeded to offer her opinions on a variety of issues. Her most note-worthy address as a House Member was delivered on January 16, 1923, when she appealed to her colleagues to support a constitutional amendment to hold a direct pop-ular vote for future United States' involvement in any war requiring the armed forces to be sent overseas. Determined to demonstrate the lack of necessity for war, Huck declared, "In a country where the people control the gov-ernment there is no opportunity for a war to originate." One month later, Huck proposed further legislation which would have barred any American trade with or financial concessions to nations that did not permit citizens to participate in referendums on war declarations. Huck continued her antiwar stance by pleading for the release of 62 men imprisoned for what the Woodrow Wilson administration deemed to be seditious speeches and writing during the war.[5] Huck also introduced a concurrent resolution declaring the people of the Philippine Islands to be free and independent, and she championed self-government for Cuba and Ireland.[6] Critics assailed her legislation as an attack on the executive power to make war and an invitation for foreign aggression, but Huck's passion for the idea of outlawing war came to fruition later in the decade with the 1928 Kellogg–Briand Pact, which was signed by several nations condemning war as a solution for international controversies. Though out of office, Huck enthusiastically supported the pact.

Huck deviated from her antiwar stance on only two occasions. First, she voted in favor of the December 1922 Ship Subsidy Bill, legislation resulting from President Warren Harding's plan to increase American international trade presence by subsidizing the merchant marine—which, in the event of war, would transport troops and weapons.[7] Huck justified her position by noting that President Harding had not urged its passage as a necessary preparation for war.[8] Second, she appointed her son, Wallace, to the United States Naval Academy, forcing the academy to waive its height requirement in accepting the 5-foot- 2-inch youth. She defended her actions by claiming that until her legislation outlawing war passed, the nation would need a "splendid army and an efficient navy."[9]

Before the conclusion of her short term in March 1923, Huck entered another Illinois primary. She sought to fill the vacancy created by the death of Illinois Representative James Mann, who died on November 30, 1922—defending Huck's right to her seat was the last action he took on the House Floor. Huck was defeated in the February 1923 primary by former state senator Morton D. Hull. Following the primary, Huck alleged that Hull had spent $100,000 on his campaign, far exceeding the $5,000 expenditure limit imposed by Congress at the time. The House denied her request to investigate Hull's campaign. Deciding that protesting the outcome would prove futile, Huck did not contest the election.[10]

After her term expired, Huck served as the chair of the Political Council of the National Woman's Party and made her living as a writer, authoring a syndicated news-paper column and working as an investigative reporter. In 1925, posing undercover as a convict in a women's prison, she wrote a series of articles for the *Chicago Evening Post* on the criminal justice system, prison conditions, and the rehabilitation of convicts, creating a national sen-sation. In 1928 and 1929, Huck worked as a staff writer on the *Chicago Evening Sun*, and she also gave lectures. Suffering failing health during the last five years of her life, Huck lived in Chicago with her family until her death there on August 24, 1936, from complications following abdominal surgery.[11]

FOR FURTHER READING

Biographical Directory of the United States Congress,
"Winnifred Sprague Mason Huck," http://bioguide.con-
gress. gov

NOTES

1   "Mason Stirs House" 4 October 1917, *New York Times*: 12; Leonard
    Schulp, "Huck, Winnifred Sprague Mason," *American National Biography*
    (*ANB*) 11 (New York: Oxford University Press, 1999): 402.

2   "Mrs. Huck Planning To Work for Peace," 19 November 1922,
    Washington Post: 3; Hope Chamberlin, *A Minority of Members: Women
    in the U.S. Congress* (New York: Praeger, 1973): 44.

3   "Congresswoman Is To Succeed Father," 9 November 1922, *Washington
    Post*: 9; Winnifred Huck, "What Happened to Me in Congress," July
    1923, *Woman's Home Companion*: 4; "First Mother in Congress Will
    Work for World Peace," 11 May 1922, *Christian Science Monitor*: 5.

4   Schulp, "Huck, Winnifred Sprague Mason," *ANB*; David T. Canon et
    al., *Committees in the U.S. Congress, 1789–1946* (Washington, D.C.:
    Congressional Quarterly Press, 2002); "Mrs. Huck Planning To Work
    for Peace," 19 November 1922, *Washington Post*: 3; "Six Committees
    Named for 'Progressive Bloc,'" 30 December 1922, *Washington Post*: 4;
    "'Miss Alice' and Mrs. Huck Chum and Chat, But Differ at Polls," 3
    December 1922, *Washington Post*: 18.

5   Office of the Historian, U.S. House of Representatives, *Women in
    Congress, 1917–1990* (Washington, D.C.: Government Printing Office,
    1991): 109; "Mrs. Huck Pleads for Prisoners," *Christian Science Monitor*,
    11 December 1922: 2.

6   Chamberlin, *A Minority of Members*: 44; *Congressional Record,* House,
    67th Cong., 4th sess. (16 January 1923): 1828; *Congressional Record,*
    House, 67th Cong., 4th sess. (16 February 1923): 3817; "Points to
    Lesson in Irish Struggle," 1 August 1921, *Washington Post*: 2; Office of
    the Historian, U.S. House of Representatives, *Women in Congress,
    1917–1990*: 6.

7   Schulp, "Huck, Winnifred Sprague Mason," *ANB*: 402.

8   Constance Drexel, "Mrs. Huck For Ship Subsidy," 26 November 1922,
    Los Angeles Times: 13.

9   "Mother, Congresswoman Sends Son to Annapolis," 24 July 1923,
    Washington Post: 2; Quoted in Schulp, "Huck, Winnifred Sprague
    Mason," *ANB*.

10 Huck, *"What Happened to Me in Congress*: 4; "Mrs. Huck Will Not
    Contest Hull's Seat," 4 March 1923, *Washington Post*: 1; Whitehead,
    Frank Insco, "Swan Songs, Tributes," 5 March 1924, *Washington Post*: 1.

11 Schulp, "Huck, Winnifred Sprague Mason," *ANB*: 403.

Rebecca Latimer Felton
1835–1930

UNITED STATES SENATOR ★ DEMOCRAT FROM GEORGIA
1922

Rebecca Felton's brief and essentially symbolic service in the Senate stood in contrast to her decades of participation in Georgia politics and civic affairs. Outspoken, determined, and irascible, Felton was involved in public life from the 1870s through the 1920s. She first entered politics during her husband's successful campaign for the House of Representatives and went on to work as a lecturer and newspaper writer, before becoming the first woman to serve in the United States Senate.

Rebecca Ann Latimer was born on June 10, 1835, in De Kalb County, Georgia, to Charles Latimer and Eleanor Swift. She attended private schools in the area before graduating from Madison Female College in 1852. She married William Harrell Felton, a physician and Methodist preacher, in 1853. They lived on a farm near Cartersville, Georgia, and eventually had four sons and a daughter. During the Civil War, William Felton served as a surgeon despite Rebecca's opposition to secession. Following the war, they worked to restore their heavily damaged farm, and she taught school. Rebecca Felton managed her husband's successful 1874 campaign for Congress when he ran as an Independent Democrat representing up-country Georgia. William served in the U.S. House (1875–1881) and, later, the state house of representatives (1884–1890). Rebecca continued to be a close adviser during his three terms in the House, serving as congressional secretary, and later as his aide in the state legislature. In 1894 William Felton ran unsuccessfully for the U.S. House on the Populist ticket. "Though now a feeble old man," writes Robert Preston Brooks, "he was full of fire and an antagonist to be dreaded." He died in late 1909 at the age of 87.[1]

The Feltons' political partnership introduced Rebecca Felton to politics and public service. She was an active participant in her husband's campaigns. "I made appointments for speaking, recruited speakers, answered newspaper attacks, contracted for the printing and distribution of circulars and sample ballots," she recalled, "and more than all, kept a brave face to the foe and a smiling face to the almost exhausted candidate." Her presence on the campaign trail—an unusual place to find a woman then—drew fire from William's opponents. She would later recall, "I did not stop to think what a change this was for a young woman considered only an ornament and household mistress." As William's congressional secretary in "Washington City," she managed her husband's correspondence and speeches while writing columns for two local newspapers. She was soon known as "our Second Representative from the Seventh."[2]

As William's career came to an end, Rebecca began building on what she had learned and experienced. It was her participation in managing Georgia's exhibits at the World's Columbian Exposition of 1893 held in Chicago that sparked her interest in national politics. Felton had come into contact with other women activists from around the nation and endorsed many of the crusades of Southern progressivism, including temperance and prison reform. Rebecca also was a gifted writer, whose vigorous prose had made her husband's campaigns memorable. Husband and wife founded a weekly newspaper, *Cartersville Free Press*, and she wrote many of its columns. Her column, "The Country Home," appeared in the *Atlanta Journal* for nearly two decades from 1899 into the 1920s. She also wrote three books: *My Memoirs of Georgia Politics* (1911), *Country Life in Georgia in the Days of My Youth* (1919), and *The Romantic Story of Georgia's Women* (1930).[3]

It was through her writings that Felton became a visible presence in Georgia politics. She supported women's suffrage, Prohibition, and public education, especially vocational training for girls, while fighting the state's system of convict leasing. Felton was also prone to making harsh personal attacks on perceived enemies and articulated an often brutal vision of social order. She espoused conventional views about labor-management issues, defending working conditions in southern cotton mills and criticizing labor unions. Looking back on an age noted for intolerance and racism, historians have characterized Felton's judgments about African Americans as especially vicious. Black rapists were of particular concern to Felton and to southerners who shared her views. She blamed the use of liquor to purchase black votes for an increase in threats to southern womanhood. Her views drew national attention when she said in an 1897 address that "if it takes lynching to protect women's dearest possession from drunken, raving human beasts, then I say lynch a thousand a week."[4]

Felton's personal determination, if not her varied political views, was much in evidence in her fleeting Senate career. The sudden death of Senator Tom Watson, an old Populist ally of Felton's, on September 26, 1922, four days after the end of the 67th Congress (1921–1923), gave Governor Thomas Hardwick an opportunity. An earlier opponent of the 19th Amendment, Hardwick saw a chance to erase this blot among women voters while giving his own political career a boost. Announcing his candidacy in the special election to fill Watson's unexpired term, the governor decided to appoint a woman to the seat on an *ad interim* basis. He first offered the appointment to Watson's widow, and when she turned it down, he offered the post to Felton. "It is unfortunate that an elected successor will prevent her from being sworn in," the governor announced. Felton was appointed on October 3rd to serve until a successor was elected, and Hardwick scheduled for mid-October the primary that would begin the process for filling the unexpired Senate term. Felton received the appointment certificate in a public ceremony held in Cartersville on October 7th. Governor Hardwick reminded the crowd that he had originally opposed

women's suffrage but said he now believed "it was right" to extend the right to vote to women. Felton said, "the biggest part of this appointment lies in the recognition of women in the government of our country. It means, as far as I can see, there are now no limitations upon the ambitions of women. They can be elected or appointed to any office in the land. The word 'sex' has been obliterated entirely from the Constitution." The press was filled with sympathetic stories about the first woman to become Senator, but they also lambasted Governor Hardwick over his transparent political ploy. The *Pittsburgh Gazette-Times* called the appointment "merely a pretty sentiment . . . an empty gesture." Suffragists began a petition campaign requesting President Warren G. Harding to call Congress into special session and thus allow Felton to be sworn in as Senator before her successor was elected. "It would be too expensive," the president responded, "to summon Congress just to seat a single senator." On October 17, Georgia supreme court justice Walter George defeated Governor Hardwick in the primary to fill the rest of Senator Watson's term.[5]

Now the situation changed. The 17th Amendment provided for a gubernatorial appointment until a successor was elected. In Georgia, dominated by the Democratic Party, winning the primary was tantamount to winning the general election. Once George won the election in November, Felton's tenure as Senator would come to an end. This was certainly how George read the situation. He feared that Georgia would have three Senators on its payroll after the fall elections. When in early November President Harding suddenly called Congress into special session, to begin November 20, 1922, for a Ship Subsidy Bill, an opportunity for Felton to be sworn in suddenly appeared. The 87-year-old Felton convinced Senator-elect George to allow her to present her credentials during the special session. George warned her that this maneuver would be vulnerable to any Senator's objection, but Felton was willing to take the chance. She checked further with Georgia Secretary of State S.G. McLendon, who told her that he had sent the official certificate of her appointment to the Senate and saw no reason against her being sworn in. On the day of the special session, Felton took her seat in the Senate Chamber, and the following day she was sworn in as that body's first woman Member. It turned out that she was the oldest Senator, too. The swearing-in ceremony was delayed by Montana Senator Thomas J. Walsh, who in a careful address examined the objections to seating Felton and the arguments from Senate precedents that seemed to allow it. Walsh's position was that if the Senate chose to seat her, it should be done because "she was entitled to take the oath" rather than "as a favor, or as a mere matter of courtesy or being moved by the spirit of gallantry." A day later, when the Senate first proceeded to business beneath a gallery filled with women assembled for the occasion, Felton made some brief remarks in which she made a prediction: "When the women of the country come in and sit with you, though there may be but a very few in the next few years, I pledge you that you will get ability, you will get integrity of purpose, you will get exalted patriotism, and you will get unstinted usefulness." Felton then gave her seat to George, who was present for the occasion. She thus gained the further and dubious distinction of being the Senator with the shortest term of service.[6]

Felton returned to Cartersville, Georgia, and continued to write on public affairs. The "grand old woman of Georgia" made a brief appearance at the Capitol in 1927 when Georgia added a statue of Alexander Stephens to the National Statuary Hall Collection. She died in Atlanta on January 24, 1930, at the age of 95.[7]

FOR FURTHER READING

Biographical Directory of the United States Congress, "Rebecca Latimer Felton," http://bioguide.congress.gov

Felton, Rebecca L. *My Memories of Georgia Politics* (Atlanta, GA: Index Printing Co., 1911).

Talmadge, John Erwin. *Rebecca Latimer Felton: Nine Stormy Decades* (Athens, GA: University of Georgia Press, 1960).

MANUSCRIPT COLLECTION

University of Georgia Libraries (Athens, GA), Hargrett Rare Book and Manuscript Library. *Papers:* 1851–1930, 22 linear feet. The papers include correspondence, speeches, articles, and scrapbooks. These materials reflect Rebecca Felton's career as politician, author, newspaper columnist, and lecturer. The papers also document her involvement in the World's Columbian Exposition (1893), the Cotton States Exposition in Atlanta (1895), and as a delegate to the Progressive Republican Convention in Chicago in 1912. Due to preservation concerns, researchers are required to use the microfilm copy. A finding aid is available in the repository.

NOTES

1 Robert Preston Brooks, "Felton, Rebecca Latimer," *Dictionary of American Biography on CD-ROM* (New York: Charles Scribner's Sons, 1998; originally published in 1931). The children were John, Mary Eleanor (died in infancy), William Harrell, Jr., Howard Erwin, and Paul Aiken (died in infancy); Hope Chamberlin, *A Minority of Members: Women in the U.S. Congress* (New York: Praeger, 1973): 25–26.

2 Chamberlin, *A Minority of Members*: 26–27.

3 Ibid., 28–29; W. Fitzhugh Brundage, "Felton, Rebecca Latimer," *American National Biography,* 7 (New York: Oxford University Press, 1999): 808–810.

4 Brundage, "Felton, Rebecca Latimer," *ANB.*

5 Chamberlin, *A Minority of Members*: 19–21.

6 Ibid., 21–22; 34–36.

7 "Statue Unveiled to Vice President of Confederacy," 9 December 1927, *Washington Post*: 2; "Mrs. Felton, Once Senator, Is Seriously Hurt in Crash," 4 March 1929, *Washington Post*: 10 ; "Georgians Mourn Mrs. Rebecca Felton," 27 January 1930, *New York Times*: 19.

Mae Ella Nolan
1886–1973

UNITED STATES REPRESENTATIVE ★ REPUBLICAN FROM CALIFORNIA
1923–1925

As the first woman to succeed her husband in Congress, widow Mae Ella Nolan set a precedent by championing the legislative agenda of her late husband, John I. Nolan. Congresswoman Nolan's example influenced many future widows. But her career, which included the distinction of being the first woman to head a congressional committee and all the attendant media attention, proved short-lived.

Mae Ella Hunt was born on September 20, 1886, to Irish immigrants in San Francisco, California, and grew up in its working-class neighborhoods. She attended the public schools in San Francisco, St. Vincent's Convent, and Ayers Business College of San Francisco. After earning a certificate in stenography, she went to work at Wells Fargo Express. In 1913, she married John I. Nolan—a former iron molder and labor activist—shortly after he was elected to the 63rd Congress (1913–1915) on the Bull Moose Party ticket. The couple raised a daughter named Corlis. John Nolan, a San Francisco native and former member of the city's board of supervisors, had been active in the city labor movement and political scene for years. He entered the iron molding trade at age 14 and moved into the ranks of union leadership—as a member of the national executive board of the molders' union, as a delegate to the San Francisco Labor Council, and as a lobbyist representing the labor council in Sacramento. He played a prominent role in the Union Labor Party, at the height of its influence in San Francisco politics during the Progressive Era. In the House, representing a district that covered southern San Francisco, Nolan eventually chaired the Labor Committee and was considered the GOP's leading labor advocate, fighting aggressively against child labor and working for protections for women in industrial jobs.[1]

He was considered for Labor Secretary in President Warren G. Harding's Cabinet. Mae Nolan was his constant companion. Corlis was known as the "Daughter of the House of Representatives," and became a regular on the House Floor and a favorite of Speakers Joe Cannon of Illinois and Champ Clark of Missouri.[2]

John Nolan was elected unopposed to a sixth term in November 1922 but died weeks after the election. The Union Labor Party quickly nominated Mae Ella Nolan to succeed her husband. She also received the support of the executive committee of the California Women's Republican League.[3] While campaigning, Nolan embraced a platform that called for relaxing Prohibition laws and supported labor interests. Though the campaign was pushed back two weeks to allow prospective candidates to gather signatures for their nomination, Nolan was the odds-on favorite. She was elected to the remainder of the 67th Congress (1921–1923) and the full term in the 68th Congress (1923–1925) on January 23, 1923, out-polling her nearest opponent, San Francisco Supervisor Edwin G. Bath, by more than 4,000 votes.[4]

Nolan was an immediate novelty because she was the first widow to serve in Congress. As the *Los Angeles Times* observed at the time of her election, Mae Nolan was "intimately associated with the Washington chapters of her husband's life" and familiar with the "pangs and diversions" of congressional politics. In announcing her platform, Nolan likened her program to a memorial for her husband. "I owe it to the memory of my husband to carry on his work," Nolan told the *San Francisco Examiner*. "His minimum-wage bill, child labor laws and national education bills all need to be in the hands of someone who knew him and his plans intimately. No one better knows than I do his legislative agenda."[5]

Though Nolan ran as an Independent, she served as a

OFFICE OF HISTORY AND PRESERVATION,
U.S. HOUSE OF REPRESENTATIVES

Republican. On February 12, 1923, she was escorted by California Congressman Charles F. Curry to take the oath of office. "I come to Washington, not as a stranger, but as one among friends," Nolan said. "I come with new responsibilities and in a new attitude, however. I can not forget that my election was a tribute to the memory of my late husband . . . and in the belief and expectation that I, who was his close associate in his legislative work for many years, could best carry that work on in his place." To help manage her office, she employed her sister, Theresa Hunt Glynn, who had worked for six years as John Nolan's secretary. Nolan also relied on Representative Julius Kahn, San Francisco's other Congressman, and a personal friend of her husband, for counsel and advice.[6]

In the 67th Congress, Nolan was appointed to the Committee on Woman Suffrage. When the 68th Congress convened in late 1923, she received an assignment on the Committee on Labor. Nolan also was appointed to chair the Committee on Expenditures in the Post Office and received national press attention as the first woman to chair a congressional committee.

Claiming that the workload with her additional assignments was too much, she dropped the Woman Suffrage Committee assignment. It was a convenient moment for Nolan to distance herself from the women's rights movement with which she had a relatively cool relationship, largely because her core labor constituency was unsupportive. In particular, the American Federation of Labor vigorously denounced the Equal Rights Amendment (introduced in Congress during Nolan's first year) because of perceptions that it would erode Progressive Era workplace protections for women in industrial jobs. As the only woman in the 68th Congress, Nolan minimized gender differences. "A capable woman is a better representative than an incapable man, and vice versa," Nolan said. "After all, the chief responsibility in legislative matters rests with the electorate. If it is alert, informed, and insistent, it will get good representation in Washington from either a man or a woman Member of Congress."[7]

Nolan sought to improve wage conditions for laborers, taking up the fight for John Nolan's minimum daily wage

bill for federal employees. "Uncle Sam should be a model employer," Mae Nolan said in late 1923. "Wages and working conditions in the Government service should conform to a proper American standard of living. I am in complete sympathy with the movement to increase the compensation of the postal workers and to provide a more generous retirement system." Nolan also supported lowering taxes on working-class Americans and raising them on the wealthy. Further, she championed a bonus for World War I veterans (an idea approved by Congress in 1922 but vetoed by President Harding). "The men who risked their lives in the trenches of Europe should receive their adjusted compensation before we undertake to reduce the tax burden of the very rich," Nolan declared.[8] In her one complete term in Congress, Congresswoman Nolan also gained passage of several bills related to her district, including one transferring the Palace of Fine Arts from the federal government's Presidio to the city of San Francisco and another authorizing construction of a federal building.[9]

Despite her ability to secure solid committee positions, Nolan seems to have had problems stepping from behind her husband's shadow into the full glare of the public spotlight. She expressed frustration at the unblinking press attention lavished on her during her early House career, claiming that she was misquoted and misrepresented regularly. The press also mercilessly derided Nolan's figure—noting at one point that she had taken up golf as a form of exercise to lose weight. She made relatively few floor speeches and soon withdrew from the reporters who sought her out for interviews. By her second year in Congress, the *Washington Post* reported that Nolan "retired into her shell and lobbyists say it is with difficulty that they can obtain a few words with her." When she left the House, a *Washington Post* headline claimed (not quite accurately) that "in Congress 2 years, she did no 'talking.'"[10]

Representative Nolan declined to run for re-election to the 69th Congress (1925–1927), citing the time-consuming workload and her responsibilities as a single parent: "Politics is entirely too masculine to have any attraction for feminine responsibilities." Mae Ella Nolan retired from Congress and returned to San Francisco. In later years, she moved to Sacramento, California, where she died on July 9, 1973.[11]

FOR FURTHER READING

Biographical Directory of the United States Congress, "Mae Ella Nolan," http://bioguide.congress.gov

NOTES

1   Kenneth Martis, *The Historical Atlas of Political Parties in the United States Congress, 1789–1989* (New York: Macmillan, 1988).

2   For a concise history of the Union Labor Party in San Francisco politics see, William Issel and Robert W. Cherny, *San Francisco, 1865–1932: Politics, Power and Urban Development* (Berkeley: University of California Press, 1986): 139–164. See also, Sally Sloane, "Only Woman in Congress," 16 December 1923, *Washington Post*: F3.

3   Office of the Historian, U.S. House of Representatives, *Women in Congress; 1917–1990* (Washington, D.C.: Government Printing Office, 1991) indicates that Nolan ran as an Independent. All other referenced sources indicate that she ran as a Republican. See, for example, Michael J. Dubin et al., *U.S. Congressional Elections, 1788–1997* (Jefferson, NC: McFarland & Company, Inc., 1998): 448; "Mae Ella Nolan," *Biographical Directory of the U.S. Congress*, available: http://bioguide.congress.gov (accessed 11 January 2005); and Hope Chamberlin, *A Minority of Members: Women in the U.S. Congress* (New York: Praeger, 1973): 46–47.

4   "Congressman Nolan Is Dead," 19 November 1922, *Los Angeles Times*: I10; "Representative Nolan Dies in California Home," 19 November 1922, *Washington Post*: 3; "Widow Sees Nolan's Seat," 30 November 1922, *Washington Post*: 9; "Delay California Election," 11 December 1922, *Washington Post*: 6; "Mrs. Nolan Goes to Congress to Succeed Her Late Husband," 24 January 1923, *New York Times*: 1.

5   "Women in Congress," 27 January 1923, *Los Angeles Times*: II4; quoted in Suzanne Pullen, "First Female California Representatives From the City," 10 November 2000, *San Francisco Examiner*: A7.

6   "Mrs. Nolan Takes Her Place in House," 13 February 1923, *Washington Post*: 4; Chamberlin, *A Minority of Members*: 46. See Mae Ella Nolan's memorial speech at the time of Julius Kahn's (husband of Florence Prag Kahn) death; *Congressional Record*, House, 68th Cong., 2nd sess. (22 February 1925): 4385.

7   "First Woman Named as House Chairman," 14 December 1923, *Washington Post*: 1; Pullen, "First Female California Representatives From the City."

8   Sloane, "Only Woman in Congress"; Steven V. Stathis, *Landmark Legislation, 1774–2002* (Washington, D.C.: Congressional Quarterly Press, 2003): 186.

9   Sloane, "Only Woman in Congress."

10 Constance Drexel, "Mrs. Nolan No 'Crusader'; Mrs. Barrett Gains Note," 24 February 1924, *Washington Post*: ES 3; "In Congress 2 Years, She Did No 'Talking,'" 5 March 1925, *Washington Post*: 9.

11 Susan Tolchin, *Women in Congress* (Washington, D.C.: Government Printing Office, 1976): 57.

Mary T. Norton
1875–1959

UNITED STATES REPRESENTATIVE ★ DEMOCRAT FROM NEW JERSEY
1925–1951

For a quarter century in the House, colleagues knew Mary T. Norton as "Battling Mary," a reformer who fought for the labor and the working-class interests of her urban New Jersey district. An apprentice with one of the most notorious Democratic political machines in America, Norton emerged from Jersey City as the first woman to represent an eastern state and eventually chaired four House committees. Norton's career was defined by her devotion to blue-collar concerns.

Mary Teresa Hopkins was born on March 7, 1875, in Jersey City, New Jersey. She was the second surviving child of Thomas Hopkins, a road construction contractor, and Maria Shea, a governess.[1] Mary kept house after her mother died and graduated from Jersey City High School. She moved to New York City in 1896 and attended Packard Business College. She later worked as a secretary and stenographer until she married Robert Francis Norton in April 1909. To cope with the death of her one-week-old son, Robert, Jr., in 1910, she began working at the Queen's Daughters Day Nursery and, within three years, became its secretary. By 1916, she was elected nursery president. It was in her capacity as a fundraiser for the nursery that she made a large number of political contacts. Robert Norton, who died in 1934, supported her career to the end.

After World War I, in search of municipal support for the nursery, she met Jersey City's mayor and powerful political boss, Frank "I Am the Law" Hague. Mayor Hague took office in 1917 and controlled Hudson County politics for three decades with a mixture of patronage, programs for his labor constituency, and, at times, direct intimidation of his opponents. Eager to bring newly enfranchised women into the Democratic Party (and under his political machine), the mayor pressed Norton to enter politics as his protégé. "It's your duty to organize the women of Jersey City," Hague commanded.[2] When Norton, who had not been involved in the suffrage movement, protested that she didn't know politics, Hague snapped back, "Neither does any suffragist."[3] In 1920, with Hague's backing, Norton was the first woman named to the New Jersey Democratic Committee and, in 1921, was elected its vice chairman, serving in that capacity until 1931. She became the first woman to head any state party when she was elevated to chairman in 1932 (she served until 1935 and was again named chairman from 1940 to 1944).

On November 5, 1924, with Hague's key endorsement, Norton won election to a Jersey City U.S. House seat—recently vacated by the retiring Representative Charles O'Brien. As the first woman to represent an eastern state, she beat Republican Douglas Story by more than 18,000 votes (62 percent of the total vote). Re-elected in 1926 by a landslide 83 percent of the vote, she dominated her subsequent 11 elections appealing to a heavily Democratic constituency, increased by reapportionment in 1932.[4]

During her first term, Norton received an assignment on the World War Veterans Legislation Committee. She would later serve on and eventually chair four committees: Labor, District of Columbia, Memorials, and House Administration. As a freshman she also encountered head-on the House patriarchy. Once, when a colleague deferred to her as a "lady," Norton retorted, "I am no lady, I'm a Member of Congress, and I'll proceed on that basis."[5]

Although she befriended Hague for life, Norton maintained that the mayor had not sought to influence her vote in Congress. She shared fundamentally, however, in Hague's desire to promote the interests of the district's mostly working-class and Roman Catholic constituency.

Norton's crowning legislative
achievement came with
the passage of the
Fair Labor Standards Act
of 1938, which she
personally shepherded
through committee
and onto the House Floor
for a vote. "I'm prouder of
getting that bill through
the House than anything
else I've done in my life,"
Norton recalled.

In keeping with the views of the American Federation of Labor, Norton opposed the Equal Rights Amendment which, she feared, would erode legislative protections for women in industry. While rejecting such a constitutional amendment, however, Norton embraced a role as a leading advocate for legislation to improve the lives of working-class families and women. She favored labor interests, introducing legislation to exempt the first $5,000 of a family's income from taxation, creating mechanisms to mediate labor-management disputes in the coal mining industry, raising survivor benefits for women whose sons were killed in World War I, and opposing the Smoot–Hawley Tariff in the late 1920s. Norton also was the first legislator to introduce bills to investigate and, later, to repeal Prohibition as codified in the 18th Amendment. It was eventually repealed in 1933. In 1929 she opposed the Gillett Bill, which would have eased restrictions on the dissemination of birth control information. A staunch Catholic, Norton argued that birth control literature would not be required if "men and women would practice self-control."[6]

When Democrats won control of the U.S. House in 1931, Norton, as ranking Democrat of the Committee on the District of Columbia, became its chairwoman. When a male member exclaimed, "This is the first time in my life I have been controlled by a woman," Norton replied, "It's the first time I've had the privilege of presiding over a body of men, and I rather like the prospect."[7] She was dubbed the "Mayor of Washington" during her tenure as chair from 1931 to 1937. It was an immense job. Since the federal government then administered the District of Columbia, all bills and petitions related to city management (an average of 250 per week) came across Norton's desk. She was acclaimed, however, for her support for a bill to provide the District of Columbia with self-government. Though she failed in that endeavor, Norton won Public Works Administration funds to build a hospital for tuberculosis patients, improved housing, secured the first old-age pension bill for District residents, and legalized liquor sales and boxing.[8]

In 1937, when Labor Committee Chairman William P. Connery, Jr., died, Norton resigned her chairmanship of the District Committee to succeed him as head of the powerful Labor Committee. She had been the second-ranking Democrat on the panel since 1929. When the Democrats gained the majority in 1931, Norton exercised increased influence over the evolution and passage of major legislation. By the time she became chair in June 1937, the so-called Second New Deal was in full swing. While much of the legislation passed during the first phase of the New Deal (1933–1935) focused on economic recovery, the second wave of programs sought to alleviate poverty and provide a social safety net that included Social Security benefits and unemployment insurance.

Norton's crowning legislative achievement came with the passage of the Fair Labor Standards Act of 1938, which she personally shepherded through committee and onto the House Floor for a vote. The only significant New Deal reform to pass in President Franklin Roosevelt's second term, the act provided for a 40-hour work week, outlawed child labor, and set a minimum wage of 25 cents per hour. To get the controversial bill out of the Rules Committee, which determined what legislation was to be debated on the floor and which was controlled by "anti-New Deal" conservative Democrats, Norton resorted to a little-used parliamentary procedure known as the discharge petition.[9] She got 218 of her colleagues (half the total House membership, plus one) to sign the petition to bring the bill to a vote. The measure failed to pass, but Norton again circulated a discharge petition and managed to get a revised measure to the floor, which passed. "I'm prouder of getting that bill through the House than anything else I've done in my life," Norton recalled.[10] In 1940, she teamed up with Majority Leader John McCormack of Massachusetts to fight off revisions to the act and scolded her colleagues for trying to reduce the benefits to working-class Americans, among which was a $12.60 weekly minimum wage. Norton declared, it "is a pittance for any family to live on . . . I think that when Members get their monthly checks for $833 they cannot look at the check and face their conscience if they refuse to vote for American workers who are getting only $12.60 a week."[11]

During World War II, Norton used her position on the Labor Committee to fight for equal pay for women laborers. She pushed for the creation of a permanent Fair Employment Practice Committee to prevent racial and gender discrimination in hiring and to secure pensions for elective and executive offices by extending the federal employee's retirement system. But she found much of her experience as Labor Committee chair in wartime frustrating because of encroachments on the panel's oversight and the bleak prospects of women's place in the postwar work-force. Critics charged that her committee was "ineffectual" because the War Labor Board and the War Manpower Commission largely determined labor policies.[12] Even House committees, in particular Naval Affairs, wrote legislation that fell properly under Labor's jurisdiction. She blamed part of these intrusions on the fact that the Labor Committee was headed by a woman.[13] "Those who really know our social system, know that women have never had very much opportunity," she said. She forecast that after the war, women would be pressed to vacate jobs and back into the home to make way for demobilized GIs seeking employment.[14]

In 1947, when Republicans regained control of the House and Norton lost her chairmanship to New Jersey's Fred H. Hartley, she resigned her Labor Committee seat in protest. "He has attended only 10 meetings of this committee in 10 years," Norton declared. "I refuse to serve under him." During her final term in Congress, when the Democrats wrested back majority control, she chaired the House Administration Committee.

At age 75, after serving 12 terms, Norton declined to run for re-election in 1950. She served briefly as a consult-ant to the Women's Advisory Committee on Defense Manpower at the Department of Labor in 1951 and 1952. She left Washington to settle in Greenwich, Connecticut, to live near one of her sisters. Norton died there on August 2, 1959.

FOR FURTHER READING

Biographical Directory of the United States Congress, "Mary T. Norton," http://bioguide.congress.gov

Mitchell, Gary. "Women Standing for Women: The Early Political Career of Mary T. Norton." *New Jersey History 96* (Spring–Summer 1978): 27–42.

Rees, Maureen. "Mary Norton: A Grand Girl." *Journal of the Rutgers University Libraries 47* (December 1985): 59–75.

Tomlinson, Barbara J. "Making Their Way: A Study of New Jersey Congresswomen, 1924–1994." Ph.D. diss., Rutgers, The State University of New Jersey–New Brunswick, 1996.

MANUSCRIPT COLLECTION

Rutgers University (New Brunswick, NJ), Alexander Library Department of Special Collections and Archives. *Papers:* 1920–1960, 10 volumes and 10 boxes. Correspondence includes letters from Franklin D. Roosevelt, Eleanor Roosevelt, and Harry S. Truman. Also includes congressional political subjects file, speeches and writings, biographical data, photographs, and scrapbooks. The unpublished memoirs of Mary T. Norton and corre-spondence concerning possible publication are included. A finding aid is available in the repository.

NOTES

1   It is unclear how many siblings were in the Hopkins family. There were as many as seven, though at least three died in infancy. See, Hope Chamberlin, *A Minority of Members: Women in the U.S. Congress* (New York: Praeger, 1973): 55; "Mary Norton," Marcy Kaptur, *Women of Congress: A Twentieth-Century Odyssey* (Washington, D.C.: Congressional Quarterly Press, 1996): 34. Carmela A. Karnoutsos, "Mary Teresa Norton," in "Jersey City Past and Present," published online at http://www.njcu.edu/programs/jchistory (accessed 13 November 2003).

2   "Mary T. Norton," *Current Biography, 1944* (New York: H.W. Wilson Co., 1944): 500–503.

3   Helen C. Camp, "Norton, Mary Teresa Hopkins," *American National Biography (ANB)* 16 (New York: Oxford University Press, 1999): 529–530.

4   "Election Statistics, 1920 to Present," http://clerk.house.gov/members/electionInfo/elections.html .

5   "Mary T. Norton," *Current Biography, 1944*: 500.

6   Chamberlin, *A Minority of Members*: 54.

7   Ibid.

8   "Mary T. Norton," *Current Biography, 1944*: 501; Camp, "Mary Teresa Hopkins Norton," *ANB*.

9   For further reading on the Fair Labor Standards Act as part of the New Deal, see Michael E. Parrish, *Anxious Decades* (New York: Norton, 1992): 382–383.

10 Kaptur, *Women of Congress*: 46.

11 "Mary T. Norton," *Current Biography, 1944*: 501.

12 Amy Porter, *Collier's*, August 1943, Vol. 112: 22.

13 "Mary T. Norton," *Current Biography, 1944*: 502. See also, John Whiteclay Chambers II, "Norton, Mary Teresa Hopkins," *Dictionary of American Biography*, Supplement 6 (New York: Scribners, 1981): 480.

14 "Mary T. Norton," *Current Biography, 1944*: 502.

Florence P. Kahn
1866–1948

UNITED STATES REPRESENTATIVE ★ REPUBLICAN FROM CALIFORNIA
1925–1937

Succeeding her husband, Florence Prag Kahn used charisma and humor to carve out her own political accomplishments as a California Representative. Going well beyond her husband's service on the Hill, Kahn quickly earned the respect of her colleagues; according to one contemporary observer, "Congress treats her like a man, fears her, admires her, and listens to her."[1] Kahn used her successful career as an example of why the Republican leadership should encourage women to participate in party politics.

Florence Prag was born in Salt Lake City, Utah, on November 9, 1866. The daughter of Polish-Jewish immigrants Conrad and Mary Goldsmith Prag, Florence and her family relocated to San Francisco when her father's business failed. Mary Prag served as an important influence on her daughter. As one of the first Jewish members of the San Francisco board of education, Mary Prag formed political connections with the city's most prominent leaders—these ties invariably assisted her daughter in her future congressional career.[2] After graduating from Girls' High School in 1883, Florence enrolled in the University of California at Berkeley, where she graduated with an A.B. in 1887.[3] Unable to pursue a law degree because she needed to help support her family, Florence Prag taught for more than a decade at Lowell High School in San Francisco.[4] On March 19, 1899, she married Julius Kahn, a former Broadway actor, state legislator, and, at the time, a first-term U.S. Representative from San Francisco.[5] The couple had two sons, Julius, Jr., and Conrad.[6]

For the next quarter century, Florence Kahn helped her husband manage his congressional workload. She acted as his aide and confidante, increasingly so as he fought a long illness late in his career while serving as chairman of the Committee on Military Affairs. Julius Kahn was re-elected in 1924 to the 69th Congress (1925–1927) but died on December 18, 1924. Local Republican Party leaders asked his widow to run for the vacant seat. Steeped in a tradition in which Jewish politicians from San Francisco typically aligned with the GOP, Kahn accepted the invitation to enter the special election because she felt she had already "carried on the work alone" during her husband's prolonged sickness.[7] As she noted, "I feel that through a sense of obligation and duty to my late husband I should accept the responsibility of continuing his work for the people of his district." [8] Kahn won the special election on February 17, 1925, for the San Francisco district, earning 48 percent of the vote against three opponents: Raymond Burr, H.W. Hutton, and Henry Claude Huck.[9] At age 58, she became the first Jewish woman elected to Congress, and was re-elected with little opposition five times.[10]

Kahn had prestigious committee assignments during her House career, positions she received because of her insider's knowledge of the institution, since her years as a political aide and adviser to her husband made her an unusually savvy freshman Member. "One of the things I learned during twenty-five years as the wife of a Congressman is not to meet the issues until they come up and not to talk too much," Kahn told the *International Herald Tribune*. "So I am not going to say that I will do any particular things except to represent my district the best I am able."[11] She also knew enough to avoid being assigned to a committee that pertained little to her district's needs. When first relegated to the Indian Affairs Committee (a fairly common committee for Congresswomen of the period), she protested publicly: "The only Indians in my district are in front of cigar stores."[12] Republican leaders

relented, and in the 71st and 72nd Congresses (1929–1933), Kahn succeeded her late husband on the Military Affairs Committee, becoming the first woman to serve on the panel. In her first term, she was on three committees: Census, Coinage, Weights, and Measures; Education; and Expenditures in the War Department. She also served on the War Claims Committee in the 70th Congress (1927–1929). Finally, Kahn earned the distinction of being the first woman appointed to the influential Appropriations Committee, one of the two most desired committees during that era, serving on the panel in the 73rd and 74th Congresses (1933–1937).[13]

Pursuing her husband's commitment to military preparedness, Kahn managed to secure expanded military installations in the Bay Area, including Hamilton Air Force Base and the Naval Air Depot in Alameda. A devout proponent of a strong military even in the face of a strengthening peace movement, Kahn defended her stance when she said, "Preparedness never caused a war, un-preparedness never prevented one."[14] While in Congress, she played a major role in appropriating federal funding for the Bay Area's two simultaneous bridge projects in the 1930s, the Golden Gate, connecting San Francisco with the Marin headlands to the north, and the Bay Bridge, which connected the city to Oakland and the East Bay. Kahn's political skill in helping to garner the unanimous congressional support necessary to build bridges over navigable waterways paved the way for the substantial boost to the economic development of San Francisco and the surrounding areas of northern California. Her support for the Federal Bureau of Investigation (FBI) was so reliable that she became a personal friend of its director, J. Edgar Hoover, who nicknamed Kahn the "Mother of the F.B.I."[15] She also opposed the Volstead Act, which prohibited the production, sale, and possession of alcohol. Believing that the government should not attempt to legislate virtues, Kahn worked to ease Prohibition strictures by permitting the manufacture of beer and wine.

As one of only a handful of women in Congress, Kahn once remarked that "the woman in political office must remember her responsibility toward other women." Heeding her own advice, Kahn worked to institute pensions for army nurses and establish a program honoring the mothers of fallen soldiers; she also publicly expressed concern about low wages for female government employees.[16] Nonetheless, despite passionately believing that women should actively participate in politics, she never considered herself a feminist. "I am not specifically interested in so-called women's questions as all national positions are sexless," Kahn noted.[17] More concerned with the welfare of the Republican Party than with promoting women's rights, Kahn urged Republican leaders to recognize the potential of women (both as voters and as possible candidates) in party politics. Regardless of her motives, Kahn illustrated the significant role women could play in the government. Originally doubted by some colleagues because of her gender, her effective service revealed that women and, in particular, widows who succeeded their husbands, could leave a mark on Congress. "This is theoretically a government of the majority," Kahn noted in a 1939 interview. "We can't let the majority be so indifferent that we will be ruled by a minority. Women must be made to realize the importance of their voice."

Much of Kahn's effectiveness in the House resulted from a vibrant and witty personality that made her presence known from the earliest days of her term. When asked how she managed such a successful legislative record, Kahn snapped back, "Sex appeal!" She usually voted with the Republican leadership, but one line that circulated around the House was: "You always know how Florence Kahn is going to vote (Republican), but only God has the slightest inkling of what she's going to say."[18] Once, New York Representative and future Mayor Fiorello La Guardia attacked her for being "nothing but a stand-patter following that reactionary Sen. [George H.] Moses," a stalwart Republican from New Hampshire. Playing off her Jewish heritage, Kahn quipped, "Why shouldn't I choose Moses as my leader? Haven't my people been following him for ages?"[19]

Electoral shifts within Kahn's district and national politics brought her House career to a close. From 1928 to 1932, the Democratic Party could not find a viable candidate and, thus, did not run any opposition against Kahn in the general election. In 1934, however, a strong challenge from Democrat Chauncy Tramutolo cut Kahn's winning share of the vote to 48 percent. FDR's 1936 re-election landslide swept congressional Democrats into office, and the San Francisco district was no exception to that trend. Progressive-Democrat Frank Havenner unseated Kahn by 58 percent to 40 percent of the vote.

In 1937, Kahn retired to San Francisco and her Nob Hill home was a gathering place for the city's political elite. During the 1939 Golden Gate Exposition, she was named one of the 12 outstanding women in the state's history. She remained active in civic affairs after she left Congress as a member of the National Council of Jewish Women and co-chair of the northern California chapter of the American Women's Voluntary Service, a World War II citizen's organization. Kahn continued her efforts to involve women in the political process and to assert their rights as citizens. "Women," she argued, "must assume the responsibility of maintaining freedom of speech in this land. They must assume also the responsibility of the ballot through government study."[20] Kahn died in San Francisco, on November 16, 1948.

FOR FURTHER READING

Biographical Directory of the United States Congress, "Florence Kahn," http://bioguide.congress.gov

Matthews, Glenna. "'There Is No Sex in Citizenship': The Career of Congresswoman Florence Prag Kahn," in Melanie Gustafson et al., *We Have Come to Stay: American Women and Political Parties, 1880–1960* (Albuquerque, NM: University of New Mexico Press, 1999).

MANUSCRIPT COLLECTION

Western Jewish History Center, Judah L. Magnes Memorial Museum (Berkeley, CA). *Papers:* In Julius and Florence (Prag) Kahn Papers, 1866–1948, two feet. An unpublished inventory is available in the repository.

NOTES

1   Quote from "Pictorial Review" used in Hope Chamberlin, *A Minority of Members: Women in the U.S. Congress* (New York: Praeger, 1973): 50.

2   Glenna Matthews, "'There Is No Sex in Citizenship': The Career of Congresswoman Florence Prag Kahn," in *We Have Come to Stay: American Women and Political Parties, 1880–1960* (Albuquerque, NM: University of New Mexico Press, 1999): 132; 134.

3   Matthews, "There Is No Sex in Citizenship": 131–132.

4   Suzanne Pullen, "First Female California Representatives from the City; In '20s, Two Women Succeeded Their Husbands in the House," 10 November 2000, *San Francisco Examiner*: A7.

5   Dorothy M. Brown, "Kahn, Florence Prag," *American National Biography* (*ANB*) 12 (New York: Oxford University Press, 1999): 334–335.

6   "Julius Kahn Dies; Was Ill for a Year," 19 December 1924, *New York Times*: 19.

7   David G. Dalin, "Jewish and Non-Partisan Republicanism in San Francisco, 1911–1963," *American Jewish History* 68(1978): 492–495. In his article, Dalin argues that San Francisco Jews flocked to the Republican Party out of an interest to curb machine politics and because Jewish politicians had a history of holding prominent political positions in the region. He also contends that Jews of German descent such as Julius Kahn had a strong tradition of supporting the GOP.

8   Matthews, "There Is No Sex in Citizenship": 134–135.

9   Ibid., 134; "Mrs. Kahn Elected to Seat in House," 18 February 1925, *Washington Post*: 1.

10   "Election Statistics, 1920 to Present," http://clerk.house.gov/members/electionInfo/elections.html .

11   "In Our Pages 100, 75 and 50 Years Ago: 1925: Female Politician," 3 March 2000, *International Herald Tribune*: opinion section, 6.

12   Susan Tolchin, *Women in Congress* (Washington, D.C.: Government Printing Office, 1976): 41; between the 67th and 76th Congresses (1921–1941), five women served on the Indian Affairs Committee.

13   Charles Stewart III, "Committee Hierarchies in the Modernizing House, 1875–1947," *American Journal of Political Science* 36 (No. 4, November 1992): 835–856.

14   Chamberlin, *A Minority of Members*: 50.

15   Brown, "Kahn, Florence Prag," *ANB*.

16   Matthews, "There Is No Sex in Citizenship": 137.

17   Frances Parkinson Keyes, "Seven Successful Women," *Delineator* (July 1928): 16.

18   "Obituary," 17 November 1948, *San Francisco Chronicle*; see also Brown, "Kahn, Florence Prag," *ANB*.

19   Pullen, "First Female California Representatives from the City."

20   Crete Cage, "Attack on Press Held Way to End Career," 9 February 1939, *Los Angeles Times*: A7.

Edith Nourse Rogers
1881–1960

UNITED STATES REPRESENTATIVE ★ REPUBLICAN FROM MASSACHUSETTS
1925–1960

As a nursing volunteer and advocate for veterans across the country during and after World War I, Edith Nourse Rogers was thrust into political office when her husband, Representative John Jacob Rogers, died in 1925. During her 35-year House career, the longest congressional tenure of any woman to date, Rogers authored legislation that had far-reaching effects on American servicemen and women, including the creation of the Women's Army Corp and the GI Bill of Rights. "The first 30 years are the hardest," Rogers once said of her House service. "It's like taking care of the sick. You start it and you like the work, and you just keep on."[1]

Edith Nourse was born in Saco, Maine, on March 19, 1881. She was one of two children born to Franklin T. Nourse, an affluent textile plant magnate, and Edith Frances Riversmith.[2] She received a private school education at Rogers Hall School in Lowell, Massachusetts, and finished her education abroad in Paris, France. Returning to America in 1907, she married John Jacob Rogers, a Harvard-trained lawyer. The couple was childless and settled in Lowell, Massachusetts. In 1912, John Rogers was elected as a Republican to the 63rd Congress (1913–1915) and was successfully re-elected to the House for six succeeding terms. He eventually served as Ranking Majority Member on the Foreign Affairs Committee and authored the 1924 Rogers Act, which reorganized and modernized the U.S. diplomatic corps.[3] During World War I, Edith Nourse Rogers inspected field hospitals with the Women's Overseas Service League. "No one could see the wounded and dying as I saw them and not be moved to do all in his or her power to help," she recalled.[4] In 1918 she joined the American Red Cross volunteer group in Washington, D.C. Her work with hospitalized veterans earned her the epithet the "Angel of Walter Reed Hospital."[5] When the war was over, three Presidents— Warren Harding, Calvin Coolidge, and Herbert Hoover—appointed Rogers as their personal ombudsman for communicating with disabled veterans. She also continued to work in her husband's congressional offices in Lowell and Washington. The Congressman considered his wife his chief adviser on policies and campaign strategy.[6] Their home on 16th Street in northwest Washington became a fashionable salon where the Rogers entertained powerful politicians and foreign dignitaries.

On March 28, 1925, Representative John Rogers died in Washington, D.C., after a long battle with cancer. Edith Rogers declared her plan to run for her husband's seat a week later.[7] Her chief Republican competition for the nomination was James Grimes, a former Massachusetts state senator who ran on a "dry," Prohibition and pro-law-and-order platform. During the campaign, Rogers noted that she had always been a prohibitionist and believed in strict enforcement of the 18th Amendment to the Constitution—a position that won her the support of temperance advocates. In the GOP primary of June 16, 1925, Rogers dispatched Grimes with 13,086 votes to 1,939.[8] Democrats nominated Eugene N. Foss of Boston, a former Massachusetts governor, to challenge Rogers in the June 30th special election. Foss believed the GOP was vulnerable because it did not support stringent tariff policies—a matter of concern especially in the strongly Democratic district which encompassed textile mill cities such as Lowell. Local political observers had nicknamed the northeastern Massachusetts district the "fighting fifth" because of its equal proportions of registered Democrats and Republicans. Having come from a family

OFFICE OF HISTORY AND PRESERVATION,

U.S. HOUSE OF REPRESENTATIVES

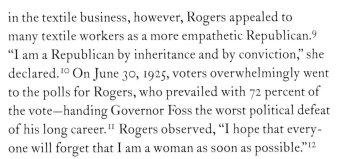
in the textile business, however, Rogers appealed to many textile workers as a more empathetic Republican.[9] "I am a Republican by inheritance and by conviction," she declared.[10] On June 30, 1925, voters overwhelmingly went to the polls for Rogers, who prevailed with 72 percent of the vote—handing Governor Foss the worst political defeat of his long career.[11] Rogers observed, "I hope that everyone will forget that I am a woman as soon as possible."[12]

Rogers was returned to the House by increasingly large margins, eclipsing those of her husband, in her subsequent 17 re-election campaigns. She was charismatic, and her sense of humor endeared her to voters and colleagues. Noting her 18-hour days, the press dubbed her "the busiest woman on Capitol Hill."[13] She was attentive to textile and clothing manufacturers—economic engines in her district, which was a hub of the U.S. textile industry— by allocating federal money to create new international markets and by advocating protective legislation.[14] With her trademark orchid or gardenia pinned to her shoulder, Rogers became a congressional institution and was never seriously challenged during her 18 consecutive terms. In 1950, on the 25th anniversary of her first election, GOP colleagues hailed her as "the First Lady of the Republican Party."[15]

When Rogers was sworn into the 69th Congress (1925–1927), she did not receive any of her husband's former committee appointments, which included Foreign Affairs and the powerful Appropriations panel. Instead, she received middling committee assignments: Expenditures in the Navy Department, Industrial Arts and Expositions, Woman Suffrage, and World War Veterans' Legislation (later renamed Veterans' Affairs). In the 70th Congress (1927–1929), she dropped the first three committees and won seats on the Civil Service and Indian Affairs panels (she stayed on the latter for only one term).

In the 73rd Congress (1933–1935), Rogers won back her husband's seat on the more coveted Foreign Affairs Committee.[16] Her concern with veterans' issues went hand-in-hand with her interest in foreign affairs. Well-traveled and attuned to international affairs, Rogers

seemed a natural appointment to that panel. Soon after taking her seat, Rogers began to address the dangers of fascism in Nazi Germany and in Italy. She was one of the first Members of Congress to denounce Nazi racial policies. In 1937 she broke with fellow Republicans to vote against the Neutrality Act, which had won wide support from GOP isolationists. In 1939, Rogers and Democratic Senator Robert Wagner of New York cosponsored a measure to increase the quota for Jewish immigrants in an effort to rescue Jewish refugee children fleeing Nazi persecution. In 1940, she again crossed party lines to vote for the Selective Service Act—creating the nation's first peacetime draft. Rogers eventually rose to the number two Ranking Minority Member post on the Foreign Affairs Committee before she voluntarily retired from it in late 1946, when the Legislative Reorganization Act reduced the number of committee assignments a Member could hold.

In 1947, Rogers gained the chairmanship of the newly renamed Veterans' Affairs Committee when the Republicans took control of the House in the 80th Congress (1947–1949). She again chaired it when power briefly transferred back to the GOP in the 83rd Congress (1953–1955). Veterans' issues had long defined Rogers's House career. In 1926, she secured pensions for army nurses and later helped create a permanent nurse corps in the Veterans' Administration.[17] In the spring of 1930, as chair of the World War Veterans' Legislation Committee's subcommittee on hospitals, Rogers inserted a $15 million provision for the development of a national network of veterans' hospitals into the Veterans' Administration Act. She did so over the objections of the committee chairman, but her diligence was applauded by veterans' groups. "Expecting much from her, veterans always receive much," one wrote. "She never disappoints."[18]

Congresswoman Rogers's crowning legislative achievements came during World War II and in the immediate postwar years. In May 1941, Rogers introduced the Women's Army Auxiliary Corps Act, to create a voluntary enrollment program for women to join the U.S. Army in a noncombat capacity. Her proposal, she explained to

In May 1941, Rogers
introduced the Women's
Army Auxiliary Corps Act,
to create a voluntary
enrollment program
for women to join
the U.S. Army in a
noncombat capacity.

colleagues, "gives women a chance to volunteer to serve their country in a patriotic way," as medical care professionals, welfare workers, clerical workers, cooks, messengers, military postal employees, chauffeurs, and telephone and telegraph operators, and in hundreds of other capacities.[19] On May 14, 1942, the WAAC Act was signed into law, creating a corps of up to 150,000 women for noncombatant service with the U.S. Army. A year later that measure was supplanted by Rogers's Women's Army Corps Bill, which granted official military status to the volunteers by creating the Women's Army Corps (WAC) within the Army. Rogers's success opened the way for other uniformed women's services in the Navy (WAVEs) and the Air Force (WASPs).

Congresswoman Rogers, who had witnessed some of the difficulties of post–World War I demobilization and its effects on veterans, sought to ease that transition by putting in place programs to assist servicemen and women who would soon return from Europe and the Pacific. As the Ranking Minority Member of the World War Veterans Legislation Committee, she sponsored a package of measures, later dubbed the GI Bill of Rights, which passed the House in 1944. Among the chief provisions of the legislation were tuition benefits for college-bound veterans and low-interest home mortgage loans. During the 82nd Congress (1951–1953), Rogers spearheaded the Veterans Re-adjustment Assistance Act of 1952, which extended the GI Bill provisions to Korean War veterans.[20] Late in the war, Rogers also proposed the creation of a Cabinet-level Department of Veterans Affairs. The proposal was not adopted in her lifetime but eventually came to fruition in 1989. So beloved by veterans was Rogers that the American Legion conferred upon her its Distinguished Service Cross—making her the first woman to receive the award.

Rogers's intense patriotism and conservative ideology led her to embrace postwar anticommunism. In the early years of the Cold War, she feared the potential insurgency of communism in the United States, making public addresses and floor speeches on the subject.[21] She supported the investigations of the House Committee on Un-American Activities and the loyalty program undertaken by President Harry S. Truman's administration. She later supported the initial investigations conducted by Republican Senator Joseph McCarthy of Wisconsin. Her concern about the influence of the "red menace" extended to international organizations. Though she supported the creation of the United Nations, Rogers advocated in 1953 that if China were admitted to the U.N. that the U.S. should withdraw from the organization and evict the organization's headquarters from New York City.

Late in her career, Rogers was mentioned as a possible challenger against Democratic Senator John F. Kennedy of Massachusetts, who came up for re-election in 1958. Observers believed Rogers was the only potential Republican who could defeat Kennedy. But the 77-year-old Congresswoman declined the opportunity. On September 10, 1960, three days before the primary for the 87th Congress (1961–1963), Congresswoman Rogers died of pneumonia in a Boston hospital.[22]

FOR FURTHER READING

Biographical Directory of the United States Congress, "Edith Nourse Rogers," http://bioguide.congress.gov

MANUSCRIPT COLLECTIONS

Massachusetts Historical Society (Boston, MA). *Papers:* 1926–1935, one folder. Letters from Edith Nourse Rogers to various constituents discussing the Grant memorial, labor issues such as the 30-hour workweek, and various bills pending in Congress.

Radcliffe College Institute for Advanced Study, Harvard University (Cambridge, MA), Schlesinger Library, http://www.radcliffe.edu/schles. *Papers:* 1854–1961, 11 linear feet. The papers include correspondence Edith Nourse Rogers received as chair of the Committee on Veterans' Affairs. Also includes correspondence with constituents, speeches, campaign material, memorabilia, recordings, motion picture film, photographs, newspaper clippings, and sympathy letters concerning her death. Scrapbooks are available on microfilm. A finding aid is available in the repository.

NOTES

1 Phil Casey, "Rep. Edith Rogers, 79, Dies; Served in House 35 Years," 11 September 1960, *Washington Post*: B12.

2 Rudolf Engelbarts, *Women in the United States Congress, 1917–1972* (Littleton, CO: Libraries Unlimited, 1974): 33.

3 "John Jacob Rogers, Bay State Member of Congress, Dead," 29 March 1925, *Washington Post*: 1; "A Friend of the Foreign Service," 31 March 1925, *New York Times*: 18.

4 Frances Mangum, "Congresswoman Good Friend to War Veterans," 23 January 1934, *Washington Post*: 11.

5 Elisabeth Ellicott Poe, "'Angel of Walter Reed' to Return to Washington as Congresswoman," 12 July 1925, *Washington Post*: SM1.

6 "Mrs. Rogers Seeking Election to Congress on Service Goal," 26 June 1925, *Christian Science Monitor*: 5.

7 "J.J. Rogers' Widow Seeks His House Seat," 8 April 1925, *Washington Post*: 3.

8 "Election of Mrs. Rogers Wins Praise of State Dry League," 1 July 1925, *Christian Science Monitor*: 7; "J.J. Rogers' Widow Nominated for House," 17 June 1925, *Washington Post*: 1; "House Election Primaries Near," 10 June 1925, *Christian Science Monitor*: 5.

9 Poe, "'Angel of Walter Reed' to Return to Washington as Congresswoman."

10 "Women Office Holders Are Now Coming From the Home," 12 July 1925, *New York Times*: X3.

11 Special election statistics from Michael J. Dubin et al., *U.S. Congressional Elections, 1788 to 1997* (Jefferson, NC: McFarland & Company, Publishers Inc., 1998): 458; "Mrs. Rogers Beats Foss by Two-to-One Vote In Bay State Election for Representative," 1 July 1925, *New York Times*: 1; "Mrs. Rogers Wins Election to House," 1 July 1925, *Washington Post*: 1.

12 Dorothy M. Brown, "Rogers, Edith Nourse," *American National Biography (ANB)* 18 (New York: Oxford University Press, 1999): 752–753; "Election of Mrs. Rogers Wins Praise of State Dry League."

13 "Bay State Congress Woman Most Tireless Worker on Hill," 18 October 1933, *Washington Post*: 9; "Women Office Holders Are Now Coming From the Home."

14 Annabel Paxton, *Women in Congress* (Richmond, VA: Dietz Press, 1945): 46; "Would Dress Up Soldiers and Aid Manufacturers," 20 June 1929, *New York Times*: 22; "Women House Members End Session With Achievement," 28 February 1931, *Washington Post*: 8; "Mrs. Rogers Seeks Tariff Findings on Japanese Textiles," 22 December 1936, *Christian Science Monitor*: 9.

15 "House Hails 'First G.O.P. Lady,'" 1 July 1950, *New York Times*: 8.

16 David T. Canon et al., *Committees in the U.S. Congress, 1789–1946*, vol. 3 (Washington, D.C.: Congressional Quarterly Press, 2002): 894. Based on Charles Stewart's relative rankings in "Committee Hierarchies in the Modernizing House, 1875–1947," *American Journal of Political Science* 36 (No. 4, November 1992): 835–856.

17 Brown, "Edith Nourse Rogers," *ANB*; "Offers Revisions in Veterans' Care: Mrs. Rogers Suggests Nursing and Physicians Corps as a Permanent Adjunct," 27 August 1943, *New York Times*: 14.

18 "Veteran's Tribute to Representative Edith Nourse Rogers," 15 May 1930, *Washington Post*: 6; Hope Chamberlin, *A Minority of Members: Women in the U.S. Congress* (New York: Praeger, 1973): 59.

19 *Congressional Record*, House, 77th Cong., 1st sess. (28 May 1941): 4531–4533; *Congressional Record*, House, 77th Cong., 1st sess. (12 December 1941): 9747.

20 In the 60 years after passage of the original GI Bill of Rights, more than 21 million veterans and servicemen received $75 billion in benefits for education and job training. The Veterans' Administration and Department of Veterans' Affairs also had guaranteed nearly 17 million home loans since the program's inception. Department of Veterans Affairs, "Fact Sheet: Facts About the Department of Veterans Affairs," (April 2003).

21 "Rep. Edith Rogers Seeks Loans for Homeless G.I.'s," 6 November 1947, *Los Angeles Times*: 11; see also, *Congressional Record*, House, 80th Cong., 1st sess. (27 March 1947): 2785–2786.

22 Chamberlin, *A Minority of Members*: 61.

Katherine Gudger Langley
1888–1948

UNITED STATES REPRESENTATIVE ★ REPUBLICAN FROM KENTUCKY
1927–1931

The career of Congresswoman Katherine Gudger Langley illustrates a highly unusual route to Congress. Her husband, John Langley, resigned his House seat after being convicted of violating Prohibition laws. Katherine Langley then defeated her husband's successor and won election to the House in a "vindication campaign" designed to exonerate her disgraced spouse.

Katherine Gudger was born near Marshall, North Carolina, on February 14, 1888, to James Madison Gudger and Katherine Hawkins.[1] Gudger graduated in 1901 from the Woman's College in Richmond, Virginia, and went on briefly to Emerson College of Oratory in Boston. A short teaching job in speech in Tennessee ended when she left for Washington, D.C., in 1904 to become her father's secretary when he was elected U.S. Representative from North Carolina on the Democratic ticket. That same year she met and later married John Langley, a former state legislator and attorney working for the Census Bureau. The couple settled in Pikeville, Kentucky, where John Langley successfully ran as a Republican for the House of Representatives in 1906. He eventually won re-election nine times in a safely Republican district that was an old unionist stronghold in eastern Kentucky.

Katherine Langley was well known in Washington society and on Capitol Hill, working as her husband's secretary and administrative assistant. From 1919 to 1925 she was clerk to the Committee on Public Buildings and Grounds while John Langley was chairman. At the same time, Katherine Langley also was an active member in party politics, serving as the first woman member of the state central committee and founder of the Women's Republican State Committee. She served as a delegate to the Republican National Convention in 1924.[2]

Katherine Langley claimed her husband's seat in the House of Representatives under very unusual circumstances. "Pork Barrel John" Langley was convicted of "conspiracy to violate the Prohibition Act" by trying to sell 1,400 bottles of whiskey.[3] He won re-election in 1924 while his conviction was being appealed. When the U.S. Supreme Court refused to overturn the decision, he resigned from the 69th Congress (1925–1927) on January 11, 1926, and was sentenced to the federal penitentiary in Atlanta for two years. "They believe he was the victim of a political conspiracy," reported the *Lexington Leader* of the district's reaction. The disaffection of Republicans in eastern Kentucky over the lack of effort by Senator Richard P. Ernst to defend John Langley contributed to Ernst's re-election defeat in 1926 to Alben Barkley.[4] Langley's district manifested a persistent sense that Kentuckians were "drinking wet and voting dry."[5] On February 13, 1926, Republican Andrew J. Kirk succeeded Congressman Langley in a special election to fill out the remainder of his term in the 69th Congress.

Katherine Langley resolved to clear her husband's name by running for his seat in the 70th Congress (1927–1929). With John Langley's active help from prison, his wife defeated Kirk in the Republican primary. Langley asked voters to "send my wife, the mother of our three children, to Washington" because "she knows better than anyone else my unfinished plans."[6] Katherine Langley was active on the stump, drawing upon her experience as a speech teacher. She impressed voters with her efforts. "John Langley wears the breeches," one voter commented, "but the lady has the brains."[7] Basking in the glow of her primary victory, she announced that her win

proved her fitness for office and vindicated her husband. That fall she won election to the House with 58 percent of the vote.[8] A little more than a month later, on December 18, 1926, John Langley was paroled from the Atlanta Penitentiary, having served 11 months of his sentence.[9] Katherine Langley's re-election in 1928 with 56 percent of the vote was more than respectable.[10]

John Langley's conviction and resignation in disgrace left his wife socially ostracized in the conservative Washington social scene. Capital elite did not approve when Langley extended her family's practice of patronage within the congressional office by hiring her married daughter as her secretary.[11] Observers were quick to notice that the former speech teacher followed a more archaic rhetorical style than was favored at the time. "She came from the 'heart of the hills,'" writes Hope Chamberlin. "Coal, 'king of energy,' was dug by 'stalwart and sturdy miners.'" Sometimes given to verse, she described the Kentucky mountaineer as "'a man whose grip is a little tighter, whose smile is a little brighter, whose faith is a little whiter.'"[12] Her reputation grew when she interrupted a debate on tax legislation to praise a Kentucky basketball team.[13] Her committee assignments were not impressive. She was appointed to the Committee on Claims, the Committee on Immigration and Naturalization, and the Committee on Invalid Pensions. In the 71st Congress (1929–1931) she also served on the Committee on Education.

In early 1930 Langley achieved an important first. She became the first woman Member to serve on the Republican Committee on Committees, succeeding John M. Robsion when he was appointed as U.S. Senator.[14] As a member of the Committee on Committees, Langley served on the body that assigned Republican Members to the standing committees. The Republican conference specified that each state delegation with a party member would have a seat on the committee. The state's representative on the committee would have a vote equivalent to the size of the state's Republican delegation. Furthermore, each state party caucus would select its committee representative.[15] Langley's achievement is cast in a different

light as a result. She was the most senior member of the Kentucky Republican caucus after Robsion left, and her appointment came after the committee assignments were made for the 71st Congress. To take full advantage of this position of influence, she would need to win re-election.

Throughout her House career, Langley continued her efforts to vindicate her husband. She succeeded in convincing President Calvin Coolidge to grant John Langley a pardon. It was issued on December 20, 1928, shortly after Katherine Langley had won her second term. The pardon apparently included an informal proviso that John Langley never run for public office again. Nevertheless, during the holidays in late 1928, he circulated a Christmas message to her constituents.[16] A week later, John Langley declared his intention to seek his House seat again, denying that any condition had been set for his clemency. Katherine Langley issued a statement in Washington that she would not step aside "for John or anyone else," and all talk of John Langley running for his old seat died away.[17]

The election of 1928, with Governor Al Smith of New York, a Catholic and an opponent of Prohibition, running as the Democratic presidential nominee, was devastating to the Democratic Party in Kentucky. Of 11 congressional districts where only two typically went Republican, all but two were lost by the Democrats in 1928. Without Smith at the head of the ticket, Kentucky Democrats expected to do much better in 1930. The continuing impact of the Great Depression hurt Republican congressional candidates, however, especially those from traditionally Republican districts. In those districts the longtime agricultural depression combined with the depressed coal industry to turn the voters against the Republican administration of President Herbert Hoover. Under these circumstances, Katherine Langley took her time to come to a decision about running for another term in the House. In late February 1930, she announced her plans for re-election.[18] In the August primary, Langley faced two opponents.[19] By the fall of 1930, she faced a growing Democratic tide at the polls, and some observers had placed her on the list of vulnerable incumbents.[20]

She narrowly lost to Andrew Jackson May, a Democrat, in her bid for a third term, gaining only 47 percent of the vote.[21] Later the *New York Times* would characterize the 1930 Republican losses in Kentucky as "one of the biggest political form reversals of its history."[22]

Congresswoman Langley retired to Pikeville, Kentucky, where John Langley had earlier resumed his law practice. John Langley died in January 1932 of pneumonia, still arguing that he had been sent to prison unjustly.[23] Katherine Langley served as a postmistress and was twice elected as a district railroad commissioner. She died in Pikeville, Kentucky, on August 15, 1948.[24]

FOR FURTHER READING

Biographical Directory of the United States Congress, "Katherine Gudger Langley," http://bioguide.congress.gov

NOTES

1 Francesco L. Nepa, "Langley, Katherine Gudger," *American National Biography (ANB)* 13 (New York: Oxford University Press, 1999): 156–157. There is the possibility that the 1888 birth date may have been in error. Langley may actually have been born in 1883.

2 Nepa, "Langley, Katherine Gudger," *ANB.*

3 James C. Klotter, *Kentucky: Portrait in Paradox,* 1900–1950 (Frankfort: Kentucky Historical Society, 1996): 283.

4 Hope Chamberlin, *A Minority of Members: Women in the U.S. Congress* (New York: Praeger, 1963): 64; Klotter, *Kentucky:* 283.

5 John Ed Pearce, *Divide and Dissent: Kentucky Politics, 1930–1963* (Louisville: University Press of Kentucky, 1987): 11.

6 Chamberlin, *A Minority of Members:* 64.

7 Ibid.

8 Nepa, "Langley, Katherine Gudger," *ANB;* "Election Statistics, 1920 to Present," http://clerk.house.gov/members/electionInfo/elections.html.

9 "Mrs. Langley to Retire From Politics in 1930," 25 December 1928, *Washington Post:* 5.

10 "Election Statistics, 1920 to Present," http://clerk.house.gov/members/electionInfo/elections.html.

11 Chamberlin, *A Minority of Members:* 65; Susan Tolchin, *Women in Congress* (Washington, D.C.: Government Printing Office, 1976): 46.

12 Chamberlin, *A Minority of Members:* 64–65; "'Lady from Kentucky' Wins Her First Plea," 25 January 1928, *Washington Post:* 4.

13 Chamberlin, *A Minority of Members:* 65.

14 "Woman on Committee on Committees," 19 January 1930, *New York Times:* 25.

15 William L. Morrow, *Congressional Committees* (New York: Scribners, 1969): 45.

16 Chamberlin, *A Minority of Members:* 65. In a Christmas message that year sent to her constituents, John Langley announced that his wife would not be a candidate for re-election in 1930. Whether or not John Langley would take advantage of the pardon to run for his old seat and resume his political career was left ambiguous. A newspaper photo caption suggested that the issue would "be a matter for the family council." See, "Mrs. Langley to Retire From Politics in 1930," 25 December 1928, *Washington Post:* 5; and "Langley May Return to Politics," 2 January 1929, *Washington Post:* 4.

17 Chamberlin, *A Minority of Members:* 65. Toward the end of 1929, John Langley finished a manuscript entitled "They Tried to Crucify Me, or the Smoke Screen of the Cumberland," dedicated to his deceased parents and to his wife. The book sought to prove that his conviction was an attempt by the scandal-ridden Attorney General Harry M. Daugherty to distract the public from the growing scandals of the Harding administration. See, "Langley Issues Book on His 'Persecution,'" 9 December 1929, *New York Times:* 32.

18 "Gentlewomen of the Congress Find the House More Stimulating Than the Home; Try for Reelection," 2 March 1930, *Washington Post:* S3.

19 "Kentucky Election Surprise Forecast," 4 August 1930, *Washington Post:* 5; "Former Kentucky Governor Defeated," 5 August 1930, *Washington Post:* 1; "Kentucky Renames Congress Members," 5 August 1930, *New York Times:* 4.

20 "Republican Upset in House Foreseen," 15 October 1930, *New York Times:* 5; "Kentucky Campaign Marked by Apathy," 26 October 1930, *New York Times:* 17.

21 "Election Statistics, 1920 to Present," http://clerk.house.gov/members/electionInfo/elections.html; "Nip and Tuck for the House," 6 November 1930, *New York Times:* 17.

22 "Laffoon Has Best Chance in Kentucky," 13 September 1931, *New York Times:* E8.

23 "John W. Langley Dies in Kentucky," 18 January 1932, *Washington Post:* 1.

24 "Mrs. J.W. Langley, Once in Congress," 16 August 1948, *New York Times:* 19; "Mrs. Langley, Ex-Member of Congress, Dies," 16 August 1948, *Washington Post:* B2.

Pearl Oldfield
1876–1962

UNITED STATES REPRESENTATIVE ★ DEMOCRAT FROM ARKANSAS
1929–1931

Pearl Oldfield succeeded her late husband, Democratic Whip William A. Oldfield, in the House of Representatives. During her tenure, Representative Oldfield sought to remedy the threats that natural disaster and economic depression posed to the livelihood and welfare of her rural Arkansas constituency. Though she had years of experience in Washington as the wife of a powerful politician, Oldfield left Congress after little more than one term, content to retire "to the sphere in which I believe women belong—the home."[1]

Fannie Pearl Peden was born on December 2, 1876, in Cotton Plant, Arkansas, one of five children born to J.A. Peden and Helen Hill Peden. The daughter of a prominent Southern family, Pearl Peden attended Arkansas College in Batesville. In 1901, she married William Allan Oldfield, a Spanish-American War veteran, lawyer, and district attorney for Izard County, Arkansas. William Oldfield was elected to the U.S. House of Representatives in 1908 and went on to win election to 10 additional consecutive terms in Congress. Representative Oldfield served as Democratic Whip for eight years, from 1920 to 1928, and as chairman of the Democratic Congressional Committee from 1924 to 1928. He also attained the chairmanship of the Patents Committee and served on the powerful Ways and Means Committee. "Equivocation and compromise were not in his nature," the *Washington Post* observed. "Party loyalty was his byword." He also was considered a top prospect to head the Democratic National Committee, but he passed on the chance to stand for the post.[2] During her husband's House career, Pearl Oldfield lived with him in an apartment in northwest Washington, D.C., returning occasionally to their Arkansas home in Batesville. After Pearl Oldfield's mother came to live

with them in 1914, the Congressman's wife stopped regular travel back to the district to provide for her mother's health-care needs. In the 1920s, a fire destroyed the Oldfields' Batesville home.[3]

William Oldfield had been in poor health since 1925, and the stress and strain of campaigning nationally for Democratic House candidates took its toll on him. Shortly after election day, on November 19, 1928, he passed away after surgery for gallstones.[4] Less than a week later, local Arkansas Democratic Party leaders—seeking a temporary replacement until a candidate could be groomed to replace the powerful Congressman—asked his wife to run for his seat.[5] Originally, leaders wanted Pearl Oldfield just to fill in the remaining four months on her husband's term in the 70th Congress (1927–1929), set to expire in March 1929. They later asked her to campaign for the full term in the 71st Congress (1929–1931) to which her husband had just been elected. Pearl Oldfield agreed. "I am deeply appreciative of the good will shown toward Mr. Oldfield's memory and the expression of confidence in me," she told reporters.[6] On December 8, 1928, the Arkansas Democratic central committee nominated Oldfield— which was tantamount to victory in the southern one-party system.[7]

In the early 20th century, Arkansas politics embodied "the one-party system in its most undefiled and undiluted form." So dominant was the Democratic Party that elections revolved less around issues or political ideology than around petty rivalries, charismatic personalities, and raw emotions.[8] Conservative Democrats commanded the political apparatus and on most major public policy issues differed little from Republican counterparts. Pearl Oldfield tapped into her husband's influential political

OFFICE OF HISTORY AND PRESERVATION,

U.S. HOUSE OF REPRESENTATIVES

connections as well as public sympathy for her bereavement. On January 9, 1929, Oldfield won election without opposition to fill out the remaining months of his term in the 70th Congress. Voters also sent her to the 71st Congress against Independent candidate R.W. Tucker; turnout was light and surprisingly close, considering the Democratic endorsement of Oldfield. She defeated Tucker with fewer than 500 votes, 4,108 to 3,641 (53 to 47 percent). "I came back to the office to look after things because no one was here to keep things going," Oldfield later said.[9]

Upon being sworn into office on January 11, 1929, Pearl Oldfield became the first woman from the South to serve in the House. In one of her first actions as a Representative, she expressed support for a $24 million appropriation to provide for federal departments' funding of the enforcement of Prohibition laws. "I'm for that $24,000,000 and as much more as they ask for," Congresswoman Oldfield told the *New York Times*. "I don't want them to have any excuse for not carrying out the Prohibition enforcement program."[10] She did not receive committee assignments until the 71st Congress convened on March 4, 1929. As a member of the minority party (the GOP gained 32 seats in the House during the 1928 elections to further solidify their dominance in the Chamber), Oldfield received assignments on three committees: Coinage, Weights and Measures; Expenditures in the Executive Departments; and Public Buildings and Grounds.

"Miss Pearl," as constituents affectionately called her, primarily tended to the needs of her district that covered large portions of northern and central Arkansas. She sponsored legislation to continue federal aid for the rehabilitation of farmland damaged by the severe Mississippi River floods of 1927. Unemployment caused by the Great Depression compounded the economic misery of residents from rural Arkansas. "I want to say that the situation is distressing and most grave with cold, sickness, and actual starvation present in many sections" of the district, Congresswoman Oldfield reported to colleagues in January 1931. Oldfield asked her House colleagues to approve a $15 million food appropriation to alleviate malnutrition in drought-affected areas where Red Cross

relief efforts were inadequate to meet the demands for food. "Some Members object to passing the $15,000,000 appropriation for food. They call it the dole system," Oldfield said. "Under ordinary conditions I also would oppose it, but under ordinary conditions Arkansans would not be compelled to make the appeal. But this is an extraordinary situation, and I feel that the end sought to be accomplished justifies any honorable means."[11] She also sponsored legislation to authorize the Arkansas Highway Commission to construct toll-free bridges across the Black River and White River in her district. She described herself as a district caretaker, fastidious about answering constituent mail and regularly attending floor debates. When Arkansas Congressman Otis Wingo passed away in 1930, Oldfield memorialized him on the House Floor as a family man and longtime friend.[12] Several months later, she welcomed his widow, Effiegene Wingo, when she succeeded her husband in a special election. It marked the first time two women from the same state served simultaneously.

Ultimately, however, Oldfield spurned the limelight and preferred anonymity—claiming that she felt unable to govern without her husband's counsel. Just months into her term, she announced she would not run for reelection in 1930. "I accepted the nomination believing I should serve only a few weeks . . . I announced my old-fashioned belief about women and the home, and that belief I still hold," Oldfield admitted.[13] She expressed her "traditional" views over the course of her term. "There are so many things a woman can do that a man can't," Oldfield remarked, in discussing her decision to leave Congress. "Why not do them and let the men do what they can?"[14] Nevertheless, Congresswoman Oldfield understood that a younger generation of women would play a greater role in politics, and she encouraged them to do so with the admonition that they not make their gender a central consideration in weighing a public career.[15]

Oldfield retired from the House in March 1931, and though she often visited Batesville, she remained in the nation's capital caring for her mother, who died in 1933. Although she had no children of her own, she looked forward to devoting herself to a niece and nephew in retirement, as well as to charitable causes "for children." Pearl Peden Oldfield passed away in Washington, D.C., on April 12, 1962.

FOR FURTHER READING

Biographical Directory of the United States Congress, "Pearl Peden Oldfield," http://bioguide.congress.gov

NOTES

1   "Mrs. Oldfield to Quit Congress at Term End," 30 May 1929, *New York Times*: 8. See also, Hope Chamberlin, *A Minority of Members: Women in the U.S. Congress* (New York: Praeger, 1973): 65–66.

2   "W.A. Oldfield, Whip of the House, Dies Here," 20 November 1928, *Washington Post*: 1; "William A. Oldfield," 20 November 1928, *Washington Post*: 6; "W.A. Oldfield Dies; A Leader in the House," 20 November 1928, *New York Times*: 28.

3   "Mrs. Oldfield to Retire," 30 May 1929, *Los Angeles Times*: 4.

4   "W.A. Oldfield Dies; A Leader in House."

5   "Mrs. Oldfield May Run for Seat in Congress," 24 November 1928, *Washington Post*: 3.

6   "Arkansas to Elect Widow of Oldfield," 27 November 1928, *Washington Post*: 5.

7   "Oldfield's Widow Wins House Seat Nomination," 8 December 1928, *Washington Post*: 2.

8   V.O. Key, Jr., *Southern Politics in State and Nation* (Knoxville: University of Tennessee Press, 1984): 183; 185–187.

9   "Mrs. Oldfield to Retire."

10 "Dry League Pushes Big Fund in House," 29 January 1929, *New York Times*: 13.

11 *Congressional Record*, House, 71st Cong., 3rd sess. (12 January 1931): 2019.

12 *Congressional Record*, House, 71st Cong., 3rd sess. (19 February 1931): 5418.

13 "Mrs. Oldfield to Retire."

14 "Leave Politics to Men, Woman in House Says," 31 December 1929, *Washington Post*: 1.

15 "Mrs. Oldfield Decries Feminist in Politics," 19 February 1931, *New York Times*: 3.

Ruth Hanna McCormick
1880–1944

UNITED STATES REPRESENTATIVE ★ REPUBLICAN FROM ILLINOIS
1929–1931

For more than three decades Ruth Hanna McCormick constantly campaigned as the daughter of Republican kingmaker and Ohio Senator Marcus Alonzo "Mark" Hanna, as the wife of U.S. Representative and Senator Medill McCormick, and as a Grand Old Party (GOP) leader herself. In the late 1920s she forged a personal political machine, a network of Illinois Republican women's clubs potent enough to propel her into elected office. "I don't want to be appointed to anything," McCormick said when asked if she would accept a prominent diplomatic or government post. "That wouldn't appeal to me. I want to be elected in a fair fight on a clean-cut issue."[1]

Ruth Hanna was born in Cleveland, Ohio, on March 27, 1880, one of three children born to Marcus Hanna and Charlotte Augusta Rhodes Hanna. Born into privilege, Ruth Hanna received an elite private school education. In 1896, Ruth accompanied her father while he waged successful campaigns as a U.S. Senate candidate and as manager for Republican presidential candidate, William McKinley.[2] Instead of heading off to college, Ruth followed Senator Hanna to Washington, D.C., where she served as his personal secretary. On June 10, 1903, Ruth Hanna married Joseph Medill McCormick, scion of the family that owned the *Chicago Tribune*.[3] The McCormicks raised three children: Katherine (Katrina), John, and Ruth. Medill McCormick served for eight years as the *Tribune* publisher. The couple participated in various progressive reform activities and lived in the University of Chicago Settlement House, an experience that deepened Ruth McCormick's concern for the welfare of women and children. Unable to purchase a special type of milk needed by one of her children, and appalled by the unsanitary conditions in Illinois dairies, she opened a dairy and breeding farm near Byron, Illinois, to produce sanitary milk for invalids and children.[4]

In 1912, Medill McCormick won the first of two terms in the Illinois legislature as a Progressive-Republican. In Springfield, Ruth was a lobbyist who helped to pass the Illinois Equal Suffrage Act in 1913, a measure ensuring women the vote in municipal and presidential elections. It marked the first time a state east of the Mississippi granted that right.[5] In 1913, McCormick succeeded the confrontational Alice Paul as chair of the Congressional Committee of the National American Woman Suffrage Association (NAWSA). She promoted pro-suffrage congressional candidates at the state level. Medill McCormick, meanwhile, was elected in 1916 to the U.S. House from Illinois and, in 1918, to the U.S. Senate by defeating Democratic Whip James Hamilton Lewis.

Despite her progressive experimentalism, McCormick was a GOP stalwart.[6] When it became apparent that women would soon achieve the vote, she quickly secured her spot within the framework of partisan politics—a move that distinguished her from many other suffragists. In September 1918, Ruth McCormick was appointed to direct the newly created Republican Women's National Executive Committee. Her main task was to organize women voters for the GOP.[7] In 1924, when the Republican National Committee (RNC) reorganized, she became the GOP's first elected national committeewoman from Illinois. That same year, Medill McCormick lost the GOP renomination to the Senate to Charles S. Deneen and committed suicide in 1925. Convinced that her husband lost his seat in part due to low turnout among Republican women, Ruth McCormick devoted herself to organizing women voters statewide. From 1924 to 1928, she raised her visibility and created an important network of GOP women's clubs in Illinois, setting up 90 entities in the state's 102 counties—a ready-made organization that later propelled her to statewide office.[8]

In 1928, McCormick left the RNC to run for one of Illinois' two At-Large U.S. House seats. She was a tireless campaigner and an engaging speaker who addressed crowds extemporaneously. McCormick advertised her party experience, not her gender. "The first and most important thing that I want to drive home is this: I haven't gone into this as a woman," McCormick told the *New York Times*. "I am a politician. I have been a political worker for more years than most of the men in the party today."[9] McCormick's platform was straightforward: favoring Prohibition and military preparedness, but with an isolationist tilt. She also supported the McNary–Haugen Bill to extend to American farmers tariff protections afforded to big industry.[10] Meanwhile, McCormick remained neutral in a violent battle between GOP factions: the political machine of Chicago Mayor William Hale "Big Bill" Thompson and opposition led by Illinois Senator Charles Deneen.[11] With thousands of Chicago police and precinct "watchers" guarding polls, primary voters turned out in record numbers, propelling McCormick into the general election. She canvassed the state, traveling more than 34,000 miles in a car and making hundreds of speeches. With her motto of "No Promises and No Bunk," she was the top vote-getter in a field of 10 candidates—winning 1.7 million votes—36 percent of the total.[12]

When she arrived in the capital, McCormick's supporters believed she might get a seat on the Agriculture Committee, considering her experience with farm operations and a large agricultural constituency.[13] But she was appointed to the Committee on Naval Affairs—chaired by Illinois Representative Fred L. Britten, one of the most influential House committees and a coveted panel where no woman had yet served.

Though handed a plum assignment, McCormick, who harbored aspirations for the U.S. Senate or the Illinois governor's office, refused to become ensconced in the House. In an experience typical for a freshman, she did not deliver any floor speeches, though she did push for passage of a farm bill to help relieve overproduction as well a tariff revision. McCormick also supported President Herbert Hoover's call to repeal the National Origins clause of the Immigration Act of 1924—an issue important to labor that concerned a large part of

McCormick's constituency.[14] Much of her time in Washington was spent attending to constituent requests, primarily from Spanish-American War veterans seeking help with pensions.

In September 1929, McCormick announced that she would seek the Republican nomination to the U.S. Senate against the freshman incumbent, Senator Deneen.[15] McCormick won the endorsement of Chicago's Mayor Thompson and Illinois Governor "Lop Ear" Lou Emmerson, who assigned an aide to manage her Cook County campaign. In "Downstate" Illinois, the candidates divided over the World Court issue, with Deneen supporting it and McCormick, the confirmed isolationist, arguing that it would draw America into European wars. In the end, the World Court debate proved decisive.[16] McCormick swamped Deneen with a nearly 200,000-vote plurality on April 8, 1930, becoming the first woman to receive a major party nomination for the U.S. Senate.

In the general election, McCormick faced former Senator James Hamilton Lewis, whom Medill McCormick defeated in 1918. Lewis's flat rejection of American adherence to the World Court deprived McCormick of a key issue.[17] Without a signal campaign issue with which to challenge Lewis, McCormick faced sustained assaults on her Prohibition stand, the economy, and her primary campaign expenses.[18] McCormick vowed to abide by the decision of Illinois voters, who also were scheduled to vote on a Prohibition referendum at the November polls.[19] This position angered women temperance zealots. McCormick's prospects were dimmed when her nemesis, Lottie O'Neill, former vice president of the Illinois Women's Club and a critic of McCormick's "bossism," ran as an Independent Republican and siphoned off a sizeable portion of the women's vote.[20] The failing economy proved most important.[21] Against the backdrop of economic depression and spreading unemployment, the disclosure of McCormick's lavish nomination campaign expenses proved damaging. McCormick told a Senate investigating committee that she had spent $252,000—10 times more than Deneen. McCormick argued the expenditures were necessary to "overcome the organized [political] machines."[22] Eventually the investigation was suspended, but the damage was done.[23] McCormick polled just 31 percent in a state that gave Hoover nearly a half-million vote plurality two years earlier. Nationally, Republicans lost 53 House seats and eight Senate seats.

Although her career as an elective officeholder came to an end, McCormick had no intention of retiring from public affairs. In March 1932, she married Albert Gallatin Simms, a former New Mexico Congressman who also served in the 71st Congress (1929–1931)—marking the first time two concurrent Members married.[24] McCormick managed two newspapers and a radio station and founded an Albuquerque girls school in 1934. In 1937, she sold her Rock River dairy farm and purchased a 250,000-acre cattle and sheep operation, Trinchera Ranch, in south-central Colorado. In 1940, she helped to manage Thomas E. Dewey's presidential campaign. A horse-riding accident put McCormick in the hospital in the fall of 1944. Shortly after being discharged, she was diagnosed with pancreatitis and died from complications in Chicago on December 31, 1944.

FOR FURTHER READING

Biographical Directory of the United States Congress, "Ruth Hanna McCormick," http://bioguide.congress.gov

Miller, Kristie. *Ruth Hanna McCormick: A Life in Politics, 1880-1944* (Albuquerque: University of New Mexico Press, 1992).

———."Ruth Hanna McCormick and the Senatorial Election of 1930." *Illinois Historical Journal* 81 (Autumn 1988): 191–210.

MANUSCRIPT COLLECTION

Library of Congress (Washington, D.C.), Manuscript Division. *Papers:* In the Hanna–McCormick Family Papers, 1792–1985, 66.4 linear feet. Includes materials relating to Ruth McCormick's political activities 1918–1944. The bulk of the material, 125 of 136 boxes, pertains to McCormick's correspondence between two date ranges: 1927–1930 and 1942–1944. An inventory is available in the repository. Her suffrage activities are extensively covered in the National American Woman Suffrage Association (NAWSA) Papers, also housed at the Library of Congress.

NOTES

1   "Current Magazines," 20 March 1927, *New York Times*: BR27. This article excerpts from the March 1927 *Century Magazine* article by Ida Clyde Clarke, "A Woman in the White House."

2   "Ruth Hanna Simms; Republican Figure," 1 January 1945, *New York Times*: 19.

3   "Ruth Hanna Simms; Republican Figure." See also, Kristie Miller, "McCormick, Ruth Hanna," *American National Biography (ANB)* 14 (New York: Oxford University Press, 1999): 923–925, and James P. Louis, "Simms, Ruth Hanna McCormick," *Dictionary of American Biography (DAB)* Supplement 3 (New York: Scribners, 1973): 710–711.

4   "Then Along Came Ruth—to Congress," 14 April 1929, *Washington Post*: SM3.

5   Kristie Miller, *Ruth Hanna McCormick: A Life in Politics* (Albuquerque: University of New Mexico Press, 1992): 93–98.

6   *ANB, DAB*, and Miller all accord on this point.

7   Melanie Gustafson, *Women and the Republican Party, 1854–1924* (Urbana: University of Illinois Press, 2003): 180.

8   Louis, "Ruth Hanna McCormick Simms," *DAB*.

9   S. J. Woolf, "Mark Hanna's Daughter Chooses to Run," 16 October 1927, *New York Times*: SM10.

10 Miller, *Ruth Hanna McCormick*: 186–187.

11 Ibid., 191.

12 "Election Statistics, 1920 to Present," http://clerk.house.gov/members/electionInfo/elections.html.

13 "Then Along Came Ruth—To Congress."

14 Miller, *Ruth Hanna McCormick*: 201.

15 Ibid.

16 This is Miller's sound conclusion, see *Ruth Hanna McCormick*: 220–221. The *Washington Post* concluded much the same soon after the election: "Ruth McCormick," 10 April 1930, *Washington Post*: 6.

17 "World Court Foes, Women and the Drys Hail Mrs. McCormick," 10 April 1930, *Washington Post*: 1; Miller, *Ruth Hanna McCormick*: 232.

18 "The Illinois Campaign," 11 April 1930, *Washington Post*: 6.

19 "Ruth and Jim," 24 August 1930, *Washington Post*: S1.

20 "Mrs. O'Neill to Oppose Bitter Rival, Running as Independent," 5 September 1930, *Washington Post*: 1; Hope Chamberlin, *A Minority of Members: Women in the U.S. Congress* (New York: Praeger, 1973): 70.

21 Miller, *Ruth Hanna McCormick*: 231.

22 Ibid., 225–229.

23 Ibid., 233.

24 "McCormick Congratulated by Colleagues," 10 March 1932, *New York Times*: 18.

Ruth Bryan Owen
1885–1954

UNITED STATES REPRESENTATIVE ★ DEMOCRAT FROM FLORIDA
1929–1933

Ruth Bryan Owen, daughter of "The Peerless Leader," three-time Democratic presidential candidate William Jennings Bryan, inherited her father's political gifts as a communicator and, like him, pursued a reform agenda in the House of Representatives. Known for her strenuous campaign efforts, oratory, and devotion to constituent services, Representative Owen became the first woman to serve on the House Foreign Affairs Committee.

Ruth Bryan was born on October 2, 1885, in Jacksonville, Illinois. The family moved in response to her father's rising political fortunes—first, upon his election to the Nebraska legislature, to Lincoln when Ruth Bryan was two years old. At age five, she moved to Washington, when her father was elected to the U.S. House of Representatives. Her mother, Mary E. Baird, was a lawyer who had been admitted to the bar and, as Owen recalled years later, "I would like to emulate her. She is a thoroughly feminine woman with the mind of a thoroughly masculine man."[1] Ruth also doted on her father, often accompanying him on the House Floor. During the ferocious tariff debates of the 1890s, Ruth's frequent appearances led Members to name her "the sweetheart of the House."[2]

Ruth Bryan attended public schools in Washington, D.C., and the Monticello Female Academy in Godfrey, Illinois. She entered the University of Nebraska in 1901 and took two years of classes before marrying the artist William Homer Leavitt in 1903. They had two children, Ruth and John. In 1908, she served as her father's traveling secretary during his third presidential campaign. Despite her fundamentalist father's objections, she divorced Leavitt and, in 1910, married Reginald A. Owen, an officer of the Royal British Engineers. The couple had two more children, Reginald and Helen. The family lived at Reginald Owen's numerous overseas duty posts. In Cairo in 1915, Ruth Owen joined the British Volunteer Aid Detachment as a nurse to care for convalescent soldiers. Owen also established a volunteer entertainment troupe, the "Optimists," that performed at military hospitals in the Middle East.[3] When her husband's health failed in 1919, she moved the family to Miami, Florida, to be near her parents. For the next 10 years, she spoke on a professional lecture circuit and served as a faculty member and on the board of regents at the University of Miami.

A year after her father's death in 1925, Ruth Bryan Owen decided to run for the House of Representatives in a district along Florida's Atlantic coast. In a state that refused to ratify the 19th Amendment, she narrowly lost in the Democratic primary to six-term incumbent William J. Sears by 800 votes. When Owen was widowed the next year, she had apprehensions about her role in politics: that "there was not the friendliest feeling toward any woman taking her place in political life."[4] Yet, Owen did not leave the political arena; she ran again for the same seat in 1928. In an effort to "meet the voters" before the primary election, she reached out to dozens of newspaper editors with promotional materials.[5] Her relief work after a devastating hurricane ripped through Miami in 1927 also drew attention to the determined candidate. Owen's efforts were not in vain, and she triumphed over Sears in the 1928 Democratic primary by more than 14,000 votes.

In the 1926 and 1928 elections, Owen adopted the high-energy campaigning tactics, complete with spirited oratory, which once distinguished her father's campaigns. She was determined to reach as many citizens as possible in the district, then one of the largest geographic districts in the country, stretching more than 500 miles along the Atlantic seaboard from Jacksonville to Key West. She cruised the coastline in a green Ford coupe dubbed "The Spirit of Florida," logging more than 10,000 miles to give 500 stump speeches. Despite her growing popularity, Owen angered Democratic Party leaders for refusing to endorse the presidential nominee, Al Smith, or to appear with him during his campaign stops in Florida. She understood that her connection to the Catholic Smith would be unpopular in the then violently anti-Catholic state. Her attention to constituents' opinions served her well, and Owen easily defeated Republican William C. Lawson with 65 percent of the vote—while the Republican presidential candidate, Herbert Hoover, scooped up Florida's electors with a 17 percent margin of victory.[6] Upon victory, Owen referred humorously to her father's three unsuccessful bids for President: "There! I am the first Bryan who ran for anything and got it!"[7]

The campaign fight, however, was not over for Owen. Lawson contested the election, charging that Owen had lost her American citizenship upon her marriage to an Englishman and then living outside the United States. He claimed that she was ineligible for election to Congress because she had not recovered her citizenship under the provisions of the 1922 Cable Act, which allowed women married to foreign men to petition for repatriation upon their return to the United States, until 1925. This did not allow for the seven years' citizenship required by the Constitution to run for U.S. Representative. Unfazed, Owen put her oratorical skills to work. She offered a persuasive and successful defense of her eligibility before the House Elections Committee, exposing the deficiencies of the Cable Act and leading to an eventual amendment to the law. Her audience convinced, she was sworn in at the start of the 71st Congress (1929–1931) on March 4, 1929. Owen won the Democratic nomination and ran unopposed in the 1930 general election.

Owen swiftly established herself as fiercely loyal to the needs of her Florida constituents. She quickly secured more than $4 million in federal funding to combat the Mediterranean fruit fly pest, which threatened Florida's citrus crop. After a tour of the southern areas of her district, she introduced legislation to set aside thousands of acres of the Everglades as a national park. The measure failed but provided the basis for a later successful designation of the area. Owen also used her position in Congress to argue for federal aid for flood control on Florida's Okeechobee River. During her tenure, she supported the establishment of a new Coast Guard Station and a U. S. District Court in eastern Florida. In perhaps the most controversial move of her time in Congress, Owen voted in favor of the Smoot–Hawley Tariff, which raised duties on imports in May 1929. Considering her father's staunch opposition to tariffs, many political observers expressed shock. Owen insisted she was only following the wishes of the pro-industrialist vote in her district. "To vote 'No' when I know without a doubt that my constituents want me to say 'Yes,'" she said, "would be a form of political treason."[8]

The early success of the fruit fly measure was testament to the novel manner in which Owen kept in touch with her constituents in Florida. In a time before congressional Members maintained district offices, Owen maintained a "resident secretary," Walter S. Buckingham, who remained in Florida and kept her abreast of local events. Buckingham also passed out questionnaires to constituents, polling their wants and needs.[9] Although Owen also developed an intricate plan to visit all 18 counties in her massive district on congressional breaks, she was determined to bring some of her constituents to the nation's capital.[10] She established an annual program (using some of her own money) to bring high school boys and girls from her district to Washington, D.C., for training as future leaders.

Legislation in favor of children and family was a priority in Owen's agenda. She criticized the labyrinthine process of securing help for indigent families in her district. As a remedy, she proposed the creation of a Cabinet-level department to oversee the health and welfare of families and children, a "Department of Home and Child." Owen used her position on the Foreign Affairs Committee—in December 1929 she became the first woman to win a seat on that influential body—to secure funding to send U.S. delegations to international conferences on health and child welfare.[11] With her well-traveled background, Owen advocated American attendance at international conferences, including the Geneva Disarmament Conference in February 1932.[12] Owen pressed U.S. officials to abide by the resolutions coming out of the 1930 Hague Conference on the Codification of International Law, a conference seeking to enumerate international laws regarding gender, marriage, and nationality, an issue Owen experienced firsthand.[13]

Like her father, Owen maintained a "dry" position, supporting Prohibition and the 18th Amendment. As

comic poem Owen had written, entitled, "The Last Will and Testament of a Lame Duck."[15]

Owen's political career did not end after she left Congress. In April 1933, President Franklin Roosevelt appointed Owen, a longtime family friend, as Minister to Denmark—making her the first American woman to head a diplomatic legation. Ironically, one of her first duties was to ease Danish concerns about the high duties created by the Smoot–Hawley Tariff, one of Owen's controversial votes. On July 11, 1936, Owen married Captain Borge Rohde of the Danish Royal Guards. Because her marriage

"I believe that woman's place is in the home. But I believe that the modern mother considers the world her home. The community in which she lives and the children grow is her home and for that reason she should assure herself of the opportunity of getting good government."

—RUTH BRYAN OWEN, *NEW YORK TIMES*, MARCH 8, 1929

temperance became more unpopular, particularly among her Florida constituents, Owen's support slipped. She lost the 1932 Democratic nomination to James M. Wilcox, who went on to lose to Sears in the general election. Owen lamented after the election, "I did not turn 'wet' fast enough to suit my constituents."[14] She wished to resign, rather than remain a "lame duck," during the second session of the 72nd Congress (1931–1933), but House Speaker John N. Garner of Texas convinced her to remain until the end of the Congress. Ever true to the wishes of her constituents, Owen voted in favor of repealing the 18th Amendment, despite her personal convictions. In the waning days of the 72nd Congress, she issued a lament fitting to her clever sense of humor. Owen's colleague, Congresswoman Florence Kahn, a Republican from California, read on the House Floor a

meant that she was a citizen of both Denmark and the United States, she had to resign her diplomatic post, but Owen spent the fall of 1936 campaigning for Roosevelt's re-election. From 1938 to 1954, she served on the Advisory Board of the Federal Reformatory for Women. In 1949, President Harry Truman appointed her as an alternate delegate to the United Nations General Assembly. Owen lived in Ossining, New York, lecturing and publishing several well-received books on Scandinavia. She died in Copenhagen on July 26, 1954, during a trip to accept the Danish Order of Merit from King Frederick IX recognizing her contributions to American–Danish relations.

OWEN ADOPTED THE HIGH-ENERGY

CAMPAIGNING TACTICS, COMPLETE

WITH SPIRITED ORATORY, WHICH

ONCE DISTINGUISHED HER FATHER'S

CAMPAIGNS. UPON VICTORY IN

1928, OWEN REFERRED HUMOR-

OUSLY TO HER FATHER'S THREE

UNSUCCESSFUL BIDS FOR

PRESIDENT: "THERE! I AM THE

FIRST BRYAN WHO RAN FOR

ANYTHING AND GOT IT!"

FOR FURTHER READING

Biographical Directory of the United States Congress, "Ruth Bryan Owen," http://bioguide.congress.gov

Owen, Ruth Bryan. *The Duties of a Congressman / Remarks of Ruth Bryan Owen in the House of Representatives, December 18, 1929* (Washington, D.C.: Government Printing Office, 1930).

————. *Leaves from a Greenland Diary* (New York, NY: Dodd, Mead & Company, 1935).

————. *Look Forward, Warrior* (New York, NY: Dodd, Mead & Company, 1942).

Vickers, Sarah Pauline. "The Life of Ruth Bryan Owen: Florida's First Congresswoman and America's First Woman Diplomat." Ph.D. dissertation, Florida State University, 1994.

MANUSCRIPT COLLECTIONS

Library of Congress (Washington, D.C.), Manuscript Division. *Papers:* In the William Jennings Bryan Papers, 1877–1940, 24.8 linear feet. Subjects covered include Ruth Bryan Owen. A finding aid is available in the repository.

Radcliffe Institute for Advanced Study, Harvard University (Cambridge, MA), Schlesinger Library, http://www.radcliffe.edu/schles. *Papers:* ca. 1928–1934, one folder. Two letters, one to Mr. Blodgett regarding her Florida campaign for Congress, 1928; one to "Cora" regarding her work as a diplomat in Denmark and the "cold reception" by Secretary of the Interior Harold Ickes to the idea of becoming his assistant, 1934.

University of Miami (Miami, FL), Archives & Special Collections, Otto G. Richter Library. *Papers:* In the Carrie Dunlap Papers, 1907–1929, 58 letters. Contains approximately 15 letters between Ruth Bryan Owen and Carrie Dunlap.

University of Pennsylvania (Philadelphia, PA), Special Collections, Van Pelt Library. Papers: 1933–1942, 6 items. Correspondence between Ruth Bryan Owen and Marian Anderson.

NOTES

1 Hope Chamberlin, *A Minority of Members: Women in the U.S. Congress* (New York: Praeger, 1973): 74.
2 J. Elliot Ramsey, "Double Helpings of Fame," *Delineator*, January 1937: 11. Also quoted in, Dorothy M. Brown. "Rohde, Ruth Bryan Owen," *American National Biography* 18 (New York: Oxford University Press, 1999): 782–783.
3 Karen Foerstel, *Biographical Dictionary of Congressional Women* (Westport, CT: Greenwood Press, 1999): 213.
4 *Current Biography, 1944* (New York: H.W. Wilson Co., 1944): 522–525.
5 Current Biography, *1944*: 523.
6 "Election Statistics, 1920 to Present," http://clerk.house.gov/members/electionInfo/elections.html.
7 Atherton, "'The Lady From Florida' Works Fast," 20 October 1929, *Washington Post*: SM7.
8 Chamberlin, *A Minority of Members*: 73.
9 *Congressional Record*, House, 71st Cong., 2nd sess. (18 December 1929): 925.
10 Atherton, "'The Lady From Florida' Works Fast."
11 David T. Canon et al., *Committees in the United States Congress, 1789–1946*, Volume I (Washington, D.C.: Congressional Quarterly, Inc., 2002): 572. Political scientist Charles Stewart III rated the committee as the ninth most "attractive" panel of the 29 committees extant between 1875 and the major congressional reorganization in 1947. See Stewart, "Committee Hierarchies in the Modernizing House, 1875–1947," *American Journal of Political Science*, 36 (No. 4, November 1992): 835–856; especially 848.
12 *Congressional Record*, House, 72nd Cong., 1st sess. (11 January 1932): 1719.
13 *Congressional Record*, House, 71st Cong., 2nd sess. (21 May 1930): 9314–9323.
14 Susan Tolchin, *Women in Congress* (Washington, D.C.: Government Printing Office, 1976): 62.
15 *Congressional Record*, House, 72nd Cong., 2nd sess. (31 January 1933): 3051.

Ruth Sears Pratt
1877–1965

UNITED STATES REPRESENTATIVE ★ REPUBLICAN FROM NEW YORK
1929–1933

Ruth Pratt, a New York City icon of government reform and fiscal conservatism, won election to the House of Representatives on the eve of the worst economic disaster ever to befall the country. Congresswoman Pratt's support for the Herbert Hoover administration's cautious programs to remedy the Great Depression held firm, even as the national crisis worsened and Americans, in ever-greater numbers, looked to the federal government for relief.

Ruth Sears Baker was born on August 24, 1877, in Ware, Massachusetts, daughter of the cotton manufacturer Edwin H. Baker and Carrie V. Baker. Ruth Baker attended Dana Hall in Wellesley, Massachusetts, and Wellesley College, where she majored in mathematics. She also studied violin at the Conservatory of Liege in Belgium.[1] In 1904, Ruth Baker married John Teele Pratt, a lawyer and the son of Charles Pratt, a pioneer Standard Oil Company executive and founder of the Pratt Institute in Brooklyn. The couple settled in New York City's Upper East Side and raised five children: Virginia, Sally, Phyllis, Edwin, and John, Jr. Ruth established strong ties with the community by engaging in a range of philanthropic activities. When her husband died in 1927, he left Ruth Pratt a fortune estimated at more than $9 million.

Pratt's involvement in Republican politics in New York began during World War I, when she worked with the Woman's Liberty Loan Committee. She served on the mayor's wartime food commission and met Herbert Hoover, then head of the National Food Administration.[2] She remained a Hoover devotee throughout her political life, working for his presidential nomination in 1920 and helping to deliver the New York state delegation to Hoover's side at the 1928 GOP convention.[3] Pratt initially balked at the notion of elective office, choosing instead to focus on the upbringing of her five children. In January 1924, she was chosen as the associate GOP leader of New York's Upper East Side Assembly district—providing her a powerful political base for the next decade.

When she overcame her reluctance to enter the political limelight and campaigned for city alderman against Democrat James O'Gorman, the race received national attention because no woman in New York City history had ever served on the city's governing body. With a heavily Republican constituency, Pratt won by a wide majority on November 4, 1925.[4] As alderman, she clashed repeatedly with Tammany Hall, the Democratic political machine, particularly over the budget, which she believed could be slashed by millions if spending, patronage positions, and rampant graft were curtailed. She became known as the "Watchdog of the Treasury."[5] In 1928, after winning re-election by an even larger margin, she introduced measures to authorize construction of the Triborough Bridge and tunnels under the East River.

Pratt entered the race for an open U.S. House seat in September 1928, when Democratic incumbent William Cohen declined the nomination. Her combination of wealth, social standing, and knowledge of local politics suited New York's "Silk Stocking District," an area that cut a geographical East–West swath across midtown Manhattan and included the city's wealthy parts of the theater district, and the westside docks and shipping businesses. Running on a platform that called for modifying the Volstead Act and the 18th Amendment (Prohibition) to allow for the production of light wines and beer but no hard alcohol, Pratt comfortably won the September 28 primary with 62 percent of the vote.[6] In the general election, she emphasized her credentials as an alderman against Democratic opponent Phillip Berolzheimer, who ran as a "wet" anti-Prohibition candidate.[7] She defeated Berolzheimer with 50 to 44 percent of the vote—despite the fact that the Democrats had a strong ticket, featuring New York Governor Al Smith as the party's presidential candidate. "That puts the Seventeenth District, back where it belonged, in the Republican column and I am glad that a woman did it," Pratt rejoiced on election night. "But I did not run as a woman. I ran for the Board of Aldermen and for Congress not as a woman but as a citizen."[8] When she took her seat in the 71st Congress (1929–1931), Ruth Baker Sears Pratt became the first woman to represent New York in the national legislature.

During Pratt's first term, she received assignments on the Banking and Currency Committee, the first for a woman and a nod to her work on New York City's budget and the Library Committee. In her first House speech, she criticized a proviso of the Smoot–Hawley Tariff Bill that raised the duty on sugar imports, arguing that the increase would be needlessly passed on to consumers and would fail to improve the wages and conditions of sugar workers.[9] Pratt's first House bill sought to increase benefits for permanently disabled World War I veterans, though she would later oppose an across-the-board bonus for all veterans.[10] She also favored repealing the 18th Amendment and, after the onset of the Depression in 1929, noted that liquor production, transportation, and sales would create new jobs.[11] In January 1930, from her seat on the Library Committee, Pratt introduced a bill for a $75,000 annual appropriation to acquire and publish books for the blind. With the public backing of Helen Keller, a nationally recognized advocate for the blind, it eventually passed the House and Senate, providing the Library of Congress $100,000 annually to procure Braille books. Pratt also presided over the House as Speaker *pro tempore* on numerous occasions during her first term.

On the Banking and Currency Committee, Pratt and her colleagues contended with the effects of the Stock Market Crash of 1929 and a severe midwestern drought, catalysts for the Great Depression. Pratt introduced a bill

amending the Federal Reserve Act to streamline the rules guiding the election of officers of Federal Reserve banks. She also advocated balancing the federal budget and limiting government intervention, once remarking that, "There is a real need for the people once more to grasp the fundamental fact that under our system of government they are expected to solve many problems themselves through their municipal and state governments."[12] In the 72nd Congress (1931–1933), with little fanfare, Pratt was assigned to the Education Committee and left Banking and Currency. She remained a fiscal conservative, however, refusing to countenance federally backed programs to alleviate the nation's economic woes. Pratt praised Hoover's reliance on private funding to curb unemployment. By 1932, as the administration considered additional measures to address the Depression, Pratt rejected the General Relief Bill as a "crowning folly" which would "unbalance the Budget." The bill sought to broaden the powers of the Reconstruction Finance Corporation, the central organizational response of the Hoover administration, and to create a public works program to employ large numbers of idle workers. A few hours after Pratt's speech, the House passed the bill, 216–182.[13] She also opposed the Steagall Bill, which called for the creation of a federal insurance guarantee fund to protect individuals' bank deposits.[14]

As a woman alderman and one of the few Republicans in the Democratically controlled Tammany Hall, Pratt and her reform efforts gained the attention of the press. In Congress, however, Pratt's appeal as a crusader diminished as she joined a group of women and became part of the Republican majority and an ardent defender of the Hoover administration. She spoke rarely on the House Floor and the impression of many voters was that she was ineffectual, if not somewhat disinterested in national politics. "New York circumstances put her in the position of an outspoken objector," a *New York Times* writer observed in 1932. "In Washington circumstances have made it possible to play the game with the rest of the team and be good. And in politics as in morals it is hard to find a spectacular way of being good."[15] Nevertheless, her name was mentioned prominently as a possible New York City mayoral candidate in 1930 and as a GOP candidate for the U.S. Senate in 1932.[16]

Internal politics within her district threatened to derail Pratt's 1930 re-election bid. Able to secure the Republican nomination despite dissension in the party ranks, Pratt faced Tammany Hall's handpicked Democratic candidate, City Magistrate Louis B. Brodsky, in the general election and the journalist Heywood Broun running on the Socialist ticket.[17]

became the presidential election. Disenchanted with Hoover's economic policies, American voters swept New York Governor Franklin Delano Roosevelt and his Democratic coalition into the federal government. In what had been an evenly divided House, the Democrats gained a commanding majority as the GOP hemorrhaged—losing 111 seats. In her Manhattan district race, Pratt lost to Peyser in a four-way race by a margin of 53 percent to 44 percent.

"You know politics is nothing but theory with a lot of people, and that's the trouble. To my mind, politics, or at least the thing that makes politics move, is personality. I happen to be one of those who like people, people of all sorts and conditions . . . It seems to me that unless you have some sort of feeling like that, unless you like people and have a sincere interest in them, you ought not to be in the active work of politics. It also seems to me that if you have that sort of feeling you can know what people really need and puzzle out whatever way there may be through public agencies to help them."

—RUTH PRATT, *NEW YORK TIMES*, NOVEMBER 5, 1925

Though she polled only about half the total of her first election, Pratt held on to win by a bare margin—695 votes out of some 45,000 cast. In 1932 she faced yet another tough battle to win re-election to the House. Prior to the 1932 GOP National Convention, a faction in the New York delegation, disenchanted with Hoover, attempted to unseat Pratt as a delegate. The move failed but seemed to weaken her base of support heading into the fall elections.[18] In the Republican primary, she weathered charges from opponents that she had abused the House franking privilege. After securing the Republican nomination, Pratt squared off against Democratic challenger Theodore A. Peyser.[19] With the two candidates agreeing on the substantive issues, the decisive factor in the race

After Congress, Ruth Pratt served as chair of the Fine Arts Foundation, a forerunner of the National Endowment for the Humanities, and was appointed to the Republican Builders, a group formed to renew the party after the defeats of 1932 and 1934. She continued to live in New York City and was president of the Women's National Republican Club from 1943 to 1946. On August 23, 1965, a day before her 88th birthday, Pratt died in Glen Cove, New York.

"New York circumstances put
her in the position of an
outspoken objector. In
Washington circumstances
have made it possible to play
the game with the rest of the
team and be good. And in
politics as in morals it is hard
to find a spectacular way
of being good."

— *New York Times* on Ruth Pratt's
House Career, June 19, 1932

FOR FURTHER READING

Biographical Directory of the United States Congress, "Ruth Sears Baker Pratt," http://bioguide.congress.gov

NOTES

1   "Then Along Came Ruth—To Congress," 14 April 1929, *Washington Post*: SM3.
2   "Then Along Came Ruth—To Congress."
3   *Ruth Baker Pratt: A Sketch of Her Activities* (n.p., 1930) in Library of Congress as a pamphlet: E748. P87R8.
4   "Woman Alderman Surveys Victory," 8 November 1925, *New York Times*: XX6.
5   "Then Along Came Ruth—To Congress."
6   "Mrs. Pratt for Wine and Beer by Change in Volstead Law," 9 August 1928, *New York Times*: 1; "Endorse Mrs. Pratt for Congress Seat," 20 July 1929, *New York Times*: 5; "Mrs. Pratt To Begin Campaign Next Week," 28 July 1928, *New York Times*: 2.
7   "Mrs. Pratt Debates Issues," 16 October 1928, *New York Times*: 20.
8   "Mrs. Pratt Victor in Congress Fight," 7 November 1928, *New York Times*: 20.
9   *Congressional Record*, House, 71st Cong., special sess. (20 May 1929): 1546–1547.
10 *Ruth Baker Pratt: A Sketch of Her Public Activities*: 13.
11 "Ruth Pratt in Fight for Repeal Bars Saloon; Would Sponsor Bill to Modify the Volstead Act," 18 October 1932, *New York Times*: 10.
12 *Congressional Record*, House, 71st Cong., special sess. (6 May 1929): 912.
13 *Congressional Record*, House, 72nd Cong., 1st sess. (7 June 1932): 12207.
14 *Congressional Record*, House, 72nd Cong., 1st sess. (27 May 1932): 11460–11462.
15 Mildred Adams, "Congresswomen Are Just Congressmen," 19 June 1932, *New York Times*: SM7.
16 Jean Eliot, "Many Favor Mrs. Pratt in Mayor's Race," 2 August 1929, *Washington Post*: 7; "Ruth Pratt Favored for Seat in Senate," 17 February 1931, *Washington Post*: 3.
17 Jean Eliot, "G.O.P. Split May Defeat Mrs. Pratt," 24 June 1930, *Washington Post*: 8.
18 W.A. Warn, "Fight on Mrs. Pratt Is Growing Sharper," 14 June 1932, *New York Times*: 1.
19 "Women Form Group to Work for Peyser," 16 October 1932, *New York Times*: 31.

Effiegene Locke Wingo
1883-1962

UNITED STATES REPRESENTATIVE ★ DEMOCRAT FROM ARKANSAS
1930-1933

Overcoming personal tragedy, Effiegene L. Wingo succeeded her late husband in Congress to help her Arkansas constituents cope with an appalling national emergency. In the early days of the Great Depression, Wingo relied on her experience and connections as an active congressional wife to bring relief to her drought-stricken and impoverished Arkansas district.

Effiegene Locke, the eldest of seven children raised by Irish parents and the great-great-great-granddaughter of Representative Matthew Locke of North Carolina, was born on April 13, 1883, in Lockesburg, Arkansas. She attended both public and private schools and received a music diploma from the Union Female College in Oxford, Mississippi. Effiegene Locke then graduated with a B.A. degree from the Maddox Seminary in Little Rock, Arkansas, in 1901. Shortly after graduation she met lawyer Otis Theodore Wingo, in De Queen, Arkansas, at a Confederate veterans' reunion. The couple soon married and raised two children, Blanche and Otis, Jr. In 1907 Otis Wingo was elected to a term in the Arkansas state senate, where he served until 1909 before returning to private business. He won election to the U.S. House of Representatives in 1912 and to the eight succeeding Congresses. During Otis Wingo's political career, his wife became immersed in the social side of political life in Washington, D.C.

In 1926, a car accident severely injured Representative Wingo, thrusting Effiegene into a far more active role. For four years she worked as an unpaid assistant in her husband's office, becoming his point of contact during long absences as he sought to recuperate from his injuries. That direct experience—tending to constituent requests—gave her valuable exposure to voters and a keen under-standing of the district's political and business networks. Following an emergency operation, Otis Wingo (who was serving his ninth term in Congress) died in Baltimore, Maryland, on October 21, 1930. His dying wish was that his wife be chosen as his successor.[1] That appeal prompted Otis Wingo's friend and the chief Democratic contender for the vacant seat, A.B. Du Laney, to peremptorily with-draw from the race and back Effiegene Wingo. Newspapers described that act as "gallant" and "chivalrous."[2] Less than a week after Otis Wingo's death, the Arkansas Democratic and Republican central committees, both of which earlier that year had nominated Otis Wingo for the seat, chose Effiegene Wingo to replace her late husband. Several speakers at the GOP meeting spoke up to offer eulogies for her husband.[3] According to the standard study on Southern politics in the early 20th century, comi-ty between the major parties was a regular occurrence in Arkansas politics. The state's political network was con-trolled largely by conservative Democrats, who differed little from their Republican counterparts on major issues of public policy. Political scientist V.O. Key explained Arkansas elections by paraphrasing a prominent local politician who described them as "'rivalries' that turn around 'personalities and emotions' of the moment" fea-turing candidates with "connections" within the political network.[4] Effiegene Wingo, a congressional widow with whom voters empathized, and who enjoyed wide name recognition, fit the pattern well. Facing no competition, she was elected simultaneously on November 4, 1930, to complete her husband's term in the 71st Congress (1929–1931) and to a full term 72nd Congress (1931–1933). She garnered 21,700 votes, more than four of the state's six other Representatives.

OFFICE OF HISTORY AND PRESERVATION,

U.S. HOUSE OF REPRESENTATIVES

Reflecting on Wingo's election, the *Richmond Times-Dispatch* observed that "heart impulses in Arkansas overwhelmed the impulses of the mind." Without crediting Wingo's four years' work in her husband's office, the *Times-Dispatch* surmised that sentimentality had overcome Arkansas voters. The editors wrote disapprovingly, "In this country public office is not a thing to be bequeathed to one's next of kin or one's best friend. Supposedly, it is won on merit, and it should descend through a like channel."[5] Debate was fueled by the fact that Wingo seemed to be part of a larger pattern: She served alongside yet another Arkansas widow, Pearl Oldfield, who was filling out the remainder of her late husband's term in the 71st Congress.

Sworn in on December 1, 1930, Effiegene Wingo received a post on the Committee on Accounts and Committee on Insular Affairs for the remaining months of the 71st Congress. In the following Congress, she served on another coveted and influential committee, Foreign Affairs.[6]

Wingo, like her colleagues, was consumed by the effects of the Great Depression. Natural disasters exacerbated the economic plight of her 11-county district on the western edge of the state, bordering Oklahoma. A severe cold snap in the winter of 1929–1930, followed by a scorching drought in the summer of 1930 created "Dustbowl" conditions. Peach orchards, the leading agricultural commodity, and the poultry industry were decimated. Many farmers lost their livelihoods and had to beg for food to feed their own families. "The failure of many banks because of these conditions has made the situation more difficult," Wingo remarked. "It will take years for the State to rehabilitate herself. The economic situation is so thoroughly demoralized that farmers will lose their cattle, their lands, their homes. People who have known wealth all their lives have nothing. This is a gloomy picture, but a true one."[7] Wingo suspended her social activities in Washington, D.C., to focus on raising relief funds for her district. Appealing to Washington society and working through the American Red Cross, she opened a channel of supplies into her district. Among those who pitched in to help was the humorist Will Rogers, who delivered talks

in the district and donated all proceeds and some of his personal money for relief efforts.[8] In Washington, Wingo relied on her daughter, the newly married Blanche Sawyer, and the same staff that her husband had employed, to attend to her busy appointment schedule.

Wingo believed that only federal aid would revitalize the Arkansas economy. In the days before the establishment of New Deal programs, she steered as many projects and as much federal money as she could into her district. She sponsored a bill to complete construction of a railroad bridge across the Little River near Morris Ferry, Arkansas.[9] In addition, she helped guide federally funded programs back home to build additional railroad bridges, a veterans' hospital, a federal building, and other large construction projects, as well as federal loans for public and private building and for welfare grants. Wingo also proposed using federal money to establish a game refuge in the Ouachita National Forest and to establish Ouachita National Park.[10]

In February 1932, citing her physician's directions, Wingo announced that she would not be a candidate for re-election. She remarked to her constituents that it had been a "sweet privilege to serve my people."[11] Wingo spent much of December 1932 at her son's hospital bedside in Connecticut, where he was recuperating from a car wreck.

After Congress, Wingo cofounded the National Institute for Public Affairs. The organization provided college students internship opportunities to enter public service through on-the-job training programs in federal departments. She resided in De Queen, Arkansas, and spent a good deal of time in Washington, D.C., tending to her educational work. On September 19, 1962, while visiting her son, Effiegene Wingo died in Burlington, Ontario.

FOR FURTHER READING

Biographical Directory of the United States Congress, "Effiegene Locke Wingo," http://bioguide.congress.gov

NOTES

1   "Society Awaits Election Returns of Its Women Representatives," 2 November 1930, *Washington Post*: S3.
2   "Political Life Is Embraced By Mrs. Wingo," 29 October 1930, *Washington Post*: 9.
3   "Both Parties in Arkansas Back Wingo's Widow for Congress," 28 October 1930, *New York Times*: 1.
4   V.O. Key, Jr., *Southern Politics in State and Nation,* 2nd ed. (Knoxville: University of Tennessee Press, 1984): 183; 185–187.
5   "Pro and Con," 5 November 1930, *Washington Post*: 6.
6   Charles Stewart III, "Committee Hierarchies in the Modernizing House, 1875–1947," *American Journal of Political Science* 36 (1992): 845–846. The paper includes rankings of House committees before the Legislative Reorganization Act of 1946 and makes a connection between committee transfers and the relative attractiveness of committee assignments.
7   *Congressional Record,* House, 71st Cong., 3rd sess. (7 February 1931): 4246.
8   *Congressional Record,* House, 71st Cong., 3rd sess. (12 February 1931): 4712.
9   *Congressional Record,* House, 72nd Cong., 2nd sess. (28 January 1933): 2790.
10 *Congressional Record,* House, 72nd Cong., 2nd sess. (16 January 1933): 1907.
11 "Pro and Con," 18 June 1932, *Washington Post*: 6.

Hattie Wyatt Caraway
1878–1950

UNITED STATES SENATOR ★ DEMOCRAT FROM ARKANSAS
1931–1945

Hattie Wyatt Caraway served for 14 years in the U.S. Senate and established a number of "firsts," including her 1932 feat of winning election to the upper chamber of Congress in her own right. Drawing principally from the power of the widow's mandate and the personal relationships she cultivated with a wide cross-section of her constituency, "Silent Hattie" was a faithful, if staid, supporter of New Deal reforms, which aided her largely agricultural state.

Hattie Ophelia Wyatt was born on February 1, 1878, on a farm near Bakerville, Tennessee. Her parents William Carroll Wyatt, a farmer and shopkeeper, and Lucy Mildred Burch Wyatt raised four children. Hattie Wyatt briefly attended Ebenezer College in Hustburg, Pennsylvania. At age 14 she entered the Dickson (Tennessee) Normal College and received a B.A. in 1896. She taught school for several years in rural Arkansas, along with her Dickson fiancé, Thaddeus Horatio Caraway. The couple married in 1902 and raised three sons, all future West Point cadets: Robert, Paul, and Forrest.[1] Thaddeus Caraway rose quickly through the political ranks in Arkansas, serving as a prosecuting attorney, winning election to four terms in the U.S. House and two terms in the U.S. Senate. A fiery orator, he earned the epithets "Fighting Thad" and "Caustic Caraway."[2]

Throughout this period, Hattie Caraway's public role was limited. Behind the scenes, however, friends recalled she played a critical part in her husband's political career. In 1920, during Thaddeus's first run for the Senate, Hattie Caraway worked in his campaign headquarters, spoke on his behalf, and received much of the credit for his election. She was her husband's close political confidante, knew his positions on all important issues affecting Arkansas, and

held Thaddeus's "profound respect" as an adviser.[3] While the Caraways tended to avoid social functions in Washington, Hattie often returned home to Arkansas to speak before women's political groups. Years later, in trying to cultivate votes by appealing to voters' sympathies for her plight as a "poor, little widow," Hattie Caraway played down her experience as a congressional wife. "After equal suffrage in 1920," she recalled, "I just added voting to cooking and sewing and other household duties."[4]

On November 6, 1931, Thaddeus Caraway died in office, prompting immediate speculation that his widow would be named to succeed him.[5] A few days after his funeral, Governor Harvey Parnell named Caraway's widow to fill the junior Senator's seat. "I have appointed Mrs. Caraway as United States Senator because I feel she is entitled to the office held by her distinguished husband, who was my friend," Parnell explained. "The office belonged to Senator Caraway, who went before the people and received their endorsement for it and his widow is rightfully entitled to the honor."[6] The *Washington Post* blasted Parnell's rationale. "Representation in Congress belongs to the people of the State," the *Post* editors wrote. "Mrs. Caraway should have been given the appointment on her own merit and not on the basis of sentimentality or family claim upon the seat."[7] Hattie Caraway, however, offered Governor Purnell a safe choice to sidestep choosing from a field of Arkansas politicians who coveted the seat: W.F. Kirby, state supreme court justice; Frank Pace, a lawyer; Hal L. Norwood, state attorney general; and Heartsill Ragon, U.S. Representative. Parnell, whose term as governor expired in January 1933, also was considered a contender for the seat in the 1932 elections.[8]

IMAGE COURTESY OF THE UNITED STATES SENATE CURATOR

On December 8, 1931, Hattie Caraway claimed her Senate seat. Her first observation upon entering the Senate was: "The windows need washing!"[9] Thus did the second woman to serve in the Senate enter the upper chamber of Congress. But behind the façade of the dutiful widow was a woman who had every intention of not surrendering her seat to a chosen male successor. Parnell's endorsement for the Democratic nomination in the one-party Arkansas system guaranteed Hattie Caraway's election to the remaining 14 months of her husband's term, which expired in early 1933. Caraway won the special election on January 12, 1932, crushing two Independent candidates with 92 percent of the vote.[10] The election forged the creation of the Arkansas Women's Democratic Club, which threw its support behind Caraway and sought to get out the vote and raise money.

Almost immediately after the special election, Caraway faced the daunting prospect of mounting a re-election campaign in the fall of the 1932 without the support of the Arkansas political establishment. But on May 10, the day of the filing deadline for the August 10 Democratic primary, Caraway shocked Arkansans and her six male contenders by announcing her candidacy. She explained to reporters, "The time has passed when a woman should be placed in a position and kept there only while someone else is being groomed for the job."[11] She confided in her journal that she planned to test "my own theory of a woman running for office."[12]

It was an uphill battle against a field of contenders that included a popular former governor and former U.S. Senator. But Caraway had an important ally in Louisiana Senator and political boss Huey Long, with whom Thaddeus Caraway had often allied and whose legislative proposals Hattie Caraway supported. Long had presidential ambitions and wanted to prove his popularity outside his home state by campaigning in the state of his chief rival, Caraway's Arkansas colleague, Senate Minority Leader Joseph T. Robinson. On August 1, nine days before the election, the "Kingfish" mobilized a small armada of cars and a host of Louisiana state employees to canvass Arkansas on Caraway's behalf. Long and Caraway logged

more than 2,000 miles and made 39 joint speeches—with the charismatic Louisianan doing most of the talking. "We're out here to pull a lot of pot-bellied politicians off a little woman's neck," Long told audiences. "She voted with you people and your interests in spite of all the pressure Wall Street could bring to bear. This brave little woman Senator stood by you."[13] For the more than 200,000 people who came out to listen in courthouses, town halls, and city parks, Long effectively portrayed Caraway as a champion of poor white farmers and workers and as a Senator whom the bankers were unable to control.[14] In the seven-way primary, Caraway won 44.7 percent of the vote, carrying 61 of the state's 75 counties.[15] Far less surprising was Caraway's landslide victory in the general election that November: In the one-party, Democratic system she out-polled her hapless Republican rival by a nearly nine-to-one margin.

Known as "Silent Hattie" because she spoke on the floor just 15 times in her career, Caraway nonetheless had a facile wit. She once explained her tendency to avoid speeches: "I haven't the heart to take a minute away from the men. The poor dears love it so."[16] Throughout her 14 years in the Senate, she was a strong supporter of President Franklin Roosevelt and his New Deal reforms, most especially farm relief and flood control. "He fumbles," Caraway once said of FDR, "but he fumbles forward."[17] She harbored deep reservations about American intervention in World War II but backed Roosevelt's declaration of war after the attack on Pearl Harbor in 1941. She was a strict prohibitionist, a critic of lobbyists, and a sympathetic friend to veterans groups. During her tenure in the Senate, Caraway secured $15 million to construct an aluminum plant in her home state and the first federal loan funding for an Arkansas college. During her second term, she voted several times against the Roosevelt administration when she sided with the farm bloc to override the presidential veto of the Bankhead Farm Price Bill, to restrict the administration's use of subsidies to lower food prices, and to readjust the price cap on cotton textiles.[18] She also proved instrumental in preventing the elimination of an U.S. House seat from Arkansas to reapportionment in 1941 and methodically attended to constituent requests.

Once ensconced in the Senate, Caraway set a number of firsts for women. In 1933, she was named chair of the Enrolled Bills Committee; the first woman ever to chair a Senate committee, she remained there until she left Congress in 1945. Caraway became the first woman to preside over the Senate, the first senior woman Senator (when Joe Robinson died in 1937), and the first woman to run a Senate hearing. She also received assignments on the Commerce Committee and the Committee on Agriculture and Forestry.[19] It was from the latter that she was most attentive to the needs of her largely rural and agricultural constituency.

contaminated as possible," Caraway quipped.[21] Race was another matter entirely, largely because she voted with the unified bloc of her southern colleagues. Caraway voted against the antilynching law of 1938 and, in 1942, joined other southern Senators in a filibuster to block a proposed bill that would have eliminated the poll tax.

Most observers, including some of her supporters, believed Caraway would retire in 1939. But she upset expectations again by declaring her candidacy for the 1938 election. In the Democratic primary, Caraway faced two-term Representative John L. McClellan, a 42-year-old lawyer who declared, "Arkansas Needs Another Man in

"Sometimes I'm really afraid that tourists are going to poke me with their umbrellas! And yet there's no sound reason why women, if they have the time and ability, shouldn't sit with men on city councils, in state legislatures, or in the House and Senate.... Women are essentially practical because they've always had to be. From the dawn of time it's been our job to see that both ends meet. And women are much more realistic than men, particularly when it comes to public questions. Of course, having had the vote for such a short time is a distinct advantage, for we have no inheritance of political buncombe."

—HATTIE CARAWAY, *CURRENT BIOGRAPHY*, 1945

Caraway's record on civil rights was mixed. In one respect she was progressive, as the first woman to endorse and vote for the Lucretia Mott Equal Rights Amendment in 1943—a measure that had been presented to the Senate on 11 prior occasions and which Caraway herself had worked for since 1937.[20] Hattie Caraway chafed at the Senate's institutional prohibitions against women, at one point noting in her journal that she had been assigned the same desk as Felton. "I guess they wanted as few [desks]

the Senate." McClellan adopted the antics and soaring oratory that Huey Long once employed to get Caraway elected.[22] Senator Caraway ran on her record of supporting New Deal legislation to alleviate the economic hardships for the state's largely agrarian economy. Throughout the campaign she was forced to defend not only her gender but her age as well. But she held two advantages. The first was wide name recognition and personal contact with voters, especially women. More importantly, although Huey Long was no longer there to support her, Caraway benefited from the support of the state's Federal Internal Revenue collector and future Arkansas governor, Homer Atkins. She also garnered endorsements from a number of key federal judges, the federal marshal, and several trade and labor unions and a mild endorsement from President Roosevelt, which she advertised widely.[23] In the August 9 primary, which many observers considered another referendum on the New Deal, Caraway prevailed by just 8,000 votes out of more than 260,000 cast.[24]

Though she went on to win the general election in 1938, it was clear that Caraway spoke even less for the Arkansas political establishment than she had in her first term. By 1944, Caraway faced a tough field of Democratic primary challengers in her bid for renomination. Her campaign was uninspired, and she finished last among the four contenders. The winner, a dynamic freshman Representative and former University of Arkansas president, J. William Fulbright, was eventually elected and served for three decades as one of the Senate's most influential Members.

Caraway was still a part of the capital city in her post-congressional years. Franklin Roosevelt nominated her in early 1945 as a member of the Federal Employees' Compensation Commission, where she served for a year. In 1946, President Harry S. Truman elevated her to the commission's appeals board, where she remained until her death on December 21, 1950, in Falls Church, Virginia.

FOR FURTHER READING

Biographical Directory of the United States Congress, "Hattie Wyatt Caraway," http://bioguide.congress.gov

Kincaid, Diane, ed. *Silent Hattie Speaks: The Personal Journal of Senator Hattie Caraway* (Westport, CT: Greenwood Press, 1979).

Malone, David. *Hattie and Huey: An Arkansas Tour* (Fayetteville: University of Arkansas Press, 1989).

Towns, Stuart. "A Louisiana Medicine Show: The King Fish Elects an Arkansas Senator." *Arkansas Historical Quarterly* 25 (Summer 1966): 117–127.

MANUSCRIPT COLLECTION

University of Arkansas (Fayetteville, AR). *Papers:* 1884–1950, 82 items. Includes correspondence (1919–1950), a journal (1931–1934), clippings, photographs, and other papers pertaining to the political career of Hattie Caraway and members of her family. A finding aid is available in the repository. *Additional Papers:* In various collections including letters to her son in the Forrest Caraway Papers, 1931–1941; and correspondence in the Clyde Taylor Ellis Papers, 1933–1976, and the Walter John Lemke Papers, 1821–1969.

NOTES

1 Sons' names cited in an Associated Press article, "Caraway's Remains Arrive at Old Home," 9 November 1931, *Washington Post*: 4.

2 Diane Kincaid, ed., *Silent Hattie Speaks: The Personal Journal of Senator Hattie Caraway* (Westport, CT: Greenwood Press, 1979): 6.

3 "Says Widow Favors Taking Caraway Seat," 10 November 1931, *New York Times*: 13; "Mrs. Caraway's Wit Matched Husband's," 15 November 1931, *Washington Post*: N1.

4 *Current Biography, 1945* (New York: H.W. Wilson and Co., 1945): 89–92.

5 *Current Biography, 1945*: 90.

6 "Gov. Parnell Names Mrs. Caraway to Senate; Asks Party to Back Her for Jan. 12 Election," 14 November 1931, *New York Times*: 1.

7 "A Woman Senator," 14 November 1931, *Washington Post*: 6.

8 "Mrs. Caraway's Wit Matched Husband's."

9 *Current Biography, 1945*: 90.

10 Kincaid, *Silent Hattie Speaks*: 8–9.

11 Susan M. Hartmann, "Caraway, Hattie Ophelia Wyatt," *American National Biography (ANB)* 4 (New York: Oxford University Press, 1999): 369–370.

12 Quoted in Karen Foerstel, *Biographical Dictionary of Women in Congress* (Westport, CT: Greenwood Press, 1999): 50.

13 Foerstel, *Biographical Dictionary of Congressional Women*: 50; and Susan Tolchin, *Women in Congress* (Washington, D.C.: Government Printing Office, 1976): 15.

14 After the death of Long, Caraway spoke at the 1941 ceremony in which the Louisiana Senator's statue was unveiled in National Statuary Hall. She reflected upon their friendship and commented that, "While I did not always agree with Senator Long, I respected his judgment and sincerity of purpose." Moreover, although grateful for his help during the 1932 campaign, she did not blindly follow his bidding in the Senate. For example, when Long asked her to vote against the World Court, she refused. See the *Congressional Record*, Senate, 77th Cong., 1st sess. (25 April 1941): 3322–3323.

15 Kincaid, *Silent Hattie Speaks*: 10.

16 *Current Biography, 1945*: 90.

17 "Hattie Caraway, Ex-Senator Dies," *Washington Post*, December 22, 1950: 1; B2.

18 *Current Biography, 1945*: 91.

19 Thaddeus Caraway served on both of these committees during his tenure in the Senate.

20 "Amendment for Equal Rights for Women Favorably Reported by Senate Committee," 24 June 1937, *New York Times*: 8; "Women in Capital Hail Mrs. Caraway," 8 December 1931, *New York Times*: 16.

21 Foerstel, *Biographical Dictionary of Congressional Women*: 51.

22 Sidney Olson, "Mrs. Caraway Faces Fight in Vote Tuesday," 6 August 1938, *Washington Post*: X1. McClellan later went on to win election to the Senate in 1942, where he served for 34 years and eventually chaired the Appropriations Committee.

23 Kincaid, *Silent Hattie Speaks*: 10.

24 Olson, "Mrs. Caraway Faces Fight in Vote Tuesday"; Sidney Olson, "Machine Bosses Hold Balance in Arkansas Race," 7 August 1938, *Washington Post*: M6; "New Dealers Lose 1, Win 2 Senate Tests," 11 August 1938, *Washington Post*: 1.

Willa McCord Blake Eslick
1878–1961

UNITED STATES REPRESENTATIVE ★ DEMOCRAT FROM TENNESSEE
1932–1933

In June 1932, Willa B. Eslick watched as her husband, Representative Edward Eslick, collapsed on the House Floor while speaking in support of the Patman Veterans' Bonus Bill. A moment that otherwise would have been a high point of the four-term Congressman's career instead turned tragic. Willa Eslick soon became the latest widow to succeed her husband. In completing the final fraction of Congressman Eslick's term in the 72nd Congress (1931–1933), she supported legislation to alleviate the economic woes of Depression-stricken farmers and to combat concerns of internal subversion.

Willa McCord Blake was the eighth child born to G.W. and Eliza Blake in Fayetteville, Tennessee, on September 8, 1878. She attended private schools for her primary education and later went to Dick White College and Milton College in Fayetteville. She also attended Winthrop Model School and Peabody College in Nashville, Tennessee. The only time in her early adult life that Willa Blake left Tennessee was to study at the Metropolitan College of Music and Synthetic School of Music in New York City. After her college career, she became active in Democratic politics, served on the Tennessee Democratic Committee, and became a civic activist. Willa Blake married Edward Everett Eslick, a lawyer from Pulaski, Tennessee, on June 6, 1906.[1] Edward Eslick eventually served as a government appeal agent for Giles County, Tennessee, during World War I. In 1924, he was elected as a Democrat to the 69th Congress (1925–1927) and won re-election to the three succeeding Congresses. Eslick represented a Tennessee district that encompassed a sprawling expanse of 11 agricultural counties in the western part of the state. Rooted in the Civil War and Reconstruction Era, Tennessee developed a solid partisan nature in which western and central portions of the state evolved into Democratic strongholds, whereas eastern Tennessee traditionally backed the GOP.[2] In 1930, Speaker Nicholas Longworth of Ohio appointed four Members, including Eslick and New York Representative Hamilton Fish, to a special House committee on communist activities, which garnered national attention.[3] Meanwhile, Willa Eslick accompanied her husband to Washington, D.C., where she followed his career with interest.

As a member of the House Ways and Means Committee in the 72nd Congress, Edward Eslick supported cash payments for American veterans who had served in World War I.[4] On June 14, 1932, the Tennessee Representative began an impassioned speech on the House Floor urging passage of the Patman Veterans' Bonus Bill. With his wife and a ragtag collection of World War I veterans watching from the House Gallery, Eslick slumped over in mid-sentence from a massive heart attack. "We hear nothing but dollars here. I want to go from the sordid side—," he said before collapsing.[5] Willa Eslick attempted to revive her 60-year-old husband as he lay on the floor, but he died soon thereafter.

Only four days later, Tennessee Democratic officials prevailed upon the widow Eslick to seek the nomination for the August special election to fill the vacant seat. William Fry, a former World War I serviceman and Columbia, Tennessee, lawyer, made the appeal on behalf of veterans, friends, and family.[6] She agreed. Eslick defeated three opponents in the August 14, 1932, special election (on the same day as the Democratic primary statewide), garnering 51 percent of the vote to become the first woman to represent Tennessee in Congress.[7] With Congress in extended recess for the fall 1932 general

elections, Eslick was not officially sworn in until the House reconvened on December 5, 1932. A special lame duck session of Congress, called to deal with the soaring federal deficit and foreign debt, enabled Eslick to serve three months, until March 3, 1933.[8] As a Representative, she received assignments on two committees: the Committee on Public Buildings and Grounds—a position her husband held throughout his tenure in the House—and the Committee on World War Veterans' Legislation.

Although Eslick's committee assignments allowed her to further the legislative interests of her husband, they deprived her of a prime platform from which to assist directly the most pressing needs of her constituents, most of whom were farmers struck hard by the Great Depression. Nevertheless, in an effort to improve the lot of Tennessee farmers, she supported a plan aimed at preventing farm-mortgage foreclosures. "There are few comforting words that we who represent agricultural districts may give to our people," Eslick noted in a floor speech. "One is that everybody now recognizes that something should be done for them without delay." She also gave voice to agriculture's traditional mistrust of big industry. "Among those who now advocate succor to the producers of our food products are even included the makers of their machinery and steel tools who are still gouging farmers with war prices," Eslick told colleagues. "They brazenly ask for more tariffs, so that no one can force a moratorium for their excessive costs. They are the source of much corruption in some parts of the land. The farmer can not continue to buy in a protected market and sell in a free one."[9]

Eslick and dozens of other Representatives from rural districts brainstormed during late-night sessions to create other legislative solutions to alleviate the economic burdens imposed on farmers: immediate farm relief measures, efforts to curb overproduction, and voluntary measures that farmers themselves could enact. She voted for the emergency farm parity plan proposed by Texas Congressman Marvin Jones. Representative Eslick also supported a bill that offered federal relief to cotton farmers who reduced their production. She strongly endorsed in-

coming President Franklin Roosevelt's plans for Tennessee River Valley development and the construction of an electrical-generating plant at Muscle Shoals, Alabama. "For our immediate section of Tennessee," she observed, "much of the gloom has been lifted by the hope which the President elect has given us."[10]

Eslick also carried on her husband's efforts to pass antisubversive legislation aimed principally at communist fellow travelers, radical immigrants, and union organizers. On February 2, 1933, she urged dire penalties for those who sought to undermine the U.S. government.[11] Two weeks later the Judiciary Committee reported on the House Floor a measure (later named the Eslick Bill, after Edward Eslick) directed at any person who "by word of mouth or in writing" advocates "the overthrow or subversion of the government of the United States by force."[12] The legislation had gained added momentum after Giuseppe Zangara, a naturalized Italian bricklayer, attempted to assassinate President-elect Franklin D. Roosevelt during a February 15, 1933, public rally in Miami, Florida. Chicago Mayor Anton J. Cermak was killed in the fusillade of bullets. Zangara, who spoke broken English, was quickly linked with radical extremists and communist groups. The Eslick Bill was related to other legislation aimed at preventing "criminal syndicalism," or union organizing, in both the agricultural and industrial sectors. The 72nd Congress adjourned in early March, before the measure was taken up on the House Floor.

Willa Eslick was not eligible for re-election to the 73rd Congress (1933–1935), since Edward Eslick died after the filing deadline for the 1932 congressional primary—and his opposition for the party primary already was set. In 1932, redistricting in Tennessee shifted most of Congresswoman Eslick's district into a newly created district, where Clarence Wyly Turner, a county judge and a former U.S. Representative, won the Democratic nomination on the same day Willa Eslick won her special election. With Tennessee's one-party system, capturing the Democratic nomination was tantamount to winning the election itself, and Turner went on to serve several terms in the House. Representative Fritz G. Lanham of Texas, chairman of the

Committee on Public Buildings and Grounds, had known Willa Eslick socially for years. But in his farewell commemorating her departure, it was her work as a committee colleague that he highlighted: "her outstanding ability, her keen intellect, which have enabled her so faithfully to carry on for her people and for the Nation work of the same efficient character" as her husband. "We part with her with regret ... because of the service she has rendered and could render to our common country," Lanham added.[13] Aside from not having qualified for nomination and the redistricting issue, however, Eslick seemed disinclined to seek a second term. She retired from public life and later returned to her home state. Willa Eslick died at age 82 on February 18, 1961, in Pulaski, Tennessee.

FOR FURTHER READING

Biographical Directory of the United States Congress, "Willa McCord Blake Eslick," http://bioguide.congress.gov

NOTES

1 "Eslick Dies in House Pleading for Bonus," 15 June 1932, *New York Times*: 1.

2 V.O. Key, Jr., *Southern Politics in State and Nation* (Knoxville: University of Tennessee Press, 1977): 75.

3 "Eslick Dies in House Pleading for Bonus."

4 "Money Issue Urged for Soldier Bonus," 14 May 1932, *Washington Post*: 15.

5 "Eslick's Death Holds Up House Vote on Bonus," 15 June 1932, *Washington Post*: 1.

6 "Mrs. Eslick to Seek Husband's Seat," 19 June 1932, *New York Times*: 16; "Widow Decides to Seek Eslick's Congress Seat," 19 June 1932, *Washington Post*: 19.

7 See Michael J. Dubin et al., *United States Congressional Elections, 1788–1997* (Jefferson, NC: McFarland & Company, Inc., Publishers, 1998): 487. Mrs. Eslick's victory was not well-documented in her state's history. Only the statistics from the State Coordinator of Elections in Nashville, Tennessee, provide evidence of her victory in the 1932 special election. Many believed that she was appointed to the position.

8 "Congress to Tackle Debts and Economy," 14 November 1932, *New York Times*: 9.

9 *Congressional Record*, House, 72nd Cong., 2nd sess. (2 March 1933): 5417–5418.

10 Ibid.

11 "Yesterday in Congress," 3 February 1933, *Washington Post*: 2. Reported as HR 8378 on 22 February 1933, see *Congressional Record*, House, 72nd Cong., 2nd sess. (22 February 1933): 4766.

12 "House Bill Aimed at Reds Gets Legislative Priority," 23 February 1933, *New York Times*: 18.

13 *Congressional Record*, House, 72nd Cong., 2nd sess. (3 March 1933): 5586.

Kathryn O'Loughlin McCarthy
1894–1952

UNITED STATES REPRESENTATIVE ★ DEMOCRAT FROM KANSAS
1933–1935

In Republican-controlled, predominantly Protestant, and traditionally oriented northwestern Kansas, Kathryn O'Loughlin McCarthy was an unusual politician: a Democrat, a Catholic, and a single woman. But her political roots, connection with farmers and cattlemen devastated by the Great Depression, and a strong Democratic tide in the 1932 elections helped her win election to the U.S. House of Representatives.

The daughter of John O'Loughlin, a Kansas state representative and cattleman, and Mary E. O'Loughlin, Kathryn Ellen O'Loughlin was born on April 24, 1894, in Hays, Kansas. She grew up on the family ranch and remembered a childhood shaped by farm chores—feeding livestock, milking cows, and familiarizing herself with the latest farm equipment.[1] She graduated from Hays High School in 1913 and, four years later, received a B.S. degree in education from the State Teacher's College in Hays. After she received a University of Chicago LL.D. in 1920, she passed the Kansas and Illinois bar exams.[2] O'Loughlin began positioning herself for a career in elective office. She returned briefly to Kansas and served as a clerk for the Kansas house of representatives' judiciary committee while John O'Loughlin was a member of the legislature. "Sometimes I could hardly sit still at the debates," she recalled. "I wanted to get in there and argue, too."[3] O'Loughlin returned to Chicago, where she participated in legal aid and social welfare work. In 1929, she resettled in Kansas and, a year later, was elected to the state legislature.

In 1932, O'Loughlin defeated eight men for the Democratic nomination in the race for a sprawling 26-county House district that covered the northwestern quarter of Kansas—compelled largely by her desire to seek progressive reform at the national level.[4] Only one Democrat had

ever represented the district since its creation in 1885. Republicans, and briefly Populists in the 1890s, dominated the elections. O'Loughlin challenged two-term incumbent Republican Charles I. Sparks, a former state judge. She focused on the devastated agricultural economy of western Kansas and proposed federal relief for farmers and ranchers. She logged more than 30,000 miles and delivered a dozen speeches daily. She stanched a "whisper campaign" against her religion, "wet" position on Prohibition, and status as a single woman. "A large part of the population of Kansas consists of German farmers who are terribly opposed to women in public life," O'Loughlin recalled after the election. "In fact the slogan of my county [Ellis County] in regard to women invading politics is '*Kinder und cookin*'—meaning 'children and cooking.' ... But I soon discovered that when I proved to the people that I knew what I was talking about, and was better informed than the average man, they gradually dropped their prejudices."[5]

On November 8, 1932, O'Loughlin defeated Sparks with 55 percent of the total vote, thanks in good part to concerns about the Great Depression and Franklin Roosevelt's long coattails in the presidential election. When she took her seat in the 73rd Congress (1933–1935) in January 1933, she became the first Kansan woman and first woman lawyer to serve in Congress. She also changed her name, to Kathryn O'Loughlin McCarthy, when she wed Daniel McCarthy, a newly elected Kansas state senator, whom she met on the campaign trail, and who initially opposed women holding public office. "I want it understood that I am not out of politics," the Congresswoman-elect declared on her wedding day, February 4, 1933. "I consider marriage an asset and not a liability in the political field."[6]

IMAGE COURTESY OF THE ELLIS COUNTY (KS) HISTORICAL SOCIETY

From the beginning, Congresswoman Kathryn O'Loughlin McCarthy faced an almost insuperable obstacle to re-election when House leaders rejected her appeal for a seat on the Agriculture Committee and instead assigned her to the Committee on Insular Affairs—in charge of U.S. overseas territories. "Where, pray tell, are the islands of Kansas?" she protested.[7] Outraged, she demanded an assignment more useful to her constituents. Her challenge caught House leaders off guard. Contending with an avalanche of freshman Democrats elected from traditionally Republican districts, they denied her request for an Agriculture seat. The decision disappointed farm constituents, who had hoped to have a stronger voice in federal projects for the state. Instead, McCarthy was reassigned to the Education Committee. She also received posts on the Public Buildings and Grounds and the World War Veterans' Legislation committees.

The repeal of Prohibition was one of the first issues McCarthy confronted. Long-standing Kansan support for temperance conflicted with the needs of the state's cash-strapped wheat and barley farmers—shaping her middling position. The issue was contentious in a state that had produced Carry Nation, a petite grandmotherly figure who had led the militant forefront of the Prohibition movement at the turn of the century. Her "Home Defenders" network of temperance zealots descended on saloons in Wichita, Topeka, and other Kansas towns, smashing them up with canes, bricks, and stones in a series of attacks that became known as "hatchetations." Against this backdrop, McCarthy steered her course. Her home county permitted the production of alcoholic beverages, but not all the counties in her district did. Shortly after her election she pledged to modify the 18th Amendment to allow "wet" states to have liquor if states that wished to prohibit alcohol were still protected. In her largely agricultural district, grain growers insisted that the alcohol market could generate revenue for devastated farming operations. Many Kansans, including some former temperance advocates, agreed the 18th Amendment should be relaxed.[8] When the Cullen Beer Bill, which legalized beer production, advertising, and distribution,

overwhelmingly passed the House on March 14, 1933, however, McCarthy joined her six Kansas colleagues to vote against the measure.[9] "You may expect me to be an ardent supporter of this bill; but I think this bill is premature, will not accomplish its purpose, and will not raise the revenue desired," she explained. "It is a discrimination in favor of big business. . . I do not think all the home-brewers in my county could raise the $1,000 license fee."[10] Later in 1933, the 21st Amendment repealed Prohibition altogether.

In Congress, McCarthy generally endorsed New Deal legislation, though she had none of the contacts with the Roosevelt administration that were enjoyed by several women colleagues. She made the best of her seat on the Education Committee, fighting for an emergency grant of $15 million in federal assistance for private, denominational, and trade schools. In particular, she hoped to boost teacher pay and put money into home economics and agriculture instruction courses. "The children of today cannot wait for the passing of the Depression to receive their education," McCarthy told colleagues.[11] By January 1, 1934, more than 2,600 schools nationwide, and more than 300 in Kansas, had been closed because of the Great Depression. Realizing that many Members would object to federal aid for nonpublic schools on the grounds of separation of church and state, McCarthy said, "That is all well and good and must be continued as a permanent policy, but this is temporary emergency legislation, to meet a time of stress."[12]

McCarthy zeroed in on the needs of her farm constituents. She recommended extending experimental Agricultural Department programs to promote better "dry land" farming practices: crop rotation, soil erosion prevention, water conservation, and summer fallowing.[13] In arguing on behalf of low interest rates for direct credits authorized under the 1933 Farm Bill, better known as the Agricultural Adjustment Act (AAA), she blasted bankers and business interests as the root cause of agricultural economic collapse. "If we had not had the high protective-tariff rates which compelled the farmer to buy everything he used in a protected market and to sell everything he produced in a world market, he would not be in the

"A LARGE PART OF THE
POPULATION OF KANSAS CONSISTS
OF GERMAN FARMERS WHO ARE
TERRIBLY OPPOSED TO WOMEN IN
PUBLIC LIFE.... BUT I SOON
DISCOVERED THAT WHEN I PROVED
TO THE PEOPLE THAT I KNEW WHAT
I WAS TALKING ABOUT, AND WAS
BETTER INFORMED THAN THE
AVERAGE MAN, THEY GRADUALLY
DROPPED THEIR PREJUDICES."

— KATHRYN O'LOUGHLIN MCCARTHY,
WASHINGTON POST, JANUARY 17, 1934

condition he is in today," she said to applause on the House Floor.[14] McCarthy fervently supported the AAA, which she believed would bring relief to farmers through a combination of federal loans, parity pricing, and quota restrictions on basic farm commodities. In 1934, McCarthy introduced bills setting compulsory caps for wheat production and taxing extra wheat crops on new land that was brought into production. For decades farmers had suffered from a market that had been deflated by overproduction, and regulation seemed to hold out hope for improved profits. Through 1933 McCarthy had argued that frequent meetings with her constituents convinced her that they broadly supported federal intervention in agriculture.[15] But by late 1934 that support had begun to erode as farmers felt AAA programs were bureaucratic and intrusive. By 1936, the Supreme Court had ruled the AAA unconstitutional.

Kansas Governor Alf Landon tapped into that growing resentment during the 1934 campaign season. Landon, a wealthy oilman elected in 1932, led the effort to unseat Kansas's congressional Democrats. He targeted McCarthy as an obedient tool of Washington New Dealers. "I believe the people of Kansas are opposed to the licensing of agriculture to the extent that each man can be told what he is going to plant," Landon said.[16] McCarthy countered that Landon misrepresented her record. "Those misrepresentations will be corrected [in Kansas], when I get on the stump," she predicted on the House Floor, "but when he throws down the gauntlet on my own doorstep, I am going to fight back. Remember my initials are K.O.— and 'Knock Out' McCarthy is on the job."[17]

McCarthy sailed through the Democratic primary unopposed. In the general election she faced Frank Carlson, Landon's handpicked challenger, who had been the governor's 1932 campaign manager and chaired the Kansas Republican Party. Carlson effectively turned the election into a referendum to endorse or to repudiate the New Deal programs.[18] McCarthy defended the federal programs and ran on her record as a friend of farmers. Public opinion, however, had already shifted. In late October, Kansas livestock producers voted against a proposal to limit corn and hog production— one of the first revolts against the AAA legislation. McCarthy's claims that most farmers supported the administration's policies were substantially weakened.[19] In a close campaign, Carlson edged out McCarthy, winning by a margin of 2,796 votes out of more than nearly 123,000 cast, or 51 percent of the vote.

After leaving Congress, McCarthy returned to her law practice in Hays and to attend to the businesses once managed by her father, who passed away in the summer of 1933.[20] In 1937, she led a reform effort to stop the wholesale practice of sterilizing young girls at state correctional facilities.[21] She paid the tuition for dozens of low-income students to attend Fort Hays State University, including several African Americans to whom she also extended free room and board in her home.[22] In 1940 and 1944, McCarthy attended the Democratic National Conventions as a Kansas delegate.[23] On January 16, 1952, she passed away in Hays, Kansas, after an extended illness.

FOR FURTHER READING

Biographical Directory of the United States Congress, "Kathryn O'Loughlin McCarthy," http://bioguide.congress.gov

MANUSCRIPT COLLECTIONS

Ellis County Historical Society (Hays, KS), Thomas More Prep Center for Research. *Papers:* 1900–1948, quantity unknown. The papers contain personal papers including announcements, a scrapbook pertaining to her term in the U.S. House of Representatives, materials on Fort Hays Frontier Park, Fort Hays Kansas State College, corporate farming, and sterilization of inmates at the State Industrial School for Girls. Also includes a scrapbook of her wedding to Daniel M. McCarthy.

Kansas State Historical Society (Topeka, KS). One reel of microfilm.

NOTES

1 Frances Mangum, "Congresswoman McCarthy Says a Word—About Cupid," 17 January 1934, *Washington Post*: 15.
2 "Kathryn McCarthy Much Entertained," 12 March 1933, *Washington Post*: S2.
3 Mangum, "Congresswoman McCarthy Says a Word—About Cupid."
4 For motivations, see Hope Chamberlin, *A Minority of Members: Women in the U.S. Congress* (New York: Praeger, 1973): 101–102; Susan Tolchin, *Women in Congress* (Washington, D.C.: Government Printing Office, 1976): 53.
5 Mangum, "Congresswoman McCarthy Says a Word—About Cupid."
6 "Weds 'Foe,'" 5 February 1933, *Washington Post*: 2. During the primary O'Loughlin met Daniel McCarthy, a candidate for the Kansas state senate opposed to women holding public office. He introduced himself to O'Loughlin by saying that it was "perfectly ridiculous" for a woman to run as a Democrat in a Republican state. Nevertheless, McCarthy introduced O'Loughlin to local Democratic leaders and endorsed her when she won the primary. Shortly after their simultaneous election victories, he proposed marriage. See Mangum, "Congresswoman McCarthy Says a Word—About Cupid."

7 Chamberlin, *A Minority of Members*: 101.
8 W.G. Clugston, "Kansas Wheat Men See Hope in Barley," 18 December 1932, *New York Times*: E6.
9 "Legal Beer Is Speeded," 15 March 1933, *New York Times*: 1.
10 *Congressional Record*, House, 73rd Cong., 1st sess. (14 March 1933): 394.
11 *Congressional Record*, House, 73rd Cong., 2nd sess. (26 April 1934): 7468–7469.
12 *Congressional Record*, House, 73rd Cong., 2nd sess. (23 May 1934): 9390–9391.
13 *Congressional Record*, House, 73rd Cong., 2nd sess. (1 March 1934): 3529–3530.
14 *Congressional Record*, House, 73rd Cong., 1st sess. (12 April 1933): 1613.
15 *Congressional Record*, House, 73rd Cong., 1st sess. (21 March 1933): 687–688.
16 Raymond Clapper, "Warns Bureaucracy AAA Grows," 12 June 1934, *Washington Post*: 2.
17 *Congressional Record*, House, 73rd Cong., 2nd sess. (18 June 1934): 1934–1935.
18 Roy Buckingham, "Republicans Start NRA Row in Kansas," 24 June 1934, *New York Times*: E6. For more on Landon's position on farm relief, see Donald R. McCoy, *Landon of Kansas* (Lincoln: University of Nebraska Press, 1966): 144–149; 197–201.
19 Roy Buckingham, "Kansans Opposed to Regimentation," 14 October 1934, *New York Times*: E1.
20 "John O'Loughlin Dies From Heart Disease," 3 July 1933, *Washington Post*: 9.
21 "Kansas Puts Stop to Sterilizing of Industrial School Children," 24 October 1937, *Washington Post*: 1.
22 Bobbie Athon, "The First Kansas Congresswoman: Kathryn O'Loughlin McCarthy," *Kansas Historical Society*, March 2001, online at http://www.kshs.org/features/feat301.htm (accessed 3 September 2003).
23 Chamberlin, *A Minority of Members*: 102.

Virginia Ellis Jenckes
1877–1975

UNITED STATES REPRESENTATIVE ★ DEMOCRAT FROM INDIANA
1933–1939

Water, liquor, and communism stirred Virginia E. Jenckes's considerable passions and spurred her into elective politics, where she unseated a 16- year veteran Congressman to become the first Indiana woman to serve in the U.S. House of Representatives. Jenckes's expressions of commitment to creating flood control for her constituents, abolishing Prohibition, and routing communist influences from American society made her one of the more colorful Washington politicians during the New Deal.

Virginia Ellis Somes was born on November 6, 1877, in Terre Haute, Indiana, to James Ellis, a pharmacist, and Mary Oliver Somes. She attended public schools in Terre Haute and took one year of coursework at Coates College.[1] In 1912, Virginia Somes married Ray Greene Jenckes, a Terre Haute businessman 34 years her senior.[2] A year later, Virginia Jenckes gave birth to a daughter, Virginia. The couple operated a 1,300-acre family farm along the banks of the Wabash River in western Indiana. Ray Jenckes died in 1921, leaving his widow to manage the farm and raise their child.

Flooding posed a constant problem in western Indiana. In 1927 a new dike along the Wabash River failed, threatening lives and Jenckes's $15,000 crop. She mobilized local residents and participated in a 3,000-sandbag effort that successfully contained the breach. That experience led her to found and serve as secretary and lobbyist for the Wabash and Maumee Valley Improvement Association, an organization that proposed flood control programs and projects. In 1928, Jenckes achieved a major political triumph when party leaders adopted one of her association's flood control plans into the Democratic National platform.[3] Success emboldened Jenckes, and within several years she had committed herself to running for Congress.

In 1932, the road to Washington was not an easy one. A year earlier, reapportionment had reshuffled Indiana politics, leaving Jenckes the task of ousting two incumbents. The new Indiana district, tucked along much of the western portion of the state that bordered Illinois, included 10 counties and Jenckes's hometown. In the primary, she faced Democrat Courtland C. Gillen, a one-term incumbent from Greencastle. Acting as her own campaign manager, Jenckes developed a simple strategy and platform: abolish Prohibition. "Get rid of Prohibition and you will have a market for your corn," she told farmers.[4] Prohibition had closed Terre Haute's distilleries after 1919 and contributed to a slide in commodities prices that accelerated with the onset of the Great Depression. The message resonated in the presumed dry sections of the Indiana district. She also reminded the voters of her strong record and personal experience with flood control.[5]

In the Democratic primary in May 1932 she unseated Gillen. In the general election, her 19-year-old daughter, Virginia, chauffeured her on a speaking tour that logged 15,000 miles.[6] Jenckes faced Fred Sampson Purnell, an eight-term incumbent, who had represented the northern counties prior to redistricting. Purnell, who voted down a proposal to loosen Prohibition laws in the 72nd Congress (1931–1933), found himself in the political battle of his life as the Democratic Party embraced the repeal of the legislation. Jenckes ultimately prevailed with 54 percent of the vote to Purnell's 46 percent. In Indiana the four GOP incumbents lost and the state's 12-seat House

THOUGH JENCKES BROADLY
SUPPORTED NEW DEAL RELIEF
PROGRAMS, HER RELATIONSHIP
WITH THE ROOSEVELT
ADMINISTRATION WAS FROSTY. . . .
SHE BELIEVED FDR TO BE TOO
CONSERVATIVE, TOO PATRICIAN,
AND TOO WILLING TO
SUBORDINATE THE DEMOCRATIC
PARTY'S INTERESTS TO HIS OWN
"SELFISH AMBITIONS."

delegation went all-Democratic, thanks to presidential candidate Franklin D. Roosevelt's long coattails. Hoping to capitalize on farmers' discontent with the Agricultural Adjustment Act (AAA), Purnell challenged Jenckes again in 1934. But she won by a hair's breadth, polling just 383 more votes than Purnell out of 135,000 cast.

Securing all-important committee assignments was another matter entirely. In 1933, Congresswoman Jenckes failed to persuade Democratic leaders to give her a seat on either the coveted Agriculture Committee or the Rivers and Harbors Committee, which would have given her the opportunity to effect change for her farming constituents through crop relief programs or flood control. Instead, she received assignments on three lower-tier committees: Mines and Mining, Civil Service, and District of Columbia.[7] She kept the latter two assignments throughout her House career but dropped Mines and Mining after the 74th Congress (1935–1937). The District of Columbia Committee assignment brought plenty of work but few rewards, as it did not remotely benefit any of her constituents. Nevertheless, Jenckes devoted herself to giving D.C. voters a greater voice in their government, reducing the workload on city firefighters, and monitoring developments in city schools. In 1937, she became the first American woman appointed as a delegate to the Interparliamentary Union in Paris.[8]

During her first term, Jenckes made good on her promise to seek an end to Prohibition—a task made easier by a compliant Congress and President. One of her first House votes was to support the Cullen Beer Bill— allowing for the production, transportation, and sale of the beverage—which passed by a wide margin in March 1933.[9] She also managed to secure $18 million in funding during the following Congress for a series of flood control projects along the Wabash River Basin.[10]

Jenckes emerged as an advocate for American veterans and workers. In one of her first floor speeches, she urged her colleagues to support a comprehensive "rehabilitation" program for U.S. veterans.[11] A year later, Jenckes voted for the Patman Bill to extend a bonus to World War I veterans. She also encouraged Congress to adopt the

Railroad Retirement Act, which nationalized rail workers' pensions, an important step toward creating universal old-age pensions.[12] Having voted for the first AAA to relieve drought and Depression-stricken farmers, Jenckes supported efforts to develop substitute legislation after the Supreme Court had invalidated the original act.[13] Jenckes believed New Deal programs particularly affected women and that it was important that she was in Congress to speak for women's interests. "For the first time in history, there's an electric connection between Congress and the home," Jenckes said.[14]

Though Jenckes broadly supported New Deal relief programs, her relationship with the Roosevelt administration was frosty. She had faith in her convictions but not always the requisite tact of a Washington insider. She believed FDR to be too conservative, too patrician, and too willing to subordinate the Democratic Party's interests to his own "selfish ambitions."[15] Jenckes soon clashed with Harry Hopkins—one of President Roosevelt's most trusted advisers, chief administrator of the Federal Emergency Relief Administration and director of the Works Progress (later Projects) Administration—over the disbursement of federal money in her district.[16] While Jenckes embraced federal programs to ease her constituents' economic burdens, she was more hesitant than other New Dealers about reinventing the role of government either in the direction of a planned economy or the creation of the welfare state. In 1934, she expressed concern that small factions of organized labor would use the National Industrial Recovery Administration as a vehicle to dominate certain trades.[17] Despite her efforts to protect the retirements of many different American workers, Jenckes seemed ambivalent about the role government should play in that regard. She voted in 1935 for the Social Security Act, which established unemployment insurance and old-age pensions. As a senior citizen, however, she refused social security payments, noting, "I think when you give dole to people you take away their self respect."[18]

With the implementation of the New Deal relief measures, Jenckes turned her attention to other matters. Her interest in stemming subversive activities in America dominated her work and made her something of a controversial figure in the nation's capital. As a strong supporter of J. Edgar Hoover's Federal Bureau of Investigation, she often defended the agency's budget requests on the House Floor. She also was an unremitting anticommunist. When many government buildings were erected in the 1930s without provision for display of the American flag, Jenckes suspected a conspiracy and introduced a measure requiring that the Stars and Stripes be flown atop every federal building.[19] Jenckes pursued her anticommunist crusade by using her seat on the District of Columbia Committee to expound on the dangers of communist indoctrination in the public schools. In 1935, she supported an amendment—later dubbed the "red rider"—to a D.C. appropriations bill which outlawed the teaching, advocacy, or mere mention of communism in the capital's public schools.[20] She locked horns with New York Representative Fred J. Sisson, who introduced an amendment to repeal the "red rider." Sisson claimed that Jenckes made her allegations without "a scintilla of evidence."[21] Jenckes would not relent, however, warning that "Washington is the hotbed of international propagandists."[22] The dispute eventually brought Jenckes into conflict with other committee members, including Chairwoman Mary Norton of New Jersey. In May 1937 the House overwhelmingly repealed her amendment.

Jenckes's tumultuous third term and growing resentment over New Deal programs foreshadowed a difficult 1938 re-election campaign. Noble Johnson, a former GOP Indiana Congressman, proved a formidable challenger. Johnson benefited from Jenckes's inability to secure a key committee assignment, as well as public backlash against President Roosevelt's failed "court packing plan." Jenckes ran unopposed in the primary but lost the general election by a 1,755-vote margin. Seven of Indiana's 12 House seats swung to GOP insurgents in 1938. After Jenckes's defeat, *New York Times* editors noted that she had "served with distinction."[23]

Retiring from Congress in early 1939, Jenckes settled in Washington, D.C., where she volunteered extensively for the American Red Cross.[24] She helped five priests escape Hungary during the 1956 uprising, setting up a behind-the-scenes network and funneling communist opposition messages to then-Secretary of Defense Charles E. Wilson. Late in life she returned to Indiana and eventually resettled in her native Terre Haute. After a long life of public service, Virginia Jenckes died in Terre Haute on January 9, 1975, at the age of 98.

FOR FURTHER READING

Biographical Directory of the United States Congress, "Virginia Ellis Jenckes," http://bioguide.congress.gov

MANUSCRIPT COLLECTIONS

Indiana State Library (Indianapolis, IN). *Papers:* 1918–1951, two linear feet. Chiefly congressional papers, including correspondence, reports, materials relating to efforts to help farmers during the Depression, campaign files, the meeting of the 1937 Interparliamentary Union, newspaper and clippings. Topics covered include flood control, railroads, women's rights, education, and communists in America. Described in published guide. Also papers: In the New Deal in Indiana Records, n.d., 88 pages. Includes correspondence between Virginia Jenckes and Franklin D. Roosevelt. *Oral History:* October 1967, 88 pages.

Vigo County Public Library (Terre Haute, IN). *Oral History:* 1972, 88 pages. A transcript of an interview with Virginia Jenckes by Tom Krasean, conducted October 11–12, 1967, in the Terre Haute House, Terre Haute, Indiana. *Papers:* Assorted scrapbooks containing newspaper clippings and copy of a letter (March 29, 1938) from Speaker William Bankhead are available on microfilm.

NOTES

1   Susan Lennis, "Virginia Jenckes: A Hoosier Ex-Congresswoman Reminisces," *Indianapolis Star Magazine*, 7 December 1969: 48–53.

2   Lennis, "Virginia Jenckes": 53.

3   Ibid., 48–53.

4   "Indiana Democrats Nominate Two Drys," 6 May 1932, *Washington Post*: 5.

5   Hope Chamberlin, *A Minority of Members: Women in the U.S. Congress* (New York: Praeger, 1973): 97–98.

6   Until her daughter Virginia's tragic death from tuberculosis in September 1936, she was a constant companion in Washington, serving as her mother's unpaid office secretary and keeping house in their rented apartment. Lennis, "Virginia Jenckes": 48–53; "Rep. Jenckes Succeeds Gillett as the Bridge Ace of Congress," 28 April 1935, *Washington Post*: SMB7.

7   Charles Stewart III, "Committee Hierarchies in the Modernizing House, 1875–1947," *American Journal of Political Science* 36 (No. 4, November 1992): 835–856.

8   *Terre Haute Tribune*, January 9, 1975. Established in 1889, the Interparliamentary Union is an international organization of sovereign states with the aim of promoting peace, cooperation, and representative governments.

9   "Roll Call on Beer Bill," 15 March 1933, *New York Times*: 3.

10 Labeling flood control projects in her district as one of her "pets," Jenckes requested that $18 million of the more than $3 billion marked for public works and recovery projects be set aside to pay for and prevent damage caused by flooding in her district. "Mrs. Jenckes Wars on Flood Peril," 19 January 1934, *Washington Post*: 11.

11 *Congressional Record*, House, 73rd Cong., 1st sess. (24 May 1933): 4093–4094.

12 *Congressional Record*, House, 73rd Cong., 2nd sess. (15 June 1934): 11889.

13 *Congressional Record*, House, 74th Cong., 2nd sess. (20 February 1936): 2512.

14 "Mrs. Jenckes, Indiana, Is Home Protagonist," 24 January 1935, *Washington Post*: 12.

15 Lennis, "Virginia Jenckes": 49.

16 Ibid., 49–50. Jenckes also resented First Lady Eleanor Roosevelt's efforts to promote close women friends for Congress.

17 *Congressional Record*, House, 73rd Cong., 2nd sess. (9 June 1934): 10962–10964.

18 Lennis, "Virginia Jenckes": 48–52.

19 *Congressional Record*, House, 74th Cong., 1st sess. (8 February 1935): 1761–1762; see also, "Ex. Rep. Virginia E. Jenckes, 97, Indiana Anti-Communist, Dead," 10 January 1975, *New York Times*: 40.

20 "Congress to Debate Communism Issue," 17 May 1936, *Washington Post*: B1.

21 "Sisson Scores Jenckes' Stand on Rider Issue," 10 March 1936, *Washington Post*: 1; *Congressional Record*, House, 74th Cong., 2nd sess. (19 June 1936): 10307–10309.

22 *Congressional Record*, House, 75th Cong., 1st sess. (11 February 1937): 1161; James D. Secrest, "Teacher Foes of Red Rider Are Assailed," 12 February 1937, *Washington Post*: 17. See also, Jenckes's statement in the *Congressional Record*, House, 75th Cong., 1st sess. (11 March 1937): 2130–2132.

23 "Congresswomen," 12 November 1938, *New York Times*: 14.

24 Peggy Preston, "Ex-Congresswoman Jenckes Says Walk for 'War Nerves,'" 3 November 1942, *Washington Post*: B7; see also Lennis, "Virginia Jenckes": 48–52.

Isabella S. Greenway
1886–1953

UNITED STATES REPRESENTATIVE ★ DEMOCRAT FROM ARIZONA
1933–1937

Isabella Greenway, a charismatic businesswoman, philanthropist, and politician, served as Arizona's first woman in Congress. Elected to the House during the depths of the Great Depression, Representative Greenway used her experience and extensive political connections to bring economic relief to her strapped state.

Isabella Selmes was born on March 22, 1886, in Boone County, Kentucky, daughter of Tilden Russell Selmes, a lawyer, general counsel for the Northern Pacific Railroad, and sheep rancher, and Martha Macomb Flandrau Selmes. The family lived briefly in North Dakota, where Tilden Selmes established ranching operations. He also befriended Theodore Roosevelt who, from that day forward, took a special interest in the young Isabella. Eventually, Selmes moved his family to St. Paul, Minnesota. After his death in 1895, Martha Selmes moved to New York City with the adolescent Isabella to enroll her in the elite Miss Chapin's School, where she made a lifelong friendship with Roosevelt's niece, Eleanor Roosevelt. In March 1905, Isabella Selmes was a bridesmaid at the marriage of Eleanor and Franklin D. Roosevelt.[1] Weeks later, 19-year-old Isabella married Robert H. Munro Ferguson, a former member of Theodore Roosevelt's military unit from the Spanish-American War, with little notice. They raised two children, Martha and Robert. Ferguson, 19 years Isabella's senior, developed tuberculosis, and the family moved in 1909 to a ranch home in the dry climate of the Burro Mountains near Silver City, New Mexico. Robert Ferguson died in 1922. A year later, Isabella married another former "Rough Rider," John Campbell Greenway, a decorated veteran of World War I, mining engineer, and copper magnate. The Greenways raised one child, John, and with Isabella's two other children, settled in the mining town of Aho, Arizona, which they helped develop alongside their Cornelia surface copper mine. John Greenway died in 1927, and Isabella relocated to Tucson with her children. She established the Arizona Hut, a woodcraft factory that employed convalescent veterans. She later built a successful hotel resort, the Arizona Inn, and owned a cattle ranch and Gilpin Airlines, based in Los Angeles, California.

Greenway was a peculiar blend of Eastern Establishment aristocracy and frontierswoman: cultured and charming, yet rugged and self-reliant. She relished meeting people and was a seemingly inexhaustible campaigner and student of the issues: "I always felt the open door of human contacts was more important than an open book."[2] Greenway also held firm convictions about the wisdom and resiliency of average Americans and believed political leaders needed to be forthright in discussing national issues. "I believe they are not only anxious to know the truth and will welcome it but that they have the courage to face it, whatever it is."[3] Western influences, she once observed, gave her something she called a "liberty of living"—a desire and an opportunity to know the wide spectrum of experiences from emotion and aesthetics to intellectual pursuits. "The West is so much less afraid of the things we may have to do and the changes we may have to make in order to save the values in American life that are worth saving," Greenway remarked, "that sometimes I think this courage of the West to dare new adventures—even if all that are proposed are not all strictly wise adventures—may be our final salvation."[4]

Isabella Greenway's political career began during the First World War. In 1918, she chaired the Women's Land Army of New Mexico, which tended to agricultural tasks traditionally performed by men then serving in the military. Her marriage to the widely revered John Greenway opened up a constellation of political connections. As tribute to her husband's memory, state Democratic elders elected Isabella Greenway a Democratic National committeewoman in 1928. Most expected she would accept it as a ceremonial honor. Instead, she treated it as a serious full-time job.[5] That year Greenway campaigned for Al Smith's presidential bid. She did the same for her longtime friend Franklin D. Roosevelt in 1932, as the only woman among Roosevelt's state leaders. To recognize Greenway's part in delivering Arizona's delegation to Roosevelt at the 1932 Democratic National Convention in Chicago, party leaders chose her to second FDR's nomination. Greenway was particularly close to Eleanor Roosevelt, whose children knew her as "Aunt Isabella." Once, when Eleanor campaigned in Los Angeles for her husband, Isabella Greenway flew on half an hour's notice to visit her friend for the evening, packing only her toothbrush in her briefcase. The two stayed up late into the night talking politics. "We've done lots of mad things together," Eleanor Roosevelt recalled.[6] Theirs was a genuine friendship that weathered Isabella's eventual political conflicts with Franklin.[7]

When Arizona's Representative At-Large, Lewis W. Douglas, resigned in March 1933 to become Director of the Bureau of the Budget, Greenway ran for his seat. Her platform included support for veterans' benefits and the implementation of a copper tariff to revive Arizona's flagging mining industry. On the same day in August that Arizonans voted 3–1 to repeal Prohibition, Greenway overwhelmingly won the Democratic primary.[8] The nomination was tantamount to election. In the October 3, 1933, special election, Greenway triumphed with 73 percent of the vote over Socialist candidate D.E. Sumpter and GOP opponent, H.B. Wilkinson.[9] She dismissed accusations during and after the campaign that her viability as a candidate depended on her ties to Roosevelt. "A great deal has been said about my being a friend of the Roosevelts," she observed. "I did not ask for votes on the basis of friendship but on the basis I was qualified to do the work. And it is on that basis that I am getting the job done."[10]

Sworn in and seated on January 3, 1934, Greenway was a persuasive and quickly successful advocate for New Deal programs to help her 450,000 constituents, who suffered from an unemployment rate in excess of 25 percent. Greenway was concerned mostly with improving the lives of workers and industrial laborers. Her chief priorities were veterans' relief, the rehabilitation of unemployed copper miners, and the development of the several flood-control projects. "Whatever happens, I must succeed for Arizona," she confided to a friend.[11] Ten days after being elected, she met with Interior Secretary Harold L. Ickes, who also served as director of the Public Works Administration. As she began to make her case for much-needed federal money for her state, Ickes told her: "Mrs. Greenway, my time is very valuable. Can you compress all that Arizona wants onto one page?" She shot back, "Mr. Secretary, Arizona would never forgive me if I could get all it wanted onto one page."[12] She left the meeting with Ickes agreeing to fund three major projects that would employ more than 9,000 Arizonans—including the development of a large irrigation system on the Verde River and the construction of a post office in Phoenix. "I know we're right," Greenway said, "when we weigh projects in terms of human beings first and dollars second."[13] She also went to work on the press, telling the *Washington Post*, "The situation is desperate. Our one industry, copper mining, is closed."[14] She plied her colleagues for information, too. One Capitol observer noted her elevator habits: "She never gets on here without two other Representatives. And you know what they're doing? Answering questions: and she can ask them fast—all about different laws."[15]

During her two terms in Congress, Greenway served on three committees important to her Arizona constituency: Public Lands, Irrigation and Reclamation, and Indian Affairs. Given her statewide district, each assignment gave Congresswoman Greenway a powerful post from which to

"The West is so much less afraid of things we may have to do and the changes we may have to make in order to save the values in the American life that are worth saving, that sometimes I think this courage of the West to dare new adventures — even if all that are proposed are not all strictly wise adventures — may be our final salvation."

—Isabella Greenway
New York Times
April 21, 1935

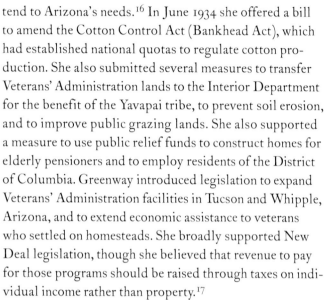

tend to Arizona's needs.[16] In June 1934 she offered a bill to amend the Cotton Control Act (Bankhead Act), which had established national quotas to regulate cotton production. She also submitted several measures to transfer Veterans' Administration lands to the Interior Department for the benefit of the Yavapai tribe, to prevent soil erosion, and to improve public grazing lands. She also supported a measure to use public relief funds to construct homes for elderly pensioners and to employ residents of the District of Columbia. Greenway introduced legislation to expand Veterans' Administration facilities in Tucson and Whipple, Arizona, and to extend economic assistance to veterans who settled on homesteads. She broadly supported New Deal legislation, though she believed that revenue to pay for those programs should be raised through taxes on individual income rather than property.[17]

Greenway demonstrated her political independence by opposing two significant pieces of Roosevelt's New Deal legislation. She broke with FDR over the Economy Act of 1933, which sought to cut veterans' pensions, rejecting World War I servicemen's call for a $2 billion bonus in benefits. Roosevelt maintained that he needed the money for his economic recovery programs. Greenway wanted to move the bonus bill beyond its "political football status" and sided with veterans, arguing that it would amount to an economic stimulus in its own right. The House passed a grant of additional money for veterans, but the Senate rejected the measure; it eventually passed during Greenway's second term. She also supported the concept of old-age pensions. "Self-reliance is the cornerstone upon which every nation must build, if it is to succeed," Greenway said on the House Floor. "To my mind, self-reliance means the use of human capacity, coupled with natural resources, in such a manner as to insure the liberty of living for all people."[18] But she opposed the provisions of the 1935 Social Security Act, sweeping legislation which eventually passed Congress and instituted unemployment insurance, pensions, and other social welfare programs. Greenway believed the legislation would be impossible to implement; "sustaining employment

through artificial channels" required the government to tax businesses, which would further hamper economic recovery. "I do not believe anybody in Congress thinks that this country can continue to carry millions of people on welfare and not eventually run on the rocks," Greenway declared.[19]

On March 22, 1936, on her 50th birthday, Greenway announced her decision to retire from the House. Not only did she wish to leave Washington politics, but despite being considered the front-runner for the Arizona governorship in 1934, she precluded any further public service.[20] She cited the need to spend more time with her family; her son John was a young teenager. Her biographer surmised family responsibilities and sheer exhaustion from congressional travel were decisive factors in her retirement.[21] Greenway expressed pride in having "been allied with the courageous experiments of this administration, many of which I feel will be continued on their merits."[22] Still, some observers perceived that her rift with the White House—first apparent in the veterans' bill—had widened since 1933.[23]

Greenway gave tacit confirmation of the break with President Roosevelt by actively campaigning for the 1940 Republican presidential candidate, Wendell L. Willkie, as chair of the Arizona chapter of Democrats for Willkie. In 1939, Greenway married Harry O. King, a former National Recovery Administration manager for the copper industry. She also went on to chair the American Women's Volunteer Service during World War II, a national group dedicated to providing civil defense training to women. Later, she participated in international cultural exchange programs. Following a long illness, Greenway died in Tucson, on December 18, 1953.

FOR FURTHER READING

Biographical Directory of the United States Congress, "Isabella Selmes Greenway," http://bioguide.congress.gov

Miller, Kristie. *Isabella Greenway: An Enterprising Woman* (Tucson, AZ: The University of Arizona Press, 2004).

MANUSCRIPT COLLECTIONS

Arizona Historical Society (Tucson, AZ). *Papers:* 1860–1953, 117 linear feet. The papers of Isabella Greenway include state and national political material covering her years in the U.S. Congress, personal correspondence, and business papers relating to the Arizona Inn in Tucson. An inventory is available in the repository.

U.S. Capitol (Washington, D.C.), Office of the Architect of the Capitol Manuscript Collection. *Papers:* February 1930–July 1932. Correspondence and other papers relating to the placement of the statue of Isabella Greenway's husband, John Campbell Greenway, in Statuary Hall.

NOTES

1   "Victory of Mrs. Greenway Cheers First Lady of Land," 5 October 1933, *Washington Post:* 5.
2   "Mrs. Greenway Tackles Work Enthusiastically," 16 March 1934, *Washington Post:* 14.
3   Duncan Aikman, "Mrs. Greenway Charts Her Own Course," 21 April 1935, *New York Times:* SM9.
4   Aikman, "Mrs. Greenway Charts Her Own Course."
5   Bernice Cosulich, "A Congresswoman Out of the West," 22 October 1933, *New York Times:* XX2.
6   "Victory of Mrs. Greenway to Add Sixth Name to 'Feminine Bloc,'" 12 August 1933, *Washington Post:* 4; see also, Blanche Wiesen Cook, *Eleanor Roosevelt,* Vol. 2 (New York: Viking, 1999): 73.
7   Cook, *Eleanor Roosevelt,* Vol. 2: 313–314.

8   See Kristie Miller, *Isabella Greenway: An Enterprising Woman* (Tucson, AZ: University of Arizona Press, 2004): 192–194; "Roosevelt's Friend Chosen," 10 August 1933, *Washington Post:* 10.
9   Michael Dubin et al., *U.S. Congressional Elections, 1788–1997* (Jefferson, NC: McFarland & Company, Inc., Publishers, 1998): 498.
10 Hope Chamberlin, *A Minority of Members: Women in the U.S. Congress* (New York: Praeger, 1973): 105.
11 See Kristie Miller, "Greenway, Isabella," *American National Biography* 9 (New York: Oxford University Press, 1999): 552–553. A variant appears in Cosulich, "A Congresswoman Out of the West."
12 Chamberlin, *A Minority of Members:* 104. Ickes's diaries do not record the encounter, nor do any of his biographies. The Miller biography of Greenway touches on other meetings between Greenway and Ickes but not on this particular encounter; see especially, Miller, *Isabella Greenway:* 201.
13 Susan Tolchin, *Women in Congress* (Washington, D.C.: Government Printing Office, 1976): 35.
14 "Mrs. Greenway Here, Eager for Job in Congress," 11 October 1933, *Washington Post:* 10.
15 "Mrs. Greenway Tackles Work Enthusiastically."
16 Her Irrigation and Reclamation assignment was, according to one study, a moderately powerful post for the era. Political scientist Charles Stewart ranks it the 11th most attractive committee during a span of 70 years from the Gilded Age to the post–World War II reorganization of Congress. See Charles Stewart III, "Committee Hierarchies in the Modernizing House, 1875–1947," *American Journal of Political Science* 36 (No. 4, November 1992): 835–856. Public Lands ranked in the bottom 10 of about 30 committees in continual existence during that era, but it was uniquely important to Greenway since the federal government owned large tracts of Arizona. Likewise, Indian Affairs was a middling committee on Stewart's scale, but Arizona contained so many Native American tribal reservations that it was an important assignment to Congresswoman Greenway.
17 "Mrs. Greenway Advocates Action on New Deal Bills," 26 January 1935, *Washington Post:* 12.
18 *Congressional Record,* House, 74th Cong., 1st sess. (13 April 1935): 5604–5605.
19 *Congressional Record,* House, 74th Cong., 2nd sess. (30 April 1936): 6480–6481.
20 "Mrs. Roosevelt's Girlhood Chum To Leave Public Life," 24 March 1936, *Christian Science Monitor:* 4.
21 Miller, *Isabella Greenway:* 228–230.
22 "Mrs. Greenway Will Quit House," 23 March 1936, *New York Times:* 21.
23 Cook, *Eleanor Roosevelt,* Vol. 2: 225–226.

Marian Williams Clarke
1880–1953

UNITED STATES REPRESENTATIVE ★ REPUBLICAN FROM NEW YORK
1933–1935

Marian Clarke won election to the U.S. House of Representatives less than two months after the death of her husband, Representative John D. Clarke, in an automobile crash. Shortly after being sworn into office, Congresswoman Clarke confided to the *Washington Post*: "I wanted dreadfully to come, of course. I felt the need of some absorbing work."[1] While coping with her own loss, Clarke attended to the needs of individuals and industry in her local district struggling with the effects of the Great Depression.

Marian K. Williams was born on July 29, 1880, in Standing Grove, Pennsylvania, the daughter of Ripp and Florence K. Williams.[2] Her parents moved her and her older brother, Kingsley, to Cheyenne, Wyoming, in 1891, and the Williamses spent their childhood in various states. Marian Williams attended art school at the University of Nebraska and graduated with a B.A. from Colorado College in 1902. As an undergraduate at Colorado College, she enrolled in a public speaking class taught by John Clarke. "At the end of the course he called me to him and said he hated to discourage me but he felt duty bound to tell me I never would be an orator," Marian recalled. "In fact, he explained that he really shouldn't pass me in the course but he would stretch a point and let me by on my written work." Years later she would deliver campaign speeches on his behalf.[3] With her strength as a writer, she worked three years as a reporter for a Colorado Springs newspaper. Marian Williams married Clarke in 1905, and the couple moved to New York City, where John worked for several mining companies before graduating from Brooklyn Law School in 1911. After earning his law degree, John Clarke worked in the mining department

of the Carnegie Steel Corporation and for several other mining interests. The Clarkes raised one son, John Duncan. In 1915, they moved to John Clarke's native Delaware County, in upstate New York. He pursued a newfound interest in agriculture and forestry, operating "Arbor Hill," a farm near Dehli, New York. He became president of the New York State Forestry Association and vice president of the New York Conservation Association.[4]

In 1920, John Clarke easily won election as a U.S. Representative from a conservative New York district covering the city of Binghamton and surrounding counties. Except for the 69th Congress (1925–1927), for which he was an unsuccessful candidate, he represented this district from 1921 to 1933. A strong believer in environmental conservation, he cosponsored the Clarke–McNary Reforestation Bill with Oregon Senator Charles L. McNary in 1924, creating a comprehensive national reforestation policy.[5] The bill authorized the President to set aside national forests on military and other federal lands and established a federally funded seedling planting program to assist "the owners of farms in establishing, improving, and in growing and renewing useful timber crops." Marian Clarke played an active role in her husband's congressional career in Washington, D.C. "You see I was always interested in my husband's work and followed his activities very closely," Clarke told the *Washington Post*. "It was a rare day that didn't find me in the gallery all eyes and ears for what was going on."[6] She recalled that her political experience also included her work as a "general factotum" in her husband's office.[7]

On November 5, 1933, while returning home from a wedding along snowy back roads, John Clarke died in a

head-on auto wreck. Less than a month after her husband's death, Marian Clarke was selected at a meeting of district Republican leaders in Sidney, New York, as the GOP nominee to fill out John Clarke's vacant term.[8] It is not clear whether she sought the nomination actively or whether GOP leaders simply offered it to her. She was a compromise candidate, however, chosen on the 11th ballot.[9] The heavily Republican New York district encompassed a largely agricultural swath of the state and the city of Binghamton near the border with Pennsylvania. Despite the high number of registered GOP voters residing in the district, New York Democrats felt optimistic about the odds of their candidate, John J. Burns, a retired shoe manufacturer and Binghamton city councilman. Burns boasted strong support among businessmen and expected to benefit from a low rural voter turnout in the dead of winter.[10] On December 28, 1933, in a blizzard, constituents—many of them driving to polling places on treacherous roads from their farms—comfortably elected Marian Clarke. Turnout was low, less than 20 percent, but Clarke ran slightly ahead across the entire district and received a large plurality in her Delaware County precincts. With that boost she beat Burns by about 5,000 votes out of approximately 30,000 cast, giving her roughly 60 percent of the total.[11] "It has been a life-saver," she said of the election. "It means that I can go right on with the same interests."[12] Clarke became one of just three Republican women—Edith Nourse Rogers of Massachusetts and Florence Kahn of California were the others—elected to Congress during the first six years of the New Deal. She also held the distinction of being the only woman among the 45 members of the New York congressional delegation.

When Clarke took her seat in the House on January 3, 1934, she received assignments on three minor committees: Civil Service, Claims, and Invalid Pensions.[13] In her first floor speech, Representative Clarke introduced a measure to raise the equipment allowance for rural mail carriers to cover winter and early spring months. In a district with many dirt roads, Clarke insisted such an extension would greatly aid postal carriers forced to navigate icy roads on snowmobiles or muddy springtime lanes by car. Increased

allowances also would help offset increased insurance expenses and a new four-cent gas tax. "No one is more aware than I of the necessity for economy at the present time, but it seems to me as though there might be other ways to save this amount that would be more humanitarian than taking it from these men whose lives are already so hard," Clarke said to applause from the floor and gallery.[14] Despite passing the House, the bill languished in committee in the Senate.[15] In March 1934, Clarke introduced a bill to reimburse Army personnel for personal property losses incurred during the infamous 1915 hurricane which struck Texas's Gulf Coast.[16] Having lived for more than a decade in the capital, Clarke also played an active role in several Washington, D.C., women's organizations.

Like her Democratic counterparts, Clarke remained preoccupied with the economic needs of her constituents during the depths of the Great Depression. Since her New York district included more than 22 shoe factories that employed 17,000 workers, Clarke urged her House colleagues to add an amendment to the Tariff Act of 1930 to protect shoe manufacturers from cheaply produced and inferior products imported from foreign countries.[17] "I am not one of those who believe that Congress can or should attempt to legislate prosperity," Clarke told her colleagues in a floor speech. "I think that is the wrong way of looking at the whole problem. I urge that it is not the function of Congress and it is not the intent of the government to lift any group bodily from a particular economic condition through economic means. . . . But I think we are all agreed, Mr. Speaker, to this general proposition: That it is the function of Congress to insure equal opportunity." Clarke argued that without protecting such large employers and preserving an industry tax base, the Franklin D. Roosevelt administration would undercut its efforts to stimulate the economy.[18]

During her short stint as a Representative, Clarke exhibited limited legislative effectiveness due to her relative political inexperience and because Democrats greatly outnumbered Republicans in the House. In 1934, she declined to run for the GOP renomination. The eventual Republican nominee, Bert Lord, a lumber business-

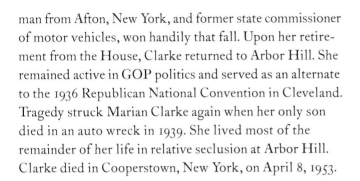
man from Afton, New York, and former state commissioner of motor vehicles, won handily that fall. Upon her retirement from the House, Clarke returned to Arbor Hill. She remained active in GOP politics and served as an alternate to the 1936 Republican National Convention in Cleveland. Tragedy struck Marian Clarke again when her only son died in an auto wreck in 1939. She lived most of the remainder of her life in relative seclusion at Arbor Hill. Clarke died in Cooperstown, New York, on April 8, 1953.

FOR FURTHER READING

Biographical Directory of the United States Congress, "Marian Williams Clarke," http://bioguide.congress.gov

MANUSCRIPT COLLECTION

New York State Historical Association Library (Cooperstown, NY). *Papers:* In the John Davenport Clarke papers, 1921–1933, approximately 2,000 items. Includes correspondence reflecting opinions on political and social issues, photograph albums, and news clippings. Also contains papers of Marian Clarke.

NOTES

1 "Congresswoman Clarke Finds Pleasure in Legislative Job," 20 January 1934, *Washington Post*: 11.

2 Though Marian K. Williams's father's name is nearly illegible in the *1900 Federal Census*, it appears to be "Ripp."

3 "Congresswoman Clarke Finds Pleasure in Legislative Job."

4 "J.D. Clarke Killed in a Motor Crash," 6 November 1933, *New York Times*: 16.

5 David J. Weber, with a foreword by Senator Gaylord A. Nelson, *Outstanding Environmentalists of Congress* (Washington, D.C.: U.S. Capitol Historical Society, 2002): 48–49.

6 "Congresswoman Clarke Finds Pleasure in Legislative Job."

7 Susan Tolchin, *Women in Congress* (Washington, D.C.: Government Printing Office, 1976): 17; Hope Chamberlin, *A Minority of Members: Women in the U.S. Congress* (New York: Praeger, 1973): 103.

8 "Nominated for Congress," 7 December 1933, *New York Times*: 15.

9 "Democrats Predict Up-State Victory," 17 December 1933, *New York Times*: N1.

10 "Democrats Predict Up-State Victory."

11 "Mrs. Clarke Wins Seat in Congress," 29 December 1933, *New York Times*: 2.

12 Tolchin, *Women in Congress*: 17.

13 Charles Stewart III, "Committee Hierarchies in the Modernizing House, 1875–1947," *American Journal of Political Science* 36 (1992): 845–846. The paper includes rankings of House committees before the Legislative Reorganization Act of 1946 and makes a connection between committee transfers and the relative attractiveness of committee assignments; Karen Foerstel, *Biographical Dictionary of Congressional Women* (Westport, CT: Greenwood Press, 1999): 59.

14 *Congressional Record*, House, 73rd Cong., 2nd sess. (26 January 1934): 1421–1422.

15 *Congressional Record*, House, 73rd Cong., 2nd sess. (21 May 1934): 9196–9197.

16 *Congressional Record*, House, 73rd Cong., 2nd sess. (1 June 1934): 10275.

17 Tolchin, *Women in Congress*: 17; Chamberlin, *A Minority of Members*: 103.

18 *Congressional Record*, House, 73rd Cong., 2nd sess. (28 March 1934): 5682–5683.

Onto the National Stage

CONGRESSWOMEN IN AN AGE

OF CRISES, 1935–1954

THIRTY-SIX WOMEN ENTERED CONGRESS BETWEEN 1935 AND 1954, a tumultuous two decades that encompassed the Great Depression, World War II, and the start of the Cold War. Women participated in America's survival, recovery, and ascent to world power in important and unprecedented ways; they became shapers of the welfare state, workers during wartime, and members of the military. During this time the nation's capital took on increasing importance in the everyday lives of average Americans. The Great Depression and the specter of global war transformed the role of the federal government, making it a provider and protector. Like their male counterparts, women in Congress legislated to provide economic relief to their constituents, debated the merits of government intervention to cure the economy, argued about America's role in world affairs, and grappled with challenges and opportunities during wartime.

Distinct trends persisted from the pioneer generation of women in Congress. Second-generation women still made up only a small fraction of the total congressional membership. At their peak, 15 women served in the 83rd Congress

Senators Joseph T. Robinson (far left) and Hattie W. Caraway of Arkansas at the June 1936 Democratic National Convention in Philadelphia, Pennsylvania, at which President Franklin Roosevelt was nominated to a second term. Caraway was a supporter of the Roosevelt administration's New Deal economic recovery programs, many of which benefited constituents in her agriculture-based state.

(1953–1955)—about 2.8 percent. These numbers afforded women scant leverage to pursue a unified agenda, though few seemed inclined to champion what would later be called "women's issues." The widow-familial succession remained for women a primary route to political office.

Subtle changes, however, slowly advanced women's status on Capitol Hill. By and large, women elected to Congress between 1935 and 1954 had more experience as politicians or as party officials than did their predecessors. In the postwar era, they were appointed more often to influential committees, including those with jurisdiction over military affairs, the judiciary, and agriculture. Also, several women emerged as national figures and were prominently featured as spokespersons by their parties; this was a significant break from tradition.

CHANGE AND CONTINUITY:
Political Experience, Committee Assignments, and Familial Connections

Compared with the pioneer generation, the women Members elected during this period had far more political experience. Half the women in the second generation (18) had served as public officeholders or as party officials. Six served in state legislatures or other statewide offices. Chase Woodhouse of Connecticut served two terms as a popular secretary of state. Four women held local political office, and 11 served as party officials at the state and national levels. The level of education of this group of Congresswomen mirrored that of the pioneer generation; two-thirds (24 of 36) had received some kind of postsecondary education. Political experience made women more attractive as candidates for national office. In 1934, Caroline O'Day of New York told campaign crowds that the "political apprenticeship" of women had come to an end. With 31 women running for the U.S. House of Representatives in 1934—and a record 38 in 1936 (12 of them nominated by the major parties)—O'Day's contention seemed validated.[1]

The median age at which women were elected to Congress (49 years) was slightly lower. This figure is important largely because it determines a Member's ability to accrue the seniority requisite for leadership positions. By comparison, the average

Congresswoman Nan Honeyman of Oregon joins members of the House Naval Affairs Committee during an inspection tour of the Naval Air Station at Seattle, Washington. Honeyman, an ally of the Franklin Roosevelt administration, had advocated the construction of a major naval facility along the Columbia River in Oregon.

IMAGE COURTESY OF THE NATIONAL ARCHIVES AND RECORDS ADMINISTRATION

age of all House Members entering Congress from 1931 to 1950 was 45 years; nearly 30 percent of the men were 39 or younger. The median age at retirement during this era ranged from 53 to 57 years.[2] Three women, all during World War II, were elected in their 30s—Winifred Stanley of New York, 33, the youngest woman elected to Congress to that date; Katharine Byron of Maryland, 37; and Clare Boothe Luce of Connecticut, 39. The oldest woman elected to Congress during this period was 66-year-old Hazel Abel of Nebraska, a distinguished state official who served a brief Senate term in 1954.

The Franklin D. Roosevelt administration, through the direct and indirect efforts of First Lady Eleanor Roosevelt, helped boost the number of Democratic women in Congress. Many of the women who rose in the 1930s to prominent positions in the federal government had known the First Lady since the days when she worked in Greenwich Village settlement houses and registered women voters across New York state.[3] In making these appointments, President Roosevelt broke with precedent; Frances Perkins was the first woman to serve in the President's Cabinet (Labor Secretary), former House Member Ruth Bryan Owen was the first woman to serve as U.S. Ambassador (to Sweden), and Florence Allen was the first woman judge on the U.S. Circuit Court of Appeals.

Connections to Eleanor Roosevelt proved to be influential in several Congresswomen's careers. Caroline O'Day, for example, was among Eleanor Roosevelt's confidantes. The pair had traversed New York in the 1920s, organizing women voters and working on Governor Al Smith's 1928 presidential campaign. In the 1934 midterm elections, Roosevelt made campaign appearances on O'Day's behalf, becoming the first First Lady to stump for a candidate. O'Day's campaign was successful, and she remained in Congress for nearly a decade. Congresswoman Nan Wood Honeyman of Oregon, an unflagging supporter of FDR, had known Eleanor Roosevelt since their days at finishing school in New York City. Helen Gahagan Douglas of California conferred often with the First Lady. Eleanor Roosevelt campaigned for successful Democrats Katharine Byron of Maryland and Chase Woodhouse, among others, and she inspired young women to consider political life. Coya Knutson of Minnesota recalled that a June 1942 radio address by Eleanor Roosevelt prodded her to become active in civic affairs. "It was as if the sun burned into me that day," Knutson said.[4]

Impressive political résumés helped more women secure influential committee assignments, particularly during and after the Second World War, when women were assigned to prominent panels such as Agriculture, Armed Services, Naval Affairs, Public Works, Rivers and Harbors, Merchant Marine and Fisheries, Judiciary, and Interior and Insular Affairs. Five women were assigned to the Foreign Affairs Committee, and four served on the Banking and Currency Committee during this era. Other assignments reinforced patterns set during the first generation of women in Congress, when women legislated on second- or third-tier panels like Education, Veterans' Affairs, Post Office and Civil Service, and Government Operations. Many of these committees dealt with issues that had long been considered part of a woman's sphere. Women served on more than 30 House committees during this era. In the Senate, where only two women served an entire term or longer, women won appointments to roughly 20 committees.[5] A trailblazer, Margaret Chase Smith of Maine was a member of the powerful Appropriations and Armed Services panels. Four women chaired six congressional committees during the period from 1935 to 1954: Representative Mary Norton of New Jersey—District of Columbia (1935–1937), Labor (1937–1947), Memorials (1941–1943), and House Administration (1949–1951); Representative O'Day—Election of the President, Vice President and Representatives in Congress (1937–1943); Representative Edith Nourse Rogers of Massachusetts—Veterans' Affairs (1947–1949 and 1953–1955); and Senator Hattie Caraway of Arkansas—Enrolled Bills (1933–1945).

House leaders, particularly Speakers Joe Martin of Massachusetts and Sam Rayburn of Texas, promoted women to key positions. As Republican Minority Leader in 1943, Martin secured seats for Margaret Chase Smith and Clare Boothe Luce on Naval Affairs and Military Affairs, respectively, to recognize women's contributions to the war effort and to bring "a woman's viewpoint" to traditionally all-male committees.[6] Rayburn steered several women onto important committees, including Chase Woodhouse, with whom he had a frank and warm relationship. "You get the same pay as we do, don't you?" Rayburn once asked her. "Yes, sir, for a change," Woodhouse replied. "And you worked three times as hard to get here as any of us did," he said.[7] Speaker Rayburn, who shared Woodhouse's disdain for fundraising and admired her efforts to keep lobbyists at arm's length, confided to her, "If I had twenty-four like you, I'd be happy."[8] Later in his Speakership, Rayburn helped persuade reluctant committee chairmen to accept Coya Knutson and Martha Griffiths of Michigan as members of powerful panels.

The widow's mandate, or familial connection, remained prevalent in the second generation of women in Congress. Fourteen of the 36 women who were elected or appointed directly succeeded their husbands. Another woman, Leonor Sullivan of Missouri, won election in 1952 to the St. Louis district served by her late husband for much of the 1940s. Dixie Graves of Alabama was appointed to the U.S. Senate in 1937 by her husband, Governor Bibb Graves. In all, 44 percent of the women from this generation came to Congress through familial connections. The persistence of this trend explains another statistic—nearly half the women elected or appointed in this era (17) served one term or less. This was particularly true of southern widows like Willa Fulmer of South Carolina, Florence Gibbs of Georgia, Elizabeth Gasque of South Carolina, Rose Long of Louisiana, and Clara McMillan of South Carolina, who were chosen by party leaders as temporary placeholders until a permanent male successor could be found. For the first time in both chambers, a woman succeeded a woman; Representative Stanley succeeded retiring Congresswoman O'Day in a New York At-Large seat in 1943, and Hazel Abel was elected Senator from Nebraska in 1954, succeeding Republican appointee Eva Bowring.

Legislative Interests and Achievements:
Ongoing Great Depression

Between 1933 and 1938, Congress passed the New Deal, a sweeping package of regulatory and economic recovery policies to alleviate the effects of the Great Depression. These changes affected virtually every facet of American life—transportation, banking, stock market regulation, agricultural practices, labor practices (including the minimum wage, the maximum length of the workday, and collective bargaining), public works, and even the arts. Many of President Franklin Roosevelt's

With many men away on overseas military duty during World War II, American women played an increasingly important role in the national economy during the war. Some, like this woman, filled nontraditional roles. She is working as a riveter on an aircraft assembly line.

IMAGE COURTESY OF THE LIBRARY OF CONGRESS

proposals were approved by Congress in the first 100 days of his term, including the Emergency Banking Relief Act, the Agricultural Adjustment Act, the Federal Emergency Relief Act, the Tennessee Valley Authority, the Civilian Conservation Corps, and the National Recovery Act.

A "second" New Deal began in 1935, as the focus on shoring up the economy shifted to providing a long-term economic safety net for all Americans. In 1935, congressional passage of the Social Security Act created unemployment insurance, old-age pensions, and public assistance programs such as Aid to Families of Dependent Children.[9] These programs helped the American family and were particularly critical to women, who often silently bore the brunt of the Great Depression. Unmarried women, single mothers, and wives in need of jobs to support their families were disadvantaged not only by the scarcity of employment but also by the widespread belief that a woman's place was at home tending to the family.[10] As chair of the Labor Committee, starting in 1937, Representative Mary Norton shaped late New Deal legislation, particularly the 1938 Fair Labor Standards Act, which she personally shepherded through committee and onto the House Floor for a vote. The act provided for a 40-hour workweek, outlawed child labor, and set a minimum wage of 25 cents per hour. Norton later helped establish a permanent Fair Employment Practice Committee to prevent racial and gender discrimination in hiring and helped secure pensions for elective and executive offices by expanding the retirement system for federal employees.

After his overwhelming re-election victory in 1936, President Roosevelt hatched an aggressive legislative plan to place as many as six additional Justices on the Supreme Court. Made public in February 1937, FDR's proposal was a thinly disguised effort to add Justices favoring his economic policies to the high court, which had recently nullified key New Deal programs such as the National Recovery Administration and the Agricultural Adjustment Administration. Public controversy ensued, and Congress refused to restructure the judiciary.[11] The court-packing episode is widely viewed as the beginning of the end of the New Deal reforms, as southern Democrats aligned with Republicans to block the administration's initiatives at home. The First Lady and Interior Secretary Harold Ickes stumped in Congresswoman Honeyman's Portland district during her 1938 re-election campaign, which she lost largely because of her unflagging support for FDR. During the next three elections, Republican women critics of the New Deal won election to Congress—Jessie Sumner of Illinois (1938), Frances Bolton of Ohio (1940), Smith (1940), Luce (1942), and Stanley (1942).

Intervention Versus Isolation

By the late 1930s, with European countries arming for war and tensions increasing due to Japanese expansion in the Pacific, Congress shifted its focus to preparing for war and to America's role in world affairs. In the years after World War I, a strong isolationist movement spearheaded by Members of Congress from midwestern states gripped the country. The isolationists believed that the Woodrow Wilson administration's pro-Allied slant and big business interests had drawn the United States into World War I, and they were committed to avoiding another world war. From 1935 to 1937, Congress passed a series of neutrality acts that incrementally banned arms trade with belligerent countries, the extension of credit to warring countries, travel on belligerent ships, and the arming of American

A World War II recruiting poster for the Women's Army Corp (WAC). Legislation authored by Congresswoman Edith Nourse Rogers created the WAC shortly after America entered World War II. In the Army and other military branches, women took on important assignments, among them roles as support staff, nurses, and pilots.
IMAGE COURTESY OF THE LIBRARY OF CONGRESS

merchant ships. The final bill, the Neutrality Act of 1937, provided that at the President's discretion, belligerent countries could purchase nonembargoed goods on a "cash-and-carry" basis, that is, the goods would be paid for when they were purchased and transported on the belligerent country's own vessels.

Opposition to American intervention in a potential world conflict centered in the late 1930s around two groups, pacifists and isolationists. In addition to monitoring the growing fascist threat in Europe and Asia, the FDR administration was waging a protracted battle at home with a core group of isolationists in Congress who resisted increasing pressure to provide economic and military support for America's traditional partners in the Atlantic Alliance.[12] Jessie Sumner epitomized the isolationist perspective. Elected to the first of four terms in 1938, Sumner was especially critical of American foreign policy in the months immediately after war broke out in Europe in September 1939. She lashed out at the Roosevelt administration for what she viewed as a pro-British bias, insisting, "our historical experience warns us that we cannot safely become an arsenal for belligerents."[13]

Caroline O'Day, a member of the Women's International League for Peace and Freedom in the 1920s, was the most significant female voice for pacifism in the late 1930s. In 1939, after Germany invaded Poland, beginning the Second World War, O'Day opposed the amendment of earlier neutrality acts that prohibited selling arms or extending credit to belligerent nations. Joining isolationists like Sumner, she also voted against the 1940 Selective Service Act, the nation's first peace-time draft, saying, "As mothers whose sons would be obliged to go to war; as women who, with the children, would remain at home to be the victims of air raids and bombing of cities, we should have the right to vote against it, and express our desire for peace."[14] However, O'Day ultimately supported the war effort when she learned about the nature of the Nazi atrocities in Europe. "We as individuals and as a nation must consent to play our proper role in world affairs," said O'Day, who was at heart, more an internationalist than an isolationist.[15]

Congress eventually voted to repeal the arms embargo against countries fighting Nazi Germany and, for the first time, allowed American merchant ships to convoy arms and equipment to Great Britain. The majority of the women in Congress supported the Roosevelt administration's foreign policy. Clara McMillan of South Carolina, a mother of five young sons, reasoned that preparing for America's seemingly imminent entry into the war would best preserve her sons' safety. Congresswoman Rogers broke with fellow Republicans to vote against the neutrality acts and for the 1940 Selective Service Act, citing the danger posed by Adolf Hitler's Germany. The Selective Service Bill passed Congress and was extended by a narrow margin a year later. Between 1940 and 1947, more than 10 million conscripts served in the U.S. military.

Japan's surprise attack against the U.S. Pacific Fleet at Pearl Harbor, Hawaii, on December 7, 1941, unified the country for war. More than 2,400 persons were killed, and 19 U.S. Navy ships were sunk or disabled. An anticlimactic but oft-celebrated event in the pacifist crusade occurred the next day, when Jeannette Rankin of Montana cast the lone vote against declaring war on Japan. During her previous term, in 1917, Rankin had voted against U.S. entry into World War I. A devoted pacifist, she served in a variety of peace organizations before being re-elected to Congress in 1940. Rankin's vote against war on Japan effectively ended her House career. "When in a hundred years from now, courage, sheer courage based upon

Willa L. Fulmer of South Carolina, wife of the late Congressman Hampton P. Fulmer, stands next to Speaker of the House Sam Rayburn for a photo commemorating her swearing-in as a Representative in November 1944. Fulmer, like many other widows elected to Congress, served only as a temporary placeholder for her party, filling out the brief remainder of her husband's term.

moral indignation is celebrated in this country," editor William Allen White observed, "the name of Jeannette Rankin, who stood firm in folly for her faith, will be written in monumental bronze, not for what she did but for the way she did it."[16]

Expanding Women's Responsibilities in Wartime

Once the nation was committed to war, women in Congress legislated to make available unprecedented opportunities for women as members and supporters of the U.S. armed services. Congresswoman Rogers authored the May 1942 Women's Army Auxiliary Corps (WAAC) Act, which created up to 150,000 noncombat positions (primarily in nursing) for women in the U.S. Army. Nearly 350,000 women eventually served as WAACs and in similar groups in other branches of the military, including the navy (WAVES), the coast guard (SPAR), and the marines (MCWR). Another 1,000 women became Women's Airforce Service Pilots (WASPs).[17] Representative Rogers also shaped the landmark Servicemen's Readjustment Act of 1944 (commonly known as the G.I. Bill of Rights), which authorized the Veterans' Administration to help servicemen adjust to civilian life by providing financial aid for school and job training, employment programs, federal housing loans, and medical care. Frances Bolton, a moderate isolationist before the war, soon embraced military preparedness. She authored the Bolton Act of 1943, creating the U.S. Cadet Nurse Corps, which was responsible for training nearly 125,000 women as military nurses. Bolton later toured Europe to observe these women at work in field hospitals. After the war, she advocated a greater role for women in the military and even suggested they be made eligible for future drafts. Margaret Chase Smith also strongly supported women's participation in the military. Her landmark Women's Armed Forces Integration Act, passed in 1948, ensured the permanent inclusion of women in the military.

The war provided new opportunities for some groups of American women. By 1942, so many men had been taken out of the economy to fill the military ranks that

"... the name of Jeannette Rankin, who stood firm in folly for her faith, will be written in monumental bronze, not for what she did but for the way she did it."

—WILLIAM ALLEN WHITE

Congresswoman Helen Gahagan Douglas of California addresses the 1945 World Youth Rally in New York City. Douglas, elected in the fall of 1944, was a staunch internationalist and an advocate for the creation of the United Nations Organization.

IMAGE COURTESY OF THE LIBRARY OF CONGRESS

women were recruited to make up for the "manpower" shortage. The War Manpower Commission created an enduring image of the era with its "Rosie the Riveter" campaign, which aimed to bring women—single and married—into the workforce. Posters of Rosie's muscular, can-do image as a production line worker at an armaments plant projected an unconventional image of women as a source of physical strength. Between 1941 and 1945, some 6 million new women entered the workforce—swelling their ranks to about 19 million and a then-all-time high of 36 percent of the U.S. workforce.[18]

Labor Committee Chairwoman Mary T. Norton urged women not to retreat into the home when the men returned from war. "This is the time for women everywhere to prove that they appreciate the responsibility they have been given," Norton said at the war's end. "Women can't be Sitting-Room Sarahs or Kitchen Katies. They have homes to keep up, food to prepare, families to clothe . . . but they have their world to make. . . . American women today stand on the threshold of a glorious future . . . .They can grasp it . . . or they can let it slide." Norton spoke passionately about the pressure on women from industry and labor unions to vacate jobs for GIs seeking employment: "Women are going to be pushed into a corner, and very soon at that." It would be, she predicted, a "heartbreaking" setback.[19]

Two women work at a clip spring and body assembly line for .30 caliber cartridges at an arsenal in Pennsylvania during World War II. Women filled numerous jobs on the wartime home front that were essential to equipping troops deployed overseas.

IMAGE COURTESY OF THE FDR LIBRARY/NATIONAL ARCHIVES AND RECORDS ADMINISTRATION

Shaping the Postwar Peace

Women Members were involved not only in preparing for and waging war, but also in creating the framework for a lasting peace. In 1944, women rode a wave of internationalist sentiment to Congress, partially signaling the triumph of FDR's foreign policy over the prewar isolationists. Three prominent internationalists—Emily Taft Douglas of Illinois, Chase Going Woodhouse, and Helen Gahagan Douglas—were elected to the House of Representatives. Emily Douglas was a forceful and articulate advocate for the implementation of the Dumbarton Oaks accords that created a postwar United Nations (UN). From her seat on the Banking and Currency Committee, Woodhouse helped execute the Bretton Woods Agreements, which created the World Bank and the International Monetary Fund. Helen Douglas, a former Hollywood actress, enthusiastically endorsed postwar U.S. reconstruction aid to Europe and supported the creation of the Atomic Energy Commission to ensure that civilians, as well as the military, would have some control over atomic technology. At the opposite end of the spectrum, isolationist Jessie Sumner retired from the House in 1947, citing her frustration with the President's power to set an expansive global U.S. foreign policy.

Civil Rights

The social and economic dislocation that resulted from the Second World War reopened a long-running debate about civil rights in America.[20] Reformers believed that the African-American contributions to the war effort underscored the moral imperative of repealing segregationist laws in the United States. Frances Bolton challenged her colleagues on this point during a debate on outlawing the poll tax used to disenfranchise African Americans:[21] "Even at painful cost, America must be true to her own vision, to her own soul, to her responsibility to tomorrow's world. We talk so much of democracy, of freedom. Can we have either so long as great sections of our land withhold freedom?" Congresswomen took public and, often, conflicting positions on civil rights. In the late 1930s, Senator Dixie Bibb

Graves received national press attention as an opponent of federal action against lynching; she insisted that the practice was in decline and that federal statute would intrude on states' rights. Her colleague Hattie Caraway agreed and later opposed efforts to outlaw poll taxes. Representative O'Day supported antilynching laws. Representative Helen Mankin of Georgia, elected to an abbreviated term in 1946, was an outspoken opponent of the politics of Governor Eugene Talmadge and of Jim Crow laws that disenfranchised southern blacks. Widely popular with the black community in her Atlanta-based district, Mankin was unseated in the fall 1946 elections, when Talmadge officials altered the rules for the Democratic primary. Marguerite Church of Illinois and Helen Douglas challenged segregationist dining policies in the Capitol. At the very end of the period, Iris Blitch of Georgia, a Talmadge protégé, won election to the first of four House terms and signed the "Southern Manifesto," opposing federal efforts to end racial segregation in the South.

The Cold War and McCarthyism

As the Second World War ended, the victorious alliance between Washington and Moscow began to weaken. Soviet forces, which had broken the backbone of the German army, occupied virtually every Eastern European capital. Soviet Premier Joseph Stalin believed Russian security interests required control of western invasion routes used by the Germans to invade his homeland twice during his lifetime. Rather than evacuate Eastern Europe and East Germany, the Soviet Red Army tightened Moscow's grip and installed pliant communist regimes. A war of words and mutual suspicions developed. By 1947, officials in Washington had decided to try to contain communism by economic and military means—implementing the Marshall Plan to rebuild Western Europe and West Germany and helping countries plagued by communist insurgencies. The first Soviet test of an atomic bomb in 1949, the founding of the communist People's Republic of China the same year, and communist North Korea's invasion of South Korea in June 1950 seemed to confirm Americans' worst fears about the expansion of international communism.[22]

Several women in Congress were vocal advocates of a hard-line American policy toward the Soviet Union. Jessie Sumner raised concerns early on about the nature of Stalinist foreign policy, arguing that Americans should beware of supporting postwar international organizations because, she believed, they would be co-opted by communist powers. Congresswoman Luce also criticized Soviet motives, especially in regard to Polish sovereignty and, along with other Members of Congress, accused the Roosevelt administration of capitulating to Stalin's demands for a Russian sphere of influence in Eastern Europe. Congresswoman Edna Kelly of New York, elected to the House in 1949, was an ardent anticommunist who gained the influential post of head of the European Affairs Subcommittee on the Foreign Affairs panel. Kelly and others, such as Woodhouse, backed the creation of the North Atlantic Treaty Organization (NATO) in 1949, supported the Marshall Plan, and advocated large foreign-aid packages to help governments resist communist insurgents.

The restructuring of U.S. national security policy and the billions of dollars spent on the global war on communism changed America's international role. Not all Congresswomen agreed that such expenditures were in the best interests of the American people. Maude Kee of West Virginia questioned the urgency of giving multibillion-dollar aid packages to foreign countries when residents of her rural

Madame Chiang (left), wife of Chinese Nationalist leader Chiang Kai-shek, confers with Congresswoman Marguerite Church of Illinois. Church took a keen interest in how American foreign aid dollars were spent in the effort to win the global struggle against communism.
IMAGE COURTESY OF THE NATIONAL ARCHIVES AND RECORDS ADMINISTRATION

"Grable" was a 15-kiloton atomic weapon—stronger than the nuclear blasts that leveled Hiroshima and Nagasaki at the end of World War II—detonated in 1953, at a Nevada test site. The nuclear mushroom cloud became a symbol of the Cold War and a constant reminder that the superpower confrontation between the United States and the Soviet Union could spiral into nuclear destruction.
IMAGE COURTESY OF THE DEPARTMENT OF ENERGY NATIONAL NUCLEAR SECURITY ADMINISTRATION

Congresswomen were more likely to bring a domestic perspective to the national security debate, arguing that improved economic and educational opportunities would best protect Americans' freedoms.

Appalachian district suffered from high unemployment and a low standard of living. Vera Buchanan of Pennsylvania publicly raised concerns about the threats of officials in the Dwight D. Eisenhower administration to annihilate the Soviet Union, using nuclear weapons in "massive retaliation" for military provocation. Marguerite Stitt Church of Illinois questioned expenditures of vast sums on military hardware for foreign countries, instead of on job-training and economic programs for women in developing countries. Other women from this period, such as O'Day and Woodhouse (and later in the Cold War, Edith Green and Coya Knutson) brought a domestic perspective to the national security debate, arguing that improved economic and educational opportunities would best protect Americans' freedom. Helen Douglas linked U.S. civil rights reforms with Cold War national security objectives. Winning the support of potential allies in the global struggle against communism required fundamental changes at home. Racial segregation in America, Douglas said on the House Floor, "raises the question among the colonial peoples of the earth . . . as to whether or not we are really their friends, whether or not we will ever understand their longing and right for self-determination."[23]

Indeed, the domestic consequences of the Cold War were profound. American officials had to garner public support for huge outlays for the containment policy and, in making their case about the dangers of communism abroad, stoked fears of communist infiltration at home. The House Committee on Un-American Activities (HUAC), which held numerous high-profile public hearings, became a soapbox from which anticommunist Members of Congress called attention to the "red menace."[24]

During its 37-year history, no woman served on HUAC (later renamed the Internal Security Committee), though several, including Edith Nourse Rogers and Edna Kelly, supported its usefulness. Both Helen Douglas and Emily Douglas attacked HUAC for its brusque tactics, which included publicizing unsubstantiated rumors. "No men are pure and unbiased enough to have this immense power to discredit, accuse and denounce which this committee wields," Helen Douglas declared. "It is un-American in-itself to be condemned in the press or before the public without trial or hearing."[25] In a speech entitled "My Democratic Credo," Douglas identified the real dangers to democracy as demagoguery and repressive domestic controls justified in the name of national security.[26] "Have we talked about communists so much that we have begun to imitate them?" she asked.[27] In a 1950 campaign for one of California's seats in the U.S. Senate, Representative Richard Nixon of California, a member of HUAC, successfully employed smear tactics to defeat Congresswoman Douglas, whom he labeled a communist sympathizer. Representative Reva Bosone of Utah, formerly a Salt Lake City judge, was turned out of office two years later, partly because her opponent attacked her for opposing a bill granting wide-ranging powers to the newly created Central Intelligence Agency.

Communist-hunting Senator Joseph McCarthy of Wisconsin (center) confers with his two principal aides, G. David Schine (left) and Roy Cohn in this June 1954 photo. McCarthy came to prominence in February 1950 when he accused the State Department of being infiltrated by dozens of communists. In 1953, McCarthy became chairman of the Government Operations Committee's Permanent Subcommittee on Investigations—a prime perch from which to pursue alleged communist activities in the U.S. government. McCarthy's sweeping and unsubstantiated accusations, carried widely by the press, produced no communists but ruined many careers and perpetuated public fears about domestic subversives.

IMAGE COURTESY OF AP/WIDE WORLD PHOTOS

Margaret Chase Smith, a freshman Senator, directly challenged McCarthy in a Senate Floor speech that demonstrated great moral courage.

In the U.S. Senate, Joseph McCarthy of Wisconsin made the shocking claim in a February 1950 speech in Wheeling, West Virginia, that he possessed a list of 205 communists employed at the State Department. He then labeled World War II hero and Secretary of Defense George C. Marshall a traitor and rebuked President Harry Truman and Secretary of State Dean G. Acheson for being "soft" on communism. As chairman of the Government Operations Committee's Subcommittee on Investigations in the 83rd Congress (1953–1955), McCarthy commenced hearings to root out "subversive activities" in the federal government. His tactics received widespread attention from the press but ferreted out no communists. However, many of the government employees and private citizens who were called before his committee had their careers and reputations ruined.[28]

Few of his contemporaries publicly countered McCarthy's unsubstantiated charges. Outgoing Representative Woodhouse told the *New York Times*, "It is the job of every balanced, conscientious person to steer us away from the dangers of hysteria and to label as traitors those in public positions who attempt to gain personal benefit from playing on the fears of the masses of the people."[29] Margaret Chase Smith, a freshman Senator, directly challenged McCarthy in a Senate Floor speech that demonstrated great moral courage. In an address she later called her "Declaration of Conscience," Senator Smith said, "those of us who shout the loudest about Americanism . . . are all too frequently those who, by our own words and acts, ignore some of the basic principles of Americanism—the right to criticize; the right to hold unpopular beliefs; the right to protest; the right of independent thought." Although she did not mention McCarthy by name, her meaning was unmistakable. She also took her colleagues to task for condoning the permissive context in which

McCarthyism was allowed to flourish and in which Senate debate had been "debased to the level of a forum of hate and character assassination."[30] McCarthy's downfall came in the spring of 1954 when he investigated the U.S. Army in televised hearings; his ruthless and exaggerated tactics were broadcast to millions of viewers. In December 1954, the Senate censured McCarthy. Voting with the majority were his Republican colleagues Senator Smith and Senator Abel.

CRAFTING AN IDENTITY

Second-generation women in Congress legislated sporadically on issues of special importance to their gender and on the initiative of individuals rather than that of a group. The paucity of Congresswomen inhibited the development of a coherent women's-issues agenda until the 1970s. Few embraced a "feminist" agenda —preferring to work within the prescribed institutional channels.

There were exceptions, however. Congresswoman Winifred Stanley introduced the first equal-pay legislation in Congress, arguing that women and men should receive the same compensation for the same type of work. "Merit, regardless of sex, should be the basis of employment," Stanley said. "Jobs should be filled by those best qualified by ability, training and experience, with the consideration given to men and women of the armed services."[31] Unsuccessful equal pay measures were introduced repeatedly in the decades that followed, notably by Representative Kelly in 1951 and by Representative Cecil Harden of Indiana in 1957. Stanley, along with then-Representative Margaret Chase Smith, also renewed the drive for the passage of the Equal Rights Amendment in 1943 to mark the 20th anniversary of its introduction to Congress.

House veteran Mary Norton realized that there were not enough women in Congress to support such an agenda. In the months immediately following the war, she despaired that a quarter century after earning the vote, women had failed to organize as an effective political bloc. "We won't see a dozen women in Congress in our day because women won't vote for women," Norton lamented.[32] More than a dozen women did serve in the 83rd Congress, two years after Norton retired. But women did not consistently hold even two dozen seats in Congress (about 5 percent of the total membership) until the mid-1980s.

Chase Woodhouse, one of Norton's contemporaries, recalled that she and her women colleagues in the House earnestly pursued individual projects but did not reach a consensus on legislation about issues that were particularly relevant to women, namely, education, employment, childcare, reproductive rights, and health issues. Norton, Woodhouse observed, worked hard to minimize distinctions between women and men in everyday House activities, insisting that the men treat the women as "Congressmen"; there were no "ladies first" in the line for the elevator, and women Members would wear plain business suits and no "frillies" or hats on the House Floor. "None of us were women's women," Woodhouse recalled years later of colleagues like Emily Douglas, Helen Douglas, Sumner, and Luce.[33] Woodhouse secured federal money for programs and organizations that were important to women, particularly prenatal clinics and child welfare agencies.[34] Acutely concerned with helping women in the workplace, Woodhouse nevertheless distanced herself from vocal feminists. "I always say I never attack a brick wall," she observed years later. "I try to go around it, and the people who are defending

Former First Lady Eleanor Roosevelt (left) and Senator Margaret Chase Smith of Maine on the set of the political television program Face the Nation *in Washington, D.C., on November 11, 1956. Both women were leading figures in the Democratic and Republican parties, respectively.*

IMAGE COURTESY OF THE FDR LIBRARY/NATION-AL ARCHIVES AND RECORDS ADMINISTRATION the other side are so surprised to see me that they even say, 'How do you do? What can I do for you?'"[35] Her colleague Frances Bolton chafed at the term "Congresswoman." "It doesn't exist" in the dictionary, she once snapped. "We've had Congressmen here for a good many generations. But we've never had Congresswomen. You're a woman Congressman. It's just like a chairman. Some people say chairwoman. But that's just silly."[36]

Importantly, however, a new legislative style for women in Congress was being pioneered by celebrities-turned-politicians—a "show horse," or publicity-driven style.[37] Capitalizing on their fame, Luce and Helen Douglas chose to become partisan champions of the issue *du jour* rather than to specialize in areas of legislative interest. Congresswoman Luce, a glamorous playwright, delivered the keynote address at the 1944 GOP National Convention; it was the first time a woman was accorded this honor by a major party.[38] Several weeks later, Douglas, an actress and a singer and the wife of film star Melvyn Douglas—then making her first run for the House—was featured prominently at the Democratic National Convention.[39] The energy these women derived from the intense media coverage of their House careers became part of their style. Reflecting late in life on her move to a career in politics, Douglas remarked, "I never felt I left the stage."[40] While neither Luce nor Douglas used this legislative style to advance a "women's-issues" agenda, later generations of women in Congress adopted their style to become public advocates for feminist concerns, particularly Bella Abzug of New York and, to a lesser degree, Martha Griffiths of Michigan and Patricia Schroeder of Colorado. In the late 1940s, California Congressman Jerry Voorhis marveled at the precarious balancing act of his women colleagues, who charted "a course midway between two fatal mistakes." Voorhis observed that "the woman member must take care that she does not base her appeal for the cause in which she is interested on the fact of her womanhood. She cannot expect chivalry from the male members when it comes to casting their votes. Neither, on the other hand, can she hope to gain a strong position for herself if she attempts the role of a hail fellow well met and tries to be like the men. What she has to do is to be simply a member of the House who quite incidentally happens to belong to the female sex."[41]

Institutional and cultural barriers added to the precariousness of women's new foothold in national political life. The Cold War, enduring paternalistic social patterns, and the temporary decline of feminist reform blunted women's drive for political power, leaving the third generation of Congresswomen—those elected from the 1950s to the early 1970s—to begin fundamentally altering the legislative landscape.

Accompanied by U.S. Marine officers, Senator Margaret Chase Smith tours a U.S. military facility. Smith was the first woman to serve on the Armed Services Committee in both the House and the Senate.

IMAGE COURTESY OF THE LIBRARY OF CONGRESS

1   "Mrs. O'Day Pledges Opposition to War," 29 October 1934, *New York Times*: 4; "38 Women Run for House," 3 November 1936, *New York Times*: 9.

2   Allan G. Bogue, Jerome M. Clubb, Carroll R. McKibbin, and Santa A. Traugott, "Members of the House of Representatives and the Processes of Modernization, 1789–1960," *Journal of American History* 63 (September 1976): 275–302.

3   The standard biography of Eleanor Roosevelt is Blanche Wiesen Cook's *Eleanor Roosevelt*, two volumes (New York: Viking Press, 1992, 1999). For more on Roosevelt's connections to prominent women activists and politicians, see Lillian Faderman, *To Believe in Women* (Boston: Houghton Mifflin, 1999).

4   Gretchen Urnes Beito, *Coya Come Home: A Congresswoman's Journey* (Los Angeles and London: Pomegranate Press, Inc.): 65–66.

5   Committee attractiveness during this period is based on Charles Stewart III, "Committee Hierarchies in the Modernizing House, 1875–1947," *American Journal of Political Science* 36 (No. 4, November 1992): 835–856. At the beginning of this period, there were 47 House committees; the Senate had 33 standing committees (see, for example, committee listings in the *Congressional Directory* for the 75th Congress, 1st Session, 1937). The Legislative Reorganization Act of 1946 restructured the committee system. After its implementation in 1947, the number of standing House committees was reduced to 19 and standing Senate committees to 15. The process of streamlining was achieved by eliminating the number of panels altogether and by renaming, reconfiguring, or broadening the jurisdiction of others. Committee structure has been modified since 1947, with the addition of the Budget Committee in the early 1970s, and again after the Republicans came to power and enacted institutional reforms in 1995. Currently in the 109th Congress, the House and Senate have 20 and 16 permanent standing committees, respectively. The House also has the Permanent Select Committee on Intelligence. The Senate has three permanent select committees. In addition, House and Senate Members serve on four joint committees.

6   "Military Affairs Mrs. Luce's Post," 19 January 1943, *New York Times*: 21; "Urge House Women on War Committees," 15 January 1943, *New York Times*: 15.

7   Chase Going Woodhouse, Oral History Interview, U.S. Association of Former Members of Congress (hereinafter USAFMOC), Manuscript Division, Library of Congress, Washington, D.C.: 225.

8   Woodhouse, USAFMOC, Oral History Interview: 237.

9   The New Deal policies enacted in the 1930s by the Roosevelt administration and Congress dominated American political life and were, in some measure, a culmination of the welfare and social work efforts that had engaged women for a century. Many New Deal programs benefited from the experience of women reformers of the Progressive Era. The professionalization and institutionalization of "1920s" women's reform groups, such as the League of Women Voters and the Women's Bureau in Labor Department, prepared women for having a voice within the administration. See, for example, Robyn Muncy, *Creating a Female Dominion in American Reform, 1890–1935* (New York: Oxford University Press, 1991).

10 Sara M. Evans, *Born for Liberty: A History of Women in America* (New York: Free Press, 1989): 202.

11 See, for example, William E. Leuchtenburg, "Franklin D. Roosevelt's Supreme Court 'Packing' Plan," in *Essays on the New Deal*, Harold M. Hollingsworth and William F. Holmes, eds. (Austin: University of Texas Press, 1969): 69–115.

12 See, for example, Wayne Cole, *Roosevelt and the Isolationists, 1932–1945* (Lincoln: University of Nebraska Press, 1983).

13 Jessie Sumner, "We Are Right To Be Safe," Address to the Republican League of Women, 2 October 1939, reprinted in the *Congressional Record*, House, 76th Cong., 2nd sess. (2 October 1939): A 91–92.

14 Jessie Ash Arndt, "Rep. O'Day Offers Plan Against War," 15 July 1937, *Washington Post*: 19.

15 *Congressional Record*, House, 77th Cong., 1st sess. (11 December 1941): A 5565.

16 Norma Smith, *Jeannette Rankin: America's Conscience* (Helena: Montana Historical Society, 2002): 185.

17 David Kennedy, *Freedom From Fear: The American People in Depression and War, 1929–1945* (New York: Oxford University Press, 1999): 776.

18 These rising wartime employment statistics masked surprisingly resilient traditional views of women's place in society. The surge appears far less dramatic in light of the fact that about half these women had recently graduated from school and would have soon joined the workforce anyway. By 1947, moreover, women's participation in the national workforce had decreased to 28 percent. In addition, "Rosie the Riveter" was atypical; most women had secretarial or clerical jobs. While defense plants employed some two million women, the vast majority (95 percent) held unskilled positions. Ironically, few were riveters, since this position required specialized skills, and employers were hesitant to train women they expected to be temporary employees. Indeed, government propagandists and business made it abundantly clear to

women that their employment would end when the men returned from war. See Kennedy's discussion, *Freedom From Fear:* 776–782; also Alice Kessler-Harris, *Out to Work: A History of Wage-Earning Women in the United States* (New York: Oxford University Press, 1982): 276–277; 294; Rosalind Rosenberg, *Divided Lives: American Women in the Twentieth Century* (New York: Hill and Wag, 1992).

19 Annabel Paxton, *Women in Congress* (Richmond, VA: Deitz Press, 1945): 37; see also Norton's obituary from the 1959 *Current Biography.*

20 Kennedy, *Freedom From Fear:* 857–858. For a comprehensive discussion of the African-American experience and the civil rights struggle, see John Hope Franklin and Alfred Moss, *From Slavery to Freedom: A History of African Americans,* 8th edition (New York: Knopf, 2000); see 475–504 for a discussion of African Americans and World War II. For more context on the emergence of the civil rights movement in the postwar era, see Taylor Branch, *Parting the Waters: America in the King Years, 1954–1963* (New York: Simon and Schuster, 1989).

21 *Congressional Record,* House, 78th Cong., 1st sess. (25 May 1943): 4849.

22 For more on the origins of the Cold War and American foreign policy during this era, see Melvyn P. Leffler, *The Specter of Communism: The United States and the Origins of the Cold War, 1917–1953* (New York: Hill and Wang, 1994) and John Lewis Gaddis, *Strategies of Containment: A Critical Appraisal of Postwar American National Security Policy* (New York: Oxford University Press, 1982).

23 *Congressional Record,* House, 79th Cong., 1st sess. (8 June 1945): 5810.

24 For more on HUAC, see Walter Goodman, *The Committee: The Extraordinary Career of the House Committee on Un-American Activities* (New York: Farrar, Straus, and Giroux, 1968).

25 *Congressional Record,* House, 79th Cong., 1st sess. (24 October 1945): 10036.

26 *Congressional Record,* House, 79th Cong., 2nd sess. (29 March 1946): 2856–2859; quote on 2857.

27 *Congressional Record,* House, 80th Cong., 2nd sess. (18 May 1948): 6030–6031.

28 For more on McCarthy and "McCarthyism"—the term coined by *Washington Post* cartoonist Herblock to describe his red-baiting tactics—see David M. Oshinsky, *A Conspiracy So Immense: The World of Joe McCarthy* (New York: Free Press, 1983). See also the *Executive Sessions of the Senate Permanent Subcommittee on Investigations of the Committee on Government Operations,* Volumes I–V, edited by Donald A. Ritchie and Elizabeth Bolling (Washington, D.C.: GPO, 2003).

29 "Smear Campaigns Laid to 'Traitors,'" 19 November 1950, *New York Times:* 38.

30 *Congressional Record,* Senate, 81st Cong., 2nd sess. (1 June 1950): 7894–7895. For an account of the episode and its effect on Smith's career, see Janann Sherman, *No Place for a Woman: A Life of Senator Margaret Chase Smith* (New Brunswick, NJ: Rutgers University Press, 2000): 104–126.

31 "Miss Stanley Backs Bill and Plank on Equal Pay," 20 June 1944, *New York Times:* 22.

32 Quoted in Norton's obituary in the 1959 *Current Biography.*

33 Chase Going Woodhouse, oral history interview with Joyce Pendry, 31 January 1981, Center for Oral History and Women's Study Programs, University of Connecticut, Storrs: 63–69.

34 *"Chase Going Woodhouse," Current Biography, 1945* (New York: H. W. Wilson and Company, 1945): 690–692.; see also on the housing issues, *Congressional Record,* House, 79th Cong., 2nd sess. (28 June 1946): 7894–7897; on the OPA and price controls see, *Congressional Record,* House, 79th Cong., 2nd sess. (16 April 1946): 3798–3800; *Congressional Record,* House 79th Cong., 2nd sess. (17 April 1946): 3892–3893.

35 Chase Going Woodhouse, Oral History Interview, USAFMOC: 31.

36 Peggy Lampson, *Few Are Chosen: American Women in Political Life Today* (Boston: Houghton Mifflin Company, 1968): 33.

37 For more on the differences between the "work horse" and the "show horse" styles, see Donald R. Matthews, "The Folkways of the United States Senate: Conformity to Group Norms and Legislative Effectiveness," *American Political Science Review* 53 (December 1959): 1064–1089. The same pattern has been observed in the House; see Charles L. Clapp, *The Congressman: His Work As He Sees It* (Garden City, NY: Doubleday, 1964): 22–23. See also James L. Payne, "Show Horses and Work Horses in the United States House of Representatives," *Polity* 12 (Spring 1980): 428–456.

38 Kathleen McLaughlin, "Mrs. Luce Assails 'Bumbledom' Trend," 28 June 1944, *New York Times:* 15.

39 "'Fencing' with Mrs. Luce Barred by Miss Gahagan," 16 July 1944, *New York Times:* 26; "Republican 'Double Talk' Assailed by Mrs. Douglas," 21 July 1944, *Christian Science Monitor:* 14; "Roosevelt Needed, Mrs. Douglas Says," 21 July 1944, *New York Times:* 11.

40 Ingrid Winther Scobie, *Center Stage: Helen Douglas, A Life* (New Brunswick, NJ: Rutgers University Press, 1995): 306.

41 Jerry Voorhis, *Confessions of a Congressman* (Garden City, NY: Doubleday & Company, 1947): 35.

Visual Statistics III

Congressional Service[1]

This timeline depicts the span of congressional service for women first sworn in between 1935 and 1954.

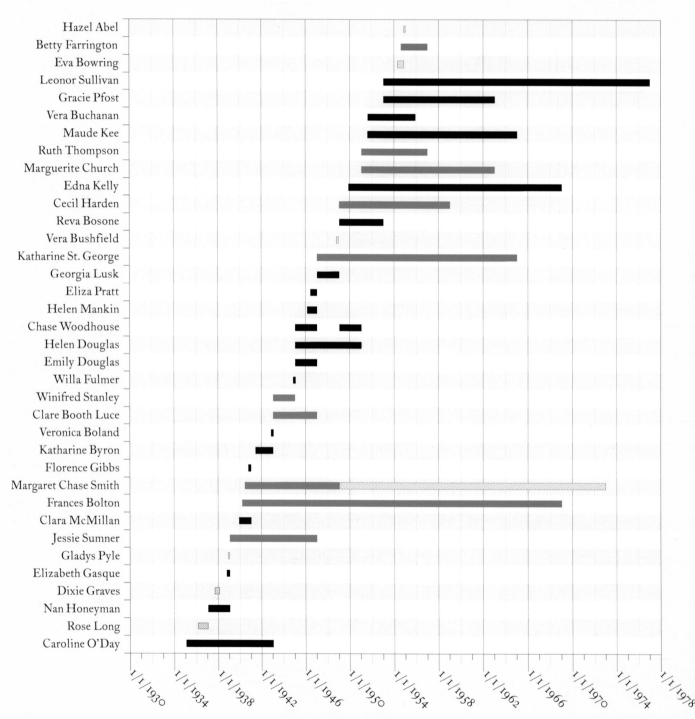

---

1. Source: *Biographical Directory of the United States Congress, 1774–2005* (Washington D.C.: Government Printing Office, 2005); also available at http://bioguide.congress.gov.

House and Senate Party Affiliation[2]

74TH–83RD CONGRESSES
(1935–1955)

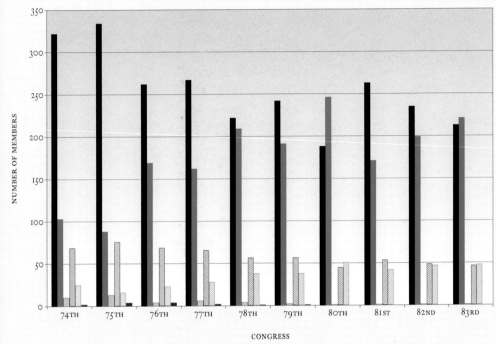

This chart depicts the party affiliation of all Members of Congress from 1935 to 1955. The following chart depicts a party breakdown only for women Members during this time period.

Party Affiliation: Women in Congress

74TH–83RD CONGRESSES (1935–1955)

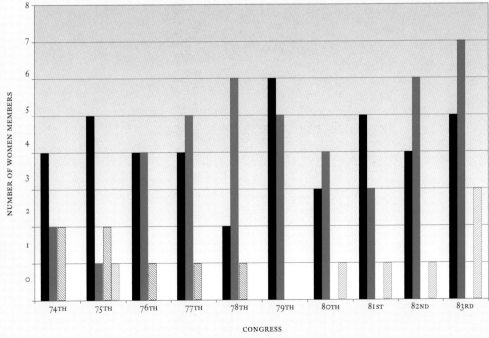

2. House numbers do not include Delegates or Resident Commissioners. Sources: Office of the Clerk, U.S. House of Representatives; U.S. Senate Historical Office.

Caroline O'Day
1875–1943

UNITED STATES REPRESENTATIVE ★ DEMOCRAT FROM NEW YORK
1935–1943

A longtime suffragist with strong ties to New York politics and First Lady Eleanor Roosevelt, Caroline O'Day was an unwavering supporter of New Deal legislation and a fervent pacifist during her four terms in the House. Once, when asked what she would do if the United States became embroiled in a war, she declared, "I would just kiss my children good-bye and start off for Leavenworth."[1] Those convictions changed, however, when O'Day realized the aims of Nazi Germany.

Caroline Love Goodwin was born on June 22, 1875, on a plantation in Perry, Georgia, daughter of Sidney Prior Goodwin and Elia Warren. Caroline Goodwin graduated from the elite Lucy Cobb Institute in Athens, Georgia, and for eight years studied art in Paris (with James McNeill Whistler), Munich, and Holland, and briefly at the Cooper Union. In 1902, she married Daniel T. O'Day, son of a Standard Oil Company executive, whom she met in Europe. They settled in Rye, New York, and had three children: Elia, Daniel, and Charles.

Caroline O'Day first became interested in politics after witnessing a suffrage parade with her husband, who turned to his wife and asked why she wasn't marching with the procession.[2] She later joined the Westchester (NY) League of Women Voters, where she became an officer and first met Eleanor Roosevelt. After the death of her husband in 1916, Caroline O'Day dedicated herself to improving the lives of working-class poor in the inner city. She served on the board of directors and volunteered at Lillian Wald's Henry Street Settlement on Manhattan's Lower East Side. A pacifist who opposed U.S. entry into World War I, O'Day became vice chair of the Women's International League for Peace and Freedom. In 1917, she joined Jeannette Rankin in support of the enfranchisement of New York women. Her first political appointment came in 1921 when New York Governor Alfred E. Smith named her to the state board of social welfare, supervising care for dependent juveniles. In 1923, O'Day became associate chair of the New York state Democratic Committee and directed its women's division—holding both positions until her death. She traversed New York, logging more than 8,000 miles with Eleanor Roosevelt and other women leaders to organize voters. As a reward, the party appointed her chair of the New York delegation to the 1924 Democratic National Convention.[3] Together, O'Day and Roosevelt led delegations of women to Albany to press the legislature to adopt Governor Smith's programs. She worked for Smith's presidential campaign in 1928 and for Franklin Roosevelt's successful 1932 campaign. After Roosevelt's inauguration, O'Day was named New York's director of the National Recovery Administration.

O'Day's 1934 race for one of two New York At-Large seats in the U.S. House of Representatives drew national attention because of the candidate's highly placed supporter: First Lady Eleanor Roosevelt.[4] O'Day secured the nomination when Roosevelt allies ousted the first-term incumbent, John Fitzgibbon (former mayor of Oswego) from the ticket, citing his insufficient support for New Deal initiatives.[5] Eleanor Roosevelt backed O'Day and, in the process, became the first First Lady to actively campaign for a congressional candidate—making a half dozen speeches and even chairing her campaign committee.[6] GOP leaders were incensed at the break with tradition and labeled O'Day as a "Yes" vote for the Roosevelt administration. Eleanor Roosevelt defended her actions on personal and political grounds.[7] "I am doing this as an individual," she said. "I believe in certain things, and . . . I feel I am justified in making this effort in my own state, because I know its problems."[8]

While Republicans howled at Eleanor Roosevelt's involvement, O'Day's principal opponent, Nyack lawyer Natalie F. Couch, refused to go on the attack and stuck to a vague nine-point platform that promised to fight unemployment and support "humane" public relief programs while balancing the federal budget.[9] O'Day's platform stressed better wages and working conditions for laborers, strong support for federal intervention to relieve the effects of the Great Depression, and the need to involve women in local and national government.[10] O'Day also tapped into a state network of Democratic women's groups and arranged for prominent national women's figures to canvass New York on her behalf. Self-styled as the "Flying Squadron," the group included such luminaries as the aviator Amelia Earhart (O'Day's Rye neighbor), Elizabeth Wheeler (daughter of Montana Senator Burton K. Wheeler), and Josephine Roche, a prominent Colorado politician.[11] O'Day topped a slate of 12 candidates with 27.6 percent of the vote, just barely ahead of Democrat Matthew J. Merritt and only a few percentage points in front of Couch. O'Day's platform had broad appeal for Depression-Era New Yorkers: "Higher standards for wage earners, adequate relief at lowest cost to the taxpayer, a sound policy, and wider opportunity for women in government."[12] The GOP ran women candidates in the next three elections in unsuccessful attempts to unseat O'Day. None could close O'Day's and Merritt's several-hundred-thousand-vote margins.[13]

Once in the House, O'Day received assignments on the Immigration and Naturalization Committee and on the Insular Affairs Committee. She also chaired the Committee on Election of President, Vice President, and Representatives in Congress from 1937 to 1943. She, along with Mary T. Norton and Isabella S. Greenway was one of the most popular and recognizable women in Congress. O'Day's trademark was her collection of hand fans. Known as "The Lady of the Fans", she carried them into committee hearings and onto the House Floor.[14]

Congresswoman O'Day's first passion was the pursuit of world peace. Her affiliation with the group World Peaceways, led O'Day to propose several measures she believed would deter world conflict: the adoption of a national referendum to allow voters to decide for or against a war; federal government control of the arms industry; and a government-backed educational campaign about the horrors of war. Women played a particularly important role in the protest movement, O'Day noted, because as mothers they "pay the first and greatest cost of war."[15] She represented the Women's International League for Peace and Freedom at the International Conference for the Maintenance of Peace in Buenos Aires, Argentina, in 1936.[16] She was concerned with the prospect of "total war," in which civilian targets—urban and industrial, in particular—were as important to strategists as traditional military targets. The Spanish Civil War, then raging in Spain, as well as Japanese and Nazi tactics in the opening years of World War II, would confirm O'Day's fears. O'Day urged that the U.S. and other nations adopt a "standard of ethics" that would outlaw mass killings.[17]

O'Day's work extended beyond pacifist principles. National security, she observed, derived from stable domestic life.[18] She was a staunch supporter of the New Deal and looked to advance the cause of labor and children's issues. O'Day's first major legislative victory was in winning the delay of the deportation of 2,600 immigrants (many of them with dependents who had citizenship rights in the U.S.), pending a thorough review by Congress.[19] She helped attach a child labor amendment to the 1936 Walsh–Healy Act, which set employment standards for federal contracts, and to the 1938 Fair Labor Standards Act, which fixed minimum wages for employment. The Congresswoman also called for a dramatic expansion of the government's aid to the dependent children program, which she described as a "national investment."[20] In 1940, O'Day urged colleagues to adopt federal aid programs for migrant workers, especially for children of migrants, who often toiled in the fields alongside their parents.[21] O'Day also fought to keep funding for federal arts projects in theater, music, and writing, initiated by the Works Progress Administration.[22]

Representative O'Day consistently championed progressive civil rights causes. She supported an antilynching bill that came before Congress in 1935, noting that "I have been interested in the efforts Southern women have been making to curb this horrible thing."[23] She backed a 1937 version of the bill that passed the House. She also criticized the Daughters of the American Revolution in 1939 when they refused to allow African-American singer Marian

lobby in the nation."[26] Eventually, however, when Nazi forces overran Western Europe and intensified atrocities against Jews and other minorities in Germany and the occupied countries, O'Day changed her position. She supported increased armaments for the American military. After the Japanese attack on Pearl Harbor on December 7, 1941, Congress voted overwhelmingly to declare war on Japan. O'Day, who by that time suffered from a chronic long-term illness, was absent for the vote. She later told House colleagues that, had she been present, she would

"Women will no longer consent to war. There is no problem affecting humanity that cannot be settled without recourse to the battlefield."

—Caroline O'Day, International Conference for the Maintenance of Peace, Buenos Aires, Argentina, 1936

Anderson to perform at Constitution Hall. In 1939, O'Day opposed legislation to create detention camps for aliens, a plan that foreshadowed later wartime internment camps for Japanese Americans. She derided the bill as "a negation of every idea and policy and principle that our country holds dear."[24] Her suffrage background and her tireless work on behalf of underrepresented minorities, however, did not translate into support for an equal rights amendment. Like many of her women colleagues, O'Day publicly rejected the idea, fearing that it would undermine protective laws she had helped implement for single women and working mothers in the labor force.[25]

Her pacifist views threatened to bring her into open conflict with the Roosevelt administration as America's entry into World War II grew imminent. O'Day opposed modification of the Neutrality Acts to authorize arms sales to nations at war with Nazi Germany and voted against the 1940 Selective Training and Service Act. She lashed out against the U.S. military as the "most powerful

have voted for the war resolution. "Japan, Germany, and Italy have decided the issue of peace or war," O'Day said.[27]

Poor health brought O'Day's career to a premature end. Her 1940 election had been carried on largely by her daughter, Elia, who made campaign appearances for her convalescing mother. O'Day declined to run for a fifth term in 1942, after she suffered complicating injuries from a fall. She was succeeded by Republican Winnifred Stanley, who prevailed against Democratic candidate Flora Dufour Johnson in the 1942 general elections. O'Day died on January 4, 1943, a day after the end of her congressional service.

In 1939, O'Day opposed
legislation to create
detention camps for aliens,
a plan that foreshadowed
later wartime internment
camps for Japanese Americans.
She derided the bill as "a
negation of every idea and
policy and principle that our
country holds dear."

FOR FURTHER READING

Biographical Directory of the United States Congress, "Caroline Love Goodwin O'Day," http://bioguide.congress.gov

NOTES

1 "Mrs. O'Day Pledges Opposition to War," 29 October 1934, *New York Times*: 4.

2 "Mrs. O'Day, Ill, Won Solely on Record," 6 November 1940, *New York Times*: 4.

3 Anne O'Hagan Shinn, "Politics Still Masculine, Convention Women Discover," 29 June 1924, *New York Times*: XX3.

4 At-Large districts in states entitled to more than one Representative were outlawed by Congress in 1967. *Congressional Quarterly's Guide to Congress,* Vol. 2 (Washington, D.C.: Congressional Quarterly Press, 2000): 910.

5 "Women Delegates Cheer Mrs. O'Day," 28 September 1934, *New York Times*: 11; "Labor Fights Mrs. O'Day," 18 October 1934, *New York Times*: 18.

6 "President's Wife Raising O'Day Fund," 16 October 1934, *New York Times*: 1; "Mrs. Roosevelt in Last Plea for Mrs. O'Day Whose Rival 'Crashes' Dinner Futilely," 2 November 1934, *New York Times*: 1.

7 Despite the criticism she received for campaigning for her friend, the First Lady apparently had the support of President Roosevelt and New Deal proponents such as Louis Howe. Blanche Wiesen Cook, *Eleanor Roosevelt,* Vol. 2 (New York: Viking, 1992; reprint 1999): 221.

8 "First Lady Opens Mrs. O'Day's Drive," 26 October 1934, *New York Times*: 1; "Mrs. O'Day Called Roosevelt 'Victim,'" 28 October 1936, *New York Times*: 20.

9 "President's Wife Raising O'Day Fund."

10 Martha H. Swain, "O'Day, Caroline Love Goodwin," *American National Biography,* 16 (New York: Oxford University Press, 1999): 616.

11 "Flier to Aid Mrs. O'Day," 30 October 1934, *New York Times*: 14; "Miss Roche Will Aid Mrs. O'Day in Fight," 19 October 1934, *Washington Post*: 1; "Elizabeth Wheeler Stumps for Mrs. O'Day," 31 October 1934, *Washington Post*: 4.

12 Susan Tolchin, *Women in Congress* (Washington, D.C.: Government Printing Office, 1976): 60.

13 "Election Statistics, 1920 to Present," http://clerk.house.gov/members/electionInfo/index.html .

14 "Caroline O'Day," 6 January 1943, *Washington Post*: 8.

15 "Mrs. O'Day in Peace Plea," 22 September 1936, *New York Times*: 32.

16 "Hull Advances 8-Point Plan as Peace Basis," 6 December 1936, *Washington Post*: M1; Carrie A. Foster, *The Women and the Warriors: The U.S. Section of Women's International League for Peace and Freedom, 1915–1946* (Syracuse, NY: Syracuse University Press, 1995): 218–219.

17 "Rep. Caroline O'Day Urges Standard of Ethics to Make Mass Killings in War as Wrong as Individual Murder," 27 January 1938, *Washington Post*: 13.

18 "Congresswomen Show They Can Take It," 8 December 1940, *Washington Post*: S10.

19 "Victory for Mrs. O'Day," 24 August 1935, *New York Times*: 2.

20 *Congressional Record,* House, 76th Cong., 1st sess. (22 May 1939): appendix A2143–2144.

21 "Federal Aid for Migrants Is Urged by Congresswoman," 1 August 1940, *Christian Science Monitor*: 8.

22 *Congressional Record,* House, 76th Cong., 1st sess. (13 January 1939): 339–340.

23 "Mrs. O'Day Indorses Anti-Lynching Bill," 16 January 1935, *Washington Post*: 3.

24 *Congressional Record,* House, 76th Cong., 1st sess. (5 May 1939): 5164.

25 Hope Chamberlin, *A Minority of Members: Women in the U.S. Congress* (New York: Praeger, 1973): 110.

26 Karen Foerstel, *Biographical Dictionary of Congressional Women* (Westport, CT: Greenwood Press, 1999): 211.

27 *Congressional Record,* House, 77th Cong., 1st sess. (11 December 1941): appendix A 5565.

Rose McConnell Long
1892–1970

UNITED STATES SENATOR ★ DEMOCRAT FROM LOUISIANA
1936–1937

Rose Long emerged from behind the long shadow of her flamboyant husband, the slain Louisiana populist Huey P. Long, to fill his Senate seat for an abbreviated term. Accompanied by her children, Long diligently assumed her husband's committee duties while, in Baton Rouge, the shattered remnants of the Long political machine vied for a permanent successor.

Rose McConnell was born in Greensburg, Indiana, on April 8, 1892. She was the first child born to Peter McConnell, a farmer, and Sally B. McConnell, who came from a long line of southern planters. The McConnell family moved to Shreveport, Louisiana, in 1901, where Rose attended the public schools and later became a local schoolteacher. In 1910, she entered a cake baking contest with a "bride loaf cake." One of the judges, a traveling salesman who had sponsored the contest to pitch the lard substitute he was selling, was named Huey Pierce Long. Rose McConnell won the contest, struck up a long correspondence with the itinerant Long, and, in 1913, in Memphis, Tennessee, she married him. The Longs moved to New Orleans, where Rose worked as a secretary to pay Huey's way through the Tulane Law School. After finishing a three-year program in seven months, he was admitted to the bar in 1915. Rose Long put her stenography skills to use on behalf of her husband's early political campaigns and served as a political adviser. Meanwhile she raised their three children: Rose, Russell, and Palmer. In 1928, after serving on the state railroad commission, Huey Long was elected Louisiana governor. As the state's political boss, he introduced sweeping legislation that ushered in large public works programs. Two years later, he won election to the U.S. Senate where, in the early years of the Depression, he gained a large populist

following of farmers and laborers who rallied around his "Share the Wealth" initiative.

Rose Long distanced herself from her husband's political work during his years as governor, though she remained supportive.[1] Unlike her egomaniacal husband, Rose shied from the spotlight and served as the anchor for her young family. She was so unobtrusive as Louisiana's First Lady as to be largely unknown to many of her husband's constituents. While Long traveled in large caravans and constantly in the company of bodyguards, Rose Long routinely drove the family car on long trips with the children, recalling that she occasionally stopped to pick up hitchhikers, whom she and her daughter would pepper with questions about politics without revealing their identities.[2]

Huey Long's political ambitions stretched all the way to the White House. He won election as Louisiana governor by tapping into voter discontent with conservative rule and pledging a tax-the-rich program. In the Senate, he eventually charged that FDR's New Deal programs had been co-opted by conservative business interests. In the fall 1932 elections, as a jab at his chief Senate rival, Long led a last-minute campaign blitz in Arkansas to help elect Hattie Caraway, who bucked the political establishment by refusing to retire after a brief appointment to succeed her late husband. With Long's help, she won a full six-year term. Huey Long became a national figure in opposition to FDR with his "Share the Wealth" program, which called for a radical redistribution of wealth to afford every American a decent standard of living. By 1935, he was a serious contender for the presidency.[3]

Long had made a host of enemies. On September 8, 1935, the Senator was shot while visiting the Louisiana state capitol and died early on the morning of September 10th. The scramble to name a successor to the "Kingfish" made for pure political spectacle throughout the fall of 1935. Long organization leaders settled on a slate of candidates for the January 21, 1936, primary and the April 21, 1936, special election. Governor O.K. Allen, Long's successor, was nominated to fill out the remainder of Long's Senate term, set to expire in January 1937. Meanwhile, the speaker of the Louisiana state house of representatives, Allen Ellender, was chosen to run for the succeeding six-year term. Richard W. Leche was named as the gubernatorial candidate, and Earl Long, Huey's brother, displaced Acting Lieutenant Governor James A. Noe on the ticket. But the plan crumbled from the top down. Governor Allen died before the primary, and Noe, his slighted subordinate, succeeded him for a four-month term.[4]

Though snubbed by the Long organization, Noe had been one of the Kingfish's closest protégés. He bypassed Ellender and chose Long's widow, Rose, to succeed her husband. In making his announcement on January 31, 1936, Noe crowed, "It is the happiest moment of my life." He also promised Rose Long that she would receive unanimous backing from state party leaders—which she soon did. To the press, he was more mellifluous: "The love of Huey Long binds us together as a solid Gibraltar... we're united and there isn't a hint of dissension in the party."[5]

Critics charged Noe with "political trickery" and attempting to advance his own ambitions for national office. Newspapers speculated that Rose Long was a mere compromise candidate who would hold the seat until a victor emerged from the swamp of Louisiana politics. The *Washington Post* denounced the move as destructive to the advancement of women in politics because it seemed to advance a family political dynasty rather than democratic interests. "Women have as much right as men to seek and fill political office," the editors wrote. "But every time a woman is elevated to a position of great influence merely for sentimental reasons it becomes more difficult for those who are really trained for effective public work to win recognition." Remembering Caraway's election, they further noted, "The fact that the two women now in the

Senate owe their positions largely to Huey Long is a tragic commentary upon the success of the feminist movement."[6]

On February 10, 1936, Rose Long was sworn into the Senate and took a seat alongside Hattie Caraway at the back of the chamber. Upon taking office, she received credentials made out to "Mrs. Huey Pierce Long," which she insisted be changed to "Rose McConnell Long." After the ceremony, at which Vice President John Nance Garner administered the oath of office before virtually the entire Senate and packed galleries, Long got right down to business, attending a floor speech on U.S.– Japanese relations. She told reporters that she intended to carry on her husband's "Share the Wealth" programs. "I am having all of our files and records sent up, and will study them before making any announcements. I am 100 percent for labor and the farmers, and will vote for everything to help them."[7] Long settled into several suites in a hotel on Connecticut Avenue in the northwest part of the city—the same hotel that Huey had occupied. She also brought her daughter, Rose, and youngest son, Palmer, to stay with her in Washington. On April 21, 1936, Rose Long won the special election to serve the remainder of her husband's term. With a sparse crowd in the gallery that included Rose and several schoolmates, she was sworn in a second time on May 19, 1936.

Senator Long's daughter, Rose, whom she brought to Washington, was more than just a supportive family member. The younger Rose possessed the political acumen to help her mother, who was sometimes awkward in public-speaking situations, adjust to her new role. The daughter first had urged her mother to accept the nomination because, she recalled, it seemed "the right thing to do."[8] The immediate family members believed that Russell was best equipped to eventually carry out his father's work— and eventually he would, serving as Louisiana Senator from 1948 to 1987 and chairing the Finance Committee. Huey, Rose, and Russell were the only father-mother-child combination in Senate history. In later years, despite her apparent abilities, the younger Rose Long did not enter public service.[9]

Though her husband's term did not expire until January 3, 1937, Rose Long's stint as a Senator was further abbreviated when the second (and final) session of the 74th Congress (1935–1937) adjourned on June 20, 1936—four months after she came to Washington. She worked hard during that stint, however, preferring the routine of committee work to the public forum of the Senate Chamber. In stark contrast to her husband, Rose Long shied from the limelight and made few floor speeches. She fit comfortably into the committee work that Huey Long often neglected. Rose Long received five assignments: Claims, Immigration, Interoceanic Canals, Post Offices and Post Roads, and Public Lands and Surveys. Her efforts on the Committee on Public Lands led to the enlargement of Chalmette National Historic Park on the site of the Battle of New Orleans in the War of 1812. "Had we not won the battle," she said in one of her rare speeches, "we would have a British Colony west of the Mississippi." [10] In March of 1936, she joined her Louisiana colleague, John H. Overton, and the Senators from Arkansas and Texas to seek authorization of the attendance of the Marine Band at the centennial celebration in Arkansas and Texas and at the 46th Confederate Reunion in Shreveport, Louisiana.

Long's brief Senate career, so representative of her behind-the-scenes approach to life, fit the pattern of her postpolitical life. She made few floor speeches and quietly left the Senate when the 74th Congress adjourned on January 3, 1937, and Allen Ellender, who had won the general election, succeeded her. Rose Long retired to private life in Shreveport. On May 27, 1970, she died in Boulder, Colorado, where, after a long illness, she had gone to live with her daughter.

FOR FURTHER READING

Biographical Directory of the United States Congress, "Rose McConnell Long," http://bioguide.congress.gov

MANUSCRIPT COLLECTIONS

Emory University (Atlanta, GA), Robert W. Woodruff Library. *Papers:* In the Huey Pierce Long Collection, 1926–1938. The collection includes a portrait of Rose McConnell Long.

Louisiana State University (Baton Rouge, LA), Louisiana and Lower Mississippi Valley Collections. *Papers:* Items are scattered throughout the Huey Long collections. Finding aids are available in the repository.

NOTES

1   F. Raymond Daniell, "Mrs. Long Emerges Modestly," 9 February 1936, *New York Times*: SM11; Martin Weil, "Ex-Sen. Rose Long Dies, Widow of Huey," 29 May 1970, *Washington Post*: B16.
2   Daniell, "Mrs. Long Emerges Modestly."
3   See T. Harry Williams, *Huey Long* (New York: Alfred A. Knopf, 1969) and Alan Brinkley, *Voices of Protest: Huey Long, Father Coughlin, and the Great Depression* (New York: Alfred A. Knopf, 1982).
4   See Thomas A. Becnel, *Senator Allen Ellender of Louisiana* (Baton Rouge: Louisiana State University Press, 1995).
5   "Mrs. Long, Speeding to Capital, Says She'll Need Luck in Senate," 10 February 1936, *Washington Post*: 7.
6   "Huey Long's Proxy," 3 February 1936, *Washington Post*: 8; see also "Mrs. Long as a Senator," 15 September 1935, *Washington Post*: B6.
7   "Mrs. Long Takes Oath in a Crowded Senate; Will Carry on 'Share-the-Wealth' Campaign," 11 February 1936, *New York Times*: 3.
8   "Long's Widow Assumes Duties as U.S. Senator," 11 February 1936, *Washington Post*: 4.
9   Daniell, "Mrs. Long Emerges Modestly."
10 Susan Tolchin, *Women In Congress* (Washington, D.C.: Government Printing Office, 1976): 47.

Nan Wood Honeyman
1881–1970

UNITED STATES REPRESENTATIVE ★ DEMOCRAT FROM OREGON
1937–1939

A Roosevelt family friend and New Deal stalwart, Nan Wood Honeyman of Oregon won election to the House of Representatives during the 1936 landslide re-election of President Franklin D. Roosevelt. As an unreconstructed supporter of the President, Honeyman experienced the promises and pitfalls of hitching her political wagon to executive programs that did not always rest well with her constituents.

Nan Wood was born in West Point, New York, on July 15, 1881. Her father was Charles Erskine Scott Wood, Indian fighter, poet, and former adjutant of the United States Military Academy. In 1883, he resigned from the army and moved his family to Portland, Oregon. "Nanny" attended private schools and graduated from St. Helen's Hall in 1898. She later attended the Finch School in New York City for three years, where she studied music and established a lifelong friendship with Franklin and Eleanor Roosevelt. In 1907, she married David Taylor Honeyman, secretary-treasurer of the Honeyman Hardware Company in Portland, and they raised three children: Nancy, David, and Judith. David Honeyman, whom his wife described as a "Roosevelt Republican," was supportive of her nascent political career though he was determined to "keep my wife's politics out of my business."[1]

Nan Honeyman became active in local and state politics in her late 40s as an anti-Prohibition activist. Though a teetotaler herself, Honeyman rejected the idea that "any law governing people's personal conduct should be a part of the Constitution."[2] In 1928, she became head of the Oregon division of the Women's National Organization for Prohibition Reform. Two years later, she aligned with liberal interests in the state and became vice chair of the Oregon Democratic Committee. The party asked her to run for Congress in 1930 as Portland's U.S. Representative. It was a testament to what party leaders believed Honeyman's potential was as a vote getter. Since the district was created through reapportionment in 1912, only one Democrat had ever won election there and, then, only for a single term. Honeyman declined the offer but campaigned actively for the eventual Democratic candidate, General Charles H. Martin. Martin won election to two consecutive terms. In 1933, Honeyman served as president of the state constitutional convention which ratified the 21st Amendment, repealing Prohibition. A year later, when Martin won election as Oregon governor, party leaders again prevailed on Honeyman to run for the Portland seat. She again declined, according to one newspaper account, because she was apprehensive about her lack of experience in elective office.[3] She instead campaigned for and won a seat in the Oregon house of representatives. Honeyman later served as a delegate to the Democratic national conventions of 1936 and 1940.

In 1936, Honeyman challenged freshman incumbent Republican William A. Ekwall in the race for the Portland seat. Honeyman embraced the New Deal platform of President Roosevelt and supported the plan championed by Eleanor Roosevelt and Labor Secretary Frances Perkins, which called for a pension drawn from taxing an individual's lifetime income. Honeyman refused to endorse a competing proposal—the so-called Townshend Plan. Francis Townshend, a California doctor, had advocated "universal" old-age pensions of $200 per month to every American 65 years or older. A faction of the Democratic Party, "Townshendites," ran John A. Jefferey as an Independent candidate after Honeyman scooped up the nomination.[4] Honeyman held two advantages, in particular: a strong network of women's groups from her anti-Prohibition work and a door-to-door campaign style. Honeyman visited Portland factories to talk with workers on their lunch breaks. She canvassed the city, walking block by block to speak with housewives and retirees. "Don't ever think that the day of personal campaigning is past," Honeyman declared. "Voters want to know who is representing them. And women running for office can overcome much masculine prejudice by meeting the men voters face to face."[5] At the 1936 Philadelphia convention, she gained valuable publicity by seconding FDR's nomination. In a state where two-thirds of voters preferred FDR to Republican Alf Landon in the fall elections, Honeyman benefited from presidential coattails. She captured 53 percent of the vote, while Ekwall, her closest competitor, managed only 31 percent.[6] She became the first woman to represent Oregon in Congress. Honeyman's youngest daughter, 20-year-old Judith, came to work for her mother in Washington.[7]

On January 4, 1937, when Honeyman took the oath of office she told a reporter that she intended to "keep my eyes and ears open and my mouth shut," during the first session.[8] She largely fulfilled that pledge. During her House service, Honeyman staunchly supported the New Deal. She was assigned to three committees: Indian Affairs, Irrigation and Reclamation, and Rivers and Harbors. The latter assignment was a valuable one, considering the port business of her district. Honeyman supported a range of federal programs that benefited her constituents. She voted for a resolution to continue loans to farmers in 1937 for crop production and harvesting, noting that about 10,000 Oregon farmers had benefited from the program since Roosevelt had taken office.[9] Honeyman supported the President's neutrality policies, including the 1937 Neutrality Act, which created a "cash and carry" program whereby belligerents could purchase strategic goods in the U.S. and ship them back on non-American carriers. She was uncomfortable, however, with America becoming an arsenal for Atlantic allies. U.S. security, she declared, might be "accomplished more effectively and quickly by concentrating our naval and

military programs to this end and by eliminating all phases of that program which might constitute needless preparation for aggressive warfare."[10] In 1938, Honeyman sponsored a bill authorizing the federal government to acquire lands along the Columbia River on which to build a large naval port and air base. Referred to the Naval Affairs Committee, it did not pass.[11]

But for all Honeyman's connections and her key committee post, she seemed a bit adrift in Washington. Her forays onto the House Floor were infrequent, and her legislative interests were eclectic, ranging from strengthening the nation's defenses to proposing that the federal government create a national award for poetry. Honeyman seemed at times curiously aloof to the interests of her district's constituents. For instance, during Irrigation and Reclamation Committee debate over appropriations for the completion and operation of the Bonneville Dam along the Columbia River, she often deferred from delivering her opinion, noting only that she unreservedly supported whatever actions President Roosevelt recommended. The Bonneville Dam was one of the great public works projects of the New Deal. Construction commenced in 1933, and by its completion five years later, the dam, combined with its system of locks, promised to open navigation along vast stretches of the Columbia River (with its mouth at the Pacific in Portland) and to generate electricity for large swaths of the Northwest. Honeyman did weigh in on the nascent issues of private versus public power, fighting to make a greater share of the hydroelectric power generated by the Bonneville Dam available to publicly owned cooperatives. To that end, Congresswoman Honeyman fought for congressional funding for more transmission lines to meet the projected increase in demand for power from the facility.[12] In an effort to limit the role of private utility companies, Honeyman also sought to keep Bonneville's power-generating function securely under the oversight of the Interior Department.[13]

The critical turning point for the freshman Representative seems to have been her unflinching support for Roosevelt in the midst of the "court-packing" fight in 1937, when the President sought to create a Supreme Court more favorable to his New Deal programs. Critics accused FDR of under-mining the independence of the judiciary. In support of Roosevelt's plan, Honeyman mailed out a mimeographed letter to constituents. She declared her allegiance to FDR, telling voters in her district that she would not oppose the President's effort "to liberalize the judiciary." Pouncing on this episode, critics described Honeyman as a "stencil for the White House duplicating machine."[14]

When Honeyman ran for re-election in 1938, she beat William J. Pendergast, Jr., by a wide margin in the Democratic primary. But in the general election she faced a formidable candidate—liberal Republican Homer D. Angell. Trained as a lawyer, Angell was in the state senate after three terms in the Oregon house of representatives and enjoyed wide name recognition in Portland. Despite the Roosevelt administration's efforts to aid her re-election—the First Lady endorsed Honeyman in her syndicated newspaper column and Interior Secretary Harold Ickes, who admired the Congresswoman's stand on public power, stumped on her behalf during the campaign's home stretch—Honeyman lost to Angell by a thin margin of about 2,500 votes, 51 to 49 percent.[15] Overall, Democrats lost 78 congressional seats in the 1938 mid-term elections. In 1940, Honeyman again challenged Angell with the support of Eleanor Roosevelt. However, with two Independent candidates drawing off about 4,000 votes, Angell won re-election by a slender margin, about 3,000 votes, or less than two percent of the total turnout.

After Congress, Honeyman stayed active in politics and government. From August 1941 to May 1942 she was the senior Pacific Coast representative of the Office of Price Administration. In late 1941, she also was appointed by the Multnomah County commissioners to fill a vacant seat for a brief term in the Oregon state senate, but she resigned several months later. Honeyman's loyalty to the Roosevelt administration was rewarded when FDR appointed her the collector of customs in the 29th District, Portland, in May 1942. She served in that position for 11 years, retiring in July 1953. Honeyman moved to Woodacre, California, in the mid-1960s and died there on December 10, 1970.

FOR FURTHER READING

Biographical Directory of the United States Congress, "Nan Wood Honeyman," http://bioguide.congress.gov

MANUSCRIPT COLLECTIONS

Huntington Library (San Marino, CA), Manuscripts Department. C.E.S. Wood Papers, ca. 1829-1980, approx-imately 30,000 pieces. Other authors include Nan Wood Honeyman.

Oregon Historical Society (Portland, OR). *Papers:* 1900-1965, nine volumes and one box. Correspondence, speeches, voting records, abstracts, political convention memorabilia, scrapbooks relating to Franklin D. Roosevelt, and documents relating to her terms as Oregon customs collector.

University of Oregon Library (Eugene, OR). *Papers:* 1932-1950, 0.5 cubic foot. Includes correspondence concern-ing political campaigns and district improvement projects.

NOTES

1 James J. Cullinane, "Mrs. Honeyman in Eight Years Heads Democrats of Oregon," 18 January 1937, *Washington Post*: 2.
2 Hope Chamberlin, *A Minority of Members: Women in the U.S. Congress* (New York: Praeger, 1976): 113.
3 Cullinane, "Mrs. Honeyman in Eight Years Heads Democrats of Oregon."
4 Ibid.
5 Malvina Lindsay, "Mrs. Honeyman Direct Exponent of Democracy," 11 November 1936, *Washington Post*: X 16.
6 "Election Statistics, 1920 to Present," http://clerk.house.gov/members/electionInfo/elections.html.
7 Cullinane, "Mrs. Honeyman in Eight Years Heads Democrats of Oregon."
8 "Congress' Women Veterans Show New Sister the Ropes," 5 January 1937, *Christian Science Monitor*: 3.
9 *Congressional Record*, House, 75th Cong., 1st sess. (25 January 1937): 101–102.
10 *Congressional Record*, House, 75th Cong., 1st sess. (2 March 1937): 1756.
11 *Congressional Record*, House, 75th Cong., 3rd sess. (11 April 1938): 5291.
12 *Congressional Record*, House, 75th Cong., 3rd sess. (28 February 1938): 2559–2560; *Congressional Record*, House, 75th Cong., 3rd sess. (17 January 1938): 232–233.
13 *Congressional Record*, House, 75th Cong., 1st sess. (23 July 1937): 7523.
14 Chamberlin, *A Minority of Members*: 114.
15 "Election Statistics, 1920 to Present," http://clerk.house.gov/members/electionInfo/elections.html.

Dixie Bibb Graves
1882–1965

UNITED STATES SENATOR ★ DEMOCRAT FROM ALABAMA
1937–1938

Dixie Bibb Graves, the first woman to serve in Congress from Alabama, came to Washington through an unusual route. When President Franklin Roosevelt surprised the country by nominating Senator Hugo Black to the U.S. Supreme Court in 1937, Alabama Governor Bibb Graves provoked a storm of criticism by naming his 55-year-old wife, Dixie Bibb Graves, to fill the Senate seat. "She has as good a heart and head as anybody," the governor told the press.[1]

Dixie Bibb was born on July 26, 1882, on a plantation near Montgomery, Alabama, to Payton and Isabel Bibb. The family was long associated with Alabama politics. Two of her ancestors had served as the first and second state governors. Dixie was raised with an orphaned cousin, Bibb Graves, and the two married in 1900 after Bibb Graves graduated from Harvard University and was serving as a state legislator. Although Dixie Graves's political power was clearly derivative, she boasted a long career in state and regional women's clubs, such as the Women's Christian Temperance Union and the Alabama Federation of Women's Clubs. From 1915 to 1917, while her husband served overseas in the army, she was president of the United Daughters of the Confederacy. She also campaigned for women's suffrage in Alabama. Bibb Graves was governor twice, 1927–1931 and 1935–1939; Alabama's constitution prohibited consecutive terms in the statehouse.[2] Dixie Graves was comfortable enough on the stump to fill in for her husband, beginning with the 1934 campaign. Press accounts described her as a woman who was "at home with deep-sea fishing tackle, a shotgun, a garden spade, or a silver ladle at the banquet table." She also was credited with drafting some of her husband's speeches and influencing key decisions. Her campaign skills impressed enough people that she was mentioned as a potential gubernatorial candidate for 1938.[3]

Governor Graves's appointment of his wife in August 1937 provoked great controversy, but it also made political sense. Alabama, like other southern states at the time, was dominated by the Democratic Party, and power within the party was divided among local organizations and machines. Senator Hugo Black's departure for the Supreme Court had presented Governor Graves with an unexpected problem. The state constitution precluded Graves from filling the Senate vacancy himself, and there was an impressive list of viable claimants to the seat, each representing a substantial political constituency or faction in the state. One historian listed a former U.S. Senator, five U.S. Representatives, a state senator, an industrialist, and a lawyer as likely appointment prospects.[4] For Graves, described by associates as "a natural-born dealer," to appoint his wife meant that he did not have to choose among political factions within the state; he had left it to the voters to choose.[5] In addition, Dixie Graves's income as a Senator would be a welcome addition: the Senate rate was twice the governor's salary.[6]

Dixie Graves's appointment, however, was opposed by women's groups, newspapers, and many Alabama constituents. "In the Senate of the United States, where matters of such grave importance arise as to try the ability (and the souls) of veterans of many years, there is no place for a woman appointee unless her past experience would justify such action," one woman wrote to a Birmingham newspaper.[7] The *Birmingham Age-Herald* judged the governor's decision "repellent to the point of being offensive."[8] Dixie Graves was sworn in before the Senate on August 20, 1937, days before the first session of the 75th Congress

(1937–1939) ended.[9] She was seated in the "Cherokee Strip," the row of Democratic desks that took up the last row on the Republican side of the aisle due to the large Democratic majority. Graves suspected the seating was meant to send a message. "I'm supposed to be seen, perhaps," she said in a radio talk, "but certainly not heard."[10] During her five months in office she served on the Committee on Claims, the Committee on Education and Labor, and the Committee on Mines and Mining. In the Senate, she was not able to capitalize on her organizational background—she was regarded by her colleagues for what she was: an interim appointee, without her own political base and without a future. Her political acumen, however, stood her in good stead. When controversy broke out over revelations that her predecessor, Justice Hugo Black, had belonged to the Ku Klux Klan, she refrained from commenting on the issue. "That has nothing to do with me or with my office," she said.[11] "After a good look, shocked Washingtonians decided that Governor Graves could have made a worse appointment," *Time* soon reported.[12] During her brief Senate service Dixie Graves compiled a near-perfect attendance record and supported New Deal programs.[13]

For her part Senator Graves gained celebrity for her maiden Senate speech of November 19, 1937, during the southern filibuster against the Wagner–Van Nuys Anti-Lynching Bill. Originally, no one expected Graves to have a chance at participating much in Washington, but President Roosevelt had called a special session of Congress that fall. When she arrived back in the Capitol, she was anticipating supporting the administration in aiding farmers and expanding wage and hours benefits.[14] Instead, she found herself facing an angry Senate roiled during this filibuster. "I abhor lynching," she stated repeatedly as she related a brief history of lynching. "Mr. President, I rejoice, too, that in the South the constituted authorities, diligent about their business and strengthened by public opinion, are banishing the crime of lynching." She observed that lynchings had fallen by two-thirds during the previous decade, and she suggested that the crime would disappear in another few years. Graves concluded that there was no

compelling reason for federal intervention in a local law-enforcement issue: "surely only a compelling emergency should cause this body to strike down the sovereignty of an indestructible State and utilize the forces of the Federal Government to insure law and order. No such emergency exists. The problem is being solved." The appearance of the bill before the Senate, she judged, was not due to political maneuverings. If neither the facts nor political advantage had brought the bill before the Senate, she blamed the media. "When one case of lynching occurs in the South, the press of these United States blazons that fact forth throughout the length and breadth of the land, and in all of its details it reiterates all of the circumstances, and harps on the same thing so long that the average person in remote sections who himself does not know the truth is very apt to believe that an isolated case is a typical one," she said. Observers in the Senate Gallery said they saw tears in her eyes as Senator Graves appealed to her colleagues to defeat the bill. After her speech, Senators from both parties gathered around to congratulate her.[15]

Graves's speech evoked strong support in the South. "It was a hit," reported the *Washington Herald*.[16] "SHE SPOKE AS A DAUGHTER OF THE DEEP SOUTH" blared the *Montgomery Advertiser*.[17] The *Washington Post* pronounced the speech one of the best on the subject, making Graves the session's best "surprise."[18] While northern newspapers denounced Graves's remarks, Governor Graves distributed 10,000 copies of the speech throughout Alabama and bragged to reporters that he was "prouder than ever of my appointment and appointee. She's won her spurs by herself without help from anyone. She didn't need any."[19] Dixie Graves's popularity in Alabama rose to such an extent that a write-in campaign was started to elect her to the Senate seat. She made it very clear, though, that she was not interested. "I would not consider serving here for any protracted length of time," she said. "My husband's work keeps him in Alabama, and I want to be there."[20] Representative Lister Hill won the special election on January 4, 1938, defeating former Senator J. Thomas Heflin.

On January 10, 1938, Graves resigned from the Senate so that her husband might appoint Hill to the seat immediately. This customary practice provided added seniority for Hill over those Senators who would be first elected in November 1938. In a farewell floor speech, Graves took special care to thank her lone female colleague, Senator Hattie Caraway of Arkansas. "I am grateful indeed, to my fellow woman Senator, a woman who, though she first came to the Senate by appointment, yet has made such a name for herself and for womanhood that her own people have honored her with election to this great office," Graves noted, "and I do devoutly hope that in time to come their example will be followed in other states."[21] Senate Democratic Leader Alban Barkley added "no Senator, whether man or woman, who has come into this body in recent years, has made a more favorable impression." Barkley went on to add, "the Senator from Alabama has conducted herself with dignity and poise, with an intelligent and alert interest...."[22]

Back in Alabama, Dixie Graves resumed her civic activities while taking on new causes, such as the United Service Organization (USO), the American Red Cross, and a statewide recruitment drive for the Women's Army Auxiliary Corps during World War II. She also became the state advisor to the National Foundation for Infantile Paralysis.[23] When her husband died in 1942 while campaigning for a third term as governor, she did not step up to take his place. Bibb Graves had crafted a very personal political machine that did not survive his death.[24] While she was in Washington, Dixie Graves had put limits on her political future. "I have always been interested in public affairs and will continue to be, but I am not a candidate for office," she had said in 1937.[25] Dixie Graves remained active in local civic activities until her death in Montgomery, Alabama, on January 21, 1965.

FOR FURTHER READING

Biographical Directory of the United States Congress, "Dixie Bibb Graves," http://bioguide.congress.gov

Watson, Elbert "Dixie Bibb Graves," in *Alabama U.S. Senators* (Huntsville, AL: Strode Publishers, 1982): 127–131.

NOTES

1   Hope Chamberlin, *A Minority of Members: Women in the U.S. Congress* (New York: Praeger, 1973): 121.

2   V.O. Key, Jr., *Southern Politics in State and Nation* (Knoxville, University of Tennessee Press, 1949, 1984): 50.

3   "New Senator Knows Politics," 21 August 1937, *Christian Science Monitor*: 5 Chamberlin, *A Minority of Members*: 123; Elbert L. Watson, *Alabama United States Senators* (Huntsville, AL: Strode Publishers, 1982): 129.

4   Virginia Van der Veer Hamilton, *Lister Hill: Statesman from the South* (Chapel Hill: University of North Carolina Press, 1987): 76.

5   Key, *Southern Politics*: 51; "Keeping It in the Family: Governor's Wife for Senate?" 19 August 1937, *Christian Science Monitor*: 1; Watson, *Alabama United States Senators*: 129.

6   Chamberlin, *A Minority of Members*: 121.

7   Ibid., 122.

8   "Alabama Resents Its New Senator," 23 August 1937, *New York Times*: 5.

9   "Mrs. Graves Sworn; Heflin Out for Post," 21 August 1937, *New York Times*: 4; Chamberlin, *A Minority of Members*: 122.

10   Chamberlin, *A Minority of Members*: 123.

11   "Dixie Graves Refuses to Comment on Black," 20 September 1937, *New York Times*: 6

12   Chamberlin, *A Minority of Members*: 122.

13   Ibid., 125; Christine Sadler, "Woman Senator Finds Her Voice in Congress," 28 November 1937, *Washington Post*: B4; "Mrs. Graves Ends Service in Senate," 11 January 1938, *New York Times*: 19.

14   Sadler, "Woman Senator Finds Her Voice in Congress."

15   *Congressional Record*, Senate, 75th Cong., 2nd sess. (19 November 1937): 172–173; "Mrs. Graves Calms Stormy Senate By Appeal Against Lynching Bill," 20 November 1937, *New York Times*: 2; "Lynch Bill Foes Set to Talk All Plans to Death," 20 November 1937, *Washington Post*: 2.

16   Chamberlin, *A Minority of Members*: 124.

17   Ibid.

18   Watson, *Alabama United States Senators*: 130.

19   Chamberlin, *A Minority of Members*: 124; Sadler, "Woman Senator Finds Her Voice in Congress."

20   Sadler, "Woman Senator Finds Her Voice in Congress."

21   *Congressional Record*, Senate, 75th Cong., 2nd sess. (10 January 1938): 274.

22   Ibid., 274–275; "Mrs. Graves Ends Service in Senate."

23   Chamberlin, *A Minority of Members*: 125.

24   Key, *Southern Politics in State and Nation*: 52.

25   Sadler, "Woman Senator Finds Her Voice in Congress."

Elizabeth H. Gasque
1886–1989

UNITED STATES REPRESENTATIVE ★ DEMOCRAT FROM SOUTH CAROLINA
1938–1939

Elizabeth Hawley Gasque, the first woman U.S. Representative from South Carolina, carried on a lifelong love affair with Washington's social scene. The death of her husband, Representative Allard Gasque, briefly added a political dimension to her activities. "She was a Congressman's wife 20 years and a Congressman's widow," one journalist wrote in 1939, "who wound up his affairs and took care of his district as though it were her life's work."[1] Thereafter, she never broke her ties to the city.

She was born Elizabeth "Bessie" Mills Hawley near Blythewood, South Carolina, on February 26, 1886, daughter of John Meade and Emina Nelson Entzminger Hawley. Bessie Hawley was a member of the southern aristocracy and spent her childhood on the expansive "Rice Creek" plantation, which covered 4,000 acres.[2] She attended the South Carolina Coeducational Institute in Edgefield, South Carolina, and graduated with a degree in expression (drama) from Greenville Female College (now Furman University) in 1907. She married Allard H. Gasque, a teacher and school administrator, in 1907, and they had four children: Elizabeth, Doris, John, and Thomas.[3] Bessie Gasque became interested in politics through her social connections. Later she would boast that she had been personally acquainted with every President from Woodrow Wilson to Franklin Roosevelt.[4] In 1923, Allard Gasque won election to the first of eight terms as a U.S. Representative from South Carolina, eventually becoming the chairman of the Committee on Pensions and a champion of war veterans and their dependents.[5] It was during her husband's congressional service that Bessie Gasque fell in love with Washington, plunging into the social scene. She became one of the regular hosts of an annual ball to raise funds to fight polio, held on President Franklin Roosevelt's birthday. Washington became her "natural home."[6]

Chairman Gasque entered Walter Reed Hospital in Washington in May 1938 and died there on June 17, the day after the 75th Congress (1937–1939) adjourned.[7] At the time of his death, Gasque was unopposed for re-election. The district encompassed eight counties in northeastern South Carolina, including Gasque's home county of Florence. State and local Democratic leaders persuaded Bessie Gasque to run for her husband's unexpired term; even the filing fee was provided for her.[8] In the perfunctory one-party special election of September 13, 1938, Elizabeth Gasque succeeded her late husband in little more than name. The election took place on the same day as that for her successor. John L. McMillan, a former secretary to Allard Gasque, was elected to the full term in the 76th Congress (1939–1941).[9] The 75th Congress had already adjourned, and although there was always the possibility that the President would call for a special lame duck session, observers considered that highly unlikely.[10] She captured 96 percent of the vote compared to a combined four percent by her two male Democratic opponents.

Following the election, Congresswoman Gasque returned to Washington. The fall races, however, went badly for the Democrats nationwide. Earlier that summer, President Roosevelt had led unsuccessful efforts to campaign against opponents of the New Deal in Democratic Party primaries. The failure of the highly public "purge," along with losses for Roosevelt proponents in many northern races, signaled the beginning of the end of the New Deal.[11] This chain of events also ended any possibility for a special lame duck session.

OFFICE OF HISTORY AND PRESERVATION,
U.S. HOUSE OF REPRESENTATIVES

GASQUE "WAS A CONGRESSMAN'S WIFE 20 YEARS AND A CONGRESSMAN'S WIDOW," ONE JOURNALIST WROTE IN 1939, "WHO WOUND UP HIS AFFAIRS AND TOOK CARE OF HIS DISTRICT AS THOUGH IT WERE HER LIFE'S WORK."

Gasque never received any committee assignments, and she was never sworn into office. She did, however, continue to be a presence on Washington's social scene, attending a presidential reception held in honor of the new Secretary of Commerce, Harry Hopkins, in December 1938.[12]

After she left Congress in January 1939, Gasque returned to South Carolina. She maintained her social ties in Washington, remaining active largely through her membership in the Congressional Club. After former South Carolina Senator Nathaniel Dial died in Washington in 1940, Gasque shared a Washington home with Dial's widow, who was noted for her parties. Locally, Gasque was active in dramatics and was an author and lecturer. At one point she served as the head of the Fine Arts Department of South Carolina's Federation of Women's Clubs. In her many travels, she was a constant booster of South Carolina as a vacation destination.[13] She eventually married A.J. Van Exem. The couple lived at Cedar Tree Plantation in Ridgeway, South Carolina, where she became a master tree farmer. She died on November 2, 1989, at the age of 103.

FOR FURTHER READING

Biographical Directory of the United States Congress, "Elizabeth Hawley Gasque," http://bioguide.congress.gov

MANUSCRIPT COLLECTION

University of South Carolina (Columbia, SC), South Caroliniana Library. *Papers*: In the Allard Henry Gasque Papers, 1920–1938, 8.75 feet (14,406 items). Chiefly constituent correspondence relating to the Depression, politics, the appointment of postmasters, and the Inland Waterway. A finding aid is available in the repository and online: http://www.sc.edu/library/socar/mpc/gasque.html

NOTES

1 "Elizabeth G. Van Exem," 31 May 1979, *The State*: C1.
2 "Elizabeth G. Van Exem."
3 *Congressional Directory*, 68th Cong., 2nd sess. (December 1924): 104.
4 "Deaths: Mrs. Van Exem," 9 November 1989, *The Herald-Independent*: 12.
5 "Allard H. Gasque, Congressman, 65," 18 June 1938, *New York Times*: 15.
6 Hope Chamberlin, *A Minority of Members: Women in the U.S. Congress* (New York: Praeger, 1973): 115; "Elizabeth G. Van Exem."
7 "Allard H. Gasque, Congressman, 65."
8 "Elizabeth G. Van Exem."
9 *Congressional Record*, House, 76th Cong., 1st sess. (30 May 1939): 2458; John Lanneau McMillan Papers, Modern Political Collections, South Caroliniana Library, University of South Carolina. Available online at http://www.sc.edu/library/socar/mpc/ mcmillan.html (accessed 1 October 2003).
10 "Elected to Congress," 22 September 1938, *Washington Post*: x12; Bascom N. Timmons, *Garner of Texas: A Personal History* (New York: Harper, 1948): 235.
11 Michael Barone, *Our Country: The Shaping of America from Roosevelt to Reagan* (New York: Free Press, 1990): 120–122; Michael E. Parrish, *Anxious Decades: America in Prosperity and Depression, 1920–1941* (New York: Norton, 1992): 383–385.
12 "Elizabeth G. Van Exem."
13 Ibid.

Gladys S. Pyle
1890–1989

UNITED STATES SENATOR ★ REPUBLICAN FROM SOUTH DAKOTA
1938–1939

The short Senate career of Gladys S. Pyle stood in marked contrast with her long and influential participation in her native South Dakota's politics. A daughter of a leading suffragist and state attorney general, Pyle was oriented to public service from an early age. Her brief time as Senator, nevertheless, stood as a signal moment in a life of commitment to South Dakotans. "Citizenship," she once observed, "is service."[1]

Gladys Shields Pyle was born on October 4, 1890, in Huron, South Dakota, the youngest of four children of John L. Pyle and Mamie Shields Pyle. Her father was a lawyer, the South Dakota attorney general, and a patron of Huron College. Mamie Pyle led the Universal Franchise League, which eventually won the vote for South Dakota women in 1918. Both parents fostered in their children a commitment to public service from which young Gladys drew for the rest of her long life. After graduating with a liberal arts degree with a music emphasis from Huron College in 1911, Gladys Pyle took graduate courses at the American Conservatory of Music and the University of Chicago. In 1912, she returned to Huron, where she taught high school until 1918, when she accepted a position as principal of a school in Wessington, North Dakota. Two years later she left teaching to work briefly as a lecturer for the League of Women Voters, traveling to several midwestern states to deliver talks on citizenship and voter participation.[2] Pyle never married.

Gladys Pyle made the transition to politics in order to put into practice what she had preached in the classroom. Years later she described her lifelong political philosophy as being that of a Progressive, moderate Republican.[3] "Politics . . . is like sailing a boat," Pyle observed. "You have to learn to tack, going from one side of the river to the other. It takes a little longer, but you can make good

progress."[4] Political activism was requisite for her.[5] Ironically, she embarked on her new career against the advice of her mother, who had reservations about Gladys running for elective office, perhaps because she believed it would make her daughter vulnerable to charges of riding her mother's coattails.[6] Undeterred, 32-year-old Gladys Pyle ran for the state legislature in 1922, winning election to the South Dakota house of representatives by a slender 350 votes. Pyle, the first woman elected to the state legislature, served an additional two terms and was instrumental in gaining South Dakota's ratification of the Child Labor Amendment to the U.S. Constitution.[7] During her time in the legislature, Pyle also served as assistant secretary of state. In 1926, she became the first woman elected as South Dakota secretary of state. She served for two terms from 1927 to 1931, introducing some of the nation's first safety codes for automobiles and motorcycles.[8]

In March 1930, Pyle made national headlines when she entered the GOP primary for South Dakota governor against four men, including former Governor Carl Gunderson and Brooke Howell, a favorite of state financiers. Pyle refused to take to the campaign trail, citing her responsibilities as secretary of state. She did, however, launch a targeted public relations blitz at newspaper editors, state delegates, and GOP county chairmen. Her campaign centered on the issue of banking reform and tighter control of miscellaneous state funds. Her slogan was, "Clean up the banks." Pyle surprised observers by winning more votes than any of her rivals—and topping her nearest contender, Gunderson, by about 1,600 votes. The 28 percent she polled, however, fell short of the 35 percent minimum required by law. The nomination was decided at a special state GOP convention in Sioux Falls in May 1930. Howell, Pyle's chief rival, eventually withdrew from the race and on the 12th ballot threw his support behind Warren E. Green, a dirt farmer who had won just seven percent of the primary vote.[9] Green prevailed. For Pyle, the episode revealed that her public career had reached something of a political glass ceiling, as the state's political old guard refused to back her.[10] From 1931 to 1933, Pyle served by appointment as secretary of the securities commission of South Dakota.[11] As secretary of the commission, she became the first woman in the state to run an executive department and the first woman permitted onto the floor of the New York Curb Market.[12] Except for her brief time in Washington, from 1933 until the 1980s, Gladys Pyle went into business as an insurance agent for two national companies.

Pyle took a circuitous route to the U.S. Senate, shaped by tragedy and peculiarities in South Dakota election laws. In late December 1936, Progressive-Republican Senator Peter Norbeck of South Dakota died after a long illness. Outgoing Democratic Governor Tom Berry, who had been defeated by a Republican in the November elections, quickly appointed Democrat Herbert Hitchcock to fill the vacancy. However, by state law, Hitchcock had to step down once the next regularly scheduled general election took place in November 1938. While a new Senator would be elected for the full term from 1939–1945, technically the seat would remain vacant from November 1938 until a successor was sworn into office in January 1939. The 75th Congress (1937–1939) had adjourned in June 1938 to prepare for the elections, and it was customary that it would not reconvene until the start of the 76th Congress (1939–1941) in January 1939. Normally, such a vacancy would provoke little concern. But as the 1938 elections took shape, rumors swirled that President Roosevelt would call for a special session after the elections to capitalize on the existing Democratic margins in both chambers of Congress. In response, the South Dakota Republican Party, which dominated the congressional delegation, pushed for a special election and sought a candidate to fill the two-month term. GOP candidate Chandler Gurney had won the nomination for the full term, but state laws prevented his name from appearing twice on the ballot.[13]

GOP leaders turned to Gladys Pyle because she had enough name recognition and support to win without the party having to invest considerable resources in the race. She traveled the state to campaign on behalf of the entire GOP ticket, with support from the Republican National Committee, arguing that the New Deal had not done enough for South Dakotans. Pyle also tapped into a strong statewide network of Republican women's clubs.[14] Recognizing that her term would be brief, voters went to the polls on November 8, 1938, and chose the 48-year-old Pyle seemingly as a gesture of appreciation for her service to the state. She registered a resounding win over Democrat John T. McCullen, 58 to 42 percent of the vote, garnering nearly 10,000 votes more than the next-best vote getter on the ticket—Gurney, who won the election for the full term. It also made her the first Republican woman elected to the Senate and the first woman from either party to win election to the Senate in her own right, without having first been appointed to fill a vacancy.

Because Congress already had adjourned, and FDR never did call a special session, Pyle was never officially sworn in to the Senate. Despite the lack of committee assignments and legislative duties, she left Huron the day after Thanksgiving and drove to Washington, D.C., with her mother and an aide and spent the next five weeks in the capital as South Dakota's Senator. She paid her own travel expenses because Members only received mileage costs if they were commuting to and from a session of Congress.[15] Once in Washington, she and an interim appointee from California shared an office space customarily reserved for one Senator.[16]

Pyle did not lack for things to do. She rallied support for her Depression-burdened state by pushing various highway and Works Progress Administration (WPA) programs. Pyle intervened with the Department of the Interior on behalf of landholders on Indian reservations who had suffered years of ruined crops and fallen far behind on mortgage payments. She also handled cases with the Bureau of Indian Affairs, investigated the sale of land inside a state park, and worked to expand funding for WPA projects within her state. Pyle tended to individual constituent needs ranging from pensions and hospitalization to civil service ratings.[17] In addition, she persuaded Norwegian officials to schedule a June 1939 visit to South Dakota of the crown prince and princess of Norway during their North American travels, delighting thousands of South Dakotans of Scandinavian heritage.[18] "I wish I had come the day after the election," Pyle admitted as her term expired. "Just because the Senate is not in session is no sign a Senator cannot be of service to her constituents."[19]

In January 1939, Pyle returned to her insurance business and stayed closely involved in public service work. At the 1940 GOP Convention in Philadelphia, she became the first woman to nominate a presidential candidate, backing South Dakota Governor Harlan J. Bushfield.[20] During that same year, she also made an unsuccessful bid for mayor of her hometown of Huron.[21] From 1943 to 1957, Pyle served on the South Dakota board of charities and corrections. In 1947, she and five other women became the first in state history to serve on a jury, as South Dakota dropped its all-male requirement. Pyle lived in Huron and was involved in numerous charities and civic organizations. In 1980, on her 90th birthday, the town named Pyle its "First Citizen." At the age of 98, Gladys Pyle died on March 14, 1989, in Huron.

FOR FURTHER READING

Biographical Directory of the United States Congress, "Gladys Pyle," http://bioguide.congress.gov

Kinyon, Jeanette, and Jean Walz. *The Incredible Gladys Pyle* (Vermillion: Dakota Press, University of South Dakota, 1985).

MANUSCRIPT COLLECTION

University of South Dakota (Vermillion, SD), I.D. Weeks Library, Richardson Archive. Pyle Family Papers: six feet. The collection includes correspondence. A finding aid is available in the repository.

NOTES

1 Hope Chamberlin, *A Minority of Members: Women in the U.S. Congress* (New York: Praeger, 1976): 126.

2 Although Gladys Pyle enjoyed her time as a teacher, she opted not to return to the classroom after taking a hiatus to care for her ailing sister-in-law. Rejecting offers to return to teaching in her hometown because of low pay and few advancement possibilities, Pyle transformed her love of civics into a profession, teaching women how to become politically active. Jeannette Kinyon and Jean Walz, *The Incredible Gladys Pyle* (Vermillion: University of South Dakota, 1985): 28–29.

3 Kinyon and Walz, *The Incredible Gladys Pyle*: 36.

4 Kim Ode, "From Equal Rights to Elm Trees," 6 July 1980, *Sioux Falls Argus Leader*: 2B.

5 Chamberlin, *A Minority of Members*: 127; a variation may be found in Kinyon and Walz, *The Incredible Gladys Pyle*: 72.

6 Kinyon and Walz, *The Incredible Gladys Pyle*: 36.

7 In 1924 both the House and Senate adopted the Child Labor Amendment. The proposed amendment authorized Congress to "limit, regulate and prohibit the labor of persons under eighteen years of age." It failed to be ratified by the necessary three-fourths of the states. David E. Kyvig, *Explicit and Authentic Acts: Amending the Constitution, 1776–1995* (Lawrence: University of Kansas Press, 1996): 254–261.

8 Kinyon and Walz, *The Incredible Gladys Pyle*: 35.

9 Richard V. Oulahan, "Republicans Face South Dakota Test," 9 October 1930, *New York Times*: 18; "Green Takes South Dakota Race," 21 May 1930, *Washington Post*: 2; Kinyon and Walz, *The Incredible Gladys Pyle*: 39–41.

10 Kinyon and Walz, *The Incredible Gladys Pyle*: 42.

11 Pyle was appointed by Governor Green, who had earlier pledged to clean up banking laws in the state.

12 Founded in 1842 and later named the American Stock Exchange.

13 Kinyon and Walz, *The Incredible Gladys Pyle*: 43.

14 Ibid., 44.

15 "Two Senators Elected to 2 Months' Pay Only," 10 November 1938, *New York Times*: 1.

16 "The Political Arena," 16 November 1938, *Washington Post*: 2.

17 "Two Months' Senatorship Costly, Says Miss Pyle," 2 January 1939 *New York Times*: 24.

18 Kinyon and Walz, *The Incredible Gladys Pyle*: 45–46.

19 "Senate Terms to End for 3 Before They Ever Take Seats," 28 December 1938, *Washington Post*: X15.

20 Kathleen McLaughlin, "Women Are Divided Over Merits of Proposed Equal Rights Plank in Platform," 28 June 1940, *New York Times*: 5; "Only Woman Nominator Names South Dakota's 'Favorite Son,'" 28 June 1940, *Christian Science Monitor*: 8.

21 Kinyon and Walz, *The Incredible Gladys Pyle*: 59.

Jessie Sumner
1898–1994

UNITED STATES REPRESENTATIVE ★ REPUBLICAN FROM ILLINOIS
1939–1947

Few Members of Congress so vocally denounced the Franklin Roosevelt administration and American intervention in World War II as Illinois Representative Jessie Sumner. Sumner not only advocated American isolationism, she reveled in it—using her biting wit and animated floor speeches to skewer wartime policies, America's major allies, and plans for U.S. participation in the postwar United Nations. By war's end, however, as an internationalist mood took hold in the country, it was Congresswoman Sumner who found herself increasingly isolated.

Jessie Sumner was born in Milford, Illinois, on July 17, 1898, to Aaron Taylor Sumner and Elizabeth Gillan Sumner. Her ancestors included such distant relations as General Zachary Taylor, who became the 12th American President, and outspoken antislavery Senator Charles Sumner of Massachusetts. Jessie Sumner graduated from the Girton School in Winnetka, Illinois, in 1916. She earned an economics degree at Smith College in Northampton, Massachusetts, in 1920. Jessie Sumner never married and relished the freedom that unwed life afforded her.[1] She studied law at the University of Chicago, Oxford University in England, and Columbia University and briefly at the University of Wisconsin at Madison. In 1923 she passed the Illinois bar and commenced practice as a private lawyer in Chicago. On the eve of the Great Depression, Sumner took a job with Chase National Bank in New York City. By 1932, she had returned to Milford, Illinois, to resume her law practice and work as a director at Sumner National Bank, which her father had founded. Her move into politics was abetted, in part, by bank robbers who abducted her brother. After the kidnappers were apprehended, she worked

feverishly to secure their convictions and was inspired to run for the office of state's attorney. Sumner lost in the GOP primary but, with the passing of her uncle, John H. Gillan, the Iroquois County judge, she ran a successful campaign in 1937 to succeed him. Sumner received national notoriety by becoming the first woman to hold a county judgeship in her state.[2]

Iroquois County was one of six jurisdictions along Illinois' eastern border with Indiana, incorporating the district once represented by "Uncle" Joe Cannon, the autocratic Republican leader and House Speaker. In 1938, Sumner used her new political influence to secure the district's GOP nomination. In the general election, serving as her own campaign manager, she faced three-term incumbent Democrat James A. Meeks, a 74-year-old lawyer. Rather than smothering her audiences with platitudes, Sumner pledged nothing more than to work hard for good government.[3] Her primary theme was a consistent attack against New Deal programs which, she argued, overtaxed Americans and intruded on their individual liberties. In particular, she singled out Roosevelt as practicing "one-man government," a charge that resonated with an electorate outraged by the President's ham-handed attempt to pack the Supreme Court with justices favorable to his programs. With the backing of the anti-Roosevelt *Chicago Tribune*, Sumner defeated Meeks with 55 percent of the vote. She joined 76 new Republicans when the 76th Congress (1939–1941) convened in January 1939.

Within weeks, Sumner emerged as a darling of the Washington press, tossing out "Sumnerisms" which provoked her opponents and delighted extreme proponents of isolationism and rolling back the New Deal.[4] The day she was sworn in, reporters asked for her evaluation of

President Roosevelt as a politician. "I am here to bury Caesar—not to praise him," Sumner quipped.[5] She referred to FDR as "Papa Roosevelt" and the "Great Spender."[6] Popular among Members for her self-deprecating style, Sumner even took to joking about her marital status and wardrobe.[7] After failing to secure a seat on the Agriculture Committee, Sumner earned a spot on the Banking and Currency Committee—her single committee assignment during her eight years in the House. Though an Agriculture seat may have more directly benefited the many farmers in her district, voters did not seem to mind that Sumner's committee assignment conferred fewer prizes. She made several speeches pressing the case that New Deal relief programs failed to alleviate the tax burden that beset American farmers.[8]

While opposition to domestic policies got her elected, the imperatives of military preparedness absorbed Sumner's attention in Congress. After World War II erupted in September 1939, Sumner opposed amending the Neutrality Act to lift the arms embargo in favor of a "cash and carry" policy, whereby belligerents could buy American war materials and transport them in their own ships. In the fall of 1940 she opposed the Burke–Wadsworth Selective Service Bill, which established the first peacetime draft in the country's history. A year later she voted against its extension and against the arming of American merchant ships ferrying war materials to Europe. She also rejected direct American aid to the British, expressing grave reservations that the President was nudging the country to war, having struck a secret alliance with London. Sumner laced her speeches with anglophobia and subtle admiration for Nazi Germany's militarization.[9] In 1939, she introduced a joint resolution to prevent U.S. participation in foreign combat without congressional consent. "We have more to fear from an American invasion of Europe," Sumner declared, "than from a European invasion of America."[10]

President Roosevelt was Sumner's target of opportunity, but her attacks also sought to rouse Congress to preserve its oversight powers and prerogative to shape American foreign policy. Sumner hoped to rein in FDR's powers by using the House's authority to originate and pass appropriations, even over the President's veto. "Today when the White House endeavors to control your votes as Representatives, by promising to approve or threatening to withhold projects for your district, they are using a power which you delegated to the Executive very recently," Sumner warned colleagues. "It is an abuse of that power. It robs you of your right and duty to vote your convictions."[11]

Sumner's isolationism mirrored that of her constituency. In her first bid for re-election in 1940, Sumner again defeated Meeks with 53 versus 47 percent of the vote. She won against two other candidates by even wider margins in 1942 and 1944, with 62 percent and 57 percent, respectively.[12] Increasingly, however, the Illinois Congresswoman found herself moving against the current in Washington.

Sumner's strident attacks on the FDR administration were only amplified after America joined the war. Most significantly, she opposed opening a Western Europe front to relieve pressure on the Soviet Union. In March 1944, Sumner took to the House Floor to declare that it made no difference whether Hitler or Stalin dominated Europe and warned an invasion might cost a million lives. "The difference between these two ambitious tyrants is not worth the life of a single American boy," she declared.[13] That spring Sumner offered an amendment to postpone the long anticipated D-Day, calling the proposed invasion a "quixotism." Simultaneously, she submitted a bill to enlarge the Pacific campaign, vesting all military authority in General Douglas MacArthur.[14]

One of Sumner's few legislative achievements during the Second World War came during consideration of a $20 billion naval appropriations bill in January 1942, when she secured an amendment (passed without dissent) that prohibited the use of parties, champagne, or gifts during the launching of new ships.[15] She introduced a bill for an Equal Rights Amendment with language modified to help women to enter the wartime workforce.[16] Sumner also urged passage of a bill to provide childcare facilities in war industry factories, to permit more women to join the job market.[17]

"TODAY WHEN THE WHITE HOUSE ENDEAVORS TO CONTROL YOUR VOTES AS REPRESENTATIVES, BY PROMISING TO APPROVE OR THREATENING TO WITHHOLD PROJECTS FOR YOUR DISTRICT, THEY ARE USING A POWER WHICH YOU DELEGATED TO THE EXECUTIVE VERY RECENTLY. IT IS AN ABUSE OF THAT POWER. IT ROBS YOU OF YOUR RIGHT AND DUTY TO VOTE YOUR CONVICTIONS."

—JESSIE SUMNER
U.S. HOUSE OF REPRESENTATIVES FLOOR SPEECH
JUNE 29, 1939

As the debate shifted from waging war to structuring the peace, Sumner's enthusiasm grew for withdrawing completely from world affairs and retreating into "fortress America." She opposed American involvement in a world organization, echoing Joe Cannon's reservations about the old League of Nations that it might become a "league of appropriations" financed by Washington.[18] Sumner denounced Representative J. William Fulbright's 1943 resolution endorsing U.S. participation in the establishment of international machinery to maintain peace, as "the most dangerous bill ever presented to an American Congress."[19] The House approved the measure, 360 to 29. In December 1945, the House overwhelmingly ratified participation in the postwar United Nations, 344 to 15. Sumner was one of 14 Republicans and one Progressive to vote against it.

In Stalin's hands, Sumner insisted, such a world government would be put to more sinister uses. Fearing that the Soviet Union might use its supervisory power over relief operations to influence the policies of countries it had liberated from German occupation, Sumner also rejected the establishment of the United Nations Relief and Rehabilitation Administration (UNRRA).[20] The House strongly supported UNRRA, which housed, clothed, and fed millions of refugees in Europe after the war. In June 1945, Sumner criticized legislation authorizing the Bretton Woods Agreements, which established the World Bank and the International Monetary Fund. Describing both agencies as the worst fraud in American history, she warned that foreign governments would have unrestricted access to American capital.[21] Her former professor at Smith College, now fellow committee member, Chase Woodhouse of Connecticut, debated her on the merits of the Bretton Woods Agreements. When Sumner proposed to join the Bank but not the Fund, her amendment went down to defeat, 328 to 29. Sumner again was in the distinct minority when the measure to enter both agencies came before the House —just one of 18 Republicans in the "No" column.

Sumner had publicly announced in early 1944 that she would not seek re-election to the 79th Congress (1945–1947). "Being a Congressman in war-time is a heartbreaking job," she observed, citing her "growing sense of frustration."[22] She lamented the fact that Congress exercised little power over foreign policy.[23] Weeks later she recanted her decision, noting her determination to oppose administration policies she believed would precipitate war with Russia. Though she won re-election in November 1944, national results, including FDR's re-election to an unprecedented fourth term, convinced Sumner that the President's internationalist policies had triumphed.[24] In 1946, she chose to retire to private life in Milford as a director and, after 1966, as president of Sumner National Bank. Jessie Sumner worked there until her death on August 10, 1994, in Watseka, near Milford.

FOR FURTHER READING

Biographical Directory of the United States Congress, "Jessie Sumner," http://bioguide.congress.gov

NOTES

1   *Current Biography, 1945* (New York: H.W. Wilson Company, 1945): 579–581.

2   "Illinois Woman Elected Judge," 8 December 1937, *Christian Science Monitor*: 7.

3   Christine Sadler, "Rep. Sumner Is Here With Quips Falling Everywhere—Principally on the New Deal," 15 January 1939, *Washington Post*: B4.

4   Pauline Frederick, "Epigrams Coined By Woman Solon," 5 February 1939, *New York Times*: D4.

5   Edward T. Folliard, "Chastened Air of Democrats Marks Opening of Congress," 4 January 1939, *Washington Post*: 1.

6   *Congressional Record,* House, 76th Cong., 1st sess. (19 June 1939): 7469.

7   "Will Illinois M.C. Primp? No!" 16 November 1938, *Christian Science Monitor*: 1; Frederick, "Epigrams Coined By Woman Solon."

8   *Congressional Record,* House, 76th Cong., 1st sess. (24 March 1939): 3266.

9   *Congressional Record,* House, 76th Cong., 1st sess. (1 November 1939): 1258–1259; *Congressional Record,* House, 76th Cong., 1st sess. (2 October 1939): 91–92; see also, Kathleen McLaughlin, "Hail Mrs. Willkie in Women's Party: Miss Sumner Says New Deal Is Keeping Its Foreign Policy Secret," 1 October 1940, *New York Times*: 14.

10 *Congressional Record,* House, 76th Cong., 1st sess. (1 November 1939): 1258; Jessie Ash Arendt, "Rep. Sumner Demands Strict U.S. Neutrality," 3 October 1939, *Washington Post*: 13.

11 *Congressional Record,* House, 76th Cong., 1st sess. (29 June 1939): 8286.

12 "Election Statistics, 1920 to Present," http://clerk.house.gov/members/electionInfo/elections.html. Sadler, "Rep. Sumner Is Here With Quips Falling Everywhere—Principally on the New Deal."

13 "Miss Sumner Protests Invasion," 30 March 1944, *New York Times*: 11.

14 "Rep. Sumner Denied Hearing on Bills to Postpone Invasion," 27 March 1944, *Washington Post*: 7; "Miss Sumner Backs Bills to Shift War," 15 March 1944, *New York Times*: 4.

15 *Congressional Record,* House, 77th Cong., 2nd sess. (27 January 1942): 755.

16 *Congressional Record,* House, 77th Cong., 2nd sess. (21 July 1942): 6474–6476.

17 *Current Biography, 1945*: 580.

18 *Congressional Record,* House, 78th Cong., 1st sess. (10 March 1943): 1809.

19 *Congressional Record,* House, 78th Cong., 1st sess. (20 September 1943): 7681–7682.

20 *Congressional Record,* House, 78th Cong., 2nd sess. (20 January 1944): 471–472.

21 *Congressional Record,* House, 79th Cong, 1st sess. (17 July 1945): 7656–7657; 7542–7544.

22 Annabel Paxton, *Women In Congress* (Richmond: Dietz Press, 1945): 62.

23 "Miss Sumner Won't Seek Re-Election to Congress," 6 January 1944, *New York Times*: 21.

24 "Woman Representative Decides to Run Again," 8 February 1944, *Christian Science Monitor*: 9.

Clara G. McMillan
1894–1976

UNITED STATES REPRESENTATIVE ★ DEMOCRAT FROM SOUTH CAROLINA
1939–1941

A one-term Representative from South Carolina, Clara G. McMillan faced the growing menace of war in Europe from the perspective of being a recent widow and a mother of five young sons.

Clara E. Gooding was the second daughter born to William and Mary Gooding in Brunson, South Carolina, on August 17, 1894. She graduated from the public schools in her hometown and later attended the Confederate Home College in Charleston and the Flora McDonald College in Red Springs, North Carolina. She married Thomas Sanders McMillan, a lawyer who served in the South Carolina house of representatives from 1917 to 1924. During his last two years, he served as speaker of the South Carolina house. In 1924, he won election to the U.S. House of Representatives, where he served eight terms and eventually became a high-ranking member of the Appropriations Committee. Throughout her husband's congressional service, Clara McMillan remained in Charleston, South Carolina, raising their five sons: Thomas, Jr., James, William, Edward, and Robert.[1] From a distance, she nevertheless kept in "close contact and cooperation" with Thomas's legislative policies.[2]

When Thomas McMillan died on September 29, 1939, South Carolina Democratic Party leaders chose Clara McMillan to run in the special election to fill her husband's coastal Carolina seat. Like most southern states, South Carolina operated under a one-party system in the early 20th century, wherein winning the Democratic nomination was tantamount to winning the general election. Less from a sense of chivalry toward a widow than the need to head off an intraparty fight among aspirants for the seat, local political leaders chose McMillan to fill out the remaining year of her husband's term. Against two weak opponents, Shep Hutto of Dorchester and James De Fieville of Walterboro, she won election to the House with 79 percent of the vote on November 7, 1939, to represent a sprawling district that covered Charleston and nine adjacent low-country counties.[3] Afterward, McMillan, who had campaigned on her familiarity with her husband's work, said she "felt it would come out as it did" because "I told the voters I would carry on his work."[4] A group of Berkeley County voters filed a protest to invalidate the special election because, they argued, the secrecy of the ballot was not maintained.[5] The South Carolina supreme court overruled the protest in late December, and McMillan took her seat in Congress at the opening of the third session of the 76th Congress (1939–1941) on January 3, 1940.

In a session that lasted a full year, McMillan served on the Committee on Patents; the Committee on Public Buildings and Grounds; and the Committee on the Election of the President, Vice President, and Representatives in Congress. In addition to answering constituent requests, some minor work engaged her interests. She introduced legislation to provide for the designation of individual domiciles in income tax returns and to allow local police officers to mail firearms for repairs. But these were secondary considerations.

The threat of American involvement in the war in Europe dominated the business of the final session of the 76th Congress. The Second World War had erupted in Europe on September 1, 1939, with the German invasion of Poland. In advocating for military preparedness, McMillan, like many of her colleagues, insisted that federal resources be devoted to defensive measures. "Perhaps it is true that geographically we are so situated that a serious invasion by any one of the powers engaged in present world conflicts is virtually impossible," McMillan told colleagues in a floor speech. "But conditions change rapidly ... press, radio, and motion pictures bring us every day new and more striking evidence of the futility of invoking treaties, covenants, and moral sanctions against a well-prepared aggressor. He understands only one language and we must learn to speak that language well. I believe firmly in military and naval preparedness."[6]

Conditions in Europe outpaced the push for preparedness in America. In the months following McMillan's speech, the situation for the Allies grew grim as German troops invaded France and, within six weeks, occupied Paris and forced the capitulation of the French army. Berlin's "blitzkrieg" warfare had swept resistance out of western Europe and isolated Great Britain, America's closest traditional ally.

These developments forced McMillan and her colleagues to countenance not only how to create an effective deterrent force but how to raise an army to fight a war that, daily, America seemed less able to avoid. McMillan took to the House Floor and, in an impassioned speech that drew much applause, spoke in favor of the Burke–Wadsworth Selective Service Bill of 1940, which established the nation's first peacetime draft. The concept of universal military training ("UMT," as it was known at the time) marked a radical departure for many Americans. Looking to past traditions as well as modern totalitarian governments abroad, many had believed that domestic liberties could not coexist with a large standing army that might be used to quash internal dissent. McMillan disagreed for both political and personal reasons. She supported President Franklin Roosevelt's foreign policy broadly and realized that Charleston, the district's largest city, would have a major role to play as a center for naval operations. But there were other reasons, too, which compelled her support for UMT. "I have five sons. The oldest will come immediately under the operation of the bill and be subject to its provisions, as he is past 21 years," McMillan told her colleagues. "My second son is almost 19 years old and is now taking military training in a school organized for that purpose. If and when my sons are needed for the defense of their country, I do not want them to go up against experienced soldiers, untrained and unskilled."[7] Three days later, the draft bill passed Congress and was signed into law.

Meanwhile, by the summer of 1940, South Carolina Democratic leaders had found their favored strong horse, Lucius Mendel Rivers, to replace their interim candidate. McMillan declined re-nomination for a full term when local politicos threw their support behind Rivers. Mendel Rivers, a young lawyer and South Carolina state representative from 1933 to 1936, went on to represent the district for nearly 30 years and eventually rose to chair the Committee on Armed Services. In the process he helped make Charleston the locus of one of the largest military establishments on the East Coast. When McMillan left Congress in 1941, she continued her government service with the National Youth Administration, the Office of Government Reports in the Office of War Information, and, from 1946 to 1957, as information liaison officer in the Department of State. Clara McMillan retired to Barnwell, South Carolina, where she died on November 8, 1976.

FOR FURTHER READING

Biographical Directory of the United States Congress, "Clara Gooding McMillan," http://bioguide.congress.gov

MANUSCRIPT COLLECTION

The University of South Carolina (Columbia, SC), Modern Political Collections, South Caroliniana Library. The Thomas S. and Clara G. McMillan Papers, ca. 1870–1980, 0.5 linear foot. The papers include general papers, speeches, photographs, clippings, and ephemera for Thomas and Clara McMillan. Of particular interest is correspondence from Clara McMillan to her son Edward after her retirement, as well as photographs documenting her Mother of the Year ceremonies, 1960, and highway dedication, 1980.

NOTES

1   *Congressional Directory*, 70th Cong., 2nd sess., 1929 (Washington, D.C.: Government Printing Office, 1929): 110.
2   "Mrs. McMillan to Carry on Husband's Work in Congress," 9 November 1939, *Washington Post*: 2.
3   Michael Dubin et al., *United States Congressional Elections, 1788–1997* (Jefferson, NC: McFarland & Company Publishing, Inc., 1998): 529.
4   "Mrs. McMillan to Carry on Husband's Work in Congress."
5   "Court Upholds Mrs. McMillan's Election to House," 28 December 1939, *Washington Post*: 1.
6   *Congressional Record*, House, 76th Cong., 3rd sess. (3 April 1940): 3954.
7   *Congressional Record*, House, 76th Cong., 3rd sess. (4 September 1940): 11448–11449.

Frances Payne Bolton
1885–1977

UNITED STATES REPRESENTATIVE ★ REPUBLICAN FROM OHIO
1940–1969

At one time celebrated as the richest woman in America, Frances Payne Bolton of Ohio shed the comfortable life of a trust fund beneficiary to enter the political arena. Her cosmopolitan upbringing and range of interests—from public health to Buddhism to economic development in sub-Saharan Africa—shaped much of her long career in Congress. From her seat on the House Foreign Affairs Committee, Representative Bolton influenced American foreign policy from World War II to the Vietnam War.

Frances Payne Bingham was born in Cleveland, Ohio, on March 29, 1885, to Charles W. Bingham and Mary Perry Payne Bingham. Her family's ties to the Standard Oil fortune permitted them to travel widely and to provide schooling for Frances at elite finishing schools and with private tutors. Her family also had a long history of public service. Mary Bingham's father, Henry B. Payne, served as an Ohio Representative and Senator in the late 1800s. On September 14, 1907, Frances Bingham married attorney Chester Castle Bolton. Mrs. Frances Bolton later became involved with a visiting nurses' program in Cleveland's tenements. During World War I, the couple and their three sons—Charles, Kenyon, and Oliver—moved to Washington, where Chester Bolton served on the War Industries Board and his wife worked with various nursing groups. During the war, she also inherited a trust fund established by her uncle, Oliver Hazard Payne, a founder of Standard Oil. The bequest made Bolton one of the world's wealthiest women and allowed her to establish the Payne Fund, which eventually distributed grants into areas of particular interest to her. In 1919, Bolton and her newborn daughter fell victim to a worldwide influenza epidemic. The baby died, and she barely survived, adopting a strict regimen of yoga exercises to aid her recovery. She also acquired an interest in eastern religions, shaping her spiritual life around Buddhism.[1]

While in Washington, Chester Bolton established himself as a powerful politician. From 1923 to 1928, he served in the Ohio state senate before winning election in 1928 to the first of five terms in the U.S. House of Representatives from a district representing outlying Cleveland. The family lived in Washington until his defeat in the 1936 elections and returned to Ohio, where Frances Bolton served on the state Republican Central Committee. Though in poor health, Chester Bolton regained his House seat in 1938 and again relocated the family to Washington for the opening of the 76th Congress (1939–1941) in January 1939. On October 29 of that year, Chester Bolton died. When Frances Bolton decided to seek her late husband's House seat, the Ohio GOP gave her a muted reception but eventually backed the nomination out of a sense of obligation to Chester Bolton's memory. "A few of [the party leaders] opposed my nomination," Bolton recalled, "but most of them thought it would be a graceful gesture which would do them no harm since they were sure I would get tired of politics in a few months, and flit on to something else."[2] Her deep pockets, both for her own campaign and the party's statewide effort, factored into her initial 1940 campaign success. She won the February 27, 1940, special election by a 2–1 margin, a greater plurality than her husband had enjoyed in any of his campaigns. Later, in the fall of 1940, Bolton defeated her Democratic challenger with 57 percent of the vote, polling more total votes than any other House candidate in the state. Bolton was never seriously challenged in her subsequent 13 re-elections in her district, the largest by population in the country, boasting a mix of shipbuilding, foreign-born residents as well as long-standing, wealthy inhabitants.[3] The first woman elected from Ohio, she also became the only mother to serve simultaneously with her son, Oliver H. Bolton, when he represented a district east of his mother's for three terms in the 1950s.

As a Member of the 76th Congress, Bolton served on the Committee on Indian Affairs; the Committee on Expenditures in the Executive Departments; and the Committee on Election of the President, Vice President and Representatives. After her re-election to the succeeding Congress, the well-traveled Bolton resigned those minor assignments for a better seat on the Committee on Foreign Affairs, where she served throughout her tenure in the House. Eventually, Bolton rose to the Ranking Minority Member post of Foreign Affairs. In addition to her standing committee assignments, Bolton served from 1955 to 1965 on the House Republican Policy Committee, which determined committee assignments and party positions on issues before the House.

Bolton entered the House in March 1940, little more than six months into the Second World War. Though starting as a moderate isolationist, she slowly came to support military preparedness. Yet, she held out late hope that America could avoid intervention. With some reservation, she supported the Lend-Lease program to sell weapons and warships and to provide monetary aid to the Allies in 1940. She opposed revision of the 1939 Neutrality Act, arguing that while she supported making America the "arsenal of Hitler's foes," President Roosevelt was obliged to "make no move to precipitate us into war."[4] As late as November 1941, Bolton still was reluctant to commit American forces to the conflict. "I beg you, think most carefully before you commit this land of ours . . . to go into a war [to] which most of her people are opposed, and to do so secretly under the cover of promises of peace," she appealed to her colleagues. "I can follow the President a long way, and I have done my best to help him keep his word to . . . our people that we shall not go into war."[5] The Japanese attack on Pearl Harbor moved Bolton firmly into

the internationalist camp. "I have not agreed with the foreign policies of the administration," Bolton admitted. "But all that is past. We are at war and there is no place in our lives for anything that will not build our strength and power, and build it quickly."[6] So complete was her turn that by June 1943, Bolton took to the House Floor to voice her support for the Fulbright Resolution, which passed the House and declared America's intention to participate in postwar international organizations.[7]

Bolton's primary wartime focus was in the realm of health care, a subject that had interested her since World War I. As early as May 1940, she had broached the idea of an army school of nursing on the House Floor.[8] In 1943, she authored the $5 million Bolton Act, creating a U.S. Cadet Nurse Corps, which one year later, had trained some 124,000 nurses. In exchange for the education, these nurses committed to a tour of duty in the armed services or in an essential civilian posts for a period of time after their training. The Bolton Act also demonstrated the Congresswoman's sympathy for African-American civil rights, as it stipulated that funding be allocated without regard to race or ethnicity. "What we see is that America cannot be less than herself once she awakens to the realization that freedom does not mean license and that license can be the keeping of others from sharing that freedom," Bolton noted.[9] In 1944, Bolton traveled to Europe to observe firsthand the military hospitals and the nurses she helped to put in place. Her efforts to bring women into greater positions of responsibility in the military extended into the 1950s. Bolton's belief in war preparedness led her to conclude that women should be drafted into noncombat roles. "I am afraid that gallantry is sorely out of date, and as a woman I find it rather stupid," she said. "Women's place includes defending the home."[10]

Bolton's work on Foreign Affairs consumed much of her postwar career and allowed her a series of firsts. At the invitation of the Soviet Ambassador, she became the first committee member to travel to the Soviet Union. On her initiative as part of the 1946 Legislative Reorganization Act, the full committee reorganized into five permanent subcommittees, corresponding with the State Department's

"Prejudice [must be put down]
wherever it raises its head,
whether we are victims or not.
[An] attack on any group
endangers everyone's freedom."

—Frances Bolton
Address to the
United Nations General Assembly, 1954

divisions of the globe. As the chair of the Near East and Africa Subcommittee of Foreign Affairs, she became the first woman to lead a congressional delegation overseas in 1947. Bolton's frequent trips to the African continent (paid out of her own pocket) led the press to dub her the "African Queen"—a reference to the 1951 film.[11] In 1953, President Dwight Eisenhower appointed her as the first woman congressional Delegate to the United Nations.[12] In the last three months of 1955, at the age of 70, Bolton undertook her longest journey to Africa. She survived an attempted charge on her car by a bull elephant, hiked up mountains, and visited remote native villages.[13] She was not distracted from serious aspects to the trip: the development of health care programs and food and aid distribution. After meetings with high-ranking South African officials in Johannesburg, Bolton denounced that nation's system of racial apartheid, which she described as "contrary to the universal law of evolution."[14] The South African foreign minister claimed that Bolton had delivered a "distorted picture" of apartheid and added, "A more flagrant intrusion into the political affairs of another country... would be difficult to imagine."[15] Bolton, undeterred, continued to press her case in Congress.

Her interest in African issues, particularly the effects of decolonization in Africa, reinforced her own convictions about the need to dismantle segregation in America. Bolton persisted in her core belief that for the United States to wage the Cold War effectively, it had to live up to its democratic rhetoric to attract developing nations to its cause. It was, moreover, a matter of personal principle and conviction. In 1954 Bolton delivered an address before the U.N. General Assembly, attacking the apartheid practices in South Africa and, again, alluding to America's failure to live up to its rhetoric of democracy. "Prejudice [must be put down] wherever it raises its head, whether we are victims or not," Bolton declared. "[An] attack on any group endangers everyone's freedom."[16]

Bolton's sense of adventure was matched by her humor, work ethic, and loyalty to women colleagues. In the late 1940s, the U.S. Navy invited "Congressmen" "Francis" Bolton, Cecil Harden, and Chase Woodhouse to make an overnight visit aboard the U.S.S. *Midway*. Navy rules, in fact, prohibited women from spending the night aboard ship, but the invitations nevertheless were sent out to the three women because they had masculine-sounding names. Bolton and her two women colleagues debated whether to accept. Finally, Woodhouse declared, "Of course, we ought to. After all, aren't you a Congressman?" Bolton replied, "You bet your life I am, and I work twice as hard as most of the men."[17] Bolton earned accolades for supporting her women colleagues, regardless of party affiliation. With the death of Edith Nourse Rogers of Massachusetts in 1960, she became the dean of women Members in the House; her 29 total years of service still rank her behind only Rogers for the longest term of service for a woman in the House.

In her final campaign in 1968, Bolton was caught in a redistricting battle. Democratic Congressman Charles Vanik, first elected to the House to represent another Cleveland seat in 1954, challenged Bolton in her newly redrawn, majority-Democratic district. Vanik defeated the 83-year-old Bolton with 55 percent of the vote. After the election, the Richard M. Nixon administration considered rewarding her long career with an ambassadorship. Bolton demurred, "No... I'm retired. Now I can do what I please."[18] She returned to Lyndhurst, Ohio, where she resided until her death on March 9, 1977, shortly before her 92nd birthday.

FOR FURTHER READING

Biographical Directory of the United States Congress, "Frances Payne Bolton," http://bioguide.congress.gov

Loth, David. *A Long Way Forward: The Biography of Congresswoman Frances P. Bolton* (New York: Longmans, Green, 1957).

MANUSCRIPT COLLECTION

Western Reserve Historical Society (Cleveland, OH). *Papers:* 1939–1977, 175 feet, 30 oversize volumes, and one oversize folder. Correspondence, reports, publications, clippings, and other materials generated during or pertaining to Frances Bolton's service in the U.S. House of Representatives, particularly reflecting her interest in nursing, work on the Committee on Foreign Affairs, travel on behalf of the committee, and work with the United Nations. Finding aid in repository. *Papers:* In the Chester Castle Bolton Papers, 1916–1943, 6.62 linear ft. Other authors include Frances Payne Bolton. *Papers:* Frances Payne Bolton Audio-Visual Collection, approximately 5,400 prints and 1,300 negatives and positive transparencies, 111 film titles, 287 audio discs, and 80 audio tapes. Includes extensive documentation from Frances Payne Bolton's African trips and other official congressional travel, campaigns, and the United Nations General Assembly. Also includes photographs of family, friends, and government officials. Audio tapes contain campaign spots, radio broadcasts, and speeches. A finding aid is available in the repository.

NOTES

1 Martha Griffiths, Oral History Interview, U.S. Association of Former Members of Congress (hereinafter cited as USAFMOC), Manuscript Room, Library of Congress, Washington, D.C.: 157; David Loth, *A Long Way Forward: The Biography of Congresswoman Frances Payne Bolton* (New York: Longmans, Green, 1957): 289–290.
2 Loth, *A Long Way Forward*: 193.
3 Hope Chamberlin, *A Minority of Members: Women in the U.S. Congress* (New York: Praeger, 1973): 131–132.
4 *Congressional Record,* House, 77th Cong., 1st sess. (16 October 1941): 7974.
5 *Congressional Record,* House, 77th Cong., 1st sess. (12 November 1941): 8803.
6 Spoken on the House Floor (*Congressional Record,* House, 77th Cong., 1st sess. [11 December 1941]: 9670) and earlier inserted into the "Extension of Remarks," *Congressional Record,* House, 77th Cong., 1st sess. (8 December 1941): A5523–5524.
7 *Congressional Record,* House, 78th Cong., 1st sess. (16 June 1943): 5944.
8 *Congressional Record,* House, 76th Cong., 3rd sess. (24 May 1940): 6865; *Congressional Record,* House, 76th Cong., 3rd sess. (24 May 1940): 3240.
9 *Congressional Record,* House, 78th Cong., 1st sess. (25 May 1943): 4849.
10 Chamberlin, *A Minority of Members*: 133.
11 George Weller, "Dust Saves Mrs. Bolton From Charging Elephant," 18 December 1955, *Washington Post*: A20.
12 Chamberlin, *A Minority of Members*: 133.
13 Weller, "Dust Saves Mrs. Bolton From Charging Elephant."
14 Rep. Frances P. Bolton, "Africa Today: Burning Issue–'Apartheid,'" 24 January 1956, *Washington Post*: 29.
15 Richard P. Hunt, "U.S. Legislators Irk South Africa," 11 June 1957, *New York Times*: 20
16 Karen Foerstel, *Biographical Dictionary of Congressional Women* (Westport, CT: Greenwood Press, 1999): 32.
17 Chase Going Woodhouse, Oral History Interview, USAFMOC, Manuscript Room, Library of Congress, Washington, D.C.: 41.
18 Chamberlin, *A Minority of Members*: 137.

Margaret Chase Smith
1897–1995

UNITED STATES REPRESENTATIVE ★ 1940–1949
UNITED STATES SENATOR ★ 1949–1973
REPUBLICAN FROM MAINE

For more than three decades, Margaret Chase Smith served as a role model for women aspiring to national politics. As the first woman to win election to both the U.S. House and the U.S. Senate, Smith cultivated a career as an independent and courageous legislator. Senator Smith bravely denounced McCarthyism at a time when others feared speaking out would ruin their careers. Though she believed firmly that women had a political role to assume, Smith refused to make an issue of her gender in seeking higher office. "If we are to claim and win our rightful place in the sun on an equal basis with men," she once noted, "then we must not insist upon those privileges and prerogatives identified in the past as exclusively feminine."[1]

Margaret Madeline Chase was born on December 14, 1897, in Skowhegan, Maine—the oldest of six children—to George Emery, the town barber, and Carrie Murray Chase, a waitress, store clerk, and shoe factory worker.[2] After graduating from Skowhegan High School in 1916, Chase took jobs as a teacher, telephone operator, and office manager for a woolen mill and on the staff of a small newspaper. In 1930, she married Clyde Harold Smith, an accomplished local politician.[3] In 1936, Clyde Smith was elected as a Republican to the House of Representatives for the 75th Congress (1937–1939). Margaret Smith managed his Washington office and also served as president of the Business and Professional Women's Club of Maine. She also worked on behalf of the Maine GOP committee.

In the spring of 1940, Representative Clyde Smith fell ill with a life-threatening heart condition. Realizing that he could not survive the rigors of an election campaign, he persuaded his wife to run for his seat in the general election the following November. Before his death on April

8, 1940, the Congressman told voters, "I know of no one else who has the full knowledge of my ideas and plans or is as well qualified as she is, to carry on these ideas or my unfinished work for the district."[4] His seat left vacant with his passing, Margaret Chase Smith declared her candidacy for the special election to serve out his unexpired term in the 76th Congress (1939–1941).[5] In the May 13, 1940, Republican special primary, Smith topped her challenger by a more-than 10-to-1 margin, virtually assuring her election to the House in the heavily Republican district.[6] Without a Democratic challenger, she won the June 3 special election, becoming Maine's first woman Member of Congress. On June 17, 1940, only a week after being seated in the House, Congresswoman Smith won the GOP primary for the full term in the 77th Congress (1941–1943), garnering more than 27,000 votes and amassing more than four times the total of her nearest competitor.[7] Her second primary triumph dispelled a popular notion that voters would abandon her—having believed that by electing her to a brief term they had fulfilled their obligation to seeing her husband's programs through to conclusion.

In the 1940 general election, Smith ran on a platform of military preparedness (including expansion of the navy, which played well in her shipbuilding district) and support for old-age pensions and assistance, which appealed to the state's large elderly population. She portrayed herself as a moderate who, in contrast to liberal feminists, would work within the established order; she employed that argument for many later campaigns. Smith drew upon her experiences campaigning with her husband, particularly his ability to strike up personal relationships with voters.[8] Smith won the general election over Democrat Edward Beauchamp, with 65 percent of the vote. After her 1940 campaigns,

Smith was re-elected to the three succeeding Congresses with relatively little challenge, defeating her opponents with 60 percent or more of the vote.[9]

As a freshman in 1940, Representative Smith had hoped to carry on her husband's work on the Labor Committee, but she was instead pushed onto four low-level committees: War Claims; Revision of the Laws; Invalid Pensions; and the Election of the President, Vice President, and Representatives in Congress.[10] Though she often broke with her GOP colleagues on important votes, party leaders answered her persistent request for a better committee assignment in the 78th Congress (1943–1945). Smith received a position on the prominent House Naval Affairs Committee—a fair compromise after her strategic request for the highly coveted Appropriations panel. "When I asked for a committee, I asked for Appropriations, knowing that I would not get it," Smith recalled, "I asked for it, because that was the thing to do in those days. You didn't expect to get what you asked for, so you would ask for something that was impossible.... And Naval Affairs was what I wanted; I didn't want Appropriations ... I think I was smart."[11] In addition to her Naval Affairs duties, Smith served on the Education Committee and the Post Office and Post Roads Committee. After the Legislative Reorganization Act of 1946 merged disparate committees with military jurisdictions, the Congresswoman was assigned to the Armed Services Committee.

Smith was an active member of the Naval Affairs and Armed Services Committees. Her position gave her power to award shipbuilding projects in Maine. It also made her an expert on military and national security matters, leading to her participation in an investigation of the construction of destroyers and the inspection of bases in the South Pacific. In addition, Smith participated in a trip to observe the postwar reconstruction in Europe, North Africa, and the Middle East. Though she expressed concern for the spread of Soviet influence in Eastern Europe, Smith remained wary of domestic communist fears. She voted against legislation to make the House Select Committee on Un-American Activities permanent.

As a member of the Armed Services Committee, Smith passed her landmark legislative achievement in the House: the Women's Armed Forces Integration Act. With a wartime peak enrollment of about 350,000, women were still considered volunteers for the armed services and did not receive any benefits.[12] In April 1947, while chairing the Armed Services' Subcommittee on Hospitalization and Medicine, Smith passed a bill giving regular status to navy and army nurses—well-accepted by her House colleagues because it covered women in traditional, "angel of mercy" roles.[13] When the Armed Forces Integration Act, providing for the permanent inclusion of all uniformed women in the military, easily passed the Senate in July 1947, Smith faced a greater challenge pushing the bill through the House. Opponents on the Armed Services Committee amended it over Smith's lone dissenting vote, significantly curtailing women's rights and benefits by offering them reserve status. The House passed the committee's version. In an effort to restore the bill's original intent in the conference committee, Smith appealed to her personal friend, Secretary of Defense William Forrestal, who gave her his full backing. Smith prevailed when the House conferees accepted a version of the legislation granting women regular status on July 2, 1948. President Harry Truman signed the bill into law 10 days later, just weeks before he racially integrated the armed forces by Executive Order.[14]

In 1947, when Maine's senior U.S. Senator, Republican Majority Leader Wallace White, announced he would not seek a fourth term, Smith entered the hotly contested 1948 primary to succeed him. The state Republican Party, stung by Smith's many votes across party lines, opposed her candidacy and supported Maine Governor Horace A. Hildreth in the four-way race. Running on the slogan, "Don't trade a record for a promise," Smith insisted that her legislative achievements in the House were worth more than the campaign promises of her opponents.[15] The personal touch that marked her House campaigns also aided in her senatorial bid. As she crisscrossed the state making speeches and meeting personally with constituents, many simply addressed her by her first name, "Margaret," with the kind of intimacy indicative of an old friendship.[16] A large corps of Maine women volunteers also greatly aided her shoestring, grass-roots campaign.[17] In the June 21 primary, Smith received nearly 64,000 votes, a greater margin the combined votes of her three challengers. After capturing the primary, Smith won a lopsided election, defeating Democrat Adrian Scolten with 71 percent of the vote. Smith's election marked the first time a woman won election to the Senate without the widow or appointment connection and the first time a woman served in both chambers. Smith was re-elected to the Senate three more times by comfortable majorities.[18]

Despite her experience in the House, Smith needed to

Senate came on June 1, 1950, when she took the Senate Floor to denounce the investigatory tactics of the redbaiting Wisconsin Senator Joseph R. McCarthy. In a speech she later called a "Declaration of Conscience," Smith charged that her Republican colleague had "debased" Senate deliberations "through the selfish political exploitation of fear, bigotry, ignorance and intolerance." She said, "The American people are sick and tired of being afraid to speak their minds lest they be politically smeared as 'Communists' or 'Fascists' by their opponents. Freedom of speech is not what it used to be in America. It has been so abused by some that it is not exercised by others."[20] Although the speech

"The American people are sick and tired of being afraid to speak their minds lest they be politically smeared as 'Communists' or 'Fascists' by their opponents. Freedom of speech is not what it used to be in America. It has been so abused by some that it is not exercised by others."

—MARGARET CHASE SMITH, SENATE FLOOR SPEECH, JUNE 1, 1950

earn her seniority in the Senate. In her first term, she received three less powerful assignments: Committee on the District of Columbia, Committee on Rules and Administration, and the Committee on Expenditures in the Executive Departments (after the 83rd Congress [1953–1955], named Government Operations). When Republicans briefly controlled the chamber in the 83rd Congress, Smith earned seats on two prominent committees which no woman had held before: Appropriations and Armed Services. She gave up Government Operations for an assignment on the Aeronautical and Space Sciences Committee in the 86th Congress (1959–1961)—a particularly influential panel at the dawn of the space race with the Soviet Union.[19] She maintained a place on these three key panels for the remainder of her Senate career.

Margaret Chase Smith's defining moment in the U.S.

attracted favorable nationwide attention and was endorsed by six fellow Republicans in the Senate, it did little to restrain Senator McCarthy and his supporters. McCarthy ridiculed Senator Smith on the Senate Floor, and he poured political capital into the campaign of Smith's 1954 GOP rival. Late in 1954, the Senate censured McCarthy for his conduct of the Army–McCarthy hearings, effectively silencing him. Despite Smith's bravery in standing up to McCarthy, her reputation as a political maverick limited her later potential in the Senate. Among the costs were her removal from the Republican Policy Committee and a drop in seniority on the Permanent Investigations Subcommittee of the Government Operations Committee.[21]

In the Senate, Smith remained more of an independent than a party-line Republican vote. The Senator's meticulous and independent nature was most evident in her rejection of several high-profile presidential nominees. In 1957, after President Dwight D. Eisenhower nominated Hollywood actor, decorated World War II veteran, and army reservist James ("Jimmy") Stewart for promotion to brigadier general, Senator Smith recommended against his promotion. She led an unexpected rejection of Commerce Secretary nominee Lewis L. Strauss in 1959, marking the third time in a century that a Cabinet appointment was rejected and deeply angering the Eisenhower administration.[22] Nearly a decade later, Smith enraged the Richard M. Nixon White House when she and fellow Senators rejected Supreme Court nominee G. Harrold Carswell. Smith's independence on high-visibility issues made it hard to categorize her politics and somewhat diminished her influence. On the domestic front, the Senator supported legislation for primarily Democratic initiatives on educational funding and civil rights. However, Smith supported a much more aggressive foreign policy than that of the John F. Kennedy administration. After the Berlin Crisis of 1961, she accused President Kennedy of lacking the resolve to use nuclear weapons against the Soviet Union, chiding the President on the Senate Floor, "In short, we have the nuclear capability but not the nuclear credibility."[23] In her long career, Smith became a Senate institution in her own right. From June 1, 1955, to September 6, 1968, she cast 2,941 consecutive roll call votes. Her streak was interrupted only by recovery from hip surgery.

After months of denying rumors that she would seek the top of the Republican ticket or the vice presidential nomination, Senator Margaret Chase Smith announced her run for President in January 1964. "I have few illusions and no money, but I'm staying for the finish," she noted, "When people keep telling you, you can't do a thing, you kind of like to try."[24] Smith embarked on her typical grass-roots campaign—losing every primary but picking up a surprising high of 25 percent of the vote in Illinois.[25] At the 1964 Republican Convention, she became the first woman to have her name put in for nomination for the presidency by a major political party. Receiving the support of just 27 delegates and losing the

nomination to Senate colleague Barry Goldwater, it was a symbolic achievement.

To the surprise of many across the country, Maine voters turned the venerable septuagenarian out of office in 1972, during her bid for a fifth consecutive term. Prior to the election, Smith had given serious consideration to retiring, but charges that she was too old—at age 74—to serve as a Senator had motivated her to run for re-election. The Democratic nominee, Maine U.S. Representative William D. Hathaway, emphasized Smith's age. He also claimed Smith was inaccessible and inattentive to Maine's concerns, citing the fact that she did not maintain an office in the state. Smith lost the election by 27,230 votes, a margin of 53 to 47 percent.[26]

Smith resettled in Skowhegan to oversee the construction of the Margaret Chase Smith Library Center, the first of its kind to focus its collection on the papers of a female Member of Congress. In 1989, President George H.W. Bush awarded her the Presidential Medal of Freedom, the nation's highest civilian honor. Margaret Chase Smith died on May 29, 1995, at the age of 97, in her hometown of Skowhegan.

FOR FURTHER READING

Biographical Directory of the United States Congress, "Margaret Chase Smith," http://bioguide.congress.gov

Schmidt, Patricia L. *Margaret Chase Smith: Beyond Convention* (Orono: University of Maine Press, 1996).

Sherman, Janann. *No Place for a Woman: A Life of Senator Margaret Chase Smith* (New Brunswick, NJ: Rutgers University Press, 2000).

Smith, Margaret Chase. *Declaration of Conscience*, edited by William C. Lewis, Jr. (New York: Doubleday Co., 1972).

Wallace, Patricia Ward. *The Politics of Conscience: A Biography of Margaret Chase Smith* (Westport, CT: Praeger, 1995).

MANUSCRIPT COLLECTIONS

Library of Congress (Washington, D.C.). *Oral History:* 1958. Interview with Senator Margaret Chase Smith.

Lyndon Baines Johnson Library (Austin, TX). *Oral History:* August 20, 1975. 49 pages.

Margaret Chase Smith Library (Skowhegan, ME), http://www.mcslibrary.org. *Papers:* 1930–1995, approximately 275 feet. Includes personal, business, and congressional papers, as well as correspondence, scrapbooks, speeches, and news releases documenting Margaret Chase Smith's service in the U.S. House of Representatives and U.S. Senate and activities after her retirement. Additional materials include photographs, portraits, motion picture film, videotape, sound recordings, and memorabilia. A finding aid is available in the repository.

NOTES

1   *Congressional Record*, House, 79th Cong., 2nd sess. (24 July 1946): A4378–A4379.

2   On parents' employment, Mary Kaptur, *Women of Congress: A Twentieth-Century Odyssey* (Washington, D.C.: Congressional Quarterly Press, 1996): 85.

3   "Rep. Clyde H. Smith of Maine, Was 63," 9 April 1940, *New York Times*: 29.

4   Quoted in Janann Sherman, *No Place for a Woman: The Life of Senator Margaret Chase Smith* (New Brunswick, NJ: Rutgers University Press, 2000): 42.

5   "Mrs. Smith To Seek Place of Husband," 9 April 1940, *Washington Post*: 9; "Clyde Smith's Widow Files," 16 April 1940, *New York Times*: 15.

6   "Rep. Clyde Smith's Widow Nominated by Maine G.O.P.," 14 May 1940, *Washington Post*: 1.

7   Patricia Schmidt, *Margaret Chase Smith: Beyond Convention* (Orono: University of Maine Press, 1996): 108–113; Sherman, *No Place for a Woman:* 47.

8   Sherman, *No Place for a Woman:* 44–45.

9   "Election Statistics, 1920 to Present," http://clerk.house.gov/members/electionInfo/elections.html.

10 Susan Tolchin, *Women in Congress* (Washington, D.C.: Government Printing Office, 1976): 75.

11 Kaptur, *Women of Congress:* 86.

12 David M. Kennedy, *Freedom From Fear* (New York: Oxford University Press, 1999): 776.

13 Schmidt, *Margaret Chase Smith:* 163.

14 Harry S. Truman, "Executive Order 9981," Truman Presidential Museum and Library, http://www.trumanlibrary.org/9981.htm (accessed 22 February 2005).

15 Hope Chamberlin, *A Minority of Members: Women in the U.S. Congress* (New York: Praeger, 1973): 143.

16 Helen Henley, "Maine GOP Nominates Mrs. Smith for Senator," 22 June 1948, *Christian Science Monitor:* 5; Josephine Ripley, "Women Hail Smith Victory in Maine," 23 June 1948, *Christian Science Monitor:* 7.

17 Schmidt, *Margaret Chase Smith:* 181–182.

18 "Election Statistics, 1920 to Present," http://clerk.house.gov/members/electionInfo/elections.html.

19 The space race began when the Russians successfully launched the first satellite into space. *Sputnik I* orbited the earth in October 1957. The Russian satellite was followed by the January 1958 launch of the American *Explorer I*, a small satellite used for collecting scientific data (National Aeronautics and Space Administration, "Sputnik and the Dawn of the Space Age," http://www.hq.nasa.gov/office/pao/History/sputnik/ (accessed 18 February 2005).

20 *Congressional Record*, Senate, 81st Cong., 2nd sess. (1 June 1950): 7894–7895.

21 Sherman, *No Place for a Woman:* 117–118.

22 Chamberlain, *A Minority of Members:* 146.

23 *Congressional Record*, Senate, 87th Cong., 1st sess. (23 September 1961): 20626.

24 Tolchin, *Women in Congress:* 76.

25 "The 1964 Elections," *Congress and the Nation, 1945–1964*, Vol. 1-A (Washington, D.C.: Congressional Quarterly Press, 1965): 54.

26 "Election Statistics, 1920 to Present," http://clerk.house.gov/members/electionInfo/index.html.

Florence Reville Gibbs
1890–1964

UNITED STATES REPRESENTATIVE ★ DEMOCRAT FROM GEORGIA
1940–1941

Election Day 1940 was just a month away, and the Members of the 76th Congress (1939–1941) saw no sign that they would adjourn for the election. As Members began leaving Washington to campaign, Florence Reville Gibbs arrived from Georgia, having just been elected to serve out the term of her late husband, Representative W. Ben Gibbs. Georgia's first woman elected to Congress served three months in the U.S. House of Representatives.

Florence Reville was born in Thomson, Georgia, on April 4, 1890, the oldest child of a country doctor, Thomas Porter Reville, and Sallie Printup Reville.[1] Florence Reville grew up in Thomson and left to attend Brenau College in Gainesville, Georgia. She married a lawyer, Willis Benjamin Gibbs, and the couple settled in Jesup, Georgia, and had two children.[2] Ben Gibbs carved out a career as a government attorney at various local and county agencies. Eventually, he was elected unopposed to a Georgia seat in the U.S. House of Representatives for the 76th Congress. His initial term in Congress was successful enough that a district rival, John S. Gibson, informed Gibbs that he would go unchallenged at the next primary election.[3] But Gibbs never stood for re-election, dying of a sudden stroke on August 7, 1940, in Washington, D.C., just 19 months into his freshman term.[4]

Florence Gibbs acceded to the wishes of the local Democratic county leaders, who asked her to run for her husband's vacant seat. She won the uncontested October 1, 1940, special election called by Georgia Governor E.D. Rivers. Turnout for the special election was typically light—from the 20-county district in the state's southeast corner, fewer than 2,500 voters went to the polls.[5] The turnout was smaller than that of 1938, when her husband had first been elected to Congress unopposed with fewer than 5,000 votes. Just more than a month later, John S. Gibson was elected unopposed to the 77th Congress (1941–1943) with more than 24,000 votes.[6]

Florence Gibbs was sworn in two days after her election, October 3, 1940, in the midst of Franklin Roosevelt's campaign for a third term as President, the resumption of the military draft, and the expansion of the Axis Powers into the Balkans.[7] Representative Carl Vinson of Georgia, the dean of the state delegation and chairman of the Naval Affairs Committee, arranged for Gibbs to be sworn in before her certificate of election had been filed by the House.[8] This was because Gibbs's term encompassed the last three months of the 76th Congress, whose third session extended throughout 1940 and recessed only for the Democratic and Republican national conventions during the summer. The following weekend was turning into an informal recess, as Members began streaming home to campaign for re-election.[9] For many Democrats, the prospects for retaining their majority status had been eroding. If Gibbs wasn't sworn in that week, the ceremony probably would have been delayed for weeks. She never received a committee assignment. Gibbs, who had no previous professional experience, was unaccustomed to such a public position. She has been described as softspoken and unassertive. A constituent recalled, "She was good for political patronage—mainly post office appointments. The job wasn't really to her liking."[10] Early on, Gibbs had made it clear that she would not be a candidate for re-election.[11]

Gibbs returned to Jesup, Georgia, at the conclusion of her House term. She died there 23 years later, on August 19, 1964.

IMAGE COURTESY OF AP/WIDE WORLD PHOTOS

A CONSTITUENT RECALLED, GIBBS "WAS GOOD FOR POLITICAL PATRONAGE—MAINLY POST OFFICE APPOINTMENTS. THE JOB WASN'T REALLY TO HER LIKING." EARLY ON, GIBBS HAD MADE IT CLEAR THAT SHE WOULD NOT BE A CANDIDATE FOR RE-ELECTION.

FOR FURTHER READING

Biographical Directory of the United States Congress, "Florence Reville Gibbs," http://bioguide.congress.gov

NOTES

1   *Congressional Directory*, 76th Cong., 1st sess., 1939 (Washington, D.C.: Government Printing Office, 1939): 21.

2   "Rep. W.B. Gibbs, of Georgia, Dies Here After Stroke," 8 August 1940, *Washington Post*: 1; "Representative Gibbs," 9 August 1940, *New York Times*: 15. Both sources identify the children as Mrs. J.A. Leaphart and Warner B. Gibbs. So does the *Congressional Directory* from 1939.

3   *Congressional Record*, House, 77th Cong., 1st sess. (18 June 1941): appendix 2920. Gibbs received an assignment to the Judiciary Committee.

4   "Rep. W.B. Gibbs, of Georgia, Dies Here After Stroke"; "Representative Gibbs."

5   The election results are incomplete in Michael J. Dubin et al., *U.S. Congressional Elections, 1788–1997* (Jefferson, NC: McFarland & Company, Inc., Publishers, 1998): 530. Dubin reports totals from just two counties. The vote figure of about 2,500 comes from Hope Chamberlin's *A Minority of Members: Women in the U.S. Congress* (New York: Praeger, 1973): 156; and press reports.

6   "Election Statistics, 1920 to Present," http://clerk.house.gov/members/electionInfo/elections.html.

7   Michael Barone, *Our Country: The Shaping of America From Roosevelt to Reagan* (New York: Free Press, 1990): 141.

8   "Mrs. Gibbs Takes Oath of Office," 5 October 1940, *Washington Post*: 28.

9   Robert A. Caro, *The Years of Lyndon Johnson: The Path to Power* (New York: Vintage, 1981, 1982): 623.

10   Chamberlin, *A Minority of Members*: 156.

11   "Takes Husband's Place in Congress," 6 October 1940, *Washington Post*: 9.

Katharine Edgar Byron
1903–1976

UNITED STATES REPRESENTATIVE ★ DEMOCRAT FROM MARYLAND
1941–1943

Maryland's first woman Member in Congress, Katharine Edgar Byron, came to the House through the "widow's mandate," after an airplane crash had killed her husband. Congresswoman Byron became a firm supporter of President Franklin Roosevelt's foreign policies during World War II.

Katharine Edgar was born on October 25, 1903, to Brigadier General Clinton Goodloe and Mary McComas Edgar in Detroit, Michigan, where General Edgar was posted. Katharine's mother, Mary, belonged to a prominent political family from western Maryland. Her father, Louis Emory McComas, had served in the House and Senate during the late 19th century. Katharine, one of two children, spent an affluent and politically connected childhood based in the McComas estate, Springfield Farm, in western Maryland.[1] She attended elite private schools such as the Westover School in Middlebury, Connecticut, and the Holton Arms School in Montgomery County, just outside Washington, D.C. In 1922, Katharine met and married William D. Byron, a World War I aviator and the owner of a leather manufacturing business. The couple had five sons: William, James, Goodloe, David, and Louis. William Byron was mayor of Williamsport, Maryland, a member of the state senate, and a member of the Maryland Roads Commission. In 1938 he successfully ran for the U.S. House as a Democrat in a district that covered western Maryland, including the towns of Frederick and Hagerstown. Byron won a tight re-election race in 1940 against the legendary professional baseball pitcher Walter "Big Train" Johnson. Katharine Byron aided her husband's political career through her activities with local organizations such as the Red Cross flood disaster committee. She also served as town commissioner for Williamsport

during William's House service. Additionally, Katharine was one of Washington's well-known Democratic hostesses from the Byron family home in northwest Washington.

Less than two months into his second term, Representative Byron died in an airplane accident on February 27, 1941, near Atlanta, Georgia, that killed six others and severely injured World War I flying ace Eddie Rickenbacker.[2] With only tepid support from local Democratic leaders, Katharine Byron decided within a month to seek her husband's seat in a special election scheduled for late May 1941. She said she hoped to "carry on Bill's work."[3] Among those rumored to be interested in the Democratic nomination were former Congressman David J. Lewis, Maryland Democratic National Committeeman William Preston Lane, State Senator John B. Funk, and Earl Cobey, a western Maryland attorney and an associate of U.S. Attorney General William C. Walsh. Lewis, a Progressive liberal and the former chairman of the Labor Committee, had represented the district for 14 years, from 1911 to 1917 and again from 1931 to 1939. In 1938, he made an unsuccessful bid for the U.S. Senate, thus opening the seat which William Byron had won. Lane, a close associate of William Byron and the spouse of a Byron family member, refused to run against Katharine, although he also withheld his endorsement from her.[4] Women's groups in Montgomery County, one of the district's largest counties, did not support Byron because they did not believe she could defeat the presumptive Republican candidate, A. Charles Stewart from Frostburg, Maryland.[5] Meanwhile, Katharine Byron pressed party leaders for the nomination, telling them that she wanted to complete her husband's programs, but pledging that if she won she would not seek re-election to

IMAGE COURTESY OF THE HONORABLE BEVERLY BYRON

the 78th Congress (1943–1945). On April 19, 1941, 30 Democratic committeemen gathered in Hagerstown, Maryland, to choose their candidate. After a long deadlock, Byron prevailed when an Alleghany County committeeman swung his vote to her, giving her a 16–14 edge and the support of three of the district's five counties.[6]

Katharine Byron's campaign for the general election was equally contentious. Stewart, age 62, was a considerable opponent and a political veteran. In 1938, he lost narrowly to William Byron in a heated contest that centered on the New Deal—falling a little less than 1,500 votes short out of 91,000 cast.[7] In 1941, the new Byron–Stewart contest centered on the nation's response to war in Europe. The Democratic candidate backed the Roosevelt administration's foreign policies and pledged to support in Congress "all aid to Britain, short of war."[8] Stewart, tapping into isolationist sentiment in the rural areas of the state, accused Byron of being a rubber stamp for an administration trying to "spill blood of our boys in the squabbles of Europe." On Stewart's behalf, Walter Johnson stumped throughout the district, drawing large crowds of workers and baseball enthusiasts.[9]

But Katharine Byron had her own marquee speakers and a built-in edge in party registration. In campaign appearances with nationally known Democrats like First Lady Eleanor Roosevelt and Representative Estes Kefauver of Tennessee, Byron endorsed U.S. support for nations fighting against the Nazis and recommended greater military preparedness. Byron, the state's first woman candidate for Congress, proved a durable campaigner and rallied the support of women's Democratic groups.[10] Two days before the election, Eleanor Roosevelt swung through the district to provide her unqualified endorsement for Byron. "Her popularity in Government circles and her contacts in Washington will prove a real benefit to her constituents," Roosevelt assured voters. "We need not only more women in Congress but more Representatives of the high qualifications possessed by Katharine Byron."[11] The widow candidate also benefited from a 4–1 advantage in registered Democrats within the district. She closed the campaign with a "caravan tour" in

Stewart's stronghold in Alleghany and Garrett counties, which included musical performances by three of her sons, who offered a rendition of a song they called "Beautiful Ka-a-aty."[12] On May 27, 1941, Byron defeated Stewart by an even slenderer margin than had her husband, a little more than 1,000 votes. "My election, I feel, is a very fitting tribute to my late husband and it is my only hope to do the utmost to carry on the work he has begun," she told reporters on election night.[13] On June 11, 1941, Katharine Byron was sworn in as U.S. Representative and assigned to the Civil Service and War Claims committees.

Katharine Byron's career in the House was shaped by international exigencies which produced a climate far different from that when her husband had won election as a Democrat just a few years earlier. Most of her 18 months in office were devoted to issues arising from American aid to nations fighting Nazi Germany and, then, U.S. intervention in the Second World War. In a debate on the amendment to the Neutrality Act in November 1941, Byron urged her colleagues to accelerate the delivery of war material to Great Britain and the Soviet Union by repealing the neutrality law that forbade American ships from delivering such equipment to belligerents. On the House Floor she recounted a conversation with her only draft-age son, William. "How should I vote?" she asked him. "Mother, there is only one thing to do and that is to vote for the repeal of the act, and I will be very proud of you," he replied. She added, "I feel it is my duty to my sons, to my late husband, and to those I represent to vote for this measure so that our country will remain the democracy it is today and not be dominated by Hitler."[14] That same month she christened the Liberty Fleet freighter *Francis Scott Key* at a Baltimore shipyard. Three weeks later, on 8 December, the day following the Japanese attack on Pearl Harbor, Speaker Sam Rayburn of Texas recognized Byron and four other Representatives to declare on the House Floor their support for a declaration of war. "I am willing to give my sons to their country's defense," Byron told colleagues. "I am 100 percent in favor of avenging the wrong done our country and maintaining our country's honor. We must go into this thing to beat the Japanese aggressor. I shall do everything by voice, by vote, everything within my power to bring about this end."[15]

The war shaped Byron's subsequent work, even where she dealt with issues of local interest. In 1942 she argued for the maintenance of Works Projects Administration (WPA) programs within her district as a necessary adjunct to national defense projects. WPA funds were supporting the construction of two airfields in the district as well as the housing and childcare needs of construction workers and their families. "We have many projects started in the district very necessary to the defense program," Bryon said, "and if these had to be abandoned it would endanger our war effort."[16]

Contrary to her earlier promise not to seek re-election, Congresswoman Byron filed for the Democratic primary in the summer of 1942, but she withdrew shortly thereafter, leaving the nomination to Lieutenant Colonel E. Brooke Lee, who eventually lost in the general election.[17] Byron had already delivered her first campaign speech, in William D. Byron Park in Williamsport, when a call went out for women to support the war effort. Her governess, a registered nurse, decided to quit and volunteer as a military nurse. Byron later claimed that she could neither stand in the way of that decision nor find a replacement and, thus, abandoned her re-election campaign to take care of her children, the youngest of whom was five.[18] In October 1947, she married Samuel Bynum Riddick, head of public relations for the Federal Housing Administration.[19] Much of Byron's postcongressional career was spent as a Red Cross volunteer. In 1970, Katharine Byron took to the campaign trail again, helping her son, Goodloe Byron, win election to the U.S. House in a district that covered much of the region that hers had 30 years earlier.[20] Katharine Byron, still active in the capital's elite social circuit, died in Georgetown on December 28, 1976.

FOR FURTHER READING

Biographical Directory of the United States Congress, "Katharine Edgar Byron," http://bioguide.congress.gov

NOTES

1 Hope Chamberlin, *A Minority of Members: Women in the U.S. Congress* (New York: Praeger, 1973): 158.
2 "Byron Killed in Air Crash Fatal to Seven," 28 February 1941, *Washington Post*: 3.
3 William O. Varn, "Contest Hot, Sixth District Votes Today," 27 May 1941, *Washington Post*: 27.
4 "Lewis May Seek Byron's Seat," 17 March 1941, *Washington Post*: 6; "Lane Denies Endorsement of Mrs. Byron," 9 April 1941, *Washington Post*: 12.
5 "Lewis May Seek Byron's Seat."
6 "Caucus Names Widow to Run for Byron Seat," 20 April 1941, *Washington Post*: B3.
7 Varn, "Contest Hot, Sixth District Votes Today."
8 "Mrs. Byron Marks Victory Amid Hubbub of Congratulations and Household Duties," 30 May 1931, *Washington Post*: 13.
9 "Walter Johnson Backs Stewart at Montgomery Rally," 8 May 1941, *Washington Post*: 7.
10 Chamberlin, *A Minority of Members*: 157.
11 "First Lady Urges Election of Mrs. Byron," 26 May 1941, *Washington Post*: 22.
12 "Mrs. Byron Marks Victory Amid Hubbub of Congratulations and Household Duties."
13 "Mrs. Byron Elected Maryland's First Congresswoman," 28 May 1941, *Washington Post*: 1.
14 Ruth Cowan, "House Women Back Change in Neutrality," 14 November 1941, *Washington Post*: 2; *Congressional Record*, House, 77th Cong., 1st sess. (13 November 1941): 8853.
15 "Katharine Byron Dies, Former Md. Legislator," 29 December 1976, *Washington Post*: C8; *Congressional Record*, House, 77th Cong., 1st sess. (8 December 1941): 9521.
16 *Congressional Record*, House, 77th Cong., 2nd sess. (11 June 1942): 5163.
17 "Coalition May Fight for Charter," 10 August 1942, *Washington Post*: 13; and "Elections Statistics, 1920 to Present," http://clerk.house.gov/members/election_information/1942election.pdf
18 Chamberlin, *A Minority of Members*: 158.
19 "Mrs. Byron, Mr. Riddick To Be Wed," 28 September 1947, *Washington Post*: S5.
20 Chamberlin, *A Minority of Members*: 158.

Veronica Grace Boland
1899-1982

UNITED STATES REPRESENTATIVE ★ DEMOCRAT FROM PENNSYLVANIA
1942-1943

The first woman to serve in Congress from Pennsylvania, Veronica Grace Boland, only served for two months, completing the term of her late husband, Patrick J. Boland, the popular Democratic Whip, who had died just before winning a primary election. "I've always preferred the background," Congresswoman Boland had told the press upon her election.[1] But her victory served as a tribute to her husband. Postmaster General Frank C. Walker, a family friend, told the *Scranton Tribune* that her election "came as a deserved recognition of Mr. Boland's long public service."[2]

Veronica Grace Barrett was born in Scranton, Pennsylvania, on March 18, 1899, a daughter of Patrick and Winifred Barrett, immigrants from Ireland. She graduated from the Scranton Technical High School in 1918. She later married Patrick J. Boland, a carpenter and building contractor. They had two sons: Patrick, Jr., and Eugene. Patrick Boland went on to a political career, elected to Scranton's city council and school board before serving as Lackawanna County commissioner from 1915 to 1919. In 1930 he was elected to a House seat as the nominee of the Republican, Democratic, and Labor parties. This left Boland free to choose which party caucus to join. He chose to organize with the Democratic Caucus, which held a narrow majority in the 72nd Congress (1931–1933). By his third term, Boland became Democratic Whip and was briefly a contender for Democratic Leader against Representative John McCormack of Massachusetts, the eventual winner, in 1940.[3] Senator Joseph F. Guffey, the Democratic leader of Pennsylvania, made retention of Boland as Whip a condition before throwing the state's House delegation

behind Sam Rayburn of Texas in his run for House Speaker in 1937.[4] Boland was credited with creating an effective Whip organization, and he was praised for his ability to determine how a vote would come out quickly and accurately. One of his triumphs was assisting Speaker Rayburn to extend the selective service system by one vote just months before the Pearl Harbor attack in 1941.[5]

On May 18, 1942, Patrick Boland died suddenly of a heart attack at home in Scranton, the morning before he won nomination in the Pennsylvania primaries for another House term. Majority Leader McCormack announced Boland's death by suggesting that wartime demands had made Boland "a casualty of the present conflict."[6] His death came at a time when Pennsylvania politics were quite volatile. New Deal policies had made the Democrats competitive in this predominantly Republican state, and the Democrats were particularly concerned with avoiding any potential fractures in their ranks.[7] The executive committee of the Pennsylvania Democratic Committee turned to Veronica Boland, Patrick's wife, to fill his unexpired term on June 5, 1942. Running unopposed, she won November 3, during the first congressional elections held after American intervention in World War II. "I really can't get excited about it," Boland told a group of reporters upon her election as Pennsylvania's first woman Representative. "I would rather have Mr. Boland there, of course."[8] She chose not to run for a full term to the 78th Congress (1943–1945), an election that was held the same day as her special election. At the same time, her willingness to serve out her husband's term bought the party's executive committee some time to settle upon a more experienced candidate for the next Congress.

"I've always preferred the background," Congresswoman Boland told the press upon her election. Boland was sworn in and seated on November 19, 1942, less than a month before the 77th Congress adjourned. As a consequence, she received no committee assignments and made no floor speeches.

Boland was sworn in and seated on November 19, 1942, less than a month before Congress adjourned on December 16.[9] As a consequence, she received no committee assignments and made no floor speeches.

After retiring from Congress, Veronica Boland returned to Scranton and worked as an executive secretary for the Dutch Manufacturing Company until 1957. She retired when she underwent eye surgery.[10] Boland died in Scranton on June 19, 1982.

FOR FURTHER READING

Biographical Directory of the United States Congress, "Veronica Grace Boland," http://bioguide.congress.gov

NOTES

1   Hope Chamberlin, *A Minority of Members: Women in the U.S. Congress* (New York: Praeger, 1976): 159.
2   Chamberlin, *A Minority of Members*: 159.
3   "Capital Leaders Mourn Boland," 19 May 1942, *Washington Post*: 1.
4   D.B. Hardeman and Donald C. Bacon, *Rayburn: A Biography* (Austin: Texas Monthly Press, 1987): 212; Joseph F. Guffey, *Seventy Years on the Red-Fire Wagon: From Tilden to Truman, From New Freedom Through New Deal* (n.p., 1952): 114. Rayburn lost the campaign but in September 1940, was elected Speaker after the death of William B. Bankhead of Alabama.
5   "Capital Leaders Mourn Boland"; Hardeman and Bacon, *Rayburn*: 265.
6   "Capital Leaders Mourn Boland."
7   Guffey, *Seventy Years on the Red-Fire Wagon*: 74–81; Philip S. Klein and Ari Hoogenboom, *A History of Pennsylvania*, second and enlarged edition (University Park: Pennsylvania State University Press, 1980): 465–470; David R. Contosta, "Reforming the Commonwealth, 1900–1950," in Randall M. Miller and William Pencak, eds., *Pennsylvania: A History of the Commonwealth* (University Park: Pennsylvania State University Press, 2002): 300.
8   Chamberlin, *A Minority of Members*: 159.
9   "Mrs. Boland Begins Service in House," 20 November 1942, *Washington Post*: B 11.
10 Chamberlin, *A Minority of Members*: 159.

Clare Boothe Luce
1903–1987

UNITED STATES REPRESENTATIVE ★ REPUBLICAN FROM CONNECTICUT
1943–1947

Clare Boothe Luce conquered the political sphere in much the same way that she stormed the publishing industry and elite society—with quick intelligence, a biting wit, and a knack for publicity that, along with her celebrity and beauty, made her a media darling. Luce won a Connecticut U.S. House seat in 1942, despite never having stood for elective office. Though she was critical of President Franklin D. Roosevelt, Luce's internationalist bent led her to back the broad outlines of the administration's plans for the postwar world. She once described her philosophy as, "America first but not only."[1]

Clare Ann Boothe was born on April 10, 1903, in New York City, to William Boothe and Ann Clare Snyder Boothe, both involved with the theater. The family moved from New York City to Memphis, Tennessee, but after her parents divorced in 1913, Clare, her mother, and her brother, David, returned to New York City to build a new life. To help pay bills, Clare worked in several play productions and did not attend school until she was 12, studying at the Cathedral School of St. Mary on Long Island and at Miss Mason's School in Tarrytown. Her mother eventually married Albert Austin, a wealthy doctor who later served in the Connecticut state legislature and the U.S. House. In 1923, Clare Boothe married George Brokaw, scion of a clothing fortune. They had one daughter, Ann Clare, but were divorced in 1929. Clare set her sights on writing and was hired by publisher Conde Nast at *Vogue*. By 1933 she served as managing editor at Nast's *Vanity Fair* magazine. On November 21, 1935, Clare Boothe married Henry R. Luce, founder of *Time*, *Life*, and *Fortune* magazines. Shortly thereafter Clare Boothe Luce came into her own as a successful playwright. In 1936, she wrote a Broadway hit, *The Women* (1936), a satire about the lives of idle rich

women. Other commercial successes followed. When war broke out in Europe, she toured the world as a *Life* correspondent. Luce eventually wrote dispatches from the North African and Chinese theaters.

Clare Boothe Luce's interest in politics developed during the Great Depression. In 1932, she worked as the executive secretary of the National Party, which united conservatives with moderately liberal plans for rescuing the economy. Through her relationship with the financier Bernard Baruch, Luce for a brief time became a Franklin Roosevelt supporter. She eventually broke with the FDR administration over New Deal economic programs. Her first active participation in Republican politics came with her energetic support of Wendell Willkie's 1940 presidential campaign. Her travels during World War II changed the focus of her criticisms of FDR from domestic to foreign policies. By 1942, Connecticut political leaders lobbied Luce to run for a U.S. House seat encompassing Fairfield County and the wealthy town of Greenwich, where Luce had a home. Initially reluctant because she thought she did not possess a temperament suited to politics and was unfamiliar with the district, she later accepted.[2] In the GOP primary, opponents attacked her as a carpetbagger but she prevailed at the nominating meeting by a nearly unanimous vote.[3] Luce based her platform on three goals: "One, to win the war. Two, to prosecute that war as loyally and effectively as we can as Republicans. Three, to bring about a better world and a durable peace, with special attention to post-war security and employment here at home."[4]

In the general election she ran against Democratic incumbent Leroy Downs, a local newspaper publisher who had defeated her stepfather, Albert Austin, in 1940.

She dismissed Downs as a Roosevelt "rubber stamp."[5] Nevertheless, her internationalist orientation differentiated Luce from isolationists. On that basis the influential syndicated columnist and FDR supporter Dorothy Thompson endorsed Luce.[6] Former GOP presidential candidate Wendell Willkie also campaigned for her.[7] With support from labor unions, Downs held his core Democratic voters together, but Luce defeated him by a 46 to 42 percent margin.[8] If Socialist candidate David Mansell had not skimmed away 15,000 votes that likely would have gone to Downs, Luce would not have been elected. Still, she portrayed her victory as a mandate. "I have campaigned for fighting a hard war—not a soft war," Luce declared. "Therefore this election proves how the American people want to fight this war.... They want to fight it efficiently and without bungling. They want to fight it in an honorable, all-out, plain-spoken partnership with our Allies."[9]

Luce originally hoped to get a seat on the Foreign Affairs Committee, but Republican Minority Leader Joe Martin steered her onto the Committee on Military Affairs. Impatient with the arduous process of creating and passing legislation, she used her Military Affairs assignment as a soapbox from which to criticize the wartime policies of the Roosevelt administration. Her first floor speech attracted half the House Members—an unprecedented draw for even the most powerful veteran. In an address entitled "America in the Postwar Air World," Luce advocated postwar U.S. air dominance, both commercial and military. In the same way that the British Navy controlled the world's oceans in the 19th century, Luce suggested, U.S. airpower would control global airspace. She warned against British and Russian competition and attacked the administration's "freedom of the skies" plan for postwar international aviation cooperation as "globaloney."[10] The speech had the effect Luce seemed to intend, stirring domestic and foreign controversy.[11] From London, Member of Parliament Lady Astor mused, "People who start out to be sensational usually don't last long."[12] Luce later clarified that she believed "every nation has sovereignty of its skies" and that the U.S. must extend aid to allied nations to reinvigorate the aviation industry and spur competition.[13]

Despite her status as a leading GOP spokesperson, Luce voted to support the general outlines of FDR's foreign policy. She described an Anglo-American bilateral alliance as the "foundation stone" of any postwar international organization.[14] She supported the so-called Fulbright Resolution in 1943, sponsored by Representative J. William Fulbright of Arkansas, which envisioned American participation in a postwar international organization—later the United Nations. She introduced resolutions to study the problem of postwar refugees and to create a U.N. agency to oversee arms control.[15] Unlike isolationist Republicans in the House, Luce backed American involvement in the United Nations Refugee Relief Agency, though she wanted separate U.S. oversight of aid distribution in recipient countries.[16] Luce also supported the creation of a Jewish state in Palestine.[17]

On domestic policy, Congresswoman Luce was more centrist than her rhetoric implied. In 1943, she supported the Equal Rights Amendment on the 20th anniversary of its introduction in the House. Luce also endorsed the development of the Women's Army Auxiliary Corps, arguing that, "We have always been fighting women and never afraid to do our part."[18] She advocated a heavy wartime tax on the rich: "those who can afford it, the well-to-do and the rich, must be taxed almost to the constitutional point of confiscation."[19] In 1946, Luce introduced a bill to create a Labor Department bureau to ensure women and minority workers equal pay for equal work.[20]

Republican leaders most valued Luce for her wit, sharp intellect, and ability to turn a phrase, especially when singling out Roosevelt's policies for criticism. Party leaders selected Luce as the keynote speaker at the 1944 Republican National Convention in Chicago, the first woman so honored by either party. Her "G.I. Joe and G.I. Jim" speech largely consisted of her charge that Roosevelt had been duplicitous in handling foreign policy as war grew imminent in both Europe and Asia, and, through wartime mismanagement, had caused undue American fatalities.[21] Aiming squarely at Roosevelt's habit of making one-man diplomacy, Luce charged that American democracy was "becoming a dictatorial bumbledom."[22]

Luce's re-election bid in the fall of 1944 was buffeted by intraparty fighting, resulting in the abrupt resignation of her top backer, J. Kenneth Bradley, from his GOP state chairmanship.[23] Luce survived the primary and entered the general election against a 29-year-old Democrat challenger—Deputy Secretary of State of Connecticut Margaret E. Connors.[24] Connors attacked Luce as a late and opportunistic convert to the cause of a postwar international organization.[25] Meanwhile, Luce intensified her rhetoric against President Roosevelt during a national speaking tour to support the GOP presidential candidate, Governor Thomas Dewey of New York. Luce declared FDR to be "the only American President who ever lied us into a war because he did not have the political courage to lead us into it," arguing that Roosevelt had not halted the transport of vital strategic materials to imperial Japan soon enough as it waged war against China.[26] She also insisted that from 1933 to 1939, as Hitler and Mussolini rose to power in Europe, FDR was "the world's leading isolationist and appeaser" because he had failed to confront fascism more forcefully.[27] Critics assailed her. Mary Norton, dean of Democratic women in the House, accused Luce of "complete ignorance" of the facts. Vice President Wallace dismissed her as a "sharp-tongued glamour girl of forty" who "when running around the country without a mental protector, 'put her dainty foot in her pretty mouth.'"[28] Connors portrayed Luce's "lies" as proof of her core isolationist beliefs.[29] Connors eventually carried industrial sections of the district by wide margins.[30] In an election year when prominent isolationists such as Hamilton Fish of New York went down to defeat, the Democratic message that conflated Luce's criticisms with isolationism proved potent. Luce barely edged Connors by 49.9 to 48.9 percent. A Socialist candidate polled 2,448 votes, a little more than Luce's margin of victory.[31]

In early 1945, Representative Luce expressed grave concerns about Soviet foreign policy objectives, particularly in Eastern Europe. She traveled to liberated Europe and toured the Buchenwald concentration camp where Nazis had murdered thousands of Jews and Soviet war prisoners.

As the German threat receded, Luce perceived a growing menace in Soviet communism. She argued that the Kremlin had "incorporated the Nazi technique of murder" and that Washington should halt the spread of communism in Europe.[32] Returning to the United States, Luce authored a bill to acknowledge American "national responsibility" for the Yalta Agreements of February 1945. Hers was a particularly resonant attack on FDR's compromise with Joseph Stalin over the division of postwar Europe. Recognizing the role the Soviet Army played in crushing German occupation forces in Eastern Europe, FDR had conceded Moscow's sphere of influence in the region. Stalin, whose chief security interest was to prevent another German invasion through a weak Polish state, soon reneged on his promises for free elections and a coalition government in that country. Nevertheless, Luce and other critics described the accords as capitulation on the part of the FDR administration and as "a partition of Poland and overthrow of its friendly, recognized constitutional Government."[33] Her position played well in her district, home to a large Polish and Eastern European community.

Luce's interest in political office, however, steadily eroded. In January 1944, her daughter, Ann, a student at Stanford University, died in an auto wreck.[34] Friends noted that the tragedy sent Luce on a three-year search for closure and greatly diminished her enthusiasm for politics. In January 1946 she declined to run for re-election and retired in January 1947.[35] She did not, however, drop out of politics. Luce addressed the 1948 Republican National Convention.[36] In 1953, President Dwight Eisenhower appointed her U.S. Ambassador to Italy, making her the fifth woman to represent the United States in a foreign country and the first posted to a major European nation.[37] She served until 1957, eventually arranging a conference that settled the disposition of Trieste, a city on the Adriatic Sea, claimed by both Italy and Yugoslavia. In 1959, she was confirmed overwhelmingly to become the U.S. Ambassador to Brazil. But, following a bitter public exchange with Senator Wayne Morse of Oregon that undermined her standing, she resigned her ambassadorship after just three days.[38] The Luces settled in

Honolulu, Hawaii, where Clare remained after Henry's death in 1967. In 1983, she accepted a post on President Ronald Reagan's Foreign Intelligence Advisory Board and received the Presidential Medal of Freedom as "a persistent and effective advocate of freedom, both at home and abroad." After a long battle with cancer, Clare Boothe Luce died on October 9, 1987, in Washington, D.C. Upon her death, the *Washington Post*, which often stood at odds with Luce's politics, eulogized her. "She raised early feminist hell. To the end she said things others wouldn't dare to—cleverly and wickedly—and seemed only to enjoy the resulting fracas . . . Unlike so many of her fellow Washingtonians she was neither fearful nor ashamed of what she meant to say."[39]

FOR FURTHER READING

Biographical Directory of the United States Congress, "Clare Boothe Luce," http://bioguide.congress.gov

Luce, Clare Boothe, ed. *Saints for Now* (San Francisco, CA: Ignatius Press, 1993).

Lyons, Joseph. *Clare Boothe Luce* (New York: Chelsea House, 1989).

Martin, Ralph G. *Henry and Clare: An Intimate Portrait of the Luces* (New York: Putnam's Sons, 1991).

Morris, Sylvia Jukes. *Rage for Fame: The Ascent of Clare Boothe Luce* (New York: Random House, 1997).

Shadegg, Stephen C. *Clare Boothe Luce; A Biography* (New York: Simon and Schuster, 1970).

Sheed, Wilfred. *Clare Boothe Luce* (New York: E.P. Dutton, 1982).

MANUSCRIPT COLLECTION

Library of Congress (Washington, D.C.), Manuscript Division. *Papers:* ca. 1930–1987, 319 linear feet. The papers of Clare Boothe Luce include correspondence (1914–1987) particularly relating to politics, religion, and literary and artistic endeavors; secretarial file (1933–1987); literary file (1919–1987) containing business records, articles, essays, reviews, commentaries, journals, notebooks, memoirs, novels, short stories, plays, nonfiction writings; congressional and ambassadorial correspondence and subject files; Booth and Luce family and personal papers; speech files scrapbooks (141 volumes); and other papers. The collection (dating chiefly from 1930 to 1987) documents Clare Boothe Luce's multifaceted career. Topics in the papers include diplomacy, intelligence service, international relations, national defense and security, public roles for women, and Luce's conversion to Roman Catholicism in 1946. A finding aid is available in the library and online.

NOTES

1   The standard biography for the early years of Luce's life and her transition from publishing to politics is Sylvia Jukes Morris, *Rage for Fame: The Ascent of Clare Boothe Luce* (New York: Random House, 1997). Quote is from Annabel Paxton, *Women in Congress* (Richmond, VA: Dietz Press, 1945): 86.

2   Morris, *Rage for Fame:* 459–460; "Mrs. Luce Decides She Will Seek Nomination as Congress Candidate," 1 September 1942, *New York Times:* 14.

3   "Fight Is Pledged by Miss Kellems," 5 September 1942, *New York Times:* 28; "G.O.P. 'Tempest' Over Mrs. Luce in Connecticut," 5 September 1942, *Christian Science Monitor:* 4.

4   James A. Hagerty, "Mrs. Luce Winner Over 6 Opponents," 15 September 1942, *New York Times:* 25.

5   Libby Lackman, "Mrs. Luce Caustic About Her Rival," 19 September 1942, *New York Times:* 10; Morris, *Rage for Fame:* 469.

6   "Dorothy Thompson Backs Clare Luce," 24 October 1942, *New York Times:* 13.

7   "Willkie Endorses Mrs. Luce in Race," 3 November 1942, *New York Times*: 15.

8   "Election Statistics, 1920 to Present," http://clerk.house.gov/members/electionInfo/elections.html.

9   Milton Bracker, "Mrs. Luce Wins Race for House; Pledges Work for 'Fighting War,'" 4 November 1942, *New York Times*: 1.

10 *Congressional Record*, House, 78th Cong., 1st sess. (9 February 1943): 759–764; "American Air Rule Urged By Mrs. Luce," 10 February 1943, *New York Times*: 27; "Spotlight Performance: Rep. Luce Urges U.S. to Plan for Postwar Air Supremacy," 10 February 1943, *Washington Post*: 1.

11 "Masaryk Rebukes Mrs. Luce," 12 February 1943, *New York Times*: 8; Sydney M. Shalett, "Mrs. Luce in the Limelight Since Her Free-Air Speech," 21 February 1943, *New York Times*: E10; "Clare Boothe Luce Upsets Capital with First Speech," 11 February 1943, *Los Angeles Times*.

12 "Lady Astor Gibes at 'Globaloney,'" 13 February 1943, *New York Times*: 13.

13 "Mrs. Luce Defines Freedom of the Air," 25 February 1943, *New York Times*: 3.

14 *Congressional Record*, House, 78th Cong., 1st sess. (24 June 1943): 6428–6434.

15 *Congressional Record*, House, 79th Cong., 2nd sess. (17 July 1946): 9261–9271; quote on 9262.

16 *Congressional Record*, House, 79th Cong., 2nd sess. (27 June 1946): 7763–7764.

17 *Congressional Record*, House, 79th Cong., 1st sess. (19 December 1945): 12391–12392.

18 "Mrs. Luce Presses Equal Rights Bill," 23 February 1943, *New York Times*: 16; *Congressional Record*, House, 78th Cong., 1st sess. (22 April 1943): 3728.

19 "Mrs. Luce Demands Heavy Tax on Rich," 18 April 1943, *New York Times*: 40.

20 *Current Biography, 1953* (New York: H.W. Wilson and Company, 1953): 375–378; *Congressional Record*, House, 79th Cong., 2nd sess. (31 January 1946): A 378.

21 Kathleen McLaughlin, "Mrs. Luce Assails 'Bumbledom' Trend," 28 June 1944, *New York Times*: 15. Includes a transcript of the complete speech.

22 "Luce Wit: Caustic Clare Can't Resist a Wisecrack," 30 April 1959, *Washington Post*: C1.

23 "Party Rift Threat to Luce Candidacy," 31 July 1944, *New York Times*: 1; "Mrs. Luce to Stand for Re-Election," 1 August 1944, *New York Times*: 12; "Griswold Assails New Deal Policies," 8 August 1944, *New York Times*: 30.

24 "Rival Happy to Make Race," 10 August 1944, *New York Times*: 13.

25 "Offers Plan for Peace," 7 October 1944, *New York Times*: 9.

26 "Roosevelt 'Lied Us Into War,' Mrs. Luce Declares in Chicago," 14 October 1944, *New York Times*: 9.

27 "Mrs. Luce Attacks Chief 'Isolationist,'" 15 October 1944, *New York Times*: 36; "Mrs. Luce Declares Reds Plot Against Labor and Democrats," 17 October 1944, *New York Times*: 14.

28 "Defeat of Mrs. Luce Is Urged by Wallace," 3 November 1944, *New York Times*: 18; "Mrs. Luce Advised to Study Record," 15 October 1944, *New York Times*: 36; "Calls Mrs. Luce Shallow," 11 October 1944, *New York Times*: 22.

29 "Woman Opponent Says Mrs. Luce 'Lied' in Accusing President of Falsehoods," 16 October 1944, *New York Times*: 11; "Miss Connors Predicts Election by 5,000; Asks Mrs. Luce Some Questions in Telegram," 1 November 1944, *New York Times*: 40.

30 "Mrs. Luce is Re-elected," 8 November 1944, *New York Times*: 2; "Fish Is Defeated; Clare Luce Wins," 8 November 1944, *New York Times*: 1.

31 "Election Statistics, 1920 to Present," http://clerk.house.gov/members/electionInfo/elections.html.

32 "Mrs. Luce Likens Russians to Nazis," 28 May 1945, *New York Times*: 5.

33 "Asylum for Poles Urged by Mrs. Luce," 20 February 1943, *New York Times*: 12.

34 "Ann Brokaw Dies in Auto Collision," 12 January 1944, *New York Times*: 25.

35 "Mrs. Luce Decides Against House Race," 31 January 1946, *New York Times*: 17; "Senate Attracts Mrs. Luce?" 28 January 1946, *Christian Science Monitor*: 4. Another reason for Luce's decision not to run for re-election was the attention given her conversion to Catholicism in early 1946. Fearing that opponents would capitalize on her conversion, she told the press that, "Therefore, I have chosen to be unavailable by design or draft for elective office." See, "Mrs. Luce Turns Roman Catholic," 18 February 1946, *Christian Science Monitor*: 7.

36 Bart Barnes, "Clare Boothe Luce, Renaissance Woman, Dies at 84," 10 October 1987, *Washington Post*: C8.

37 W.H. Lawrence, "Rome Envoy's Post Seen for Mrs. Luce," 24 January 1953, *New York Times*: 10; "Mrs. Luce Chosen as Envoy to Rome," 8 February 1953, *New York Times*: 1; Edward F. Ryan, "Mrs. Luce Appointed Ambassador to Italy," 8 February 1953, *Washington Post*: M1; "Eisenhower to Nominate Mrs. Luce to Rome Post," 9 February 1953, *Christian Science Monitor*: 14.

38 Russell Baker, "Mrs. Luce Wins in Senate; Husband Asks Her to Quit," 29 April 1959, *New York Times*: 1; Edwin L. Dale, Jr., "Mrs. Luce Quits; Declares Morse 'Poisoned' Task," 2 May 1959, *New York Times*: 1.

39 "Clare Boothe Luce," 11 October 1987, *Washington Post:* H6.

Winifred Claire Stanley
1909–1996

UNITED STATES REPRESENTATIVE ★ REPUBLICAN FROM NEW YORK
1943–1945

During her one term as a New York Congress-woman, Winifred Stanley tirelessly championed women's rights. The former prosecutor and the first female assistant district attorney in Erie County, New York, urged Americans to contemplate and begin planning for the imperatives of peacetime demobilization and new international responsibilities after World War II.

Winifred Stanley was born on August 14, 1909, in the Bronx, New York. The eldest of six children, she was raised by her mother, Mary, who once was an English and a music teacher, and her father, architect John Francis Stanley, in Buffalo, New York. Winifred Stanley graduated from Lafayette High School and earned her bachelor's degree with honors from the University of Buffalo in 1930. Stanley went on to receive her L.L.B. and J.D. from the same institution in 1933, graduating first in her class. In 1934, she commenced her law practice.

Stanley's reputation as a lawyer was impeccable, but her greatest precongressional accomplishment proved to be the root of her future defense of women's rights while serving in Congress. When going to court one morning, she found the courtroom closed to women because of the nature of the crime being tried. She considered this an intolerable affront to women, especially because her gender also had been barred from New York juries, regardless of the crime. Stanley considered jury duty "second in importance only to the right to vote" and mobilized women's clubs, church societies, and political organizations to press for women's right to participate in the courtroom as citizen peers.[1] Her actions not only won the right for participation on a jury panel for women in New York but also caught the attention of then-District Attorney Leo J. Hagerty. He subsequently

named 28-year-old Stanley the first female assistant district attorney of Erie County.

Following the 1940 Census, New York stood to lose two seats in Congress. The Republican Party searched for an effective short-term Representative to win the state's At-Large seat slated for elimination. Once redistricting occurred, their ideal candidate would choose not to run against a higher-ranking Republican in the following election. Winifred Stanley, by then a successful assistant district attorney, was the perfect choice. Stanley was elected to the 78th Congress (1943–1945) in 1942, winning in a landslide and topping eight other candidates with a final total of nearly two million votes.[2]

With a strong legal background, she sought a spot on the Judiciary Committee. Despite her qualifications, the Congresswoman was denied a position because she lacked seniority and because sexism still prevailed among her mostly male colleagues. James W. Wadsworth, Jr., a New York Representative in charge of committee assignments, flatly opposed women in the workplace. He believed that, "a woman's place is in the home."[3] Other Republican leaders seemed disinclined to assist Stanley, perhaps because of her short-term status.[4] Instead of the Judiciary Committee, she was appointed to the Patents and Civil Service committees, both lower-rung panels.[5]

The imminent end of World War II created the challenge for the 78th Congress to provide for victory and plan for the subsequent peace. Citing the overwhelming support of her constituents, Stanley supported economist Beardsley Ruml's plan in 1943—a suggestion to forgive all 1942 federal income taxes, while instating a withholding tax on all 1943 wages.[6] The withheld tax would allow for a quick source of revenue for the federal government's war effort,

and Americans would not have to pay the previous year's taxes alongside their present dues.

Stanley also gained a reputation for being a pragmatic postwar planner who was more interested in the "prose" of the readjustment to peacetime, than in the "poetry" of victory.[7] She commented that, "Maintaining peace is like maintaining democracy. It's a full time job."[8] On January 24, 1944, Stanley introduced a concurrent resolution calling for a special joint committee to deal with postwar employment. Citing the national problem of returning soldiers who would flood the job market, she insisted that the committee be bipartisan and consist of Members from different parts of the country.[9] In a speech on the House Floor, she also proposed a resolution in support of an American delegation to the proposed United Nations.[10] In addition, Stanley looked out for the interests of war veterans and her constituents by pushing for the establishment of more Veterans' Administration hospitals in upstate New York.

Stanley continued to advocate women's rights during her congressional service, becoming the first Member of Congress to introduce an equal pay for equal work bill. On June 19, 1944, Stanley proposed a bill to amend the National Labor Relations Act to make it unlawful "to discriminate against any employee, in the rate of compensation paid, on account of sex."[11] She wanted to maintain in "peacetime the drive and energy which women have contributed to the war effort" and further declared that, "we shall only be paying lip service to those glorious and fundamental guarantees of our nation's heritage."[12] She vigorously worked for the Equal Rights Amendment (ERA) to both the U.S. Congress and the New York state constitution. Along with Margaret Chase Smith of Maine, Stanley was one of the first House Members to push for a renewed effort at passing ERA in 1943, the 20th anniversary of its introduction in the House.[13] In addition, she argued that women should be commissioned as surgeons in the U.S. Army. "It has often been remarked that this is a 'man's world,'" she once noted, "It's 'our world,' and this battered old universe needs and will need the best brains and the ability of both men and women."[14] Stanley also

introduced a joint resolution calling for a constitutional amendment to eliminate the poll tax, and she also backed increasing wages for postal employees.[15]

In line with her party, Congresswoman Stanley was a vocal critic of the Roosevelt administration's New Deal programs. During the 1944 campaign, while losing her own seat to reapportionment, she nevertheless remained busy, taking to the campaign trail in 15 states to urge election of the GOP presidential candidate, New York Governor Thomas Dewey. During one rally, Stanley told the crowd: "American voters are sick of the New Deal's mismanagement, which results in two agencies doing the work of one. They are tired of the countless alphabetical agencies and bureaus which have sprung up like mushrooms. They want the alphabet given back to the children. They want the Government of this country restored to the people. They want intelligence and integrity restored to the White House."[16] Stanley, however, was not above urging government intervention when New York's interests were at stake. In February 1943, responding to a meat shortage crisis in New York City, Stanley asked the wartime Office of Price Administration to aid independent meat packers who were suffering from high livestock prices.[17]

Despite her reputation as a tenacious worker, Stanley also was active in the Washington, D.C., social scene. She received a Fashion Academy Award for being one of the nation's best-dressed public women. She also served as an adviser to the "Eight Girls to Every Man" club, an organization finding homes and proper social engagements for young women working for the federal government.[18] Rumor linked Stanley romantically with Republican Whip, Congressman Leslie Arends of Illinois. Both parties publicly denied any such relationship.[19]

After leaving Congress in 1945, Stanley accepted an appointment in New York Governor Dewey's administration. She was later appointed counsel for the State Employees Retirement System and subsequently returned to the position of assistant district attorney, this time in the Albany office of the state law department. She retired from state service in 1979 but remained in private practice until 1986. After a brief illness, Winifred Stanley died on February 29, 1996, in Kenmore, New York.

FOR FURTHER READING

Biographical Directory of the United States Congress, "Winifred Claire Stanley," http://bioguide.congress.gov

NOTES

1   Hope Chamberlin, *A Minority of Members: Women in the U.S. Congress* (New York: Praeger, 1973): 161.

2   "Election Statistics, 1920 to Present," http://clerk.house.gov/ members/electionInfo/index.html.

3   Chamberlin, *A Minority of Members*: 162.

4   Republican Leader Joe Martin seems not to have come to Stanley's assistance. No mention is made in his autobiography. He occasionally intervened on behalf of House GOP women, as was the case in the 1950s when he helped block efforts to redistrict Edith Nourse Rogers' Massachusetts seat.

5   Charles Stewart III, "Committee Hierarchies in the Modernizing House, 1875–1947," *American Journal of Political Science*, 36 (No. 4, November 1992): 835–856.

6   *Congressional Record*, House, 78th Cong., 1st sess. (15 March 1943): A1196.

7   Chamberlin, *A Minority of Members*: 160.

8   Chamberlin, *A Minority of Members*: 160.

9   "Joint Action," 4 February 1944, *Washington Post*: 8.

10   *Congressional Record*, House, 78th Cong., 2nd sess. (15 December 1944): 9555.

11   "Miss Stanley Backs Bill and Plank on Equal Pay," 20 June 1944, *New York Times*: 22.

12   Chamberlin, *A Minority of Members*: 160.

13   "Mrs. Luce Presses Equal Rights Bill," 23 February 1943, *New York Times*: 16.

14   "Move Started for Equal Pay After the War," 20 June 1944, *Christian Science Monitor*: 9.

15   "Submits Poll-Tax Ban Amendment," 18 May 1944, *New York Times*: 22. *Congressional Record*, House, 78th Cong., 2nd sess. (12 December 1944): A4721.

16   "Anti-New Deal Tide Seen," 6 November 1944, *New York Times*: 16.

17   "Miss Stanley Asks OPA to Aid Packers," 12 February 1943, *New York Times*: 17.

18   "Stanley Joins Group to Advise Government Girls," 29 April 1943, *Washington Post*: B1.

19   Hope Ridings Miller, "Oddments of Interest Picked Up in Passing—About Persons of More Than Passing Importance," 12 January 1944, *Washington Post*: B5.

Willa Lybrand Fulmer
1884–1968

UNITED STATES REPRESENTATIVE ★ DEMOCRAT FROM SOUTH CAROLINA
1944–1945

Like several other congressional widows from the South, Willa Lybrand Fulmer filled her late husband's seat long enough for party officials to successfully insert a long-term successor. Mrs. Fulmer did not participate actively in the long career of her powerful husband, Hampton P. Fulmer, author of the Agricultural Adjustment Act (AAA) of 1933. But her name recognition with voters secured her a short term in the final months of the 78th Congress (1943–1945), helping to preserve a narrow Democratic majority in the House.

Willa Essie Lybrand was born in Wagener, South Carolina, on February 3, 1884. She attended public schools in Wagener and the Greenville Female Seminary. In 1901, at age 17, she married Hampton Pitts Fulmer, a successful cotton farmer, merchant, and banker. Hampton Fulmer would eventually serve in the South Carolina state house and then go on to a 23-year career in the U.S. House of Representatives that included the chairmanship of the influential Agriculture Committee. Congressman Fulmer was a tireless advocate for farmers and a major figure in New Deal efforts to alleviate their economic woes. He authored the AAA, which dealt with the problem of low farm commodities prices by controlling surplus crops and providing low-interest farm mortgage refinancing. Congressman Fulmer also authored the U.S. Cotton Grading Act, which standardized cotton-grading methods and he was well-known for helping to draft a $1.3 billion bill to build a national veterans' hospital network.[1] Willa Fulmer raised their three daughters—Margie, Ruby, and Willa—and, by the 1930s, was a fixture at many capital society events. Although she and her husband maintained a home in Orangeburg, South Carolina, Mrs. Fulmer spent much of her time in Washington, D.C., where two of her daughters settled into married life. On a roster of Representatives with family members working in their congressional offices, the name Willa Fulmer appears as an aide to Congressman Fulmer in the early 1930s; she earned $266 dollars per month, which put her in the upper salary bracket for Capitol Hill staff at the time.[2]

The day after Hampton Fulmer died suddenly of a heart attack on October 19, 1944, South Carolina Democratic officials phoned Willa Fulmer to ask her to run in a special election to fill her husband's vacant seat, which encompassed six counties in the southeastern part of the state, including the city of Orangeburg.[3] Congressman Fulmer's death had reduced the Democratic advantage in the closely divided House to just two seats, sending party leaders scrambling for a sure-fire successor for the remainder of the 78th Congress. But the process was complicated because Congressman Fulmer had already been nominated, and his death occurred less than three weeks before the general election. Party leaders were forced to call a nominating convention for November 1, a week before the general election.

From the start, it was clear that Willa Fulmer would be a placeholder. While agreeing to seek the nomination, she stated she had no intention of running in the concurrent election for the following Congress. Fulmer later recalled that she acquiesced to the party's wishes but "with a deep sense of improbability."[4] She had never been active in her husband's political career and had little desire to pursue a public career. In the November 1, special primary, she ran unopposed for the short term in the final two months of the 78th Congress.[5] For years the widely popular Hampton Fulmer had run unopposed, easily winning the Democratic

OFFICE OF HISTORY AND PRESERVATION,

U.S. HOUSE OF REPRESENTATIVES

The *Washington Post* described Congresswoman Willa Fulmer as "more of a southern gentlewoman than a career type," who, nevertheless, "surprises you with her knowledge of politics and world events."

nominations which, in the one-party South, were tantamount to winning the general election. While Willa Fulmer ran unopposed and enjoyed name recognition among the constituency whom her husband had served for nearly a quarter century, voter participation in the November 7 special election was extremely low; she received 7,943 votes out of the district with a population of nearly 362,000.[6] Also on that November 7 ballot was the contest for the full term in the 79th Congress (1945–1947); the winning candidate, Democrat John J. Riley, received nearly 20,000 votes (97 percent) against his GOP challenger.

Days before Congresswoman Fulmer was sworn in on November 16, 1944, the *Washington Post* described her as "more of a southern gentlewoman than a career type," who, nevertheless, "surprises you with her knowledge of politics and world events."[7] Whatever her aptitude for the job, however, Willa Fulmer never got a chance to demonstrate her abilities. Events were so rushed, that when House Speaker Sam Rayburn of Texas administered the oath of office to Representative Willa Fulmer on November 16, her election credentials had not yet arrived from South Carolina. Thus, Representative James P. Richards of South Carolina asked special permission from his colleagues to conduct the swearing-in; they consented.[8] She moved into her husband's Cannon House Office Building quarters, but during her lame duck term, Representative Fulmer made no floor speeches and received no committee assignments. Congress adjourned a month after she took her seat.

Fulmer's two-month term ended on January 3, 1945, when John J. Riley was sworn into Congress as the district's new Representative—the first of his eight straight terms in the House. Mrs. Fulmer returned to private life, retiring to a home in northwest Washington, D.C.[9] She returned occasionally to South Carolina, engaged in agricultural pursuits, and also became an avid traveler. Willa Lybrand Fulmer died aboard a luxury liner en route to Europe on May 13, 1968.

FOR FURTHER READING

Biographical Directory of the United States Congress, "Willa Lybrand Fulmer," http://bioguide.congress.gov

NOTES

1   "Congressman H.P. Fulmer Dies at Home," 20 October 1944, *Washington Post*: 1.

2   Based on numerous society page articles from the *Washington Post*. For the congressional office citation see, "List of Representatives and Their Employees with Identical Names as Shown by Payroll," 21 May 1932, *New York Times*: 16.

3   This is according to Hope Chamberlin, *A Minority of Members: Women in the U.S. Congress* (New York: Praeger, 1973): 164.

4   Chamberlin, *A Minority of Members*: 164.

5   "John J. Riley Named to Seat in Congress," 2 November 1944, *The State* (Columbia, SC): 1.

6   Michael Dubin et al., *U.S. Congressional Elections, 1788–1997* (Jefferson, NC: McFarland and Company, Inc., Publishers, 1998): 549.

7   Genevieve Reynolds, "Nation's Feminine Eyes Are on a Distaff Contingent Named as Representatives," 12 November 1944, *Washington Post*: S1.

8   "Mrs. Fulmer Is Sworn In," 17 November 1944, *The State* (Columbia, SC): 10-A.

9   "Willa L. Fulmer, Served Two Months in Congress," 26 May 1968, *Washington Post*: D4.

Emily Taft Douglas
1899–1994

UNITED STATES REPRESENTATIVE ★ DEMOCRAT FROM ILLINOIS
1945–1947

In 1944, Emily Taft Douglas, a proponent of overseas humanitarian projects and a postwar United Nations Organization, defeated one of the most strident isolationists in the House of Representatives—heralding, as some observers believed, the triumph of American internationalism. "We, ourselves, must have faith in the doctrine of collective security as a bulwark against another war and chaos," Representative Douglas said. "We must be prepared to make whatever compromises and sacrifices that security demands."[1]

Emily Taft was born in Chicago, Illinois, on April 10, 1899, one of three daughters of the famous sculptor Larado Taft and Ada Bartlett Taft. President William Howard Taft was a distant cousin. She grew up in Chicago and traveled widely with her father during his frequent lecture and teaching tours in the United States and Europe. President Woodrow Wilson's effort to coax the United States into the League of Nations, though unsuccessful, convinced Emily Taft to register as a Democrat.[2] She graduated with honors a year early, in 1920, from the University of Chicago, with a B.A. in economics and political science. After graduating, she embarked on a theatrical career. She studied at the American Academy of Dramatic Art in New York City. Emily Taft joined national theatrical tours, winning acclaim as the lead in a Broadway production of *The Cat and the Canary*. She also became active in Illinois politics, as a protégé of pioneer women state legislators.[3] She served as the organizing secretary for the Illinois League of Women Voters and, in that capacity, met her future husband, Paul Douglas, a University of Chicago economics professor and future U.S. Senator. They married in 1931 and raised one daughter, Jean.

The Douglases took up the internationalist cause after a 1935 trip to Europe convinced them of the dangers of fascism in Benito Mussolini's Italy and Adolf Hitler's Germany. The couple returned to Chicago, where they began a public campaign to warn fellow citizens about the growing menace in Europe. In 1938, Paul Douglas won election as a Chicago alderman, and in 1942 he mounted an unsuccessful campaign as an independent Democrat for a U.S. Senate seat from Illinois. Ten days later, Paul Douglas enlisted in the Marines as a 50-year-old private, where he served in the Pacific theater in World War II and became a decorated combat veteran. Emily Douglas returned from the 1935 trip abroad to organize and chair the government and foreign policy department of the Illinois League of Women Voters. In 1942, she became executive secretary of the International Relations Center in Chicago. During the war, she also traveled widely to raise funds for the Red Cross organization.

It was Douglas's work as an advocate of internationalism, touring the state and the country, which brought her into her first campaign for public office. Illinois Democratic leaders approached Douglas to run for the state's lone At-Large seat (with what was then the fourth-largest constituency in the nation) in the winter of 1943–1944. Douglas was shocked by the proposal, recalling that her first response was, "Gentlemen, this is so sudden!"[4] In February 1944, after turning down the initial offer, Douglas reconsidered and accepted and won the Democratic primary. In the general election, she challenged two-term incumbent Republican Stephen A. Day, a staunch isolationist. Day was controversial even among the party faithful for his Nazi sympathies and his authorship of a 1941 book, *We Must Save the Republic Now*, which argued against intervention in the European war.[5] Day enjoyed an enormous media advantage with the endorsement of the anti-FDR *Chicago Tribune* and its powerful publisher, Colonel

Robert McCormick. Douglas charged that "by his voting record [Day] stands convicted as the worst obstructionist in Congress."[6] Douglas also ran as a supporter of Franklin Roosevelt's New Deal programs and foreign policies, including his plan for American participation in the post-war United Nations organization. Observers speculated that Douglas would have to ride FDR's coattails to win her seat; in fact, she defeated Day by a greater margin than FDR's over GOP presidential candidate Thomas Dewey, taking 52 percent of the vote, with most of her support concentrated in Chicago. "Building a permanent, workable peace is the big job of this generation," Douglas said shortly afterward. "It is evident that the electorate made a definite decision to get rid of extreme isolationists and obstructionists."[7] Syndicated columnist Marquis Childs hailed her victory as symbolizing the receding of isolationism," in some ways more significant than the defeat of [isolationist Representative] Ham Fish in New York."[8]

Representative Douglas registered her greatest influence in international relations. She received her lone committee assignment on Foreign Affairs and was widely recognized as a specialist in the field. Douglas became a forceful and erudite proponent of the Dumbarton Oaks plan for the creation of the United Nations. "My election was, without question, a mandate from the people of Illinois for the ideal of world cooperation," Douglas told the *New York Times*. "In Congress, and especially in my work on the Foreign Affairs Committee, I am going to proceed on the thesis that the will to get along with the other nations of the world is of greater importance than the machinery. Failure to see that, I think, lies at the root of our not having achieved a permanent peace after the last war."[9] In marked contrast to her isolationist Illinois colleague, Jessie Sumner, Douglas voted with the vast majority of the House to support the United Nations and the Bretton Woods Agreements, which established the World Bank and the International Monetary Fund. Along with California Representative Jerry Voorhis, she proposed legislation to put the United Nations in charge of international programs for arms control and the abolition of atomic weaponry. "With our new powers of destruction so vast and immediate, we have no time for fumbling," Douglas said in a floor speech. "The

ominous race must be halted at once.... The speed and firmness with which the [United Nations] acts, may determine the fate of mankind."[10]

Having worked on behalf of the Red Cross during the war, she was an ardent supporter of the United Nations Relief and Rehabilitation Administration (UNRRA), which provided food, shelter, and clothing to millions of displaced European postwar refugees. In August 1945, she joined several committee colleagues on a visit to Europe to inspect the work of UNNRA, particularly in occupied Germany and Italy. The spectacle of devastation in Europe convinced her that UNRRA, backed principally by American dollars, had a crucial role to play in the early reconstruction of the continent. "As the only major power which was neither bombed nor invaded, we must bear the chief burden of relief," Douglas declared during House debates in the late fall of 1945. Furthermore, she believed UNRRA was the first experiment in making the international organization a reality. "Before men can cooperate politically, they must have bread, shelter, clothes, and medical care," Douglas said in a floor speech. "By meeting elemental needs, the United Nations can save the lives of millions, [and] undermine the pull of violent nationalisms which emerge like fascism after every war."[11] Based on her visit to a refugee camp, she later proposed a program for the rehabilitation of European youth who were reared under fascist regimes. In the spring of 1946, as the threat of famine hung over Western Europe, Douglas urged Americans to return to wartime rationing to save food for donations.[12]

In the 1946 midterm elections, Douglas's re-election campaign was seen as a bellwether race for the state and for Democrats nationally. Her opponent was William G. Stratton, a navy veteran and former one-term House Member and a staunch isolationist who pledged opposition to any foreign loans and ran on the GOP platform of lowering taxes and slashing federal expenditures.[13] Douglas ran on a platform which supported President Harry S. Truman's domestic policies and his expanded foreign aid programs. Weary and frustrated by wartime controls, high prices, commodity shortages, and the economic dislocations caused by demobilization, voters took their anger out on the Truman administration and its Democratic supporters in the House. At the polls, Americans ousted 54 House Democrats, returning control of the chamber to the GOP in the 80th Congress (1947–1949). Among those voted out of office was Douglas, losing 55 to 44 percent to Stratton, who ran a weak second to Douglas in Chicago but carried all but four of the downstate counties. The trend carried over statewide, where Republicans picked up six seats to take 20 of the 26 House delegation spots.[14]

Douglas was active in politics for much of her post congressional life. In 1948, she campaigned on behalf of her husband, Paul, who won election to the first of his three terms as a U.S. Senator from Illinois. Emily Douglas was appointed in 1950 as U.S. Representative to the U.N. Educational, Scientific, and Cultural Organization (UNESCO), an organization for international cultural and scientific exchange that she had supported during her House career.[15] She later served on the legislative committee of the Unitarian Fellowship for Social Justice and as vice president and moderator of the American Unitarian Association, its highest lay office. In 1965, she marched in the Selma, Alabama, civil rights protest with the Reverend Martin Luther King, Jr. Emily Douglas also authored several books during her lifetime, including *Margaret Sanger* (1970), a biography of the pioneer in family planning, and *Remember the Ladies* (1966), a book of essays on famous American women. After Paul Douglas died in 1976, she resided in White Plains, New York, where she passed away on January 28, 1994.

FOR FURTHER READING

Biographical Directory of the United States Congress, "Emily Taft Douglas," http://bioguide.congress.gov

Douglas, Emily Taft. *Margaret Sanger; Pioneer of the Future* (New York: Holt, Rinehart, and Winston, 1970).

———. *Remember the Ladies; The Story of Great Women Who Helped Shape America* (New York: G.P. Putnam's Sons, 1966).

MANUSCRIPT COLLECTIONS

Columbia University (New York, NY), Oral History Research Office. *Oral History:* In the Paul Howard Douglas Interview, 1975, 52 pages. Includes reminiscences of Paul Howard Douglas. Subjects covered include Emily Taft Douglas.

Library of Congress (Washington, D.C.), Manuscript Division. *Oral History:* Transcript in the Oral History Collection of the U.S. Association of Former Members of Congress. Sound recording in the Library's Motion Picture, Broadcasting and Recorded Sound Division.

NOTES

1   Cabell Phillips, "Presenting Mrs. Douglas and Mrs. Douglas," 18 February 1945, *New York Times*: SM 11.
2   Hope Chamberlin, *A Minority of Members: Women in the U.S. Congress* (New York: Praeger): 178.
3   Only the married names of two mentors (Mrs. J. Paul Goode and Mrs. Henry W. Cheney) are known; see Annabel Paxton, *Women in Congress* (Richmond, VA: Dietz Press, 1945): 110.
4   *Current Biography, 1945* (New York: H.W. Wilson Company, 1945): 159; Genevieve Reynolds, "Nation's Feminine Eyes Are on Distaff Contingent Named as Representatives," 12 November 1944, *Washington Post*: S1.
5   Drew Pearson, "The Washington Merry-Go-Round," 25 October 1944, *Washington Post*: 14.
6   *Current Biography, 1945*: 159.
7   Chamberlin, *A Minority of Members*: 176–180.
8   Marquis Childs, "Washington Calling: New Congress," 11 November 1944, *Washington Post*: 4.
9   Phillips, "Presenting Mrs. Douglas and Mrs. Douglas."
10   *Congressional Record*, House, 79th Cong., 1st sess. (17 December 1945): 12223.
11   *Congressional Record*, House, 79th Cong., 1st sess. (5 December 1945): 11502–11503; *Congressional Record*, House, 79th Cong., 1st sess. (31 October 1945): 10228–10229.
12   "Rep. Douglas Urges Return to Food Rationing in U.S.," 2 April 1946, *Washington Post*: 3; for full speech, see *Congressional Record*, House, 79th Cong., 2nd sess. (1 April 1946): 2920.
13   "Illinois GOP Gets 3 Seats in House," 6 November 1946, *New York Times*: 6; James Reston, "Midwest Cities Political Question; Republicans Work Hardest There," 17 October 1946, *New York Times*: 12.
14   "Illinois GOP Wins 5 Congress Seats," 7 November 1946, *New York Times*: 9.
15   *Congressional Record*, House, 79th Cong., 2nd sess. (21 May 1946): 5383–5384.

Helen Gahagan Douglas
1900–1980

UNITED STATES REPRESENTATIVE ★ DEMOCRAT FROM CALIFORNIA

1945–1951

Decades before Ronald Reagan, stage star and California celebrity Helen Gahagan Douglas made the transition from acting to politics to become one of her party's standard-bearers. In an era when Cold War priorities often marginalized domestic reforms, Douglas became a beacon to New Deal liberals, who hoped to push economic and social legislation into the post–World War II period.[1] Impatient with the institutional pace and intricacies of the House, Representative Douglas used her skills as an actress and her fame to speak passionately about topics ranging from equal rights for women to civil rights for African Americans and protections for the American worker.

Helen Gahagan was born in Boonton, New Jersey, on November 25, 1900, one of five children raised by Walter Hamer Gahagan II and Lillian Rose Mussen Gahagan. Her father owned a prosperous construction and shipyard business, and the family lived in the upper-middle-class section of Park Slope in Brooklyn, New York. Helen Gahagan attended the prestigious Berkeley School for Girls in Brooklyn. She later studied at the Capen School for Girls in Northampton, Massachusetts, and then at Barnard College in New York City. Against her father's wishes, Gahagan left school before earning a degree. From 1922 to 1938, she pursued a career as an opera singer and an actress, starring in a variety of shows and plays. In a 1930 Broadway hit, *Tonight or Never*, Helen Gahagan met and costarred with her future husband, Melvyn Douglas. They married on April 5, 1931, and left New York City to relocate in Los Angeles as Melvyn pursued a film career. There, the Douglases raised two children, Peter and Mary Helen.

The move west, made in the early years of the Great Depression, exposed Helen Douglas to the suffering and deprivations wreaked by a disastrous drought and economic crash. It also inspired her to become active in public service on behalf of migrant farm workers and others whom the Depression had dislocated. "I became active in politics because I saw the possibility, if we all sat back and did nothing, of a world in which there would no longer be any stages for actors to act on," she recalled.[2] Domestic woes were compounded by foreign dangers. Douglas and her husband traveled frequently and witnessed firsthand Japanese militarism and European fascism in the 1930s.[3] With international tensions on the rise, Helen Douglas set entertainment work aside and threw herself into public-service projects, becoming a member of the national advisory committee of the Works Progress Administration and a member of the California state committee of the National Youth Administration. She traveled frequently to the White House to meet with Eleanor Roosevelt. In 1940, she became a California Democratic national committeewoman—a post she held until 1944—serving as the vice chair of the California Democratic central committee and as head of the women's division. From 1942 to 1943, she was on the board of the California Housing and Planning Association.

In 1944, when six-term incumbent Democrat Thomas Ford announced he would retire from his seat encompassing downtown Los Angeles, Douglas entered the race to succeed her political ally. With Ford's endorsement, she prevailed in the primary as the only woman among eight candidates, receiving more than 14,000 votes, versus about 5,200 for the runner-up.[4] In the general election, Douglas appealed to African-American voters in her urban district. Her platform called for equal rights, labor rights, food subsidies, unemployment insurance for

IMAGE COURTESY OF THE LIBRARY OF CONGRESS

returning GIs, a revitalized farm security program, and income-based taxation for farmers and small business owners. She also advocated international cooperation. Her candidacy drew attention to equality for women. When asked about a woman's place in Congress, Douglas replied, "Politics is a job that needs doing—by anyone who is interested enough to train for it and work at it. It's like housekeeping; someone has to do it. Whether the job is done by men or women is not important—only whether the job is done well or badly."[5] Douglas ultimately prevailed over her Republican opponent, William D. Campbell, by a slim margin, 51.5 to 48.5 percent. As she established a reputation in the House, Douglas's electoral support increased. In her subsequent bids for re-election in 1946 and 1948, she defeated her GOP challengers with 54 percent and 65 percent, respectively.[6]

Douglas had little interest in mastering legislative processes, preferring instead to call attention to her agenda while using her celebrity to gain public exposure and awareness for specific programs.[7] Her busy congressional schedule was complemented by an equally hectic speech-making itinerary around the country. Repeatedly during her congressional years, Douglas acted as a publicist for key liberal issues by making major speeches, both on and away from the House Floor, on issues ranging from postwar price controls to civil rights to the international regulation of atomic energy.

Douglas's sole committee assignment throughout her six years in the House reflected one of her many areas of focus: Foreign Affairs. At the center of her philosophy on U.S. foreign policy was Douglas's abiding internationalism. Douglas believed that America's dominant military and economic "strength carries responsibilities and obligations which we must fulfill."[8] Consequently, she backed American participation in the United Nations, supported the implementation of the Bretton Woods Agreements, which created the World Bank and the International Monetary Fund, and consistently challenged U.S. policy early in the Cold War which, she believed, contributed to tensions with the Soviet Union. Douglas also supported Philippine independence and the creation of a Jewish state in Israel.[9] President Harry S. Truman appointed her as an alternate U.S. Delegate to the United Nations Assembly.

In early October 1945, as debate raged over control and oversight of atomic energy, Douglas weighed in with a major floor speech that called for civilian, rather than military, control over the developing science. "We cannot keep this knowledge to ourselves," she warned. "The air needs to be cleared of suspicion and doubt and fear. The United Nations, through the Security Council, should have the right to find out and know what is going on in every research laboratory in the world."[10] In the winter of 1945–1946, Congresswoman Douglas and Senator Brien McMahon of Connecticut introduced nearly identical bills which aimed at developing peaceful uses of atomic energy through U.S. civilian control. Douglas fought to strike out amendments during House passage which granted far-ranging powers to military developers. Many of these provisions did not appear when the House and Senate versions were reconciled, and the measure was passed in 1946. The Atomic Energy Act created the Atomic Energy Commission, charged with oversight of the development and testing of atomic weapons, as well as with peaceful applications of atomic power.[11]

Douglas's House career also drew from her devotion to domestic priorities, including the continuation of New Deal economic policies and the pursuit of civil rights reform. In 1948, she trooped onto the House Floor toting a bag of groceries, to demonstrate the reduced buying power of housewives after the government lifted wartime price controls.[12] A vocal and consistent defender of labor and unions, Douglas vehemently opposed the Taft–Hartley Act. Officially known as the Labor–Management Relations Act, the bill encompassed a series of amendments to the New Deal-era National Labor Relations Act, weakening the power of organized labor. Among its most controversial provisions was an amendment requiring union leaders to sign loyalty oaths attesting that they were not Communist Party members.[13] Douglas also was a major proponent of federal efforts to provide affordable housing for Americans in the postwar era, an issue central to her constituency in booming California.[14]

During a period when the Jim Crow laws still applied in the nation's capital, Helen Douglas used her outsider status to challenge prevailing racial attitudes. The first white Representative with African Americans on her staff, she also sought to desegregate Capitol restaurants. Douglas also attacked the practice of poll taxes, which effectively prevented many southern African Americans from voting, and she urged passage of antilynching legislation.[15] When Mississippi Democrat John Rankin, chairman of the Committee on World War Veterans' Legislation, charged that black regiments performed incompetently during key

used in many quarters to blind us to our real problems."[18] In her 1948 re-election campaign, Douglas's GOP opponent used redbaiting tactics to try to unseat her. The strategy failed, as she won by the widest margin of her career, but it set a troubling pattern in motion.

In 1950, Representative Douglas opted to run for one of California's U.S. Senate seats. When incumbent Senator Sheridan Downey abruptly withdrew from the race, Manchester Boddy, editor of the Democratic-leaning *Los Angeles Times*, became Douglas's principal opponent. Despite Boddy's attempts to smear Douglas during the

"The first step toward liberation for any group is to use the power in hand. . . . And the power in hand is the vote."

—HELEN GAHAGAN DOUGLAS, *MS. MAGAZINE*, OCTOBER 1973

World War II battles, Douglas fiercely fought the allegation using military records. African-American servicemen, she reminded colleagues, fought "for a freedom which [they have] not as yet been permitted fully to share."[16]

Douglas's role as a spokesperson for liberal causes made her beloved by liberals and reviled by conservatives. In October 1945, Douglas lashed out at the House Un-American Activities Committee, which was investigating alleged communist sympathizers and which would eventually focus on many Hollywood writers and artists. Douglas argued that such a panel was unconstitutional.[17] Critics charged that she was a communist fellow traveler. Douglas countered that the gravest danger to American society was not the threat of internal, or even external, communist subversion but that of demagoguery and repressive domestic controls justified in the name of national security. "The fear of communism in this country is not rational," Douglas exhorted. "And that irrational fear of communism is being

Democratic primary by labeling her a communist sympathizer, or a "pink lady," Douglas ultimately prevailed by a 2–1 margin.[19] The negative campaign begun by Boddy—particularly the "pink lady" epithet—resonated in the general election, as Douglas's Republican opponent, Representative Richard M. Nixon, employed a similar strategy. Nixon's ample campaign purse permitted him to wage a massive public relations campaign against Douglas. Nixon accused her of being "pink down to her underwear"; he distributed hundreds of thousands of pink flyers comparing Douglas's liberal voting record with those of other congressional liberals. Douglas defended her voting record and returned Nixon's verbal volleys; in one speech she referred to Nixon as "Tricky Dick," a name that stuck with him for the remainder of his political career.[20] But when Douglas tried to redirect the debate to compare their congressional careers and positions on issues, Nixon's whispering campaign of unsubstantiated innuendos kept voter interest focused on allegations against Douglas. Nixon won with 59 percent of the vote, a nearly 700,000-vote plurality.[21]

Douglas retired to private life as a lecturer and a successful author. She later returned to the theater and performed in two Broadway plays. In 1964 she was again in the political spotlight when President Lyndon Johnson appointed her as the Special Ambassador to head the United States delegation to the inauguration ceremonies for President William V.S. Tubman of Liberia. She also authored a book based on her close friendship with Eleanor Roosevelt. She resided in New York City, succumbing to cancer on June 28, 1980.

FOR FURTHER READING

Biographical Directory of the United States Congress, "Helen Gahagan Douglas," http://bioguide.congress.gov

Douglas, Helen Gahagan. *A Full Life* (Garden City, NY: Doubleday, 1982).

Scobie, Ingrid Winther. *Center Stage: Helen Gahagan Douglas, A Life* (New York: Oxford University Press, 1992, reprinted by Rutgers University Press, 1995).

MANUSCRIPT COLLECTIONS

Columbia University (New York, NY), Oral History Research Office. *Oral History:* 1973–1976, 345 pages. Includes reminiscences of Helen Gahagan Douglas.

Franklin D. Roosevelt Library (Hyde Park, NY). *Oral History:* 1979, 26 pages. In the interview, Helen Gahagan Douglas discusses the Roosevelts in the White House.

Lyndon B. Johnson Library (Austin, TX). *Oral History:* A November 10, 1969, interview (52 pages) and a November 1972 interview (13 pages) with Helen Gahagan Douglas.

University of California, Berkeley (Berkeley, CA), Bancroft Library. *Oral History:* 1973–1978, 1,371 pages, including index. Copies of four volumes of oral histories conducted with Helen Gahagan Douglas from the Regional Oral History Office.

University of Oklahoma (Norman, OK),Carl Albert Center Congressional Archives http://www.ou.edu/special/albertctr/archives/douglas.htm. *Papers:* ca. 1922–1980, 110 cubic feet. Also includes files relating to the careers of Helen Gahagan Douglas, on the stage and in the U.S. House of Representatives, as well as materials on her postcongressional life and drafts of her autobiography. Includes correspondence, printed materials, photographs, sound recordings, and memorabilia. An inventory is available in the repository and online

NOTES

1   Ingrid Winther Scobie, *Center Stage: Helen Douglas, A Life* (New Brunswick, NJ: Rutgers University Press, 1995): xv.

2   Shirley Washington, *Outstanding Women Members of Congress* (Washington, D.C.: U.S. Capitol Historical Society, 1995): 24.

3   Cabel Phillips, "Presenting Mrs. Douglas and Mrs. Douglas: As Freshmen in Congress They Have Already Broken Down Some Time-Honored Traditions," 18 February 1945, *New York Times*: SM11.

4   Scobie, *Center Stage*: 151.

5   Hope Chamberlin, *A Minority of Members: Women in the U.S. Congress* (New York: Praeger, 1973): 183.

6   "Election Statistics, 1920 to Present," http://clerk.house.gov/members/electionInfo/index.html.

7   Scobie, *Center Stage*: xvi. For example, see Richard Fenno, *Home Style: House Members in Their Districts* (Boston: Little, Brown, 1978). Fenno writes, "Dramatic analogies are appropriate to politics because politicians, like actors, perform before audiences and are legitimized by their audiences"; see his "U.S. House Members and Their Constituencies: An Exploration," *American Political Science Review* 71, part 2, (September 1977): 898. See also, Ralph Huitt and Robert L. Peabody, *Congress: Two Decades of Analysis* (New York: Harper and Row, Publishers, 1969): 170.

8   Phillips, "Presenting Mrs. Douglas and Mrs. Douglas: As Freshmen in Congress They Have Already Broken Down Some Time-Honored Traditions."

9   For the latter, see *Congressional Record*, House 79th Cong., 1st sess. (16 October 1945): 9692–9694.

10 *Congressional Record*, House, 79th Cong., 1st sess. (4 October 1945): 9460–9461. See also, *Congressional Record*, House, 79th Cong., 1st sess. (15 November 1945): 10740; *Congressional Record*, House, 79th Cong., 1st sess. (23 November 1945): 10940–10945; *Congressional Record*, House, 79th Cong., 2nd sess. (18 July 1946): 9350–9379; and *Congressional Record*, House, 79th Cong., 2nd sess. (25 July 1946): 10108–10111.

11 Though Cold War prerogatives led the *AEC* to focus on weapons development, frustrating its creators, it did set the precedent for U.S. civilian control that later became embodied in the *AEC's* successors—the Department of Energy and the Nuclear Regulatory Commission.

12 *Congressional Record*, House, 80th Cong., 2nd sess. (28 April 1948): 5011–5024; quote on 5011.

13 Alexander R. George, "Federal Efficiency First–Then Housing: Hoover Reorganization Plan Ranks No. 1 on Lady Legislators' Lists," 3 July 1949, *Washington Post*: S4.

14 George, "Federal Efficiency First–Then Housing: Hoover Reorganization Plan Ranks No. 1 on Lady Legislators' Lists." See also Douglas's statement in the *Congressional Record*, House, 80th Cong., 2nd sess. (5 August 1948): 9904–9913.

15 *Congressional Record*, House, 79th Cong., 1st sess. (12 June 1945): 5977; *Congressional Record*, House, 79th Cong., 2nd sess. (2 August 1946): 10771–10772.

16 *Congressional Record*, House, 79th Cong., 2nd sess. (1 February 1946): A428–443.

17 *Congressional Record*, House, 79th Cong., 1st sess. (24 October 1945): 10036.

18 *Congressional Record*, House, 79th Cong., 2nd sess. (29 March 1946): 2856–2859; quote on 2857.

19 Scobie, *Center Stage*: 248–252; Stephen Ambrose, *Nixon: The Education of a Politician 1913–1962* (New York: Simon and Schuster, 1987): 209–210.

20 Scobie, *Center Stage*: 265; Ambrose, Nixon: 215–218; Greg Mitchell, *Tricky Dick and the Pink Lady: Richard Nixon vs. Helen Gahagan Douglas—Sexual Politics and the Red Scare, 1950* (New York: Random House, 1998): 183–185.

21 "Election Statistics, 1920 to Present," http://clerk.house.gov/members/electionInfo/index.html.

Chase Going Woodhouse
1890–1984

UNITED STATES REPRESENTATIVE ★ DEMOCRAT FROM CONNECTICUT
1945–1947, 1949–1951

Chase Going Woodhouse, an economics professor-turned-politician, served for two nonconsecutive terms, representing a competitive district spanning eastern Connecticut. In recognition of her longtime advocacy for women in the workplace, the Democratic leadership awarded Woodhouse a prominent post on the Banking and Commerce Committee. Linking American domestic prosperity to postwar international economic cooperation, she put forward a powerful argument on behalf of U.S. participation in such organizations as the International Monetary Fund (IMF) and the World Bank. "Only the fighting is over," Woodhouse said in November 1945. "We still have got to win the war. And winning the war means working out a system of economic cooperation between nations."[1]

Chase Going was born on March 3, 1890, in Victoria, British Columbia, the only child of American parents Seymour Going, a railroad developer and an Alaska mining pioneer, and Harriet Jackson Going, a teacher. Chase's maternal grandmother particularly influenced her political development, taking her young granddaughter to polling places each election day to protest her inability to vote.[2] In 1908, Chase Going graduated from Science Hill High School in Shelbyville, Kentucky. She studied economics at McGill University in Montreal, Canada, and graduated in 1912. A year later she earned her M.A. in economics from McGill. Chase Going pursued advanced studies in political economy at the University of Berlin and, after the outbreak of the First World War, at the University of Chicago. In 1917 she married Yale political scientist Edward James Woodhouse. The couple raised two children, Noel and Margaret, and pursued their academic careers simultaneously, obtaining faculty positions at Smith College and

then at the University of North Carolina. At Chapel Hill, Woodhouse founded the Institute of Women's Professional Relations (IWPR) to study the status of working women and trends in employment. For several years, she was employed as an economist for the Bureau of Home Economics at the U.S. Agriculture Department. In 1934, she became a professor of economics at Connecticut College and initiated a series of IWPR conferences in Washington, D.C.[3]

Woodhouse vented her frustration with the ongoing Depression by running for political office. In 1940, the Connecticut Democratic Party convinced an initially reluctant Woodhouse to join the ticket.[4] By a larger margin than any other elected official in the state, she won a two-year term as secretary of state.[5] From 1943 to 1948, Woodhouse presided over the Connecticut Federation of Democratic Women's Clubs. She served on key wartime labor boards in Connecticut, the Minimum Wage Board and the War Labor Board, chairing the latter.[6] From 1942 to 1943, she also chaired the New London Democratic Town Committee.

Woodhouse later recalled that her desire for social change and economic justice for women convinced her to run for a seat in the U.S. Congress in 1944. Though she first was interested in a U.S. Senate seat, the Connecticut Democratic Party instead nominated her as a Representative.[7] At the state convention, Woodhouse defeated William L. Citron, a former Congressman At-Large, by a vote of 127 to 113 among party officials.[8] She earned a reputation as an indefatigable campaigner and talented public speaker, supported by an active network of labor and women's organizations. In the general election Woodhouse faced one-term GOP incumbent John D.

McWilliams, a Norwich builder and town selectman. She described the central campaign issue as the development of a postwar United Nations and international redevelopment system "that will make permanent peace possible." Woodhouse also advocated tax reform, a plan for full peacetime employment, and more federal money for education and rural electrification programs.[9] In the 1944 elections, voter turnout was high and President Franklin D. Roosevelt carried the state by a slim margin of 52 percent. Woodhouse ran even with the President, edging out McWilliams with a plurality of about 3,000 votes.

Her male House counterparts, Woodhouse recalled years later, made her feel more a colleague than part of a distinct minority. Speaker Sam Rayburn of Texas steered Woodhouse onto the Committee on Banking and Currency, an influential assignment for a freshman Member and one he thought would best put her talents to use. Woodhouse's daughter, Margaret, then in her early 20s, worked in the Washington office as executive secretary.[10] Woodhouse also was innovative in that her chief political adviser, John Dempsey, was based in the district rather than in Washington, D.C. He eventually became a powerful Connecticut governor and one of the state's longest serving chief executives.

In her first term, Woodhouse fought for the maintenance of wartime price controls as a protection against inflation for consumers and for more affordable housing for returning veterans. "I have no illusions of what a new Member of Congress can do the first year," she told reporters. "I'm going to evaluate every piece of legislation in terms of how many jobs there will be after the war. Feed them first and reform them later!" The Harry S. Truman administration failed to heed her warnings on the issue and rolled back price controls.

The bulk of Woodhouse's work in the 79th Congress (1945–1947) centered on issues before the Banking and Currency Committee. The committee played a large role in House approval of the $3.75 billion loan to the British government in 1946, the Bretton Woods Conference agreements, and the creation of the World Bank and the IMF. Woodhouse supported the controversial British loan, as she would the Marshall Plan later in her career, by dismissing the opposition as largely "emotional" and "psychological." Woodhouse told colleagues in a floor speech that, "We do not, as yet, always think of ourselves in terms of the responsibilities of the greatest and richest country in the world, the country which alone has the power to determine whether or not the democratic, free enterprise system will expand or decline."[11] She was an ardent supporter of the implementation of the accords for the IMF and the World Bank, arguing that these were indispensable tools for postwar redevelopment. Even while fighting still raged in the Pacific theater, Woodhouse argued for acceptance of Bretton Woods as an important "first step" toward economic integration. "This war is being won not only by military and political cooperation, but also by economic cooperation," Woodhouse said.[12]

Standing for re-election to the 80th Congress (1947–1949) in 1946, Woodhouse and other Democrats faced serious challenges at the polls. Unemployment problems created by rapid demobilization, as well as soaring prices for groceries and other staples, roiled voters. Her opponent in the general election was Horace Seely-Brown, a World War II Navy veteran who married into a family that operated a lucrative apple orchard in eastern Connecticut.[13] Disaffected Democratic voters did not turn against so much as they simply stayed at home in large droves. Seely-Brown captured about 60,000 votes, roughly the same number as McWilliams had in 1944. But Woodhouse polled nearly 15,000 fewer votes than in the prior election, as her opponent won with a comfortable 55 to 45 percent margin. Backlash against Democrats was further aided by the presence of voting machines, which allowed for voting a straight party ticket with the push of a single button. Republicans swept all five Connecticut House seats, turning three Democratic incumbents out of office.

During her hiatus from Congress, Woodhouse served as executive director of the Women's Division of

"WE DO NOT, AS YET, ALWAYS THINK
OF OURSELVES IN TERMS OF THE
RESPONSIBILITIES OF THE GREATEST
AND RICHEST COUNTRY IN THE
WORLD, THE COUNTRY WHICH
ALONE HAS THE POWER TO
DETERMINE WHETHER OR NOT THE
DEMOCRATIC FREE ENTERPRISE
SYSTEM WILL EXPAND OR DECLINE."

—CHASE GOING WOODHOUSE
HOUSE FLOOR SPEECH
JULY 12, 1946

the Democratic National Committee (DNC), and lectured widely on the topic of women in politics.[14] Eager to escape the patronage and politicking required at the DNC, Woodhouse sought a position as a staff expert for the Allied Military Governor of Germany, General Lucius Clay.[15] As Clay's economic adviser, she toured the Allied zones of occupied western Germany and kept closely informed about reconstruction and rehabilitation efforts. The DNC post provided Woodhouse public visibility, while the economic advisory role in Germany offered her input into policymaking.[16] That combination made her a formidable comeback candidate in 1948 when she challenged Seely-Brown. She benefited from a larger voter turnout for the presidential election, in which she ran ahead of incumbent President Truman. Woodhouse collected nearly 70,000 votes, outpolling Seely-Brown 52 to 48 percent. Statewide, Democrats regained a majority of Connecticut's House seats.[17]

During her second term in the House, Woodhouse regained her seat on the Banking and Currency Committee and received an additional assignment on the House Administration Committee. She remained a confirmed supporter of Truman administration foreign policies. In 1949, she endorsed the ratification of the North Atlantic Pact that created America's first permanent overseas military alliance, the North Atlantic Treaty Organization (NATO). "The Marshall Plan has proven its value as an effective tool of economic recovery in Europe and as a bulwark against the threatened onrush of communism," Woodhouse told reporters, adding that the Atlantic Pact was the "next logical step."[18] Based on her extensive travels in Germany, she declared that the 1948 Berlin Airlift—which supplied blockaded Soviet-occupied East Berlin with food and supplies—was "worth every cent of the cost," because it proved to Moscow that the Western Allies "mean business" in protecting open access to the German capital.[19]

In 1950, Woodhouse again faced Horace Seely-Brown in her fourth congressional campaign. Much of the midterm election focused on the Truman administration's

foreign policy, particularly the decision to intervene with military force on the Korean peninsula to halt North Korea's invasion of South Korea. Following a trend in which the GOP regained control of Connecticut, Woodhouse lost by fewer than 2,300 votes out of 135,000 cast.[20]

After Congress, Woodhouse served as head of congressional relations for the Office of Price Stabilization, where she worked from 1951 until 1953. She was an early and harsh critic of McCarthyite anti-communism, especially when used for political gain.[21] From 1953 until she retired in 1980 at age 90, Woodhouse served as head of the Connecticut Service Bureau for Women's Organizations in Hartford. Woodhouse also was the first chair of the Connecticut Committee on the Status of Women and was a delegate to the Connecticut constitutional convention in 1965. She retired to a circa-1726 home on a 390-acre farm near Baltic, Connecticut. On December 12, 1984, Chase Woodhouse died in New Canaan, Connecticut.

FOR FURTHER READING

Biographical Directory of the United States Congress, "Chase Going Woodhouse," http://bioguide.congress.gov

MANUSCRIPT COLLECTIONS

Library of Congress (Washington, D.C.), Manuscript Division. *Oral History:* three folders. Transcript in the Oral History Collection of the U.S. Association of Former Members of Congress. Restricted. Sound recording in the Library's Motion Picture, Broadcasting and Recorded Sound Division.

University of Connecticut Libraries (Storrs, CT), Archives and Special Collections at the Thomas J. Dodd Research Center. *Papers:* 1922–1984, 50 linear feet. Papers reflecting Chase Going Woodhouse's activities and interests in women and family issues, service to the state of

Connecticut and her local community, and other career activities (excluding her duties as secretary of state and U.S. Representative). Includes published and unpublished writings; office files, scrapbooks, and annual reports of Auerbach Service Bureau, a women's service organization, Hartford, Conn.; reference files and reports of U.S. Work Projects Administration, Trends in Occupations Project; reference files, newsletters, and reports on the status of women and the women's movement; records of the Connecticut constitutional convention (1965) to which she was a delegate; Juvenile Justice Standards Project records and publications; and citations, commissions, awards, and photos. Donated by Mrs. Woodhouse, 1983. A finding aid is available in the National Inventory of Documentary Sources in the United States, microfiche 3.78. *Papers:* In the Political Women in Connecticut Collection, ca. 1934–1981, five linear feet. Includes photocopies of transcripts of oral history tapes held by University of Connecticut, Center for Oral History, Storrs, Conn. Interviewees include Chase Going Woodhouse. A finding aid is available in the National Inventory of Documentary Sources in the United States, microfiche 3.78.35.

NOTES

1   *Current Biography, 1945* (New York: H.W. Wilson and Company, 1945): 690–692.

2   Andree Brooks, "A Pioneer Feminist Savors Grandmother Role," 10 May 1981, *New York Times*: CT 1.

3   *Current Biography, 1945*: 691; see, for example, Marjorie Shuler, "University Women to Review Rights and Duty in New Fields," 30 March 1927, *Christian Science Monitor*: 3.; "Jessie Ash Arndt, "Mrs. Woodhouse Tells of Studies in Trends," 21 May 1940, *Washington Post*: 13.

4   Chase Going Woodhouse, Oral History Interview, U.S. Association of Former Members of Congress (hereinafter cited as USAFMOC), Manuscript Room, Library of Congress, Washington, DC: 161–165.

5   "Connecticut Woman Seeks U.S. Senate Seat," 22 July 1944, *Christian Science Monitor*: 5.

6   Susan Tolchin, *Women in Congress* (Washington, D.C.: Government Printing Office, 1976): 83.

7   "Connecticut Women Back Mrs. Woodhouse for Democratic Nominee Against Danaher," 12 June 1944, *New York Times*: 11; "Connecticut Woman Seeks U.S. Senate Seat," 22 July 1944, *Christian Science Monitor*: 5.

8   "Mrs. Woodhouse in Race," 13 August 1944, *New York Times*: 34.

9   *Current Biography, 1945*: 691.

10 "Daughter Serves Mother," 27 July 1950, *Christian Science Monitor*: 5; a stand-alone photo and caption. See Woodhouse's extensive recollections about Margaret in her Oral History Interview, USAFMOC.

11 *Congressional Record*, House, 79th Cong., 2nd sess. (12 July 1946): 8861–8864; quote on 8861.

12 *Congressional Record*, House, 79th Cong., 1st sess. (5 June 1945): 5584.

13 Woodhouse, Oral History Interview, USAFMOC: 203–205.

14 "Democrats Give Post to Mrs. Woodhouse," 15 February 1947, *New York Times*: 3; "Political Apathy Decried by Women," 17 April 1948, *Washington Post*: B4; see also, "Mrs. Woodhouse Off on Democratic Tour of 17 States With a Gibe at Mrs. Taft," 3 October 1947, *New York Times*: 4.

15 Woodhouse, Oral History Interview, USAFMOC: 261–262.

16 Ibid.

17 "Election Statistics, 1920 to Present," http://clerk.house.gov/members/electionInfo/index.html.

18 Alexander R. George, "Hoover Reorganization Plans No. 1 on Lady Legislators' Lists," 3 July 1949, *Washington Post*: S4.

19 "Rep. Woodhouse Finds Berlin Lift a Bargain," 4 March 1949, *Washington Post*: C5.

20 "Election Statistics, 1920 to Present," http://clerk.house.gov/members/electionInfo/index.html.

21 "Smear Campaigns Laid to 'Traitors,'" 19 November 1950, *New York Times*: 38.

Helen Douglas Mankin
1896–1956

UNITED STATES REPRESENTATIVE ★ DEMOCRAT FROM GEORGIA
1946–1947

During her brief U.S. House term, Helen Douglas Mankin of Georgia brought national attention to her longtime political cause: advocating on behalf of poor and disenfranchised southern voters. "I earnestly believe that the election of a woman from this State to the House of Representatives will mean to the rest of the country another note of progress out of the South," Mankin declared after her victory in a February 1946 special election in which she benefited from the support of African-American voters. Mankin's bid for re-election later that summer, however, revealed the limits of voting reform in the South: the political machine of segregationist Governor Eugene Talmadge blocked her renomination to a full term.

Helen Douglas was born on September 11, 1896, in Atlanta, Georgia, the daughter of Hamilton Douglas and Corrine Williams Douglas. Her parents were teachers who had studied law together at the University of Michigan. Corrine became involved in education when the family moved to Georgia, where state laws prevented women from joining the bar. Hamilton eventually founded the Atlanta Law School. Their home was an intellectual parlor for the likes of reformer Jane Addams and former President and Supreme Court Justice William Howard Taft. Helen Douglas attended Rockford College in Illinois, following in the footsteps of her mother and maternal grandmother. She graduated in 1917 with an A.B. degree but interrupted her law studies to join the American Women's Hospital Unit No. 1 in France, where she served as an ambulance driver for more than a year. When Douglas returned to the United States, she resumed her academic career, graduating from Atlanta Law School in 1920. A year later, the state of Georgia

admitted her to the bar along with her 61-year-old mother when the state legislature lifted the bar's ban on women. For two years, she and her sister toured North America by car before she opened a law office in 1924, specializing in aid to poor and black clients while supplementing her income as a lecturer at the Atlanta Law School.

Her first political experience came as the women's manager of I.N. Ragsdale's campaign for mayor of Atlanta in 1927. That year Helen Douglas married Guy M. Mankin, a widower with a seven-year-old son, Guy, Jr. After traveling to several overseas locations following Guy Mankin's job assignments, the family settled in Atlanta, where Helen Mankin resumed her legal career in 1933.[1] In 1935, as chair of the Georgia Child Labor Committee, she unsuccessfully urged the state legislature to ratify a proposed child labor constitutional amendment. The next year she won a seat in the legislature, serving for a decade as a critic of Governor Eugene Talmadge's administration and as a supporter of constitutional, educational, electoral, labor, and prison reforms. In the process, she became an ally of liberal Governor Ellis Arnall, who had succeeded Talmadge in 1942. In 1945, Mankin and Arnall successfully steered a measure through the Georgia house of representatives to repeal the poll tax, a method southern states frequently employed to disenfranchise African-American voters too poor to pay a requisite tax in order to vote.[2]

When Georgia Representative Robert Ramspeck resigned from the U.S. House at the end of 1945, Mankin entered the race to succeed him in a February 1946 special election. The only woman in the crowded contest for the three-county district, which included both Atlanta and Decatur, Mankin used a series of radio addresses to talk about the central issue of her campaign: the equalization of freight rates, which varied greatly from section to section of the country and which she believed inhibited southern industry and agriculture. She also used these opportunities to criticize her leading opponent, Thomas Camp, the handpicked successor of Ramspeck, warning voters that Camp was a "railroad employee" and therefore a part of the conspiracy to keep the people of Georgia trapped in poverty. Pledging to support price controls, federal housing programs, and federal aid to education, Mankin won the backing of Governor Arnall, women's groups, and the Congress of Industrial Organizations (CIO). [3] Her determination to pursue voting reforms, seen in her support for a constitutional amendment to abolish the poll tax, earned her the solid backing of African Americans.[4] This bloc of voters was barred from primaries, but not from special elections, and black voters helped Mankin prevail on February 12, 1946. Trailing Camp until the reporting of the final precinct tallies from the predominantly black Ashby Street, Mankin ended up winning the election by nearly 800 votes. Of the 1,039 registered voters in the African-American neighborhood, 963 cast their vote for Mankin.[5] The African-American *Atlanta Daily World* newspaper noted that the election marked the first time in Atlanta history that blacks served as precinct managers and clerks in a congressional contest.

Mankin's election sent shock waves through segregationist Georgia. Her coalition of minority voters and white liberals caused great unease in the state. When Eugene Talmadge came out of political retirement that fall to run for re-election as governor of Georgia, he inveighed against "the spectacle of Atlanta Negroes sending a Congresswoman to Washington."[6] During his campaign, he mocked Mankin, nicknaming her the "Belle of Ashby Street." Rather than retaliating, the Congresswoman adopted the title as a point of pride, as if she had invented the name herself.[7]

During her short term on the Hill, Mankin championed reform in Georgia politics and looked to give African Americans a greater voice in their government. She served on four committees—Civil Service, Claims, Elections,

and Revision of Laws—but was not appointed to her first choice, the House Education Committee. Mankin exhibited loyalty to the Democratic Party, voting with the party 92 percent of the time—an uncharacteristic trait for the typically conservative South of the period. As a Representative, she supported price controls, a federal housing program, and the Hobbs Bill directed against the CIO's Teamsters' Union. Mankin voted against the Case Anti-Labor Bill, opposed funding for the House Committee on Un-American Activities, and favored an end to the poll tax. "I am a liberal but not a radical," Mankin said, when opposing plans for national health insurance.[8] She also backed an internationalist foreign policy in which the United States played a greater role in maintaining world stability after World War II.[9]

In the Georgia Democratic primary of July 1946, which the Supreme Court opened to African Americans for the first time, Mankin outpolled her opponent, James C. Davis, by more than 11,000 votes.[10] But to offset the African-American vote, state officials, unhappy with Mankin's liberal voting record, revived Georgia's county unit system, which had been out of use in the district since 1932. Designed to favor rural precincts and to mitigate the urban vote by awarding the winner of the popular vote in each county a designated amount of unit votes, it was employed—as a former Georgia Representative observed—"to beat Mrs. Mankin, nothing else."[11] The strategy also gave Talmadge, a leading spokesman of white supremacy in the South, a large lead over Governor Ellis Arnall's endorsed candidate, James Carmichael, in the gubernatorial primary—despite the fact that more than 100,000 African Americans went to the polls.[12] Mankin received six unit votes for carrying Fulton County (encompassing much of Atlanta's suburbs), while Davis received eight for carrying two less-populous counties.

Citing her popular mandate, Mankin declared her intention to run as an independent in the general election. She refused to allow "anybody [to] frisk me out of my victory."[13] A special three-judge tribunal in the U.S. District Court in Atlanta upheld the unit system and rejected the Congresswoman's petition to annul the primary results.[14]

Mankin appealed the decision while Governor Arnall and Georgia Democratic Executive Committee members loyal to him made the unprecedented move of putting Mankin's name on the ballot as a Democrat alongside Davis's. But Mankin suffered from a series of setbacks in October 1946. First, after Talmadge won official confirmation as the Democratic gubernatorial nominee at the October 9 party convention, he wrested control of the executive committee from Arnall and promptly acted to remove Mankin's name from the ballot, an effort that succeeded just fours days before the election.[15] The Georgia state democratic convention approved a plan to create an all-white primary to exclude blacks from future nomination processes.[16] On October 29, in a 6–3 decision, the U.S. Supreme Court upheld the Georgia unit rule, dimming Mankin's prospects.[17] She remained in the race as a write-in candidate, despite threats from white supremacy groups and reports of voting fraud. She won 38 percent of the vote but lost by a margin of almost 12,000 votes to Davis. When she challenged the election results before the House Administration Committee's Subcommittee on Privileges and Elections, the subcommittee rejected her charges.[18] Bitterly disappointed when she realized she had no further legal recourse to contest the election, Mankin angrily commented, "I was written in and counted out, they stole my seat in Congress."[19]

Mankin mounted one more challenge to Davis in the 1948 election. But by that time, as a proponent of civil rights reforms, she had become a magnet for southern segregationist anger. She lost by a wide margin in the Democratic primary. Mankin returned to her law practice and waged a fight against the county unit system. When she initiated a federal suit (*South v. Peters*), the U.S. District Court in Atlanta ruled against her, and the decision was upheld by the U.S. Supreme Court, which would not rule the practice unconstitutional until 1962. She nonetheless remained active politically, volunteering on the presidential campaign of Adlai Stevenson in 1952. On July 25, 1956, Mankin died in College Park, Georgia, from injuries sustained in an automobile accident.

FOR FURTHER READING

Biographical Directory of the United States Congress, "Helen Douglas Mankin," http://bioguide.congress.gov

Spritzer, Lorraine Nelson. *The Belle of Ashby Street: Helen Douglas Mankin and Georgia Politics* (Athens: University of Georgia Press, 1982).

MANUSCRIPT COLLECTIONS

Emory University (Atlanta, GA), Special Collections Department, Robert W. Woodruff Library. *Papers:* In the James C. Davis Papers, 1937–1966, 217 feet. The campaign series (approximately 10 feet, ca. 1946–1962) includes materials (correspondence, clippings, printed matter, sound recordings) on the race between James C. Davis and Helen Mankin.

Georgia State University Library (Atlanta, GA), Special Collections & Archives. *Papers:* In the Georgia Government Documentation Project, 1946–1948, amount unknown. The project includes a series of interviews conducted by Lorraine Nelson in preparation of her book on Helen Douglas Mankin, *The Belle of Ashby Street.* A finding aid is available in the repository and online.

State officials, unhappy with Mankin's liberal voting record, revived Georgia's county unit system, which had been out of use in the district since 1932. Designed to favor rural precincts and to mitigate the urban vote . . . it was employed—as a former Georgia Representative observed—"to beat Mrs. Mankin, nothing else."

NOTES

1   The family moved frequently during their early years together, as Guy Mankin worked as an electrical system designer in Cuba, Brazil, and Argentina.

2   *Current Biography, 1946* (New York: H.W. Wilson and Company, 1946): 379–381.

3   "Work for Better Legislation Promised Anew by Mrs. Mankin," 21 February 1946, *Christian Science Monitor*: 16; Lorraine Nelson Spritzer, *The Belle of Ashby Street: Helen Douglas Mankin and Georgia Politics* (Athens, GA: University of Georgia Press, 1982): 67.

4   Hope Chamberlin, *A Minority of Members: Women in the U.S. Congress* (New York: Praeger, 1976): 191.

5   "Negro Vote Decisive In Election, Paper Says," 14 February 1946, *New York Times*: 19.

6   Lorraine Nelson Spritzer, "Mankin, Helen Douglas," *American National Biography (ANB)* 14 (New York: Oxford University Press, 1999): 415–416.

7   Spritzer, *The Belle of Ashby Street*: 74.

8   Chamberlin, *A Minority of Members*: 192; see also Jay Walz, "'Congressman Helen': Mrs. Mankin of Atlanta, Lawyer and State Legislator, Is an Active Freshman," 28 April 1946, *New York Times*: SM13.

9   Susan Tolchin, *Women in Congress* (Washington, D.C.: Government Printing Office, 1976): 50.

10 Harold B. Hinton, "Talmadge Leading as 100,000 Negroes Vote in Primary," 18 July 1946, *New York Times*: 1.

11 Spritzer, "Mankin, Helen Douglas," *ANB*. Proponents of the system claimed the unit vote helped to prevent the rise of political machines. See "Ga. Unit Vote System Upheld in U.S. Court," 27 August 1946, *Washington Post*: 2.

12 As part of his primary victory speech, Talmadge declared, "I had to win for the good of the South and the Nation. No Negro will vote in Georgia for the next four years." Quoted in "Victory of Talmadge Called Reversion to Old Traditions," 19 July 1946, *Washington Post*: 1.

13 "Two Representatives Lose in Georgia Court," 19 July 1946, *Los Angeles Times*: 5.

14 "Unit-Vote System Upheld By Court," 27 August 1946, *New York Times*: 14.

15 "Party Shelves Rep. Mankin in Favor of Davis," 1 November 1946, *Washington Post*: 2.

16 "Negroes Excluded by Georgia Party," 10 October 1946, *New York Times*: 24.

17 Lewis H. Hood, "High Court Backs Georgia Unit Rule," 2 October 1946, *New York Times*: 19.

18 See also, Mankin's letter to the editors of the *Washington Post*: "Rep. Mankin's Contest," 20 January 1947, *Washington Post*: 6.

19 Spritzer, *The Belle of Ashby Street*: 130. Years later, Mankin's chief rival in the 1946 special election, Thomas Camp, confirmed that account: "The people who controlled the situation just didn't want any more of her and out she went." Quoted in Spritzer, *The Belle of Ashby Street*: 73.

Eliza Jane Pratt
1902–1981

UNITED STATES REPRESENTATIVE ★ DEMOCRAT FROM NORTH CAROLINA
1946–1947

A longtime House legislative aide for a string of Congressmen from a south-central North Carolina district, Eliza Pratt developed a rapport with voters and knowledge of legislative interests in the district that eventually exceeded that of most other local politicians. When her boss, Congressman William O. Burgin, died in April 1946, Pratt seemed a natural choice to succeed him. Her election a month later, by a far wider margin than any of her predecessor's victories, made Pratt the first woman to represent her home state in Congress.

She was born Eliza Jane Pratt in Morven, North Carolina, on March 5, 1902, one of seven children of James Pratt and Lena Little Pratt. James Pratt was a merchant and farmer who instilled in Eliza a passion for gardening. She enrolled at Queens College in Charlotte, North Carolina, planning to study music, but she left school to seek employment after her father's health failed. She later attended Kings Business College in Charlotte and Temple Secretarial School in Washington, D.C.[1] Pratt never married and raised no children. She became editor of the *Montgomerian* (Troy, North Carolina) newspaper in 1923. In 1924 she resigned her position to accept an offer to serve in Washington, D.C., as an administrative assistant to North Carolina Congressman William C. Hammer, who represented a large swath in the southwestern part of the state. When Hammer died in 1930, Pratt went on to work for a succession of North Carolina Representatives from the same district: Hinton James, J. Walter Lambeth, and William O. Burgin. During the 1930s and 1940s, Pratt was active in various clubs and social programs for North Carolinians who worked on Capitol Hill.

Following Congressman Burgin's death, North Carolina Democratic Party leaders began the search for a successor. Unlike most other southern states during that era, North Carolina was not a one-party state. While the congressional delegation remained solidly Democratic, an active Republican Party had its stronghold in the western piedmont of the state. It had been key when the state voted for the GOP presidential candidate, Herbert Hoover, in 1928.[2] Preparing for the 1946 elections, Republicans hoped to capitalize on voter discontent with the Harry S. Truman administration's postwar economic policies.

Eliza Jane Pratt had built-in advantages in the scramble for the Democratic nomination, primarily her strong base in the district. Pratt's hometown, Lexington, was located in a narrow band in the oddly shaped district stretching south to northwest between Charlotte and Greensboro. After working 22 years for four successive Congressmen, she knew the needs of the constituency better than any of her challengers and voters knew her. In a special meeting held in Troy to nominate a candidate, Pratt's supporters pushed her name against six other candidates. Though Pratt was ill with the flu and unable to make her own case, the North Carolina Democratic Party executive committee debated only 30 minutes before nominating her for the remainder of Congressman Burgin's term in the 79th Congress (1945–1947).[3] Following a five-week campaign in which she paid all her own expenses, Pratt won a lopsided victory over Republican candidate, lumberman H. Frank Hulin of Lexington, on May 25, 1946, to fill the remainder of Burgin's term. Pratt tallied 31,058 votes to Hulin's 8,017—for an 80 percent margin of victory, a percentage well above that of Burgin in any of his four election campaigns.[4]

IMAGE COURTESY OF THE LIBRARY OF CONGRESS

It was an impressive but temporary triumph. A nearby newspaper, the *Greensboro Record*, seemed to sum up expectations when, in explaining her special election, the editors remarked that in the fall elections "the man to fill the post for the regular congressional term will be chosen."[5] *Charlotte Observer* Washington correspondent Red Buck Bryant, who understood Pratt's special qualifications, saw things somewhat differently. "With her background and training," Bryant wrote, "Miss Pratt would make a worthy Congressman for years instead of a few months." While Pratt had the experience, she later observed that she had little money to mount political campaigns.[6] Moreover, the party had settled on its preferred candidate for the full term in the 80th Congress (1947–1949). On the day Pratt won the special election, Charles B. Deane of Rockingham secured the Democratic nomination by a slender margin against another male candidate. Pratt was not a candidate in that race. In the fall elections, Deane (compiler of the *Congressional Directory*) survived a strong effort by GOP candidate Joseph H. Wicker, Sr., winning by a margin of 54 to 46 percent.[7]

Pratt became the first woman to represent North Carolina when she took the oath of office on June 3, 1946, escorted by Members of the state delegation into the House Chamber. Three of her sisters looked on as House Speaker Sam Rayburn of Texas administered the oath.[8] Congresswoman Pratt was appointed to three committees: Pensions, Territories, and Flood Control. Her work as a longtime congressional aide gave her an intimate knowledge of pending legislation and taught her to manage her office and efficiently handle constituent requests. During the brief eight weeks that the House was in session during her term (Congress recessed on August 2), Pratt made no floor speeches and introduced no bills.

Pratt retired from Congress on January 3, 1947, but remained close to the capital scene for more than a decade after leaving Congress. She worked in Washington for several federal agencies. From 1947 to 1951, she was employed in the Office of Alien Property. She later served in the Agriculture Department, from 1951 to 1954, and the

Library of Congress, from 1954 to 1956. She returned to Capitol Hill as a secretary to Representative Alvin P. Kitchin, serving her former district, from 1957 to 1962. Afterward, she resettled in North Carolina and worked as a public relations executive for the North Carolina Telephone Company. Reflecting on the role of women in North Carolina politics, Pratt later found reason for hope. "The men here were slow to accept suffrage, and the majority have not yet fully recognized women as equal political partners," she said. "But, looking back, I can remember the time when only a handful of women would turn out for a rally. Now they sometimes outnumber the men. And they work as regular members of a campaign organization. Unfortunately, when a campaign ends, they are all too often relegated to their former roles as second-class politicians."[9] She resided in Wadesboro, North Carolina, until her death in Charlotte on May 13, 1981.

FOR FURTHER READING

Biographical Directory of the United States Congress, "Eliza Jane Pratt," http://bioguide.congress.gov

MANUSCRIPT COLLECTION

East Carolina University (Greenville, NC), J.Y. Joyner Library, http://www.lib.ecu.edu. *Papers:* 1946, two scrapbooks. One scrapbook mainly including congratulatory messages to Eliza Pratt on the nomination and election to fill out the term of Representative William Burgin. The other scrapbook contains mostly clippings on her activities during her six months in office. The scrapbooks are also available on microfilm. A finding aid is available in the repository.

NOTES

1   Hope Chamberlin, *A Minority of Members: Women in the U.S. Congress* (New York: Praeger, 1973): 194.
2   V.O. Key, Jr., *Southern Politics in State and Nation* (Knoxville: The University of Tennessee Press, 1997): 205–228.
3   "Only Woman Elected to Congress From N.C. Dies," 16 May 1981, *Charlotte Observer*: 2C; Chamberlin, *A Minority of Members*: 194.
4   Michael J. Dubin et al., *United States Congressional Elections, 1788–1997* (Jefferson, NC: McFarland Publishing Company, 1998): 558.
5   "State Democrats Vote for Candidates Today," 25 May 1946, *Greensboro Record*: A1.
6   Chamberlin, *A Minority of Members*: 195.
7   For the *Congressional Directory* reference, see Jerry Kluttz, "The Federal Diary," 20 October 1946, *Washington Post*: M2.
8   Mary James Cottrell, "She's the First N.C. 'Jane' In Congress," 4 June 1946, *Charlotte Observer*: A1.
9   Chamberlin, *A Minority of Members*: 195.

Georgia Lee Lusk
1893–1971

UNITED STATES REPRESENTATIVE ★ DEMOCRAT FROM NEW MEXICO
1947–1949

Georgia Lee Lusk was the first woman elected to the United States Congress from New Mexico. Representative Lusk entered the 80th Congress (1947–1949) determined to improve the education system, but as the mother of three World War II servicemen, one of whom was killed in action, she also fought for increased benefits for returning war veterans and supported the foreign policy of the Harry S. Truman administration.

On May 12, 1893, Georgia Lee Witt was born to George and Mary Isabel Witt in Carlsbad, New Mexico. In 1914, Georgia graduated from New Mexico State Teacher's College after also attending New Mexico Highlands University and Colorado State Teacher's College. She worked as a teacher for a year before marrying Dolph Lusk, a cattleman, in 1915. Dolph Lusk died in 1919, leaving Georgia with three young sons. While also running the family ranch, the young widow resumed her teaching career to support her family. In 1924, Lusk became school superintendent of Lea County, New Mexico. After an unsuccessful bid in 1928, she was elected state superintendent of public instruction in 1930, serving until 1935. A year later, she took on the superintendent position for rural Guadalupe County, before serving as New Mexico state superintendent again from 1944 until 1947. During her long tenure in school administration, Lusk often witnessed discouraging circumstances in New Mexico classrooms, such as severe book shortages and schoolroom overcrowding. A shrewd administrator, she found state funding, even during the Depression, to improve school conditions. Her eight years of leadership as state superintendent moved New Mexico from near the bottom of the nationwide school financing list to the top.[1]

After her children were grown, Lusk turned her sights on improving education on the national level. In 1944, she served as a delegate to the White House Conference on Rural Education.

Georgia Lusk's political zeal led her to seek one of two At-Large seats in the U.S. House of Representatives, left open after Congressman Clinton Anderson resigned his seat when appointed Secretary of Agriculture in 1946. In the June primary, she led six other candidates, barely beating popular Lieutenant Governor J.B. Jones by fewer than 300 votes.[2] In the general election, she garnered more statewide votes than the well-seasoned incumbent candidate, Congressman Antonio Fernandez, the other At-Large winner. In an election where the Republicans gained 55 seats and took control of the House of Representatives, Lusk, a staunch Democrat, also bucked a Republican trend when she took her seat in the 80th Congress in January 1947.[3] She was one of seven women elected to that Congress.

Like any typical freshman, Lusk defended the interests of her constituents, weighing in on debates concerning copper mining and national policy on the maintenance of arid land, both economic concerns for New Mexico voters.[4] However, her background as a teacher and superintendent inspired Lusk to use her national office to promote educational measures. She supported the establishment of a Cabinet-level department of education, remarking that, "If it's important for the government to give financial assistance to transportation, why not to education?"[5] In June, 1947, she lent her support to a bill necessitating the foreign broadcast of pro-American messages via "Voice of America" radio programs. Although opponents during the early Cold War Era were concerned about the reception of such "propaganda" broadcasts in budding communist regimes, Lusk argued that this plan was a peaceful form of education and outreach to other nations. Lusk also backed federal aid to education, including support for funding hot lunch programs in schools and defending teachers against salary cuts proposed by Governor Thomas E. Dewey of New York, the Republican presidential candidate in 1948.[6]

Georgia Lusk's support for educational measures was second only to her concern for veterans' benefits and civil defense. Lusk's sons—Virgil, Morgan, and Thomas Eugene—served in World War II; Virgil, a fighter pilot,

worked closely with Republican Congresswoman Edith Nourse Rogers to obtain many of these increased benefits.

Despite cooperating with Rogers on veterans' benefits, Lusk maintained her Democratic loyalties. She was a staunch backer of the Truman administration's foreign policy proposals, voting in favor of financial and military aid for governments in Greece and Turkey and endorsing universal military training (UMT). Lusk saw UMT as an insurance policy on the country's future, disagreeing with critics that training all young men for combat was an act of aggression. She stressed the educational component of UMT, claiming that it would teach discipline and fight

"If it's important for the government to give financial assistance to transportation, why not to education?"

—GEORGIA LUSK, 1946

was killed in action in North Africa.[7] Because of her experience as the mother of veterans, Lusk was appointed to the Veterans' Affairs Committee. She took her role on this committee very seriously, believing that with the recent end of hostilities, the Veterans' Affairs Committee would likely touch more American lives than any other committee in Congress.[8] Lusk introduced several bills increasing the benefits provided by the 1944 Servicemen's Readjustment Act, popularly known as the G.I. Bill of Rights. Her legislation specifically called for a larger stipend for students under the bill's jurisdiction, benefits for widows and dependents of servicemen who were killed or wounded in battle, and better housing benefits for returning veterans to accommodate the increased cost of living.[9] Lusk also supported legislation to increase retirement benefits for servicemen and to provide on-the-job training to veterans returning to civilian life. Lusk

provincialism, as it would allow young men to interact with others from different parts of the country.[10] Lusk supported the majority of the Truman administration's domestic programs, most significantly backing the President's unpopular opposition to income tax reduction. She turned away from President Truman, however, when she voted in favor of the Taft–Hartley Act, a piece of anti-labor legislation, which passed over the President's veto.

In the June 1948 Democratic primary, Georgia Lusk sought renomination for her At-Large seat but fell short in a three-way election split. Winner and former Governor John E. Miles, also an education reformer, went on to win the general election, serving one term in the 81st Congress (1949–1951).[11] Incumbent colleague, Congressman Antonio Fernandez, won back his seat, to take the other At-Large bid. Lusk's loss was by a narrow margin of only 2,451 votes, and rumors of an illegal move by a political machine-backed candidate led her to weigh demanding a recount.[12] Lusk declined a recount, however, citing the financial obligation of the process, and later quipped, "I thought they'd only say 'a woman can't take a lickin.'"[13] In September 1949, President Truman appointed her to the War Claims Commission, where she served with other Democratic appointees until their dismissal by President Eisenhower in 1953. Lusk returned to Albuquerque and continued her crusade for education, serving again as the state superintendent of public schools. Lusk retired from public service in 1960. She died on January 15, 1971, in Albuquerque, New Mexico.

FOR FURTHER READING

Biographical Directory of the United States Congress, "Georgia Lee Lusk," http://bioguide.congress.gov

MANUSCRIPT COLLECTION

New Mexico State Records Center and Archives (Santa Fe, NM), Archives and Historical Services Division. *Papers*: 1931–1958, six linear feet and 10 volumes. The collection includes political and private papers of Georgia L. Lusk that relate to the 80th Congress, the Veterans' Affairs Committee (1947–1955), War Claims Commission (1947–1953), and education in New Mexico (1931–1958). Also included are 10 scrapbooks pertaining to her tenure as Superintendent of Public Instruction for New Mexico.

NOTES

1 Hope Chamberlin, *A Minority of Members: Women in the U.S. Congress* (New York: Praeger, 1973): 202.
2 "Warren is Chosen By Both Primaries" 6 June 1946, *New York Times*: 15.
3 Statistics taken from Kenneth C. Martis, *The Historical Atlas of Political Parties in the United States Congress, 1789–1989* (New York: Macmillan, 1989).
4 *Congressional Record*, House, 80th Cong., 1st sess. (12 March 1947): 1991; *Congressional Record*, House, 80th Cong., 2nd sess. (24 April 1947): 3995.
5 Chamberlin, *Minority of Members*: 201.
6 *Congressional Record,* House, 80th Cong., 2nd sess. (18 March 1948): 3102; *Congressional Record*, House, 80th Cong, 2nd sess. (28 July 1948): 9527.
7 "7 Women on Rolls of New Congress," 4 January 1947 *New York Times*: 3.
8 *Congressional Record,* House, 80th Cong., 1st sess. (6 March 1947): 1743.
9 *Congressional Record,* House, 80th Cong., 1st sess.: H.R.2172; H.R. 4754; 80th Cong., 2nd sess.: H.R. 5825, H.R. 5851.
10 *Congressional Record,* House, 80th Cong., 1st sess. (13 June 1947): 6960–6961.
11 Judith Boyce DeMark, "Lusk, George Lee Witt," *American National Biography* 14 (New York: Oxford, 1999): 149–150; see also the entry for John Miles, *Biographical Directory*, http://bioguide.congress.gov
12 Chamberlin, *Minority of Members*: 202.
13 Ibid.

Katharine St. George
1894-1983

UNITED STATES REPRESENTATIVE ★ REPUBLICAN FROM NEW YORK
1947-1965

orn to privilege, Katharine St. George became involved in the family business—politics. During her 18 years in the House, she rose into the GOP leadership because of her fiscal conservatism and commitment to limiting the size of government, two beliefs that distinguished her from her famous cousin, President Franklin Delano Roosevelt. Though she spurned the feminist label, St. George became an outspoken advocate for women's economic equality, coining the phrase "equal pay for equal work."

Katharine Delano Price Collier was born on July 12, 1894, in Bridgnorth, England, one of four children born to Price Collier, an Iowa-born Unitarian minister and later the European editor of *Forum* magazine, and Katharine Delano, an aunt of Franklin Delano Roosevelt. When she was just a toddler, her family moved to Tuxedo Park, New York, a posh haven for millionaires located northwest of the city. At age 11, Collier returned to Europe, where she was schooled in France, Switzerland, and Germany.[1] In April 1917, Katharine Collier married George St. George who, by 1919, operated a wholesale coal brokerage on Wall Street. The couple had one daughter, Priscilla. Katharine St. George opened and managed a highly successful kennel business that bred setters and pointers.

St. George also was active in civic affairs as a longtime chair of the area's Red Cross chapter, a town board member from 1926 to 1949, and a member of the local education board from 1926 to 1946. St. George, who also had been a member of the Republican county committee in the 1920s, distanced herself from Republican politics during President Franklin Roosevelt's first two terms out of deference to her cousin. She opposed his third term in 1940, however, and that break marked her reentry into politics (in Congress, she would vote for the 22nd Amendment, which limited Presidents to a maximum of two terms in office).[2] In 1942 she lost her bid for the Republican nomination to the state assembly, but that only seemed to provide motivation. St. George recalled that "a politician ought to know how it feels to be licked."[3] That fall she chaired the Orange County campaign committee and worked for the successful re-election of longtime New York Representative Hamilton Fish.

Congressman Fish's political misfortune spurred St. George to run for a seat in the U.S. House. In 1944, the isolationist Congressman lost his seat, representing a vast district in the Hudson River Valley north of New York City, to Augustus W. Bennet, a Republican who had lost to Fish in the primary but then ran successfully on the Democratic and American Labor Party ticket in the general election. On April 1, 1945, St. George decided to face Bennet in the 1946 Republican primary. She campaigned for 14 months, giving speeches and courting the Republican establishment. She campaigned on a labor-oriented platform: promising jobs for returning veterans, meeting farmers' agricultural needs, and preserving labor's gains during the New Deal. The "ultimate goal" seemed to be to make the system so bountiful as to make, in St. George's words, "every union member a capitalist."[4] With the strong support of Fish, St. George defeated Bennet in the primary and, with 60 percent of the vote in the general election, dispatched Democrat James K. Welsh.[5] Though she faced significant primary opposition again in 1948, St. George won another eight terms without being seriously challenged, despite the fact that her district was twice redrawn, in 1952 and 1962.

POCKET CONGRESSIONAL DIRECTORY, 84TH CONGRESS

During her 18-year tenure, she served on the Committee on Post Office and Civil Service, the Committee on Government Operations, and the influential Committee on Armed Services. St. George later claimed that the Post Office and Civil Service assignment was a key one for her, because it allowed her to bring high-profile projects to her district that would benefit her constituents. She also served as president of the American delegation to the Inter-Parliamentary Union. In 1961, as a reward for her seniority and fidelity to the party, the Republican leadership made St. George the first woman to serve on the powerful House Rules Committee, which prioritizes bills that come to the floor and sets the conditions of debate.

Congresswoman St. George had a keen interest in foreign affairs and was more of an internationalist than her predecessor. But she realized that her district, with pockets of wealthy communities surrounded by dairy farming counties, had been isolationist for generations and had little interest in overseas policies. Therefore, as a junior Member she focused on local needs. Only later, after she had seniority, did she attend to national issues. In May 1953, as chair of a Post Office and Civil Service subcommittee, she proposed legislation to grant the Postmaster General, rather than Congress, authority to increase postal rates. In a legislative effort important to local dairy farmers, she authored bills to allow the Defense Department to use surplus butter in military food rations and to limit reductions in dairy price controls. St. George also wrote legislation to establish a federal safety division in the Labor Department, to supply a code of ethics for government service, and to prohibit payment of Veterans' Administration benefits to persons belonging to groups advocating the overthrow of the U.S. government.

Representative St. George's seniority gave her a prominent position in the party hierarchy: She earned seats on the Republican Policy Committee and the Committee on Committees, which determined assignments for Republicans. As her state's representative on the committee, St. George was responsible for committee assignments to Republican Members from New York. Once, when New York Representative John Lindsay requested a post on

Foreign Affairs, St. George turned him down. Noting that he had little background for it, she instead placed him on the Judiciary Committee, where eventually he oversaw much of the civil rights legislation of the period. "You know what you'd be if you go on Foreign Affairs?" St. George told Lindsay. "You'd just be a cookie-pusher around Washington cocktail parties. You're a lawyer. Now go on a good committee where you can do something."[6] After his service in the House, Lindsay was elected mayor of New York City. St. George also served as a regional whip, tracking votes for Republican legislation.[7] She reveled in her congressional service, once telling a colleague, "It is the only place on earth where neither wealth nor parentage counts for anything. . . . You may inherit your father's seat . . . but you do not inherit his position in the House of Representatives. You earn it on your own."[8]

Though St. George did not embrace the feminist label, she became a champion of two decidedly reformist causes—equal rights and equal pay for women. Women's rights were the one area in which she dissented from her GOP colleagues. She was unable in 1950 to convince the Judiciary Committee to report out to the full House a proposed Equal Rights Amendment (ERA). She also failed in her attempt to get 218 signatures from House Members on a discharge petition that would have brought the bill to the floor. At the core of her work on this issue was an abiding conviction that if women were to achieve equality and fully participate in American society, they needed a base of economic strength. St. George persevered, and her 1959 proposal to outlaw sex discrimination in the payment of wages became law in the form of the Equal Pay Act of 1963. "What you might mean by 'equal rights' might be totally different to what I believe is 'equal rights,'" St. George said. "I always felt . . . women were discriminated against in employment . . . I think women are quite capable of holding their own if they're given the opportunity. What I wanted them to have was the opportunity."[9] In 1964, she joined ranks with other women lawmakers, led by Democrat Martha Griffiths of Michigan, to demand inclusion of a "sexual discrimination" clause in Title VII of the Civil Rights Act. "We are entitled to this little crumb of equality,"

St. George told male colleagues in a floor speech. "The addition of that little, terrifying word 's-e-x' will not hurt this legislation in any way. In fact, it will improve it. It will make it comprehensive. It will make it logical. It will make it right."[10]

St. George's traditional notions about women's place at home became magnified as she witnessed the radicalization of the feminist movement of the 1960s. Her early work on legislation calling for an end to discrimination in the workplace and equality under the law appeared incongruous with her later statements about women's role in society. She once told a reporter, "A good mother at home is twice as effective as one at a meeting." She also discouraged women from running for federal office, noting that in any circumstance politics "should certainly not be undertaken until her children are grown."[11]

In her 1964 election bid for a 10th consecutive term, St. George ran into a problem that plagued many Republicans. GOP presidential candidate Barry Goldwater had a polarizing effect on the electorate with his pro-war, arch-conservative platform. Nevertheless, she campaigned actively for Goldwater in her district, more so than for her own re-election.[12] President Lyndon B. Johnson crushed Goldwater in the general election winning by more than 15 million votes. The New York Republican Party suffered tremendously, losing eight incumbents in the state delegation.[13] St. George was one of those political casualties, losing a narrow race to previously unknown liberal Democrat John G. Dow by about 6,000 votes out of 188,000 cast (52.5 percent to 48.5 percent). "I was under a mistaken idea that my situation was pretty well established," St. George recalled.[14] At age 68 she returned to Tuxedo Park, where she remained active in local politics as chair of the Republican town committee. Katharine St. George died in Tuxedo Park on May 2, 1983.

FOR FURTHER READING

Biographical Directory of the United States Congress, "Katharine Price Collier St. George," http://bioguide.congress.gov

MANUSCRIPT COLLECTIONS

Cornell University Library (Ithaca, NY), Department of Manuscripts and University Archives. *Papers:* 1939–1964, 84 feet. Correspondence, speeches, reports, memoranda, itineraries, press releases, campaign files, newsletters, guestbooks, clippings, scrapbooks, records and tape recordings, films, and photographs, chiefly from the service of Katharine St. George in Congress. Topics covered include appropriations, agriculture, alien property, civil rights, conservation, flood control, foreign affairs and aid, space program, health insurance, public housing, poverty, veterans' benefits, immigration claims, service academy appointments, post offices, ERA, and Republican Party matters. A finding aid is available.

Library of Congress (Washington, D.C.), Manuscript Division. *Oral History:* Transcript in the Oral History Collection of the Association of Former Members of Congress. Sound recording in the Library's Motion Picture, Broadcasting and Recorded Sound Division.

NOTES

1   Katharine Price Collier St. George, Oral History Interview, 10 May 1979, U.S. Association of Former Members of Congress (hereinafter cited as USAFMOC), Manuscript Reading Room, Library of Congress, Washington, D.C.: 2, 5–6.
2   St. George, Oral History Interview, USAFMOC: 7.
3   Hope Chamberlin, *A Minority of Members: Women in the U.S. Congress* (New York: Praeger, 1973): 203.
4   *Current Biography, 1947* (New York: H.W. Wilson and Company, 1947): 559–561.
5   "Election Statistics, 1920 to Present," http://clerk.house.gov/members/electionInfo/index.html.
6   St. George, Oral History Interview, USAFMOC: 47.
7   Karen Foerstel, *Biographical Dictionary of Congressional Women* (Westport, CT: Greenwood Press, 1999): 240.
8   For St. George's remark to Martha Griffiths, see Martha Griffiths, Oral History Interview, 30 October 1979, USAFMOC Manuscript Room, Library of Congress, Washington, D.C.: 137.
9   St. George, Oral History Interview, USAFMOC: 32.
10 *Congressional Record*, House, 80th Cong., 2nd sess. (8 February 1964): 2580–2581.
11 Chamberlin, *A Minority of Members*: 206–207.
12 St. George, Oral History Interview, USAFMOC: 20.
13 Robert L. Peabody, *Leadership in Congress* (Boston: Little, Brown and Company, 1976).
14 St. George, Oral History Interview, USAFMOC: 20.

Vera Cahalan Bushfield
1889–1976

UNITED STATES SENATOR ★ REPUBLICAN FROM SOUTH DAKOTA
1948

Vera Bushfield's brief Senate service in the autumn of 1948 never brought her to the Capitol, where the 80th Congress (1947–1949) had recessed for the general elections. Instead, she stayed in her native South Dakota tending to constituent services after being appointed to the final weeks of the term of her late husband, Harlan J. Bushfield.

Vera Sarah Cahalan was born in Miller, South Dakota, on August 9, 1889, the year the state was admitted to the Union. Her parents, Maurice Francis Cahalan and Mary Ellen Conners Cahalan, were farmers who had recently resettled from Iowa. They raised three daughters and a son. Vera Cahalan grew up in Miller, attended the public schools, and, in 1912, graduated with a degree in domestic science from Stout Institute in Menominee, Wisconsin. She later attended Dakota Wesleyan University and the University of Minnesota. On April 15, 1912, Vera Cahalan married Harlan J. Bushfield, a lawyer born and raised in Miller. The Bushfields had three children: Mary, John, and Harlan, Jr.

Harlan Bushfield became involved in state politics and eventually chaired the South Dakota GOP, guiding it into Alf Landon's win column during the 1936 presidential election. He later served as governor of South Dakota from 1939 to 1943. Elected to the U.S. Senate in November 1942, Bushfield served on the Rules and Finance committees, as well as the District of Columbia, the Agriculture and Forestry, and the Indian Affairs committees. Bushfield earned a reputation as a leading isolationist and an outspoken opponent of President Franklin Roosevelt's New Deal programs.[1]

During her husband's political career, Vera Bushfield became a noted speaker throughout South Dakota,

specialized in women's and children's issues, and was her husband's most trusted adviser. She was a member of the Hand County (SD) child welfare commission. The Bushfields' political ideologies were closely aligned.[2] While governor, Harlan Bushfield reformed the state tax laws and sought to keep government small. A strong believer in small and decentralized government, Governor Bushfield cut the state budget by a quarter and put South Dakota on a pay-as-you-go basis.[3] The couple gained national recognition when Harlan Bushfield was nominated as a GOP presidential candidate during the 1940 Republican National Convention. Wendell Willkie eventually won the nomination.

In early 1948, Harlan Bushfield announced that due to ill health, he would not seek re-election.[4] On September 27, 1948, with Congress out of session, he passed away. The Republican Governor of South Dakota, George T. Mickleson, appointed Vera Bushfield to fill her husband's unexpired term on October 6 to "permit the late Harlan J. Bushfield's office to function normally and without interruption." Mickleson added that the appointment was made "with the understanding that shortly before the 80th Congress reconvenes [Vera Bushfield] will resign."[5] Earlier in the year Karl E. Mundt, a five-term U.S. Representative, won the Republican nomination for the full term, beginning in the 81st Congress (1949–1951).[6]

Vera Bushfield's qualifications as a political adviser to a prominent politician put her in good stead to tend to the needs of the people of her state. With the Senate in temporary recess, she chose to remain in South Dakota with a small staff in Pierre rather than relocate to Washington, D.C., for what she knew would be an abbreviated term. She noted that "I can serve the constituency best by making

"ON MANY OCCASIONS A WOMAN IS

MORE CONSCIOUS OF THE PULSE OF

THE PEOPLE THAN A MAN. SHE HAS

A BETTER UNDERSTANDING OF

WHAT LIFE IN THE HOME IS LIKE.

SHE IS CLOSER TO THE YOUTH.

WITH INTELLIGENCE AND EFFORT,

SHE CAN EASILY LEARN THE

FUNDAMENTALS OF GOVERNMENT,

ESPECIALLY NOWADAYS WHEN

EDUCATION IS AVAILABLE TO

ANYONE WHO HAS THE AMBITION

TO PURSUE IT."

—VERA BUSHFIELD, 1971

myself as accessible as possible," but reportedly admitted that she had more interest in her grandchildren than in "political oratory."[7] Senator Bushfield received no committee assignments and made no floor speeches. She was not even sworn in to office in a traditional Senate Chamber ceremony.

When the Senate reconvened late in the year, Vera Bushfield tendered her resignation, effective December 26, 1948, to give a seniority edge to Senator-elect Mundt. She retired to her family and grandchildren and never sought elective office again. Asked years later about the role of women in politics, she observed that women in public service had inherent advantages over men. "On many occasions a woman is more conscious of the pulse of the people than a man," Bushfield explained in 1971. "She has a better understanding of what life in the home is like. She is closer to the youth. With intelligence and effort, she can easily learn the fundamentals of government, especially nowadays when education is available to anyone who has the ambition to pursue it. More than ever the political odds are in a woman's favor."[8] Vera Bushfield died in Fort Collins, Colorado, on April 16, 1976.

FOR FURTHER READING

Biographical Directory of the United States Congress, "Vera Cahalan Bushfield," http://bioguide.congress.gov

Pressler, Larry. "Vera Bushfield," in *U.S. Senators From the Prairie* (Vermillion, SD: Dakota Press, 1982): 129–130.

MANUSCRIPT COLLECTION

South Dakota State Historical Society (Pierre, SD). *Papers:* Several letters in the Harlan Bushfield Papers.

NOTES

1 Larry Pressler, *U.S. Senators From the Prairie* (Vermillion, SD: Dakota Press, 1982): 125–126; "Senator Bushfield of S. Dakota Dead," 28 September 1948, *New York Times*: 27.
2 Hope Chamberlin, *A Minority of Members: Women in the U.S. Congress* (New York: Praeger): 197.
3 "Senator Bushfield of S. Dakota Dead"; see also Frank L. Perrin, "Bushfield Condemns Pessimism," 11 September 1939, *Christian Science Monitor*: 3.
4 "Bushfield Quits S.D. Senatorial Primary Race," 24 January 1948, *Washington Post*: 11.
5 Chamberlin, *A Minority of Members*: 196–199; "Woman Is Named Senator by South Dakota Governor," 7 October 1948, *Washington Post*: 1.
6 "Mundt Overwhelmingly Nominated to the Senate," 3 June 1948, *Washington Post*: 4.
7 Chamberlin, *A Minority of Members*: 197; "Mrs. Vera Bushfield," 5 December 1948, *Washington Post*: M9.
8 Chamberlin, *A Minority of Members*: 199.

Reva Beck Bosone
1895–1983

UNITED STATES REPRESENTATIVE ★ DEMOCRAT FROM UTAH
1949–1953

A former Salt Lake City municipal judge and Utah legislator (the state's first woman to serve in both capacities), Congresswoman Reva Beck Bosone blended a jurist's authority and impartiality with a reformer's commitment to improving people's lives. "Do right and fear not," Judge Bosone once advised a group of college graduates.[1] As a two-term Representative who specialized in land reclamation, water projects, and the reform of the Indian Affairs Bureau, she legislated according to that motto.

The granddaughter of Danish immigrants and Mormon pioneers, Reva Beck was born in American Fork, Utah, on April 2, 1895, to Christian M. Beck and Zilpha Ann Chipman Beck, hotel proprietors. Raised in a comfortable household that encouraged learning, Reva Beck attended public schools and eventually graduated from Westminster Junior College in 1917.[2] Two years later she received a Bachelor of Arts degree from the University of California at Berkeley. Reva Beck married the son of a prominent Utah politician, but the union soon failed.[3] From 1920 until 1927, Beck taught high school English, speech, and drama in several Utah schools. When she enrolled at the University of Utah, College of Law, in Salt Lake City, she met Joseph P. Bosone. For a brief stint, she taught English at the university. Reva Beck married Joseph Bosone in 1929 and, a year later, shortly before the birth of their only child, a daughter named Zilpha, Reva Beck Bosone graduated with her L.L.B. The Bosones relocated to Helper, a coal-mining community in central Utah, where they opened a law practice together.[4]

Bosone remembered that the origins of her interest in political office derived from her mother's admonition: "If you want to do good, you go where the laws are made because a country is no better than its laws."[5] In 1932, she became the first woman to serve in the state legislature when she was elected as a Democrat to the Utah house of representatives from a rural district.[6] She won re-election in 1934, this time from Salt Lake City, where she and her husband had moved their law practice. Bosone rose quickly to the majority party floor leader's post and chair of the sifting committee, which controlled the flow of bills to the floor. She secured passage of a women's and children's wage and hour law, a child labor amendment to the Utah constitution, and an unemployment insurance law. In 1936, she left the legislature and won election as the first woman to hold a Salt Lake City judgeship. Initially, she held a post in the traffic court and earned a reputation as a scrupulous jurist, leveling fines sometimes twice those of other judges and instituting a thriving traffic school and programs to treat alcohol abuse. "Repeaters," Bosone told the Associated Press, "go to jail."[7] After a year, she took over the Salt Lake City police court. The city's traffic accident rates plummeted, and Bosone became a public favorite and a darling of the press for her tough approach. She won re-election in 1940 and 1944 and served in that capacity until her election to Congress. A talented public speaker, she also hosted a local radio program, "Her Honor—the Judge."[8] In 1945, Bosone was an official observer at the United Nations' founding conference at San Francisco. She also served as the first director of the Utah state board for education on alcoholism.

In 1948 Bosone challenged one-term incumbent Republican William A. Dawson for the U.S. congressional seat encompassing Salt Lake City and a sliver of the state that ran northwest of the city to the Nevada border. She recalled phoning the *Salt Lake Tribune* on impulse from her chambers: "I'm going to have my announcement in the paper tomorrow. I'm going to run for the U.S. Congress."[9] The campaign cost $1,250 and drew heavily on volunteers, Utah women's organizations, and several women state legislators. Dawson had been a member of the Utah senate from 1940 to 1944. In 1946, he ran a successful campaign for Congress as nationwide the GOP gained 56 seats in the House and took a solid majority. Bosone ran as a "Fair Deal" Democrat, campaigning with President Harry S. Truman during his whistle stop train tour through Utah and broadly supporting his domestic and foreign policies, especially U.S. involvement in the United Nations.[10] She also took a keen interest in soil conservation and reclamation, important issues for her Utah constituency. Enjoying wide name recognition, Bosone ran ahead of Truman on the ticket, winning 57 percent of the vote and becoming the first woman to represent her state in Congress. Nationally, Democrats regained their House majority.

When Bosone took her seat in the House for the 81st Congress (1949–1951) in January 1949, she was offered a spot on the Judiciary Committee, a plum assignment for a freshman with her background and a panel on which no woman had served. But she turned it down and persuaded reluctant Democratic leaders to put her onto the Public Lands Committee (later named Interior and Insular Affairs), a seat more important to her western district.[11] In the 82nd Congress (1951–1953), Bosone also served on the House Administration Committee.

The bulk of Congresswoman Bosone's legislative initiatives came from her Interior and Insular Affairs assignments on the Public Lands and Indian Affairs subcommittees. In April 1950, she introduced a bill "to start the wheels turning to take American Indians off Government wardship."[12] Though unacquainted with the issue prior to coming to Congress, she was inspired by Native Americans' testimony before the committee and several visits to reservations. The measure authorized the Secretary of the Interior to commission a study to determine which Native-American tribes should be removed from under the supervision of the Indian Bureau and granted control and management of their affairs. Critics warned it would repeal vital federal protections for Native Americans enacted in the 1934 Indian Reorganization Act, but the measure still passed the House.[13] It failed, however, to gain Senate approval.

From her Interior seat, Bosone hoped to promote land management, reclamation, and water control efforts through proposals such as her Small Water Projects Bill, which would have established a revolving fund to pay for modest reclamation projects.[14] She also helped pass the Weber Basin Project, which provided water to northern Utah. In a move unpopular with conservation groups, Bosone tried to include the proposed Echo Park Dam as part of the Colorado River Project, though the plan eventually was rejected because Dinosaur National Monument, in the upper reaches of Grand Canyon National Park, would have been submerged.[15] During Bosone's congressional career, she also aided the unsuccessful effort to build Hell's Canyon Dam on Idaho's Snake River. In addition, Bosone took an interest in overseas territories, supporting Hawaiian and Alaskan statehood and voting for a Puerto Rican constitution in 1952 which contained a controversial provision that opponents labeled as socialistic.[16]

Congresswoman Bosone supported a range of legislation that did not always accord with her conservative-leaning Salt Lake constituency. She favored extension of Social Security and funding for public housing for military personnel, as well as the creation of a national healthcare system.[17] Bosone voted against the Subversive Activities Control and Communist Registration Act, believing the government had overstepped its bounds. In 1949, she opposed the Central Intelligence Agency (CIA) Act on the grounds that it invested too much power in an agency that operated under minimal congressional oversight.[18] While fellow Members feared they would be tarred as communist sympathizers if they opposed the measure, Bosone was one of only four 'No' votes for the bill. She declared, "I vote my conscience."[19] In December 1950, weeks after the Chinese intervention in the Korean War, she argued that mandatory price and wage controls be put into place to check the rising cost of groceries and to stem inflation.[20] Bosone once observed of the role of a Representative, "the job should be done, whether the required course of action is popular or not. The biggest need in politics and government today is for people of integrity and courage, who will do what they believe is right and not worry about the political consequences to themselves."[21]

Shifting electoral sands and Bosone's only significant stumble during two decades of public office conspired to bring her House career to a sudden close. In 1950, she had won a second term by defeating Republican National Committeewoman and future U.S. Treasurer Ivy Baker Priest, with 53 percent of the vote. In May 1952, as Bosone geared up to campaign for a third term in a "grudge fight" rematch with GOP candidate William Dawson, reports emerged that she had illegally accepted $630 in campaign contributions from two staffers.[22] Bosone and her aides claimed the contributions were voluntary, that Bosone had been unaware of the law, and that the money was unspent. The Justice Department eventually cleared Bosone of wrongdoing, but press coverage proved damaging. Dawson pounced on the allegations of campaign malfeasance and also implied that Bosone was sympathetic to communism because of her support for social welfare programs and her opposition to the CIA Bill.[23] He also benefited from GOP presidential candidate Dwight Eisenhower's long coattails. Bosone ran better than Democratic presidential candidate Adlai Stevenson but lost 53 to 47 percent. The entire Utah delegation went Republican, and the House swung back to GOP control.

After leaving Congress, Bosone resumed law practice in Salt Lake City. She hosted a four-day-a-week award-winning television show, "It's a Woman's World," which highlighted topics of interest to women. In 1954, she again ran for Congress in her old district, winning the Democratic primary by a more than 2-to-1 margin. She lost, however, in the general election to Dawson, 57 percent to 43 percent of the vote, despite the fact that Democrats ran well nationally and wrested control of

both chambers of Congress back from the GOP. From 1957 to 1960, Bosone served as legal counsel to the Safety and Compensation Subcommittee of the House Committee on Education and Labor. In 1961, President Kennedy named Bosone the U.S. Post Office Department's judicial officer and chair of its contract board of appeals.[24] She held these posts until her retirement in January 1968. Late in life, Bosone lived with her daughter in Vienna, Virginia, until her death on July 21, 1983.

FOR FURTHER READING

Biographical Directory of the United States Congress, "Reva Beck Bosone," http://bioguide.congress.gov

Clopton, Beverly B. *Her Honor, the Judge: The Story of Reva Beck Bosone* (Ames: Iowa State University Press, 1980).

MANUSCRIPT COLLECTIONS

Library of Congress (Washington, D.C.), Manuscript Division. *Oral History:* Transcript in the Oral History Collection of the U.S. Association of Former Members of Congress. Sound recording in the Library's Motion Picture, Broadcasting and Recorded Sound Division.

University of Utah Libraries (Salt Lake City, UT), Special Collections Department. *Papers:* 1927–1977, 18 feet. Includes correspondence, speeches, articles, autobiographical and biographical material, newspaper clippings, photographs, and phonograph records of Reva Beck Bosone. A register is available in the repository.

BOSONE ONCE OBSERVED OF THE
ROLE OF A REPRESENTATIVE, "THE
JOB SHOULD BE DONE, WHETHER
THE REQUIRED COURSE OF ACTION
IS POPULAR OR NOT. THE BIGGEST
NEED IN POLITICS AND GOVERN-
MENT TODAY IS FOR PEOPLE OF
INTEGRITY AND COURAGE, WHO
WILL DO WHAT THEY BELIEVE IS
RIGHT AND NOT WORRY ABOUT THE
POLITICAL CONSEQUENCES TO
THEMSELVES."

NOTES

1   American Mothers Committee, *Mothers of Achievement in American History, 1776–1976* (Rutland, VT: C.E. Tuttle and Company, 1976): 531.

2   Reva Beck Bosone, Oral History Interview, U.S. Association of Former Members of Congress (hereinafter USAFMOC), Manuscript Room, Library of Congress, Washington, D.C.: 61.

3   Bosone, Oral History Interview, USAFMOC: 94.

4   Bosone's early life is amply covered in several chapters in Beverly B. Clopton's *Her Honor, the Judge: The Story of Reva Beck Bosone* (Ames: Iowa State University Press, 1980).

5   Bosone, Oral History Interview, USAFMOC: 1.

6   Mary Van Rensselaer Thayer, "Ex-Alcoholic Gave Reva Bosone a Cocktail Shaker; She Won't Use It," 4 January 1949, *Washington Post*: B6.

7   "Woman Judge Routs Speeders," 25 September 1937, *Washington Post*: 3.

8   Jean Bickmore White, "Bosone, Reva Beck," *American National Biography (ANB)* 3 (New York: Oxford University Press, 1999): 222–223.

9   Bosone, Oral History Interview, USAFMOC: 3.

10   For more on this aspect of the election, see Clopton, *Her Honor, the Judge*: 132–134.

11   Bosone, Oral History Interview, USAFMOC: 11; 4–5.

12   "Measure to 'Free' Indians Is Offered," 22 April 1950, *New York Times*: 10.

13   *Congressional Record*, House, 82nd Cong., 2nd sess. (18 March 1952): 2492. See also, Robert C. Albright, "Lady Legislator Has Indian Bureau Lobbying Itself Out of Business," 13 August 1950, *Washington Post*: B2; *Congressional Record*, House, 82nd Cong., 2nd sess. (9 May 1952): 5450–5451. Bosone argued that her bill would force the Indian Affairs Bureau to "shift its 100-year-old basic policy from taking care of the Indian to a policy of letting the Indian take care of himself as soon as he is able." For criticism, see Harold Ickes, "Bosone Plan for Indians: Attack on Rights," 17 September 1950, *Washington Post*: B4.

14   "Reclamation Bill Filed," 15 February 1951, *Washington Post*: 31.

15   For an account of the proposed dam project, see David J. Webber, *Outstanding Environmentalists of Congress* (Washington, D.C.: U.S. Capitol Historical Society, 2002): 73–74.

16   *Congressional Record*, House, 82nd Cong., 2nd sess. (28 May 1952): 6172–6173.

17   Alexander R. George, "Hoover Reorganization Plan Ranks No. 1 on Lady Legislators' Lists," 3 July 1949, *Washington Post*: S4.

18   Karen Foerstel, *Biographical Dictionary of Congressional Women* (Westport, CT: Greenwood Press, 1999): 34.

19   Bosone, Oral History Interview, USAFMOC: 9.

20   *Congressional Record*, House, 81st Cong., 2nd sess. (15 December 1950): 16649.

21   Hope Chamberlin, *A Minority of Members: Women in the U.S. Congress* (New York: Praeger, 1973): 208.

22   "Slates Are Chosen for Utah Primary," 4 August 1952, *New York Times*: 9; "Mrs. Bosone Admits Gifts in House Race," 24 May 1952, *New York Times*: 26; "Josephine Ripley," McGranery Fraud Blast Fired with Modest Pop," 28 May 1952, *Christian Science Monitor*: 7; "Justice Drops Probe of Bosone Case," 5 September 1952, *Washington Post*: 44; "Legal Bar Prevents Bosone Prosecution," 15 October 1952, *Washington Post*: 17. See also Bosone's recounting of the episode in her Oral History Interview, USAFMOC: 43–46.

23   For more on this episode, see Clopton, *Her Honor, the Judge*: 199–218.

24   Alvin Schuster, "Woman Is Chosen Postal Law Aide," 24 February 1961, *New York Times*: 8.

Cecil Murray Harden
1894–1984

UNITED STATES REPRESENTATIVE ★ REPUBLICAN FROM INDIANA
1949–1959

Cecil M. Harden rose through the ranks of the Republican Party in her state and nationally before winning her first campaign for elective office to the House of Representatives. Harden eventually served five terms, making her one of the longest-serving women at the time of her retirement in 1959. "There is no game more fascinating, no game more important, than the great game of politics as we play it here in America," Harden said early in her public career. "The more interest you take in politics, the more you meet your responsibilities as a citizen."[1]

Cecil Murray was born November 21, 1894, in Covington, Indiana, daughter of Timothy J. Murray, a real estate broker and longtime local Democratic leader, and Jennie Clotfelter Murray. She attended public schools in Covington and entered Indiana University. Later that year she left to teach school in Troy Township, Indiana, and in the public schools in Covington. On December 22, 1914, she married Frost Revere Harden, who eventually became a Covington automobile dealer. They had one son, Murray.

Cecil Harden took an active interest in politics after President Herbert Hoover appointed her husband postmaster of Covington. A year later, when the new President, Franklin D. Roosevelt, appointed a Democrat to the position, she became involved in the local Republican committee, which often held its meetings in the hall above her husband's automobile showroom.[2] In 1932, Harden was elected the Republican precinct vice chairman, a position she held until 1940. In 1938, she won the vice chairmanship of the Fountain County GOP (which she held until 1950) and was made vice chair of an Indiana congressional district. She became a member of the

Republican National Speakers Bureau in 1940. From 1944 to 1959, Harden served as a Republican National Committeewoman from Indiana. She was an At-Large delegate to the Republican National Conventions in 1948, 1952, 1956, and 1968. In 1949, GOP National Chairman Hugh Scott named Harden to a special steering group to map Republican strategy in between regular meetings of the whole committee.[3] "I believe that the American people are basically opposed to the trend our domestic affairs has been taking," Harden said, reflecting on 16 years of Democratic Party rule in the White House. "I am confident that once the Republican Party advances a concrete program for a revision of this trend toward socialism, the American people will rally behind us in overwhelming numbers."[4]

When western Indiana GOP Representative Noble J. Johnson resigned in July 1948 to accept a federal judgeship, Harden won the Republican nomination for the general election that fall. The vacant seat—which stretched west of Indianapolis and south to include Terre Haute—had been held by Johnson since he defeated three-term Democrat Virginia Jenckes in 1938. Harden's Democratic opponent, Jack J. O'Grady, had been campaigning a full three months before she ever entered the race. Despite years of work behind the scenes in the Republican Party, Harden was little-known by the public. She decided to canvass the district in her station wagon on a seven-day-a-week speaking tour and to buy space on roadside billboards.[5] Harden stuck to generalities and laid out few specific initiatives in her platform. She spoke about the dangers of communism and the importance of balancing the federal budget.[6] In what proved to be an unusually close race, Harden prevailed with a margin of just 483 votes out of more than 132,000 cast, with O'Grady taking his hometown of Terre Haute but Harden winning the surrounding rural counties. A third-party Prohibition candidate captured about twice Harden's plurality. In the ensuing four elections, Harden won slightly more comfortable margins of victory ranging from 52 to 56 percent.[7]

When Harden was sworn in as a freshman Representative in January 1949, she was appointed to the Veterans' Affairs Committee. She transferred to the Committee on Expenditures in Executive Departments (later Government Operations) in the following term and served on the Committee on the Post Office and Civil Service in the 83rd through the 85th Congresses (1953–1959). In the 83rd Congress, while the GOP briefly held the majority, Harden chaired the Inter-Governmental Relations subcommittee of Government Operations. Her responsibilities on the Republican National Committee also required a great deal of travel. In Washington, she took up residence in the Congressional Hotel (later named the O'Neill House Office Building), while her husband, Frost, remained in Covington. Though supportive of his wife's work, he kept his distance from it. "I have nothing whatever to do with my wife's congressional office," Frost Harden once told reporters. "I used to dabble in politics once, myself. When my wife got in, she passed me fast."[8]

Harden was an early advocate of women's rights. At a time of GOP recriminations over losing the 1948 presidential election, she teamed with Senator Margaret Chase Smith of Maine and Representative Frances Bolton of Ohio to criticize the "male dominance" of the Republican Party. The group proposed a voter education program, and Harden called for "better salesmanship for Republicanism and Americanism," urging the party to promote women's issues in its future platforms.[9] In 1957, along with Representative Florence Dwyer of New Jersey, Harden offered a bill to provide equal pay for women, one of a series of proposals that women had championed starting with Winifred Stanley of New York in 1943.[10] Harden believed women had an important part to play in politics, particularly in local organizations and volunteer groups, which would provide the kind of experience they needed to move into higher offices. "It cannot be denied that there

is prejudice in varying degrees on the part of men toward women in high positions of governmental or party authority," Harden observed in 1949. But "before we women start making any real progress in politics, we must somehow develop a genuine conviction of our own worth to the world . . . we must feel in our hearts that women are as competent to assess problems and meet situations as men."[11]

Congresswoman Harden represented the district in much the same manner as Virginia Jenckes had during the 1930s, by paying close attention to its economic needs. Harden promoted flood control for the Wabash Valley and secured funding for a dam and recreational facility. She criticized the Defense Department's 1956 plan to close the Atomic Energy Commission's heavy water plant in Dana, Indiana, claiming that 900 people would lose jobs and be added to her district's already long unemployment rolls. As a member of the Committee on Expenditures in Executive Departments, she toured military supply installations in the U.S. and Asia to study ways of improving the armed forces' procurement procedures.[12] As chair of the Intergovernmental Relations Subcommittee of the Government Operations Committee, Harden pushed to have the armed forces and other government branches stop performing work that could be outsourced to private companies. All this was related to a bigger push by the Dwight D. Eisenhower administration to trim the military budget and the overall federal budget. "The Department of Defense," Harden said, echoing a statement by Defense Secretary Charles E. Wilson, "supports the basic principle that free competitive enterprise should be fostered by the government."[13] She also authored legislation which repealed the excise tax on leather goods and took an interest in traffic safety and legislation to provide for a uniform national system of highway signage and signals.[14]

Like so many other Republican politicians during the 1950s, Harden's political fortunes were hitched to the wagon of popular war hero and two-term GOP President Dwight D. "Ike" Eisenhower. As a GOP national committeewoman she had supported Senator Robert Taft of Ohio for the nomination at the contentious 1952 Republican

Convention, but also had played an active part as a member of the credentials committee in allowing the pro-Eisenhower delegates to be seated. She aligned herself closely with Eisenhower once he took office.[15] One political commentator noted that Harden had come to Congress by campaigning and assuring her constituents that she "has always been a forthright woman with a mind of her own." The commentator observed that "now all she seems to want [voters] to know is that she stands all right with the man in the White House. Ike and his personal popularity have taken the temper out of her steel."[16]

That strategy could cut both ways, as Harden found out in 1958. The election was something of a referendum on President Eisenhower's economic policies and an expression of voter frustration with an economic recession. Her district, with industry centralized in Terre Haute, was particularly hard hit by unemployment. Harden lost her campaign for re-election in a tight race to Democrat Fred Wampler, a Terre Haute high school football coach, who prevailed by little more than two percent of the vote. She was one of seven Indiana Republican incumbents who lost in a national Democratic sweep which cost the GOP 47 House seats that fall. Overnight, Indiana's House delegation swung from a 9–2 GOP advantage to a 9–2 Democratic advantage.

Two months after leaving office in January 1959, Harden was appointed special assistant for women's affairs to Postmaster General Arthur E. Summerfield and served until March 1961.[17] In August 1970 President Richard M. Nixon appointed her to the National Advisory Committee for the White House Conference on Aging. Afterward, she retired to her home in Covington. Cecil Harden died on December 5, 1984, in a nursing home in Lafayette, Indiana.

FOR FURTHER READING

Biographical Directory of the United States Congress, "Cecil Murray Harden," http://bioguide.congress.gov

MANUSCRIPT COLLECTION

Indiana Historical Society (Indianapolis, IN). *Papers:* ca. 1938–1984, 12 feet. The collection consists largely of Cecil Harden's personal and political correspondence. Arranged chronologically, these folders contain cards and letters from family and friends as well as correspondence between constituents and colleagues. Also included is correspondence regarding Harden's six congressional campaigns (1948–1958) and her work as special assistant to the postmaster general, as well as five letters from President Eisenhower congratulating her for her congressional work. Also includes Republican committee and convention correspondence and information as well as election results, and legislation sponsored by Harden. Also comprising a substantial part of the collection are her speeches and news releases. Other items in the collection include political and personal expense accounts, appointment books, and calendars. Military academy appointments made by Harden when in Congress, issues such as aging, health and nutrition, and women in politics are also covered. Clippings from various newspapers document her personal and political life. Republican material including Richard M. Nixon speeches and election material are among the miscellaneous items. Speech notes, expense books, check books, note pads, address books, and diaries also are contained in the collection. A finding aid is available in the repository and online: http://www.indianahistory.org/library/manuscripts/collection_guides/harden.html.

"... BEFORE WE WOMEN START
MAKING ANY REAL PROGRESS IN
POLITICS, WE MUST SOMEHOW
DEVELOP A GENUINE CONVICTION
OF OUR OWN WORTH TO THE WORLD
... WE MUST FEEL IN OUR HEARTS
THAT WOMEN ARE AS COMPETENT
TO ASSESS PROBLEMS AND MEET
SITUATIONS AS MEN."

—CECIL HARDEN
WASHINGTON POST
MARCH 5, 1949

★ CECIL MURRAY HARDEN ★

NOTES

Joan Cook, "Ex-Rep. Cecil Harden Dies; Worked for Women's Rights," 8 December 1984, *New York Times*: 17.

2 Cook, "Ex-Rep. Cecil Harden Dies."

3 "Five to Map GOP Strategy," 5 June 1949, *New York Times*: 42.

4 *Current Biography, 1949* (New York: H.W. Wilson and Company, 1949): 243–245; quote on 244.

5 Hope Chamberlin, *A Minority of Members: Women in the U.S. Congress* (New York: Praeger, 1973): 210.

6 *Current Biography, 1949*: 244.

7 "Election Statistics, 1920 to Present," http://clerk.house.gov/members/electionInfo/index.html.

8 Elizabeth Ford, "'My Wife Went to Congress,'" 5 January 1955, *Washington Post*: 29.

9 "'Male Dominance' of GOP Criticized," 5 February 1949, *New York Times*: 12; Cook, "Ex-Rep. Cecil Harden Dies."

10 Marie Smith, "Women Legislators: Plan to Push Equal Pay Bill," 27 March 1957, *Washington Post*: C3.

11 "Women Blamed By Rep. Harden for Own Plight," 5 March 1949, *Washington Post*: B3.

12 "Wilson Tells Armed Forces to Stop Work That Private Firms Can Do," 16 December 1953, *Wall Street Journal*: 2.

13 "Wilson Tells Armed Forces to Stop Work That Private Firms Can Do"; "U.S. Urged to Quit Coffee Roasting," 24 December 1953, *New York Times*: 21.

14 Susan Tolchin, *Women in Congress* (Washington, D.C.: Government Printing Office, 1976): 36.

15 Chamberlin, *A Minority of Members*: 212.

16 George Dixon, "Washington Scene: Strain on the Coattail," 16 June 1955, *Washington Post*: 15.

17 "Mrs. Harden Gets Post Office Job," 11 April 1959, *Washington Post*: B4.

FORMER MEMBERS | 1935–1954 ★ 277

Edna Flannery Kelly
1906–1997

UNITED STATES REPRESENTATIVE ★ DEMOCRAT FROM NEW YORK
1949–1969

Edna Flannery Kelly, a 20-year veteran of the U.S. House and the first woman to represent Brooklyn, New York, in Congress, made her mark on the Foreign Affairs Committee supporting a broad sweep of American Cold War policies ranging from the creation of the North Atlantic Treaty Organization (NATO) to intervention in the Vietnamese civil war. As chair of the Subcommittee on Europe, Congresswoman Kelly took a hard-line approach to America's rivals in the Kremlin and in Soviet-sponsored regimes throughout the world.

Edna Patricia Kathleen Flannery was born on August 20, 1906, in East Hampton, Long Island, New York, the youngest of five daughters raised by Irish immigrants Patrick Joseph Flannery, a horticulturalist, and Mary Ellen McCarthy Flannery. Edna Flannery graduated from East Hampton High School in 1924 and, in 1928, received a B.A. in history and economics from Hunter College in New York City. In the fall of 1928, Edna Flannery married Edward Leo Kelly, a Brooklyn lawyer. The couple raised two children, William and Maura. In January 1942, New York Governor Herbert Lehman appointed Edward Kelly as a judge on the New York City court. Less than eight months later, however, Kelly was killed in an automobile accident.

Only after her husband's death did Edna Kelly seriously consider a career in politics. She had a powerful ally in Irwin Steingut, then the minority leader in the New York Assembly and Brooklyn's political boss. Steingut encouraged her to become active in local political organizations.[1] She reorganized the women's auxiliary of the ailing Madison Democratic Club and served as a research director for the New York state legislature from 1943 until 1949.[2] In 1944 she was elected to the first of three

terms on the Democratic executive committee of Kings County, New York, and joined Steingut as a co-leader of the 18th assembly district.

On July 15, 1949, Kings County Democratic leaders chose Kelly as their nominee to fill the vacancy caused by the death of Brooklyn-based U.S. Representative Andrew L. Somers. Local leaders were eager to put a woman on the ballot. "They felt that this was the time to recognize the work of women," Kelly later explained. "I had been a long time working in the Democratic Party."[3] The district contained large Catholic and Jewish populations and was heavily Democratic. Kelly supported President Harry S. Truman's domestic and foreign policies, pledging to back U.S. participation in the United Nations as well as continued financing for the Marshall Plan, aid to Israel, and entry into NATO.[4] On the domestic side, Kelly focused on issues of interest to women, advocating federal dollars for the development of childcare centers and an investigation into high milk prices, as well as her opposition to excise taxes on cosmetics.[5] She defeated her nearest competitor, Liberal Party candidate Jules Cohen, by a 2–1 margin.[6] Kelly became the first Democratic woman to represent New York City in Congress. From the start, however, she stressed her credentials as Representative for all district constituents, not just women. "Please don't describe me as attractive," she chided reporters. "Just say I have common sense!"[7]

Upon her arrival in Congress, Kelly sought an assignment on the Foreign Affairs Committee. Kelly's 44 New York colleagues backed her candidacy to fill a vacancy on the committee, but prominent figures—Speaker Sam Rayburn of Texas, former First Lady Eleanor Roosevelt, and President Truman—asked Kelly to defer that post to

Franklin Roosevelt, Jr. Kelly refused. Ultimately, the Democratic Caucus of the Ways and Means Committee controlled the assignments, and that group was dominated by Kelly supporters. She received the assignment; FDR, Jr., got a seat, too, when the committee expanded its roster.[8] Kelly served there for her entire House career. She eventually chaired a special Subcommittee on the Canada–United States Interparliamentary group and was Secretary of the House Democratic Caucus. In 1967, she was appointed to the newly formed Committee on Standards of Official Conduct and helped draft its procedures.[9]

Kelly's lasting contributions came in international affairs. Her first vote in Congress was in favor of a bill in early 1950 to increase aid to South Korea. It failed by one vote, and Kelly recalled John McCormack of Massachusetts lamenting, "We're going to resent this vote."[10] Later that year, North Korean communists invaded South Korea. Kelly soon established herself as an implacable foe of communism. In the summer of 1955, she visited the ongoing Geneva Peace talks—the first Soviet-Atlantic Alliance summit of the Cold War—culminating with a great power meeting that included President Dwight Eisenhower, Soviet Premier Nikolai Bulganin, British Prime Minister Anthony Eden, and French President Edgar Faure. In the midst of the conference, Kelly confronted Secretary of State John Foster Dulles about revelations of massive Russian weapons shipments to Middle Eastern countries. "Mr. Secretary, you leave this ministers' conference and tell the world what the Russians are doing," she demanded. Dulles, no friend of Moscow, answered curtly, "Edna, you want war?" Kelly replied, "You're going to get war if you don't do it."[11] On the home front, she supported the House Committee on Un-American Activities, arguing that it "performed good service."[12] Among her legislative achievements was her successful amendment to President Truman's 1952 bill requesting $7.9 billion in foreign aid, suspending funding to Communist Yugoslavia. The House also approved her amendment to the Agricultural Trade Development and Assistance Act of 1954, which outlawed the sale of surplus commodities to the Soviet Union or its satellites.

Voters seemed to agree with her hard-line anti-commu-

nist positions. In her 1954 campaign, Kelly defeated Republican Abraham Sher, who campaigned for U.S. diplomatic recognition of Communist China, with 73 percent of the vote. Two years later, she defeated Sher by a similar margin.[13] In fact, Kelly never faced serious opposition in the 10 general elections during her two decades in the House.[14]

After she became chair of the Foreign Affairs Subcommittee on Europe in 1955, Kelly led the first of five fact-finding missions to Europe and the Middle East. Based upon information gleaned from these trips and from her careful study of postwar Europe, Kelly recommended a wide variety of legislation. She was particularly successful introducing resolutions deploring religious persecutions in Eastern Europe. Throughout the 1950s and 1960s, from the vantage of her committee, she urged the United States to play a more aggressive role in mediating Arab–Israeli peace accords through the aegis of the United Nations, though to little effect. In 1963, President John F. Kennedy appointed her a member of the U.S. delegation to the United Nations, where she worked closely with her friend U.N. Ambassador Adlai Stevenson. At the time of her retirement, she was the third-ranking Member on the Foreign Affairs Committee. Her sources in Europe were legendary. A colleague recalled trips with Kelly were "like going abroad with Mata Hari. She had innumerable contacts . . . that were not available at all to the State Department."[15]

Kelly's influence even touched on U.S. foreign policy in East Asia. During a fact-finding trip to Yugoslavia, Kelly attended a dinner with a senior communist official who had visited Viet Minh leader Ho Chi Minh (who had not been seen in public for months). "Oh, you mean my old friend, Ho? How is he?" Kelly deadpanned, fishing for information. The Yugoslav official warmed to her and reported that Ho had been gravely ill for months, information which the American government had not been able to confirm previously.[16] Kelly personally knew some of the principals in the Saigon government waging civil war with Hanoi during the 1950s. In 1954, she met Ngo Dinh Diem, the Eisenhower administration's hand-picked

KELLY'S LASTING CONTRIBUTIONS
CAME IN INTERNATIONAL AFFAIRS.
AT THE TIME OF HER RETIREMENT,
KELLY WAS THE THIRD-RANKING
MEMBER ON THE FOREIGN AFFAIRS
COMMITTEE. HER SOURCES IN
EUROPE WERE LEGENDARY.
A COLLEAGUE RECALLED TRIPS
WITH KELLY WERE "LIKE GOING
ABROAD WITH MATA HARI. SHE
HAD INNUMERABLE CONTACTS . . .
THAT WERE NOT AVAILABLE AT ALL
TO THE STATE DEPARTMENT."

leader in the newly formed Republic of South Vietnam. She remained an ardent backer of Diem, despite later misgivings about corruption within the Saigon government.[17] By 1965, two years after Diem was killed in a U.S.-backed coup, Kelly supported direct American military intervention and remained an unwavering supporter.[18]

By the 1960s, shifting demographics and the decline of the once-powerful New York City Democratic machine threatened Kelly's safe seat. Political alliances were shifting as reformers sought to topple New York City's entrenched Democratic organization.[19] By 1966, Kelly's pro-Vietnam War position had become controversial enough to make her a vulnerable incumbent. She narrowly survived a primary challenge from a Flatbush politician who attacked her pro-Vietnam votes and what he described as Kelly's "anti-Israel" position in the Middle East.[20] In the general election, however, Kelly trounced her GOP opponent and a third-party peace candidate with 73 percent of the vote.[21]

The ethnic and racial composition of Representative Kelly's section of Brooklyn also shifted dramatically.[22] By 1968, the New York legislature had folded Kelly's district into two new ones. A new black majority district, drawing from the Bedford-Stuyvesant neighborhood Kelly once represented, elected Shirley Chisholm, the first African-American woman to serve in Congress. The other new district went to the dean of the New York state delegation and chair of the Judiciary Committee, Representative Emanuel Celler, a 45-year House veteran. Rather than retire, Kelly mounted the first primary challenge against Celler since he entered Congress in 1923. But with her power base scattered between the two districts, she received only 32 percent of the vote, losing by about 8,500 votes. She later charged that Democratic Party leaders and Celler supporters tried to intimidate her: "It was rougher and dirtier than ever before."[23]

When Kelly retired in January 1969, Representative Mel Laird, a Wisconsin Republican and Secretary-Designate of Defense, observed that the Congresswoman's personal "strength" contributed to America "being strong and being prepared and being willing to stand up and be

counted when the chips were down in vital areas of the world."[24] Kelly returned to her home in the Crown Heights section of Brooklyn and helped coordinate a Library of Congress oral history project with former U.S. Representatives. Residing in Brooklyn until 1981, Kelly suffered a stroke and moved to Alexandria, Virginia, to live with her daughter. She died there on December 14, 1997.

FOR FURTHER READING

Biographical Directory of the United States Congress, "Edna Flannery Kelly," http://bioguide.congress.gov

MANUSCRIPT COLLECTION

Library of Congress, Manuscript Division, Washington, D.C. *Oral History:* Transcript in the Oral History Collection of the U.S. Association of Former Members of Congress. Restricted. Sound recording in the Library's Motion Picture, Broadcasting and Recorded Sound Division.

NOTES

1   *Current Biography, 1950* (New York: H.W. Wilson and Company, 1950): 290.

2   *Current Biography, 1950*: 290.

3   Edna Kelly, Oral History Interview, U.S. Association of Former Members of Congress (hereinafter cited as USAFMOC), Manuscript Room, Library of Congress, Washington, D.C.: 1.

4   "Mrs. Kelly's Program," 7 October 1949, *New York Times*: 21.

5   "On Her Way to Congress," 3 December 1949, *Cue*; also cited in Marcy Kaptur's, *Women of Congress: A Twentieth-Century Odyssey* (Washington, D.C.: Congressional Quarterly Press, 1996).

6   "Brooklyn Woman Sent to Congress," 9 November 1949, *New York Times*: 7; "Election Statistics, 1920 to Present," http://clerk.house.gov/members/electionInfo/index.html.

7   Martin Weil, "Edna F. Kelly Dies at 91; Longtime Member of Congress," 17 December 1997, *Washington Post*: C6.

8   Kelly, Oral History Interview, USAFMOC: 2.

9   Ibid., 51–52.

10 Ibid., 6.

11 Ibid., 10.

12 Ibid., 22.

13 William M. Farrell, "Mrs. Kelly and G.O.P. Rival Split Sharply Over Red China," 22 October 1954, *New York Times*: 18; Edith Evans Ashbury, "Mrs. Kelly in the 10th District Won in '54 by 50,000 Votes," 26 October 1956, *New York Times*: 22.

14 "Election Statistics, 1920 to Present," http://clerk.house.gov/members/electionInfo/elections.html ; Kelly, Oral History Interview, USAFMOC: 52–53.

15 See Martha Griffiths, Oral History Interview, 29 October 1979, USAFMOC, Manuscript Room, Library of Congress, Washington, D.C.: 155.

16 Griffiths, Oral History Interview, USAFMOC: 155–156.

17 Kelly, Oral History Interview, USAFMOC: 7–9; 12–13.

18 Elizabeth Shelton, "Rep. Kelly Says Threats Helped Defeat Her," 10 October 1966, *Washington Post*: C3.

19 "Reform Democrats Plan Brooklyn Bid for House Seat," 12 February 1964, *New York Times*: 21.

20 Richard Reeves, "Brooklyn Contests Aim at Jewish Vote," 12 June 1966, *New York Times*: 55; Warren Weaver, Jr., "House Contests Shake Democrats," 30 June 1966, *New York Times*: 25; Alfred E. Clarke, "Edna Kelly Vote Upheld By Court," 26 August 1966, *New York Times*: 21.

21 "Election Statistics, 1920 to Present," http://clerk.house.gov/members/electionInfo/elections.html; Edward Hudson, "Two Leftists Among Mrs. Kelly's Rivals in the 12th," 26 October 1966, *New York Times*: 51.

22 Richard L. Strout, "Mrs. Kelly of Flatbush," 26 May 1967, *Christian Science Monitor*: 18.

23 Elizabeth Shelton, "Rep. Kelly Says Threats Helped Defeat Her," 10 October 1968, *Washington Post*: C3.

24 Weil, "Edna F. Kelly Dies at 91."

Marguerite Stitt Church
1892–1990

UNITED STATES REPRESENTATIVE ★ REPUBLICAN FROM ILLINOIS
1951–1963

After years of assisting the political career of her husband, Ralph Church, and working for various charities, Marguerite Stitt Church won election to the House of Representatives to succeed Congressman Church after his death in 1950. Congresswoman Church sought and gained a seat on the Foreign Affairs Committee, traveling to more than 40 countries and seeing firsthand how U.S. foreign aid was employed in them.

Marguerite Stitt was born in New York City on September 13, 1892, the daughter of William and Adelaide Stitt. She developed an interest in foreign countries at an early age when her parents took her abroad each summer as a child. She attended St. Agatha School in New York City and, later, as a member of Phi Beta Kappa, earned an A.B. in psychology with a minor in economics and sociology from Wellesley College in 1914. After graduation, she taught a biblical history course at Wellesley for a year before enrolling in a masters program in economics and sociology at Columbia University.[1] She completed her graduate degree in 1917 and worked for a year as a consulting psychologist with the State Charities Aid Association of New York City. In 1918, she traveled to Chicago and met Illinois state legislator Ralph Church.[2] The couple married that December and settled in Evanston, Illinois, where they raised three children: Ralph, William, and Marjory. Marguerite Church worked in a succession of organizations devoted to family and children's welfare. In 1934, Ralph Church was elected to the U.S. House of Representatives to the first of seven terms in a seat representing the densely populated suburbs just north of Chicago. Marguerite embarked with him on investigative trips, making her own speaking tour on behalf of Republican presidential campaigns in 1940 and 1944. During and after World War II,

at her husband's request, she made several inspection tours of Europe. In Washington she served as president of the Congressional Club, a group of wives and daughters of Members of Congress, the Cabinet, and the Supreme Court. But she later recalled that while he was alive she never seriously considered a political career. "My political life was one of adaptation to his life," Church observed. Nevertheless, her experience as a congressional spouse was critical to her later success, making her "a realist as regards the practical operation of Congress."[3]

Ralph Church died suddenly of heart failure during a House committee hearing in March 1950.[4] Shortly thereafter, GOP leaders in Illinois persuaded Marguerite Church to run for her husband's vacant seat. "If a man had been nominated and made a mistake, you would have said he is stupid," Church said at the time. "If I make a mistake, you will say she is a woman. I shall try never to give you reason to say that."[5] In the general election that fall, she defeated Democrat Thomas F. Dolan with 74 percent of the vote. In her next five re-election bids, she was never seriously challenged, winning between 66 and 72 percent of the vote. "The [local GOP] organization, of course, never considered anybody else after I got in," Church recalled. "They just went along."[6] Much of her success was due to her attention to district needs. She returned to Illinois frequently, opened her home to voters, and personally dictated replies to an average of 600 letters per week. Her cardinal rule was if anyone came asking for help, "never let yourself ask, 'Is he a Republican or a Democrat?' . . . We never made any political distinction whatsoever, and I think that was one reason that in the long run people began to trust me."[7] Church's independence also earned her the respect of colleagues.[8]

When Church took her seat in the 82nd Congress (1951–1953), she was assigned to the Committee on Expenditures in Executive Departments (later Government Operations), where she chaired a special subcommittee investigating President Dwight Eisenhower's reorganization of the Council of Economic Advisers.[9] Church was instrumental in helping to pass recommendations offered by the Second Hoover Commission on efficiency in government.[10] In 1957, Church supported the Civil Rights Bill. She also was one of the first Members to bring African-American guests into the House dining room, when she treated six young newsboys to lunch. Capitol staff told her she would never get through the door. "Well," she replied, the boys have worked hard selling newspapers "and I certainly do not intend to tell them they can't luncheon in the dining room of their own Capitol."[11] The group ate lunch in the dining room. Though not "militant about a woman's rights," Church supported women's rights legislation, including the Equal Pay Bill. She encouraged women entering politics to think of themselves as public servants rather than advocates of feminism. She believed in "equal protection under the law for both men and women, period."[12]

Church left Government Operations in the 84th Congress (1955–1957) to focus exclusively on her Foreign Affairs Committee assignment (which she had received two years earlier). After winning re-election in 1952, she had been offered a spot on the prestigious Appropriations Committee, where her husband once sat and, in fact, where only one woman had previously served. The committee chairman made the offer, but Church declined. "I'm awfully sorry," she replied. "I've spent all summer trying to persuade people that it would be a loss to the country if they didn't put me on the Foreign Affairs Committee. That has become my major interest." She later claimed that she did not want to accept an assignment that, she believed, was made partly as a tribute to her husband.[13] She served on Foreign Affairs until she retired from Congress.

Church's chief interests and influence flowed from her work on the Foreign Affairs Committee, where she was assigned to the Subcommittee on Foreign Economic Policy. She was a skeptic of large foreign-aid bills appropriated for many of America's Cold War allies in Asia, the Middle East, and Africa. "The idea that you can win friends and influence people merely by pouring out millions—and it's amounted by this time to billions—never caught my attention or my faith," she recalled.[14] As a member of the Subcommittee on the Far East and the Pacific, she traveled widely to witness firsthand the implementation of American programs. "Some officials protested that this was no place for a lady," Church told a reporter. "I told them I was not a lady. I was a Member of Congress."[15] In 1959, while Ranking Republican Member on the Foreign Economic Policy Subcommittee, she logged more than 40,000 miles in 17 countries.[16] Her experience with a group of tribal women in a remote sub-Saharan African village shaped her view of how foreign aid should be targeted. "These women, I found, didn't want guns; they didn't want atomic plants; they didn't want navies," Church said. "They wanted someone who could show them the next step up from where they were to where they'd like to be."

During the first year of the John F. Kennedy administration, that memory factored into her championing of the Peace Corps, which sought to provide educational and technological support to developing countries through the work of trained college-aged American volunteers.[17] During a September 14, 1961, debate, seven-term Representative H.R. Gross of Iowa launched a verbal diatribe against the Peace Corps program. Gross described it as a "Kiddie Korps," reminiscent of Hitler's youth corps in Nazi Germany, and a "utopian brainstorm" that would exacerbate the U.S. deficit. In response, Congresswoman Church entered the well of the House to speak on behalf of the program, recounting her numerous trips abroad where she had seen foreign-aid dollars misspent and misdirected in the battle for the developing world. "Here is something which is aimed right," Church told colleagues, "which is American, which is sacrificial—and which above all can somehow carry at the human level, to the people of the world, what they need to know; what it is to be free; what it is to have a next step and be able to take it; what it is to have something to look forward to, in an increase of human dignity and confidence." A GOP colleague recalled that Church's floor speech was critical in persuading a number of reluctant Republicans to support the measure. "You quite literally could see people who had been uncertain or perhaps who had already decided to vote against the Peace Corps sit there, listen to her very quietly and start to rethink," Representative Catherine May of Washington State said."[18] Later that afternoon, the Peace Corps legislation passed the House by a wide margin, 288 to 97.[19]

In 1962, as an advocate of mandatory retirement for Members of Congress and facing reapportionment in her district, Church set her own example by retiring at age 70 after the close of the 87th Congress (1961–1963) in January 1963. She worked on behalf of the Republican presidential campaigns of Barry Goldwater in 1964 and Richard M. Nixon in 1968. She later served on the boards of directors for the Girl Scouts of America and the U.S. Capitol Historical Society. In 1971, President Nixon selected Church to serve on the planning board for the White House Conference on Aging. Marguerite Church resided in Evanston, Illinois, where she died on May 26, 1990.

FOR FURTHER READING

Biographical Directory of the United States Congress, "Margaret Stitt Church," http://bioguide.congress.gov

MANUSCRIPT COLLECTIONS

Evanston Historical Society (Evanston, IL). *Papers:* 1919–1981, 2.5 linear feet. Chiefly personal and political papers, including letters of congratulations from Members of the House of Representatives for Marguerite Church's retirement from office in 1962. Also includes scrapbooks containing newspaper clippings relating to her husband Ralph Church's political career, her husband's death, programs and announcements for official events, press clippings and releases, speeches, and a book relating to a special political committee. A finding aid is available in the repository.

Library of Congress (Washington, D.C.), Manuscript Division. *Oral History*: Transcript in the Oral History Collection of the U.S. Association of Former Members of Congress. Sound recording in the Library's Motion Picture, Broadcasting and Recorded Sound Division.

NOTES

1   Marguerite Stitt Church, Oral History Interview, 25 November 1978, U.S. Association of Former Members of Congress (hereinafter USAFMOC), Manuscript Room, Library of Congress, Washington, D.C.: 16.

2   Kerry Luft, "Marguerite Stitt Church, Ex-Congresswoman," 27 May 1990, *Chicago Tribune*: 8.

3   Genevieve Reynolds, "Charming Mrs. Ralph Church, A Model of Cultured Intellect," 13 February 1949, *Washington Post*: S8; Marie McNair, "Mrs. Church Dons New Role," 21 January 1951, *Washington Post*: S1; Church, Oral History Interview, USAFMOC: 1; 23.

4   "Rep. Church Dies Testifying in Committee," 22 March 1950 *Washington Post*: 1.

5   Luft, "Marguerite Stitt Church, Ex-Congresswoman."

6   Church, Oral History Interview, USAFMOC: 5.

7   Ibid., 6.

8   Ibid., 8–9.

9   "Politics Won't Sway Him, Economic Chief Asserts," 15 July 1953, *New York Times*: 13; "No Politics in His Advice, Chief Economic Aide Says," 15 July 1953, *Wall Street Journal*: 20.

10 Hope Chamberlin, *A Minority of Members: Women in the U.S. Congress* (New York: Praeger, 1973): 221–222; Karen Foerstel, *Biographical Dictionary of Congressional Women* (Westport, CT: Greenwood Press, 1999): 59; *Congress and the Nation, 1945–1964*, Vol. I-B (Washington, D.C.: Congressional Quarterly Press, 1965), 1466.

11 Church, Oral History Interview, USAFMOC: 28–30.

12 Luft, "Marguerite Stitt Church, Ex-Congresswoman."

13 Church, Oral History Interview, USAFMOC: 9.

14 Ibid., 12.

15 Jane Eads, "Congresswoman Church Back From Far East," 31 January 1954, *Washington Post*: S3.

16 Joan Cook, "Marguerite Church, Ex-Congresswoman, Dies at the Age of 97," 30 May 1990, *New York Times*: B20.

17 Church, Oral History Interview, USAFMOC: 13–14.

18 Catherine Dean May, Oral History Interview, 20 April 1979, USAFMOC, Manuscript Room, Library of Congress, Washington, D.C.: 216–217.

19 *Congressional Record*, House, 87th Cong., 1st sess. (14 September 1961): 19502–19504; 19535–19536.

Ruth Thompson
1887–1970

UNITED STATES REPRESENTATIVE ★ REPUBLICAN FROM MICHIGAN
1951–1957

Ruth Thompson, a longtime lawyer and judge, became the first woman to represent Michigan in Congress and the first to serve on the House Judiciary Committee. Her legislative interests were eclectic, ranging from a proposal to create a Department of Peace to the establishment of a congressional Page academy. Representative Thompson's career ended abruptly following a contentious fight over the development of a jet fighter base in her northwestern Michigan district.

Ruth Thompson was the first child born to Thomas and Bertha Thompson in Whitehall, Michigan, on September 15, 1887. She attended public schools and graduated from the Muskegon Business College in Muskegon, Michigan, in 1905. Beginning in 1918, she worked in a law office and studied law in night school for six years before she was admitted to the bar in 1924, becoming the first female lawyer in Muskegon County. She also served as the registrar of the county's probate court for 18 years. Thompson was elected judge of probate in Muskegon County in 1925, a position she held for 12 years. In 1938 she won election to a term in the Michigan state house of representatives as the state's first woman legislator. From 1941 to 1942, Thompson worked for the Social Security Board's Old Age and Survivor's Insurance Division in Washington, D.C. She then worked for three years in the Labor Department's Wage and Hour Division. In 1945, Thompson went to Headquarters Command of U.S. occupation forces in Frankfurt, Germany, and Copenhagen, Denmark, where she worked on the adjutant general's staff. A year later, she returned to private law practice in Michigan.

In 1950, when Michigan's GOP Representative Albert J. Engel, a 16-year House veteran, declined to run for re-election to campaign for the governorship, Thompson entered the race to fill his vacant seat. In the Republican primary, she topped challenges from the Muskegon County GOP chairman and a former lieutenant governor, relying on grass-roots campaigning and her name recognition from years as a judge. "I started out in my car and stopped all over, ringing doorbells, visiting business places, talking with the people on the streets, and addressing countless gatherings," Thompson recalled, traveling around the northwestern Michigan district. "Many of those whom I met were people I had known when I was probate judge—I'd handled their estates, helped them when they wanted to adopt children, or placed young wards of the court in their homes for boarding."[1] In the general election, she defeated Democrat Noel P. Fox, chairman of the state Labor Mediation Board, with 55 percent of the vote in the rural and Republican-leaning district bordering Lake Michigan. She won comfortable re-election campaigns in 1952 and 1954 with 60 and 56 percent of the vote, respectively. In the latter campaign, Thompson turned back a GOP primary challenge from Robert Engel, son of the former Representative from the district.[2]

When she took her seat in the 82nd Congress (1951–1953) in January 1951, Thompson won a coveted spot on the House Judiciary Committee, becoming the first woman to serve on that panel. There was initial resistance to her appointment, but her work as a judge and as chair of the Michigan prison commission for women, from 1946 to 1950, helped override objections. Admired by colleagues for her work ethic, she remained on the Judiciary Committee throughout her House career, serving as a member of the subcommittees on Bankruptcy and

Immigration and Naturalization. In the 84th Congress (1955–1957), Thompson also was appointed to the Joint Committee on Immigration and Nationality Policy.

A proponent of limited federal spending, Thompson opposed much of the Harry S. Truman administration's domestic program. She voted to curtail housing construction provided for under the Public Housing Administration, supported a measure to shrink the size of the federal workforce, and joined other GOP Congresswomen in an effort to publicize how inflation limited the ability of housewives to buy groceries for their families.[3] Thompson also was a critic of President Truman's foreign policy. In the wake of military reverses in the protracted Korean War, she joined conservative Republicans in calling for the removal of Secretary of State Dean G. Acheson and, occasionally, voted against military and economic assistance to Western Europe. In 1953, Thompson proposed the creation of a Department of Peace, which would be represented in the presidential Cabinet. She explained, "All the guns, all the tanks, and all the bombs we are building during these hectic times are not going to save us from our enemies at home or abroad." As a potential secretary for the department, Thompson proposed the evangelist Billy Graham.[4]

Thompson also played a major role in shaping a Capitol Hill institution by introducing a bill to establish a formal academy for House and Senate Pages which would have provided a central dormitory and adult supervision. The Pages, a group of about 75 blue-coated teenage boys who ran errands for Members in the chambers and the congressional offices, came to Washington on patronage appointments from around the country. In addition to their official duties, they took classes at the Library of Congress. But the Pages were responsible for securing their own room and board. "A boy 15 years old isn't old enough to choose his own home and determine his own hours," Thompson said.[5] The reforms that Thompson proposed, however, were not enacted for another 30 years.[6]

Congresswoman Thompson generally preferred committee work to speechmaking. She spent little time on the House Floor and, when she did, it was normally to offer her succinct support for measures introduced by the Judiciary Committee. Thompson supported a "submerged lands" bill, which sought to retain state control from the federal government over coastal waters with oil and mineral deposits. She argued, in part, that if the states lost revenue from the development of these deposits, a principal revenue source for educational programs would decline.[7] In 1953, based on her own experience in an accident with fireworks, she supported a measure by colleague Marguerite Stitt Church of Illinois seeking to restrict the sale of out-of-state, "bootleg" fireworks in jurisdictions in which they were illegal.[8] As a member of the Judiciary Subcommittee on Immigration and Naturalization, she supported a 1952 revision of immigration law that came out of her committee.[9]

Thompson's congressional career began to unravel when the Air Force announced that it planned to build a new fighter-interceptor base outside her district, despite her private and public protest that Defense Department officials had originally promised her repeatedly that the base would be located inside her northwestern Michigan district. Thompson also revealed that she had been offered a $1,000 campaign bribe to agree to have the base built in Cadillac, Michigan, outside her congressional district. She had informed Harold E. Talbott, the Secretary of the Air Force, of the bribe and was assured that Cadillac would not be chosen under any circumstances. When that city was named in favor of two others, Thompson protested vigorously to Carl Vinson of Georgia, chairman of the House Armed Services Committee. Vinson sided with the Congresswoman, and the base was eventually built in Manistee, inside her district.[10] But the political fallout resulting from the delay and additional construction costs, which totaled $5 million, created resentment among Thompson's constituents. In August 1955 local Democratic leaders drew up a recall petition against Thompson, charging that she was "jeopardizing the safety of the nation by prolonging the jet base decision."[11] Though the recall drive failed, it demonstrated just how much the episode had roiled the district. In the August 1956 GOP primary, the 70-year-old Thompson lost narrowly to Robert P. Griffin (who won the general election and later went on to serve in the U.S. Senate).

After Congress, Thompson returned to Whitehall, Michigan. She died on April 5, 1970, in Allegan County, Michigan.

FOR FURTHER READING

Biographical Directory of the United States Congress, "Ruth Thompson," http://bioguide.congress.gov

MANUSCRIPT COLLECTION

University of Michigan (Ann Arbor, MI), Michigan Historical Collections, Bentley Historical Library. Includes a scrapbook containing clippings, greeting cards, telegrams, correspondence, programs, photographs, and miscellaneous loose scrapbook materials. Two phonograph records, "Report from Congress, 1951" and "1956 Republican Congressional Campaign," are stored in the library's record collection.

NOTES

1 Hope Chamberlin, *A Minority of Members: Women in the U.S. Congress* (New York: Praeger, 1973): 222–225.

2 "Michigan Unions Clash in Primary," 18 July 1954, *New York Times*: 37; "Election Statistics, 1920 to Present," http://clerk.house.gov/members/electionInfo/elections.html.

3 Karen Foerstel, *Biographical Dictionary of Congressional Women* (Westport, CT: Greenwood Press, 1999): 268–270; *Congressional Record*, House, 82nd Cong., 1st sess. (15 March 1951): 2502; "A Problem for the Housewife," 16 March 1951, *New York Times*: 12.

4 *Congressional Record*, House, 83rd Cong., 2nd sess. (13 July 1954): 10452.

5 "Rep. Thompson: Proposes Academy for Pages," 16 February 1954, *Washington Post*: 24; "Senate, House Pages Take Dim View of Proposed Academy for Them," 23 February 1954, *Washington Post*: 17; *Congressional Record*, House, 83rd Cong., 2nd sess. (16 February 1954): 1850; Donald Bacon et al., *The Encyclopedia of the United States Congress*, Vol. 3 (New York: Simon and Schuster, 1995): 1517–1518.

6 The first girl Page entered service in 1971; the first female House Page was admitted in 1973. Congressionally operated Page dorms were opened in the 1980s.

7 *Congressional Record*, House, 82nd Cong., 1st sess. (27 July 1951): 9096; *Congressional Record*, House, 83rd Cong., 1st sess. (30 March 1953): 2505.

8 *Congressional Record*, House, 83rd Cong., 1st sess. (20 July 1953): 9288.

9 *Congressional Record*, House, 82nd Cong., 2nd sess. (23 April 1952): 4308.

10 For Thompson's explanation of this tortuous process, see *Congressional Record*, House, 84th Cong., 2nd sess. (12 April 1956): 6251–6253.

11 "Recall Move Prompted by Jet Base Row," 2 August 1955, *Washington Post*: 8.

Maude Elizabeth Kee
1895–1975

UNITED STATES REPRESENTATIVE ★ DEMOCRAT FROM WEST VIRGINIA
1951–1965

Maude Elizabeth Kee made history as West Virginia's first woman Member of Congress and as a critical part of that state's Kee family dynasty in the U.S. House, stretching from the start of the New Deal to the Watergate Era. Succeeding her late husband, John Kee, in 1951, Elizabeth Kee went on to chair the Veterans' Affairs Subcommittee on Veterans' Hospitals and became a leading advocate for the coal-mining industry, a major employer in her district. When she left Congress in 1965, her son, James, won her seat, accounting for one of a handful of father-mother-son combinations in Congress.

Maude Etta "Elizabeth" Simpkins was born in Radford, Virginia, on June 7, 1895, the seventh of 11 children born to John Jesse Wade Simpkins and Cora French Hall Simpkins. Her father was a policeman and a railway company employee before moving into real estate and resettling the family in Roanoke, Virginia. Raised in a conservative Republican, Baptist household, she quickly challenged her parents' politics and religion. Her siblings later recalled that she converted to Catholicism and became a Democrat, "as soon as she was old enough."[1] She attended the National Business College and, during World War I, took her first job as a secretary for the business office of the *Roanoke Times* and, later, as a court reporter for a law firm. Elizabeth Simpkins married James Alan Frazier, a railway clerk. They had three children: Frances, James, and a child who died in infancy. The marriage soon fell apart, and James Frazier's attorney during the divorce was John Kee, who fell in love with Elizabeth. In 1925 she moved to Bluefield and, a year later, she married him.[2] John Kee was elected to the 73rd Congress (1933–1935) in the 1932 Roosevelt landslide, as a Democrat from a southeastern West Virginia district. Elizabeth Kee served as his executive secretary throughout his congressional career, including his service after 1949 as

chairman of the Committee on Foreign Affairs.[3] She once described her job on Capitol Hill as "being all things to all constituents," a combination of "clergyman, lawyer, psychiatrist and family friend."[4] Meanwhile, Kee authored "Washington Tidbits," a weekly column that was syndicated to West Virginia newspapers.

John Kee died suddenly on May 8, 1951, during a committee meeting. Four days later, Elizabeth Kee announced that she planned to seek nomination to fill her late husband's seat.[5] Initially, she was the underdog behind such powerful politicians as Walter Vergil Ross, who had served several terms in the West Virginia legislature, and Sheriff Cecil Wilson. Party leaders proposed that she should be retained as a secretary for the eventual nominee, a suggestion that infuriated her. Her son, James, campaigned heavily with United Mine Workers Association leaders in the district, convincing them that John Kee had several projects developing in Congress and that Elizabeth Kee could attend to them unlike any outsider. That strategy worked as the United Mine Workers Union—a powerhouse in her district which encompassed seven coal-mining counties and the famous Pocahontas coal fields—threw its weight behind the widow Kee. She still faced a formidable challenge from Republican Cyrus H. Gadd, a Princeton, West Virginia, lawyer. Gadd tried to turn the campaign into a referendum on the Harry S. Truman administration, which was at the nadir of its popularity. Gadd also attacked Kee as being beholden to oil interests after Oklahoma Senator Robert Kerr, an oilman and old ally of John Kee's, campaigned for her in the district. The Kee campaign turned the table on Gadd, exposing his major campaign contributors with ties to the oil industry. Kee won the July 17, 1951, special election with a plurality of about 8,500 votes, receiving 58 percent of the total.[6] She was sworn in to office on July 26, 1951, becoming the first woman to represent West Virginia in the U.S. Congress.[7]

Later that year, Kee announced she would not seek re-nomination for the seat, but she reversed herself several weeks later when a flood of requests convinced her to remain in Congress.[8] In the 1952 general election, she again faced GOP challenger Cyrus Gadd, dispatching him with a 35,000-vote margin, capturing 64 percent of the total. She won by a greater plurality than any of her West Virginia House colleagues. She subsequently was re-elected five times by sizable majorities, winning her next two campaigns with more than 60 percent of the vote or more; in 1958, she was unopposed.[9] One local paper's endorsement summed up the depth of her support: "it is absolutely unthinkable . . . for the voters to even consider anyone else to represent them than Mrs. Kee. We don't want her to have to waste valuable time in campaigning, when she could be devoting her energy and 'know how' in furthering legislation and certain projects for the benefit of southern West Virginia."[10]

John Kee had crafted a reputation as a progressive-liberal Democrat in Congress, and it was a political pattern that Elizabeth Kee followed.[11] Throughout her 14 years in Congress, she served on the Veterans' Affairs Committee, eventually chairing the Subcommittee on Veterans' Hospitals. She also was appointed to the Government Operations Committee in the 85th through 87th Congresses (1957–1963) and to the Committee on Interior and Insular Affairs in the 88th Congress (1963–1965). From her Veterans' Affairs seat, Kee became an advocate on behalf of former servicemen and servicewomen, noting, "more attention should be devoted to the welfare of this country's veterans. . . . You just can't economize at the expense of the veteran. And I know the American people—no matter how much they want Government spending cut—I know they feel that way."[12]

Kee generally was a firm supporter of Cold War foreign policy. Of her own volition and on her own dime, she toured seven South American countries in 1952 on a 16,000-mile trip that, in part, fulfilled one of her husband's aspirations.[13] In the 82nd Congress (1951–1953) she voted for an extension of the Marshall Plan's economic aid program to Europe in the form of a $7.5 billion assistance package. In the following

two years, she supported $4.4 billion and $5 billion foreign aid bills.[14] Kee would come to question such extravagant outlays during the Dwight Eisenhower administration, particularly when economic conditions deteriorated within her home state. Representative Kee was particularly critical of proposed tariff reductions, which she feared would affect her constituents.[15]

Representing the second largest coal-producing district in the country, Kee became a major advocate for coal miners and related businesses. West Virginia mines accounted for about one-third of the national output by 1957.[16] But the industry suffered heavily from foreign fossil fuel competition and, for much of the 1950s, recession plagued the state economy. Throughout her time in the House, Kee repeatedly defended U.S. coal operations from foreign energy imports, particularly "residual" (heating) fuel oil from South America and natural gas from Canada. "We do not intend to stand idly by and see American workers thrown out of employment by unnecessary concessions to foreign countries," Kee declared.[17] Congresswoman Kee addressed this issue, often casting it as a threat to U.S. national security because it took away American jobs and made the country reliant on imports of critical materials. "If we are to be prudent in our efforts to safeguard the basic security of our country, our own self-preservation, then the Congress of the United States must, now, face up to its responsibility and pass legislation to protect in a fair and just manner our own basic coal industry," she said in a floor speech.[18] Still, Kee could do little to stanch the flow of foreign oil into the U.S. market.

Kee was successful, however, developing a program of economic rejuvenation for West Virginia that mirrored the "Point Four" technological and economic aid that U.S. officials extended to developing nations.[19] Given little support from the Eisenhower administration, Kee and other Catholic supporters threw their full weight behind the candidacy of John F. Kennedy in 1960, playing an influential part in helping Kennedy win the critical West Virginia primary.[20] During the first year of the Kennedy administration, Kee's economic program was adopted as part of the Accelerated Public Works Act, which sought to head off recession by providing federal dollars for public works projects in vulnerable districts. The legislation created the Area

Redevelopment Administration (ARA), which pumped millions of dollars into recession-prone regions in the form of industrial loans, job retraining programs, and grants for water systems. In southern West Virginia, which became a model for the program, ARA money created recreational facilities, parks, and tourist attractions.[21] Kee reminded her colleagues that despite pressing concerns abroad that required huge allocations of American aid, immediate problems at home still needed to be addressed. Foreign aid bills were important, Kee admitted, "But not more important than bread and milk for coal miners' children, good jobs for their fathers, new industries and increased business activities for economically depressed American towns and cities," she said.[22]

In 1964, Kee declined to seek an eighth term in the House due to poor health.[23] Her son and longtime administrative assistant, James, won the Democratic nomination. That November, when he won easy election with 70 percent of the vote, Maude Kee became the first woman in Congress to be succeeded directly by one of her children. From 1933 to James Kee's retirement, when the district was reapportioned out of existence prior to the 1972 elections, the Kee family represented West Virginia in the House. Elizabeth Kee retired to Bluefield, where she died on February 15, 1975.

FOR FURTHER READING

Biographical Directory of the United States Congress, "Maude Elizabeth Kee," http://bioguide.congress.gov

Hardin, William H. "Elizabeth Kee: West Virginia's First Woman in Congress," *West Virginia History* 45 (1984): 109–124.

MANUSCRIPT COLLECTION

West Virginia University Libraries, West Virginia and Regional History Collection (Morgantown, WV). *Papers*: 1963–1966, 13 feet. Includes congressional papers and correspondence. Finding aid available in repository.

NOTES

1 William H. Hardin, "Elizabeth Kee: West Virginia's First Woman in Congress," *West Virginia History* 45 (1984): 109–123; quotes pp. 109–110.

2 Hardin, "Elizabeth Kee": 110–111.

3 Ibid.

4 Hope Chamberlin, *A Minority of Members: Women in the U.S. Congress* (New York: Praeger, 1973): 226; Genevieve Reynolds, "Congressional Capers," 28 August 1949, *Washington Post*: S3.

5 "Mrs. Kee Willing to Run," 13 May 1951, *New York Times*: 61.

6 "Grandmother Runs for Seat in Congress," 22 July 1951, *New York Times*: 45; this is a story on Vera Buchanan in which Kee is mentioned. See also, Hardin, "Elizabeth Kee": 109–123; and Michael Dubin et al., *U.S. Congressional Elections, 1788–1997* (Jefferson, NC: McFarland & Company, Inc., Publishers, 1998): 585.

7 "Taking Her Husband's Place in Congress," 27 July 1951, *New York Times*: 19.

8 "Mrs. Kee to File for Renomination to Seat in House," 5 January 1952, *Washington Post*: 12.

9 "Election Statistics, 1920 to Present," http://clerk.house.gov/members/electionInfo/elections.html.

10 Chamberlin, *A Minority of Members*: 226.

11 Hardin, "Elizabeth Kee": 109–123.

12 *Current Biography, 1954* (New York: H.W. Wilson and Company, 1954): 370–371; *Congressional Record*, House, 87th Cong., 1st sess. (27 February 1961): 2743.

13 *Current Biography, 1954*: 371.

14 Ibid.

15 *Congressional Record*, House, 85th Cong., 2nd sess. (25 February 1958): 2804; *Congressional Record*, House, 84th Cong., 2nd sess. (19 April 1956): 6708–6709.

16 *Congressional Record*, House, 85th Cong., 1st sess. (1 April 1957): 4953–4954.

17 *Congressional Record*, House, 83rd Cong., 2nd sess. (28 January 1954): 975; *Congressional Record*, House, 85th Cong., 1st sess. (3 June 1957): 8276–8277.

18 *Congressional Record*, House, 83rd Cong., 2nd sess. (28 June 1954): 9115; *Congressional Record*, House, 87th Cong., 1st sess. (18 August 1961): 16333; *Congressional Record*, House, 87th Cong., 2nd sess. (29 March 1962): 5504; *Congressional Record*, House, 85th Cong., 2nd sess. (17 June 1958): 11546–11547.

19 Hardin, "Elizabeth Kee": 121; see also, *Congressional Record*, House, 85th Cong., 1st sess. (18 July 1957): 12116.

20 Hardin, "Elizabeth Kee": 122.

21 Hardin, "Elizabeth Kee": 121–122.

22 *Congressional Record*, House, 85th Cong., 1st sess. (23 May 1957): 7598.

23 "Rep. Kee Retiring at End of Term," 5 January 1964, *Washington Post*: A4.

Vera Daerr Buchanan

1902–1955

UNITED STATES REPRESENTATIVE ★ DEMOCRAT FROM PENNSYLVANIA

1951–1955

Bookended by tragedy, Vera Buchanan's brief tenure in the U.S. House of Representatives began in 1951 as an extension of her late husband's legislative efforts representing blue-collar steel workers in southwest Pittsburgh. But by the time she stood for re-election 18 months later in the newly reapportioned, more center-city district, Buchanan demonstrated that she was not merely a caretaker of the office her husband once held, but a skilled politician in her own right.

Vera Daerr was born in Wilson, Pennsylvania, on July 20, 1902, daughter of John Daerr and Jennie Leasure Daerr.[1] She grew up in the steel mill town of Duquesne, Pennsylvania, and attended local public and parochial schools. After high school, she worked as a secretary for a Duquesne steel company. In 1929, Vera Daerr married Frank Buchanan, an automobile dealer and teacher, and the couple raised twin daughters, Jane and Joan. In 1942, Vera Buchanan helped her husband win election as mayor of McKeesport, a post which he held for four years. Vera operated a beauty shop and was a member of the Democratic Women's Guild. As the first lady of McKeesport, she conducted a listening campaign to familiarize herself with the needs of constituents and began cultivating a support base for future election campaigns. In May 1946, Frank won the special election to fill the vacancy left in the 79th Congress (1945–1947) by the resignation of Representative Samuel Weis. The Congressman was re-elected to the next three consecutive terms. Serving on the Banking and Currency Committee, Frank Buchanan became an expert in housing legislation and earned a reputation as a bright, candid, and liberal Member of the House. He chaired a select committee that brought to light extensive corporate and union lobbying efforts on Capitol Hill.[2] Vera Buchanan served as her husband's secretary during his five-year tenure in Congress.

Vera Buchanan's leap into elective politics came unexpectedly when Congressman Buchanan died suddenly on April 27, 1951, at the age of 48. The Pennsylvania Democratic Party chose his widow to run for the vacated seat; she accepted the invitation. "We were a very close-knit family," Buchanan later explained. "Frank's death was a great shock. I decided to run because I wanted to see the things he believed in carried on."[3] Part of Buchanan's motivation was to clear her husband's name after he had been attacked by a redbaiting columnist. Prior to his death, Frank Buchanan had developed a lengthy refutation which he was never able to deliver on the House Floor— and Vera Buchanan wanted to put it on the record herself.[4]

Critics suggested that Vera Buchanan was running as a contender based strictly on her husband's name. The *Pittsburgh Post-Gazette* despaired that "Mrs. Buchanan's foremost attribute was that she was the widow of Frank Buchanan."[5] Vera Buchanan dispelled any question of her legitimacy in a tough, quick-witted campaign that echoed her husband's positions. "I'll be proud to support a President—Harry S. Truman—who has labored and devoted the highest office in the land to restoring law and order in the world," Buchanan told supporters days before the election. Her opponent, Republican Clifford W. Flegal, the McKeesport city controller, attacked Truman and Secretary of State Dean G. Acheson for being soft on communism and for the unpopular Korean War. When Flegal challenged Buchanan to a debate, she retorted: "The oldest saw in politics is 'Let's debate.' This is no time for hot air. It's time for decision. If my opponent hasn't made up his mind at this late date, it's just too bad.

My mind is made up."[6] In the July 24, 1951, special election, Buchanan defeated Flegal with nearly 62 percent of the vote and was sworn into Congress by House Speaker Sam Rayburn of Texas a week later, on August 1.[7] Following the 1950 Census, Pennsylvania lost three congressional seats. In the redrawn district, which encompassed heavily unionized sections of Pittsburgh, her native McKeesport, and other steel-making communities, Buchanan proved an even more powerful incumbent. In 1952 and 1954, she defeated GOP opponents by 2–1 margins.[8]

In the House, Vera Buchanan served on three committees: Banking and Currency, Merchant Marine and Fisheries, and Public Works. In early 1952, she resigned her Merchant Marine and Fisheries post to concentrate on her remaining assignments.[9] As had her husband, Congresswoman Buchanan employed her daughter, Jane, to serve as her secretary.

A solid supporter of most Truman administration policies, Buchanan became a critic of the Dwight Eisenhower administration's efforts to roll back domestic welfare programs. Vera Buchanan, like her husband, took a special interest in housing legislation. In 1954, she criticized Eisenhower's plan to halve the number of annual public housing projects over a four-year period. Noting that federal housing in McKeesport and Pittsburgh had been a success, she urged the Republican majority in the House to restore the figure to 75,000 per year, where it had been under President Truman. "An American family . . . should have a chance to live in decent housing," Buchanan said in a floor speech. "Housing is one of the most important factors in a child's environment. We have ample evidence that juvenile delinquency flourishes out of all proportion in slum areas, and out of juvenile delinquency grows vicious adult crime."[10] She attacked efforts to remove price controls on grocery commodities and rental units, noting that the "cost of living is nearing an all-time high, but the legislation to deal with the problem is nearing an all-time low."[11] For these and other of her legislative forays, Buchanan earned a reputation as a trusted ally among her district's union members and other laborers. Buchanan also pushed for the study of the flood problems plaguing her district, insisting on federal funding for the Turtle Creek Valley Flood Control Project, after a series of floods devastated local housing and industry.[12]

Congresswoman Buchanan demonstrated an independence from parochial interests. She supported the development of the St. Lawrence Seaway Project, and her appointment to the Public Works Committee in 1952 led to open speculation that the long-stalled piece of legislation would begin moving through the House.[13] Initially, opinion in her district had been against its development, but it became more evenly split after the discovery of the large Labrador iron ore deposits in Canada (iron was a critical raw material for steel production). Buchanan's reasoning was simple and extended beyond the narrow focus of her district. She argued that since the seaway would be built either jointly with Canada or without any U.S. involvement, that it was in the "national self-interest and the self-interest of every industry and business in the United States [to] require that our Government have a full, equal voice in the construction and operation of so important a waterway—a full and equal voice on every aspect of the operation."[14] The House eventually approved U.S. participation in the St. Lawrence project in 1956.

When President Eisenhower took office in 1953, Buchanan raised concerns about the bellicose rhetoric of his new Secretary of State, John Foster Dulles. Dulles was then developing his concept of "massive retaliation," which threatened Soviet leaders in the Kremlin with instant nuclear annihilation for any military provocations—whether conventional or nuclear—at any point around the globe.[15] While suspicious of Moscow's designs, Buchanan nevertheless expressed concern that Washington officials were relying too much on the threat of nuclear deterrence. "But are we doing enough, trying hard enough to restore sanity and peace—real peace—to the world?" she said in a floor speech. "Have we tried every possible avenue of approach? Have we left anything undone which could possibly—even as a long chance—mean enduring peace and the end of the constant danger of atomic incineration of mankind?"[16]

In June of 1955, during her third term in Congress, Buchanan became ill. A condition initially diagnosed as bronchial pneumonia turned out to be terminal late-stage cancer. Despite the diagnosis, Buchanan tried to carry on her congressional work from her hospital bed—first at the Bethesda Naval Hospital and, later, for the final three months of her life, in a hospital in McKeesport. During her final days, House Speaker John McCormack of Massachusetts visited Buchanan. When he rose to leave, Buchanan said, "Good-bye, my friend." The Speaker replied, "I won't say 'good-bye,' just 'so long.' I'll see you up in the Gallery."[17] Buchanan passed away on November 26, 1955, becoming the first woman Member to die in office. "I learned to know Vera Buchanan as I had known Frank Buchanan, loyal, hard-working, intelligent, and considerate," eulogized Representative Abraham Multer of New York. "I can think of no greater tribute . . . they had a keen sense of devotion to the services of the people of this country—not only their district but of the country."[18]

FOR FURTHER READING

Biographical Directory of the United States Congress, "Vera Daerr Buchanan," http://bioguide.congress.gov

NOTES

1   "Vera Buchanan, Lawmaker, Dies, 27 November 1955, *New York Times*: 88.

2   "Frank Buchanan," 30 April 1951, *Washington Post*: 10.

3   "Mrs. Buchanan Dead; In Congress 4 Years," 27 November 1955, *Washington Post*: A16.

4   Hope Chamberlin, *A Minority of Members: Women in the U.S. Congress* (New York: Praeger): 228.

5   Chamberlin, *A Minority of Members*: 227.

6   "Grandmother Runs for Seat in Congress," 22 July 1951, *New York Times*: 45.

7   *Congressional Record*, House, 82nd Cong., 1st sess. (26 July 1951): 8986.

8   "Election Statistics, 1920 to Present," http://clerk.house.gov/members/electionInfo/elections.html.

9   *Congressional Record*, House, 82nd Cong., 2nd sess. (29 January 1952): 593.

10 *Congressional Record*, House, 83rd Cong., 2nd sess. (30 March 1954): 4111–4112; see also, *Congressional Record*, House, 83rd Cong., 2nd sess. (20 July 1954): 11106–11107.

11 *Congressional Record*, House, 82nd Cong., 2nd sess. (28 June 1952): 8536–8537.

12 *Congressional Record*, House, 84th Cong., 1st sess. (15 June 1955): 8336–8337; *Memorial Services for Vera Daerr Buchanan*, 84th Cong., 2nd sess. (Washington, D.C.: Government Printing Office, 1956): 33.

13 "Chances for St. Lawrence Seaway Brighten as Friend of Project Joins House Committee," 31 January 1952, *New York Times*: 19.

14 *Congressional Record*, House, 83rd Cong., 2nd sess. (6 May 1954): 6160.

15 *Congress and the Nation, 1945–1964*, Vol. 1-A, (Washington, D.C.: Congressional Quarterly Press, 1965): 108; for more on "massive retaliation," see John Lewis Gaddis, *Strategies of Containment* (New York: Oxford University Press, 1982).

16 *Congressional Record*, House, 83rd Cong., 1st sess. (3 August 1953): A5324–A5325.

17 Chamberlin, *A Minority of Members*: 228; McCormack's account of this episode is similar, although he provides no direct quotations; see *Memorial Services for Vera Daerr Buchanan*: 21–24.

18 *Memorial Services Vera Daerr Buchanan*: 19.

Gracie Bowers Pfost
1906–1965

UNITED STATES REPRESENTATIVE ★ DEMOCRAT FROM IDAHO
1953–1963

A five-term Representative from Idaho, Gracie Pfost was a consistent critic of private gain at the expense of the public interest. The press dubbed Congresswoman Pfost "Hell's Belle" for her unremitting crusade to develop the proposed Hells Canyon High Dam and hydroelectric facility as a federally managed program. The massive project, which would have been situated along the Snake River in her northern Idaho district, took advantage of one of the longest gorges in the country. "It is a natural dam site," Pfost declared. "All we need is to plug up that river with some concrete."[1]

Gracie Bowers was born in an Ozark Mountain log cabin on March 12, 1906, in Harrison, Arkansas, daughter of William L. Bowers and Lily E. Wood Bowers. Her family, which included four siblings, moved to Idaho in 1911. She quit high school at age 16 and took a job as a milk analyst for the Carnation Milk Company in Nampa, Idaho. A year later, in 1923, Gracie Bowers married John W. "Jack" Pfost (pronounced "post"), her supervisor and a master mechanic who was twice her age.[2] During their long marriage, Jack Pfost remained an enduring source of support for his wife's political career which, she admitted, was "more or less a joint venture with him."[3] The couple had no children. In 1929, Gracie Pfost graduated from the Link's Business School in Boise, Idaho. During this time, she became involved in politics on the local level, working as a temporary replacement for the Canyon County clerk, auditor, and recorder. She ended up working full-time in this position for a decade after her predecessor resigned.[4] In 1941, after losing her first bid by 1,500 votes, Pfost was elected treasurer of Canyon County, a post she held for another decade. She also served as a delegate to five consecutive Democratic National Conventions, beginning in

1944. Throughout the late 1940s and into the 1950s, she and her husband owned and operated a real estate business.

In 1950, Gracie Pfost won the Democratic nomination in the race for the open congressional seat which represented all of northern Idaho, including the panhandle area up to the Canadian border. She lost the election by 783 votes to GOP contender John T. Wood, a 72-year-old doctor and World War I veteran. In 1952, at the urging of her husband, Pfost again challenged Wood.[5] She entered the Democratic primary and easily trumped three male challengers. With enthusiasm, Pfost ran an exhaustive general election campaign. There were no television stations on which to advertise, so she and her husband canvassed the 400-mile long district in their Pontiac car, logging more than 20,000 miles.[6] Pfost received a boost from Eleanor Roosevelt, who used her syndicated column to attack Wood's record in Congress, particularly his efforts to derail the United Nations. Her slogan contained a pun on her name: "Tie Your Vote to a Solid Post—Gracie Pfost for Congress."[7] In a state that went for Dwight Eisenhower on a 2–1 basis (her district favored Eisenhower by 25,000 votes), she narrowly edged out Wood by 591 votes of about 109,000 cast.[8]

When she was seated in the House in January 1953 as Idaho's first woman in Congress, Pfost earned assignments on the Public Works, the Post Office and Civil Service, and the Interior and Insular Affairs committees. Jack Pfost worked as an unpaid assistant in his wife's office and was her constant companion. Her assignment on Interior and Insular Affairs was a plum for a junior Member from the West because of the vast tracts of public land which fell under the panel's jurisdiction. From 1955 to 1961, Gracie Pfost chaired the Interior and Insular

Affairs Subcommittee on Public Lands, which had oversight of more than 450 million acres of federally managed land.[9] She first attracted national attention as a member of the Select Committee to Investigate Tax-Exempt Foundations, which probed the finances of such philanthropic organizations as the Ford Foundation and the Fund for the Republic, to determine if grants were distributed for "un-American" activities. On May 24, 1954, Pfost and Wayne Hays of Ohio walked out of the hearings and accused the committee of permitting unreliable testimony against foundation employees and failing to require witnesses to submit prepared statements or digests of testimony prior to their appearances. As a result of their withdrawal, the committee voted in July to end its hearings. Pfost dissented from the final committee report, which concluded that several foundations had unwittingly subsidized subversive ventures.

Pfost was an adept and calculating campaigner. During the 1954 campaign, she attended a county fair and challenged GOP opponent, Erwin H. Schwiebert, to a log-rolling contest. "If a man dumps me, he's no gentleman," she observed. "If I dump him, I'm a superwoman."[10] She fell off the log first but won the election by about 9,000 votes. She fastidiously cultivated her constituent base, sending personal congratulatory notes to each high school graduate in her district and a card and childcare book to new parents.[11] From 1954 through the next three elections, she won by pluralities of 55 percent or more and ran ahead of the Democratic presidential ticket in 1956 and 1960. In 1956, she beat Louise Shattuck, a staffer for a former GOP Idaho governor, by 10 percentage points. In 1958, Pfost won a personal-best 65 percent of the vote. After 1952, she was not challenged in the Democratic primaries until 1960 and, then, won handily.[12]

A dam became the defining point of Pfost's political work. It was during the 1952 campaign that she had earned the nickname, "Hell's Belle," because of her stalwart support for the construction of a publicly funded and operated dam at Hells Canyon. As part of the Snake River project on the Idaho–Oregon border, the proposed dam would provide hydroelectric power and irrigation for a

large section of the Northwest. Advocating publicly funded construction, she fought stubbornly against private power interests and their political allies, whom she branded "the gimmie-and-get boys in the private electric utilities."[13]

Throughout the 1950s, the subject of Snake River development was a divisive issue in the politics of the Northwest. Characteristic of a national debate during the decade, grounded in the legitimacy of federally operated programs such as the Tennessee Valley Authority, advocates of regional development through low-cost public power squared off against those backing private utilities.[14] In April 1953, Pfost introduced the first of several bills that proposed construction of a massive, multi-purpose dam across the Snake River at Hells Canyon to provide cheap electricity and construction jobs to spur Idaho's flagging economy. Regional power companies objected, lobbying instead for the development of a series of three smaller dams. "There can be no argument that the high dam at Hells Canyon will give the people the most for the least expenditure on their part," Pfost told colleagues in a floor speech.[15] Later, the Congresswoman claimed that she was the target of a smear campaign by private utilities companies in her own state—as she dubbed it, the effort to "Get Gracie Pfost." "I don't intend to be bluffed, bullied or frightened by the private monopolies," she declared.[16]

But the Congresswoman could only bitterly protest in August 1955 when the Federal Power Commission granted the Idaho Power Company a license to construct the three-dam proposal. Pfost charged that the Dwight D. Eisenhower administration was dominated by the big business interests which scuttled federal oversight. When President Eisenhower sought U.S. funding to construct the High Aswan Dam in Egypt, she protested that Hells Canyon should come first. "I think it is time for the administration to stop double-talking and get the high Hells Canyon Dam under construction," she said.[17] Pfost and her supporters suffered a final defeat in July 1957 when a majority of the Interior and Insular Affairs Committee, all the Republicans and two swing Democrats— with firm backing from President Eisenhower—voted to discard her dam construction bill. Pfost claimed that the rejection of federal funding was "strangling the lifeblood of the Pacific Northwest."[18]

Hells Canyon did not completely eclipse other legislative interests for Pfost. She also had a critical hand in making sure that the legislation approving Alaskan statehood in 1958 passed the House.[19] Pfost was an outspoken advocate of a 10 percent pay hike for postal employees.[20] In 1956, she supported a school construction bill to provide for new schools to meet the millions of "Baby Boom" grade-schoolers who were just then entering the educational system.[21] That same year she pushed for passage of a farm bill to help relieve a sagging agricultural commodities market.[22] In 1962, Congress passed a bill that Pfost authored to construct the $3.5 million Mann Creek irrigation project in Idaho.[23] Pfost also supported the Equal Rights Amendment.[24]

With Jack Pfost's sudden death in 1961, Gracie Pfost lost not only her husband, but her closest political confidant. In 1962, when Idaho Senator Henry C. Dworshak died, Pfost chose to leave her safe House seat to run as the Democratic candidate in the fall election to fill the remainder of Dworshak's unexpired term. Pfost ran against former Governor Len B. Jordan, a Boise rancher who had been appointed three months earlier by Idaho's GOP governor to an interim position in the Senate. Pfost lost narrowly by only 4,881 votes (51 to 49 percent), failing to carry her home county of Canyon. After her political defeat, she was appointed Special Assistant for Elderly Housing at the Federal Housing Administration (FHA). Gracie Pfost, suffering for several years from Hodgkin's disease, served at the FHA until she died at age 59 on August 11, 1965, at Johns Hopkins Hospital in Baltimore, Maryland.

FOR FURTHER READING

Biographical Directory of the United States Congress, "Gracie Bowers Pfost," http://bioguide.congress.gov

MANUSCRIPT COLLECTIONS

Idaho State Historical Society (Boise, ID). *Papers:* 1940–1962, 4.5 cubic feet. Correspondence, clipping files, campaign material, and miscellaneous papers relating to the political career of Gracie Bowers Pfost, including her campaigns for re-election as Canyon County (Idaho) treasurer (1940–1950), her service as U.S. Representative from Idaho (1952–1958); and her campaign for a U.S. Senate seat, 1962. A finding aid is available in the repository.

University of Idaho Library (Moscow, ID), Special Collections. *Papers:* 1950–1962, 61 cubic feet. Administrative records including interoffice memoranda and procedure statements, constituent correspondence, personal correspondence, records of committees, bills sponsored, speeches, news releases, and audiotapes of radio talks. Finding aid in repository.

A DAM BECAME THE DEFINING
POINT OF PFOST'S POLITICAL
WORK. IT WAS DURING THE 1952
CAMPAIGN THAT SHE HAD EARNED
THE NICKNAME, "HELL'S BELLE,"
BECAUSE OF HER STALWART
SUPPORT FOR THE CONSTRUCTION
OF A PUBLICLY FUNDED AND
OPERATED DAM AT HELLS CANYON.
AS PART OF THE SNAKE RIVER
PROJECT ON THE IDAHO–OREGON
BORDER, THE PROPOSED DAM
WOULD PROVIDE HYDROELECTRIC
POWER AND IRRIGATION
FOR A LARGE SECTION
OF THE NORTHWEST.

NOTES

1 "Rep. Pfost Speaks: 'Hell's Belle' Gives the GOP Likewise," 19 May 1953, *Washington Post*: 23.

2 Karen Bossick, "Idaho's First Woman in Congress; Gracie Pfost Took Humanitarian Attitude from Nampa to D.C.," 25 July 1999, *Idaho Statesman*: 1 E.

3 Hope Chamberlin, *A Minority of Members: Women in the U.S. Congress* (New York: Praeger, 1976): 230.

4 Bossick, "Idaho's First Woman in Congress."

5 Ibid.

6 Mary Van Rensselaer Thayer, "Gracie and Louise Will Battle to Finish in Hills of Idaho," 1 July 1956, *Washington Post*: F 11; Georgette Ross Howard, "Gracie Pfost Never Forgets Idaho," 17 September 1954, *Christian Science Monitor*: 8; *Congressional Record*, House, 84th Cong., 1st sess. (11 May 1955): 6182–6183, reprint of article by Anne Cottrell Free, "Petticoats in Our Government—Representative Gracie Pfost Tagged 'Hell's Belle' as She Fights for Dam at Hells Canyon," publication and date are unidentified.

7 "Gracie Pfost Dies; Idaho Democrat," 12 August 1965, *New York Times*: 27.

8 "Election Statistics, 1920 to Present" http://clerk.house.gov/members/electionInfo/elections.html.

9 Despite a high level of satisfaction among Members serving on the Interior and Insular Affairs Committee (due in great part to a good record of securing legislation originating in the committee), turnover was not uncommon. Some Members, most especially those not from the West, viewed it as a short-term committee assignment, which could explain why Pfost was able to rise through the ranks to chair a subcommittee so quickly. Richard F. Fenno, Jr., *Congressmen in Committees* (Boston: Little, Brown, and Company, 1973): 274–275.

10 Bossick, "Idaho's First Woman in Congress."

11 Ibid.

12 "Rep. Gracie Pfost Wins Easily in Idaho," 8 June 1960, *Washington Post*: A2; "Election Statistics, 1920 to Present" http://clerk.house.gov/members/electionInfo/elections.html.

13 Susan Tolchin, *Women In Congress* (Washington, D.C.: Government Printing Office, 1976): 63.

14 William H. Chafe, *The Unfinished Journey: America Since World War II* (New York: Oxford, 2003): 139.

15 *Congressional Record*, House, 83rd Cong., 1st sess. (3 August 1953): A5233–5235; *Congressional Record*, House, 83rd Cong., 1st sess. (16 April 1953): 3232–3235; *Congressional Record*, House, 84th Cong., 1st sess. (8 March 1955): 2530–2537.

16 *Congressional Record*, House, 83rd Cong., 2nd sess. (14 April 1954): 5181–5184.

17 *Congressional Record*, House, 84th Cong., 2nd sess. (6 June 1956): 9709.

18 "House Unit Kills Hells Canyon Bid: Blocks Pfost Bill for Federal Dam," 25 July 1957, *New York Times*: 1, 10; see also, *Congressional Record*, House, 85th Cong., 1st sess. (29 April 1957): 6130–6133.

19 Bossick, "Idaho's First Woman in Congress"; *Congressional Record*, House, 85th Cong., 2nd sess. (26 May 1958): 9510–9511.

20 *Congressional Record*, House, 85th Cong., 1st sess. (22 July 1957): 12348; *Congressional Record*, House, 84th Cong., 1st sess. (31 March 1955): 4155.

21 *Congressional Record*, House, 84th Cong., 2nd sess. (29 June 1956): 11465.

22 *Congressional Record*, House, 84th Cong., 2nd sess. (11 April 1956): 6154–6156; *Congressional Record*, House, 84th Cong., 2nd sess. (9 April 1956): 5955.

23 Marie Smith, "Gracie Pfost Sets Bonnet for Seat in the Senate," 3 August 1962, *Washington Post*: C5.

24 *Congressional Record*, House, 87th Cong., 1st sess. (20 July 1961): 13122; *Congressional Record*, House, 84th Cong., 2nd sess. (20 February 1956): 2922–2923.

Leonor K. Sullivan
1902–1988

UNITED STATES REPRESENTATIVE ★ DEMOCRAT FROM MISSOURI
1953–1977

A s one of America's early consumer advocates, Leonor K. Sullivan authored many of the protective laws that Americans have come to take for granted. Initially, it was a lonely undertaking. As Representative Sullivan recalled of her early years in Congress, "Those of us interested in consumer legislation could have caucused in an elevator."[1] During her 12 terms in Congress, Sullivan left her mark on a variety of issues, becoming one of the more influential Congresswomen to serve in the U.S. House of Representatives.

Leonor Alice Kretzer was born on August 21, 1902, in St. Louis, Missouri, one of nine children of Frederick William Kretzer and Nora (Jostrand) Kretzer. Her father was a second-generation German tailor. Since her parents did not have the resources to send her to college, Kretzer worked at a local telephone company and took night classes at Washington University in St. Louis, focusing on vocational psychology. During the 1930s, she worked as an instructor in business and accounting at the St. Louis Comptometer School; she later became placement director there before becoming director of the St. Louis Business School.[2] On December 27, 1941, she married John Berchmans Sullivan, a freshman Congressman from St. Louis. Leonor Sullivan worked as her husband's administrative assistant and campaign manager in five primary and election campaigns; during that stretch of time, her husband was defeated twice, only to be returned to office in the subsequent election.[3]

When John Sullivan died on January 29, 1951, Missouri Democratic leaders refused to nominate Leonor Sullivan to run in the special election to fill the vacancy. "We don't have anything against you," they told Sullivan, "we just want to win."[4] Their chosen candidate, Harry Schendel, lost to

Republican Claude I. Bakewell. Leonor Sullivan, meanwhile, took a year-long position as an administrative aide to Missouri Representative Theodore Irving because she lacked the funds to amass her own congressional campaign without the backing of the Democratic Party. In 1952, Sullivan announced her candidacy for her husband's reapportioned district. She defeated seven contenders in the Democratic primary, including the party-endorsed candidate, who made a campaign promise that if elected, he would give Sullivan a job on his staff. Running in the general election as "Mrs. John B. Sullivan," she defeated her Republican opponent, Bakewell, by a 2–1 margin, to earn a seat in the 83rd Congress (1953–1955). During the campaign, Sullivan claimed greater experience and qualification than the incumbent because of her years in Washington working for her husband's office, a message that resonated with many of the late Congressman's former supporters. After that campaign, Sullivan, the first woman elected to Congress from her state (and the only one until the 1990s), was never seriously challenged; she captured her next 11 elections with between 65 and 79 percent of the vote.[5]

Congresswoman Sullivan quickly established herself as a protector of working Americans and consumers. In 1953, she urged her colleagues to amend the income tax law to allow widows and working mothers to make deductions for childcare. Sullivan also delivered a speech on the House Floor against proposed cuts to the Women's Bureau of the Department of Labor. In 1957 she wrote and successfully guided into law the first Federal Poultry Products Inspection Act. She also sponsored legislation to protect consumers from hazardous substances, harmful food color additives, and cosmetics. A committed consumer advocate, in 1962 Sullivan urged her House colleagues to pass stricter consumer protection legislation. "You are faced with an arena of supreme importance to the lives and health and safety and well being of the American people—all of the foods we eat, all of the drugs and devices we use for health purposes, all of the cosmetics used not only by women but in increasing numbers by men, as well."[6]

In 1959, working with Senator Hubert Humphrey, Sullivan authored the Food Stamp Act. Under the new legislation, low-income Americans would no longer have to rely upon disbursements of surplus food, but instead would be able to use coupons to buy food at grocery stores. During the second Dwight D. Eisenhower administration, however, the Agriculture Department refused to allocate funds for the program, which the conservative Secretary of Agriculture, Ezra Taft Benson, considered improper. Upon the urging of Sullivan, the John F. Kennedy administration reinstated an experimental food stamp program in 1961. In 1964, Sullivan authored legislation to increase the scope of the Kennedy initiative, making food stamps available for poor Americans nationally. On the House Floor, she maintained, "The States and localities, which now bear a heavy financial burden under the direct distribution system, would save added millions under the food stamp plan. Who loses, then, under the plan? Hunger. Only hunger loses."[7] President Lyndon Johnson incorporated the legislation into his "War on Poverty" in 1964, but not before a sharp partisan battle within the Agricultural Committee and the President's decision to couple the food stamp measure with increased subsidies for wheat and cotton farmers.

One of Sullivan's great legislative triumphs came when she served as the House Floor manager for the 1968 Consumer Credit Protection Act. The bill established "truth in lending" provisions, requiring lenders to provide consumers with information about the cost of credit. "Now we come to the moment of truth in truth in lending," Sullivan declared to her colleagues during debate. "Will we give the consumer the whole truth in lending, or just part of the truth?"[8] When President Johnson signed the groundbreaking legislation, he praised "that able Congresswoman from Missouri," noting that Sullivan "fought for a strong effective bill when others would have settled for less."[9] Two

years later, Sullivan continued her efforts to protect American consumers when she authored the Fair Credit Reporting Act, a bill prohibiting credit companies from distributing false credit information.

By 1969, after 15-term veteran Representative Frances Bolton of Ohio had retired, Sullivan emerged as the doyenne of women in Congress. The first woman appointed to the House Democratic Steering Committee, which determines Democratic committee assignments, she also was elected secretary of the House Democratic Caucus, an organization to determine party strategy and consensus, for five terms. During her 24 years in the House, Sullivan served on the Banking and Currency Committee, the Committee on Merchant Marine and Fisheries, and the Joint Committee on Defense Production. During the 93rd and 94th Congresses (1973–1977), she chaired Merchant Marine and Fisheries, making her only the sixth woman in congressional history to chair a committee. As chairwoman, her accomplishments included passage of the 1976 Fishery and Conservation Management Act, an environmental bill which established a 200-mile fisheries conservation zone off the coasts of the United States.

Though she defended the rights of women consumers, Sullivan did not embrace the larger feminist agenda. She was the only woman Member to vote against the Equal Rights Amendment (ERA) in the 92nd Congress (1971–1973), because she thought it threatened home life and existing legislation which protected women in the workplace. "I believe that wholesome family life is the backbone of civilization," Sullivan said. Passage of the ERA would "accelerate the breakup of home life."[10] She also feared that the amendment would break down hundreds of protective labor, marital, and family statutes in the states. Finally, the ERA offended her sensibilities. The "ERA says you are my equal," she once observed, but "I think I'm a whole lot better."[11] Sullivan also opposed efforts by younger women Members to create a special caucus for women's issues, which came about only after her retirement.[12] Nevertheless, Sullivan supported the Equal Pay Act of 1963, a first step toward the equal pay for equal work doctrine. She also backed an amendment to the 1964

Civil Rights Act that stipulated an end to sexual discrimination in the workplace. In 1961, Sullivan and her fellow Congresswomen marched into Speaker Sam Rayburn's office to request the appointment of Representative Martha Griffiths of Michigan to the influential Joint Economic Committee.[13]

In 1976, at age 74, Sullivan declined to seek a 13th term and was succeeded by Richard A. Gephardt, who eventually became Democratic Leader in the House. Her age, but principally her disaffection with the institution of Congress, accounted for her decision to retire. She explained in a post-Watergate interview that despite contemporary attempts at congressional reform, she was "disturbed at what's happening to the whole government . . . the corruption that always goes on . . . the lack of morals . . . too many people thinking, 'So what?'"[14] She returned to St. Louis and moved into a home she had bought long before on the south side of the city, atop a bluff overlooking the Mississippi River. Passing riverboat captains often blew their ships' horns to salute Sullivan, who had been a benefactor of the barge industry during her time on the Merchant Marine and Fisheries Committee.[15] In 1980, she married retired millionaire businessman Russell L. Archibald. He died in March 1987. Sullivan died in St. Louis on September 1, 1988.

FOR FURTHER READING

Biographical Directory of the United States Congress, "Leonor Kretzer Sullivan," http://bioguide.congress.gov

MANUSCRIPT COLLECTIONS

Georgetown University Library (Washington, D.C.). *Papers*: 1943–1976, three feet. Concerns material on the Panama Canal. Includes photocopies of materials in the St. Louis University Library. A finding aid is available .

Radcliffe Institute for Advanced Study, Harvard University (Cambridge, MA), Schlesinger Library,

http://www.radcliffe.edu/schles. *Oral History:* 1974–1976, four folders. An interview of Leonor Sullivan by Katie Louchheim.

St. Louis University School of Law (St. Louis, MO). *Papers:* 1953–1976, 350 linear feet. Congressional papers and correspondence, including materials relating to her work on the Merchant Marine Committee, the Banking and Currency Committee, food and drug laws, and issues relating to St. Louis. The collection contains access restrictions. A finding aid is available in the repository.

NOTES

1 Hope Chamberlin, *A Minority of Members: Women in the U.S. Congress* (New York: Praeger, 1973): 238.

2 *Current Biography, 1954* (New York: H.W. Wilson and Company, 1954): 590.

3 "Election Statistics, 1920 to Present," http://clerk.house.gov/members/electionInfo/elections.html.

4 Susan Tolchin, *Women in Congress* (Washington, D.C.: Government Printing Office, 1976): 106.

5 "Election Statistics, 1920 to Present," http://clerk.house.gov/members/electionInfo/index.html.

6 Chamberlin, *A Minority of Members*: 236.

7 Marcy Kaptur, *Women of Congress: A Twentieth-Century Odyssey* (Washington, D.C.: Congressional Quarterly Press, 1996): 108.

8 Tolchin, *Women in Congress*: 234.

9 Chamberlin, *A Minority of Members*: 234.

10 Quoted in Chamberlin, *A Minority of Members*: 234.

11 Tolchin, *Women in Congress*: 107.

12 See Irwin N. Gertzog, *Congressional Women: Their Recruitment, Integration, and Behavior* (Westport, CT: Praeger, 1995): 166–167.

13 Leonor Sullivan's former administrative assistant claimed that she led the Congresswomen on a march to Speaker Rayburn's office to demand that he fulfill Griffiths's request for a Ways and Means position in 1962. However, Griffiths recalls her colleagues aiding her on capturing the Joint Economic position in 1961. See, Kaptur, *Women of Congress*: 110; Martha Griffiths, Oral History Interview, 29 October 1979, *U.S. Association of Former Members of Congress*, Manuscript Room, Library of Congress, Washington, D.C.: 51; 136.

14 "Leonor K. Sullivan," obituary, 2 September 1988, *Los Angeles Times*: 28.

15 "Leonor K. Sullivan," obituary, 2 September 1988, *Washington Post*: C4.

Eva Kelly Bowring
1892–1985

UNITED STATES SENATOR ★ REPUBLICAN FROM NEBRASKA
1954

In 1954, Eva Bowring arrived in the Senate with the vocabulary of a witty cattle wrangler and impressive credentials as a state political figure and prosperous businesswoman. Appointed to fill the vacancy resulting from the death of Senator Dwight Griswold of Nebraska, Bowring had become one of Nebraska's wealthiest women through her ranching enterprises and was a leading GOP figure in the state. Her transition from riding the range on her sprawling ranch to the U.S. Senate Chamber was abrupt and somewhat unexpected. "I'm going to have to ride the fence a while until I find where the gates are," Bowring told a reporter shortly after arriving at the Capitol.[1]

Eva Kelly was born on January 9, 1892, in Nevada, Missouri. She attended school in Kansas City, Missouri. In 1911, at age 19, she married Theodore Forester, a grain and feed salesman, and the Foresters settled in Kansas City. When Theodore Forester died in 1924, Eva was left to raise the couple's three young sons: Frank, Harold, and Donald.[2] To support her family, Eva moved to Lincoln, Nebraska, and took up Theodore's work selling livestock feed; she drove as many as 40,000 miles a year around rural Nebraska roads in an unreliable old car. Once, near Merriman, Nebraska, the car broke down. A homesteader named Art Bowring happened to be driving by and stopped to help. In 1928, Eva married Bowring, who had served as county commissioner and went on to win election as a representative and senator in the state legislature. The family settled on Art Bowring's ranch, the Barr-99, near Merriman in the Sand Hill Country of Cherry County. The couple expanded their land-holdings and eventually managed a prosperous 13,000-acre operation. After Arthur's death in 1944, Eva Bowring operated the Barr-99, becoming the first woman to chair the Nebraska

Stockgrowers Association Brand Committee. In her capacity as a rancher, Bowring became involved with Nebraska Republican politics, eventually serving as the state's first woman county GOP chair. From 1946 to 1954, Bowring served as vice chair of the Nebraska Republican Central Committee and as its director of women's activities.

Bowring's transition to public office was sudden. Governor Robert B. Crosby appointed Bowring on April 16, 1954, to fill the vacancy caused by the death of Senator Dwight Palmer Griswold. Bowring, who described herself as a "forward looking Republican," refused the offer initially. She was reluctant to leave her 1,200 head of cattle and the calving and branding work that she still enjoyed and actively participated in at age 62. "This is one cross I don't think I have to bear, Bob," Bowring told the governor. But Crosby was persuasive. After a private meeting with the governor, Bowring emerged from the office to tell reporters she accepted the appointment. She explained that after years of exhorting GOP women into politics, she could not now reverse course herself, noting that, "when a job is offered to you, take it. Men can refuse but women are increasingly important in political life."[3] Bowring was sworn in as the first Nebraska woman to serve in Congress on April 26, 1954, for the term that would end, according to state law, at the next general election. In November 1954 a candidate would be selected to finish out the final two months of Griswold's term, as well as a successor to the full six-year term starting in the 84th Congress (1955–1957). At the time of her appointment, Bowring joined the Senate's only other woman Member, Margaret Chase Smith of Maine. Smith wrote that Bowring's appointment "did the women of America as well as the women of Nebraska a great honor."[4] For her

part, Bowring expressed hope that her Senate colleagues would "remember I'm just a girl from cow country."[5] Her guiding philosophy was succinct: "I've not been one who thought the Lord should make life easy; I've just asked Him to make me strong."[6] According to custom, the state's senior Senator, Hugh Butler, accompanied her to the front of the chamber for the swearing in. Vice President Richard Nixon, presiding over the ceremony, relayed a message from Butler to viewers in the gallery: "The senior Senator from Nebraska has asked the chair to announce that no implication should be drawn from the fact that the senior Senator from Nebraska is a widower and the junior Senator from Nebraska is a widow."[7]

Bowring was appointed to three committees: Interstate and Foreign Commerce, Labor and Public Welfare, and Post Office and the Civil Service. The needs of Nebraska's agricultural constituents were familiar to Bowring and were the focus of her only two major floor speeches. Bowring declared her backing for a program of flexible agricultural price supports proposed by the Dwight D. Eisenhower administration to reduce production fluctuations that often resulted in surplus food staples. She argued that the measure would "cushion farmers against wide breaks in the market on basic commodities," economize land use, and produce a more stable market. "In the long run, rigid price supports take from the farmer more than he receives," Bowring concluded. "They encourage him to deplete his soil. They saddle the markets with surpluses which give him no opportunity to realize full parity. They destroy the normal relationship of feed and livestock prices. . . . They place the farmers in such a position

that they lose much of their freedom to make management decisions." A number of her colleagues who attended the speech, including Prescott Bush of Connecticut and Albert Gore, Sr., of Tennessee, praised her "incisiveness" and "intimate grasp" of the workings of the agriculture market.[8] In addition to the commodities pricing bill, Bowring and Senator Butler introduced a measure for the construction of the Red Willow Dam and Reservoir as part of the Missouri River Basin Project. Bowring also sponsored legislation providing for flood control works in the Gering Valley of Nebraska. On August 18, 1954, Bowring had the distinction of joining a select handful of women who presided over the Senate when she was named acting president *pro tempore* for the day's debates.[9]

In June 1954, Bowring announced that she would not seek election to the full six-year term or the short term to follow the November general election. After Hugh Butler's death on July 1, 1954, she became Nebraska's senior Senator. On November 8, she was succeeded by another woman, Republican Hazel Abel, whom she presented before the Senate. After leaving office, Bowring returned to her Barr-99 ranch and later served on the national advisory council of the National Institutes of Health from 1954 to 1958 and from 1960 to 1961. President Dwight Eisenhower also appointed Bowring to the Board of Parole at the Department of Justice, where she served from 1956 to 1964. Eva Bowring died on January 8, 1985, in Gordon, Nebraska.

FOR FURTHER READING

Biographical Directory of the United States Congress,
"Eva Kelly Bowring," http://bioguide.congress.gov

MANUSCRIPT COLLECTION

Nebraska State Historical Society (Lincoln, NE). *Papers:*
Scrapbook of clippings about her career in the Paul Riley
scrapbook collection and photographs.

NOTES

1   Evelyn Simpson, "Senator in a Hustle: She'll Probably Put Her Brand
    on Congress," 25 April 1954, *Washington Post*: S1; Josephine Ripley,
    "Senator's in New Saddle: Nebraskan Doubles Distaff Strength," 3
    May 1954, *Christian Science Monitor*: 12.
2   Boys identified in: Ripley, "Senator's in New Saddle: Nebraskan
    Doubles Distaff Strength."
3   "Nebraska Woman Named to Griswold Senate Seat," 17 April 1954,
    New York Times: 1; Simpson, "Senator in a Hustle: She'll Probably Put
    Her Brand on Congress."
4   Hope Chamberlin, *A Minority of Members: Women in the U.S. Congress*
    (New York: Praeger, 1973): 240.
5   "Woman Joins Senate Today," 26 April 1954, *New York Times*: 27;
    "Nebraska's Senator Is Sworn In," 27 April 1954, *New York Times*: 27.
6   "Nebraska Woman Named to Griswold Senate Seat."
7   "Random Notes from Washington," 2 May 1954, *New York Times*: 16.
8   *Congressional Record*, Senate, 83rd Cong., 2nd sess. (24 June 1954):
    8836–8838; Aubrey Graves, "Ike to Press Farm Fight on Floors of
    Congress," 25 June 1954, *Washington Post*: 1; see also, *Congressional
    Record*, Senate, 83rd Cong., 2nd sess. (6 August 1954): 13554–13555.
9   *Congressional Record*, Senate, 83rd Cong., 2nd sess. (18 August 1954):
    14921.

Mary E. "Betty" Farrington
1898–1984

DELEGATE ★ REPUBLICAN FROM HAWAII
1954–1957

Mary Elizabeth "Betty" Farrington emerged in the mid-1950s as the leading advocate for Hawaiian statehood, serving three years in the House as a territorial delegate. Her political partnership with her husband, Joe Farrington, another champion of statehood, spanned decades and prepared her to succeed him in Congress after his death in 1954. Years before she was elected to Congress, *McCall's* magazine chose Farrington, publisher of the *Honolulu Star-Bulletin* and director of the National Federation of Republican Women's Clubs, as one of "Washington's 10 Most Powerful Women," a list that included Eleanor Roosevelt, Margaret Chase Smith, and Bess Truman.[1]

Mary Elizabeth Pruett was born to American missionaries Robert Lee and Josie Baugh Pruett, native Tennesseans—on May 30, 1898, in the Tsukiji (foreign resident) section of Tokyo, Japan. She attended the Tokyo Foreign School before the family resettled in 1906 in Hollywood, California. After Mary Pruett graduated from Hollywood High School, she enrolled at the exclusive Ward-Belmont Women's Junior College in Nashville, Tennessee. Two years later, she transferred to the University of Wisconsin at Madison and earned a journalism B.A. in 1918. During her studies, she met Joseph Farrington, son of Wallace R. Farrington, publisher of the *Honolulu Star Bulletin*, and an early advocate of Hawaiian annexation and statehood.[2] They married in May 1920 and, three years later, when President Warren G. Harding appointed Wallace Farrington territorial governor of Hawaii, Joe and Mary returned to the islands to manage the *Star Bulletin*. The couple raised two adopted children, John and Beverly.[3] In the early 1930s, Joe Farrington was elected to the Hawaii territorial senate and began a long political career in which

he relied heavily on his wife for advice. "He didn't make a move without talking to me," Mary Farrington recalled.[4] Joe Farrington soon succeeded his father as the newspaper's general manager. By the mid-1940s, Betty Farrington assumed her husband's duties as publisher and president of the *Honolulu Star-Bulletin*, a position she held until the 1960s.

In 1942, Joe Farrington, was elected to the first of six consecutive terms in the U.S. House as a Republican territorial delegate from Hawaii, propelling Betty Farrington into national politics, too. Throughout Joe Farrington's dozen years in Washington, the Farringtons were frequent entertainers and popular on the capital's society circuit.[5] Betty Farrington immersed herself in party politics, serving as president of the District League of Republican Women from 1946 to 1948. On January 1, 1949, she became president of the National Federation of Women's Republican Clubs (later named the National Federation of Republican Women), which included more than 500,000 members.[6] Farrington energized the group by creating a school of politics in 1950 at which precinct workers received briefings on party history, current initiatives, and political techniques.[7]

Joe Farrington suffered from a heart ailment throughout his congressional service but remained dedicated to bringing Hawaii into the Union. In June 1954, while intensively lobbying colleagues to support a statehood bill, he collapsed and died in his office. Shortly afterward, the *Washington Post* predicted that Hawaiian statehood "will be Mr. Farrington's monument."[8] Betty Farrington had just returned to Honolulu to orchestrate the funeral services when Governor Sam King, Joe Farrington's friend and political ally, began pressing her to succeed her husband. She replied, "For heaven's sake, no!" King relented but came back a week later, asking her to run "for Joe" and the cause of statehood. Betty Farrington agreed.

Being on the campaign trail was restorative for the widow Farrington. "I was just kind of numb, you know. I think it saved my life," she recalled. "I was doing something for him; carrying on for him, you know."9 Farrington won the GOP nomination to succeed her husband, and in the July 31 special election she defeated Democrat Delbert Metzger and independent Helene Hale by garnering 66 percent of the vote in a light turnout. She topped Metzger, her nearest competitor, by more than 20,000 votes.10

Farrington took the oath of office and joined the 83rd Congress (1953–1955) on August 4, 1954, to a standing ovation. She immediately moved to the well and addressed the 200 Members in attendance. "Someday, somehow, I hope that by action and deed I can prove to you how deeply I have appreciated the many expressions of sympathy during the past few weeks," Farrington said. "It has given me the courage and the strength to carry on in the manner that I know Joe would have me do, in the manner that I know the people of Hawaii would have me do."11 Parliamentarians could not remember a newly sworn-in Member ever having given such an address.12 Farrington got an immediate boost when she inherited her husband's top-tier committee assignments on the Armed Services, the Agriculture, and the Interior and Insular Affairs committees. She retained these posts for the duration of her House tenure. Farrington's service on the Agriculture Committee marked the first by a woman.

Delegate Farrington immediately got to work on the issue of statehood, which was the central and defining facet of her House career. The day after her swearing-in, longtime friend John Saylor, a Pennsylvania Representative and key member of the Interior and Insular Affairs Committee, arranged a meeting with President Dwight Eisenhower to discuss statehood. During her Oval Office visit, Farrington pushed a plan for dual admittance: Hawaii and Alaska. In fact, she recalled that she spent more time pitching the concept of Alaskan statehood to President Eisenhower than that of Hawaii.13

Days after meeting with the President, Farrington took to the House Floor to push for debate for Hawaiian statehood. Critics objected that Hawaii was vulnerable to communist infiltration from Asian "subversives" and labor agitators in California. With World War II still a potent memory, opponents also doubted the loyalty of the large Japanese population living on the island. Farrington countered that a vote for statehood "would be an act of vision because, even at this late hour, it would tell the freedom-loving peoples of Asia, who are engaged in a great struggle against communism, that we Americans do practice what we preach."14 The bill for Hawaiian statehood alone had passed the House in the 80th (1947–1949), 81st (1949–1951), and 83rd Congresses but had never been reconciled with the Senate version. In the 83rd Congress, the Senate added on an amendment that also sought statehood for Alaska. It was that version of the bill that the House Rules Committee refused to allow out onto the floor for debate. It lapsed at the end of the Congress.

Simultaneous with that development, Farrington contended with another electoral campaign. In the 1954 general election, she faced Democrat John A. "Jack" Burns, chairman of the Honolulu traffic safety commission, whom her husband had resoundingly defeated in 1948.15 Democrats in territorial and local offices, however, surged to power in the 1954 midterm elections, campaigning on a platform of better employment, higher taxes for social services, and better schools. For the first time in Hawaii's 54 years as a territory, Democrats seized control of the legislature.16 Farrington, who had won by a 2–1 margin in the special election just three months earlier, barely defeated Burns, with a margin of 890 votes out of more than 138,000 cast.17

After returning to Washington, Farrington renewed her call for joint Hawaiian–Alaskan statehood. Still, powerful House leaders and the Rules Committee, despite the change in party control in the 84th Congress (1955–1957), opposed the proposal.18 Appearing before the Rules Committee, Farrington blasted redbaiting tactics as "extravagant, undocumented and unsupported" and as "an insult to the majority of Hawaii's traditionally loyal population."[19] Eventually, after extensive hearings before the Rules Committee in which numerous allegations were made about communist influences in Hawaii, the bill came to the House Floor for sharply curtailed debate. The measure went down to defeat by a vote of 218 to 170 on May 10, 1955.

As a Delegate, Farrington could not vote on the House Floor, but she could participate in virtually every other capacity. Alliance building became critical to her success.[20] She enjoyed a number of minor legislative victories for her district, including the creation of the Geophysics Institute at the University of Hawaii, the creation of the "City of Refuge" on the Island of Hawaii as a national historic park, the repeal of an expensive travel tax from the mainland to Hawaii that opponents believed hurt tourism, and the return of Fort Armstrong to the Territory of Hawaii. Farrington also managed to secure the reapportionment of the Territorial Legislature, allowing more equitable representation for the higher population areas.

Farrington ran for re-election in 1956, again facing Jack Burns and a groundswell of support for Democratic candidates. Voter discontent, spurred by the partisan actions of Governor King, who repeatedly used his veto to block Democratic legislative programs, helped bring about an abrupt end to Farrington's congressional career. Burns campaigned on a simple platform—aimed as much at King as at Farrington. He called for the right of Hawaiians to elect their own governor if Congress again refused to grant statehood. He also suggested a congressional investigation of King's practices was in order.[21] Farrington garnered only 45 percent of the vote in an election which polled the largest turnout ever cast for a Hawaii Delegate. Her defeat sent a Democrat to the House for the first time since Hawaii was awarded a Delegate's seat in 1932.

After leaving Congress, Farrington resumed her newspaper work, serving as president of the *Star Bulletin* until 1961. Farrington lived to see her husband's dream of statehood for Hawaii realized in 1959. She was invited to the ceremony at which President Eisenhower signed the legis-

lation that made Hawaii the 50th state to enter the Union.[22] She also directed and chaired the Honolulu Lithograph Company, Ltd., from 1957 to 1961 and was president of the Hawaiian Broadcasting System, Ltd., from 1960 to 1963. In 1969, President Richard Nixon appointed Farrington Director of the Office of the Territories in the Department of the Interior. When the Department of the Interior abolished the post in 1971, she worked in the congressional liaison office until 1973. After retirement, Betty Farrington returned to Honolulu, where she lived until her death on July 21, 1984.

FOR FURTHER READING

Biographical Directory of the United States Congress, "Mary Elizabeth Pruett Farrington," http://bioguide. congress.gov

Whitehead, John S. *Completing the Union: Alaska, Hawaii, and the Battle for Statehood* (Albuquerque, NM: University of New Mexico Press, 2004).

MANUSCRIPT COLLECTIONS

Hawaii Public Archives (Honolulu, HI). *Papers:* 1942–1956, 80 feet. Includes files with Mary Elizabeth Pruett Farrington and Joseph Farrington as Territorial Delegates to the U.S. Congress.

Library of Congress (Washington, D.C.), Manuscript Division. *Oral History:* Transcript in the Oral History Collection of the U.S. Association of Former Members of Congress. Sound recording in the Library's Motion Picture, Broadcasting and Recorded Sound Division.

DELEGATE FARRINGTON ARGUED
THAT A VOTE FOR HAWAIIAN
STATEHOOD, "WOULD BE AN ACT OF
VISION BECAUSE, EVEN AT THIS
LATE HOUR, IT WOULD TELL THE
FREEDOM-LOVING PEOPLES OF
ASIA, WHO ARE ENGAGED IN A
GREAT STRUGGLE AGAINST
COMMUNISM, THAT WE AMERICANS
DO PRACTICE WHAT WE PREACH."

NOTES

1   Susan Tolchin, *Women In Congress* (Washington, D.C.: Government Printing Office, 1976): 24.

2   Mary Elizabeth Pruett Farrington, Oral History Interview, U.S. Association of Former Members of Congress (hereinafter USAF-MOC), Manuscript Room, Library of Congress, Washington, D.C.: 9.

3   *Current Biography, 1955* (New York: H.W. Wilson and Company, 1955): 197.

4   Farrington, Oral History Interview, USAFMOC: 14.

5   Ibid., 19.

6   Sonia Stein, "GOP to School Women in Political Tactics," 9 April 1950, *Washington Post*: S3.

7   Nicha Searle, "'Mrs. Republican': Mrs. Farrington Heads 500,000 Women," 11 February 1951, *Washington Post*: S5; "GOP School Trains Workers for Door-to-Door Vote Drives," 2 May 1950, *Christian Science Monitor*: 12.

8   "Deaths in Congress," 21 June 1954, *Washington Post*: 6; see also, "J.R. Farrington of Hawaii Is Dead," 20 June 1954, *New York Times*: 84.

9   Farrington, Oral History Interview, USAFMOC: 26–27.

10 Newspaper reports indicate that less than 65 percent of the eligible voters went to the polls; previous races produced 85 percent turnout. See, "Widow Wins Farrington's Delegate Seat," 2 August 1954, *Washington Post*: 2. See also, "Mary Elizabeth Pruett Farrington," *Current Biography, 1955*: 196.

11 *Congressional Record*, House, 83rd Cong., 2nd sess. (4 August 1954): 13282.

12 Elizabeth Ford, "Mrs. Farrington Makes Thank-You Speech; New Hawaii Delegate Is Sworn In," 5 August 1954, *Washington Post*: 41; "Hawaii Delegate Sworn," 5 August 1954, *New York Times*: 29.

13 Drew Pearson, "A Plea for Hawaiian Statehood," 17 August 1954, *Washington Post*: 39. Apparently Farrington herself was the source for Pearson's article because her oral history account of the meeting with Eisenhower matches this account and, in some places, is verbatim. See Farrington, Oral History Interview, USAFMOC: 45–46.

14 *Congressional Record*, House, 83rd Congress, 2nd sess. (12 August 1954): 14303.

15 "Election Statistics, 1920 to Present," http://clerk.house.gov/members/electionInfo/elections.html. See also, Burns's entry in the online *Biographical Directory*, at http://bioguide.congress.gov.

16 Republicans expressed surprise at the election results; however, many observers attributed the change in party control to a backlash against Republican policies on a variety of local issues such as taxes and unemployment. "Democrats Upset G.O.P. Hawaii Rule," 4 November 1954, *New York Times*: 22.

17 "Election Statistics, 1920 to Present," http://clerk.house.gov/members/electionInfo/elections.html.

18 Democrats gained 19 seats to take control of the House from the Republicans at the beginning of the 84th Congress. See "Party Divisions," http://clerk.house.gov/histHigh/Congressional_History/partyDiv.html.

19 "Statehood Duo Starts Again—At the Bottom," 11 May 1955, *Christian Science Monitor*: 18; "Hawaiian Red Peril Charge Called Insult," 20 April 1955, *Washington Post*: 32; "Statehood Urged by Delegate," 25 March 1955, *Washington Post*: 64; see also, Farrington's lengthy defense of Hawaii statehood in the *Congressional Record*, House, 84th Cong., 1st sess. (10 May 1955): 5921–5925.

20 Farrington, Oral History Interview, USAFMOC: 19; 58.

21 "Hawaii Delegate in Close Contest," 14 October 1956, *New York Times*: 62; "Election Revises Hawaii Strategy," 11 November 1956, *New York Times*: 53.

22 Farrington, Oral History Interview, USAFMOC: 65.

Hazel Hempel Abel
1888–1966

UNITED STATES SENATOR ★ REPUBLICAN FROM NEBRASKA

1954

Hazel Hempel Abel, an accomplished business-woman and Republican Party official, was elected to the U.S. Senate from Nebraska to fill a two-month term created by a technicality in the state's election law. Though her service was brief, Abel participated in an historic censure of fellow Republican Senator Joseph McCarthy of Wisconsin for his aggressive redbaiting tactics.

Hazel Pearl Hempel was born in Plattsmouth, Nebraska, on July 10, 1888. Her mother was Ella Beetison Hempel, and her father, Charles Hempel, worked as a railroad official. Hazel Hempel went to Omaha High School and graduated in 1908 from the University of Nebraska with a B.A. and a teaching certificate. Prior to her marriage to George Abel in 1916, she worked as a teacher instructing high school students in mathematics, English, Latin, and German. The Abels raised five children: Helen, George, Hazel, Alice, and Annette. While managing family responsibilities, Hazel Abel later served as a high school principal in three Nebraska towns. She left teaching to work for the Abel Construction Company as secretary-treasurer for 20 years, assuming the company's presidency after her husband's death in 1937. She served in that capacity until 1951 and once observed that her education and managerial experience made the transition into those responsibilities of company head somewhat easier. "These assets compensated somewhat for my lack of knowledge about cement mixing," she quipped. Hazel Abel also served as a trustee for four colleges, including the University of Nebraska, and became a driving force in reforms in the juvenile probation system and juvenile courts and in a broad recodification of the state's children's laws.[1] Abel also was an active member of the

Nebraska Republican Party, eventually chairing the state's GOP Central Committee.

A quirk in Nebraska election laws launched Abel's brief career in elective politics. Eva Bowring, who had been appointed in April 1954 to fill the vacancy caused by the death of Dwight Griswold, was barred by law from serving past the date of the first general election following her appointment. That fall, a special election open only to candidates not seeking the six-year term in the Senate was set for November 2, 1954. Hopefuls from both parties seized on the opportunity to run for the brief, 60-day term. Sixteen Republicans and three Democrats jumped into the race. The 66-year-old Abel outran the field. Dubbed "Hurricane Hazel," she waged a high-energy campaign conducted from the driver's seat of her automobile as she crisscrossed the state.[2] Her platform was centered on support for the Dwight D. Eisenhower administration's foreign and domestic policies. She beat her nearest GOP rival by nearly 20,000 votes and swept past her chief opponent, William Meier, the state's Democratic chairman, by carrying 86 of Nebraska's 93 counties and 58 percent of the total vote.[3] Nebraska election law would not certify the election, however, until November 22, which posed a problem because immediately after the elections, the Senate determined that it would come back into session to hold censure proceedings against Wisconsin Senator Joseph McCarthy. Governor Robert Crosby, therefore, took the unusual step of appointing Abel to succeed Bowring, which allowed her to be seated immediately.[4]

On November 8, 1954, with her five children and other family members looking on, Abel became the first woman to succeed a woman in the Senate.[5] On November 30, she was appointed to the Finance Committee and the Interstate and Foreign Commerce Committee, the latter assignment having been held by her predecessors, Bowring and Griswold.[6] Her only floor speech during the Senate's abbreviated three-week session was a eulogy of former Nebraska Senator Hugh Butler, whom she had known through her work as a trustee of Doane College.[7] Abel's presence, however, was widely noted simply because she and Margaret Chase Smith were the only women in the Senate. Her presence created some confusion in Washington social circles. Shortly after taking office, she received an invitation to the British Embassy for a reception for the visiting Queen Mother Elizabeth. Upon arriving at the embassy door and identifying herself, a British diplomat refused her entry, insisting that he thought Smith was the only woman in the Senate. Eventually Abel's daughter, Helen, a writer for the *San Diego Union*, who also was attending, came to the door and identified her mother, who was then allowed to enter.[8]

Just days after taking her seat, Abel participated in the historic censure of Joseph McCarthy, whose hearings into the activities of alleged communists in the U.S. government mesmerized the American public and intimidated federal employees and many politicians in Washington. Political observers believed that she would join her Nebraska colleague, Senator Roman Hruska, in voting against censure. Before the proceedings, Abel told the *Washington Post*, "I came to Washington to hear the discussion during the session. I have not made up my mind either way."[9] She did not participate in the rancorous floor debates that raged between McCarthy's critics and defenders but instead carefully studied the evidence.

Poring over the thousands of words of testimony and remaining on the Senate Floor on the final day of the debate without taking a break, Abel voted with the majority—67 to 22—to reprimand McCarthy on December 2, 1954, for his sensational and redbaiting investigatory tactics. That day the Senate adjourned, bringing Abel's active work in the upper chamber to a close.[10]

Hazel Abel resigned her seat on December 31, 1954, three days before the expiration of her term, to give fellow Republican Carl Curtis of Nebraska, elected to the six-year term in November, a seniority advantage. She later observed that she campaigned for the two-month term to raise the visibility of women in political office. "To me it was more than just a short term in the Senate," Abel recalled for *Newsweek*. "I wanted Nebraska voters to express their approval of a woman in government. I was sort of a guinea pig."[11]

Abel returned to an active civic life in Nebraska. She chaired the Nebraska Republican state delegation at the 1956 national convention. In 1957, Abel was chosen the "American Mother," an honor which included an invitation to the Brussels International Exposition to address the Mothers of the World. She also served as the chairwoman of the board of trustees of Doane College in Lincoln, Nebraska. She unsuccessfully sought the Republican nomination for governor of Nebraska in 1960. In 1963 the University of Nebraska conferred an honorary LL.D. to Abel for her work as a teacher and political leader. Hazel Abel died in Lincoln on July 30, 1966.

FOR FURTHER READING

Biographical Directory of the United States Congress,
"Hazel Hempel Abel," http://bioguide.congress.gov

NOTES

1   American Mothers Committee, *Mothers of Achievement in American History, 1776–1976* (Rutland, VT: C.E. Tuttle and Company, 1976): 388.

2   Hope Chamberlin, *A Minority of Members: Women in the U.S. Congress* (New York: Praeger, 1973): 244.

3   Michael J. Dubin et al., *United States Congressional Elections, 1788–1997* (Jefferson, NC: McFarland and Company, Inc., Publishers): 596.

4   "Distaff Senators Are Firsts," 6 November, 1954, *Washington Post*: 23.

5   Elizabeth Ford, "Abel Clan Sees Senator Sworn In," 9 November 1954, *Washington Post*: 31; "Distaff Senators Are Firsts."

6   For committee assignments, see Garrison Nelson, *Committees in the U.S. Congress, 1947 to 1992* (Washington, D.C.: Congressional Quarterly Press, 1993). Her successor, Curtis, did not receive posts on either of these committees. See also, "Random Notes From Washington: President Seeks a Liberal G.O.P.," 27 December 1954, *New York Times*: 7.

7   *Congressional Record*, Senate, 83rd Cong., 2nd sess. (9 November 1954): 15895.

8   "Random Notes From Washington: High Court Gives Itself Hearing," 15 November 1954, *New York Times*: 20.

9   "3 New Senators To Act on Censure," 5 November 1954, *New York Times*: 6; Ford, "Abel Clan Sees Senator Sworn In."

10 *Congressional Record*, Senate, 83rd Cong., 2nd sess. (2 December 1954): 16392.

11 Chamberlin, *A Minority of Members*: 246.

A Changing of the Guard

TRADITIONALISTS, FEMINISTS, AND THE NEW FACE OF WOMEN IN CONGRESS, 1955–1976

THE THIRD GENERATION OF WOMEN IN CONGRESS, the 39 individuals who entered the House and the Senate between 1955 and 1976, legislated during an era of upheaval in America. Overlapping social and political movements during this period —the civil rights movement of the 1950s and 1960s, the groundswell of protest against American intervention in the Vietnam War in the mid- to late 1960s, the women's liberation movement and the sexual revolution of the 1960s and 1970s, and the Watergate Scandal and efforts to reform Congress in the 1970s—provided experience and impetus for a new group of feminist reformers. Within a decade, an older generation of women Members, most of whom believed they could best excel in a man's world by conforming to male expectations, was supplanted by a younger group who challenged narrowly prescribed social roles and long-standing congressional practices.[1]

Several trends persisted, however. As did the pioneer generation and the second generation, the third generation of women accounted for only a small fraction of the total population of Congress. At the peak of the third generation, 20 women served in the 87th Congress (1961–1963)—about 3.7 percent. The latter 1960s were the nadir for new women entering the institution; only 11 were elected or appointed to

Representatives Bella Abzug (left) and Shirley Chisholm of New York confer outside a committee hearing room in the early 1970s. Abzug and Chisholm represented a new type of feminist Congresswoman who entered Congress during the 1960s and 1970s.

office during the entire decade. Moreover, the widow-familial succession, though less prevalent than in earlier generations, remained a primary route for women to Congress.

Yet, this group of Congresswomen began to embrace a unique legislative identity and an agenda that distinguished them from their predecessors. Representative Martha Griffiths, a central figure in the passage of gender-based civil rights legislation, vocalized this new mindset. First elected in 1954, Griffiths chafed at the deference senior Congresswomen showed to the traditions of the male-dominated institution. "The error of most women was they were trying to make the men who sat in Congress not disapprove of them," Griffiths recalled years later. "I think they wanted to be liked, they didn't want to make enemies. So they didn't try to do things they thought the men would disapprove of. I didn't give a damn whether the men approved or not."[2] More often than not, the women elected to Congress after Griffiths shared her sentiment.

New Patterns
Political Experience, Committee Assignments, and Familial Connections

Outwardly, the greatest change in women's participation in Congress was in their racial makeup. In 1964 Hawaii Representative Patsy Mink became the first Asian-American woman and the first woman of color in Congress; all 72 Congresswomen who preceded her were white. In 1968 Shirley Chisholm of Brooklyn, New York, became the first African-American woman elected to Congress. An unprecedented 17 African Americans were elected in the 93rd Congress (1973–1975), including three more women: Yvonne Burke of California, Cardiss Collins of Illinois, and Barbara Jordan of Texas. "There is no longer any need for any one to speak for all black women forever," Burke told the *Washington Post* shortly before she and Jordan were elected to Congress. "I expect Shirley Chisholm is feeling relieved."[3] The first Hispanic-American woman in Congress, Ileana Ros-Lehtinen of Florida, was elected to the House nearly two decades later in 1989.

However, race and ethnicity were not the only dramatic changes in the characteristics of the women entering Congress; in the decades between 1955 and 1976, a new type of well-educated, professional candidate emerged. Women's precongressional experiences merged reform backgrounds with specialized training, lengthy résumés and, increasingly, elective experience. Before 1955, just seven women in Congress held law degrees (the first was Kathryn O'Loughlin McCarthy of Kansas, elected in 1932). From 1955 through 1976, 10 of the women elected to Congress were lawyers, and several were graduates of the nation's premier law schools. Of the 39 women who were elected or appointed to Congress during this period, 34 (87 percent) had postsecondary education.

Significantly, 14 of these women had served in state legislatures, making the third generation of women in Congress the first in which women elected with legislative experience outnumbered women who were elected as widows. For many women, service in the state legislature was an invaluable introduction to parliamentary procedure and legislative process. "I felt like a fish in just the right temperature of water, learning where the currents were and how to move with them when you wanted to get things done," Millicent Fenwick recalled of her experience in the

From left, Congresswoman Martha Griffiths of Michigan, journalist May Craig, House Rules Committee Chairman Howard W. Smith of Virginia, and Congresswoman Katharine St. George of New York pose for a photo shortly after the House added a sexual discrimination amendment to Title VII of the Civil Rights Act of 1964. Led by Representative Griffiths, Congresswomen argued that employment laws should include both gender and race protections.

IMAGE COURTESY OF THE LIBRARY OF CONGRESS

New Jersey assembly.[4] Several women were legislative leaders: Ella Grasso of Connecticut was elected Democratic floor leader in the Connecticut house in 1955, Julia Hansen of Washington served as speaker *pro tempore* in the Washington house of representatives from 1955 to 1960, Florence Dwyer of New Jersey was appointed assistant majority leader of the New Jersey assembly in the 1950s, and Barbara Jordan was elected speaker *pro tempore* of the Texas senate in 1972. These achievements were considerable in 1969, when just 4 percent of all state legislators were women. By the end of the 1970s that figure had more than doubled to 10.3 percent.[5] Women's increased participation in state legislatures fueled their growing membership in Congress during the latter decades of the 20th century.

Other women, including Mink, Chisholm, Burke, Bella Abzug of New York, Elizabeth Holtzman of New York, and Patricia Schroeder of Colorado, gained valuable political experience as civil rights advocates or as Vietnam War dissenters. Though each had her own style of advocacy and her own public persona, these women were connected by the thread of modern feminism—assertively pursuing their agendas. Catherine Dean May of Washington, who served from 1959 to 1971 and whose legislative style was that of an earlier generation of women Members, noted the feminists' immediate impact on Congress. "The arrival of personalities like Shirley Chisholm and Bella Abzug on the congressional scene shook our august body to its foundations," May recalled. "Shirley and Bella were not what the male members of Congress had come to expect from a female colleague. They got just as demanding and as noisy and as difficult as men did!"[6]

The widow's mandate, or familial connection, remained for women a significant route to Congress. Of the 39 women who entered Congress between 1955 and 1976, 12 directly succeeded their husbands. Charlotte Reid of Illinois replaced her late husband, GOP candidate Frank Reid, on the ballot when he died just weeks before the 1962 general election. Elaine Edwards of Louisiana was appointed by her husband, Louisiana Governor Edwin Edwards, to briefly fill a Senate vacancy in 1972. In all, 14 women in the third generation (36 percent) reached Congress via a familial connection. While many women served only as temporary placeholders (eight served a term or less), several, including Reid, Cardiss Collins, and Lindy Boggs of Louisiana, had long and distinguished careers. Moreover, as a group, the women in Congress during this era served an average of 4.5 House terms or 1.5 Senate terms (9 years)—longer, on average, than their predecessors from the second generation, who served 3.5 House terms, or slightly more than one Senate term.

The median age of the women elected to Congress between 1955 and 1976 rose one year, on average, to 50.1 years, despite the fact that five women were elected in their 30s (including the youngest woman ever elected to the House, Elizabeth Holtzman, at age 31 years, 7 months). The oldest woman elected to Congress during this period was 68-year-old Corrine Riley of South Carolina, who briefly succeeded her late husband to serve the remainder of his term during the 87th Congress (1961–1963). In the House, where all but two of the women elected during this period served, the average age of all new Members tended to be lower. In the late 1950s, the average age of new Members was 43 years. By the first three elections of the 1970s, the median age of all new House Members was 42.1. But even during the 1970s youth movement in the chamber, the women (at 47.9 years) still lagged behind the men by nearly 6 years. Moreover, 43 percent of the new male Representatives (93 of 216) elected in these elections were in their 20s or 30s.[7]

Irene Baker of Tennessee, widow of Howard Baker, Sr., poses for a ceremonial picture of her swearing-in as a U.S. Representative on March 10, 1964. Speaker John McCormack of Massachusetts (left) administers the oath. Looking on is Majority Leader Carl Albert of Oklahoma.

IMAGE COURTESY OF THE HOWARD H. BAKER CENTER FOR PUBLIC POLICY, UNIVERSITY OF TENNESSEE, KNOXVILLE

A poster from one of Congresswoman Patsy Mink's early election campaigns. In 1964 Mink won her campaign for a U.S. House seat from Hawaii, becoming the first woman of color to serve in Congress.

The practical result was that the men had a considerable advantage in accruing seniority at a younger age.

More explicitly than their predecessors, the women elected between 1955 and 1976 legislated regarding issues that affected women's lives. Their feminism—their belief in the social, political, and economic equality of the sexes–shaped their agendas. Patsy Mink, a Representative from Hawaii and one of the first modern feminists elected to Congress, discovered early in her House career that, concerning women's issues, she was a spokesperson, or a "surrogate representative," for all American women.[8] Mink recalled that "because there were only eight women at the time who were Members of Congress . . . I had a special burden to bear to speak for [all women], because they didn't have people who could express their concerns for them adequately. So, I always felt that we were serving a dual role in Congress, representing our own districts and, at the same time, having to voice the concerns of the total population of women in the country."[9] The Congresswomen of this era tended to perceive themselves, and women in general, as being united by common bonds and life experiences as mothers, primary caregivers, and members of a patriarchal culture.[10] These experiences led to interest in legislation to redress long-standing gender-based inequities in areas like health care and reproductive issues, hiring practices and compensation in the workplace, consumer advocacy, access to education, childcare, and welfare programs for single parents.

Congresswomen thus sought committee assignments, particularly on committees that allocated federal money, that would permit them to effect these changes. An unprecedented four women served on the powerful Appropriations Committee during this period—Julia Hansen of Washington, Edith Green of Oregon, Charlotte Reid, and Yvonne Burke. Lindy Boggs and Virginia Smith of Nebraska joined the committee at the beginning of the 95th Congress (1977–1979), just after the third generation. At the behest of a group of Congresswomen, Speaker Sam Rayburn appointed Martha Griffiths to the Joint Economic Committee in 1960 and to the prestigious Ways and Means Committee in 1961; these assignments had never been held by a woman. Martha Keys of Kansas won appointment to the Ways and Means Committee as a freshman after reforms in the mid-1970s opened prominent panels to junior Members. Marjorie Holt of Maryland, Patsy Mink, and Elizabeth Holtzman served on the newly created Budget Committee in the early 1970s. Women also had a growing voice in defense decisions as Patricia Schroeder and Marjorie Holt gained seats on the influential Armed Services Committee. Holtzman and Jordan served on the Judiciary Committee after their 1972 elections, and at the beginning of the 95th Congress, Shirley Chisholm became the first Democratic woman to sit on the Rules Committee. The most common committee assignments for women were Education and Labor and Government Operations, followed by Interior and Insular Affairs, Banking and Currency, District of Columbia, Public Works, Post Office and Civil Service, and Veterans' Affairs.

Women also made advances in leadership in caucuses and committees. Most notably, a woman was Secretary for the Democratic Caucus—then the party's fifth-ranking position—for most of the period from the mid-1950s to the mid-1980s.[11] Edna Kelly served as Caucus Secretary in the 83rd (1953–1955), 84th (1955–1957), and 88th (1963–1965) Congresses. Leonor Sullivan of Missouri held the post in the 86th and 87th Congresses (1959–1963) and in the 89th through the 93rd Congresses (1965–1975). Patsy Mink succeeded Sullivan in the 94th Congress

(1975–1977). In the Senate, Margaret Chase Smith chaired the Republican Conference from the 90th through the 92nd Congresses (1967–1973); she was the highest-ranking woman in the party leadership in that chamber. While Leonor Sullivan was the only woman to chair a full committee during this period (Merchant Marine and Fisheries in the 93rd and 94th Congresses, from 1973 to 1977), a total of 10 women chaired 13 congressional subcommittees from 1955 to 1976. Julia Hansen quickly advanced to chair the Interior and Related Agencies Subcommittee of the powerful Appropriations Committee, becoming the first woman to serve in that capacity. Other women who chaired subcommittees included Gracie Pfost of Idaho, who headed the Public Lands Subcommittee of the Interior and Insular Affairs Committee, and Katherine Granahan of Pennsylvania, who chaired the Postal Operations Subcommittee of the Post Office and Civil Service Committee. Sullivan chaired the Merchant Marine and Fisheries' Panama Canal Subcommittee and the Consumer Affairs Subcommittee of the Banking and Currency Committee. Maude Kee of West Virginia led three panels on the Veterans' Affairs Committee: Education and Training, Administration, and Hospitals.[12]

Legislative Interests

Two key pieces of legislation—Title VII of the 1964 Civil Rights Act and the debate on the Equal Rights Amendment (ERA)—forged a unique bond of cooperation between women Members during this period. The emphasis on gender-based equality in these measures was echoed in a number of other legislative efforts, particularly in those aimed at creating opportunities for women in education and the workplace. Women Members continued to play a prominent part in legislation on diverse national concerns, ranging from Cold War defense strategy to internal congressional reforms. Central to this period was a group of federal reform programs known collectively as the Great Society. Initiated by President Lyndon

Johnson in the mid-1960s, these measures were in many ways an extension of the social programs created during the New Deal. Great Society legislation marked the zenith of federal activism—addressing civil rights, urban development, the environment, health care, education, housing, consumer protection, and poverty. This legislation ranged from the Civil Rights Act of 1964 and the Voting Rights Act of 1965, which ended racial segregation in America, to the enactment of a Medicare program for the elderly and a Medicaid program for the poor that provided access to hospitalization, optional medical insurance, and other health care benefits.[13] Women participated in these efforts, decisively shaping some of them, often with a conscious eye toward improving the welfare of all American women.

Representative Martha Griffiths was the prototype for many young activists of the 1970s. One of the first career women elected to Congress, Griffiths had practiced law, served in the state legislature, and presided as a judge in her home state of Michigan. In the U.S. House, she honed in on sexual discrimination in the workplace. While Griffiths believed initially that taking cases to the Supreme Court could result in equality for women, she became so disillusioned with the high court's rulings, she decided only gender-specific legislation could give women access to education, job security, and comparable pay for comparable work.[14]

As the Civil Rights Act of 1964 moved through committee and onto the House Floor for debate, Griffiths, joined by Catherine May, Edna Kelly, Frances Bolton of Ohio, and Katharine St. George of New York, resolved that Title VII, which contained language banning employers from discrimination in hiring on the basis of race, color, religion, or national origin, should also contain language banning discrimination in hiring on the basis of sex. The Congresswomen believed this language was necessary to protect women, reasoning that without it, they would be especially vulnerable to discrimination in hiring on the basis of their gender.[15]

In a parliamentary maneuver designed to derail the entire Civil Rights Act, powerful Rules Committee chairman Howard W. Smith of Virginia freighted the bill with controversial provisions and then proposed to extend protection against discrimination to women. Realizing that Smith could get more than 100 southern votes behind the amendment, Griffiths decided to let him introduce it. When he did, on February 8, 1964, the men on the House Floor erupted into guffaws that grew louder as the women Members rose to speak on behalf of the bill.

Debate on the amendment forged strange alliances; conservatives and segregationists lined up with progressive women. Opposing these unlikely allies were moderate and liberal northern Representatives who were fearful that the entire bill would be defeated. Griffiths stood in the well of the House and scolded the raucous Members, saying, "I suppose that if there had been any necessity to have pointed out that women were a second-class sex, the laughter would have proved it." She touched on the history of enfranchisement for African-American men in the 19th century, noting that women—white and

Lera Thomas of Texas, who succeeded her late husband, Albert Thomas, for the remainder of his term in the 89th Congress (1965–1967), meets with President Lyndon B. Johnson in this White House photo. Albert Thomas was one of President Johnson's close political allies. Lera Thomas continued many of her husband's legislative programs and inspected U.S. efforts in Vietnam during a six-week tour.

black—were denied the basic rights of citizenship guaranteed under the 14th and 15th Amendments. "A vote against this amendment" by a male Representative, she warned, "is a vote against his wife, or his widow, or his daughter, or his sister." Other Congresswomen followed her lead. Only Edith Green objected to the amendment, noting that it was more important to first secure African-American civil rights: "For every discrimination I have suffered, I firmly believe that the Negro woman has suffered 10 times that amount of discrimination," Green said. "She has a double discrimination. She was born as a woman and she was born as a Negro."[16]

The debates were followed by a teller vote, in which Members filed down the aisles of the chamber to cast their votes. Smith chose Griffiths to count the "yes" votes. With many Members absenting themselves from the vote, the amendment passed 168 to 133. When this result was announced, a woman in the House Gallery cried out, "We made it! We are human!"[17] Eventually, Smith's tactic backfired, as the House and the Senate voted the full civil rights measure into law later that summer. Griffiths worked feverishly behind the scenes to ensure that the amended version of Title VII was left intact. Years later, after Smith had retired and was visiting the House Chamber, Griffiths greeted him with a hug, saying, "We will always be known for our amendment!" Smith replied, "Well, of course, you know, I offered it as a joke."[18]

Griffiths also played a key role in the passage of another piece of landmark legislation—the Equal Rights Amendment. The ERA, drafted by suffragist Alice Paul and supported by the National Woman's Party, was introduced to Congress in 1923 to commemorate the 75th anniversary of the 1848 Seneca Falls Convention.[19] The original language of the ERA stated that "men and women shall have equal rights throughout the United States and in every place subject to its jurisdiction."

For decades the ERA languished in the House Judiciary Committee and was a deeply divisive issue for many former suffragists and feminists. Advocates believed it would equalize conditions for women. Opponents insisted it would negate an accumulation of laws that protected working women. Earlier Congresswomen, such as Mary Norton of New Jersey and Caroline O'Day of New York, refused to endorse the ERA on the grounds that it would adversely affect labor laws. In 1940 the GOP adopted the ERA as part of its platform, and Winifred Stanley of New York and Margaret Chase Smith sponsored measures to bring it up for a vote on the 20th anniversary of the introduction of the original amendment. But passing the ERA out of committee was especially difficult, since the longtime chairman of the Judiciary Committee, Emanuel Celler of New York (1949–1953 and 1955–1973), opposed the measure on the traditional grounds that it would undermine labor protections. During this period, the language of the ERA was modified, making it less a crusade for change than an affirmation of existing constitutional guarantees. The new wording stipulated that "equal rights under the law shall not be abridged or denied . . . on account of sex."

In 1970, Griffiths changed parliamentary tactics, using a discharge petition that required her to get a majority (218 of the 435 House Members) to support her effort to bring the bill out of committee and onto the floor for general debate and a vote. Griffiths obtained the 218 signatures and on August 10, 1970, opened debate on the bill on the House Floor, where it passed by a wide margin.[20] Later that fall the Senate voted to amend the ERA with a clause exempting women from the draft.

"For every discrimination I have suffered, I firmly believe that the Negro woman has suffered 10 times that amount of discrimination," Representative Edith Green said. "She has a double discrimination. She was born as a woman and she was born as a Negro."

Congresswoman Martha Griffiths of Michigan stands outside the House wing of the Capitol shortly after the House passed the Equal Rights Amendment in August 1970. Griffiths used a long-shot parliamentary maneuver to dislodge ERA from the Judiciary Committee, where it had languished for years. Eventually, ERA passed the Senate and went to the states for ratification in 1972, where it failed to muster the necessary support to become a constitutional amendment.

IMAGE COURTESY OF THE LIBRARY OF CONGRESS

However, the House and the Senate failed to work out their differences in conference committee before Congress adjourned for the year, forcing Griffiths to begin anew. Throughout this legislative battle, Griffiths received the nearly unanimous backing of liberal and conservative women Members. Congresswoman Louise Hicks of Massachusetts dismissed critics who suggested the law would force women into direct combat roles in places like Vietnam.[21] "There is no reason why women should not carry equally the burdens as well as the rights of full citizenship," she responded. "Indeed, most are willing or eager to do so." The ERA was necessary, Hicks argued, because, "discrimination against women—on the job, in education, in civil and criminal law—is a disgrace to a nation which has long proclaimed its belief in equality before the law and individual dignity for all citizens."[22] After Representative Griffiths again successfully maneuvered the ERA onto the House Floor, it won wide approval. The Senate accepted it without revisions in March 1972.

However, the battle over the ERA had just begun and would continue into the early 1980s. By law, the constitutional amendment required the approval of three-quarters of the state legislatures within seven years. By the end of 1973, 30 states had ratified it. Five more states approved the amendment between 1974 and 1976, but "Stop ERA," a grass-roots movement led by conservative activist Phyllis Schlafly, organized opposition, and several signatory states considered rescinding their support. Schlafly portrayed herself as a defender of women's traditional roles as mothers and homemakers. During the 1970s, Schlafly (who ran for Congress as a Republican, unsuccessfully, in 1952 and 1970) declared that the small number of women in Congress "does not prove discrimination at all." Rather, she said, it "proves only that most women do not want to do the things that must be done to win elections."[23] Schlafly argued that the ERA would destroy protections for women in divorce law and child custody law, weaken laws for sex crimes against women, lead to women being drafted into the military, and undermine the institution of marriage. In a televised debate in 1976, Millicent Fenwick argued with Schlafly and her allies, who wanted the ERA stripped from the Republican Party platform.[24] Fenwick's frustration was palpable: "I think it is sad and a little comic . . . in the Bicentennial year to be wondering about whether we ought to admit that 51 percent [to] 52 percent of the citizens of America are really citizens."[25] By 1977, the ERA was still three states shy of the 38 it needed for ratification. The debate continued and later provided the crucial momentum Congresswomen needed to organize themselves as a formal group.

Economic Equality

The efforts associated with Title VII and the ERA were only the tip of the iceberg; legislation affecting women extended into virtually every facet of American life. A major goal was to achieve economic equality. Since World War II, Congresswomen had been promoting legislation to require equity in pay for men and women in similar jobs. Winifred Stanley introduced such a measure in 1943, but it failed to pass the House. Later, Edna Kelly, Florence Dwyer, Katharine St. George, and Katherine Granahan introduced equal-pay bills, which met with similar outcomes despite support from Presidents Harry Truman and Dwight Eisenhower, largely because of opposition from big business and its congressional allies. Congresswoman Granahan had introduced a measure to end gender-based wage discrimination in the 85th Congress (1957–1959). "When two workers, side by side, performing the same sort of work are doing it equally well, there is no justification under law or moral justice that they should not be accorded an equal opportunity for equal pay," she said in a floor speech.[26] Women Members persisted. With Edith Green of Oregon shepherding it through Congress, the legislation passed the House in 1962 and eventually became law in 1963 when the House and the Senate agreed on a revised bill. The Equal Pay Act, which built on the Fair Labor Standards Act of 1938, decreed that no employer could pay a woman "at a rate less than the rate at which he pays wages to employees of the opposite sex . . . on jobs the performance of which requires equal skill, effort, and responsibility, and which are performed under similar working conditions." The law allowed wage differences based on factors such as seniority and merit.[27]

Economic opportunity had a racial component as well. Title VII of the 1964 Civil Rights Act created the Equal Employment Opportunity Commission (EEOC) to investigate unlawful employment practices and to report findings to Congress and the President. It also authorized the Attorney General to file a civil suit when employers showed a pattern of discrimination.[28] The EEOC became an important recourse for women and racial minorities. Yvonne Burke, who represented a large constituency of African Americans in the Los Angeles area, insisted that civil rights include economic equality as well as political equality. "True dignity, true freedom, are economic in 1974," she said.[29] Congresswoman Burke championed the cause of minority women, eventually authoring the Displaced Homemakers Act to provide financial assistance and job training for divorced women and single mothers entering the job market.

Because they often managed the household budget and did most of the household shopping, women took a special interest in consumer affairs. Representative Leonor Sullivan was the leading advocate for consumer protection in the House. Sullivan's signal piece of legislation was the 1968 Consumer Credit Protection Act, which established truth in lending provisions, requiring financial institutions to fully disclose the conditions and costs of borrowing. In the Senate, Maurine Neuberger advocated honest labeling on consumer items. She challenged the meat packing industry regarding its additives and criticized bedding manufacturers that sold flammable blankets. Neuberger also led the fight to regulate tobacco advertising and to require health warning labels on cigarette packaging.

Education

Education was another area in which women, long considered authorities, wrote and shepherded major measures through Congress. Coya Knutson of Minnesota and Edith Green were instrumental in developing the National Defense Education Act (NDEA) of 1958, which passed just one year after Russia's successful launch of the *Sputnik* satellite sparked concern that American students lagged behind those in communist countries in critical subject areas. The NDEA provided $1 billion in federal loans and grants to subsidize science, mathematics, and foreign language study in U.S. universities and created the first federal college loans based on student need.

Federal aid for education was expanded dramatically during the Great Society, and two women played prominent legislative roles in the process. Patsy Mink helped shape Head Start legislation, which provided federal money to help

"*...true dignity, true freedom, are economic in 1974.*"

—YVONNE BURKE

communities meet the needs of disadvantaged preschool-aged children. Administered by the Department of Health and Human Services, Head Start provided comprehensive child development programs for children up to age five and their families. Mink's Women's Education Equity Act, which passed as part of a 1974 education bill, mandated the removal of gender stereotypes from school textbooks and provided federal incentives to educational programs that promoted gender equity. Edith Green, a former teacher, became known as the Mother of Higher Education for her leadership on school issues during her two decades in the U.S. House. Among Green's landmark legislative achievements was the Higher Education Act of 1965, which created the first federal program providing financial assistance to undergraduates. In 1972, Congresswoman Green held the first hearings on discrimination against women in college sports programs. Both Green and Mink sponsored Title IX, one of the 1972 federal education amendments, which provided that "No person in the United States shall, on the basis of sex, be excluded from participation in, be denied the benefits of, or be subjected to discrimination under any education program or activity receiving federal financial assistance."

Foreign Policy

The Cold War dominated U.S. foreign policy throughout the period from 1955 to 1976. During the Eisenhower administration, the United States stockpiled nuclear weapons and enhanced its missile and aircraft delivery systems to deter Soviet leaders from carrying out aggressive military actions around the globe. The Soviets, too, developed nuclear capabilities and engaged Washington in a game of strategic brinksmanship. This policy nearly resulted in a nuclear exchange in 1962 during the Cuban Missile Crisis, when the John F. Kennedy administration instituted a naval "quarantine" of Cuba after discovering that the Soviet government, under Nikita Khrushchev, had secretly placed intermediate-range nuclear missiles on the communist-controlled island. After backing away from nuclear apocalypse, the two superpowers tacitly agreed to avoid direct confrontations.

However, the Cold War had moved into a new phase in the developing world, as the Soviets and Americans vied for the support of postcolonial governments in Africa, the Middle East, and Asia. Though careful not to challenge one another directly, Washington and Moscow poured economic and military aid into these regions and underwrote "proxy wars" fought by indigenous peoples. Beginning in 1954, America became the primary benefactor of the Ngo Dinh Diem regime in South Vietnam in a civil war against the communist-controlled government of Ho Chi Minh in North Vietnam. A decade later, in July 1965, after it became clear that the South could not win alone, the United States intervened directly against North Vietnamese forces and communist rebels. By late 1967, more than 485,000 U.S. troops were stationed in Vietnam. Eventually, some 2 million Americans served in Vietnam, and more than 58,000 of them died. Vietnamese losses were staggering; during the civil war from 1954 to 1975, more than 1.1 million North Vietnamese soldiers and Viet Cong rebels were killed and nearly 2 million North and South Vietnamese civilians perished. U.S. intervention spurred a massive anti-war protest movement that had spread by the late 1960s from college campuses to large cities, drawing Americans from all walks of life.[30]

A number of women who entered Congress during this period won election as antiwar candidates: Mink, Chisholm, Abzug, and Schroeder among them.

The Vietnam War divided women Members. Charlotte Reid and Edna Kelly were ardent supporters of military intervention. Edith Green was one of a handful to oppose her party and the President when the Johnson administration sought funding for the initial American intervention. A number of women who entered Congress during this period, including Mink, Chisholm, Abzug, and Schroeder, won election as antiwar candidates. With much fanfare, Abzug introduced legislation to withdraw U.S. troops from South Vietnam and to impeach President Richard Nixon for his prosecution of the war. Schroeder, who became in 1973 only the third woman ever to sit on the House Armed Services Committee, was in the 1970s and 1980s a particularly vocal advocate of reining in defense spending and securing new arms control accords. She was determined to bring women's perspectives to a debate from which they had been largely excluded. "When men talk about defense, they always claim to be protecting women and children," Schroeder said, "but they never ask the women and children what they think."[31] Other Congresswomen advocated more vigorous U.S. support for international human rights. Two New Jersey Representatives emerged as critics of authoritarian governments allied with America in the Cold War against the Soviets. Helen Meyner criticized human rights abuses by Ferdinand Marcos's government in the Philippines, seeking to cut U.S. aid to the regime. Millicent Fenwick helped craft the Helsinki Accords on Human Rights, which investigated abuses behind the communist iron curtain, and openly challenged American support for dictatorial regimes in the Middle East and Africa.

Reform and Congressional Accountability

Women also participated in several efforts to make congressional operations more transparent and accountable and to circumvent procedural attempts to block legislation. For example, in 1961, Representative Florence Dwyer of New Jersey was one of about two dozen northern Republicans from urban districts who sided with Speaker Sam Rayburn and liberal Democrats as the House pushed through a measure to expand the membership of the Rules Committee, which controlled the flow of legislation to the House Floor. Chairman Howard Smith, a conservative Democrat from Virginia, had used his power to block social legislation. By assigning more liberal Members to the committee, the House paved the way for the consideration in subsequent years of major bills like the Civil Rights Act of 1964.

Later in the 1960s, the Committee on Standards of Official Conduct (commonly known as the Ethics Committee) was formed to provide Members with ethics guidelines and to investigate violations of House practice. Like many other Members, Congresswoman Edna Kelly had financed her campaigns out of her own pocketbook. She recalled that that practice changed in the 1960s as an increasing number of her colleagues relied on fundraising events to pay for the costs of biannual elections. Believing this new system could be abused, Kelly became a founding member of the Ethics Committee in 1967 and helped draft the committee's operating procedures.[32] Representative Millicent Fenwick earned the epithet Conscience of Congress for her repeated appeals to colleagues to reform the campaign finance system. Elected in 1974, Fenwick had a tendency to speak out on the House Floor that prompted Wayne Hays of Ohio, the powerful chairman of the House Administration Committee, to threaten to withhold her staff's paychecks "if that woman doesn't sit down and keep quiet."[33] Undeterred, Fenwick directly challenged Hays, who shortly afterward fell victim to scandal and left the House.

Judiciary Committee member Barbara Jordan of Texas was a freshman when the House began impeachment inquiries against President Richard M. Nixon in 1974, at the height of the Watergate Scandal. Television coverage of committee proceedings—which included her statements about the constitutional gravity of the crisis—instantly made Representative Jordan a national figure. Here, she is shown during Judiciary Committee proceedings.

IMAGE COURTESY OF TEXAS CHRISTIAN UNIVERSITY, BARBARA JORDAN COLLECTION

The Watergate Scandal was one of the defining political events of the 20th century and a moment of constitutional crisis. It grew out of the culture of suspicion within the Nixon administration, the obsession with secrecy that characterized Cold War national security imperatives, and the related expansion of presidential power.[34] Clandestine Central Intelligence Agency and Federal Bureau of Investigation surveillance operations had been authorized by President Nixon in 1970 against domestic opponents, antiwar protestors, and government officials suspected of leaking classified material about the planning for the Vietnam War. In 1972, the Committee to Re-Elect the President (CREEP), headed by former Attorney General John Mitchell, approved a plan to wiretap the phones of the Democratic National Committee in the Watergate complex in Washington, D.C. The June 17, 1972, break-in was botched, and the perpetrators were arrested. The ensuing cover-up involved senior administration officials and even the President himself.

Over a period of nearly two years, the details of the story gradually came to light through a combination of investigative journalism, judicial action, and legislative inquiries. In February 1973, the Senate created the Committee on Presidential Campaign Activities (widely known as the Ervin Committee, after its chairman, Sam Ervin of North Carolina) to investigate the break-in. By 1974, after a series of indictments and resignations involving top officials in the Nixon administration, the House Judiciary Committee initiated formal proceedings to impeach the President. When the committee voted to support articles of impeachment, President Nixon resigned on August 9, 1974. Two first-term Congresswomen, Barbara Jordan and Liz Holtzman, served on the Judiciary Committee during the impeachment process. A large television audience was mesmerized by Jordan's eloquence on the immense constitutional questions that hung in the balance. Her work on the committee transformed her into a national figure. Holtzman, too, earned a reputation as an erudite member of the panel, particularly for her sharp questioning of President Gerald Ford, who later testified before the committee to explain his pardon of Nixon in September 1974.

Watergate and mounting concerns over the abuse of power in federal agencies spurred Congresswomen like Bella Abzug to make government more accountable

President Gerald R. Ford signs a proclamation marking Women's Equality Day on August 26, 1974. Present are a group of Congresswomen: (from left) Yvonne Burke of California, Barbara Jordan of Texas, Elizabeth Holtzman of New York, Marjorie Holt of Maryland, Martha Keys of Kansas, Patricia Schroeder of Colorado, Cardiss Collins of Illinois, and Lindy Boggs of Louisiana.

IMAGE COURTESY OF THE NATIONAL ARCHIVES
AND RECORDS ADMINISTRATION

to the public. As chair of a Government Affairs subcommittee, Abzug shepherded through the House the Privacy Act of 1974, which expanded "sunshine laws," making government records more available for public scrutiny. A companion to the Freedom of Information Act of 1966, which allowed private citizens access to government records, the Privacy Act permitted individuals to view federal records about themselves and to amend inaccuracies. The Privacy Act also required government agencies to publish descriptions of their record-keeping systems and prohibited the disclosure of personal information to third parties.[35]

Much of the effort to reform government during this era was focused on Capitol Hill itself. One of the most important attempts to reform House practices and procedures was undertaken by the Democratic Caucus's Committee on Organization, Study, and Review, later known as the Hansen Committee for its chair, Representative Julia Hansen. The Hansen Committee was part of a larger effort to overhaul internal congressional procedures, a task begun by liberal reformers as far back as the 1930s. For several decades, most of these efforts were consistently blunted by conservative southern Democrats, who held the most powerful committee posts and perceived reform as a threat to their autonomy. Reformers sought to centralize the Democratic Party's decision-making process, to diminish the power of autocratic committee chairs, to provide better resources for subcommittees and, generally, to make the system more responsive to rank-and-file Members and the public.[36] By the early 1970s, junior Members like Ella Grasso argued that the tenure-based committee system had to be reformed so that chairs would be chosen "on the basis of intelligence and leadership." Grasso explained that the party would be best served by permitting "all the qualities of intelligence and vigor in the House Democratic membership to have full effect."[37]

Members' respect for Hansen and her moderate approach made her a logical choice to head the panel, which reviewed radical proposals put forward by a select committee led by Representative Richard Bolling of Missouri in 1973–1974. The Bolling Committee recommended altering committee jurisdictions, abolishing some panels entirely, and expanding resources for subcommittees. But the House approved the recommendations of the Hansen Committee in the fall of 1974, leaving jurisdictions intact but weakening chairmen by further curbing the power of the Rules Committee and expanding the membership and the resources of subcommittees.[38] Reform efforts during this period resulted in better committee assignments for new Members and allowed them to participate more directly in the formulation of party strategy and legislation. Gladys Spellman of Maryland, one of the early leaders of the House freshman class of 1974, the so-called "Watergate Babies," helped conduct a review of entrenched committee chairmen. Several of the most powerful—W.R. Poage of Texas of the Agriculture Committee, Felix Edward Hébert of Louisiana of the Armed Services Committee, and Wright Patman of Texas of the Committee on Banking and Currency—were forced from their positions in rapid succession.

By the early 1970s, junior Members like Ella Grasso argued that the tenure-based committee system had to be reformed so that chairs were chosen "on the basis of intelligence and leadership." Grasso explained that the party would best be served by permitting "all the qualities of intelligence and vigor in the House Democratic membership to have full effect."

IDENTITY: CHANGING SOCIAL AND INSTITUTIONAL PERCEPTIONS ABOUT WOMEN

After the disruption, alienation, and insecurity of the Great Depression and the Second World War, the family, more so than ever before, became the center of American life. Couples wed early (in the late 1950s the average age of American women at marriage was 20) and in proportions that surpassed those of all previous eras and have not been equaled since. They reared large families. Many moved to sprawling, affordable tract housing developments in the suburbs, bought modern conveniences ranging from cars to dishwashers, and enjoyed more leisure time.

Postwar prosperity made the banalities of housework less taxing but often came at a cost to the women who gave up careers to maintain the domestic sphere. This lifestyle stressed the importance of a one-income household, with the husband working and the wife staying at home to raise the children. Historian Elaine Tyler May called it a kind of "domestic containment": In seeking to nurture their families in the suburbs of the 1950s, housewives and mothers often gave up their aspirations for fulfillment outside the home.[39] For instance, the decline in the proportion of women who sought higher education degrees can be attributed in large part to marital and familial priorities. In 1920, 47 percent of college students were women; by 1958, that figure stood at 38 percent, despite the availability of more federal aid to pay for university education.[40]

Social expectations for what constituted a woman's proper role outside the home constrained women Members of Congress as well. When asked if women were handicapped in the rough-and-tumble of political campaigns because society held them to different standards than men, Maurine Neuberger, who served for years in the Oregon legislature before succeeding her late husband in the U.S. Senate, replied, "Definitely. . . . A woman enters into a man's world of politics, into backfighting and grubbing. Before she puts her name on the ballot, she encounters prejudice and people saying, 'A woman's place is in the home.' She has to walk a very tight wire in conducting her campaign. She can't be too pussyfooting or mousy. Also, she can't go to the other extreme: belligerent, coarse, nasty."[41] Congresswoman Gracie Pfost observed that a woman seeking political office "must be willing to have her every motive challenged, her every move criticized," and added that she "must submit to having her private life scrutinized under a microscope . . . and [being] the subject of devastating rumors every day."[42]

The primacy of family responsibilities and the power of society's expectations of what constituted a "woman's sphere" in the 1950s is aptly illustrated by the demise of Coya Knutson's congressional career. The first woman to represent Minnesota, Knutson was an early advocate for the creation of a food stamp program, funding for school lunches, and federal student loans. But after two terms, her abusive husband sabotaged her promising career by conspiring with her opposition to publicly embarrass Knutson. He accused her (falsely) of neglecting their family, which included a young adopted son, and of having an affair with a Washington aide. The press sensationalized the story, along with Andy Knutson's plea, "Coya come home." In the 1958 elections, Knutson's opposition subtly exploited this theme, and her constituents voted her out of office by a slim 1,390-vote margin. Although the House elections subcommittee agreed with Knutson's complaint that the accusations had contributed to her defeat, the damage had been done. Knutson's 1960 bid for re-election failed by an even wider margin.

> *Social expectations for what constituted a woman's proper role outside the home also constrained women Members of Congress. . . . The primacy of family responsibilities and the power of society's expectations of what constituted a "woman's sphere" in the 1950s is aptly illustrated by the demise of Coya Knutson's congressional career.*

Knutson's experience reinforced the widely held perception that women politicians could not manage both a career and family. The debate over balancing domestic responsibilities and professional life lasted well into the 1990s, and though male political opponents were less inclined to exploit it in latter decades, women politicians were repeatedly put on the defensive by the media and constituents who raised the issue.

Shifting social norms quickly altered staid notions of domesticity. Amidst the routine of household duties, many postwar wives and mothers were frustrated by their lack of professional fulfillment. Betty Friedan memorably identified this malaise as "the problem with no name" in her landmark book *The Feminine Mystique* (1963). The book's popularity attested to Friedan's connection with a feeling of discontent. Daughters who came of age in the 1960s were determined to make their lives less constrained than those of their mothers. Consequently, the women's rights movement and the sexual revolution of the 1960s challenged many of the traditional notions of motherhood and marital relationships.[43] Many young women rejected the sexual conventions of their parents' generation. Open discussion of sexuality and cohabitation outside marriage became more socially accepted. As birth control became more widely available, women exercised greater control over when, or if, they would have children. In the landmark *Roe v. Wade* (1973) decision, the Supreme Court upheld on the grounds of privacy a woman's constitutional right to terminate her pregnancy.

Sexual and reproductive freedom provided more options for women, who previously chose either a career or marriage. By the 1970s, many marriages involved two careers, as both the husband and the wife worked and, increasingly, shared familial duties. These added stress to family life. The divorce rate rose, and the phenomenon of the single, working mother became more commonplace. Yet, throughout this period, more young women pursued careers in traditionally male-dominated fields such as law, medicine, and business—loosening their bonds to home and hearth and preparing the way for a new and larger generation of women in state and national politics.

These changes profoundly altered the characteristics of the women who were elected to Congress from the 1970s onward. As younger women entered the institution, they faced questions about motherhood and family. Like many of their contemporaries outside politics, some Congresswomen chose motherhood as well as a career. In November 1973, a year after winning election to the U.S. House, Yvonne Burke gave birth to a daughter, Autumn, becoming the first sitting Member of Congress to become a mother.

Young mothers in Congress entered territory where few, if any, of their predecessors could provide guidance. Representative Schroeder recalled that several weeks after her first election, Congresswoman Bella Abzug telephoned to congratulate her. Abzug then asked incredulously how Schroeder, the mother of two young children, planned to maintain two careers: Representative and mom. "I told her I really wasn't sure and had hoped she would give the answer, not ask the question!"[44] Schroeder said. Service in Congress, she recalled, placed many extra demands on her family and required some creativity on her part—bringing diapers onto the House Floor in her handbag, keeping a bowl of crayons on her office coffee table, moving the family wholesale from Denver to Washington, and contending with her husband's decision to leave his career to follow hers.[45] Schroeder's

In November 1973, a year after winning election to the U.S. House, Yvonne Burke gave birth to a daughter, Autumn, becoming the first sitting Member of Congress to become a mother.

contemporaries and later women Members often echoed her descriptions of the disruption and uprooting of familial rhythms.

Challenging the Institution

The younger generation of feminist lawmakers also tended to buck many of Capitol Hill's most visible discriminatory and patronizing practices. In the 1960s, Patsy Mink publicly protested the House gym's exclusionary policy towards women by marching on the facility with Charlotte Reid and Catherine Dean May. "It was just a symbolic gesture that there are so many ways in which sex discrimination manifests itself in the form of social custom, mores or whatever, that you really have to make an issue whenever it strikes to protest it," Mink recalled. "You can't tolerate it."[46] The women also complained that the only bathroom facilities directly off the House Floor were for men. By the early 1960s, there were nearly 20 women Members sharing a single lavatory. Congresswoman Edith Green appealed to the House Administration Committee to set aside a space for the women, and in 1962, they were assigned a suite off the Old House Chamber that included a powder room, a kitchen, and a sitting area. Eventually the suite was named the Lindy Claiborne Boggs Congressional Women's Reading Room in honor of Representative Boggs's long service to the institution.[47]

Deviating from traditional dress codes was another way women challenged congressional custom. Bella Abzug broke long-standing tradition when she insisted on wearing her trademark hat onto the House Floor. Others followed her lead, often contending with resistance and outright scorn. "The day I wore a pants suit onto the floor you'd have thought I asked for a land base for China," Armed Services member Pat Schroeder told a local newspaper. "I just want to do my job. Does it make any difference if I have a bow in my hair or not?"[48]

Feminists not only challenged their male colleagues; they also questioned the conviction, prevalent among the older generation of Congresswomen, that they should not organize to champion their own agenda. In 1971, Bella Abzug and Shirley Chisholm helped organize the National Women's Political Caucus to promote greater participation of women in all aspects of U.S. politics. More than 320 women attended the founding conference in Washington, D.C.[49] Abzug, Chisholm, and other new Members, including Schroeder and Holtzman, pushed to create a formal congressional women's caucus, both to organize women and to educate the rank-and-file Membership about issues of special importance to women. Early efforts floundered, however, without the sanction of senior women leaders. The most influential among them—Leonor Sullivan, Julia Hansen, and Edith Green—subscribed to more-traditional views and generally hoped to avoid the establishment of a women's caucus.[50]

This clash was primarily generational rather than ideological, pitting older Democratic Members against a younger cadre of party members. By 1970, the dean of congressional women was 68-year-old Representative Sullivan, who proved far more traditional than many of her younger colleagues. She was the only Congresswoman to vote against the Equal Rights Amendment, not only because she believed it was a threat to labor laws, but because she believed it would jeopardize the family. "I believe that wholesome family life is the backbone of civilization," Sullivan said. Passage of the ERA would "accelerate the breakup of home life."[51] She added, "There are differences between male and female roles in our

> "The day I wore a pants suit onto the floor you'd have thought I asked for a land base for China," Armed Services member Pat Schroeder told a local newspaper. "I just want to do my job. Does it make any difference if I have a bow in my hair or not?"

society and I hope there always are."[52] Sullivan refused to countenance a women's caucus because she believed it unnecessary and a possible affront to male colleagues. Julia Hansen, a pioneer at virtually every level of Washington state government, also showed little support for a women's caucus. Having made her way in the male political world principally by hard work, talent, and determination, without benefit of caucuses or women's groups, Hansen was reluctant to advocate a caucus that would distinguish her based on her gender.[53] Caucus advocates also received no support from Edith Green. Like Sullivan, Representative Green viewed a potential women's caucus as a polarizing force that would do little to ease divisions and might even hinder legislation that addressed inequities for women and minorities.[54]

Other factors added to the reluctance to create a women's group. The leadership's lack of support for the effort led some women to question the legitimacy and staying power of a women's caucus. Others, elected by more-conservative constituencies, feared they might alienate voters by joining a group that likely would advocate nontraditional issues. Also, many Members were particularly concerned with the probable participation of Bella Abzug, a domineering and highly partisan Member some feared might quickly become the public face of the caucus.

New impetus for organization came after Sullivan, Green, and Hansen retired in the mid-1970s and Abzug left the House to run for the Senate in 1976. By 1977, the deans of House women—Republican Margaret Heckler of Massachusetts and Democrat Shirley Chisholm of New York, elected in 1966 and 1968, respectively— had only about a decade of seniority.[55] These changes enabled a renewed effort to form a women's caucus and continued emphasis on legislation that addressed women's economic, social, and health concerns.

NOTES

1   For further reading, see Jo Freeman's *A Room at a Time: How Women Entered Party Politics* (Lanham, MD: Rowan & Littlefield Publishers, Inc.): 227–235.

2   Elizabeth Kastor, "A Woman's Place; The 1950s Were Not Easy for Females in Congress," 17 November 1996, *Washington Post:* F01.

3   Leroy F. Aarons, "Legislator With a Subtle Touch," 22 October 1972, *Washington Post:* K1.

4   Louise Sweeney, "Congress's Millicent Fenwick: A Blueblood With a Social Conscience," 25 June 1975, *Christian Science Monitor:* 17.

5   Center for American Women and Politics (Rutgers University, New Brunswick, NJ), "Women in Sta Legislatures, 2003," http://www.cawp.rutgers.edu/Facts/StLegHistory/stleghist.pdf (accessed 30 March 2005).

6   Catherine Dean May, Oral History Interview, 1 March 1979, 9 March 1979 and 20 April 197' Association of Former Members of Congress (hereinafter cited as USAFMOC), Manusc Library of Congress, Washington, D.C.: 148–149.

7   For the 1955–1960 period, see Allan G. Bogue, Jerome M. Clubb, Carroll R. McKib¹ Traugott, "Members of the House of Representatives and the Processes of Moder *Journal of American History* 63 (September 1976): 275–302. For the 1970, 1972, an' were compiled using birth dates from the *Congressional Directory.* Two hundre⸍ were elected to the House in the 92nd, 93rd, and 94th Congresses; 17 were elected in their 30s, and 11 men were elected in their 20s.

8   Jane Mansbridge, "The Many Faces of Representation," Working Pa' of Government, Harvard University; and Jane Mansbridge, "Shou' Women Represent Women? A Contingent 'Yes,'" *Journal of Politics* 61

9   Patsy T. Mink, Oral History Interview, 6 March 1979, 26 March 1979, ai. Manuscript Division, Library of Congress, Washington, D.C.: 43.

10 Susan J. Carroll, "Representing Women: Congresswomen's Perceptions of Their ι Roles," paper delivered at the 13–15 April 2000, conference on "Women Transformin⸝

Albert Congressional Research and Studies Center, University of Oklahoma, Norman.

11 Mildred Amer, "Major Leadership Election Contests in the House of Representatives, 94th–108th Congresses," 3 September 2003, Congressional Research Service (CRS) Report for Congress, Library of Congress, Washington, D.C.; Amer, "Women in the United States Congress, 1917–2004," 1 July 2004, CRS Report for Congress, Library of Congress, Washington, D.C.

12 For lists of women committee chairs and subcommittee chairs and a list of women elected to leadership positions, see Appendices E, F, and G.

13 For more on the origins and history of the Great Society, see James T. Patterson, *Grand Expectations: The United States, 1945–1970* (New York: Oxford University Press, 1996): 524–592; Robert Dallek, *Flawed Giant: Lyndon Johnson and His Times, 1961–1973* (New York: Oxford University Press: 1998).

14 *Congressional Record,* House, 91st Cong., 2nd sess. (10 August 1970): 28005; see also Martha Griffiths, Oral History Interview, 29 October 1979, USAFMOC, Manuscript Division, Library of Congress, Washington, D.C.: 82–83.

15 This effort is explained in detail in Griffiths's USAFMOC oral history.

16 All quotes from the *Congressional Record,* House, 88th Cong., 2nd sess. (8 February 1964): 2578–2583.

17 Unpublished article by Martha Griffiths on sex in the Civil Rights Act, Appendix I, Griffiths USAFMOC Oral History Interview; see also 73–76.

18 Griffiths, USAFMOC, Oral History Interview: 73–76.

19 See Joan Hoff-Wilson, *Rights of Passage: The Past and the Future of the ERA* (Bloomington: Indiana University Press, 1986).

20 *Congressional Record,* House, 91st Cong., 2nd sess. (10 August 1970): 28004–28005; Martha Griffiths's letter to House colleagues, 2 September 1970, included in her USAFMOC interview.

21 Quoted in *Current Biography, 1974* (New York: H.W. Wilson and Company, 1974); also available at http://vweb.hwwilsonweb.com; Mark Feeney, "Louise Hicks, Icon of Tumult, Dies," 22 October 2003, *Boston Globe.*

22 *Congressional Record,* House, 92nd Cong., 1st sess. (6 October 1971): 35324–35325.

23 Karen Foerstel and Herbert N. Foerstel, *Climbing the Hill: Gender Conflict in Congress* (Westport, CT: Praeger, 1996): 186; for Schlafly's election results in 1952 and 1970, see "Election Statistics, 1920 to Present," http://clerk.house.gov/members/electionInfo/elections.html.

24 Shirley Washington, *Outstanding Women Members of Congress* (Washington, D.C.: U.S. Capitol Historical Society, 1995): 29.

25 Amy Schapiro, *Millicent Fenwick: Her Way* (New Brunswick, NJ: Rutgers University Press, 2003): 177.

26 *Congressional Record,* House, 85th Cong., 1st sess. (25 July 1957): 12780.

27 *Congress and the Nation, 1945–1964,* Volume IA (Washington, D.C.: Congressional Quarterly, 1965): 640; see also Stephen Stathis, *Landmark Legislation: 1774–2002* (Washington, D.C.: Congressional Quarterly Press, 2003): 261.

28 *Congress and the Nation, 1945–1964,* Volume IB (Washington, D.C.: Congressional Quarterly, 1965): 1640.

29 David Winder, "Jobs, Pay Become Blacks' Top Priority," 31 July 1974, *Christian Science Monitor:* 3.

30 For a useful overview of the Vietnam War, see George C. Herring, *America's Longest War: The United States and Vietnam, 1950–1975,* 4th ed. (New York: McGraw-Hill Inc., 2002); for a recent treatment of early dissent against the war and the crucial series of decisions by the Johnson administration to "Americanize" the war, see Fredrik Logevall, *Choosing War: The Lost Chance for Peace and the Escalation of War in Vietnam* (Berkeley: University of California Press, 1999).

31 "Patricia Schroeder," *Current Biography,* 1978 (New York: H.W. Wilson and Company, 1978): 368.

32 Edna Kelly, Oral History Interview, USAFMOC, Manuscript Division, Library of Congress, Washington, D.C.: 50–52.

33 Bruce Lambert, "Millicent Fenwick, 82, Dies; Gave Character to Congress," 17 September 1992, *New York Times:* D25.

34 For an overview of Watergate and its origins in the political culture of the Cold War, see Keith W. Olson, *Watergate: The Presidential Scandal That Shook America* (Lawrence: University Press of Kansas, 2003). A standard history of the episode is Stanley Kutler's *The Wars of Watergate: The Last Crisis of Richard Nixon* (New York: W.W. Norton and Company, 1992).

35 See House Report 108–172, Committee on Government Reform, "A Citizen's Guide on Using the Freedom of Information Act and the Privacy Act of 1974 To Request Government Records," http://thomas.loc.gov/cgi-bin/cpquery/T?&reportffihr172&dbnamefficp108&.

36 Julian Zelizer, *On Capitol Hill: The Struggle to Reform Congress and Its Consequences, 1948–2000* (New York: Cambridge University Press, 2004): for example, 125–155.

37 Susan Bysiewicz, *Ella: A Biography of Governor Ella Grasso* (The Connecticut Consortium for Law and Citizenship Education, Inc., 1984): 56.

38 See Zelizer, *On Capitol Hill:* 139–151.

39 See Elaine Tyler May, *Homeward Bound: American Families in the Cold War Era* (New York: Basic Books, 1988): especially 16–36.

40 Figures cited in Betty Friedan, *The Feminine Mystique* (New York: Norton, 1963), chapter one, "The Problem That Has No Name."

41 Myrna Oliver, "Maurine Neuberger; One of First Women in the Senate," 24 February 2000, *Los Angeles Times*: A20.

42 Hope Chamberlin, *A Minority of Members: Women in the U.S. Congress* (New York: Praeger, 1973): 230.

43 For more on the sexual revolution, see David Garrow's *Liberty and Sexuality: The Right to Privacy and the Making of* Roe v. Wade (New York: Macmillan Company, 1994).

44 Patricia Schroeder with Andrea Camp and Robyn Lipner, *Champion of the Great American Family: A Personal and Political Book* (New York: Random House, 1989): 15.

45 Schroeder, *Champion of the Great American Family:* 16–17.

46 Mink, USAFMOC, Oral History Interview: 111.

47 "History of the Lindy Claiborne Boggs Congressional Women's Reading Room, H-235, United States Capitol," prepared by the Architect of the Capitol; see also, William Allen, *History of the United States Capitol: A Chronicle of Design, Construction, and Politics* (Washington, D.C.: Government Printing Office, 2001): 432.

48 Joan A. Lowy, *Pat Schroeder: A Woman of the House* (Albuquerque: University of New Mexico Press, 2003): 85.

49 See the National Women's Political Caucus history page, http://www.nwpc.org/index.php?displayffiShowSpecialPage&nameffiHistory (accessed 1 April 2005).

50 See Irwin N. Gertzog, *Congressional Women: Their Recruitment, Integration, and Behavior* (Westport, CT: Praeger, 1995): 165–169.

51 Both quotes from Chamberlin, *A Minority of Members:* 234.

52 Lowy, *Pat Schroeder:* 86.

53 Susan Tolchin, *Women in Congress* (Washington, D.C.: Government Printing Office, 1976): 35; Gertzog, *Congressional Women:* 167–168.

54 Gertzog, *Congressional Women:* 167–169.

55 Ibid.

VISUAL STATISTICS IV

Congressional Service[1]

This timeline depicts the span of congressional service for women first sworn in between 1955 and 1976.

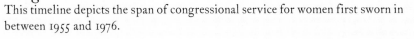

---

1. Source: *Biographical Directory of the United States Congress, 1774–2005* (Washington D.C.: Government Printing Office, 2005); also available at http://bioguide.congress.gov.

House and Senate Party Affiliation[2]

84TH–94TH CONGRESSES
(1955–1977)

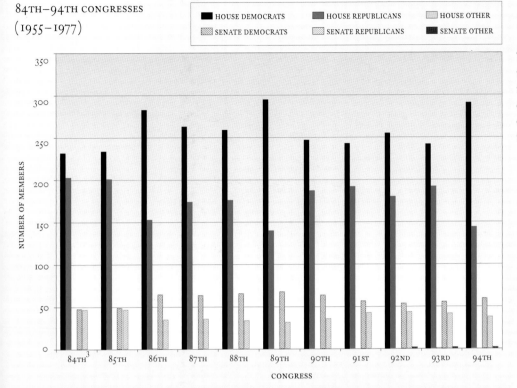

This chart depicts the party affiliation of all Members of Congress from 1955 to 1977. The following chart depicts a party breakdown only for women Members during this time period.

Party Affiliation: Women in Congress

84TH–94TH CONGRESSES (1955–1977)

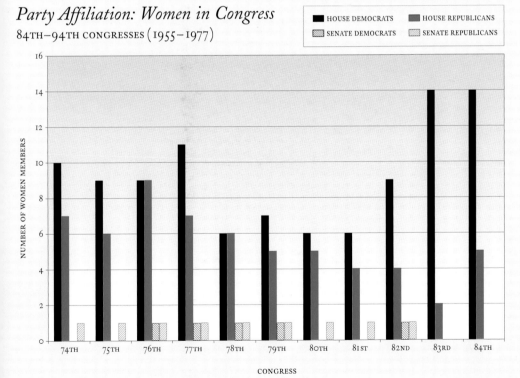

2. House numbers do not include Delegates or Resident Commissioners. Sources: Office of the Clerk, U.S. House of Representatives; U.S. Senate Historical Office.

3. Strom Thurmond (SC) was an Independent Democrat during the 84th Congress (1955–1957) until his resignation on April 4, 1956. In November of that year he was elected as a Democrat to fill the vacancy created by his resignation. The Independent Member listed above was Wayne Morse (OR), who changed from an Independent to a Democrat on February 17, 1955. [U.S. Senate Historical Office]

Iris Faircloth Blitch

1912–1993

UNITED STATES REPRESENTATIVE ★ DEMOCRAT FROM GEORGIA
1955–1963

Representative Iris Blitch of Georgia embodied a peculiar mixture of progressive feminism and southern conservatism during her long political career, which included four terms in the U.S. House. As a Georgia state legislator she pushed women's rights concerns. In the U.S. House, while displaying considerable legislative ability, she hewed to more traditional lines, advocating on behalf of agricultural interests in her rural district while denouncing federal efforts to enforce civil rights in the South. Over the span of her career, Blitch earned a reputation as a quick-tongued legislator who enjoyed the give-and-take of debate. "I can't remember a time when I wasn't interested in politics," she once recalled.[1]

Iris Faircloth was born near Vidalia, Georgia, on April 25, 1912, daughter of James Louis Faircloth and Marietta Ridgdill Faircloth. She attended public elementary schools in Georgia. Both of her parents died by the time she was nine, so Iris Faircloth moved to Frederick, Maryland, to live with her two older sisters. She graduated from Hagerstown High School and returned to Georgia in 1929 to attend the University of Georgia at Athens. After her first year of school, Iris Faircloth married businessman Brooks Erwin Blitch, Jr. The couple raised two children, Betty and Brooks, while working together in their pharmacy, lumber, cattle, and fertilizer businesses, as well as tending to the family farm in Homerville.

Iris Blitch became involved in politics during the Great Depression, out of concern for the lack of assistance for people suffering from the economic disaster. At the time, Georgia politics were controlled at the executive level by Democratic Governor Eugene Talmadge's political machine, characterized by its popular conservative, rural,

and anti–New Deal stance.[2] In this context, Blitch first ran for elective office as a Democratic candidate for the Georgia state house of representatives in 1940. Although she was unsuccessful, she later won a seat in the Georgia state senate in 1946. Two years later, Blitch was elected to the state house of representatives. While in the legislature, she managed to pass a bill to allow women to serve on Georgia juries. When opponents objected that women were too delicate for "indecent" courtroom responsibilities, Blitch shot back, "then it is time to bring women into the court rooms to clean them up."[3] Blitch also returned to school in 1949 and attended South Georgia College at Douglas, where she studied political science, accounting, and English. After losing her 1950 re-election campaign, she was elected to the state senate in 1952 and served until December 1954 as a close ally of the administration of Governor Herman Talmadge (Eugene's son) and was soon recognized as a top leader in the Talmadge machine.[4] During this time she also was heavily involved with the national Democratic Party, serving from 1948 to 1956 as one of the eight members of the Democratic National Committee's executive committee.

In 1954, Iris Blitch set her sights on the U.S. House of Representatives. In the race for the Democratic nomination for a southeastern Georgia seat, Blitch faced four-term incumbent Representative William McDonald "Don" Wheeler, an Alma, Georgia, native, Air Force veteran, and lawyer. Wheeler had made headlines in June 1953 when he introduced a motion to impeach Supreme Court Justice William O. Douglas after Douglas granted a temporary stay of execution to Julius and Ethel Rosenberg. The Rosenbergs had been convicted of passing along classified atomic information to the Soviet Union.[5] Blitch blasted Wheeler for his absence during a number of House votes and for what she described as his failure to protect the district's large agricultural constituency. She also advocated a major water conservation program for the South, along with the development of the harbor in Brunswick, Georgia.[6] In the September 1954 Democratic primary, Blitch won by about 1,400 votes—46 to 44 percent in a three-way race—carrying 13 of the district's 20 counties. In the then-one-party system in place in Georgia, the nomination was tantamount to election, and Blitch had no opposition in the general election. The Congresswoman also was unopposed in each of her three succeeding elections.[7] Throughout her House career, Blitch ran a district office from her converted garage at her Homerville residence.[8] The family bought a Washington, D.C., residence, but Brooks Blitch commuted to Homerville to tend to his cattle and timber businesses.

Benefiting from her strong party ties, and from her connections to powerful southern Congressmen, Blitch was given a seat on the popular Public Works Committee, where she served on three subcommittees: Roads, Rivers and Harbors, and Public Buildings and Grounds. As a member of Public Works, she steered a series of federal projects into her district including the construction of many post office and public buildings and the development of a major port at Brunswick Harbor. Blitch also proved to be something of a conservationist and won appropriations to protect the Okefenokee Swamp from overdevelopment and the threat of reduced water levels. During her first year, she introduced a bill providing for the conservation of water on small farms and the drainage of lowlands to make them suitable for growing timber. Her amendment to the Watershed Protection and Flood Prevention Act encouraged small water conservation projects by providing individual property owners with federal funds.[9] The bill was passed during her second term in the House. "The management of soil and water resources must be the concern of everyone who loves his Nation," Blitch once remarked in a floor speech.[10]

Much of her focus was devoted to the agricultural issues that affected her rural district. Working closely with the Agriculture Committee, she tried to meet the needs of farmers of wheat, tobacco, and jute, a fibrous material used for carpet backing. Seeking to protect the jute-backing industry in her district and to encourage its growth throughout southern Georgia, Blitch favored amending the 1930 Tariff Act to make it more difficult for foreign-made jute to enter the country.[11] Business-oriented as well, she expended much effort on attracting other industries to her district.[12] Blitch was a fiscal conservative who opposed federal funding for education. She described efforts to allocate federal money for public schools and universities as "a naked lust for national power, rather than a pious beneficence"; an intrusion of federal oversight on local, particularly southern, school systems.[13] Along similar lines, she argued throughout her four terms that the U.S. should not provide large foreign aid packages to its Cold War allies and other developing nations. "We cannot continue throwing good money after bad just hoping that it will save us," she told House colleagues. "It is up to the people of the different countries, including the United States of America, to assume some responsibility for themselves."[14]

In March 1956, Blitch was part of a group of 100 Members of Congress—19 Senators and 81 Representatives—from 11 southern states who signed the "Southern Manifesto." The document pledged the signatories to work to reverse the Supreme Court's 1954 *Brown v. Board of Education* decision outlawing racial segregation in public schools. Many southerners viewed the decision as infringing on state's rights, and the "Manifesto" denounced it as a "clear abuse of judicial powers."[15] Blitch also attacked a proposed voting rights amendment then on the House Floor as "iniquitous, infamous" and a "cancer of indecencies." In reaction to federal efforts to enforce civil rights legislation in the South, Blitch argued that "in an age where millions have died to preserve freedom, the executive, the judiciary, the legislative branches of the United States are destroying it."[16] She blasted a proposed 1956 Civil Rights Bill as a measure designed to sow internal discord between southern blacks and whites. "If you do not think that this bill is a Communist plan, then you are

B LITCH DESCRIBED EFFORTS TO

ALLOCATE FEDERAL MONEY FOR

PUBLIC SCHOOLS AND UNIVERSITIES

AS "A NAKED LUST FOR NATIONAL

POWER, RATHER THAN A PIOUS

BENEFICENCE"; AS AN INTRUSION

OF FEDERAL OVERSIGHT ON LOCAL,

PARTICULARLY SOUTHERN,

SCHOOL SYSTEMS.

not using the brain that God gave you," she declared in a floor speech. "Russia would rejoice at the passage of this bill because it would accomplish what she wants. It would divide and separate us."[17] During debate on federal aid to education in 1956, Blitch went so far as to argue that "a grave cloud of doubt" hung over the "legality" of the post-Civil War amendments to the Constitution, including those outlawing slavery, guaranteeing citizenship rights for all Americans, and conferring voting rights to African-American men.[18] She also argued against the legislation which eventually was signed into law as the Civil Rights Bill of 1957.[19]

Due to severe arthritis, Blitch declined to run for renomination for a fifth term in 1962. Among the 10 colleagues who spoke about her retirement on the House Floor, Majority Leader Carl Albert of Oklahoma remarked, "I have never known anyone more persistent in her devotion to duty. I have seen her sit here on the floor attending to every item of duty when she was ill and in pain. She is a real soldier."[20] Not long after she left Congress, however, Blitch once again made headlines. In August 1964, she announced her decision to leave the Democratic Party to support the Republican presidential candidacy of Senator Barry M. Goldwater. "In my political lifetime," Blitch said during her endorsement of Goldwater, "only one leader has come forward to give the American people a choice between a more centralized state and the complete dignity of the individual."[21] Afterward, Blitch retired from active politics and settled on St. Simons Island off the southeastern coast of Georgia. Late in life, Blitch moderated her stance on civil rights and supported then-Governor of Georgia Jimmy Carter when he declared that "the time for racial discrimination is over."[22] In 1988, she moved to San Diego, California, to be nearer to her daughter. Iris Blitch died there on August 19, 1993.

FOR FURTHER READING

Biographical Directory of the United States Congress, "Iris Faircloth Blitch," http://bioguide.congress.gov

MANUSCRIPT COLLECTIONS

Georgia State University (Atlanta, Georgia), Special Collection Department, William Russell Pullen Library. *Oral History:* In the Helen Bullard Oral History Interview, July 25, 1977, one audiotape and transcript (54 pages). Individuals discussed include Iris Blitch. A funding aid is available in the repository.

University of Georgia (Athens, GA), Richard B. Russell Library for Political Research and Studies. *Papers:* 1954–1985, 80.5 linear feet. The Iris F. Blitch Papers document her four terms representing Georgia's Eighth District in the U.S. Congress and, to a lesser extent, her campaigns and personal life. Well-documented throughout the entire collection, particularly in the Legislative Series and the Subject Series, are the issues that were important to Blitch and to the 20 counties that composed her district, such as agriculture, conservation, and the environment. The papers provide insight into the political climate for women in the second half of the 1950s and the early 1960s as well as into social mores regarding their participation. As one of only 15 women Members (and the only southern woman) in the House of Representatives in 1958, the challenges faced by Blitch and other women in Washington, as well as the public's perceptions, are well-documented throughout the papers, mainly in feature newspaper articles and interviews. Iris Blitch's personal beliefs and opinions of women in government and politics, as well as their roles and responsibilities, are evident in speeches and interviews she gave throughout her career and can be found primarily in both the Subject and Personal Series. Also documented in the papers, particularly in the Subject Series, is her position on segregation and an integrated society. To a lesser extent, and primarily through correspondence found in the Personal Series, is information relating to her immediate and extended family as well as her fragile health, which ultimately forced her retirement in 1963. A finding aid is available in the repository and online.

NOTES

1   Catherine Harrington, "83rd Chugs In: Senate Is 'Home' Again," 7 November 1954, *Washington Post*: S1.

2   V.O. Key, Jr., *Southern Politics in State and Nation*, 2nd ed. (University of Tennessee Press, 1977): 107–129; Corey T. Lesseig, "Talmadge, Eugene" *American National Biography* 21 (Oxford University Press, 1999): 283.

3   "Georgia Senate Votes Jury Duty for Women," 26 February 1947, *New York Times*: 17.

4   Karen Foerstel, *Biographical Dictionary of Congressional Women* (Westport, CT: Greenwood Press, 1999): 27. A peculiar county-unit voting system, which empowered rural counties, bolstered both Eugene and Herman Talmadge's strength in their gubernatorial races. This strength did not transfer to legislative or local races (Key, *Southern Politics*: 109–110). Though Blitch was aligned with the Talmadge machine, Clinch County (containing Homerville) was one of the persistent weaknesses for Eugene Talmadge during the 1940s and might explain Blitch's inconsistent career in the state legislature (see Figure 21 in Key, *Southern Politics*: 112).

5   Murrey Marder, "Introduced by Wheeler: Motion to Impeach Douglas Brings Applause in House," 18 June 1953, *Washington Post*: 1.

6   Harrington, "83rd Chugs in: Senate Is 'Home' Again."

7   "Election Statistics, 1920 to Present," http://clerk.house.gov/members/electionInfo/elections.html.

8   James Carberry, "Rep. Blitch Collects Rent for Her Garage," 1 April 1959, *Washington Post*: A1; see also, "Reporter Berated by Congresswoman," 15 April 1959, *Washington Post*: 65; "Rep. Blitch Hits Press on Payroll News," 15 April 1959, *Washington Post*: A3; *Congressional Record*, House, 86th Cong., 1st sess. (14 April 1959): 5842–5843.

9   *Congressional Record*, House, 84th Cong., 2nd sess. (24 April 1956): 6886–6887.

10 *Congressional Record*, House, 85th Cong., 2nd sess. (23 August 1958): 19725–19726.

11 *Congressional Record*, House, 84th Cong., 1st sess. (14 March 1955): 2835.

12 Susan Tolchin, *Women in Congress* (Washington, D.C.: Government Printing Office, 1976): 6.

13 *Congressional Record*, House, 86th Cong., 2nd sess. (26 May 1960): 11297–11298.

14 *Congressional Record*, House, 84th Cong., 2nd sess. (11 July 1956): 12370–12371; *Congressional Record*, House, 84th Cong., 2nd sess. (7 June 1956): 9829–9830; *Congressional Record*, House, 86th Cong., 1st sess. (24 March 1959): 5083–5084.

15 Robert E. Baker, "Anti-Court Manifesto Stirs Row," 13 March 1956, *Washington Post*: 1; Joseph C. Harsch, "The Southern Manifesto," 13 March 1956, *Christian Science Monitor*: 1; Numan Bartley, *Rise of Massive Resistance* (Baton Rouge: Louisiana State University Press, 1965); Gilbert C. Fite, "Southern Manifesto," *Encyclopedia of the United States Congress*, Vol. 4 (New York: Simon and Schuster, 1995): 1855.

16 *Congressional Record*, House, 85th Cong., 1st sess. (27 August 1957): 16104; similar quote in Hope Chamberlin's *A Minority of Members: Women in the U.S. Congress* (New York: Praeger, 1973): 250.

17 *Congressional Record*, House, 84th Cong., 2nd sess. (17 July 1956): 13183.

18 *Congressional Record*, House, 84th Cong., 2nd sess. (5 July 1956): 11872–11873.

19 *Congressional Record*, House, 85th Cong., 1st sess. (10 June 1957): 8706–8707; *Congressional Record*, House, 85th Cong., 1st sess. (27 August 1957): 16104.

20 *Congressional Record*, House, 85th Cong., 2nd sess. (10 October 1962): 23088.

21 "Ex-Representative Switches to the G.O.P. in Georgia," 12 August 1964, *New York Times*: 20.

22 Chamberlin, *A Minority of Members*: 251.

Edith Starrett Green
1910–1987

UNITED STATES REPRESENTATIVE ★ DEMOCRAT FROM OREGON
1955–1974

Few women in Congress have left such a substantial legacy as did Edith Green, and few have demonstrated such independence of mind and deed. From the time that she was elected to the 84th Congress (1955–1957), through her service in the nine succeeding Congresses, she left her mark on almost every education bill enacted and subsequently gained considerable influence in the Democratic Party despite her refusal to support the party's Presidents on all issues. Though Representative Green originally supported federal aid to education and the antipoverty programs, she grew disillusioned with what she perceived as an inefficient federal bureaucracy. Her increased frustration with "big government" contributed to her eventual drift from the liberal agenda of the Democrats.

The daughter of two schoolteachers, James Vaughn and Julia Hunt Starrett, Edith Louise Starrett was born on January 17, 1910, in Trent, South Dakota. At the age of six, she and her family moved to Oregon, where she went to public schools in Salem. She attended Willamette University from 1927 to 1929 and later enrolled at the University of Oregon, where she eventually graduated in 1939. While teaching school in Salem, Oregon, in 1933, she married Arthur N. Green. The Greens raised two sons, James and Richard, but later divorced. After 11 years as an educator, Edith became an announcer at KALE radio station in Portland, Oregon, and also served as legislative chairperson of the Oregon Congress of Parents and Teachers for three years. In this leadership position, Green gained experience in state politics, advanced her knowledge of national and regional educational issues, and learned the importance of lobbying—all of which served as a valuable foundation for her future career in Congress.[1]

Upon the urging of friends and Democratic officials, Green ran for secretary of state of Oregon in 1952. Although unsuccessful in her bid, she garnered enough public exposure to make a competitive run for the House seat encompassing much of Portland, Oregon, and its eastern suburbs in 1954.[2] After winning by a wide margin against her closest competitor, C.S. Johnston, in the Democratic primary, Green subsequently defeated the state's future governor, Republican Tom McCall, in the general election with 52 percent of the vote.[3] She became the second woman to represent Oregon in the House of Representatives. (Nan Wood Honeyman was the first in 1937.) Green went on to win her nine succeeding elections with ease, rarely facing any serious opposition.[4] Although offered the opportunity to run for the U.S. Senate on three separate occasions, she opted to continue serving in the House. Citing a fondness for the seniority system, which she believed allowed women the capacity to wield power that otherwise would remain unattainable because of gender discrimination, Green also feared the steep cost of a Senate campaign would require accepting contributions with "strings attached."[5]

As a recognized expert on educational policy, Green was appointed to the Committee on Education and Labor during her freshman term in the House. She served on that committee for 18 years, eventually becoming the second-ranking Democrat, a prominent position that enabled her to shape much of the social legislation of the United States. During her final term in Congress, she stepped down from her coveted committee assignment to take a seat on the influential Committee on Appropriations because, according to Green, the latter had more "action."[6] Green also served various terms on other House committees, including Interior and Insular Affairs, House Administration, Merchant Marine and Fisheries, and the District of Columbia.

Green's legislative interests were focused on education, so much so that she earned the epithets "Mrs. Education" and "the Mother of Higher Education."[7] Due in great part to her own experience with financial hardship that forced her to withdraw from college, Green dedicated herself to drafting and endorsing legislation to provide students of all economic backgrounds the opportunity to pursue higher education. Early in her political career, Green helped secure the passage of the National Defense Education Act (1958), a bill designed to ensure that American students kept pace with their Soviet counterparts by improving science and math education. The measure established a series of loans for impoverished students and allocated graduate fellowships for prospective college instructors.[8] According to Green, the deliberate addition of the word "defense" to the bill ensured its success. Conscious of the political climate of the Cold War, Green and other liberal backers of the legislation used the prevailing fear of the Soviet Union to convince conservative Members of the House that additional funds for education would strengthen American national defense. Green later speculated that the launching of the Soviet satellite *Sputnik* in 1957, which set off intense fear in Washington that the Soviets were winning the nascent space race, "did more for American education than the Congress was ever able to do up to that time."[9]

Green also authored two significant bills that changed the face of secondary education: the Higher Education Facilities Act (1963) and the Higher Education Act (1965). Labeled by President Lyndon B. Johnson as the "greatest step forward in the field" in 100 years, the Higher Education Facilities Act allocated federal funds for the expansion and improvement of college and university libraries, classrooms, and laboratories.[10] Two years later, Green guided the passage of the Higher Education Act, which authorized the first-ever federal financial

assistance for undergraduate students. She also worked to improve the Vocational Rehabilitation Act (1965) by adding a series of amendments (commonly referred to as the Green Amendments) to provide further employment training opportunities for urban youth.[11]

Despite insisting that she avoided feminist causes because she would "become too emotionally involved," Green's legislative record in Congress demonstrated a genuine commitment to advancing the rights of women. Advised as a young woman not to pursue a career as an electrical engineer because of her gender, Green spent much of her adult life attempting to eliminate the social and legal obstacles that prevented women from achieving equality. Because she believed that "a woman has to work twice as hard as a man to prove that she can do the job," she focused on drafting legislation that would even the scales between the sexes.[12] Two of her perennial concerns as a Representative, pay equity and gender equality in postsecondary education, resulted in the passage of landmark legislation that vastly improved the opportunities for American women. Signed into law in 1963, the Equal Pay Act mandated that women and men receive equal pay for equal work. Although pleased by the passage of the groundbreaking bill, Green bemoaned that it took "eight years to persuade Congress that a woman doing identical work with a man ought to be paid the same salary!"[13]

One of Green's most enduring legislative triumphs was Title IX, a part of the 1972 Higher Education Act that prohibited federally funded colleges and universities from discriminating against women. As chair of the Subcommittee on Higher Education of the Education and Labor Committee, Green presided over seven days of hearings in which a wide range of witnesses explained the various ways women faced discrimination in postsecondary education. She set the tone for the proceedings when she exclaimed, "Let us not deceive ourselves. Our educational institutions have proven to be no bastions of democracy."[14] Green overcame opposition from many university administrators, as well as from conservative Congressmen who feared the proposed bill would force school officials to construct unisex locker rooms and admit an equal number of male and female students. When reflecting upon the passage of Title IX, she stated: "I don't know when I have ever been so pleased, because I had worked so long and it had been such a tough battle."[15] Although Green did much to advance the rights of women, she did not always place this issue ahead of all others. For instance, because of her ardent commitment to civil rights legislation, she voted against the inclusion of the word "sex" in the Civil Rights Act (the only Congresswoman to do so), because she feared it might "help destroy" the bill.[16]

Early in her career, Green's liberal record made her a recognized asset to the Democratic Party. As evidence of her high standing within the party, Green seconded the presidential nomination of Adlai Stevenson at the Democratic National Convention in 1956, and four years later she performed the same honor for John F. Kennedy. As a show of thanks for successfully managing his presidential campaign in Oregon, Kennedy offered Green the position of U.S. Ambassador to Canada. Green declined the offer but later accepted an appointment to Kennedy's Presidential Committee on the Status of Women.

Over time, however, Green distanced herself from the Democratic Party agenda. Though originally a vocal supporter of Lyndon Johnson's Great Society social welfare package, Representative Green grew increasingly disenchanted with the expanded role of the federal government.[17] Her mistrust of big government caused her to reject much of the legislation she had worked for during the previous two decades. Fearful that federal programs had done little to alleviate the plight of the poor or to improve the quality of American education, Green advocated shifting responsibilities to state and local governments.[18]

At times, Green even retreated from legislation she helped push through the House, as was the case when she proposed denying federal aid to universities that failed to control student riots. Even though Green considered her suggestion "moderate," liberal members of the Education Committee branded it repressive.[19] Her ideological drift from the mainstream beliefs of her party, as well as her willingness to align with conservative southern Democrats and Republicans, triggered animosity and hostility in

many of her former allies, including President Johnson.[20] When asked about her shifting political stance, Green protested that she had not become more conservative, but that "ultra-liberals have moved so far to the left that they have distorted the position of all other liberals."[21] Former Oregon Senator Mark Hatfield, a political contemporary and friend of Green, described the Congresswoman as a "political maverick" who crossed party lines, at times to even support the candidacy of Republican candidates such as Hatfield.[22]

As an independent thinker and as a Congresswoman who believed in remaining true to her principles, Green often represented the minority opinion. Throughout her career, Green had shown a propensity for staking out positions that exposed her to political criticism. As one of only seven House Members to vote against Johnson's 1965 request for increased funds for the escalation of military involvement in Vietnam, Green remarked, "I cannot in good conscience lend myself to that kind of usurpation of congressional power." After the measure passed, Green expressed her discontent with her congressional colleagues and with the President: "I find it impossible to understand why an admittedly unnecessary appropriation request need be mantled in a cloak of urgency and secret meaning, with full, free, and frank discussion of its merits denied."[23] Green's steadfast determination, straightforward approach (as evidenced by her recurring campaign motto: "You Get Straight Answers from Edith Green"), and ability to make stirring speeches frequently worked to her advantage. These qualities, in conjunction with her sharp intellect, oftentimes enabled Green to persuade her colleagues to support her political agenda.[24]

Although virtually assured of re-election for the indefinite future, Green refused to stand for renomination to the 94th Congress (1975–1977) and resigned from the House on December 31, 1974. Two years prior to her retirement from congressional politics, Green quipped, "One thing is for certain. They won't have to drag me out of here in a coffin—I don't have Potomac fever."[25] Determined to leave Congress at an "appropriate time," Green declared that "twenty years in any one job is a reasonably long time."[26] After leaving the House of Representatives, Green taught at Warner Pacific College, served as co-chair of the National Democrats for Gerald Ford, and in 1979 was appointed to the Oregon Board of Higher Education. When asked to comment on her political career, Green succinctly noted, "It was plain hard work."[27] Green resided in Portland, Oregon, until her death in Tulatin, Oregon, on April 21, 1987.

FOR FURTHER READING

Biographical Directory of the United States Congress, "Edith Starrett Green," http://bioguide.congress.gov

Gates, Robert Edwin, Jr. "The Development of Title IX of the Educational Amendments of 1972 and Its Current Application to Institutional Athletic Programs." Ph.D. diss., University of Louisville, 1984.

Green, Edith. *Fears and Fallacies: Equal Opportunities in the 1970's*. Ann Arbor: Graduate School of Business Administration, University of Michigan, 1975.

Rosenberg-Dishman, Marie C. Barovic. "Women in Politics: A Comparative Study of Congresswomen Edith Green and Julia Butler Hansen." Ph.D. diss., University of Washington, 1973.

Ross, Naomi Veronica. "Congresswoman Edith Green on Federal Aid to Schools and Colleges." Ph.D. diss., Pennsylvania State University, 1980.

MANUSCRIPT COLLECTIONS

John F. Kennedy Library (Boston, MA). *Oral History*: 14 pages. *Oral History*: 33 pages. Part of Robert F. Kennedy Oral History Project.

Library of Congress (Washington, D.C.), Manuscript Division. *Oral History:* Transcript in the Oral History Collection of the U.S. Association of Former Members of Congress. Sound recording in the Library's Motion Picture, Broadcasting and Recorded Sound Division.

Lyndon B. Johnson Library (Austin, TX). *Oral History:* 82 pages. Restricted.

Oregon Historical Society (Portland, OR). *Papers:* 1954–1974, 200 cubic feet. Congressional papers and correspondence, photographs, and memorabilia. Unprocessed; a preliminary inventory available. Restricted. *Oral History:* December 1978, 1 cassette; interview with Representative Green regarding her career.

Radcliffe Institute for Advanced Study, Harvard University (Cambridge, MA), Schlesinger Library, http://www.radcliff/edu/schles. *Oral History*: 1974–1976. Interview of Edith Green by Katie Loucheim.

NOTES

1   Marcy Kaptur, *Women of Congress: A Twentieth-Century Odyssey* (Washington, D.C.: Congressional Quarterly Press, 1996): 112.

2   Hope Chamberlin, *A Minority of Members: Women in the U.S. Congress* (New York: Praeger, 1973): 256.

3   "Election Statistics, 1920 to Present" http://clerk.house.gov/members/electionInfo/elections.html; "Rep. Angell Trailing in Oregon Primary," 23 May 1954, *Washington Post*: M2.

4   "Election Statistics, 1920 to Present" http://clerk.house.gov/members/electionInfo/elections.html.

5   Chamberlin, *Minority of Members*: 257.

6   Bart Barnes, "Former Rep. Edith Green of Oregon Dead at 77," 23 April 1987, *Washington Post*: D6.

7   Barnes, "Former Rep. Edith Green of Oregon Deat at 77."

8   Steven Stathis, *Landmark Legislation, 1774–2002: Major U.S. Acts and Treaties* (Washington, D.C.: Congressional Quarterly Press, 2003): 249–250.

9   Edith Green, Oral History Interview, U.S. Association of Former Members of Congress (hereinafter cited as USAFMOC), Manuscript Room, Library of Congress, Washington, D.C.: 62.

10   Chamberlin, *Minority of Members*: 251.

11   Ibid.

12   Green, Oral History Interview, USAFMOC: 58.

13   Chamberlin, *Minority of Members*: 257; Sue Cronk, "Battle to Better Women's Wages Still Goes On," 14 January 1964, *Washington Post*: F9.

14   Susan Tolchin, *Women in Congress* (Washington, D.C.: Government Printing Office, 1976): 32.

15   Green, Oral History Interview, USAFMOC: 103.

16   Marie Smith, "Should Sex Amendment Be in the Rights Bill?" 11 February 1964, *Washington Post*: 35.

17   William C. Selover, "Mrs. Green's Role Credited in Antipoverty Victory," 20 November 1967, *Christian Science Monitor*: 3.

18   Barnes, "Former Rep. Edith Green of Oregon Dead at 77."

19   Kaptur, *Women of Congress*: 116.

20   Mason Drukman, *Wayne Morse: A Political Biography* (Portland: Oregon Historical Society Press, 1997): 395.

21   Norman C. Miller, "Rep. Edith Green, a Bareknuckle Fighter," 3 December 1969, *Wall Street Journal*: 18.

22   *Congressional Record*, Senate, 100th Cong., 1st sess. (22 April 1987): 9204; Green even served as the honorary chairwoman of Hatfield's 1984 campaign. See Mark O. Hatfield, *Against the Grain: Reflections of a Rebel Republican* (Ashland, OR: White Cloud Press, 2001): 9.

23   *Congressional Record*, House, 89th Cong., 1st sess. (5 May 1965): 9536.

24   Chamberlin, *A Minority of Members*: 255; Dennis Hevesi, "Ex-Rep. Edith Green, 77, Is Dead; Early Opponent of Vietnam War," 23 April 1987, *New York Times*: D31.

25   Gayle Tunnell, "Edith Green: 'A Smiling Cobra' or 'Mrs. Education?'" 9 August 1970, *Washington Post*: 240.

26   Mary Russell, "Rep. Edith Green Joins List of Retirees From Congress," 16 February 1974, *Washington Post*: A3.

27   Kaptur, *Women of Congress*: 116.

Martha Wright Griffiths

1912–2003

UNITED STATES REPRESENTATIVE ★ DEMOCRAT FROM MICHIGAN
1955–1974

Known as the "Mother of the ERA," Martha W. Griffiths, a peppery and quick-witted Detroit Representative, was a key figure in bringing women's rights legislation to successful passage in Congress. During her 20 years in the U.S. House, Representative Griffiths compiled a distinguished record on tax reform and civil rights. She was the first woman to serve on the powerful Ways and Means Committee.

Martha Edna Wright was born on January 29, 1912, in Pierce City, Missouri. She was one of two children reared by Charles Elbridge Wright, a mailman, and Nell Sullinger Wright. Martha Wright graduated from Pierce City High School in 1930. Realizing that without an education her daughter would eventually be dependent on her future husband, Nell Wright took on extra jobs to pay for Martha's college tuition.[1] Her mother's foresight and her paternal grandmother's struggle to raise three children after the death of her husband inspired Martha Wright to pursue equal rights for women. She attended the University of Missouri at Columbia, earning an A.B. in political science in 1934. In college she met and married Hicks G. Griffiths, a future Michigan Democratic Party chairman and her husband of 62 years until his death in 1996. The couple studied law at the University of Michigan, where Martha Griffiths worked on the staff of the *Michigan Law Review*. She graduated with an LL.B. in 1940 and was admitted to the bar the next year. Her first job was working in the legal department of the American Automobile Insurance Association in Detroit. During World War II she worked as a contract negotiator in the Detroit district for Army Ordnance. In 1946, Griffiths opened her own law practice; Hicks joined a few months afterward. A year later, G. Mennan "Soapy" Williams,

heir of the Mennan toiletries fortune and a former college classmate, became a partner in the firm.

Martha Griffiths entered politics at her husband's suggestion by making an unsuccessful bid for a seat in the Michigan house of representatives in 1946. She later won election to the state legislature in 1948 and 1950. During her first term she and her husband organized the Michigan Democratic Club, which engineered the election of G. Mennan Williams as governor. In the fall of 1952, Griffiths captured the Democratic nomination for a seat in the U.S. Congress from a Michigan district encompassing northwest Detroit and some outlying suburbs but lost the general election by a margin of 10,500 votes (or about six percent of the total) to Republican Charles G. Oakman. In April 1953, Governor Williams appointed her a recorder and judge of recorders court in Detroit. The following November she was elected as judge and served until 1954. At the time, she observed, "It is at least an unusual experience to assist for four years in making the laws of this state, and then sit as a judge of people charged with breaking those laws."[2] During her brief tenure she conducted more than 430 criminal examinations, including a highly publicized teamsters' conspiracy case.

The name recognition Griffiths garnered as a 1952 candidate and as a judge helped her mount another bid for the Detroit seat in the U.S. House in 1954. She revived from her initial campaign a district-wide tour by house-trailer—meeting tens of thousands of voters in their neighborhoods and serving them refreshments. Facing Oakman in the general election, Griffiths unseated the incumbent with about a 7,000-vote margin, 52 to 48 percent. Griffiths's victory came without the support of organized labor and the state's Democratic Party, as both backed other candidates.3 Despite this opposition, Griffiths never was seriously challenged again, winning nine more terms and gradually increasing her margins of victory: 53 percent in 1956, 69 percent in 1966, and 80 percent in 1970.4

The second woman from Michigan elected to the U.S. House, Griffiths was appointed to the Banking and Currency and Government Operations committees. During the 91st Congress (1969–1971) she served on the Select Committee on Crime, and she also had a seat on the Joint Study Budget Control Committee during the 92nd (1971–1973) and 93rd (1973–1975) Congresses. In the 90th (1967–1969) through 93rd Congresses, Griffiths chaired the Select Committee on the House Beauty Shop, a largely ceremonial assignment which oversaw the institution's operations.

In a move that astonished many observers, Griffiths ran for her former position as judge of the Detroit recorders court but was defeated in the April 1959 election. She later explained that she was motivated by a desire to return to Detroit and by her frustration with the protocols and pace of the committees, particularly the Banking and Currency Committee.5 Griffiths retained her House seat, however, and a year later she was re-elected to Congress with 58 percent of the vote.

Congresswomen had lobbied Speaker Sam Rayburn of Texas in 1961 to assign a woman to the prominent Ways and Means Committee, extracting a pledge from him that an appointment would be made at the next vacancy. Rayburn died in November 1961, but his promise was fulfilled in 1962 when Griffiths became the first woman Representative to win appointment to Ways and Means. Eventually, she became the fourth-ranking Member on that powerful panel. She also was assigned to the Joint Economic Committee, where she served through the 93rd Congress and eventually chaired the Subcommittee on Fiscal Policy. From both of these prominent positions, Congresswoman Griffiths pursued tax reform and proposed legislation to repeal the excise tax on automobiles, to provide tax relief for single parents, to amend tax laws to aid married couples and widows, and to reduce social

security taxes paid by low-income families. Her skills as a former judge, solid preparation, and ability to pick apart arguments, along with her sometimes blunt style, made her a fearsome opponent. She was especially attentive to frequent requests from women on how to circumvent discrimination in the workplace. On one occasion, when it came to light that a major airline fired a flight attendant on the grounds that she was going to be married soon, Griffiths grilled the airline's personnel manager: "You point out that you are asking a bona fide occupational exception that a stewardess be young, attractive, and single. What are you running, an airline or a whorehouse?"6

In 1964, Griffiths made one of her two greatest contributions to the women's rights movement. As the House Judiciary Committee began to deliberate a landmark civil rights bill pertaining to racial discrimination, Griffiths argued that sexual discrimination must be added to it. She did much to frame the sex discrimination amendment to Title VII of the 1964 Civil Rights Act and later prompted the new Equal Employment Opportunity Commission to enforce the act more vigorously. She relied on a deft legislative move to secure her amendment. The chairman of the powerful Rules Committee, Democrat Howard Smith of Virginia, was preparing to make his own sexual discrimination amendment to the bill, in hopes of making the bill so controversial as to derail the entire Civil Rights Act. Griffiths, realizing that Smith would easily bring 100 southern votes if he introduced the amendment on the floor, held back on introducing the amendment herself. When Smith made the argument in the well of the House, Members erupted in laughter and jeers.7 Griffiths immediately took to the floor to make her case. "I presume that if there had been any necessity to point out that women were a second-class sex, the laughter would have proved it," she scolded colleagues. The chamber fell silent.8 With a southern bloc voting for the amendment and Griffiths's own efforts to line up votes, the measure was passed and added to the act. Though many of the southern lawmakers who passed the amendment voted against the whole Civil Rights Act of 1964, the House and Senate eventually passed the bill, and President Lyndon Johnson signed it into law that year.

Griffiths also was pivotal in bringing the Equal Rights Amendment (ERA) to a vote, eventually steering it to successful passage in the House. Though she originally thought that the way to secure women's rights was to bring case after case before the Supreme Court, Griffiths eventually came to believe that a constitutional amendment was the only way to overcome the high bench's history of decisions which, in her view, denied that women were "'persons' within the meaning of the Constitution."9

sure that when I had Number 199 signed up, I rushed to his office, and Hale Boggs became Number 200."10 Griffiths got the 218 signatures in the required time, and on August 10, 1970, took to the House Floor to open debate. "Mr. Speaker, this is not a battle between the sexes—nor a battle between this body and women," Griffiths said. "This is a battle with the Supreme Court of the United States."11 With 62 Members not voting, the House passed the ERA by a vote of 352 to 15.12 Later that fall the Senate voted to amend the ERA with a clause exempting women from the draft. The House and Senate

"My grandmother wanted to live long enough to vote for a woman President. I'll be satisfied if I live to see a woman go before the Supreme Court and hear the Justices acknowledge, 'Gentlemen, she's human. She deserves the protection of our laws.'"

—MARTHA W. GRIFFITHS

Every year since she entered the House in 1955, she had introduced ERA legislation, only to watch while the bill died in the Judiciary Committee.

In 1970, Congresswoman Griffiths relied on the discharge petition, a little-used parliamentary procedure which required that she get a majority (218 of the House's 435 Members) to support her effort to bring the bill out of committee and onto the floor for general debate and a vote. For nearly 40 days, Griffiths stalked reluctant Congressmen, cornering them on the House Floor after roll call votes, visiting their offices, and calling in favors in order to add names to the petition. At one point, she approached the Democratic Whip, Hale Boggs of Louisiana, for his signature. Boggs at first demurred. "But he promised to sign as Number 200, convinced that I would never make it," Griffiths recalled. "You may be

failed to work out their differences in conference committee before Congress adjourned for the year. Griffiths began the process again, and this time the amendment cleared the House in 1971 and was approved by the Senate in March 1972 without revision. The ERA, however, was ratified by only 35 of the requisite 38 states and never became part of the Constitution. Despite the amendment's ultimate failure, Griffiths's recognition soared after her work on ERA. In 1970, she was rumored to be in consideration for Majority Whip and, therefore, the first woman to hold a major leadership post; however, she never was selected for that position.13

Griffiths declined to run for an 11th term in 1974, citing age and a wish to spend time with her family as her reasons for leaving. She did not disappear from politics, however, returning in 1976 as the chair of the Rules Committee for

THOUGH SHE ORIGINALLY
THOUGHT THAT THE WAY TO
SECURE WOMEN'S RIGHTS WAS TO
BRING CASE AFTER CASE BEFORE
THE SUPREME COURT, GRIFFITHS
EVENTUALLY CAME TO BELIEVE
THAT A CONSTITUTIONAL AMEND-
MENT WAS THE ONLY WAY TO
OVERCOME THE HIGH BENCH'S
HISTORY OF DECISIONS WHICH, IN
HER VIEW, DENIED THAT WOMEN
WERE "'PERSONS' WITHIN THE
MEANING OF THE CONSTITUTION."

the Democratic National Convention, and in 1982, becomingMichigan's first elected lieutenant governor on a ticket with Michigan Representative James J. Blanchard. In 1986, the pair was re-elected, but Blanchard decided to drop the 78-year-old Griffiths from the ticket for a third term because of her age. "Ridiculous!" she retorted. She then told a crowd of reporters: "The biggest problem in politics is that you help some s.o.b. get what he wants and then he throws you out of the train."[14] Blanchard lost in the general election to Republican John Engler, an outcome many observers attributed to disaffected women and senior votes that Griffiths had helped swing to Blanchard in the previous two elections. After her terms as lieutenant governor, Griffiths resumed practicing law. Martha Griffiths died of pneumonia at her home in Armada, Michigan, on April 22, 2003.

FOR FURTHER READING

Biographical Directory of the United States Congress, "Martha Wright Griffiths," http://bioguide.congress.gov

George, Emily. *Martha W. Griffiths* (Washington, D.C.: University Press of America, 1982).

MANUSCRIPT COLLECTIONS

Library of Congress (Washington, D.C.), Manuscript Division. *Oral History:* two folders. Transcript in the Oral History Collection of the U.S. Association of Former Members of Congress. Sound recording in the Library's Motion Picture, Broadcasting and Recorded Sound Division.

Radcliffe Institute for Advanced Study, Harvard University (Cambridge, MA), Schlesinger Library, http://www.radcliffe.edu/schles. *Oral History:* 1974–1976. Interview of Martha Griffiths by Katie Louchheim. Closed.

University of Michigan (Ann Arbor, MI), Michigan Historical Collections, Bentley Historical Library. *Papers:* 1956–1976, 60 linear feet and eight oversized volumes. The collection consists primarily of correspondence with constituents and lobbying groups on matters on legislation. Subjects covered include civil rights, assistance to the poor, health care for the aged, and environmental protection. Other subjects include the war in Vietnam, tension among the races, and the Watergate crisis. Of particular interest are files documenting Griffiths's work on the Ways and Means Committee, notably of her efforts for equity in benefits accorded to American women. A finding aid is available in the repository and online: http://www.hti.umich.edu.

NOTES

1 Martha Griffiths, Oral History Interview, 29 October 1979, U.S. Association of Former Members of Congress (hereinafter cited as USAFMOC), Manuscript Room, Library of Congress, Washington, D.C.: 3–4.
2 *Current Biography, 1955* (H.W. Wilson and Company, 1955): 244–245.
3 Griffiths, USAFMOC, Oral History Interview: 3–4.
4 "Election Statistics, 1920 to Present," http://clerk.house.gov/members/electionInfo/elections.html.
5 Griffiths, Oral History Interview, USAFMOC: 32–34.
6 Emily George, *Martha W. Griffiths* (Lanham, MD: University Press of America, 1982): 154.
7 Griffiths, Oral History Interview, USAFMOC: 74–75; David E. Kyvig, *Explicit and Authentic Acts: Amending the U.S. Constitution, 1776–1995* (Lawrence: University Press of Kansas, 1996): 402–403.
8 Karen Foerstel, *Biographical Dictionary of Congressional Women* (Westport, CT: Greenwood Press, 1999): 109–110.
9 *Congressional Record*, House, 91st Cong., 2nd sess. (10 August 1970): 28005; see also the Griffiths Oral History Interview, USAFMOC: 82–83.
10 Chamberlin, *A Minority of Members*: 260.
11 *Congressional Record*, House, 91st Cong., 2nd sess. (10 August 1970): 28004–28005.
12 *Congressional Record*, House, 91st Cong., 2nd sess. (10 August 1970): 28036–28037; Kyvig, *Explicit and Authentic Acts*: 402–404.
13 "A Woman as House Whip?" 7 July 1970, *Washington Post*: B3.
14 "Michigan: Throw Mama from the Train," 17 September 1990, *Newsweek*: 34.

Coya Knutson
1912–1996

UNITED STATES REPRESENTATIVE ★ DEMOCRAT FROM MINNESOTA
1955–1959

Unlike so many women whose marriage connection catapulted them to Congress, Coya Knutson's familial ties brought her promising political career to a premature close. Knutson's work in the House, devoted largely to protecting the family farm and opening educational opportunities, unraveled after her husband publicly called on her to resign. "I am not a feminist or anything else of that sort," Knutson once explained. "I do not use my womanhood as a weapon or a tool. . . . What I want most is to be respected and thought of as a person rather than as a woman in this particular job. I would like to feel that I am respected for my ability, my honesty, my judgment, my imagination, and my vision."[1]

Cornelia "Coya" Genevive Gjesdal was born on August 22, 1912, in Edmore, North Dakota, to Christian and Christine (Anderson) Gjesdal, Norwegian immigrant farmers. She attended the public schools of Edmore, worked on her father's farm, and, in 1934, earned a B.S. degree from Concordia College in Moorhead, Minnesota. Coya completed postgraduate work at the State Teachers College in Moorhead. In 1935, she briefly attended the Julliard School of Music in New York City. An unsuccessful appearance on a national amateur hour radio show convinced her to abandon a career as a professional singer. For the next dozen years, she taught high school classes in North Dakota and Minnesota. In 1940, Coya Gjesdal married Andy Knutson, her father's farm hand. The young couple moved to Oklee, Minnesota, his hometown, where they eventually operated a hotel and grain farm. In 1948 the Knutsons adopted an eight-year-old boy, Terry.[2]

Coya Knutson's involvement in politics developed through community activism. During World War II, Knutson served as a field agent for the Agricultural Adjustment Administration, investigating issues of price support. She helped establish the Oklee Medical Clinic, a local Red Cross branch, and the Community Chest Fund. She became a member of the Democratic-Farmer-Labor (DFL) Party, created in 1944 when state Democrats, a minority party, merged with a third party composed of agricultural and factory workers. In 1948, Knutson became a member of Red Lake County Welfare Board and was appointed chair of the DFL's Red Lake County organization. In the fall of 1950, she won election as a DFL candidate to the Minnesota house of representatives. Meanwhile, Andy Knutson resented his wife's burgeoning political career and lent little support. Moreover, their marriage deteriorated because of his alcoholism.

In 1954, Coya Knutson decided to make a run for the U.S. House, against the wishes of DFL Party leaders, who preferred she remain in the Minnesota legislature. Undeterred, Knutson crisscrossed the northwestern Minnesota district covering most of the Red River Valley, trying to meet as many farmers as possible to discuss agricultural issues and commodity prices. Knutson polled 45 percent to 24 percent against Curtiss Olson, the closest of her four rivals. In the general election, she challenged Republican Harold Hagen, a six-term incumbent. Knutson proved an adept and tireless campaigner, traveling more than 25,000 miles by car to stump in each of the district's 15 counties, at times delivering a dozen speeches per day.[3] The state DFL organization ignored her, and Knutson funded the campaign from her own savings. She favored farm supports and higher price levels for staples such as poultry, eggs, and milk.[4] She also attacked President Dwight Eisenhower and Secretary of Agriculture Ezra Taft Benson for pushing a plan for lower agricultural

IMAGE COURTESY OF THE LIBRARY OF CONGRESS

commodities pricing. She defeated Hagen by a 2,335-vote plurality out of more than 95,500 votes cast, interpreting her triumph as a "protest vote" against the Eisenhower administration's farm program.[5] When Knutson took her seat on January 3, 1955, she became the first Minnesota woman to serve in Congress.

With her background and largely rural constituency, Knutson followed the advice of neighboring Minnesota Representative John Blatnik and immediately wrote to Speaker Sam Rayburn of Texas and Majority Leader John McCormack of Massachusetts to express her interest in serving on the Agriculture Committee. Delegate Elizabeth Farrington of Hawaii had just been on the Agriculture Committee as its first woman Member in the previous Congress. But Chairman Harold Cooley of North Carolina, a 22-year veteran of the committee, had no intention of allowing another woman to serve with him. Speaker Rayburn intervened on Knutson's behalf.[6] Less than six months later, Cooley took to the House Floor to explain his newfound respect for Knutson. "Frankly, I would not swap her for one-half dozen men," Cooley admitted.[7]

During her tenure on Agriculture, Knutson's only committee assignment, she fought for a variety of programs to increase the distribution and profitability of farm commodities. She advocated higher price supports for farm products, an extension of the food stamp program into which farm surpluses could be channeled, and a federally supported school lunch program, including free milk for primary school students. Knutson also urged U.S. officials to reinvigorate the international export of foodstuffs, which had slackened between 1951 and 1954.[8] "American agriculture cannot prosper if it can only produce the food and fiber needed for the people of the United States. Agriculture must export or die," she said on the House Floor. One of her more inventive proposed measures would have permitted farmers to place fallow land into a national "conservation acreage reserve" and still be paid rent on the unproductive acreage from federal funds. Knutson argued that this would help replenish the soil, protect it from overuse, and, ultimately, boost future

yields.[9] As the economy went into recession in 1957–1958, Knutson was a caustic critic of the spending priorities of the Eisenhower White House. "All this talk about 'conquering outer space' is just jibberish if Congress and the administration do nothing about conquering the vast inner space in the hearts of young Americans—from the family farm, or whatever their origin—who have lost their jobs," she said.[10] Knutson authored 61 bills during her four years in the House, 24 of which addressed agricultural issues.[11]

The Minnesota Congresswoman's greatest legislative triumph, however, came in educational policy. She wrote a measure creating the first mechanisms for a federal student financial aid program. It drew on her experience as a teacher, work in the Minnesota state legislature, and deep desire to find a way for "poor country kids to go to college."[12] Based on government-administered loan programs in Norway, Knutson's measure, first introduced in 1956, called for federal loans for higher education based on a student's economic needs. "Educational freedom and progress are most dear to my heart," Knutson told colleagues on the House Floor. "We can't take the risk of limiting education to only those who can afford it. As our Nation grows, so should our democracy grow, and our thinking along educational lines should and must grow with it."[13] The legislation received a boost in 1957 when the Soviet Union launched *Sputnik*, the first man-made object to orbit the earth. Public debate swirled around whether or not the United States had fallen behind the Russians in education and the sciences. Knutson's bill passed in September 1958 as Title II of the National Defense Education Act (NDEA). The NDEA established a seven-year, $1 billion loan and grant program. Knutson's contribution was the creation of a program of loans for needy students. Among its other provisions were graduate fellowship programs for aspiring college instructors (Knutson called it "dollars for scholars") and a series of grants for college guidance programs, educational television, and the construction of vocational schools.[14]

Though popular and unusually effective as a new Member of Congress, Knutson had a tenuous grasp on her seat because of her strained relations with the DFL. Local leaders still resented Knutson's defeat of their hand-picked candidate in the 1954 primary. In 1956, against the wishes of party leaders, Knutson supported Senator Estes Kefauver of Tennessee for the Democratic presidential nomination, serving as his Minnesota state co-chair. DFL officials had lined up behind Adlai Stevenson of Illinois, the Democrats' 1952 nominee. Stevenson eventually won the presidential nomination, but DFL leaders privately fumed at Knutson. Still, in the 1956 primaries, Knutson was unopposed and benefited from public notoriety generated by her tour with Kefauver. Knutson turned back a challenge from Harold Hagen with 53 percent of the vote, a 6,000-vote plurality out of almost 112,000 cast.

Congresswoman Knutson's political problems mushroomed when angry DFL leaders conspired with Andy Knutson to subvert her political career. As early as 1957, DFL politicians approached her husband for his help in supporting an alternative candidate in the 1958 primaries. Jealous of his wife's success, broke, and deeply suspicious of her principal legislative aide, Bill Kjeldahl, Andy Knutson threw his support behind local DFL leader Marvin Evenson. At the district convention in May 1958, Coya Knutson's supporters mounted a frenzied defense and managed to retain the nomination for a third term. Days after the convention, Andy Knutson released a letter to the press (written by DFL officials) which asked his wife not to run for re-election. The *Fargo Forum* reprinted the letter and coined the phrase, "Coya, Come Home." The Associated Press picked up the story and sent it over the national wires. Andy Knutson then sent another letter, a press release also drafted by DFL leaders, which publicized the Knutsons' marital problems. These revelations, along with Andy Knutson's accusations that Kjeldahl exercised "dictatorial influence on my wife" (hinting at a love affair between Kjeldahl and the Congresswoman) were political dynamite.

Coya Knutson was hamstrung because she believed that public expectations of duty to family prevented her from attacking her husband's charges frontally. She settled on a policy of refusing to discuss her married life, submerging from public view a long history of physical and mental abuse by her spouse.[15] "It has always been my belief that an individual's family life is a personal matter," Knutson told the *Washington Post*.[16] House colleagues rallied to her support. The first time she entered the chamber after the story broke, she recalled, "I was so busy shaking hands I had no time for anything else."[17]

Representative Knutson survived another challenge from Evenson (who again received Andy's endorsement) in the September DFL primary, defeating him by more than 4,000 votes.[18] But she entered the general election severely compromised and without DFL support. Her opponent was Odin E. Langen, a Minneapolis native and the Republican leader in the state legislature. Pitching himself as a "family man," Langen brought his wife and son to campaign events, in stark contrast to Andy Knutson's absence from his wife's re-election rallies.[19] Langen won with a 1,390-vote margin out of slightly more than 94,300 cast. Knutson, the only incumbent Democrat nationwide to be unseated by a Republican in 1958, filed a formal complaint with the Special House Elections Subcommittee, arguing that she had the victim of a "malicious conspiracy" between her husband, DFL opponents, and associates of Langen.[20] Coya and Andy Knutson testified before a subcommittee on campaign expenditures, with Andy expressing regret that his wife's political opponents had "duped" him.[21] A majority of the committee agreed that "the exploitation of the family life of Mrs. Knutson was a contributing cause to her defeat."[22] But the committee found no evidence to link Langen directly to the alleged conspiracy and thus ended its investigation.[23]

Coya Knutson challenged Langen again in 1960, this time with Andy Knutson's support. She managed to defeat the DFL's handpicked candidate in the September primary, State Senator Roy Wiseth.[24] In the general election, however, she lost to the incumbent, 52 to 48 percent. In June 1961 President John F. Kennedy appointed Knutson the liaison officer for the Department of Defense in the Office of Civil Defense, where she served from 1961 to 1970. In 1962, the Knutsons were divorced; Andy died in

1969. In 1977, Knutson ran for Congress again but failed to capture the DFL Party nomination in a special election primary. Retiring from the political scene, Knutson lived with her son's family and helped raise her grandchildren.[25] On October 10, 1996, Coya Knutson died at the age of 82.

FOR FURTHER READING

Beito, Gretchen Urnes. *Coya Come Home: A Congresswoman's Journey* (Los Angeles: Pomegranate Press, Ltd., 1990).

Biographical Directory of the United States Congress, "Coya Gjesdal Knutson," http://bioguide.congress.gov

MANUSCRIPT COLLECTION

Minnesota Historical Society (St. Paul, MN). *Papers:* 1952–1980, 1.25 cubic feet. Includes constituent correspondence, news releases, speeches, clippings, legislative and campaign material, and newspaper and magazine articles about her. A finding aid is available in the repository. *Papers:* Gretchen Urnes Beito's research materials on Coya Knutson, 1930–1990, 0.75 cubic foot. Correspondence, theses, research materials, and a manuscript draft.

NOTES

1 *Congressional Record,* House, 85th Cong., 2nd sess. (15 May 1958): 8791–8792.

2 For more on her early life, see the biography by Gretchen Urnes Beito, *Coya Come Home: A Congresswoman's Journey* (Los Angeles: Pomegranate Press, Inc., 1990). A number of detailed obituaries also marked Knutson's death in 1996: Chuck Haga, "'Come Home' Coya Dies; Husband's Plea Probably Caused Congresswoman's Defeat," 11 October 1996, *Minneapolis Star Tribune:* 1A; "Coya Knutson, Minnesota's Only Woman Elected to Congress, Dies," 12 October 1996, *Saint Paul Pioneer Press:* 1B; Robert McG. Thomas, Jr., "Coya Knutson, 82, Legislator; Husband Sought Her Defeat," 12 October 1996, *New York Times:* 52; "Coya Knutson Dies at 82; Served 2 Terms in Congress," 13 October 1996, *Washington Post:* B4.

3 Beito, *Coya Come Home:* 147; "Gals Tell How They Got Elected," 20 January 1955, *Washington Post:* 44.

4 Catherine Harrington, "Congresswomen: Results Show Gals Are Better Vote Getters," 4 November 1954, *Washington Post:* 52.

5 "Election Statistics, 1920 to Present," http://clerk.house.gov/members/electionInfo/elections.html; Harrington, "Congresswomen: Results Show Gals Are Better Vote Getters."

6 Beito, *Coya Come Home:* 160; see also, Hope Chamberlin, *A Minority of Members: Women in the U.S. Congress* (New York: Praeger, 1973): 266; and, C.P. Trussell, "House Democrats Are Assigned to Their Seats on Committees," 14 January 1955, *New York Times:* 10.

7 *Congressional Record,* House, 84th Cong., 1st sess. (30 July 1955): 12445. Cooley also inserted a very favorable report on Knutson into the *Congressional Record.* See *Congressional Record,* House, 84th Cong., 2nd sess. (24 July 1956): 14313.

8 See, for example, *Congressional Record,* House, 84th Cong., 1st sess. (12 July 1955): 10338–10339.

9 *Congressional Record,* House, 84th Cong., 1st sess. (13 April 1955): 4416.

10 *Congressional Record,* House, 85th Cong., 2nd sess. (22 April 1958): 6965–6966.

11 Beito, *Coya Come Home:* 262–263.

12 Susan Tolchin, *Women in Congress* (Washington, D.C.: Government Printing Office, 1976): 45; see also, Eileen Summers, "Lady Solons Find Alarm But No Sputnik Hysteria," 7 January 1958, *Washington Post:* B4.

13 *Congressional Record*, House, 85th Cong., 1st sess. (27 February 1957): 2734.

14 Steven Stathis, *Landmark Legislation: 1774–2002* (Washington, D.C.: Congressional Quarterly Press, 2003): 249–250; *Congressional Record*, House, 85th Cong., 2nd sess. (8 August 1958): 16743; James L. Sundquist, *Politics and Policy: The Eisenhower, Kennedy, and Johnson Years* (Washington, D.C.: Brookings Institute, 1968).

15 Detailed in Beito, *Coya Come Home*.

16 Marie Smith, "Mrs. Knutson Sidesteps Mate's Plea To Quit Congress and Return Home," 9 May 1958, *Washington Post*: A1.

17 "Lady Lawmakers Vote Coya 'Aye,'" 13 May 1958, *Washington Post*: B4; Jean White, "Working Wives' Mates Dispute [Andy] Knutson's View," 11 May 1958, *Washington Post*: A3; Maxine Cheshire, "Rep. Knutson, as 'Breadwinner,' Rejects Husband's Plea to Quit," 10 May 1958, *Washington Post*: A1.

18 John C. McDonald, "Mrs. Knutson Pulls Ahead," 10 September 1958, *Christian Science Monitor*: 18.

19 Peg Johnson, "Coya's Ode to 'Mr. Sam' All Part of Campaign Plan," 12 September 1958, *Washington Post*: C15.

20 One other Democratic Representative, Brooks Hays of Arkansas, was unseated by a segregationist write-in candidate. Austin C. Wehrwein, "Minnesota Says: Coya, Come Home," 6 November 1958, *New York Times*: 23. See also Knutson's comment on the episode in Maxine Cheshire, "Plea to 'Come Home' Just 'Fraud' to Coya," 29 November 1958, *Washington Post*: A1; and "Inquiry Is Asked By Mrs. Knutson," 29 November 1958, *New York Times*: 44.

21 Hearings before the Special Committee to Investigate Campaign Expenditures, *Matter of Complaints Filed Relative to the Elections Held in the 5th Congressional District of Arkansas and the 9th Congressional District of Minnesota*, U.S. House of Representatives, 85th Cong., 2nd sess., 15–17 December 1958 (Washington, D.C.: Government Printing Office, 1959).

22 Karen Foerstel, *Biographical Directory of Congressional Women* (Westport, CT: Greenwood Press, 1999): 152–153.

23 Tom Nelson, "Coya Is Denied Full-Scale Quiz," 18 December 1958, *Washington Post*: A2.

24 "Comeback Sought by Mrs. Knutson," 11 September 1960, *New York Times*: 54.

25 Chuck Haga, "Coya Knutson: A 'Fighter' and 'Loving Soul,'" 15 October 1996, *Minneapolis Star Tribune*: 7B.

Kathryn E. Granahan
1894–1979

UNITED STATES REPRESENTATIVE ★ DEMOCRAT FROM PENNSYLVANIA
1956–1963

The widow of Philadelphia Democratic Congress-man William Granahan, Kathryn Granahan suc-ceeded her late husband and followed his example as a liberal New Dealer who supported workers' rights, welfare legislation, and civil rights. From her post as chair of the Post Office and Civil Service Subcommittee on Postal Operations, however, Granahan embarked on a moral mission to halt the spread of pornography. "The peddling of smut to children is a heinous crime that must be stopped," Granahan explained, noting that many par-ents and localities "are seemingly unaware of the size and seriousness of this problem."[1] During her congressional service, Granahan linked obscenities in literature and sex-ual content in movies to juvenile delinquency and even communism.[2]

On December 7, 1894, Kathryn Elizabeth O'Hay was born to James and Julia (Reily) O'Hay in Easton, Pennsylvania. She graduated from Easton High School and Mount St. Joseph Collegiate Institute (later Chestnut Hill College) in Philadelphia, Pennsylvania. She became the supervisor of public assistance in the state auditor general's department and liaison officer between that department and the department of public assistance, Commonwealth of Pennsylvania, from 1940 to 1943. In that job, O'Hay met William T. Granahan, a World War I veteran, member of the state Democratic committee, Democratic ward leader in Philadelphia, and chief dis-bursing officer for the Pennsylvania treasury. In 1943, the couple married. A year later, William Granahan won election as a Democrat to a U.S. congressional district encompassing Philadelphia's west end. He lost his bid for re-election in the national Republican sweep of 1946, but recaptured his seat from the incumbent, Robert N.

McGarvey, and returned to office in 1949. Congressman Granahan earned a reputation as a progressive liberal dur-ing his years of service as Ranking Member on the House Interstate and Foreign Commerce Committee. He was an original sponsor of the Full Employment Act and also had been an author of a Fair Employment Practices Bill and other antidiscrimination legislation.[3] Representative Granahan caused something of a stir when, in 1945, he broke with precedent and refused to resign his post as ward leader; he held the position throughout his House service.[4] Having no children, the Granahans worked closely together on the needs of the district's constituents. Kathryn assisted her husband both within the district and in his Washington office, residing with him in their Mayflower Hotel apartment for much of his decade of service. She also served as chair of the board of governors of the Women's Democratic Club of Philadelphia and was a trustee of several other civic service associations.

Shortly after winning the 1956 primary, Congressman Granahan passed away unexpectedly on May 25, 1956. A week after his death, local committeemen elected Kathryn Granahan to succeed William Granahan as ward leader. Several days later Philadelphia's Democratic powerbro-kers chose her to run for her husband's vacant seat in the House, both for the remainder of the 84th Congress (1955–1957) and for the full term in the 85th Congress (1957–1959).[5] Mrs. Granahan was a natural choice to replace her husband. She understood the needs of her community and was accustomed to commuting and work-ing between Washington, D.C., and the district. As the new political leader in western Philadelphia, Granahan sought to change the manner in which politics were con-

POCKET CONGRESSIONAL DIRECTORY, 85TH CONGRESS

ducted in the old Democratic ward. She eliminated the traditional beer barrel at political meetings and replaced it with tea and cookies. "I believe that only the highest type of people should be in politics-even in the lowest echelons," Granahan declared.[6] A self proclaimed "mad hatter," she campaigned wearing a lucky hat which she would not change until after her election. On November 6, 1956, Kathryn Granahan won the special election to the remainder of the 84th Congress and at the same time was elected to serve a full term for the 85th Congress, winning 62 percent of the vote against GOP candidate Robert Frankenfield. Her service began with the special election, thus giving her seniority over incoming freshmen in the 85th Congress. In 1958 and 1960, Granahan topped her Republican challengers by ever-wider margins—66 percent and 72 percent, respectively.[7]

Granahan made an unsuccessful bid to replace her late husband and become the first woman to serve on the Interstate and Foreign Commerce Committee. Instead, she received appointments to two committees: District of Columbia and Post Office and Civil Service. After a year, she left the District of Columbia Committee to accept a seat on Government Operations. In 1959, she became chair of the Post Office and Civil Service Subcommittee on Postal Operations, where she served for the remainder of her House career. In 1960, she was selected as a delegate to the Democratic National Convention which nominated Massachusetts Senator John F. Kennedy as the party's presidential candidate.

Granahan's primary legislative undertaking was an effort to halt the spread of pornographic materials through the U.S. mail, specifically those which worked their way into the hands of children and teenagers. Legislating for public morality seemed to contradict her liberal credentials, but Granahan nevertheless pressed on with two months of hearings in 1959 that broadly addressed the dangers pornography presented in American society. "There are many things we don't allow our juveniles to do," she said. "We don't allow them to drink, carry guns or drive vehicles. So why allow these filth merchants to sell youngsters material which is a contributing cause of juvenile delin-

quency?"[8] In April 1959, using her clout as a subcommittee chair, she appealed to private citizens and organizations to help take the lead in crushing the pornography trade. Granahan charged that the Post Office Department had been "lax in halting the circulation of pornography" and called on Postmaster General Arthur Summerfield to appear as a witness before her committee.[9] In August, she introduced legislation requiring mandatory jail sentences for persons found guilty of operating pornographic mail order businesses. At the time, she told the *Christian Science Monitor*, "I don't want to repeal the Constitution or deny a free press. It is a most difficult problem to solve."[10] Granahan also was a chief sponsor of a bill passed by the House in September 1959 that strengthened the post office's power to impound mail addressed to recipients suspected of mailing pornographic materials.

In 1961, Congresswoman Granahan tried to counsel the Supreme Court to issue stricter guidelines to help authorities determine if publications were obscene. The high court eventually rendered a decision in *Manual Enterprises v. Postmaster General Day*, a case in which the postmaster of Alexandria, Virginia, had determined that hundreds of magazines were unfit for delivery. The Justices ruled that post office officials could not arbitrate what constituted pornography. Granahan, disappointed by the finding, delivered a speech that lambasted the decision and implied that Congress itself must curtail the distribution of pornography. "It is my earnest hope that prompt and vigorous action will now be taken to strengthen the criminal laws and close the U.S. mails to muck merchants and vendors of pornography and propaganda of perverts," she told colleagues.[11] She also tried her best to link pornography to national security: "There is a campaign of filth and smut aimed at the nation's youth," she once warned, "that might well prove to be communist inspired."[12]

Meanwhile, Representative Granahan also used her Postal Operations chair to wage a campaign to clean up motion pictures, an industry over which her panel had no jurisdiction, except as movies were often sent through the mails. Nevertheless, for three days in February 1960, her subcommittee interviewed witnesses. Granahan urged motion picture officials to follow a policy of "effective self-regulation." She argued that the core question at stake was not one of "censorship, but of propriety," that is, whether movie content was "degrading or objectionable when tested against the moral standards of the American public."[13]

When the 1960 Census revealed that Pennsylvania would lose three of its House seats, a political fight erupted among state party officials. U.S. Representative Bill Green, who also served as the powerful Democratic chairman of Philadelphia, wanted to keep the city's six seats in the House. But as part of a compromise plan, Green and other Democratic leaders chose Granahan's seat for elimination. As the only woman among the Philadelphia Representatives and, moreover, the only potential woman candidate statewide for the 1962 election, Granahan and her supporters (including women's groups) protested bitterly but kept their dissent within the confines of the party.[14] Granahan eventually agreed to the plan and promised not to run against the incumbent whose new district would encompass her old one. As recompense, Green (who had orchestrated a huge voter turnout for John F. Kennedy in Philadelphia which helped him carry the state in 1960) convinced the President to appoint Kathryn Granahan Treasurer of the United States after the post was vacated in April 1962.

Granahan finished the House term for the 87th Congress (1961–1963) on January 3, 1963, and began her Cabinet appointment on January 9, 1963. Among her proposals as the fourth woman to head the Treasury was the return of the two-dollar bill to circulation. In May of 1965, Mrs. Granahan underwent brain surgery for a blood clot caused by an accidental fall. While the surgery was successful, Granahan worked a reduced schedule and her capacity to serve as Treasurer eventually was called into question. On June 10, 1966, a Philadelphia judge set aside a petition to have her declared incompetent and to appoint a guardian to her estate. Four months later, Granahan submitted her resignation to Treasury Secretary Henry H. Fowler. Kathryn Granahan died in Norristown, Pennsylvania, on July 10, 1979.

FOR FURTHER READING

Biographical Directory of the United States Congress, "Kathryn Elizabeth Granahan," http://bioguide.congress.gov

NOTES

1 "Pornography Scored: Nation-wide Drive Is Asked to 'Smash' Business," 19 May 1959, *New York Times*: 18; "Moral Sabotage Seen: Church Leader Says Reds Use Pornography as Weapon," 23 May 1959, *New York Times*: 25.

2 Susan Tolchin, *Women In Congress* (Washington, D.C.: Government Printing Office, 1976): 29.

3 "Rep. Granahan Dies Serving Fifth Term," 26 May 1956, *Washington Post*: 18; "W.T. Granahan, House Democrat," 26 May 1956, *New York Times*: 17.

4 "Kathryn E. Granahan," *Current Biography, 1959* (New York: H.W. Wilson and Company, 1959): 157.

5 "Mrs. Granahan Named," 12 June 1956, *New York Times*: 18.

6 George Dixon, "Washington Scene: A Sweet Ward Leader," 16 April 1957, *Washington Post*: A19; George Dixon, "Washington Scene: A Gentlewoman Ward Leader," 18 May 1957, *Washington Post*: A13.

7 "Election Statistics, 1920 to Present" http://clerk.house.gov/members/electionInfo/elections.html.

8 Joan Cook, "Kathryn O'Hay Granahan Dies; A Former Head of U.S. Treasury," 13 July 1979, *New York Times*: A14.

9 Richard Peason, "Kathryn Granahan, 82, U.S. Treasurer," 13 July 1979, *Washington Post*: D7.

10 "Study Urged to Rid Mails of Obscenity," 28 August 1958, *Christian Science Monitor*: 2.

11 *Congressional Record*, House, 87th Cong., 2nd sess. (28 June 1962): 12119.

12 Tolchin, *Women in Congress*: 29.

13 Richard L. Lyons, "House Group Urges Less Sex in Movies, Film Ads," 5 February 1960, *Washington Post*: A19.

14 "Seat of Rep. Granahan Slated for Elimination," 10 January 1962, *Washington Post*: A9; Kenneth G. Gehret, "Political Sparks Start in Key Year in Pennsylvania," 24 January 1962, *Christian Science Monitor*: 3.

Florence P. Dwyer
1902-1976

UNITED STATES REPRESENTATIVE ★ REPUBLICAN FROM NEW JERSEY
1957-1973

Florence Price Dwyer, a New Jersey Representative who described herself as a "progressive" Republican, pushed for civil rights legislation, consumer protection measures, and institutional reform during her 16-year House career. Though she did not consider herself a feminist, Dwyer was a consistent champion of women's rights who supported the Equal Rights Amendment (ERA) and an "equal pay for equal work" bill modeled after one she had initially steered through the New Jersey state assembly.

Florence "Flo" Louise Price was born on July 4, 1902, in Reading, Pennsylvania. Educated in the public schools of Reading and Toledo, Ohio, she briefly attended college at the University of Toledo. Price left college to marry M. Joseph Dwyer, the Toledo football coach and, later, an industrial relations executive. The couple raised a son, Michael, and moved to Elizabeth, New Jersey. Florence Dwyer's role as a member of the local Parent Teacher Association initiated her interest in politics. She joined the Republican Club in Elizabeth in the 1930s: "At the time women were used to lick envelopes and take messages," she recalled.[1] A delegate to the Republican National Convention in 1944, Dwyer subsequently worked as a lobbyist in Trenton, the state capital, for the New Jersey Business and Professional Women's Clubs. State Assemblyman Joseph Brescher, who served as majority leader and speaker, hired Dwyer as his secretary. When Brescher retired in 1949, Dwyer succeeded him, serving from 1949 to 1957 and eventually rising to the assistant majority leader post.

In 1956, at the urging of New Jersey Senator Clifford Case, Dwyer entered the Republican primary for a U.S. House district just south of Newark. The district coincided with the Union County boundaries and encompassed the most industrialized part of the state. Dwyer's chief competitor was Irene T. Griffin, a former assemblywoman. But Dwyer's name recognition, her support across the party from moderates to conservatives, and her longtime base of support in Elizabeth, which sat in the eastern section of the district, helped her secure the nomination.[2] She faced a two-term incumbent Democrat, Harrison A. "Pete" Williams, Jr., in the general election. Historically a Republican stronghold, beginning in 1951, factionalism within the party had weakened the GOP's grip on the district. The 1956 campaign quickly became a contest over which of the candidates could best court the voters who supported President Dwight Eisenhower. Dwyer centered her campaign on domestic issues such as more funding for education and pressing for an equal-pay bill in Congress.[3] Vice President Richard Nixon campaigned for Dwyer, while Democratic presidential candidate Adlai Stevenson stumped for Williams. Dwyer's campaign literature read: "Ike Wants Flo" and "A Vote for Flo Is a Vote for Ike."[4] The incumbent President carried the district by nearly 80,000 votes, while Dwyer edged out Williams by a little more than 4,000. (Williams would go on to serve in the U.S. Senate for more than two decades.)

Dwyer quickly proved she could get votes on her own.[5] In her next four campaigns, she won increasingly by larger margins, garnering between 51 and 59 percent of the vote. Redistricting in 1966 cost Dwyer her traditional Elizabeth base, so she sought re-election in another newly realigned district, which included part of Union County and eastern Essex County to the north.[6] In the middle-class, suburban district, she crushed her opponents by margins of 33 to 50 percentage points.[7] In all, Dwyer won eight consecutive terms in the House. Throughout her career, she described herself to voters as a "moderate or

progressive Republican" who did not follow the party line "unless the measure benefits the people I represent and the national interest."[8] The Congresswoman was not afraid to stand apart from other Republicans. She once told House Minority Leader Charlie Halleck of Indiana, "When you see me walk on the floor wearing pink, you'll know I'm going to step to the left and vote with the Democrats. But if I'm wearing black or white, you'll know I'm with the Republicans."[9]

Dwyer served on the Committee on Government Operations throughout her term in the House. She particularly concerned herself with institutional reforms. In 1961, Dwyer gained notoriety as the leader of the "saintly seven," a group of GOP Members who voted with House Speaker Sam Rayburn of Texas and the Democrats to increase the membership of the Rules Committee, which controlled the flow of legislation on the House Floor.[10] The episode involved a bitter power struggle between Speaker Rayburn and Rules Committee Chairman Howard Smith of Virginia. The "saintly seven" were actually part of a group of 22 northern Republicans who supported the reform and declared their intention to "repudiate" a GOP alliance with southern Democrats "to attempt to narrow the base of our party, to dull its conscience, to transform it into a negative weapon of obstruction. . . ."[11] By a margin of 217 to 212, Rayburn prevailed. The vote changed House rules and undercut the power of a coalition of southern Democrats and conservative Republicans who used their influence on the committee to prevent major social legislation—including civil rights measures—from reaching the House Floor. In 1965, Dwyer authored legislation that called for a four-year term for Members of the House. A longer term "could greatly improve the quality of representation," Dwyer told the *New York Times*. "Under the present two-year system, most House Members must spend an excessive amount of time politicking and campaigning—simply to survive. A term of three or four years would give us time to think and plan and produce a more consistent and constructive legislative program."[12] During consideration of the Legislative Reorganization Act of 1970, she was author of an amendment requiring the

recording of individual teller votes. Prior to that rule change, Members merely walked down the aisle and were counted, but their names were not recorded.

Congresswoman Dwyer was an early supporter of civil rights reform. Just a month into her first term in 1957, she introduced a version of the Dwight D. Eisenhower administration's Civil Rights Bill.[13] The measure called for, among other things, the creation of a bipartisan Commission on Civil Rights to secure voting rights for African Americans in the South. It also provided for an assistant attorney general at the Department of Justice, tasked solely to civil rights issues. The New Jersey Congresswoman supported a constitutional amendment to outlaw the poll tax, which discriminated against African-American and poor white voters in the South. In 1960, Dwyer introduced a bill to create a "Commission on Equal Job Opportunity Under Government Contracts," which aimed at providing for fair contract award processes for minority businesses and individuals.[14] She often cast the necessity for civil rights reforms at home against the backdrop of the Cold War abroad. "If freedom has any meaning at all, if our opposition to world communism is at all justifiable, then we have no alternative but to make secure for all Americans—regardless of race or color or religion or national origin or economic status—the practice and opportunity of full freedom," she said on the House Floor. Equal opportunity in voting, education, work, and housing were essential, she argued.[15]

Dwyer championed women's issues in Congress in a consistent but unadorned manner. True to her initial campaign promise, she pursued a pay equity bill for women during her first term in the House. In March 1957, Representative Dwyer and colleague Cecil Harden of Indiana introduced "Equal Pay for Equal Work" legislation. "The need for equal pay is a matter of simple justice," Dwyer said. "Women are contributing more and more to the economic life of our country. And yet they are expected to accept a second-class role as far as wages are concerned."[16] Dwyer also was a firm and early supporter of the ERA, endorsing it during her first term in office on the observance of Susan B. Anthony Day.[17] Nevertheless, she refused to run her campaigns by appealing to her gender. "I am campaigning on my record," Dwyer once told group of New Jersey women. "I have never campaigned as a woman; if I can't take on any man running against me, I don't deserve to represent the women and men of the county."[18] When Republican Richard Nixon became President in 1969, she and four other GOP women from the House urged him to appoint more women to federal office. "None of us are feminists," Dwyer told Nixon. "We do not ask for special privileges. . . . Our sole purpose is to suggest ways and means by which women's rights as citizens and human beings may be better protected, discrimination against women be eliminated and women's ability to contribute to the economic, social and political life of the Nation be recognized."[19]

Dwyer decided not to run for re-election in 1972 to the 93rd Congress (1973–1975). Health issues, her age (she was 70), and yet another reconfiguration of her district convinced her to leave the House "with some reluctance."[20] Dwyer maintained, "The time has come to rearrange my priorities—to spend more time with my family and to devote myself to a number of matters which have not received my attention during my years in Congress."[21] Dwyer retired as Ranking Republican on the Government Operations and Banking and Currency committees. In the 1972 elections she campaigned actively for Republican candidate and State Senator Matthew J. Rinaldo, who won the seat to succeed her. Dwyer retired to Elizabeth, New Jersey, where she resided until her death on February 29, 1976.

FOR FURTHER READING

Biographical Directory of the United States Congress, "Florence Price Dwyer," http://bioguide.congress.gov

Tomlinson, Barbara J. "Making Their Way: A Study of New Jersey Congresswomen, 1924–1994." Ph.D. diss., Rutgers, The State University of New Jersey - New Brunswick, 1996.

MANUSCRIPT COLLECTION

Kean College of New Jersey (Union, NJ), Nancy Thompson Library. *Papers:* 1955–1972, 362 cubic feet.

Congressional papers, including correspondence, bills, speeches, photographs, radio broadcasts, campaign records, and memorabilia.

NOTES

1 "Jersey Honors Representative Dwyer," 24 September 1972, *New York Times*: 48.

2 George Cable Wright, "G.O.P. Split Spurs Two Jersey Races," 13 April 1956, *New York Times*: 15.

3 Edith Evans Asbury, "Close Race Seen as Woman Acts to Oust Democrat in 6th," 11 October 1956, *New York Times*: 34.

4 Asbury, "Close Race Seen as Woman Acts to Oust Democrat in 6th."

5 Hope Chamberlin, *A Minority of Members: Women in the U.S. Congress* (New York: Praeger, 1973): 269.

6 Martin Arnold, "Congresswoman Is the Favorite Over Professor Allen," 10 October, 1966, *New York Times*: 44.

7 Michael J. Dubin et al., *United States Congressional Elections, 1788–1997* (Jefferson, NC: McFarland & Company, Publishing, Inc., 1998); "Election Statistics, 1920 to Present," http://clerk.house.gov/members/electionInfo/index.html.

8 Milton Honig, "Mrs. Dwyer, G.O.P., Opposed in 6th by Mrs. Egolf," 10 October 1962, *New York Times*: 43.

9 Patricia Camp, "Florence Price Dwyer Dies, Supported Women's Rights," 1 March 1976, *Washington Post*: C6.

10 Marie Smith, "Ladybird Likes to Drive–No Limousine for Her," 26 February 1961, *Washington Post*: F2. Other members of the "saintly seven": Thomas B. Curtis of Missouri, John V. Lindsay of New York, Silvio O. Conte of Massachusetts, Perkins Bass of New Hampshire, Seymour Halpern of New York, and William T. Cahill of New Jersey.

11 Julian E. Zelizer, *On Capitol Hill: The Struggle to Reform Congress and Its Consequences, 1948–2000* (New York: Cambridge University Press, 2004): 56–60.

12 William V. Shannon, "Reforming the House—A Four Year Term?" 10 January 1965, *New York Times*: SM22.

13 "Rep. Dwyer Introduces Civil Rights Bill," 7 February 1957, *Washington Post*: C17.

14 *Congressional Record*, House, 87th Cong., 2nd sess. (27 August 1962): 17663; *Congressional Record*, House, 86th Cong., 2nd sess. (28 April 1960): 8932–8933.

15 *Congressional Record*, House, 86th Cong., 2nd sess. (11 March 1960): 5316.

16 *Congressional Record*, House, 85th Cong., 1st sess (25 March 1957): 4347–4348.

17 *Congressional Record*, House, 85th Cong., 1st sess. (19 July 1957): 12238.

18 Marybeth Weston, "Ladies' Day on the Hustings," 19 October 1958, *New York Times*: SM32.

19 Marie Smith, "Nixon Eyes Women," 9 July 1969, *Washington Post*: D1.

20 "Representative Dwyer to Retire After Her 8th Term in House," 15 April 1972, *New York Times*: 12; Ronald Sullivan, "G.O.P. Is Aided By Districting," 16 April 1972, *New York Times*: 71.

21 "Representative Dwyer to Retire After Her 8th Term in House."

Catherine Dean May

1914–2004

UNITED STATES REPRESENTATIVE ★ REPUBLICAN FROM WASHINGTON
1959–1971

The first woman to represent Washington state in the U.S. House of Representatives, Catherine May, entered public service after her father insisted that she not repeat his example of avoiding the political arena. Congresswoman May established herself as a moderate. She advocated for the needs of her agrarian district, congressional ethics, and women's rights, supporting such measures as the Equal Rights Amendment (ERA) and the inclusion of the sex discrimination clause in the 1964 Civil Rights Act.

Catherine Dean Barnes was born on May, 18, 1914, in Yakima, Washington, to Charles H. Barnes, a deparment-store owner and real estate broker, and Pauline Van Loon Barnes. She attended Yakima Valley Junior College and, in 1936, graduated from the University of Washington with a B.A. in English and speech. Catherine Barnes taught high school English in Chehalis, Washington. In 1940, she pursued a radio broadcasting career in Tacoma and Seattle. On January 18, 1943, she married James O. May. The following year, while waiting for her husband to be discharged from the U.S. Army, Catherine May worked as a writer and assistant commentator for the National Broadcasting Company in New York City. The couple returned to Yakima in 1946, where James May established a real estate and insurance business while she worked as a women's editor for a local radio station. The Mays raised a son and daughter, Jamie and Melinda. The couple became active in politics after Charles Barnes, whose department store went bankrupt in the Great Depression, revealed that his great regret in life was not participating in local government to address public problems.[1] The Mays joined the Young Republicans and became active precinct workers. In 1952, at James's urging, Catherine May ran for a seat as Yakima's representative in the Washington legislature.[2] Elected as a Republican, she served for six years.

When eight-term U.S. Representative Otis H. Holmes declined to seek re-election for his U.S. House seat in 1958, May entered the race against heavily favored Democrat Frank Le Roux (who had nearly unseated Holmes in 1956). The sprawling Washington state district was bordered by Idaho to the east, Oregon to the south, and the Cascade Mountain range to the west and extended into the Columbia River basin in the north. Running on a lean budget, May resorted to distributing handbills and going door-to-door to meet voters, while Le Roux bought billboards to reach the district's thinly spread electorate. May turned LeRoux's advertising against him, challenging him to a debate (which he declined) and delivering campaign speeches in which she declared: "Come out from behind those billboards."[3] May defeated Le Roux by a margin of 10,000 votes, tallying 54 percent of the total. That was the closest race Congresswoman May encountered in six successful campaigns, as she steadily increased her margins of victory: 59 percent in 1960, 65 percent in 1964, and 67 percent in 1968.[4] The 1964 election was especially noteworthy since the strong turnout against Republican presidential candidate Barry Goldwater cost four incumbent Washington Republicans their House seats.

May entered the 86th Congress (1959–1961) as the first Washington woman ever to serve in the U.S. Congress. Part of her campaign pledge to the farmers and poultry producers had been that she could secure a seat on the prestigious House Agriculture Committee. May's break came when Representative Katharine St. George of New York won a seat on the Republican Committee on Committees.

As a committee member, St. George could cast her state delegation's votes to select membership to various committees. For the Republicans, states were awarded a number of votes equal to the number of that delegation's GOP representatives. Committee members typically reserved their votes for Members of their own state delegations; however, St. George made an exception for May. With the clout of the largest congressional delegation at the time— including 25 Republicans—St. George secured May one of just three openings on the Agriculture Committee, where she served throughout her career.[5]

May also served briefly on the Committee on the District of Columbia, earning appointment at the opening of the 91st Congress (1969–1971) in January 1969. She left the District of Columbia Committee after just six months when she was offered a seat on a panel she long had sought because of the important Hanford Nuclear Power Plant located in her district: the Joint Committee on Atomic Energy. May established a record as a moderate Republican who generally backed the economic policies of the Dwight D. Eisenhower and Richard M. Nixon administrations and sought to curb the Great Society programs of the Lyndon B. Johnson administration.[6] In 1965, she was rewarded for her party loyalty with spots on the Republican Policy and Research Committee, which determined GOP positions on future legislation, and the Committee on Committees. Only on rare occasions, usually when agrarian and western power and utility issues were involved, did May break with her party.

Much of Congresswoman May's agenda focused on her assignment to the Agriculture Committee, where she tended to her district's farming interests. She championed domestic beet sugar production, a key agricultural industry in Washington. She favored establishment of a special fee on imported sugar and, in 1964, proposed a higher permanent quota for domestic beets. May cosponsored a joint resolution in 1967 to establish the U.S. World Food Study and Coordinating Commission, which examined the market structure of the food production industry. In addition, May also took an interest in using agricultural surpluses to help feed poor families and children. She amended the

1966 Child Nutrition Act to include children in overseas American-run schools in the school milk program. In 1970, Representative May sponsored the Nixon administration's proposal to provide free food stamps to families with monthly incomes of less than 30 dollars.

Another focus for May was the Hanford Nuclear Plant located on the Columbia River in her district. Originally built in secret to provide plutonium for the Manhattan Project and subsequent weapons projects, the Hanford Plant was targeted as a facility to produce nuclear energy for Washington state. In the early 1960s, May sought to preserve the reactor from reduced output or deactivation—a move urged by environmentalists concerned about the effects on local aquatic life. May countered that it provided cost-effective electric power and jobs. The reactor remained open, though the plutonium reactor was eventually shut down (the creation of steam power from uranium continued).[7] Eventually, opposition from coal power interests in Congress led the Nixon administration to deactivate the plant in the early 1970s.[8]

In the fall of 1966, May sponsored a measure to establish the House Select Committee on Standards of Official Conduct, serving on it briefly before it became a standing committee in early 1967. A series of congressional scandals—May specifically cited proceedings related to Representative Adam Clayton Powell's misuse of congressional funds as "the tip of the iceberg"—and her own experience with lobbyists and outside interest groups convinced her that the House needed an ethics committee.[9] "It concerned me," May later recalled, "I certainly had no claim to morality, I didn't feel superior, but I knew it was hurting Congress and that it was going to hurt the very institutions of freedom themselves."[10] Noting that the late 1960s was a time of social unrest in the United States, May emphasized that Americans needed to be able to trust their public officials: "The great danger was the people of America losing faith in their institutions—that is the beginning of the end of a nation."[11]

May supported women's rights legislation during her House career, noting after her first election that she had a "tremendous feeling of responsibility toward all women."[12]

May supported
women's rights legislation
during her House career,
noting after her first
election that she had
a "tremendous feeling
of responsibility
toward all women."

Nevertheless, she avoided defining herself as an activist. In part, she had to educate herself about discrimination at the national level. "I wondered what women were screaming about when I went to Congress, because we had had equal rights in the state of Washington for years," May recalled, concluding, "Boy, I learned."[13] She became active in a legislative sense, fighting on behalf of the Equal Pay Act of 1963, and joined a group of women lawmakers who demanded access to the then-all-male House gym. May supported the insertion of Title VII in the 1964 Civil Rights Act that prohibited discrimination based on sex. She also backed the ERA, which remained bottled up in the Judiciary Committee for most of her House career. Asked if America was a "woman's country" early in her career, May replied, "No, if it were a woman's country, it would give priority to the humane side of problems that seem like details to men. But sometimes these details have big implications in regard to the safety, comfort, or health of the people."[14]

Like other Washington state Republicans in the 1970 election, May faced voter discontent with the stagnant local economy and rising jobless rate for which Democrats successfully blamed the GOP and the Nixon administration. She lost her re-election bid to Democrat Mike McCormack, a former Hanford scientist, by a plurality of about 7,000 votes out of more than 125,000 cast, a 55 to 45 percent margin. Months before the election, May had divorced her husband after six years of legal separation. She married a management consultant, Donald Bedell, in November 1970. President Nixon appointed her as chair of the U.S. International Trade Commission, where she served from May 1971 to 1981. In 1982, the Ronald W. Reagan administration named May a special consultant to the President on the 50 States Project, an effort to weed out gender-discriminatory state laws. Catherine May Bedell passed away in Rancho Mirage, California, on May 28, 2004.

FOR FURTHER READING

Biographical Directory of the United States Congress, "Catherine Dean May," http://bioguide.congress.gov

Pidcock, Patricia Graham. "Catherine May: A Political Biography." Ph.D. diss., Washington State University, 1992.

MANUSCRIPT COLLECTIONS

Library of Congress (Washington, D.C.), Manuscript Division. *Oral History:* Transcript in the Oral History Collection of the U.S. Association of Former Members of Congress; 236 pages, March 1–April 20, 1979, recorded by Fern S. Ingersoll. Sound recording in the Library's Motion Picture, Broadcasting and Recorded Sound Division.

The Pennsylvania State University (University Park, PA), Special Collections, Paterno Library. *Oral History:* In "A Few Good Women" Oral History Collection, ca. 1997–1998, two folders.

Washington State University (Pullman, WA). *Papers:* 1959–1970, 275 linear feet. Correspondence, notes, memoranda, radio broadcasts, clippings, photographs, and other papers relating to her congressional service. A published guide is available in the repository and online.

NOTES

1 Catherine Dean May (Bedell), Oral History Interview, 1 March 1979, 9 March 1979, 20 April 1979, U.S. Association of Former Members of Congress (hereinafter cited as USAFMOC), Manuscript Division, Library of Congress, Washington, D.C.: 6–7. See also, Hope Chamberlin, *A Minority of Members: Women in the U.S. Congress* (New York: Praeger, 1973): 275; *Current Biography, 1960* (New York: H.W. Wilson and Company, 1960): 269–271.

2 *Current Biography, 1960*: 270.

3 May, Oral History Interview, USAFMOC: 29–34; see also, George Dixon, "Washington Scene: New Congresswoman Calls on Ike," 15 December, *Washington Post*: A 19.

4 "Election Statistics, 1920 to Present," http://clerk.house.gov/members/electionInfo/index.html.

5 May, Oral History Interview, USAFMOC: 105–106.

6 Dixon, "*Washington Scene*: New Congresswoman Calls on Ike."

7 Chamberlin, *A Minority of Members*: 276–277.

8 "Hanford Reactor," *Congress and the Nation*, 1945–1964, Vol. 1-A (Washington, D.C.: Congressional Quarterly Press, 1965): 936–937.

9 May, Oral History Interview, USAFMOC: 120.

10 Ibid.

11 Ibid., 123.

12 Alice Myers Winther, "Seattle Congresswoman Has Family Backing," 30 December 1958, *Christian Science Monitor*: 6.

13 May, Oral History Interview, USAFMOC: 35.

14 Betty Beale, "A Woman's World? 'Nays' Have It," 28 August 1961, *Los Angeles Times*: A 1.

Edna O. Simpson
1891–1984

UNITED STATES REPRESENTATIVE ★ REPUBLICAN FROM ILLINOIS
1959–1961

Edna O. Simpson, the wife of Congressman Sid Simpson of Illinois, was unexpectedly thrust into public life when her husband collapsed and died less than two weeks before the 1958 midterm elections. A day after Sid Simpson's death, Edna Simpson agreed to replace him as the GOP nominee in the western Illinois congressional district. Virtually unknown in Washington prior to her election, Simpson remained an outsider during her single term in the House. In 1960, she declined to stand for renomination.

She was born Edna Borman, daughter of John and Emily Armstrong Borman, in Fieldon, Illinois, on October 26, 1891. On February 1, 1920, Edna Borman married Sidney E. Simpson, an automobile dealer and longtime GOP chairman of Greene County, in western Illinois. The Simpsons raised two daughters, Martha and Janet. In 1942, Sid Simpson was elected as a Republican to the House of Representatives for a seat encompassing Greene County and 13 other counties situated between the Mississippi River and the capital of Springfield in the central part of the state. He went on to serve a total of eight terms in Congress and, from 1953 to 1955, chaired the District of Columbia Committee when Republicans controlled the House. As chair and later as Ranking Republican Member, Simpson helped to create a long-range public works program for the capital.[1] He also rose to the third-ranking spot on the Agriculture Committee. Simpson was re-elected by sizeable majorities and, in his final four elections, carried each county in his district.[2] During her husband's 16 years in the House, Edna Simpson and her daughters resided primarily in Carrollton, Illinois, Sid Simpson's hometown.

Ten days before the November 4, 1958, election, Sid Simpson collapsed and died while presiding over the dedication of a new hospital wing in Pittsfield, Illinois. Edna Simpson was seated beside him and watched as doctors tried unsuccessfully to revive him. Only a day later, on October 27, the congressional district's GOP committee convinced Edna Simpson to put her name on the ballot in place of her husband's.[3] With congressional redistricting looming on the horizon—Illinois eventually lost a House seat with the reapportionment that transpired after the 1960 Census—party leaders may have found it difficult to recruit a seasoned politician to replace Sid Simpson in the House. Additionally, Edna Simpson's candidacy most likely held appeal for the GOP due to potential voter sympathy for the grieving widow and the significance of name recognition in such an abridged election campaign.[4] Her opponent was Democratic nominee Henry W. Pollack, an attorney from Quincy, Illinois, whom Congressman Simpson had defeated by a wide margin in 1956. Edna Simpson did not campaign or make a single speech, but won a seat to the 86th Congress (1959–1961) by easily defeating Pollack with 55 percent of the vote.[5]

In Washington, Edna Simpson chose to remain an obscure figure. She brought her daughter, Janet, who had worked in Sid Simpson's office and for Dwight D. Eisenhower's adviser Sherman Adams, to act as her principal legislative aide. During her two years in the House, Edna Simpson never made a speech on the floor, remaining virtually unknown to her colleagues. Nevertheless, her Illinois colleague Marguerite Stitt Church observed that during her single term, Simpson compiled "an admirable record of service" on the House Administration

During her two years in the House, Edna Simpson never made a speech on the floor, remaining virtually unknown to her colleagues. Nevertheless, her Illinois colleague Marguerite Stitt Church observed that during her single term, Simpson compiled "an admirable record of service" on the House Administration Committee and the Interior and Insular Affairs Committee.

Committee and the Interior and Insular Affairs Committee.[6] The reclusive Congresswoman proposed an amendment to the Railroad Retirement Act that allowed retirees who received veterans' benefits to collect their full annuities. Apparently, one of the only times she wielded her official prerogative was in a dispute with the Office of the Clerk of the House about the name that would appear on her congressional stationery. The Clerk planned to print "Edna Oakes Simpson" (Oakes was the name of her first husband, who died less than a year after they were married). Over the Clerk's objection, the Congresswoman received her preference: "Edna (Mrs. Sid) Simpson."[7] In serving as a "Mrs.", she set a precedent, since previous women, both married and single, served under their given names without a salutatory title.[8]

In December 1959, Edna Simpson announced she would not seek re-election in 1960, choosing instead to retire to a quiet private life in Illinois. She died in Alton, Illinois, on May 15, 1984.

FOR FURTHER READING

Biographical Directory of the United States Congress, "Edna Oakes Simpson," http://bioguide.congress.gov

NOTES

1   "Rep. Simpson Dead at 64," 27 October 1964, *Washington Post*: A1.
2   "Sid Simpson Dead; House Member, 64," 27 October 1958, *New York Times*: 27.
3   "Simpson's Widow Put on Illinois G.O.P. Ballot," 28 October 1958, *New York Times*: 29.
4   "Illinoisan Plans Race," 27 December 1961, *New York Times*: 23; Joseph D. Mathewson, "Two Incumbents Fight Each Other in Unusual Illinois House Battle," 18 October 1962, *Wall Street Journal*: 1.
5   "Election Statistics, 1920 to Present," http://clerk.house.gov/members/electionInfo/elections.html.
6   Hope Chamberlin, *A Minority of Members: Women in the U.S. Congress* (New York: Praeger, 1973): 279.
7   Chamberlin, *A Minority of Members*: 279.
8   Marie Smith, "86th Congress Finds There's a 'Mrs.' in the House," 6 January 1959, *Washington Post*: B3.

Jessica McCullough Weis
1901–1963

UNITED STATES REPRESENTATIVE ★ REPUBLICAN FROM NEW YORK
1959–1963

A gregarious socialite from a well-to-do family, Jessica Weis originally became involved in upstate New York Republican organizations because she was concerned with the scope of New Deal reforms in the 1930s. "I really went into politics because I got tired of sitting around the sitting room objecting to the ways things were being run," Weis recalled. "I decided I ought to do something about it or stop objecting to it."[1] Working her way through the local GOP hierarchy, she eventually became a national committeewoman and spokesperson on the party's lecture circuit. Speaking before numerous audiences and working closely with party activists came naturally to her. "Politics, after all, is a matter of human relationships," she once said.[2] Weis eventually represented her Rochester district in the U.S. House of Representatives, where she defended local agricultural interests and championed women's equality in the workplace.

Jessica "Judy" McCullough was born on July 8, 1901, in Chicago, Illinois, daughter of Charles H. McCullough, Jr., and Jessie Martin McCullough. Her father was president of the Lackawanna Steel Company in Buffalo, New York. Born into privilege, Judy McCullough attended elite finishing schools in Pennsylvania and New York. In September 1921, McCullough married Charles W. Weis, Jr., who went on to become president of a lithography company in Rochester, New York.[3] They settled there and raised three children: Charles, Jessica, and Joan. Judy Weis joined the Rochester Junior League and participated in other local charities, often joking that a "deep-seated hatred of housework" drove her to politics.

Weis became active in the New York Republican Party during the 1930s when she "got upset about those who

worried about the New Deal and didn't do anything about it."[4] She first served on the local GOP finance committee and, during the 1936 presidential election, organized motorcar caravans throughout the state to support GOP nominee Alf Landon. In 1937, Weis was appointed vice chair of the Monroe County Republican Committee, where she served for the next 15 years. In 1940, Weis was elected president of the National Federation of Republican Women and was chosen by the state's "Committee of 48" to notify Wendell Willkie of his nomination for the presidency.[5] In the early 1940s she traveled on the GOP's national speaking circuit, addressing groups on a range of topics from women's issues to the need for an internationalist foreign policy.[6] When former New York Congresswoman Ruth Baker Pratt resigned as New York's committeewoman to the national GOP in January 1943, Weis was named to succeed her.[7] From 1940 through 1956 she also was a delegate at-large to GOP conventions. In 1948, Weis seconded the nomination of New York Governor Thomas Dewey for the presidency and then became the first woman to work as associate manager of a national campaign when she joined the Dewey-for-President team.[8]

Throughout this period, her chief base of operations was her Rochester home, "just like the party symbol, a big ungainly gray elephant," she once observed. When asked if she would consider elective office in 1954 she demurred, "I'm not interested—I think it would affect my amateur standing."[9] In 1953, President Dwight D. Eisenhower appointed Weis to the National Defense Civil Advisory Council; he reappointed her in 1956 and 1960. In 1956, Weis worked as the planning chair for the GOP National Convention in San Francisco, gaining additional national attention.

With more than 20 years' experience in Republican politics in 1958, Weis was one of a dozen New York GOP members considered for the party nomination to fill the vacancy created when U.S. Senator Irving M. Ives announced his retirement in 1958; other candidates included Congresswoman Katharine St. George and Representative Kenneth Keating, who had represented Rochester and Monroe County for a dozen years.[10] Keating eventually was nominated for and won the vacant Senate seat; however, Weis won a hard-fought four-way race for the nomination to Keating's old House seat. "I can outlast any man," she declared afterward. In the general election she faced Democrat Alphonse L. Cassetti. Weis's name recognition and her network of women's GOP groups throughout the state made her a strong candidate. During the campaign she described herself as a "middle of the road" Republican, although she added, "I hate all labels." Her platform had few specifics, though she spoke broadly of "peace and the economy."[11] She coasted past Cassetti, garnering 58 percent of the vote in the heavily Republican district. In 1960, Weis was re-elected by the same margin against Democrat Arthur B. Curran, Jr.[12]

In her first term, Congresswoman Weis served on the Government Operations and the District of Columbia committees. She was a solid supporter of the Dwight D. Eisenhower administration's legislative program. In one of her first votes on a major piece of legislation, she supported the 1959 Landrum–Griffin Act, which was designed to control illegal practices by labor unions. "I am convinced that the bill will go a long way toward routing out the corruption and racketeering which had worked its way into the labor–management relations field," Weis said. "I do not believe that this bill will harm the clean, democratically run union; it will, in fact, protect and promote honest trade unionism."[13] As a fiscal conservative, she opposed domestic spending initiatives for veterans' housing, airports, power plant construction, and water pollution control. As a Representative from an agricultural district, however, Weis did not regard aid to farmers as inflationary and lent her support to agricultural subsidies. She opposed a proposal to increase parcel post rates, arguing that mail order nurseries in her district would be adversely affected by the rate hike.[14]

During her second term, Weis was appointed to the newly created Committee on Science and Astronautics. As part of her new assignment, she worked on provisions for the Apollo Space Project that eventually sent manned missions to the moon. "We have been in the space age now for only a very short time and we are just on the threshold of a vast and largely unknown universe," she said in a 1962 floor debate on space technology appropriations. She urged her colleagues to vote for a provision to boost federal money to the National Aeronautics and Space Administration's program developing meteorological and communications satellite capabilities.[15]

On issues of women's rights, Weis supported the proposed Equal Rights Amendment to the Constitution, and urged an end to wage discrimination against women. Weis took to the House Floor in 1959 and 1962 to support the proposed Equal Pay Act, which provided for pay equity between men and women in the workplace. "Mental capacity, talent, imagination, and initiative are not parceled out on the basis of sex," Weis declared, shortly before passage of the bill. "In the space age, with the premium on excellence in these various qualities, this Nation cannot afford to waste its human resources by discriminatory pay practices which demean and cheapen the contributions of women."[16] Weis also returned home to Rochester each year to participate in the annual celebrations commemorating one the city's most famous natives, Susan B. Anthony. Weis helped raise funds and awareness for the preservation of the leading suffragist's home. Weis used these activities to inspire other women to become involved in politics.[17] She encouraged young women to "get started early in politics and be noisy about it."[18]

Congresswoman Weis's career was cut short by terminal cancer. In June 1962 Weis informed the New York Republican State Committee that her health prevented her from running for a third term. She was succeeded by Republican Frank J. Horton. In a final effort to inspire young women, Weis donated her congressional papers to the women's history archives at Radcliffe.[19] Judy Weis died on May 1, 1963, in Rochester.

FOR FURTHER READING

Biographical Directory of the United States Congress, "Jessica McCullough Weiss," http://bioguide.congress.gov

MANUSCRIPT COLLECTION

Radcliffe Institute for Advanced Study, **Harvard University** (Cambridge, MA), Schlesinger Library, http://www.radcliffe.edu/schles. *Papers:* 1922–1963, 7.25 feet. Correspondence, speeches, articles, scrapbooks, photographs, clippings, and other materials relating to Weis's political career. The bulk of collection is from her congressional service and consists of correspondence with constituents, other Members of Congress, government departments, nongovernmental organizations, and the Republican Party. The papers are also available on microfilm. A finding aid is available in the repository.

NOTES

1 "Jessica McCullough Weis Dead; G.O.P. Committeewoman, 62," 2 May 1963, *New York Times*: 30.

2 "'Judy' Weis Mounts Political Ladder," 3 September 1942, *Christian Science Monitor*: 15.

3 Charles Weis died in July, 1958, shortly before Jessica Weis was elected to Congress.

4 Estelle Jackson, "Not Looking for a Job: Meet GOP Committeewoman," 7 February 1954, *Washington Post*: S2; Phyllis Battelle, "Planning Chairman Promises: Convention Will Be 'Entertaining,'" 20 August 1956, *Washington Post*: 23.

5 "'Judy' Weis Mounts Political Ladder."

6 See for example, James A. Hagerty, "Young Republicans Condemn Isolation," 16 May 1942, *New York Times*: 14.

7 "Mrs. Pratt Quits Republican Group," 23 January 1943, *New York Times*: 28.

8 Jackson, "Not Looking for a Job: Meet GOP Committeewoman."

9 Ibid.

10 Leo Egan, "G.O.P. Senate List Includes 2 Women," 21 August 1958, *New York Times*: 49.

11 Elizabeth Ford, "GOP Campaign Tune in New York: Judy's Playing It By Ear," 24 September 1958, *Washington Post*: C3.

12 "Election Statistics, 1920 to Present," http://clerk.house.gov/members/electionInfo/elections.html.

13 *Congressional Record*, House, 86th Cong., 1st sess. (14 September 1959): 19952–19953.

14 *Congressional Record*, House, 86th Cong., 2nd sess. (2 February 1960): 1828–1829.

15 *Congressional Record*, House, 87th Cong., 2nd sess. (23 May 1962): 9083–9084.

16 *Congressional Record*, House, 87th Cong., 2nd sess. (25 July 1962): 14755; *Congressional Record*, House, 86th Cong., 1st sess. (2 February 1959): 1601.

17 Hope Chamberlin, *A Minority of Members: Women in the U.S. Congress* (New York: Praeger, 1973): 281; see also, *Congressional Record*, House, 87th Cong., 1st sess. (28 August 1961): 17263–17264; *Congressional Record*, House, 86th Cong., 1st sess. (16 February 1959): 2419.

18 Elizabeth Ford, "Start 'Noisy,' Early, but Small in Politics," 2 August 1961, *Washington Post*: B7.

19 Chamberlin, *A Minority of Members*: 282.

Julia Butler Hansen
1907–1988

UNITED STATES REPRESENTATIVE ★ DEMOCRAT FROM WASHINGTON
1960–1974

Julia Butler Hansen's seven terms in the House capped a 43-year career in elective office on the city, state, and federal level. Her legislative interests focused on issues affecting western states, such as transportation infrastructure, resource management, and improving the quality of life of Native Americans. As the first woman to chair an Appropriations subcommittee, Hansen thoroughly enjoyed the workings of Congress, once commenting, "I have a knack for legislation, and I like the rough and tumble of legislation."[1] Admired by her House colleagues, Congresswoman Hansen chaired a Democratic Caucus committee in 1974 which recommended procedural reforms that reined in committee powers and made exclusive committees more accessible to junior Members.

Julia Caroline Butler was born in Portland, Oregon, on June 14, 1907. Her father was a carpenter and her mother a schoolteacher. "I was raised by my mother and my New England grandmother, who believed that idle hands were the devil's workshop and I was always raised to keep busy," she recalled.[2] Julia Butler attended Oregon State College from 1924 to 1926, and while working as a dietician and swimming instructor eventually graduated from the University of Washington in 1930 with a degree in home economics. A year before marrying lumberman Henry Hansen in July 1939, she was elected to the city council of Cathlamet, Washington, where she served until 1946. The lack of a transportation infrastructure in Washington state brought Hansen into politics: "You couldn't help but be interested in transportation when you came from this area because we did not have a road in or out of here until 1930," she recalled.[3] Between 1939 and 1960, Julia Hansen served in the Washington state house of representatives, eventually rising to speaker *pro tempore*

from 1955 to 1960 and chairing several committees: education, highways, and elections and privileges. One of the major transportation projects that Hansen helped develop was the state's extensive ferry system. She also chaired the Eleven Western States Highway Policy Committee from 1951 to 1960, managed a title and casualty insurance business from 1958 to 1961, and, all the while, helped to raise her only child, David.

In 1960, Hansen won the Democratic primary for the special election to fill the southwestern Washington seat held by Representative Russell V. Mack, who had died in office. On November 8, 1960, Hansen defeated Republican Dale M. Nordquist, 53 to 47 percent, to fill Mack's unexpired term in the 86th Congress (1959–1961).[4] On the same November 8 ballot, Hansen prevailed by the same margin against Nordquist for the full term to the 87th Congress (1961–1963). Hansen's election was impressive, considering that she was one of just two Democrats from Washington who won election to the House in the 87th Congress. Representative Don Magnuson had won by fewer than 200 votes in his Seattle district and, in the presidential balloting, Richard M. Nixon led John F. Kennedy by about 30,000 votes statewide. In Congresswoman Hansen's six subsequent bids for re-election, she was never seriously challenged, winning a range from 57 to 70 percent of the vote, including a 66–34 percent win in her final campaign in 1972.[5]

Although Hansen's House service commenced on the date of her special election, she was not sworn in to office until January 1961 at the start of the 87th Congress. She received assignments on three committees: Veterans' Affairs, Education and Labor, and Interior and Insular Affairs. Within a month, she left Veterans' Affairs, at the request of Speaker Sam Rayburn of Texas, who planned to place her on the influential Ways and Means Committee.[6] That position never developed but, when a spot opened in the following Congress on the powerful Appropriations Committee, Hansen was on the short list of potential candidates for the exclusive post. Only one other woman, Representative Florence Kahn of California in the 1930s, had served on the committee. Representative Hansen used the political prowess she had developed during three decades in state and local politics to lobby for the assignment. Appropriations Committee Chairman Clarence Cannon of Missouri had told her in a letter, "I'd love to have a woman on my committee." Hansen's chief competition, Representative Arnold Olsen of Montana, lobbied Cannon by saying, "You don't want a woman on your committee." From Hansen's perspective, Chairman Cannon wavered and appeared ready to deny her the post. An intense competition developed, with Hansen threatening Cannon through an emissary, "You wouldn't want your opposition to women and your letter to me to appear in the press, would you?" To Olsen she said directly, "If you want to run versus me on the basis of knowledge, experience, and what votes we can get, fine. But if you are going to run versus me on grounds that I'm a woman, I'll go out to Montana where I often go to make speeches to Democratic women, and I'll cut you to pieces out there."[7] The next day Olsen conceded, and Hansen secured the post that she held for the duration of her time in Congress.

In 1965, Hansen became the first woman in House history to chair one of the Appropriations Committee's 13 subcommittees—and the only one until Barbara Vucanovich of Nevada in 1995.[8] When she was under consideration for the chairmanship of the Interior and Related Agencies Subcommittee on Appropriations, Chairman George Mahon of Texas, who succeeded Cannon, privately polled other committee members as to whether or not a woman was an appropriate candidate for the position. Hansen cornered him: "Mr. Chairman, have you ever run around and asked the members of the committee if a man would make a good chairman?" She recollected years later that Mahon "looked kind of sheepish" and quit his surveying.[9]

As one of the 13 Appropriations "cardinals," Hansen relied on her legislative experience to master floor procedure and to navigate the deal making that went on behind committee doors. An allusion to the "College of Cardinals," who elect and advise the Pope of the Roman Catholic Church, the cardinal title was meant to convey the power and authority vested in the handful of Appropriations members who shaped federal appropriations. As the Interior and Related Agencies chair, Hansen thoroughly grounded herself in floor procedure. "If you know your parliamentary procedures you've got no problems," she observed. "The parliamentarian said to me after I handled my bill for the first time, 'Julia, I'm going to quit worrying about you.'"[10] Martha Griffiths of Michigan later recalled that Hansen "probably understood more of how to deal with power than any other woman who was ever in Congress." When she brought her first bill as subcommittee chair to the full committee, Chairman Mahon decided to test her. "Oh, Julie, you're going to have to cut at least $2 million out of that bill," Mahon said. Hansen complied. The next morning, after conferring with her subcommittee, she reported to Mahon that she had cut $2.5 million from the bill. "Julie, that's wonderful," Mahon said. "Where did you take it out of the bill?" She replied, "Right out of your district, Mr. Chairman."[11] The episode only enhanced Hansen's popularity and stature on the Appropriations Committee.

From her Appropriations seat, Hansen helped parcel out federal funds for government-owned land for each of the annual budgets for a decade. Her subcommittee, which Hansen claimed "had a deep interest in the environment long before it was fashionable" was the first to appropriate funds for the development of the Alaska Pipeline and helped pass the stipulation that oil companies pay for the cost of any environmental cleanup—a requirement that she said was responsible for the careful construction and development of the project. In addition, she used her position to promote and protect federal forests and national parks. Hansen's interest in protecting the environment often caused friction with developers from her home state, especially in her timber-rich district.[12]

WHEN HANSEN WAS UNDER
CONSIDERATION FOR THE
CHAIRMANSHIP OF THE INTERIOR
AND RELATED AGENCIES
SUBCOMMITTEE ON
APPROPRIATIONS, CHAIRMAN
GEORGE MAHON OF TEXAS
PRIVATELY POLLED OTHER
COMMITTEE MEMBERS AS TO
WHETHER OR NOT A WOMAN WAS AN
APPROPRIATE CANDIDATE FOR THE
POSITION. HANSEN CORNERED HIM:
"MR. CHAIRMAN, HAVE YOU EVER
RUN AROUND AND ASKED THE
MEMBERS OF THE COMMITTEE IF A
MAN WOULD MAKE A
GOOD CHAIRMAN?"

Hansen did not share the focus on women's issues of the younger feminists who came to serve in Congress during the 1970s. Hard work and determination shaped her career and her outlook. "Women of my generation who entered public office had a very different kind of experience than those who come in today," she recalled. "There was little women's movement . . . and one had to work one's way up the political ladder without too much assistance from either men or women. When I was one of four women in the Washington state house of representatives, in 1939, the other 95 members could not have cared less whether we were there or not."[13] In 1972, however, she did vote for the Equal Rights Amendment. Though sympathetic to efforts in the early to mid-1970s to create a formal caucus for women's issues, Hansen ultimately did not support the proposal.[14]

During her final term, Hansen chaired the Democratic Caucus Committee on Organization, Study, and Review (also known as the Hansen Committee), which recommended the first changes in committee structure since passage of the Legislative Reorganization Act of 1946.[15] It was a delicate task, and Hansen's role in the project demonstrated her colleagues' admiration for her work and her sense of fairness as a widely respected moderate. The "Hansen Committee" reviewed a controversial plan to change committee jurisdictions and to reform procedures proposed in 1974 by the Select Committee on Committees, headed by Richard Bolling of Missouri. Hansen's alternative plan, which passed the House by a vote of 203 to 165 on October 8, 1974, included provisions to expand permanent committee staff, to prohibit voting by proxy in committee, to require committees of more than 15 Members to have at least four subcommittees, to empower the Speaker to refer bills to more than one committee (to resolve jurisdictional disputes), and to mandate that the House meet in December of election years to organize itself for the next Congress. The Hansen Committee, however, abandoned most of the far-reaching jurisdictional changes proposed by the Bolling Committee.[16]

The episode pitted much of the House leadership and senior Members against the Bolling plan, while many junior Members, including half of the Democratic freshmen, were against the more conservative reforms enacted by the Hansen plan.[17] Though Representative Hansen herself believed in the need to restrict the number of committees on which a Member could serve, she had reservations about radically altering the seniority system to more quickly advance younger Members. One reporter asked her if she supported an age limit for committee chairs. Hansen snapped, "Would [you] suggest that the Democratic Party should be the first group to go down to the office of discrimination and explain why, against the law, they have discriminated against anybody over 65?" Years later she observed, "They've got young people in Congress now to a large extent, and I don't see that they've done a damn bit better than the old boys did. That's where—you know, there is a great thing for experience. You know, with age comes some wisdom and some experience and some knowledge."[18]

Even before the Hansen Committee circulated its proposals, Congresswoman Hansen announced in February 1974 that she would not run for renomination to an eighth term and resigned her seat on the last day of the year. She cited overwork and the grind of being "pursued by an endless string of people who want everything from post offices to gasoline."[19] Hansen had been a prize-winning author long before entering politics, writing a work of juvenile fiction, *Singing Paddles* (1935). In retirement she continued her writing endeavors as an author and playwright. She also stayed active in government administration. In 1975 she was appointed to a six-year term on the Washington state toll bridge authority and state highway commission, which she had helped create during her years in the state legislature. She chaired the Washington state transportation commission from 1979 until her resignation in 1980. Julia Hansen resided in Cathlamet until her death on May 3, 1988.

FOR FURTHER READING

Anderson, Lynda Ring. "Julia Butler Hansen: The Grand Lady of Washington Politics." Ed.D. diss., Seattle University, 1992.

Biographical Directory of the United States Congress, "Julia Butler Hansen," http://bioguide.congress.gov

Rosenberg, Marie C. Barovic. "Women in Politics: A Comparative Study of Congresswomen Edith Green and Julia Butler Hansen." Ph.D. diss., University of Washington, 1973.

MANUSCRIPT COLLECTIONS

Library of Congress (Washington, D.C.), Manuscript Division. *Oral History:* Transcript in the Oral History Collection of the U.S. Association of Former Members of Congress. Sound recording in the Library's Motion Picture, Broadcasting and Recorded Sound Division.

Radcliffe Institute for Advanced Study, Harvard University (Cambridge, MA), Schlesinger Library, http://www.radcliffe.edu/schles. *Oral History:* 1974–1976, four folders. Interview of Julia Butler Hansen by Katie Louchheim.

University of Washington Library (Seattle, WA), Manuscripts and University Archives Division. *Papers:* 1961–1974, 218 feet. Congressional office files, including correspondence, legislation and subject files, speeches, and material relating to committee work. An unpublished guide is available in the library.

NOTES

1 Julia Butler Hansen, Oral History Interview, 3 March 1980, U.S. Association of Former Members of Congress (hereinafter referred to as USAFMOC), Manuscript Room, Library of Congress, Washington, D.C.: 19.

2 Hansen, Oral History Interview, USAFMOC: 21.

3 Ibid., 3.

4 Michael J. Dubin et al., *United States Congressional Elections, 1788–1997* (Jefferson, NC: McFarland & Company, Publishing, Inc., 1998): 620.

5 "Election Statistics, 1920 to Present," http://clerk.house.gov/members/electionInfo/elections.html.

6 Hansen, Oral History Interview, USAFMOC: 4.

7 Interview with Representative Julia Butler Hansen, May 1968, Research Interview Notes of Richard F. Fenno, Jr., with Members of the U.S. House of Representatives, 1959–1965, National Archives and Records Administration. Carl Albert recalls a different competition between Hansen and another Member, apparently when she was still being considered for the Ways and Means Committee.

8 Karen Foerstel, *Biographical Dictionary of Congressional Women* (Westport, CT: Greenwood Press, 1999): 113.

9 Hansen, Oral History Interview, USAFMOC: 9.

10 Ibid.

11 See Martha W. Griffiths's Oral History Interview with the USAFMOC, also at the Library of Congress.

12 Hansen, Oral History Interview, USAFMOC: 5–7; Hope Chamberlin, *A Minority of Members: Women in the U.S. Congress* (New York: Praeger, 1973): 282; Karen and Herbert Foerstel, *Climbing the Hill: Gender Conflict in Congress* (Westport, CT: Praeger, 1996): 24.

13 Susan Tolchin, *Women in Congress* (Washington, D.C.: Government Printing Office, 1976): 35.

14 Irwin N. Gertzog, *Congressional Women: Their Recruitment, Integration, and Behavior* (Westport, CT: Praeger, 1995): 167–168.

15 Tolchin, *Women in Congress*: 35; John Kornacki, "Julia's Committee: Overlooked Impact," 9 September 2003, *The Hill*: 7.

16 For more on the Bolling Committee and the Hansen Committee, see Julian Zelizer, *On Capitol Hill: The Struggle to Reform Congress and Its Consequences, 1948–2000* (New York: Cambridge University Press, 2004): 139–151.

17 Zelizer, *On Capitol Hill*: 150.

18 Hansen, Oral History Interview, USAFMOC: 15.

19 Mary Russell, "Rep. Julia Butler Hansen to Retire," 7 February 1974, *Washington Post*: A3; Foerstel, *Biographical Dictionary of Congressional Women*: 113.

Maurine B. Neuberger
1907–2000

UNITED STATES SENATOR ★ DEMOCRAT FROM OREGON
1960–1967

With her husband Richard Neuberger, Maurine B. Neuberger was part of a "mediagenic power couple" that together reformed the Oregon Democratic Party and emerged onto the national scene.[1] After her husband's death in 1960, Maurine Neuberger succeeded him in the U.S. Senate to become a leading advocate for consumer rights and reform and an outspoken critic of the tobacco industry.

Maurine Brown was born in coastal Cloverdale, Oregon, on January 9, 1907, the daughter of Walter T. Brown, a country doctor, and Ethel Kelty Brown, a schoolteacher. She had one brother, Robert.[2] Brown graduated from Bethel High School in Polk County, Oregon, and in 1924 earned a teacher's certificate at the Oregon College of Education in Monmouth. She taught physical education and modern dance at private and public schools before returning to college. She earned a B.A. in English and physical education in 1929 from the University of Oregon in Eugene. She later took graduate courses at the University of California at Los Angeles. For 12 years Maurine Brown taught public school in Oregon, before returning to the family dairy farm during World War II. While teaching in Portland in 1936 she had met Richard (Dick) L. Neuberger, a young writer who aspired to politics. After Neuberger's tour in the U.S. Army during World War II, the couple married on December 20, 1945. They had no children.

Maurine Neuberger's political career began in 1946 when she helped her husband during his campaign as a Democratic candidate to the Oregon senate. Richard Neuberger lost the race but was elected to the state senate in 1948. Inspired by her husband's victory, Maurine Neuberger won election to the state house of representatives

in 1950, making the Neubergers the first husband and wife to serve simultaneously in both chambers of a state legislature.[3] When the couple arrived in Salem, Richard Neuberger once told an associate, there were so few Democrats that, "Maurine and I can caucus in bed!"[4] Together the Neubergers played an important role in the revival of Oregon's Democratic Party, which previously had been overshadowed by the Republicans.[5] Maurine Neuberger focused on consumer rights and education reform, successfully arguing for the repeal of a state ban on colored oleomargarine (she won her wide notoriety for her demonstration of the process of making the product on the Oregon house floor) and initiating programs for students with special needs. She was wildly popular among Oregon voters, who often came to her husband's campaign appearance especially to see her. Richard Neuberger once observed that his wife went further in politics than anyone else who regularly spoke their mind. In 1952 she outpolled President Dwight D. Eisenhower and, in 1954, collected more votes than anyone on the state ticket. In 1954, the Neubergers chronicled their rise in state politics in a book, *Adventures in Politics: We Go to the Legislature*. That same year, Richard Neuberger defeated the Republican incumbent for a U.S. Senate seat. Maurine Neuberger, who had been his chief strategist, joined him as an unpaid aide in Washington in 1955 after completing her final term in the Oregon house. Despite her husband's ascension into national politics, when asked if she would run for the United States Congress in 1956, Maurine Neuberger replied, "One member of Congress in the family is enough. I find my duties as a wife and official hostess keep me occupied full time."[6]

Maurine Neuberger changed her mind about running

IMAGE COURTESY OF THE U.S. THE SENATE HISTORICAL OFFICE

for national office when, on March 10, 1960, Richard Neuberger, who had suffered from cancer, died of a brain hemorrhage just months before his bid for re-election. "I couldn't think of anything except going back to Washington and getting Muffet, our cat, closing the office, and moving out of our apartment," she recalled. "But as I thought more about it, I began to realize I was probably as qualified as any other potential candidate. And, above all, I knew in my heart that Dick would have wanted me to run."7 Despite the pleas from many Democrats, Oregon Governor Mark O. Hatfield passed over Maurine Neuberger as the appointee for the last nine months of her husband's term running up to the general election. Wanting to choose someone who would not be seeking the full term the following November, Hatfield selected longtime Oregon state supreme court judge Hall Stoner Lusk.8 Against steep odds, Maurine Neuberger sought and won the Democratic nomination and defeated Republican Elmo Smith, a former governor, for both the unexpired term (November 9 to January 3, 1961) and the full term ending January 3, 1967. In the general election, Neuberger capitalized on her wide name recognition and the vocal support of Oregon Representative Edith Green and her personal friend, former Democratic presidential nominee Adlai E. Stevenson. She polled about 55 percent of the total vote.

Neuberger carried on her husband's emphasis on reform legislation, though she specialized in consumer issues. She eventually served on three standing committees: Agriculture and Forestry, Banking and Currency, and Commerce. Neuberger also was appointed to the Special Committee on Aging and the Committee on a Parliamentary Conference with Canada. She is best remembered as a reformed pack-a-day smoker who took on the tobacco industry by initiating a nationwide anti-smoking campaign even before the U.S. Surgeon General had publicly linked cigarettes with cancer. Her position enraged the tobacco industry but put momentum behind an eventually successful campaign to get the Federal Trade Commission to regulate tobacco advertising. Neuberger sponsored one of the first bills to require warning labels on cigarette

packaging. In 1961, she voted for a two-year extension of federal payments to states which regulated billboards along highways as part of her attempt to fight cigarette sales. "The question is whether the view from the highway will be 'purple mountain majesties' or ads for cigarettes," Neuberger said in a speech on the Senate Floor.9 In 1963, she followed up this legislation by publishing a scathing book on industry practices that popularized her efforts: *Smoke Screen: Tobacco and the Public Welfare*.

Neuberger's emphasis on reform led to her eventual transfer to the Commerce Committee, where she authored and cosponsored a range of consumer protection legislation. She pushed for honest packaging and labeling techniques on food products, challenged the meat packing industry for its additives, and criticized bedding manufacturers that sold flammable blankets. "No industry I know of has ever been able to regulate itself to the interest of the consumer public," she once observed.10 One of her earliest bills, in May 1961, proposed authorizing federal contributions to presidential and congressional candidates and placing spending caps on campaign expenditures.11 In 1962, she cosponsored legislation with New Jersey Senator Clifford Case that required Members of Congress and the executive branch to make periodic public disclosures of their financial interests. Neuberger also worked to protect women's roles in the workplace by ensuring that the Labor Department received funding to establish the President's Commission on the Status of Women. In 1964, she introduced an amendment to the Revenue Act, making it easier for taxpayers to deduct expenses for childcare. She also supported reformed immigration laws which ended the national origins quota system, one of the first bills to reduce automobile emissions levels, and a bill to establish the Oregon Dunes National Seashore.

Neuberger worked on behalf of farming and, especially, lumber interests within her state, advocating higher soybean price supports and sponsoring a bill to enable foreign ships to convey U.S. lumber to Puerto Rico. She recalled later, however, that her short term on the Agriculture Committee was largely "four miserable years, fruitless years."12 Neuberger chafed under the control of the committee by prominent southerners who focused their attention on crops such as tobacco, rice, and peanuts. Forestry concerns were rarely, if ever, addressed.

On November 1, 1965, Neuberger announced that she would not seek re-election to a second full term. Concerned about her health after undergoing abdominal surgery in 1961 to remove a malignant tumor, Neuberger also was somewhat disillusioned with the Senate procedures and her chilly relationship with Oregon's senior Senator, Wayne Morse. Morse, a fellow Democrat, had become outspoken in his opposition to American intervention in

raising the money that I knew it was going to take," Neuberger told an interviewer. "Each year it got more and more expensive, and I just didn't have the heart to go out and buttonhole people in various organizations from New York to California to Florida and Seattle to build a campaign chest. That was the hardest thing about the whole job, raising the money. I just decided I didn't want to do it, so I just bided my time."[15]

After leaving the Senate, Neuberger chaired the Commission on the Status of Women and was a lecturer on consumer affairs and the status of women and taught

---

"To many people, 'politician' is a dirty word. But if we don't encourage our children and friends to enter politics, the professional politicians depicted in the cartoons will take over."

—Maurine Neuberger, Speech to the faculty women's club at George Washington University, February 4, 1956

---

the Vietnam War; Neuberger typically supported President Lyndon Johnson's administration, once commenting "When it came to foreign policy, I did whatever Bill Fulbright said I should do."[13] Despite her eventual ideological shift concerning Vietnam (from voting for the Gulf of Tonkin Resolution to publicly criticizing the war), Neuberger still considered Morse "impossible to work with," citing his indifference to her political agenda and his expectation that she defer to the senior Senator.[14] "But the real, actual, hard core reason I didn't run was

American government at Boston University, Radcliffe Institute, and Reed College. She briefly remarried, to the Boston psychiatrist Philip Solomon in 1964, but they were divorced in 1967. She retired to Portland, Oregon, tending to her garden and mentoring scores of young Democratic politicians. When Democratic Representative Ron Wyden visited her in 1994 and they talked about congressional investigations of tobacco advertising she told Wyden, "Stay after them."[16] She lived in Portland until her death there on February 22, 2000.

OF HER DECISION NOT TO STAND
FOR RE-ELECTION IN 1966,
NEUBERGER REMARKED: "THE
REAL, ACTUAL, HARD CORE REASON
I DIDN'T RUN WAS RAISING THE
MONEY I KNEW IT WAS GOING TO
TAKE. EACH YEAR IT GOT MORE
AND MORE EXPENSIVE, AND I JUST
DIDN'T HAVE THE HEART TO GO OUT
AND BUTTONHOLE PEOPLE IN
VARIOUS ORGANIZATIONS FROM
NEW YORK TO CALIFORNIA TO
FLORIDA AND SEATTLE TO BUILD
A CAMPAIGN CHEST."

FOR FURTHER READING

Biographical Directory of the United States Congress, "Maurine Brown Neuberger," http://bioguide.congress.gov

Neuberger, Maruine B. *Smoke Screen: Tobacco and the Public Welfare* (Englewood Cliffs, NJ: Prentice-Hall, 1963).

Neuberger, Maurine B. and Richard Neuberger, *Adventures in Politics: We Go to the Legislature* (New York: Oxford Press, 1954).

MANUSCRIPT COLLECTIONS

John F. Kennedy Library (Boston, MA). *Oral History:* 1970, 33 pages.

Library of Congress (Washington, D.C.), Manuscript Division. *Oral History:* 1979, 92 pages. An interview of Maurine Neuberger by the U.S. Association of Former Members of Congress.

Oregon Historical Society (Portland, OR). *Papers:* In the Richard and Maurine Neuberger Papers, 1954–1966, 13 boxes. Senate files and other papers including press releases and speeches. Topics include agriculture in Oregon, commerce, conservation, public lands, and social security. Finding aid. Also miscellaneous items in various collections.

University of Oregon (Eugene, OR). *Papers:* 1950–1967, 54 feet. Chiefly Senate office files (1960–1967), including correspondence, press releases, newsletters, statements, campaign records, minor legislative files, manuscripts of speeches, scrapbooks, and tape recordings. Topics include conservation, public power, reclamation, public health, and social security. A finding aid is available in the repository.

NOTES

1 Op-Ed, "Sen. Maurine Neuberger," 24 February 2000, *Portland Oregonian*: D10.
2 *Current Biography, 1961* (New York: H.W. Wilson and Company, 1961): 339–340.
3 *Current Biography, 1961*: 339.
4 Jeff Mapes, "Politician Maurine Neuberger Dies at 94; The Oregon Democrat, the Third Woman Elected to the U.S. Senate, Fought Tobacco and Championed Consumer Causes," 23 February 2000, *Portland Oregonian*: A1.
5 Mapes, "Politician Maurine Neuberger Dies at 94"; Mason Drukman, *Wayne Morse: A Political Biography* (Portland: Oregon Historical Society, 1997): 261.
6 Eileen Summers, "Run For Congress? Answer Is No!" 4 February. 1956, *Washington Post*: 19.
7 Interview with Maurine Neuberger, *Saturday Evening Post*, 7 January 1961.
8 "Oregon Justice, Democrat Gets Neuberger's Seat in U.S. Senate," 16 March 1960, *New York Times*: 28.
9 Adam Bernstein, "Sen. Maurine Neuberger, 93, Dies; 3rd Woman to Win Full Term," 25 February 2000, *Washington Post*: B7.
10 Mapes, "Politician Maurine Neuberger Dies at 94."
11 *Current Biography, 1961*: 340.
12 Maurine Neuberger, Oral History Interview, 5 April 1979, 17 April 1979, 1 May 1979, 10 May 1979, 15 May 1979, U.S. Association of Former Members of Congress (hereinafter cited as USAFMOC), Manuscript Room, Library of Congress, Washington, D.C.: 49.
13 Drukman, *Wayne Morse*: 413.
14 Op-Ed, "Sen. Maurine Neuberger"; Neuberger, Oral History Interview, USAFMOC: 59.
15 Neuberger, Oral History Interview, USAFMOC: 84.
16 Mapes, "Politician Maurine Neuberger Dies at 94."

Catherine D. Norrell
1901–1981

UNITED STATES REPRESENTATIVE ★ DEMOCRAT FROM ARKANSAS
1961–1963

Having worked alongside her husband, William Frank Norrell, as his legislative assistant for three decades, Catherine D. Norrell succeeded him as an Arkansas Representative in a special election after his death. Her experience as a congressional wife and aide helped to prepare her for new legislative responsibilities. But Norrell was confronted by an almost insuperable barrier to her re-election, as reapportionment carved up her southeastern Arkansas district between two powerful incumbents.

Catherine Dorris was born on March 30, 1901, in Camden, Arkansas. Her father, William Franklin Dorris, was an itinerant Baptist preacher, and he moved his wife, Rose Whitehead Dorris, and their family from congregation to congregation in Texas, Tennessee, and Arkansas. Catherine attended Ouachita Baptist College in Arkadelphia, Arkansas, and the University of Arkansas in Fayetteville, training as an accomplished pianist and organist. Before her 1922 marriage to William Frank Norrell, a World War I veteran and Monticello, Arkansas, lawyer, Catherine Dorris was a music teacher and director at the music department of Arkansas A&M College. The Norrells raised one daughter, Julia Jean, nicknamed Judy. After eight years in the Arkansas state senate, William Norrell was elected to the U.S. House in November 1938—the first of 12 consecutive terms representing a southeastern Arkansas district. He would eventually become the sixth-ranking Democrat on the powerful Appropriations Committee and chairman of its Legislative Appropriations Subcommittee.[1] During her husband's tenure in Little Rock and in the U.S. House, Catherine Norrell worked as his unpaid assistant, learning the workings of the legislative process. She also served as

president of the Congressional Wives Club and was a close friend of Hattie Wyatt Caraway, the Arkansas Senator and first woman elected to the U.S. Senate.

Reapportionment after the 1960 Census cost Arkansas two of its six House seats. William Norrell's district was carved into two parts, the first being lumped into a northeastern district represented by Wilbur Mills, chairman of the powerful Ways and Means Committee. The bulk of the Norrell's old district, including his home county, was placed into the district represented by Democrat Oren Harris, a formidable, 20-year incumbent who chaired the Committee on Interstate and Foreign Commerce. Norrell, who claimed Harris was behind the redistricting effort, vowed to fight him in the 1962 Democratic primary for a seat in a new district which spanned the southern half of the state.[2] He never got that chance. On February 15, 1961, William Norrell died a few days after being discovered unconscious in his office; he had suffered a stroke. Arkansas Democratic leaders soon approached Catherine Norrell to fill the vacancy in a special election. Like many widows running for their husbands' seats, Norrell campaigned on the promise of continuing her husband's policies. Her daughter Judy, on leave from George Washington University Law School, managed the campaign. Norrell's slogan was direct: "Keep Your Congressional Power Up! Elect Mrs. W. F. Norrell . . . the Only Candidate Prepared to Step In."[3] She faced four Democratic men in the campaign, including the top contender, John Harris Jones, a young attorney from Pine Bluff. Jones attacked Norrell for attempting to claim two congressional salaries, one as a widow receiving survivor's compensation and one as a Member were she to be elected. But his efforts to undercut wide sympathy for the widow Norrell

were to no avail. In the special election held on April 18, 1961, Norrell prevailed with 43 percent of the vote to 25 percent for Jones and 23 percent for M.C. Lewis.[4]

Catherine Norrell took the oath of office on April 25, 1961, and received an assignment on the Committee on Post Office and Civil Service. Despite her experience as a congressional wife, her new duties seemed daunting. She admitted to President John F. Kennedy during a conversation, "Having the responsibility squarely on your shoulders is not quite the same as watching someone else do it."[5] Also clouding the issue was the decision Norrell would soon have to face about challenging Oren Harris in the 1962 primary, a decision that hinged on her ability to raise sufficient finances.

Once in office, Catherine Norrell concentrated her legislative efforts on the promotion of economic prosperity in her district. She was especially interested in protecting the area's clay, textile, and lumber industries through tariffs and other government controls. In August 1961, Norrell supported a bill that eased Internal Revenue Service efforts to collect retroactive taxes from businesses in the clay brick and tile industry.[6] A month later, Norrell joined with Representative Cleveland M. Bailey of West Virginia in insisting that the Kennedy administration was not adequately protecting American industry under the framework of the General Agreement on Trade and Tariffs. Norrell complained particularly that the wood product industry in her district suffered from a reduction in U.S. tariff rates that foreign countries had failed to reciprocate.[7]

Norrell used her new prominence to acknowledge the contributions women had made to American political life. In May 1961, she sponsored a joint resolution calling for passage of the Equal Rights Amendment, a measure long stuck in the House Judiciary Committee.[8] In August 1961, to commemorate the ratification of the 19th Amendment that gave women the right to vote, Norrell told colleagues that the Arkansas state constitutional convention in 1868 considered a measure to grant the vote to "all citizens, 21 years of age." Arkansas also had been home to Catherine Campbell Cunningham, editor of the *Woman's*

Chronicle, a weekly newspaper that agitated for women's suffrage. "Woman's place in public life has evolved slowly," Norrell observed. The 19th Amendment, which followed various state suffrage initiatives, "was the result of a lengthy crusade in which thousands of persons endeavored to convince the public that the franchise should not be restricted to men."[9]

Norrell also supported the Kennedy administration's Cold War policies. She cast her first vote in Congress on behalf of a foreign aid bill to Latin American countries, despite feeling that it went "almost against my own conscience." Norrell believed her husband would have voted for the measure, too, though she vowed: "I expect in the future my vote will be more conservative than liberal."[10] She sponsored legislation prohibiting interstate and foreign commerce in goods imported into the United States from Cuba. In July 1962, she marked "Captive Nations Week," recalling her piano idol, the Polish musician-statesman Jan Paderewski, whose remains were interred at Arlington National Cemetery until, as he had wished, Poland was freed from Soviet occupation.[11]

Even as she was elected in April 1961, Norrell faced the impending reapportionment. Political, familial, and, most importantly, financial considerations convinced her not to challenge Harris. Her decision was influenced, ironically, by her campaign manager, daughter Judy, who was concerned about the stress the hotly contested campaign would have on her mother. Judy Norrell explained that she did not want "to lose two parents to the political scene of things. . . . I was of the opinion she should not run—which I think she always regretted."[12] Privately, Catherine Norrell told friends that she could not afford to challenge Harris. Upon her retirement, Catherine Norrell told her House colleagues, "This has been the most challenging and interesting experience of my life. Never having expected to serve in elective office of any kind, I feel a deep sense of gratitude to the people of the Sixth Congressional District."[13]

Shortly after Norrell left Congress, President Kennedy named her as Deputy Assistant Secretary of State for Educational and Cultural Affairs, a post she held from

1963 to 1965. When President Lyndon Johnson won election to a full term, he appointed Norrell the director of the State Department's reception center in Honolulu, Hawaii, where she served from 1965 to 1969. Upon her arrival at the post, reporters cornered Norrell to remind her that her husband had voted against Hawaii's statehood in the 1950s. "But that was my husband and not me," she replied. "I'm delighted to be here."[14] Norrell stayed in Hawaii for most of her retirement, employed as a church musician, before returning to her hometown of Monticello, Arkansas. She died in Warren, Arkansas, on August 26, 1981.

FOR FURTHER READING

Biographical Directory of the United States Congress, "Catherine Dorris Norrell," http://bioguide.congress.gov

MANUSCRIPT COLLECTION

University of Arkansas Libraries (Fayetteville, Arkansas), Special Collections Division. *Papers:* In the William F. and Catherine D. Norrell Papers, 1932–1981, 39 boxes. Includes materials relating to Congresswoman Norrell's personal life, her activities during her husband's congressional career, and her own term in Congress. Includes correspondence and texts of speeches made by Norrell from 1961 to 1965. Also includes items relating to the Congressional Club, materials addressing the status of women, files from her tenure with the Bureau of Educational and Cultural Affairs, including files of materials accumulated during her trip to Europe and the Middle East in 1963. There are also scrapbooks containing materials dating from her term in Congress. A finding aid is available in the repository and online.

NOTES

1   "Rep. Norrell Dead; Served 22 Years," 17 February 1961, *Washington Post*: B8; "Rep. W.F. Norrell of Arkansas Dead," 16 February 1961, *New York Times*: 31.
2   "Rep. Norrell Dead; Served 22 Years"; *Congressional Record*, House, 87th Cong., 2nd sess. (13 October 1962): 23547.
3   Hope Chamberlin, *A Minority of Members: Women in the U.S. Congress* (New York: Praeger, 1973): 286.
4   Michael J. Dubin et al., *United States Congressional Elections, 1788–1997* (Jefferson, NC: McFarland & Company, Publishers, Inc., 1998): 629; Chamberlin, *A Minority of Members*: 287.
5   Chamberlin, *A Minority of Members*: 288.
6   *Congressional Record*, House, 87th Cong., 1st sess. (21 August 1961): 16532.
7   *Congressional Record*, House, 87th Cong., 1st sess. (14 September 1961): 19569.
8   *Congressional Record*, House, 87th Cong., 1st sess. (9 May 1961): 7686.
9   *Congressional Record*, House, 87th Cong., 1st sess. (28 August 1961): 17272–17273.
10 "Lobbying Ladies Bend 320 Ears," 28 April 1961, *Washington Post*: C1.
11 *Congressional Record*, House, 87th Cong., 2nd sess. (16 July 1962): 13713–13714.
12 Phyllis D. Brandon, "Julia J. Norrell: Judy Norrell's Art Collection Documents the Good and Bad Days of the South; She Can Also Reflect on the Good and Bad of Arkansas Politics," 18 February 2001, *Arkansas Democrat-Gazette*: D1.
13 *Congressional Record*, House, 87th Cong., 2nd sess. (13 October 1962): 23547.
14 Brandon, "Julia J. Norrell."

Louise G. Reece
1898–1970

UNITED STATES REPRESENTATIVE ★ REPUBLICAN FROM TENNESSEE
1961–1963

Louise G. Reece, an inseparable political companion during her husband Carroll Reece's long service as a Tennessee Representative, won a special election to succeed him after his death in 1961. Her brief career in Congress was a direct product of decades of experience in support of his busy schedule—running Carroll Reece's re-election campaigns, scouting key legislation, and, in his absence, making important contacts on his behalf. During her 19 months on Capitol Hill, Louise Reece followed her husband's example as a fiscal conservative and defender of business interests in eastern Tennessee.

Louise Despard Goff was born in Milwaukee, Wisconsin, on November 6, 1898, the only child of Guy Despard Goff, a lawyer who had left his native Clarksburg, West Virginia, for Milwaukee, and Louise Van Nortwick Goff, a graduate of Wells College. In April 1905, her mother died of a paralytic stroke.[1] Born to a wealthy family of bankers and lawyers, Louise Goff was educated at private schools in Milwaukee and at the prestigious Miss Spence's School in New York City. In 1912, her grandfather Nathan Goff, a former U.S. Representative from West Virginia and a U.S. circuit court judge, was elected to the U.S. Senate. In 1917, Louise Goff moved to Washington, D.C., with her family when her father was appointed a special assistant to the U.S. Attorney General. He worked in that capacity intermittently for six years, while also serving as the general counsel of the U.S. Shipping Board and, during the war, as a commissioned army colonel in the Judge Advocate General's Department. In 1924, Guy Goff won election to his father's old Senate seat from West Virginia. The Goff family lived in Washington, and Louise Goff became immersed in the capital's social life. She left the comforts of home in 1920, to volunteer for an

American relief effort in France spearheaded by Anne Morgan, daughter of financier J.P. Morgan. While in France, Goff drove ambulances through areas of the country that had been ravaged by World War I.[2]

In 1923, Louise Goff married Brazilla Carroll Reece, initiating an almost-four-decade-long political union. Carroll Reece, then a second-term Republican Representative from Tennessee, had been a highly decorated World War I serviceman and university administrator. The couple settled into a home in Washington, D.C., and spent their summers and recess breaks in Johnson City, Tennessee, until World War II, when Louise Reece and the couple's only child, a daughter named Louise, moved back full-time to Tennessee. Carroll Reece served 18 total terms in the House (1921–1931; 1933–1947; 1951–1961). He represented the formerly Unionist, and safely Republican, upper-eastern section of the state. Reece was deeply conservative and an isolationist, and forged a close political alliance with Senator Robert A. Taft of Ohio. He helped to shape and to amend such measures as the Food and Drug Act and the Federal Communications Act, opposed much of the New Deal, and was a fervent anti-communist during the early Cold War years.[3] Reece also was the acknowledged leader of the Tennessee GOP and the most prominent of southern Republicans.[4] In 1947, he relinquished his House seat to chair the Republican National Committee (RNC), supporting Taft at the 1948 Republican National Convention and resigning his seat after the nomination of Thomas Dewey. He returned to the House in 1951 to serve another decade.[5]

During her husband's lengthy service in the House, Louise Reece made regular appearances on the campaign trail and acted as his chauffeur during campaign swings.

IMAGE COURTESY OF THE LIBRARY OF CONGRESS

During several of his re-election campaigns, she later recalled, "he stayed in Washington and I came home and ran things. In those days he only had to show at just one county rally to clinch another term. But all I knew about politics, I learned from him."[6] She also worked as Carroll Reece's eyes and ears in Washington, tracking legislation in caucus meetings or congressional committees, and as an observer and point of contact at GOP meetings, including the national conventions. Even after Louise Reece moved away from the capital in the early 1940s, she returned often to assist her husband while living out of a hotel. One congressional aide recalled that "most East Tennesseans thought of them as Mr. and Mrs. Republican." Their daughter, who, as a licensed pilot, also transported Carroll Reece around eastern Tennessee, recalled of her parents' political partnership, "They were a team."[7]

Following a long battle with cancer, Congressman Carroll Reece died on March 19, 1961.[8] Less than a week after his death, Louise Reece announced her intention to seek the GOP nomination to fill out the remainder of his term.[9] Two days later, local Republican committeemen unanimously chose her as their candidate to succeed Carroll Reece and simultaneously called for a nominating convention for April 15.[10] Reece was opposed in the GOP convention by Leland Davis, a 38-year-old oilman with no previous experience in politics.[11] Reece prevailed handily and, for the next five weeks, campaigned extensively throughout the district, much as she had nearly 20 years earlier on behalf of her husband. "I thought of a lot of back roads my husband had forgotten," she remarked.[12] The first returns on the evening of the May 16, 1961, special election came from Carroll Reece's home county, Johnson County, where Louise won with 1,800 votes out of 2,000 cast. That trend carried over throughout the district. In the three-way race, Louise Reece defeated her nearest competitor, Democrat William Faw, who had been endorsed by Senator Estes Kefauver, by a two-to-one margin.[13] Shortly after winning, she told a reporter, "I am a conservative. You can count on me to be on that side. I'm going with the Republican leaders." She noted that her interests would be in the areas of juvenile delinquency and school building projects. Reflecting on her victory

further, Reece said that being a Member of Congress was "the last thing I ever thought of." From her earliest days, such aspirations had, apparently, been discouraged. She recalled her father's exclusionary practices as a Senator: "No woman ever got inside his office door."[14]

Louise Reece took the oath of office on May 23, 1961, and was assigned to the Committee on Public Works. In an effort to protect her district's glass industry, Reece paired with West Virginia Representative Cleveland Bailey in urging President John F. Kennedy to restore tariff rates on certain glass products.[15] She joined the other Republicans on the Public Works Committee in issuing a report in opposition to the Public Works Acceleration and Coordination Act that they thought would needlessly increase federal spending and overburden the bureaucracy. Though she supported government aid to build schools, she opposed federal dollars going towards increasing teachers' pay. "If that comes, the next thing they will do is to tell us what to teach," she said.[16] In a special order marking the 45th anniversary of the 19th Amendment guaranteeing women the right to vote, Reece dedicated one of her rare floor speeches to recalling the role of Tennessee in providing the final vote for ratification. "I feel highly honored to be a Member of the present delegation from the great Volunteer State that made this contribution to the progress of our country and to women in particular," Reece said, joining most of her women colleagues in a round of celebratory speeches.[17]

A severe arthritic condition cut her congressional career short.[18] The 63-year-old Congresswoman announced in January 1962 that she would not be a candidate for re-election. "A younger person, who can start building up some seniority for the district, ought to be here in Washington," Reece told reporters.[19] Her successor, Republican James Quillen, did just that, winning election in 1962 to the first of 17 consecutive terms in the House. Louise Reece returned to her business interests in Tennessee and West Virginia and succeeded her late husband on the RNC. She was still a member of the RNC when she died in Johnson City, Tennessee, on May 14, 1970.

FOR FURTHER READING

Biographical Directory of the United States Congress, "Louise Goff Reece," http://bioguide.congress.gov

MANUSCRIPT COLLECTION

East Tennessee State University Library (Johnson City, TN), Archives of Appalachia. *Papers:* In the James H. Quillen Papers, ca. 1918–1999, 566 linear feet. The collection also includes some of the papers of James Quillen's predecessors, Brazilla Carroll and Louise Goff Reece. A finding aid is available in the repository and online.

NOTES

1   Gerald Wayne Smith, *Nathan Goff, Jr.: A Biography; With Some Account of Guy Despard Goff and Brazilla Carroll Reece* (Charleston, WV: Education Foundation, Inc., 1959): 304–305.

2   Peggy Preston, "Political Pow-Wows Old Story to GOP Chairman's Wife," 5 April 1946, *Washington Post*: 14; Eugene L. Meyer, "Congressman Louise Reece, GOP National Chief's Widow," 16 May 1970, *Washington Post*: B4; "Still Helping France," 5 December 1920, *New York Times*: 98.

3   "B. Carroll Reece," 21 March 1961, *Washington Post*: A12.

4   Smith, *Nathan Goff, Jr.*: 341–347.

5   Ibid., 342.

6   Elizabeth Ford, "New Rep. Reece: First Returns Were Happy Ones for Her," 19 May 1961, *Washington Post*: C2.

7   Hope Chamberlin, *A Minority of Members: Women in the U.S. Congress* (New York: Praeger, 1973): 290.

8   "B. Carroll Reece, Legislator, Dead," 20 March 1961, *New York Times*: 29.

9   "Reece's Widow Plans to Seek His House Seat," 25 March 1961, *Washington Post*: 49.

10 "Mrs. Reece Endorsed," 26 March 1961, *New York Times*: 45.

11 "Jobber Opposes Mrs. Reece," 6 April 1961, *New York Times*: 22.

12 Meyer, "Congresswoman Louise Reece, GOP National Chief's Widow."

13 "Reece's Widow Wins Election for His Seat," 17 May 1961, *New York Times*: 25; Michael J. Dubin et al., *United States Congressional Elections, 1788–1997* (Jefferson, NC: McFarland & Company, Publishing, Inc.): 629.

14 Ford, "New Rep. Reece: First Returns Were Happy Ones for Her."

15 *Congressional Record*, House, 87th Cong., 1st sess. (29 June 1961): 11918.

16 Ford, "New Rep. Reece: First Returns Were Happy Ones for Her."

17 *Congressional Record*, House, 87th Cong., 1st sess. (28 August 1961): 17264–17265.

18 Meyer, "Congresswoman Louise Reece, GOP National Chief's Widow."

19 "Mrs. Reece to Retire," 18 January 1962, *New York Times*: 13.

Corinne Boyd Riley
1893–1979

UNITED STATES REPRESENTATIVE ★ DEMOCRAT FROM SOUTH CAROLINA
1962–1963

Riding on the tradition of a "widow's mandate" in South Carolina, Corinne Boyd Riley, without making a single stump speech, appearing at an election rally, or even facing a bona fide opponent, won the special election to fill the last nine months of the term of her late husband, John J. Riley. She became the fourth widow to represent South Carolina and the second from a district in the south-central part of the state. She held the seat long enough to vote for several projects benefiting local interests in the district her husband had represented during his eight terms in the House.

Corinne Anderson Boyd was born in Piedmont, South Carolina, on July 4, 1893. The daughter of a Methodist preacher, Reverend George Boyd, she was named for her mother. She graduated from Converse College in Spartanburg, South Carolina, in 1915 and taught high school for the next 22 years. In 1917, she married John Jacob Riley, a World War I veteran, real estate broker, and insurance businessman. The couple raised a daughter, Helen, and a son, O. Beverley. From 1938 to 1942, Corinne Riley worked as a field representative for the South Carolina textbook commission. During World War II, she joined the civilian personnel office at Shaw Air Force Base in Sumter, South Carolina. In November 1944, John Riley won election as a Democrat to the 79th Congress (1945–1947) as a south-central South Carolina Representative. He succeeded Willa Lybrand Fulmer, the widow of longtime Representative Hampton Pitts Fulmer. Riley served two terms before being defeated for the 81st Congress (1949–1951) in 1948; however, he was re-elected to the 82nd Congress (1951–1953) and then to five succeeding terms.[1] He voted in line with other conservative southern Democrats, opposing foreign aid

expenditures and seeking a balanced budget. He eventually served on the Appropriations Committee, working on its defense and public works subcommittees.

When John Riley died on January 1, 1962, local and national leaders from both parties urged Corinne Riley to run in the special election to fill her husband's seat.[2] She initially resisted the invitation to represent the state's largest district, but reversed herself and announced her candidacy in mid-January. "I want to finish the work John started," she told reporters. "Women do have a place in politics, of course, but it's not one of leadership. It is one of helping her husband."[3] Nominating a deceased Congressman's widow had become tradition in South Carolina starting in the 1930s, with the precedent set by previous widows Elizabeth Gasque, Clara McMillan, and Willa Fulmer. Both parties respected this gesture of sympathy as a political code.[4] They further announced that if Riley won the nomination, neither party would run another candidate against her with the expectation that she would retire at the end of the term.

However, South Carolina political leaders did not expect another more experienced woman politician to challenge the tradition. Riley faced an 11-term member of the state house of representatives, Martha T. Fitzgerald, in the February 1962 Democratic primary. Fitzgerald claimed her credentials as an able state legislator made her a more suitable candidate than Riley. Still in official mourning for her husband, Riley made no campaign appearances and sent surrogates to read her speeches at various political meetings. She promised only to pursue the conservative agenda of her husband and to retire at the end of his unexpired term. "I know just what my husband thought about foreign aid, the United Nations, the Peace

Corps and federal aid to education, and I'll vote his views," she declared, ticking off a series of programs which John Riley had opposed.[5] In the end, tradition won out. Riley triumphed by more than a two-to-one plurality, carried all eight counties in the district, and described the nomination as "a tribute to the voters' confidence in my husband and their faith in me." Despite the strength of precedent and outpouring of sympathy on her behalf, Riley admitted that her defeat of Fitzgerald was "rather surprising."[6] Shortly after Riley's nomination, the *Columbia State* observed that she "would bring to the office a considerable knowledge of its requirements gained through her close association with it through her late husband. Also, since she shares the conservative views of her husband, and since this district is largely (not totally) one of that bent, there would be considerable satisfaction from the service of Mrs. Riley, a dedicated South Carolinian and a woman of considerable force and ability."[7] Corrine Riley faced no challenger in the April 10, 1962, special election.

After taking the oath of office two days later, Congress-woman Riley was assigned a seat on the Committee on Science and Astronautics. Though her husband had served on the Appropriations Committee, she had no illusions about getting on that sought-after committee.[8] She did, however, resist initial offers for the Education and Labor Committee and the Committee on Post Office and Civil Service, convincing House Speaker John McCormack of Massachusetts and Majority Leader Carl Albert of Oklahoma that the Science and Aeronautics assignment would be "more useful" to voters in her district. She also expressed satisfaction that the assignment "might mean a trip to Europe."[9] During her brief eight-month term, Riley introduced a bill authorizing the General Services Administration to transfer surplus property to the Aiken (South Carolina) Historical Society for use as a historical monument. She also supported authorizing the Federal Communications Commission to require that television sets be equipped with high-frequency channels, a proposal she hoped would benefit an educational television system operating in her district. "We in South Carolina have worked long and hard to preserve this valuable resource

which we call our VHF channel in Columbia," Riley noted in her brief and only floor speech as a Member.[10]

True to her campaign promise, Riley declined to seek re-election in the fall of 1962. Years later she described her congressional career as "a pleasant interlude."[11] Riley retired to Sumter, where she died on April 12, 1979.

FOR FURTHER READING

Biographical Directory of the United States Congress, "Corrine Boyd Riley," http://bioguide.congress.gov

NOTES

1   "Rep. Riley Dies; Served Eight Terms," 3 January 1962, *Washington Post*: B5; "Rep. John J. Riley, 15 Years in House," 3 January 1962, *New York Times*: 33. See also "Election Statistics, 1920 to Present," http://clerk.house.gov/members/electionInfo/elections.html.

2   "Widow Will Seek Riley House Seat," 14 January 1962, *New York Times*: 52; "Widow Backed for House Seat," 5 January 1962, *New York Times*: 21.

3   "Congress Time for Mrs. Riley," 16 April 1962, *Christian Science Monitor*: 5.

4   Hope Chamberlin, *A Minority of Members: Women in the U.S. Congress* (New York: Praeger, 1973): 290.

5   Marie Smith, "Mrs. John J. Riley: She'll Vote Husband's Views," 16 February 1962, *Washington Post*: C2.

6   "Mrs. Riley Wins Nomination," 14 February 1962, *Christian Science Monitor*: 11; Smith, "Mrs. John J. Riley: She'll Vote Husband's Views."

7   *Congressional Record*, House, 87th Cong., 2nd sess. (5 February 1952): A1075. In the above-referenced speech, Representative Robert W. Hemphill of South Carolina included the 14 February 1962 editorial of the *Columbia (SC) State*.

8   Smith, "Mrs. John J. Riley: She'll Vote Husband's Views."

9   Chamberlin, *A Minority of Members*: 291.

10 *Congressional Record*, House, 87th Cong., 2nd sess. (1 May 1962): 7444–7445.

11 Chamberlin, *A Minority of Members*: 291.

"I KNOW JUST WHAT MY HUSBAND THOUGHT ABOUT FOREIGN AID, THE UNITED NATIONS, THE PEACE CORPS, AND FEDERAL AID TO EDUCATION, AND I'LL VOTE HIS VIEWS," CORRINE RILEY DECLARED, TICKING OFF A SERIES OF PROGRAMS WHICH JOHN RILEY HAD OPPOSED.

Charlotte T. Reid

1913–

UNITED STATES REPRESENTATIVE ★ REPUBLICAN FROM ILLINOIS
1963–1971

Charlotte T. Reid had already enjoyed a career as a nationally acclaimed singer before she began her second career relatively late in life as the widow and successor of a congressional candidate who died in mid-campaign. Opponents objected that Reid's celebrity did not prepare her for public office. But Reid, a fiscal conservative who opposed President Lyndon Johnson's Great Society programs while supporting American intervention in Vietnam, demonstrated her political aptitude by gaining a seat on the prestigious Appropriations Committee in her third term.

Charlotte Leota Thompson was born on September 27, 1913, in Kankakee, Illinois, the only child of Edward Charles Thompson and Ethel (Stith) Thompson. She attended public schools in Aurora and the Illinois College in Jacksonville, Illinois. In 1932, she left Illinois College, without taking a degree, to pursue her musical interests. In 1936, Thompson auditioned and won a spot on a popular, Chicago-based show, Don McNeill's "Breakfast Club." Thompson sang under the name Annette King for nearly three years as the show's featured vocalist and became a voice familiar to millions of Americans who listened on the National Broadcasting Company network. On January 1, 1938, she married Frank Reid, Jr., an Aurora attorney. They had four children: Patricia, Frank, Edward, and Susan. Charlotte Reid left her music career for marriage and motherhood, pursing several civic interests in Illinois, including the March of Dimes, the Child Welfare Society, and the Girl Scouts.

In 1962, Frank Reid, Jr., won the Republican nomination for an Illinois seat in the House of Representatives but died suddenly of a heart attack in August during the campaign. Republican leaders in the traditionally conservative district just west of Chicago persuaded Charlotte Reid to run in her husband's place. Though she had little political experience, Reid was an effective campaigner. With the support of retiring Illinois Congresswoman Marguerite Church, she won the general election against Democrat Stanley Cowan, a Dundee, Illinois, businessman, with 60 percent of the vote. Reid was sworn in to the House on January 3, 1963.[1]

Reid faced only one serious challenge, during the 1964 election cycle. Democratic opponent Poppy Mitchell, a mother and college graduate who had never held political office, ran on a pro-Lyndon B. Johnson, Great Society platform, charging that Reid was "unconcerned" about educational improvements and welfare programs. Mitchell managed a grass-roots door-to-door campaign, serving coffee to constituents from an old mail truck and an armored car painted white with red and blue lettering, converted into "Poppy Wagons."[2] Reid's duties in the House kept her from campaigning actively until late in the summer, but she remained the favorite, given the district's traditional conservatism. Moreover, her celebrity and national name recognition from her show business years made her a popular figure among GOP candidates, who heavily recruited her to canvass their districts and stump on their behalf. Among the nearly 20 invitations she received from House colleagues on the campaign trail, Reid campaigned in the districts of House Minority Leader Charlie Halleck of Indiana and GOP Whip Leslie Arends of Illinois.[3] Reid ran on a platform opposed to President Johnson's proposed expansion of federal welfare programs. On the campaign trail, Reid countered, "The federal government has grown big and powerful, and in my way of thinking, exercises far too much control over

each of us."[4] She also suggested that Congress needed to provide funding for a strong military force to achieve "peace with honor" in Vietnam. Reid prevailed with 58 percent of the vote, an impressive result considering the size of Lyndon Johnson's electoral landslide and his lengthy coattails, particularly in Illinois, where Johnson piled up a nearly 900,000-vote margin over Republican nominee Barry Goldwater. After that election, Reid never again was seriously challenged, winning in 1966, 1968, and 1970 with 72 percent, 68 percent, and 69 percent of the vote, respectively.[5]

In Congress, Reid favored fiscal austerity and shrinking the size and scope of the federal government. "I dislike labels as such, but if I have to have one," she once said, "it would be as a conservative Republican."[6] She served in the 88th Congress (1963–1965) on the Committee on Interior and Insular Affairs. In later terms, she also served on the Public Works and the Standards of Official Conduct committees. In 1967, Reid received an assignment on the Appropriations Committee, just the third woman ever to serve on that panel. During the 88th Congress, she introduced a constitutional amendment to allow public school students to engage in noncompulsory prayer, noting that prayers preceded the daily business of Congress. The Supreme Court decision to ban prayer in public schools, Reid contended, "encourages agnosticism and atheism."[7] She opposed antipoverty measures such as the Economic Opportunity Act of 1964 and voted against community renewal programs, increased aid to education, and support for low-income home buyers, largely on the basis of reining in the federal budget. "My guiding principles on all questions are economy, decentralization of federal power and freedom of the individual," Reid said in a *New York Post* interview in July 1964. "Not many bills offered today pass that check list."[8]

Reid was an unwavering supporter of the military policies of Presidents Lyndon Johnson and Richard Nixon in Vietnam. In December 1965, she became one of the first Members of Congress to visit South Vietnam after the dramatic expansion of U.S. military forces earlier that summer. Reid paid the costs of the four-day trip on her own, rode helicopters into the war zone, visited the sprawling American bases at Da Nang and Bien Hoa, and boarded the aircraft carrier *U.S.S. Ticonderoga* in the South China Sea. "I want to reassure our fighting men that the overwhelming majority of loyal Americans stand back of them 100 percent," Reid said. Her support did not waver, even as American forces became mired in an intractable conflict that eventually drew more than a half-million troops into Southeast Asia. In 1968, Reid voted for the Scherle Amendment to a higher education bill that banned student protesters from receiving federal loans. She also opposed the Cooper–Church Bill, which stipulated that the President could not expand the war into Cambodia without congressional approval.

Reid's conservatism, however, did not cross over into several significant social issues. Though she did not seek out the label, Reid was a strong supporter of women's rights. "I don't like to think I am interested just in women's issues," she once said.[9] Nevertheless, Reid advocated the proposed Equal Rights Amendment, which was sponsored by Democrat Martha Griffiths of Michigan. Reid, Patsy Mink of Hawaii, and Catherine May of Washington state made international headlines for their efforts to open up the House gym to women lawmakers. She regularly encouraged women to enter politics. "You have to work hard, and you don't have time to see the latest shows or read everything on the best seller's list, but you have the satisfaction of seeing some of your ideas enacted into law," she once told a gathering of the League of Republican Women.[10] "Men respect our opinions and ideas," Reid said. "Small as our numbers are [in the House], we create a needed balance in the complicated business of adapting our governmental processes to the requirements of a changing society."[11]

On July 2, 1971, President Richard M. Nixon appointed Reid to the Federal Communications Commission (FCC) to succeed fellow Illinois Republican Thomas J. Houser. Reid, with some reservations, resigned her seat and accepted the appointment. Nixon was eager to place a woman on the FCC, and Reid was only the second in its history. Reid acknowledged wanting the relative security afforded by the seven-year appointment. But perhaps the most compelling reason was electoral and derived from imminent redistricting changes after the 1970 Census. In 1971, the Illinois state legislature agreed on a reapportionment plan that split her district in two. A portion went into Republican Robert McClory's district northeast of Chicago. But the vast majority of Reid's old district was merged with a portion of the old district south of the city, which had for nearly three decades elected House Minority Whip Leslie Arends to Congress. Had Reid remained in the House for the 1972 elections, she would have had the unenviable task of facing Arends in the GOP primary or of challenging McClory in a district where she had almost no base of support.[12] The Senate confirmed her appointment on July 22, 1971, with little debate, though the Nixon administration asked her to remain in the House until several pieces of its legislative program cleared the floor. Reid resigned from Congress on October 7, 1971.

During her FCC tenure, Reid was a strong proponent of a hands-off approach to regulation, suggesting that the market, rather than federal overseers, should determine media content. Shortly after marrying H. Ashley Barber, a manufacturer of construction equipment from Aurora, Illinois, on May 26, 1976, Reid resigned from the FCC. Later, she was a member of the President's Task Force on International Private Enterprise from 1983 to 1985. She also served on the board of overseers of the Hoover Institution from 1984 to 1988. Reid resides in Frankfort, Michigan.

FOR FURTHER READING

Biographical Directory of the United States Congress, "Charlotte T. Reid," http://bioguide.congress.gov

NOTES

1 "Election Statistics, 1920 to Present," http://clerk.house.gov/members/electionInfo/elections.html.

2 "Women Candidates Avow Their Battle Will Be Ladylike," 8 July 1964, *Washington Post*: C2.

3 Joseph D. Mathewson, "Two Women Vie in Illinois Race," 23 October 1964, *Wall Street Journal*: 14.

4 Mathewson, "Two Women Vie in Illinois Race."

5 "Election Statistics, 1920 to Present," http://clerk.house.gov/members/electionInfo/elections.html.

6 "Congresswoman Reid Says She's a Conservative G.O.P.," 8 January 1963, *Washington Evening Star*: B8.

7 *Current Biography, 1975* (New York: H.W. Wilson and Company, 1975): 345.

8 *Current Biography, 1975*: 345.

9 "Congresswoman Reid Says She's a Conservative G.O.P.,"

10 "Rare Birds Outnumber Congresswomen," 7 February 1967, *Washington Post*: C1.

11 Hope Chamberlin, *A Minority of Members: Women in the U.S. Congress* (New York: Praeger, 1973): 306–307.

12 See James M. Graham and Victor H. Kramer, *Appointments to the Regulatory Agencies: The Federal Communications Commission and Federal Trade Commission, 1949 to 1974* (Washington, D.C.: Government Printing Office , 1976): 320–325; located as a Senate committee print, CIS-NO: 76-s262-7.

Irene Bailey Baker

1901–1994

UNITED STATES REPRESENTATIVE ★ REPUBLICAN FROM TENNESSEE
1964–1965

Irene Bailey Baker came to Congress as part of the widow's mandate, succeeding a powerful and well-connected husband who died so suddenly that party leaders were caught unprepared to name a long-term successor. Mrs. Baker had long before established herself as a politician in her own right, serving as a Tennessee GOP national committeewoman and chairing the state's Grass Roots Organization of Republican Women. An adept campaigner, she nevertheless ran on the reputation of her late husband, Tennessee Congressman Howard Baker, in a special election to fill his vacant seat. "I stand on Howard's record," Irene Baker declared, on her way to winning election to a 10-month term in which her chief goal was to provide continuity for her husband's legislative agenda.

Edith Irene Bailey was born in Sevierville, Tennessee, on November 17, 1901. She attended public schools in Maryville and Sevierville, and studied music. She served in local government as a court clerk from 1918 to 1924, eventually becoming the deputy clerk and master in the chancery court in Sevierville. Her first husband died, and she was hired by the Tennessee Valley Authority (TVA) as an abstractor of titles in the early 1930s. She met Howard Henry Baker, a widower, and they were married in 1935. The couple raised Baker's two children from his first marriage—Howard H. Baker, Jr., and Mary Elizabeth Baker—and one of their own, Beverly Irene Baker.[1]

Howard Baker was a lawyer who had served briefly in the Tennessee legislature before working as the attorney general for a judicial circuit that encompassed six counties in the northeastern part of the state. He also published the weekly *Cumberland Chronicle* in his hometown of Huntsville, Tennessee. In the 1930s, he became a powerful player in

state GOP politics, working as a party official while establishing his own law firm in Huntsville. He was a delegate to the 1940 GOP convention and, in 1948 and 1952, was chairman of the Tennessee delegation at the Republican National Convention. Irene worked on her husband's unsuccessful campaigns for governor in 1938 and for U.S. Senator in 1940. When Howard Baker won election to the U.S. House of Representatives in 1950 in an eastern Tennessee district which encompassed Knoxville, Irene worked in his Washington, D.C., office. Congressman Baker eventually became Tennessee's leading GOP power broker and the number-two Republican on the powerful Ways and Means Committee. In his subsequent six re-election campaigns he never faced serious competition, either within his party or from Democrats.[2] Since the founding of the Republican Party in 1856, Baker's district had always voted Republican.

Though aligned with the conservative wing of the party (Congressman Baker had supported Senator Robert Taft for the presidency in 1952), he supported the Democratic majority on such key issues as Social Security entitlements, the TVA, and the Atomic Energy Commission (AEC). The latter two programs were of special interest to eastern Tennesseans, for whom the TVA provided much of the industrial infrastructure. The AEC, which managed the Oak Ridge Nuclear Laboratories, provided many jobs to the local economy. Baker once described the TVA as "a part of our Second District everyday life."[3] In 1959, Congressman Baker played a key part in the passage of a TVA self-financing act that renewed the agency's authority to generate power for seven states. He also was instrumental in helping the TVA retain its forestry and conservation programs.[4]

When Congressman Baker died of a sudden heart attack on January 7, 1964, the Tennessee Republican leadership chose Irene Baker to run in the March 10, 1964, special election. The decision was motivated in part by the desire to stave off intraparty rivalry. It worked exceedingly well. Baker pledged only to fill the remaining 10 months of her husband's term, allowing GOP leaders to select a candidate for the fall 1964 elections. Irene Baker campaigned on her husband's reputation. "Why need I say I am for full employment at Oak Ridge, in the coal mining regions, in more industry for the district, for a balanced budget and fiscal responsibility and for a reduction in taxes based on a reduction in federal expenditures?" she said during a campaign rally. She also supported her husband's resolution to amend the Constitution to permit the reading of the Bible and prayers in public schools. "To say these things could possibly create questions of how I stand, and there can be no question of that."[5] Potential Republican contenders stepped aside, and Baker ran an efficient campaign against her Democratic rival, Willard Yarbrough, the assistant city editor of the *Knoxville News-Sentinel*. Despite light voter turnout, Baker won the special election by a margin of 55 percent to 43 percent, a plurality of about 9,000 votes out of 72,000 cast.[6]

Congresswoman Baker was sworn in to the 88th Congress (1963–1965) on March 19, 1964. During her short term she served on the Committee on Government Operations. In that position Representative Baker continued many of her husband's policies: advocating a balanced federal budget, looking to protect jobs in her district's major industries of coal mining and nuclear research laboratories, and supporting the TVA. She also advocated cost of living increases for Social Security recipients and criticized the Lyndon Johnson administration for risking inflation through excessive government spending. "I feel that we owe it to Social Security beneficiaries to increase their benefits," Baker explained to colleagues in a floor speech. "It [the economy] is not their fault."[7]

As promised, Baker declined to run for the 89th Congress (1965–1967), returning to private life in Knoxville. She was succeeded by yet another family dynasty, headed by the former mayor of Knoxville, John James Duncan. Duncan served from 1965 until his death in June 1988; he was succeeded by his son, John J. Duncan, Jr. Irene Baker served as Knoxville's director of public welfare from 1965 to 1971. Her stepson, Howard H. Baker, Jr., continued the family political tradition by winning election in 1966 as a U.S. Senator from Tennessee. He served from 1967 to 1985, becoming Senate Majority Leader in 1981. Irene Baker died in Loudon, Tennessee, on April 2, 1994.

FOR FURTHER READING

Biographical Directory of the United States Congress, "Irene Bailey Baker," http://bioguide.congress.gov

MANUSCRIPT COLLECTION

University of Tennessee Libraries (Knoxville, TN), Special Collections. *Papers:* In the Howard and Irene Baker Papers, 1933–1965, 49.5 feet. Congressional papers, as Irene Baker completed the term of her deceased husband, Howard H. Baker. An unpublished finding aid is available in the repository.

NOTES

1   Hope Chamberlin, *A Minority of Members: Women in the U.S. Congress* (New York: Praeger, 1973): 308.

2   "Election Statistics, 1920 to Present," http://clerk.house.gov/members/electionInfo/elections.html.

3   David Walker, "Rep. Baker Dies of Heart Attack," 8 January 1964, *Washington Post*: D4.

4   "Howard H. Baker, Representative: Tennessee Republican Dies–Supporter of T.V.A.," 8 January 1964, *New York Times*: 37.

5   "Tennessee Area to Vote Tuesday: Rep. Baker's Widow Running for House in 2nd District," 8 March 1964, *New York Times*: 72.

6   Michael J. Dubin et al., *United States Congressional Elections, 1788–1997* (Jefferson, NC: McFarland and Company, Publishing, Inc., 1998): 638.

7   Susan Tolchin, *Women in Congress* (Washington, D.C.: Government Printing Office, 1976): 5.

Baker advocated
cost of living increases for
Social Security recipients
and criticized the
Lyndon B. Johnson
administration for risking
inflation through excessive
government spending. "I feel
that we owe it to Social
Security beneficiaries to
increase their benefits," Baker
explained to colleagues in a
floor speech. "It [the econo-
my] is not their fault."

Patsy T. Mink

1927–2002

UNITED STATES REPRESENTATIVE ★ DEMOCRAT FROM HAWAII
1965–1977, 1990–2002

Patsy T. Mink, the first woman of color elected to Congress, participated in the passage of much of the 1960s Great Society legislation during the first phase of her congressional career. After a long hiatus, Mink returned to the House in the 1990s as an ardent defender of the social welfare state at a time when much of the legislation she had helped establish was being rolled back. As a veteran politician who had a significant impact on the nation during both stints in the House of Representatives, Mink's legislative approach was premised on the belief, "You were not elected to Congress, in my interpretation of things, to represent your district, period. You are national legislators."[1]

Patsy Matsu Takemoto was born in Paia, Hawaii Territory, on December 6, 1927, one of two children raised by Suematsu Takemoto, a civil engineer, and Mitamia Tateyama Takemoto. She graduated from Maui High School in 1944 as class president and valedictorian and went on to attend Wilson College in Chambersburg, Pennsylvania, and the University of Nebraska at Lincoln, before graduating with a B.A. in zoology and chemistry from the University of Hawaii in 1948. Three years later, she earned a J.D. from the University of Chicago Law School. In 1951 she married John Francis Mink, a graduate student in geology at the university. The couple had one child, a daughter named Gwendolyn, and moved to Honolulu, where Patsy T. Mink went into private law practice and lectured on business law at the University of Hawaii. In 1954 Mink founded the Oahu Young Democrats and worked as an attorney for the territorial house of representatives in 1955. Mink served as a member of the territorial house of representatives in 1956 and 1958 and was

elected to the Hawaii senate, serving from 1958 to 1959 and again from 1962 to 1964, where she eventually chaired the education committee. In 1959, when Hawaii achieved statehood, Mink unsuccessfully sought the Democratic nomination for the state's At-Large seat in the U.S. House of Representatives, which was captured by future Senator Daniel Inouye.

In 1964, after reapportionment created a second seat for Hawaii in the U.S. House, Mink again mounted a grass-roots campaign that relied on a staff of unpaid volunteers; her husband, John, served as her campaign manager, "principal sounding board," and "in-house critic."[2] She ran without the blessing of the state Democratic Party leadership, raising campaign funds largely in small individual contributions. Throughout her career, Mink never had a warm relationship with the state leaders of her party; she attributed their lack of support to her unwillingness to allow the party to influence her political agenda.[3] With help from President Lyndon Johnson's landslide victory in the presidential race, Mink was elected as one of two At-Large Representatives. In a four-way race, she received 27 percent of the total to become the first Asian-American woman and the first woman from Hawaii to serve in Congress. In her subsequent five campaigns for re-election Mink faced a number of difficult primaries in which the local Democratic Party tried to oust her, twice by running women candidates to, in Mink's view, deprive her of the gender issue.[4] She proved a durable candidate in the general elections, however. In 1966 and 1968, in a four-way race for the two House seats, she garnered slightly more than 34 percent of the vote; in the 1966 race she collected more votes than any of the other three candidates. In the subsequent three elections, after Hawaii had been divided into two congressional districts, Mink ran unopposed in 1970, won 53 percent of the vote in 1972 and 63 percent in 1974.[5]

In the House, Mink successfully sought a seat on the Committee on Education and Labor, on which she served from the 89th Congress (1965–1967) through the 94th Congress (1975–1977). In her second term she also joined the Committee on Interior and Insular Affairs and, in the 93rd (1973–1975) and 94th Congresses, served on the Budget Committee. Mink's committee assignments allowed her to concentrate on the same issues that had been the focus of her attention in the Hawaii legislature. Among the education acts Mink introduced or sponsored were the first childcare bill and legislation establishing bilingual education, student loans, special education, and Head Start. As a member of the Interior and Insular Affairs Committee, she supported the economic and political development of the Trust Territory in the Pacific. As chair of the Subcommittee on Mines and Mining, she helped author the landmark Surface Mining Control and Reclamation (Strip Mining) Act of 1975 and the Mineral Leasing Act of 1976. The House failed to override President Gerald R. Ford's veto of the Surface Mining Control and Reclamation Act, though a similar measure was eventually signed into law in 1977.

During the Johnson presidency, Mink strongly supported the administration's domestic programs that were part of the Great Society legislation, but she was a critic of the Americanization of the Vietnam War. In September 1967, she refused to support the President's request for an income tax increase because of her fear that the new revenues would be used for military action rather than the expansion of social programs. It was, she said, like "administering aspirin to a seriously ill patient who needs major surgery."[6] If inflation threatened the economy, she suggested, the administration should tax big business and not just the average working taxpayers.[7] Her views clashed with those of the three other Members of the Hawaii congressional delegation, as well as those of many of her constituents in a state with a heavy military presence. Years later, however,

Mink recalled, "It was such a horrible thought to have this war that it really made no difference to me that I had a military constituency. It was a case of living up to my own views and my own conscience. If I was defeated for it, that's the way it had to be. There was no way in which I could compromise my views on how I felt about it."[8]

Mink also advocated many women's issues in Congress, including equal rights. One of her great legislative triumphs was the Women's Education Equity Act, passed as part of a comprehensive education bill in 1974. It provided $30 million a year in educational funds for programs to promote gender equity in schools, to increase educational and job opportunities for women, and to excise sexual stereotypes from textbooks and school curricula. Mink garnered critical support for Title IX of the 1972 Education Amendments, which barred sexual discrimination in institutions receiving federal funds and opened up opportunities for women in athletics. She realized early in her House career that "because there were only eight women at the time who were Members of Congress, that I had a special burden to bear to speak for [all women], because they didn't have people who could express their concerns for them adequately. So, I always felt that we were serving a dual role in Congress, representing our own districts and, at the same time, having to voice the concerns of the total population of women in the country."[9]

In 1976, passing up a bid for what would have been certain re-election to a seventh term in the House, Mink sought the Democratic nomination for a seat in the U.S. Senate. Mink lost the nomination to fellow House Member Spark Matsunaga.[10] She remained active in politics, however, serving as Assistant Secretary of State for Oceans and International Environmental and Scientific Affairs from 1977 to 1978. For the next three years she was president of the Americans for Democratic Action, a liberal political lobbying organization founded in 1947 by an array of scholars, activists, and politicians.[11] Mink returned to Hawaii and was elected to the Honolulu city council, serving there from 1983 to 1987 (from 1983 to 1985 as its chair). She ran unsuccessfully for governor in 1986 and for mayor of Honolulu in 1988.

In 1990, Mink returned to the U.S. House of Representatives when she won a special election on September 22, 1990, to fill the vacancy in the Hawaii congressional district left by the resignation of Daniel Akaka after his appointment to the Senate. On the same day she won the Democratic nomination to fill Akaka's seat, Mink also won nomination to the race for a full term in the 102nd Congress (1991–1993). She won both races and was reelected comfortably to five subsequent terms with winning percentages ranging from a high of 73 percent in 1992 to a low of 60 percent in 1996.[12]

der discrimination still persisted in the United States 20 years after the passage of Title IX, Mink asserted that targeting gender bias in elementary and secondary education would help reduce inequalities between the sexes. She told the House, "We must assure that schools all across this country implement and integrate into their curriculum, policies, goals, programs, activities, and initiatives to achieve educational equity for women and girls."[13] Mink continued to crusade for women's rights by organizing and leading the Democratic Women's Caucus in 1995.

Throughout her political career, Mink remained true

"America is not a country which needs to punish its dissenters to preserve its honor. America is not a country which needs to demand conformity of all its people, for its strength lies in all our diversities converging in one common belief, that of the importance of freedom as the essence of our country."

—PATSY T. MINK, HOUSE FLOOR SPEECH, 1967

Mink was once again appointed to the Committee on Education and Labor (later Education and the Workforce) and also was assigned to the Government Operations (later Government Reform) Committee. During the 103rd Congress (1993–1995), she was on the Natural Resources and Budget committees, serving on the latter through the 105th Congress (1997–1999).

Mink continued to pursue legislative reform in health care and education. Believing that voters cared more about quality health coverage than any other domestic issue, she advocated a universal health care plan that would allow people of all economic backgrounds to receive medical treatment. Mink combined two of the longstanding interests during her congressional career when she co-sponsored the Gender Equity Act in 1993. Disturbed that gen-

to her liberal ideals. Previously in the majority, both in her party affiliation and her political ideology, she often found herself in the minority during her second stretch in the House. During the 1990s, Mink expended considerable effort opposing conservative legislation that challenged the liberal agenda she had promoted. An outspoken critic of the welfare overhaul legislation that the Republican Congress and the William J. Clinton administration agreed upon in 1996, Mink exclaimed, "Throwing people off welfare and forcing them to take the lowest-paying jobs in the community has created a misery index for millions."[14] She also raised concerns about the establishment of the Department of Homeland Security (DHS) in 2002. Created in response to the terrorist attacks against the United States on September 11, 2001,

Of her opposition to the
Vietnam War, Mink recalled, "It
was such a horrible thought to
have this war that it really
made no difference to me that I
had a military constituency. It
was a case of living up to my own
views and my own conscience. If
I was defeated for it, that's the
way it had to be."

the DHS was charged with preventing further domestic terrorist strikes. Mink feared the DHS might undermine civil liberties by violating the privacy of American citizens in the name of national security. In favor of full disclosure of government attempts to safeguard the nation from international threats, she proposed that no secrets be kept from the public.[15] As Ranking Member of the Education and the Workforce Subcommittee on Oversight and Investigations during the 105th Congress (1997–1999), Mink butted heads with conservative Republicans regarding a proposed $1.4 million investigation of alleged fraud within the Teamsters Union. A loyal supporter of organized labor, Mink accused Republican leadership of sponsoring a "fishing expedition" that wasted "taxpayers' money for sheer partisan political purposes."[16]

On September 28, 2002, after a month-long hospitalization with pneumonia, Patsy T. Mink died in Honolulu, Hawaii. Her name remained on the November ballot, and she was re-elected by a wide margin. Democrat Ed Case defeated Patsy Mink's husband and more than 30 other candidates in the special election to succeed Mink in the 107th Congress (2001–2003) and later won election to a full term in the 108th Congress (2003–2005).[17] Shortly after Mink's death, John Boehner of Ohio, chairman of the Education and Workforce Committee, reflected upon Mink's congressional service: "Patsy Mink was a vibrant, passionate, and effective voice for the principles she believed in. Her passing is a significant loss for our committee, the people of Hawaii and the people of the United States."[18]

FOR FURTHER READING

Biographical Directory of the United States Congress, "Patsy Takemoto Mink," http://bioguide.congress.gov

MANUSCRIPT COLLECTIONS

Library of Congress (Washington, D.C.), Manuscript Division. *Papers:* 1965–2002, 935,000 items. Collection has not yet been processed. *Oral History:* Patsy T. Mink,

Oral History Interview, 6 March 1979, 26 March 1979, 7 June 1979, conducted by the U.S. Association of Former Members of Congress.

Wichita State University (Wichita, KS), Special Collections and University Archives. *Papers,* ca. 1956–1972, three linear feet. The Patsy Mink collection contains congressional reports, copies of bills, speeches and addresses given by Mink, and an oral history transcript. The material in this collection displays Mink's political concerns, including affirmative action and strip mining legislation.

NOTES

1   Patsy T. Mink, Oral History Interview, 6 March 1979/26 March 1979/7 June 1979, U.S. Association of Former Members of Congress (hereinafter referred to as USAFMOC), Manuscript Room, Library of Congress, Washington, D.C.: 74

2   Mink, Oral History Interview, USAFMOC: 31.

3   Ibid., 16.

4   Ibid., 25.

5   "Election Statistics, 1920 to Present" http://clerk.house.gov/members/electionInfo/elections.html.

6   *Current Biography, 1968* (New York: H.W. Wilson and Company, 1968): 255.

7   *Current Biography, 1968*: 255.

8   Mink, Oral History Interview, USAFMOC: 98.

9   Ibid., 43.

10   *Politics in America, 2002* (Washington, D.C.: Congressional Quarterly Press, 2001): 290–291.

11   James T. Patterson, *Grand Expectations: The United States, 1945–1974* (New York: Oxford, 1996): 146.

12   "Election Statistics, 1920 to Present," http://clerk.house.gov/members/electionInfo/elections.html.

13   *Congressional Record,* House, 103rd Cong., 1st sess. (21 April 1993): 8021.

14   *Politics in America, 2002*: 290–291.

15   *Congressional Record,* House, 107th Cong., 2nd sess. (26 July 2002): 5852.

16   *Politics in America, 2000*: 403–404.

17   James Gonser, "Case Wins; Set Sights on Jan. 4," 2 December 2002, *Honolulu Advertiser*: 1A.

18   Erin P. Billings, "Rep. Mink, First Asian-American Woman Elected to the House Dies," 30 September 2002, *Roll Call*; also Elissa Gootman, "Patsy Mink, Veteran Hawaii Congresswoman, Dies at 74," 30 September 2002, *New York Times*: B10.

Lera Millard Thomas

1900–1993

UNITED STATES REPRESENTATIVE ★ DEMOCRAT FROM TEXAS

1966–1967

For more than 30 years, Lera Millard Thomas worked behind the scenes to cultivate the political career of her husband, Albert Thomas, who became one of the most powerful Members in the House. Upon Congressman Thomas's death in 1966, however, Lera Thomas opted to run for the vacant seat out of a desire to provide continuity for constituents and to further her husband's political agenda. In her brief nine-month term, Thomas worked on legislation affecting Houston from her Merchant Marine and Fisheries Committee seat. A descendant of Texas territory pioneers, Thomas was the state's first woman to serve in Congress.

Lera Millard was born in Nacogdoches, Texas, on August 3, 1900, the daughter of Jesse Wadlington Millard and Annie Donnell Watkins Millard. She attended Brenau College in Gainesville, Georgia, and the University of Alabama. In 1922, Millard married her high school sweet-heart, Albert Thomas. The couple moved from Nacogdoches to Houston, where Albert took a position as assistant U.S. district attorney for the southern district of Texas. The Thomases had three children: Jim, Ann, and Lera.

Originally, Lera Thomas did not want her husband to become involved in politics. But when Jim died at a very young age in 1934 (he was then their only child), the Alberts decided "to throw ourselves completely away from everything that we had done or where we lived or anything like that."[1] In 1936, Albert left his district attorney post to campaign for a seat in the U.S. House, covering most of Houston, in the 75th Congress (1937–1939). Since radio advertisement time was scarce and prohibitively expensive, Albert and Lera Thomas divided up campaign duties to make the rounds at political events: "He'd go in one direction to picnics and barbeques and I would go in the other direction. Just to meet people." Lera Thomas frequently debated her husband on political issues to help him sharpen his positions. He "used to say I was his severest critic."[2] Thomas won election to the House as a Democrat against a longtime popular mayor of Houston. He went on to win 14 consecutive elections after that and became a senior member of the House Appropriations Committee. Beginning in 1949, he headed the Subcommittee on Defense Appropriations, which eventually controlled funding for the National Aeronautics and Space Administration (NASA) and the Atomic Energy Commission, among other Cold War appropriations. Congressman Thomas helped make Houston a center for manned space flight operations, often opposed his party on generous foreign aid packages during the Cold War, and was considered an ally of labor unions. Lera Thomas, meanwhile, raised the family in Washington, D.C., and often commuted back to Houston for events in the district. Though Albert Thomas's name was not widely known to the public outside Texas, he worked closely with three Democratic Presidents—Harry S. Truman, John F. Kennedy, and Lyndon B. Johnson. At the time of his death in February 1966, the *New York Times* described him as a "quiet power in the Capitol."[3]

Days after Albert Thomas died from cancer, district party leaders asked Lera Thomas to run for her husband's vacant seat, and she agreed to accept the nomination. In the March 26, 1966, special election, Thomas won with more than 74 percent of the vote against Republican Louis Leman, who himself had encouraged voters to go to the polls for the widow Thomas.[4] Constituents identified with the Thomas name and seemed inclined to believe that Lera Thomas would carry on in her husband's tradition. "We see in her, the modesty and integrity that personified her late husband," one supporter observed.[5] Party leaders seemed equally as interested in encouraging her candidacy because she was a safe placekeeper who was familiar with the Washington office operations. It was believed that her presence would create stability to keep experienced staff in place until a long-term successor could be chosen.

Once ensconced in Washington, Congresswoman Thomas was faced with deciding whether or not to run for a full term in the succeeding Congress. Texas election law kept Albert Thomas's name on the May 7 primary ballot for the Democratic nomination to the 90th Congress (1967–1969). A victory for the deceased Congressman would have permitted the Harris County Democratic Executive Committee to name Lera Thomas as the party's candidate in the fall election, but she discouraged the movement to gain her another term in office.[6] Bob Eckhardt, an eight-year veteran of the Texas state legislature, eventually won the nomination and went on to win the general election in 1966.[7]

Sworn in and seated four days after the election on March 30, 1966, Thomas continued her husband's dedicated service to the district during her abbreviated term. She received a single committee assignment: Merchant Marine and Fisheries. Thomas's principal legislative task was to further the support her husband had gained for the space program and other economic interests of the urban Texas district. She petitioned Congress to appropriate funds for the construction of NASA's lunar sample receiving laboratory in Houston. The Congresswoman appealed to her colleagues, "If the lunar laboratory were to be placed at some location other than the spacecraft center . . . administrative and technical support would add considerably to the costs . . . . Who would build a house with a pantry at the opposite end from the kitchen?"[8] From her Merchant Marine and Fisheries seat, she also sought additional funding of the Houston Ship Channel, the waterway connecting Houston with the Gulf of Mexico, which had been another of her husband's projects.[9]

Thomas undertook her most ambitious work as she prepared to leave office. In late 1966, she traveled to Vietnam as a Member and, after the expiration of her term on January 3, 1967, continued on as a journalist to gain an understanding of the prospects of victory in the war. A few days before she was scheduled to leave, she received an urgent message from the White House: She was to meet President Johnson at his plane at Andrews Air Force Base just outside the capital and fly with him on a trip to Texas. Setting aside her packing chores, Thomas complied, though she had no idea why the President needed to see her on such short notice. In mid-flight, Johnson summoned her to the front of the plane. "What do you mean—going to Vietnam?" he demanded. Thomas sensed Johnson's concern about growing congressional criticism of the war and sought to ease his fears that she would join the chorus of dissenters. She replied, "Mr. President you went to Vietnam and I'm not nearly as important as you are." Johnson told her, "All right, then, go on and go."[10] On her six-week trip, Thomas personally delivered letters to U.S. troops. Some of her observations, based on meetings with South Vietnamese, were published by the *Houston Chronicle* and were later reprinted in the *Congressional Record*. In one account, Thomas wrote: "One fact is clear to me: Unless a stable economy is established in South Vietnam and the people are given an incentive to maintain that economy, we will lose what we are fighting for here."[11]

After returning to Washington in February 1967, Thomas served for six months as a consultant in the Vietnam Bureau of the U.S. State Department's Agency for International Development. She eventually returned to Texas and managed the family farm and an antique shop. One of Thomas's legacies was her part in the establishment of the Millard Crossing Historical Center on the north side of Nacogdoches, culminating years of work to preserve buildings and structures dating from the pioneer days of Texas to the Victorian Era.[12] Lera Thomas died of cancer on July 23, 1993, in her hometown of Nacogdoches.

FOR FURTHER READING

Biographical Directory of the United States Congress, "Lera Millard Thomas," http://bioguide.congress.gov

MANUSCRIPT COLLECTIONS

Lyndon B. Johnson Library (Austin, TX). *Oral History:* October 11, 1968. 32 pages. Available online.

Rice University Library (Houston, TX), Woodson Research Center. *Papers:* In the Albert Thomas Papers, 1937–1965, 11 feet. Subjects covered include Lera Millard Thomas. A finding aid is available in the repository.

NOTES

1   Lera Millard Thomas, Oral History, 11 October 1968, Lyndon Baines Johnson Library (hereinafter referred to as LBJL), Austin, TX: 4.
2   Thomas, Oral History, LBJL: 9.
3   "Rep. Albert Thomas Dies at 67; Texan a Quiet Power in the Capitol," 16 February 1966, *New York Times*: 43.
4   Michael J. Dubin et al., *United States Congressional Elections, 1788–1997* (Jefferson, NC: McFarland & Company, Publishing, Inc., 1998): 647.
5   Hope Chamberlin, *A Minority of Members: Women in the U.S. Congress* (New York: Praeger, 1973): 316.
6   Martin Waldron, "Texas Democrats In Key Vote Today," 7 May 1966, *New York Times*: 15; see also, Thomas, Oral History, LBJL: 20.
7   "Election Statistics, 1920 to Present," http://clerk.house.gov/members/electionInfo/elections.html.
8   *Congressional Record*, House, 89th Cong., 2nd sess. (10 May 1966): 10225.
9   Chamberlin, *A Minority of Members*: 316; Thomas, Oral History, LBJL: 5.
10 Thomas, Oral History, LBJL: 18–19.
11 *Congressional Record*, House, 90th Cong., 1st sess. (February 13, 1967): A619.
12 Candace Leslie, "Collecting Culminates in Millard's Crossing," 7 July 1996, *Houston Chronicle*: 10.

Margaret M. Heckler

1931–

UNITED STATES REPRESENTATIVE ★ REPUBLICAN FROM MASSACHUSETTS
1967–1983

Margaret Mary Heckler served eight restless terms in the House, as she was frequently mentioned for state office while moving through six standing committees. "Her seniority and bargaining ability were weakened by these frequent moves," observed a colleague, "and she was forced most often to carry her agenda directly to the House Floor."[1] Such activity may have been due to the fact that Heckler was a moderate Republican from one of the nation's most liberal and Democratic states.

Margaret Mary O'Shaughnessy was born on June 21, 1931, in Flushing, New York. She was the only child of John O'Shaughnessy, a hotel doorman, and Bridget McKeon O'Shaughnessy, Irish-Catholic immigrants. She graduated from Albertus Magnus College in 1953, marrying John Heckler, an investment banker, in 1954. Theirs would be a commuter marriage that eventually produced three children: Belinda, Alison, and John, Jr. The marriage ended in 1985 after she left Congress. Heckler went on to Boston College School of Law, where she was the only woman in her class. She graduated in 1956, forming a law office with fellow law school graduates. Shortly afterward she began volunteering in local Republican campaigns, and in 1958 she became a member of the Republican committee for Wellesley, Massachusetts, a position she held for eight years. Heckler became the first woman elected to the eight-person governor's council (an elected advisory body mandated by the state constitution) in 1962, serving two terms. Thereafter, she was frequently mentioned as a possible candidate for statewide office.

In 1966, Heckler dismayed the Republican establishment when she announced her candidacy against Representative Joseph W. Martin, the venerable 81-year

-old House incumbent, whose seat encompassed southeastern Massachusetts. Martin had served in Congress since 1925 and was Speaker of the House twice. Heckler's energetic campaign was a marked contrast to the performances of her elderly opponent, who had missed more than half of the votes in the previous Congress.[2] She narrowly won the Republican primary by 3,200 votes.[3] Heckler went on to win the general election against labor lawyer Patrick H. Harrington, Jr., with 51 percent of the vote, to become the first woman from Massachusetts elected to Congress without succeeding her husband. "The men kept saying I couldn't make it," she later recalled, "but the women convinced them that a woman, even if she was the underdog, deserved their backing."[4]

Early in her House career, Heckler quickly moved to build her support. She concentrated on building a reputation as her district's champion in the capital by setting up a toll-free hot line to facilitate communication between her constituents and her Washington office. She also scheduled weekly visits to her district. In addition, Heckler took care to be a policy advocate for her constituents: calling for an end to foreign oil import quotas in order to gain cheaper fuel oil, protecting the New England textile industry, demanding protection of U.S. fishermen from Soviet harassment on the seas, and calling for tax credits to help parochial schools. Four days into her first term, Heckler ignored the chamber's tradition that freshman Members remain silent, when she publicly demanded the release of a constituent, a naturalized citizen, who had been arrested for espionage in Czechoslovakia.[5] Former staffer Jack Horner recalled, "She would never take no for an answer when it came to her constituents."[6]

Heckler struggled to balance party loyalty with the prevailing viewpoints of her district. Moving beyond issues clearly tied to her constituents, she seemed uncertain to some observers, who believed she cast votes based on the lead of other Members rather than her own convictions.[7] A former aide defended her, noting that she survived "in a district that rightfully should have had a Democrat [as] Representative. And she did it by very close calculations on how to vote. She's an astute, careful politician."[8] The liberal Americans for Democratic Action's roll call votes scorecard for Heckler ranged from 47 percent to 74 percent support of their favored issues. The conservative Americans for Constitutional Action issued scorecards for Heckler that ranged from 12 percent to 48 percent support for their issues. That Heckler had entered Congress by deposing her party's favorite and had achieved a level of popularity that resulted in two races, 1972 and 1976, where she ran unopposed, writes Marcy Kaptur, suggested that "she felt no obligation to toe the party line."[9] One colleague in the Massachusetts delegation told the *Washington Post*, "People don't give her credit for being a woman in a man's world, a Republican in a Democratic state, a moderate in liberal country. She's never been in the mainstream, always an outsider. . . . Yes, she's shrill and she doesn't work well with people. But she had to be all those things to get where she is."[10]

Congresswoman Heckler demonstrated a sincere interest in increasing the number of women in politics. During her first term, she described why she had run for Congress. Besides contributing to making good policy, she added, "I also felt very strongly that there should be more women in Congress."[11] Heckler made a fervent and consistent commitment to women's issues, ranging from combating rape, curbing domestic violence, protecting pension rights for women on maternity leave, and prohibiting discrimination based on gender or marital status in acquiring credit. In 1976, she began working to organize a caucus of all women House Members, efforts which were initially rebuffed. In April 1977, she and Representative Elizabeth Holtzman of New York became the first co-chairs of the bipartisan Congresswomen's Caucus. The goal of the caucus

was to promote legislation beneficial to women and to encourage women appointments. Fifteen of the 18 women in Congress joined. Heckler served as the Republican chair until 1982, the year the caucus changed its name to the Congressional Caucus for Women's Issues. "The Women's Caucus is making a difference and it's very important to continue," Heckler remarked on the caucus's 25th anniversary. "The hard struggles have been won, but there will always be small struggles. I have to believe the Caucus was a part of that."[12]

Heckler played a balancing role when it came to abortion. While opposing the use of federal funds for abortions, she also opposed a pro-life constitutional amendment or any requirement for federally funded clinics to notify parents of teenagers receiving birth control prescriptions. The National Women's Political Caucus endorsed Heckler's opponents in 1980 and 1982 because of her stand on abortion.[13] Two years later the National Organization for Women also refused to endorse her. "It was very hurtful to me psychologically," Heckler recalled in 2002. "It was very important to have a Republican component in the advancement of women because these women knew without a Republican, these issues wouldn't be taken seriously. Abortion is difficult, and it has divided women, but I don't think women's identity should focus on that one issue."[14]

A level of restlessness existed during Heckler's House career that is reflected in her committee history. She came to Congress seeking appointment to the Committee on the Judiciary; instead, she was put onto the Committee on Veterans' Affairs. She remained on Veterans' Affairs during her entire House service, rising to Ranking Member in 1975. Her second committee assignment, though, was unusually variable. Originally, Heckler was on the Committee on Government Operations. In her second term she moved to the Committee on Banking and Currency. After serving there for six years, Heckler took the opportunity to move to the Committee on Agriculture. Once again, her tenure lasted six years. During her final term she transferred to the Committee on Science and Technology. Heckler also took a position in the 94th Congress (1975–1977) on the Joint Economic Committee.

Her tenure there lasted eight years. She further served on the Ethics Committee for the 95th Congress (1977–1979), the Committee on Aging in the 97th Congress (1981–1983), and the largely ceremonial House Beauty Shop Committee in the 92nd and 93rd Congresses (1971–1975). Heckler had been characterized as impatient and uncomfortable with the more deliberative pace of the legislative process.[15]

Heckler's congressional career ended unexpectedly in 1982 while she was the most senior Republican woman in the House. The Massachusetts legislature redrew its con-

and tax cuts. A sagging economy—district unemployment was more than 13 percent—made Heckler vulnerable to Frank's charges, and in response she could only argue that she was not "a Reagan clone." "I've served under five Presidents, unbossed and unbought," she proclaimed.[17] But observers found her campaign poorly organized. Negative TV ads by the Heckler campaign may have hurt her by creating a sympathy vote for Frank. The result was considered a surprise: Barney Frank won re-election with 59 percent of the vote to Heckler's 40 percent.[18]

"I felt the Congress was the office where I could make the best contribution. I was really concerned about the issues of the day, not only in the traditional areas of education and consumer protection, in criminal justice, social security, conservation, air and water pollution. I also felt very strongly that there should be more women in Congress and that the government should be brought closer to the people."

— MARGARET M. HECKLER, 1968

gressional districts after the 1980 Census, facing the task of losing one House seat. Heckler's decision to forego challenging Senator Edward Kennedy for re-election pitted her against Representative Barney Frank, a Democratic freshman, in a new and economically diverse district encompassing wealthy Boston suburbs and working-class communities in southeastern Massachusetts. In the match-up, Heckler was so heavily favored that Frank considered retiring.[16] Frank worked hard to make the race a referendum on President Ronald Reagan's conservative policies. His campaign repeatedly concentrated on Heckler's support of Reagan's 1981 budget and economic plan, which combined spending

In the aftermath of Heckler's defeat, President Ronald W. Reagan nominated her as Secretary of Health and Human Services. Nearly a week after the Senate confirmed her appointment, Justice Sandra Day O'Connor swore Heckler into the Cabinet on March 9, 1983. During her tenure she oversaw the establishment of new disability guidelines for Social Security and increased federal funding for Alzheimer's disease. But her greatest challenge was dealing with the emerging HIV/AIDS crisis. Heckler came under attack from conservatives in late 1985 as an ineffective administrator and as weak in her support of the Reagan administration's programs. She accepted President Reagan's offer to be U.S. Ambassador to

Heckler survived "in a district that rightfully should have had a Democrat [as] Representative," noted one of her former aides. "And she did it by very close calculations on how to vote. She's an astute, careful politician."

Ireland and served from December 1985 through October 1989. She currently resides in Wellesley, Massachusetts.

FOR FURTHER READING

Biographical Directory of the United States Congress, "Margaret Heckler," http://bioguide.congress.gov

Kaptur, Marcy. "Margaret M. Heckler," in *Women of Congress: A Twentieth-Century Odyssey* (Washington, D.C.: Congressional Quarterly Press, 1996).

MANUSCRIPT COLLECTION

Boston College (Boston, MA), John J. Burns Library Congressional Archives, Chestnut Hill, MA. *Papers:* ca. 1966–1987, approximately 237 linear feet. The collection of Margaret Heckler contains personal, business, and congressional papers and correspondence, including photographs, portraits, video tape, sound recordings, and memorabilia, documenting her career in Congress and in the Department of Health and Human Services. The collection also includes material relating to the Republican Party. Most of the collection is currently restricted.

NOTES

1 Marcy Kaptur, *Women in Congress: A Twentieth-Century Odyssey* (Washington, D.C.: Congressional Quarterly Press, 1996): 133.

2 *Current Biography, 1983* (New York: H.W. Wilson and Company, 1983): 183.

3 Hope Chamberlin, *A Minority of Members: Women in the U.S. Congress* (New York: Praeger, 1973): 318–319.

4 *Current Biography, 1983*: 183.

5 Marie Smith, "She's for a Strong Ethics Code," 14 May 1967, *Washington Post*: K3.

6 Lois Romano, "Heckler: Tough Campaigner for HHS," 13 February 1983, *Washington Post*: L12.

7 "Heckler," 13 February 1983, *Washington Post*: L11.

8 *Current Biography, 1983*: 185.

9 Romano, "Heckler."

10 Ibid.

11 *Current Biography, 1983*: 183.

12 Lynn Olanoff, "Silvery Anniversary," 18 April 2002, *Roll Call*: 42.

13 Robert Pear, "Reagan Chooses Ex-Rep. Heckler To Be the New Secretary of Health," 13 January 1983, *New York Times*: D22.

14 Olanoff, "Silver Anniversary."

15 Romano, "Heckler."

16 "Frank Will Take On Margaret Heckler," 14 January 1982, *Roll Call*.

17 Juan Williams, "President Names Ex-Rep. Heckler as Head of HHS," 13 January 1983, *Washington Post*: A8; *Current Biography, 1983*: 185.

18 "Election Statistics, 1920 to Present," http://clerk.house.gov/members/electionInfo/elections.html.

Shirley Anita Chisholm
1924–2005

UNITED STATES REPRESENTATIVE ★ DEMOCRAT FROM NEW YORK
1969–1983

Shirley Anita Chisholm was the first African-American woman to serve in Congress, representing a newly reapportioned U.S. House district centered in Brooklyn. Elected in 1968 because of her local roots in the Bedford-Stuyvesant neighborhood, Chisholm nevertheless served as a national figure—catapulted into the limelight by virtue of her race, gender, and outspoken personality. In 1972, in a largely symbolic undertaking, she campaigned for the Democratic presidential nomination. But "Fighting Shirley" Chisholm's frontal assault on many congressional traditions and her reputation as a crusader limited her influence as a legislator. "I am the people's politician," she once told the *New York Times*. "If the day should ever come when the people can't save me, I'll know I'm finished. That's when I'll go back to being a professional educator."[1]

Shirley Anita St. Hill was born on November 20, 1924, in Brooklyn, New York. She was the oldest of four daughters of Charles St. Hill, a factory laborer from Guyana, and Ruby Seale St. Hill, a seamstress from Barbados. For part of her childhood, Shirley St. Hill lived in Barbados on her maternal grandparents' farm, receiving a British-system education while her parents worked during the Great Depression to make money to settle the family in Bedford-Stuyvesant. The most outward manifestation of her West Indies roots was her slight, clipped, British accent that she retained throughout her adult life. She attended public schools in Brooklyn and graduated with high marks. Accepted to Vassar and Oberlin colleges, Shirley St. Hill attended Brooklyn College on scholarship and graduated *cum laude* with a B.A. in sociology in 1946. From 1946 to 1953, Chisholm worked as a nursery school teacher and then as director of two day care centers. St. Hill married Conrad Q. Chisholm, a private investigator, in 1949.

Three years later, Shirley Chisholm earned an M.A. in early childhood education from Columbia University. She served as an educational consultant for New York City's Division of Day Care from 1959 to 1964. In 1964, Chisholm was elected as an assemblywoman in the New York state legislature—the second African-American woman to serve in Albany.

A court-ordered reapportionment, which created a new Brooklyn congressional district carved out of Chisholm's Bedford-Stuyvesant neighborhood, convinced her to run for Congress. The influential Democratic political machine, headed by Stanley Steingut, declared its intention to send an African American to the House from the new district. The endorsement of the machine usually meant victory in the primary which, in the heavily Democratic area, was tantamount to election. In the primary, Chisholm faced three African-American challengers: civil court judge Thomas R. Jones, a former district leader and New York assemblyman; Dolly Robinson, a former district co-leader; and William C. Thompson, a well-financed state senator. Chisholm roamed the new district in a sound truck which pulled up outside housing projects while the candidate announced: "Ladies and Gentleman . . . this is fighting Shirley Chisholm coming through." Chisholm capitalized on her personal campaigning style. "I have a way of talking that does something to people," she noted. "I have a theory about campaigning. You have to let them feel you."[2] In the primary in mid-June 1968, Chisholm defeated Thompson, her nearest competitor, by about 800 votes in an election marked by light voter turnout.

In the general election, Chisholm faced the Republican-Liberal candidate James Farmer, a civil rights activist. Both candidates held similar positions on housing, employment, and education issues and also were united in their opposition to the Vietnam War. Farmer charged that the Democratic Party "took [blacks] for granted and thought they had us in their pockets. . . . We must be in a position to use our power as a swing vote."3 But the election turned on the issue of gender. Farmer hammered away, arguing that "women have been in the driver's seat" in black communities for too long and that the district needed "a man's voice in Washington," not that of a "little schoolteacher."4 Chisholm, whose campaign motto was "unbought and unbossed," met that charge head-on, using Farmer's rhetoric to highlight discrimination against women and to explain her unique qualifications. "There were Negro men in office here before I came in five years ago, but they didn't deliver," Chisholm countered. "People came and asked me to do something . . . I'm here because of the vacuum." Chisholm portrayed Farmer as an outsider (he lived in Manhattan) and also used her fluent Spanish to appeal to the growing Hispanic population in the Bedford-Stuyvesant neighborhood; Puerto Rican immigrants accounted for about 20 percent of the district vote. The deciding factor, however, was the district's overwhelming liberal tilt: More than 80 percent of the voters were registered Democrats. Chisholm won the general election by a resounding 67 percent of the vote. Thereafter, she was never seriously challenged for her seat in six subsequent general elections.5

Chisholm was part of a freshman class that included African Americans of future prominence: Louis Stokes of Ohio and William L. Clay of Missouri. Chisholm's class boosted the number of African Americans in the House from five to 10, the largest total up to that time. She also was the only new woman to enter Congress in 1969.

Chisholm's welcome in the House was not warm, due to her immediate outspokenness. "I have no intention of just sitting quietly and observing," she said. "I intend. . . to focus attention on the nation's problems." She did just that, lashing out against the Vietnam War in her first floor speech on March 26, 1969. Chisholm vowed to vote against any defense appropriation bill "until the time comes when our values and priorities have been turned

right-side up again."6 She was assigned to the Committee on Agriculture, a decision which she appealed directly to House Speaker John McCormack of Massachusetts (bypassing Wilbur Mills of Arkansas, the chairman of the Democratic selection committee). McCormack told her to be a "good soldier," to which Chisholm responded by bringing her complaint to the House Floor. She was reassigned to the Veterans' Affairs Committee which, though not one of her top choices, was more in tune with her district's makeup. "There are a lot more veterans in my district than trees," she quipped.7 From 1971 to 1977 she served on the Committee on Education and Labor, winning a place on that panel with the help of Hale Boggs of Louisiana, for whom she had voted as Majority Leader.8 She also served on the Committee on Organization Study and Review (known as the Hansen Committee), which recommended reforms in the selection process for committee chairmen that were adopted by the Democratic Caucus in 1971. From 1977 to 1981, Chisholm served as Secretary of the Democratic Caucus. She eventually left her Education Committee assignment to accept a seat on the Rules Committee in 1977. She was the first black woman (and only the second woman ever) to serve on that powerful panel. Chisholm also was a founding member of the Congressional Women's Caucus in 1977.

Chisholm's congressional career was marked by continuity with her earlier community activist causes. She sponsored federal funding increases to extend daycare facility hours and a guaranteed minimum annual income for families. She was a fierce defender of federal assistance to education, serving as a primary backer of a national school lunch bill and leading her colleagues in overriding President Gerald R. Ford's veto on this measure. By her own admission, however, Chisholm did not view herself as a "lawmaker, an innovator in the field of legislation." Rather, in her efforts to address the needs of the "have-nots," she often chose to work outside the established system. At times she criticized the Democratic leadership in Congress as much as she did the Republicans in the White House. She played more the role of an explorer and a trailblazer than she did the role of a legislative artisan.9

CHISHOLM'S WELCOME IN THE
HOUSE WAS NOT WARM, DUE TO HER
IMMEDIATE OUTSPOKENNESS. "I
HAVE NO INTENTION OF JUST
SITTING QUIETLY AND OBSERVING,"
SHE SAID. "I INTEND TO SPEAK OUT
IMMEDIATELY IN ORDER TO FOCUS
ATTENTION ON THE NATION'S
PROBLEMS."

True to this approach, Chisholm declared her candidacy for the 1972 Democratic nomination for President, charging that none of the other candidates represented the interests of blacks and the inner-city poor. She campaigned across the country and got her name on the ballot in 12 primaries, becoming as well known outside her Brooklyn neighborhood as she was inside it. At the Democratic National Convention she received 152 delegate votes, or 10 percent of the total, a respectable showing, given her low funding. A 1974 Gallup Poll listed her as one of the top 10 most-admired women in America—ahead of Jacqueline Kennedy Onassis and Coretta Scott King and tied with Indian Prime Minister Indira Gandhi for sixth place.[10] But while the presidential bid enhanced Chisholm's national profile, it also stirred controversy among House colleagues. Chisholm's candidacy split the Congressional Black Caucus. Many male colleagues felt she had not consulted them or had betrayed the group's interests by trying to create a coalition of women, Hispanics, white liberals, and welfare recipients.[11] Pervasive gender discrimination, Chisholm noted, cut across race lines: "Black male politicians are no different from white male politicians. This 'woman thing' is so deep. I've found it out in this campaign if I never knew it before."[12] Her campaign also strained relations with other women Members of Congress, particularly Bella Abzug of New York, who instead endorsed George McGovern.

By 1976, Chisholm faced a stiff challenge from within her own party primary by a longtime political rival, New York City Councilman Samuel D. Wright. Wright, born and raised in Bedford-Stuyvesant, was a formidable opponent who had represented Brooklyn in the New York assembly for a number of years before winning a seat on the city council. He criticized Chisholm for her absenteeism in the House, brought on by the rigors of her presidential campaign, and a lack of connection with the district. Chisholm countered by playing on her national credentials and role as a reformer of Capitol Hill culture. "I think my role is to break new ground in Congress," Chisholm noted. She insisted that her strength was in bringing legislative factions together. "I can talk with legislators from the South, the West, all over. They view me as a national figure and that makes me more acceptable."[13] Two weeks later Chisholm turned back Wright and Hispanic political activist Luz Vega in the Democratic primary, winning 54 percent of the vote to 36 percent and 10 percent, respectively, for Wright and Vega.[14] She won the general election handily with 83 percent of the vote.[15]

From the late 1970s forward, speculation among Brooklyn Democrats was that Chisholm was losing interest in her House job. Her name was widely floated as a possible candidate for several education-related jobs, including president of the City College of New York and chancellor of the New York City public school system.[16] In 1982, Chisholm declined to seek re-election. "Shirley Chisholm would like to have a little life of her own," she told the *Christian Science Monitor*, citing personal reasons for her decision to leave the House.[17] She wanted to spend more time with her second husband, Arthur Hardwick, Jr., a New York state legislator whom she had married about six months after divorcing Conrad Chisholm in 1977. Hardwick, who sustained serious injuries in an automobile accident a year after their marriage, died in 1986.

Other reasons factored into her decision. In part, she had grown disillusioned over the conservative turn the country had taken with the election of President Ronald W. Reagan in 1980. Also, there were tensions with people on her side of the political fence, particularly African-American politicians who, she insisted, misunderstood her efforts at alliance building. Chisholm maintained that many in the black community did not understand the need for negotiation with white politicians. "We still have to engage in compromise, the highest of all arts," Chisholm noted. "Blacks can't do things on their own, nor can whites. When you have black racists and white racists it is very difficult to build bridges between communities."[18]

After leaving Congress in January 1983, Chisholm helped cofound the National Political Congress of Black Women and campaigned for Jesse Jackson's presidential campaigns in 1984 and 1988. She also taught at Mt. Holyoke College in 1983. Though nominated by President William J. Clinton for U.S. Ambassador to Jamaica,

Chisholm declined due to ill health. Chisholm lived in Palm Coast, Florida, where she wrote and lectured. She died on January 1, 2005, in Ormond Beach, Florida.

FOR FURTHER READING

Biographical Directory of the United States Congress, "Shirley Anita Chisholm," http://bioguide.congress.gov

Brownmiller, Susan. *Shirley Chisholm* (New York: Doubleday, 1970).

Chisholm, Shirley. *The Good Fight* (Boston: Houghton Mifflin, 1973).

———. *Unbought and Unbossed* (Boston: Houghton Mifflin, 1970).

MANUSCRIPT COLLECTION

Rutgers University Library, Center for American Women and Politics, Eagleton Institute of Politics (New Brunswick, NJ). *Papers:* 1963–1994, approximately 3.7 cubic feet. The papers of Shirley Chisholm consist of speeches, 1971–1989, on a wide variety of topics; congressional files, 1965–1981, composed primarily of complimentary letters received and presidential campaign materials; general files, 1966–1986, consisting chiefly of biographical materials, including information on Chisholm's record in Congress; newspaper clippings, 1969–1990, in the form of editorials written by Chisholm, as well as coverage of her speeches, writings, and retirement; constituent newsletters, 1969–1982, complemented by selected press releases; photographs (including photocopies and other reproductions), 1969–1990, many of which depict Chisholm with other political figures; publications, 1969–1992, with additional coverage of Chisholm's political career and her retirement; and campaign miscellany, 1969 and 1972, including buttons from her presidential campaign and political posters.

NOTES

1 Susan Brownmiller, "This Is Fighting Shirley Chisholm," 13 April 1969, *New York Times*: SM32.

2 Brownmiller, "This Is Fighting Shirley Chisholm."

3 John Kifner, "G.O.P. Names James Farmer For Brooklyn Race for Congress," 20 May 1968, *New York Times*: 34; John Kifner, "Farmer and Woman in Lively Bedford-Stuyvesant Race," 26 October 1968, *New York Times*: 22.

4 Shirley Washington, *Outstanding Women in Congress* (Washington, D.C.: U.S. Capitol Historical Society, 1995): 17.

5 "Election Statistics, 1920 to Present," http://clerk.house.gov/members/electionInfo/elections.html.

6 *Current Biography, 1969* (New York: H.W. Wilson and Company, 1969): 94; Hope Chamberlin, *A Minority of Members: Women in Congress* (New York: Praeger, 1973): 325

7 Karen Foerstel, *Biographical Dictionary of Congressional Women* (Westport, CT: Greenwood Press, 1999): 56.

8 Jane Perlez, "Rep. Chisholm's Angry Farewell," 12 October 1982, *New York Times*: A24.

9 Marcy Kaptur, *Women of Congress: A Twentieth-Century Odyssey* (Washington, D.C.: Congressional Quarterly Press, 1996): 150–151; see also, Shirley Chisholm, *Unbought and Unbossed* (Boston: Houghton Mifflin, 1970): 70, 112.

10 "The Gallup Poll: Meir, Betty Ford Are Most Admired," 2 January 1975, *Washington Post*: B3.

11 Kaptur, *Women of Congress*: 150; William L. Clay, Sr., *Just Permanent Interests* (New York: Armistead Press, 1993): 222.

12 Karen Foerstel and Herbert Foerstel, *Climbing the Hill: Gender Conflict in Congress* (Westport, CT: Praeger, 1996): 30.

13 Charlayne Hunter, "Chisholm-Wright Feud in Brooklyn Is Eroding Blacks' Political Power," 20 March 1976, *New York Times*: 24; Ronald Smothers, "Rep. Chisholm Battling Wright in Showdown Race in Brooklyn," 30 August 1976, *New York Times*: 26; Ronald Smothers, "Wright, Mrs. Chisholm Trade Charges in Face-to-Face Debate in Brooklyn," 3 September 1976, *New York Times*: A14.

14 "Voting in Primaries for U.S. House and State Legislature," 16 September 1976, *New York Times*: 34.

15 "Election Statistics, 1920 to Present," http://clerk.house.gov/members/electionInfo/elections.html.

16 Marcia Chambers, "School Post Weighed for Mrs. Chisholm," 18 February 1978, *New York Times*: B13; Samuel Weiss, "Rep. Chisholm Is a Candidate for College Job," 19 February 1981, *New York Times*: B12.

17 Julia Malone, "Advice From Retiring Insiders on Shaping Better Congress," 3 November 1982, *Christian Science Monitor*: 1.

18 Malone, "Advice From Retiring Insiders on Shaping Better Congress."

Bella Savitzky Abzug
1920–1998

UNITED STATES REPRESENTATIVE ★ DEMOCRAT FROM NEW YORK
1971–1977

Bella Abzug, feminist and civil rights advocate, embodied many Americans' discontent with the political establishment in the tumultuous Vietnam War era. She gained notoriety as one of the most colorful and controversial House Members during the 1970s. Once quoted as saying "women have been trained to talk softly and carry a lipstick," the feisty New York Congresswoman spent much of her life refuting the notion that women should remain on the political sidelines.[1] Despite only serving in Congress for three terms, Abzug's political flair and unwavering determination helped inspire an entire generation of women and created a new model for future Congresswomen. "She was such a trailblazer," a former aide noted after Abzug's death in 1998, "It wasn't that she was the first woman in Congress. It was that she was the first woman to get in Congress and lead the way toward creating a feminist presence."[2]

The daughter of Russian-Jewish immigrants Emmanuel and Esther Tanklefsky Savitsky, she was born Bella Savitsky in the Bronx, New York, on July 24, 1920. She received an A.B. from Hunter College in Manhattan in 1942 and immediately entered Columbia University Law School. In 1944, Bella Savitsky married Martin Abzug. As a stockbroker and novelist, her husband had little inclination toward politics. Nevertheless, Bella Abzug counted him as her closest confidant and supporter: "one of the few un-neurotic people left in society."[3] The Abzugs raised two children: Eve and Liz. After interrupting her studies to work in a shipyard during World War II, Bella Abzug served as editor of the *Columbia Law Review*, and graduated with an LL.B. in 1947. For the next two decades Abzug practiced law on behalf of people whom the existing legal and social structures bypassed, citizens she once described as being "on the outside of power."[4] She defended Willie McGee, an African-American man convicted and sentenced to death in Mississippi for raping a white woman. She also represented individuals whom Senator Joseph McCarthy's investigatory committee tarred as communist agents. In 1961 Abzug cofounded Women Strike for Peace, a group which protested the nuclear arms race and, later, the American military commitment in Vietnam. She served as a leader in the "Dump Johnson" movement to remove embattled President Lyndon B. Johnson from the 1968 Democratic ticket. Reflecting on this long record, Abzug later conceded that she was at heart an activist rather than a politician.[5]

In 1970, at the age of 50, Abzug made her first attempt at elected office, when she decided to enter the race for a U.S. House of Representatives seat in Manhattan's wealthy, liberal Upper West Side. Employing the campaign slogan "This woman's place is in the House . . . the House of Representatives!" Abzug ran on an antiwar and pro-feminist platform. Her insistence that she would have a stronger voice and more active presence on Capitol Hill than her opponent helped Abzug earn 55 percent of the vote in the Democratic primary and unseat the seven-term incumbent, Leonard Farbstein.[6] In the general election, Abzug defeated Republican-Liberal Barry Farber, a radio talk show host, in a three-way election, with 52 percent to Farber's 43 percent.[7] Throughout the campaign, Abzug benefited from the support of celebrity entertainers and New York City Mayor John Lindsay. The national media focused on her effort, foreshadowing the publicity she would attract as a sitting Representative.[8]

After taking the official oath of office for the 92nd Congress (1971–1973) on January 3, 1971, Abzug took a "people's oath" on the House steps administered by her New York colleague Shirley Chisholm. Onlookers cheered, "Give 'em hella, Bella!" By seeking a seat on the coveted Armed Services Committee, Abzug also flaunted House decorum, which expected freshman to accept lower-level committee assignments. The request was denied (she eventually accepted positions on the Government Operations and Public Works committees). Undeterred, she worked on devising methods to dismantle the entrenched House seniority system that prevented most newly elected Representatives from receiving influential assignments. Despite her freshman status, Abzug made waves in Congress by supporting a variety of controversial causes. On the first day of the session, she introduced legislation demanding the withdrawal of U.S. forces from Vietnam. She authored a bill to end the draft, an institution she likened to "slavery" motivated by "insane priorities," and she asked for an investigation into the competence of widely feared Federal Bureau of Investigation Director J. Edgar Hoover.[9] "I spend all day figuring out how to beat the machine and knock the crap out of the political power structure," Abzug wrote in her journal, published in 1972.[10] "Battling Bella," an epithet she earned because of her tenacity and confrontational demeanor, also had the distinction of being one of the first politicians to publicly call for the impeachment of President Richard Nixon, even before the 1973 congressional outcry about his Vietnam policy in early 1972.[11]

Writer Norman Mailer once described Abzug's voice as an instrument that "could boil the fat off a taxicab driver's neck."[12] Cognizant that her personality often prompted discussion and, at times, dismay from onlookers, Abzug retorted, "There are those who say I'm impatient, impetuous, uppity, rude, profane, brash and overbearing. Whether I'm any of these things or all of them, you can decide for yourself. But whatever I am—and this ought to be made clear from the outset—I am a very serious woman."[13] Easy to spot in her trademark wide-brimmed hat (which she began wearing as a young female professional because she believed it was the only way men "would take you seriously"), Abzug waged a highly publicized battle to protect her right to wear it on the House Floor. Her colorful style attracted as many dedicated opponents as it did admirers and allies. A 1972 report by Ralph Nader estimated that Abzug's sponsorship of a bill often cost it as many as 30 votes.[14] Nevertheless, she inspired young women, many of whom became prominent politicians. "Let's be honest about it: She did not knock politely on the door," New York Representative Geraldine Ferraro said. "She took the hinges off of it." The 1984 Democratic vice presidential candidate conceded, "If there never had been a Bella Abzug, there never would have been a Gerry Ferraro."[15]

In 1972, when Abzug's district was merged with a neighboring one, she decided to run against popular reform Democrat William Fitts Ryan in a newly created district which extended her former west Manhattan district's boundaries farther south and east. The primary was a bitter contest, even by New York City's standards. Ryan defeated Abzug but died two months before the general election. The Democratic committee appointed Abzug as its replacement candidate. She defeated Ryan's widow, Priscilla, who ran on the Liberal Party ticket in another divisive campaign. Abzug took 56 percent of the vote to Ryan's 28 percent in a five-way race. In 1974, Abzug easily defeated her GOP opponent, Stephen Posner, with 79 percent of the vote.[16]

Abzug's sustained clash with the conventions of Congress and her party's political machine mitigated her ability to fulfill her ambitious political agenda, but she did achieve some solid results. Her most noteworthy contributions, particularly the "sunshine" laws under the Freedom of Information Act, came as a member of the Government Operations Committee. She worked to make government, particularly national security policies, more transparent. The "sunshine law," which required government hearings to be held in public, came out of the Subcommittee on Government Information and Individual Rights, which she chaired.[17] During her first term, she coauthored the Child Development Act with Brooklyn Congresswoman Shirley Chisholm. When promoting the legislation on the floor of the House, she emphasized that the bill concerned women as much as children, commenting, "Without adequate, low-cost day care facilities, women are doomed to occupy low-paying, low-prestige jobs; without day care, women must remain economic serfs."[18] Abzug also introduced ground-breaking legislation aimed at increasing the rights of lesbians and gays. The bill called for amending the Civil Rights Act of 1964 "to prohibit discrimination on the basis of sexual or affectional preference."[19]

In 1976, Abzug chose not to run for a fourth House term, instead waging a close but unsuccessful campaign against Daniel Patrick Moynihan in the Democratic primary for an open Senate seat. In 1977, she also failed in her bid for the New York City Democratic mayoral nomination. When the winner of the mayor's race, Ed Koch, resigned from Congress, Abzug tried but failed to win his vacant seat on New York's Upper East Side. President Jimmy Carter named her the co-chair of the National Advisory Committee on Women in 1978, though Abzug later was replaced when she criticized the administration's economic policies. In 1986, Abzug made another bid for the House of Representatives, this time in Westchester County, New York. After winning the Democratic primary, however, she lost in the general election to the Republican incumbent, Joseph DioGuardi.[20] Her last attempt to regain a place in Congress came six years later when Abzug announced her intention to run for the open seat in her old district on the Upper West Side of Manhattan, following the death of Congressman Ted Weiss. Abzug's desire to return to politics was cut short when party leaders failed to back her candidacy.[21]

In her two-decade, postpolitical career, Abzug remained a respected and visible figure in the feminist movement. She addressed international women's conferences in Beijing, Nairobi, and Copenhagen. She also established the Women USA Fund and the Women's Environment and Development Organization, both non-profit advocacy groups that worked to give women's issues more prominence on the United Nations' agenda. New York Mayor David Dinkins appointed her to chair his Commission on the Status of Women from 1993 to 1995. Her health declined as she battled breast cancer and heart disease. Abzug died in New York City on March 31, 1998.

FOR FURTHER READING

Abzug, Bella. *Bella! Ms. Abzug Goes to Washington* (New York: Saturday Review Press, 1972).

Abzug, Bella, and Mim Kelber. *Gender Gap: Bella Abzug's Guide to Political Power for American Women* (Boston: Houghton-Mifflin, 1984).

Biographical Directory of the United States Congress, "Bella Savitsky Abzug," http://bioguide.congress.gov

Faber, Doris. *Bella Abzug* (New York: Lothrop, 1976).

MANUSCRIPT COLLECTION

Columbia University (New York, NY), Rare Book & Manuscript Library, Butler Library. *Papers*: 1970–1976, ca. 554,100 items. Congressional papers consisting of correspondence, memoranda, speeches, reports, photographs, and printed materials relating to Abzug's terms in Congress. The collection contains general correspondence and administrative files, as well as extensive subject files on a wide variety of topics with which Abzug was involved while in Congress. Also included are legislative files, being the chronological files of background material for legislation considered on the House Floor, and printed versions of legislation by Abzug and others. The casework files documenting Abzug's advocacy on behalf of constituents involved in cases related to civil rights, housing, military, and employment, are closed. Among the major correspondents are Carl Albert, Abraham D. Beame, Hugh L. Carey, Gerald R. Ford, Edward I. Koch, John V. Lindsay, Nelson A. Rockefeller, and Gloria Steinem. Materials added in 1981 include draft transcripts of an oral history, appointment books, speeches and subject files (particularly on privacy and freedom of information). These materials are interfiled in the collection with campaign materials, press releases, and newspaper clippings. Casework files, selected correspondence, and administrative files were opened in 2005. Selected correspondence

COGNIZANT THAT HER
PERSONALITY OFTEN PROMPTED
DISCUSSION AND, AT TIMES, DISMAY
FROM ONLOOKERS, ABZUG
RETORTED, "THERE ARE THOSE WHO
SAY I'M IMPATIENT, IMPETUOUS,
UPPITY, RUDE, PROFANE, BRASH, AND
OVERBEARING. . . . BUT WHATEVER I
AM—AND THIS OUGHT TO BE MADE
CLEAR FROM THE OUTSET—I AM A
VERY SERIOUS WOMAN."

and administrative files are closed. Campaign materials, press releases, and newspaper clippings from the 1981 addition require the donor's permission. A register to the papers is available.

NOTES

1   Michele Ladsberg, "Bella Abzug Was 'Alive to Her Fingertips,'" 12 April 1998, *Toronto Star*: A2.

2   Susan Baer, "Founding, Enduring Feminist Bella Abzug is dead at 77," 1 April 1998, *Baltimore Sun*: 1A.

3   Laura Mansnerus, "Bella Abzug, 77, Congresswoman and a Founding Feminist, Is Dead," 1 April 1998, *New York Times*: A1.

4   Hope Chamberlin, *A Minority of Members: Women in the U.S. Congress* (New York: Praeger, 1973): 334.

5   Edward L. Lach, Jr., "Abzug, Bella," http://www.anb.org/articles/ 07/07-00714.html, *American National Biography (ANB)* online (accessed 19 June 2002).

6   Lach, "Abzug, Bella," *ANB* online.

7   "Election Statistics, 1920 to Present," http://clerk.house.gov/members/ electionInfo/elections.html.

8   *Almanac of American Politics, 1972* (Washington, D.C.: National Journal, Inc., 1972): 546.

9   Karen Foerstel, *Biographical Dictionary of Congressional Women* (Westport, CT: Greenwood Press, 1999): 19.

10 Bella Abzug, *Bella! Ms. Abzug Goes to Washington* (New York: Saturday Review Press, 1972).

11 Foerstel, *Biographical Dictionary of Congressional Women*: 19; Spencer Rich and Richard L. Lyons, "President Rebuffed by Democrats," 10 May 1972, *Washington Post*: A1.

12 Chamberlin, *A Minority of Members*: 334.

13 Abzug, *Bella! Ms. Abzug Goes to Washington*.

14 Mansnerus, "Bella Abzug, 77, Congresswoman and a Founding Feminist, Is Dead."

15 Adam Nagourney, "Recalling Bella Abzug's Politics and Passion," *New York Times*, 3 April 1998: D17.

16 *Almanac of American Politics, 1974* (Washington, D.C.: National Journal, Inc., 1974): 696–697; see also, "Election Statistics, 1920 to Present," http://clerk.house.gov/members/ electionInfo/elections.html.

17 Mansnerus, "Bella Abzug, 77, Congresswoman and a Founding Feminist, Is Dead."

18 *Congressional Record*, House, 92nd Cong., 1st sess. (7 December 1971): 45091–45092.

19 *Congressional Record*, House, 94th Cong., 1st sess. (25 March 1975): 8581.

20 "Election Statistics, 1920 to Present," http://clerk.house.gov/members/ electionInfo/elections.html.

21 Mansnerus, "Bella Abzug, 77, Congresswoman and a Founding Feminist, Is Dead."

Ella Tambussi Grasso
1919–1981

UNITED STATES REPRESENTATIVE ★ DEMOCRAT FROM CONNECTICUT
1971–1975

Connecticut Representative Ella Grasso's brief House career bridged two decades of service in state government and two trailblazing terms as the state's governor. In Congress she concerned herself primarily with combating rampant unemployment in her district while preparing for her triumphant return to Connecticut politics. Throughout her long career in state and national politics, on issues ranging from civil rights to campaign finance reform, Grasso sensed the public mood and positioned herself at the forefront of the legislative response.[1]

Ella Rose Giovanna Oliva Tambussi was born on May 10, 1919, in Windsor Locks, Connecticut, the only child of Italian immigrants Giacomo and Maria Oliva Tambussi. Ella Tambussi, who spoke fluent Italian, attended St. Mary's School in Windsor Locks, and the Chaffee School in Windsor. She received a B.A. in 1940 from Mount Holyoke College in South Hadley, Massachusetts, and was elected to Phi Beta Kappa. Two years later, she received a master's degree in both economics and sociology from Mount Holyoke. After graduating in 1942, Ella Tambussi married Thomas Grasso, a schoolteacher and principal. The couple raised two children, Susane and James. Ella Grasso served as a researcher and, then, assistant director of research for the war manpower commission of Connecticut from 1943 to 1946.

Grasso first became involved in politics as a member of the League of Women Voters. She later credited that experience with helping her develop "a real understanding of issues." She recalled, "I realized early on that if I was concerned with problems, the best way of getting them solved was to be part of the decision-making process."[2]

The veteran of local campaign organizations and a protégé of Connecticut's legendary Democratic leader John Bailey (a close ally of John F. Kennedy and future chairman of the Democratic National Committee), Grasso entered electoral politics in 1952 when she won a seat in the state house of representatives. According to politicians familiar with both Grasso and Bailey, the Connecticut political boss saw Grasso as an important draw for women voters and, as an Italian-American, a prominent member of an increasingly important ethnic minority in state politics long dominated by Irish Americans.[3]

According to her biographer, Grasso took to heart Bailey's central political philosophy: "The mark of a successful politician is one that finds out where the parade is going, takes one step out in front of the band and declares himself the leader." During her service in the state legislature, Grasso fought for equal rights and a law forbidding housing discrimination. In her second term she rose to assistant Democratic leader of the state legislature, and in 1955 she became the first woman elected floor leader. In 1958, Grasso was elected secretary of state of Connecticut; she won her two subsequent bids in 1962 and 1966. The office provided a level of visibility and constituent contact that helped Grasso, like Chase Going Woodhouse before her, to create a strong political network.[4] During her time in the state legislature, Grasso remained active in the Democratic Party, serving as a member of the Democratic Platform Committee in 1960 and as co-chair of the Resolutions Committee for the 1964 and 1968 conventions.

As early as 1966, when the incumbent Democrat in Ella Grasso's home congressional district lost to Republican opponent Thomas Meskill, party insiders began speculating that she could be a contender for the House seat. Citing family considerations (her husband had recently suffered two major heart attacks), she declined to seek the nomination. In 1970, however, Meskill vacated the seat to make a run for the Connecticut governorship. With the backing of John Bailey, Grasso entered the race and handily beat two rivals, Arthur Powers of Berlin and Andrew Denuzee of New Britain, for the Democratic nomination.[5] The district, located in northwest Connecticut, was created after the 1960 Census, when the resulting reapportionment eliminated the state's At-Large seat. It also straddled two very different groups of constituents, working-class voters in several industrial towns in Hartford County and an affluent, intellectual class that resided in rural Litchfield County. Grasso's Republican opponent in the general election, Richard Kilborne, labeled her "Spender-Ella" and attacked her liberal record as dedicated to government spending to "help the un-helpable."[6] But Grasso's two decisive advantages, wide name recognition and the blessing of Bailey, helped her defeat Kilborne with 51 percent of the vote.[7] Grasso's victory was noteworthy in the sense that Meskill won the governor's race, overwhelming his Democratic opponent by nearly 35,000 votes in Grasso's district.[8]

After entering the House in January 1971, Representative Grasso appealed to Speaker Carl Albert of Oklahoma for seats on the Committee on Education and Labor and the Committee on Veterans' Affairs. She had served with Albert as co-chair of the Resolutions Committee at the 1964 Democratic Convention, and impressed by Grasso's political skills, he had promised that if she ever won election to the House of Representatives, she would receive the committee assignments she desired. He was as good as his word, granting both requests.

With her district reeling from unemployment, Grasso sponsored a variety of legislation designed to increase employment, boost the minimum wage, hike Social Security payments, and protect workers. In 1971, she authored amendments to the Fair Labor Standards Act, which raised the minimum wage and brought an additional six million workers under benefit coverage. As a conferee of that year's Emergency Employment Act, she managed to secure 600 new jobs within her district. On the Veterans' Affairs Committee she worked to pass a $272-per-month education benefit to veterans returning from Vietnam; while the measure failed, it helped raise the sights of a subsequent bill that passed the House and boosted the benefits to more than $200 per month.[9] Arguably the most important accomplishment of her two terms came with her part in drafting the Comprehensive Employment and Training Act, which again provided relief to hundreds of workers in her economically distressed district.

In 1972, Grasso was re-elected with a margin of 60 percent of the vote over her opponent Republican John Walsh. The results were made even more impressive by the fact that Republicans surged in the state delegation—taking control of half the House seats in the wake of incumbent President Richard Nixon's strong electoral showing. In her Connecticut district, where Nixon ran ahead of Democratic candidate George McGovern by nearly 50,000 votes, Grasso topped Walsh by a plurality of about 40,000.[10]

While she earned a reputation as a "moderate-liberal," the diversity of Grasso's district often kept her on the middle of the road on key issues. For instance, though she opposed the Vietnam War, she did so while treading lightly. Arguing that a cut-off date was needed for bringing the troops home, she nevertheless made no floor speeches on the subject and, twice in 1971, skipped two votes on measures to end the war. Part of this stance acknowledged the importance of defense sector jobs located in her district, as well as blue-collar support for the war effort.[11]

The press portrayed Grasso as one of the group of new-style feminist women who entered the House in 1971. At a Washington Press Club address along with Bella Abzug of New York and Louise Hicks of Massachusetts, Grasso stressed their commonalities with a self-deprecating joke: "We're all fat, we're all middle-aged and we spend most of our time together talking about our children."[12] On women's rights issues, however, she remained largely ambivalent and distanced herself from feminists like

Grasso's experience in Congress was not typical of those of most of her women colleagues. "For most of them . . . it was their baptism into politics," one Grasso aide observed, "but for her it was merely a continuation of something that had been going on for 20 years. . . . She was very much the old-school politician."

Abzug on such issues as abortion and childcare. Her biographer notes that Grasso's tack toward the feminist agenda demonstrated "how she skillfully manipulated her position so she could simultaneously identify and disassociate herself with a popular cause." Significantly, her experience was not typical of those of most women then entering Congress. "For most of them . . . it was their baptism into politics," one Grasso aide observed, "but for her it was merely a continuation of something that had been going on for 20 years. . . . She was very much the old-school politician."[13] Grasso worked quietly on the Education and Labor Committee to ensure women's parity in schools and the workplace, allaying some of the criticisms that she did not do enough to advance the feminist cause. In 1971, Grasso supported passage of the Equal Rights Amendment, noting that "Congress must provide the constitutional framework upon which to build a body of law to achieve the goal of equal rights."[14] In the final analysis, however, she correctly calculated that personal political success made her an appealing figure for feminists eager to draw women into politics and that, at the end of the day, women's groups would support her even if she was not the loudest voice in the feminist chorus.[15]

Grasso was never as captivated by the work of Capitol Hill as she had been by Connecticut politics. Privately she complained to colleagues that the legislative process in the House frustrated her.[16] In the Connecticut legislature she had been a senior lawmaker and part of the party leadership, but in the House, she could not work her way out of the rank and file. Eventually, she turned her attention back to the Connecticut statehouse. "I can be a gadfly here," she complained. "But you can't make a long-term career out of Congress at age fifty."[17]

By early in her second term, Grasso largely viewed her House service as a way to raise her political profile in Connecticut. She ran her office much like she had during her time as Connecticut secretary of state, opening a toll-free phone service to her New Britain office (the "Ellaphone") for constituents to speak more readily with her aides. She also held "office hours" by regularly traveling to towns in her district and meeting with a variety of citizens.[18] By early 1973, the press and state political insiders regularly mentioned her name as a likely candidate for Connecticut governor.[19]

In January 1974, Grasso announced her gubernatorial candidacy, which ensured that by the following January she would retire from the House.[20] With the support of Bailey's statewide Democratic organization, Grasso won the gubernatorial race against a GOP House colleague, Representative Robert Steele, and became the first woman to be elected a U.S. governor without succeeding a husband. Grasso's four-year term commenced in January 1975. The fiscal problems of Connecticut forced Grasso to follow a far more conservative policy as governor than she had as a Member of Congress. Despite budget cuts, Grasso maintained her popularity and won re-election in 1978 against another House GOP veteran, Ronald Sarasin. Grasso was diagnosed with ovarian cancer in early 1980, and her condition deteriorated as doctors were unable to stem the spread of the disease. On December 4, 1980, she announced her resignation, effective December 31, after which she returned to her hometown of Windsor Locks. Grasso died in Hartford on February 5, 1981.

FOR FURTHER READING

Biographical Directory of the United States Congress, "Ella Tambussi Grasso," http://bioguide.congress.gov

Bysiewicz, Susan. *Ella: A Biography of Governor Ella Grasso* (Hartford: Connecticut Consortium for Law and Citizenship Education, Inc., 1984).

Purmont, Jon E. "Ella Grasso: As She Saw Herself," *Connecticut Review* 17 (Spring 1995): 23–29.

MANUSCRIPT COLLECTION

Mount Holyoke College (South Hadley, MA), Archives and Special Collections. *Papers:* 1919–1981, 108 linear feet. The bulk of the collection dates from 1970 to 1974 and primarily documents Grasso's work as a Member of the House. The collection contains primary source material on veterans' affairs, the Vietnam War, President Richard Nixon's impeachment, gas prices and fuel shortages, family planning and birth control, and education legislation. A finding aid is available at http://asteria.fivecolleges.edu/findaids/mountholyoke/mshm301.html.

NOTES

1 Susan Bysiewicz, *Ella: A Biography of Governor Ella Grasso* (Hartford: Connecticut Consortium for Law and Citizenship Education, Inc., 1984): especially, 133–139.

2 Jo Ann Levine, "Ella Grasso on Move: A Governor's Chair May Be in Her Future," 26 July 1974, *Christian Science Monitor*: 10; Shirley Washington, *Outstanding Women Members of Congress* (Washington, D.C.: U.S. Capitol Historical Society, 1995): 35.

3 Matthew L. Wald, "Ex-Gov. Grasso of Connecticut Dead of Cancer," 6 February 1981, *New York Times*: A1; Joseph I. Lieberman, *The Power Broker: A Biography of John M. Bailey Modern Political Boss*: 230, 257–259.

4 Emily S. Rosenberg, "Grasso, Ella Tambussi," *American National Biography* 9 (New York: Oxford University Press, 1999): 427–428.

5 Bysiewicz, *Ella*: 53.

6 Washington, *Outstanding Women Members of Congress*: 36.

7 "Election Statistics, 1920 to Present" http://clerk.house.gov/members/electionInfo/elections.html.

8 Bysiewicz, *Ella*: 53–54.

9 Bysiewicz, *Ella*: 58–60; *Congressional Record*, House, 93rd Cong., 2nd sess. (10 October 1974): 35154; *Congressional Record*, House, 93rd Cong., 2nd sess. (19 February 1974): 3264.

10 "Election Statistics, 1920 to Present" http://clerk.house.gov/members/electionInfo/elections.html.

11 See, for instance, Bysiewicz, *Ella*: 52–55.

12 Sally Quinn, "Ella, Bella and Louise," 10 February 1971, *Washington Post*: B2.

13 Bysiewicz, *Ella*: 60. "Ex-Gov. Grasso of Connecticut Dead of Cancer." This is not to say that Grasso did not experience discrimination, even in the state legislature, where she was on the "inside track" with her connections to Bailey. She recalled, "There was a committee I very much wanted to be on and I was clearly the best qualified. But the men caucused in the men's room! What was I to do?" See Anita Shreve and John Clemens, "The New Wave of Women Politicians," 19 October 1980, *New York Times*: SM30.

14 *Congressional Record*, House, 92nd Cong., 1st sess. (12 October 1971): 35799.

15 Bysiewicz, *Ella*: 60.

16 Wald, "Ex-Gov. Grasso of Connecticut Dead of Cancer."

17 Bysiewicz, *Ella*: 57.

18 Ibid., 61–62.

19 Jo Ann Levine, "Ella Grasso on Move: A Governor's Chair May Be in Her Future," 26 July 1974, *Christian Science Monitor*: 10.

20 Lawrence Fellows, "Rep. Ella Grasso Plans to Enter Connecticut Governorship Race," 9 January 1974, *New York Times*: 32; Lawrence Fellows, "Mrs. Grasso Opens Race for Governor," 20 January 1974, *New York Times*: 22.

Louise Day Hicks
1916–2003

UNITED STATES REPRESENTATIVE ★ DEMOCRAT FROM MASSACHUSETTS
1971–1973

A controversial critic of busing to achieve racial deseg-regation in the Boston public schools, Louise Day Hicks won election in 1970 to fill the Massachusetts congressional seat of retiring Speaker John McCormack. Expectations were that Hicks would become a prominent opponent in Congress of federal efforts to enforce busing programs. But Congresswoman Hicks instead spent much of her single term in the House working to return to power in her home city.

Anna Louise Day was born on October 16, 1916, in South Boston, Massachusetts. Her parents, William J. Day and Anna McCarron Day, raised their four children in a three-story, 18-room house in the predominantly Irish-Catholic community. Louise Day lived there her entire life. William Day eventually became a popular Democratic district court judge. Anna Day died when Louise was just 14, leaving her husband as the principal role model for the children. Years later Louise recalled, William Day was "the greatest influence in my life . . . my first and only hero. My father must have been the creator of women's lib because he felt there were no limitations to what I could do or to the opportunities I should be exposed to."[1] Louise Day graduated from Wheelock Teachers' College in 1938 and taught first grade for sever-al years. On October 12, 1942, she married John Hicks, a design engineer. The couple raised two sons, William and John. As a young mother, Louise Day Hicks earned a B.S. degree in education in 1952 from Boston University. In 1955, as one of just nine women in a class of 232, Hicks graduated with a J.D. from Boston University's School of Law. She was admitted to the Massachusetts bar the fol-lowing year and, with her brother John, established the law

firm of Hicks and Day in Boston. She served as counsel for the Boston juvenile court in 1960.

Hicks's first foray into political office came when she won election to the Boston school committee, which she chaired from 1963 to 1965. At the time, she clashed with the local chapter of the National Association for the Advancement of Colored People (NAACP) over a proposal to integrate Boston schools by busing students to different districts to achieve racial balance. Hicks gained national attention as a stalwart opponent of busing and as the leading defender of "neighborhood schools." Hicks's position on busing brought her notoriety, including a *Newsweek* cover story and local and national condemnation. Under constant threat, she sought a permit to carry a handgun and was regularly accompanied by bodyguards. "No one in their right mind is against civil rights," she remarked at the time. "Only, let it come naturally."[2] She criticized white liberals who lived outside the city but supported busing as a remedy for educational inequalities in urban neigh-borhoods. "Boston schools are a scapegoat for those who have failed to solve the housing, economic, and social problems of the black citizen," she declared.[3] Congress of Racial Equality leader James Farmer denounced Hicks as "the Bull Conner of Boston," alluding to the police com-missioner of Birmingham, Alabama, who turned fire hoses and police dogs on peaceful civil rights marchers.[4] Despite the protestations of the NAACP and the Boston media, she was handily re-elected to the school committee in 1964. In 1967, armed with the slogan "You Know Where I Stand," she ran against Kevin White for Boston mayor and drew 30 percent of the vote in a 10-candidate race, but ended up losing to White by 12,000 votes. In 1969, she won election to the Boston city council by an overwhelming majority.

When U.S. House Speaker John W. McCormack announced his plans to retire at the end of the 91st Congress, Hicks launched a campaign for his seat. The Massachusetts congressional district encompassed a sliver of Boston running north to south through ethnically diverse neighborhoods that included the Italian North End, Irish-dominated sections of South Boston, the African-American enclave of Roxbury, and the racially mixed Dorchester area. Hicks held a great name recognition advantage over the other chief candidates for the Democratic primary nomination—a prominent African-American attorney, David E. Nelson, and widely respected State Senator John Joseph "Joe" Moakley. Voters were so familiar with Hicks that she was able to avoid such racially divisive issues as busing, to embrace a general platform of "law and order" and to campaign at a less frenetic pace than her opponents. She reprised her old slogan, "You know where I stand," skipped television ads, kept the press at arm's length, and refused to appear in debates with Moakley or Nelson. The primary largely became a referendum on Hicks, supported by stalwarts on the busing issues and opposed by those who dismissed her as a bigot.[5] Nelson's appeal to black constituents was simple: "Get it together or Louise will."[6] But Moakley and Nelson split the anti-Hicks vote, allowing her to win the September 15 primary; she beat Moakley, the runner-up, by a margin of about 10 percent.[7] Nomination in the heavily Democratic district was tantamount to certain election. During the fall campaign for the general election, Hicks ratcheted up her platform of law and order, attacking Mayor Kevin White for the city's high crime rate. She promised to "do more for Boston on the federal level" and dominated a three-way race by capturing 59 percent of the vote against Republican Laurence Curtis and Independent Daniel J. Houton.[8]

In the 92nd Congress (1971–1973), Hicks was assigned to the Committee on Education and Labor and the Committee on Veterans' Affairs. Particularly interested in issues of education, she proposed a system of tax credits for parents of children in private schools, a precursor to the school voucher proposals of the late 1990s, and backed the Higher Education Act of 1971, which expanded federal aid to public universities and colleges.[9] During her time in Congress, Hicks generally supported the Richard M. Nixon administration's conservative agenda, which was based on the premise that a "silent majority" of Americans eschewed 1960s liberalism and supported traditional values instead. She publicly defended the American incursion into Cambodia and, despite calling for the "orderly withdrawal" of troops from Vietnam, Hicks told an audience in Boston, "The disgrace of this war is not our being in Vietnam, but rather in those who oppose our boys while they are there."[10]

Nevertheless, Hicks remained unusually aloof in her role as a U.S. Representative and evinced more interest in Boston political developments than in issues before the House. Her reticence to leave Boston politics was notable from the outset.[11] She had kept her position on the Boston city council for several weeks after being sworn in to the House, hoping to manage both jobs.[12] Five months after taking office she confided to the *New York Times*, "Some mornings, I wake up and I'm positive I'm going to run for mayor [of Boston] again. Then other times I'm not sure at all. If I could only take the Congress to Boston I'd be perfectly happy."[13] Colleagues who had expected her to be a counterpart to "Battling" Bella Abzug, a fellow freshman Representative, were baffled by Hicks's reticence to make floor speeches or join in debates. Her office staff in Washington totaled three—the smallest Hill operation of any Member—while her Boston office employed nine aides. Her efforts to impose a federal ban on busing were, at best, halfhearted. Hicks was not even present for a debate on whether to strike an anti-busing provision from an education appropriations bill. By June 1971, Hicks publicly declared her candidacy for the 1971 mayoral race, challenging incumbent Kevin White.[14] This time, White overwhelmed Hicks by a margin of 40,000 votes. "Being mayor of Boston is the only job she's ever wanted," a friend confided to a writer profiling Hicks.[15]

In her 1972 bid for re-election to the House, Hicks confronted a district race in which reapportionment (based on 1970 Census figures), had reshaped her constituency. Her Boston district had been reconfigured to include more than 100,000 suburban constituents, while the Dorchester area, an Irish working-class stronghold for Hicks, had been stripped out.[16] Though she easily won the Democratic primary, she lost narrowly in a four-way general election to Joe Moakley, who ran this time on the Independent-Conservative ticket. Moakley edged Hicks out with 70,571 to 67,143 votes (43 percent to 41 percent of the total vote).[17] In 1973, Moakley switched his affiliation to the Democratic Party and was re-elected to 14 consecutive terms.

Hicks returned to her law practice in Boston and headed an anti-busing group called "Return Our Alienated Rights" (ROAR) until a 1976 federal court instituted busing. In 1973 Hicks was re-elected to the Boston city council, describing it as her "sabbatical year for the people." She promised to challenge Moakley for the 1974 Democratic nomination but later chose to stay in Boston politics.[18] In 1976, she was elected the first woman president of the city council. After serving on the city council for four terms, Hicks retired from public life entirely in 1981. Louise Day Hicks died in her South Boston home on October 21, 2003.

FOR FURTHER READING

Biographical Directory of the United States Congress, "Louise Day Hicks," http://bioguide.congress.gov

NOTES

1   Mark Feeney, "Louise Hicks, Icon of Tumult, Dies," 22 October 2003, *Boston Globe*: A1; see also, Katie Zezima, "Louise Day Hicks, Who Led Fight on Busing in Boston, Dies at 87," 23 October 2003, *New York Times*: C15; and Adam Bernstein, "Louise Day Hicks Dies at 87; Led Anti-Busing Effort in Boston," 23 October 2003, *Washington Post*: B4.

2   *Current Biography, 1974* (New York: H.W. Wilson and Company, 1974): 174.

3   *Current Biography, 1974*: 174.

4   Feeney, "Louise Hicks, Icon of Tumult, Dies."

5   Liz Roman, "Unspoken Issue Helps Mrs. Hicks Campaign for Seat in Congress," 31 August 1970, *Wall Street Journal*: 1; Jules Witcover, "'Louise' Is Issue in Boston Race,'" 15 September 1970, *Washington Post*: A5.

6   Witcover, "'Louise' Is Issue in Boston Race."

7   David S. Broder, "Mrs. Hicks Nominated for McCormack's Seat," 16 September 1970, *Washington Post*: A5.

8   "Election Statistics, 1920 to Present," http://clerk.house.gov/members/electionInfo/elections.html.

9   *Congressional Record*, House, 92nd Cong., 1st sess. (27 October 1971): 37811–37812.

10   Marjorie Hunter, "A Quiet Mrs. Hicks Baffles Congress," 16 May 1971, *New York Times*: 26.

11   "Louise Hicks Runs in Boston for McCormack's House Seat," 9 June 1970, *Washington Post*: A2.

12   "Louise Hicks Quits Boston City Council," 25 January 1971, *Washington Post*: A3.

13   Hunter, "A Quiet Mrs. Hicks Baffles Congress."

14   "Rep. Hicks in Mayor's Race; Says Boston Is at a Low Point," 15 June 1971, *New York Times*: 41.

15   Hope Chamberlin, *A Minority of Members: Women in the U.S. Congress* (New York: Praeger, 1973): 341.

16   Peter C. Stuart, "Rebel Congressmen Redistricted," 14 December 1971, *Christian Science Monitor*: 1.

17   "Election Statistics, 1920 to Present," http://clerk.house.gov/members/electionInfo/elections.html.

18   Richard Weintraub, "Mrs. Hicks Seeks Office in Boston," 16 June 1973, *Washington Post*: A3.

Elizabeth Bullock Andrews

1911–2002

UNITED STATES REPRESENTATIVE ★ DEMOCRAT FROM ALABAMA
1972–1973

Elizabeth Andrews was schooled in elective politics as the wife of a longtime and powerful Member of Congress. When her husband, George W. Andrews, died suddenly in late 1971, friends convinced her to seek election for the remainder of his term to further his legislative agenda. "All I want is to do the best I can for the rest of the term," Elizabeth Andrews told reporters on New Year's Day 1972. "I simply want to complete George's plans as best I can."[1]

Leslie Elizabeth Bullock was born in Geneva, Alabama, on February 12, 1911. Her father, Charles Gillespie Bullock, was a businessman. Elizabeth Bullock attended school in her hometown of Geneva. In 1932 she graduated from Montevallo College, majoring in home economics. Bullock subsequently taught high school home economics in Livingston, Alabama. During the Depression, she relocated to a school in Union Springs for better pay.[2] There she met her future husband, George William Andrews, whom she married in 1936. They raised two children, Jane and George, Jr.

During the 1930s, George W. Andrews served as district attorney in the Alabama circuit court system. He held the position until 1943, when he served as an officer in the U.S. Naval Reserve and was stationed in Pearl Harbor, Hawaii Territory. When longtime Representative Henry B. Steagall of Alabama died in November 1943, Andrews announced his candidacy for the vacant seat in the rural, 12-county southeastern Alabama district. Elizabeth Andrews, at home raising the couple's young daughter, got her first taste of elective politics. With her husband thousands of miles away in the Pacific, she became a lead member of his campaign team, taking to the hustings to make speeches on his behalf. Running as a Democrat,

Andrews won the March 1944 special election for a seat in the 78th Congress (1943–1945) while still overseas. He was re-elected to the 14 succeeding Congresses. The couple eventually relocated to Washington, D.C., where Elizabeth became active in the Congressional Club, made up of spouses of Members of Congress. Eventually, she served as vice president of the organization in 1971. George Andrews, meanwhile, became a senior and powerful member of the Appropriations Committee, eventually chairing its Legislative Subcommittee. He was a fiscal conservative, a critic of civil rights legislation, a friend of controversial Alabama Governor George Wallace (whose hometown was in Andrews's district), and a defense hawk. By his final term in office, he was among the top 20 House Members in terms of seniority.

On Christmas Day 1971, George Andrews died after complications from heart surgery. "I had no idea of running for George's office," Elizabeth Andrews later recalled, "until friends encouraged me to do so." One in particular, Lera Thomas, a congressional widow-turned-Representative from Texas, proved most convincing. Thomas, who served out the remainder of her husband's term in the 89th Congress (1965–1967) in 1966, and Andrews had known each other for years; their husbands had served on the Appropriations Committee together. After George Andrews's funeral, Lera Thomas approached Elizabeth: "Don't rule out going to Capitol Hill yourself. You know more about his plans than any other living person, and I personally know what it will mean to the constituency."[3] Andrews told Democratic state party leaders that she would consider running for the office.[4]

On January 1, 1972, Andrews announced her candidacy. Due to the fact that Alabama lost one seat after the 1970

IMAGE COURTESY OF AUBURN UNIVERSITY

Census, George Andrews's district was set to be reapportioned out of existence before the November 1972 elections. Andrews's death made the district's boundaries even more vulnerable, as districts of retiring or deceased long-term incumbents were often divided in the case of reapportionment. The impending change in district lines brought in new voters, which also threatened the traditional Democratic dominance in the district; no Republican had served southeastern Alabama since the end of Reconstruction in 1877. (In fact, the new district, which incorporated more central territory, including Montgomery, eventually elected a GOP candidate in November 1972.)[5] A number of Democratic contenders showed some initial interest in the nomination, but the problems created by the impending reapportionment dampened their enthusiasm.[6] This did not bother Andrews, as she also firmly announced her intention not to run for a term in the succeeding Congress.[7] Moreover, Andrews's name recognition and powerful supporters added to the long-term historical trends that favored her candidacy.[8]

When the Alabama Democratic Executive Committee convened to choose a nominee, a group of progressive members opposed Andrews's candidacy, pushing for Lucius Amerson, the state's first elected African-American sheriff since Reconstruction. Amerson seemed to be a symbolic choice given his race, but he also appealed to local Democrats who wanted a strong candidate to seek re-election in November and retain the party's control over the new district.[9] Success in Alabama politics in the early 1970s, however, often depended on the support of personal connections.[10] Andrews's supporters included the powerful Governor George Wallace, formerly an ardent segregationist, who intervened on behalf of his late friend's wife. Though distancing himself from his previous racial views in preparation for a 1972 presidential bid, Wallace endorsed Elizabeth Andrews over Amerson and insisted that if Democrats did not nominate her, he would back her as an Independent.[11] Based largely on the influential Wallace's warning, the committee favored Andrews 72 to 17. Afterward, the state GOP Executive Committee allowed her to run unopposed in the general election if

Democrats nominated her, ostensibly to focus on the November campaign for a full term in the next Congress.[12]

On April 4, 1972, facing no opposition, Andrews easily won election to fill out the remainder of her husband's term.[13] The cost of her bid was so low that she was able to return most of the donations to her campaign.[14] She became the first woman from Alabama ever elected to Congress; two previous women had been nominated to serve brief terms in the Senate. Andrews, however, minimized the significance of her gender. "Womanhood per se was never an issue," she said. "In Alabama today, if a woman is qualified and capable, she can obtain political support."[15]

In the 92nd Congress (1971–1973), Elizabeth Andrews served on the Committee on Post Office and Civil Service, occupying the same office space as George Andrews had from 1950 to 1964. From her committee post, Congresswoman Andrews introduced several amendments to protect medical and Social Security benefits. One of her amendments to Social Security legislation increased recipients' earned income limits; another abolished proposed cuts in welfare aid scheduled because of coincident increases in Social Security payments. Andrews also secured funding for cancer and heart disease research centers in Birmingham, a special pet project of her husband's. Along with Alabama Representative William Nichols, she sponsored a bill establishing a Tuskegee Institute National Historic Park. The site commemorated the teachers' school that Booker T. Washington founded in the late 1880s that later became a center for African-American education and home to an aeronautics program and flight school which produced the legendary Tuskegee Airmen of World War II.

Andrews also favored the Richard M. Nixon administration's plan for withdrawing U.S. troops from Vietnam, the so-called "Vietnamization" of the war effort, noting that "military victory has been abandoned as a goal."[16] Andrews made only one floor speech during her nine months in office, taking to the well of the House to denounce "professional dissenters" and protestors the day after presidential candidate and Alabama Governor George Wallace was critically wounded in an assassination attempt while campaigning in Laurel, Maryland. "Failure to maintain order for all presidential candidates during their public appearances has resulted in an ominous atmosphere of tension, hostility, and clear danger in which a presidential contender like George Wallace takes life in hand when he goes to the people with the true but unpleasant message that lawless elements in this country are being pampered by our courts, that schoolchildren are being cruelly used by liberal social experimenters, and that our nation's defenses are being undermined from within," Andrews told colleagues. "All Americans, regardless of philosophy or party affiliation, should be dismayed at this vicious assault on a man who dared to go out among the people in his quest for support in a presidential campaign."[17]

When Andrews's term expired, her House colleagues praised her service. Fellow Alabama Representative William J. Edwards noted, "In serving her constituents this year she worked harder than most freshmen Members running for re-election . . . furthering the programs her husband worked so hard for." Jamie Whitten of Mississippi observed that Andrews "carried on in the style her district has been accustomed to."[18] Prior to retiring, the 62-year-old Congresswoman told a reporter that "the district needed the mantle to fall on someone younger."[19] After she left Congress in January 1973, Andrews retired to Union Springs and remained active in civic affairs for several decades. On December 2, 2002, Congresswoman Andrews passed away in Birmingham.

FOR FURTHER READING

Biographical Directory of the United States Congress, "Elizabeth Bullock Andrews," http://bioguide.congress.gov

MANUSCRIPT COLLECTION

Auburn University Library (Auburn, AL). *Papers:* In George W. Andrews Papers, 1943–1972. Unpublished finding aid in repository.

NOTES

1   "Rep. Andrews' Widow Seeks His Hill Seat," 2 January 1972, *Washington Post*: A32.

2   Hope Chamberlin, *A Minority of Members: Women in the U.S. Congress* (New York: Praeger, 1973): 345.

3   Chamberlin, *A Minority of Members*: 344.

4   Vicki McClure, "Elizabeth Andrews, Once in Congress, Dies," 4 December 2002, *Birmingham News*.

5   See *Congressional Directory*, 92nd Cong., 2nd sess. (Washington, D.C.: Government Printing Office, 1972); *Congressional Directory*, 93rd Cong., 2nd sess. (Washington, D.C.: Government Printing Office, 1974); for subsequent representation of southeastern Alabama, see Kenneth Martis, *Historic Atlas of Political Parties in the United States Congress: 1789–1989* (New York: McMillan, 1989).

6   Chamberlin, *A Minority of Members*: 343.

7   "Rep. Andrews' Widow Seeks His Hill Seat."

8   Irwin N. Gertzog, *Congressional Women: Their Recruitment, Integration, and Behavior* (Westport, CT: Praeger, 1995): 20–22.

9   Chamberlin, *A Minority of Members*: 344.

10 David R. Mayhew, *Placing Parties in American Politics* (Princeton University Press, 1986): 118–120.

11 For Wallace's segregation platform in 1972, see Dan T. Carter, *Politics of Rage* (New York: Simon and Schuster, 1995): 417–418.

12 McClure, "Elizabeth Andrews, Once in Congress, Dies"; Alvin Benn, "Ex-Congresswoman Dies," 4 December 2002, *Montgomery Advertiser*: C3; "Mrs. Andrews Likely to Fill Husband's Seat in Congress," 7 February 1972, *New York Times*: 37.

13 Michael J. Dubin et al., *United States Congressional Elections, 1788–1997* (Jefferson, NC: McFarland and Company, Publishers, Inc., 1998): 675.

14 Chamberlin, *A Minority of Members*: 343.

15 Ibid., 344.

16 Cited in Karen Foerstel, *Biographical Dictionary of Congressional Women* (Westport, CT: Greenwood Press, 1999): 21–22; Rudolf Engelbarts, *Women in the United States Congress, 1917–1972: Their Accomplishments; With Bibliographies* (Littleton, CO: Libraries Unlimited, 1974): 118.

17 *Congressional Record*, House, 92nd Cong., 2nd sess. (16 May 1972): 17391.

18 *Congressional Record*, House, 92nd Cong., 2nd sess. (16 October 1972): 36715; *Congressional Record*, House, 92nd Cong., 2nd sess. (17 October 1972): 36910.

19 Death Notices, 4 December 2002, *Birmingham News*.

Elaine S. Edwards

1929–

UNITED STATES SENATOR ★ DEMOCRAT FROM LOUISIANA

1972

Senator Elaine Edwards of Louisiana came to Congress by way of her matrimonial connection, traveling a political path frequented by earlier southern women. Rather than succeeding her husband, however, Edwards was appointed to a U.S. Senate seat by her husband, Louisiana Governor Edwin Edwards. Though not unprecedented, the move was controversial. Yet it allowed Governor Edwards to sidestep a thorny political problem in backing other aspirants to the seat. It also provided Elaine Edwards a chance to practice the political craft she first learned as a congressional spouse and the first lady of Louisiana. Though she served only three months during the frenetic end of the 92nd Congress (1971–1973), Edwards counted a number of admirers. Upon her retirement, Senator Mike Mansfield of Montana described her work as "quietly effective."[1]

Elaine Lucille Schwartzenburg was born on March 8, 1929, in Marksville, Louisiana, to Errol Schwartzenburg, a grocery store owner, and Myrl Dupuy Schwartzenburg. When she was nine years old, she contracted a bacterial bone infection in one leg, underwent several surgeries, and spent five years recuperating.[2] She graduated from Marksville High School and, in 1949, she married her childhood sweetheart Edwin W. Edwards, a Marksville, Louisiana, native and a lawyer. They raised four children: Anna, Vicki, Stephen, and David. Edwin Edwards embarked on a long political career in which he served as a Crowley, Louisiana, city councilman and a state senator. In a 1965 special election, Edwards was elected as a Democrat to the first of four U.S. House terms as a Louisiana Representative. Elaine Edwards was active in her husband's political campaigns at the district and state level. She remained at the family home in Crowley while

her husband was in the House of Representatives, but she answered phone calls at home on a second line, working with individual constituents to resolve Social Security and veterans' requests and relaying the information to Congressman Edwards's Washington office.[3] As her husband's political career developed, Elaine Edwards participated in a variety of civic and philanthropic pursuits ranging from the Special Olympics to a project that raised $1 million for the Crippled Children's Hospital of New Orleans.[4] Congressman Edwards left the House in May 1972 to serve as governor of Louisiana, where he remained for a total of four terms.

When longtime Louisiana Senator Allen Ellender died on July 27, 1972, Governor Edwards appointed his wife to fill the vacancy. The governor claimed that the appointment was a "meaningful, symbolic gesture" against decades of discrimination of women in politics.[5] It was not the first time a woman had received a U.S. Senate seat in this manner. Almost exactly 35 years earlier, Alabama Governor Bibb Graves named his wife Dixie to fill Hugo Black's Senate seat after he was appointed to the Supreme Court. Principally, Edwards made the controversial decision in order to avoid the politically tricky endorsement of a successor to Ellender, a 35-year Senate veteran, and the difficulty of finding an interim candidate who would step down shortly after a full-term successor was elected. Among the contenders for the seat were three of his gubernatorial campaign's top backers and his two brothers.[6]

Elaine Edwards was initially reluctant to accept the post, admitting at one point, "I never wanted to be liberated from sewing, cooking, or even gardening." Critics charged that she was merely a "caretaker" or "seat-warmer" who represented the views of the Louisiana governor's mansion in the Senate by consulting Baton Rouge before each vote.[7] The *New York Times* editors described it as a "hollow interim appointment" and also decried the fact that Edwards's "function . . . will be to represent other women by supinely taking orders—and from men at that." Edwards conceded, "I'm no U.S. Senator" and said she believed she would "get along fine" under the guidance of her state delegation and its dean, Senator Russell Long.[8] After a brief meeting with President Richard Nixon in the White House, she took the oath of office on August 7, 1972. Asked if she was likely to vote against her husband's advice, Edwards replied, "I doubt it."[9] She also pledged not to run for the full Senate term.

In Congress, Edwards served on the Agriculture and Forestry Committee and the Public Works Committee. She joined Senator Hubert Humphrey in introducing a bill to establish an educational fellowship in Senator Ellender's name that appropriated $500,000 in fellowships for low-income high school students and teachers. She also cosponsored an amendment to the Federal Environmental Pesticide Control Act and another to increase the allowable amount of outside income for Social Security recipients. She took particular pride in securing federal funding for highways in Louisiana, including a 70/30 federally financed toll road. "My proudest moment was convincing members of the Public Works Committee to vote funds for a north-south highway to connect the two east-west interstates in Louisiana," Edwards said. "Now the prospects are very real that we can lure much-needed industry to the central part of the state."[10] In her only floor speech, Edwards spoke on behalf of a motion to vote on the proposed Equal Education Opportunities Act, which would have restricted the use of busing to achieve school integration. Edwards described the bill as a "reasonable, just, and adequate remedy at law to help resolve the critical problems which have arisen from the excessive zeal and bad judgments of U.S. district court judges in the exercise of their discretionary powers."[11] In late September 1972, Edwards voted with a slim majority composed of Republicans and southern Democrats to kill a proposed Vietnam War fund cutoff which would have halted all money for U.S. military expenditures.[12] On October 3, Edwards presided over an evening Senate debate in which a heated confrontation occurred between two of the chamber's elder statesmen.[13]

The senatorial role seemed to suit Elaine Edwards. A month into her new job she told the *Washington Post*: "I like being a Senator very much. I would have liked to have been able to run and keep the seat this fall, had I not been the first lady of Louisiana. . . . But I am going to stay with Ed and do whatever he's doing."[14] Acceding to her husband's wishes, Edwards resigned her seat on November 13, 1972, in order to provide Louisiana Senator-elect J. Bennett Johnston an edge in seniority by finishing the remainder of Ellender's term. As she prepared to retire, nine colleagues, including Henry "Scoop" Jackson of Washington and Hubert Humphrey of Minnesota, delivered tributes to Edwards on the Senate Floor. "It is unfortunate that Mrs. Edwards will not be in the Senate for a longer period of time," Jackson said. "It is obvious, even during her short tenure, that she has the ability and capacity to become one of the more influential Members of this body."[15] Elaine and Edwin Edwards divorced in 1989 after 40 years of marriage. Elaine Edwards retired to Baton Rouge, where she continues to reside.

FOR FURTHER READING

Biographical Directory of the United States Congress, "Elaine Schwartzenburg Edwards," http://bioguide.congress.gov

NOTES

1   *Congressional Record,* Senate, 92nd Cong., 2nd sess. (17 October 1972): 36738.
2   American Mothers Committee, *Mothers of Achievement in American History, 1776–1976* (Rutland, VT: C.E. Tuttle & Co, 1976): 233–234.
3   Hope Chamberlin, *A Minority of Members: Women in the U.S. Congress* (New York: Praeger, 1973): 347.
4   See, for instance, *Mothers of Achievement*: 233–234.
5   "Lady From Louisiana," 4 August 1972, *New York Times*: 30; Chamberlin, *A Minority of Members*: 346.
6   Chamberlin, *A Minority of Members*: 346–347.
7   See, for instance, "Seatwarmers," 15 April 1982, *Washington Post*: A24.
8   'Liberated' quote in Karen Foerstel, *Biographical Dictionary of Congressional Women* (Westport, CT: Greenwood Press, 1999): 79; "Lady From Louisiana," 4 August 1972, *New York Times*: 30.
9   "New Senator Sworn," 8 August 1972, *New York Times*: 39.
10 Chamberlin, *A Minority of Members*: 348.
11 *Congressional Record,* Senate, 92nd Cong., 2nd sess. (12 October 1972): 35329.
12 Spencer Rich, "Senate Kills Viet Fund Cutoff," 27 September 1972, *Washington Post*: A1.
13 "Angry Scene on the Senate Floor," 4 October 1972, *New York Times*: 94.
14 Jeannette Smyth, "Louisiana Get-Together," 15 September 1972, *Washington Post*: B3.
15 *Congressional Record,* Senate, 92nd Cong., 2nd sess. (18 October 1972): 37713–37714.

Yvonne Brathwaite Burke

1932–

UNITED STATES REPRESENTATIVE ★ DEMOCRAT FROM CALIFORNIA
1973–1979

Yvonne Brathwaite Burke was a rising star in California and national politics years prior to winning a U.S. House seat. She was the first African-American woman elected to the California assembly in 1966. At the 1972 Democratic National Convention she served as vice chair of the platform committee, gaining national television exposure. That same year she became the first black woman from California (and only the third ever) elected to the House. Her meteoric career continued with a prime appointment to the Appropriations Committee and her election as the first woman to chair the Congressional Black Caucus (CBC). But her most notable distinction for much of the public came in 1973, when Burke became the first serving Congresswoman to give birth and be granted maternity leave.

Perle Yvonne Watson was born on October 5, 1932, in Los Angeles, California, the only child of James Watson, a custodian at the MGM film studios, and Lola (Moore) Watson, a real estate agent in East Los Angeles. Yvonne (she rejected the name Perle) grew up in modest circumstances and at first was enrolled in the public schools.[1] At the age of four she was transferred to a model school for exceptional children. Watson became class vice president at Manuel Arts High School in Los Angeles. She enrolled at the University of California at Berkeley in 1949 but transferred to the University of California at Los Angeles, where she earned a B.A. in political science in 1953. She became only the second black woman to be admitted to the University of California School of Law, earning her J.D. and passing the California bar in 1956. After graduating, she found that no law firms would hire an African-American woman and, thus, entered her own private practice specializing in civil, probate, and real estate law. In addition to her private practice, she served as the state's deputy corporation commissioner and as a hearing officer for the Los Angeles Police Commission. In 1957, Yvonne Watson wed mathematician Louis Brathwaite; their marriage ended in divorce in 1964. Yvonne Brathwaite organized a legal defense team for Watts rioters in 1965 and was named by Governor Edmond Brown to the McCone Commission, which investigated the conditions that led to the riot. A year later she won election to the California assembly. She eventually chaired the assembly's committee on urban development and won re-election in 1968 and 1970.[2]

Brathwaite eventually grew impatient with the pace of social legislation in the California assembly and, when court-mandated reapportionment created a new congressional district, decided to enter the race for the seat. The district encompassed much of southwest Los Angeles, was nearly 75 percent registered Democrat, and had a large African-American constituency. In the Democratic primary, Brathwaite faced Billy Mills, a popular African-American Los Angeles city councilman. She amassed 54 percent of the vote to defeat Mills and three other challengers. Just days after the primary, on June 14, 1972, Yvonne Brathwaite married businessman William Burke, who had been an aide to Mills. Less than a month later, Yvonne Brathwaite Burke garnered national media attention as the vice chair of the Democratic National Convention in Miami Beach that nominated George McGovern. She spent much of the convention controlling the gavel during the long and sometimes raucous platform deliberations, eventually helping to pass revised rules that gave minorities and young voters a greater voice in shaping party policy.[3]

The convention exposure only added to her luster,

YVONNE BURKE BECAME THE
FIRST MEMBER TO GIVE BIRTH
WHILE SERVING IN CONGRESS.
AT THE TIME, SHE OBSERVED
THAT IT WAS "A DUBIOUS HONOR."
SPEAKER OF THE HOUSE
CARL ALBERT SUBSEQUENTLY
GRANTED BURKE MATERNITY
LEAVE, ANOTHER FIRST
IN CONGRESSIONAL HISTORY.

though it was hardly a factor in the general election that November in the heavily Democratic district. Burke faced 31-year-old Gregg Tria, a recent law school graduate, who ran on an anti-busing and anti-abortion platform. Burke defeated Tria easily, winning 73 percent of the vote. In Burke's subsequent re-election bids in 1974 and 1976, in a newly reapportioned California district, she won 80 percent of the vote against Republicans Tom Neddy and Edward Skinner, respectively.[4]

In Burke's first term during the 93rd Congress (1973–1975), she received assignments on two committees: Public Works and Interior and Insular Affairs. She gave up both of those panels in December 1974 to accept a seat on the powerful Appropriations Committee, where she served for the duration of her House career. Burke's appointment to the panel signaled the first time that African Americans simultaneously were on the most influential House committees: Appropriations (Burke), Ways and Means (Charles Rangel of New York), and Rules (Andrew Young of Georgia).[5] In the 94th Congress (1975–1977), Burke was appointed chair of the Select Committee on the House Beauty Shop, an honorific position that rotated among the women Members.

Burke made national headlines again as a freshman Member when she revealed in the spring of 1973 that she was expecting a child. When Autumn Roxanne Burke was born on November 23, 1973, Yvonne Burke became the first Member to give birth while serving in Congress. At the time, she observed that it was "a dubious honor."[6] Speaker of the House Carl Albert of Oklahoma subsequently granted Burke maternity leave, another first in congressional history.[7] The Burkes also had a daughter, Christine, from William Burke's previous marriage.

Representative Burke recognized that the civil rights struggle had shifted to a phase in which less overt discrimination must be confronted. "The kinds of things we faced in my generation were easy to understand," she explained. "Your parents said, 'They don't let you sit down here, they don't let you go to that place.' Everybody knew. But now it is so complex, so frustrating to young people when they are led to believe that everything is fine, yet at

the same time it is not fine."[8] Minority interests were always in the forefront of Burke's legislative agenda. During her first term in office she fought the Richard M. Nixon administration's efforts to unravel some of the programs established under Lyndon Johnson's Great Society, particularly the Office of Economic Opportunity (OEO), which Nixon stripped of many of its programs. One of Burke's earliest House Floor speeches was a defense of the OEO.[9]

Burke also fought on behalf of equal opportunities for minority owned businesses in the construction of the Trans-Alaskan Pipeline by adding two amendments to the bill that provided the framework for the nearly 800-mile-long project. One amendment required that affirmative action programs be created to award some pipeline contracts to minority businesses. A version of that amendment later would require that any project funded with federal dollars must provide affirmative action incentives, reminiscent of the legislative technique used by Adam Clayton Powell of New York, in which he attached antidiscrimination riders to legislation involving federal funding. "The construction of the Alaskan Pipeline will create substantial employment opportunities, and it therefore seems desirable and appropriate to extend the existing programs for non-discrimination and equal employment opportunity" to that project, Burke told colleagues on the House Floor.[10] Burke's second amendment to the bill, the "Buy America Act," required that the materials to construct the pipeline "to the maximum extent feasible" would be manufactured in the United States.[11] Despite voicing strong concerns about potential environmental problems, Burke continued to back the Alaska pipeline project, believing it would help the impending energy crisis in the United States.[12]

In the House, Burke earned a reputation as a legislator who avoided confrontation and controversy, yet nevertheless worked with determination behind the scenes to effect changes she believed to be important. "I don't believe in grand-standing," she once explained, "but in the poverty areas, if there is something we need, then I'll go after it."[13] Using her experience as a former state legislator in the California assembly, Burke chose her positions carefully and usually refrained from partisan rhetoric in debates. She also seemed to take to heart the advice of former President Lyndon Johnson, who had advised her as a freshman Member, "Don't talk so much on the House Floor."[14]

With quiet determination, Representative Burke supported most major feminist issues and joined the Congressional Women's Caucus when it was founded in 1977. In that capacity she served as the group's first treasurer.[15] She was part of a successful effort to extend the time limitation for the Equal Rights Amendment by an additional three years.[16] That same year, the California Congresswoman introduced the Displaced Homemakers Act, which authorized the creation of job training centers for women entering the labor market, particularly middle-aged women who had for years been out of the job market but through divorce or the death of a spouse were left to support themselves. The purpose of the bill, which also provided health and financial counseling, was "to help displaced homemakers make it through a readjustment period so that they may have the opportunity to become productive, self-sufficient members of society," Burke explained.[17] In 1977, she vigorously criticized the Hyde Amendment, which prohibited the use of federal Medicaid funds for abortions. "The basic premise which we cannot overlook is that if the Government will not pay for an indigent woman's abortion, she cannot afford to go elsewhere," Burke wrote in a *New York Times* op-ed piece.[18] In 1978, Burke introduced a bill to prohibit sex discrimination in the workplace based on pregnancy, particularly employer policies that kept women out of their jobs for long periods of time both before and after childbirth.[19]

Despite her prominent committee assignments and role as chair of the CBC, which she assumed in 1976, Congresswoman Burke never seemed completely at home on Capitol Hill. Publicly, she expressed her desire to have a more direct and administrative effect on policy than the demands of being one of 435 House Members allowed her. Privately, however, associates believed that by 1977

the distance from her husband and her 4-year-old daughter in Los Angeles, not to mention the toll of the 3,000-mile biweekly commute, had left her exhausted and unhappy.[20]

In 1978, Burke declined to run for re-election to the 96th Congress (1979–1981), in order to campaign for the office of California attorney general, a position that no woman in America had ever been elected to in state government. She won the Democratic nomination but lost to Republican State Senator George Deukmejian in the general election. In June 1979, California Governor Jerry Brown appointed Burke to the Los Angeles County board of supervisors, making her the first black person to sit on the panel. In 1980, she lost her bid to a new four-year term and returned to private law practice. In 1984, Burke was the vice chair of the Los Angeles Olympics Organizing Committee. Burke became the first African American to win outright election as an L.A. County supervisor in 1992, defeating future Congresswoman Diane Watson by a narrow margin.[21] A year later, she became the first woman and the first minority to chair the board. Burke has been re-elected twice and most recently chaired the board of supervisors in 2002 and 2003. She resides in her native Los Angeles.[22]

FOR FURTHER READING

Biographical Directory of the United States Congress, "Yvonne Brathwaite Burke," http://bioguide.congress.gov

Gray, Pamela Lee. "Yvonne Brathwaite Burke: The Congressional Career of California's First Black Congresswoman, 1972-1978." Ph.D. diss., University of Southern California, 1987.

MANUSCRIPT COLLECTIONS

University of California (Berkley, CA), The Bancroft Library. *Oral History:* 1982, 46 pages. The title of the interview is "New Arenas of Black Influence." Includes discussion of Congresswoman Burke's political offices, including her drive for social legislation, her entry into Democratic Party politics, her tenure in the California assembly during Governor Ronald W. Reagan's administration, as well as a discussion on minorities and women.

University of Southern California (Los Angeles, CA), Regional Cultural History Collection, Department of Special Collections, Doheny Memorial Library. *Papers:* 1966–1980, 452 feet. Correspondence, photographs, sound recordings, and memorabilia relating to Congresswoman Burke's years in the California assembly, U.S. Congress, and Los Angeles County board of supervisors. Also included are materials relating to her campaign for attorney general of California. Some restrictions pertain to the collection. A finding aid is available in the repository.

NOTES

1 Leroy F. Aarons, "Legislator With a Subtle Touch," 22 October 1972, *Washington Post*: K1.

2 "Yvonne Brathwaite Burke," *Notable Black American Women*, Book 1 (Detroit, MI: Gale Research: 1992).

3 Leroy F. Aarons, "That Woman in the Chair Aims for Hill," 14 July 1972, *Washington Post*: A8.

4 "Election Statistics, 1920 to Present" http://clerk.house.gov/members/electionInfo/elections.html.

5 "Committee Sizes Shift in the House," 13 December 1974, *Washington Post*: A2.

6 "Rep. Burke: 'A Dubious Honor,'" 5 July 1973, *Washington Post*: C7; "7-lb. 9-oz. Girl for Rep. Burke," 24 November 1973, *New York Times*: 19.

7 "Congressional First," 24 November 1973, *Washington Post*: D3.

8 "'The World I Want for My Child,'" 27 March 1974, *Christian Science Monitor*: 20. This is an op-ed piece based on excerpts of an *Ebony* article from March 1974 that Burke had authored.

9 *Congressional Record*, House, 93rd Cong., 1st sess. (31 January 1973): 2835–2836.

10 *Congressional Record*, House, 93rd Cong., 1st sess. (2 August 1973): 27655.

11 *Congressional Record*, House, 93rd Cong., 1st sess. (2 August 1973): 27710; "Trade Proposals Causing Concern," 3 September 1973, *New York Times*: 23.

12 *Congressional Record*, House, 93rd Cong., 1st sess. (2 August 1973): 27653–27655.

13 "2 Black Women Head for House," 7 October 1972, *New York Times*: 18.

14 Dorothy Gilliam, "He'd Have Said, 'Go 'Head,'" 25 January 1973, *Washington Post*: C1.

15 Irwin Gertzog, *Congressional Women: Their Recruitment, Integration, and Behavior* (Westport, CT: Praeger, 1995): 186.

16 *Congressional Record*, House, 95th Cong., 2nd sess. (15 August 1978): 26226–26232.

17 *Congressional Record*, House, 94th Cong., 2nd sess. (25 May 1976): 15449–15450; *Congressional Record*, House, 94th Cong., 1st sess. (21 October 1975): 33482–33483.

18 Yvonne Brathwaite Burke, "Again, 'Back-Alley and Self-Induced Abortions,'" 22 August 1977, *New York Times*: 23.

19 *Congressional Record*, House, 95th Cong., 2nd sess. (18 July 1978): 21442.

20 Lacey Fosburgh, "Women's Status a Key Factor in Race by Rep. Burke," 13 May 1978, *New York Times*: 10.

21 "Ex-Lawmaker Seems Victor in Los Angeles," 22 November 1992, *New York Times*: 29.

22 "Biography of the Honorable Yvonne B. Burke," available at http://burke.co.la.ca.us/pages/Bioybb.htm (accessed 4 April 2006).

Marjorie Sewell Holt

1920–

UNITED STATES REPRESENTATIVE ★ REPUBLICAN FROM MARYLAND
1973–1987

As a member of the newly formed Budget Committee, Congresswoman Marjorie Sewell Holt was the champion of fiscal conservatism in Congress, seeking to cap federal spending—with the exception of a defense budget—across the board. Famous for her sponsorship of legislation to end busing as a means of racial desegregation, Holt was a consistent supporter of the conservative social politics of the Richard M. Nixon, Gerald R. Ford, and Ronald W. Reagan administrations.

Marjorie Sewell was born on September 17, 1920, in Birmingham, Alabama, to Edward and Juanita Sewell. The oldest of four sisters, Marjorie Sewell spent most of her youth in Jacksonville, Florida. She graduated from Jacksonville Junior College in 1945. In December 1946, Sewell married Duncan Holt, an electrical engineer, and the couple raised three children: Rachel, Edward, and Victoria. That same year, she entered law school at the University of Florida at Gainesville, earning her L.L.B. in 1949. The family moved to Maryland in 1950, where Marjorie Holt practiced law in Annapolis and became involved with GOP state politics. In 1963, Holt was appointed to the Anne Arundel County board of elections and served as supervisor of elections until 1965.[1] She was elected Anne Arundel County circuit court clerk a year later, defeating longtime local Democratic leader, Louis Phipps, Jr. She served as clerk until 1972.

When reapportionment created a new Maryland seat in the U.S. House in 1972, Holt decided to pursue her longtime desire to serve in Congress.[2] As a conservative, Marjorie Holt confronted some challenges in the new district which included a portion of minority-populated Prince George's County and a 5–2 ratio of registered Democrats to Republicans.[3] Holt, however, also enjoyed some advantages. The district's Democratic voters had a recent history of electing local Republican officials.[4] The United States Naval Academy in Annapolis and Andrews Air Force Base, moreover, provided Holt pockets of conservative military voters.[5] Holt later commented on her first campaign, "I saw the perfect district, the timing was right. I started early, amassed support, and muscled [my opponents] out."[6]

After she handily defeated two challengers in the Republican primary, the general election race between Holt and her Democratic opponent, former state legislator and agency head Werner Fornos, was immediately dubbed a contest between conservatism and liberalism. Although both Holt and Fornos opposed busing as a means of desegregating schools, a particularly volatile issue in Prince George's County, both candidates differed considerably on other issues, such as wage and price controls, taxes, the role of federal employees in political campaigns, and the war in Vietnam.[7] Holt summarized her platform, saying, "My whole pitch is for less government."[8] She promised to reduce the size of the federal government through cutbacks in all nonmilitary government spending. Holt defeated Fornos, with 59 percent of the total vote.[9] The aftermath of the election was bitter, as Fornos accused Holt of running a "hate campaign" and later charged Holt's backers with violating campaign laws by spreading anonymous and false charges that Fornos was going to be indicted by a state grand jury.[10] An Anne Arundel County grand jury later acquitted Holt of these charges.[11] Holt easily was re-elected to the six succeeding Congresses, winning by no less than 58 percent of the total votes and, in 1980, taking a career best 71 percent of total returns.[12]

IMAGE COURTESY OF THE LIBRARY OF CONGRESS

Holt soon established herself as one of the House's staunchest defenders of local control over education. She led the charge in Congress to end the busing of children to different school districts in order to achieve desegregation.[13] After the 1964 Civil Rights Act granted the Department of Health, Education, and Welfare (HEW) the power to withhold federal money from school districts that did not meet certain racial percentage quotas, busing became a solution for creating greater diversity in schools. Holt called the busing system, which often placed middle-class and primarily white students in poorer schools, "the new racism." "We should get back on the track and start making every school a good school in providing education for the children," she countered.[14] In 1974, the House passed Holt's measure that prevented HEW from classifying schools by student and teacher racial quotas in order to determine federal funding, a move that Holt believed would end the need for busing.[15] Although it was eventually rejected by the Senate, Holt's amendment set precedent for a proposed amendment to the U.S. Constitution, introduced by Ohio Democrat Ronald M. Mottl in 1979.[16]

In 1976, Holt left her seat on the House Administration Committee after serving only a partial term for a prestigious appointment to the Budget Committee. Created in 1974, the committee was charged with drafting the federal budget each April. It also featured a rotating membership, allowing Members to serve only six years in a 10-year period. In 1978, Holt countered the Democratic majority's budget proposal by offering an alternative Republican plan, including an amendment that would slow spending by as much as seven percent over the previous year.[17] Although her proposal failed by a 198–203 roll call vote, the practice of offering a substitute budget thereafter became standard strategy for the minority party.[18] A career-long member of the Armed Services Committee, Holt also acted as the unofficial spokesperson for the military from her position on the Budget panel by attempting to protect military spending. Even after her departure from the Budget Committee in 1980, Holt often pushed her Armed Services Committee colleagues to ask for bigger

defense allotments, despite apparent opposition on the Budget Committee. "Where are we going to get additional budgetary authority if we don't ask for it?" she said.[19] Holt returned to the forefront in economic policy when she gained a position on the Joint Economic Committee in 1983, serving until 1986.

Holt's tough conservative policies were well respected among her Republican colleagues. However, she suspected that gender discrimination and her conservative "inflexibility" often kept her from attaining leadership positions.[20] In 1975, Holt vied for the vacant chair of the Republican Research Committee, a congressional caucus which served as a legislative conservative think tank. Just before the vote, Minority Whip Robert Michel of Illinois endorsed Minnesota Representative Bill Frenzel, arguing that the conservative bent of the rest of the Republican leaders had to be balanced by a moderate. Though Michel later championed women's participation in the party, some House Members suggested that he did not support Holt's ascendancy based on her gender.[21] She lost another race in 1981 to fill the vacant chairmanship of the Republican Policy Committee. Holt was the favorite for the position until popular freshman and former White House Chief of Staff Dick Cheney of Wyoming, made a last minute pitch for the chairmanship, defeating Holt in 99–68 vote.[22]

Marjorie Holt was reticent to embrace the political cause of women's rights and liberation. "I've always thought of myself as a person and I certainly haven't been discriminated against," she told voters in her first House race.[23] She warned feminists, "I don't think we should de-emphasize the satisfaction of raising children."[24] Consistent with her fight for a smaller federal government, Holt voted in 1976 against providing federal money for daycare centers and abortions.[25] In 1980, she joined other anti-abortionists in barring federal employees from using their health insurance to pay for abortions.[26] After its creation in April 1977, Holt declined to join the Congressional Caucus on Women's Issues. In order to gain the membership of all women in Congress, caucus co-chairs Elizabeth Holtzman and Margaret Heckler convinced Holt to join the caucus in 1979 by assuring her that Members would

HOLT CALLED THE BUSING

SYSTEM, WHICH OFTEN

PLACED MIDDLE-CLASS AND

PRIMARILY WHITE STUDENTS

IN POORER SCHOOLS,

"THE NEW RACISM," SAYING,

"WE SHOULD GET BACK

ON THE TRACK AND START

MAKING EVERY SCHOOL A GOOD

SCHOOL IN PROVIDING

EDUCATION FOR THE CHILDREN."

be allowed to ally with or distance themselves from the caucus as they saw politically fit. Moreover, the caucus would not publicly endorse any issue that was not agreed to unanimously.[27] Holt resigned her membership in 1981, when the caucus altered some of the rules that persuaded her to join.[28]

Citing a desire to spend more time with her family, Holt retired from Congress in 1986, at the age of 66, and returned to practicing law at a firm in Baltimore, Maryland. Holt remained active in the Republican Party. She was nominated by President Ronald W. Reagan as a member of the General Advisory Committee on Arms Control and Disarmament in July 1987. In 2000, Holt served as the Maryland state co-chair for the George W. Bush and Richard Cheney presidential campaign and was named a member of the Maryland campaign leadership team seeking to re-elect the Bush ticket in 2004.[29]

FOR FURTHER READING

Biographical Directory of the United States Congress, "Marjorie Sewell Holt," http://bioguide.congress.gov

Holt, Marjorie. *The Case Against the Reckless Congress* (Ottawa, IL: Green Hill Publishers, 1976).

———, ed. "The Poverty of Equality," In *Can You Afford This House?*, edited by David Treen (Ottawa, IL: Green Hill Books, 1978).

MANUSCRIPT COLLECTION

University of Maryland Libraries (College Park, MD), Archives and Manuscript Department, http://www.lib.umd.edu/UMCP/ARCV/archives.html. *Papers:* 1972–1986, 20 feet. Congressional papers and correspondence, including speeches, voting records, schedule books, bills sponsored or cosponsored, press clippings, photographs and political cartoons, and legislative files (chiefly on environmental issues of the Chesapeake Bay region). A preliminary inventory is available in the repository.

NOTES

1 "Marjorie Sewell Holt," Associated Press Candidate Biographies, 1986.

2 Holt noted that she first expressed her desire to run for Congress in seventh grade. See, "Holt: 'Inefficiency' Rife," 10 September 1972, *Washington Post*: D1.

3 Douglas Watson, "Two Busy in Md. 4th District," 20 August 1972, *Washington Post*: B1.

4 Douglas Watson, "Anne Arundel Finally To Get Representative," 18 May 1972, *Washington Post*: B7.

5 *Almanac of American Politics, 1984* (Washington, D.C.: Congressional Quarterly, Inc., 1985): 673.

6 *Politics in America, 1986* (Washington, D.C.: Congressional Quarterly, Inc., 1985): 673.

7 Douglas Watson, "4th District Congressional Rivals Oppose School Busing," 1 October 1972, *Washington Post*: A14.

8 Douglas Watson, "Victory Is No Surprise to Woman in Hill Race," 9 November 1972, *Washington Post*: A7.

9 *Politics in America, 1986*: 673; Watson, "Victory Is No Surprise to Woman in Hill Race."

10 Douglas Watson, "Md. Loser Blames 'Hate Campaign,'" 19 November 1972, *Washington Post*: D4; Paul G. Edwards, "Campaign Violations Laid to Holt Backers," 20 September 1973, *Washington Post*: A1.

11 Charles A. Krause, "Jury Clears Holt Campaign," 6 March 1974, *Washington Post*: C1.

12 "Election Statistics, 1920 to Present," http://clerk.house.gov/members/electionInfo/index.html; Sandra Sugawara, "Reagan, Maryland Congressional Delegation Frequently Crash," 15 August 1985, *Washington Post*: MDA11.

13 Watson, "4th District Congressional Rivals Oppose School Busing."

14 *Politics in America, 1986*: 672; Watson, "4th District Congressional Rivals Oppose School Busing."

15 "House Revotes Aid-Cutoff Ban Over Busing," 5 December 1974, *Washington Post*: A9.

16 Steven Green, "Senate Kills Holt's School Amendment," *Washington Post*, 15 December 1974: A1; *Politics in America, 1986*: 671–672; Felicity Barringer, "The Battle Over a Busing Ban: P.G. Congresswomen on Opposite Sides as Measure Fails," *Washington Post*, 25 July 1979: C4.

17 Mary Russell, "House GOP to Offer Bigger Tax Cut, Spending Trims in Battle of Budget," *Washington Post*, 29 April 1978: A2.

18 *Politics in America, 1986*: 671.

19 *Almanac of American Politics, 1984*: 521; *Politics in America, 1986*: 671; Mary Russell, "House Defeats GOP Proposals to Cut Budget," 10 May 1979, *Washington Post*: A24.

20 Irwin N. Gertzog, *Congressional Women: Their Recruitment, Integration, and Behavior* (Westport, CT: Praeger, 1995): 122.

21 Gertzog, *Congressional Women*: 123 (see quoted text at the top of the page). Particularly notable is Michel's later endorsement of Illinois Representative Lynn Martin for a coveted seat on the Budget Committee in her freshman term. He later appointed her to the powerful Rules Committee.

22 *Politics in America, 1982*: 672.

23 "Holt: 'Inefficiency' Rife," 10 September 1972, *Washington Post*: D1.

24 "Holt: 'Inefficiency' Rife."

25 Paul Hodge, " Md. Congressmen's Voting Records on Consumer Issues," 28 October 1974, *Washington Post*: MD2.

26 Martin Weil and Victor Cohn, "Anti-Abortionists In House Attack Insurance Plans," 22 August 1980, *Washington Post*: A1.

27 Gertzog, *Congressional Women*: 197.

28 Ibid., 208.

29 "Bush–Cheney '04 Announces Maryland Campaign Leadership Team," 6 March 2004, PR Newswire Association.

Elizabeth Holtzman

1941-

UNITED STATES REPRESENTATIVE ★ DEMOCRAT FROM NEW YORK
1973–1981

A self-proclaimed political outsider, Elizabeth "Liz" Holtzman defeated a 50-year House veteran and powerful chairman to win a seat in the U.S. House of Representatives. During her four terms in the House, Holtzman earned national prominence as an active member of the Judiciary Committee during the Richard M. Nixon impeachment inquiry and as a cofounder of the Congressional Caucus on Women's Issues.

Elizabeth Holtzman and her twin brother, Robert, were born on August 11, 1941, in Brooklyn, New York, to Russian immigrants Sidney Holtzman, a lawyer, and Filia Holtzman, a faculty member in the Hunter College Russian Department. Elizabeth Holtzman graduated *magna cum laude* from Radcliffe College in 1962 as a member of Phi Beta Kappa and received her J.D. from Harvard Law School in 1965, one of 15 women in her class of more than 500. After graduation, she returned to New York to practice law and became active in state Democratic politics. From 1967 to 1970, Holtzman managed parks and recreation as an assistant to New York City Mayor John Lindsay. From 1970 to 1972, she served as a New York state Democratic committee member and as a district leader from Flatbush. She also cofounded the Brooklyn Women's Political Caucus.

In 1972, Holtzman mounted a long-shot campaign to unseat incumbent Congressman Emanuel Celler, who had represented central Brooklyn for half a century and was chairman of the powerful House Judiciary Committee.[1] Though she lacked the funding that Celler mustered for the Democratic primary, Holtzman mounted an energetic grass-roots campaign by canvassing the urban district. "If I had known how little money we could raise, I would

never have gotten into it," Holtzman recalled. "But it was possible to use shoe leather and win a race."[2] She often introduced herself to patrons in lines outside movie theaters, emphasizing her commitment to constituent needs. "There was no hostility to the fact that I was a woman. I remember truck drivers leaning out of their trucks and saying, 'I think it's great . . . it's fantastic that a woman is running,'" she recalled. "I found mothers taking their daughters up to me. They wanted their daughters to have a different conception of the possibilities for them."[3] Holtzman noted that the 84-year-old Celler had become increasingly distant from local affairs and had no Brooklyn district office. She further played on her substantive policy disagreements with the incumbent, who had for years bottled up the Equal Rights Amendment (ERA) in the Judiciary Committee and had been an unwavering supporter of the war in Vietnam, an unpopular stance in the Democratic district. Holtzman won the nomination by a narrow margin of 635 votes, whereupon *Time* magazine dubbed her "Liz the Lion Killer."[4] In the general election, Holtzman was the sound winner, with 66 percent to Republican Nicholas R. Macchio, Jr.'s 23 percent. Running as a Liberal Party candidate, Celler left the race in September, endorsing Holtzman; however, he still received 7 percent of the vote.[5] "My victory says that no political figure, no matter how powerful, can forget about the people he was elected to serve," Holtzman declared.[6] In her subsequent three re-election bids, Holtzman never was seriously challenged, winning with margins of 70 percent or more.[7]

When Liz Holtzman took her seat in the 93rd Congress (1973–1975), at the age of 31, she became the youngest woman ever to serve in the House. Immediately after her

election, Representative Holtzman obtained a seat on the powerful Judiciary Committee, where she served all four terms of her service. In the 94th Congress (1975–1977), she was assigned to the Budget Committee, where she remained through the 96th Congress (1979–1981). Holtzman also served on the Select Committee on Aging in the 96th Congress.

From her seat on the Judiciary Committee, Holtzman gained notoriety through her participation in the Nixon impeachment hearings as a freshman Representative. Of her role in reaching a verdict, Holtzman said, "It's the most serious decision I'll ever have to make."[8] She later aggressively questioned President Gerald R. Ford about his pardon of Nixon and defended the government's claim over the Nixon tapes and papers.[9] In 1973, Holtzman filed suit to halt American military action in Cambodia, on the grounds that it had never been approved by Congress. A district court ruled the Cambodian invasion unconstitutional, but the court of appeals reversed the decision.

Like many of her Democratic colleagues, Holtzman challenged military spending levels and weapons programs in the post-Vietnam era. Holtzman praised the Jimmy Carter administration's decision not to pursue a neutron bomb. "I think the people of the world have a right not to see life jeopardized by nuclear holocaust, and that means not only Russian life and American life but all life on this earth," she said in a floor speech. "The development of the neutron bomb and the deployment of countless unnecessary nuclear weapons will simply take us further down the road to such a holocaust."[10]

In 1977, Congresswomen Holtzman and Margaret Heckler of Massachusetts cofounded the Congressional Caucus for Women's Issues. As co-chairs, they persuaded 13 other House women to join (three declined), and the group held its first meeting on April 19, 1978. Though the women Members had met informally since the early 1970s to discuss women's issues, Holtzman had to allay the fears of many colleagues who were reluctant to join a formal caucus because they "felt their constituents wouldn't understand working on women's issues. Some were very worried that they would be embarrassed politically."[11]

The organizers agreed that the caucus would be used as a forum to create momentum for legislation on which Members could find consensus rather than as a disciplined unit that spoke with one voice on all issues.[12] One of the group's first battles was for passage of the ERA. In 1978, Holtzman led the fight to secure a seven-year extension of the March 1979 ratification deadline, a move that many Members considered to be on shaky constitutional grounds when it was introduced in committee.[13] Congress eventually added three-and-a-half years to the deadline. Holtzman also helped secure a prohibition on sex discrimination in federal programs during her time in the House. In a *New York Times* interview, Holtzman reflected on her role as a female legislator, "The vast majority of the legislation that's been introduced affecting the status of women was introduced by women."[14]

In 1980, rather than seek re-election for a fifth term in the House, Representative Holtzman entered the Democratic primary for nomination to the Senate. She won the heated contest for the nomination against Bess Myerson, a former Miss America-turned-consumer advocate, and Holtzman's former boss, John Lindsay. The Congresswoman portrayed herself as a candidate who was not beholden to special interests and who stood up to the political machine: "I have never been handpicked by the bosses. I have never been handpicked by anyone." It also marked the first time that a major party had nominated a woman to run for the Senate in New York. Holtzman ran on her record in the House stating that, "While others kept silent, I asked Gerald Ford the hard questions about whether the Nixon pardon was a deal," and that she, "got Congress to pass the bill extending the time limit ratifying the Equal Rights Amendment."[15] In the general election, she ran in a three-way race that included the incumbent Republican Jacob Javits, who had lost the GOP primary but ran on the Liberal ticket, and the man who beat Javits, a little-known Long Island politician named Alfonse D'Amato. Despite her distinguished record in Congress, Holtzman narrowly lost to Republican candidate D'Amato, 44.8 percent to 43.5 percent, with Javits drawing off about 11 percent of the vote.[16]

RECALLING HER FIRST CAMPAIGN FOR THE HOUSE, HOLTZMAN NOTED, "I FOUND MOTHERS TAKING THEIR DAUGHTERS UP TO ME. THEY WANTED THEIR DAUGHTERS TO HAVE A DIFFERENT CONCEPTION OF THE POSSIBILITIES FOR THEM."

A year after the loss of the Senate seat, Holtzman was elected district attorney of Brooklyn and served in that office until she was elected comptroller of New York City in 1989.[17] In 1992, she entered the Democratic Senate primary against former House colleague Geraldine Ferraro and State Attorney General Robert Abrams for the nomination to challenge Senator D'Amato in the general election. In an internecine primary squabble, Holtzman accused Ferraro of ethics violations during her House career and of ties to the mafia.[18] Abrams eventually won the Democratic nomination. Many observers believed that Holtzman's campaign tactics had effectively ended her political career. In 1993, she failed in her bid for the Democratic nomination for city comptroller. Holtzman entered private law practice in New York City and published her memoirs in 1996.

FOR FURTHER READING

Biographical Directory of the United States Congress, "Elizabeth Holtzman," http://bioguide.congress.gov

Holtzman, Elizabeth J., with Cynthia L. Cooper, *Who Said It Would Be Easy?: One Woman's Life in the Political Arena* (New York: Arcade, 1996).

MANUSCRIPT COLLECTION

Radcliffe Institute for Advanced Studies, Harvard University (Cambridge, MA), Schlesinger Library, http://www.radcliff.edu/schles. *Papers:* 1970–1981, 295 linear feet. Correspondence, speeches, financial records, scheduling books, telephone logs, campaign literature, awards, clippings, photographs, records of casework, community work, and the Judiciary Committee, and administrative and legislative files cover primarily Holtzman's election to and service in the U.S. House of Representatives and her unsuccessful campaign for election to the U.S. Senate. Subject files pertain to abortion, Cambodia, employment, environment, energy, housing and urban development, national security and the Central Intelligence Agency, New York City, rape privacy, social security, public welfare, transportation, and the Congressional Women's Caucus. Included are questionnaire responses from constituents on Watergate, the energy crisis, wage and price controls, Nixon's pardon, Rockefeller's vice presidency, amnesty, and mail services; material on Nixon's impeachment hearings; and testimony from hearings on immigration and refugee policy. Finding aid in repository. The bulk of the papers are restricted. *Video tapes:* 1987–1993, 20 video tapes. Consists mainly of media coverage of Holtzman. Included are news reports, talk show interviews, and press conferences. Also contains several speeches by Holtzman and a debate among U.S. Senate candidates. A finding aid is available in the repository. Appointment required for viewing video tapes. *Oral History:* 1973. 63 pages. Interview with Holtzman, by Marilyn Shapiro, sponsored by the William E. Wiener Oral History Library of the American Jewish Committee.

NOTES

1   In 1972, reapportionment changed Celler's district, extending the
    boundaries farther south. His constituency did not change dramatical-
    ly. See Kenneth Martis, *The Historical Atlas of Political Parties in the
    United States Congress: 1789–1989* (New York: MacMillan, 1989);
    Congressional Directory, 92nd Cong., 2nd sess. (Washington, D.C.:
    Government Printing Office, 1972); *Congressional Directory*, 93rd Cong.,
    1st sess. (Washington, D.C.: Government Printing Office, 1973).

2   Howard Kurtz, "The Private Public Prosecutor: Elizabeth Holtzman,
    Tough and Guarded as Brooklyn's DA," 27 October 1987, *Washington
    Post*: D1.

3   Susan Tolchin, *Women in Congress* (Washington, D.C.: Government
    Printing Office, 1976): 95.

4   "Liz the Lion Killer," *Time*, 3 July 1972, *Time*; see also, Hope
    Chamberlin, *A Minority of Members: Women in the U.S. Congress* (New
    York: Praeger, 1973): 353.

5   Lucia Johnson Leith, "In Congressional Races—'At Least 10 May Be
    Winners,'" 3 November 1972, *Christian Science Monitor*: 14; "Election
    Statistics, 1920 to Present," http://clerk.house.gov/members/
    electionInfo/index.html.

6   Chamberlin, *A Minority of Members*: 353.

7   "Election Statistics, 1920 to Present," http://clerk.house.gov/members/
    electionInfo/index.html.

8   "Tough Year for Freshman Class in Congress," 20 June 1974, *Christian
    Science Monitor*: 5A.

9   "Miss Holtzman Will Seek to Set Up Panel on Tapes," 7 November
    1974, *New York Times*: 26.

10 *Congressional Record*, House 95th Cong., 2nd sess. (11 April 1978):
    9668–9669.

11 "The Women's Caucus, 20 and Roaring," 20 October 1997, *Washington
    Post*: C3.

12 Irwin N. Gertzog, *Congressional Women: Their Recruitment, Integration, and
    Behavior* (Westport, CT: Praeger, 1995): 185–187; and generally chap-
    ters 9 through 11.

13 Larry Steinberg, "The Long Haul for ERA—And Now, Division in the
    Ranks," 31 December 1977, *National Journal* 9(no.52–53): 2006.

14 "Women in Office: How Have They Affected Women's Issues?" 4
    November 1980, *New York Times*: B8.

15 "Miss Holtzman Announces Bid for Javits's Senate Seat" 9 January
    1980, *New York Times*: B1.

16 "Election Statistics, 1920 to Present," http://clerk.house.gov/members/
    electionInfo/elections.html.

17 Selwyn Raab and Dennis Hevesi, "Holtzman's 6 Years: Innovations
    and Antagonism," 5 January 1998, *New York Times*: B1; Kurtz, "The
    Private Public Prosecutor: Elizabeth Holtzman, Tough and Guarded
    as Brooklyn's DA."

18 Helen Dewar, "Political Sisterhood Sours in N.Y. Race: Bitter Rivalry
    of Ferraro, Holtzman Seen Benefiting Male Opponent," 13 September
    1992, *Washington Post*: A21.

Barbara Jordan
1936–1996

UNITED STATES REPRESENTATIVE ★ DEMOCRAT FROM TEXAS
1973–1979

During the Watergate impeachment investigation, a time when many Americans despaired about the Constitution and the country, Barbara Jordan emerged as an eloquent and powerful interpreter of the crisis. Her very presence on the House Judiciary Committee, as one of the first African Americans elected from the Deep South since 1898 and the first black woman ever from that region, lent added weight to her message.

Barbara Charline Jordan was born in Houston, Texas, on February 21, 1936, one of three daughters of Benjamin M. Jordan and Arlyne Patten Jordan. Benjamin Jordan, a graduate of Tuskegee Institute, worked in a local warehouse before becoming pastor of Good Hope Missionary Baptist Church, which his family had long attended. Arlyne Jordan was an accomplished public speaker. Barbara Jordan was educated in the Houston public schools and graduated from Phyllis Wheatley High School in 1952. She earned a B.A. from Texas Southern University in 1956 and a law degree from Boston University in 1959. That same year she was admitted to the Massachusetts and Texas bars, commencing practice in Houston in 1960. To supplement her income (her law office was, for a while, in her parents' home), she worked as an administrative assistant to a county judge.[1]

Barbara Jordan's political turning point came when she worked on the John F. Kennedy presidential campaign in 1960. She eventually helped manage a highly organized get-out-the-vote program that served the 40 African-American precincts in Houston. In 1962 and 1964, Jordan ran for the Texas house of representatives but lost both times. So, in 1966, she ran for the Texas senate when court-enforced redistricting created a district largely consisting of minority voters. Jordan won, defeating a white liberal and

becoming the first African-American state senator since 1883 and the first black woman ever elected to that body.[2] The 30 other, male, white senators received her coolly. But Jordan won them over as an effective legislator who pushed through bills establishing the state's first minimum wage law, antidiscrimination clauses in business contracts, and the Texas Fair Employment Practices Commission. On March 28, 1972, Jordan's peers elected her president *pro tempore* of the Texas legislature, making her the first black woman in America to preside over a legislative body. In seconding the nomination, one of her male colleagues stood and singled Jordan out from across the chamber, spread his arms open, and said, "What can I say? Black is beautiful."[3] One of the functions of that job was to serve as acting governor when the governor and lieutenant governor were out of the state. When Jordan filled that largely ceremonial role on June 10, 1972, she became the first black chief executive in the nation.

In 1971, Jordan entered the race for the Texas congressional seat covering downtown Houston. The district had been redrawn after the 1970 Census and was composed of a predominantly African-American and Hispanic-American population. In the 1972 Democratic primary, Jordan faced Curtis Graves, another black state legislator, who attacked her for being too close to the white establishment. Jordan blunted Graves's charges with her legislative credentials. "I'm not going to Washington and turn things upside down in a day," she told supporters at a rally. "I'll only be one of 435. But the 434 will know I am there."[4] Jordan took the primary with 80 percent of the vote. In the general election, against Republican Paul Merritt, she won 81 percent of the vote. Along with Andrew Young of Georgia, Jordan became the first African American elected to

Congress from the Deep South in the 20th century. In the next two campaign cycles, Jordan simply overwhelmed her opposition, capturing 85 percent of the total vote in both general elections.[5]

Congresswoman Jordan's political philosophy from her days in the state legislature led her to stick closely to local issues. Civil rights and women's rights activists sometimes criticized her when she chose to favor her community interests rather than theirs. She followed this pattern in the House. "I sought the power points," she once said. "I knew if I were going to get anything done, [the congressional and party leaders] would be the ones to help me get it done."[6] Jordan was reluctant to commit herself to any one special interest group or caucus, such as the Congressional Black Caucus (CBC), of which she was a member. House women met informally too, but Jordan's attendance at those meetings was irregular, and she was noncommittal on most issues brought before the group. She was especially careful not to attach herself too closely to an agenda over which she had little control and which might impinge on her ability to navigate and compromise within the institutional power structure. "I am neither a black politician nor a woman politician," Jordan said in 1975. "Just a politician, a professional politician."[7]

In both her Texas legislative career and in the U.S. House, Jordan made the conscious decision to pursue power within the established system. One of her first moves in Congress was to establish relations with Members of the Texas delegation which, itself, had strong institutional connections. Her attention to influence inside the House was demonstrated by where she sat in the House Chamber's large, theatre-like arrangement. CBC members traditionally sat to the far left of the chamber. But Jordan chose the center aisle because she could hear better, be seen directly by the presiding officer, and save an open seat for colleagues who wished to stop and chat. Her seating preferences, as well as her loyalty to the Texas delegation, agitated fellow CBC members, but both fit perfectly into Jordan's model of seeking congressional influence.[8]

Jordan also believed that an important committee assignment, one in which she would be unique because of her gender and race, would magnify her influence. She, thus bypassed suggestions that she accept a seat on the Education and Labor Committee and pursued an assignment to the Judiciary Committee. Jordan, who had been a guest of fellow Texan Lyndon Johnson at the White House during her time as a state legislator, used that connection to secure this plum committee assignment. Securing President Johnson's intercession with Wilbur Mills of Arkansas, chairman of the Committee on Committees, she landed a seat on the Judiciary Committee, where she served for her three terms in the House. In the 94th and 95th Congresses (1975–1979), she also was assigned to the Committee on Government Operations.

It was as a freshman Member of the Judiciary Committee, however, that Jordan earned national notoriety. In the summer of 1974, as the committee considered articles of impeachment against President Richard M. Nixon for crimes associated with the Watergate Scandal, Jordan delivered opening remarks that shook the committee room and moved the large television audience tuned into the proceedings. "My faith in the Constitution is whole, it is complete, it is total," Jordan said. "I am not going to sit here and be an idle spectator to the diminution, the subversion, the destruction of the Constitution." She then laid out her reasoning behind her support of each of the five articles of impeachment against President Nixon. If her fellow committee members did not find the evidence compelling enough, she concluded, "then perhaps the eighteenth-century Constitution should be abandoned to a twentieth-century paper shredder."[9] Reaction to Jordan's statement was overwhelming. Jordan recalled that people swarmed around her car after the hearings to congratulate her. Impressed by her articulate reasoning and knowledge of the law, many people sent letters of praise to the Texas Congresswoman, with one person even resorting to a series of billboards in Houston declaring, "Thank you, Barbara Jordan, for explaining the Constitution to us."[10] The Watergate impeachment hearings helped transform Jordan into a recognizable and respected national politician.

From her first days in Congress, Jordan encouraged colleagues to extend the federal protection of civil rights to more Americans. She introduced civil rights amendments to legislation authorizing law enforcement assistance grants and joined seven other Members on the Judiciary Committee in opposing Gerald R. Ford's nomination as Vice President, citing what they considered to be a mediocre civil rights record. In 1975, when Congress voted to extend the Voting Rights Act of 1965, Jordan sponsored legislation which broadened the provisions of the act to include Hispanic Americans, Native

improve on the system of government, handed down to us by the founders of the Republic, but we can find new ways to implement that system and to realize our destiny."[12] Amidst the historical perspective of the national bicentennial year, and in the wake of the shattering experiences of the Vietnam War and Watergate, Jordan's message, like her commanding voice, resonated with Americans. She campaigned widely for Democratic presidential candidate James Earl "Jimmy" Carter, who defeated President Ford in the general election. Though Carter later interviewed Jordan for a Cabinet position, he

---

"'We the People.' It is a very eloquent beginning. But when [the Constitution] was completed on the seventeenth of September in 1787 I was not included in that 'We the People.' I felt somehow for many years that George Washington and Alexander Hamilton, just left me out by mistake. But through the process of amendment, interpretation, and court decision I have finally been included in 'We the People.'"

—BARBARA JORDAN, STATEMENT TO THE HOUSE JUDICIARY COMMITTEE ON IMPEACHMENT OF RICHARD M. NIXON, 25 JANUARY 1974

Americans, and Asian Americans. Although she voted for busing to enforce racial desegregation in public schools she was one of the few African-American Members of Congress to question the utility of the policy.[11]

Jordan's talent as a speaker contributed more and more to her national profile. In 1976, she became the first woman, as well as the first African American, to keynote a Democratic Party National Convention. Appearing after a subdued speech by Ohio Senator John Glenn, Jordan energized the convention with her oratory. "We are a people in search of a national community," she told the delegates, "attempting to fulfill our national purpose, to create and sustain a society in which all of us are equal. . . . We cannot

was not prepared to give her the one post she said she would accept: U.S. Attorney General.

By 1978, downplaying reports about her poor health, Jordan nevertheless declined to run for what would have been sure re-election to a fourth term. She cited her "internal compass," which she said was pointing her in a direction "away from demands that are all consuming."[13] She also said she wanted to work more directly on behalf of fellow Texans. Jordan was appointed the Lyndon Johnson Chair in National Policy at the LBJ School of Public Affairs at the University of Texas in Austin, where she taught into the early 1990s. She continued to speak widely as a lecturer on national affairs. In 1988 and 1992,

JORDAN WAS ESPECIALLY CAREFUL
NOT TO ATTACH HERSELF TOO
CLOSELY TO AN AGENDA OVER
WHICH SHE HAD LITTLE CONTROL
AND WHICH MIGHT IMPINGE ON
HER ABILITY TO NAVIGATE AND
COMPROMISE WITHIN THE
INSTITUTIONAL POWER STRUCTURE.
"I AM NEITHER A BLACK POLITICIAN
NOR A WOMAN POLITICIAN," SHE
SAID IN 1975. "JUST A POLITICIAN,
A PROFESSIONAL POLITICIAN."

she delivered speeches at the Democratic National Convention. Her 1992 keynote address took place in the midst of a lengthy battle with multiple sclerosis; she delivered her speech from a wheelchair. And, in 1994, President William J. Clinton appointed her to lead the Commission on Immigration Reform, a bipartisan group that delivered its findings in September of that year. Jordan received nearly two dozen honorary degrees and, in 1990, was named to the National Women's Hall of Fame in Seneca, New York. She never married and carefully guarded her private life. Jordan died in Austin, Texas, on January 17, 1996, from pneumonia as a complication of leukemia.

FOR FURTHER READING

Biographical Directory of the United States Congress, "Barbara Charline Jordan," http://bioguide.congress.gov

Bryant, Ira Babington. *Barbara Charline Jordan: From the Ghetto to the Capital* (Houston: D. Armstrong, 1977).

Fenno, Richard F. *Going Home: Black Representatives and Their Constituents* (Chicago, IL: University of Chicago Press, 2003).

Jordan, Barbara, and Shelby Hearon. *Barbara Jordan: A Self Portrait* (Garden City, N.Y.: Doubleday, 1979).

Rogers, Mary Beth. *Barbara Jordan: American Hero* (New York: Bantam Books, 1998).

MANUSCRIPT COLLECTIONS

Lyndon B. Johnson Library (Austin, TX). *Oral History:* March 28, 1984. 16 pages. Description in library.

Texas Southern University (Houston, TX). *Papers:* 1966–1996, 462 linear feet. The papers are divided into three major groups: State Senate Papers, U.S. House of Representatives Papers, and Personal Papers. A finding aid is available in the repository and online: http://www.tsu.edu/about/ library/specialCollections.pdf. The processing of the papers has not yet been completed.

NOTES

1   For information on Jordan's early life, see *Barbara Jordan and Shelby Hearon, Barbara Jordan: A Self Portrait* (Garden City, N.Y.: Doubleday, 1979) and Mary Beth Rogers, *Barbara Jordan: American Hero* (New York: Bantam Books, 1998).

2   *Current Biography, 1993* (New York: H.W. Wilson and Company, 1993): 291; Rogers, *Barbara Jordan.*

3   Richard Fenno, *Going Home: Black Representatives and Their Constituents* (Chicago: University of Chicago Press): 106–109.

4   Fenno, *Going Home:* 89–92.

5   "Election Statistics, 1920 to Present," http://clerk.house.gov/members/electionInfo/elections.html.

6   Susan Tolchin, *Women in Congress* (Washington, D.C.: Government Printing Office, 1976): 96–97.

7   Fenno, *Going Home:* 106–109.

8   Ibid.

9   Quotations from Barbara Jordan and Shelby Hearon, "Barbara Jordan: A Self-Portrait," 7 January 1979, *Washington Post:* A1.

10 Jordan and Hearon, "Barbara Jordan: A Self-Portrait."

11 *Current Biography, 1993:* 291. See also, Tolchin, *Women in Congress:* 96–97.

12 *Current Biography, 1993:* 292.

13 Ibid.

Patricia S. Schroeder

1940–

UNITED STATES REPRESENTATIVE ★ DEMOCRAT FROM COLORADO
1973–1997

Though political rivals and some male colleagues at first dismissed her as "little Patsy," Pat Schroeder became the forceful doyenne of American liberals on issues ranging from arms control to women's reproductive rights during her 24-year House career. Congresswoman Schroeder's biting wit and political barbs—from her seat on the Armed Services Committee, she once told Pentagon officials that if they were women, they would always be pregnant because they never said "no"—helped to make her a household name and blazed a trail for a new generation of women onto Capitol Hill.[1]

Patricia Scott was born in Portland, Oregon, on July 30, 1940, daughter of Lee Scott, an aviation insurance salesman, and Bernice Scott, a public-school teacher. Her great-grandfather had served alongside William Jennings Bryan in the Nebraska legislature, lending a reform-populist cast to her political heritage. As part of a military family that moved from post to post, she was raised in Texas, Ohio, and Iowa. Pat Scott earned a pilot's license and operated her own flying service to pay her college tuition. She graduated from the University of Minnesota in 1961, a member of Phi Beta Kappa majoring in philosophy, history, and political science. She earned a J.D. from Harvard Law School in 1964, though, as one of just 15 women in a class of more than 500, she felt "submergedin sexism."[2] On August 18, 1962, she married a law school classmate, James Schroeder, and the couple moved to Denver, eventually rearing two children, Scott and Jamie.[3] While in law school, a professor told Schroeder that most corporations shunned women lawyers, so she took a job with the federal government for two years as a field attorney for the National Labor Relations Board. She later moved into private practice, taught law, and volunteered as counsel for Planned Parenthood.

Schroeder, at her husband's encouragement, entered the 1972 race for the predominantly Democratic but conservative congressional district encompassing most of Colorado's capital city of Denver. Running without the support of the state Democratic Party or the Democratic National Committee, Schroeder campaigned as an anti-Vietnam War candidate. When asked to explain the motivation behind her unlikely congressional bid, Schroeder replied, "Among other things the need for honesty in government." She added, "It's an issue that women can speak best to—and more should be given the chance."[4] Schroeder ran a grass-roots campaign that seemed as overmatched as those of her political idol, Adlai Stevenson; she believed she would "talk sense to the American people and lose."[5] Voters, however, embraced her antiwar, women's rights message. She beat out her Democratic primary opponent Clarence Decker by 4,000 votes and, in the general election, defeated first-term incumbent Republican Mike McKevitt with 52 percent of the vote. Schroeder was the first woman elected to Congress from Colorado, a state that had granted women the vote in 1893.[6] In her subsequent 11 elections, she rarely faced serious opposition, typically garnering more than 60 percent of the vote.[7]

Claiming her seat in Congress proved thornier than the campaign. One of only 14 women in the House of Representatives, Schroeder confronted a male-dominated institution that frowned not only on her feminist agenda but on her mere presence. She likened the atmosphere there to that of "an over-aged frat house."[8] One male colleague remarked, "This is about Chivas Regal, thousand-dollar bills, Lear jets and beautiful women. Why are you here?"[9] Another asked how she could be a mother of two small children and a Member of Congress at the same time.

CONGRESSIONAL PICTORIAL DIRECTORY, 97TH CONGRESS

She replied, "I have a brain and a uterus and I use both."[10] Still another male colleague sneered, "I hope you aren't going to be a skinny Bella Abzug!"[11]

As the second-youngest woman ever elected to Congress (her Harvard Law School classmate Elizabeth Holtzman was the youngest, at 31) and the 32-year-old mother of a six- and a two-year-old, Schroeder received considerable attention from the media, her congressional colleagues, and the general public. Few other women had served in Congress while caring for such young children, and Schroeder did little to hide the fact that she was juggling two occupations, politician and mother. Known to keep diapers in her bag while on the floor of the House and crayons on her office coffee table, she bristled when criticized about her choice to undertake two careers. "One of the problems with being a working mother, whether you're a Congresswoman or a stenographer or whatever, is that everybody feels perfectly free to come and tell you what they think: 'I think what you're doing to your children is terrible.' 'I think you should be home.' They don't do that to men."[12] Although Schroeder defended her decision to run for political office while caring for her children, she did harbor some doubts early in her career. She recalled that shortly before beginning her first day on the job, she pondered, "My gosh, what's a mother like me doing here? I'm about to be sworn into Congress and I haven't even potty-trained my daughter."[13]

Schroeder received a rude introduction to the power of entrenched committee chairmen. She sought and earned a seat on the all-male Armed Services Committee because, according to the newly elected Congresswoman, "When men talk about defense, they always claim to be protecting women and children, but they never ask the women and children what they think."[14] Eager to identify and curb defense appropriations which, at the time, totaled nearly 40 percent of the national budget, Schroeder represented a minority viewpoint on the conservative Armed Services Committee.[15] Infuriated that a young woman sat on his committee, Chairman F. Edward Hébert of Louisiana, a Dixiecrat and 30-year veteran of Congress, made Schroeder share a chair with Ron Dellums, an African-American Democrat from California, during the organizational meeting for the committee. As Schroeder recalled, she and Dellums sat "cheek to cheek" because the chairman declared "that women and blacks were worth only half of one regular Member" and thus deserved only half a seat.[16] Dellums later commented that he and Schroeder acted as if sharing a chair was "the most normal thing in the world," in an effort to undermine Hébert's obvious attempt to make them uncomfortable. When Schroeder sought a spot on a delegation to a Strategic Arms Limitation Treaty disarmament conference on chemical warfare, Hébert declined her request noting, "I wouldn't send you to represent this committee in a dogfight."[17] Undeterred, Schroeder and her Democratic Caucus colleagues managed to oust Hébert in 1975, during the height of congressional reform efforts which included rules changes that weakened the power of long-standing committee leaders. Schroeder remained on the panel throughout her congressional career.

Representative Schroeder quickly became a driving force in the 1970s and 1980s as Democrats sought to rein in Cold War expenditures. In unison with a more like-minded chairman, Les Aspin of Wisconsin, she fostered an era of Democratic defense budgets that, in Schroeder's estimate, supported "reasonable strength" rather than "unreasonable redundancy."[18] She also asserted herself as a major advocate for arms control, opposing, among other programs, the MX ("Missile Experimental") program. Arguing against the philosophy that the U.S. Air Force's mobile MX rockets would serve as a deterrent to nuclear war, Schroeder suggested instead that "everyone in the world would be more impressed if we didn't deploy the weapon and showed common sense."[19] Schroeder worked to improve benefits, health care, and living conditions for military personnel, crafting the 1985 Military Family Act and eventually chairing the Subcommittee on Military Installations. Toward the end of her career, she convinced the Armed Services Committee to recommend that women be allowed to fly combat missions. In 1991, Schroeder spearheaded demands for reform in the military after two highly publicized sexual harassment scandals:

Schroeder sought and earned a seat on the all-male Armed Services Committee because, according to the newly elected Congresswoman, "When men talk about defense, they always claim to be protecting women and children, but they never ask the women and children what they think."

the navy "Tailhook" and a later case involving an army sergeant's abuse of female recruits. Schroeder also served as spokesperson for those in Congress who believed that American allies should bear more of the global defense burden.

The area in which Schroeder specialized, however, was women's rights and reforms affecting the family. In many respects, she made these issues, shared by many middle-class Americans, the blueprint for her work: women's health care, child rearing, expansion of Social Security benefits, and gender equity in the workplace. She was a vocal pro-choice advocate and a supporter of the Equal Rights Amendment. In 1977, Schroeder cofounded the Congressional Women's Caucus, subsequently co-chairing it for 10 years. She helped pass the 1978 Pregnancy Discrimination Act, which mandated that employers could not dismiss women employees simply because they were pregnant or deny them disability and maternity benefits. Later she created and chaired the Select Committee on Children, Youth and Families (which was dismantled in 1995). She also served on the Judiciary Committee and the Post Office and Civil Service Committee, where she eventually chaired the Subcommittee on Civil Service. In 1993, Schroeder scored her biggest legislative successes with the passage of the Family and Medical Leave Act and the National Institutes of Health Revitalization Act. For nearly a decade, she had toiled on the Family and Medical Leave Act, which in its final form provided job protection of up to 18 weeks of unpaid leave for the care of a newborn, sick child, or parent.

By the late 1980s, Schroeder was one of the most recognizable faces on Capitol Hill, battling Republicans on military spending, reproductive rights, or workplace reform measures. She became a master at using the media to publicize an issue, often in staunchly partisan terms. Schroeder dubbed President Ronald Reagan the "Teflon President," a reference to his popularity despite high-profile scandals such as the Iran-Contra Affair. She chaired Senator Gary Hart's presidential campaign in 1987 before it fell apart because of revelations of his marital infidelities. Incensed at Hart's behavior, Schroeder decided for a brief

time to seek the Democratic nomination for President, promising a "rendezvous with reality" that would bring to center the issues of underrepresented Americans.[20] She broke down while announcing her withdrawal, however, spurring many feminists to charge her with undermining women's political advances with her emotional display. Those criticisms proved spurious, since in 1992 Schroeder, as the House's elder stateswoman, welcomed a record number of women elected in the "Year of the Woman." She described the event as an "American perestroika."[21]

Despite being the longest-serving woman in the House at the time of her retirement, Schroeder never chaired a full committee. In line to become chair of the Post Office and Civil Service Committee, Schroeder lost the opportunity at a leadership position when Republicans eliminated the panel once they gained control of the House after a 40-year hiatus. As a Member of the minority party, Schroeder lost much of her institutional power base when the switch in power occurred in the 104th Congress (1995–1997). No longer the chair of any subcommittees, she also failed to earn the distinction of Ranking Democrat on any House committees.[22]

Though she held less political influence than in previous terms, Schroeder remained in the spotlight due to her public disputes with newly elected Speaker of the House, Newt Gingrich of Georgia. On opposite ends of the political spectrum, both politicians looked to the media to promote the interests of their respective parties and clashed on an array of issues. Schroeder blamed Gingrich for impairing the clout of the Congressional Women's Caucus by dismantling its staff, and she was one of the key players in the ethics investigation against the Speaker during the mid-1990s. Apparently frustrated by the growing partisan nature of the House, Schroeder ignored the pleas of her husband and liberal colleagues to seek re-election for a 13th term, commenting, "I always said I wasn't going to be here for life, and life was ticking by."[23] Shortly before leaving office, Schroeder revealed her dissatisfaction with the progression of gender equality in Congress. "I think women still should never kid themselves that they're going to come [to Congress] and be part of the team.

And you ought to come here with a very clear definition of what it is you want to do, and that you will not be deterred. There's a whole group of little harpies out there every day trying to talk you out of it. They really don't want you pushing the envelope, because then it becomes choose-up-sides time for everybody."[24]

After a brief teaching stint at Princeton University's Woodrow Wilson School of Public and International Affairs, Schroeder was appointed president and CEO of the Association of American Publishers in June 1997. She also was selected to lead a multi-year study for the Institute on Civil Society to identify and promote social programs to encourage social cohesion and restore a sense of community for Americans.

FOR FURTHER READING

Biographical Directory of the United States Congress, "Patricia Scott Schroeder," http://bioguide.congress.gov

Lowey, Joan. *Pat Schroeder: Woman of the House* (Albuquerque: University of New Mexico Press, 2003).

Schroeder, Patricia S. *Champion of the Great American Family* (New York: Random House, 1989).

———. *24 Years in the House . . . and the Place Is Still a Mess* (New York: Andrews McMeel, 1998).

MANUSCRIPT COLLECTION

Colorado Historical Society (Denver, CO). *Papers:* ca. 1970s–1996. The collection is unprocessed and its size is unknown. Consult the Curator of Books and Manuscripts regarding use. Contains campaign material.

NOTES

1   Lloyd Grove, "Laying Down Her Quip; For Rep. Pat Schroeder, A Hard-Hitting Decision," 1 December 1995, *Washington Post:* F1.

2   Patricia Schroeder, *Champion of the Great American Family* (New York: Random House, 1989): 43.

3   *Current Biography, 1978* (New York: H.W. Wilson and Company, 1978): 367.

4   Hope Chamberlin, *A Minority of Members: Women in the U.S. Congress* (New York: Praeger, 1973): 355.

5   John Brinkley, "A Brave Woman Leaves Her Mark; Pat Schroeder Exits Congress," 31 December 1996, *Cleveland Plain-Dealer:* 1E.

6   Marcy Kaptur, *Women in Congress: A Twentieth-Century Odyssey* (Washington, D.C.: Congressional Quarterly Press, 1996): 174; see also, *Current Biography, 1978:* 368.

7   "Election Statistics, 1920 to Present," http://clerk.house.gov/members/electionInfo/elections.html; *Politics in America, 1996* (Washington, D.C.: Congressional Quarterly Press, 1995): 221.

8   Patricia Schroeder, *24 Years of House Work . . . and the Place Is Still a Mess* (NY: Andrews McMeel, 1998).

9   Melissa Healy, "Patricia Schroeder: Fighting for 24 years to Expand Women's Role in Government," *Los Angeles Times,* 1 December 1996: M3.

10   *Current Biography, 1978:* 368.

11   Schroeder, *24 Years of House Work.*

12   Marilyn Gardner, "A One-Woman, Pro-Family Lobby," 15 March 1989, *Christian Science Monitor:* 14; Joan A. Lowy, *Pat Schroeder: A Woman of the House* (Albuquerque: University of New Mexico Press, 2003): 61–62.

13   Lowy, *Pat Schroeder:* 189.

14   *Current Biography, 1978:* 368.

15   Ibid.

16   Schroeder, *24 Years of House Work;* Jane Gross, "Critic as Chairman Gets Praise as Both," 8 February 1993, *New York Times:* A12; Ronald V. Dellums and H. Lee Halterman, *Lying Down With the Lions: A Public Life From the Streets of Oakland to the Halls of Power* (Boston: Beacon Press, 2000): 149–150; "Critic as Chairman Gets Praise as Both," 8 February 1993, *New York Times:* A12.

17   *Current Biography, 1978:* 369.

18   Ibid.

19   Steven V. Roberts, "Gambling on the Russian Response to MX Missile," 4 June 1983, *New York Times:* 8; "A Strategic-Arms Glossary," 6 April 1979, *New York Times:* A10.

20   Melissa Healy, 1 December 1996, *Los Angeles Times:* M3; Clara Bingham, *Women on the Hill: Challenging the Culture of Congress* (New York: Times Books, 1997).

21   *Almanac of American Politics, 1994* (Washington, D.C.: National Journal Group Inc., 1993): 222–225.

22   Lowy, *Pat Schroeder:* 172.

23   Ibid., 172–173; 187, 189.

24   Interview, 1 December 1996, *Los Angeles Times:* Opinion Section, 3.

Corinne Claiborne (Lindy) Boggs
1916-

UNITED STATES REPRESENTATIVE ★ DEMOCRAT FROM LOUISIANA
1973–1991

When 14-term Representative and House Majority Leader Hale Boggs's airplane vanished without a trace over the vast Alaska landscape, Democratic leaders in Louisiana immediately turned to his wife, Corrine "Lindy" Boggs. After three decades of serving as her husband's political confidante, strategist, and surrogate campaigner, Lindy Boggs possessed more political acumen than any conceivable challenger. After winning a special election to succeed her husband, Congresswoman Boggs went on to serve 18 years in the House, becoming an advocate for women's equality, economic opportunity for minorities, and the preservation of House heritage.

Marie Corinne Morrison Claiborne was born in Pointe Coupee Roads, Louisiana, on March 13, 1916. Her father Roland Claiborne, a prominent lawyer, died when she was only two years old. She so resembled her father that she was nicknamed "Lindy," short for Rolinde, the French feminine version of Roland. Her mother, Corinne Morrison Claiborne, remarried several years later to George Keller, a cotton plantation owner. Lindy Claiborne's stepfather saw to it that she was educated by a series of private tutors. At age 15, Lindy Claiborne attended Newcomb College of Tulane University in New Orleans. A history and education major, she was an editor of the student newspaper, and in that capacity met her future husband, Hale Boggs, who was then the paper's general editor. She married her college sweetheart on January 22, 1938, a short time before he graduated from law school. After their wedding, Lindy Boggs focused her energy on supporting her husband's political career and raising three children: Barbara, Tommy, and Corrine ("Cokie").

Hale Boggs won election to the U.S. House of Representatives in 1940. Lindy moved with her husband to become a member of his Washington, D.C., staff. Hale Boggs lost his 1942 re-election bid but later returned to the seat representing Jefferson Parish (including New Orleans), where he served continually from 1947 until his death in 1973. Lindy Boggs was his chief political adviser. She set up her husband's district office in New Orleans, orchestrated his re-election campaigns, canvassed voters, arranged for her husband's many social gatherings, and often acted as his political surrogate as demands on his time became greater the further he climbed in the House leadership.

By 1971, Hale Boggs had ascended to the House Majority Leader position and was widely expected to one day become Speaker. As the Majority Leader, he campaigned on behalf of other Democrats. On an October 1972 campaign trip in Alaska, Boggs's plane disappeared; the wreckage was never found. Hale Boggs won the re-election three weeks later, but the House was forced to declare the seat vacant on January 3, 1973. On January 12, Lindy Boggs announced her candidacy for the March 20 special election to fill the vacancy. At the time she noted, "I know the job and am humbled by its proportions."[1] In the February 3 Democratic primary, Boggs easily outpolled her nearest competitor by a nearly 4–1 margin.[2] Boggs received strong support from her late husband's colleagues. "She's the only widow I know who is really qualified—damn qualified—to take over," said the cantankerous Armed Services Chairman F. Edward Hébert of Louisiana.[3] In the special election, Boggs easily defeated Republican challenger Robert E. Lee, a lawyer from the

SHORTLY AFTER HER FIRST
election to the House, when
asked if she ever had doubts
about running for her
husband's seat, Boggs replied,
"The only thing that almost
stopped me was that I didn't
know how I could do it
without a wife."

New Orleans suburb of Gretna, by a count of 42,583 to 10,352 votes (an 80 percent margin).[4] Boggs's victory made her the first woman ever to represent Louisiana in the House (Rose Long and Elaine Edwards had previously served in the Senate). Shortly after the election, when asked if she ever had doubts about running for her husband's seat, Boggs replied, "The only thing that almost stopped me was that I didn't know how I could do it without a wife."[5]

Unlike most freshman Members, Lindy Boggs came to Congress thoroughly prepared for the challenge. Not only did she know Capitol Hill, she enjoyed long-standing personal relationships with virtually every committee chairman, some of whom owed their positions to her late husband. Knowing that most of committee assignments had already been made in January, shortly after her election, she asked Speaker Carl Albert of Oklahoma, which panels still had vacancies. Albert countered, "What committees do you want to be on?" She asked for a spot on the Committee on Banking and Currency, the same panel that Hale Boggs had served on in his freshman term. The House leadership created an extra seat on the committee to accommodate her request.[6] In the 94th Congress (1975–1977), Boggs also received an assignment to the Committee on House Administration. Beginning with the 95th Congress (1977–1979), she gave up both of those standing committee assignments for a seat on the Committee on Appropriations, becoming one of just a handful of women ever to serve on that powerful panel. She held that post until her retirement at the end of the 101st Congress (1989–1991). During her House career, Boggs was instrumental in creating the Select Committee on Children, Youth, and Families on which she served from the 99th through the 101st Congresses (1985–1991). As part of her duties on the select committee, she chaired the Crisis Intervention Task Force, which examined social and economic issues concerning American families.[7]

As a former history teacher, Lindy Boggs used her educational background to great effect as a lead member of other non-standing committees. She chaired two commemorative panels: the Joint Bicentennial Arrangements Committee (94th Congress, 1975–1977) and the Commission on the Bicentenary of the U.S. House (99th through the 100th Congresses, 1985–1989). In July 1987, she presided over a congressional meeting at Independence Hall in Philadelphia in commemoration of the Great Compromise of the Federal Convention.[8] Boggs's persistence eventually led to the creation of the House Historian's Office in the early 1980s. She also was instrumental in securing funding for the repair and upkeep of the historic Congressional Cemetery in Southeast Washington, D.C.

In 1977, Representative Boggs helped cofound the Congressional Woman's Caucus and later served as its secretary. As she perceived it, a Caucus was necessary to concentrate Congresswomen on common issues. "If we met regularly there would be mutual concerns that would be revealed that we may not think of as compelling now," she said.[9] Unlike other colleagues, she did not view the Caucus as a mechanism for battling discriminatory institutional practices; in fact, Boggs later claimed that she had never experienced discrimination as a woman in the House.

Nevertheless, Boggs considered herself a champion of women's issues and always maintained that the most important of these were economic rather than the more divisive and sensational social issues. "Almost all women's issues are economic issues, a stunning idea to those persons who want to hear about 'Great Women's Issues' and expect us to be preoccupied with the ERA or abortion or sexual harassment," she observed. "The major issues of importance that I've worked for are economic ones: equal rights for women in business, banking, and home ownership; the promotion of women in the workplace; better jobs in government contracts; and equal opportunities for higher education, especially in science and medicine. Women vote their pocketbooks . . . it boils down to that."[10] When the Banking and Currency Committee began to mark up the Equal Credit Opportunity Act of 1974, Boggs noted it secured people from discrimination on the basis of "race and age, and their status as veterans." Her experience as a newly widowed woman seeking credit and managing her own finances convinced her that the words "or sex or marital status" should be added to that provision. Without informing the other Members, she inserted those words, walked to the photocopying machine, and made copies for her colleagues. "Knowing the Members composing this committee as well as I do, I'm sure it was just an oversight that we didn't have 'sex' or 'marital status' included," Boggs said after distributing the revisions. "I've taken care of that, and I trust it meets with the committee's approval." It did, passing unanimously 47–0.[11] A Roman Catholic, Boggs parted company with her women colleagues in 1977 to vote for the so-called Hyde Amendment, which barred Medicaid funding for abortions; Boggs was one of six House women out of a total of 18 who voted "Aye."[12] While this position opened her to criticism from reproductive rights groups, Boggs did support family planning legislation.

In 1976, Boggs became the first woman to preside over a national political convention when she chaired the Democratic National Convention that nominated James Earl "Jimmy" Carter for the presidency. In 1984, when Democratic presidential candidate Walter Mondale sought a vice presidential running mate, his party encouraged him to select a woman.[13] Boggs's name was added to a high-profile list of current, former, and future Members of Congress, including Senator Barbara Mikulski of Maryland, future Senator Dianne Feinstein of California, Representative Pat Schroeder of Colorado, and former Representative Martha Griffiths of Michigan. Mondale eventually picked Boggs's House colleague, rising Democratic star Representative Geraldine Ferraro of New York. Observers believed that the choice of Ferraro had as much to do with her pro-abortion position (in contrast with Boggs), as it did her potential for delivering a larger electoral college state.[14] "[The party's] confidence was pleasing, but I knew that my age and my feelings regarding abortion . . . would preclude any serious consideration of me," Boggs later recalled. "I stayed within the mainstream of the consideration and talked to various groups, never about myself but always about the fact that a woman could be President or Vice President. I wanted people to remain interested in the possibility."[15] The possibility

passed in 1984, however, when the Mondale–Ferraro ticket was handily defeated by the Ronald Reagan–George H.W. Bush team in November.

Representative Boggs had relatively few challenges in her eight re-election bids. Only three times, in 1974, 1976, and 1982, was she even opposed in the general election, winning each with margins of 61 to 93 percent of the vote.[16] The toughest challenge to Boggs's House career came in 1984, when her district was reapportioned in response to a federal court order to create the state's first majority-black congressional district. The redrawn district was 56 percent black and, in the primary, she faced Judge Israel M. Augustine, Jr., a longtime Boggs family friend. (In 1969, with the help of Hale Boggs, Augustine became the first African American to receive a state district judgeship in Louisiana history.) The candidates agreed on virtually every issue. Though the contest was friendly, it was animated largely by race, with Augustine framing the election as an opportunity for voters to elect the first black to Congress in state history. But the Boggs family had developed a loyal African-American constituency during its 40-year tenure in the House and, of great significance, New Orleans' first black mayor, Ernest N. "Dutch" Morial, refused to support either candidate; political observers noted that his neutrality benefited Boggs.[17] The incumbent won by a margin of 60 to 39 percent of the vote, polling more than one-third of the African-American vote. "I hope we've all laid to rest that the people in this city are ever divided about what's right . . . or what's good for this city," Boggs declared.[18] She was re-elected two more times in the district, defying conventional political wisdom. "She is the only white Congress Member representing a black voter majority in the United States," one political observer noted. "And she is more popular among blacks than among whites in that district, but she's also extremely popular among whites."[19]

In July 1990, at age 74, Lindy Boggs announced that she would not be a candidate for re-election to the 102nd Congress (1991–1993). Her daughter, Barbara, mayor of Princeton, New Jersey, was dying of cancer, and Boggs hoped to spend more time with her. Barbara succumbed to the disease in November 1990. After leaving Congress in January 1991, Lindy Boggs did not retire from the political spotlight. She maintained homes in Washington, D.C., and New Orleans, and wrote her autobiography. The House named a room off the Rotunda for her, the Lindy Claiborne Boggs Congressional Women's Reading Room, in July 1991.[20] In 1997, President William J. Clinton appointed the 81-year-old as U.S. Ambassador to the Vatican, where she served until 2001. In July 2002, Congress honored Boggs for "her extraordinary service" to Louisiana and the country. The occasion marked the 25th anniversary of the Congressional Women's Caucus.

FOR FURTHER READING

Biographical Directory of the United States Congress, "Corinne Claiborne (Lindy) Boggs," http://bioguide.congress.gov

Boggs, Lindy, with Katherine Hatch. *Washington Through a Purple Veil: Memoirs of a Southern Woman* (New York: Harcourt Brace and Co., 1994).

Ferrell, Thomas H., and Judith Haydel. "Hale and Lindy Boggs: Louisiana's National Democrats," *Louisiana History* 35 (Fall 1994): 389–402.

MANUSCRIPT COLLECTION

Tulane University (New Orleans, LA). *Papers:* 1941–1991, 300 linear feet.

NOTES

1 "Widow to Run for Boggs' Seat," 13 January 1973, *Washington Post*: A8.

2 "Mrs. Boggs Wins Race in Louisiana," 4 February 1974, *New York Times*: 21.

3 Myra McPherson, "Lindy Boggs, Heir to the House," 4 March 1973, *Washington Post*: K1.

4 "Widow of Boggs Wins His Seat in the House by a Large Margin," 21 March 1973, *New York Times*: 24.

5 Marion Bell Wilhelm, "Lindy Boggs Shifts Professionalism From Politician's Wife to Congress," 21 September 1973, *Christian Science Monitor*: 10.

6 Lindy Boggs with Katherine Hatch, *Washington Through a Purple Veil: Memoirs of a Southern Woman* (New York: Harcourt Brace, 1994): 274–275.

7 Hearing Before the House Select Committee on Children, Youth, and Families, *Teenagers in Crisis: Issues and Programs*, 98th Cong., 1st sess., 27 October 1983; Hearing Before the House Select Committee on Children, Youth, and Families, *Families in Crisis: The Private Sector Response*, 98th Cong., 1st sess., 12 July 1983.

8 *Congressional Record*, Senate, 100th Cong., 1st sess. (23 June 1987): 10099.

9 Peggy Simpson, "Women Weighing Caucus," 26 December 1974, *Washington Post*: C22.

10 Boggs, *Washington Through a Purple Veil*: 331.

11 Ibid., 277–278.

12 Martin Tolchin, "House Bars Medicaid Abortions and Funds for Enforcing Quotas," 18 June 1977, *New York Times*: 1.

13 William V. Shannon, "Election of 1984," in Arthur M. Schlesinger, Jr., et al., eds. *History of American Presidential Elections, 1789–1984*, Vol. 10 (Philadelphia: Chelsea House Publishers, 2002): 4157–4158.

14 Marcy Kaptur, "Corinne Claiborne 'Lindy' Boggs," in *Women of Congress: A Twentieth-Century Odyssey* (Washington, D.C.: Congressional Quarterly Press, 1996): 166.

15 Boggs, *Washington Through a Purple Veil*: 342.

16 "Election Statistics, 1920 to Present," http://clerk.house.gov/members/electionInfo/elections.html.

17 John Pope, "Rep. Boggs Faces Old Friend in Tough Race," 29 September 1984, *Washington Post*: A6.

18 "Boggs Takes Primary Race in Louisiana," 30 September 1984, *Washington Post*: A17; Frances Frank Marcus, "Boggs Is Re-Elected to House in Louisiana Voting," 1 October 1984, *New York Times*: B11.

19 Frances Frank Marcus, "Lindy Boggs to Quit House, Ending a Louisiana Dynasty," 21 July 1990, *New York Times*: 7.

20 Donnie Radcliffe, "A Room With a Past for Lindy Boggs," 30 July 1991, *Washington Post*: C2.

Cardiss Collins

1931–

UNITED STATES REPRESENTATIVE ★ DEMOCRAT FROM ILLINOIS
1973–1997

By the end of her congressional career, Cardiss Collins was the longest-serving black woman in the history of Congress. She served 12 consecutive terms, a decade of which she was the only African-American woman in Congress. After succeeding her late husband, George Collins, in the House of Representatives after his death in 1972, Cardiss Collins continued his legacy as a loyal politician in the Chicago Democratic organization under the direction of Mayor Richard Daley. As one of a handful of women to serve in Congress for more than 20 years, Representative Collins evolved into a dedicated legislator who focused on the economic and social needs of her urban district.

Cardiss Hortense Robertson was born on September 24, 1931, in Saint Louis, Missouri, to Finley, a laborer, and Rosia Mae Robertson, a nurse. Upon graduating from the Detroit High School of Commerce in Michigan, she began work in a factory tying mattress springs, while living with her maternal grandmother in Chicago. She later found employment as a stenographer at a carnival equipment company. Her drive for advancement pushed her to attend night classes at Northwestern University, where she earned a business certificate in 1966 and a diploma in professional accounting one year later.[1] After graduation, Cardiss Robertson remained in Chicago, where she worked for the Illinois department of labor as a secretary and later with the Illinois department of revenue. She worked for the latter office as an auditor until her election to Congress.

Robertson gained her first political experience in the party organization of Chicago, when she served as a committeewoman for the ward regular Democratic organization. In 1958 she married George Washington Collins and

participated in his various campaigns for alderman, committeeman, and U.S. Representative, while raising their son Kevin.[2] On November 3, 1970, George Collins won a special election to fill a U.S. House seat representing Chicago, which became vacant after the death of Illinois Representative Daniel J. Ronan. In his one term in Congress, he served on the House Government Operations and Public Works committees. As a World War II veteran, the Democratic Congressman worked to improve the conditions of African Americans serving in the military. Known as a diligent but quiet Member who rarely spoke on the House Floor, Collins had close political ties to Richard Daley.[3]

In December 1972, shortly after George Collins won election to his second term in Congress, he died in an airplane crash near Chicago's Midway Airport. His widow later recalled, "I never gave politics a thought for myself. When people started proposing my candidacy right after the crash, I was in too much of a daze to think seriously about running."[4] Collins overcame her initial reluctance, however, and announced her candidacy for the special election to fill the vacant congressional seat that encompassed the predominantly African-American west side of Chicago.[5] Created in the apportionment of 1947, the inner-city district was one of five congressional seats located in Chicago, each of which was a product of the local political machine.[6] With the solid backing of Mayor Daley's Cook County Democratic organization, Collins handily defeated her opponents Otis Collins, a former state representative, and Milton Gardner, a Columbia University law student, in the Democratic primary, winning 84 percent of the vote.[7] On June 5, 1973, she became the first African-American woman to represent the state of Illinois in Congress by defeating Republican contender Lar Daly and Angel Moreno, an Independent, in convincing fashion, with 92 percent of the vote.[8]

Although anxious to continue the work begun by her husband in Congress, Collins admittedly had much to learn about her new job. Her lack of political experience, made worse by entering office midterm, led to unfamiliarity with congressional procedures. During her early tenure, Collins often relied upon her colleagues in the House to assist her in learning more about the basic rules of Congress. Collins also had to overcome her reserved demeanor. A few years after taking office, she noted that "once people learned I had something to say, I gained confidence."[9]

During her first term in Congress, Collins served on the Committee on Government Operations (later Government Reform and Oversight). As a member of the panel throughout her tenure in Congress, Collins chaired two Government Operations subcommittees: Manpower and Housing and Government Activities and Transportation. As chair of the latter subcommittee from 1983 to 1991, Collins worked to improve air travel safety and fought for stricter controls on the transportation of toxic materials. She eventually rose to the position of Ranking Democrat of the full committee during the 104th Congress (1995–1997). Collins also served on the Committee on International Relations (later Foreign Affairs) from 1975 to 1980, the District of Columbia Committee during the 95th Congress (1977–1979), and the influential Committee on Energy and Commerce (later Commerce) from the 97th through the 104th Congresses (1981–1997). Collins also earned distinction as the first African American and woman selected as a Democratic Whip At-Large.

Four years after taking office in 1973, Collins commented that her primary objective as a Congresswoman was to "provide better living and working conditions for people [on Chicago's west side] and other low and moderate income people throughout the country." Known for her commitment to the issues directly affecting her constituents, Collins spent eight days each month in her district to ensure she stayed abreast of the concerns of her voters.[10] The close attention she paid to her district reaped benefits

at the polls. For more than two decades, Collins won by comfortable margins in the strongly Democratic district, typically defeating her Republican opponents by more than 80 percent.[11] Collins did, however, experience some difficult primary races during the mid-1980s—a consequence of the declining power of the Cook County Democratic organization that accelerated with the death of Daley in 1976.[12] She proved resilient without the influential machine that helped launch her congressional career; devoid of such strict local party control, Collins had the ability to develop as a politician and pursue her own legislative interests.

Collins increased both her presence and notoriety in the House when she assumed the role of chairwoman of the Congressional Black Caucus (CBC) during the 96th Congress (1979–1981). As the second woman to hold the leadership position in the CBC and as the fourth black woman ever to serve in the U.S. House of Representatives, Collins found herself in the spotlight. The high visibility encouraged her to become more outspoken. At one fundraiser, for instance, Collins voiced the growing disillusionment of the CBC when she declared, "We will no longer wait for political power to be shared with us, we will take it."[13] Members of the CBC praised Collins, citing her ability to lead with fairness and to create an atmosphere that encouraged unity through debates rather than arguments.[14] As leader of the CBC, Collins voiced disapproval with President James Earl "Jimmy" Carter's record on civil rights. She criticized the President for not gathering enough congressional support to pass legislation making the birthday of Martin Luther King, Jr., a federal holiday. Collins also disparaged the House for its failure to pass the bill, alleging that "racism had a part in it."[15]

Throughout her 24 years in Congress, Collins dedicated herself to the advancement of African Americans and other minorities. According to Collins, some federal agencies, such as the National Endowment for the Humanities, the Federal Trade Commission, and the U.S. Justice Department, were not upholding the provisions of the Civil Rights Act requiring agencies that received federal funding to provide

COLLINS COMMENTED THAT HER

PRIMARY OBJECTIVE AS A

CONGRESSWOMAN WAS TO

"PROVIDE BETTER LIVING AND

WORKING CONDITIONS FOR PEOPLE

[ON CHICAGO'S WEST SIDE] AND

OTHER LOW AND MODERATE

INCOME PEOPLE THROUGHOUT

THE COUNTRY."

information on the scheduling of their affirmative action programs. As the result of her 1985 findings as the chair of the House's Subcommittee on Government Activities and Transportation, she called for Congress to curb funding to the specific agencies, arguing, "Laws that have been debated and passed by the courts cannot arbitrarily be negated by individuals." In the 1980s, she continued her defense of affirmative action by drawing attention to the hiring practices of U.S. airlines, which rarely placed African Americans in professional positions.[16] Congresswoman Collins's push for equality in the aviation industry helped pave the way for an amendment to the Airport and Airway Safety, Capacity, and Expansion Act of 1987, requiring that 10 percent of all concession stands in airports be run by minority- and women-owned businesses.

Collins also worked to prevent federal tax write-offs for advertising firms that discriminated against minority-owned media companies. Hoping to "provide black and other minority station owners with a mechanism for redress," Collins argued that financial penalties for offending agencies would help combat discrimination and level the playing field for all media organizations. She crusaded against gender and racial inequality in broadcast licensing as well. On several occasions, Collins introduced legislation to preserve Federal Communications Commission policies designed to increase the number of women and minorities owning media companies.[17]

In an effort to promote equal opportunities for women in sports at colleges and universities, Collins introduced the Equality in Athletic Disclosure Act on February 17, 1993. The amendment to the Higher Education Act of 1965 directed colleges and universities to publicize the rate of program participation by gender. In recognition of her commitment to gender equity in athletics, Collins was inducted into the Women's Sports Hall of Fame in 1994.[18] Collins also cosponsored the Universal Health Care Act and the Health Security Act in 1993 and urged the National Institutes of Health to focus on the health issues that concern minorities, since "little use has been made of studies on minority prone diseases despite the significant

disproportionate array of health conditions."[19] A longtime advocate of increasing breast cancer awareness, Collins drafted legislation to help elderly and disabled women receive Medicare coverage for mammograms and introduced a law designating October as National Breast Cancer Awareness Month.

Collins declined to run for re-election to the 105th Congress (1997–1999). Vowing to remain active in Democratic politics, she nonetheless decided that the time had come to end her career in elective office. Collins cited age as a principal motivation for leaving office, telling reporters, "I'm going to be 65 next year, and that's the time many people retire."[20] After the completion of her last term, she returned to Chicago, Illinois, and, later, moved to Alexandria, Virginia.

FOR FURTHER READING

Biographical Directory of the United States Congress, "Cardiss Collins," http://bioguide.congress.gov

NOTES

1 "Cardiss Collins," in *Notable Black American Women*, edited by Jessie Carney Smith, (Detroit, MI: Gale Research, 2003): 204.

2 "Cardiss Collins," *Notable Black American Women*: 204.

3 "Rep. George Collins (D-Ill.) Killed in Chicago Jet Crash," 10 December 1972, *Washington Post*: B4.

4 "Cardiss Collins," *Notable Black Women*: 205.

5 Joel Weisman, "Congressman's Widow Elected in His Place," 6 June 1973, *Washington Post*: A7.

6 Leo M. Snowiss, "Congressional Recruitment and Representation," *American Political Science Review* 60 (1966): 628–629.

7 "House Race Won By Widow," 18 April 1973, *Washington Post*: A22.

8 "Widow Wins a Bid for Husband Seat," 18 April 1973, *New York Times*: 42; Andrew H. Malcolm, "Illinois Elects Its First Black Woman to Congress, on 92% of Vote," 7 June 1973, *New York Times*: 11; "Election Statistics, 1920 to Present," http://clerk.house.gov/members/electionInfo/elections.

9 Jacqueline Trescott, "The Coming Out of Cardiss Collins," 21 September 1979, *Washington Post*: C1.

10 "Cardiss Collins," *Notable Black American Women*: 205, 208.

11 "Election Statistics, 1920 to Present," http://clerk.house.gov/members/electionInfo/elections.

12 Roger Biles, *Richard J. Daley: Politics, Race and the Governing of Chicago* (DeKalb, IL: Northern Illinois University Press, 1995): 221–222, 232; *Politics in America, 1994* (Washington, D.C: Congressional Quarterly Press, 193): 474–475.

13 Jacqueline Trescott and Elisabeth Bumiller, "The Raucous Caucus," 24 September 1979, *Washington Post*: B1.

14 Trescott, "The Coming Out of Cardiss Collins."

15 *Politics in America, 1990* (Washington, D.C.: Congressional Quarterly Inc., 1989): 345.

16 "Cardiss Collins," *Contemporary Black Biography*, Vol. 10 (Farmington Hills, MI: Gale Group, 2002). Reproduced in the Biography Resource Center, http://www.galenet.com/servlet/biorc; see also *Congressional Record,* House, 99th Cong., 1st sess. (26 February 1985): E633.

17 *Congressional Record*, House, 102nd Cong., 1st sess. (3 January 1991): E32.

18 Karen Foerstel, *Biographical Dictionary of Congressional Women* (Westport, CT: Greenwood Press, 1999): 63; "Colleges Told to Publish Sports Costs," 3 December 1995, *New York Times*: 37.

19 "Cardiss Collins," *Contemporary Black Biography*.

20 "A Chicago Democrat is Quitting Congress," 9 November 1995, *New York Times*: B14.

Millicent Fenwick

1910–1992

UNITED STATES REPRESENTATIVE ★ REPUBLICAN FROM NEW JERSEY
1975–1983

Millicent Fenwick, an outspoken patrician who served four terms in the U.S. House, earned the epithet "Conscience of Congress" with her fiscal conservatism, human right's advocacy, and dedication to campaign finance reform. Fenwick's blueblood mannerisms, which were inspiration for a popular comic strip character, belied her lifelong commitment to liberal activism on behalf of consumers, racial minorities, and women's rights. Representative Fenwick's humor and independence—she voted against her House GOP colleagues 48 percent of the time—made her one of the most colorful Members of Congress during the 1970s.[1]

Millicent Vernon Hammond was born in New York City, on February 25, 1910. Her father, Ogden Haggerty Hammond, was a wealthy financier and New Jersey state legislator; her mother, Mary Picton Stevens Hammond, died aboard the U.S.S. *Lusitania* in 1915 after a German U-boat torpedoed the ship.[2] Millicent Hammond attended the elite Foxcroft School in Middleburg, Virginia, from 1923 until 1925. She then accompanied her father to Madrid when President Calvin Coolidge appointed him U.S. Ambassador to Spain. In 1929, she attended Columbia University and later studied with the philosopher Bertrand Russell at the New School for Social Research. In 1934, Hammond married businessman Hugh Fenwick, and they raised two children, Mary and Hugh. The Fenwicks separated four years later, however; they eventually divorced in 1945. Millicent Fenwick refused financial assistance from her family and, instead, found a job to support her children. She modeled briefly for *Harper's Bazaar* and then took a job as associate editor on the staff of Condé Nast's *Vogue* magazine. From 1938 to 1952, Fenwick worked on several Nast publications.[3] In 1948, she wrote

Vogue's Book of Etiquette, a 600-page "treatise in proper behavior." It sold more than a million copies. Fenwick left *Vogue* in 1952 and inherited a fortune when her father passed away a few years later.

Fenwick's earliest encounter with political issues came during the 1930s with the rise of fascism in Europe. "Hitler started me in politics; when I became aware of what he was doing to people, I fired up," she recalled.[4] She joined the National Conference of Christians and Jews in an attempt to counter anti-Semitic propaganda in the United States, speaking out in public for the first time in her life. Fenwick served on the Bernardsville, New Jersey, board of education from 1938 to 1947. She supported Wendell Willkie for President in 1940 and joined the National Association for the Advancement of Colored People in 1946. She worked on the 1954 campaign of Republican Senate candidate Clifford Case. She also chaired the Somerset County Legal Aid Society and the Bernardsville Recreation Commission. From 1958 to 1964, she was a member of the Bernardsville borough council and served on the New Jersey committee to the U.S. Commission on Civil Rights from 1958 to 1972. Her first campaign for state office was in 1970 when she won a seat in the New Jersey assembly at the age of 59. Fenwick served several years in the assembly before New Jersey Governor William Cahill appointed her the state's first director of consumer affairs. She sought to restrict auto dealers' misleading advertising and to require funeral homes to offer advance itemization of bills.

In 1974, when her friend Peter Frelinghuysen decided to retire from the affluent congressional district in north central New Jersey which he had held for 22 years, Fenwick entered the race for his open seat. In the June GOP primary

ELEGANT AND PATRICIAN,
SPEAKING IN A RASPY VOICE,
FENWICK NEVERTHELESS
CONNECTED WITH AVERAGE
PEOPLE. A LONGTIME AIDE
DESCRIBED HER AS "THE KATHARINE
HEPBURN OF POLITICS. WITH HER
DIGNITY AND ELEGANCE, SHE COULD
GET AWAY WITH SAYING THINGS
OTHERS COULDN'T."

for the most solidly Republican district in New Jersey, Fenwick narrowly defeated another friend and close ideological counterpart, Assemblyman Thomas Kean, the future governor of New Jersey, polling a margin of 76 votes out of nearly 25,000 cast.[5] In the general election, she campaigned on a liberal platform: civil rights, consumer rights, campaign finance, and public housing assistance.[6] Fenwick handily defeated her Democratic opponent, Frederick Bohen, by a 53 percent to 43 percent margin. At the age of 64, Fenwick became one of a handful of women elected to Congress past their 60th birthdays; the press dubbed her victory a "geriatric triumph."[7] Subsequently, Fenwick won increasingly large majorities, making her one of New Jersey's most popular officials.[8]

Fenwick's wry humor and idiosyncrasies quickly made her one of the most recognizable faces in American politics. Once, during a debate in the New Jersey assembly over the Equal Rights Amendment (ERA), a colleague told her: "I just don't like this amendment. I've always thought of women as kissable, cuddly and smelling good." Fenwick retorted, "That's the way I feel about men, too. I only hope for your sake that you haven't been disappointed as often as I have."[9] Elegant and patrician, speaking in a raspy voice, she nevertheless connected with average people. One of her trademark habits was pipe smoking, which she adopted when her doctor warned her to curb her cigarette intake. Her refined mannerisms, coupled with her outspokenness and wit, made her both appealing and the object of public curiosity. Garry Trudeau, the creator of the socially satirical *Doonesbury* cartoon, drew inspiration from Fenwick for one of the strip's most popular characters, Lacey Davenport. A longtime aide described Fenwick as "the Katharine Hepburn of politics. With her dignity and elegance, she could get away with saying things others couldn't."[10] In Congress, she counted among her close friends the equally colorful Bella Abzug of New York; both were drawn to their shared commitment to women's rights.[11] Subsequently, supporters and detractors alike nicknamed Fenwick the "Bella Abzug of Somerset County."

During four terms in the House, Fenwick served on several committees. She was first assigned to the Committee on Banking, Currency, and Housing and the Committee on Small Business. She also served on the Committee on the District of Columbia, the Committee on Education and Labor, and the Select Committee on Aging. Though she was fluent in three languages and more cosmopolitan than the vast majority of her colleagues, it took her years to convince House leaders to let her onto the Committee on Foreign Affairs. But she persisted in her efforts, and they relented, giving her a seat in 1979. Though committee work engaged her, Fenwick also was renowned for the amount of time she spent on the House Floor listening to debate, always from her perch in the third row back on the Republican side of the center aisle. She once explained her rationale to a woman colleague: "Get to know [your colleagues], not only in committee, but on the floor when debates are going on. It is then you can learn to judge those whose opinions you can trust, and whose opinions you must be skeptical of. Be able to evaluate them."[12]

Fiscal conservatism, for Fenwick an extension of civic responsibility and her personal frugality, shaped a large portion of her House agenda. She was an early and consistent advocate for ending the so-called "marriage-tax penalty," a higher income tax that occurred when two wage earners married and filed a joint return instead of separate returns. "Under the present law, if the wife decides to work to help support the family, her first dollar of income will be taxed at the same rate as the last dollar earned by her husband. In effect, her income will be taxed at a much higher rate," Fenwick explained.[13] During her four terms in the House, Fenwick returned more than $450,000 in unspent office allowances to the U.S. Treasury. Likewise, she returned $35,000 in congressional pay raises that made her feel uncomfortable.[14]

Although she was a fiscal conservative, on other matters Fenwick differed from many of her Republican colleagues. She supported women's issues such as the ERA, federal funding for abortions, and the food stamp program. At the 1976 Republican National Convention in Kansas City, Fenwick successfully fought to keep the ERA plank in the party's platform.[15] In 1980, when the GOP dropped its 40-year support for ERA, a reporter asked Fenwick to describe her feelings. "Absurd is the only word," she scoffed.[16] Fenwick, a founding member of the Congressional Women's Caucus, eventually withdrew from the group because of its increasing partisanship. "I don't like to act only on behalf of women," she explained. "Wherever injustice occurs, we all need to be concerned."[17]

A champion of human rights, Fenwick worked vigorously to create the 1975 Helsinki Agreement on Human Rights, which investigated human rights abuses behind the Iron Curtain in Eastern Europe and the Soviet Union. In particular, she wrote the bill that established the U.S. Commission on Security and Cooperation in Europe, which monitored implementation of the Helsinki Accords. She later described that work as her proudest achievement in Congress. She also questioned American foreign aid policy to authoritarian regimes during the Cold War and was particularly disturbed by Iraqi ties to Middle East terrorist groups, Zambia's military arms trade with the Soviets, and repressive practices and human rights violations in Mozambique.[18]

Fenwick extended her promise to pursue campaign finance reform into a sustained appeal to House colleagues to dedicate themselves to rehabilitating the image of Washington politics, damaged in the mid-1970s by the Watergate Crisis and congressional scandals. In 1976, she demanded the overhaul of the campaign finance system, having become alarmed at the influence of powerful donors on voting patterns. "When every candidate is asked—repeatedly—which organizations he or she had accepted money from, and how much, I think we will begin to see some changes," Fenwick wrote. "Candidates will see that voters care. . . . We have a sturdy governmental system—Thomas Jefferson called it 'the strongest government on earth.' But no system can withstand this kind of abuse forever."[19] She also spoke out against the widespread practice of Members using their franking privileges to send out campaign mailings.[20] Fenwick served on the Ethics Committee during the investigation of Tongsun Park's attempts to influence Members of Congress, the so-called "Koreagate" affair. For her independence and determination to speak her mind, the CBS

news anchor Walter Cronkite soon took to calling Fenwick the "Conscience of Congress."[21] "I suppose the hope of furthering justice is really my main thing," Fenwick said during an introspective moment. "I think about my town, my district, my state, my country, my planet, and then I think we're all in this together and somehow we've got to try to work out a just and a peaceful society."[22]

In 1982, the 72-year-old Fenwick chose to forgo certain re-election to her House seat to seek a U.S. Senate seat vacated when longtime Senator Harrison Williams of New Jersey resigned his office in the wake of his conviction on bribery charges related to the Federal Bureau of Investigation's Abscam sting.[23] When she was not appointed to the post to fill out the remainder of Williams's term, Fenwick chose to run for the full term in the next Congress. She faced millionaire businessman Frank Lautenberg, who portrayed Fenwick as an "eccentric," out of touch with New Jersey voters. Fenwick remained unruffled and true to her style, scolding her opponent: "How can you be so awfully naughty?"[24] Early on, Fenwick was favored to win, but Lautenberg outspent her by a wide margin.[25] Refusing to accept money from any political action committees or corporate donors because it might stymie her independence, Fenwick noted, "Nobody pressures me! And nobody has the right to . . . say, 'We supported you, didn't we? You'd better vote for this.'"[26] But high unemployment and dissatisfaction with the Ronald W. Reagan administration's economic policies worked against the GOP candidate; Lautenberg won 51 to 48 percent.[27] The day after her defeat, the *Washington Post* took note of Fenwick's protest about the cost of the campaign. She spent nearly $3 million to Lautenberg's $5.5 million. "She fought the good fight," the *Post* editors wrote, "and she went out the same way she came in: with class."[28]

After Fenwick left office in January 1983, President Reagan appointed her to the United Nations Agencies for Food and Agriculture, where she served as United States Representative with rank of ambassador from 1983 to 1985. Millicent Fenwick retired to Bernardsville, where she lived until her death on September 16, 1992.

FOR FURTHER READING

Biographical Directory of the United States Congress, "Millicent Hammond Fenwick," http://bioguide.congress.gov

Fenwick, Millicent. *Speaking Up* (New York: Harper and Row, 1982).

Schapiro, Amy. *Millicent Fenwick: Her Way* (New Brunswick, NJ: Rutgers University Press, 2003).

MANUSCRIPT COLLECTIONS

Rutgers University (New Brunswick, NJ), Alexander Library Department of Special Collections and Archives. *Papers:* 1975–1982, approximately 310 cubic feet. Includes correspondence, administrative files, legislative research files, sponsored and cosponsored bills, project files, political and campaign files, financial documents, photographs, press releases, constituent newsletters, and other papers. Restricted.

University of Oklahoma (Norman, OK), Carl Albert Center Congressional Archives, http://www.ou.edu/special/albertctr/archives/fenwick.htm. *Papers:* 1975–1978, 28 cubic feet. Personal and congressional papers and correspondence; letters of invitation, congratulations, and regret; military academy files; and other documents.

NOTES

1 *Current Biography, 1977* (New York: H.W. Wilson and Company, 1977): 153–156; see also Amy Shapiro's biography, *Millicent Fenwick: Her Way* (New Brunswick, NJ: Rutgers University Press, 2003). For a typical press feature story from the period, see Louise Sweeney, "Congress's Millicent Fenwick: A Blueblood with a Social Conscience," 25 June 1975, *Christian Science Monitor*: 17.
2 Bruce Lambert, "Millicent Fenwick, 82, Dies; Gave Character to Congress," 17 September 1992, *New York Times*: D25.
3 Judy Bachrach, "Millicent Fenwick," 23 February 1975, *Washington Post*: 137.
4 S.J. Horner, "Millicent Fenwick Remembers," 9 December 1979, *New York Times*: NJ45.
5 Ronald Sullivan, "Mrs. Fenwick Edges Out Kean in Jersey Primary," 5 June 1974, *New York Times*: 89.
6 Schapiro, *Millicent Fenwick*: 141, 143.
7 *Current Biography, 1977*: 155.
8 "Election Statistics, 1920 to Present," http://clerk.house.gov/members/

electionInfo/elections.html; Edward C. Burks, "Millicent Fenwick: Personal Diplomacy," 9 July 1978, *New York Times*: NJ1.
9 Lambert, "Millicent Fenwick, 82, Dies; Gave Character to Congress."
10 Ibid.
11 Martin Tolchin, "An Odd Couple on Capitol Hill: Daughter of the Bronx and Well-Bred Jersey Lady," 5 March 1976, *New York Times*: 65. Abzug said of Fenwick: "I like people who have emotions and feelings. I always like style and she has style. We both have a sense of ourselves. We're both women of the world. I have crossed many boundaries, and I'm sure she has, too."
12 Schapiro, *Millicent Fenwick*: 153.
13 Edward C. Burks, "Rep. Fenwick: Basics Her Forte," 13 May 1979, *New York Times*: NJ4; see also, Edward C. Burks, "Mrs. Fenwick Sees Marriage Tax's End," 1 March 1981, *New York Times*: NJ1.
14 Amy Schapiro, *Millicent Fenwick*: 193.
15 Spencer Rich, "GOP Panel Adopts A Pro-ERA Plank," 13 August 1976, *Washington Post*: A1.
16 Leslie Bennetts, "Republicans and Women's Issues: For Some, A Painful Conflict," 2 September 1980, *New York Times*: B12.
17 Deborah Churchman, "Congresswomen's Caucus Wields Clout Beyond Its Size," 11 June 1981, *Christian Science Monitor*: 17.
18 Edward C. Burks, "'Fenwick Doctrine' Altering Foreign Aid," 13 April 1980, *New York Times*: NJ4.
19 Millicent Fenwick, "Congressional Reform: A View From the Inside," 24 August 1976, *Washington Post*: A17.
20 Millicent Fenwick, "Congress Must Give Up Its 'Royalty Complex,'" 5 October 1978, *Christian Science Monitor*: 23.
21 Schapiro, *Millicent Fenwick*: 161.
22 Shirley Washington, *Outstanding Women Members of Congress* (Washington, D.C.: U.S. Capitol Historical Society, 1995): 30.
23 Abscam was a U.S. scandal that followed a 1978 investigation by the Federal Bureau of Investigation (FBI). FBI agents, posing as associates of a fictitious wealthy Arab sheik, tried to pay U.S. officials in exchange for political favors. The media derived the name Abscam from the name of the fake company set up by the FBI to conduct its investigation, "Abdul Enterprises, Inc." Five Representatives and Senator Williams were indicted and convicted in 1981 for bribery and conspiracy.
24 Margot Hornblower, "Fighting Fenwick 'Legend,' Lautenberg Takes to the Airwaves," 27 October 1982, *Washington Post*: A14.
25 Michael Norman, "Lautenberg Pictures Mrs. Fenwick as 'Eccentric' Who Can't Do Job," 21 October 1982, *New York Times*: B9.
26 Ward Morehouse III, "Millicent and the Millionaire: Big Bucks, Tough Talk Mean Lively Race," 20 September 1982, *Christian Science Monitor*: 5.
27 Joseph Sullivan, "Jersey Democrat, in First Contest, Upsets Rep. Fenwick for the Senate," 3 November 1982, *New York Times*: A1; "Election Statistics, 1920 to Present," http://clerk.house.gov/members/electionInfo/index.html.
28 "Millicent Fenwick's Defeat," 4 November 1982, *Washington Post*: A18; see Fenwick's own editorial "In Congress: Buy Your Seat Or Sell Your Vote," 9 November 1982, *Washington Post*: A1.

Martha Elizabeth Keys

1930–

UNITED STATES REPRESENTATIVE ★ DEMOCRAT FROM KANSAS

1975–1979

In many respects, Kansas Representative Martha Keys's two-term House career provides a window on a transitional moment in the story of women in Congress. As a freshman in 1975, Keys benefited from significant institutional changes that helped land her a plum assignment on one of the House's most powerful committees. Simultaneously, however, her divorce from her husband of 25 years (and marriage to a House colleague) tested the limits of public aversion to turmoil in the personal lives of their elected officials and highlighted long-standing social double standards to which women were held.

On August 10, 1930, Martha Elizabeth Ludwig was born to S.T. and Clara Krey Ludwig in Hutchinson, Kansas. Martha Ludwig graduated from Paseo High School in Kansas City, Missouri, in 1945. She attended Olivet College in Kankakee, Illinois, from 1946 to 1948. Ludwig received her A.B. in music from the University of Missouri in Kansas City, Missouri, in 1951. In 1949, Martha Ludwig married Sam Keys, a university professor and later the dean of education at Kansas State University, and they raised four children: Carol, Bryan, Dana, and Scott. In 1973, Keys served as co-chair of the Manhattan–Riley (Kansas) County United Way campaign and also was appointed to a special committee that examined the city's recreational needs. Keys's brother-in-law, Gary Hart, a campaign aide to presidential candidate George McGovern, persuaded her to join the McGovern campaign in 1972. Then a 42-year-old housewife with limited political experience—as a volunteer coordinator in the 1964 and 1968 presidential campaigns—Martha Keys eventually ran the McGovern campaign in Kansas. Though McGovern lost the state by a wide margin, Keys's tact and organizational skills left a positive impression with many Democrats.[1]

In 1974, when Gary Hart launched his successful campaign for Colorado senator, Keys announced her intention to seek a seat in the U.S. House of Representatives vacated by Representative William Roy. The two-term Democratic incumbent left the House to challenge incumbent Robert Dole for a U.S. Senate seat. The district was traditionally Republican-leaning, and the GOP considered the seat to be highly competitive. Only once since the Civil War had the district's voters sent a Democrat to Congress for more than one term, and that was Congressman Roy.[2] On a shoestring budget, Keys defeated four men in the Democratic primary. "You have to overcome the woman thing," she told a reporter during the campaign. "I think being a woman is basically beneficial in this campaign. It helps you get the attention you need. It's up to you to keep it."[3] In the general election Keys faced a 26-year-old GOP state legislator, John C. Peterson. The candidates conducted a series of debates on inflation, campaign reform, and government spending. Keys, while supporting social programs, also stressed federal fiscal responsibility. In particular, she tried to connect with ordinary housewives. Both candidates stuck to the issues and avoided personal attacks, and Keys spent only $75,000 total for her operations. One reporter for a national newspaper described the campaign as "a model of what American campaigning could be—but rarely is."[4] Voters chose Keys by a 55 to 44 percent majority.[5]

Keys entered Congress at a time when a series of post-Watergate institutional reforms re-ordered many of the traditions and power structures within the House. When Democrats gathered just before the start of the 94th Congress (1975–1977), they agreed to name two freshmen to the Ways and Means and the Appropriations committees.

Longtime Ways and Means Chairman Wilbur Mills of Arkansas stepped down and the committee lost its role of assigning Democrats to committees to the Steering and Policy Committee. Keys directly benefited from these changes, becoming only the second woman, and one of only a handful of freshman Members in House history, who received an assignment on Ways and Means.[6] Keys served on two of its subcommittees: Health and Unemployment Compensation. Ways and Means was her only assignment, and she retained it for the duration of her House career.

During her first term, Keys was a strong supporter of the Title IX Amendment to create equal opportunities for female athletes at both the high school and college level. Title IX prohibited institutions that received federal funding from practicing gender discrimination in educational programs or activities. Although Congress had approved the basis for Title IX legislation in 1972 and President Richard M. Nixon signed it into law in 1973, lawmakers needed several more years to hammer out the details. After a trial period in which suggested modifications were incorporated, President Gerald R. Ford submitted revised regulations to Congress in May 1975. When she arrived in Washington in 1975, Keys recalled, there was "the heavy lobbying going on" and "it was very dramatic." She remembered being lobbied by major college sports coaches for a variety of men's teams who opposed the bill on the basis that it would drain money from men's programs.[7] Undeterred, Keys and other women Members worked across party lines to pass the new provisions. In high schools alone, the number of women in sports programs increased dramatically over the next quarter century—from fewer than 300,000 in 1971 to more than 2.4 million in 1996.[8]

Keys used her Ways and Means seat to help broaden women's economic base for equality. Along with Representative Don Fraser of Minnesota, Keys sponsored a measure that provided Social Security coverage for women who had spent their lives working in the home rather than in paying jobs.[9] The bill stipulated that in determining Social Security credits, all earnings should be split between husband and wife and credited to separate old-age pension accounts, specifically seeking special protections for women following a divorce. Keys observed that "the structure of the [Social Security] system was based upon a different time and a different era. It is based upon the idea that most workers are male and most workers support women and children. In today's life that is no longer true . . . these needs should be recognized in a restructuring of our system."[10]

During her first term, Keys's personal life made national headlines when she divorced her husband Sam and married Democratic Congressman Andrew Jacobs, Jr., of Indiana. Keys and Jacobs had met on the Ways and Means Committee. After Keys's divorce became official in July 1975, the couple announced their engagement and were married a year later. Their union marked the first time in history that two Members of Congress married while serving together.[11]

Some observers expected the 1976 election to be a referendum on Keys's divorce and Middle America's attitude toward the personal problems of elected officials. One prominent Kansas Republican openly worried, "I don't think Kansas wants a Representative who lives in Washington and is married to an Indianan."[12] Keys maintained there was a double standard at work: No one expressed similar concerns about her husband's ability to carry out his duties. "Our voting records are very different," she pointed out. "We are both totally committed in our own way to the public interest."[13] Keys spoke frankly with voters: "Marriage isn't a good reason to oppose me politically."[14] The couple maintained separate residences in their respective districts and shared a Washington, D.C., home. Keys's GOP opponent, Ross Freeman, an attorney and insurance company executive, insisted that he would not make a campaign issue of the "tragedy of divorce." Freeman prominently displayed pictures of his family on campaign literature, however, and made frequent indirect references to Keys's marital problems by advertising his "deep family ties to Kansas." He also campaigned on a platform that called for curbing social programs, balancing the federal budget, and boosting defense spending.[15] The incumbent carried the district, but not by much—fewer than

6,000 votes out of 150,000 cast, for a 52 to 48 percent edge.[16]

In the 1978 election Keys was initially favored in her general election race against conservative Republican businessman and World War II veteran Jim Jeffries. But Jeffries ran an aggressive campaign that focused on Keys's liberal voting record and suggested that she was no longer in tune with the district's voters. He also raised and spent more than his Democratic opponent, producing radio ads in which a New York resident offered a "thank you" to Keys for voting with other Democrats to give millions of dollars in loan guarantees to New York City.[17] Keys lost 52 to 48 percent, as House Democrats lost 15 seats in the midterms. Shortly thereafter, she and Jacobs sought a divorce.[18]

After Keys left Congress in January 1979, President Jimmy Carter appointed her as special adviser to the Secretary of Education and Welfare from 1979 to 1980. She served from June 1980 to January 1981 as assistant secretary of education. During the balance of the 1980s and 1990s, Keys remained involved with education issues as a consultant with several Washington-based firms.[19] In 1990, she and several other former Members of Congress created the Council for the National Interest, a nonprofit that sought to highlight issues important to Palestinians. Martha Keys remained invested in the social development of young women. More than two decades after helping to extend Title IX legislation, she observed, "It's exciting to see the opportunities girls and women have now. I see my own granddaughter involved in all kinds of sports."[20]

FOR FURTHER READING

Biographical Directory of the United States Congress, "Martha Elizabeth Keys," http://bioguide.congress.gov

MANUSCRIPT COLLECTION

Kansas State University (Manhattan, KS). *Papers:* ca. 1975–1979, 90 linear feet. Keys's papers are divided into two primary series: 1) legislative papers and 2) casework papers. The casework papers are sealed until 2029.

NOTES

1 Lou Cannon, "Campaign '74: A Model Race in Kansas," 27 October 1974, *Washington Post*: C4.

2 June Kronholz, "For Congresswoman, Issue in Kansas Race Is a 'Messy' Divorce," 7 October 1976, *Wall Street Journal*: 1.

3 Cannon, "Campaign '74."

4 Ibid.

5 "Election Statistics, 1920 to Present," http://clerk.house.gov/members/electionInfo/elections.html.

6 Mary Russell, "Rep. Mills Gives Up Hill Post," 11 December 1974, *Washington Post*: A1; Richard D. Lyons, "Ways and Means in Liberal Shift," 12 December 1974, *New York Times*: 38; Eileen Shanahan, "Ways and Means Panel Enters a New and Open Era," 11 February 1975, *New York Times*: 1.

7 Pete Goering, "Keys to the Future," *Topeka Capital-Journal*, March 17, 2002.

8 U.S. Department of Education, "Title IX: A Sea Change in Gender Equity in Education," available at http://www.ed.gov/pubs/TitleIX/part3.html (accessed 4 December 2003); see also, Goering, "Keys to the Future."

9 Spencer Rich, "Social Security Sex 'Reform' Seen Costly," 12 March 1978, *Washington Post*: A13; see also *Congressional Record*, House, 95th Cong., 2nd sess. (25 July 1978): 22622–22623.

10 *Congressional Record*, House, 95th Cong., 1st sess. (26 October 1977): 35261–35262.

11 Ruth Hanna McCormick of Illinois had served in Congress with her future husband, Albert Gallatin Simms of New Mexico. They married after McCormick left the House. Emily Taft Douglas, an Illinois Representative, served in the House several years prior to her husband's election to the Senate. In the 1990s, Susan Molinari and Bill Paxon, both of New York, became the second couple to wed while serving together in the same Congress.

12 Kronholz, "For Congresswoman, Issue in Kansas Race Is a 'Messy' Divorce."

13 Myra McPherson, "Careers and Conflicts: Perspective on the Dilemma of Political Spouses," 28 January 1976, *Washington Post*: C1.

14 Kronholz, "For Congresswoman, Issue in Kansas Race Is a 'Messy' Divorce."

15 Ibid.

16 "Election Statistics, 1920 to Present," http://clerk.house.gov/members/electionInfo/elections.html.

17 Billy Curry and Ward Sinclair, "GOP Turns in Strong Showing," *Washington Post*: A21.

18 "Election Statistics, 1920 to Present," http://clerk.house.gov/members/electionInfo/elections.html; J. McIvor Weatherford, "Capitol Hill 'Clans'," 13 December 1981, *New York Times*: 29.

19 "Hart Asking Supporters to Help Found Think Tank," 20 April 1985, Associated Press.

20 Goering, "Keys to the Future."

Marilyn Lloyd

1929–

UNITED STATES REPRESENTATIVE ★ DEMOCRAT FROM TENNESSEE

1975–1995

Personal tragedy brought Marilyn Lloyd into the House of Representatives where, for 20 years, she represented the science and technology interests of her Tennessee district. When her husband, Mort Lloyd, died shortly after winning a Democratic nomination to the U.S. House of Representatives in 1974, local leaders named Marilyn Lloyd to succeed him as the party candidate, despite the fact that she had no elective experience. When she defeated the GOP incumbent, Lloyd won a string of relatively easy re-election campaigns. But her political fortunes were tied to the fate of several large federal projects in the district as well as its shift toward a more competitive makeup in the early 1990s.

Rachel Marilyn Laird was born in Fort Smith, Arkansas, on January 3, 1929, daughter of James Edgar Laird and Iva Mae (Higginbotham) Laird. Marilyn Laird attended schools in Texas and Kentucky and studied at Shorter College in Rome, Georgia. She married Mort Lloyd, who eventually became a well-known Chattanooga, Tennessee, television newsman. The couple raised three children: Nancy, Mari, and Mort. Marilyn Lloyd and her husband owned and managed WTTI, a radio station in Dalton, Georgia, and an aviation company in Tennessee.

Mort Lloyd ran for Congress in 1974 as the Democratic candidate in a southern Tennessee district including Chattanooga, but was killed just weeks after securing the nomination when the light airplane he was piloting crashed. The district's Democratic leaders convinced Marilyn Lloyd to run in her husband's place. Her supporters wore buttons from her husband's campaign with a piece of black tape covering "Mort," leaving visible the words "Lloyd for Congress."[1] When her principal competitor, Chattanooga millionaire Franklin Haney, dropped out of

contention rather than split the party, Lloyd's nomination was sealed. Though she had no prior political experience and was running in a district that regularly voted Republican in presidential elections, Lloyd benefited from public backlash against the Watergate Scandal. She unseated two-term incumbent Republican Lamar Baker with 51 percent of the vote.

For her entire career, Lloyd served on the Committee on Science, Space and Technology, which had jurisdiction over much of the legislation related to the atomic energy facilities at Oak Ridge in her district. During the 97th Congress (1981–1983), she began chairing the Subcommittee on Energy Research and Development—a post she held until she retired from Congress in 1995, when she was the second-ranking Democrat of the full committee. Lloyd also served on the Committee on Public Works (later Public Works and Transportation) from the 94th through the 99th Congresses (1975–1987). From the 98th Congress through the 103rd Congress (1983–1995), she had a seat on the Armed Services Committee, serving on its Subcommittee on Military Acquisition. Lloyd also served on the House Select Committee on Aging for much of her congressional career, and was appointed chair of its Subcommittee on Housing and Consumer Interests in January 1990. In 1978, Lloyd married engineer Joseph P. Bouquard, and she served for several Congresses under the name Bouquard. In 1983 the couple divorced, and she went back to using the name Marilyn Lloyd. In 1991, she married Robert Fowler, a physician.[2]

Lloyd had a voting record that largely was moderate on social and economic issues but hawkish on defense and foreign policy matters.[3] In 1979, she successfully steered through the House legislation for completion of the controversial Tellico Dam in Tennessee, despite President James Earl "Jimmy" Carter's threat to veto the bill because of the danger the dam might pose to the snail darter fish.[4] In 1989 Lloyd was elected as the first woman to chair the Congressional Textile Caucus. She advocated for textile quotas to make American garment makers more competitive against overseas manufacturers. "I think the textile issue is a women's issue," Lloyd said. "Clearly there are more women employed in textile-apparel production than there are men. You have women with only one skill, who do not have the education that allows them to transfer to another occupation. Many of these women are also the breadwinners in their families."[5] However, when the Congressional Women's Caucus was founded in 1977, Lloyd was one of three women Members who did not join, citing the fact that she felt she did not have the time to make the commitment. Patricia Schroeder, a Caucus cofounder, speculated that Lloyd and Republicans Marjorie Holt of Maryland and Virginia Smith of Nebraska might have been hesitant to join because they would be "labeled" as feminists.[6] Yet, relatively late in her congressional career, Lloyd began to advocate women's issues. In 1992, she spoke out about accusations of sexual abuse in the military, noting, "Men must accept women as human beings, not sex objects."[7] Her own experience with breast cancer led her to work for the Breast Cancer Screening Safety Act and to introduce the Breast Implant Informed Decision Act. It was her experience in seeking treatment for her cancer which led her to switch to a pro-choice position on abortion in 1992. "I have had to fight to make decisions about my own options for recovery, which I feel should have been mine alone," she said, "I have made my own choices and have been blessed by a full recovery. This has led me to take a long, hard look at the position I have held so long against access to abortion services."[8]

Lloyd's principal work was to care for and augment the Oak Ridge atomic energy facilities, as well as to support the construction of the Tennessee Valley Authority's (TVA) controversial Clinch River breeder reactor. The breeder reactor created the by-product plutonium, a highly toxic substance used to create atomic weapons. Critics

argued that, besides posing an environmental threat, the breeder would increase the risk that terrorists or rogue states could acquire more readily the ingredients for a nuclear bomb.[9] Opponents also complained about the reactor's exorbitant costs. More than $1 billion was spent on project planning, and millions more would be required once construction was scheduled to begin. From 1974 to 1982, Lloyd was one of the Clinch River project's principal advocates, but a coalition of antinuclear environmentalists and fiscal conservatives in Congress eventually killed off the project. Lloyd, who had been elected comfortably in the five prior elections (by as much as 89 percent of the vote in 1978), suddenly found herself in a series of relatively tight races—winning by 52 percent in 1984, 54 percent in 1986, and 53 percent in 1990 and edging out a win in 1992 with one percent of the vote (about 3,000 votes out of roughly 216,000 cast). In 1987, poor health had caused her to announce she would not run in 1988, but she reversed her decision and ran, winning 53 percent of the vote.

In 1990, Lloyd had gained enough seniority to make a bid for the chairmanship of the Science, Space, and Technology Committee, but she was defeated easily by George Brown of California, 166 to 33.[10] Following the 1992 elections, Lloyd and New Jersey Congressman William Hughes became the top-ranking Members on the Select Committee on Aging, which held little legislative influence on the House Floor but provided a high-profile position from which to advance issues important to elderly constituents. Lloyd solicited support from her colleagues for a bid to chair the committee in the 103rd Congress (1993–1995); however, Speaker Tom Foley selected Hughes over Lloyd, reasoning that "H" came before "L" in the alphabet. Lloyd expressed her outrage and frustration with the seemingly arbitrary decision, which she attributed to gender discrimination. As a conservative Democrat, however, Lloyd's frequent breaks with the majority had often put her at odds with the leadership. When the House convened in 1993, however, the select committee was abolished.[11]

In October 1993, Lloyd announced she would not run

for re-election, citing a desire to "enjoy my family, friends, and community." She also told reporters, "During my congressional career, I maintained one goal. That goal was to work for the good of Tennesseans with the energy and honesty that all my constituents deserve."[12] At the time, she was the third-ranking woman in the House, behind Democrats Cardiss Collins of Illinois and Patricia Schroeder of Colorado. The following year, in a controversial and surprising political move, she supported the Republican candidate whom she had barely defeated for re-election in 1992, Zach Wamp. Wamp went on to defeat Democrat Randy Button with 52 percent of the vote. Lloyd resides in Chattanooga, Tennessee.

FOR FURTHER READING

Biographical Directory of the United States Congress, "Marilyn Laird Lloyd," http://bioguide.congress.gov

MANUSCRIPT COLLECTION

University of Tennessee at Chattanooga, Lupton Library. *Papers:* 1974–1994, 130 linear feet. The collection documents the work of Lloyd on the following House panels: Armed Services Committee, Select Committee on Aging, Subcommittee on Housing and Consumer Interests, Science, Space and Technology Committee, Subcommittee on Energy Research and Development, TVA Caucus, and Textile Caucus. The collection also includes press clippings, floor information from each congressional session, voting record, legislative correspondence, subject files, district projects, speeches, and other legislative activities. Additional materials include plaques and artwork, as well as files relating to the Oak Ridge facility and energy legislation. This acquisition supplements her earlier donation of 96 cubic feet of office files from 1975 to 1994, including materials on the TVA, Department of Energy, Oak Ridge and Clinch River Breeder Reactor, the Armed Services Committee, foreign affairs, and childcare.

NOTES

1   Patrick Riordan, "Widow of Candidate To Run in His Place," 7 September 1974, *Washington Post*: A6.

2   "Lloyd's Husband Kills Himself," 29 August 1996, *Memphis Commercial Appeal*: 17A; "Ex-Rep. Lloyd Sues Estate," 23 July 1997, Chattanooga Times: B7. The *Chattanooga Times* notes that Fowler was Lloyd's fourth marriage.

3   *Almanac of American Politics, 1994* (Washington, D.C.: National Journal Inc., 1993): 1183–1184.

4   *Politics in America, 1982* (Washington, D.C.: Congressional Quarterly Press, 1981): 1129–1130.

5   Robert LaRussa, "The Congresswoman Takes Issue with Textile Imports; Marilyn Lloyd, Head of Congressional Textile Caucus," 6 March 1989, *Daily News Record* 19 (No. 6): 20.

6   Donnie Radcliffe, "The Women's Caucus," 27 April 1978, *Washington Post*: B12.

7   *Almanac of American Politics, 1998*: 1183.

8   Joel Connelly, "Once-Guaranteed Right Eroding Quickly," 22 June 1992, *Seattle Post-Intelligencer*: A1.

9   "Breeder Reactor Officials Expect Clinch River Project to Be Built," 16 November 1980, *New York Times*: 62.

10 Tim Curran, "Rep. Lloyd Is Fourth Democrat to Depart," 4 October 1993, *Roll Call*.

11 Irwin N. Gertzog, *Congressional Women: Their Recruitment, Integration, and Behavior* (Westport, CT: Praeger Publishers, 1995): 123–125.

12 Curran, "Rep. Lloyd Is Fourth Democrat to Depart."

Helen Stevenson Meyner

1929–1997

UNITED STATES REPRESENTATIVE ★ DEMOCRAT FROM NEW JERSEY
1975–1979

Politically connected by both birth and marriage, Helen Stevenson Meyner entered elective politics for the first time to serve New Jersey for two terms in the U.S. House of Representatives. Congresswoman Meyner developed a reputation as a thoughtful internationalist and advocate of human rights issues. She also became a well-respected charter member of the Congresswomen's Caucus during her short tenure in the House.

Helen Day Stevenson was born on March 5, 1929, to William E. and Eleanor B. Stevenson. She had one sister, Priscilla. The Stevensons worked for the American Red Cross, establishing units in Europe and Africa during World War I. William Stevenson later served as the president of Oberlin College in Ohio and also as U.S. Ambassador to the Philippines. After graduating from Rosemary Hall High School in Greenwich, Connecticut, in 1946, Helen Stevenson earned her bachelor's degree from Colorado College in 1950. Immediately following graduation, she served as a field worker for the Red Cross in Korea from 1950 to 1952 and then as a tour guide at the United Nations. From 1953 to 1956 she was hired by a major airline to travel around the globe on a promotional tour under the name Mary Gordon. In 1956, Stevenson volunteered for the presidential campaign for her mother's distant cousin, Adlai Stevenson. During the campaign, she met New Jersey Governor Robert Meyner, and they married in 1957. In 1970, Meyner lost a baby in childbirth, and the couple had no other children. After Robert Meyner left office in 1962, Helen Meyner began writing a twice-weekly column for the *Newark Star-Ledger*, which she continued until 1969. She also hosted a New York–New Jersey television interview program from 1965 to 1968. Beginning in 1971, Meyner was appointed to the New Jersey rehabilitation commission.

Admittedly more comfortable in the role of politician's wife, Meyner began her improbable political career in July 1972.[1] The Democratic nominee for a northeastern New Jersey congressional district, Irish immigrant Joseph O'Dougherty withdrew from the race because he had failed to meet the U.S. Constitution's seven-year citizenship criterion. The state Democratic committee convinced Meyner, who was at the time working on a biography of writer Katherine Mansfield, to enter the race as the new Democratic nominee in the heavily Republican district. Despite her experience in politics, she admitted that, "in the beginning, the adjustment to stand on my own and projecting myself in public was very difficult."[2] Initially overshadowed by accusations that she supported an expensive dam project because it benefited her own investments, Meyner lost to Republican Joseph J. Maraziti by a margin of 56 to 43 percent in the general election.

Two years later, Meyner challenged Maraziti again. In 1974, her GOP opponent was compromised by revelations that he kept a woman who did not work in his office on his congressional payroll.[3] This, coupled with the backlash resulting from the Watergate investigation, gave Meyner the edge. She defeated Maraziti, reversing the 1972 results for a seat in the 94th Congress (1975–1977). Following her victory, Meyner discussed the demands of a grueling campaign: "They [the Democratic Party] package a candidate like they're selling some underarm deodorant. Now I feel like I'm re-entering life after a long stay in a hospital or prison."[4] Nevertheless, Representative Meyner fought another close battle in 1976, barely holding off Republican challenger William F. Schluter in the general election. In a four-way race, Meyner emerged with 50 percent of the vote to Schluter's 48 percent. She quickly accustomed herself to her position as politician, rather than politician's wife. "I was always on the back stage like most every other politician's wife. And I was always introduced as 'Bob Meyner's lovely wife, Helen,'" she admitted to reporters. "I am still waiting, incidentally, for someone to introduce my husband and me as 'Helen Meyner and her lovely husband, Bob.'"[5]

During her two terms in the House, Meyner served on the Committee on the District of Columbia, the Committee on Foreign Affairs, and the Select Committee on Aging. She also was appointed to a relatively ceremonial position on the House Beauty Shop Committee. In order to take the seat on the prestigious Foreign Affairs Committee (later International Relations), Meyner turned down an assignment on the powerful Ways and Means Committee, as the latter required Members to resign all other assignments.[6] While serving on the Foreign Affairs Committee, Meyner criticized the nuclear arms race and, most memorably, opposed attempts by nonaligned nations to suspend or expel Israel from the United Nations. She condemned the 1975 U.N. resolution that equated Zionism with racism; however, she argued against using the incident as a pretext for U.S. withdrawal from the world organization.[7] Meyner voted in favor of forming a State Department board to oversee the creation of a center for conflict resolution. She amended an aid bill to the Philippines which cut about $5 million in assistance to punish Ferdinand Marcos's authoritarian regime for human rights abuses. Meyner told House colleagues in a floor speech, "I believe that it is very important that we send a concrete signal, and this would only be a signal, of our concern for the serious human rights situation in the Philippines. Words do not seem to have any effect. We must show our concern in a more substantive way."[8]

Meyner also used her seat on Foreign Affairs to tend to New Jersey's economic needs. She worked with her Garden State colleagues to save her district's Picatinny Arsenal from closure; soon after, it was designated as the headquarters for the Army's Armament Research and Development Command. She also sought to sustain New

Jersey's ailing textile industry in the face of competition from foreign imports. In late 1976, Meyner lobbied Democrats in the New Jersey senate, urging them not to rescind the state's endorsement of the Equal Rights Amendment to the Constitution. She subsequently participated in the 1978 Select Committee on Aging hearings on poor conditions in boarding homes for senior citizens.

Meyner actively promoted women's rights and their increased involvement in politics. "A woman's viewpoint is different," Meyner said upon her 1974 election, "perhaps more intuitive and sensitive to people's needs in the special areas like day care, environment and education."[9] In her first term, she supported legislation that aided destitute women, including a vote to provide federal funding for abortions through Medicare.[10] As an active member of the newly founded Congresswomen's Caucus, Meyner served as the organization's resident expert on foreign policy. She developed a reputation as an even-tempered, thoughtful, and effective legislator, somewhat overshadowed by her New Jersey colleague, Millicent Fenwick. In what was later dubbed New Jersey's "Year of the Woman," the more flamboyant Fenwick was elected to Congress alongside Meyner in 1974; however, the two had an uneasy relationship.[11] After the caucus traveled to China in 1977, the fiscally conservative Fenwick publicly rebuked Meyner for spending taxpayers' money to bring her husband on the trip. Other Congresswomen, whose family members also accompanied them, defended Meyner.[12]

In 1978, Meyner faced Republican James A. Courter in another close election. High inflation, soaring gas prices, and a lagging economy under the Jimmy Carter administration were prime issues during the midterm elections. Running on a platform to improve economic opportunities, Courter defeated Meyner by fewer than 6,000 votes, winning 52 to 48 percent. After leaving Congress, Meyner returned to Princeton, New Jersey, where she again worked for the state rehabilitation commission. She also served on the boards of several major corporations, where she developed a reputation for pushing women's equality in corporate management. After her husband's death in

1990, she moved to Captiva Island, Florida. Meyner subsequently oversaw the establishment of the Robert B. Meyner and Helen S. Meyner Center for the Study of State and Local Government at her husband's alma mater, Lafayette College, in Easton, Pennsylvania. Helen Meyner died on November 2, 1997, in Captiva Island.

FOR FURTHER READING

Biographical Directory of the United States Congress, "Helen Stevenson Meyner," http://bioguide.congress.gov

Tomlinson, Barbara J. "Making Their Way: A Study of New Jersey Congresswomen, 1924–1994." Ph.D. diss., Rutgers, The State University of New Jersey–New Brunswick, 1996.

MANUSCRIPT COLLECTIONS

Lafayette College (Easton, PA), David Bishop Skillman Library Special Collections and College Archives, http://ww2.lafayette.edu/filibrary/special/meyner/meyner.html. *Papers:* In the Robert B. and Helen Stevenson Meyner Papers, 1910–1990, 93 linear feet. The collection documents the work of Helen Stevenson Meyner and includes correspondence, committee files, bill files, press files, materials documenting her voting record, special projects, district offices, and her four campaigns (1972–1978). Also includes personal and business papers, photographs, motion picture film, video tape, sound recordings, and memorabilia. Also includes 13 diaries (1955–1977). Some material is restricted.

Princeton University Library (Princeton, NJ). *Papers:* 1974–1978, 86 cubic feet. Consists of legislative correspondence, casework, invitations, requests, and campaign and project material. Also includes references to her services on the Subcommittee on Education, Labor and Social Services (1976) and the Select Committee on Aging (1977–1978).

NOTES

1   Mary C. Churchill, "Helen Meyner Adjusting to Life in Politics," 17 November 1974, *New York Times*: 90.
2   Churchill, "Helen Meyner Adjusting to Life in Politics."
3   Joseph F. Sullivan, "Maraziti Describes Duties For 'No Show' Aide," 19 October 1974, *New York Times*: 35.
4   Churchill, "Helen Meyner Adjusting to Life in Politics."
5   Jo Ann Levine, "Women Plot Campaign Course," 2 August 1974, *Christian Science Monitor*: 12.
6   "Helen Meyner, Lawmaker, Kin of Oberlin College Chief," 3 November 1997, *Cleveland Plain Dealer*: 9B; Steven S. Smith and Christopher Deering, *Committees in Congress,* 2nd ed. (Washington D.C.: Congressional Quarterly Press, 1990): 37.
7   "Zionism Resolution Assailed," 16 November 1975, *New York Times*: 92.
8   *Congressional Record,* 95th Cong., 2nd sess. (3 August 1978): 24221–24222.
9   Churchill, "Helen Meyner Adjusting to Life in Politics."
10 *Almanac of American Politics, 1978* (Washington, D.C.: National Journal Inc., 1977): 541.
11 David M. Halbfinger, "Ex-Rep. Helen S. Meyner, 69; Born Into Democratic Politics," 3 November 1997, *New York Times*: B7; "In Record Year for Women Candidates, New Jersey Lags Far Behind," 24 October 1994, State News Service.
12 Irwin N. Gertzog, *Congressional Women: Their Recruitment, Integration, and Behavior* (Westport, CT: Praeger, 1995): 201.

Virginia Dodd Smith
1911–2006

UNITED STATES REPRESENTATIVE ★ REPUBLICAN FROM NEBRASKA
1975–1991

Virginia Dodd Smith's House career owed much to her 40 years on a Nebraska farm and experience as a spokesperson for agricultural issues. As the first woman elected to Congress from Nebraska, Smith steered federal money toward farm programs from her seat on the powerful Appropriations Committee. Widely popular in her state, she also exercised a great deal of influence on political developments there, both because of her western Nebraska district's size and her personal connection with constituents, whom she visited regularly.

Virginia Dodd was born in Randolph, Iowa, on June 30, 1911, to Clifton Clark Dodd and Erville (Reeves) Dodd. She graduated from Shenandoah High School in Shenandoah, Iowa. Virginia Dodd met Haven Smith while attending the University of Nebraska. The two wed on August 27, 1931, taking a hiatus from school to earn tuition money. The Smiths settled in Chappell, Nebraska, in the western portion of the state near the Colorado border and worked on Haven's family wheat farm during the depths of the Great Depression. They both returned to school and received their bachelor of arts degrees from the University of Nebraska in 1936. The Smiths eventually expanded their wheat farming business into poultry, seed potatoes, and other crops.[1] From 1950 until 1960, Virginia Smith worked for the Home Economics Research Advisory Committee for the U.S. Department of Agriculture. She became involved in a wide variety of farm organizations, such as the American Farm Bureau Federation (AFBF), spending 20 years on its board of directors and serving as the national chair of the AFBF women's bureau from 1955 to 1974. Meanwhile, Smith was active in the state's Republican Party.

Smith's extensive participation in farming organizations and civic affairs in Nebraska provided an invaluable network for her first run for elective office in 1974, when seven-term incumbent Republican Dave Martin retired from the U.S. House of Representatives. Martin represented what was then the nation's largest congressional district, consisting of 61 counties and 307 towns spread over the western three-quarters of the state, an area dominated by the wheat, corn, and cattle businesses. A political observer described it as "one of the most macho districts" in America.[2] It certainly was one of the most historically Republican regions. The farmers and ranchers of western Nebraska had voted for Republican House Members with only one significant interruption—from 1932 to 1942 during the heyday of the New Deal agricultural programs.

Name recognition in the massive district was no problem for Smith. Already a familiar face in many of the district's small farm towns, she defeated eight candidates in the GOP primary. In the general election, Smith faced Democratic candidate Wayne W. Ziebarth, a former state senator. Ziebarth, too, had name recognition, after having run a statewide race in 1972 for the Democratic nomination to the U.S. Senate. Smith was a formidable campaigner who engaged individuals in the crowds in one-on-one conversations and had an "extraordinary" capacity for names, faces, and issues.[3] She relied on the wholehearted support of her husband, Haven. "It was a two-person job," Virginia Smith recalled. "He was just my righthand man all the way."[4] Ziebarth aided Smith's cause when he made a crucial mistake late in his campaign, publicly stating that women were not cut out for politics.[5] Smith defeated her opponent by a margin of just 737 votes out of more than 161,000 cast.[6] When she took her seat in the 94th Congress (1975–1977), she did so as the first Nebraska woman elected to the U.S. House. In her subsequent bids for re-election, voters returned Smith to office for seven more terms by increasingly wide margins, from 73 to 84 percent of the vote.[7]

During Smith's freshman year, she served on the Education and Labor and the Interior and Insular Affairs committees. In her second term in Congress, she managed to get a seat on the powerful Appropriations Committee—an assignment she held until her retirement in 1991. She served on two Appropriations subcommittees: Rural Development, Agriculture, and Related Agencies and Energy and Water Development. She also was assigned to the GOP policy committee in 1977, which advised House Republicans on key issues.

Throughout her tenure, Smith focused on agricultural matters. Fiscally conservative on most issues, she nevertheless routinely favored spending federal money on farm programs. As Ranking Member of the Rural Development, Agriculture, and Related Agencies Subcommittee of the Appropriations Committee, she had a strong position from which to steer federal dollars into that sector, and into her district in particular. In 1984, for instance, more than $162 million dollars in federal payments for corn growers flowed into her district, by far the largest amount of any other congressional district for a region that, in fact, produced more corn than any other in the nation.[8] In 1987, she managed to exempt U.S. agriculture exporters from having to ship a certain percentage of their product on American vessels, which charged higher shipping costs. In 1989, as the United States began to send food aid to Eastern European countries emerging from communist rule, Smith was one of several midwestern Representatives to argue that the U.S. government should continue to allow shipments to be made on foreign vessels—at about one-third of the transportation rates on American-registered ships. The differential could then have been applied to buying more foodstuffs, which would have further benefited American farmers.[9] Smith also supported the creation of more domestic land and air transportation routes, in order to keep rural America connected to urban centers. "The revitalization of rural America

cannot and will not occur unless we guarantee mobility."[10] In a 1989 Appropriations Committee vote, her amendment to restore subsidies to airline companies as an incentive to fly to small towns was narrowly defeated, with the vote breaking down not along party lines, but between rural and urban legislators.[11] In 1988, she helped secure federal funding for a bus line that connected remote parts of western Nebraska with South Dakota.[12] That same year she also successfully fended off efforts to cut funding to the Davis Creek Dam which, when completed, would provide irrigation water in her district.[13]

Smith's farming constituents showed their approval for her policies with her overwhelming success at the polls. "I think people know I fight very hard to get a fair share of federal revenues for Nebraska," she once said. "I visit every one of the counties in my district every year and I visit most of them quite a lot of times. I work seven days a week on this job. I do my homework . . . I love this job and I love the people of my district, and I think that when you have the privilege of representing 500,000 of the finest people on earth, you ought to work hard."[14]

Focusing on the needs and traditions of her agricultural constituents, Smith did not embrace feminist issues during her House career. As a new Member of Congress, for instance, she had requested that she be known as "Mrs. Haven Smith."[15] In 1977, though she often encouraged women to enter politics, Smith was one of three Members who did not join the Congressional Women's Caucus during its inaugural meetings.[16]

Smith did not stand for re-election in 1990 and retired the following January. In retirement, she and her husband settled in Sun City West, Arizona. Three years later, the community named Virginia Smith one of its favorite leaders. Haven Smith died on May 12, 1997, after the couple had reached their milestone 65th wedding anniversary. Approaching age 90, Virginia Smith was still active in Nebraska politics. In 2000, she agreed to work on the campaign for a promising Republican candidate in her old district.[17] Virginia Smith died on January 23, 2006, in Sun City West, Arizona.[18]

FOR FURTHER READING

Biographical Directory of the United States Congress, "Virginia Dodd Smith," http://bioguide.congress.gov

MANUSCRIPT COLLECTION

University of Nebraska–Lincoln (Lincoln, NE), University Libraries Archives and Special Collections. *Papers:* 1974–1990, 463 linear feet. Includes correspondence, legislation and congressional committee reports, speeches, office records and schedules, press clippings and releases, photographs, audiotapes, and films. A finding aid is available in the repository.

NOTES

1 David C. Beeder, "Virginia Smith's 'Right-Hand-Man,' Haven Smith, Dies," 14 May 1997, *Omaha World-Herald*: 1.

2 Douglas E. Kneeland, "Rep. Thone Is Victor in Nebraska Election," 10 May 1978, *New York Times*: A19.

3 David Hendee, "Virginia Smith Celebrates Her 90th," 3 July 2001, *Omaha World-Herald*: 9.

4 Beeder, "Virginia Smith's 'Right-Hand-Man,' Haven Smith, Dies."

5 *Politics in America, 1982* (Washington, D.C.: National Journal Inc., 1981): 791.

6 "Election Statistics, 1920 to Present," http://clerk.house.gov/members/electionInfo/index.html; "Republican Wins Neb. House Seat," 19 November 1974, *Washington Post*: A8.

7 "Election Statistics, 1920 to Present," http://clerk.house.gov/members/electionInfo/index.html.

8 Agricultural subsidy statistics, 16 October 1985, *Washington Post*: A21.

9 "Aid to Poland Sets Off a Fight Over Shipping," 8 December 1989, *New York Times*: A19.

10 "Rural Transit Hurting, Says Congresswoman," *Chicago Tribune*, August 24, 1988: 3.

11 Dan Morgan, "Geography Shoves Ideology Aside in Money Fights," 13 August 1989, *Washington Post*: A1.

12 William Robbins, "On the Road to Ending Rural Isolation by Forging Bus Links," 27 August 1988, *New York Times*: 5.

13 *Politics in America, 1990* (Washington, D.C.: National Journal Inc., 1989): 897.

14 "Virginia Dodd Smith," Associated Press Candidate Biography, 1990.

15 *Politics in America, 1990*: 898.

16 Donnie Radcliffe, "A Show of Support for Women's Issues," 26 April 1978, *Washington Post*: B3.

17 "Yes, Virginia, There Is an Open Seat," Associated Press, 10 January 2000; "Smith Backs Gale in 3rd District Race," Associated Press, 9 January 2000.

18 Bill Hord, "Virginia Smith, 1911–2006, A 'Legend' Remembered: Longtime 3rd District Representative Dies at 94," 24 January 2006, *Omaha World-Herald*: 1A.

Gladys Noon Spellman
1918–1988

UNITED STATES REPRESENTATIVE ★ DEMOCRAT FROM MARYLAND
1975–1981

Gladys Noon Spellman rose through the ranks of Maryland politics to become an influential advocate for the federal workforce in the U.S. House of Representatives. Elected in 1974 to a large freshman class of Democrats, Spellman joined the front ranks of the "freshman revolt" bent on reforming congressional practices. Very quickly, however, she settled into a role as a Representative dedicated to district work, securing what had been a tenuous first victory.[1] Within a short span of six years she became a widely popular local politician in the Maryland suburbs of Washington, D.C., before suffering a heart attack that left her permanently incapacitated.

She was born Gladys Blossom Noon in New York City on March 1, 1918, daughter of Henry and Bessie Noon, and was educated in the New York City and Washington, D.C., public schools.[2] After attending George Washington University and the graduate school of the U.S. Department of Agriculture, Spellman taught in the public schools of Prince George's County, Maryland, a suburban area northeast of Washington, D.C. Gladys Noon married Reuben Spellman, and they raised three children: Stephen, Richard, and Dana. Gladys Spellman made her mark as a crusading Parent Teacher Association leader before winning election to the Prince George's County board of commissioners in 1962. At first, she faced a cool reception from her colleagues. One remarked, "You think just like a man." Spellman took that as a compliment, at first. "Then I got angry and said, 'Well, I guess today was an off-day for me. Tomorrow I'll be myself and do better.'"[3] A county executive recalled years later that his nickname for Spellman—"Madame Tinkerbell"—derived from her ability to use her ebullient personality, her broad smile, and

her uncanny ability to recall names to engage voters and work a room.[4] She was re-elected in 1966 and chaired the board for two years, the first woman ever to lead the county. In 1970, when Prince George's County changed to a charter form of government, Spellman won election to the county council as an at-large member, serving from 1971 to 1974.

In 1974, when U.S. Representative Lawrence J. Hogan declined to run for re-election in order to seek the party's nomination as Maryland gubernatorial candidate, Spellman entered the race to succeed the three-term Republican. Historically, the congressional district which wrapped around Washington's northern and eastern suburbs and swung into southern Maryland had been solidly Democratic since the mid-1920s. To the south and east it was composed of farms and rural communities, while on the northern and western side it was made up of suburban communities wedged between the capital and Baltimore. The federal government, which had major installations in the district, employed a large number of workers. Only two Republicans ever had held the seat: a one-termer who rode Dwight D. Eisenhower's presidential coattails in 1952 and Hogan who won in 1968 when Richard Nixon and Maryland native son Spiro Agnew made up the winning GOP presidential ticket (they nearly carried Maryland as well and, in 1972, won it convincingly).

Spellman easily won the September 1974 Democratic primary with 67 percent against Karl H. Matthes, a political unknown, accumulating more total votes than Matthes and the two GOP primary contenders combined, including Prince George's County Councilman John B. Burcham, Jr., the eventual Republican winner.[5] The seat was hotly contested with prominent politicians from both parties campaigning in the district—House Speaker Carl Albert and Senator Ted Kennedy of Massachusetts for Spellman and President Gerald R. Ford and Representative Hogan for Burcham.[6] The candidates divided on some hot-button issues. While both candidates opposed a plan by President Ford to add a five percent federal surtax to bring inflation under control, Spellman attacked the GOP, arguing that the election "ought to be a referendum on the Republican handling of the economy." Instead, it was a referendum on an issue neither of the candidates addressed squarely: the Watergate Scandal that had forced the resignation of President Nixon in August 1974. According to a *Washington Post* poll conducted in late October 1974, nearly a quarter of all suburban Maryland voters said that they would be less likely to cast their vote for a Republican.[7] Nationally, the scandal contributed to a string of GOP losses in five 1974 special elections and the November general elections. Republicans lost a total of 48 seats, creating an even larger Democratic majority in Congress. Nevertheless, Spellman only narrowly defeated Burcham, 53 percent to 47 percent of the vote.[8]

Spellman entered the House as one of seven leaders of the so-called "freshman revolt" of the class of 1974, which sought to extend reforms of congressional procedure to secure better committee assignments for first-term Members and to weaken the power of committee chairmen. Spellman was appointed to the Democratic Steering and Policy Committee, a panel reinstituted in 1973 to allow party leaders to assert more control over the committee assignment process and to shape legislative policy.[9] Congresswoman Spellman avowed, "We may be new kids on the block, but we're not stupid"—an allusion to her frustration with chairmen who underestimated the expertise and clout of freshman "Watergate Babies."[10] Many reforms already had been pushed through at the end of the preceding Congress and, in January 1975, the freshmen Members of the 94th Congress (1975–1977) provided momentum to help depose three entrenched southern committee chairmen and appoint new Members to prominent committees.

Yet, within six months, Representative Spellman's focus rested almost entirely on issues pertinent to her district from which her office received hundreds of phone calls and as many letters each day. "You don't always want to stay in kindergarten," Spellman explained about her decision to decline the chairmanship of the freshman caucus. "We accomplished a great deal, and now we've been made a part of the establishment. We don't always have to be just freshmen." But observers noted that political necessity changed Spellman's focus. Vague statements by former Representative Hogan that he would challenge her in 1976, her thin margin of victory in 1974, and the demands of constituent service for a district located astride the capital forced her reconsideration. Spellman hinted that the latter concern more than any other caused her to reorient her attention from institutional reform to district caretaking. "Mine is the kind of district," she said, "that requires a lot of time and attention."[11] She dedicated herself to attending citizen meetings across the district, answering constituent mail personally, developing a newsletter, and distributing "listening post reports" (that included her home phone number) which requested suggestions from local residents.[12]

Over time, Spellman became one of the most popular figures in Maryland politics. In a 1976 rematch against Burcham, the Congresswoman ran on her record as a reformer and as a politician closely attuned to the needs of her constituents. She declared that she had participated in a movement that had "opened the doors wide and pumped fresh air back into the smoke-filled rooms" of the Capitol.[13] In the 1976 election she widened her margin of victory against Burcham to 57 percent. In subsequent campaigns against other GOP opponents, Spellman widened her margins: 77 percent in 1978 and 80 percent in 1980.[14]

During her three terms in Congress, Spellman served on the Committee on Banking, Currency, and Housing (renamed the Banking, Finance, and Urban Affairs Committee after the 94th Congress) and the Committee on Post Office and Civil Service. In 1977 she favored legislation to establish a bank to make loans to cooperatives owned by consumers and legislation to extend the federal revenue-sharing program. She also voted in 1975 for $7 billion in loan guarantees to aid financially troubled New York City.

Nearly 40 percent of the workforce in Spellman's district was employed by the federal government, at the time, the largest percentage of any congressional district in the country. Spellman was carefully attuned to its needs. As chair of the Subcommittee of Compensation and Employee Benefits of the Post Office and Civil Service Committee, she frequently used her position to advance the interests of federal employees. She sought to derail President James Earl "Jimmy" Carter's 1978 reform of the civil service, which planned to merge the federal retirement program with Social Security. Spellman also pushed for cost of living adjustments and opposed hiring freezes. She was particularly critical of the proposed Senior Executive Service, which she feared would politicize the civil service. Spellman also favored an amendment to the 1970 Intergovernmental Personnel Act which would have authorized a subsidy to train civil servants in management–labor relations. She was especially sensitive to the morale of the federal workforce which, in the post-Watergate years, became a favorite target for "anti-Washington" candidates. In her newsletter, she often devoted a "Beautiful Bureaucrat" column to praise federal workers and insist that the vast majority of them were people who "far from slowing down the wheels of government are really the people who keep them churning."[15]

On October 31, 1980, two days before the general election in which she was re-elected to a fourth term, Spellman suffered a severe heart attack. She survived but lapsed into a coma from which she never regained consciousness.[16] House Resolution 80, passed on February 24, 1981, declared Spellman's seat vacant, since she was unable to discharge the duties of her office. It marked the first time the House had ever vacated the seat of a Member who had become mentally or physically impaired. The next day the *Washington Post*, while observing that the move "was only right" for representation of her district, celebrated Spellman's "brilliant" career: it "remains a classic for all who would seek public office and serve successfully."[17] Her husband, Reuben, was a Democratic candidate in the April 1981 special primary to choose nominees to succeed her. He finished second out of a field of six candidates; the winner of

the primary, Steny Hoyer, also won the general election. Gladys Spellman died in Rockville, Maryland, on June 19, 1988.

FOR FURTHER READING

Biographical Directory of the United States Congress, "Gladys Noon Spellman," http://bioguide.congress.gov

NOTES

1   Karen DeYoung, "They Say Gladys Spellman Is as Good as She Says," 25 October 1976, *Washington Post*: B1.

2   Parents' names come from Spellman's death notice, printed in the 21 June 1988, *Washington Post*: B4.

3   Karen Foerstel, *Biographical Dictionary of Congressional Women* (Westport, CT: Greenwood Press, 1999): 260.

4   Bart Barnes, "Former Md. Representative Gladys N. Spellman, 70, Dies," 20 June 1988, *Washington Post*: A1.

5   Douglas Watson, "Barbara Mikulski Scores Big in Md. Primary," 12 September 1974, *Washington Post*: B1.

6   Charles A. Krause, "Speaker of House Aids Md. Candidate," 13 September 1974, *Washington Post*: A10; Charles A. Krause, "Sen. Kennedy Makes Big Hit as Backer of Mrs. Spellman," 7 October 1974, *Washington Post*: C5; Donald F. Baker, "Hogan Campaigns for Burcham," 28 September 1974, *Washington Post*: D4.

7   Douglas Watson, "Watergate Hurt GOP in Nearby Md.," 28 October 1974, *Washington Post*: A1.

8   "Election Statistics, 1920 to Present," http://clerk.house.gov/members/electionInfo/elections.html.

9   Richard L. Lyons, "Democrats Eye Reform in the House," 5 January 1973, *Washington Post*: A1; Julian E. Zelizer, *On Capitol Hill: The Struggle to Reform Congress and Its Consequences, 1948–2000* (New York: Cambridge University Press, 2004): 137–138.

10 Richard L. Lyons, "Freshmen Assess House Chairmen," 14 January 1975, *Washington Post*: A2.

11 Helen Dewar, "Rep. Spellman Drops 'Freshman Revolt' for Political Survival," 27 July 1975, *Washington Post*: 21.

12 Dewar, "Rep. Spellman Drops 'Freshman Revolt' for Political Survival."

13 Cynthia Gorney, "Spellman Will Seek Re-election," 7 March 1976, *Washington Post*: 25.

14 "Election Statistics, 1920 to Present," http://clerk.house.gov/members/electionInfo/elections.html.

15 DeYoung, "They Say Gladys Spellman Is as Good as She Says."

16 See, for example, "Friends of Spellman Mourn Life Lost in Coma," 15 October 1987, *Washington Post*: MDA5.

17 "Gladys Spellman's Brilliant Career," 25 February 1981, *Washington Post*: A16.

Shirley N. Pettis

1924-

UNITED STATES REPRESENTATIVE ★ REPUBLICAN FROM CALIFORNIA
1975–1979

Shirley Pettis, a successful California businesswoman and congressional spouse, won election to the U.S. House of Representatives to succeed her husband, who died in 1975. During two terms in Congress, Pettis sought to continue Jerry L. Pettis's conservative legislative agenda and sponsored an environmental bill that vastly expanded the "wilderness" boundaries of the Joshua Tree National Monument east of Los Angeles.

Shirley Neil McCumber was born in Mountain View, California, on July 12, 1924, to Harold Oliver and Dorothy Susan O'Neil McCumber. Shirley McCumber studied at Andrews University in Berrien Springs, Michigan, and at the University of California at Berkeley. After the death of her first husband, Dr. John McNulty, in World War II, she married Jerry L. Pettis, a World War II flight instructor who would go on to become a self-made millionaire and a professor of economics at Loma Linda University. They raised two children, Peter and Deborah.[1] Along with her husband, Shirley Pettis was a founder and manager of the Audio Digest Foundation, a nonprofit affiliate of the California Medical Association which placed abstracts of medical journals and lectures on audiocassette tapes.[2] The couple also owned Magnetic Tape Duplicators. In addition, Pettis assisted her husband in the operation of their southern California ranch and, when he was elected to Congress, wrote a regular newspaper column for the *San Bernardino Sun-Telegram*. Jerry Pettis was elected as a Republican Representative from California to the 90th Congress (1967–1969) and eventually earned a spot on the influential Ways and Means Committee. He served in the House from 1967 until his death on February 14, 1975, in a private aircraft crash in Banning, California.[3]

Immediately after the accident, friends and associates began encouraging Shirley Pettis to run for her husband's vacant congressional seat, which included vast tracts of desert and mountain areas east of Los Angeles in San Bernardino and Riverside counties. "'Shirley, you have to run,'" she recalled them saying to her. "'You have name recognition and everybody knows you.'" But it was not until her daughter, then 16 years old, and her 19-year-old son encouraged her that Pettis filed for candidacy.[4] Campaigning as her late husband's "working partner," Pettis won more than 60 percent of the vote against a field of 12 other candidates in the April 29, 1975, special election to fill his seat. "I think the people definitely felt that Jerry Pettis' philosophy and mind—that government should serve the people and not that people should serve the government—was the philosophy they wanted to continue to represent them," she said the night of her victory.[5] After taking the oath of office on May 6, 1975, she was appointed to the Committee on Interior and Insular Affairs. In 1976, district voters elected Pettis to a full term in the 95th Congress (1977–1979); she defeated Democrat Douglas C. Nilson, Jr., with 71 percent of the vote.[6] In January 1977, Pettis was assigned to the Committee on Education and Labor and the Committee on International Relations.

During her first term in the House, Pettis used her seat on Interior and Insular Affairs to advance legislation protecting desert lands in her district. She secured wilderness status for nearly half a million acres in the Joshua Tree National Monument, which limited vehicular access and prohibited development. In 1994, Joshua Tree became a national park. Pettis also worked to have the California desert established as a conservation area. During her short tenure in Congress, she took up her late husband's

IMAGE COURTESY OF THE LIBRARY OF CONGRESS

fight to win federal funding for a cleanup of the Salton Sea, a large lake in her congressional district that was home to migratory birds. The initial interest that Jerry Pettis had raised in such a project had waned. "It kind of dribbled away," Shirley Pettis recalled. The California Congresswoman also helped to bring the first solar power plant in the nation to her district.[7]

On nonenvironmental issues during her two terms, she voted with her GOP colleagues to oppose federal funding for abortions and the creation of a federal consumer rights agency, and she proposed cuts to America's military and economic assistance to South Korea.[8] As a Representative with 16 Native-American tribes in her district, Pettis remained a consistent advocate of legislation aimed at improving the health and welfare of Native Americans.

Pettis, who helped cofound the Women's Caucus in 1977, recalled that her reception as a woman in Congress was initially somewhat rocky. She recalled one elevator ride in which she was chatting with a senior House committee chairman. When the doors opened and they exited, the Congressman turned to Pettis and asked, "So whose secretary did you say you were?" Such experiences led Pettis to encourage young women to enter politics not only to fight gender discrimination but to fulfill their responsibilities as good citizens. "Politics isn't a far off thing that happens in a state capital or in Washington," she once remarked. "It is the road you drive on, the schools you attend; it's the groceries you buy. It isn't far away from you. It's important that everyone become involved in the issues central to their lives."[9]

Citing difficulty with keeping in touch with her constituents from the sprawling 27,000-square-mile

California district, Pettis declined to run for renomination in 1978.[10] From 1980 to 1981, she served as vice president of the Women's Research and Education Institute in Washington, D.C. Following that, Pettis was a member of the Arms Control and Disarmament Commission for two years. President George H.W. Bush appointed her to the Commission on Presidential Scholars, where she served from 1990 to 1992. In 1979, Pettis also began a long term of service on the board of directors of a major insurance company. She married Ben Roberson in February 1988, and resides in Rancho Mirage, California.

FOR FURTHER READING

Biographical Directory of the United States Congress, "Shirley Neil Pettis," http://bioguide.congress.gov

MANUSCRIPT COLLECTION

Loma Linda University Libraries (Loma Linda, CA). *Papers:* In the Jerry and Shirley Pettis Papers, 1966–1978, 350 feet. Items include nearly 150 archival boxes of official and personal papers of both Representatives, numerous correspondence files, House committee- and bill-related materials, photographs, plaques, and other memorabilia. A finding aid is available in the repository.

NOTES

1   Information about her first marriage appeared in a Loma Linda University newsletter, http://www.llu.edu/news/today/june0602/grad.html (accessed 26 May 2004).

2   Gary Libman, "Audiocassette Tapes Have a Way With Words," 28 December 1987, *Los Angeles Times*: 1("View" section); Information about the Audio Digest Foundation appeared in a Meetingnet.com article, Tamar Hosansky, "An Ear for CME," 1 January 2002, http://mm.meetingsnet.com/ar/meetings_ear_cme/ (accessed 18 March 2005).

3   "Rep. Pettis Dies in Crash of His Plane," 15 February 1975, *Washington Post*: A4.

4   Interview, *Women in Public Service*, video (Washington, D.C.: U.S. Capitol Historical Society, 1998); "Widow Is Running in California to Fill Seat Husband Held," 28 April 1975, *New York Times*: 21.

5   "Mrs. Pettis Elected to House Vacancy," 1 May 1975, *Washington Post*: A2; see also, Michael J. Dubin et al., *United States Congressional Elections, 1788–1997* (Jefferson, NC: McFarland & Company, Publishers, Inc., 1998): 694.

6   "Election Statistics, 1920 to Present," http://clerk.house.gov/members/electionInfo/elections.html.

7   "Country's First Solar Power Plant Planned for California Area," 20 August 1977, *Washington Post*: D3; "Around the Nation," 12 August 1977, *New York Times*: 8.

8   Karen Foerstel, *Biographical Dictionary of Congressional Women* (Westport, CT: Greenwood Press, 1999): 218.

9   *Women in Public Service*, video.

10 "The Capitol," 28 January 1978, *Washington Post*: A3.

Assembling, Amplifying, and Ascending

RECENT TRENDS AMONG
WOMEN IN CONGRESS, 1977–2006

THE FOURTH WAVE OF WOMEN TO ENTER CONGRESS—FROM 1977 TO 2006—
was by far the largest and most diverse group. These 134 women accounted for more
than half (58 percent) of all the women who have served in the history of Congress.
In the House, the women formed a Congresswomen's Caucus (later called the
Congressional Caucus for Women's Issues), to publicize legislative initiatives that
were important to women. By honing their message and by cultivating political
action groups to support female candidates, women became more powerful. Most
important, as the numbers of Congresswomen increased and their legislative interests expanded, women accrued the seniority and influence to advance into the ranks
of leadership.

Despite such achievements, women in Congress historically account for
a only a small fraction—about 2 percent—of the approximately 12,000 individuals
who have served in the U.S. Congress since 1789, although recent trends suggest
that the presence of women in Congress will continue to increase. Based on gains
principally in the House of Representatives, each of the 13 Congresses since 1981
has had a record number of women Members.

(From left) Marilyn Lloyd, Tennessee; Martha Keys, Kansas; Patricia Schroeder, Colorado;
Margaret Heckler, Massachusetts; Virginia Smith, Nebraska; Helen Meyner, New Jersey;
and Marjorie Holt, Maryland, in 1978 in the Congresswomen's Suite in the Capitol—now
known as the Lindy Claiborne Boggs Congressional Reading Room. Schroeder and
Heckler co-chaired the Congresswomen's Caucus, which met here in its early years.

2003

One of the major legislative triumphs for women in Congress during the 1990s was the passage of the Violence Against Women Act (VAWA) of 1994, which allocated more than a billion dollars to prevent domestic abuse and other violent crimes against women. Such legislation also raised awareness about a scourge long kept out of the national dialogue. This stamp, released by the U.S. Postal Service a decade later, was part of the continuing effort to educate the public about family violence.

A defining moment of change was the general election of 1992 dubbed the "Year of the Woman." The arrival of 28 new women in Congress resulted from the confluence of historic circumstances that have not recurred since. Yet, the doubling of the number of women in Congress virtually overnight had far-reaching effects on the way women were perceived in the institution. Elected to the House in 1992, Lynn Schenk of San Diego, aptly summarized the changes. "After years in the trenches, more women are finally moving up to the front lines."[1] The elections of 1992 inaugurated a decade of gains for women in Congress—in regard to their number and their seniority. These gains were capped by the election of Representative Nancy Pelosi as House Democratic Leader in 2002. It was the first time a woman held the top post in a major U.S. political party.

New Patterns: Familial Connections and Political Experience

During this period, the number of women elected to Congress via a familial connection—particularly widows of Congressmen—while still statistically significant, was far smaller. Of the 134 women who came to Congress during this period, just 12 (9 percent) were widows who succeeded their late husbands. Three women directly succeeded their fathers: Representatives Susan Molinari of New York, and Lucille Roybal-Allard of California, and Senator Lisa Murkowski of Alaska. In all, 11 percent of the Congresswomen from this period arrived in Congress through a familial connection.

The elections of Jo Ann Emerson of Missouri, Lois Capps of California, and Mary Bono of California—each succeeding her late husband—to the House between January 1997 and April 1998 were portrayed by the national media as a testament to the power of the marital connection. But an important factor distinguished this trio and the modern congressional widows: their professional and political résumés were more evolved than those of their predecessors. Earlier widows in Congress, such as Mae Ella Nolan of California, Katharine Byron of Maryland, and Irene Baker of Tennessee, were to various degrees involved in their husbands' political careers. But the widows of the late 20th century had their own careers distinct from their husbands'. Whereas earlier widows, even if they were politically savvy, tended to run for office to complete their husbands' legislative agenda—in effect, to honor their husbands' memory—later widows were more likely to pursue interests related to careers they established before coming to Congress. For example, in 1998, Lois Capps succeeded her late husband, Walter, a theology professor-turned politician. Having worked as a nurse and medical administrator for decades, Capps eschewed her husband's focus on religious issues and became an advocate for health care professionals and reform within the industry. In March 2005, Doris Matsui of California won a special election to succeed her late husband, Robert, head of the Democratic Party's congressional campaign committee, after years as a White House staffer in the William J. Clinton administration.

Since many present-day congressional marriages unite partners with impressive political résumés, the influence of the widow's—or perhaps the widower's—mandate will likely persist.[2] But while personal tragedy and matrimonial connections will undoubtedly continue to bring women into Congress, candidates will be judged less on familial ties than on prior political experience and professional accomplishments.

A matrimonial role reversal occurred in the U.S. Senate early in the new millennium. In the 1990s, President Bill Clinton of Arkansas and Senator Bob Dole of Kansas emerged as party leaders and faced off against each other in the 1996 presidential election. By 2001, both had retired from politics. Their departure marked a moment of arrival for their wives, Hillary Rodham Clinton of New York and Elizabeth Hanford Dole of North Carolina, who had subordinated their own political aspirations to further their husbands' careers. In November 2000, Hillary Clinton won election as New York's first woman Senator, becoming the first First Lady to hold political office. Elizabeth Dole, who had served as Secretary of Transportation and Secretary of Labor, contended for the GOP presidential nomination in 2000 and was elected to the Senate two years later, becoming the first woman to represent North Carolina in the Senate. While their husbands were guests on political talk shows on network television, Hillary Clinton and Elizabeth Dole debated policy on the Senate Floor as spokespersons for their respective parties.

While the importance of the widow's mandate waned, the number of women elected to Congress with federal, state, and local electoral experience surged. Sixty-four women elected since 1976 (48 percent) had served in state legislatures; 12 had held state executive office positions including lieutenant governor, treasurer, and secretary of state; eight had held federal positions ranging from U.S. Ambassador to Cabinet Secretary to head of the Equal Employment Opportunity Commission; and several had been mayors of large cities. In all, nearly 60 percent had held elective or appointed office at the state or federal level.[3]

Moreover, the level of education of women in Congress, which had always been higher than average, exceeded that of previous generations. All but two of the women from this period (98.5 percent) had some postsecondary education, and the vast majority of these had four-year degrees. By contrast, according to the 2000 Census, just 51 percent of Americans had at least some college education. Moreover, 60 of the women (45 percent) elected to Congress during this period had held graduate degrees (among them were 23 lawyers, five doctors of philosophy, and one medical doctor), again far eclipsing the level of education in the general population (in 2000 eight percent of the U.S. population held a masters degree or a more advanced degree).[4] The average age at which women were first elected or appointed to Congress between 1977 and 2006 dropped nearly two years from that of the third generation, to 48.4 years.[5] The youngest woman elected to Congress in this period was Susan Molinari of New York, at age 31 years, 9 months. The oldest woman to enter Congress during this period was Jocelyn Burdick of North Dakota—a 70-year-old widow appointed to the Senate to succeed her late husband, Quentin Burdick, for the brief remainder of his term.

A significant number of the women who were elected had young families and thus were required to balance their careers with their family life. The structure of the modern congressional workweek, the necessity of frequent trips to the district, and increasing demands on Members' time strained family life. As in American society generally, divorce became more prevalent in Congress during the third and fourth generations of women. Many Members' families remained behind in the district instead of moving to Washington, D.C., increasing the time families were separated. Representative Lynn Martin of Illinois became an influential House Member in the 1980s, with a seat on the powerful Budget Committee and an elective position in the GOP leadership. But family concerns competed with political responsibilities. "The first time I was in Ronald Reagan's office, I called Caroline, my 9-year-old, and I said, 'I have just been in with President Ronald Reagan,'" Martin recalled. Her daughter replied, "'Are you going to be here tomorrow for the carpool?' And I said, 'I have just been . . .' and she said, 'I heard you. Are you going to be here tomorrow for the carpool?' I mean, oh my Lord: 'I'm deciding the fate of the Western World and you're worrying about a carpool?' And the answer was, 'Yes, I am.'"[6] Some Congresswomen chose not to raise a family in order to devote themselves to the rigorous demands of public office. "I think one of the reasons I've never married and had children is because of the guilt I would feel taking time from them," Marcy Kaptur of Ohio said in 1992. "To me, one of the great achievements of my life has been not wounding a child. To raise children in this job? You can count on one hand the number of women in this job who have."[7] Three incumbent Congresswomen gave birth later in the decade—Utah Republican Enid Greene Waldholtz (a daughter in 1995), New York Republican Susan Molinari (a daughter in 1996), and Arkansas Democrat Blanche Lambert Lincoln (twin boys in 1996).

ORGANIZATIONAL EFFORTS:
Congressional Women's Caucus

After the dean of women in the House, Leonor Sullivan of Missouri, retired in 1977, momentum for a women's caucus developed rapidly. Sullivan had energetically opposed the formation of a caucus, fearing it would increase tensions with male colleagues and undo decades of women's efforts to work their way into the institutional power structure. Her departure, along with the retirements of veterans like Edith Green of Oregon and Julia Butler Hansen of Washington, removed the greatest roadblock to forming a caucus. Organizers acted quickly. Among the core founders were Elizabeth Holtzman of New York, Margaret Heckler of Massachusetts, Shirley Chisholm of New York, and Barbara Mikulski of Maryland. The Congresswomen's Caucus convened for its first meeting on April 19, 1977. Its primary purposes were to 1) inform Members about women's issues, 2) identify and create women's legislation, 3) follow floor action and support caucus legislation by testifying before committees and 4) monitor federal government initiatives affecting women.[8] Holtzman and Heckler served as the first co-chairs, imparting the bipartisan cast the group would retain. Fifteen women joined the caucus. Three women— Marilyn Lloyd of Tennessee, Marjorie Holt of Maryland, and Virginia Smith of Nebraska—initially declined membership because they felt their constituents would disapprove but later joined the caucus. The group also received a boost from important noncongressional entities, winning the enthusiastic endorsement of advocacy groups like the National Organization for Women (NOW) and the National Women's Political Caucus (NWPC), which had long sought a forum to convey policy ideas to women Members.

The Women's Caucus waged its first battle in 1977, obtaining an extension for the Equal Rights Amendment (ERA). The statute proposing the amendment passed Congress in March 1972, pending that three-quarters of state legislatures, ratified the amendment within seven years. By the end of 1973, 30 states had ratified it. Five more states approved the amendment between 1974 and 1976. In the meantime, four of the states that had approved the ERA indicated their intention to rescind support.

Thus, in 1977 the ERA was still short of the 38 states it needed for ratification before its expiration in 1979. In October 1977, Holtzman introduced legislation to obtain a seven-year extension. The Women's Caucus campaigned to win support for the measure when it was taken up before the House Judiciary Committee. In the end, the House voted 230 to 189 to extend the deadline for ratification three years to June 30, 1982. The Senate concurred, 60 to 36. However, the ERA lapsed, failing to obtain approval in any other state, and was not incorporated into the Constitution.

The Women's Caucus experienced a transition several years after its creation, as ideological differences emerged among Members and several key Members left Congress. In 1979, Millicent Fenwick of New Jersey resigned when the organization accepted outside contributions at a fundraiser for the Women's Research and Education Institute (WREI), which provided resources for education and outreach for the caucus and published the caucus newsletter, *Update*. "I don't think it's appropriate for Members of Congress to form a group and get deductibility for contributions made to that group," Fenwick said later.[9] Congresswoman Holtzman, one of the founders of the caucus, left Congress in 1981 when she lost a bid for a U.S. Senate seat from New York. In addition, Representative Gladys Spellman of Maryland, the caucus secretary and an important mediator among Members, suffered a heart attack in late 1980 and slipped into a coma from which she never regained consciousness.[10]

Caucus membership stagnated as the four Congresswomen elected in 1980—Lynn Martin of Illinois, Marge Roukema of New Jersey, Paula Hawkins of Florida, and Bobbi Fiedler of California—initially refused to join. Senator Hawkins asserted, "I don't believe in a women's caucus, black caucus, or any special interest caucus."[11] The conservative Hawkins also objected to key items on the caucus agenda. She called the Equal Rights Amendment "irrelevant" and "oversold, vaguely worded and ambiguous."[12] Hawkins added, "As women we're all for equality—or superiority. But there are better ways to attack the problems which have come to be known as women's issues. Elect more women to the United States Senate. It's women's fault for not running for office."[13] Other potential caucus members were disturbed by the fact that Schroeder, an outspoken liberal, had informally assumed the role of the group's spokesperson. "The dues were too high, and I don't need to pay that for a Pat Schroeder show," Lynn Martin said.[14] The four Republican women initially distanced themselves from the caucus to avoid the political costs of alienating the new Ronald Reagan administration and its large constituency. Eventually, four other conservative women—Beverly Byron of Maryland, Marilyn Lloyd, Marjorie Holt, and Virginia Smith, all among the least active caucus members—resigned for the same reason. By late 1981, only 10 of the 20 Congresswomen belonged to the Women's Caucus.

Declining enrollment and changes in the House rules forced the group to adopt new membership procedures, further altering its composition.[15] In October 1981, the House Administration Committee wrote new regulations that affected all 26 Legislative Service Organizations (LSOs), including the Women's Caucus, that operated in the institution. The new procedures stipulated that an LSO using House office space, supplies, and equipment could no longer receive funding from outside sources such as corporations or nonprofit foundations. With subscriptions to *Update* now defined as a source of outside revenue, the Women's Caucus was forced to either adopt new rules for dues and membership to retain its status as an LSO

Reproductive rights continued to be a political flashpoint in the late 20th century—and a major item on the legislative agenda of many women in Congress. In this 1993 photo, protestors from both sides of the debate gather outside the Supreme Court in Washington, D.C., as the Justices hear arguments in a case pertaining to pro-life supporters who picketed abortion clinics.

IMAGE COURTESY OF AP/WIDE WORLD PHOTOS

associated with the House or to cut its ties with the House and fund the WREI as a separate, off-site entity.

Thus, in March 1982, the Women's Caucus changed its name to the Congressional Caucus for Women's Issues and opened its ranks to male Members of Congress. "The Congresswomen's Caucus has gone co-ed," reported the *New York Times* when the policy was first approved.[16] Women paid $2,500 per year in dues, and men paid $500 per year in dues, for which they received a subscription to *Update* and a circumscribed role in the caucus meetings. Within months, more than 100 men had joined. The decision to allow men to join the caucus was not only financially advantageous, but also politically expedient. "We've known for some time that we had to broaden our base of support," Schroeder explained. "We knew that separatism was not the way to go. We need partnership with men in the women's movement." She added, "The money helps, of course, but it's much more than money we're interested in. We need allies on changing the multitude of discriminatory and inequitable laws."[17] The caucus kept its office in the Rayburn House Office Building and dropped outside funding.[18] By 1985, 110 men and 15 women were members of the caucus.[19]

By the 103rd Congress (1993–1995) the caucus had an annual budget of $250,000 and six full-time staff members who drafted and tracked a variety of bills related to women's issues. The 1992 elections doubled the caucus membership as 24 new women won election to the House. However, when the Republicans gained control of the House in 1995, the GOP leadership eliminated LSOs, forcing all caucuses—regardless of party affiliation—to operate without resources from the House. The Congressional Caucus for Women's Issues created Women's Policy, Inc., a nonprofit group that was moved out of House facilities. Like its predecessor, WREI, Women's Policy, Inc. was tasked with providing resources for outreach and education. Men were no longer allowed to be caucus members.[20] By the late 1990s, the caucus included virtually every woman House Member and had weathered its early divisions over issues like abortion. As Congress generally became more partisan, the caucus retained its bipartisanship, partly by keeping the co-chair structure, moving further from the divisive abortion issue, setting a working agenda at the start of each Congress, and pairing women from both parties to work jointly on introducing relevant legislation.

Women's Organizations and PACs

Historically, a lack of money had discouraged many women from seeking political office. Jeannette Rankin's 1916 campaign depended significantly on the largesse of her wealthy brother. Many of the early women in Congress—including Ruth Pratt of New York, Ruth Hanna McCormick of Illinois, Caroline O'Day of New York, Frances Bolton of Ohio, Clare Boothe Luce of Connecticut, and Katharine St. George of New York—won their first elections because they were independently wealthy. Campaign funding was a source of concern even for incumbent women in Congress. In 1962, Catherine D. Norrell of Arkansas, who had succeeded her late husband a year earlier, faced reapportionment and a campaign against a powerful incumbent. She seriously considered seeking a second term but, at the filing deadline, announced she would not seek re-election due to the exorbitant cost of campaigning. The expense of running campaign commercials on television, Norrell lamented, was transforming politics into "a rich person's game."[21] Senator Maurine Neuberger of Oregon left office after one term, citing health concerns. "But the real,

... in March 1982, the Women's Caucus changed its formal name to the Congressional Caucus for Women's Issues and opened its ranks to male Members of Congress.

actual, hard core reason I didn't run was raising the money I knew it was going to take," she recalled years later. "Each year it got more and more expensive, and I just didn't have the heart to go out and buttonhole people in various organizations from New York to California to Florida and Seattle to build a campaign chest."[22] Neuberger calculated that a 1966 Senate race would have cost at least $250,000. During the next four decades, campaign costs soared because of the expense of advertising on television, radio, and the Internet and because of the expense of hiring large, professional campaign staffs.

Norrell's and Neuberger's contemporaries outside government soon began to organize political groups to raise public awareness about women's issues and to generate the resources to field more women candidates. On June 30, 1966, the National Organization for Women was created at the Third National Conference of the Commission on the Status of Women. With Betty Friedan as its first president, NOW committed itself "to take action to bring women into full participation in the mainstream of American society now, exercising all privileges and responsibilities thereof in truly equal partnership with men."[23] The group organized mass rallies and protests, lobbied government officials, and initiated class-action lawsuits and other forms of litigation. Among its major aims were to champion women's reproductive freedom and economic equality, as well as to combat racial injustice and violence against women. NOW figured prominently in debates during the 1970s about the ERA and about a woman's right to seek an abortion. It became a powerful political and educational force, enrolling more than 500,000 members in more than 500 chapters nationwide by the first part of the 21st century.

In the late 1980s and early 1990s women's political action committees (PACs) played a critical role in raising money for candidates.[24] No single PAC surpassed the achievements of EMILY's List (an acronym for "Early Money Is Like Yeast" [it makes the dough rise]). Frustrated with Democratic women's lack of progress in gaining and retaining congressional seats, 25 women founded the group in 1985, culling their first donors from their personal contacts. EMILY's List raised money for pro-choice women candidates, whose numbers in the House had declined since the 1970s. Under the leadership of founder and president Ellen Malcolm, the group provided its membership with information on selected candidates and encouraged donors to contribute money directly to their campaigns. "Money is the first rule, the second rule, and the third rule" of campaign success, Malcolm observed.[25] In 1986, EMILY's List raised $350,000 from its 1,155 members to help Representative Barbara Mikulski of Maryland become the first Democratic woman to win election to the Senate without having her husband precede her. By the 2004 elections, more than 100,000 members had raised $10.1 million and EMILY's List had become America's largest PAC.[26] During the 1990s, the group went international, with EMILY's List UK established in 1993, followed in 1996 by EMILY's List Australia.

"Each year it got more and more expensive, and I just didn't have the heart to go out and buttonhole people in various organizations from New York to California to Florida and Seattle to build a campaign chest," recalled Senator Maurine Neuberger of Oregon about her decision to retire.

Institutional Developments

American politics in the late 20th century were shaped largely by the Vietnam War and the Watergate Scandal. Public approval of government plummeted as many Americans accused officials of secretly enlarging and then mismanaging the war in Southeast Asia and of abusing the constitutional powers of the presidency. Poll after poll revealed that Americans felt dissatisfied with and disconnected from their elected leaders.

In Congress, major changes resulted from the turbulent era of the 1960s and 1970s. Post-Watergate reforms opened congressional proceedings to the public, and committee hearings were largely opened to the public and to broadcasters. In 1979, the House began televising live broadcasts of House Floor proceedings with the Senate following suit several years later. This publicity not only made government more transparent, but it also exposed the partisanship of debates once settled behind closed doors.[27]

In 1994, during the "Republican Revolution," the GOP gained control of the House for the first time in 40 years—running on a national platform that featured a conservative document called the "Contract with America." Led by Speaker Newt Gingrich, the Republicans passed through the House large parts of their Contract, which promised to cut back welfare and entitlement programs, shrink federal bureaucracy, and reform House procedures. These efforts resulted in sharp ideological debates that were exacerbated by a shutdown of the federal government in 1995. In 1998, the partisanship in the closely divided Congress reached a new level of rancor, as the House impeached President Clinton based on his testimony about his extramarital relationship with a White House intern. However, the Senate failed to gain the two-thirds majority necessary to remove the President from office.

It was against this backdrop that the fourth generation of women entered Congress. An unprecedented ability to bring national attention to women's issues helped these Congresswomen pass laws that affected women's health, education, and

Representative Patricia Schroeder of Colorado (center) leads a delegation of Congresswomen on October 8, 1991, from the House side of the Capitol to the Senate to voice their concerns on the nomination of Clarence Thomas to the Supreme Court. Accompanying Schroeder (beginning second from left) are Congresswomen Louise Slaughter of New York, Barbara Boxer of California, Eleanor Holmes Norton of the District of Columbia, Nita Lowey of New York, Patsy Mink of Hawaii, and Jolene Unsoeld of Washington.

concerns in the workplace as well as family life. Moreover, women emerged from the struggle for women's rights in the 1960s and 1970s with a greater voice about a larger range of national issues. Over time, women Members authored legislation affecting every facet of American life—transportation and infrastructure, military affairs, international relations, economics, and social policy.

Committee Assignments

Unlike the Congresswomen of previous eras, the Congresswomen of this period had access to virtually all the committees in both Chambers, including the elite panels. A dozen of the women who entered the House from 1977 to 2005 served on the Appropriations Committee, 17 served on the Armed Services Committee, six women won seats on the Ways and Means Committee and also were assigned to on the Rules Committee. The most common committee assignments in the House reflected women's changing role in American society in the latter part of the 20th century—particularly the trend of more women entering the workforce. More than two dozen women served on committees with jurisdiction over finance and business—the Budget Committee, the Financial Services Committee (formerly Banking and Financial Services), and the Small Business Committee. Barbara Mikulski became the first woman to gain a seat on the influential Commerce Committee in 1977; more than a dozen women followed her. The Transportation and Infrastructure Committee—long a vehicle for Representatives seeking federal funding for local projects—was the most popular committee assignment for women in this era; more than 30 women served on the panel. More than two dozen women also served on the Science Committee and on the Government Reform Committee, which has oversight of the federal workforce.

Although women in the House continued to serve on committees that were traditionally part of their province such as Veterans' Affairs and Education and the Workforce (formerly Education and Labor), the number of women on these panels no longer outnumbered the number on the aforementioned panels. Moreover, while women still accounted for only a small number of the total membership of any given committee, their representation on key committees roughly equaled and, in some instances, exceeded their percentages in the chamber.[28]

Women's ability to secure better committee posts was most dramatic in the Senate, where the number of women in the chamber increased from one to 14 between 1977 and 2005. There were a number of "firsts." Most notably, Nancy Kassebaum of Kansas served on four committees to which women had not been assigned—Budget (1979), Foreign Relations (1977), Environment and Public Works (1977), and Select Intelligence (1979). In 1977, Maryon Allen of Alabama, a widow who served a brief portion of her late husband's term, was the first woman assigned to the influential Senate Judiciary Committee. The first women to serve a full term on that panel were Dianne Feinstein of California and Carol Moseley-Braun of Illinois. Moseley-Braun was also the first woman to serve on the powerful Senate Finance Committee (1993). As recently as 1997, Patty Murray of Washington became the first woman to serve on the Veterans' Affairs Committee. As in the House, the most common committee assignments for women in the Senate—Armed Services; Banking, Housing, and Urban Affairs; Commerce; Budget; Appropriations; Energy and Natural Resources; Foreign Relations; and Health, Education, Labor, and Pensions—reflected American women's expanded participation in the workplace and the military and in the formulation of foreign policy.

Over time, women Members authored legislation affecting every facet of American life—transportation and infrastructure, military affairs, international relations, economics, and social policy.

Legislative Interests

The Soviet bloc unraveled in the late 1980s as Moscow faced significant economic problems and resistance from its traditional Eastern European allies, particularly Poland. In the fall of 1989, the Berlin Wall—an internationally recognized symbol of the division of Europe—was opened, and the flow of people and commerce between West Germany and East Germany was renewed. By the early 1990s, the Soviet Union had disintegrated under the weight of a global struggle against the Western Alliance. For the first time in at least two generations, international affairs became less important to the ordinary American. (However, this temporary shift was radically altered by the terrorist attacks of September 11, 2001.)

With the end of the Cold War, the national focus turned to domestic matters, particularly the direction of the economy and the viability of large federally funded social programs. Welfare reform, nationalized health care, campaign finance reform, and the reduction of the federal deficit were hotly debated in the 1990s. Many of the federal programs initiated under the Great Society of the 1960s were sharply curtailed or eliminated. The issue of health care reform was debated but left largely unresolved, as the cost of medical insurance and prescription drugs skyrocketed. A technology boom, driven by the commercialization of Cold War military technologies such as computers and wireless communications, led to relative economic prosperity and lower federal deficits in the late 1990s.

With positions on key committees that allocated federal money, a caucus to educate and inform Members and the public, and public focus shifting to domestic policy, women in Congress spearheaded a number of successful efforts to pass legislation affecting women, both in the home and in the workplace. In 1978, the Women's Caucus rallied support for passage of the Pregnancy Discrimination Prohibition Act. The measure outlawed employers from discriminating against women on the basis of pregnancy, childbirth, or related medical conditions and required employers to provide health insurance for pregnant employees. Two measures—the Family Support Act of 1988 and the Child Support Recovery Act of 1992—implemented stricter procedures for enforcing child support and stiffened the penalties for delinquent parents. The Family Support Act of 1988 also extended childcare and medical benefits for families that had recently stopped receiving government assistance. In 1988, Congress passed the Women's Business Ownership Act, which created a program targeting service-related businesses owned by women and helped guarantee commercial bank loans of up to $50,000. This legislation also established the National Women's Business Council to monitor federal, state, and local programs aimed at helping women-owned businesses.

One of the most heralded pieces of legislation initiated by women in Congress—notably Patricia Schroeder and Marge Roukema—was the Family and Medical Leave Act. Passed by Congress in February 1993, this measure required employers to grant employees up to 12 weeks of unpaid leave each year for a chronic health problem, for the birth or adoption of a child, or for the care of a family member with a serious illness. Some Congresswomen observed afterward that men were quick to take credit for an issue that women had pushed initially and consistently. At the presidential bill signing ceremony, only male Senators and Representatives shared the stage with President Clinton and Vice President Al Gore. Schroeder, who was seated in the second row of the audience, complained that Congresswomen often received no acknowledgment for their contributions to legislation. "Often you see women start the issue, educate on the issue, fight for the issue, and then when it becomes fashionable, men push us aside," Schroeder observed, "and they get away with it."[29]

More major successes followed, however. In 1994, with the help of California Senator Barbara Boxer (who had spearheaded the effort as a House Member in the early 1990s), the Violence Against Women Act (VAWA) passed as part of a major omnibus crime bill. VAWA allocated $1.6 billion to prevent domestic abuse and other violent crimes against women—creating an Office on Violence Against Women in the U.S. Justice Department, disbursing funds for victims of abuse, and educating the public about a scourge that had been missing from the national dialogue.

Through the efforts of the Congressional Caucus for Women's Issues and the bipartisan work of leading Democratic and Republican women, major legislation was passed that altered research into diseases affecting women. In 1993, Congress passed the National Institutes of Health (NIH) Revitalization Act, which created the Office of Women's Health Research at NIH. This legislation appropriated funding for research on breast cancer, ovarian cancer, sexually transmitted diseases, and other disorders affecting women. Funding increased over the course of the 1990s, and informational campaigns raised public awareness. For example, in 1997 Congress passed the Stamp Out Breast Cancer Act, introduced by Representative Susan Molinari. The measure authorized the creation of a first-class postage stamp that raised millions of dollars for additional NIH programs.

The Decade of Women, 1992–2002

On election Tuesday 1992, American voters sent as many new women to Congress as were elected in any previous *decade*, beginning a decade of unparalleled gains for women in Congress. In November 2002, women attained another historic milestone when the House Democratic Caucus elected 15-year veteran Nancy Pelosi of California as Democratic Leader—making her the highest ranking woman in congressional history.

Expectations for a "breakthrough" year for women had been high since the late 1970s; in fact, 1984 had been hopefully, but prematurely, advertised as the "Year of the Woman." Political observers discussed the rise of a "gender gap," predicting that 6 million more women than men would vote in the 1984 elections.[30] When Congresswoman Geraldine Ferraro of New York was chosen as the Democratic candidate for Vice President that year—the first woman to appear on a major party ticket—expectations soared for a strong turnout by women at the polls. Jan Meyers of Kansas, one of a group of women running for national office in 1984, credited Ferraro's high profile with having "a very positive impact" on her campaign in suburban Kansas City for a House seat. Ferraro put women in the headlines, increased their credibility, and forced the Republican Party to focus on women voters, Meyers said shortly after winning a seat in Congress.[31] Some expected women to vote as a bloc on the hot-button issues that were important to them—reproductive rights, economic equality, and health care; the emergence of a women's voting bloc had been predicted since the passage of the 19th Amendment. But this bloc failed to materialize in 1984, and Ferraro and Democratic presidential candidate Walter Mondale of Minnesota lost in a landslide to the incumbent President Reagan.

Through the efforts of the Congressional Caucus for Women's Issues and the bipartisan work of leading Democratic and Republican women, major legislation was passed that altered research into diseases affecting women.

In 1992, women went to the polls, energized by a record-breaking number of women on the federal ticket. The results were unprecedented; the 24 women who won election to the U.S. House of Representatives for the first time that November comprised the largest number elected to the House in any single election, and the women elected to the Senate tripled the number of women in that chamber.[32] Dubbed the "Year of the Woman," 1992 also marked the beginning of a decade of remarkable gains for minority women. Twenty-three of the 34 African-American, Hispanic-American, and Asian-Pacific-American women who have served in Congress were elected between 1992 and 2005.

California's 1992 congressional races were a microcosm of the changes beginning to take place nationally. During the 102nd Congress, from 1991 to 1993, women held three seats on the California congressional delegation—roughly 6 percent. In 1992, a record 71 California women were nominated to run in the fall elections for federal and state offices; nationally 11 women won major party nominations for Senate races, while 106 women contended for House seats in the general election.[33] "The days of cold lonely fights of the '60s and '70s, when women were often laughed at as we tried to push for new opportunities, are over," said Lynn Schenk, a congressional candidate from San Diego. "No one's laughing now. If people truly want someone to be an agent of change, I'm that person. And being a woman is part of that."[34] Six new women Members from California, including Schenk, were elected to the House in the fall of 1992 alone. Two others, Representative Barbara Boxer and former San Francisco Mayor Dianne Feinstein, won election as U.S. Senators, making California the first state with two women in the Senate. By the 109th Congress in 2005, 21 members of the California congressional delegation were women—38 percent of the state's total representation in Congress.

Women's impressive gains in 1992 were not the product of any one galvanizing event, but rather the confluence of several long-term trends and short-term election year issues. Demographics, global politics, scandal, and the ripple effect of the women's liberation movement all played a part in the results of that historic election.

In 1992, the incumbent candidates faced a tougher-than-usual contest for re-election. An economic downturn that had begun in 1991 was predicted to be the leading edge of a long-term recession. American business mired as the country transitioned to a peace-time economy after the fall of the Soviet Union and the end of the Cold War. The national focus shifted from the Soviet–American conflict and national security to areas where women's influence was more established—education, health care, welfare reform, and the economy. While Americans worried about their jobs, they watched apprehensively the resurgent Japanese economy and the reunification of Germany. The check-writing scandal in the House "bank" (operated by the Sergeant at Arms), where a large number of Representatives had overdrawn their accounts—in some cases on hundreds of occasions—also contributed to the anti-incumbent sentiment within the electorate that disdained business-as-usual politics in Washington. Moreover, the debate over the abortion issue had reached a divisive point, with a pro-life President in the White House and the Supreme Court considering a ruling that could have reversed *Roe v. Wade*.

The issue of whom President George H. W. Bush's administration would appoint to replace retiring Supreme Court Justice Thurgood Marshall became a galvanizing one for women candidates. Bush nominated Clarence Thomas, a con-

servative he had earlier appointed to the U.S. Court of Appeals. Thomas's antiabortion stance, as well as his opposition to affirmative action, made him a lightning rod for liberal groups and Democratic Senators. But his confirmation hearings became a public forum on sexual harassment in the workplace when Thomas's former aide Anita Hill accused him in televised hearings before the Senate Judiciary Committee of making unwanted advances. Beamed into millions of homes, the spectacle of the all-male Judiciary Committee offering Hill little sympathy and at moments treating her with outright hostility reinforced the perception that women's perspectives received short shrift on Capitol Hill. Seven Democratic women from the House marched in protest to address the caucus of their Democratic Senate colleagues, but they were rebuffed.

While controversy stirred by the Thomas–Hill episode provided good campaign rhetoric and a convenient media explanation for the "Year of the Woman," other contributing factors included the availability of funding, the growing pool of women candidates with elective experience, and the presence of a Democratic presidential candidate, who shared their beliefs on many of the issues (24 of the 27 women elected that fall were Democrats). Also significant were the effects of redistricting after the 1990 Census, the large number of retiring Members, and the casualties of the House banking scandal; the combination of these effects created 93 open seats in the U.S. House during the 1992 elections.[35] Candidates of both genders embraced the popular theme of change in government by stressing their credentials as Washington outsiders, but women benefited more from this perception, because they had long been marginalized in the Washington political process. As Elizabeth Furse, a successful candidate for an Oregon House seat, pointed out during her campaign: "People see women as agents of change. Women are seen as outsiders, outside the good old boy network which people are perceiving has caused so many of the economic problems we see today."[36]

For all the media attention paid to the "Year of the Woman," it was but a part of the larger trend of women's movement into elective office. A number of women expressed exasperation with the media focus that hyped the sensational news story but largely ignored more enduring trends and influences. "The year of the woman in retrospect was a small gain, but it was the start of what was a big gain," Senator Barbara Boxer observed a decade later. "I don't even think it was the year of the woman then, but it started the trend of electing more women."[37] Others felt the label diminished women's achievement and reinforced perceptions that their impact on Congress was temporary. As Senator Barbara Mikulski of Maryland said: "Calling 1992 the Year of the Woman makes it sound like the Year of the Caribou or the Year of the Asparagus. We're not a fad, a fancy, or a year."[38]

The trend that culminated in the 1990s had begun decades earlier in the state legislatures, where women began to accumulate political experience that prepared them to be legislators. The first Congresswoman with elective experience in a state legislature was Kathryn O'Loughlin McCarthy of Kansas. For decades McCarthy proved the exception to the rule; between her election to Congress in 1932 and 1970, when great numbers of women began to serve in state capitols, hardly more than a dozen Congresswomen had held a seat in the state legislature or a statewide elective office. It was only in the last 30 years of the 20th century that women made significant gains in state legislatures and, subsequently, the U.S. Congress. For example, in 1970 women held about four percent (301 seats) of all the seats in state legislatures nationwide. In 1997 that figure plateaued at around 1,600, and for the next five years women made up about 22 percent of state legislators nationally. In 2003, 1,648 (22.3 percent) of the 7,382 state legislators in the United States were women.[39]

Ultimately, however, the "Year of the Woman" spawned expectations that women candidates in subsequent elections could not realistically meet. Contrary to widely held beliefs, women were not about to change the political culture overnight—especially not on seniority-based Capitol Hill. Later political battles over issues such as reproductive rights, welfare reform, and the federal deficit dashed hopes that women would unite across party lines, subordinate ideology to pragmatism, and increase their power.

Moreover, the belief that sexism would be eradicated proved overly optimistic, as old stereotypes persisted. Along with Representatives Barbara Boxer and Marcy Kaptur of Ohio, Mary Rose Oakar of Ohio led a 1985 protest of House women demanding equal access to the House gym and fitness facilities. Unhappy that the women's gym lacked the modern exercise equipment, swimming pool, and basketball court accessible to the male Members, the three lawmakers made their pitch in a song belted out to the tune of "Has Anyone Seen My Gal?" before a meeting of the House Democratic Whips.[40] However, women still contended with unequal access to gym facilities and other indications of sexism.[41] Once when fellow freshman Leslie Byrne of Virginia entered an elevator full of Members, a Congressman remarked, "It sure is nice to have you ladies here. It spiffs up the place." Exasperated, Byrne quipped, "Yup, chicks in Congress."[42] Another Member of the class of '92 observed that Congress had failed to keep pace with changes in American society. "Out in the real world, we took care of a lot of these basic issues between men and women years ago," said Lynn Schenk. "But this place has been so insulated, the shock waves of the '70s and '80s haven't quite made it through the walls."[43]

After the 1992 elections, women Members were still in a distinct minority, although for the first time in congressional history they accounted for more than 10

The trend that culminated in the 1990s had begun decades earlier in the state legislatures, where women began to accumulate the kind of political experience that prepared them as campaigners and as legislators.

percent of the total membership. Subsequent growth was slower, though steady. On average since 1992, 10 new women have been elected to Congress each election cycle, while incumbency rates have remained well above 90 percent. In August 2005, women made up 15.5 percent of Congress—an all-time high. Some women noted that although they had failed to achieve numerical parity in Congress, they had dramatically altered the political culture within the electorate. "In previous years, when I have run for office, I always had to overcome being a woman," said Texas Senator Kay Bailey Hutchison. "All I've ever wanted was an equal chance to make my case, and I think we're getting to that point—and that's the victory."[44]

COMMITTEE AND PARTY LEADERSHIP

The women who entered office in record numbers in the 1990s soon accrued seniority in committees and catapulted into top leadership posts. This trend ran counter to historical precedent, although arguably the most powerful and influential woman to head a committee was one of the first: Mary T. Norton chaired four House committees during the 1930s and 1940s—Labor, House Administration, District of Columbia, and Memorials. However, Norton's experience was unusual and, tellingly, she never held a top leadership job in the Democratic Party during her 25 years in the House. As late as the spring of 1992, the iconic feminist Congresswoman Pat Schroeder observed that the wheels of sexual equality on Capitol Hill turned slowly. "It's not revolutionary, it's evolutionary," Schroeder said. "We get some appointments, we get some this, we get some that. But to think that women get any power positions, that we've become the bull elephants, that we're the kahunas or whatever, well, we're not."[45]

Unlike the third generation of women in Congress, the fourth generation often chose to confront the institution less directly. Whereas Bella Abzug's generation worked against the congressional establishment to breach gender barriers, many women in the fourth generation worked for change from within the power structure. Women in the 1980s and early 1990s who moved into leadership posts did so largely by working within traditional boundaries—a time-honored approach that extended back to Mary Norton and Edith Nourse Rogers in the first generation of Congresswomen. The careers of Lynn Martin and Barbara Kennelly of Connecticut illustrate this tendency: Martin served as Vice Chair of the GOP Conference; Kennelly served as the Democratic Party's Chief Deputy Whip (a position created for her) and eventually became Vice Chair of the Democratic Caucus. Congresswoman Geraldine Ferraro also possessed an ability to work with the House leadership, particularly Speaker Tip O'Neill of Massachusetts, in a way her male colleagues perceived as "nonthreatening." As Ferraro's colleague Marge Roukema observed, Ferraro "takes a feminist stand but works only within the art of the possible."[46] The Congresswoman's pragmatism struck a balance that was pleasing to both Capitol Hill insiders and feminists. Betty Friedan, founder of NOW, judged that Ferraro was "no cream puff; she's a tough dame."[47] Other women who were influential in their parties followed a similarly pragmatic approach. "I worry about marginalizing women in the institution," said freshman Rosa DeLauro of Connecticut in 1992. "It's a very competitive place, and what you need to do is build coalitions, and since there are 29 women who don't think alike, you build coalitions among women, and you build coalitions among men. If you sit

After the 1992 elections, women Members were still in a distinct minority, although for the first time in congressional history they accounted for more than 10 percent of the total membership.

there and say, 'I'm a woman, we're in the minority here,' then you're never going to get anywhere in this body."[48]

Nevertheless, until 1992, women had been on the margins of institutional leadership. Fewer than 10 women had chaired full congressional committees, and just eight House and Senate women had held positions in the party leadership. The two highest-ranking women in House were still at considerable remove from the levers of power: Mary Rose Oakar was Vice Chair of the Democratic Caucus and Lynn Martin was Vice Chair of the Republican Conference in the 99th and the 100th Congresses (1985–1989). The highest-ranking woman in Senate history was Margaret Chase Smith of Maine, whom GOP peers elected Chair of the Republican Conference in the 90th through the 92nd Congresses (1967–1973).

Three women led committees in the 104th Congress (1995–1997): Jan Meyers chaired the House Small Business Committee, Nancy Johnson chaired the House Committee on Standards of Official Conduct, and Nancy Landon Kassebaum chaired the Senate Labor and Human Resources Committee. Kassebaum's post was particularly noteworthy, as she was the first woman in Senate history to head a major standing committee. However, by the end of the 104th Congress, Meyers, Johnson, and Kassebaum had either left their posts or retired from Congress. The only other women to chair congressional committees during this period were Senators Olympia Snowe (Small Business) and Susan Collins (Governmental Affairs) in the 108th and 109th Congresses (2003–2007).

But gradual changes in the 1990s had begun to alter the leadership makeup in ways that portended greater involvement for women. From the 103rd through the 108th Congresses (1993–2005), 12 more women moved into the leadership ranks. Representatives Susan Molinari, Jennifer Dunn of Washington, Tillie Fowler of Florida, and Deborah Pryce of Ohio served as the Vice Chair of the House Republican Conference from the 104th through the 107th Congresses, respectively. In the 108th Congress, Pryce, who first won election to Congress in the "Year of the Woman," became the highest-ranking woman in House GOP history when she was elected Chair of the Republican Conference. Her accomplishment was exceeded only by that of Congresswoman Nancy Pelosi of California, who had succeeded Representative Sala Burton of California in the House after her death in 1987. In 2001, Pelosi won the Democratic Caucus contest for Whip. Little more than a year later, when Representative Dick Gephardt of Missouri left the Democratic Party's top post, Pelosi overwhelmingly won her colleagues' support in her bid to become House Democratic Leader. This event garnered national and international attention.

Meanwhile, many of the women elected in the 1990s accrued seniority and, as a result, more important committee assignments. Though not yet apparent in the chairmanships of full committees, this power shift was evident in the chairmanships of subcommittees—a key prerequisite for chairing a full committee. Since the 80th Congress (1947–1949)—the first Congress for which such records are readily accessible—54 women have chaired House or Senate subcommittees. Three women—Margaret Chase Smith, Barbara Mikulski and Barbara Boxer—chaired subcommittees in both the House and the Senate. While just two women—Representatives Smith and Bolton—chaired House subcommittees in the 80th Congress (there were no women chairing Senate subcommittees at the time), by the 109th Congress in 2005, 10 women chaired subcommittees in the House and the

Senate. More telling, roughly half the women in congressional history who chaired subcommittees attained these posts after 1992.

Representatives Pelosi and Pryce were on the leading edge of the spike in women elected to Congress. Pryce was elected to Congress at age 41 and attained her leadership post at 51. Pelosi arrived in the House at age 47 and was elected House Democratic Leader at 62. Behind these two leaders are a host of women who were elected in the latter 1990s. When elected, some of these women were 10 years younger than Pelosi and Pryce upon their arrival in Congress, giving them additional tenure to accrue seniority and power. If present trends continue and more and younger women are elected to Congress, women will likely become better represented in high committee posts and the leadership.

NOTES

1 Barry M. Horstman, "Women Poised to Make Big Political Gains," 24 August 1992, *Los Angeles Times.*

2 At least two husbands have attempted to directly succeed their wives in the House. In 1980, Gladys Noon Spellman of Maryland suffered a heart attack and lapsed into a coma from which she never recovered. When the House declared her seat vacant in early 1981, her husband, Reuben Spellman, entered the April 1981 Democratic primary but lost. After Patsy Mink of Hawaii died in September 2002, her husband, John Francis Mink, was one of more than 30 candidates in a special election to fill her seat for the remainder of the 107th Congress. He, too, was unsuccessful.

3 Five of the aforementioned group had a combination of state legislative and state executive or federal office experience.

4 Statistics based on the 2000 U.S. Census. Figures are from chart QT-P20: "Educational Attainment by Sex: 2000." Available online at http://factfinder.census.gov.

5 For information on the average age of congressional Membership, see the *CQ Guide to Congress,* 4th ed, p. 700 and the Congressional Research Service (CRS) Profiles of the 103rd to 109th Congresses.

6 David Finkel, "Women on the Verge of a Power Breakthrough," 10 May 1992, *Washington Post Magazine:* W15.

7 Finkel, "Women on the Verge of a Power Breakthrough."

8 Irwin Gertzog, *Congressional Women: Their Recruitment, Behavior, and Integration* (Westport, CT: Praeger, 1995): 186. For a detailed analysis of the Women's Caucus that extends into the late 1990s, see Gertzog's *Women and Power on Capitol Hill: Reconstructing the Congressional Women's Caucus* (Boulder, CO: Rienner Publishers, 2004).

9 Lynn Rosellini, "Dues Plan Divides Women's Caucus," 16 July 1981, *New York Times:* C13.

10 Gertzog, *Congressional Women: Their Recruitment, Behavior, and Integration*: 200–202.

11 Rosellini, "Dues Plan Divides Women's Caucus."

12 "Paula Hawkins," *Current Biography 1985* (New York: H.W. Wilson and Company, 1985): 176.

13 Elizabeth Bumiller, "The Lady Is the Tigress: Paula Hawkins, Florida's Pugnacious New Senator," 2 December 1980, *Washington Post:* B1; Jo Thomas, "Mrs. Hawkins, the Battling Housewife, Goes to Washington," 7 November 1980, *New York Times:* 18.

14 Gertzog, *Congressional Women:* 204–205.

15 Ibid., 209–212.

16 Majorie Hunter, "Congresswomen Admit 46 Men to Their Caucus," *New York Times,* 14 December 1981, *New York Times:* D10.

17 Hunter, "Congresswomen Admit 46 Men to Their Caucus."

18 Ibid.

19 Barbara Gamarekian, "Women's Caucus: Eight Years of Progress," 27 May 1985, *New York Times:* A20.

20 Kevin Merida, "Role of House Women's Caucus Changes," 15 February 1995, *Washington Post:* A4; see also "The Women's Caucus: Caucus History," http://www.womenspolicy.org/caucus/history.html (accessed 28 April 2005).

21 Hope Chamberlin, *A Minority of Members: Women in the U.S. Congress* (New York: Praeger, 1973): 289.

22 Maurine Neuberger, Oral History Interview, April 5 and 17, 1979; May 1, 10, 15, 1979, conducted by the U.S. Association of Former Members of Congress, Inc., Manuscript Room, Library of Congress, Washington, D.C.

23 National Organization for Women Web site: http://www.now.org/organization/faq.html (accessed 17 May 2005).

24 Other influential PACs included the nonpartisan Women's Campaign Fund, created in 1974 to fund pro-choice political candidates; WISH ("Women in the Senate and House") List, which supports pro-choice Republican women; and the National Women's Political Caucus, founded in the early 1970s, to promote women's participation in the political process by supporting pro-choice women at all levels of government and providing political training for its members. In the 1990s and 2000s, a number of pro-life PACs were founded to support candidates who opposed abortion procedures. These groups included the Republican National Coalition for Life, founded by Phyllis Schlafly in 1990; the National Pro-Life Alliance; and the Pro-Life Campaign Committee.

25 Charles Trueheart, "Politics' New Wave of Women; With Voters Ready for a Change, Candidates Make Their Move," 7 April 1992, *Washington Post*: E1.

26 http://www.emilyslist.org/about/history.phtml (accessed 13 June 2003; 28 April 2005).

27 Julian E. Zelizer, *On Capitol Hill: The Struggle to Reform Congress and Its Consequences, 1948–2000* (New York: Cambridge University Press, 2004): see especially, 206–232.

28 For instance, by the 109th Congress (2005–2007), eight women served on the Appropriations Committee (12 percent of its membership), and 11 women held seats on the Energy and Commerce Committee (19 percent). The terrorist attacks of September 11, 2001, also changed the way Congress did business. A Select Committee on Homeland Security was created in the 108th Congress and was later made permanent in the 109th Congress. The new panel included eight women Members (23.5 percent).

29 Joan A. Lowy, *Pat Schroeder: A Woman in the House* (Albuquerque, NM: University of New Mexico Press, 2003): 100.

30 See, for example, Jane Perlez, "Women, Power, and Politics," 24 June 1984, *New York Times*: SM22.

31 Bill Peterson, "Reagan Did Understand Women: While Democrats Slept, the GOP Skillfully Captured Their Votes," 3 March 1985, *Washington Post*: C5.

32 Twenty-four women had been elected to the House in the decade running from 1980 to 1989; 23 were elected between 1970 and 1979.

33 Susan Yoachum and Robert B. Gunnison, "Women Candidates Win Record 71 Nominations," 4 June 1992, *San Francisco Chronicle*: A1; Jackie Koszczuk, "Year of the Woman? Political Myth Fades," 18 October 1992, *Wisconsin State Journal*: 1E. Heading into the primaries in 1992 an unprecedented 37 California women were candidates for U.S. House and Senate seats (as well as an equally exceptional number of 127 for the California Assembly); these numbers reflected the larger national trend, where 157 women were running in the Democratic and Republican primaries for the U.S. House (140) and the Senate (17). Previously, the largest number of women contenders was 10 for Senate seats (1984) and 70 for House seats (1990).

34 Barry M. Horstman, "San Diego County Elections; Women Flex Muscles in County Races," 4 June 1992, *Los Angeles Times*: B1.

35 Adam Clymer, "In 2002, Woman's Place May Be in the Statehouse," 15 April 2002, *New York Times*: A1.

36 Trueheart, "Politics' New Wave of Women; With Voters Ready for a Change, Candidates Make Their Move."

37 Lauren Whittington, "Women See Gains Slowing: Number of Female Lawmakers Not Expected to Rise Dramatically," 19 September 2002, *Roll Call:* 13, 20.

38 Barbara Mikulski et al. *Nine and Counting: The Women of the Senate* (New York: Morrow, 2000): 46–50.

39 See "Women in State Legislatures 2001," (December 2001) and "Women in Elective Office 2002," (June 2002), *Center for American Women and Politics,* Rutgers University, http://www.cawp.rutgers.edu. Of the top 10 states with the highest percentages of women legislators in 2003, seven were western states: Washington (36.7 percent), Colorado (34 percent), Oregon (31.1 percent), California (30 percent), New Mexico (29.5 percent), and Nevada (28.6 percent). Four eastern states round out the list: Maryland (33 percent), Vermont (30.6 percent), Connecticut (29.4 percent), and Delaware (29 percent).

40 Marjorie Hunter, "A Woman's Place, They Say, Is in the Gym," 16 June 1985, *New York Times:* 40.

41 Finkel, "Women on the Verge of a Power Breakthrough."

42 Rich Heidorn, "Capitol Offense: No Longer Darlings, Congress' Women Look Ahead," *Chicago Tribune,* 16 October 1994: woman news, 5.

43 Karen Ball, "Congressional Women: Wave of Change Never Made It Through Capitol Walls," 7 September 1993, Associated Press.

44 Whittington, "Women See Gains Slowing."

45 Finkel, "Women on the Verge of a Power Breakthrough."

46 "Woman in the News: Liberal Democrat from Queens," 13 July 1984, *New York Times:* A1.

47 "A Team Player, Can a Liberal from Archie Bunker Country Make a Contender of Walter Mondale?", 23 July 1984, *Newsweek.*

48 Finkel, "Women on the Verge of a Power Breakthrough."

Visual Statistics V

This chart shows the party affiliation of all Members of Congress from 1935 to 1955. The following chart shows a party breakdown only for women Members during this time period.

House and Senate Party Affiliation[1]
95TH–109TH CONGRESSES (1977–2007)

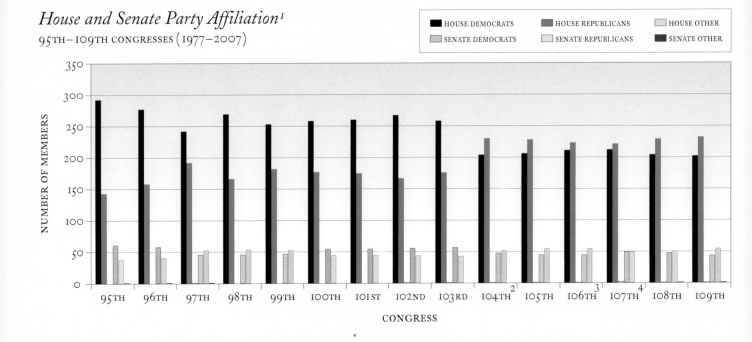

Party Affiliation: Women in Congress
95TH–109TH CONGRESSES (1977–2007)

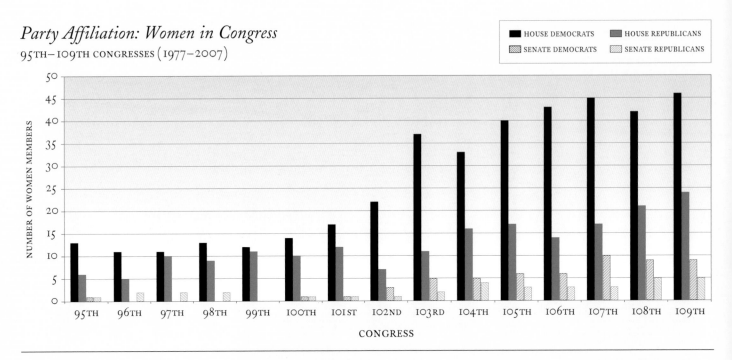

1. House numbers do not include Delegates or Resident Commissioners. Sources: Office of the Clerk, U.S. House of Representatives; U.S. Senate Historical Office.

2. Party ratio changed to 53 Republicans and 47 Democrats after Richard Shelby of Alabama switched from the Democratic to Republican party on November 9, 1994. It changed again, to 54 Republicans and 46 Democrats, when Ben Nighthorse Campbell of Colorado switched from the Democratic to Republican party on March 3, 1995. When Robert Packwood (R-OR) resigned on October 1, 1995, the Senate divided between 53 Republicans and 46 Democrats with one vacancy. Ron Wyden (D) returned the ratio to 53 Republicans and 47 Democrats when he was elected to fill the vacant Oregon seat. [U.S. Senate Historical Office]

3. As the 106th Congress began, the division was 55 Republican seats and 45 Democratic seats, but this changed to 54–45 on July 13, 1999 when Senator Bob Smith of New Hampshire switched from the Republican party to Independent status. On November 1, 1999, Smith announced his return to the Republican party, making the division once more 55 Republicans and 45 Democrats. Following the death of Senator Paul Coverdell (R-GA) on July 18, 2000, the balance shifted again, to 54 Republicans and 46 Democrats, when the governor appointed Zell Miller, a Democrat, to fill the vacancy. [U.S. Senate Historical Office]

Women Elected to Congress by Decade [5]

AS A PERCENTAGE OF THE TOTAL NUMBER OF WOMEN
WHO SERVED FROM 1917–2006

This chart illustrates women's dramatic gains in Congress, particularly in the last four decades. Two thirds of all 229 women in congressional history have entered office since 1970.

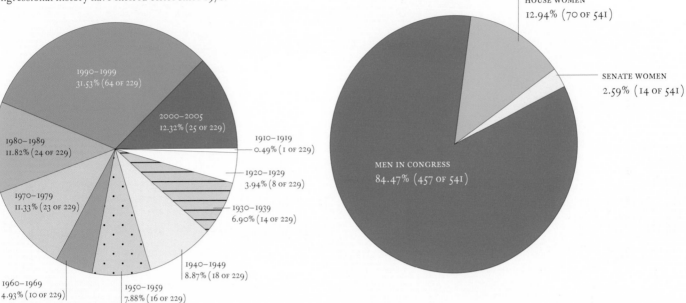

1990–1999
31.53% (64 OF 229)

2000–2005
12.32% (25 OF 229)

1910–1919
0.49% (1 OF 229)

1980–1989
11.82% (24 OF 229)

1920–1929
3.94% (8 OF 229)

1930–1939
6.90% (14 OF 229)

1970–1979
11.33% (23 OF 229)

1940–1949
8.87% (18 OF 229)

1960–1969
4.93% (10 OF 229)

1950–1959
7.88% (16 OF 229)

Women as a Percentage of Congress

109TH CONGRESS (2005–2007)

The most women in any Congress to date—a total of 84—served in the 109th Congress (2005–2007). This chart illustrates the number of seats (540 total) held by women compared to those held by men.

HOUSE WOMEN
12.94% (70 OF 541)

SENATE WOMEN
2.59% (14 OF 541)

MEN IN CONGRESS
84.47% (457 OF 541)

Women of Color in Congress [6]

89TH–109TH CONGRESSES (1965–2007)

This chart shows the number of women of color who served in Congress between 1965 and 2005 broken down by ethnic or racial group.

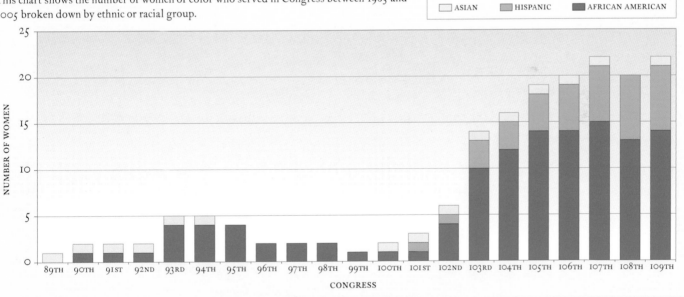

☐ ASIAN ☐ HISPANIC ■ AFRICAN AMERICAN

NUMBER OF WOMEN

CONGRESS — 89TH, 90TH, 91ST, 92ND, 93RD, 94TH, 95TH, 96TH, 97TH, 98TH, 99TH, 100TH, 101ST, 102ND, 103RD, 104TH, 105TH, 106TH, 107TH, 108TH, 109TH

4. From January 3 to January 20, 2001, with the Senate divided evenly between the two parties, the Democrats held the majority due to the deciding vote of outgoing Democratic Vice President Al Gore. Senator Thomas A. Daschle served as majority leader at that time. Beginning on January 20, 2001, Republican Vice President Richard Cheney held the deciding vote, giving the majority to the Republicans. Senator Trent Lott resumed his position as majority leader on that date. On May 24, 2001, Senator James Jeffords of Vermont announced his switch from Republican to Independent status, effective June 6, 2001. Jeffords announced that he would caucus with the Democrats, giving the Democrats a one-seat advantage, changing control of the Senate from the Republicans back to the Democrats. Senator Thomas A. Daschle again became majority leader on June 6, 2001. Senator Paul D. Wellstone (D-MN) died on October 25, 2002, and Independent Dean Barkley was appointed to fill the vacancy. The November 5, 2002, election brought to office elected Senator James Talent (R-MO), replacing appointed Senator Jean Carnahan (D-MO), shifting balance once again to the Republicans—but no reorganization was completed at that time since the Senate was out of session. [U.S. Senate Historical Office]

5. Source: *Biographical Directory of the United States Congress, 1774–2005* (Washington D.C.: Government Printing Office, 2005); also available at: http://bioguide.congress.gov. See also Mildred Amer, "Women in the United States Congress, 1774–2005," 1 July 2004, Congressional Research Service (CRS) Report.

6. Source: Appendix H –Women of Color in Congress, 1965–2006

Mary Rose Oakar
1940–

UNITED STATES REPRESENTATIVE ★ DEMOCRAT FROM OHIO
1977–1993

During her 16-year tenure, Congresswoman Mary Rose Oakar was dedicated to improving the economic welfare of women. She led the charge in Congress for women's rights, though she often came into conflict with national women's groups for her staunch pro-life position. Representative Oakar became an influential figure in the Democratic Party, climbing the leadership ladder by mastering House internal procedures and administration.

Mary Rose Oakar, the youngest of five children, was born in Cleveland, Ohio, on March 5, 1940, to parents of Lebanese and Syrian ancestry. Her father was a laborer and her mother a homemaker. Working her way through school as a telephone operator, Oakar graduated from Ursuline College in 1962 with a B.A. degree, and earned an M.A. four years later from John Carroll University, both in Ohio. She also studied at the Royal Academy of Dramatic Arts in London, Westham Adult College in England, and Columbia University in New York City. From 1963 to 1975, Oakar taught at a Cleveland high school and at Cuyahoga Community College. She served on Cleveland's city council from 1973 to 1976. As a member of the city council, Oakar became a popular local leader who earned the reputation of being an aggressive advocate for women, children, and the elderly. She won support for her personalized campaign strategy which included distributing pens decorated with roses–a tactic to remind voters of her name.[1]

Hoping to capitalize on her strong local ties and political experience, Oakar entered the 1976 Democratic primary for the heavily Democratic congressional district encompassing much of Cleveland west of the Cuyahoga River, vacated by James Stanton, who made an unsuccess-

ful bid for the U.S. Senate. During the campaign she emphasized her status as the only woman in the race, declaring the need for more women in Congress to offset what she perceived as the arrogance exuded by many Congressmen. She also highlighted her Cleveland roots when making campaign stops–via her convertible adorned with roses–in the community. "The overriding issue is that people want to feel the person who represents you at the federal level is close to you," she remarked.[2] She defeated 11 other candidates with 24 percent of the vote. Oakar then dominated the general election, capturing 81 percent of the vote against two Independent candidates. In her seven successful re-election bids through 1990 in the heavily Democratic district, she never faced a serious challenge, often receiving no opposition from Republican candidates.[3]

In the 95th Congress (1977–1979), Oakar served on the Banking, Finance, and Urban Affairs Committee, and she introduced successful legislation to commemorate the work of suffragist Susan B. Anthony by creating a $1 coin featuring her likeness.[4] She eventually chaired the Banking Subcommittee on Economic Stabilization. Oakar subsequently was appointed to several more committees, including the House Select Committee on Aging in the 96th Congress (1979–1981), the Post Office and Civil Service Committee in the 97th Congress (1981–1983), and the House Administration Committee in the 98th Congress (1983–1985). She served on these committees through the 102nd Congress (1991–1993).

Oakar developed a reputation as a liberal who worked on behalf of women's rights issues, especially economic parity. "Economic security is the truly liberating issue for women," she said. "If you're economically liberated, you're free to pursue other avenues in your life."[5] As chair

of the Post Office and Civil Service Subcommittee on
Compensation and Employee Benefits, she sponsored two
bills during the mid-1980s: the Pay Equity Act and the
Federal Pay Equity Act. Both revived a longtime effort
among women in Congress to achieve salary equity with
men for employment of comparable worth. Charging that
"employers have used gender as a determining factor when
setting pay rates," Oakar stressed the need for a comprehensive study investigating pay discrepancies between men
and women both in the private sector and in the federal
government.

The congressional debates about equal pay received
national attention. Conservative activist Phyllis Schlafly
labeled Oakar's efforts of advocating pay raises for profes-
sions typically occupied by women, such as teaching and
nursing, as an attack against blue-collar men. Oakar countered Schlafly by claiming salary increases for women
would help men because it would lead to stronger
families.[6] In a 1985 House hearing on economic parity,
Oakar received additional criticism, this time from
Clarence M. Pendleton, Jr., chairman of the U.S.
Commission on Civil Rights, who branded Oakar's proposed legislation as "Looney Tunes" and "socialism without a plan." She insisted that Congress needed to intervene
to correct gender pay inequity and dismissed Pendleton's
commission, arguing that "it has ceased to be a champion
of civil rights."[7]

Oakar dissented from the Democratic majority on two
high-profile issues. As one of the few Arab Americans
serving in Congress during the 1980s, she suggested that
the Ronald W. Reagan administration's foreign policy tilted too much toward the interests of Israel. On another
front, her pro-life stance caused friction with powerful
women's groups like the National Organization for
Women (NOW), undermining her potential to emerge as a
leading public figure in feminist circles. Although frustrated with her inability to connect with leading women's
organizations, Oakar encouraged all women, including her
colleagues on Capitol Hill, to work for equality with men.
"There are only 24 women in Congress," she declared. "It
seems to me, beyond all other issues, we're obligated to

correct inequities toward our own gender. No one else is
going to do it."[8]

Oakar built a reputation as an expert on House rules
and procedures, and it was in this capacity that she worked
her way into the Democratic leadership. On the House
Administration Committee, which she joined in 1984,
Oakar eventually rose to chair its Subcommittee on Police
and Personnel. She worked in the Democratic Whip organization and traveled around the country on behalf of fellow
Democratic candidates. Oakar was elected Secretary of the
House Democratic Caucus in the 99th Congress
(1985–1987), one of a handful of women in either party to
hold a leadership position. The previous secretary of the
Caucus and the Democratic vice presidential nominee in
1984, Geraldine Ferraro of New York, contacted Oakar
shortly after the Ohio Representative assumed her new
position. According to Oakar, Ferraro coupled congratulations with a warning that the male-dominated Democratic
leadership would exclude her from significant meetings.
Oakar informed Speaker of the House Thomas (Tip)
O'Neill, Jr., of Massachusetts that she expected to be
treated as an equal. Despite her pre-emptive strategy, she
was not invited to the first White House meeting of the
new Congress. Oakar objected with such intensity that the
Speaker made certain she always had the opportunity to
attend leadership meetings. Quite often the only woman in
attendance, she compared herself to Ferraro, commenting,
"Each of us had to break down a barrier."[9] After the position was renamed "Vice Chair" during the 100th Congress
(1987–1989), Oakar made a spirited attempt to gain the
fourth most powerful seat in the House–Chair of the
Democratic Caucus. Though her campaign employed
such innovative tactics as buttons, posters, and even a full-
page advertisement in the congressional newspaper *Roll
Call* entitled, "Mary Rose: She Earned It," Oakar failed to
achieve her goal, losing to then-Budget Chairman
William H. Gray III of Pennsylvania.[10]

In the spring of 1992, Congresswoman Oakar received
her first significant primary challenge in her newly reapportioned district in western Cleveland. Oakar had
been linked to a scandal that revolved around dozens of

Representatives (focusing on about 20) who had written more than 11,000 overdrafts in a three-year period from the House "bank"—an informal money service provided by the House Sergeant at Arms. Oakar wrote 213 overdrafts during that period for an undisclosed amount of money, and she resigned from her prominent position as co-chairwoman of the Democratic Platform Committee for that summer's Democratic National Convention.[11] After this embarrassing incident, Oakar burnished her credentials as a caretaker for the district and an advocate for health care and the elderly. Oakar defeated Tim Hagan in the June 2 primary with 30 to 39 percent of the vote (five other contenders split the remainder). Oakar described the result as "a tribute to the people I represent" and as "an outpouring of affection" from voters on her behalf.[12] In the general election, however, she faced a difficult task making inroads with voters in the two-fifths of the district that had been incorporated after apportionment. In addition, the fall 1992 elections were difficult for many congressional incumbents because of redistricting and the down-turning economy. In November, Republican challenger Martin R. Hoke defeated Oakar by a plurality of 30,000 votes, 57 to 43 percent.[13]

After Congress, Oakar was indicted on charges of receiving illegal campaign contributions. She pled guilty in March 1995 and received two years' probation, community service, and fines.[14] Oakar's work on behalf of the elderly continued, however, as President William J. Clinton appointed her in 1995 to the 25-member advisory board for the White House Conference on Aging. She went on to work as a business executive and consultant. Oakar was elected to the Ohio state house of representatives, where she served from 2001 to 2003. In June 2003, Oakar was named President of the American Arab Anti-Discrimination Committee.

FOR FURTHER READING

Biographical Directory of the United States Congress, "Mary Rose Oakar," http://bioguide.congress.gov

MANUSCRIPT COLLECTION

University of Oklahoma (Norman, OK), The Julian P. Kanter Political Commercial Archive, Department of Communication. *Video cassette*: 1988, four commercials on one video cassette. The commercials were used during Mary Rose Oakar's campaign for the 1988 U.S. congressional election in District 20 of Ohio.

NOTES

1   Michelle Ruess, "Oakar's Loss a Blunder, Not a Coup," 8 November 1992, *Plain Dealer*: 1B; Karen Foerstel, *Biographical Dictionary of Congressional Women* (Westport, CT: Greenwood Press, 1999): 209.

2   Ruess, "Oakar's Loss a Blunder, Not a Coup."

3   "Mary Rose Oakar," Associated Press Candidate Biographies 1992; "Election Statistics, 1920 to Present," http://clerk.house.gov/members/electionInfo/elections.html.

4   *Congressional Record*, House, 95th Cong., 2nd sess. (14 June 1978): 17712; *Congressional Record*, House, 95th Cong., 2nd sess. (11 July 1978): 20139; *Congressional Record*, House, 95th Cong., 2nd sess. (14 July 1978): 21044.

5   Steven V. Roberts, "Of Women and Women's Issues," 8 October 1985, *New York Times*: A20.

6   "Equal Pay Bill Labeled Anti-Family," 5 April 1984, *Washington Post*: A4.

7   Juan Williams, "Retorts Traded in Hill Hearing on Comparable-Worth Issue," 5 April 1985, *Washington Post*: A2.

8   Roberts, "Of Women and Women's Issues."

9   Ibid.

10 Chuck Conconi, "Personalities," 6 December 1988, *Washington Post*: E3.

11 Karin Schulz, "'Mary Rose' Takes Old-Fashioned View of Campaigning," 20 September 2001, *Cleveland Plain Dealer*: B1; Adam Clymer, "Congresswoman Is Facing Difficult Challenge in Ohio," 27 May 1992, *New York Times*: A19; Susan B. Glasser, "How Did Mary Rose Pull It Off?" 8 June 1992, *Roll Call*. Previously, in 1987, the Ethics Committee reprimanded Oakar for having kept a former aide on the payroll two years after she had left Oakar's office, and for giving another aide a $10,000 pay raise at the time that she and Oakar bought a house together. Oakar repaid the money and survived the incidents largely unscathed. For information on the reprimand, see the Committee on Standards of Official Conduct history of disciplinary actions at http://www.house.gov/ethics/Historical_Chart_Final_Version.htm.

12 Glasser, "How Did Mary Rose Pull It Off?"

13 "Election Statistics, 1920 to Present," http://clerk.house.gov/members/electionInfo/elections.html.

14 "Ex-Congresswoman Denies Seven Felonies," 5 March 1995, *New York Times*: 14.

Muriel Humphrey
1912–1998

UNITED STATES SENATOR ★ DEMOCRAT FROM MINNESOTA
1978

The archetypical political wife, Muriel Buck Humphrey supported her husband, Hubert Humphrey, during a career that took him from being a clerk at his father's pharmacy in North Dakota to a political powerbroker in the Minnesota Democratic-Farmer-Labor Party and national prominence in the Senate and, finally, as Vice President. But when Senator Humphrey passed away in 1978, his political partner and adviser, Muriel, emerged to fill his seat and carry out his programs. As only the second Minnesota woman ever to serve in Congress, Muriel Humphrey pursued her own interests during her brief tenure, supporting an extension of the Equal Rights Amendment (ERA) ratification deadline and advocating several programs to benefit persons with mental disabilities.

Muriel Fay Buck was born on February 20, 1912, in Huron, South Dakota, to Andrew and Jessie May Buck. Her father supported the family as a produce middleman, buying and selling such staples as cream, eggs, and poultry. Muriel Buck was raised in a Presbyterian home and was educated in public schools. From 1931 to 1932, she attended classes at Huron College. It was at that time that she met a young man tending counter at his father's pharmacy, Hubert Horatio Humphrey.[1] On September 3, 1936, Muriel Buck married Hubert Humphrey and, within a year, Muriel began helping to fund her husband's college education at the University of Minnesota and his graduate studies at Louisiana State University.[2] They raised a daughter and three sons: Nancy, Hubert III, Bob, and Douglas. Hubert Humphrey went on to teach political science at the University of Minnesota and at Macalester College during World War II. He also served as the state chief of the Minnesota war service program as assistant

director of the War Manpower Commission in 1943. Two years later he launched a long and storied political career by winning election as mayor of Minneapolis. Humphrey became a powerful force in the state's Democratic-Farmer-Labor Party (DFL). In 1948, he was elected to the first of three consecutive terms as one of Minnesota's U.S. Senators. In 1964, President Lyndon B. Johnson chose Humphrey as his running mate on the presidential ticket. After their landslide victory, Humphrey served as Vice President from 1965 to 1969.

Muriel Humphrey played an indirect part in her husband's early political career, keeping a certain distance between her role as mother and Hubert's public life, but also assisting him as an informal advisor. She recalled their talks in the kitchen: "I'd say something while taking care of my babies and later it would be part of his speech."[3] It was not until Humphrey's first Senate re-election campaign in 1954 that his wife actively participated in public appearances on his behalf.[4] From that point forward, she gradually played a more active role in her husband's political career. When President Lyndon Johnson chose Hubert Humphrey as his 1964 running mate, the *Wall Street Journal* described Muriel Humphrey as one of her husband's key advisers: "Not only is the relationship between Hubert and Muriel Humphrey a genuinely warm and close one, but he has particular respect for her judgments of people and common sense assessments of situations. Mrs. Humphrey has never 'gone Washington,' and the Vice President feels that gives added weight to her opinions."[5] During the term that Hubert served as Vice President, the press portrayed Muriel as a dutiful and supportive wife: an adoring grandmother who sewed children's clothes (and her own),

as well as an avid gardener.[6] But Muriel Humphrey also logged more than 650,000 miles on campaign trips and official visits during her husband's long political career.[7] After his unsuccessful campaign for the presidency in 1968, Hubert Humphrey was elected U.S. Senator from Minnesota in 1970. He won re-election in 1976.

In 1977, Hubert Humphrey was diagnosed with terminal cancer and passed away in January 1978. Minnesota Governor Rudy Perpich appointed Muriel Humphrey less than two weeks later, on January 25, 1978, to serve in her husband's Senate seat until a special election could be held later that fall to fill the remaining four years of his term. Widespread public sentiment supported Muriel Humphrey's appointment. It was both testament to the Humphreys' partnership and a reflection of Minnesotans' belief that she would know how best to try to bring her husband's programs to fruition.

But the move served a political purpose as well. The 1978 elections in Minnesota would occur with the top three posts on the ticket held by unelected officials—senior Senator, governor, and junior Senator. Perpich's predecessor, Wendell Anderson, had resigned his gubernatorial post in December 1976 with the understanding that Perpich would appoint him to the Senate seat vacated when Walter Mondale became Vice President. Observers believed that the appointment of another politically ambitious member of the DFL to Hubert Humphrey's seat would set off a controversy that could hurt them at the polls.[8] Muriel Humphrey debated whether or not to accept and conferred with two political confidantes, Representative Barbara Jordan of Texas and Representative Lindy Boggs of Louisiana. "They both wanted me to accept the post and run for office," Humphrey noted.[9] Humphrey denied she was acting as merely a caretaker for the seat (postponing a decision on whether she would stand for election in the fall of 1978 to the remaining four years of the term), viewing the opportunity as a chance to help the DFL Party through a troubled period. "As a Member of the Senate, I believe I can help complete some of the very important legislative business that Hubert hoped to finish," Humphrey said

during her appointment announcement.[10] Sworn in by Vice President Walter Mondale on February 6, she added modestly, "I hope I can fill Hubert's shoes."[11]

During her 10 months in office, Muriel Humphrey served on the Foreign Relations and Governmental Affairs committees. In her first speech as a Senator, Humphrey urged ratification of the treaties turning over control of the Panama Canal to Panama and guaranteeing the canal's neutrality, positions once espoused by her husband. On the Foreign Relations panel she also cast a key vote in favor of President James Earl "Jimmy" Carter's proposal to sell military aircraft to Egypt, Israel, and Saudi Arabia.[12] From her seat on Government Affairs, Humphrey sponsored a successful amendment to the Civil Service Reform Act of 1978 that extended better job security protections to federal employees who exposed waste or fraud in government. The Senator also had the opportunity to witness the completion of a major segment of her husband's work with the passage of the 1978 Humphrey–Hawkins Full Employment and Balanced Growth Act, attending the White House bill-signing ceremony.[13] The measure declared that it was the policy of the federal government to promote full employment, extend economic growth and increase real income, balance the budget, and create price stability.

Humphrey also championed liberal causes that were distinctively hers. She cosponsored a successful joint resolution to extend the deadline for ratification of the ERA by an additional three years. She also proposed a nationwide advocacy system to protect the rights of seriously disabled psychiatric patients and backed universal testing of pregnant women to prevent mental retardation in babies.[14] In September of 1978, the Senate approved her amendment to the Department of Education Organization Act that changed the Department of Health, Education, and Welfare to the Department of Health and Human Services. During her tenure she admitted that she found the Senate at first to be "frightening. Especially presiding at meetings," she noted. But she did not lose her humor. "It's awfully hard for me to rap the gavel or interrupt when someone is talking. My upbring-

ing was that you never interrupt your elders, but I'm learning."[15]

On April 8, 1978, at a dinner in St. Paul honoring her late husband, Muriel Humphrey announced her decision not to seek election to the remaining four years of his term. Speaking to reporters, Senator Humphrey remarked that it was a "difficult decision," noting that "like Hubert, I feel stirred by the purpose and the promise and the challenge" of elective office. But after spending much of the past three decades in public life, spanning 12 elections, she yearned "to return to Minnesota in November and resume life as a private person with ample time for my home, family and friends."[16] Humphrey's Senate term expired on November 7, 1978, following the election of David Durenberger to serve the remaining four years of Hubert Humphrey's unexpired term.

After completing her Senate service, Humphrey retired to Excelsior, Minnesota. In 1979, she married an old family friend and widower whom she had known since her high school days, Max Brown. The couple settled in Plymouth, Minnesota, where Humphrey-Brown spent time with her family and largely away from the political spotlight. In 1998, during Hubert Humphrey III's campaign for governor of Minnesota, she appeared on the campaign trail with him. That fall, Muriel Buck Humphrey-Brown passed away in Minneapolis on September 20, 1998.

FOR FURTHER READING

Biographical Directory of the United States Congress, "Muriel Buck Humphrey," http://bioguide.congress.gov

MANUSCRIPT COLLECTION

Minnesota Historical Society (St. Paul, MN). *Papers:* 1924–1978, 140 feet. Includes: correspondence, scrapbooks, subject files, and speeches from her Senate career and her earlier public and private life. Particular emphasis on mental health issues. Finding aid. Restricted.

NOTES

1   Carl Solberg, *Hubert Humphrey: A Biography* (New York: Norton, 1984): 52.

2   Linda Charlton, "The Newest Senator From Minnesota: Muriel Buck Humphrey," 26 January 1978, *New York Times*: A18; Marilyn Hoffman, "His 'Inspirational' Force," 9 August 1968, *Christian Science Monitor*: 6.

3   Solberg, *Hubert Humphrey: A Biography*: 195; Helen Dewar, "Important Business to Finish: Friends Unsurprised by Muriel Humphrey's Decision," 26 January 1978, *Washington Post*: A3.

4   Dorothy McCardle, "Muriel Humphrey Adds Special Campaign Spark," 27 October 1968, *Washington Post*: H1; Dorothy McCardle, "Hubert Humphrey Is Her Husband," 14 July 1968, *Washington Post*: H1; Sue Cronk, "Minnesota's Muriel: She Can't Place the Faces, But She Gets the Votes," 9 August 1964, *Washington Post*: F6.

5   Alan L. Otten, "Humphrey's Helpers: Vice President's Advisers Influence His Many Projects," 1 March 1965, *Wall Street Journal*: 10.

6   "Sharing the Distaff Ticket . . . Lady Bird and Muriel," 28 August 1964, *Christian Science Monitor*: 1.

7   Marilyn Bender, "Showing Campaign Style All Her Own," 23 September 1968, *New York Times*: 38; Hoffman, "His 'Inspirational' Force"; Irvin Molotsky, "Muriel Humphrey Brown, Senator, Dies at 86," 21 September 1998, *New York Times*: B12; Charlton, "The Newest Senator From Minnesota: Muriel Buck Humphrey."

8   See, for example, Douglas E. Kneeland, "Mrs. Humphrey Seems Assured of Offer of Senate Appointment," 18 January 1978, *New York Times*: A14; Jon Nordheimer, "Perpich to See Mrs. Humphrey," 25 January 1978, *New York Times*: A12.

9   Karen DeWitt, "Muriel Humphrey Ponders a Big Question—To Run or Retire?" 8 April 1978, *New York Times*: 11.

10 Jon Nordheimer, "Muriel Humphrey Accepts Appointment to Husband's Senate Seat," 26 January 1978, *New York Times*: A18.

11 "Senator Muriel Humphrey Is Sworn In," 7 February 1978, *Washington Post*: A2; Charlton, "The Newest Senator From Minnesota: Muriel Buck Humphrey."

12 Albert R. Hunt, "Sen. Humphrey to Give Carter Key Vote In Senate Panel on Arms Sale to Mideast," 11 May 1978, *Wall Street Journal*: 7.

13 Edward Walsh, "Humphrey–Hawkins Measure Is Signed by the President," 28 October 1978, *Washington Post*: A9.

14 DeWitt, "Muriel Humphrey Ponders a Big Question—To Run or Retire?"

15 Ibid.

16 Douglas Kneeland, "Mrs. Humphrey Decides Not to Seek Election in Fall," 9 April 1978, *New York Times*: 27; Douglas Kneeland, "Race Is Clarified as Mrs. Humphrey Declines to Run," 10 April 1978, *New York Times*: A18.

Maryon Pittman Allen

1925–

UNITED STATES SENATOR ★ DEMOCRAT FROM ALABAMA

1978

Maryon Pittman Allen, who briefly succeeded her husband upon his sudden death, is one of the few widows who remarked frankly about the shock and pain associated with serving under such circumstances. A journalist who married into politics, she was appointed to the U.S. Senate in 1978 by Alabama Governor George Wallace after the death of the skilled parliamentarian James Allen.

Maryon Pittman was born on November 30, 1925, in Meridian, Mississippi, one of four children raised by John D. and Tellie Chism Pittman. The family moved to Birmingham, Alabama, the following year, where John Pittman opened a tractor dealership. Maryon Pittman attended public schools and then went to the University of Alabama from 1944 to 1947. While still attending college, she married Joshua Mullins on October 17, 1946. The couple raised three children—Joshua, John, and Maryon—but were divorced in 1959. As a single mother, Maryon Pittman was employed as an insurance agent and then as a journalist, working as the women's section editor for five local weeklies in Alabama. As a staff writer for the *Birmingham News*, she took an assignment in 1964 to interview James Browning Allen, a widower and then the lieutenant governor of Alabama, who had just delivered a speech before the Alabama Federation of Women's Clubs. Four months later, on August 7, 1964, James Allen and Maryon Pittman married; Allen brought two children from his previous marriage, James Jr., and Mary. When Alabama Senator Lister Hill chose not to seek re-election to the 91st Congress (1969–1971), James Allen sought and won election to his seat. A longtime Alabama state legislator, Senator Allen served on the Judiciary Committee. He became a master of parliamentary procedure, helping to

revive the filibuster. Senator Allen fought the creation of a federal consumer protection agency, taxpayer financing of federal campaigns, and the 1978 treaties which ceded U.S. control of the Panama Canal. Allen, the *New York Times* observed, "was a valued ally in any fight, a man who could out-talk or out-maneuver many of the wisest and most experienced politicians in Washington. . . . If he did not beat the opposition, he wilted them."[1] Senator Alan Cranston once remarked, "He can catch other people napping, but he's not sneaky. He just plays hardball within the rules."[2] The *Washington Post* wrote that Allen "did not merely learn Jefferson's parliamentary manual; he absorbed it and employed it more doggedly, shrewdly and creatively than any other senator in years."[3] While her husband ensconced himself in the Senate, Maryon Allen continued her journalism career, writing a Washington-based news column, "The Reflections of a News Hen," that was syndicated in Alabama newspapers.

On June 1, 1978, Senator Allen died suddenly of a heart attack. Alabama Governor George Wallace, with whom James Allen served as lieutenant governor in the 1960s, appointed Maryon Allen on June 8, 1978, to succeed her husband. Wallace also called a special election to coincide with the general election on November 7, 1978, to fill the remaining two years of James Allen's term. Maryon Allen pledged to "continue to espouse the great principles of government to which Senator Allen dedicated his life. When I cast a vote on the floor of the U.S. Senate, it will reflect the philosophy he expressed so eloquently and strongly during his almost 10 years of service." She also announced her intention to run for the two-year term despite widespread speculation that Governor Wallace (who was ineligible for gubernatorial re-election) was

considering campaigning for the seat himself. On June 12, 1978, Maryon Allen was sworn into the U.S. Senate by Vice President Walter Mondale; Senator Muriel Humphrey, widow of Hubert Humphrey, embraced Allen after the ceremony.[4]

"I'm trying to do this thing with taste and dignity, I'm not sure I can do it," Maryon Allen told the *Washington Post* after two months on the job. She also confided that her husband had made her promise that if his health failed, she would consider taking his seat in the Senate. "Jim and I found each other late in life," she recalled. "We were too close. I feel like I am an open, bleeding, raw, walking wound. I cover it up all during the day here in the Senate with a front. Jim wanted me to. I hate the word widow. But if I hadn't done this I would have fallen into the poor pitiful Pearl routine and felt sorry for myself. Jim wasn't going to give me that luxury. He gave me every other one. And, I must admit, at my age it's kind of exciting to start a new career."[5] She was assigned seats on two of her husband's former committees: Agriculture, Nutrition, and Forestry and Judiciary. Though she had lobbied Senate Majority Leader Robert Byrd of West Virginia for a seat on the Rules and Administration Committee, she did not receive it.[6]

Perhaps her most important vote during her short Senate career came in October 1978, when she supported a proposal by Republican Jake Garn of Utah which would have allowed any of the 35 states that had ratified the Equal Rights Amendment (ERA) since its passage in 1972 to rescind their approval. The Senate also was considering an extension of the ERA deadline of March 1979 by an additional three years. Supporters of the Garn Amendment argued that if the extension was passed to allow more states to approve then states also should be allowed to reverse their votes within that same time frame. The proposal failed by a 54–44 vote, clearing the way for successful passage of the extension.[7]

Alabama political observers fully expected that retiring Governor George Wallace would challenge Allen for the seat in the November special election. But early in the summer he surprised supporters by declining to seek the Democratic nomination, leaving Allen as the favorite. In yet another unexpected twist, Allen's campaign began to fall apart in the wake of a July *Washington Post* interview in which the new Senator was quoted as being highly critical of Governor Wallace and his wife.[8] Allen later claimed the interviewer had distorted her comments, but the reaction in Alabama damaged her chances for election. Nevertheless, Senator Allen remained confident. She concentrated on her Senate duties and campaigned little before the Democratic primary of September 5th. Allen led the primary voting with 44 percent, but fell short of the outright majority required by state election laws. Forced into a run-off with Alabama State Senator Donald Stewart, Maryon Allen eventually lost by a margin of more than 120,000 votes on September 26, 1978. In the general election Allen supported Republican candidate James D. Martin, a U.S. Representative and close friend of her husband's. Stewart eventually defeated Martin, 55 percent to 43 percent. Allen left the Senate on November 8, 1978, the day after the election.

After her Senate career, Maryon Allen worked as a columnist for the *Washington Post*. She later worked as a public relations and advertising director for an antique and auction company in Birmingham, Alabama, where she still resides.

FOR FURTHER READING

Biographical Directory of the United States Congress, "Maryon Pittman Allen," http://bioguide.congress.gov

Watson, Elbert L. "Maryon Pittman Allen," in *Alabama United States Senators* (Huntsville, AL: Strode Publishers, 1982): 150–152.

MANUSCRIPT COLLECTION

Alabama Department of Archives and History (Montgomery, AL). *Papers:* 1978, one cubic foot. Includes files and press releases. See also, the James B. Allen Papers, 1968–1978, 92 cubic feet. Subjects covered include Maryon Allen.

NOTES

1   M.A. Farber, "Senator James B. Allen Dies; Alabamian Led Canal Pact Fight," 2 June 1978, *New York Times*: B2.
2   Martin Weil, "Sen. James Allen of Alabama Dies of Heart Attack," 2 June 1978, *Washington Post*: A1.
3   "James Browning Allen," 4 June 1978, *Washington Post*: B6.
4   "Maryon Allen Sworn In Senate," 13 June 1978, *Washington Post*: A4; Ray Jenkins, "Allen's Death Roils Politics in Alabama," 3 June 1978, *New York Times*: 8.
5   Sally Quinn, "Maryon Allen—The Southern Girl in the Senate," 30 July 1978, *Washington Post*: K1.
6   Quinn, "Maryon Allen—The Southern Girl in the Senate."
7   Chris Kendrick, "ERA Supporters Win a Round in Senate," 5 October 1978, *Christian Science Monitor*: 1.
8   Quinn, "Maryon Allen—The Southern Girl in the Senate."

Nancy Landon Kassebaum

1932–

UNITED STATES SENATOR ★ REPUBLICAN FROM KANSAS
1978–1997

Hailing from a distinguished Kansas political family, Nancy Landon Kassebaum made her own mark by winning election to the U.S. Senate and serving there for nearly two decades, eventually becoming the first woman to chair a major Senate committee. As both chair of the Labor and Human Resources Committee and a senior member of the Foreign Relations Committee, Senator Kassebaum earned a reputation as a determined and independent voice on issues ranging from Cold War policy to women's rights.

Nancy Landon was born in Topeka, Kansas, on July 29, 1932, into a family that emerged as a Midwestern dynasty. Her father was Alfred Mossman Landon, a successful oil man, two-term Kansas governor, and the 1936 Republican presidential nominee. Her mother, Theo Cobb Landon, was an accomplished pianist and harpist. Nancy Landon was born into a world of privilege, and national political figures dotted her childhood memories, including William Howard Taft and his family.[1] "I enjoyed politics and public policy so much," Kassebaum recalled years later, "that there were times in high school and college when I mused about becoming actively involved as a candidate."[2] She graduated from the University of Kansas in 1954 with a B.A. in political science and, in 1956, earned a M.A. from the University of Michigan in diplomatic history. While at the University of Michigan, Landon met Philip Kassebaum, who later pursued a law degree there. The couple married in 1956. They settled on a farm in Maize, Kansas, and raised four children: John, Linda, Richard, and William. Nancy Kassebaum served as a member of the school board in Maize. She also worked as vice president of Kassebaum Communications, a family-owned company that operated several radio stations. In

1975, Kassebaum and her husband were legally separated; their divorce became final in 1979. She worked in Washington, D.C., as a caseworker for Senator James B. Pearson of Kansas in 1975; however, Kassebaum returned to Kansas the following year.

When Senator Pearson declined to seek re-election in 1978, Kassebaum declared herself a candidate for the open seat. Though she seemed a political neophyte, the decision was a considered one, as she later reminisced, "I believed I could contribute something, that I had something to offer."[3] Philip Kassebaum, with whom Nancy Kassebaum remained close, worked on her campaign and advised her: "You have to want it enough to have a gnawing in the pit of your stomach that won't let you sleep. If you have that, then you can put up with the strenuous campaign."[4] Nancy Kassebaum proved to be a ferocious campaigner with a simple philosophy: "To be a good Senator, you need to be willing to work with people. You don't need to be a professional politician."[5]

Kassebaum's family background in professional politics was a tremendous boost to her campaign. In the race for the Republican nomination, she beat a field of eight contenders, including a politically experienced woman state senator, Jan Meyers, who later served six terms in the U.S. House. In the general election she faced Bill Roy, a lawyer and physician who had narrowly lost a bid to unseat Senator Robert Dole in 1974. The visibility generated in that campaign made him a formidable opponent in 1978. But Kassebaum wielded the Landon family name to great effect. "It has been said I am riding on the coattails of my dad," she admitted, "but I can't think of any better coattails to ride on."[6] Her campaign slogan was "A Fresh Face: A Trusted Kansas Name." Kassebaum went on to

eclipse Roy by a margin of 86,000 votes out of about 749,000 cast, winning the election with 54 percent of the vote to Roy's 42 percent. In 1984 and 1990, Kassebaum was easily returned to office with 76 and 74 percent of the vote, respectively. Though the Landon name proved crucial, Kassebaum also won because of Kansas's conservative political tradition, virtually unanimous support from major newspapers in the state, and a pattern of Republican success during the 1978 midterm elections.[7] Another supporter throughout her campaign was former Senator Margaret Chase Smith of Maine. Upon Kassebaum's victory, Smith wrote a congratulatory note in which she expressed special pride in the fact that Kassebaum "ran as a candidate first, and a woman second."[8]

Kassebaum's gender unmistakably distinguished her in the Senate, where she was the only woman among the 100 Members. She took office on December 23, 1978, filling the vacancy created when Senator Pearson resigned a few days early to give Kassebaum an edge in seniority. She later recalled that it took her a while to adjust to life in the Senate as a woman; she remembered, for instance, avoiding the Senate Members' dining room because she was "intimidated."[9] She maintained her humor, however, once quipping of her special responsibilities as a woman: "There's so much work to do: the coffee to make and the chambers to vacuum. There are Pat Moynihan's hats to brush and the buttons to sew on Bob Byrd's red vests, so I keep quite busy."[10]

Kassebaum received assignments on a number of prominent committees, including: Banking, Housing and Urban Affairs; Budget; Commerce, Science and Transportation; and the Special Committee on Aging. In 1980, when Republicans took control of the Senate, Kassebaum exchanged her seat on the Banking Committee for one on the prestigious Senate Foreign Relations Committee. She immediately was named chair of the Subcommittee on African Affairs, a position she held until the Democrats gained control of the Senate in 1987. She would remain on Foreign Relations for the duration of her tenure in Congress, and it became the focus of much of her energy. Though she knew virtually nothing

about Africa she quickly became steeped in the region and U.S. interests there.

Kassebaum became a respected member of the Foreign Relations Committee, whose individualism often led her to depart from her party's positions during the presidencies of Ronald W. Reagan and George H.W. Bush. She was a major critic of President Jimmy Carter's grain embargo against the Soviet Union in the late 1970s (Kansas was the nation's leading grain producer), though she supported the return of the Panama Canal to Panamanian rule. She initially opposed funding for parts of President Reagan's Strategic Defense Initiative (SDI) program, though she later voted to fund major portions of it in 1992. In 1986, she surprised Republican colleagues by advocating sanctions to protest the South African government's policy of racial apartheid. She also proved prescient in two significant cases during President Bush's term. In June 1990, Kassebaum, along with Kansas Democratic Representative Dan Glickman, called for the suspension of $700 million in credit guarantees for Iraq, money allocated for food relief but spent by Iraqi dictator Saddam Hussein on military armaments. Much to its regret, the Bush administration rejected the proposal. A few months later, Hussein's forces invaded Kuwait and set in motion the first Gulf War. Kassebaum also supported arming U.N. workers in Somalia in 1992 in order to more effectively carry out their food relief mission. Again, the Bush administration demurred, only to reverse course later in the year and insert troops.[11]

Overall, Kassebaum earned a reputation as a moderate who supported the broad outlines of Republican budget and defense programs but remained independent on social issues. For instance, she supported a woman's right to have an abortion. She also backed programs for international family planning, which again brought her into conflict with conservative Republicans. In 1992, she cofounded the Republican Majority Coalition, a group that sought to counter the rise of the religious right in the party. She resisted the feminist label, noting on one occasion that she thought of herself foremost as a "U.S. Senator, not a woman Senator." She added, "It diminishes

KASSEBAUM THOUGHT OF HERSELF
FOREMOST AS A "U.S. SENATOR,
NOT A WOMAN SENATOR." SHE
ADDED, "IT DIMINISHES WOMEN TO
SAY THAT WE HAVE ONE VOICE AND
EVERYTHING IN THE SENATE
WOULD CHANGE IF WE WERE
THERE."

women to say that we have one voice and everything in the Senate would change if we were there."[12] In 1994, she voted for President William J. Clinton's crime bill, a move which so enraged Republican Members that they tried, unsuccessfully, to strip her of seniority. Late in her final term, she also worked with Democratic Senator Ted Kennedy to push a bill through the Senate that would have overhauled the national health insurance system and provided coverage for people with pre-existing conditions. As a member of the Budget Committee in 1984 and 1987 she worked to enact a bipartisan deficit reduction plan.

Beginning in the 101st Congress (1989–1991), Kassebaum served on the Labor and Human Resources Committee and, when the Republican Party recaptured the Senate in 1994, Kassebaum's seniority made her chair of the committee. Her chairmanship of Labor and Human Resources during the 104th Congress (1995–1997) marked the first time that a woman had chaired a major standing Senate committee and the first time that any woman had headed a Senate panel since Margaret Chase Smith chaired the Special Committee on Rates and Compensation of Certain Officers and Employees of the Senate in 1954. Kassebaum also rose to chair the Commerce Committee's Subcommittee on Aviation. In the 99th and 100th Congresses (1985–1989), she was named to the Select Committee on Ethics.

In 1996, Kassebaum declined to run for re-election, citing the "need to pursue other challenges, including the challenge of being a grandmother."[13] That year she also married former Tennessee Senator Howard Baker, Jr. Kassebaum worked briefly as a visiting professor at Iowa State while she and Baker divided their time between homes in Kansas and Tennessee. In 2001, Kassebaum was named a co-chair of the Presidential Appointment Initiative Advisory Board which made recommendations to the Senate Governmental Affairs Committee on how to streamline the presidential nominee appointment process. Later that year, when Howard Baker was appointed U.S. Ambassador to Japan, Kassebaum accompanied him on his assignment to Tokyo.

FOR FURTHER READING

Biographical Directory of the United States Congress, "Nancy Landon Kassebaum," http://bioguide.congress.gov

Kassebaum, Nancy Landon. "To Form a More Perfect Union," *Presidential Studies Quarterly* 18 (Spring 1988): 241–249.

Marshall-White, Eleanor. *Women, Catalysts for Change: Interpretive Biographies of Shirley St. Hill Chisholm, Sandra Day O'Connor, and Nancy Landon Kassebaum* (New York: Vantage Press, 1991).

MANUSCRIPT COLLECTION

Kansas State Historical Society (Topeka, KS). *Papers:* Nancy Landon Kassebaum U.S. Senate Papers, 1979–1996, ca. 659 cu. ft. Included are alphabetical, general and department (federal agency) subject, grant notification, Correspondence Management System/ Constituent Service System, and Education Subcommittee-related correspondence; newsletters, news releases, clippings, and other press files relating to Senator Kassebaum and the Labor and Human Resources Committee; scheduling and other administrative records; speeches; files of legislative assistants on a wide variety of topics considered by Congress and as part of Senator Kassebaum's committee assignments; and records relating to her daily activities, sponsored legislation, and voting record. Major subjects represented in the papers include women's and children's issues, foreign policy and African affairs, education, and health care reform. Major components: correspondence, boxes 1–473; administrative files, boxes 474–484; speeches, boxes 485–590; press files, boxes 496, 508–513, 515–519; legislative aide files, boxes 520–636; legislative record, boxes 637–675. Access partially restricted. Unpublished finding aids available in the repository. Photographs and audio-visual materials removed to: Kansas State Historical Society, Library and Archives Division, photograph collection.

★ NANCY LANDON KASSEBAUM ★

NOTES

1   Paul Hendrickson, "His Daughter, the Senator-Elect from Kansas; Alf Landon Aimed for Washington, Now Nancy Kassebaum Is Going," 30 November 1978, *Washington Post*: G1.

2   Hendrickson, "His Daughter, the Senator-Elect from Kansas."

3   *Current Biography, 1982* (New York: H.W. Wilson and Company, 1982): 191.

4   *Current Biography, 1982*: 191–192.

5   Ibid., 192.

6   Ibid.

7   Ibid.

8   Hendrickson, "His Daughter, the Senator-Elect from Kansas."

9   Marcy Kaptur, *Women of Congress: A Twentieth-Century Odyssey* (Washington, D.C.: Congressional Quarterly Press, 1996): 198–199.

10 Interview, 4 October 1979, *Working Woman*: 62.

11 *Almanac of American Politics, 1994* (Washington, D.C.: National Journal Inc., 1993): 491–492.

12 Karen Foerstel, *Biographical Dictionary of Congressional Women* (Westport, CT: Greenwood Press, 1999): 144.

13 "Senator Kassebaum Says She'll Retire in '96," 21 November 1995, *New York Times*: A17.

Beverly Butcher Byron
1932–

UNITED STATES REPRESENTATIVE ★ DEMOCRAT FROM MARYLAND
1979–1993

After winning the election to fill the seat of her late husband, Beverly Byron went on to have a 14-year career in the House of Representatives. She used the experience she acquired as an unpaid aide to her husband and her family background to assert herself as an influential member of the Armed Services Committee. As a staunch defender of both military and defense spending, Congresswoman Byron served as one of the more conservative Democrats in Congress.

Beverly Barton Butcher was born in Baltimore, Maryland, on July 27, 1932, to Harry C. and Ruth B. Butcher. She grew up in Washington, D.C., where her father managed a radio station before becoming an aide to General Dwight Eisenhower for a short period of time in World War II. She graduated from the National Cathedral School in Washington, D.C., in 1950. In 1963, she attended Hood College in Frederick, Maryland, for one year before marrying Goodloe E. Byron. She became active in politics at about that time, serving in 1962 and 1965 as a treasurer for the Maryland Young Democrats. She eventually left her career as a high school teacher to work on her husband's campaign for the Maryland legislature and, in 1970, his successful campaign for a U.S. House seat that encompassed western Maryland. During her husband's tenure as a Representative, she worked closely with him, even debating his opponents on occasion when his official duties prevented district visits.[1]

One month before the general election in 1978, Goodloe Byron died of a heart attack while jogging along the Chesapeake and Ohio Canal. Before finding time to gain perspective on the tragedy, Beverly Byron was pressured by local Democratic leaders, who faced a seven-day deadline to name an alternate candidate. "Before I knew what was happening, the officials from Annapolis were in my living room with papers to sign," Byron recalled. "My children made the decision for me." In addition to heeding the advice of Goodloe, Jr., Barton, and Mary, Byron further explained her motivation to campaign for her husband's seat when she commented, "I knew the things he stood for and I understood how he felt. I wanted to give it a try. All you can do is try."[2] In the general election, Byron easily defeated her Republican opponent Melvin Perkins, an unemployed vagrant, capturing 90 percent of the vote.[3] In winning election to the 96th Congress (1979–1981), she succeeded her husband, just as his mother, Katharine E. Byron, had succeeded her husband (Goodloe's father), William D. Byron, following the latter's death in 1941.

Representative Beverley Byron earned a reputation as a conservative Democrat who voted for Ronald W. Reagan and George H.W. Bush administration policies, frequently breaking ranks with moderate and liberal Democrats on both fiscal and social issues. She opposed a national health care system and a woman's right to seek an abortion except in extreme cases where the mother's life was in danger. In 1981, she was one of only two northern Democrats in the House to support President Reagan's budget, declaring, "The system we've been working under has not worked. I'm willing to give the President's proposals a chance."[4] Although she often angered fellow Democrats with her conservative agenda, Byron's party-crossing habit worked well in her right-of-center district. As the fourth person of the "Byron dynasty," she, much like her late husband and his parents, adopted a political agenda that typically mirrored the conservative interests of the majority of people living in western Maryland.[5] Beverly Byron won re-election to the next six Congresses

IMAGE COURTESY OF THE HONORABLE BEVERLY BYRON

without seriously being challenged, accumulating between 65 and 75 percent of the vote.[6] She received her husband's committee assignments on Armed Services and the Select Committee on Aging. In the 97th Congress (1981–1983), she served on the Interior and Insular Affairs Committee. She held all three assignments until she left Congress in 1993.

Congresswoman Byron's legislative interests gravitated toward military policy. From 1983 to 1986, she chaired the House Special Panel on Arms Control and Disarmament, where she sought to limit the scope of nuclear test ban proposals. She also backed the development of the MX Missile (the experimental mobile nuclear missile system), supporting the Reagan administration's contention that it would serve as a bargaining chip during future arms control negotiations with the Soviet Union. In a 1984 debate, Byron urged her colleagues in the House to support funding for the weapon: "I think for this nation, at this time, to decide not to go ahead with the MX, to let down our NATO allies, to not support the continuation of the modernization of our missile program is a wrong signal."[7] During her congressional career, Byron visited numerous military facilities and built a reputation for examining military hardware firsthand during inspections. In November 1985, Byron became the first woman to fly in the military's premier spy plane, the SR-71 "Blackbird," capable of cruising at Mach 3 (three times the speed of sound) at an altitude of about 90,000 feet.

In 1987, Byron beat out Representative Pat Schroeder, a more senior member of the House Armed Services Committee, for election as chair of the influential Military Personnel and Compensation Subcommittee. Two years earlier, Representative Les Aspin of Wisconsin, chairman of the House Armed Services Committee, had deferred plans to create a new military subcommittee for fear that a "civil war" would ensue; conservative members of Armed Services wanted Byron as head of the new subcommittee rather than Aspin's political ally, Schroeder.[8] Despite his delaying tactics, Aspin failed to muster enough support for Schroeder in 1987, thereby allowing Byron to assume a leadership role. As the first woman to head an Armed Services subcommittee, Byron oversaw more than 40 percent of the Defense Department's budget and had a hand in shaping military policy that coincided with the dismantling of the Warsaw Pact (the Eastern European Communist military coalition) and the end of the Soviet Union itself. Though she rarely wavered from her support for defense expenditures, Byron openly criticized the military during the Navy's "Tailhook" sexual harassment scandal of the early 1990s.

As a Representative, Byron did not consider the advancement of women's rights a priority. Admittedly not attuned to gender discrimination, she once stated, "It's hard for me to understand people who have doors closed on them."[9] Although she joined the Congressional Women's Caucus, Byron rarely participated in the meetings and activities of the organization. When caucus leaders modified the bylaws in 1981 to bolster its effectiveness, Byron balked at the changes, such as the new mandatory annual dues. She resigned from the caucus shortly thereafter declaring that, "I can't justify it for the amount of work I get in return in my district. I think there are others that feel the same."[10] Despite her inclination to align herself with congressional conservatives in both parties, Byron voted for the Equal Rights Amendment in 1983. Undecided until the day of the vote on the floor, she divulged that she found the legislation compelling because it might lead to greater opportunities for her daughter. When asked about her decision to back the amendment, Byron proclaimed that she voted her conscience, remarking, "Eventually, you just have to make up your mind."[11]

By the early 1990s, Byron's conservatism did not rest easily with the liberal wing of her party and with some of her constituents. "I go home and I get beat up," she said at the time. "Down here [in Washington], I'm wonderful."[12] Throughout her career, Byron expended little effort or money when campaigning for re-election, rarely conducting polls or running advertisements attacking her opponents. In March 1992, Byron's hands-off approach to campaigning played a part in her surprising loss in the Democratic primary. Tom Hattery, a liberal state legislator

who insisted that Byron was out of touch with her district because she agreed to take a large congressional pay raise while western Maryland suffered from a nine percent unemployment rate, garnered 56 percent of the vote in the primary. Byron's electoral upset—she was the first incumbent woman to lose a House race since 1984 and the first sitting Member to lose in the 1992 primaries—signaled an anti-incumbent mood that proved decisive in the fall elections. It also marked the first time in more than two decades that a Byron would not represent western Maryland.[13]

After Congress, Beverly Byron returned to Frederick, Maryland, with her second husband, B. Kirk Walsh, and served on the board of directors for a major defense contractor. In 1995, President William J. Clinton appointed her to the Naval Academy Board of Visitors. Four years later, Byron became a member of the Board of Regents for the Potomac Institute for Policy Studies.

FOR FURTHER READING

Biographical Directory of the United States Congress, "Beverly Butcher Byron," http://bioguide.congress.gov

MANUSCRIPT COLLECTIONS

Dwight D. Eisenhower Library (Abilene, KS). *Papers:* In the Harry C. Butcher Papers, 1910–1959, 5.4 linear feet. Correspondents include Beverly Byron. A finding aid is available in the repository.

The Mount St. Mary's University (Emmitsburg, MD), Archives & Special Collections.

NOTES

1   Donald P. Baker, "Mrs. Byron Succeeds Husband as Candidate for Congress," 13 October 1978, *Washington Post*: C1.

2   Lois Romano, "Women in the Line of Succession," 13 October 1983, *Washington Post*: D1.

3   Baker, "Mrs. Byron Succeeds Husband as Candidate for Congress."

4   Dale Russakoff, "Beverly Byron's GOP Vote," 9 July 1981, *Washington Post*: A1.

5   Russakoff, "Beverly Byron's GOP Vote"; "Congressional Choices: Maryland," 20 October 1982, *Washington Post*: A22.

6   "Election Statistics, 1920 to Present," http://clerk.house.gov/members/electionInfo/elections.html.

7   *Congressional Record,* House, 98th Cong., 2nd sess. (16 May 1984): 12530.

8   Steven V. Roberts, "Mission: Melt the Rubber in the Pentagon Stamp," 5 February 1985, *New York Times*: A20.

9   Irwin Gertzog, *Congressional Women: Their Recruitment, Integration, and Behavior* (Westport, CT: Praeger, 1995): 261.

10   Lynn Rosellini, "Dues Plan Divides Women's Caucus," 16 July 1981, *New York Times*: C13; see also, Gertzog, *Congressional Women*: 208, 261.

11   Margaret Shapiro, "Rep. Beverly Byron's Dilemma on the ERA," 16 November 1983, *Washington Post*: A9.

12   Dan Beyers, "In 6th Byron Dynasty Fell to Young Turk," 5 March 1992, *Washington Post*: C1; see also, Dan Beyers, "6th District: A Second Match up for Hattery, Byron," 27 February 1992, *Washington Post*: M9.

13   Beyers, "In 6th Byron Dynasty Fell to Young Turk"; Beyers, "6th District: A Second Match up for Hattery, Byron."

Geraldine Anne Ferraro

1935–

UNITED STATES REPRESENTATIVE ★ DEMOCRAT FROM NEW YORK
1979–1985

I n 1984, Congresswoman Geraldine Ferraro secured the nomination as the first woman vice presidential candidate on a major party ticket. Representative Ferraro's pragmatism and political skill, coupled with her close relationships with top Washington Democrats, allowed her rapid climb up the House leadership ladder. While serving in Congress, Ferraro was able to pursue a liberal, feminist agenda without ignoring the concerns of her conservative district or alienating her mostly male colleagues.

The daughter of Italian immigrants Dominick and Antonetta Ferraro, Geraldine Anne Ferraro was born on August 26, 1935, in Newburgh, New York. The youngest child and only girl in the family, Geraldine was born shortly after her older brother Gerald, for whom she was named, died in a car accident.[1] Dominick Ferraro died from a heart attack in 1943. Antonetta Ferraro moved her three children to the Bronx, where she worked to send her daughter to Marymount Catholic School in Tarrytown, New York. Geraldine Ferraro excelled in academics, skipping the sixth through eighth grades and graduating early from high school in 1952. She earned a full scholarship to attend Marymount College in New York City, graduating with a B.A. in English in 1956.[2] While teaching in New York public schools, Ferraro attended night school at Fordham University and earned her law degree in 1960. On July 16, a week after graduation, she married a real-estate broker, John Zaccaro; however, Ferraro kept her maiden name as a tribute to her mother.[3] She practiced law part-time while raising their three children: Donna, John, and Laura.[4] In 1974, Ferraro's cousin, District Attorney Nicholas Ferraro, offered her the position of assistant district attorney in Queens, New York. Geraldine Ferraro

was later transferred to the Special Victims Bureau in 1975, where she quickly earned a reputation for her tenacity and talent in the courtroom.[5] Ferraro later said her work in the Special Victims Bureau changed her political views from moderate to liberal. Finding the work draining and citing unequal pay at the district attorney's office, she left in 1978, and set her sights on Congress.[6]

After serving as the U.S. Representative in a Queens, New York, district for nearly 30 years, Democratic Congressman James Delaney announced his retirement in 1978. An ethnically and financially diverse district, the bulk of the population, however, consisted of white middle-class and blue-collar workers, a setting that inspired Archie Bunker's neighborhood in the popular television show, *All in the Family*. Although formerly a bastion for Roosevelt and Kennedy Democrats, the district had become increasingly conservative.[7] Labeled a liberal feminist and lacking the support of local Democratic leaders, Ferraro faced long odds when she sought Delaney's vacant seat.[8] Capitalizing on her ethnic background and running on a platform of increased law and order, support for the elderly, and neighborhood preservation, she secured the party nomination with 53 percent of the vote in a three-way battle against Thomas Manton, a city councilman who had the support of the local Democratic leadership, and Patrick Deignan, a popular candidate of Irish descent.[9]

Ferraro moved on to a heated campaign in the general election against former Republican State Assemblyman Alfred DelliBovi. She quickly went on the offensive, adopting the slogan, "Finally, A Tough Democrat," when her opponent criticized her decision to send her children to private schools.[10] After Ferraro appealed to the nation-

al party for help in the close race, Speaker of the House Thomas "Tip" O'Neill of Massachusetts pressured the local Democratic leadership to lend their support.[11] She ultimately defeated DelliBovi with 54 percent of the vote earning a seat in the 96th Congress (1979–1981). As the first Congresswoman from Queens, she also was re-elected to two subsequent Congresses, winning in 1980 and 1982 with 58 and 78 percent of the vote, respectively.[12]

One of Ferraro's greatest challenges in Congress was balancing her own liberal views with the conservative values of her constituents. Especially in her first two terms, she remained mindful of the needs of the citizens in her district. Assigned to the Post Office and Civil Service Committee for the 96th and 97th Congresses (1979–1983), Ferraro earned a spot on the Public Works and Transportation Committee in 1981.[13] When appointed to the Select Committee on Aging in 1979, a post she held until 1985, she organized a forum in her district to discuss problems concerning housing, medical aid, and social support systems for the New York elderly.[14] In deference to the sentiments in her district, Ferraro voted in favor of some conservative legislation, such as a proposed constitutional amendment banning mandatory busing for school desegregation, tuition tax credits for private schools, and school prayer.[15] Early in her career, she supported a strong national defense posture.[16] Ferraro later broke from the Democratic Party leadership when she voted against a 1982 tax increase.

Ferraro generally remained loyal to the Democratic agenda, however, voting with her party 78 percent of the time in her first term and following the party line even more closely during her second and third terms.[17] She was particularly critical of the Ronald W. Reagan administration's policies towards women, disdaining what she called the White House's efforts to glorify the nonworking mother, stating, "I don't disparage that [being a stay-at-home mom], I did it myself. . . . But not every woman can afford to do that."[18] Ferraro looked after the economic needs of women, sponsoring the Economic Equity Act in 1981. The legislation reformed pension options for women, protecting the rights of widows and divorcées

and allowing homemakers to save as much as their working spouses in individual retirement accounts.[19] One of the most controversial women's issues, reproductive rights, remained a strong personal issue for Ferraro. Despite criticism by conservative Catholics and even her own mother, Ferraro supported abortion rights, vowing to not let her religious beliefs as a Catholic interfere with her constitutional obligation to a separate church and state.[20]

It was her ability to push her own agenda without abandoning her conservative constituents or taking a threatening feminist stance that caught the attention of her fellow Democratic colleagues and allowed her rapid rise within the party leadership. Representative Barney Frank, a Democrat from Massachusetts, summed up her political skill, observing that "[Ferraro] manages to be threatening on issues without being threatening personally."[21] Speaker O'Neill observed Ferraro's seemingly natural political ability and took an immediate liking to the Congresswoman, whom he described as being "solid as a rock."[22] He admired her forthright yet pragmatic style and found her liberal policies, particularly her pro-labor stance, to be parallel with his own.[23]

Congresswoman Ferraro used her friendship with Speaker O'Neill to open doors for herself and other female colleagues. At the start of the 98th Congress (1983–1985), she sought a position on the prestigious Ways and Means Committee. Ferraro was passed over, mainly because New York was already heavily represented on that committee.[24] To the surprise of many congressional veterans, however, O'Neill appointed her to the prominent Budget Committee. In addition to Ferraro's assignment, other Congresswomen received their preferred appointments. Defending the increase in appointments of women to important committees, Speaker O'Neill claimed that their placement was long overdue and was quoted as saying, "They [women] hadn't sought those spots before."[25]

Ferraro's rise within the Democratic ranks was further evidenced by her election as Secretary of the Democratic Caucus in 1980 and again in 1982. Historically an honorific position typically held by women Members, party rules had changed such that the Secretary now sat on the

Democratic Steering and Policy Committee, the panel responsible for making committee assignments and forming party strategy.[26] Ferraro also increased her visibility within the party ranks by playing a prominent role in the 1980 Democratic National Convention. At the 1980 convention, Ferraro introduced the keynote speaker, Representative Morris Udall of Arizona.[27] Two years later in 1982, she was instrumental in achieving automatic delegate status to the 1984 Democratic National Convention for three-fifths of the Democrats serving in the House and the Senate, an effort to give professional politicians a

Walter Mondale planned on selecting a female running mate, the leadership's favorite, Geraldine Ferraro, topped a list that included Representatives Lindy Boggs of Louisiana, Pat Schroeder of Colorado, and Barbara Mikulski of Maryland, along with San Francisco Mayor and future U.S. Senator Dianne Feinstein. On her chances of becoming a vice presidential nominee, Ferraro remarked, "People are no longer hiding behind their hands and giggling when they talk about a woman for national office, and I think that's wonderful."[30] In July 1984, Mondale selected Ferraro as his running mate, mak-

"The fact it is a struggle is never a good enough reason not to run. You do it because you believe you can make a difference. You do it because it's an opportunity available to you that could barely have been imagined by your ancestors."

—GERALDINE FERRARO, ON THE DECISION TO RUN FOR ELECTIVE OFFICE

chance to unify and shape the party's platform. In 1984, Ferraro became the first woman to chair the Democratic platform committee. Although she faced the arduous task of creating a unified platform for the upcoming presidential contest, the position afforded Ferraro invaluable media exposure and distinction in the Democratic Party.[28]

During the 1984 presidential campaign, political strategists and feminist groups pressured the Democratic Party to nominate a woman to the ticket. The movement, which hinged on the belief that selecting a woman as the vice presidential candidate would energize the party and help Democrats compete against popular incumbent President Ronald Reagan (by attracting women voters), gained momentum in the months preceding the convention.[29] As rumors circulated that presidential candidate

ing her the first woman to run for election for a major party on a national ticket.[31]

Ferraro's addition to the ballot was expected to appeal to the diverse audience she represented: women, Italian Americans, Roman Catholics, and the northeastern voters. Ultimately, her characteristic pragmatism won her the nomination. Her gender alone would appeal to women and progressive voters, but as fellow House Democrat Tony Coelho of California, commented, Ferraro wasn't a "threat" to the Democratic mainstream. Qualifying his statement, Coelho said, "She is not a feminist with wounds."[32] Still, some congressional colleagues criticized Ferraro as being too inexperienced on many important issues, most especially on foreign policy matters.[33] Other women, including potential candidates Representatives

Boggs and Schroeder, questioned Ferraro's selection, citing themselves as better candidates because of their long experience in Washington politics.[34] The campaign momentum stalled when allegations of financial wrong-doing by John Zaccaro emerged. In November 1984, the Mondale–Ferraro ticket was handily defeated by the incumbent Reagan–Bush team. John Zaccaro later was convicted in February 1985 of conducting fraudulent real estate transactions.[35]

After the defeat, Geraldine Ferraro returned to practicing law. She served as a fellow at the Harvard Institute of Politics from 1988 until 1992. In addition, she authored three books about her political career. Ferraro re-entered electoral politics when she ran for the U.S. Senate in 1992 and 1998. After failing to secure the Democratic Party's nomination in both unsuccessful campaigns, Ferraro vowed to never run again for public office. In 1993, President William J. Clinton appointed her to the United Nations Human Rights Convention in Geneva, Switzerland. Ferraro also was appointed vice chair of the U.S. Delegation to the Fourth World Conference on Women, held in Beijing in September, 1995.[36] She later worked as president of a global management consulting firm, and as a television analyst and syndicated columnist.

After being diagnosed with multiple myeloma, a dangerous form of blood cancer, in 1998, Ferraro spoke publicly about her illness and her use of the drug Thalidomide to treat her condition. In a plea for continued research on Thalidomide's effects on her illness, she testified at a June 2001 Senate hearing. Using herself as an exhibit, she stated, "I look great, and I feel great, and it's what early diagnosis and research can do."[37]

FOR FURTHER READING

Biographical Directory of the United States Congress, "Geraldine Anne Ferraro," http://bioguide.congress.gov

Ferraro, Geraldine A. *Changing History: Women, Power, and Politics* (Wakefield, RI: Moyer Bell Distributed by Publishers Group West, 1993).

Ferraro, Geraldine A., with Linda Bird Francke. *Ferraro: My Story* (New York: Bantam Books, 1985).

Ferraro, Geraldine A., with Catherine Whitney. *Framing a Life: A Family Memoir* (New York: Scribners, 1998).

MANUSCRIPT COLLECTION

Marymount Manhattan College (New York, NY), Thomas J. Shanahan Library. *Papers:* 1979–1984, approximately 305 cubic feet. Personal, business, and congressional papers and correspondence, including photographs, portraits, sound recordings, and memorabilia; 82 boxes of correspondence, speeches, and *Congressional Record* statements have been microfilmed.

NOTES

1   "A Team Player: Can a Liberal from Archie Bunker Country Make a Contender of Walter Mondale?" 23 July 1984, *Newsweek*.

2   "Congresswoman Ferraro: A Career of Rising from Nowhere," 13 July 1984, *Christian Science Monitor*: 1.

3   Elisabeth Bumiller, "The Rise of Geraldine Ferraro," 29 April 1984, *Washington Post*: K1.

4   Bumiller, "The Rise of Geraldine Ferraro."

5   *Current Biography, 1984* (New York: H.W. Wilson and Company, 1984): 119.

6   Bumiller, "The Rise of Geraldine Ferraro."

7   *Almanac of American Politics, 1984* (Washington, D.C.: National Journal Inc., 1983): 805–806.

8   *Current Biography, 1984*: 119.

9   "A Team Player: Can a Liberal from Archie Bunker Country Make a Contender of Walter Mondale?"

10 *Current Biography, 1984*: 119–120; "A Team Player: Can a Liberal from Archie Bunker Country Make a Contender of Walter Mondale?"; Bumiller, "The Rise of Geraldine Ferraro."

11 *Current Biography, 1984*; John E. Farrell, *Tip O'Neill and the Democratic Century* (Boston: Little, Brown and Company, 2001): 644; "Woman in the News: Liberal Democrat from Queens," 13 July 1984, *New York Times*: A1.

12 "Election Statistics, 1920 to Present," http://clerk.house.gov/members/electionInfo/elections.html.

13 "Woman in the News: Liberal Democrat from Queens."

14 Garrison Nelson et al., *Committees in the U.S. Congress, 1947–1992* (Washington, D.C.: Congressional Quarterly Inc., 1993): 293–294; Barbara Delatiner, "On the Isle," 23 Nov. 1980, *New York Times*: LI26.

15 "Congresswoman Ferraro: A Career of Rising from Nowhere."

16 Hedrick Smith, "Consistent Liberal Record in the House," 13 July 1984, *New York Times*: A10; *Current Biography, 1984*: 120.

17 The Americans for Democratic Action (ADA) compiled the cited score for Ferraro's first term in Congress. See also *Current Biography, 1984*: 120; "Congresswoman Ferraro: A Career of Rising from Nowhere"; "Woman in the News: Liberal Democrat from Queens."

18 "Woman in the News: Liberal Democrat from Queens."

19 Ibid.

20 "Ferraro: 'I'd Quit' If Faith, Duty Clash," 12 September 1984 *Washington Post*: A8; "Woman in the News: Liberal Democrat from Queens."

21 Quoted in *Current Biography, 1984*: 120. Chris Matthews, then an aide to Speaker O'Neill, reiterated Frank's sentiments, writing in his 1988 book, *Hardball*, that the secret to Ferraro's success was that, "she asked; she received; she became a player." Chris Matthews, *Hardball: How Politics Is Played, Told By One Who Knows the Game* (New York: Perennial Library, 1988): 72.

22 "A Team Player: Can a Liberal from Archie Bunker Country Make a Contender of Walter Mondale?"

23 *Current Biography, 1984*: 119.

24 "Is This the Year for a Woman VP?" 27 March 1984, *Christian Science Monitor*: 18.

25 "A Team Player: Can a Liberal from Archie Bunker Country Make a Contender of Walter Mondale?"

26 Ibid.

27 Frank Lynn, "Carey's Tactics Cut His Power at Convention," 10 August 1980, *New York Times*: 33.

28 *Current Biography, 1984*: 120.

29 Bill Peterson and Alison Muscatine, "Pressure Increasing for Woman on Ticket," 19 June 1984, *Washington Post*: A6; *Current Biography, 1984*: 119.

30 "Is This the Year for a Woman VP?"

31 Although Ferraro made history by becoming the first woman selected as the vice presidential nominee for a major party, President Gerald R. Ford considered two women as his Republican running mate in 1976: Anne Armstrong and Carla Hills. See Joseph Kraft, "Mr. Ford's Choice," 8 August 1976, *Washington Post*: 37; R.W. Apple, Jr., "President Favors a Running Mate in the Middle of the Road," 9 August 1976, *New York Times*: 1.

32 Farrell, *Tip O'Neill and the Democratic Century*: 644.

33 *Current Biography, 1984*: 119.

34 Thomas O'Neill and William Novak, *Man of the House: The Life and Times of Speaker Tip O'Neill*, (Boston: G.K. Hall, 1987): 358; see Joan A. Lowry, *Pat Schroeder: A Woman of the House* (Albuquerque, NM: University of New Mexico Press, 2003): 133–134.

35 Ralph Blumenthal, "Judge Sentences Zaccaro to Work in Public Service," 21 February 1985, *New York Times*: A1.

36 Ralph Blumenthal, "Geraldine Ferraro to Speak at CWRU's 2003 commencement convocation"; available at http://www.cwru.edu/pub-aff/univcomm/2002/11-02/ferraro.htm (accessed 30 March 2004).

37 "Ferraro Is Battling Blood Cancer with a Potent Ally: Thalidomide" 19 June 2001, *New York Times*.

Bobbi Fiedler

1937–

UNITED STATES REPRESENTATIVE ★ REPUBLICAN FROM CALIFORNIA
1981–1987

Thrust onto the public stage because of her opposition to a controversial Los Angeles busing program, Bobbi Fiedler managed to convert her local celebrity into a political career. The former housewife and businesswoman who described herself as a "fiscal conservative and a social liberal" managed to unseat a prominent incumbent to earn a seat in the U.S. House of Representatives.[1] Fiedler's congressional career ended following an unsuccessful run for the U.S. Senate.

Roberta "Bobbi" Frances Horowitz was born to Jack and Sylvia Levin Horowitz in Santa Monica, California, on April 22, 1937. After graduating from Santa Monica High School in 1955, she attended Santa Monica Technical School and Santa Monica City College through 1959. During the 1960s, she and her husband owned and operated two pharmacies in the San Fernando section of Los Angeles and had two children, Randy and Lisa.[2] The Fiedlers later divorced.

Bobbi Fiedler first entered the public spotlight when she became a vocal critic of a divisive Los Angeles busing program of the 1970s. Aimed at promoting racial integration in Southern California public schools, the mandatory busing system attracted the ire of parents throughout the district because of its tendency to force children to travel long distances to and from school. As a parent volunteer in a local elementary school, Fiedler led the charge of disgruntled parents by organizing an anti-busing group called BUSTOP. Fiedler's notoriety from her work with the protest organization helped launch her political career. In 1977, she won election to the influential Los Angeles city board of education which oversaw an urban school district encompassing more than 3 million people.[3] The high-profile leadership position spurred Fiedler's

ascent on both the state and national scene. From 1977 through 1987, Fiedler served as a delegate to the California State Republican conventions, and she also was a delegate to the Republican National Convention in 1980 and 1984. During the 1984 Republican National Convention in Dallas, Texas, Fiedler delivered a speech seconding President Ronald Reagan's nomination for re-election.[4]

Brimming with confidence from her newfound role as a leading public figure in the Los Angeles area, Fiedler decided to run for a seat in the 97th Congress (1981–1983) that represented portions of suburban Los Angeles in the San Fernando Valley, including the towns of Woodland Hills, Northridge, and Granada Hills. It was a district dominated by white-collar, middle-class families. She faced little opposition in the Republican primary, earning 74 percent of the vote against Patrick O'Brien. Despite her easy victory in the primary, Fiedler had the daunting task of running against 10-term incumbent Representative James Corman in the general election. Not intimidated by her opponent's influential position in Congress, Fiedler pronounced, "He's so out of touch he doesn't know what people in the district think."[5] Few people believed Corman, chair of the Democratic Congressional Committee and high-ranking member of the powerful Ways and Means Committee, could be unseated by an inexperienced candidate. With a straightforward campaign strategy focusing on opposition to the Los Angeles busing system—a tactic that paralleled Congresswoman Louise Hicks' (of Massachusetts) path to the House a decade earlier–Fiedler stunned experts with one of the biggest upsets of the political season, defeating Corman on November 4, 1980, by 752 votes.[6] Fiedler also was aided by Ronald W. Reagan's landslide defeat of incum-

bent President James Earl "Jimmy" Carter in the 1980 presidential election; Carter's early concession speech, given three hours before the polls closed in California, may have tilted the closely contested race in Fiedler's favor by discouraging voter turnout among Democrats.[7]

In Congress, Fiedler was rewarded handsomely for her unlikely victory, winning appointment to the Budget Committee, where she served for all three of her terms and was on the Joint Economic Committee during the 99th Congress (1985–1987). She also was the senior Republican member of task forces on defense and international affairs as well as health. As a Congresswoman, Fiedler typically backed the Reagan administration and her Republican colleagues on fiscal matters, most especially in her position as a member of the Budget Committee. Nonetheless, she strayed from the party line with respect to her views towards women's rights. Admittedly not a feminist before becoming a politician, Fiedler commented that soon after taking office she felt a "special obligation" to represent the concerns of women. She went on to remark, "I began to realize that most men have very little real knowledge of the problems women face. They don't understand the special responsibility of working full time and getting up at one or two in the morning with a sick child."[8] During her tenure in Congress, Fiedler promoted a range of issues concerning women, such as Individual Retirement Account allotments for homemakers, child support and enforcement, and welfare reform, as well as supporting the Equal Rights Amendment. However, some feminists criticized her for not assuming a more public role in advocating the equal rights of women.[9]

As a result of 1982 reapportionment, Fielder's district became a Republican stronghold in California. Re-elected to both the 98th and 99th Congresses (1983–1987) with more than 70 percent of the vote, Fiedler nonetheless opted to leave her safe seat to challenge the longtime Democratic California Senator Alan Cranston in 1986.[10] Although Cranston had easily defeated his conservative Republican opponents in his previous two re-election bids, Fiedler entered the race in part because of her belief

that her more moderate views would appeal to voters. Moreover, Cranston, a man she termed an "ultra-liberal" and the "last of the old-time big spenders," was viewed by some Republicans as vulnerable coming off his unsuccessful run for the Democratic presidential nomination in 1984.[11] During the Republican primary, Fiedler's candidacy fell apart when a grand jury indicted her and an aide for attempting to pay an opponent to withdraw from the race. Fiedler called the allegation "a political dirty trick" and maintained her innocence.[12] The indictment soon was dropped, but the political fallout was costly. Fiedler lost the primary, garnering just 15 percent of the vote.

Following the end of her third term in Congress, she returned to Northridge, California, where she married Paul Clarke, her former chief of staff, on February 15, 1987. Fiedler expressed interest in succeeding outgoing U.S. Secretary of Transportation Elizabeth Dole in the fall of 1987, but the Reagan administration did not nominate her for the Cabinet position.[13] Fiedler later worked as a lobbyist and political commentator.[14]

FOR FURTHER READING

Biographical Directory of the United States Congress, "Bobbi Fiedler," http://bioguide.congress.gov

NOTES

1   A.O. Sulzberger, Jr., "The Four New Congresswomen on the Issues," 11 January 1981, *New York Times*: 52.

2   John Balzar, "Bobbi Fiedler—She Won't Be Counted Out," 9 May 1986, *Los Angeles Times*: 3.

3   Sulzberger, "The Four New Congresswomen on the Issues."

4   *Politics in America, 1982* (Washington, D.C.: Congressional Quarterly Inc., 1981): 132; "Fiedler After Cabinet Post," 6 October, 1987, *Los Angeles Times*: 2.

5   Joel Kotkin, "Support of Busing Could Cost Calif. Congressman His Seat," 21 September 1980, *Washington Post*: A5.

6   "Election Statistics, 1920 to Present," http://clerk.house.gov/members/electionInfo/elections.html; Jim Bencivenga, "Grassroots School Government Hallmark of Nation's Strength," 28 January 1983, *Christian Science Monitor*: B6.

7   *Almanac of American Politics, 1984* (Washington, D.C.: National Journal Inc., 1983): 127.

8   Steven V. Roberts, "Congress Stages a Pre-emptive Strike on the Gender Gap," 6 May 1984, *New York Times*: 227.

9   *Almanac of American Politics, 1986* (Washington, D.C.: National Journal Inc., 1985): 148.

10 "Election Statistics, 1920 to Present," http://clerk.house.gov/members/electionInfo/elections.html; "Bobbi Fiedler," Associated Press Candidate Biographies, 1986.

11 Keith Love, "Fiedler Enters Contest for Senate, Attacks Cranston," 7 January 1986, *Los Angeles Times*: 3; "Bobbi Fiedler," Associated Press Candidate Biographies, 1986; Robert Lindsey, "Cranston Arming for Tough Fight," 1 December 1985, *New York Times*: 31; *Almanac of American Politics, 1986*: 148.

12 Robert W. Stewart and Paul Feldman, "Fiedler Calls Self Victim of 'Ridiculous' Bribe Charge; Top Aide Blasts 'Dirty Trick,'" 24 January 1986, *Los Angeles Times*: 1; Judith Cummings, "Effort to Bribe Rival Charged to Rep. Fiedler," 25 January 1986, *New York Times*: 1; Keith Love and John Balzar, "Both Fiedler, Davis Seen as Hurt; Indictment Plunges GOP Senate Race into Chaos," 25 January 1986, *Los Angeles Times*: 1.

13 "Fiedler After Cabinet Post."

14 "Digest: Local News in Brief; Bobbi Fiedler, Former Aide Paul Clarke Wed," 17 February 1987, *Los Angeles Times*: 7.

Paula Fickes Hawkins

1927–

UNITED STATES SENATOR ★ REPUBLICAN FROM FLORIDA
1981–1987

An aggressive and outspoken Republican, Paula Hawkins sailed into office in a Republican sweep led by victorious presidential candidate Ronald Reagan in 1980. A staunch defender of her ever-changing Florida constituency, she also created a public dialogue on the subject of missing, exploited, and abused children. Hawkins's vigorous work to pass the 1982 Missing Children's Act helped bring to light a long-ignored national scourge.

Paula Fickes was born in Salt Lake City, Utah, on January 24, 1927, the oldest of three children raised by Paul, a chief warrant officer in the Navy, and Leone (Staley) Fickes. In 1934, the family settled in Atlanta, Georgia, where Paul Fickes took a teaching job at Georgia Tech. The Fickes eventually separated, and Leone Fickes moved with her children to Logan, Utah. Paula Fickes graduated from Cache High School in Richmond, Utah, in 1944. She attended Utah State University before taking a job as a secretary for the university's director of athletics. Paula Fickes married Walter Eugene Hawkins on September 5, 1947. The couple settled in Atlanta, where Walter studied electrical engineering; he later owned a successful electronics business. The Hawkins raised three children: Genean, Kevin, and Kelly Ann. The family moved to Florida in 1955 where Paula Hawkins first entered public affairs as a community activist and volunteer for the local Republican Party organization. In 1966, she helped orchestrate Republican Edward Gurney's successful campaign in the GOP primary and general election for a House seat. Two years later, Hawkins co-chaired the Richard Nixon presidential campaign in Florida. Hawkins's work as a GOP regular provided her the base

from which to launch a political career, winning election to the Florida public service commission from 1972 to 1979. In 1974, she entered the primary race for the U.S. Senate seat held by Gurney, then a freshman incumbent under investigation for campaign finance improprieties.[1] Hawkins, however, failed to secure the GOP nomination. In 1978, Hawkins also lost a campaign for lieutenant governor of Florida.

In 1980, encouraged by the Republican National Committee chairman, Hawkins entered the race for the seat of incumbent Democrat Senator Richard B. Stone. She won a plurality against five other contenders in the GOP primary but fell short of the necessary majority by just a few points. In the run-off primary she overwhelmed the runner-up, former U.S. Representative Lou Frey, Jr., with 62 percent of the vote.[2] In the general election, she faced popular former U.S. Representative Bill Gunter, who had edged Senator Stone in the Democratic primary. The election seemed to hinge less on substantive issues than on the candidates' personalities, with Hawkins depicted, partly on her own volition, as being aggressive and forceful. "[Voters] don't want specifics," Hawkins said. "People are looking for somebody that will shake it up.... That's all they want. They want a fighter."[3] Observers agreed that Hawkins benefited from the long coattails of GOP presidential candidate Ronald Reagan, who won Florida with 56 percent of the vote on his way to victory. Hawkins won, too, but by a narrower margin, just 52 percent.[4] She was part of a Republican tide in the Senate, as 14 new GOP Senators were elected to the upper chamber, shifting control away from the Democrats for the first time in nearly three decades.

When Senator Stone resigned from office on December

"Paula's like a teabag,"
one Florida
GOP official observed.
"You have to put her
in hot water to
see how strong she is."

31, 1980, Hawkins was appointed to fill his seat on January 1, 1981, thus giving her a minor seniority advantage over the rest of the Senate freshmen who were sworn in two days later. Senator Hawkins was assigned to three committees when the 97th Congress (1981–1983) convened: Labor and Human Resources; Agriculture, Nutrition, and Forestry; and Joint Economic. In the 98th Congress (1983–1985), she received additional appointments to the Foreign Relations Committee and the Banking, Housing, and Urban Affairs Committee. Hawkins also served on the Special Committee on Aging.

Hawkins immediately began cultivating her image as a scrapper. Her outspoken manner, however, was not always well-received by more staid Senate colleagues. After a year in office, Hawkins altered her approach, hoping that constituents would judge her legislative achievements rather than her aggressive style. "I guess I have my dog in too many fights," she confided to the *New York Times* in late 1981.[5] Hawkins lobbied hard for federal aid to help the state defray the costs of caring for, housing, and processing thousands of Cuban and Haitian refugees in Florida. She warned that otherwise, "We just might have to dig a ditch at our northern border, erect a sign, 'Yankees, Keep Out,' and apply for foreign aid ourselves. Florida is under siege, and it's no fault of our own." In particular, Hawkins expressed concern about the effects of the 1980 Mariel boatlift, which resulted when Cuban dictator Fidel Castro temporarily lifted emigration restrictions. It was later revealed that Castro emptied some of his nation's jails, setting hardened criminals aboard the "freedom flotilla" to Florida; 23,000 of the immigrants had conviction records. State authorities were extremely taxed handling the flood of refugees. Hawkins described the boatlift people in sweeping terms; they were, she told one newspaper, "terrorists." Her solution to the problem: "Send them home."[6]

As chair of the Investigation and Oversight Subcommittee of the Senate Labor and Human Resources Committee, Hawkins initiated a year-long probe of the rising numbers of children reported missing by their families. She worked closely with a Florida couple, John and Reve Walsh, whose son, Adam, was abducted from a Florida shopping mall and was later found decapitated, a horrific episode that riveted national attention. The Walsh family had found that a number of bureaucratic road blocks hindered the search for their son and were determined to create a missing children's agency to facilitate searches. Paula Hawkins was a key ally in that effort. Her work led to the passage of the Missing Children's Act of 1982, a measure that established a national center for information about missing children. Prior to this legislation, parents had been required to wait 48 hours before the federal officials could become involved in the search for a missing child. Hawkins's bill abolished that waiting period. It also gave parents access to a Federal Bureau of Investigation database, the National Crime Information Center, where they could list their child and perform searches through records of existing reports.[7] By clearing away the red tape, Hawkins's bill helped locate more than 2,000 children in the first year of its existence.

In 1984, at the Third National Conference on Sexual Victimization of Children, Hawkins stunned the audience by revealing that she was sexually molested as a kindergartener by a trusted elderly neighbor. When the case went to court, however, the judge discounted her and other neighborhood children's testimony. The molester was set free. "I like to win," Hawkins recalled, "and it's bothered me all this time that the 'nice old man' got off and went on abusing children for the rest of his life. The embarrassment and humiliation of being called a liar will stay with me the rest of mine." For Hawkins, the effect of "going public" with this well-kept secret was personally therapeutic and rewarding in the sense that it encouraged others to do so as well. "Almost immediately, many other child abuse victims felt free to discuss their own difficult experiences," she recalled in her autobiography. "After all, if a U.S. Senator had opened up, why shouldn't they?"[8]

Hawkins's 1986 re-election campaign was judged to be a referendum not only on Hawkins's first term in office but the Reagan presidency as well. With 22 GOP seats up for election, the Republican majority in the Senate was at stake. Early on, GOP officials deemed Hawkins's contest

a key electoral battle and began putting money and resources into it. She faced the most popular politician in the state: two-term Governor Bob Graham, whose approval ratings topped 80 percent. At one point Hawkins trailed by as much as 22 percent in some of the polls, but political observers refused to count her out. "Paula's like a teabag," one Florida GOP official observed. "You have to put her in hot water to see how strong she is."[9] Nevertheless, her campaign was plagued by her ill health and poor luck. In May 1985, news reports revealed that Hawkins's estranged brother had been indicted on child abuse charges.[10] Hawkins maintained that the timing of that news release was a ploy to hurt her campaign. In early 1986, suffering pain from an old back injury, Hawkins checked herself into Duke University Hospital and was temporarily sidelined by a surgical procedure.[11] Lost weeks of campaigning hurt Hawkins in a state where voter turnover—by one estimate nearly one-third of the registered voters in 1986 had not been residents in 1980—was a perennial concern for politicians.[12] She also had the difficult task of campaigning against a Democratic opponent who supported such Republican positions as Strategic Defense Initiative, aid to the Contras in Nicaragua, and the death penalty.[13] Hawkins lost to Governor Graham by nearly 180,000 votes, or a 55 percent to 45 percent margin, as Democrats regained control of the Senate.[14]

After completing her term in the Senate, Hawkins returned to her home in Winter Park, Florida. She served for seven years as a representative for the United States on the Organization of American States Inter-American Drug Abuse Commission. In 1997, she retired from politics and joined the board of directors of a large drug and cosmetic company. Hawkins continues to serve as president of a management consulting company she founded in 1988.

FOR FURTHER READING

Biographical Directory of the United States Congress, "Paula Hawkins," http://bioguide.congress.gov

Hawkins, Paula. *Children at Risk, My Fight Against Child Abuse: A Personal Story and a Public Plea* (Bethesda, MD: Adler & Adler, 1986).

MANUSCRIPT COLLECTIONS

University of North Carolina (Chapel Hill, NC). *Oral History*: 1974, 27 pages. Subjects discussed include Watergate Affair, women in politics, U.S. and Florida politics, and the Florida Republican Party.

Winter Park Public Library (Winter Park, FL). *Papers*: 1969–1986, 294 cubic feet. The main emphasis of the collection is the service of Paula Hawkins in the United States Senate. Included is correspondence from various political figures (state and national), records of her legislative activities and materials from her various senatorial campaigns. The majority of the materials were generated by Hawkins (from her conduct of official and public duties and business) and can provide the researcher with both a survey of Florida's political environment in the 1970s and 1980s, and a profile of Senator Hawkins as a politician. On a broader scale, the collection provides a look into the activities and issues that were of interest to the Florida congressional delegation during her term in the Senate (1981–1987). Issues include the Cross-Florida Barge Canal, immigration, the citrus industry/agriculture, foreign trade, and illegal drugs.

NOTES

1   Robin D. Meszoly, "Women in Politics: Good, Bad News," 14 April 1974, *Washington Post*: A9.

2   Judith Miller, "Senator Beaten In Florida Race for Nomination," 8 October 1980, *New York Times*: B8.

3   *Current Biography, 1985* (New York: H.W. Wilson and Company, 1985): 174.

4   "Election Statistics, 1920 to Present," http://clerk.house.gov/members/electionInfo/elections.html.

5   Phil Gailey, "For Senator Hawkins, A Debatable First Year," 15 December 1981, *New York Times*: B18.

6   Art Harris, "Boatlift Bloat Sends Angry Florida Officials Into Tropical Politics," 22 December 1981, *Washington Post*: A2.

7   See especially, Paula Hawkins, *Children at Risk: My Fight Against Child Abuse—A Personal Story and a Public Plea* (Bethesda, MD: Adler & Adler, 1986): 39–45; see also *Congressional Record*, Senate, 97th Cong., 2nd sess. (24 February 1982): 2322–2325.

8   Hawkins, *Children at Risk*: 7; Sandy Rovner, "Children of Abuse: Sen. Paula Hawkins Says She Was Molested at Age 5," 27 April 1984, *Washington Post*: B1; Marjorie Hunter, "The Effects of Going Public on Sexual Abuse," 5 May 1984, *New York Times*: 11; Nadine Brozan, "A Senator Recounts Her Own Experience as an Abused Child," 27 April 1984, *New York Times*: A1.

9   John Dillin, "Florida Contest Typifies Fight for US Senate Control: Reagan Has Big Stake in Such Races as Graham vs. Hawkins," 8 September 1986, *Christian Science Monitor*: 3.

10 Bill Peterson, "Paula Hawkins, Fighter: Senator's Reelection Bid Crucial for GOP," 2 September 1985, *Washington Post*: A1; "Sen. Hawkins' Brother in Jail," 27 May 1985, *Washington Post*: C3; Fred Grimm, "Paula Hawkins and the Family Tragedy," 2 June 1985, *Washington Post*: H1.

11 Jon Nordheimer, "Hawkins Interrupting Senate Race for Operation," 7 April 1986, *New York Times*: A23; Bill Peterson, "Hawkins' Health Is Biggest Campaign Issue," 16 February 1986, *Washington Post*: A3; Bill Peterson, "Hawkins Changes Publicity Strategy," 7 April 1986, *Washington Post*: A7.

12 Jon Nordheimer, "Florida Lawmakers Face Growth Issues," 3 April 1985, *New York Times*: A16.

13 Ellen Hume, "Sen. Paula Hawkins Struggles in Reelection Bid to Overcome Challenge from Popular Governor," 20 October 1986, *Wall Street Journal*: 56.

14 Maureen Dowd, "Ads Are the Issue in Florida In Hawkins–Graham Race," 29 October 1986, *New York Times*: A23; Jon Nordheimer, "G.O.P. Elects Governor; Graham Beats Hawkins," 5 November 1986, *New York Times*: A27; see also, "Election Statistics, 1920 to Present," http://clerk.house.gov/members/electionInfo/elections.html.

Lynn Martin

1939–

UNITED STATES REPRESENTATIVE ★ REPUBLICAN FROM ILLINOIS
1981–1991

In a decade in the House, Lynn Martin's expertise on economic issues, her quick wit, moderation, and independence helped her to become the first woman House Member to attain leadership positions high within the Republican Party. As she had in the Illinois house of representatives, Congresswoman Martin earned a reputation as a liberal on women's issues but also as a stalwart fiscal conservative eager to rein in a government that, in her view, had spent beyond its means since the 1960s. "All bureaucracy doesn't have to exist forever," Martin said shortly after arriving in Congress.[1]

Judith Lynn Morely was born on December 26, 1939, in Evanston, Illinois, youngest of two daughters of William Morely, an accountant, and Helen Hall Morely, a department store clerk. She grew up on the north side of Chicago in a heavily Irish-Catholic and Democratic neighborhood and attended public schools. Her earliest political experience was in running for eighth-grade class president against her boyfriend. "I lost by one vote. My vote. You see, I voted for my opponent because I thought it was polite," she recalled years later. "Well, he voted for himself, and I learned my lesson: if you believe in yourself, vote for yourself."[2] She made Phi Beta Kappa and earned a B.A. in English at the University of Illinois at Urbana in 1960. A week after she graduated she married John Martin, an engineering student. They raised two daughters, Julia and Caroline. Lynn Martin taught at several high schools in DuPage County and Rockford, Illinois.

Martin entered public service after becoming "interested in my community" and worried that the local government was "out of touch" and "buried."[3] In 1972, Martin was elected to the Winnebago County (Illinois) board and four years later won a seat in the state house of representatives. Her political mentors were Betty Ann Keegan, a Democrat in the Illinois state senate who first encouraged her to run for office, and Republican Congressman Robert Michel of Illinois, the future U.S. House Minority Leader. There she served on the appropriations committee and earned the nickname "the Axe" for her efforts to reduce spending.[4] Martin won election to the Illinois senate in 1978. That same year she and John Martin were divorced. Lynn Martin eventually remarried in 1987 to Harry Leinenweber, a U.S. District Court judge.

When U.S. Representative John Anderson retired to run for the presidency in 1980, Martin beat four other Republicans in the primary for the open seat in the northwest Illinois district bordering Wisconsin. The largely agrarian district was anchored by the town of Rockford, and had not sent a Democrat to Congress in the 20th century.[5] Martin's platform supported the Equal Rights Amendment and was pro-choice on the abortion issue, while fiscally conservative, calling for lower taxes and business deregulation. Her socially moderate stance earned her the support of women's groups. In a state that went comfortably for Republican presidential nominee Ronald Reagan in the general election, Martin cruised to victory with 67 percent of the vote against Democratic candidate Douglas R. Aurand. Though held to less than 60 percent of the vote in 1982 and 1984, she never was seriously challenged afterward.[6] "I had an opportunity to run for the House and wrestle with some things, like the direction of growth in government," Martin said shortly after taking office. "I knew if I ignored the opportunity, then I'd never have the right to complain about these things."[7]

In Congress, Martin quickly became a leader within the Republican Party. She possessed an encyclopedic

CONGRESSIONAL PICTORIAL DIRECTORY, 100TH CONGRESS

knowledge of economic issues and a razor sharp tongue with which she skewered Democrats (and some Republicans) for what she identified as zealous spending habits. Her mentor, Minority Leader Robert Michel, got Martin a seat on the Budget Committee in the 97th Congress (1981–1983), a plum assignment for a freshman. Martin explained, "It's a little like getting sex education at age six. It's a little too soon to understand—there's a lot of stuff you shouldn't know until a lot later." Soon after, Martin was plotting budget strategy with the Reagan White House and clashing with the Defense Department, which wanted to vastly expand military spending at the expense of social programs.[8] In 1986, during the committee's budget negotiations, Martin stood in for the ailing Ranking Republican. She established a cordial working relationship with Democratic Chairman William Gray III of Pennsylvania, impressing observers with her acumen. In 1987, during a markup session on the budget, a question arose over whether the committee should restore a revenue-sharing program. Several of the men, both Republicans and Democrats, made assertive arguments for restoration. Martin balked, arguing that the deficit-strapped federal government had no money to share with local governments. "Maybe girls learn to say 'no' easier than boys," she chided her colleagues, drawing chuckles from many in the room.[9]

When Geraldine Ferraro became the Democratic vice-presidential candidate in 1984, Martin played a prominent role in steering Republican national strategy. First, she became Vice President George H. W. Bush's sparring partner, a stand-in for Ferraro to prepare for the fall debates. She adopted an aggressive style in those mock debates, throwing the Vice President off balance and convincing him that he needed to prepare more rigorously. Martin also was tapped to deliver Bush's nominating speech at the Republican National Convention in Dallas. The party further named her chair of the Reagan–Bush Illinois campaign. When Bush ran for President in 1988, she was the only woman named a national co-chair of his campaign. After the 1984 election she also won the historic distinction of being elected Vice Chair of the House Republican Conference, the first woman ever to serve in the

House GOP leadership. She was re-elected to the post two years later. In 1988, when Conference Chair Dick Cheney of Wyoming opted to run for the party's second highest position of Whip, Martin entered the race for his vacant leadership spot. She lost her bid by only three votes to Jerry Lewis of California after party conservatives mounted a campaign against her, in part, for her voting record on social issues.[10]

Martin avoided labels such as "crusader" or "feminist." She once exclaimed, "I don't walk into every meeting humming, 'I Am Woman.'"[11] In the 100th Congress (1987–1989) she waged a successful crusade to bring 30,000 congressional employees under the protection of the 1964 Civil Rights Act (from which they had been exempt). It was, in large part, an effort to raise working conditions, reduce discrimination, and to improve the pay for women staff members whom Martin demonstrated were consistently underpaid.[12] She was oriented toward helping women through providing economic opportunity rather than government aid. "In a recessive economy," Martin said in 1981, "the people the most hurt are minority women. So the best place I could help would be to get it going again. If we're in a recession—if there are no jobs—programs don't mean a thing."[13]

Martin distinguished herself on several other committees, serving on House Administration (1981–1985), Public Works and Transportation (1983–1985), Armed Services (1985–1989), and Rules (1989–1991). On a number of important issues she parted company with Republicans: arguing for a minimum wage increase, voting to override President Reagan's 1986 veto of a sanctions bill against the apartheid regime in South Africa, joining with Democrats to stiffen punishment for white-collar criminals, and supporting pro-choice legislation.

In 1990, President Bush and other Republican leaders convinced Martin to give up her House seniority to challenge incumbent Democrat Paul Simon for a U.S. Senate seat. Observers thought it would be a close race. Martin's campaign suffered from several gaffes and a lack of funding (Simon outspent her by a nearly two-to-one margin).[14] Both candidates were pro-choice, though Simon managed to

win support of the Women's Campaign Fund because of his connections to that group's major donors. It was a blow to Martin's cash-strapped campaign. Simon also was able to capitalize on wide public support for Operation Desert Shield, the military buildup leading up to the Gulf War, by generating publicity from his seat on the Senate Foreign Relations Committee; he appeared on television with the troops in Saudi Arabia.[15] Martin lost in a landslide as Simon scooped up 65 percent of the vote.[16]

Martin's supporters in the party helped her in her post-congressional career. On December 14, 1990, President Bush appointed her Secretary of Labor, despite the fact that she was at variance with the administration on social issues. "I can't imagine the only people who should work for a President are those who sycophantically agree on everything," Martin said. "It would be the most boring Cabinet in the world and it would be of no use to the President."[17] She served as Labor Secretary from February 22, 1991, until January 20, 1993, developing several programs: "Job Training 2000" for youth apprenticeships; the Pension Opportunities for Worker's Expanded Retirement; and the "Glass Ceiling" Initiative. Martin later taught at Northwestern University, worked for Deloitte & Touche's Council on the Advancement of Women, chaired a University of Illinois task force on "The Future of the Health Care Labor Force in a Graying Society," and conducted a comprehensive study on sexual harassment in the workplace for a major automobile company.[18] She lives in Chicago, Illinois.

FOR FURTHER READING

Biographical Directory of the United States Congress, "Lynn Morley Martin," http://bioguide.congress.gov

Petri, Thomas E., William F. Clinger, Jr., Nancy L. Johnson, and Lynn Martin, eds. *National Industrial Policy: Solution or Illusion* (Boulder, CO: Westview Press, 1984).

MANUSCRIPT COLLECTION

University of Oklahoma (Norman, OK), The Julian P. Kanter Commercial Archive, Department of Communication. *Video reels and video cassettes:* 1980–1990, 10 video reels and two video cassettes. Includes 33 commercials used during campaigns for 1980, 1984, 1986, and 1988 U.S. congressional elections and her 1990 U.S. senatorial election in Illinois.

NOTES

1 Deborah Churchman, "Illinois Congresswoman Brings Her Frugal Style to Washington," 8 January 1981, *Christian Science Monitor*: 17.

2 Shirley Washington, *Outstanding Women Members of Congress* (Washington, D.C.: U.S. Capitol Historical Society, 1995): 57.

3 Churchman, "Illinois Congresswoman Brings Her Frugal Style to Washington."

4 *Current Biography, 1989* (New York: H.W. Wilson and Company, 1989): 386.

5 *Politics in America, 1982* (Washington, D.C.: Congressional Quarterly Inc., 1981): 362.

6 "Election Statistics, 1920 to Present," http://clerk.house.gov/members/electionInfo/elections.html.

7 Churchman, "Illinois Congresswoman Brings Her Frugal Style to Washington."

8 *Current Biography, 1989*: 386.

9 Milton Coleman, "Lynn M. Martin: Finessing an Insider's Game in House GOP Leadership," 19 May 1986, *Washington Post*: A13.

10 Susan F. Rasky, "Parties Name House Leaders and Goals," 6 December 1988, *New York Times*: B13; Clifford D. May and David Binder, "Briefing," 24 November 1988, *New York Times*: B15; *Almanac of American Politics, 1990* (Washington, D.C.: National Journal Inc., 1989): 382.

11 Coleman, "Lynn M. Martin: Finessing an Insider's Game in House GOP Leadership."

12 Irvin Molotsky, "House Extends Job Bias Protection To Its Own Workers, With Limits," 5 October 1988, *New York Times*: A1.

13 Churchman, "Illinois Congresswoman Brings Her Frugal Style to Washington."

14 *Almanac of American Politics, 1994* (Washington, D.C.: National Journal Inc., 1993): 384.

15 Washington, *Outstanding Women Members of Congress*: 60

16 "Election Statistics, 1920 to Present," http://clerk.house.gov/members/electionInfo/elections.html.

17 Charles Trueheart, "Lynn Martin: No Yes Woman," 19 August 1992, *Washington Post*: B1. See also Karen Foerstel, *Biographical Dictionary of Congressional Women* (Westport, CT: Greenwood Press, 1999): 173–174.

18 "Mitsubishi Settles with Women in Sexual Harassment Lawsuit," 29 August 1997, *New York Times*: A14.

Margaret (Marge) Roukema

1929–

UNITED STATES REPRESENTATIVE ★ REPUBLICAN FROM NEW JERSEY
1981–2003

For more than two decades Congresswoman Marge Roukema forged a reputation as a Republican moderate in the U.S. House, focusing on family issues and welfare reform. Personal tragedy helped prompt Roukema toward a career in politics and factored into one of her great legislative successes.

Margaret Scafati was born in Newark, New Jersey, on September 19, 1929. She was named for her mother, and her father, Claude, was a first-generation Italian American who worked as an auto mechanic. Margaret Scafati earned a B.A. degree in history and political science from Montclair State College in 1951 and subsequently pursued graduate studies there. In 1975 she also did graduate work in city and regional planning at Rutgers University. She worked as a high school teacher in American history and government before marrying Richard W. Roukema, a psychiatrist. The couple raised three children: Greg, Todd, and Meg. Marge Roukema's first public service position was on the board of education in Ridgewood, New Jersey, where she served from 1970 to 1973. Her political activity was, in part, spurred by her 17-year-old son, Todd, and his battle with leukemia. Roukema put her plans to attend law school at Rutgers University aside to tend to her dying son who succumbed to the disease in October 1976. Roukema later recalled that in the aftermath she was searching for an emotional and intellectual outlet.[1] She became active in local party politics as the first woman elected president of the Ridgewood Republican Club in 1977 and 1978. In 1977, she also supported moderate Republican gubernatorial candidate Tom Kean, at first as a volunteer but quickly rising to become his campaign coordinator in 30 towns. That experience led her to launch her own campaign for federal office.[2] In 1978, she mount-

ed a challenge against incumbent Democrat Andrew Maguire for a U.S. House seat in northern New Jersey that encompassed Bergen County and included the towns of Paramus and Hackensack. But Roukema lost by a margin of about 9,000 votes, 53 percent to 47 percent.[3]

In 1980, Roukema again challenged Maguire, whom she described as a liberal "out of touch" with his constituency. Roukema, this time aided by the strong Republican turnout for Ronald Reagan, won the seat by a margin of 9,000 votes. In 1982 the district lines were redrawn, and it stretched west to include Sussex County, and Roukema was able to claim an even larger margin of victory: a plurality of 50,000 votes against Democrat Fritz Cammerzell. Indeed, in 11 re-election campaigns, she was never seriously challenged during the general elections, claiming between 65 and 71 percent of the vote. In her final two Republican primaries in 1998 and 2000, however, she faced stiff challenges from the conservative elements of her party who claimed that she was too liberal on a range of issues. Against a conservative state assemblyman in the 2000 primary, Roukema won by less than 2,000 votes, though she again dominated the general election with 71 percent of the vote.[4]

When she entered Congress in 1981, Roukema received assignments on the Committee on Education and Labor (later renamed Education and Workforce) and the Committee on Banking, Finance, and Urban Affairs (later renamed Financial Services). She sat on both committees for the duration of her career in the House, eventually rising to chair Financial Services's two subcommittees: Housing and Community Opportunity, and Financial Institutions and Consumer Credit. In addition, Roukema worked on the Education Reform and the Employer-

Employee Relations subcommittees of Education and Workforce. In the 98th Congress (1983–1985) she joined the newly formed Select Committee on Hunger as its Ranking Republican Member; she served there for a decade until the committee was disbanded in 1995.

Roukema's committee assignments led her into legislative work on behalf of job training in the private sector, child support, welfare reform, and family leave policy. Her biggest legislative achievement was the enactment of the Family and Medical Leave Act of 1993, a bill that Roukema and Democrat Patricia Schroeder of Colorado worked on for years. It required large companies to extend unpaid leave time to new parents, disabled workers, and those caring for chronically ill relatives. Roukema secured the key compromise which helped pass the bill, an exemption for small businesses. Her experience caring for her son shaped her perspective on the issue. "When my son Todd was stricken with leukemia and needed home care, I was free to remain at home and give him the loving care he needed," Roukema told colleagues in a floor speech. "But what of the millions of mothers who work for the thousands of companies that do not have family leave policies?"[5] Roukema later recalled that "the tragedy with Todd was what made me so determined about the Family and Medical Leave Act."[6] She also tended to cross party lines to vote with Democrats on social issues, supporting abortion rights and gun control, for instance. In 1994, she was one of just 11 Republicans to vote to bring a Democratic anti-crime bill to the House Floor and to vote with Democrats to ban assault weapons.[7]

As Roukema's seniority rose in the GOP, so did her criticisms of the party's conservative turn during the 1980s and 1990s. During the controversy stirred by the investigation of the fundraising practices of House Speaker Newt Gingrich, Roukema suggested that an interim Speaker be named until the House Ethics Committee finished its probe. When the House levied a $300,000 fine against Gingrich for breaking ethics rules, Roukema insisted that he pay it from personal rather than campaign funds.[8] In May 1997 she bristled on the House Floor about Republican efforts to cut $38 million in funding for a

major nutrition program for children and pregnant women. "We are not going to take food out of the mouths of little babies!" she declared. "Don't we ever learn?" In an interview at the time she warned, "Our party will either become a true majority party, or a regional party" in the South. "And the way you maintain a majority," she concluded, "is to find consensus within your party."[9]

By the 107th Congress (2001–2003), Roukema was the longest serving woman in the House and the dean of her state delegation. She also was the Ranking Republican on the Financial Services Committee, but the Republican leadership skipped over her in picking the new chair. "The fact that I was a woman had something to do with it," Roukema told the *New York Times*. Her outspokenness and the fact that she did not raise prodigious amounts of money to steer to the campaigns of fellow House Republicans also contributed to the decision, she added. "I was an Independent voter in Congress, and I voted my conscience and my state," Roukema recalled several years later. "That brought me down in [leadership's] estimation. I was not elected to do what leadership [said]. I was elected to do what my intelligence, my conscience, and my constituents needed.... That was my reason for being in Congress."[10] She was offered a position as U.S. Treasurer in the George W. Bush administration in 2001 but turned down the offer to serve as chair of the Financial Services' Housing and Community Opportunity Subcommittee.

In November 2001, Roukema announced that she would not seek re-election to a 12th term. She retired in January 2003, at age 73, and returned to New Jersey. Roukema served on the boards of several nonprofits dedicated to children's issues and planned to lecture about politics at several universities.[11]

★ MARGARET (MARGE) ROUKEMA ★

FOR FURTHER READING

Biographical Directory of the United States Congress, "Margaret Scafati Roukema," http://bioguide.congress.gov

Roukema, Marge. "Congress and Banking Reform I," in "Symposium: The Direction of New Jersey Banking," *Seton Hall Legislative Journal* 16 (1992): 481–490.

Tomlinson, Barbara J. "Making Their Way: A Study of New Jersey Congresswomen, 1924–1994." Ph.D. diss., Rutgers, The State University of New Jersey, New Brunswick, 1996.

1 Melinda Henneberger, "Preaching Moderation on Her Own Side of the Aisle," 20 July 1997, *New York Times*: Section 13NJ: 2.

3 "Election Statistics, 1920 to Present," http://clerk.house.gov/members/electionInfo/elections.html.

5 Karen Foerstel, *Biographical Dictionary of Congressional Women* (Westport, CT: Greenwood Press, 1999): 236.

6 Bob Ivry, "Home from the House: Roukema in Transition after 11 Terms in Congress," 1 December 2002, *Bergen Record*: A1; see also, *Congressional Record*, House, 103rd Cong., 1st sess. (3 February 1993): 405–407.

7 *Politics in America, 2002* (Washington, D.C.: Congressional Quarterly Inc., 2001): 637–638; Ivry, "Home from the House."

8 Foerstel, *Biographical Dictionary of Congressional Women*: 236.

9 *Congressional Record*, House, 105th Cong., 1st sess. (14 May 1997): 2603; Henneberger, "Preaching Moderation on Her Own Side of the Aisle."

11 Miles Benson, "Out of Congress, Not Down and Out; Members Depart With Pensions, Plethora of Perks," *New Orleans Times-Picayune*, 19 December 2002: 7; Joseph P. Fried, "Spending Time at Home After Career in House," 15 June 2003, *New York Times*: 23.

Claudine Schneider

1947–

UNITED STATES REPRESENTATIVE ★ REPUBLICAN FROM RHODE ISLAND
1981–1991

The first woman elected from Rhode Island to the U.S. House of Representatives, Claudine Schneider also was the first Republican Representative to serve the state in more than 40 years. During her five terms in Congress, Schneider earned a reputation as one of the House's strongest environmental advocates.[1]

Claudine Schneider was born Claudine Cmarada in Clairton, Pennsylvania, on March 25, 1947, the eldest of three children. Her father was a tailor.[2] She graduated from Pittsburgh's Winchester–Thurston High School in 1965, before studying at Rosemont College in Pennsylvania and the University of Barcelona in Spain. She received a B.A. in languages from Vermont's Windham College in 1969. She later attended the University of Rhode Island's School for Community Planning in 1975. After graduation, Cmarada moved to Washington, D.C., where she worked as executive director of Concern, Inc., a national environmental education organization. Engaged to Dr. Eric Schneider, she moved with him to Narragansett, Rhode Island, in 1970 when he took a position as a research scientist at the University of Rhode Island's Center for Ocean Management Studies. In 1973, she was diagnosed with Hodgkin's disease, a rare form of cancer in the lymph nodes, which she battled for five years. After twelve years of marriage, Claudine and Eric Schneider were divorced in 1985. Despite her continuing battle with cancer, Claudine Schneider became involved in the Rhode Island environmental movement. She founded the Rhode Island Committee on Energy in 1973, and the following year, she became executive director of the Conservation Law Foundation. In 1974, she led a group of concerned community and environmental

groups, launching the first successful campaign in the United States to halt the construction of a nuclear power plant near her home in Charlestown, Rhode Island.[3]

In the mid-1970s, Claudine Schneider aspired to run as a Democrat for one of Rhode Island's two seats in the U.S. House but found little support among party leaders. Rarely did a candidate win without the support of the statewide machine and, though both parties were well-organized at all levels in Rhode Island politics, the Democratic Party had enjoyed a strong statewide majority since the 1930s.[4] A political moderate, Schneider switched party allegiances in 1978, finding more support from the minority GOP.[5] That same year, after her husband declined to seek the GOP gubernatorial nomination, Schneider expressed her own interest. Republican leaders had a different candidate in mind; however, they offered Schneider a chance for a U.S. House seat in a district that included Providence and the state's southern beaches.[6] She ran a competitive race against Democratic incumbent Edward Beard.[7] A former house painter, Beard's blue-collar background appealed to the capital city's ethnic Italian neighborhoods.[8] Schneider won 48 percent of the turnout, coming within 9,000 votes of Beard.[9] She continued her environmental pursuits and, in addition, she attracted more publicity as a television producer and a public affairs talk show host for a statewide Sunday morning program. She challenged Beard again in 1980 when he ran for a fourth term. This time Beard's reputation for being quarrelsome and ill-informed hurt his reputation.[10] Schneider, on the other hand, garnered more ethnic appeal by taking Italian lessons. She won an upset victory, winning with 55 percent of the vote as the first woman to represent Rhode Island.[11] The first Republican to win either of the state's two House seats since 1938, Schneider was re-

elected to the four succeeding Congresses, enjoying increasingly larger margins of victory.[12] At 72 percent, her 1986 and 1988 victories were the highest percentage for a GOP candidate in Rhode Island since 1878.[13]

Claudine Schneider arrived for the 97th Congress (1981–1983) insisting that she was not a liberal Republican, but outside her economic policies, her voting record indicated otherwise.[14] Schneider tended to be a fiscal conservative, allying with her fellow Republicans on issues such as balancing the federal budget and curbing inflation.[15] "We've got to stop the government from spending more money," she said. "I don't look to the government to solve our problems."[16] Schneider stopped short of slashing the social programs on which her working-class constituents depended, claiming, "We can help them, but we can do it in a cost-efficient fashion."[17] However, Schneider quickly earned a reputation as a GOP critic of President Ronald Reagan's conservative social agenda. She opposed the President's position 75 percent of the time, more than the average for House Democrats. Her liberal district urged her in this direction; during her freshman term, she estimated that her constituent mail ran 19-to-1 against the President.[18]

Schneider's committee assignments recognized her environmental expertise. She served on the Committee on Merchant Marine and Fisheries and the Committee on Science, Space and Technology. In the 98th Congress (1983–1985), Schneider was appointed to the Select Committee on Aging—an appropriate appointment, as Rhode Island had the second oldest population in the country.[19] Her differences with President Reagan often translated into differences with the Republican Party leadership in Congress, which consequently excluded her from some important committee assignments. For the 101st Congress (1989–1991), she lost a bid to the prestigious Energy and Commerce Committee, the prime forum for the discussion of environmental issues.[20] Schneider rose to Ranking Member of the Science, Space, and Technology Committee's Subcommittee on Natural Resources, Agricultural Research, and Environment.

Given her background, protecting the environment became the predictable cornerstone of Representative Schneider's work in Congress. Her first and greatest environmental triumph was her work on a multi-year battle to close the Clinch River nuclear reactor. A private and federally funded project, the Clinch River Nuclear Reactor was scheduled to open near Oak Ridge, Tennessee, before the James Earl "Jimmy" Carter administration halted its construction in 1977. However, a powerful lobby, which included President Reagan and Tennessee Senate Majority Leader Howard Baker, Jr., all endorsed the reactor's continued construction in the early 1980s. As one of Clinch River's most vocal critics, Schneider called the project "a confederacy of corporate issues."[21] She teamed with other moderate GOP freshmen to fight its continued construction on the grounds that the project's costs outweighed its benefit. In May 1981, Schneider convinced the fiscally conservative Science Committee to cut $230 million in additional funding. In 1983, she offered legislation which eliminated the remaining federal funding for the Clinch River project. This proved to be the final blow, shutting down the severely underfunded project. Upon the Clinch River reactor's demise, Schneider proudly claimed, "We won it on the economic argument. This was a total, complete victory."[22]

As a former television host, Schneider knew how to attract attention to some of her core issues. In an effort to promote a more peaceful relationship with the Soviet Union, Representatives Schneider and George Brown of California headed a project, called "CongressBridge," to exchange live satellite transmissions on television between the Supreme Soviet and Members of Congress.[23] When the project launched in 1987, Schneider commented, "For too long we have seen each other only as warmongers. The time is ripe for new ways of thinking. [We are] getting beyond posturing."[24]

Her ability to garner the spotlight and her reputation for being feisty and independent made Schneider a well-respected politician in Rhode Island. In 1984, the state Republican Party considered her as a challenger for Senator Claiborne Pell's seat. She waited, however, until 1990 to take on the popular incumbent, boosted by her clear 1986 and 1988 House victories in a district so large

"WE'VE GOT TO STOP THE
GOVERNMENT FROM SPENDING MORE
MONEY," SCHNEIDER SAID. "I DON'T
LOOK TO THE GOVERNMENT TO
SOLVE OUR PROBLEMS." SCHNEIDER
STOPPED SHORT OF SLASHING THE
SOCIAL PROGRAMS ON WHICH HER
WORKING-CLASS CONSTITUENTS
DEPENDED, CLAIMING, "WE CAN
HELP THEM, BUT WE CAN DO IT IN A
COST-EFFICIENT FASHION."

that her elections were nearly statewide. The race between Schneider and Pell drew national attention, as Schneider ran close to the Senator in some polls.[25] A popular stalwart in Rhode Island politics, Pell mostly relied on his reputation and television spots in his bid for re-election to a sixth term. Schneider, on the other hand, campaigned vigorously, returning to Rhode Island every weekend. She boasted a grass roots campaign, even walking unescorted through a dangerous West Providence neighborhood to draw attention to its social problems. As the contest drew closer, President George H.W. Bush made a stop in Providence to speak on Schneider's behalf. On the eve of the 1991 Gulf War against Iraq, foreign policy was a popular issue among Rhode Island voters. Pell's experience on the Senate Foreign Relations Committee gave him the edge over Schneider, whose foreign policy experience included her televised debates with the Supreme Soviet and attendance at a Conference on Peace and disarmament in April 1985.[26] Rhode Islanders also strongly supported the Democratic Party, as one voter commented before heading to the polls, "I'd vote for her; she's young and she's got drive. But that might bring the Senate into Republican hands. That might prevent me from voting for her."[27] Schneider failed to unseat the popular incumbent, receiving 38 percent of the vote.[28]

After leaving Congress in 1991, Schneider remained active in the environmental protection movement. She invested in a Massachusetts-based consulting company, which sold environmentally sound energy systems in Central and South America. Schneider also accepted a teaching position at the John F. Kennedy School of Government at Harvard University. Following Democratic presidential candidate William J. Clinton's 1992 victory, she received an appointment to the Competitiveness Policy Council.[29] In 1999, Schneider was diagnosed with cancer for a second time. She sought a successful, alternative treatment. Having defeated the disease twice, she settled permanently in Boulder, Colorado.[30]

FOR FURTHER READING

Biographical Directory of the United States Congress, "Claudine Schneider," http://bioguide.congress.gov

MANUSCRIPT COLLECTIONS

University of Rhode Island (Kingston, RI), Special Collections, University Library. *Papers:* 1973–1990, 63.5 linear feet. The Claudine Schneider Papers, transferred through Schneider's office manager, were donated by the Congresswoman in 1990 and 1991. Prior to their transfer, the records were housed in Schneider's Washington, D.C., office. Included are official records from Schneider's five terms (1981–1991) as the U.S. Representative from Rhode Island's second district. The collection deals chiefly with Schneider's political campaigns and House service but includes materials predating her congressional career which relate to her later legislative work.

University of Oklahoma (Norman, OK). The Julian P. Kanter Commercial Archive, Department of Communication. *Video cassettes:* 1990, four video cassettes. Includes 35 commercials used during Schneider's campaigns for the 1990 U. S. Senatorial election in Rhode Island, Republican Party.

NOTES

1 "Schneider: Ex-Rep. Again Ill With Cancer," 8 April 1999, *National Journal*.

2 William K. Gale, "Claudine's Back in Town—Ex-Congresswoman Returning to Give a Speech," 17 April 2001, *Providence Journal Bulletin*: 1F.

3 Margot Hornblower, "Charging In," 22 December 1980, *Washington Post*: A1.

4 David R. Mayhew, *Placing Parties in American Politics* (Princeton, NJ: Princeton University Press, 1986): 24–27.

5 *Politics in America, 1990* (Washington, D.C.: Congressional Quarterly Inc., 1989): 1349; Colman McCarthy, "Bridging the East-West Gap," 28 December 1986, *Washington Post*: A1.

6 *Politics in America, 1990*: 1349.

7 Mayhew, *Placing Parties in American Politics*: 27.

8 *Politics in America, 1990*: 1349;

9 Kathy Sawyer, "More Women Seeking Office In '80 Election," 14 October 1980, *Washington Post*: A1; A.O. Sulzenberger, Jr., "More Women Than Ever May Win Congress Seats," 1 September 1980, *New York Times*: A1.

10 *Politics in America, 1990*: 1349.

11 Luica Mouat, "Women in Politics: Steady Progress," 6 November 1980, *Christian Science Monitor*: 8.

12 *Politics in America, 1990*: 1349.

13 Ibid., 1348; "Election Statistics, 1920 to Present," http://clerk.house.gov/members/electionInfo/elections.html.

14 *Politics in America, 1990*: 1347.

15 *Almanac of American Politics, 1990* (Washington, D.C.: National Journal Inc., 1989): 1090.

16 Hornblower, "Charging In."

17 Ibid.

18 *Politics in America, 1990*: 1347; Steven V. Roberts, "G.O.P. 'Gypsy Moths' Test Their Wings," 26 July 1981, *New York Times*: E4.

19 See Catherine Foster, "Rhode Island Senate Race Takes Politeness Prize," 26 October 1990, *Christian Science Monitor*: 7.

20 *Politics in America, 1990*: 1347.

21 Joanne Omang, "House Science Unit Votes to Pull Plug on Nuclear Project," 8 May 1981, *Washington Post*: A20.

22 Martin Tolchin, "Senate Vote Virtually Kills Clinch River Atom Reactor," 27 October 1983, *New York Times*: A24.

23 *Politics in America, 1990*: 1347.

24 Barbara Gamerekian, "U.S. and Soviet Legislators Are Planning to Debate on TV," 12 April 1987, *New York Times*: 12.

25 John Dillin, "GOP Likely to Gain Senate Seats," 18 April 1990, *Christian Science Monitor*: 1.

26 Judy Mann, "Defense Queens," 21 June 1985, *Washington Post*: C3.

27 Catherine Foster, "Rhode Island Senate Race Takes Politeness Prize," 26 October 1990, *Christian Science Monitor*: 7.

28 Ross Sneyd, "Democrats Sweep Rhode Island from Governor's Mansion on Down," 7 November 1990, Associated Press.

29 James M. O'Neill, "Environmentalist Schneider Finds Bully Pulpit in New Role," 19 June 1994, *Providence Journal Bulletin*: 2B.

30 "Schneider: Ex-Rep. Again Ill With Cancer," 8 April 1999, *National Journal*; Gale, "Claudine's Back in Town."

Barbara B. Kennelly

1936–

UNITED STATES REPRESENTATIVE ★ DEMOCRAT FROM CONNECTICUT
1982–1999

Raised in a prominent Connecticut political family, Barbara Bailey Kennelly became one of the highest-ranking women in the history of the Democratic Party and the U.S. House. Unlike many feminists who sought to challenge the political system from the outside, Congresswoman Kennelly capitalized on her name, "lifelong familiarity with public service," and political connections to gain positions of power in the House leadership—a coveted seat on the powerful Ways and Means Committee and the vice chairmanship of the Democratic Caucus.[1]

Barbara Ann Bailey was born in Hartford, Connecticut, on July 10, 1936, daughter of John Bailey, a Connecticut political boss and state Democratic leader and, later, chairman of the Democratic National Committee in the 1960s. He was widely credited with having engineered John F. Kennedy's presidential nomination and victory in 1960. Her mother, Barbara L. Bailey, was an advocate for women's rights and had worked as a teacher prior to marrying in 1933. Barbara Ann Bailey attended St. Joseph Cathedral School and graduated from Mount St. Joseph Academy in West Hartford in 1954. She earned a B.A. from Trinity College in Washington, D.C., in 1958, a certificate in business administration from Harvard Business School in 1959, and an M.A. in government from Trinity College in Hartford, Connecticut, in 1971. Barbara Bailey married John Kennelly, speaker of the Connecticut house. They had four children: Eleanor, Barbara, Louise, and John. Barbara Kennelly spent her early career outside of politics, however, working as the director of two social service organizations. Kennelly was nearly 40 when she was appointed in 1975 to fill a vacancy on the Hartford court of common council. She was elected to the post the

next year and served for a total of four years. In 1978, when Connecticut Secretary of State Gloria Schaffer left office, Kennelly launched her own successful campaign to win election to the post against the wishes of Democratic leaders, cobbling together a coalition that observers said was reminiscent of her father's deal-making skills.[2] The secretary of state's office had been a traditional stepping-stone for women politicians in Connecticut: in the 1940s Chase Woodhouse and, in the 1970s, Ella Grasso, both launched congressional careers from the post which had earned them wide name recognition with voters.

On September 8, 1981, six-term Democratic Congressman William R. Cotter died, leaving a vacancy in a district encompassing Hartford, and more than a dozen other small towns in central Connecticut. The largest employers were several major insurance corporations, a defense contractor, and state government agencies. Despite a large white-collar workforce, Hartford itself was rated as one of the poorest midsized cities in the nation, having suffered during the economic downturn of the late 1970s and early 1980s. Kennelly won the Democratic nomination uncontested and faced Republican Ann Uccello, the former mayor of Hartford in the special election.[3] The campaign turned on the economic policies of the Ronald Reagan administration, with Kennelly sharply criticizing the President's budget and tax plans and Uccello defending them. Kennelly had built-in advantages, running in a district safely held by Democrats for 22 years and using her name recognition to bring in big political contributions. She outspent Uccello by about a 3-to-1 margin.[4] "To me, in 1981, it is very important to be the daughter of John Bailey," Kennelly said. "I used to try to separate it. I don't try to separate it anymore because the more I am in

this business, the prouder I am of him." Nevertheless, she added, "I'm not running as John Bailey's daughter. I'm running as Barbara Kennelly, a woman who has established a record."[5] On January 12, 1982, Kennelly won a special election to the 97th Congress (1981–1983) by defeating Uccello with about 59 percent of the vote.[6] She took her seat on January 25, 1982, when she was assigned to the Committee on Government Operations and the Committee on Public Works and Transportation. Kennelly was returned to Congress later in the fall of 1982, winning 68 percent of the vote against Republican candidate Herschel Klein. She never was seriously challenged thereafter, serving a total of nine terms in the House.

Congresswoman Kennelly drew on her father's advice for working within the existing power structure and cracking the old boys' network by socializing with the Democratic leadership. She worked hard to ingratiate herself, polishing her golf game in order to mingle with the mostly male membership.[7] Her efforts paid dividends. Kennelly quickly established herself and set a number of firsts for a woman Member. In her first full term during the 98th Congress (1983–1985), she left her prior committee assignments to join the influential Ways and Means Committee, where she served on the Subcommittees on Human Resources and Select Revenue Measures. House Speaker Thomas "Tip" O'Neill of Massachusetts also named Congresswoman Kennelly to the Democratic Steering and Policy Committee which made committee appointments and set the broad outlines of the party's legislative agenda. In 1987, she became the first woman to serve on the Permanent Select Committee on Intelligence. Two years later, she was appointed Chief Deputy Majority Whip, the first woman named to that position. During the 103rd Congress (1993–1995), Kennelly ran against Louise Slaughter of New York and captured the vice chairmanship of the Democratic Caucus. At the time, it made her the highest ranking woman ever in the Democratic Party leadership. As a leader in her party, Kennelly's voting record rarely strayed from the Democratic line.

The seat on Ways and Means gave Kennelly a powerful post from which to tend to her district and other longtime legislative interests that had national reach: child support, housing credits, welfare reform, and tax reform. "Her father must have injected her and her mother must have fed her political milk," said her friend New York Congresswoman Geraldine Ferraro, "because she really has this sixth sense. Obviously she's going to be concerned about how something affects her district, but she looks at the bigger picture."[8] The Ways and Means assignment was particularly important for the insurance industry which resided in her district. Kennelly helped pass measures that both lowered its tax burden and restrained new tax regulations. In the 100th Congress (1987–1989), over the wishes of powerful Ways and Means Chairman Dan Rostenkowski of Illinois, Kennelly presented and won passage for a scaled-back plan to regulate tax-free earnings on premium payments.[9] A self-admitted "policy wonk," she pushed legislation to reduce the vesting period for pension plans, to allow the terminally ill to collect life insurance benefits early and tax-free, to increase the minimum wage, and to defeat a bill that would have denied illegal immigrants a public education.

Kennelly supported women's rights as a member of the Women's Caucus, though she admitted that it was only at the urging of her daughters that she began to pursue women's issues more vigorously during her House career. "Am I going to tell you I am going to change the world of [Ways and Means Chairman] Danny Rostenkowski? No," she said in 1983. "Am I going to try? Yes."[10] Later, reflecting on the fact that only 25 of her colleagues in the House were women, Kennelly said, "We are desperate in Congress for more women."[11] In 1983, Kennelly introduced the Child Support Enforcement Amendment, which required states to withhold earnings if child support payments were more than a month late. The House and Senate unanimously passed the bill in 1984.[12] Kennelly again supported strengthening laws against "deadbeat" parents who were delinquent on their payments in the 1996 Welfare Reform Bill.[13] She also used her seat on Ways and Means to help preserve the

childcare federal tax deduction and to expand the standard deduction for single parents.[14] She joined other women lawmakers in 1991 to protest the appointment of Clarence Thomas to the Supreme Court in the face of sexual harassment charges by Anita Hill. Kennelly also supported women's reproductive rights.

Kennelly did not run for re-election in 1998, choosing instead to give up her safe House seat for a bid to run for the governor's office in Connecticut. She easily won the Democratic nomination, but her campaign lacked funds and never found its stride.[15] Kennelly suffered a double-digit loss to the well-financed Republican incumbent John Rowland. Afterwards, Kennelly was appointed Associate Commissioner and Counselor at the Social Security Administration, overseeing the office of retirement policy. She also served as an advisor and lobbyist for a national law firm. In April 2002, Kennelly was named president and CEO of the National Committee to Preserve Social Security and Medicare. Following the death of her husband in 1995, Kennelly resided in Connecticut.

FOR FURTHER READING

Biographical Directory of the United States Congress, "Barbara Bailey Kennelly," http://bioguide.congress.gov

MANUSCRIPT COLLECTION

University of Connecticut Libraries (Storrs, CT). Archives & Special Collections, Thomas J. Dodd Research Center. *Papers:* ca. 1977–1998, 79.3 linear feet. The collection of Barbara Kennelly includes correspondence to and from constituents and colleagues, notes, research materials, speeches, official congressional documents, congressional records, press clips, photographs, audio and video tapes, and special interest reports. A finding aid is available in the repository and online.

NOTES

1   Richard L. Madden, "Candidates Seek Advantage in Their Pasts," 4 October 1981, *New York Times:* CN22.

2   *Politics in America, 1990* (Washington, D.C.: Congressional Quarterly Inc., 1989): 259.

3   "3 Women Run for House in Connecticut," 25 November 1981, *Washington Post:* A7.

4   "Barbara Kennelly Wins House Seat from Connecticut," 13 January 1982, *Washington Post:* A7.

5   Madden, "Candidates Seek Advantage in Their Pasts."

6   "Election Statistics, 1920 to Present," http://clerk.house.gov/members/electionInfo/elections.html.

7   Karen Foerstel, *Biographical Dictionary of Congressional Women* (Westport, CT: Greenwood Press, 1999): 149.

8   Todd S. Purdom, "Choices Painful for Hartford Politician," 1 July 1994, *New York Times:* A13.

9   *Politics in America, 1990:* 258.

10 Ibid.

11 Marilyn Gardner, "Women Legislators See Their Influence Grow in State Policymaking," 23 November 1987, *Christian Science Monitor:* 3.

12 Margaret Engel, "New Law Helps Parents to Collect Support Pay From Scofflaw Spouses," 1 October 1985, *Washington Post:* A9.

13 Foerstel, *Biographical Dictionary of Congressional Women:* 150.

14 *Politics in America, 1990:* 258–259.

15 "Connecticut Endorsements: Re-elect Governor Rowland," 30 October 1998, *New York Times:* A34.

Jean Spencer Ashbrook

1934–

UNITED STATES REPRESENTATIVE ★ REPUBLICAN FROM OHIO
1982–1983

Jean Ashbrook, who once described herself as "a small-town girl who enjoyed the role of wife and mother," came to Congress in a manner that by the 1980s had become less conventional for women: the widow's mandate.[1] Congresswoman Ashbrook served out the remaining seven months of John Ashbrook's term and retired when her Ohio district was reapportioned out of existence.

Emily Jean Spencer was born in Cincinnati, Ohio, on September 21, 1934. She attended schools in Newark, Ohio, and graduated from Newark High School in 1952. Spencer received a bachelor of science degree from Ohio State University in 1956. In 1974, she married John Ashbrook, a lawyer, newspaper publisher, and son of a former conservative Democratic Representative from Ohio. As a homemaker, Jean Ashbrook raised three children from a previous marriage: Elizabeth, Katherine, and John. She also served as a member of several charities and political clubs. John Ashbrook had children of his own, three daughters from a marriage to Joan Needles which ended in divorce in 1971.

John Ashbrook, who followed in his father's professional footsteps, was elected as a Republican to 11 terms as the U.S. Representative from an Ohio district that covered a large swath of the north-central part of the state, an agricultural region with the town of Mansfield as its largest population center. Congressman Ashbrook served as the Ranking Republican on the Education and Labor Committee and also on the Judiciary and Select Intelligence committees. Ashbrook earned the reputation as one of the House's most "militant and dedicated" conservatives but also one of its most independent. "I have never felt I had to go along with anything," he once remarked, "and getting along is not important to me."[2] This sentiment rang true when Ashbrook challenged President Richard Nixon for the Republican nomination in 1972. Undeterred by the opposition he received from many conservatives in the GOP, Ashbrook entered the race to draw attention to what he perceived as the "leftward drift" of the Nixon administration.[3]

John Ashbrook had entered the primary for Ohio's senatorial nomination before he died suddenly on April 24, 1982. Ohio Governor James A. Rhodes urged Jean Ashbrook, who had been campaigning across the state for her husband's Senate race, to run for his vacant House seat. "Immediately I said, 'Yes,'" she recalled. "I really don't know why." Her motivation, like that of many widows who had preceded her, became clearer during the brief campaign as she pledged to continue the conservative politics of her husband. At her announcement press conference Ashbrook emphasized her experience as a congressional spouse. "We were a team," she said. "I campaigned for eight years in the 17th District, and I do of course believe for what [John] stood for. I think John thought I was capable. I think I could do a good job."[4]

Congressman Ashbrook's district was one of two Ohio seats slated for elimination at the end of the 97th Congress (1981–1983) as a result of a redistricting plan precipitated by declining state population. His district was chosen for consolidation because of his decision to seek the Republican nomination for the Senate.[5] Aware that her tenure in Congress would be brief, Jean Ashbrook nonetheless entered the race to succeed her husband in the House.

Despite a voter turnout of only 10 percent in the June 29 special election, Ashbrook defeated Democrat Jack

Though Ashbrook's husband had been a close friend of President Reagan's, she acknowledged concerns over the economy in her district by noting that, "I'm pro-Reagan, but John Ashbrook was never a rubber stamp for anyone. I'm definitely backing the President, but I will have my eyes and ears open."

Koelbe with 74 percent of the vote. "Under the circumstances, it's a bittersweet victory for me," Ashbrook told her supporters. "But I'm very pleased that the people of the 17th District have reaffirmed their commitment to President Ronald Reagan and the principles they shared with my late husband." Though her husband had been a close friend of the President, Ashbrook acknowledged concerns over the economy in her district by noting that, "I'm pro-Reagan, but John Ashbrook was never a rubber stamp for anyone. I'm definitely backing the President, but I will have my eyes and ears open."[6] Ashbrook's election and seating in the House on July 12 set a new record for the number of women in Congress–22. "My gosh, I made history," Ashbrook said at the time. "That was rather nice."[7] After being sworn in on July 12, 1982, she received an assignment on the Committee on Merchant Marine and Fisheries. Her only ambition, she remarked, was "to carry on John's conservative philosophy."[8]

In her first speech on the House Floor, Ashbrook spoke out against President Reagan's veto of a bill to strengthen copyright laws. The legislation would have been a boon to the printing industry, which was a major employer in her district. "I hated to do that to the President," she said. "But after all, I said I wouldn't be a rubber stamp."[9]

In most other legislative matters, Ashbrook was a confirmed supporter of the Reagan administration. In July, Ashbrook introduced a bill that would have denied federal law enforcement or criminal justice assistance to any jurisdictions that implemented certain gun control ordinances. She also introduced a bill to prescribe mandatory minimum sentences for anyone convicted of federal felonies committed against senior citizens. Ashbrook supported the Enterprise Zone Tax Act of 1982, which provided tax relief and regulatory exemption for businesses that relocated to poor areas with high unemployment. She also backed a bill that would have created a U.S. Academy of Freedom to educate citizens about the dangers of communism and to promote democracy abroad.

After retiring from Congress on January 3, 1983, Ashbrook returned to Ohio. She resides in her hometown of Newark.

FOR FURTHER READING

Biographical Directory of the United States Congress, "Jean Spencer Ashbrook," http://bioguide.congress.gov

MANUSCRIPT COLLECTION

Ashland College (Ashland, OH), Ashbrook Center for Public Affairs. *Papers:* 1950–1982, 300 linear feet. Personal, business, and congressional papers and correspondence, including campaign files, photographs, portraits, motion picture film, video tape, and memorabilia. A description of the material is available at the Web site: http://archives.ashland.edu/Ashbrookmancol.html.

NOTES

1   Steven V. Roberts, "New Members Reflect Diversity of the House," 6 September 1982, *New York Times*: 18.

2   *Politics in America, 1982* (Washington, D.C.: Congressional Quarterly Inc., 1981): 968.

3   Martin Weil, "John M. Ashbrook Dies; 11-Term GOP Congressman from Ohio," 25 April 1982, *Washington Post*: B5.

4   "Widow to Run for Congressman's Seat," 29 April 1982, Associated Press.

5   "Jean Ashbrook Easily Wins Rest of Husband's Term," 30 June 1982, *Washington Post*: A2.

6   "Congressman's Widow Wins Unexpired Term," 30 June 1982, Associated Press.

7   "Washington Whispers," 12 July 1982, *U.S. News and World Report*: 16; Roberts, "New Members Reflect Diversity of the House."

8   "Congressman's Widow Wins Unexpired Term."

9   Roberts, "New Members Reflect Diversity of the House."

Katie Beatrice Hall

1938–

UNITED STATES REPRESENTATIVE ★ DEMOCRAT FROM INDIANA
1982–1985

Growing up in the pre-civil rights era South, Katie Hall could not exercise her constitutional right to vote. Subject to segregation laws, Hall felt trapped in her tiny hometown until she heard two speeches that changed her life; the speakers were African-American Congressmen Adam Clayton Powell, Jr., of New York, and William Dawson of Illinois. The experience led her to believe that she could receive a quality education and that there was a better life for her outside Mississippi.[1] Hall eventually sought public office and became the first African American elected from Indiana to serve in the House of Representatives. Among her chief accomplishments was piloting a bill through Congress to make the birthday of Martin Luther King, Jr., a national holiday.

On April 3, 1938, Katie Beatrice Green was born to Jeff and Bessie Mae Hooper Green, in Mound Bayou, Mississippi. One of twelve children, Katie attended the public schools in Mound Bayou before receiving a B.S. from Mississippi Valley State University in 1960. During her junior year of college, in 1957, she married John H. Hall. The couple had three children: Jacqueline, Junifer, and Michelle. In 1968, Katie Hall received her M.S. degree from Indiana University in Bloomington. She subsequently taught social studies in Gary, Indiana, an industrial city on the south shore of Lake Michigan. Hall's early political involvement included campaigning for black lawyer Richard Hatcher, a Gary mayoral candidate. Her experience on the sidelines encouraged her to enter electoral politics herself. Hall ran an unsuccessful campaign for the Indiana state house of representatives in 1972, but won a seat there in 1974. Two years later, Hall was elected to the state senate, where she served from 1976 until 1982. She also served as the chair of the Lake County Democratic Committee from 1978 to 1980, and chaired the 1980 Indiana Democratic convention.

In September of 1982, Indiana Democratic Representative Adam Benjamin, Jr., died suddenly of a heart attack. Katie Hall attended a public forum a week after the Congressman's death to discuss a possible successor and was surprised to hear mention of her name; however, her aspiration for national office was not new. "I had always thought about running for Congress," she admitted, but refrained because "I saw Adam as a very highly respected Congressman who did the job very well. I saw him as a person who was undefeatable."[2] Patricia Benjamin, the Congressman's widow, also expressed interest in succeeding her husband. Under Indiana law, the chairman of the district's Democratic committee selected the nominee to fill the vacancy for the remainder of the 97th Congress (1981–1983).[3] Then-chairman Richard Hatcher, whom Hall considered her political mentor, did not forget Hall's support for his mayoral campaigns.[4] He selected his protégé to run for the vacant seat which represented the northwest corner of the state, anchored by Gary. At the same time, the committee nominated Hall—with Hatcher casting the deciding vote—to a full term in the 98th Congress (1983–1985) to represent a newly reapportioned district.[5] The district's boundaries remained relatively unchanged after the reapportionment, and white northern Indiana Democrats expressed concern over Hall's electability because of her race; downtown Gary was primarily black, but the suburbs gave the district a 70 percent white constituency.[6] A legal battle ensued when Patricia Benjamin's supporters claimed that Hatcher, as chairman of the old district, did not have the

★ KATIE BEATRICE HALL ★

right to select a candidate for the new district.[7] The courts refused to overturn Hatcher's decision, and Hall's nomination as the Democratic nominee for both the vacancy and the full term stood, a position tantamount to election in the working-class, Democratic district. Hall defeated her Republican opponent, Thomas Krieger, with 63 percent to win election to the remainder of the 97th Congress.[8] She simultaneously won election with 56 percent of the vote for the 98th Congress.[9] Upon her election, Hall became the first black woman from Indiana to serve in the U.S. Congress.

When she arrived in Washington to be sworn in on November 2 1982, Representative Hall received assignments typical to freshmen Members: the Committee on Post Office and Civil Service and the Committee on Public Works and Transportation. Representative Hall voted with the Democratic majority against much of the Ronald W. Reagan administration's legislative agenda, focusing on education, labor, and women's issues. In addition, Congresswoman Hall became involved in the fight to alleviate famine in Africa when, during a congressional trip to northern Ethiopia, she was moved by the widespread suffering she witnessed. Hall also supported a variety of measures designed to reduce her urban and industrial district's high rate of unemployment and to mitigate the attendant social problems: crime, family debt and bankruptcy, and alcohol and drug abuse. As a member of the House Steel Caucus, Hall endorsed the Fair Trade in Steel Act, which was intended to revitalize Gary's ailing steel industry.

Katie Hall's most lasting legislative contribution came as chairwoman of the Post Office and Civil Service's subcommittee on Census and Population. Devoted to commemorating the memory of Dr. Martin Luther King, Jr., in July 1983, Hall introduced a bill to make King's birthday a federal holiday. Since the King assassination in 1968, similar measures had been introduced annually, but all had failed. As a nod to her negotiating abilities, Hall became the measure's floor manager. The primary argument against the bill led by fiscal conservatives was the large cost of the holiday to the federal government, esti-

mated at $18 million in holiday overtime pay and lost work time.[10] Hall courted detractors by moving the holiday from a fixed date—King's January 15 birthday—to the third Monday of January to prevent government offices from opening twice in one week, therefore saving money. Under Hall's leadership, the House Subcommittee on Census and Population passed the measure in a five-to-one vote, sending it to the House Floor. In opening the debate, Hall reminded her colleagues that "the legislation before us will act as a national commitment to Dr. King's vision and determination for an ideal America, which he spoke of the night before his death, where equality will always prevail."[11] Hall's persistence paid off. In November 1983, 15 years after King's assassination, the bill passed the House by a vote of 338 to 90.[12] Impressed by Hall's success, veteran lawmaker William Gray of Pennsylvania observed, "Sometimes when you get to the goal line it's good to go to someone fresh and new to take it over. She brought a freshness of approach, a spirit of reconciliation to what had sometimes been a bitter battle."[13]

In her 1984 bid for renomination and re-election to the 99th Congress (1985–1987), Katie Hall faced a formidable challenge. Despite her widespread support, including from Speaker Thomas "Tip" O'Neill of Massachusetts, two strong Democrats challenged Hall in her district primary, former Adam Benjamin aide Peter Visclosky and county prosecutor Jack Crawford. Hall maintained that intraparty opposition was, in some measure, based on her race and gender. During one debate Hall declared, "If I wasn't black and female, there wouldn't be a contest."[14] Reverend Jesse Jackson, whose name appeared on the primary ballot for the Democratic presidential nominee, also rallied to her aid.[15] In the May primary, Hall lost the Democratic nomination to Visclosky by a margin of 2,367 votes. Hall immediately cited racial injustice for her primary loss.[16] Most detrimental to her case, however, was that outside of Hatcher, prominent African-American officials in Gary had not rallied support behind her, resulting in only a 50 percent voter turnout in the predominately black city.[17] Hall also questioned returns in

areas where polls indicated she ran stronger than the final count.[18] The incumbent filed a petition and won a suit for a recount of the primary results; however, the recount only confirmed her losing margin.

After Congress, Hall continued to be active in Indiana Democratic politics. In 1986 and in 1990, she tried but failed to recapture the Democratic nomination in her old House district. Hall returned to Gary and served as the vice chair of the city's housing board commissioners. Hall became the Gary city clerk in 1985. She resigned in January 2003, after pleading guilty to charges of federal mail fraud.[19]

FOR FURTHER READING

Biographical Directory of the United States Congress, "Katie Hall," http://bioguide.congress.gov

Catlin, Robert A. "Organizational Effectiveness and Black Political Participation: The Case of Katie Hall," *Phylon* 46 (September 1985): 179–192.

NOTES

1 Steven V. Roberts, "Mississippi Gets a Representative from Indiana," 26 November 1982, *New York Times*: B8.

2 Jan Carroll, "Katie Hall Could Be First Black Representative From Indiana," 21 September 1982, Associated Press.

3 "Black Woman Nominated to Succeed Benjamin," 13 September 1982, Associated Press.

4 Carroll, "Katie Hall Could Be First Black Representative From Indiana."

5 James R. Dickerson, "Indiana Democrats Feud Over Benjamin's Seat," 19 September 1982, *Washington Post*: A10.

6 "Black Woman Nominated to Succeed Benjamin"; for statistics on the white majority, see *Almanac of American Politics, 1984* (Washington, D.C.: National Journal Inc., 1983): 387; Julia Malone, "Folks Back Home Speak Their Piece to Representatives," 8 September 1982, *Christian Science Monitor*: 1.

7 Dickerson, "Indiana Democrats Feud Over Benjamin's Seat."

8 "Gary Indiana Newspaper Rejects Candidate's Newspaper Ad," 27 October 1982, United Press International; Roberts, "Mississippi Gets a Representative from Indiana."

9 "Election Information, 1920 to Present," http://clerk.house.gov/members/electionInfo/index.html.

10 Larry Margasak, "Courting Conservatives to Back King Holiday," 14 August 1983, Associated Press.

11 *Congressional Record*, House, 98th Cong., 1st sess. (2 August 1983): 22208.

12 A three-year grace period also was part of the compromise (see Sandra Evans Teeley, "King Holiday Bill Approved by House Panel," 1 July 1983, *Washington Post*: A10). The United States celebrated its first Martin Luther King, Jr. holiday on January 20, 1986.

13 Margasak, "Courting Conservatives to Back King Holiday."

14 E.R. Shipp, "Rep. Katie Hall Facing Tough Fight in Indiana," 7 May 1984, *New York Times*: B8.

15 David S. Broder and Kevin Klose, "Two States' House Primaries Will Involve Interracial Battles," 5 May 1984, *Washington Post*: A7.

16 "Mrs. Hall Loses Bid for Renomination in Indiana; Racism Charged," 10 May 1984, *Washington Post*: B19.

17 "Racism, Low Voter Turnout Blamed for Black Congresswoman's Defeat," 9 May 1984, Associated Press.

18 "Black Congresswoman Seeks Recount After Loss in Democratic Primary," 22 May 1984, Associated Press.

19 Barbara Sherlock, "Gary Official Resigns After Pleading Guilty; City Clerk Accepts Mail Fraud Charges," 29 January 2003, *Chicago Tribune*: N2.

Barbara F. Vucanovich

1921–

UNITED STATES REPRESENTATIVE ★ REPUBLICAN FROM NEVADA
1983–1997

In 1982, Barbara Vucanovich became the first Nevada woman elected to federal office. At the time, Vucanovich represented one of the biggest districts in the country, covering nearly the entire state. Winning her first elective office at the age of 61, the former business owner and congressional aide won an influential seat on the Appropriations Committee (eventually chairing the Military Construction Subcommittee) and served seven terms in the House of Representatives.

Barbara Farrell was born on June 22, 1921, in Fort Dix, New Jersey, to Thomas and Ynez Farrell. Public service was a part of her life from an early age.[1] Her father was the chief civil engineer for New York under Governors Al Smith and Franklin Roosevelt. Her mother had been a volunteer ambulance driver in World War I. Barbara Farrell was raised in Albany, New York, graduating from the Albany Academy for Girls in 1938. She attended the Manhattanville College of the Sacred Heart from 1938 to 1939. In 1949, the family moved to Nevada. On March 8, 1950, Barbara Farrell married Ken Dillon and they settled in the Reno area in the northwest part of the state. The couple raised five children: Patty, Mike, Ken, Tom, and Susan, before her husband died in 1964. Barbara Farrell Dillon married George Vucanovich on June 19, 1965. While raising her family, Barbara Vucanovich also owned and operated a speed reading school and a travel agency.

Vucanovich's first experience in politics came in 1952 when she served as a delegate to the Nevada state GOP convention. Three years later, she won a one-year term as president of the Nevada Federation of Republican Women. She worked for Republican Paul Laxalt for nearly 20 years while he served as Nevada's lieutenant governor and governor. When Laxalt won election to the U.S. Senate,

Vucanovich worked for him as manager of his district office and as a campaign adviser from 1974 until 1982. It was in that capacity that she learned the nuances of constituent service, a skill that even her opponents admired. One observer noted Vucanovich "is good with people, and she can think on her feet talking to them."[2] In 1976 and 1980 she served as a delegate to the Republican National Convention.

Reapportionment after the 1980 Census split Nevada into two congressional districts, one which encompassed the expanding city of Las Vegas and the other covering the sprawling remainder of the state. Senator Laxalt encouraged Vucanovich to run for the larger district. "Good Lord, what would I be able to do?" she replied. It was a "wide-open state" she observed—open 24 hours a day for gambling and legalized prostitution. As a 61-year-old grandmother with five grown children and 15 grandchildren, she seemed an odd fit. "You would be wonderful," Laxalt responded. With that endorsement, she secured the GOP nomination and squared off in the general election against Democratic opponent State Senator Mary Gojack, who had previously challenged Laxalt for his Senate seat in 1980. Though she had lost her Senate bid by a wide margin, the race had helped increase Gojack's visibility; however, President Ronald Reagan also bolstered Vucanovich's name recognition when he made an appearance at a rally in Reno on her behalf while stumping for Nevada Republican candidates.[3] The economy was a major focus of the 1982 campaign—unemployment in Las Vegas and Reno had eclipsed 10 percent during the ongoing national recession—and the issue offered a clear dividing line between the two candidates. Gojack seized this statistic, arguing that the Republican administration had not aided Nevada during the economic downturn.

Vucanovich supported the Reagan administration's plan, one of lower taxes and reduced government spending. She also shared the President's optimism that the economy was on its way to recovery.[4] Gojack's ties to the women's rights movement and the Equal Rights Amendment (ERA) battle in the 1970s contrasted with Vucanovich, who painted herself as a social conservative. "The real choice is between a liberal and a conservative," Vucanovich said. "Mary's . . . trying to effect social change. But the people here are very conservative. They back the President and so do I. I think he's trying to turn the country around from the socialistic bent to less government and less spending."[5] Vucanovich was victorious with 56 percent of the vote.[6]

Congresswoman Vucanovich successfully secured six additional terms in Congress. Of those elections, only one was won with an overwhelming majority, 71 percent in the Reagan landslide of 1984. Another was much closer. In 1992, running against the popular mayor of Reno, Pete Sferrazza, and three minor party candidates, Vucanovich won just 48 percent of the vote. Sferrazza campaigned as a pro-choice candidate, railing against increasing congressional salaries and cost of living raises. He ran well in Reno and its surrounding counties, but Vucanovich—who outspent her opponent three-to-one—held on to her seat by a five-point margin, winning in large part because she carried the vast rural stretches of the state by a wide margin.[7] Two years later, in her final House race, Vucanovich won with 64 percent of the vote. The fact that she campaigned statewide for her enormous district made Vucanovich a logical choice for a potential gubernatorial campaign in 1990, a candidacy for which she received widespread encouragement and support. "The people of Nevada have told me they believe, as I do, that I can be elected governor and that I would make a great governor," she said; however she declined the nomination: "At the same time, [voters] feel my voice is too important in the House of Representatives, and I happen to agree with them."[8]

During her tenure in Congress, she served on four committees: Appropriations, Interior and Insular Affairs (later named the Resources Committee), House Administration, and the Select Committee on Children, Youth, and Families. At the time of her retirement, she ranked 14th out of 23 Republicans on the Appropriations Committee and was the chair of the Subcommittee on Military Construction—only the second woman ever to chair a subcommittee of that prestigious panel.[9] Her grandmotherly demeanor played to her advantage in an institution filled with men, many of whom were decades younger than she. She once entered the Republican Cloakroom to find male Congressmen sprawled on the couches, smoking cigars, and telling patronizing jokes about women. She thought to herself, "You know, I've raised three boys, why do I have to put up with this junk?" Vucanovich turned to her colleagues, "Hey, listen you guys, knock it off, will you?" The jokes stopped.[10]

Vucanovich lived up to her campaign persona as a fiscal and social conservative. She was one of a handful of women to consistently vote against any measure that permitted abortion or federal funding of the procedure and, in 1993, voted for a parental consent law. In 1984, she opposed the addition of an ERA plank in the GOP platform, arguing that if it did manage to pass, legal challenges to its exact meaning would clog the courts "for 100 years."[11] Vucanovich also supported the death penalty and was a major recipient of National Rifle Association funding for her positions against gun control.[12] Realizing that her votes sometimes conflicted with her constituents' wishes, she asked them to take a wider perspective of her House service: "I don't ask you to agree with me on every issue, but I do ask that you look at what I stand for, consider the job I have done, and decide if you believe I have earned your vote."[13]

As a Member of the House of Representatives, Vucanovich pursued a variety of issues important to Nevada's natural resources. Vucanovich opposed a federal plan to use Yucca Mountain in Nevada as the U.S. government's primary storage dump for nuclear waste. The measure eventually passed Congress after her retirement. From her seat on Interior and Insular Affairs, Vucanovich also protected the Nevada mining industry. She vigorously opposed an early 1990s overhaul of the Mining Act of 1872, arguing that it favored eastern coal interests rather

than western mining. She proposed 150 amendments to stall its progress, and the measure later lapsed at the end of the 102nd Congress (1991–1993). Vucanovich also strenuously opposed President William J. Clinton's proposed 12.5 percent gross royalty on minerals, and she went so far as to invite the President to visit mining operations in western Nevada.[14]

At the beginning of her freshman term in 1983, Vucanovich was diagnosed with breast cancer during a routine mammogram, which identified the cancer at an early stage, leading to prompt, lifesaving treatment. Thereafter, Representative Vucanovich supported all efforts to increase medical research and treatment for women, despite her fiscal conservatism. "As a breast cancer survivor, I know the importance of medical research," Vucanovich said in a floor speech. "I also know the many questions that run through your head—why, how, and why me? We need diverse research to provide us with these essential answers."[15] In 1989, she introduced the Omnibus Breast Cancer Control Act, which required Medicare and Medicaid coverage for annual mammograms for women over certain ages and increased funding for a public awareness program through the National Cancer Institute. "Breast cancer is not a partisan issue or a women's issue," Vucanovich told her colleagues. "Breast cancer must become a legislative and communications priority in the government and the private sector."[16]

In 1996, at age 75, Vucanovich announced her retirement from Congress. She told reporters that she wanted to spend more time with her family. "I look forward to returning to Nevada full time and expect to continue working on Nevada's behalf as a private citizen," she said.[17] Her husband passed away in December 1998. In 2000, a post office in Nevada was named after Vucanovich to honor the state's first female member of Congress.[18]

FOR FURTHER READING

Biographical Directory of the United States Congress, "Barbara Farrell Vucanovich," http://bioguide.congress.gov

MANUSCRIPT COLLECTION

University of Nevada (Reno, NV), Special Collections Department, http://www.library.unr.edu/specoll/. *Papers:* ca. 1982–1996, 86 cubic feet. Includes congressional papers and correspondence: press clippings and releases, Appropriations Committee files, staff files, legislative files, campaign materials, Commission on Presidential Debate materials, office administrative files, and photographs. Also includes portraits, video tape, sound recordings, memorabilia. A finding aid is available in the repository. Restricted.

NOTES

1 United States Capitol Historical Society (hereinafter cited as USCHS) *Women in Public Service,* videocassette (Washington, D.C.: U.S. Capitol Historical Society, 1998).

2 Deborah Churchman, "Nevada Congresswoman Barbara Vucanovich Brings Care, Warmth to Washington," 1 February 1983, *Christian Science Monitor:* 18.

3 James Gerstenzang, "President Plugging for GOP Candidates in Nevada," 6 October 1982, Associated Press.

4 Tom Raun, "Election '82: Nevada Race Offers Clear Test of Reaganomics," 26 October, 1982, Associated Press.

5 Joseph Kraft, "In Nevada, a Turn To Wine and Cheese," 21 October 1982, *Washington Post:* A19.

6 "Election Statistics, 1920 to Present," http://clerk.house.gov/members/electionInfo/elections.html.

7 *Almanac of American Politics, 1994* (Washington, D.C.: National Journal Inc., 1993): 786; "Election Statistics, 1920 to Present," http://clerk.house.gov/members/electionInfo/elections.html.

8 "Barbara Vucanovich," Associated Press Candidate Biographies, 1996.

9 *Politics in America, 1994* (Washington, D.C.: Congressional Quarterly Inc., 1993): 935.

10 USCHS, *Women in Public Service.*

11 Steven V. Roberts, "Panel of G.O.P. Concludes Draft of '84 Platform," 17 August 1984, *New York Times:* A1.

12 "Handguns and Money," 3 March 1986, *Washington Post:* A9.

13 "Barbara Vucanovich," Associated Press Candidate Biographies, 1996.

14 *Almanac of American Politics, 1994:* 786.

15 *Congressional Record,* House, 102nd Cong., 2nd sess. (28 May 1992): 3839.

16 *Congressional Record,* House, 101st Cong., 1st sess. (18 September 1989): 5694.

17 "Vucanovich to Retire from House," 6 December 1995, *Washington Post:* A8.

18 "Vucanovich: Ex-Rep. Has Officially Gone Postal," 10 October 2000, *The Hotline.*

Sala Galante Burton
1925–1987

UNITED STATES REPRESENTATIVE ★ DEMOCRAT FROM CALIFORNIA
1983–1987

A Polish émigré who fled the Nazis and settled in America, Sala Galante Burton succeeded her husband, the powerful California Representative Phillip Burton, after he died suddenly in 1983. In the House, Congresswoman Burton championed many of the same interests she had worked for during her decades as a leading figure in the California Democratic Party: civil rights, women's reproductive rights, the environment, and world peace.

Sala Galante was born in Bialystock, Poland, on April 1, 1925, daughter of Max Galante, a Polish textile manufacturer. With her Jewish parents she fled from Poland in 1939 at the age of 14, just before the Nazi invasion and occupation. "I saw and felt what happened in Western Europe when the Nazis were moving," Burton recalled years later. "You learn that politics is everybody's business. The air you breathe is political—it isn't just a game for certain people. We must all be vigilant in terms of whom we elect to office, vigilant in terms of our civil rights and liberties."[1] She retained those memories and a hint of her Old World accent for the remainder of her life. She attended public schools in San Francisco, and studied at San Francisco University. From 1949 to 1950, she was associate director of the California Public Affairs Institute. Galante also worked with the National Association for the Advancement of Colored People in its efforts to eliminate job and housing discrimination. Sala Galante met her future husband, Phillip Burton, at a California Young Democrats convention in 1950. They married three years later and raised a daughter, Joy, whom Sala Burton had from a previous marriage that had ended in divorce.

In the 1950s, Sala Burton embarked on an active political career that paralleled her husband's rise to influence in state and national politics. She had a lighter, more genial touch than her husband's sometimes brusque approach to issues. Phil Burton, who lost a race to be House Majority Leader in 1976 by one vote and was regarded as the dean of California politics, often referred to her as his better political half, "the popular Burton." He added, "I keep Sala busy repairing all the fences I've busted."[2] She was a founder of the California Democratic Council and served as its vice president from 1951 to 1954. Burton presided over the San Francisco Democratic Women's Forum from 1957 to 1959 and was a member of both the San Francisco County and California State Democratic Central committees. She also was a delegate to the Democratic National Conventions in 1956, 1976, 1980, and 1984. In 1964, when Phillip Burton won the first of 10 consecutive terms to the U.S. House from a San Francisco district, the Burtons moved to Washington, D.C. In Washington, Sala Burton served as president of the Democratic Wives of the House and Senate from 1972 to 1974.

Eight days after Phil Burton died suddenly in April of 1983, Sala Burton announced her candidacy to fill her husband's unexpired term as Representative for his San Francisco district. She told supporters, "I will continue in his footsteps."[3] She also minimized gender issues in the campaign. "I'm not running because I'm a woman," Burton told voters during her campaign. "I'm running because I think I can do more in Congress than anyone."[4] Her main competitors were Democratic attorney Richard Doyle, Republican real estate broker Duncan Howard, and Republican Tom Spinosa, who had lost several campaigns to Phil Burton. While her husband used the telephone to gather support, as if it were "an extension of his body" by one aide's account, Sala Burton was a tireless

CONGRESSIONAL PICTORIAL DIRECTORY, 99TH CONGRESS

door-to-door campaigner. "I want to go everywhere, she said. "I want to feel like I've earned this."[5] Turnout was light at the June 21 special election (less than 30 percent), but Burton won 55 percent of the vote in a field of 11 candidates; Howard finished second with 22 percent. In her two re-election campaigns Burton was never seriously challenged, winning 72 percent against Spinosa in 1984 and 75 percent against Republican Mike Garza in 1986.

When Sala Burton took her seat in the House on June 28, 1983, she received her husband's assignments on two committees: Education and Labor and Interior and Insular Affairs. She also received an assignment on the Select Committee on Hunger during the 98th and 99th Congresses (1983–1987). In the 99th Congress, after failing in a hard-fought effort to win a seat on the prestigious Appropriations Committee, Burton dropped her Education and Labor and her Interior assignments to get a seat on the influential House Rules Committee. She served there through the remainder of her time in Congress, working on the Subcommittee on the Legislative Process.

Burton set out, in her own words, "to represent, as my husband did, the dispossessed, the hungry, the poor, the children, people in trust territories, the aged—those people who don't have a lot of lobbying being done for them."[6] From her committee assignments, Burton was able to serve as an advocate for a broad range of policies such as social welfare programs, child nutrition assistance, bilingual education, and the Equal Rights Amendment (ERA). One of her first actions was to sign on as a co-sponsor of the ERA. Burton took a special interest in education legislation for primary-and secondary school students, helping to secure funding for federal grants to open public schools for "latch key" kids who came from households with working parents. Burton backed provisions to the Higher Education Act that provided poor women the childcare support to allow them to attend school. She also wrote an amendment to outlaw so-called "Saturday night specials"—cheap handguns—which the Rules Committee adopted but which was voted down on the House Floor.[7] Congresswoman Burton authored a

bill to create a protective breakwater for ships moored in an area of San Francisco Bay that was part of Golden Gate National Recreation Area, which her husband created.[8] Her support for environmental protection measures led her to advocate restrictions on oil drilling off California's coast. Burton was a noteworthy critic of military spending under the arms buildup of the Ronald W. Reagan administration, opposing the funding of the MX missile. She also was an opponent of Reagan's foreign policy, strongly denouncing the U.S. invasion of Grenada, voting against aid to Contra rebels in Nicaragua, and withdrawing her original support for an 18-month extension of the U.S. Marine occupation in Lebanon.[9] She spoke in defense of Soviet dissidents and Salvadoran refugees, opposing an immigration reform bill which she described as discriminatory.[10]

In the final year of her life, Sala Burton battled cancer, undergoing surgery in August 1986. Though she easily won re-election to the 100th Congress in 1986, she was too ill to take the oath of office on the House Floor and, by special resolution, was sworn in at her home by California Representative Don Edwards. The following day she entered the hospital. In her final weeks, much the same way that Phil Burton had supported her as a successor, Sala Burton said that when the seat became vacant, she would support the candidacy of her campaign chairwoman, Nancy Pelosi. Burton died in Washington, D.C., on February 1, 1987. Sala's death brought to a close the "Burton era" in the House, since in 1983 Phil had died and his brother, John, had retired from a neighboring congressional district.

FOR FURTHER READING

Biographical Directory of the United States Congress, "Sala Galante Burton," http://bioguide.congress.gov

MANUSCRIPT COLLECTION

University of California (Berkeley, CA), Bancroft Library. *Papers:* 1983–1986, 6.25 feet. Includes correspondence and other routine working files from Congresswoman Burton's tenure in the U.S. House of Representatives. Correspondence is chiefly incoming from other Members of Congress, friends, constituents, and organizations. Also includes press clippings and releases, election files, subject files, legislative and voting records, photographs, audio cassettes, and video cassettes. Finding aid in repository. Restricted. Advance notice required for access.

NOTES

1   Martin Weil, "California Democratic Rep. Sala Burton Dies," 2 February 1987, *Washington Post*: E6; Barbara Gamarekian, "'The Popular Burton' and Her Mission," 29 July 1983, *New York Times*: A 10.

2   Gamarekian, "'The Popular Burton' and Her Mission."

3   Weil, "California Democratic Rep. Sala Burton Dies."

4   "Widow of Rep. Burton Is Elected in California Congressional Race," 23 June 1983, *New York Times*: A 16.

5   Jay Mathews, "Female Politicians Gaining Power in San Francisco: Phillip Burton's Widow Likely to Win Today," 21 June 1983, *Washington Post*: A 3.

6   Gamarekian, "'The Popular Burton' and Her Mission."

7   "Sala Burton: Congresswoman Was 61," 1 February 1987, United Press International.

8   Dan Morain, "Rep. Sala Burton, Who Replaced Husband in Congress, Dies at 61," 2 February 1987, *Los Angeles Times*: 3.

9   "Sala G. Burton," Associated Press Candidate Biographies, 1988.

10   "Sala Burton: Congresswoman Was 61."

Helen Delich Bentley

1923–

UNITED STATES REPRESENTATIVE ★ REPUBLICAN FROM MARYLAND
1985–1995

As a Member of Congress representing suburban Baltimore, Helen Delich Bentley focused on the issues that were at the center of her earlier careers as a journalist and federal appointee—those affecting the maritime industry and American trade. Able to attract blue-collar and traditionally Democratic voters, despite remaining relatively conservative, Bentley's gruff style and raspy voice seemed the very embodiment of her decades of experience spent on the city docks and plying the oceans. "I am a woman who worked in men's fields for a long time. I insisted on working on the city side of the paper and not the women's pages," Bentley once explained. "I did it all on my own. Women have to be willing to work and produce and not just expect favors because they are women."[1]

Helen Delich was born to Michael Ivanesevich Delich and Mary (Kovich) Delich, Yugoslavian immigrants, in Ruth, Nevada, on November 28, 1923. She and her six siblings grew up in the neighboring town of Ely. Michael Delich, a copper miner, died of an occupational disease, silicosis, when Helen was just eight years old. Helen graduated as valedictorian from White Pine High School in Ely in 1941, earning two scholarships to attend the University of Nevada. She transferred to the University of Missouri's journalism school in the fall of 1942. In the summer of 1942, Delich managed the U.S. Senate campaign of James G. Scrugham in two Nevada counties. Scrugham, a Democrat and five-term U.S. Representative, won the election. When he was sworn into the Senate in 1943, he hired Delich as his secretary. She worked nine months in Scrugham's Capitol office, before returning to the University of Missouri in the fall of 1943. She earned a bachelor's degree in journalism in 1944 and worked newspaper jobs in Indiana and Idaho.

In June 1945, Helen Delich was hired by the *Baltimore Sun*, beginning a three-decade-long relationship with the newspaper. She specialized in labor issues and, in 1947, became the first woman to cover an American Federation of Labor convention. A year later, the *Sun*'s city editor gave her a new beat.[2] Through direct observation and the cultivation of sources ranging from dockhands to union officials to bureaucrats and local politicians, Bentley educated herself and then the public on issues related to America's maritime interests, using the port of Baltimore as a prism through which to understand the industry. Her "Around the Waterfront" column was syndicated in 15 newspapers and eventually led to the development of a popular, long-running television show on the maritime industry. She often traveled aboard ship to produce stories, taking her on the high seas around the world. Delich's demeanor and presentation were as salty and as blunt as the sailors and stevedores about whom she wrote. Over the years, she earned a national reputation as an authority on maritime issues.[3] On June 7, 1959, Helen Delich married William Bentley, a school teacher. They had no children.

In 1968, when GOP presidential nominee Richard Nixon chose Maryland Governor Spiro Agnew as his vice presidential running mate, Bentley served as an advisor on shipping matters for the Nixon–Agnew campaign. Shortly after winning the election, President Nixon named Bentley as chair of the Federal Maritime Commission. Confirmed by the Senate in October 1969, she became the highest ranking woman in the Executive Branch. She chaired the commission until 1975, calling attention to the country's aging and declining merchant fleet. She later worked as a columnist for *World Port Magazine* and as a shipping company executive.

In 1980, Bentley made her first attempt to win political office by challenging a powerful, nine-term House incumbent in a Maryland district encompassing northern Baltimore and its suburbs. After securing the Republican nomination by upsetting Baltimore County Republican Chairman Malcolm McKnight in the primary, Bentley faced Representative Clarence "Doc" Long. Congressman Long was an institution in Maryland politics and the chairman of the Appropriations Subcommittee on Foreign Operations.[4] In 1980, the overwhelmingly Democratic district encompassed the predominantly Jewish suburb of Pikesville, the upper-income community of Towson, and to its east the blue-collar towns of Sparrows Point and Dundalk. Many Democrats residing in the district, however, tended to be conservative. Bentley enjoyed wide name recognition from her work as a journalist and her time on the Federal Maritime Commission. During the campaign, she focused on her support of dredging Baltimore Harbor to accommodate larger ships, a move which she argued would boost maritime business.[5] In the general election, Long defeated Bentley with a 57 to 43 percent margin.[6]

Bentley would not relent, however, and challenged Long again in 1982. Reapportionment improved her chances as the reconfigured district included a slice of suburban, middle-class Harford County northeast of the city.[7] In a losing effort, Bentley nevertheless closed the margin to 53 percent to 47 percent.[8] In 1984, Bentley challenged Long a third time. "If we lived in the Middle Ages, she would be called Helen the Determined," observed a high-ranking state Republican. "This election is either the last hurrah or the dawn of a new day" for Bentley.[9] Long had become a GOP target, having used his Appropriations post to challenge the Ronald W. Reagan administration's foreign policy programs. In a race that drew national attention, GOP leadership sent former President Gerald Ford, Vice President George H.W. Bush and his wife Barbara, and President Reagan's daughter, Maureen, to stump for Bentley in the district. The campaign became the most expensive congressional race in state history, with the candidates collectively spending more than

$1.2 million.[10] Bentley's anti-tax and jobs creation message appealed to the working-class voters and the "Reagan Democrats" in her district. This time she prevailed with 51 percent of the vote, riding Reagan's coattails.[11] Bentley's district went for Reagan by better than a 2-to-1 margin.[12] In her subsequent four re-election campaigns Congresswoman Bentley won by wide margins, ranging from about 60 percent to 75 percent of the vote.[13]

When she took her seat in the 99th Congress (1985–1987), Bentley was assigned to the Committee on Merchant Marine and Fisheries and the Committee on Public Works and Transportation. She remained on Merchant Marine and Fisheries throughout her five terms in the House. Beginning in the 101st Congress (1989–1991), she left Public Works and Transportation to serve on the Budget Committee. In the 103rd Congress (1993–1995), she left the Budget Committee for a seat on the powerful Appropriations Committee. Bentley also served on the Select Committee on Aging from the 99th through the 102nd Congresses (1985–1992).

As a Member of Congress, Helen Bentley focused on shipping and trade issues. She immediately used her seat on the Public Works Committee to find funding for a harbor-deepening project in Baltimore. Within a year, she secured more than $17 million for the project, ensuring that the dredging was underway by the start of her second term in office. She routinely combed legislation on her various committees—in the words of one observer, like a "suspicious watchdog"—trying to ferret out bills that might be contrary to the interests of Baltimore.[14] She also concentrated on constituent services, for which she became widely known. She was such a trusted and known entity within the Baltimore maritime community, that in the winter of 1989–1990 she acted as a mediator between the local unions and shipping management to bring about a resolution to a labor dispute.[15]

As an aggressive protector of American business, Congresswoman Bentley backed numerous "Buy America" campaigns, targeting key U.S. trading partners and opposing free trade programs such as the North American Free Trade Agreement in 1993. It was in this

CONGRESSWOMAN BENTLEY WAS
AN AGGRESSIVE PROTECTOR OF
AMERICAN BUSINESS. "I'M TIRED OF
EMPLOYING FOREIGNERS ALL THE
TIME IN FOREIGN COUNTRIES AND
HELPING THEM OUT. I WANT TO
HELP OUT AMERICANS."

regard that she achieved national prominence. "I'm tired of employing foreigners all the time in foreign countries and helping them out," said Bentley, who plied her district in an American-made station wagon with the license plate, "BUY USA." "I want to help out Americans."

One particular target of her fury in the late 1980s and early 1990s was the widening U.S. trade gap with Japan. In 1987, Bentley organized a public relations stunt in which she and several GOP colleagues used sledgehammers to destroy a Japanese-made radio on the Capitol steps. The act was part protest of Japanese technology sharing with the Soviet Union and also a visible sign of U.S. frustration with rigid Japanese trade policies.[16] After taking a trip to the Far East, House Speaker Thomas Foley of Washington joked with Bentley, "Helen, you're the most famous American in Japan since Admiral Perry."[17] Bentley also assailed the Pentagon's reliance on overseas manufacturers as being contrary to "all responsible military strategies to the point where I begin to wonder if we have forgotten what defense is all about."[18] As a fiscal conservative, she backed a 1992 balanced budget constitutional amendment and counted as one of her major congressional achievements a floor debate on a measure she sponsored to cap federal spending increases at 2 percent per year (the measure lost by a wide margin).

Congresswoman Bentley's voting on social issues revealed an admixture of viewpoints. She enthusiastically supported the Equal Rights Amendment, having worked in jobs where she was paid far less than men who did less work. She also backed many federal programs that sought to advance the cause of women's health care. Yet, Bentley opposed federal funding for abortions and voted for a 1993 bill that required parental notification of minors' abortions. She also opposed the Family and Medical Leave Act.

Representative Bentley declined to run for virtually certain re-election to the 104th Congress (1995–1997); she instead sought the GOP nomination for governor of Maryland. An early favorite in the race, she was upset in the Republican primary by conservative Ellen Sauerbrey, 52 to 38 percent. In 2000, Bentley led the Maryland

"George W. Bush for President" campaign. Two years later she won the Republican nomination for her old seat—facing Baltimore County Executive Dutch Ruppersberger. Redistricting by the Democratic-controlled state legislature, however, had tilted the district toward a more liberal base. "I still have that vim for all the issues important to me," said the 78-year-old Bentley, adding that the race would come down to a single issue: "Integrity."[19] Ruppersberger eventually prevailed, with 54 percent of the vote to Bentley's 46 percent.[20] Bentley resides in her old district, leading a consulting firm specializing in transportation and trade issues.[21]

FOR FURTHER READING

Biographical Directory of the United States Congress, "Helen Delich Bentley," http://bioguide.congress.gov

MANUSCRIPT COLLECTIONS

University of Maryland, Baltimore College (Baltimore, MD), the Langsdale Library. *Papers*: 1945–1995, 596 cubic feet. Collection covers Bentley's career from her work as a maritime reporter for the *Baltimore Sun* through her five terms in the U.S. House of Representatives through her failed 1994 gubernatorial Republican primary election in Maryland. Among the items in the collection are the newspaper articles she wrote on the port of Baltimore as a *Sun* reporter, correspondence, reports, some video, campaign materials, published and unpublished reports, and hearings. A finding aid is available in the repository.

University of Oklahoma (Norman, OK), The Julian P. Kanter Commercial Archive, Department of Communication. *Sound and video reels*: 1982–1994, three sound reels and six video reels. Includes 24 commercials used during Bentley's campaigns for the 1982, 1984, 1986, and 1988 U.S. congressional elections and the 1994 gubernatorial election in Maryland, Republican Party.

★ HELEN DELICH BENTLEY ★

NOTES

1   Alison Muscatine, "GOP's Bentley Squares Off With Rep. Long," 27 October 1984, *Washington Post*: B1.

2   *Current Biography, 1971* (New York: H.W. Wilson and Company, 1971): 35–37.

3   Muscatine, "GOP's Bentley Squares Off with Rep. Long."

4   Saundra Saperstein, "Maryland Campaign Blessings From the GOP," 2 October 1980, *Washington Post*: MD1.

5   Eugene L. Meyer, "Rep. Clarence Long: Out of Tune, But in Touch," 21 September 1980, *Washington Post*: B1.

6   "Election Statistics, 1920 to Present," http://clerk.house.gov/members/electionInfo/elections.html.

7   *Politics in America, 1990* (Washington, D.C.: Congressional Quarterly Inc., 1989): 658.

8   "Election Statistics, 1920 to Present," http://clerk.house.gov/members/electionInfo/elections.html.

9   Muscatine, "GOP's Bentley Squares Off With Rep. Long."

10 Saundra Saperstein, "Bentley Edges Past Incumbent Long in Maryland's 2nd District," 7 November 1984, *Washington Post*: A32.

11 Saundra Saperstein and Alison Muscatine, "Candidate Bentley Rode Reagan-Bush Coattails," 8 November 1984, *Washington Post*: A55; "Election Statistics, 1920 to Present," http://clerk.house.gov/members/electionInfo/elections.html.

12 *Politics in America, 1990*: 658.

13 "Election Statistics, 1920 to Present," http://clerk.house.gov/members/electionInfo/elections.html.

14 *Politics in America, 1990*: 657.

15 Richard Tapscott, "Bentley's Big Stick; Tough-Minded Republican Hard to Peg in Race for Md. Governor," 26 June 1994, *Washington Post*: B1.

16 Janet Naylor, "Bentley Confident GOP Can Win MD; Foes Call Her 'Stealth Candidate,'" 9 September 1994, *Washington Times*: C4.

17 Tapscott, "Bentley's Big Stick; Tough-Minded Republican Hard to Peg in Race for Md. Governor."

18 Helen Delich Bentley, letter to editor, "Japanese Grip the Pentagon in a Chiplock," 20 November 1989, *New York Times*: A22.

19 Spencer S. Hsu, "Maryland's 2nd District Key Partisan Battleground," 29 October 2002, *Washington Post*: B1.

20 "Election Statistics, 1920 to Present," http://clerk.house.gov/members/electionInfo/elections.html.

21 Andrew A. Green, "For Bentley, Her Age Doesn't Slow The Pace," 20 October 2002, *Baltimore Sun*: 1B; James Mosher, "Former Congresswoman Bentley Not Interested in Job as Director of Port of Baltimore," 28 February 2005, *Daily Record* (Baltimore, MD).

Jan L. Meyers
1928–

UNITED STATES REPRESENTATIVE ★ REPUBLICAN FROM KANSAS
1985–1997

In 1995, Jan Meyers, a five-term Representative from Kansas, became the first Republican woman to chair a standing House committee in more than 40 years. That milestone capped Meyers's long tenure as a public servant that began on the Overland Park (Kansas) City Council and included more than a decade in the state senate. Reflecting on a political career that sometimes saw her take a stand against her party on major social issues, Meyers advised would-be politicians, "Listen to your conscience and your constituents—both. Most of the time they'll agree. If your conscience is different than your constituents', then you'll have a hard time."[1]

Janice Lenore Crilly was born on July 20, 1928, in Lincoln, Nebraska, the daughter of Howard M. Crilly, a newspaper publisher, and Lenore N. (Hazel) Crilly. Janice Crilly and her brother, Donn, were raised in Superior, Nebraska, where her father ran the local newspaper, *The Superior Express*, beginning in the mid-1930s.[2] In 1948, she graduated with an Associate Fine Arts degree from William Woods College in Fulton, Missouri, and with a B.A. in communications from the University of Nebraska in 1951. Following graduation, she worked in advertising and public relations. Crilly married Louis "Dutch" Meyers, who eventually became a Kansas City television station executive, and they raised a daughter and son, Valerie and Philip.

Jan Meyers's career in Kansas GOP politics began in 1966, when she served as Overland Park's chairwoman for Edward Lawrence "Larry" Winn, Jr.'s campaign for a U.S. House seat representing suburban Kansas City. Two years later, she was district co-chair for the first of Senator Robert Dole's string of five successful Senate races. In 1974, Meyers chaired Republican Bob Bennett's

gubernatorial campaign in Johnson County. From 1967 to 1972, she served as a member of the Overland Park City Council, presiding for two years. In 1972, Meyers won election to the Kansas state senate and served there for the next 12 years, rising to chair the public health and welfare committee as well as the local government committee. In 1978, Meyers entered the GOP primary for one of Kansas's seats in the U.S. Senate but garnered only 10 percent of the vote and finished fourth in a race eventually won by Republican Nancy Kassebaum.

When Representative Winn retired in 1984, Meyers entered the GOP primary to succeed him. By that point, the district was a narrow north-south sliver nestled in the northeast corner of Kansas across the river from the metropolis of Kansas City, Missouri. Geographically the smallest of the state's four congressional districts, it was dominated by two counties—Wyandotte, which encompassed Kansas City, Kansas, with a large blue-collar and working-class population and, to the south, Johnson County, a white-collar, suburban, affluent address which included the city of Overland Park. Meyers began the race with the best name recognition but her support for legalized abortion alienated many among the conservative Republican base. In a five-way race she won the party nomination with just 35 percent of the vote; her nearest opponent, Russell Leffel, captured 28 percent. In the general election she faced a formidable opponent in the Democratic candidate, Kansas City Mayor John Reardon. Though Reardon supported a nuclear weapons freeze, he distanced himself from most Democratic economic programs and supported a ban on abortions. Meyers hewed to budget and military issues, running on President Ronald W. Reagan's platform, calling for strong defense and a bal-

anced budget amendment. She emphasized her long experience in state politics and plastered the district with "Jan Can" posters.[3] Benefiting from being on a ticket that featured Reagan and the popular Kassebaum (who received more votes than Reagan in the November elections), Meyers won with 55 percent to Reardon's 40 percent (the district went for Reagan by a nearly 2-to-1 margin).[4]

Meyers faced little opposition in her subsequent general elections; indeed, in 1988, she defeated a Democratic challenger by a 3-to-1 margin. Meyers faced only one serious primary challenge. In 1992, a conservative Kansas state representative tried to capitalize on anti-incumbent sentiment by questioning Meyer's use of franking privileges for campaign mail. Meyers prevailed 56 to 23 percent in the primary and won the general election by a margin of 20 percentage points.[5]

When Congresswoman Meyers arrived in the House, she was determined to work her way into a position of power through traditional routes. She sought a seat on high-profile committees such as Ways and Means and Appropriations, but was unable to secure a spot on either. Instead, she was appointed to the Committee on Science and Technology, the Committee on Small Business, and the Select Committee on Aging. In the 100th Congress (1987–1989), she transferred from Science and Technology to the more prestigious Foreign Affairs Committee.

Meyers was most active on the Small Business Committee. She introduced a number of legislative measures to protect small business interests and to ensure that they had fair representation in government. She worked to bring permanent tax cuts for small businesses and exempt them from minimum wage laws and to increase the health care deductions for the self-employed to 100 percent. In 1993, Meyers opposed the Family and Medical Leave Act, which required employers to provide unpaid leave for employees tending to newborns or sick family members; she believed it would disproportionately affect small businesses. She supported the North American Free Trade Agreement, arguing that by lifting trade barriers between the U.S., Canada, and Mexico, policymakers could prevent European countries from forming a trade bloc with America's northern and southern neighbors. More importantly, she noted, her constituents supported the measure.[6]

When Republicans took control of the House in the 1994 elections, Jan Meyers was promoted to chair of the Small Business Committee. It marked the first time that a Republican woman had chaired a House committee since Edith Nourse Rogers headed Veterans' Affairs in the 83rd Congress (1953–1955). "Leadership positions come as a result of seniority," Meyers said later. "I sincerely hope that women continue to run and continue to get elected, and I think that will ultimately result in more women being elected to leadership positions."[7]

In 1995, the House leadership briefly considered disbanding the Small Business Committee. But Meyers pointed out that small business owners were a major constituency of the GOP and that they deserved a forum for their interests. She introduced legislation that would have created a Cabinet-level post for the Small Business Administration.[8] Meyers often referenced the "ingenuity and can-do attitude" of small businesses in America and the fact that by the 1990s, women and minorities represented the fastest growing segment of that business sector.[9] In 1994, during the debate over universal health care, Meyers advocated small business opposition against government mandated programs. "Small business owners, including those currently offering health care, still believe that the government that governs best, governs least," she said. "Let us heed their wisdom and real world experience."[10] Reflecting on the Congresswoman's work on behalf of small-sized employers, Kansas Senator Dole later said in a tribute on the Senate Floor, "Jan Meyers never stopped fighting to reduce the regulatory and tax burdens on America's small businessmen and women."[11]

Rising through the committee ranks via her seniority, Meyers also attempted to ascend the party leadership ladder. She often volunteered for bottom-rung partisan positions, such as serving on various task forces and policy groups. Meyers won a spot on the Republican Policy Committee (chairing a panel which helped overhaul the GOP Conference rules) and served on the Republican Task Force on Health Care Policy. In the 101st Congress

(1989–1991), she also served as a vice chair of the Energy and Environment Study Conference and, two years later, Minority Leader Robert Michel of Illinois appointed Meyers to his Economic and Health Task Force. Yet, her dutiful approach to such chores did not earn her the political capital needed to break into the elected leadership ranks. In late 1988, Meyers lost a contest for the Republican Conference Secretary's post to Representative Vin Weber of Minnesota, a protégé of Whip Newt Gingrich of Georgia.[12]

Meyer's fiscal conservatism contrasted with her moderate social positions, especially on reproductive issues and gun control. She was a regular defender of a woman's right to seek an abortion, particularly in cases of rape or dire medical threat to mothers. Meyers criticized the George H. W. Bush administration in 1992 for legislation prohibiting women's health counselors at federally funded clinics from discussing a range of options, including abortion, with patients. "It is a family planning issue. It is an issue of equity for poor women, and of free speech," Meyers said on the House Floor. "They should be able to get full information about that health care."[13] She voted against proposals to require parental notification for minors' abortions and supported funding for U.S. family planning efforts overseas. Both positions put her at odds with many GOP colleagues. From her seat on the Foreign Affairs Committee, Meyers also advocated anti-drug efforts on both the supply and the demand side of the illegal drug trafficking problem. "We must make the user's life so difficult, and the use of drugs so socially unacceptable, that people will not start drug use," she said.[14] Meyers approved of Republican efforts to overhaul the welfare system in the mid-1990s—arguing that the emphasis should be shifted from federal- to state-based aid and that those receiving entitlements should shoulder more responsibility.[15]

Meyers declined to run for re-election in 1996, noting that she wanted to spend more time with her family. "There are other things in life I want to do, and being a Member of Congress, if you take the job seriously, simply does not leave time," Meyers told the press.[16] She also said she believed that Members of Congress should serve

no more than 10 to 14 years.[17] Meyers returned to Overland Park, Kansas, where she joined foundation boards for a local library and a community college.

FOR FURTHER READING

Biographical Directory of the United States Congress, "Jan Meyers," http://bioguide.congress.gov

MANUSCRIPT COLLECTION

University of Oklahoma (Norman, OK), The Julian P. Kanter Political Commercial Archive, Department of Communication. *Video reel:* 1994, two commercials from Meyers's campaign for the U.S. Congress.

NOTES

1   Amy Kenna, "No Business Like Small Business: Meyers Reflects on Being One of Only Four Women in History to Chair a House Panel," 8 March 2001, *Roll Call*: 38.

2   *"Who's Who in Nebraska, Nuckolls County,"* http://www.rootsweb.com/fineresour/OLLibrary/who1940/co/nuckolls.htm, under the entry "Crilly, Howard M." (accessed 17 September 2004).

3   *Politics in America, 1990* (Washington, D.C.: Congressional Quarterly Inc., 1989): 566–567.

4   "Election Statistics, 1920 to Present," http://clerk.house.gov/members/electionInfo/elections.html.

5   Ibid.

6   "Janice Lenore Meyers," Associated Press Candidate Biographies, 1996.

7   Kenna, "No Business Like Small Business."

8   Karen Foerstel, *Biographical Dictionary of Congressional Women* (Westport, CT: Greenwood Publishers, 1999): 185–186.

9   *Congressional Record*, House, 102nd Cong. 2nd sess. (12 May 1992): 3138.

10 *Congressional Record*, House, 103rd Cong., 2nd sess. (23 June 1994): 4886.

11 *Congressional Record*, Senate, 104th Cong., 1st sess. (5 December 1995): 18013.

12 *Politics in America, 1994* (Washington, D.C.: Congressional Quarterly Inc., 1993): 600; *Politics in America, 1990*: 566.

13 *Congressional Record*, House, 102nd Cong., 2nd sess. (2 April 1992): 2273.

14 *Politics in America, 1990*: 566.

15 *Congressional Record*, House, 103rd Cong., 2nd sess. (26 April 1994): 2759–2760.

16 "Kansas Congresswoman Won't Run Again," 29 November 1995, *New York Times*: B14.

17 "Kansas Lawmaker to Retire," 29 November 1995, *Washington Post*: A15.

Catherine S. Long

1924–

UNITED STATES REPRESENTATIVE ★ DEMOCRAT FROM LOUISIANA
1985–1987

Catherine ("Cathy") S. Long married into Louisiana's legendary political family and spent nearly four decades immersed in state and national politics as a politician's wife. When her influential husband, Gillis Long, died suddenly in 1985, Democratic Party leaders believed Cathy Long was a logical choice to succeed him, having served as his campaign surrogate and close advisor. She easily won the special election to his seat. "The biggest change in my life is not Congress," Congresswoman Long told a reporter shortly after taking office. "It was the death of my husband."[1]

Cathy Small was born in Dayton, Ohio, on February 7, 1924. She graduated from high school in Camp Hill, Pennsylvania, and studied at Louisiana State University where she received a B.A. in 1948. In 1947, Cathy Small married Gillis Long, a decorated World War II veteran and member of one of Louisiana's most powerful political families. He was a distant cousin of the flamboyant Louisiana political boss Huey Long and longtime U.S. Senator Russell Long. In 1962, he won election to the U.S. House of Representatives from a central Louisiana district encompassing Baton Rouge. A supporter of civil rights, he was targeted in 1964 by his cousin, Speedy Long, who defeated him for renomination by charging that Gillis Long had aided the passage of the 1964 Civil Rights Bill.[2] Long had voted with the House leadership to expand the membership of the House Rules Committee, effectively giving a majority to civil rights advocates and unleashing a logjam of reforms. After his defeat, Long served in the Lyndon B. Johnson administration for two years before returning to private law practice. Gillis Long won re-election to the U.S. House in 1972 to the first of seven consecutive terms in his old

district. He became one of the most respected figures in the Democratic Party as chairman of the House Democratic Caucus in the early 1980s, a high-ranking member of the Rules Committee, and a close ally of Speaker Thomas "Tip" O'Neill of Massachusetts.

While raising their two children, George and Janis, Cathy Long's early career included nonelective political work. After college she had worked as a pharmacist's mate in the U.S. Navy. She subsequently was a staff assistant to Oregon Senator Wayne Morse and Ohio Representative James G. Polk. She also served as a delegate to Democratic National Conventions and was a member of the Louisiana Democratic Finance Council and the state party's central committee. She put that experience to work on behalf of her husband's career—campaigning, canvassing the district to hear constituent issues, and acting as an informal adviser to Gillis Long. "You couldn't have found a wife that was more active than I was," she recalled. A heart condition slowed her husband in his later years in the House, leaving Cathy Long to make the frequent trips back to the district for the "physical campaigning."[3] Throughout her husband's political career, Cathy Long recalled, she campaigned more than the candidate. "I feel thoroughly at home with campaigning, I've done it so much," she said.[4]

When Gillis Long died on January 20, 1985, the party turned immediately to his widow to run for his vacant seat. "From the very minute Gillis died, I was under terrific strain to run," Cathy Long recalled. "One person called me at 3 a.m. that morning and said, 'You have to run.' At the wake I had two people give me checks for $1000 each."[5] On February 4, 1985, she declared her intention to seek the nomination.[6] Long ran on her husband's name recognition with a central campaign pledge to fulfill

his legislative interests without offering many specific policy positions of her own. She also noted her familiarity with the institution: "I don't have to start from scratch. I already know the way Congress works."[7] The Baton Rouge-centered district contained a cross-section of Louisiana culture, with rice, soybean, and sugar farmers, as well as Cajuns, African Americans (who made up 33 percent of the constituency), and labor union interests.[8] Unemployment, which had eclipsed 12 percent in the district, emerged as the primary issue in the campaign. Long's principal competitor, Louisiana state legislator John "Jock" Scott, challenged her refusal to commit to positions on the issues: "If Cathy Long can't talk to us here, how can she talk for us in Washington?"[9] Cathy Long defeated Scott by a more than a 2-to-1 margin with 56 percent of the vote (in a field with three other candidates) and carried all but one of 15 parishes in a special election on March 30, 1985.[10] Sworn in on April 4, 1985, Cathy Long was appointed to the Committee on Public Works and Transportation and the Committee on Small Business. Among her chief allies were two longtime friends and Members of the state delegation: Representatives John Breaux and Lindy Boggs who, in 1973, succeeded her late husband, Majority Leader Hale Boggs.

As a Representative, Cathy Long hewed to the same agenda as her husband, who often criticized the Ronald W. Reagan administration.[11] Her first major vote was against aid to the Nicaraguan Contra rebels. For the most part, however, she focused on Louisiana's economic needs. She sought to preserve price supports for sugar and opposed an amendment to the Mississippi River and Tributaries Project Bill that would have required local governments in the lower Mississippi Valley to share the costs of flood control. It was a program that the federal government had for decades recognized as an issue of national concern. Long also joined her colleagues in the Louisiana delegation in introducing legislation to authorize the Legal Services Corporation to make a grant to the Gillis W. Long Poverty Law Center at Loyola University in New Orleans.

Additionally, Representative Long worked on issues impacting women and other minorities. She cosponsored the 1985 Economic Equity Act, which secured pension and health benefits for women and sought to restrict racial and sex discrimination in insurance practices. In foreign affairs, the Louisiana Representative voted for economic sanctions against South Africa for its apartheid system and worked to provide aid for Nicaraguan refugees.

Shortly after taking office, Long sought to dispel notions that she was a one-term caretaker. "I would not have run if I didn't want to stay," she told a reporter. "Of course I'm going to run again. It was part of the decision I made at the time."[12] Yet, several months later, citing the burden of remaining campaign debts from her special election and a year in which she lost nearly a half dozen close friends and family members, Long declined to run for re-election in 1986. "The decision was not an easy one," she told reporters on October 15, 1985. "I sought this seat to carry on my husband's work. I would love to continue the job, but the weight of my current debt jeopardizes the possibility of a credible campaign in 1986. I believe it better for me to step aside now to give all others the opportunity to pursue this job."[13]

After Congress, Long worked as a volunteer in Washington, D.C., area homeless shelters and as a reading tutor. She also spent time with her grandchildren, who grew up near the capital. Cathy Long resides in Washington, D.C.

FOR FURTHER READING

Biographical Directory of the United States Congress,
"Catherine Small Long," http://bioguide.congress.gov

MANUSCRIPT COLLECTION

Louisiana State University (Baton Rouge, LA), Special
Collections. *Papers:* 1984–1986, 60 cubic feet. Includes
personal and congressional papers and correspondence,
photographs, portraits, video tape, sound recordings,
and memorabilia; also includes legislative and committee
files, issue mail and computer indexes to constituent correspondence, speeches, and campaign and political files. A
preliminary finding aid is available in the repository.
Restricted.

NOTES

1   Will Scheltema, "Cathy Long: She Carries On," 16 May 1985, *Roll Call*: 8.
2   Joan Cook; "Rep. Gillis Long, 61, Louisiana Liberal, Dies," 22 January
    1985, *New York Times*: A22; Richard Pearson, "Rep. Gillis Long, 61,
    Influential Democrat," 22 January 1985, *Washington Post*: D4.
3   Suzanne Nelson, "Remembering Her Husband: Louisiana Member
    Willingly Took Her Spouse's Seat, But She's Glad To Be Out," 5
    October 2000, *Roll Call*: 46.
4   Scheltema, "Cathy Long: She Carries On."
5   Nelson, "Remembering Her Husband."
6   "Mrs. Long To Seek Office," 5 February 1985, *New York Times*: B5.
7   "Catherine S. Long," Associated Press Candidate Biographies, *1986*.
8   Paul Taylor, "Political Nonpositions: Louisiana's Cathy Long Runs on
    Artfully Vague Race," 30 March 1985, *Washington Post*: A2.
9   Taylor, "Political Nonpositions: Louisiana's Cathy Long Runs on
    Artfully Vague Race."
10 "Mrs. Long Goes to Washington," 1 April 1985, Associated Press;
    Michael J. Dubin et al., *United States Congressional Elections, 1788– 1997*
    (Jefferson, NC: McFarland and Company, Inc., Publishers, 1998): 745.
    A legacy of French colonial rule in the region, Louisiana counties still
    are referred to as parishes.
11 Scheltema, "Cathy Long: She Carries On."
12 Ibid.
13 "Rep. Cathy Long Says She Won't Seek Another Term," 18 October
    1985, Associated Press.

Constance A. Morella

1931–

UNITED STATES REPRESENTATIVE ★ REPUBLICAN FROM MARYLAND
1987–2003

Congressional politics at the end of the 20th century became more polarized, and for moderates, their plight became unenviable. Constance Morella was one of a shrinking group of moderate House Republicans who had been so numerous during the 1960s and 1970s. From the first, she built her career around her Maryland district, but the 2000 Census offered an opportunity to recast her constituency dramatically. At the same time she found herself tied more closely to her party after the Republicans took control of the House in 1995, making her vulnerable, as Democrats recruited stronger candidates to run against her.

Constance Albanese was born on February 12, 1931, in Somerville, Massachusetts, to Italian immigrants Salvatore and Christina Albanese. Her father was a cabinetmaker, and her mother worked in a laundromat. Constance Albanese attended Boston University, graduating in 1951, and marrying Anthony Morella in 1954. The couple moved to Maryland, where she taught high school. Eventually, they would have three children (Paul, Mark, and Laura) and help raise Constance Morella's sister's six children (Christine, Catherine, Louise, Paul, Rachel, and Ursula) after she died. After receiving her MA degree from American University in 1967, Morella taught at Montgomery College in Rockville, Maryland, from 1970 to 1986. Morella also became active in community organizations and was soon serving in a variety of public positions, finding herself attracted to the Republican moderates, as represented by Governor Nelson Rockefeller of New York. She was a member of the Montgomery County commission for women (1971–1975), and in 1974 she ran unsuccessfully for the Maryland general assembly. She was elected to the general assembly in 1978, serving through 1987.

Morella's first run for a seat in Congress took place in 1980. She ran unsuccessfully for the Republican nomination against former Representative Newton Steers, Jr. When incumbent Representative Michael Barnes announced in 1986 that he was retiring from the House to make what later was an unsuccessful bid for the U.S. Senate, Morella won the vacant seat over State Senator Stewart Bainum, Jr., with 53 percent of the vote. The district covered much of Montgomery County outside of Washington, with more than 60,000 federal employees and the center of Maryland's technology industry. Having run on a platform of strong ties to the district, backing from women's groups, and support for some elements of the Ronald W. Reagan administration's foreign policy, this election was crucial in setting her style as a House Member.[1] A moderate Republican had won election to Congress in a Democratic state. "[The 1986] election shows that Montgomery County voters are very independent," Morella recalled. "It proves that party label is nothing that's going to keep people from voting for a person."[2] High voter turnout in her hometown of Bethesda also gave her the edge.[3]

Morella built her House career by emphasizing those issues of greatest concern to her constituents. She also developed an intense district presence. "Three things are certain in Montgomery County," noted the *Washington Post* in 1992, "death, taxes and Connie Morella showing up for every small-town parade and public forum."[4] Morella worked hard to establish a close relationship with her district, developing a reputation for independence while muting her party affiliation in the heavily Democratic district.[5] As a result, Morella was frequently on the other side of major issues from the rest of her Republican

MORELLA FELL VICTIM TO ONE
OF THE VULNERABILITIES OF AN
INCUMBENT WHO RELIES ON A
CLOSE AND FAMILIAR RELATIONSHIP
WITH THE DISTRICT: THE VAGARIES
OF REDISTRICTING. "DON'T LOOK
AT ME AS A SYMBOL," MORELLA
APPEALED TO VOTERS WHO
CONTINUED TO LIKE HER BUT
WERE UNHAPPY WITH HER PARTY.
"LOOK AT ME."

colleagues. "We'd like her to vote with us more often," Republican Representative Henry Hyde of Illinois said in 1990. "But to get elected she must reflect her district, and she votes like her predecessors." [6] Her initial committee assignments catered to her district's greatest concerns: the Committee on Post Office and Civil Service and the Committee on Science, Space, and Technology. During the first part of her House career, she used these committee assignments as the basis of her legislative activities in areas such as federal pay, parental leave, and health care benefits for the civil service.

Morella's ability to establish a close nonpartisan bond with her district through serving the interests of her constituents allowed her to win re-election by wide margins. In the early 1990s, Morella consistently won more than 70 percent of the vote. This period of electoral popularity allowed her to begin venturing into more policies that often built on her committee assignments. She staked out positions on health care, calling for more scientific research on cancer and HIV/AIDS and affordable childcare programs. House colleagues called her the "angel of NIST"–the National Institute of Standards and Technology, based in the district.[7] She took an interest in programs to combat domestic violence and teen pregnancies. But Morella also began venturing into less safe territory relative to her own party's legislative priorities. In contrast to many Republican colleagues, Morella supported abortion and reproductive rights. In 1992 she led an unsuccessful effort to remove the anti-abortion plank at the Republican National Convention. "I would like to move the party closer to the center," she said in 1993. [8] While her stand gained her the endorsement of abortion rights groups, Morella strongly believed the issue went beyond politics. In 1996 she said of abortion that "it has to do with one's personal beliefs, and it doesn't belong on the agenda for politicians."[9]

During her tenure in Congress Morella was frequently mentioned as a possible nominee for governor or U.S. Senator.[10] She resisted, however, efforts to position herself to be able to influence the direction of her party colleagues. "Do I seek to be in leadership?" Morella told

the *Washington Post*. "No. I'll be damned if I kowtow to anyone. I need the independence. And you just don't have that in leadership. You have to do what they want."[11]

When the Republicans captured the House after the 1994 elections, Morella's status underwent a transformation. Formerly a backbench Member of a minority party, she became chair of the Subcommittee on Technology on the renamed Committee on Science. Because the Republicans eliminated the Committee on Post Office and Civil Service, Morella became a member of the Committee on Government Reform and Oversight, renamed the Committee on Government Reform in 1999. Morella later became the chair of its Subcommittee on the District of Columbia during the 107th Congress (2001–2003). Of her service as subcommittee chair, Delegate Eleanor Holmes Norton of Washington, D.C., said, "Everybody loves Connie."[12]

Becoming part of the majority was not cost-free for Morella, however. Many of the new Republican Members dismissed moderates like Morella as "squishy" and resented the ability of the senior moderates to temper some of their policy proposals.[13] Meanwhile, the still-popular Morella now confronted constituents who were unhappy with what the Republican majority was doing —particularly in the polarizing atmosphere developing between the Republican Congress and Democratic White House. In the late 1990s, Morella's re-election margins began to erode. Her opponents became better known and more experienced, and they had deeper financial pockets.[14] Past supporters of Morella began to listen sympathetically to the argument that a vote for Morella was a vote to keep Newt Gingrich as Speaker. "What I saw," charged her 1998 opponent Ralph Neas, "was someone who would vote against the Republican leadership when it no longer made a difference."[15] When the Republicans narrowly retained their majority in 1996, the news that Gingrich admitted to ethical violations led some Republican moderates to refrain from voting for Gingrich as Speaker or to vote for other candidates. Morella was among five Republicans to vote "present."[16] In one of the major battles between the Republican Congress and the

Democratic President, Morella joined a minority of Republicans who voted against impeaching William J. Clinton in 1998.[17] She would recall that Congress "did become more polarized, which is really too bad."[18]

The Maryland redistricting for the 2002 elections contributed to the erosion of Morella's base. Her new district, created by a Democratic state legislature, lopped off the northwestern portion that had supported her most strongly while adding highly Democratic territory to the east. The core of her old district (including her Bethesda base) that she retained was made up largely of voters that were becoming more Democratic over time.[19] One state senator proclaimed, "If she runs, she loses."[20] Morella agreed. "They wanted to gerrymander me into retirement."[21] She was widely viewed as the most vulnerable House Republican in the country.[22] A potentially divisive Democratic primary between State Delegate Mark K. Shriver, a member of the Kennedy family, and State Senator Christopher Van Hollen, Jr., held out the promise that Morella would face an opponent with a depleted war chest.[23] Both national parties concentrated resources on the race, raising $5.6 million, the most expensive race in Maryland history.[24]

Morella fell victim to one of the vulnerabilities of an incumbent who relies on a close and familiar relationship with the district: the vagaries of redistricting. "Don't look at me as a symbol," Morella appealed to voters who continued to like her but were unhappy with her party. "Look at me."[25] Despite national and statewide Republican gains, Van Hollen, the Democratic challenger with the greatest legislative experience, eked out a 9,000-vote victory over Morella in a race where more than 200,000 votes were cast.[26] "I had a flawless campaign," she would recall later. "Can you imagine—the only one I lost was flawless." Looking back, though, she remained philosophical about her career. "It was a great privilege," she told the *Washington Post* a year later. "It was time for me to move on."[27]

Morella returned to Montgomery County amid rumors and talk that she would become a member of the administration of President George W. Bush or of Maryland Governor Robert L. Ehrlich, Jr. In July 2003, President Bush nominated her to be U.S. Ambassador to the Organization for Economic Cooperation and Development.[28] After assuming her post on October 8, 2003, she continued to worry about the increasing polarization in Congress.[29] Moderates, she mused, "have been endangered, and I hope that changes."[30]

FOR FURTHER READING

Biographical Directory of the United States Congress, "Constance Morella," http://bioguide.congress.gov

MANUSCRIPT COLLECTIONS

University of Maryland Libraries (College Park, MD), Archives and Manuscripts Department, Special Collections. *Papers:* 1975–2002, 189 linear feet. The papers of Constance Morella document her legislative efforts on such issues as scientific research and development, education, the federal workforce, equity for women, and the environment. The files consist of correspondence, newspaper clippings, press releases, photographs, memorabilia, awards, and subject files. The collection is unprocessed, although a preliminary inventory is available.

University of Oklahoma (Norman, OK), The Julian P. Kanter Commercial Archive, Department of Communication. *Sound tape reels:* 1986, five sound tape reels. Includes seven commercials used during Morella's campaign for the 1986 U.S. congressional election in Maryland, Republican Party.

NOTES

1   R.H. Melton, "Morella: Tirelessly Tackling the Odds," 29 October 1986, *Washington Post*: B1.

2   *Current Biography, 2001* (New York: H.W. Wilson and Company, 2001): 34.

3   R.H. Melton, "Morella's Election a Triumph of Personality Over Party; Democrats Crossover Votes Played Key Role in Md. 8th District," 6 November 1986, *Washington Post* : A57.

4   *Current Biography, 2001*: 34.

5   Dan Balz and Jo Becker, "Shaping Up as an Amazing Race," June 2, 2002, *Washington Post*: A15.

6   *Current Biography, 2001*: 33.

7   Brigid Schulte, "For Morella, Independence Carries a Cost," October 15, 2002, *Washington Post*: B5.

8   *Current Biography, 2001*: 35.

9   Ibid.

10 Spencer S. Hsu, "Political Spotlight Shines On Morella's Balancing Act," 11 March 2002, *Washington Post*: C8.

11 Schulte, "For Morella, Independence Carries a Cost."

12 Ibid.

13 Linda Killian, *The Freshmen: What Happened to the Republican Revolution?* (Boulder, CO: Westview Press, 1998): 38.

14 Jo Becker and Brigid Schulte, "Party Lines Are Drawn on Morella's Home Turf," 3 November 2002, *Washington Post*: C7.

15 Dan Balz and Jo Becker, "Shaping Up As an Amazing Race," 2 June 2002, *Washington Post*: A15.

16 Killian, *The Freshmen*: 423.

17 Hsu, "Political Spotlight Shines On Morella's Balancing Act"; Schulte, "For Morella, Independence Carries a Cost."

18 Keith B. Richburg, "Morella Reshapes Local Politicking Skills for Overseas Post," 26 October 2003, *Washington Post*: A9.

19 Balz and Becker, "Shaping Up As an Amazing Race."

20 Brigid Schulte, "Sad but Stoical, Morella Is Trying to Understand," 7 November 2002, *Washington Post*: B8.

21 Richburg, "Morella Reshapes Local Politicking Skills for Overseas Post."

22 Balz and Becker, "Shaping Up As an Amazing Race."

23 Hsu, "Political Spotlight Shines On Morella's Balancing Act."

24 Jo Becker, "Van Hollen Ousts Morella as Voters Swing to Party Line," 6 November 2002, *Washington Post*: A32.

25 Schulte, "For Morella, Independence Carries a Cost."

26 "Election Statistics, 1920 to Present," http://clerk.house.gov/members/ electionInfo/elections.html.

27 Richburg, "Morella Reshapes Local Politicking Skills for Overseas Post."

28 *Congressional Record*, Senate, 108th Cong., 1st sess. (11 July 2003): 9310; *Congressional Record*, Senate, 108th Cong., 1st sess. (31 July 2003): 10527.

29 "United States' Permanent Representative to the OECD," Organization for Economic Co-operation and Development, http://www.oecd.org/ (accessed 7 January 2004).

30 Richburg, "Morella Reshapes Local Politicking Skills for Overseas Post."

Elizabeth J. Patterson

1939–

UNITED STATES REPRESENTATIVE ★ DEMOCRAT FROM SOUTH CAROLINA
1987–1993

Representative Elizabeth Patterson of South Carolina carved out a political career as a Democrat in a conservative-leaning district, portraying herself as a budget hawk and opponent of tax increases, though not at the expense of providing for working-class needs. The daughter of a powerful politician, Patterson's long experience in public service, fiscal austerity, and ability to capitalize on the South Carolina GOP's internal divisions gave her narrow majorities over her opponents. Ultimately, her middle-of-the-road approach lost its appeal in a conservative state.[1]

Elizabeth Johnston was born on November 18, 1939, to Olin DeWitt Talmadge Johnston and Gladys Atkinson Johnston in Columbia, South Carolina. Her father, Olin Johnston, was a political fixture in South Carolina politics, serving in the state house of representatives before being elected governor in 1935. He served a total of six years as governor (1935–1939; 1943–1945), before resigning in his second term after he had won election to the U.S. Senate. Johnston served 20 years in the Senate and was the longtime chairman of the Post Office and Civil Service Committee. Elizabeth Johnston attended public schools in suburban Maryland but graduated from Spartanburg High School in Spartanburg, South Carolina, in 1957. In 1961, she received her bachelor's degree at Columbia College in Columbia, South Carolina. She subsequently studied political science at the University of South Carolina. On April 16, 1967, Elizabeth Johnston married Dwight Patterson and they raised three children: Dwight, Olin, and Catherine. Elizabeth Patterson, worked as recruiting officer for the Peace Corps and VISTA, as a Head Start coordinator for the South Carolina Office of Economic Opportunity, and as a staff assistant for South

Carolina Representative James R. Mann from 1969 to 1970. Patterson made her debut in elective politics when she won an open seat on the Spartanburg County Council in 1975. She served in that capacity for two years, securing a reputation as a fiscal conservative who trimmed county expenses while opposing a tax increase.[2] In 1979, Patterson was elected to the South Carolina senate, where she served through 1986. She worked diligently on the finance committee to reduce and restructure the state budget. She also served on the governor's task force on hunger and nutrition.

Patterson declared her candidacy for a South Carolina U.S. House seat in 1986, when four-term Republican Representative Carroll A. Campbell, Jr., declined renomination in order to run for governor. The district encompassed the Greenville and Spartanburg area, which had swung Republican in the 1960s. With the exception of the 1976 election, South Carolina had voted for the GOP presidential candidate since 1964, and the district had been a mainstay of conservatives. As a stronghold of evangelical and fundamentalist conservatives, the district increasingly was contested between religiously conservative Republicans versus more "commerce-minded" Republicans and moderate to conservative Democrats.[3] Patterson campaigned as a fiscal conservative with a social conscience. As a moderate, she supported prochoice legislation citing that, "the government should not interfere with this most personal decision."[4] She advocated giving aid to the Nicaragua Contra rebels, opposed gun control, and also supported the death penalty. In the general election, Patterson faced Republican William D. Workman III, a former newspaper editor, the mayor of Greenville, and the son of a man who had once opposed

Olin Johnston for the Senate.[5] Workman had survived a heated GOP primary in which he'd been attacked by religious fundamentalist opponents as a tool of big business. Though polls favored Workman, Patterson skillfully exploited divisions in the GOP between her opponent and religious-right critics by painting him as a friend of corporations and the district's bluebloods. When Workman charged Patterson was a free-spending Democrat, she countered with television advertisements that declared, "I'm one of us"— in which she was portrayed as a homemaker and family values candidate.[6] Patterson won by a plurality of about 5,400 votes out of more than 130,000 cast, a margin of 51 percent.[7]

In subsequent elections, the district remained competitive. Less than a month on the job, Patterson was specifically targeted by the GOP for defeat.[8] Although President George H.W. Bush carried the district with 68 percent in the 1988 presidential elections (six points ahead of his statewide percentage), Patterson held on against Knox White, another business-oriented Republican, winning with 52 percent of the vote. During the 1990 midterm elections, because an economic downturn eroded support for the President Bush and Patterson cast a popular vote against a federal tax increase, South Carolina voters gave her a third term with her largest margin—61 percent against Republican Terry Haskins, the South Carolina house minority leader who was supported by religious conservatives.[9]

While in the House, Patterson sat on three committees: Veterans' Affairs; Banking, Finance and Urban Affairs; and the Select Committee on Hunger. From her Banking, Finance, and Urban Affairs post, Representative Patterson weighed in on the savings and loan industry crisis. High interest rates in the early 1980s made many of these institutions insolvent. In 1988 alone, more than 190 savings and loan banks failed, and by the time new regulatory practices were in place, the government bailout of the industry through the Federal Deposit Insurance Corporation (FDIC) was estimated to cost more than $160 billion. "We must protect the depositors. We must protect the taxpayers. And finally, we must protect the safety

and soundness of our banking industry," Patterson declared on the House Floor. She argued that uninsured deposits, foreign or domestic, should not be protected at a cost to the bank insurance fund.[10] She also opposed a radical overhaul of the FDIC, while allowing it greater power to intervene to close down insolvent banks. The Federal Deposit Insurance Corporation Improvement Act, passed in 1991, greatly revised the agency's operations.

In 1990, Patterson chaired the Conservative Democratic Forum's Task Force on Budget Reform and eventually voted against the 1990 proposed tax increase (a move which aided her re-election later that year). She also served on the Speaker's Task Force on Budget Reform, and, in 1991, introduced the Budget Simplification and Reform Act, which would have amended the Congressional Budget Act of 1974 to limit the use of continuing resolutions and expedite the rescission process. Her bill also contained a clause that would have required Members to provide explanatory statements identifying the sponsor and the cost of projects that benefited 10 or fewer people, as a means of combating pork barrel legislation. "Let us spread a little sunshine on Capitol Hill," Patterson said.[11]

Patterson also defended the beleaguered textile industry, which, until the 1980s, when it began losing to foreign competition, had been a major employer in her district. She joined the bipartisan Congressional Textile Caucus and, in 1992, Patterson was appointed chair of the panel. Patterson often expressed frustrations felt by her constituents who not only were losing jobs but were unable to "buy American." Patterson told of one occasion when her daughter went shopping in the district for a simple cotton shirt and had to resort to buying a foreign-made item. "It was made in China . . . where human rights abuses are rampant and where wages are slave wages," Patterson lamented to colleagues. "At the same time, a shirt factory in my district is closed, a factory where shirts were made of better quality and sold for a cheaper price. Those people cannot buy the clothes that I bought for my children because they are out of work."[12]

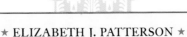

In the 1992 elections, a year eventually dominated by Democrats and women candidates, Patterson faced a tough campaign against Bob Inglis, a 33-year-old Republican challenger. Inglis, a corporate lawyer and the Greenville County GOP chairman, was highly organized and targeted 11 precincts which he believed would determine the election in the district. He also won the support of the Christian Coalition, which distributed material that accused Patterson of supporting "abortion on demand," although she had consistently opposed the procedure in all cases except rape, incest, or when the mother's life was in danger.[13] Inglis, meanwhile, depicted Patterson as a liberal on the abortion issue and as a political tool of banking interests. Inglis pledged to take "not one dime" from political action committees and declared that he would honor a pledge to serve just three terms in the House. He also attacked her for abusing the informal House "bank" maintained for Members by the Sergeant at Arms (she bounced two checks) by distributing bumper stickers in the form of a check that read, "Bounce Liz."[14] One observer noted that the Patterson campaign was slow to respond: "one problem was that she was so moderate she was hard to define. Nobody thought that she would lose."[15] Patterson eventually did lose by a margin of about 5,600 votes, 50 to 47 percent.

After leaving Congress, Patterson sought the lieutenant governorship of South Carolina in 1994. While she won the closely contested Democratic primary, she eventually lost in the general election. Patterson settled into a teaching job as a political science professor at Spartanburg Methodist College. In 1999, she received an M.A. in liberal arts from Converse College. Elizabeth Patterson resides in Spartanburg, South Carolina.

FOR FURTHER READING

Biographical Directory of the United States Congress, "Elizabeth Patterson," http://bioguide.congress.gov

MANUSCRIPT COLLECTION

University of South Carolina (Columbia, SC), Modern Political Collections, South Caroliniana Library. *Papers*: 1964–1994. Includes public papers documenting Elizabeth Patterson's service in the state general assembly and Congress. Personal papers reflect her campaigns for office and service outside of public office. Also includes audio-visual materials, consisting chiefly of video tape of campaign ads and appearances, photographs, and audio recordings. Papers are closed until 2010.

NOTES

1   Ronald Smothers, "S. Carolina Experiences Fresh Surge By G.O.P," 25 August 1994, *New York Times*: B7.
2   "Elizabeth Patterson Papers, Biography," http://www.sc.edu/library/socar/uscs/1996/patter96.htm (accessed 13 August 2002).
3   *Politics in America, 1994* (Washington, D.C.: Congressional Quarterly Inc., 1993): 1156.
4   "Elizabeth Johnston Patterson," Associated Press Candidate Biographies, 1992.
5   Steven V. Roberts, "Campaigners for House Seats Stress Local Concerns and Efficient Service," 1 November 1986, *New York Times*: 8.
6   *Politics in America, 1990*: 1368; *Almanac of American Politics, 1988* (Washington, D.C.L National Journal Inc., 1987): 1087–1088.
7   "Election Statistics, 1920 to Present," http://clerk.house.gov/members/electionInfo/elections.html.
8   "The Perils of Success," 1 February 1987, *Washington Post*: A10.
9   "Election Statistics, 1920 to Present," http://clerk.house.gov/members/electionInfo/elections.html.
10 *Congressional Record*, House, 102nd Cong., 1st sess. (31 October 1991): 8793.
11 *Congressional Record*, House, 102nd Cong., 1st sess. (1 August 1991): 6297.
12 *Congressional Record*, House, 101st Cong., 2nd sess. (2 October 1990): 8603.
13 Anthony Lewis, "Tax-Exempt Politics?" 20 November 1992, *New York Times*: A15.
14 Megan Rosenfeld, "Anatomy of a Defeat: How a Middle-of-the-Road Incumbent Got Run Over on Election Day," 12 November 1992, *Washington Post*: D1.
15 Rosenfeld, "Anatomy of a Defeat."

Patricia F. Saiki

1930–

UNITED STATES REPRESENTATIVE ★ REPUBLICAN FROM HAWAII

1987–1991

Patricia Fukuda Saiki's revitalization of the Hawaiian Republican Party propelled her to election as the first GOP Representative in the state since it entered the Union in 1959. As a Member of Congress, Saiki focused on economic and environmental legislation important to her Honolulu constituency as well as the international Asian community. In 1990, Saiki left the House to campaign for a Senate seat in a race that many political observers believed might signal a shift in the balance of political power in Hawaii. "Before Pat Saiki was elected to Congress, it was hard for us to relate to young people and tell them, 'It's great to be a Republican,'" noted a Hawaiian GOP member. "Now we can begin to spin the tale that will make people interested in supporting the Republican Party in Hawaii."[1]

Patricia Fukuda was born to Kazuo and Shizue Fukada on May 28, 1930, in Hilo, on the big island of Hawaii. She graduated from Hilo High School in 1948 and received a bachelor of science degree from the University of Hawaii at Manoa in 1952. In 1954, she married Stanley Saiki, an obstetrician, and they had five children: Stanley, Stuart, Sandra, Margaret, and Laura. Patricia Saiki taught history in Hawaii's public and private schools for 12 years. Her path to politics began with her work as a union organizer and research assistant to Hawaii senate Republicans. In the mid-1960s, Saiki served as the secretary and then the vice chair of the state Republican Party. She attended the state constitutional convention in 1968, and that year won election to the Hawaii senate, where she served for six years. In 1974, Saiki won election to the state house of representatives, where she served until 1982 and rose to the position of assistant GOP floor leader. In 1982, Saiki left the legislature and made an unsuccessful bid for

lieutenant governor. She subsequently oversaw a three-fold expansion in party membership and helped the party raise $800,000 during her two-and-a-half-year tenure as party chair. Her hand in reviving the Republican Party in the strongly Democratic state aided President Ronald W. Reagan's victory there in the 1984 presidential election (the only previous Republican presidential candidate to carry the state was Richard Nixon in 1972) and the election of Democrat-turned-Republican Frank Fasi as Honolulu mayor.

After spending nearly two decades in state politics, Saiki decided to run for the U.S. House seat vacated in July 1986 by five-term Democrat Cecil Heftel, who left to run for governor. As the state's population center, the district encompassed Honolulu, its suburbs, and the Pearl Harbor Naval base (Hawaii's only other congressional district included the rest of Oahu and the other islands). Tourism and commercial shipping were the lifeblood for the cosmopolitan population of Caucasians, Asian Americans, and native Hawaiians, most of whom were registered Democrats. The potential for influence in Washington as well as the war on drugs were the major issues leading up to the September special election to fill the remaining four months of Heftel's term in the 99th Congress (1985–1987). Liberal Democratic State Senator Neil Abercrombie was the early favorite; however, a third candidate, Democrat Mufi Hannemann, a 32-year-old corporate lobbyist and former White House fellow, entered the race, siphoning off a portion of the liberal vote. Saiki certainly benefited from the Democratic interparty warfare; however, she was unable to best Abercrombie in the September 20 special election. He prevailed over Saiki by fewer than 1,000 votes, 30 to

29 percent; Hannemann trailed by about 2,200 votes (28 percent). On the same day, Saiki won the Republican primary to run for a full term in the 100th Congress (1987–1989), while Abercrombie and Hannemann battled for the Democratic nomination for the full term. As the two Democrats faced off in the closed primary, several thousand Saiki supporters temporarily registered as Democrats in order to give Hannemann a narrow win, instantly reducing Abercrombie to lame-duck status in the 99th Congress.[2]

In the general election for the 100th Congress, Hannemann had history on his side: Since the state entered the Union in 1959, Hawaii sent only Democrats to the House of Representatives. But Hannemann also faced several obstacles. First, the acrimony from the primary carried over as Abercrombie withheld his endorsement. More importantly, Saiki's ancestral roots as a Japanese-American—one-third of the voters shared her ethnic background—helped her popularity. Saiki won the general election with 59 percent of the vote, a 33,000-vote plurality; no previous Hawaiian Republican candidate for the U.S. House had ever polled more than 45 percent of the vote.[3] She became the first Republican to represent Hawaii in the House since Elizabeth Farrington won election as a territorial delegate in 1954 (Republican Hiram Fong served in the U.S. Senate from 1959 to 1976). Two years later, Saiki went unopposed in the 1988 Republican primary. In the three-way Democratic primary, Mary Bitterman, a former director of the Voice of America, emerged as the convincing winner; however, she spent the bulk of her treasury securing the nomination, leaving her little money for the general election. She was not able to dent Saiki's record, and the incumbent won comfortably with a 55 percent majority.

Throughout her career, Saiki established a fiscally conservative voting record on economic issues, in line with most of her GOP colleagues. She also supported much of the Reagan and George H.W. Bush administration's foreign policy programs—voting for aid to the Nicaraguan Contras, funding for the Strategic Defense Initiative, and the death penalty for drug-related murders. Where she parted company with many Republicans was on her moderate stance on touchstone social issues, chief among them reproductive rights. Saiki supported women's reproductive freedom. "I don't want to be sexist about this, but anything that involves a woman's life or career, it's very personal, very close to us," Saiki told the *New York Times*. "We're the ones who experience it. We're the ones who have to pay for it."[4]

Saiki received seats on the Committee on Banking, Finance and Urban Affairs; the Committee on Merchant Marine and Fisheries; and the Select Committee on Aging. Her seat on Merchant Marine and Fisheries, with assignments on its oceanography and fisheries subcommittee, was particularly important to her ocean-side constituency. Saiki worked to preserve the islands' natural beauty and unique resources. She attempted to persuade the Bush administration to suspend military test bombing on the island of Kahoolawe, situated just offshore from Maui. Claimed by U.S. officials in the early 1950s, the island nevertheless retained significant cultural relevance for native Hawaiians.[5] In 1990, she supported an amendment to revise the annual accrual method of accounting for pineapple and banana growers, whose longer growth and production cycles distorted their income statements and exposed them to excess taxation.[6] Saiki also advocated a ban on environmentally unsound drift fishing nets in the South Pacific, urging the U.S. Secretary of State to call an international convention to discuss the topic.[7]

In 1987, Representative Saiki cosponsored legislation that called for monetary reparations and an official apology to the Japanese Americans who were interned during World War II. In September 1987, Saiki voted with the majority as one of the few Republicans to favor the bill; nearly 100 GOP Members opposed it. After the measure passed the Senate, Saiki was present when President Reagan signed it into law a year later. She subsequently pressed Congress to expedite payouts.[8] As an Asian American representing a district in the middle of the Pacific, Saiki also was involved with Pacific-Rim issues. She served on congressional delegations that visited Tonga for the South Pacific island monarch's birthday and

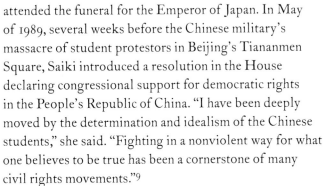
attended the funeral for the Emperor of Japan. In May of 1989, several weeks before the Chinese military's massacre of student protestors in Beijing's Tiananmen Square, Saiki introduced a resolution in the House declaring congressional support for democratic rights in the People's Republic of China. "I have been deeply moved by the determination and idealism of the Chinese students," she said. "Fighting in a nonviolent way for what one believes to be true has been a cornerstone of many civil rights movements."[9]

In April 1990, popular, long-serving Hawaii Senator Spark Matsunaga died of cancer. Urged by her friend President George H.W. Bush, Saiki entered the election to fill the Democrat's vacant seat. "Hawaii needs a Senator who can make the people on Pennsylvania Avenue and Constitution Avenue understand the people on Kamehameha Avenue," Saiki said while announcing her candidacy.[10] Democratic Governor John Waihee appointed Hawaii Congressman Daniel Akaka to serve as interim Senator until the November special election. Also the Democratic candidate in the special election, Akaka's new position made him the favorite. Yet, Saiki proved a formidable opponent. She won the primary against four other Republican candidates with a strong 92 percent of the vote. Both candidates supported the key economic issues that many Hawaiians favored: maintaining price supports for cane sugar, promoting increased tourism, and halting target practice on Kahoolawe. Saiki proved a more dynamic candidate than the sedate Akaka. She also had repeatedly proved her ability to draw votes from the Japanese-American community. Moreover, the growing suburban, conservative Caucasian population allowed her, in the words of one political strategist, to "cut into the Democratic establishment."[11] Political observers believed Saiki might be among a handful of candidates to help Republicans regain control of the Senate. However, Akaka had the support of the well-entrenched Hawaiian Democratic establishment, and his warm, pleasing personality appealed to voters. Saiki lost to Akaka by a healthy margin of about 33,000 votes, 54 percent to 45 percent.

After Saiki left Congress, President Bush appointed her director of the Small Business Administration, where she served from 1991 to 1993. In 1993, she taught at Harvard University's Institute of Politics at the John F. Kennedy School of Government. The following year, she became the first woman candidate on a major party ticket for Hawaii governor. Saiki lost a three-way race to Democratic Lieutenant Governor Ben Cayetano.[12] Patricia Saiki lives in Honolulu, where she has returned to teaching.

FOR FURTHER READING

Biographical Directory of the United States Congress, "Patricia Fukuda Saiki," http://bioguide.congress.gov

NOTES

1   "Liu: Up & Coming in Republican Politics," 13 February 1987, *Asian Week*: 5.
2   *Politics in America, 1986* (Washington, D.C.: Congressional Quarterly Inc., 1985): 389.
3   *Politics in America, 1986*: 389.
4   Robin Turner, "G.O.P. Women Raise Voices For the Right to an Abortion," 31 October 1989, *New York Times*: A1.
5   *Congressional Record*, House, 101st Cong., 2nd sess. (22 October 1990): 11512.
6   *Congressional Record*, House, 101st Cong., 2nd sess. (16 May 1990): 1560.
7   *Congressional Record*, House, 101st Cong., 1st sess. (17 November 1989): 9123.
8   *Congressional Record*, House, 101st Cong., 1st sess. (1 August 1989): 2834.
9   *Congressional Record*, House, 101st Cong., 1st sess. (23 May 1989): 2057.
10 Maralee Schwartz, "Hawaii GOP Rep. Saiki to Run Against Akaka in Senate Race," 1 June 1990, *Washington Post*: A12.
11 "Republicans Select Woman in Hawaii," 20 September 1994, *New York Times*: A19; Robert Reinhold, "Hawaii Race Tests Democratic Hold," 1 November 1990, *New York Times*: D22; Robert Reinhold, "Republicans Sense Chance in Hawaii," 9 May 1990, *New York Times*: A26.
12 "West: Despite Voter Discontent, Governors Win Re-Election in California and Colorado," 9 November 1994, *New York Times*: B8.

Jolene Unsoeld

1931–

UNITED STATES REPRESENTATIVE ★ DEMOCRAT FROM WASHINGTON
1989–1995

Jolene Unsoeld's passion for the environment and government transparency shaped a public service career that eventually took her to the U.S. House of Representatives. Serving a Washington state district that stretched from the Pacific Ocean to the Cascade Mountains, each of Unsoeld's congressional campaigns tested her ability to serve a constituency of diverse business and environmental interests. "Sometimes I feel like I'm in a marathon relay race," Unsoeld once said of her grueling campaigns. "I'm running alone, but they keep sending in replacements. I wipe them out, and they send in more."[1]

Jolene Bishoprick was born on December 3, 1931, in Corvallis, Oregon, one of four children born to Stanley and Cora Bishoprick. Her father was in the timber business and moved his family to Oregon, Canada, and China with each new job assignment, finally settling in Vancouver, Washington. From 1949 to 1951, Jolene Bishoprick attended Oregon State University in Corvallis. In college, she met mountaineer and environmental advocate William "Willi" Unsoeld, one of the first climbers to ascend Mt. Everest's treacherous west ridge. They were married at the summit of Oregon's Mount Hood, and Jolene Unsoeld, also an accomplished mountaineer, became the first woman to climb Wyoming's Grand Teton via its north face.[2] The Unsoelds eventually raised four children, two girls and two boys: Krag, Regon, Nanda Devi, and Terres. Willi Unsoeld directed the Peace Corps in Katmandu, Nepal, and served with the Agency for International Development from 1962 to 1967. Jolene Unsoeld worked as director of an English-language institute. The family returned to the United States in 1967 and settled in Olympia, Washington, in 1971.

While living in the state capital, Jolene Unsoeld took an interest in politics as a self-described "citizen meddler," recalling, "We had moved to Olympia, and there was the state Capitol, so I set out to see what was happening under that dome."[3] Unsoeld successfully lobbied for a 1972 bill in the state legislature that created Washington's public disclosure act. Subsequently serving as a self-appointed watchdog for special interest groups, she authored two editions of the book, *Who Gave? Who Got? How Much?*, which revealed major interest groups' contributions to politicians in the Washington legislature. Tragedy marked her early life in public service; twice, in a span of less than three years, Unsoeld lost family members in mountain-climbing accidents. In September 1976, 22-year-old Nanda Devi died while ascending the Himalayan mountain for which she was named.[4] In March 1979, Willi Unsoeld was one of two people killed in an avalanche while climbing Mt. Rainier.[5] "Living beyond grief is probably as hard a thing as you ever tackle," Jolene Unsoeld observed years later. "It does toughen you, which is necessary if you're going to be in this type of [public] service."[6] In 1984, Unsoeld won an open state legislature seat, where she specialized in environmental issues. From 1980 through 1988, she also served as a member of the Democratic National Committee.

In 1988, building on support from her grassroots environmental activities, Unsoeld entered the race for the open seat in a western Washington district when seven-term incumbent Representative Don Bonker, a Democrat, ran for the U.S. Senate. The district encompassed much of southwest Washington. Its boundaries stretched from the Pacific Ocean to the west to the Cascade Mountain range further east, and from the state capital Olympia in the

north to the Columbia River and border with Oregon in the south. Fishing and lumber production were the primary industries in the largely Democratic district, populated by a number of blue-collar workers. However, the district was increasingly divided between moderates concerned with job creation and liberal reformers and environmentalists.[7] In the Democratic primary, Unsoeld captured 50 percent of the vote, defeating John McKibbin, a Clark County commissioner and a moderate who portrayed Unsoeld as being too liberal for the district.[8]

In the general election, Unsoeld faced Republican Bill Wight, a retired Army lieutenant colonel and native of the area who had returned in 1988 after a long tour of duty at the Pentagon. Wight ran on an economic development and anti-drug, anti-crime platform. He portrayed Unsoeld as an environmental extremist and an ultra-liberal feminist. Unsoeld countered by stressing her local ties to the community and highlighting Wight's carpetbagger status as "the hometown boy from the Pentagon."[9] She also ran an energetic campaign, driving her own car from stop to stop around the district (usually unaccompanied by staff) to address town meetings, business gatherings, or union groups. Her willingness to stick to her convictions, especially on the environment, eventually won the admiration of even those who opposed her.[10] The election was the closest House race in the country that year. Unsoeld prevailed with a 618-vote margin of victory, out of more than 218,000 votes cast; she was declared the winner after a recount, five weeks after election day.[11]

Unsoeld received assignments to three committees: Merchant Marine and Fisheries; Education and Labor; and Select Aging. The Merchant Marine and Fisheries Committee was particularly important to Unsoeld's career-long goal to support environmental legislation while protecting the fishing and logging industries important to her district. She focused much of her energy on saving U.S. Pacific salmon runs from Japanese fishermen, who used a controversial form of drift nets (some 30 miles in length) which swept vast ocean areas of all marine life. In 1989, Unsoeld told a hearing of the Senate Commerce, Science, and Transportation Committee that foreign fishers were "stealing" $21 million in U.S. salmon annually.[12] In late 1989, when the U.N. banned all use of drift nets, Unsoeld hailed it as "a major breakthrough." She added, "The next step is to ensure strict enforcement. Drift nets are a horribly destructive technology."[13] Unsoeld also advocated restrictions on the timber industry, to prevent what she described as "over-cutting" in old-growth forests in order to sustain the business and also to protect the natural habitats of endangered species. She backed a ban on timber exports also supported by the George H.W. Bush administration, noting that as much as 25 percent of all exported logs never passed through American mills. With environmental regulations threatening several thousand jobs in her district alone, Unsoeld attempted to appease the timber industry by pushing for federal money to retrain laid off lumber workers. "Our over-cutting, our mismanagement of the forest, our export of raw logs, all are to blame for the situation we're in," Unsoeld said, noting that her grandfather and father worked in the industry. "It's a difficult and complex situation. People criticize me because they are emotional, they feel threatened. I understand that.... Nobody who knows anything about the forest believes we can continue cutting the way we have."[14] In 1991, she sought a ban on oil and gas drilling off the coast of Washington state, eventually achieving a nine-year moratorium.[15]

Unsoeld's environmental positions made her an endangered incumbent during her 1990 bid for re-election. "I know we'll have to put together an obscene amount of money," she told the *New York Times* months before the race.[16] That instinct was correct, as Unsoeld raised a record $1.3 million and took part in the most expensive House race in state history.[17] Unsoeld faced Gomer Robert Williams in the general election, a former Washington state legislator and the 1988 GOP candidate for governor. Williams had strong backing from both fundamentalist Christian groups and the timber industry. One of the most contentious campaign issues was the federal intervention to save the endangered spotted owl and its old-growth forest habitat. It was an environmental preservation policy that directly threatened the logging industry. Unsoeld supported protecting

the bird and Williams capitalized on this unpopular position as well as pegging her as a "tax-and-spend liberal."[18] In addition, Unsoeld had problems with her liberal base when she switched her position on the gun control debate midterm. After supporting restrictions in 1988, she opposed a strict assault weapons ban, instead authoring a successful amendment that banned only assault weapons assembled in the U.S. with foreign parts.[19] Despite her odds, Unsoeld eventually defeated Williams by about 13,000 votes out of nearly 178,000 cast, a 54 percent plurality. In 1992, riding Democratic presidential candidate William J. Clinton's coattails, Unsoeld defeated Republican Pat Fiske with her largest plurality—56 percent.

Unsoeld faced a tough battle for re-election in 1994. In a bruising open primary she weathered an assault by Republican Tim Moyer, a millionaire businessman and moderate who painted her as a model for a big-spending Congress. Moyer's campaign eventually fell apart when his tax record was called into question; however, in the general election, Moyer's mentor, the conservative populist Linda Smith, took up his slack. Smith was a champion of tax limits and maintained statewide recognition as the proponent of a measure that placed caps on state spending. She also had a large base of fundamentalist Christian backers, who campaigned actively on her behalf. Running on the "Contract with America," Smith won by a 14,000-vote margin out of more than 192,000 votes cast, 52 percent to Unsoeld's 45 percent. A third-party candidate who supported gun control won three percent of the vote.

Since leaving Congress in January 1995, Unsoeld has continued to advocate environmental reform and government transparency. "I believe all activism comes about because you see something that drives you crazy, and you want to do something about it," she once told an interviewer.[20] Unsoeld resides in Olympia, Washington.

FOR FURTHER READING

Biographical Directory of the United States Congress, "Jolene Unsoeld," http://bioguide.congress.gov

MANUSCRIPT COLLECTION

The Evergreen State College Archive (Olympia, Washington). Personal papers from when U.S. Representative Unsoeld was a lobbyist for the organization named "Common Cause" and papers from when she was a Washington state legislator.

NOTES

1   Michael Paulson, "Always a Fight to the Finish for Unsoeld; Liberal Incumbent Is 'A Good Target,' Says Longtime Supporter," 25 October 1994, *Seattle Post-Intelligencer*: A1.
2   Paulson, "Always a Fight to the Finish for Unsoeld."
3   See Dennis Farney, "Unsoeld, Her Mountains Climbed and Tragedies Past, Is Again Caught Between Man and Nature," 19 September 1990, *Wall Street Journal*: A24; quote is cited in Paulson, "Always a Fight to the Finish for Unsoeld."
4   "U.S. Climber Dies on Peak Whose Name She Bore," 18 September 1976, *New York Times*: 4.
5   "Willi Unsoeld, Mountaineer, In Mount Rainier," 6 March 1979, *Washington Post*: C4.
6   Paulson, "Always a Fight to the Finish for Unsoeld."
7   *Politics in America, 1990* (Washington, D.C.: Congressional Quarterly Inc., 1989): 1582.
8   David Ammons, "Two Congressmen Battle in Democratic Senate Primary; Republican Coasts," 21 September 1988, Associated Press.
9   *Politics in America, 1990*: 1582.
10 Paulson, "Always a Fight to the Finish for Unsoeld."
11 "Election Statistics, 1920 to Present," http://clerk.house.gov/members/electionInfo/elections.html.
12 Philip Shabecoff, "Pact Reached to Monitor Japan's Fishing Practices," 18 May 1989, *New York Times*: A29.
13 Paul Lewis, "Agreement Is Reached at the U.N. To End Use of Drift Fishing Nets," 14 December 1989, *New York Times*: A5.
14 Timothy Egan, "Debate Over Logging Means Trouble for Incumbent in Washington State," 25 September 1990, *New York Times*: A18.
15 "U.S. Seeks To Limit Oil Drilling Off Washington State Coast," 23 August 1991, *New York Times*: D18.
16 Robin Toner, "Freshman Legislator Girds for Bruising Campaign," 22 August 1989, *New York Times*: A20.
17 Paulson, "Always a Fight to the Finish for Unsoeld."
18 "The 1990 Campaign: The Next Congress, in the Making—West," *New York Times*, 8 November 1990: B9.
19 Martin Tolchin, "Battle Over Assault Weapons Bill," 15 October 1990, *New York Times*: B7.
20 "Jolene Unsoeld: 'An Awe of Nature.'" See http://www.olywa.net/speech/march00/Jolene.html (accessed 13 September 2002).

Jill L. Long

1952–

UNITED STATES REPRESENTATIVE ★ DEMOCRAT FROM INDIANA
1989–1995

Jill Long[1], an academic by training, rose through the ranks of Indiana politics to become an influential advocate for the state's agricultural interests. Long wrested away from Republicans a northeastern Indiana district considered a safe GOP seat. She went on to serve in the House for three terms, campaigning as a no-tax, conservative Democrat. In Congress, Long focused on farm issues and, as chair of the Congressional Rural Caucus, doubled the group's membership.

Jill Lynette Long was born on July 15, 1952, in Warsaw, Indiana. Raised on a family grain and dairy farm, she graduated from Columbia City Joint High School in Columbia City, Indiana. After receiving a B.S. at Valparaiso University in 1974, Long pursued her academic studies at Indiana University; she earned an M.B.A. in 1978 and a Ph.D. in business in 1984. From 1981 to 1988, Long taught business administration as an assistant professor at Valparaiso University. She also served as a lecturer at Indiana University at Bloomington and an adjunct at Indiana University–Purdue University at Fort Wayne from 1987 to 1989.

Long's first public service experience was as a member of the city council of Valparaiso from 1984 to 1986. She was dubbed "Jill Longshot" when she ran as a Democrat against GOP incumbent Dan Quayle in the 1986 race for a seat in the U.S. Senate. "I sort of like the nickname," Long admitted. "The more people hear it, the more they'll remember me."[2] That contention proved prophetic later in her career, though at the time Quayle beat her handily with 61 percent of the vote. In 1988, she ran in a Fort Wayne-centered U.S. House district in northeast Indiana against incumbent Dan R. Coats (a Quayle protégé who had moved on to take his mentor's old House seat). Coats

turned back Long's bid, capturing 62 percent of the vote.[3]

When Coats was appointed to fill his mentor's U.S. Senate seat after Quayle resigned to become Vice President in 1989, Long challenged the Republican candidate Dan Heath in a special election for the vacant Indiana House seat. The district had been in GOP control since 1976, and Heath, a former adviser to the Fort Wayne mayor and Representative Coats, was initially favored to win. The candidates held similar positions on the budget, military spending, and gun control. Both also grew up on farms and shared many of the same views on agriculture policy.[4] In part because of her name recognition, but also because of an anti-tax pledge and attacks on Heath's controversial connection to a proposed Fort Wayne income tax plan, Long defeated her opponent by a slim one-point margin in the March 28, 1989, special election, winning with fewer than 2,000 votes out of more than 128,000 cast.[5] Democrats trumpeted her surprise election, eager to advertise their success in what had traditionally been a "safe" seat for the GOP. In the 1990 and 1992 elections, Long defeated her Republican challengers by 61 and 62 percent, respectively. She ran effectively as a conservative Democrat, depriving her Republican challengers of issues related to taxation and fiscal conservatism. "She's done a good job of impersonating a Republican," a longtime local GOP chairman observed. "Tell the truth, she sometimes sounds more conservative than I do."[6]

After being sworn in on April 5, 1989, Long sought and received a seat on the Agricultural Committee to represent her largely rural district. She served on several of its subcommittees: Environment, Credit, and Rural Development; General Farm Commodities; and Livestock. She was successful in amending the 1990 Farm Bill to

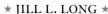

include provisions that provided incentives to farmers who employed conservation techniques and ensured fair planting flexibility for farmers. In 1993 she was elected chair of the Congressional Rural Caucus. She managed to double its membership to more than 100 and earned a reputation as a leading advocate for farm interests on Capitol Hill.

Long established herself as a fiscal conservative, opposing congressional pay raises and all tax increases (including President William J. Clinton's 1994 budget). "I'm cautious and moderate by nature," she said. "I was raised not to like taxes, to save money, to darn socks and refinish furniture—all the 4-H Club stuff."[7] On the Task Force on Government Waste, Long helped investigate dozens of government agencies to identify inefficient use of federal money. But she usually sided with liberals on social issues. She voted to increase the minimum wage and for federal funding for abortion in cases of rape and incest. She also opposed the authorization granting President George H.W. Bush to use force against Iraq in the Persian Gulf War. As a member of the Veterans' Affairs Committee and its Subcommittee on Hospitals and Health Care, she worked for better treatment of post-traumatic stress disorder and advocated the expansion of hospice care for dying veterans. She also served on the Select Committee on Hunger.

Congresswoman Long had been a Democrat popular among GOP voters, relying by one estimate on 20 percent or more of the Republican vote.[8] The Republican groundswell of 1994 and the backlash against Democratic President Clinton cut into her margins. Despite her fiscally conservative roots, Long was one of the victims of the 1994 "Republican Revolution," losing by 10 percent of the vote to Republican Mark E. Souder, an aide to Senator Dan Coats. After Congress, she served briefly as a Fellow at the Institute of Politics in the John F. Kennedy School of Government at Harvard University. President Clinton then appointed her as an Undersecretary of Agriculture, where she served from 1995 to 2001. As Undersecretary for Rural Development, Long managed 7,000 employees and an $11 billion budget. After leaving

the Department of Agriculture, she taught as the Mark E. Johnson Professor of Entrepreneurship at Manchester College in North Manchester, Indiana, and as an adjunct professor in the School of Public and Environmental Affairs at Indiana State University.

In 2002, Long easily won the Democratic primary for a newly redrawn U.S. House seat in north-central Indiana encompassing South Bend and lying just west of much of her old district. She faced business executive Chris Chocola in the general election for the open seat. In a competitive and, at times, heated race in which both candidates spent more than $1 million, Long narrowly lost to her Republican opponent, 50 to 46 percent.[9] After her defeat, she offered a conciliatory message to her backers: "It's important for us to give support to whoever is elected in this position because the top priority for all of us is to do all we can to make sure our government is as strong as it can be."[10] Long lives on a farm with her husband, Don Thompson, a former Navy pilot, near Argos, Indiana.[11]

FOR FURTHER READING

Biographical Directory of the United States Congress, "Jill Lynette Long," http://bioguide.congress.gov

NOTES

1   This essay reflects the Congresswoman's name at the time of her House service. She subsequently was married and changed her name to Jill Long Thompson.
2   Doug Richardson, "Long Sweeps Indiana Primary; LaRouche Candidate Loses," 7 May 1986, Associated Press.
3   "Election Statistics, 1920 to Present," http://clerk.house.gov/members/ electionInfo/elections.html.
4   Susan F. Rasky, "Special Race in Indiana Tests Democratic Gains," 27 March 1989, *New York Times*: B13.
5   Michael J. Dubin et al., *U.S. Congressional Elections, 1788–1997* (Jefferson, NC: McFarland & Company, Inc., Publishers, 1998): 764; "Democrat Wins Indiana Race," 29 March 1989, *New York Times*: A17; *Politics in America, 1990* (Washington, D.C.: Congressional Quarterly Inc., 1989): 501.
6   R.W. Apple, Jr., "Indiana House Race Shows Incumbency Is Still of Value," 4 November 1990, *New York Times*: 32.
7   Apple, "Indiana House Race Shows Incumbency Is Still of Value."
8   *Politics in America, 1996* (Washington, D.C.: Congressional Quarterly Inc., 1995): 464.
9   Jack Colwell, "Chocola Wins; Bush Visits Seen as Helping Bid," 6 November 2002, *South Bend Tribune*: A1; "Election Statistics, 1920 to Present," http://clerk.house.gov/members/ electionInfo/ elections.html.
10 Colwell, "Chocola Wins; Bush Visits Seen as Helping Bid."
11 Jack Colwell, "Candidate's Family Angry Over Mailing; Long Thompson's Husband, Father Denounce 'Terrorist' Reference," 22 October 2002, *South Bend Tribune*: A1.

Susan Molinari

1958–

UNITED STATES REPRESENTATIVE ★ REPUBLICAN FROM NEW YORK
1990–1997

Representative Susan Molinari crafted a meteoric political career as a moderate Republican who could reach out to an increasingly important voter demographic: young, suburban, middle-class mothers. Hailing from a Republican political dynasty that had played a role in Staten Island politics for nearly 50 years, she succeeded her father—Guy Molinari—in the U.S. House of Representatives. When the Republicans took control of the House in 1994, they quickly elevated the charismatic Molinari to prominent positions, giving her a place in GOP policy deliberations.

Susan Molinari was born on March 27, 1958, in the Bronx, New York, the only child of Guy and Marguerite Wing Molinari. The son of a politically involved family, Guy Molinari served in the New York state assembly from 1974 to 1980 and later spent 10 years in the U.S. House of Representatives representing Staten Island, New York. In 1976, Susan Molinari graduated from St. Joseph Hill Academy in Staten Island. Four years later, she graduated with a B.A. from New York State University at Albany and, in 1982, she earned a M.A. in political communications at SUNY Albany. From 1981 to 1983, Molinari worked as a finance assistant for the Republican Governor's Association. She also worked two years as an ethnic community liaison for the Republican National Committee in Washington. In 1985, she won election to the city council of New York, defeating her Democratic opponent by fewer than 200 votes.[1] As the only Republican on the 36-member council, Molinari served as minority leader and was entitled to sit on all committees. Popular among constituents, she won re-election with 75 percent of the vote.[2] In 1988, Susan Molinari married John Lucchesi of Staten Island; the couple divorced in 1992, with no children.[3]

In 1990, Representative Guy Molinari resigned his U.S. House seat to become the Staten Island borough president.[4] His district, which encompassed all of Staten Island and a portion of Brooklyn, had a nearly 2-to-1 Democratic edge in voter enrollment but was nevertheless known as New York City's most conservative enclave. Susan Molinari declared her candidacy for the March 20 special election, running on her four years' experience on the city council and the strength of her family name. She received a boost from her father's well-established political machine and a fundraising visit by President George H.W. Bush. Molinari's platform included a mix of anti-crime programs, promises to reduce taxes, reasonable defense spending, support for reproductive rights, and pro-environmental positions.[5] On the eve of the special election, the *New York Times* endorsed Molinari over Democratic candidate Robert J. Gigante because she "promises to add a moderate Republican voice to the city's Democrat-dominated congressional delegation."[6] Molinari defeated Gigante with a 24 percent margin. In her subsequent three re-election campaigns in her newly reapportioned (but largely intact) district, she won with comfortable majorities between 50 and 69 percent. In each contest Molinari topped her main Democratic challengers by 15 percentage points or more, as a sizeable number of voters went to the polls for third-party candidates.[7]

When Susan Molinari was sworn into Congress on March 27, 1990, she received assignments on the Small Business and Public Works and Transportation (later, Transportation and Infrastructure) committees. In the 102nd Congress (1991–1993), she took a seat on the Education and Labor Committee and left Small Business. When the Republicans took control of the House in the

104th Congress (1995–1997), Molinari traded in her Education and Labor seat for a place on the Budget Committee.

From her post on Education and Labor, Molinari sought to strengthen laws to prevent sexual abuse and domestic violence. She also introduced several initiatives to encourage businesses to diversify their work forces and bring more women into the management ranks. In 1993, she voted for the Family Leave Act, which required companies to grant employees a minimum of six weeks of unpaid leave for care of a newborn or a sick family member. She also used her committee assignments to tend to district business. Molinari used her Public Works and Transportation seat to impose stricter regulations on Staten Island's Fresh Kills landfill, which had a bad environmental track record. In 1990, Molinari also managed to keep federal funds flowing for the construction of the Stapleton Homeport, a U.S. Navy facility located on Staten Island. Aside from her committee work, in 1992 and 1993, Molinari traveled to Croatia, one of several states which emerged after the disintegration of Yugoslavia. Many Staten Island constituents had family ties to the Balkans, and Representative Molinari took a keen interest in urging the U.S. government to recognize the republic—a move that would facilitate expansion of aid efforts.

In August 1993, Molinari became engaged to Congressman Bill Paxon, a rising star in the GOP who represented a suburban Buffalo, New York, district. Paxon dropped to his knees on the House Floor and proposed. "I said, 'Yes—but get up,'" Molinari recalled.[8] Molinari and Paxon married July 3, 1994.[9] The next few years were heady ones for the young Washington power couple. By 1993, Molinari was the darling of the Republican Party—a smart, articulate, spokeswoman in a party with a dearth of female faces. She considered a run for New York governor in 1994, but passed on it, citing her desire to cultivate an as-normal-as-possible married life.[10] In 1996, Paxon and Molinari had a daughter, Susan, born on May 10. Representative Molinari became one of just four women to give birth while serving in Congress. Another Daughter, Katherine Mary, was born several years later.

In the 103rd Congress (1993–1995), her third term on the job, Molinari observed that conditions had improved for Congresswomen. "For the first time there's not that resentment against women Members.... There's a growing attitude among the men that they want to do what is best," she told the New York Times. But, she added, "Congress is still being run by the same people. Women have hit a glass ceiling here."[11] She began working toward a post in the Republican leadership, noting that, "I spend a lot of time trying to promote the Republican Party.... And, frankly, there has been an awful lot of discussion there should be a woman in the leadership and I don't disagree."[12]

In the late fall of 1994, Molinari won the vice chairmanship of the Republican Conference, making her the fifth-ranking Republican in the House and one of the highest-ranking women ever in the GOP leadership. In the summer of 1996, party leaders chose Molinari to deliver the keynote address at the Republican National Convention in San Diego, which nominated Senator Robert Dole of Kansas as its presidential candidate. She fit the profile that GOP leaders were seeking to appeal to: the young, middle-class, suburban mothers whom incumbent President William J. Clinton had lured away in droves in the 1992 campaign. Observers believed that by choosing Molinari, Dole was extending an olive branch to party moderates and pro-choice advocates alienated by House conservatives. Molinari took center stage at the GOP convention, while controversial congressional Republican leaders were given less prominent roles.

Congresswoman Molinari's rise into the Republican leadership, however, made her position as a moderate more precarious. By 1994, the New York Times, which had endorsed Molinari in 1990, was critical of her environmental record and her pro-business orientation, describing her as "reflexively conservative" on most major issues save abortion.[13] "Conservatives don't really look at her as one of them," said Representative John A. Boehner, an Ohio Republican. "The moderates don't really look at her as one of them. My point here is that she is not trying to walk this fine line. She has created this path based on her own per-

sonality and style."[14] Former allies were angered by her support for a ban on late-term abortion as well as for her efforts campaigning on behalf of pro-life candidates in the 1994 elections. Labor groups, smarting from GOP efforts to cut Medicaid, vowed to turn her out of office. Molinari suggested she had a pragmatic approach. "If you want to call me a moderate, I'm fine. I enjoy positive Conservative Party ratings, too. If you want to call me a feminist, that's good, too," she said. "I don't get bogged down with what that label is going to be on any particular day, because it does change."[15]

In late May 1997, Molinari announced her retirement, effective that August, to pursue her lifelong passion as a television personality and focus on raising her family. House Republicans and other colleagues were stunned by that decision, one which Molinari insisted she had been considering for more than a year.[16] Less than two months later, Bill Paxon fell out of favor with Speaker Newt Gingrich. He resigned his post as one of Gingrich's top lieutenants in July 1997 and did not seek re-election a year later.[17] Susan Molinari's career in television as cohost of the "CBS News Saturday Morning" program was short-lived. After nine months, she left to teach as a visiting Fellow at Harvard's Kennedy School of Government in the fall of 1998. In 1998, she wrote *Representative Mom: Balancing Budgets, Bill, and Baby in the U.S. Congress*, a memoir of her career on Capitol Hill. She continued to do television political commentary and opened a Washington-based consulting firm. Molinari also chaired the Century Council, a nonprofit which aimed to curb underage drinking and drunk driving. Molinari and her family reside in Alexandria, Virginia.

FOR FURTHER READING

Biographical Directory of the United States Congress, "Susan Molinari," http://bioguide.congress.gov

Molinari, Susan, with Elinor Burkett. *Representative Mom: Balancing Budgets, Bill, and Baby in the U.S. Congress* (New York: Doubleday, 1998).

MANUSCRIPT COLLECTION

University of Oklahoma (Norman, OK), The Julian P. Kanter Commercial Archive, Department of Communication. *Video cassette*: 1990, one video cassette. Includes three commercials that aired during Molinari's campaign in the New York congressional special election.

NOTES

1   Mary Voboril, "Prime Time: Susan Molinari is 38, Urban, Italian, a Working Mother and an Abortion-Rights Advocate," 12 August 1996, *Newsday*: B04.

2   "Susan Molinari," Associated Press Candidate Biographies, 1994.

3   Catherine S. Manegold, "Her Father's Daughter and Her Party's Luminary: Molinari Finds Herself on National Stage in Republican Spotlight, on Her Own Terms," 18 May 1993, *New York Times*: B1.

4   Donatella Lorch, "Molinari Sworn as New Leader on Staten Island," 15 January 1990, *New York Times*: B3.

5   *Politics In America, 1994* (Washington, D.C.: Congressional Quarterly Inc., 1993): 1057.

6   Frank Lynn, "G.O.P. Tries for Dynasty in S.I. Race for Congress," 17 March 1990, *New York Times*: 31.

7   "Serrano and Molinari for Congress," 15 March 1990, *New York Times*: A22.

8   "Election Statistics, 1920 to Present," http://clerk.house.gov/members/electionInfo/elections.html.

9   "Rep. Bill Paxon Says, 'Will You Marry Me?'" 6 August 1993, *New York Times*: A22.

10   Lois Smith Brady, "Susan Molinari and Bill Paxon," 10 July 1994, *New York Times*: 36; "Chronicle: Two Members of New York's Congressional Delegation Marry," 4 July 1994, *New York Times*: 25.

11   "Susan Molinari Will Not Run for Governor," 14 December 1994, *New York Times*: B3.

12   Maureen Dowd, "Growing Sorority in Congress Edges Into the Ol' Boys' Club," 5 March 1993, *New York Times*: A1.

13   "Susan Molinari," Associated Press Candidate Biographies, 1994.

14   "Susan Molinari," 22 May 1994, *New York Times*: CY13.

15   Ian Fisher, "Standing Out Among the Men in Suits: Molinari, an Urban Republican, Balances Power and Pragmatism," 2 May 1996, *New York Times*: B1.

16   Lawrie Mifflin, "In a Surprise Move, Molinari Is Leaving Congress for TV Job," 28 May 1997, *New York Times*: A1.

17   Jerry Gray, "Representative Paxon, in Power Struggle, Is First Casualty," 18 July 1997, *New York Times*: A1; Steven Erlanger, "Paxson Says He Doesn't Want Speaker's Post Despite Revolt," 21 July 1997, *New York Times*: A14; Lizette Alvarez, "Ex-G.O.P. Star Says He'll Quit Congress in '98," 26 February 1998, *New York Times*: A1.

Barbara-Rose Collins

1939–

UNITED STATES REPRESENTATIVE ★ DEMOCRAT FROM MICHIGAN

1991–1997

A longtime community activist and single mother, Barbara-Rose Collins was elected to Congress in 1991 on a vow to bring federal dollars and social aid to her economically depressed downtown Detroit neighborhood. In the House, Collins focused on her lifelong interest as an advocate for minority rights and economic aid as well as preserving the family in black communities.

Barbara Rose Richardson was born in Detroit, Michigan, on April 13, 1939, the eldest child of Lamar Nathaniel and Lou Versa Jones Richardson. Her father supported the family of four children as an auto manufacturer and later as an independent contractor in home improvements. Barbara Richardson graduated from Cass Technical High School in 1957 and attended Detroit's Wayne State University majoring in political science and anthropology. Richardson left college to marry her classmate, Virgil Gary Collins, who later worked as a pharmaceutical salesman to support their two children, Cynthia and Christopher.[1] In 1960, the Collins' divorced and, as a single mother, Barbara Collins was forced to work multiple jobs. Collins received public financial assistance until the Wayne State University, physics department hired her as a business manager, a position she held for nine years. Collins subsequently became an assistant in the office of equal opportunity and neighborhood relations at Wayne State. In the late 1960s, Collins heard a speech by black activist Stokeley Carmichael at Detroit's Shrine of the Black Madonna Church. Inspired by Carmichael's call to African Americans to improve their own neighborhoods, Collins purchased a house within a block of her childhood home and joined the Shrine Church, which focused on uplifting black neighborhoods via a sociopolitical

agenda. In 1971, Collins was elected to Detroit's region-one school board, earning widespread recognition for her work on school safety and academic achievement. Encouraged by the Shrine Church pastor, Collins campaigned for a seat in the state legislature in 1974. She adopted her hyphenated name ("Barbara-Rose") to distinguish herself from the other candidates.[2] Victorious, she embarked on a six-year career in the state house. Collins chaired the constitutional revision and women's rights committee, which produced, *Women in the Legislative Process*, the first published report to document the status of women in the Michigan state legislature.[3]

Bolstered by her work in Detroit's most downtrodden neighborhoods, Collins considered running for the U.S. House of Representatives in 1980 against embattled downtown Representative Charles Diggs; however, Collins heeded the advice of her mentor, Detroit Mayor Coleman Young, to run a successful bid for Detroit city council instead.[4] Eight years later, she challenged incumbent U.S. Representative George W. Crockett, who had succeeded Diggs, in the Democratic primary. In a hard-fought campaign, Collins held the respected but aging Crockett to a narrow victory with less than 49 percent of the vote. Crockett chose not to run for re-election in 1990, leaving the seat wide open for Barbara-Rose Collins. Collins's 1990 campaign focused on bringing federal money to Detroit, an economically depressed city which was losing its population to the suburbs. Her district's rapidly rising crime rate (ranked among the top three or four districts in the nation) also hit home for the candidate.[5] In 1989, Collins's teenaged son was convicted of armed robbery, and she concluded that he went astray because he lacked a strong male role model. "I could teach

a girl how to be a woman, but I could not teach a boy how to be a man," she later told the *Detroit Free Press*.[6] Drawing from this experience, Collins aimed at strengthening black families, rallying under the banner "save the black male." In a crowded field of eight candidates, Collins won her primary with 34 percent of the vote, a victory that amounted to election to Congress in the overwhelmingly Democratic district. Collins sailed through the general election with 80 percent of the vote and was twice re-elected with even greater percentages.[7]

One of three black women in her freshman class, Collins sought the influence and counsel of longtime Michigan Congressman John Dingell, Jr. Dingell aided Collins in gaining a seat on the Public Works and Transportation Committee (later Transportation and Infrastructure).[8] She also received assignments to the Committee on Science, Space, and Technology and the Select Committee on Children, Youth, and Families. She later traded these two panels for Government Operations (later named Government Reform and Oversight) and the Post Office and Civil Service Committee, where she chaired the Subcommittee on Postal Operations and Services in the 103rd Congress (1993–1995). A member of the Congressional Black Caucus and the Congressional Women's Caucus, Representative Collins also was appointed as a Majority Whip-At-Large from 1993 until 1994.

Collins's career focused on her campaign promises of economic and social aid for the urban black poor. She started in October 1992 by encouraging agricultural growers to donate excess food, which would otherwise go to waste, to urban food banks and shelters.[9] Collins generally supported President William J. Clinton's economic and job stimulus initiatives; however, she vocally opposed adopting the North American Free Trade Agreement, arguing that opening American borders to cheaper Mexican products would take domestic manufacturing jobs away from urban minority workers.[10] Though she favored the bill's final version, she voted against the President's April 1994 omnibus crime bill, objecting to its extension of the death penalty to several more federal crimes and opposing a section that guaranteed life in prison for people convicted of three felonies. Collins argued that these provisions would have the greatest impact on minorities, declaring, "I think justice is dispensed differently for people of color, be they black or Hispanic."[11] Collins's advocacy of the family unit was apparent when she expressed enthusiastic support for the October 1995 "Million Man March," a mass rally in Washington D.C., in which marchers expressed their commitment to family. Collins planned to provide water for marchers, exclaiming, "The idea is electrifying.... Black men will be reaffirming their responsibility for black women and for the black family."[12] She also advocated adding housework, childcare, volunteer work, and time put into the family business as a component for calculating the gross national product. "If you raise the status of women," she declared, "we would be more conscious of the family unit."[13]

With her domestic focus, Representative Collins generally opposed greater spending on foreign aid. "Our cities are hurting," she observed. "We must learn how to take care of America first."[14] In April 1994, however, Collins took an interest in foreign policy when she and five other Democratic House Members were arrested after staging an unlawful sit-in at the White House to protest American policy towards Haiti. In the wake of the island nation's military coup, the protestors wanted greater acceptance of Haitian refugees, and they demanded that a light embargo of the country be strengthened.[15] "What's being done to Haitians is inhumane and immoral," Collins said at the time. "The fact of the matter is we welcome Hungarians with open arms, we welcome Vietnamese with open arms, we welcome Cubans with open arms, but when it comes to black Haitians, we tell them, 'Stand back we don't want you,' the result being that hundreds are drowned at sea, children and women eaten by sharks."[16] All six Members were fined and released.

While popular among her constituents, Collins drew negative publicity when the Justice Department and the House Ethics Committee investigated her office in 1996 for alleged misuse of campaign and scholarship funds.[17]

Though previously unopposed in the 1994 primary, six opponents stepped forward following the public controversy. Challenger Carolyn Cheeks Kilpatrick defeated the incumbent in the primary by a 21-point margin and went on to win the general election. Barbara-Rose Collins remained active in local politics. In 2002, she won a seat on the Detroit city council for a term ending in 2006.

FOR FURTHER READING

Biographical Directory of the United States Congress, "Barbara-Rose Collins," http://bioguide.congress.gov

NOTES

1 The couple had a third child, who died in infancy.
2 Jessie Carney Smith, ed. *Notable Black American Women,* Vol. 2 (Detroit: Gale Research Inc., 1996): 135.
3 Smith, *Notable Black American Women:* 135.
4 Ibid.
5 *Almanac of American Politics, 1996* (Washington, D.C.: National Journal Inc., 1995): 710.
6 Smith, *Notable Black American Women:* 135.
7 "Election Statistics, 1920 to Present," http://clerk.house.gov/members/electionInfo/index.html.
8 Smith, *Notable Black American Women:* 136
9 *Congressional Record,* House, 102nd Cong., 2nd sess. (5 October 1992): 3074
10 *Congressional Record,* House, 103rd Cong., 1st sess. (21 October 1993): 8336; *Congressional Record,* House, 103rd Cong., 1st sess. (26 October 1993): 8436.
11 *Politics In America, 1996:* 685.
12 Francis X. Clines, "Organizers Defend Role of Farrakhan in March by Blacks," 13 October 1995, *New York Times:* A1.
13 Maria Odum, "If the G.N.P. Counted Housework, Would Women Count for More?" 5 April 1992, *New York Times:* E5.
14 Adam Clymer, "House Votes Billions in Aid to Ex-Soviet Republics," 7 August 1992, *New York Times:* A1.
15 Peter H. Spiegel, "Members Arrested in Haiti Protest," 25 April 1994, *Roll Call.*
16 Kenneth R. Bazinet, "Congressmen Arrested Outside White House," 21 April 1994, United Press International.
17 In January 1997, the House Standards of Official Conduct Committee found Representative Collins guilty of violating 11 different House rules and federal laws; however, the panel did not recommend disciplinary action against her because she had already left office. The committee provides a historical chart of all formal House ethics actions: http://www.house.gov/ethics/ Historical_Chart_ Final_ Version.htm. See also, Robyn Meredith, "Ethical Issues Pose Test to a Detroit Lawmaker," 2 August 1996, *New York Times:* A10; Sarah Pekkanen, "Ethics Committee Issues Scathing Report on Collins," 8 January 1997, *The Hill.*

Joan Kelly Horn
1936–

UNITED STATES REPRESENTATIVE ★ DEMOCRAT FROM MISSOURI
1991–1993

In her first attempt at elected office, Joan Kelly Horn earned a spot in the 102nd Congress (1991–1993) by securing an upset victory against a two-term incumbent. During her short tenure in the U.S. House, she focused on the needs of her district by channeling federal money into a series of local projects in her home state of Missouri. Representing an area once described as "the most unstable district in the state," Horn became part of a pattern of party turnover when she lost her bid for re-election to her Republican opponent in 1992.[1]

The daughter of an advertising executive, Horn was born on October 18, 1936, in St. Louis, Missouri. After graduating from the Visitation High School in St. Louis in 1954, she attended St. Louis University. She left school in 1956 to marry after completing three semesters. Joan Kelly Horn worked part-time as a Montessori teacher while she raised her six children: Michael, Matthew, Kelly, Stephen, Mark, and Kara. She later resumed her education, earning a B.A. and an M.A. in political science from the University of Missouri at St. Louis, in 1973 and 1975, respectively.[2] In 1987, Horn married her second husband, E. Terrence Jones, a dean at the University of Missouri at St. Louis who had one son from a previous marriage. The couple divorced in 1999.[3] Upon the completion of her academic studies, Horn worked on a variety of local projects encompassing education, conservation, and community development. She also was active in the local Democratic Party and led both the Missouri Women's Political Caucus and the Freedom of Choice Council. In 1987, Horn became committeewoman of the Clayton Township of Missouri. She also served as a political consultant in a firm she operated with her husband.[4]

Although she lacked extensive political experience, Horn decided to run for Congress in 1990. In the Democratic primary for the congressional seat representing a suburban district northwest of St. Louis, she faced John Baine, a stockbroker. During the campaign, her opponent questioned her "family values," an allusion to her decision to live with her second husband prior to marriage and to the public battle she waged with town officials in the affluent St. Louis suburb of Ladue concerning a town ordinance banning unmarried couples from occupying the same residence. She responded by reminding voters that she had a husband, six children, seven grandchildren, and the qualifications to go to Congress.[5] After easily defeating Baine in the primary, Horn had a much tougher challenge in the general election. Realizing that few experts gave her a chance to succeed against the two-term incumbent Republican Jack Buechner, she adopted an aggressive campaign strategy that included a blitz of advertisements alleging that her opponent used his position in the House for personal gain.[6] In an extraordinarily close election, Joan Kelly Horn pulled off an unexpected upset, defeating Buechner by 54 votes. After being sworn in on January 3, 1991, Horn told supporters, "It's an awesome responsibility. The people of the Second District sent me here, and they deserve to know that I'll work very hard for them."[7]

In Congress, Horn served on three committees: Public Works and Transportation; Science, Space and Technology; and Select Children, Youth and Families. Interested in "bringing the federal government to the people," Horn used her committee assignments to direct federal money to her district.[8] In addition to helping obtain funding for a light-rail system in the region, she also played an important role in increasing federal appropriations for the aerospace manufacturer McDonnell Douglas, which employed thousands of people from her district. During her one term in the House, Horn promoted the expansion of the St. Louis airport, worked to protect the benefits of Trans World Airline (TWA) employees in the St. Louis area when it became clear that the airline was in financial hardship, and succeeded in persuading the House to boost the amount of money earmarked for Pentagon programs created to assist the conversion of defense industries to civilian companies.[9]

Among the small number of women serving in the House during the 102nd Congress, Horn reflected upon her minority status when she commented, "There are just so few of us. Not that it's deliberate; it's just systematic to the institution. Since we aren't going to get equity, we have to work with men."[10] As a Representative, Horn worked closely with Democratic Majority Leader Richard Gephardt, also from Missouri. She also used her position in Congress to address issues of interest to women, in particular, abortion. Although she downplayed her record of abortion rights activism during her initial congressional bid for fear of alienating conservative voters in her district, Horn resumed her strong pro-choice stance in the House. Voting against the "gag rule" that barred physicians in government-funded clinics from advising patients on abortions, she also backed a controversial measure in 1991 that would have allowed American military women stationed overseas access to abortions in military hospitals.[11]

Horn quickly earned a reputation as "conscientious" and "diligent," compelled to perform district work vital for freshmen Members seeking re-election.[12] Making frequent trips to her district to ascertain the needs of her constituents, she continued to organize meetings, speaking appearances, and seminars to promote her message in the St. Louis area. Horn also earned credibility with many voters when she fulfilled two of her major campaign promises: her refusal to accept a pay raise and to travel at the expense of taxpayers. While she donated her share of a congressional pay hike to charity, she also funded her own business trips, such as a tour of a McDonnell Douglas plant in California.[13]

One of Horn's most controversial votes in Congress involved the balanced budget amendment, which aimed at reducing the federal deficit. Amid much criticism, Horn and 11 of her Democratic colleagues who originally cosponsored the measure later switched their position and voted against the bill; according to Horn, the budget cuts she supported derived from military spending, unlike the proposed amendment that took money from domestic programs. When President George H.W. Bush and other Republican leaders attacked Horn for her change of heart, the Missouri Congresswoman defended her position declaring, "I didn't change, the amendment changed."[14] Despite being quick to defend her record, Horn's decision to turn her back on the legislation she once supported haunted her re-election campaign.

In 1992, Horn's campaign platform included promises to reduce the federal deficit, to strengthen the local economy by increasing employment opportunities, and to promote "family-friendly policies." Already facing a difficult race against the experienced Missouri State Representative and minority floor leader James Talent, Horn also had to contend with a reapportioned district that lost several Democratic neighborhoods.[15] In the November 1992 general election, Horn narrowly failed to retain her congressional seat for the 103rd Congress (1993–1995), capturing 47 percent of the vote to Talent's 50 percent.[16]

After leaving Congress, Horn served in the Department of Commerce and resumed her local service commitment as director of the St. Louis community development agency. In 1996, she attempted a political comeback when she announced her candidacy for her old district. Declaring herself "the voice of moderation," she defeated her four opponents in the Democratic primary but lost once again to Talent in the general election, garnering just 37 percent of the vote.[17]

FOR FURTHER READING

Biographical Directory of the United States Congress, "Joan Kelly Horn," http://bioguide.congress.gov

MANUSCRIPT COLLECTION

University of Oklahoma (Norman, OK), The Julian P. Kanter Political Commercial Archive, Department of Communication. *Video cassette:* 1990, one video cassette. Includes four commercials used during Horn's campaign for the 1990 U.S. congressional election in Missouri, Democratic Party.

NOTES

1 Mark Schlinkmann, "2nd District Competition Tough Reapportionment, Unaligned Voters, 11 Debates; Challenge Candidates," 31 October 1992, *St. Louis-Dispatch*: 1B.

2 Mark Schlinkmann, "Woman Behind the Upset: Horn Is Called Calm, Focused," 11 November 1990, *St. Louis Post-Dispatch*: 1A.

3 Jerry Berger, "Joan Kelly Horn Loses Ruling as Marriage Ends," 4 June 1999, *St. Louis Post-Dispatch*: A2.

4 Schlinkmann, "Woman Behind the Upset: Horn Is Called Calm, Focused"; Karen Foerstel, *Biographical Dictionary of Congressional Women* (Westport, CT: Greenwood Press, 1999): 126.

5 *Politics In America, 1992* (Washington, D.C.: Congressional Quarterly Inc., 1991): 844; "Democrat Starts Campaign for Congress," 2 April 1990, *St. Louis Post-Dispatch*: 6A.

6 Foerstel, *Biographical Dictionary of Congressional Women*: 126; Schlinkmann, "Woman Behind the Upset: Horn Is Called Calm, Focused."

7 "Rep. Horn Sworn in to House Pledges to 'Work Hard' for People of the 2nd District," 4 January 1991, *St. Louis Post-Dispatch*: 1A.

8 Charlotte Grimes, "Horn Shows She's Learned Art of Rough-and-Tumble; Congresswoman Finds Footing Among Washington Politicians," 3 October 1992, *St. Louis Post-Dispatch*: 1B.

9 Grimes, "Horn Shows She's Learned Art of Rough-and-Tumble"; Jon Sawyer, "Congress' Appropriation Delights McDonnell Douglas," 28 November 1991, *St. Louis Post-Dispatch*: 14A.

10 "31 Women, 31 Voices on Capitol Hill," 1 April 1992, *USA Today*: 4A.

11 Foerstel, *Biographical Dictionary of Congressional Women*: 127; Mark Schlinkmann, "Democratic Rivals Split on Abortion," 8 July 1990, *St. Louis Post-Dispatch*: 1B; Schlinkmann, "Woman Behind the Upset: Horn Is Called Calm, Focused."

12 Grimes, "Horn Shows She's Learned Art of Rough-and-Tumble."

13 Ibid; Schlinkmann, "2nd District Competition Tough Reapportionment, Unaligned Voters, 11 Debates."

14 Grimes, "Horn Shows She's Learned Art of Rough-and-Tumble"; Adam Clymer, "Balanced-Budget Amendment Fails to Gain House Approval," 12 June 1992, *New York Times*: 1A.

15 Schlinkmann, "2nd District Competition Tough Reapportionment, Unaligned Voters, 11 Debates"; "2nd District Battle Highlights House Races," 1 November 1992, *St. Louis Post-Dispatch*: 3; Grimes, "Horn Shows She's Learned Art of Rough-and-Tumble."

16 "Election Statistics, 1920 to Present," http://clerk.house.gov/members/electionInfo/elections.html.

17 Jo Mannies, "Joan Horn To File for Congress," 24 March 1996, *St. Louis Post-Dispatch*: 3C; "Election Statistics, 1920 to Present," http://clerk.house.gov/members/electionInfo/elections.html.

Jocelyn Birch Burdick

1922–

UNITED STATES SENATOR ★ DEMOCRAT FROM NORTH DAKOTA
1922

Jocelyn Burdick was appointed to a brief three-month term to fill the vacancy caused by the death of her husband, Quentin Burdick, a longtime North Dakota Senator and Representative. She earned the distinction of being the first woman Senator from the state and one of a record number of women serving simultaneously in the Senate.

Jocelyn Birch was born to Albert and Magdalena Towers Carpenter Birch in Fargo, North Dakota, on February 6, 1922. Her great-grandmother, Matilda Jocelyn Gage, was a leading women's suffrage advocate in the 1870s. Jocelyn Birch attended Principia College in Elsah, Illinois, and graduated with a B.S. degree from Northwestern University in Evanston, Illinois, in 1943. She worked as a radio announcer in Moorhead, Minnesota. In 1948, she married Kenneth Peterson of Grand Forks, North Dakota. They raised two children—a son, Birch, and daughter, Leslie—before Kenneth Peterson died in 1958. Two years later, Jocelyn Birch Peterson married Quentin Northrop Burdick. Previously, a Fargo, North Dakota, lawyer, and son of former Congressman Usher Burdick, Quentin Burdick was elected to the U.S. House in 1958, serving one term before he won a special election to fill a vacant U.S. Senate seat. He served in the Senate 32 years, earning a reputation for his liberal voting record and ability to funnel federal dollars to fund projects in his home state.[1] A widower, Quentin Burdick had four children from his previous marriage: Jonathan, Jan Mary, Jennifer, and Jessica. Jocelyn Burdick raised their combined six children (plus one they had together, Gage, who died in 1978) and served as her husband's adviser and as a volunteer in his four Senate re-election campaigns.

Quentin Burdick was the third-longest-serving Senator in office (behind South Carolina's Strom Thurmond and West Virginia's Robert Byrd) when he died from heart failure on September 8, 1992. Jocelyn Burdick was appointed as a Democrat to the U.S. Senate by North Dakota Governor George Sinner on September 12, 1992. Governor Sinner noted that Burdick was "dumb-founded" when he first approached her; however, after consulting her relatives, she agreed to fill her late husband's seat temporarily until the December special election.[2] She was the first and only woman ever to serve North Dakota in the U.S. Congress. Burdick took the oath of office on September 16, 1992, telling her Senate colleagues, "I am deeply honored and I look forward to spending the next three months doing my best to carry on Quentin's agenda."[3] Burdick joined Senators Nancy Kassebaum of Kansas and Barbara Mikulski of Maryland as one of three women in the Senate, a record number at the time. Later that fall Dianne Feinstein of California also entered the Senate, raising the total to four.

During her three-month tenure, Burdick served on the Environment and Public Works Committee, which Quentin Burdick had chaired at the time of his death. The only time Burdick spoke on the Senate Floor was to say goodbye to her colleagues on October 2, 1992. "I am honored to be the first woman to represent North Dakota in Congress," she said. "I hope that the 103rd Congress will find many more women seated in this body." Jocelyn Burdick served until December 14, 1992, when her special term concluded. Fellow North Dakota Senator Kent Conrad had earlier announced his retirement from his own Senate seat, fulfilling a 1986 election vow in which he promised to vacate his seat if the federal deficit was not

"I AM DEEPLY HONORED AND I
LOOK FORWARD TO SPENDING THE
NEXT THREE MONTHS DOING MY
BEST TO CARRY ON QUENTIN'S
AGENDA," JOCELYN BURDICK TOLD
HER SENATE COLLEAGUES.

significantly reduced after his first term. Succumbing
to pressure from North Dakota Democrats, as well as
Burdick, who indicated that Conrad was the candidate
"to carry on the Burdick legacy," Conrad ran and won the
election to fill the remainder of the unexpired portion of
the term ending on January 4, 1995.[4]

After leaving the Senate, Burdick returned to North
Dakota. She resides in Fargo.

FOR FURTHER READING

Biographical Directory of the United States Congress, "Jocelyn
Burdick," http://bioguide.congress.gov

MANUSCRIPT COLLECTION

University of North Dakota (Grand Forks, ND), Chester
Fritz Library. *Papers:* Part of the Quentin Burdick Papers,
1958–1992.

NOTES

1 Wolfgang Saxon, "Quentin N. Burdick, 84, Is Dead; U.S. Senator
   From North Dakota," 9 September 1992, *New York Times*: A19;
   Marilynn Wheeler, "North Dakota Sen. Quentin Burdick Dies, Age
   84," 8 September, 1992, Associated Press.
2 "Senator Burdick's Wife Is Interim Successor," 13 September 1992,
   New York Times: 26.
3 "North Dakota: Jocelyn Burdick Appointed Interim Successor," 14
   September 1992, *The Hotline*.
4 "Burdick's Widow Urges Conrad to Run in N.D.," 21 September 1992,
   National Journal; see Kent Conrad's entry in the online *Biographical
   Directory of the United States Congress*, http://bioguide.congress.gov.

Eva M. Clayton

1934–

UNITED STATES REPRESENTATIVE ★ DEMOCRAT FROM NORTH CAROLINA

1992–2003

Eva Clayton became the first African-American woman to represent North Carolina in Congress, and the state's first black Representative since 1901. From her post on the House Agriculture Committee, Clayton advanced the interests of her rural district in the northeastern part of her state and called attention to the economic inequalities which impacted African Americans nationally.

Eva McPherson was born in Savannah, Georgia, on September 16, 1934. She grew up in Savannah and received a B.S. degree in biology from Johnson C. Smith University in Charlotte, North Carolina, in 1955. In 1962, she earned an M.S. in biology and general science from North Carolina Central University in Durham. She originally planned to become a doctor and travel to Africa to do missionary work. Shortly after receiving her undergraduate degree, Eva McPherson married Theaoseus Clayton, who became a prominent lawyer, and they raised four children: Theaoseus Jr., Martin, Reuben, and Joanne.

The civil rights movement mobilized Eva Clayton to become active in civic and political affairs. At one point, she even picketed her husband's law office to protest the fact that Theaoseus and his white law partner owned the building in which a racially segregated restaurant was open for business.[1] As early as 1968, Eva Clayton was recruited by civil rights activist Vernon Jordan to seek election to Congress in a north-central North Carolina district. Though Clayton won 31 percent of the vote in the Democratic primary, the incumbent, Lawrence Fountain, prevailed. Her campaign, however, had the intended effect of spiking black voter registration.[2] "In 1968, the timing wasn't there," she later admitted.[3] Reluctantly, Clayton withdrew from law school after the birth of her fourth child. "I wasn't super enough to be a supermom," Clayton recalled years later. "I left to be a mom. My husband was supportive, but I felt enormously guilty. I think I would do it differently now. I think I would know how to demand more of my husband."[4] In the early 1970s, she worked for several public-private ventures, including the North Carolina Health Manpower Development Program at the University of North Carolina. In 1974 she cofounded and served as the executive director of Soul City Foundation, a housing organization which renovated dilapidated buildings for use as homeless shelters and day care centers. Two years later, she worked on the successful gubernatorial campaign of Jim Hunt, who later appointed Clayton the assistant secretary of the North Carolina department of natural resources and community development. Clayton served in that capacity from 1977 until 1981. After leaving state government, she founded an economic development consulting firm. A year later, in 1982, she won election to the Warren County Board of Commissioners, which she chaired until 1990. Over the next decade, Clayton helped steer more than $550 million in investments into the county and also successfully passed a bond issue for new school construction.

When Congressman Walter Jones, Sr., announced his retirement in 1992, Clayton entered the Democratic primary to fill his seat. The district had recently been reapportioned by the state legislature, one of two congressional districts in North Carolina which consisted of black majorities. Jones died in September 1992, and his son Walter, Jr., was considered the favorite in the primary. He captured 38 percent to Clayton's 31 but fell two points shy of winning the nomination outright. In the run-off, Clayton secured the support of her other primary

opponents and won 55 percent to Jones's 45 percent. In the general election, Clayton ran on a platform of increased public investment and job training for rural areas in the district, which encompassed a large swath of eastern North Carolina, including the towns of Goldsboro, Rocky Mount, and Greenville. To lower the federal deficit, she advocated slashing the defense budget. "We went into the projects and knocked on doors and got people out" to vote, Clayton recalled.5 On November 3, 1992, she won the special election to fill the last two months of Walter Jones, Sr.'s unexpired term in the 102nd Congress (1991–1993) and defeated Republican Ted Tyler for the full term in the 103rd Congress (1993–1995). Mel Watt, an African American, also won election from a North Carolina district to the House on November 3, but Clayton, by virtue of the fact that she was elected to the 102nd, became the first African American to be seated from North Carolina since George White, who left Congress in 1901. In her subsequent four bids for re-election, she won comfortably, with 60 percent or more of the vote. She defeated Tyler three times, including in 1998 after court rulings reshaped the district once again by adding 165,000 new constituents and shrinking the African-American majority by seven percent, effectively dividing the district between black and white constituents. In 2000, the GOP ran Duane E. Kratzer, Jr., who managed just 33 percent of the vote to Clayton's 66 percent.

Clayton claimed her seat in the 102nd Congress on November 5, 1992, but did not receive committee assignments until the 103rd Congress convened in January 1993. She won spots on two committees: Agriculture and Small Business. Clayton eventually became the Ranking Democratic Member on the Operations, Oversight, Nutrition, and Forestry Subcommittee of Agriculture. Her Democratic colleagues also made her the first woman president of the freshman class. In 1995, she was appointed to the Democratic Advisory Committee to formulate party strategy. In the 105th Congress (1997–1999) she dropped her Small Business assignment for a seat on the prestigious Budget Committee. Clayton also was assigned to the Social Security Task Force.

Clayton became a staunch defender of the rural and agricultural interests of her district, which comprised 20 counties with numerous peanut and tobacco growers. Along with Missouri Republican Jo Ann Emerson, she revived the Rural Caucus and rallied more than 100 Members to pledge continued federal aid to farmers, rural job creation, and technology initiatives. In 1993 and 2000, respectively, Clayton voted against the North American Free Trade Agreement and permanent normal trade relations with China. She insisted that both would adversely affect the agricultural industry and remove low-wage jobs from her district. "Must eastern North Carolina lose in order for the Research Triangle to win?" she asked in a pointed reference to the state's booming high-tech corridor to the west of her district.6 Although Clayton advocated smaller defense budgets, she remained supportive of naval contracts for projects at the nearby Newport News shipyards which provided jobs for her constituents. From her seat on the Agriculture Committee, and in contrast with many Democratic colleagues, Clayton supported extension of tobacco subsidies to farmers at a time when critics attacked the program. "This is not about smoking," Clayton said. "This is about discriminating against the poorest of the poor of that industry.... They really are attacking the small farmer."7 She also fought successfully to preserve Section 515 of the Agriculture Department's affordable housing program, which provided federal loans for multiple-unit housing projects in rural areas.8

Clayton's district suffered a major natural disaster in 1999, when Hurricane Floyd dumped rains on the state, submerging parts of eastern North Carolina under 14 feet of swollen river water. Clayton and other Members of the state delegation secured billions in relief aid. Clayton also acquired $1.5 million in federal money for a study of a dike along the Tar River in Princeville, the nation's first town chartered by African Americans in 1885. She also assembled a volunteer force of more than 500 people, who aided flood victims throughout eastern North Carolina.

As she gained seniority and prestige in the House, Clayton created a high profile for herself as an advocate

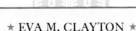
for programs to help economically disadvantaged African Americans. Throughout her career, she stressed the importance of job training. "The issue of equity in jobs and fairness of opportunities is paramount," Clayton said. "Job opportunities combined with a fair wage are key to strengthening families and communities and increasing our quality of life."[9] With fellow North Carolinian Mel Watt, Clayton, as chair of the Congressional Black Caucus Foundation, organized a campaign to get 1 million African Americans to buy homes by 2005. In 1996 she also played a key part in fighting GOP efforts to cut youth summer job programs. Declaring that she intended "to wake up" the House, Clayton said that the programs helped more than 615,000 youth in 650 cities and towns: "This is the first opportunity many of these young people have to get a job."[10]

In November 2001, Clayton declined to seek renomination to a sixth term in the House. She had been involved in intense bargaining with state legislators to make sure her majority African-American district was "protected" during reapportionment after the 2000 Census. "My heart is leading me somewhere else," Clayton explained of her retirement. "I don't know exactly where that is, but I do want to have another opportunity for public service before I really hang it up."[11] Clayton was succeeded by an African-American man, Frank Ballance, Jr., in the fall 2002 elections. After retiring in January 2003, Clayton returned to her home in Littleton, North Carolina.

FOR FURTHER READING

Biographical Directory of the United States Congress, "Eva M. Clayton," http://bioguide.congress.gov

NOTES

1 Rob Christensen, "Clayton to Retire in 2002," 21 November 2001, *Charlotte News and Observer*: A1.

2 Christensen, "Clayton to Retire in 2002."

3 Scott Mooneyham, "Clayton Announces She Will Retire From Congress," 20 November 2001, Associated Press.

4 Marian Burros, "Rep. Mom: Even in Washington's Watershed Year, Laundry Still Needs Doing," 20 June 1993, *Chicago Tribune*: woman news section, 12.

5 "Eva M. Clayton," Associated Press Candidate Biographies, 1998.

6 *Almanac of American Politics, 2002* (Washington, D.C.: National Journal Inc., 2001): 1139–1140.

7 *Politics in America, 2002* (Washington, D.C.: Congressional Quarterly Inc., 2001): 738–739.

8 *Current Biography, 2000* (New York: H.W. Wilson and Company, 2000): 121–124.

9 "Eva M. Clayton," *Contemporary Black Biography, 1998,* Volume 20 (Detroit, MI: Gale Research Inc., 1998).

10 "Congresswomen Lead Campaign for Summer Jobs for Black Youth," 15 April 1996, *Jet*: 39.

11 John Mercurio, "Going Home: Clayton Will Retire; But North Carolina Map Expected to Alter 1st District Only Slightly," 26 November 2001, *Roll Call.*

Leslie L. Byrne
1946–

UNITED STATES REPRESENTATIVE ★ DEMOCRAT FROM VIRGINIA
1993–1995

Leslie Byrne made Virginia history in 1992 by becoming the first woman elected to Congress from the Old Dominion. "I am Virginia's first Congresswoman, but now my job is not to be a historical footnote," she told reporters. "My job is to serve."[1] Elected as part of a large, reform-minded freshman class, Byrne sought to protect the northern Virginia families and federal government employees that formed her base constituency. She also proved fiercely loyal to the Democratic Party, proposing punishment for subcommittee chairmen who refused to support President William J. Clinton's economic initiatives.

Leslie Beck was born in Salt Lake City, Utah, on October 27, 1946. Her father, Stephen Beck, was a smelter, and her mother, Shirley, an office manager.[2] She attended Mount Vernon College, in Mt. Vernon, Ohio, and the University of Utah in Salt Lake City, where she majored in psychology and drama, graduating in 1965. During her sophomore year, she married Larry Byrne, and the couple eventually moved to Falls Church, Virginia, in 1971, where they raised two children, Alexis and Jason.

Leslie Byrne served as chair of the Fairfax County commission on fair campaign practices from 1978 to 1980, and as president of the Fairfax Area League of Women Voters from 1982 to 1983. Byrne was elected to the Virginia house of delegates, where she served from 1986 to 1992. Her greatest legislative triumph in the state legislature was forcing a bill out of committee, against the wishes of party leadership, requiring open container trucks to be covered with protective tarps. She gained a reputation as an outspoken legislator who often showed disdain for opponents by putting on lipstick during floor

debate.[3] When the legislature adjourned from its brief annual sessions, Byrne worked as president of a human resources consulting firm.

In 1992, Byrne ran for a U.S. House seat in a newly created northern Virginia district centered in Fairfax County. The new district contained primarily suburban, dual-income households and many federal government workers. Byrne went unopposed in the Democratic primary. In the general election, with the help of women's funding groups, such as EMILY's List, she ran the best-financed campaign in the country for an open congressional seat, raising approximately $800,000. The campaign was a brutal battle of political opposites. As one voter quipped, "There's nothing fuzzy about this race."[4] Byrne portrayed her Republican opponent, Henry N. Butler, as an archconservative and, late in the race, questioned his character while downplaying suggestions that she used her gender as a campaign issue. Byrne insisted that her platform was similar to that of Democratic presidential candidate, Bill Clinton.[5] Butler responded by painting Byrne as an antibusiness, tax-and-spend liberal destined to stymie economic growth. Byrne came under a good deal of criticism for negative TV ads which attacked her opponent. She later admitted that she was walking a fine line; however, she indicated that accusations of wrongdoing were leveled at her because of her gender. "What comes across in men as 'fighter, outspoken, champion of the people' comes across in women differently," Byrne said. "There was the constant tension between getting the facts out and going toe-to-toe with him, and not wanting to be perceived as pushy [or] brassy."[6] Byrne defeated Butler with 50 percent of the vote. He took 45 percent against two other independent candidates. District residents, however, were

ideologically split, favoring incumbent President George H.W. Bush over Clinton, 43 percent to 42 percent.[7]

Byrne was elected to the 103rd Congress (1993–1995) as part of a large, reform-minded, diverse freshman class. A rash of retirements and defeats in the 1992 election also opened more than 200 vacancies on various committees (the most in 44 years), granting ample opportunity for new Members to receive coveted assignments.[8] Byrne sought a position on the prestigious Ways and Means Committee. No new women from either party, however, won appointment to that committee. Fellow Virginian and three-term incumbent Lewis Payne gained a seat representing the state's delegation on that panel.[9] Byrne instead received two lower-level assignments: Post Office and Civil Service and Public Works and Transportation. These committees made sense in light of her constituency: 17 percent of her constituents were federal employees, and traffic and transportation problems that burdened the Washington, D.C., area were at the forefront of voters' concerns.[10] Byrne received a nod from the Democratic leadership when she was appointed an At-Large Whip.[11]

Byrne's one term in office focused on protecting and increasing benefits to the families and federal employees in her district, particularly concentrating on health care, education, and retirement benefits. She sponsored legislation that expanded childhood immunizations and provided more funding for Head Start education programs, arguing that money spent on young children would head off far more expensive problems in the future. Byrne introduced a bill that would allow penalty-free withdrawals from retirement accounts to purchase homes or to pay for education expenses. She proposed evaluating Social Security benefits providing minimum health care and health insurance for the elderly, as well as adding services to this benefit, such as in-home health care and nutritional counseling.

Byrne gained the most notoriety, however, for being a maverick within her own party. In May 1993, she led the movement to create a petition calling for the removal of House subcommittee chairs who opposed President Clinton's first budget package. Though she initially was skeptical of the President's proposed pay freeze for federal employees, knowing the effect it would have on her district, Byrne nonetheless supported President Clinton's economic initiatives and budget proposal. Byrne indicated that dissenting subcommittee chairs were poor leaders for being unwilling "to step up to the plate" and swallow some of the budget's unpopular measures, including tax increases, in order to cut the deficit. "There's a strong feeling among many [Democrats] that those who serve in a leadership position ought to be there when the country needs them," Byrne said. "This particular issue should not be decided by sticking our finger in the wind. There is no free lunch. We ate it and now we have to pay for it."[12] Gathering more than 80 signatures, she was able to force the Democratic Caucus to consider her effort at party discipline. Speaker Thomas Foley of Washington State convinced Byrne not to bring the proposal to a formal vote by promising to consider it within the Steering and Policy Committee, which determined party strategy. No changes came about, but Byrne claimed that the move had its desired effect.[13]

In the 1994 election, Byrne faced Republican challenger Thomas M. Davis III, the Fairfax County board chairman. Davis emphasized fiscal restraint and conservative values, while highlighting the need to aid the disadvantaged.[14] Byrne went on the offensive, touting her legislative achievements for families and painting Davis as unfriendly to unions.[15] In a hotly contested race, Davis defeated the incumbent in a Republican sweep in which the GOP took control over the House of Representatives for the first time in 40 years, collecting 53 percent of the vote to Byrne's 45 percent.

After leaving the House, Byrne was an unsuccessful candidate for the 1996 Democratic nomination for a Virginia seat in the U.S. Senate. From 2000 to 2003, she served as a Democrat in the Virginia senate. In June 2005, Byrne won the Democratic nomination for lieutenant governor of Virginia but lost narrowly in the general election in November 2005.

★ LESLIE L. BYRNE ★

FOR FURTHER READING

Biographical Directory of the United States Congress, "Leslie Larkin Byrne," http://bioguide.congress.gov

NOTES

1   Lorraine Woellert, "The 'Schoolyard Bully'; Byrne Expected To Be Partisan, Effective on the Hill," 1 January 1993, *Washington Times*: B1.

2   Eric Lipton, "Byrne Says Conviction of Purpose Drives Her Rough-and-Tumble Style," 20 October 1994, *Washington Post*: C4.

3   Woellert, "The 'Schoolyard Bully'; Byrne Expected To Be Partisan, Effective on the Hill."

4   Peter Baker, "Byrne Was Subtle in Trailblazer Role; Voters Considered Woman More Likely to Effect Change, Analysts Say," 5 November 1992, *Washington Post*: C12.

5   Jim Clardy, "House Hopefuls Steer Clear of Bush Coattails," 28 October 1992, *Washington Times*: B1.

6   Baker, "Byrne Was Subtle in Trailblazer Role."

7   *Politics in America, 1994* (Washington, D.C.: National Journal Inc., 1993): 1602.

8   Craig Winneker, "Women and Blacks Augment Numbers on Top Panels as Parties Fill 292 Slots," 14 December 1992, *Roll Call*.

9   Jim Clardy, "Local Legislators Take Aim at Key Hill Panels," 7 December 1992, *Washington Times*: B1; Winneker, "Women and Blacks Augment Numbers on Top Panels as Parties Fill 292 Slots."

10 *Almanac of American Politics, 1994* (Washington, D.C.: National Journal Inc., 1993): 1330.

11 *Politics in America, 1994*: 1601.

12 Timothy J. Burger, "Rosty, Dingell, Frosh Seek to Unseat 11 Chairmen Who Bucked President," 31 May 1993, *Roll Call*.

13 *Almanac of American Politics, 1994*: 1330; see also, Jim Clardy, "Byrne Draws Fire From Caucus," 10 June 1993, *Washington Times*: A4.

14 Eric Lipton, "Lessons Learned in Complex Youth Moderate Davis's Political Approach," 20 October, 1994, *Washington Post*: C4.

15 Eric Lipton, "Burnishing the Byrne Image," 6 October 1994, *Washington Post*: V3.

Patsy Ann Danner

1934–

UNITED STATES REPRESENTATIVE ★ DEMOCRAT FROM MISSOURI
1993–2001

Elected to the U.S. House by unseating an eight-term incumbent, Patsy Danner carved out a reputation as a moderate, independent Democrat. Congresswoman Danner used her seat on the Public Works and Transportation Committee to tend to aviation interests in her district. As a member of the International Relations Committee, she criticized American troop commitments in the Balkans and a series of free trade agreements favored by the William J. Clinton administration in the 1990s.

Patsy Ann "Pat" Berrer was born in Louisville, Kentucky, on January 13, 1934, daughter of Henry Joseph Berrer and Catherine Shaheen Berrer. She studied at Hannibal-LaGrange College for one year, in 1952, but did not graduate with a degree. Patsy Berrer married Lavon Danner, and together they had four children—Stephen, Shavonne, Shane, and Stephanie—but were later divorced. In 1982, Danner remarried to C. Markt Meyer, a retired airline pilot. Patsy Danner graduated with a B.A. in political science from Northeast Missouri State University in 1972.

Danner became involved in Missouri politics during the 1970s. From 1970 to 1972, she served as the vice chair for the Congressional District Democratic Committee in northeast Missouri and on the Macon County Democratic Committee. From 1973 to 1976, she acted as the chief district aide to U.S. Representative Jerry Litton. A charismatic favorite son from north-central Missouri, Litton was killed in a plane crash the night he secured the Democratic nomination from Missouri for the U.S. Senate in 1976. Danner lost in the Democratic primary to fill Litton's seat, which represented a large area of northwestern Missouri. During the James Earl "Jimmy" Carter administration, she served in a sub-Cabinet post as co-chair of the Ozarks Regional Commission from 1977 to 1981; she was the first woman to chair a regional commission. In 1983, she won election to the Missouri state senate, where she served for a decade. She eventually chaired the transportation committee and was vice chair of the education committee. In 1991, Danner's son, Steve, joined her in the Missouri senate. At the time, they were the only mother–son combination in a single legislature in the country. "I think both of us have the same philosophy," she said, "we serve our constituents first."[1]

In 1992, Pat Danner announced her candidacy for the Democratic primary in the U.S. House district her former boss, Representative Litton, once represented, encompassing northwest Missouri and the Kansas City suburbs. She won the Democratic Party's backing to face eight-term Republican incumbent Tom Coleman, a protégé of one-time Missouri Attorney General (and later U.S. Senator) John Danforth, who had won the general election in 1976 to succeed Litton. For years, Coleman had relatively little competition. Then, in 1990, his challenger, an unknown farmer, spent virtually no money and captured 48 percent of the vote. Constituents, particularly farmers, believed that Coleman, a lawyer who was the Ranking Republican on the Agriculture Committee—a key panel for the district's predominantly rural economy—had lost touch with his district. In an anti-incumbent year, Danner tapped into that sentiment. She questioned Coleman's support for a $35,000 congressional pay raise and for having one of the House's highest mailing budgets at taxpayer expense. Danner also suggested that Coleman had done little to help constituents who had suffered from the 1991–1992 recession. Coleman touted his seniority on the Agriculture Committee, appealing to voters that he could

exercise greater influence than Danner. He also sought to turn the insider label back on Danner by running television commercials which portrayed the state senate veteran as a lifetime politician. But Danner, who had assembled her own "Farmers for Danner" group, struck a chord with agricultural interests: "I know what it's like to lose a crop and I know what it's like to make a crop," Danner said during a debate with Coleman. She won the election with 55 percent of the vote. In her victory speech, Danner invoked Litton's memory: "There never will be another Jerry Litton, but I'll try my best to be the kind of Congressman for this district that he was."[2] In her three subsequent re-election campaigns, Danner steadily added to her margins of victory: 66 percent in 1994, 68 percent in 1996, and 71 percent in 1998.

When Danner took her seat in the 103rd Congress (1993–1995), she hoped to use her close connection to Majority Leader Dick Gephardt of St. Louis to win a seat on the Appropriations Committee and the Public Works and Transportation Committee. Though unable to secure the plum Appropriations assignment, she received a Public Works and Transportation (later renamed Transportation and Infrastructure) post and an assignment to the Small Business Committee. She remained on Transportation and Infrastructure for her four terms of House service, with seats on the Aviation and Ground Transportation Subcommittees. She resigned the Small Business assignment after her first term and received a seat on the International Relations Committee in the 105th and 106th Congresses (1997–2001). On International Relations, Danner served on the Subcommittee for International Economic Policy and Trade with oversight important to the farm constituency in her district.

Congresswoman Danner emerged as a moderate-to-conservative Democrat in the House. As a freshman, she voted in favor of the Family and Medical Leave Act of 1993 but opposed a nationalized health care system. Danner also voted against the Clinton administration's 1993 budget and economic stimulus package, both of which she had supported in their early stages. An abortion

opponent during her years in the Missouri legislature, Danner moderated her stance somewhat as a Member of the U.S. House, voting against a bill requiring parental notification by minors; she opposed another measure to allow federally financed abortions. Danner maintained that federal funds could only be made available in the case of rape, incest, or dire threat to the mother's life. She voted against the Brady Handgun Bill, which required a five-day waiting period for the purchase of handguns. Danner also introduced a bill that would have given states the authority to regulate out-of-state shipments of waste, a function exclusively under federal control at the time.[3] In 1994, also as a freshman, she dropped out of the Congressional Women's Caucus, claiming that it was not worth the investment of the membership fee. However, it also appeared that she was increasingly at loggerheads with the group's advocacy of abortion rights.[4]

Much of her legislative work focused on the needs of her district. In 1993 massive flooding in the Midwest affected many of her constituents. She joined with Members of her state delegation and Illinois lawmakers to secure emergency relief. She also helped pass a measure which allowed the Army Corps of Engineers to repair damaged levees that had not previously been under their mandate. Danner again got federal relief for Missouri farmers during 1997 floods. In the 105th Congress, from her seat on the Transportation Committee, Danner helped steer federal funding into her district for several major highway upgrades.[5] Since that committee also had some jurisdiction over aviation issues, Danner worked to help keep Trans World Airlines operating in Missouri, including its aircraft maintenance location near Kansas City and hub operation in St. Louis.

From her International Relations seat, Danner was a consistent critic of the Clinton administration's foreign policy, particularly its decision to send in U.S. troops for peacekeeping duty in the Balkans. In 1995, she took to the House Floor to oppose a troop deployment in Bosnia, noting she had "grave reservations" about placing U.S. peacekeepers in harm's way when neither side in the civil war had yet accepted the terms of a ceasefire.[6] In 1999,

when the Clinton administration inserted American troops as peacekeepers in Kosovo, Danner loudly objected, citing the "human" costs and impact on military families of extended tours of duty in Bosnia. Noting that the original commitment in Bosnia in 1995 was estimated at one year and costing $1 billion, Danner complained that the mission was into its fourth year at a price tag of more than $10 billion. "There is no reason to believe that a mission in Kosovo would not drag on indefinitely with a high possibility of American casualties," she told colleagues.[7] As with the administration's use of the military, Danner often dissented on trade and international economic policy. In 1993, she voted against the North American Free Trade Agreement and, later, the General Agreement on Tariffs and Trade accord. She also opposed the Clinton administration's permanent normalization of trade relations with China in 2000.

After being diagnosed with breast cancer in the fall of 1999 and receiving treatment, Danner announced in May 2000 that she would not seek re-election to a fifth term.[8] Weeks before she announced her intention to retire, Danner took to the House Floor to speak on behalf of the Breast and Cervical Cancer Prevention and Treatment Act of 2000, a bill she cosponsored with Republican Sue Myrick of North Carolina, who also had been diagnosed with breast cancer in 1999. The legislation, which eventually passed the House, expanded coverage for low-income women. Danner noted that she had been lucky to discover the disease early through checkups as an insured patient. "Unfortunately, there are many women who do not have the ability to pay for treatment after being diagnosed with breast or cervical cancer," she told colleagues. "This is a most tragic situation that this legislation seeks to address."[9] Her son, Steve, was considered an early favorite to replace her, but he did not win the Democratic primary in August 2000. Representative Danner returned to Kansas City after leaving Congress in January 2001.

FOR FURTHER READING

Biographical Directory of the United States Congress, "Patsy Ann (Pat) Danner," http://bioguide.congress.gov

NOTES

1   Joseph Coleman, "Mother and Son Both in State Senate," 21 January 1991, Associated Press; Virginia Young, "Family Ties: Steve Danner Joins Mother, Sen. At Danner, in the Only Mother-Son Duo in a State Senate," 18 November 1990, *St. Louis Post-Dispatch*: 12D.

2   J. Duncan Moore, "New Blood in Missouri's 6th District," 9 November 1992, *St. Louis Post-Dispatch*: 3B.

3   *Congressional Record*, House, 103rd Cong., 1st sess. (23 February 1993): 423.

4   Cited in *Politics in America, 1996* (Washington, D.C.: Congressional Quarterly Inc. 1995): 756–757.

5   *Politics in America, 2002* (Washington, D.C.: Congressional Quarterly Inc., 2001): 790–791; *Congressional Record*, House, 103rd Cong., 1st sess. (13 July 1993): 4515.

6   *Congressional Record*, House, 104th Cong., 1st sess. (19 December 1995): 2400.

7   *Congressional Record*, House, 106th Cong., 1st sess. (11 March 1989): 1179.

8   Steve Kraske, "Rep. Danner Decides She Won't Run Again," 23 May 2000, *Kansas City Star*: A1; Robert Schlesinger and Melanie Fonder, "In Reversal, Danner Will Not Seek Reelection," 24 May 2000, *The Hill*: 20; Mary Lynn F. Jones, "For Congressional Families, Breast Cancer Is No Statistic," 31 May 2000, *Roll Call*: 1.

9   For Danner's remarks on the "Breast and Cervical Cancer Prevention and Treatment Act of 2000," see the *Congressional Record*, House, 106th Cong., 2nd sess. (9 May 2000): 2687.

Jennifer Dunn

1941–

UNITED STATES REPRESENTATIVE ★ REPUBLICAN FROM WASHINGTON
1993–2005

Jennifer Dunn, a longtime Washington state GOP official, won election to the U.S. House in the so-called "Year of the Woman." A self-styled "Reagan conservative," Congresswoman Dunn became a prominent figure in the Republican Party as it gained control of the House in 1994, moving into the GOP leadership and securing a seat on the powerful Ways and Means Committee.[1] Her chief legislative work was in the field of tax policy.

Jennifer Blackburn was born in Seattle, Washington, on July 29, 1941, the daughter of Helen and John "Jack" Charles Blackburn. Her father was a cannery worker, fishing equipment salesman, and real estate broker. Her mother taught Native-American children but gave up her career to raise her children. Jennifer Blackburn grew up in Bellevue, Washington, and excelled at sports and outdoor activities. "Just about everything she did was full steam ahead," her brother recalled.[2] She attended the University of Washington from 1960 to 1962 and earned a B.A. in English literature from Stanford University in 1963. For five years she worked as a systems designer for a major computer company. She married Dennis Dunn, who later became the GOP chairman in King County, Washington. The Dunns raised two children, Bryant and Reagan, but were divorced in 1977. Jennifer Dunn worked as a public relations officer in the King County department of assessments from 1978 to 1980. One of her first major political posts was as the statewide coordinator for Ronald Reagan's 1976 presidential campaign. From 1980 to 1992, she chaired the state Republican Party and also served as vice chair of the Republican National Committee's executive board from 1988 to 1991. Dunn joined U.S. delegations to the United Nations Commission on the Status of Women in 1984 and in 1990.[3]

In 1992, when incumbent Washington Republican Rod Chandler left his House seat to run for the U.S. Senate, Dunn declared her candidacy. In the open primary for the district spanning many of Seattle's affluent eastern suburbs in King and Pierce counties (an area containing many of the leading technology companies), she edged out Republican state senator Pam Roach 32 to 29 percent. In the general election, she faced a Republican-turned-Democrat, businessman George Tamblyn. Dunn campaigned on a pro-abortion rights agenda that contrasted with her conservative bona fides: opposition to tax increases, support for school vouchers and the line-item veto, and a tough-on-crime platform.[4] Dunn won with 60 percent of the vote. In her subsequent five re-election bids, she equaled that margin of victory or exceeded it.[5]

When Dunn took her seat in the 103rd Congress (1993–1995), she received assignments on three committees: House Administration; Public Works and Transportation; and Science, Space, and Technology. In the 104th Congress (1995–1997), when her ally Newt Gingrich of Georgia became Speaker, Dunn began a swift rise through the Republican ranks. In just her second term, she won a seat on the influential Ways and Means Committee, which required her to relinquish her prior assignments. In the 107th Congress (2001–2003), Dunn served on the Joint Economic Committee. In the 108th Congress (2003–2005), Dunn was tasked as vice chair of the newly created Select Committee on Homeland Security.

During her freshman term, Representative Dunn advocated fiscal reform, challenging House committees to make 25 percent cuts in their own budgets. She broke ranks with her GOP colleagues to support the Violence

Against Women Act, though she later voted against the Family and Medical Leave Act in 1993, which was backed by most of her women colleagues. Dunn also consistently voted to support women's reproductive rights, though she opposed federal subsidies for the procedure and funding for international family-planning programs. On most other hot-button social issues, however, Dunn was firmly in the GOP ranks, voting for gun owners' rights and a constitutional amendment to allow school prayer. "Too often we assume that women are going to be liberals," Congresswoman Dunn said. "But there are women out there who believe we can solve our problems with non-government, non-invasive solutions."[6]

Dunn focused on issues of tax legislation, high technology, and retirement security from her Ways and Means seat. Considered one of the House's top experts on tax relief, her most prominent piece of legislation was a 2000 bill to repeal estate taxes, which won convincing bipartisan support to pass the House, though not enough to override President William J. Clinton's veto.[7] She also supported the abolition of the so-called marriage penalty, whereby married couples filing jointly were taxed at a higher rate than if they filed separately.[8]

In 1997, Congresswoman Dunn was elected Vice Chair of the House Republican Conference, the fifth-ranking position in the GOP leadership. At the time, it made her one of the highest-ranking women in the House. One of her major tasks was to overcome the rancor and partisanship of the 1990s and, as well, present the Republican Party in a more favorable light to women voters. "I have found that if you listen to the American woman and respect her advice, the answers are all right there," Dunn declared.[9] During the 1996 campaign, she pitched the GOP to women voters as being friendly to women business owners, married couples, and working families and concerned with health care and research issues. "We agree on 80 percent of the things in our party.... We ought to be able to help come out with really good legislation by including everybody, their energy, their passions, their work," Dunn said in a 1998 interview.[10] At the time, she was making history by becoming the first woman of either

party to run for House Majority Leader. Dunn used her gender as an entering wedge, noting that she was a "fresh face" with a "softer voice," who could carry "a banner for working moms." As a woman familiar with "bumping up against the glass ceiling," she nevertheless portrayed herself as effectively "working in a man's world."[11] She eventually lost her challenge against Majority Leader Dick Armey of Texas and also gave up her seat as Vice Chair of the GOP Conference.

In the 2000 presidential election, Dunn served on George W. Bush's campaign committee and raised more than $1 million for the GOP candidate. After Bush's victory, some insiders believed Dunn would be offered a Cabinet post as Secretary of Labor or Secretary of Transportation. But the offer never came, in part, because with Congress so evenly divided, the Bush administration was reluctant to pull key congressional allies out of the House or Senate, and Dunn held a powerful post on Ways and Means.[12] In early 2004, having recently married Keith Thomson, a Hanford nuclear facility executive, Dunn surprised colleagues by announcing her decision to retire from the House. "While I never took a pledge on term limits, I do believe that our nation is better served if from time to time we senior Members step aside to allow individuals with fresh ideas to challenge the status quo in Congress," Dunn said. "It is time for me to move on."[13] Dunn retired at the end of the 108th Congress in early January 2005.

FOR FURTHER READING

Biographical Directory of the United States Congress, "Jennifer Blackburn Dunn," http://bioguide.congress.gov

NOTES

1   Mike Lindblom, "Rep. Dunn, a Force in the 8th District: Candidates Views Are Right Down Party Lines," 25 October 2000, *Seattle Times*: B1.

2   Libby Ingrid Copeland, "The House's Dunn Dealer: GOP's Smooth Referee Aims for No. 2 Spot," 16 November 1998, *Washington Post*: B1.

3   For precongressional information, see Copeland, "The House's Dunn Dealer."

4   David Schaefer, "Democrat Faces Long Odds in 8th District Race–Dunn a Formidable Foe For Tamblyn," 26 October 1992, *Seattle Times*: B1; Ellis E. Conklin, "It Looks Like a Dunn Deal in 8th District," 16 September 1992, *Seattle Post-Intelligencer*: A6.

5   "Election Statistics, 1920 to Present," http://clerk.house.gov/members/electionInfo/elections.html.

6   "Jennifer Dunn," Associated Press Candidate Biographies, 2000.

7   *Politics in America, 2002* (Washington, D.C.: Congressional Quarterly Inc., 2001): 1076–1077.

8   *Congressional Record*, House, 106th Cong., 2nd sess. (10 February 2000): 291.

9   "What the GOP Has Done for Women," Jennifer Dunn campaign speech, 1996, online at: http://gos.sbc.edu/d/dunn.html (accessed 17 June 2002).

10 *Current Biography, 1999* (New York: H.W. Wilson and Company, 1999): 178.

11 Danny Westneat, "Race and Gender at Play in GOP Leadership Spots: Jennifer Dunn Appealing to Party to Place Women in Some Key Roles," 17 November 1998, *Seattle Times*: A1.

12 Barbara A. Serrano, "Despite Hopes, Dunn Likely to Stay in House," 17 December 2000, *Seattle Times*: A1.

13 Charles Pope and Larry Lange, "Dunn Says She Won't Run Again: Surprise Decision Ends 12-Year Career in Congress for Bellevue Republican," 31 January 2004, *Seattle Post-Intelligencer*: A1; David Postman, "Dunn Stuns GOP, Says She'll Retire from House: Decision Starts Speculation on Who Will Go for Her Seat," 31 January 2004, *Seattle Times*: A1.

Karan English

1949–

UNITED STATES REPRESENTATIVE ★ DEMOCRAT FROM ARIZONA
1993–1995

Karan English won election to the U.S. House as an environmental reformer from one of the nation's largest mining districts, an expansive area covering northeastern Arizona. Congresswoman English's single term in the House centered on her effort to balance strong mineral development interests among her constituency with her own convictions about the necessity of environmental protections.

Karan English was born in Berkeley, California, on March 23, 1949. She attended Shasta Junior College and the University of California at Santa Barbara, before earning a B.A. from the University of Arizona in 1973. She then worked as a conservation program director. In 1980 English was elected to the Coconino County board of supervisors, serving from 1981 to 1987. She also raised two children, Stacy and David, after divorcing her husband in 1984. She won election to the Arizona state legislature, serving from 1987 to 1991. By 1990, she had risen to the state senate, where she served a two-year term, chairing the environment committee and serving on the education and transportation panels. One of her legislative achievements in the state senate was to craft a bill that imposed a "cradle-to-grave" system for transporting, treating, and disposing of hazardous waste material.[1] In 1992, she married Rob Elliott, a rafting business owner and Flagstaff politician, with three children from a previous marriage.

English entered the 1992 race for a newly apportioned U.S. House district that stretched from the suburbs of Phoenix and Scottsdale in central Arizona to the sprawling counties of Apache, Gila, and Navajo in the northeastern corner of the state. She captured 44 percent of the vote, defeating two challengers in the Democratic primary, including her colleague in the state senate, minority leader

Alan Stephens. In the general election, she faced Doug Wead, a minister who had been the George H.W. Bush administration's liaison with religious leaders. She ran on a platform that reflected her experience in the state legislature: environmental cleanup, more funding for AIDS research and relief, and cutting the budget deficit.[2] English secured support from two key national groups: EMILY's List and the Women's Campaign Fund. But the endorsement that propelled her in the polls came from an unlikely source. As her campaign got underway, her son, David, took an unexpected phone call at their Flagstaff home. The caller was Barry Goldwater, the conservative godfather of Arizona politics, former U.S. Senator, and one-time presidential candidate. He wanted to speak to English. When her son replied she wasn't at home, Goldwater said, "Well, tell your mother, if I lived in the Sixth District, I'd vote for her." The endorsement made its way into the media, with Goldwater stating that he was concerned with Republican candidate Doug Wead's "connection to the religious right" and with the fact that Wead, having lived in the state for just two years, was something of a political carpetbagger.[3] English became only the second woman elected to Congress from Arizona (the first was Isabella Greenway in the 1930s) by defeating Wead, 53 to 41 percent.[4]

When English took her seat in the 103rd Congress (1993–1995), she was appointed to the Natural Resources and the Education and Labor committees. Following her work in the Arizona legislature, she used the Natural Resources seat to focus on environmental issues, despite the fact that her district encompassed large ranching and mining interests. In 1992, nearly half of all copper mining in the U.S. took place in English's district and the industry

was the largest employer in the district, providing jobs for nearly 30,000 people, both directly and in support trades. English spoke out in favor of the Mineral Exploration and Development Act of 1993, a bill that the mining industry and environmental groups roundly criticized. It represented Congress's effort to reform the General Mining Law of 1872 by eliminating a patenting system that priced public lands for as little as $2.50 per acre, raising operations standards, and creating a federal land reclamation fund to deal with the restoration of mined lands. Placing herself in the "pro-responsible mining camp" English declared that mining must "be accompanied by a fair return to the owners of the land: the American taxpayer. . . . Clearly what is needed here—what is always needed—is balance. Let us realize that the old acrimonious debate pitting jobs versus the environment is ultimately self-defeating. Arizonans at least know that in the long-term, we must maintain a healthy partnership between extractive uses of the public lands and environmental protection."[5] Mining interests objected that the bill would prohibit any new mining on public lands. Environmentalists believed that English had given away too much to the industry. Adding to English's difficulties with district industries, ranching and farm interests chafed at her support for a tax hike on gasoline and an increase in grazing fees.

Some of English's personal experiences shaped her legislative initiatives. In the early 1990s, she had a scare with breast cancer which led her to push for the Access to Rural Health Information Act in 1994. Her bill called for the establishment of a toll-free hotline for rural residents to receive information ranging from medical services and physician referrals to where to go for domestic violence counseling. "Rural America faces a tough challenge in providing health care to its residents," English noted. "Primarily, these problems can be attributed to the lack of primary care providers, physical and economic barriers, and the fragile nature of rural health care delivery systems dependent on a sparse population base. When a rural area loses its doctor, it often loses its health care."[6]

English faced a tough re-election campaign in the fall of 1994. Many of her votes had not resonated well with her conservative-leaning constituents. In addition to the controversial mining and ranching reforms she supported, English also had voted in favor of abortion rights, the William J. Clinton administration's 1993 budget, the Brady Handgun Bill, and the 1994 ban on assault weapons. Even Goldwater retracted his support for her. She lost to Republican J.D. Hayworth, a former television sportscaster, by a 55 to 42 percent margin. After the election, she recalled, "I didn't lose to J.D. I lost to the Christian Coalition. And they didn't beat me, they beat this image that had been created over the past two years and I couldn't turn it around." She was not alone. Sixteen of the 1992 freshman class—all Democrats—were turned out of office in the 1994 "Republican Revolution," which gave control of the House to the GOP for the first time in 40 years. In a late November meeting of the Democratic Caucus, recriminations flew over the election defeat for House Democrats, with at least one lawmaker observing that some of the damage could have been mitigated if some of the freshmen Members had not voted the way they did on politically sensitive issues. English offered a sharp retort: "To suggest that we shouldn't have taken these tough votes to save our careers . . . [is] exactly what the problem is in Congress. I came here to do something, not to be somebody." The Caucus gave her a standing ovation.[7]

After Congress, English returned to Flagstaff, Arizona, where she worked with the National Democratic Institute of International Affairs as a consultant for countries developing democratic institutions. Since 1997, English has worked at Northern Arizona University, where she currently directs its ecological monitoring and assessment program.

FOR FURTHER READING

Biographical Directory of the United States Congress, "Karan English," http://bioguide.congress.gov

MANUSCRIPT COLLECTION

Northern Arizona University (Flagstaff, AZ), Cline Library, http://www.nau.edu/ficline/speccoll/. *Papers:* 1980–1994, 91 linear feet. The collection includes files from English's six years as Coconino County supervisor, her two terms in the Arizona house, one term in the Arizona senate, and one term in the U.S. Congress. The collection includes files on northern Arizona and Arizona political issues, environmental issues, and women's issues.

NOTES

1   "The 103rd Congress: Why This Freshman Class Is Greener Than Ever Before," April 1993, *Environmental Health Perspectives*, 101 (No. 1), online at http://ehpnet.lniehs.nih.gov/docs/1993/101-1/spheres.html (accessed 18 June 2002).

2   Daniel Wood, "Two Women Take on GOP in Arizona Races," 19 October 1992, *Christian Science Monitor*, special section, "Campaign '92": 9.

3   Charles Hirshberg, "Ms. English Goes to Washington," April 1993, *Life*: 68; Steve Yozwaik, "Goldwater Jolts GOP, Backs Democrat: Wead Dealt Blow By His Hero, Who Favors Rival English," 30 October 1992, *Arizona Republic* online archive at http://www.arizonarepublic.com (accessed 18 June 2002).

4   "Election Statistics, 1920 to Present," http://clerk.house.gov/members/electionInfo/elections.html.

5   *Congressional Record*, House, 103rd Cong., 1st sess. (16 November 1993): 9739.

6   *Congressional Record*, House, 103rd Cong., 2nd sess. (21 April 1994): 751.

7   Kevin Merida, "Hill Reformers of '92 Bow to Class of '94; Turned Out After a Term, Arizona Democrat Ponders What Could Have Been," 1 December 1994, *Washington Post*: A1.

Tillie Kidd Fowler

1942–2005

UNITED STATES REPRESENTATIVE ★ REPUBLICAN FROM FLORIDA
1993–2001

Tillie Fowler, whose roots in Florida politics ran deep, rose to become one of the highest-ranking Republican women in the House. Representative Fowler served on the influential Armed Services Committee, a key assignment since her district encompassed the Jacksonville naval facilities, before honoring a term limit pledge to retire after four terms.

Tillie Kidd was born in Atlanta, Georgia, on December 23, 1942, daughter of Culver and Katherine Kidd. She was raised in a politically active family; her father served for more than 40 years in the Georgia state legislature. Kidd received an A.B. in political science from Emory University in 1964 and a J.D. from the Emory University School of Law in 1967; she was admitted to the bar that year. She moved to Washington, D.C., to work as a legislative assistant to Representative Robert G. Stephens, Jr., of Georgia from 1967 to 1970. In 1968, she married L. Buck Fowler, and the couple lived in Washington as Tillie Fowler accepted a position as a counsel in the Richard M. Nixon White House Office of Consumer Affairs from 1970 to 1971. The Fowlers moved to Jacksonville in 1971, where they raised two daughters, Tillie Anne and Elizabeth. After more than a decade as a mother and housewife, Tillie Fowler re-entered politics. She was elected to the Jacksonville city council and served from 1985 to 1992 as its first female and, later, as its first Republican president in 1989 to 1990. She also served as chair of the Duval County tourism development council from 1989 to 1990 and chair of the Florida Endowment for the Humanities from 1989 to 1991.[1]

In 1992, when Democrat Charles E. Bennett, a 22-term Representative, announced his retirement from the House, Fowler entered the race for the northeast Florida seat, which encompassed Jacksonville and portions of St. Johns and Duval counties. Her opponent in the general election was Mattox Hair, a prominent state legislator. With a well-financed campaign that focused on congressional reform and term limits, Fowler won with 56 percent of the vote. She ran unopposed in the succeeding three elections.[2] When she entered the 103rd Congress (1993–1995), Fowler was appointed to the Armed Services Committee and the Transportation and Infrastructure Committee.

Fowler soon earned a reputation as a moderate conservative who supported budgetary restraint but approved of federal funding of abortions in rape cases, an increase in the minimum wage, and federal funds for the National Endowment for the Humanities. Fowler advocated an overhaul of the welfare system, which she described as "anti-family" in 1993. She also championed increased federal funding for women's health care and cancer research.

Having first been elected to Congress in the "Year of the Woman," Fowler believed that women would have a unique impact on the institution but cautioned that most problems could not be solved through the lens of gender. "I think as mothers, home-workers, as people who usually had to juggle a lot of different priorities, we get pretty good at that. I think we bring a different view to issues such as child care," Fowler said at the time. "But I also don't believe that there is any one set of issues that is just women's issues because I think women's perspective is needed in defense; that's one of the reasons I wanted to be on the Armed Services Committee. I think women are all concerned with defense issues and I think our perspective is needed there."[3]

On the Armed Services Committee, Fowler became a regular critic of the William J. Clinton administration's

"I THINK AS MOTHERS, HOME-
WORKERS, AS PEOPLE WHO USUALLY
HAD TO JUGGLE A LOT OF
DIFFERENT PRIORITIES, WE GET
PRETTY GOOD AT THAT. I THINK
WE BRING A DIFFERENT VIEW TO
ISSUES SUCH AS CHILDCARE,"
FOWLER SAID. "BUT I ALSO DON'T
BELIEVE THAT THERE IS ANY ONE
SET OF ISSUES THAT IS JUST
WOMEN'S ISSUES."

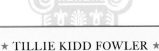
defense budgets and foreign policy during the 1990s. As defense budgets were trimmed in the post–Cold War years, Fowler maintained that the cuts were so deep that they affected the military's core capabilities. Much of her concern came as a Representative with a heavy naval presence in her district, including the Mayport Naval Station and facilities in Jacksonville. She pointed out that defense cuts occurred at a time when the military's mission had been expanded into peacekeeping and humanitarian causes. Fowler also dissented from the Clinton administration's policy in the Balkans. She twice visited American troops in the region, praising their work but criticizing the open-ended goals of Washington policymakers who, she said, were attempting an experiment in "nation-building."[4] A longtime opponent of deploying American troops to Bosnia, Fowler nonetheless did not underestimate the significance of U.S. relations with the Balkan nation. "I have supported the involvement of our sea and air forces, our intelligence and logistics assets, and our most diligent diplomatic efforts," she commented. "But I have never felt that our interests were so vital that they warranted putting our ground troops at risk."[4]

Fowler rose quickly through the ranks of the Republican Party. She served as a Deputy Whip in the 105th Congress (1997–1999). In the 106th Congress (1999–2001) she won election as Vice Chair of the GOP Conference, the fifth-ranking Republican position in the House. It made her the highest-ranking woman in the party. During that Congress she also rose to chair the Transportation Subcommittee on Investigations and Emergency Management.

Fulfilling her 1992 campaign pledge to retire after four terms, Fowler did not seek re-election to the 107th Congress (2001–2003). At the time, the move was widely praised as a highly ethical decision, in no small measure because Fowler made it despite her high profile in the Republican leadership. "I take great pride in the fact that we not only changed Congress, but we changed America," Fowler said upon announcing her retirement.[6] In 2001, Fowler joined a Washington-based law firm. In May 2004, Secretary of Defense Donald Rumsfeld appointed Fowler as one of four members of an independent panel to investigate abuse of Iraqi prisoners of war. The panel recommended a sweeping overhaul of the U.S. military's procedures for the handling of prisoners. On February 28, 2005, Fowler suffered a brain hemorrhage while in Jacksonville. She died two days later on March 2.[7]

FOR FURTHER READING

Biographical Directory of the United States Congress, "Tillie Kidd Fowler," http://bioguide.congress.gov

NOTES

1   "Tillie Fowler," Biography Resource Center Online, Gale Group (2000), http://www.galenet.com (accessed 16 August 2002); Adam Bernstein, "Florida's Rep. Tillie Fowler Dies; Defense-Minded Republican," 3 March 2005, *Washington Post*: B6.
2   "Election Statistics, 1920 to Present," http://clerk.house.gov/members/electionInfo/elections.html.
3   Liza N. Burba, "Year of the Woman Puts Washington Focus on Health and Child Care," 30 September 1993, *NCJW Journal* 16 (No. 2): 6.
4   *Politics in America, 2000* (Washington, D.C.: Congressional Quarterly Inc., 1999): 296–298.
5   *Congressional Record,* House, 104th Cong., 1st sess. (13 December 1995): 14854).
6   Bill Adair, "Rep. Fowler Won't Seek Re-election," 5 January 2000, *St. Petersburg Times*: 3A; Douglas Martin, "Tillie Fowler: 62, a Former House Leader," 3 March 2005, *New York Times*: A29.
7   Bernstein, "Florida's Rep. Tillie Fowler Dies"; Martin, "Tillie Fowler: 62, a Former House Leader."

Elizabeth Furse

1936–

UNITED STATES REPRESENTATIVE ★ DEMOCRAT FROM OREGON
1993–1999

Born a colonist in the British Empire, Elizabeth Furse became an antiapartheid activist, an advocate for migrant farm workers and Native Americans, and founder of a peace institute. She claimed her first elective office in 1992, representing a U.S. House district that encompassed suburban Portland, Oregon. Through a series of legislative initiatives, Representative Furse sought to turn the national dialogue away from its old Cold War focus to domestic reforms.

Elizabeth Furse was born a British subject in Nairobi, Kenya, on October 13, 1936. Her grandmother, Dame Katherine Furse, established the Women's Royal Naval Service (the "Wrens") during World War I. Her father was a naval lieutenant who later settled in the then-British colony of Kenya as a coffee planter. The family moved to South Africa, where Furse's mother established an anti-apartheid women's group, "Black Sash." Elizabeth Furse marched with the group at the age of 15. In 1955, she left South Africa to live in London, where she met and married an American doctor. They moved to Los Angeles, and Furse became a naturalized U.S. citizen in 1972. The couple raised two children, Amanda and John, though they eventually divorced. Furse later married John Platt. In 1974, Furse earned a B.A. at Evergreen State College, in Olympia, Washington. In California, Furse had been active in the United Farm Workers movement led by Cesar Chavez. When she relocated to Oregon in 1978, she worked as the director of the Oregon Legal Services Restoration Program for Native American tribes from 1980 to 1986. In 1985, Furse founded the Oregon Peace Institute for nonviolent conflict resolution. With her husband, she also became the owner and operator of a vineyard.

In 1992, when suburban Portland's Democratic Representative Les AuCoin left the House to run for one of Oregon's U.S. Senate seats, Furse entered the race for his seat as a long-shot candidate. The district stretched from the city westward along the Columbia River to the Pacific coast and took in Washington and Yamhill counties. Furse defeated Gary Conkling, a former AuCoin aide, in the primary 60 to 40 percent, largely with support from women voters and groups, including EMILY's List. In the general election, she faced a well-known state politician, Oregon treasurer Tony Meeker. Furse made her pro-choice position on abortion a prominent feature of her campaign, which contrasted sharply with Meeker's pro-life policy. She also used gender as a campaign theme, capitalizing on the outrage over the Clarence Thomas Senate confirmation hearings. She echoed Democratic presidential candidate William J. Clinton's promises of job creation and political change in Washington and eventually went on to edged out Meeker 52 to 48 percent.[1]

When Furse took her seat in the 103rd Congress (1993–1995), she received assignments on three committees: Armed Services; Banking, Finance, and Urban Affairs; and Merchant Marine and Fisheries. In the 104th Congress (1995–1997) she resigned from her initial assignments to join the Commerce Committee. In 1995, Furse quit the Women's Caucus to protest a Republican Member's politicking on behalf of her 1994 election opponent who was running as an anti-abortion candidate; she expressed special contempt because her GOP colleague shared her own abortion rights position.[2]

Furse supported the Clinton budget in 1993 and the 1994 crime bill but opposed the North American Free Trade Agreement, citing its danger to small businesses

in her district. She also secured funding for Portland's Westside Light Rail Project. During her first term, Furse introduced an amendment requiring European allies to pay for a large portion of the bill for American troops stationed on the continent.[3] She also supported one of Bill Clinton's lightning rod campaign issues: the recognition and further incorporation of gays and lesbians into the military.

From her seat on the Armed Services Committee, Furse spoke out about the problem of nuclear proliferation. She brought attention to the longtime American-British collaboration on weapons development, noting the existence of more than 40 joint working groups that had carried over into the post–Cold War era. She accused U.K. Prime Minister John Major's government of undercutting American nuclear nonproliferation efforts. "We feed the British nuclear weapons complex, and right now they are biting the hand that feeds them," Furse declared. "It's a tragic irony that I, as a Member of Congress and the Armed Services Committee, can be better informed on U.K. defense matters than a British Citizen or MP."[4] After the House voted on a nuclear test ban bill in 1992 to take effect in 1996, the Pentagon pushed to lift the moratorium to allow tests of nuclear weapons under one kiloton yield. Furse, in opposing that allowance, cited the nearly half-billion yearly price tag for nuclear tests and paraphrased a line from George Orwell's book *1984*: "War is peace, freedom is slavery, ignorance is strength, a small nuclear test is not a nuclear test."[5] In 1993, she joined forces with House colleague John Spratt of South Carolina in cosponsoring an amendment to ban research and development of low-yield nuclear warheads; the measure became part of the 1994 defense authorization bill. "I introduced an amendment last year that killed an entire generation of nuclear weapons," Furse recalled. "If I do nothing else, it makes going [to Washington, D.C.] worthwhile."[6]

In 1994, Furse won a razor-thin re-election campaign against Republican Bill Witt, beating him by 301 votes out of more than a quarter-million votes cast. She raised $1.1 million in campaign funds—more than twice Witt's total—but nearly succumbed to Witt's strong organiza-

tional base and an electorate that widely supported the Republican "Contract with America." In 1996, she again faced Witt but won by a more comfortable margin of 52 to 45 percent.[7] She surprised political observers in 1995 by entering the Democratic primary for the seat of resigned Oregon Senator Bob Packwood, of whom Furse had been highly critical after charges of sexual harassment were made public by some of his former aides. The nomination eventually went to U.S. Representative Ron Wyden.

Throughout her three-term House tenure, Furse was an advocate for women's issues as well as what she called their unique perspective on the meaning of "security"— both national and domestic. "The whole matter of security . . . men see it in terms of national defense. But what about domestic violence?" Furse said. "A woman who is living in a home where she is battered is living where there is a real war going on. We have to decide whether we're going to continue spending too much on the Pentagon and too little on domestic security—things like safer streets and shelters for victims of domestic violence."[8] She also supported the 1993 Freedom of Access to Clinic Entrances Act after a spate of violence outside abortion clinics. "While the decision is difficult, once it is made, women should not be prevented from or harassed while exercising their rights, and physicians must be allowed to practice medicine without fear for their lives," Furse said on the House Floor.[9] In 1997, Furse cosponsored the Children's National Security Act, an omnibus bill that included initiatives ranging from health insurance for children to health care research and education, assistance for caregivers, firearm child safety lock requirements, school construction, and economic security for families. The bill would be funded with cuts from the Pentagon budget. "I believe it's time to change the focus of our priorities, to reflect that national security means providing children a quality education, access to health care, and a safe place to live and learn," Furse told colleagues. "We cannot continue to invest in outdated Cold War weapons systems while we neglect our children."[10]

Furse became a major proponent for affordable health care coverage and greater research into women's health

issues. As early as 1993, she supported government-funded health care, speaking out in support of the American Health Security Act.[11] In 1997, she again pushed for expanded health care coverage for the then-estimated 10 million uninsured American children. Furse proposed adoption of an Oregon state program that insured children in low-income families for as little as $35 per month. Again, she cast her argument in appropriated military language: "I think what we are dealing with is a national security issue. If we do not have healthy children, we do not have healthy adults, we do not have people who can be the best and the brightest that they could be."[12] In 1996, she introduced the Women's Health Environmental Factors Research Act, which proposed greater funding for research into synthetic compounds in the environment and their effect specifically on women. Furse also pushed for greater research and funding for diabetes, a disease which afflicted her daughter, Amanda.[13]

Furse, who supported term limits, announced during her third term that she would not seek re-election in 1998. After she retired from the House in January 1999, she worked as the director of tribal programs at the Institute for Tribal Government in Portland. Furse resides in Hillsboro, Oregon, where she manages a winery with her husband.

FOR FURTHER READING

Biographical Directory of the United States Congress, "Elizabeth Furse," http://bioguide.congress.gov

NOTES

1   "Election Statistics, 1920 to Present," http://clerk.house.gov/members/electionInfo/elections.html; *Almanac of American Politics, 1994* (Washington, D.C.: National Journal Inc., 1993): 1061–1063.
2   Kevin Merida, "Role of House Women's Caucus Changes," 15 February 1995, *Washington Post*: A4.
3   *Almanac of American Politics, 1996* (Washington, D.C.: National Journal Inc., 1995): 1111–1113.
4   Martin Fletcher, "A Daughter of the Empire Takes Arms Against Britain," 27 November 1993, *London Times*.
5   *Congressional Record*, House, 103rd Cong., 1st sess. (11 May 1993): 2351.
6   Joel Connelly, "Battles for Women in the House," 9 June 1994, *Seattle Post-Intelligencer*: A1; James C. Dao, "Senate Panel Votes To Lift Ban On Small Nuclear Arms," 10 May 2003, *New York Times*: 2.
7   "Election Statistics, 1920 to Present," http://clerk.house.gov/members/electionInfo/elections.html.
8   Interview with Furse and other women Members of Congress published in *Redbook*, September 1996.
9   *Congressional Record*, House, 103rd Cong., 1st sess. (14 September 1993): 6681.
10 *Congressional Record*, House, 105th Cong., 1st sess. (21 May 1997): 3148.
11 *Congressional Record*, House, 103rd Cong., 1st sess. (28 April 1993): 2109.
12 *Congressional Record*, House, 105th Cong., 1st sess. (14 May 1997): 2657.
13 Marie McCarren, "The Expert and the Activist: When Amanda Briggs Wants to Tell Congress a Thing or Two About Diabetes, She Simply Calls Her Mom," December 1995, *Diabetes Forecast* 48 (No. 12): 14.

Marjorie Margolies-Mezvinsky

1942–

UNITED STATES REPRESENTATIVE ★ DEMOCRAT FROM PENNSYLVANIA
1993–1995

A longtime television journalist, Marjorie Margolies-Mezvinsky won election to the U.S. House in 1992. Her brief congressional career turned, quite literally, on a single vote when the Pennsylvania Congresswoman abruptly backed the William J. Clinton administration's budget after being an outspoken critic of the legislation.

Marjorie Margolies was born on June 21, 1942, in Philadelphia, Pennsylvania, daughter of Herbert and Mildred Margolies. "Margie always kept me busy," her mother said, recalling a schedule that involved multiple ballet lessons each week, sports, cheerleading, honor roll academics, and finishing junior high two years early.[1] After graduating from Baltimore's Forest Park High School in 1959, Margolies earned a B.A. from the University of Pennsylvania in 1963. She worked as a television reporter for a Philadelphia NBC affiliate in 1967 and, from 1969 to 1970, she was a CBS News Foundation Fellow at Columbia University.

In 1970, at age 28, she covered a story on Korean orphans and was so moved by the experience that she became the first single woman in the United States to adopt a foreign child, a Korean girl. Several years later she adopted a Vietnamese girl. Covering another story on adopted children, Margolies met then-Iowa Representative Edward Mezvinsky, and they married in 1975. Together the couple raised 11 children: Margolies's two children, Mezvinsky's four children from a previous marriage, two sons born to them, and three Vietnamese boys whom they adopted together. Figuring in the number of refugee families that they sponsored over the years, Marjorie Margolies-Mezvinsky estimated that her household had provided for 25 children. In 1976, she tes-

tified before Congress and was credited with helping change legislation on adoption and immigration practices incorporated into the 1976 Immigration and Nationalities Act.[2] When Edward Mezvinsky lost his re-election bid in 1976, the couple settled in Philadelphia. Margolies-Mezvinsky commuted weekly to Washington, D.C., where she worked as a correspondent for 12 years for the local NBC television affiliate, focusing on congressional issues. She also worked for a Philadelphia television station and for NBC's *Today Show* in New York City. During her career, she won five Emmy Awards. She also published three books, including *They Came to Stay* (1976), relating her experiences as an adoptive parent and a supporter of immigrant families.

When Representative Lawrence Coughlin announced his retirement from the House, two members of Pennsylvania's Montgomery County Democratic Committee approached Margolies-Mezvinsky to run for the nomination. Producing reports for four network television programs, she nevertheless felt she needed to heed her own admonition to her children: "You've got to be prepared to lose before you can win. You've got to get out of the stands and onto the playing field."[3] From the moment Margolies-Mezvinsky declared her candidacy for the open seat that encompassed most of the Montgomery County suburbs northwest of Philadelphia, it was an uphill battle, since the district was two-to-one in favor of registered Republicans and had not elected a Democrat since 1916. Her campaign focused on job creation, health care, and education and the necessity of each of these for good family life. She addressed the 1992 Democratic National Convention and later recalled as she stood on the podium: "I thought about what Barbara

Jordan had said the night before, invoking Thomas Jefferson and talking about women being in the halls and councils of power. And I thought about how important it was that we get in in numbers that can make a difference, to change the face and the body of [Congress]. And I thought, here I am, standing here, part of all this. Me. Herbert and Mildred's daughter."[4] In the general election she faced Republican Montgomery County Commissioner Jon D. Fox. During the campaign, Margolies-Mezvinsky portrayed herself as a nontraditional Democrat who sought to reduce the cost of social programs and avoid hiking taxes.[5] She won in an exceedingly close race with a margin of 1,373 votes out of more than a quarter million cast, 50.27 percent to 49.73 percent.[6]

When Margolies-Mezvinsky took her seat in the 103rd Congress (1993–1995), she received assignments on the influential Energy and Commerce Committee, as well as the Government Operations and Small Business committees. She focused on issues affecting women, from abortion to health care. Her first vote on major legislation was for the Family and Medical Leave Act. She also opposed the "Hyde Amendment," which prohibited federal funding of abortions. In 1993, Margolies-Mezvinsky joined women colleagues in the House who effectively pushed for more funding and research for breast and cervical cancer and making preventive tools available to more women. "The best mammogram means precious little to the woman who cannot afford it," she said. "The opportunity for women to save ourselves rests upon the commitment of this Congress to put the money on the line for our sisters, our daughters, and our wives."[7] She also proposed legislation to better educate doctors about diseases prevalent among women and to encourage leadership training for women in the medical field.[8]

Along with women's issues, Margolies-Mezvinsky supported much of the Democratic Party's legislative agenda. She voted for the Brady Handgun Bill, which passed the House in late 1993. It required a background check and waiting period for gun buyers. "Waiting periods work. Waiting periods save lives," Margolies-Mezvinsky noted at the time.[9] She also introduced bills

that raised the minimum retirement age to 70 by the year 2012 and set cost-of-living adjustments for Social Security recipients at a flat rate.[10]

The turning point for Margolies-Mezvinsky came when she made a last-minute switch to support the 1993 Clinton budget after months of publicly voicing her opposition to the bill because it did not contain enough spending cuts. During her campaign, she had promised not to raise taxes, and the budget proposed a hike in federal taxes, including a gasoline tax. On the day of the vote, she appeared on television and told her constituents that she was against the budget. Minutes before the vote, however, on August 5, 1993, President Clinton called to ask Margolies-Mezvinsky to support the measure. She told him that only if it was the deciding vote—in this case, the 218th yea—would she support the measure. "I wasn't going to do it at 217. I wasn't going to do it at 219. Only at 218, or I was voting against it," she recalled.[11] She also extracted a promise from Clinton that if she did have to vote for the budget package, that he would attend a conference in her district dedicated to reducing the budget deficit. He agreed (and later fulfilled the pledge). Nevertheless, Margolies-Mezvinsky told Clinton "I think I'm falling on a political sword on this one." When she finally walked onto the House Floor to cast the decisive vote, passing the measure 218 to 216, Democrats cheered while Republicans jeered, "Goodbye, Marjorie!"[12] She later recalled that "I knew at the time that changing my vote at the 11th hour may have been tantamount to political suicide. . . . [but] the vote would resolve itself into one simple question: Was my political future more important than the agenda the President had laid out for America?"[13]

Margolies-Mezvinsky's vote, coming as it did after her specific promises, created wide resentment among her district constituents. "I ran into a wall of anger," she recalled when she returned to her district throughout the fall of 1993.[14] In 1994, the Republican National Committee targeted her and 14 other vulnerable House Democrats (many of them first-term women) who had voted for the Clinton budget. That fall Margolies-Mezvinsky again

faced off against Jon Fox, who attacked her relentlessly for her vote. He won by a slim margin of 8,000 votes, with 49 percent to her 45 percent in a four-way race.[15]

After Congress, Margolies-Mezvinsky chaired the National Women's Business Council and served as the Director and Deputy Chair of the U.S. delegation to the United Nations Fourth World Conference on Women. She served as executive director of the Women's Campaign Fund, a group that supported pro-choice women candidates. In 1998, she left that post to run unsuccessfully for lieutenant governor of Pennsylvania. In 1999, Margolies-Mezvinsky initiated a challenge against incumbent U.S. Senator Rick Santorum of Pennsylvania but soon withdrew when her husband's finances came under investigation. Although Edward Mezvinsky was convicted on federal fraud charges in 2002, investigators cleared Marjorie Margolies-Mezvinsky of wrongdoing.[16]

FOR FURTHER READING

Biographical Directory of the United States Congress, "Marjorie Margolies-Mezvinsky," http://bioguide.congress.gov

Margolies-Mezvinsky, Marjorie, and Barbara Feinman. *A Woman's Place: The Freshman Women Who Changed the Face of Congress* (New York: Crown Publishers, 1994).

Margolies-Mezvinsky, Marjorie, and Ruth Gruber. *They Came to Stay* (New York: Coward, McCann & Geoghegan, 1976).

NOTES

1   Dale Russakoff, "The Mother of All Candidates: Marjorie Margolies Mezvinsky, Practicing the Soft Sell," 28 October 1992, *Washington Post*: D1.

2   "Marjorie Margolies Mezvinsky," Associated Press Candidate Biographies, 1994.

3   Russakoff, "The Mother of All Candidates."

4   Ibid.

5   *Almanac of American Politics, 1994* (Washington, D.C.: National Journal Inc., 1993): 1108–1109.

6   "Election Statistics, 1920 to Present," http://clerk.house.gov/members/electionInfo/elections.html.

7   *Congressional Record,* House, 103rd Cong., 1st sess. (14 June 1993): 3473.

8   *Congressional Record,* House, 103rd Cong., 2nd sess. (22 September 1994): 1917.

9   *Congressional Record,* House, 103rd Cong., 1st sess. (10 November 1993): 9151.

10   *Congressional Record,* House, 103rd Cong., 2nd sess. (21 July 1994): 1524.

11   Michael Janofsky, "Marjorie Margolies-Mezvinsky: After Her Pivotal 'Yes' on Budget, Now the Fallout," 11 August 1993, *New York Times*: A11.

12   Michael deCourcy Hinds, "Budget Vote Still Hounds Lawmaker," 12 December 1993, *New York Times*: 30.

13   Marjorie Margolies-Mezvinsky, *A Woman's Place: The Freshman Women Who Changed the Face of Congress* (New York: Crown, 1994); quoted in Barbara Slavin, "This Woman's Place: Freshman Representative Marjorie Margolies-Mezvinsky Is No 'Three M Girl,' and After Casting Some Controversial Votes on Key Issues, She's Shown She Can Hang With the Big Boys," 30 May 1994, *Los Angeles Times*: E1.

14   Hinds, "Budget Vote Still Hounds Lawmaker."

15   "Election Statistics, 1920 to Present," http://clerk.house.gov/members/electionInfo/elections.html.

16   Maryclaire Dale, "Democratic Power Couple's Lives Unravel Over Guilty Plea to $10 Million Fraud," 30 September 2002, Associated Press; Debbie Goldberg, "Democratic Power Couple Suddenly Rich in Troubles; Husband's Business Deals Entangle Margolies-Mezvinsky," 16 February 2000, *Washington Post*: A3; David B. Caruso, "Former Congressman, To Be Imprisoned, Says He Wants to Pay Back Fraud Victims," 10 January 2003, Associated Press.

Carrie P. Meek

1926–

UNITED STATES REPRESENTATIVE ★ DEMOCRAT FROM FLORIDA
1993–2003

Carrie P. Meek won election to the House in 1992 as one of the first African-American lawmakers to represent Florida in Congress since Reconstruction. Focusing on the economic and immigration issues of her district, Meek secured a coveted seat on the House Appropriations Committee as a freshman Representative. While able to work with Republicans on health issues, she was a sharp critic of welfare reform efforts during the mid-1990s.

Carrie Pittman, daughter of Willie and Carrie Pittman, was born on April 29, 1926, in Tallahassee, Florida. Her grandmother was born and raised in Georgia as a slave. Carrie Pittman's parents began their married life as share-croppers, though her father went on to become a caretaker and her mother a laundress and the owner of a boarding-house. She was the youngest of 12 children, a tomboy whom her siblings nicknamed "Tot." She lived near the old Florida capitol in a neighborhood called the "Bottom." Pittman was a track and field star while earning a B.S. in biology and physical education at Florida A&M University in 1946. She enrolled at the University of Michigan graduate school because blacks were banned from Florida graduate schools, though the state government would pay out-of-state tuition, "if we agreed to get out of Dodge," she later recalled.[1] She graduated in 1948 with an M.S. degree in public health and physical education. Afterward, Pittman taught at Bethune Cookman, a historically black college in Daytona Beach, where she coached basketball and taught biological sciences and physical education. She later taught at Florida A&M in Tallahassee. In 1961, as a divorced mother of two young children, Carrie Pittman Meek moved to Miami-Dade Community College, where she spent the next three

decades teaching and administrating, eventually serving as special assistant to the vice president of the college. In 1978, she won election to the Florida state house of representatives, defeating a field of 12 candidates. She served from 1979 to 1983, during which time she chaired the education appropriations subcommittee. From 1983 to 1993, Meek served in the Florida senate. She was the first African-American woman elected to that body and the first black to serve there since Reconstruction. She earned a reputation as a particularly effective legislator, passing a minority business enterprise law and other legislation to promote literacy and reduce the school dropout rate.[2]

In 1992, when incumbent Congressman Bill Lehman (a veteran 10-term Democrat) decided to retire, Meek captured the Democratic nomination for his newly reapportioned district that ran through northern Miami suburbs in Dade County. She ran unopposed in the general election. Since Meek essentially clinched the seat by winning the September primary in the heavily Democratic district, she later claimed to be the first African American elected to represent Florida in Congress since Reconstruction. Democrats Corrine Brown and Alcee L. Hastings, who prevailed over opponents in the November general election in two other Florida districts, were sworn in with Meek on January 3, 1993.

Meek entered Congress at age 66 and immediately launched into an ambitious agenda belied by her soft southern accent and grandmotherly demeanor. "Don't let her fool you. She is not a little old lady from the ghetto," a Florida political observer noted at the time of her election. "Carrie Meek is a player."[3] Meek intensively—and successfully—lobbied for a seat on the Appropriations Committee, a virtually unheard of assignment for a fresh-

man legislator. When the Republicans took control of the House in 1994, Meek was bumped off Appropriations and reassigned to the Budget Committee and the Government Reform and Oversight Committee. In 1996, she returned to the Appropriations Committee and eventually served on two of its subcommittees: Treasury, Postal Service, and General Government and VA, HUD, and Independent Agencies.

Meek focused on the needs of her district, which included issues arising from unemployment, immigration, and even natural disaster. Shortly after arriving on Capitol Hill, Meek sought federal aid for her district, which encompassed Homestead, Florida, the town that bore the brunt of Hurricane Andrew's devastation in August 1992. She used her Appropriations seat, however, principally to try to expand federal programs to create jobs and provide initiatives for blacks to open their own businesses. Meek also authored a measure to modify Social Security laws to cover household workers. On behalf of the Haitian community in her district, Meek sought to extend the period of stay in the country for immigrants and refugees excluded from two 1997 bills addressing Central American immigration. In 1999, she worked to get a more accurate census count in her district by providing a measure whereby welfare recipients familiar with their poor, traditionally undercounted neighborhoods could temporarily work as census employees without losing their benefits.[4]

On issues of national scope, Meek developed a cooperative and congenial style punctuated with partisan episodes. For instance, she was able to work with Republicans to change cigarette label warnings, to reflect the fact that a higher number of African Americans suffer from several smoking-related diseases. She also worked with Republican Anne Northup of Kentucky to increase funding for lupus disease research and to provide federal grants for college students with poor reading skills due to learning disabilities.[5] But, in early 1995, amid the controversy surrounding Speaker Newt Gingrich's $4.5 million book advance, Meek denounced him on the House Floor. "If anything, now, how much the Speaker earns has grown

much more dependent upon how hard his publishing house hawks his book," Meek said. "Which leads me to the question of exactly who does this Speaker really work for. . . . Is it the American people or his New York publishing house?" Republicans shouted Meek down and struck her remarks from the *Congressional Record*.[6] She also charged that Republicans were balancing the budget on the backs of America's working poor, elderly, and infirm by gutting the welfare system. "The spending cuts that the House approved today fall mainly on the weakest members of our society, on the sick and on the elderly," she said in June 1997. "Tomorrow we will be voting on tax cuts that mainly favor the wealthy. . . . Today, the House voted to rob from the poor so that tomorrow the majority can help the rich."[7]

In 2002, citing her age, Meek declined to seek certain re-election to a sixth term. "I wish I could say I was tired of Congress," Meek told the *Miami Herald*. "I love it still. But at age 76, understandably, some of my abilities have diminished. I don't have the same vigor that I had at age 65. I have the fire, but I don't have the physical ability. So it's time."[8] Her youngest child, 35-year-old Kendrick Meek, who served in the Florida senate, announced his candidacy for the Democratic nomination in her district. When Kendrick Meek won the November 2002 general election, he became just the second child to directly succeed his mother in Congress.[9] It also marked just the fifth time that the child of a woman Member served in Congress.[10]

FOR FURTHER READING

Biographical Directory of the United States Congress, "Carrie P. Meek," http://bioguide.congress.gov

NOTES

1   William Booth, "The Strong Will of Carrie Meek; A Florida Sharecropper's Daughter Takes Her Stand on Capitol Hill," 16 December 1992, *Washington Post*: C1.

2   "Carrie P. Meek," Associated Press Candidate Biographies, 1992; *Politics in America, 1994* (Washington, D.C.: Congressional Quarterly Inc., 1993): 310–311.

3   Booth, "The Strong Will of Carrie Meek."

4   *Almanac of American Politics, 2000* (Washington, D.C.: National Journal Inc., 1999): 409.

5   *Politics in America, 2002* (Washington, D.C.: Congressional Quarterly Inc., 2001): 240.

6   Karen Foerstel, *Biographical Dictionary of Women in Congress* (Westport, CT: Greenwood Press, 1999): 184.

7   *Politics in America, 2002*: 240–241.

8   Andrea Robinson and Tyler Bridges, "Carrie Meek to Retire: She Made History from Tallahassee to Capitol Hill," 7 July 2002, *Miami Herald*: A1.

9   James Kee of West Virginia, who succeeded his mother Maude Kee in 1965, was the first.

10 See Appendix I for the full list.

Carol Moseley-Braun

1947–

UNITED STATES SENATOR ★ DEMOCRAT FROM ILLINOIS

1993–1999

As the first African-American woman to serve in the U.S. Senate, Carol Moseley-Braun[1] also held the distinction of being only the second black Senator since the Reconstruction Era. "I cannot escape the fact that I come to the Senate as a symbol of hope and change," Moseley-Braun said, shortly after being sworn into office in 1993. "Nor would I want to, because my presence in and of itself will change the U.S. Senate."[2] During her single term in office, Senator Moseley-Braun was an advocate for civil rights issues and for legislation dealing with crime, education, and families.

Carol Moseley was born in Chicago, Illinois, on August 16, 1947. Her parents, Joseph Moseley, a policeman, and her mother, Edna (Davie) Moseley, a medical technician, divorced in 1963. The oldest of the four Moseley children in a middle-class family, Carol graduated from Parker High School in Chicago and earned a B.A. in political science from the University of Illinois in 1969.[3] Possessing early an interest in politics, she worked on the campaigns of Harold Washington, an Illinois state representative, U.S. Representative, and the first African-American mayor of Chicago, and of Illinois State Senator Richard Newhouse.[4] In 1972, Carol Moseley graduated from the University of Chicago School of Law. There she met and later married Michael Braun; she hyphenated her maiden and married names. The couple raised one son, Matthew, but the marriage ended in divorce in 1986. Moseley-Braun worked as a prosecutor in the office of the U.S. Attorney in Chicago from 1973 until 1977. In 1978, she won election to the Illinois state house of representatives, a position she held for a decade. After an unsuccessful bid for Illinois lieutenant governor in 1986, she was elected the Cook County, Illinois, recorder of

deeds in 1988, becoming the first African American elected to an executive position in Cook County.[5]

Not satisfied with her position as recorder of deeds, and believing that politicians remained out of touch with average Americans, Moseley-Braun contemplated running for Congress. Her resolve to seek national office strengthened after witnessing the questions directed at Anita Hill by Senators during the controversial confirmation hearing of Clarence Thomas for the Supreme Court in 1991. "The Senate absolutely needed a healthy dose of democracy," she observed later, adding, "It wasn't enough to have millionaire white males over the age of 50 representing all the people in the country."[6] Officially entering the race for the Senate in November 1991, her Democratic primary campaign against the two-term incumbent Alan Dixon focused on his support of the Clarence Thomas appointment and the need for diversity in the Senate. Despite campaign organizational problems and paltry fundraising, Moseley-Braun stunned experts by defeating her two opponents, Dixon and Alfred Hofeld, an affluent Chicago lawyer, when she captured 38 percent of the primary vote.[7] Shortly after her surprise victory, Moseley-Braun remarked, "This democracy is alive and well, and ordinary people can have a voice with no money."[8] In the general election, she faced Republican candidate Richard Williamson, a lawyer and former official in the Ronald W. Reagan and George H.W. Bush administrations.[9] Focusing on a message of change and diversity encapsulated by slogans such as, "We don't need another arrogant rich guy in the Senate," Moseley-Braun ultimately defeated Williamson with 53 percent of the vote.[10] In the "Year of the Woman," Carol Moseley-Braun became a national symbol of change, reform, and equality. Soon after her

election to the Senate she commented that "my job is emphatically not to be a celebrity or a full time symbol. Symbols will not create jobs and economic growth. They do not do the hard work of solving the health care crisis. They will not save the children of our cities from drugs and guns and murder."[11]

In the Senate, Moseley-Braun became the first woman to serve on the powerful Finance Committee when a top-ranking Democrat, Tom Daschle of South Dakota, gave up his seat to create a spot for her. Moseley-Braun and Senator Dianne Feinstein of California also became just the second and third women to serve on the prestigious Senate Judiciary Committee. In addition, Moseley-Braun served on the Senate Banking, Housing, and Urban Affairs Committee and the Small Business Committee. In 1993, the Illinois Senator made headlines when she convinced the Senate Judiciary Committee not to renew a design patent for the United Daughters of the Confederacy (UDC) because it contained the Confederate flag; the UDC patent had been routinely renewed by the Senate for nearly a century. Despite the Judiciary Committee's dis-approval, the Senate was poised to pass a resolution sponsored by Senator Jesse Helms of North Carolina which included a provision to authorize continuation of the federal patent. Moseley-Braun threatened to filibuster the legislation "until this room freezes over." She also made an impassioned and eloquent plea to her colleagues about the symbolism of the Confederate flag, declaring that "it has no place in our modern times, place in this body, place in our society."[12] Swayed by Moseley-Braun's convincing argument, the Senate rejected the UDC patent renewal.[13]

Moseley-Braun sparred with Senator Helms once again when managing her first bill on the Senate Floor. As one of the cosponsors of a measure for federal fund-ing for the Martin Luther King, Jr. Holiday Commission —an organization established in 1984 to promote national recognition of the holiday—Moseley-Braun helped thwart a Helms amendment to the legislation that would replace government money with private donations. The Illinois Senator evoked personal memories of her participation in

a civil rights march with King in the 1960s in an attempt to win support for the legislation.[14] The Senate eventually approved the bill. Among her other social legislation tri-umphs, Moseley-Braun played a prominent role in the passage of the Child Support Orders Act, the 1994 William J. Clinton administration crime bill, the Multiethnic Placement Act, and the Improving America's School Act.[15]

During her one term in the Senate, Moseley-Braun addressed an array of issues affecting women and African Americans. She helped create legislation to assist divorced and widowed women, because according to the Illinois Senator, "Pension laws were never written for women . . . no wonder the vast majority of the elderly poor are women."[16] She also sponsored the creation of the Sacagawea coin to recognize "women of color" and a National Park Service initiative to fund historic preservation of the Underground Railroad.[17] A consistent supporter of equal opportunity and affirmative action, Moseley-Braun also spoke out against sexual harassment —as was evidenced by her decision to join five of her women colleagues in the Senate in 1995 to call for public hearings concerning the sexual misconduct allegations against Senator Bob Packwood of Oregon.[18]

Despite the high expectations following Moseley-Braun's upset victory in 1992, controversy marked her term in the Senate. Moseley-Braun drew criticism for alleged campaign finance violations which eventually led to a Federal Election Commission investigation.[19] In 1996, the Congressional Black Caucus and human rights organizations chastised Moseley-Braun for traveling to Nigeria to attend the funeral of the son of dictator, General Sani Abacha , a private trip made despite the objections of the State Department. Previously an out-spoken critic of human rights violations in the African nation, Moseley-Braun reversed her position and defended the Nigerian government.[20]

Under great scrutiny, Moseley-Braun faced a difficult challenge in her bid for re-election to the Senate in 1998, against Republican Peter Fitzgerald, an Illinois state senator.[21] She lost, capturing just 47 percent of the vote

against her Republican opponent, who spent nearly $12 million of his own money.[22] President Clinton appointed Moseley-Braun as the United States Ambassador to New Zealand, where she served from 1999 until 2001. Moseley-Braun unsuccessfully attempted to revive her political career when she entered the race for the Democratic nomination for President in 2000. The campaign marked the second time an African-American woman sought the nomination. Since 2001, Moseley-Braun has taught political science at Morris Brown College (Atlanta) and DePaul University (Chicago) and managed a business consulting company in Chicago.[23] In 2004, Moseley-Braun again made an unsuccessful bid for the Democratic presidential nomination.

FOR FURTHER READING

Biographical Directory of the United States Congress, "Carol Moseley-Braun," http://bioguide.congress.gov

D'Orio, Wayne. *Carol Moseley-Braun* (Philadelphia, PA: Chelsea House, 2003).

Moseley-Braun, Carol. *Shared Prosperity Through Partnership* (Washington, D.C.: Division of International Studies, Woodrow Wilson International Center for Scholars, 1996).

MANUSCRIPT COLLECTIONS

Chicago Historical Society (Chicago, IL). *Papers:* 1992–1999. Senatorial papers.

University of Oklahoma (Norman, OK), The Julian P. Kanter Commercial Archive, Department of Communication. *Video reels:* 1992, eight video reels. Includes nine commercials used during Carol Moseley-Braun's campaign for the 1992 U.S. senatorial election in Illinois, Democratic Party.

NOTES

1 Senator Moseley-Braun served with a hyphenated name during her U.S. Senate term. After she left Congress, she removed the hyphen. This essay reflects the hyphenation of her name at the time of her service.

2 *Current Biography, 1994* (New York: H.W. Wilson and Company, 1994): 378.

3 Steve Johnson, "Braun's Win Turns Around a Once-Stagnant Career," 4 November 1992, *Chicago Tribune*: 19.

4 Johnson, "Braun's Win Turns Around a Once-Stagnant Career"; Sarah Nordgren, "Carol Moseley-Braun: The Unique Candidate," 26 July 1992, Associated Press.

5 *Current Biography, 1994*: 379.

6 Ibid., 380.

7 Nordgren, "Carol Moseley-Braun: The Unique Candidate"; Frank James, "Welcome to the Club: Carol Moseley-Braun's Campaign for the Senate Was Her Own Excellent Adventure," 6 December 1992, *Chicago Tribune*: 14.

8 Lynn Sweet, "A Braun Upset; First Defeat for Dixon in 42 Years," 18 March 1992, *Chicago Sun-Times*: 1.

9 Edward Walsh, "Carol Braun's Rocky Road to History; After the Upset, It's Still a Long Way to the Senate," 28 April 1992, *Washington Post*: C1.

10 James, "Welcome to the Club"; Sharon Cohen, "Carol Moseley-Braun: From Face in the Crowd to National Spotlight," 4 November 1992, Associated Press; *Current Biography, 1994*: 381.

11 *Current Biography, 1994*: 378–379; Thomas Hardy, "Clinton Elected President: Carol Moseley-Braun Sweeps to Historic Senate Victory," 4 November 1992, *Chicago Tribune*: 1.

12 Helen Dewar, "Senate Bows to Braun on Symbol of Confederacy," 23 July 1993, *Washington Post*: A1.

13 Dewar, "Senate Bows to Braun on Symbol of Confederacy"; Steve Neal, "Moseley-Braun Record Is Inconsistent," 28 July 1993, *Chicago Sun-Times*: 31.

14 Mitchell Locin, "Moseley-Braun Tangles Anew With Helms," 25 May 1994, *Chicago Tribune*: 4.

15 *Current Biography, 1994*: 381.

16 Lynn Sweet, "Bill Seeks Fair Pension Shake for Women," 12 May 1996, *Chicago Sun-Times*: 28.

17 Alaina Sue Potrikus, "Braun Has Something to Prove in Her Bid for President," 14 January 2004, *Milwaukee Journal Sentinel*: 12A.

18 Dori Meinert and Toby Eckert, "Moseley-Braun Assailed for Backing Clinton," 27 February 1998, *State Journal-Register* (Springfield, IL): 11.

19 Darryl Fears, "On a Mission in a Political Second Act; Bush's Record Forced Her to Run, Braun Says," 13 July 2003, *Washington Post*: A6.

20 Fears, "On a Mission in a Political Second Act"; *Politics in America, 1998* (Washington, D.C.: Congressional Quarterly Inc., 1997): 441–442.

21 Nordgren, "Carol Moseley-Braun: The Unique Candidate"; Jennifer Loven, "Peter Fitzgerald: He's Heading for Capitol Hill but What Will He Do There?" 7 November 1998, Associated Press.

22 "Carol Moseley-Braun Says She Won't Run for Office Again," 5 November 1998, Associated Press.

23 "Ambassador Carol Moseley-Braun to Keynote SLDN National Dinner," 7 March 2005, *U.S. Newswire*.

Lynn Schenk

1945–

UNITED STATES REPRESENTATIVE ★ DEMOCRAT FROM CALIFORNIA
1993–1995

The daughter of working-class immigrants, Democrat Lynn Schenk won a hotly contested election in a majority Republican district to become the first woman to represent San Diego, California, in the U.S. House of Representatives. During her brief service, Schenk attempted to balance a policy of environmental protection, which she forged as a local politician with the business interests and booming biotechnical industry in her district. The Congresswoman eventually succumbed to the GOP resurgence in the 1994 election.

Lynn Schenk was born in the Bronx, New York, on January 5, 1945, to Hungarian immigrants. Her parents, Sidney and Elsa Schenk, survived the Nazi Holocaust and fled to the United States before 1945. She and her one brother, Fred, were raised in a working-class household; Sidney Schenk worked as a tailor, and Elsa Schenk was a manicurist. Lynn Schenk attended the Beth Jacobs School for Girls of the East Bronx. When she was 14, her family moved to California. In 1962, she graduated from Hamilton High School, in Los Angeles. Schenk earned a B.A. from the University of California at Los Angeles in 1967. Three years later, she received her J.D. from the University of San Diego Law School. Schenk confronted a male-dominated institution and, with the support of fellow female students, pressed the law school into building female restroom facilities in convenient locations. In 1970, she pursued postgraduate studies in international law at the London School of Economics. In 1972, Lynn Schenk married a University of San Diego law professor, C. Hugh Friedman, becoming the stepmother to his three children. Schenk became the deputy attorney general in the criminal division of the California attorney general's office.

From 1972 to 1976, she worked as an attorney for the San Diego Gas and Electric Company. She cofounded the Lawyers Club of San Diego, which supported female attorneys in 1972. Schenk also founded the first California bank owned and operated by women in 1973.

Schenk dove into politics when she received a prestigious position as a White House Fellow in 1976. She subsequently worked as a special assistant to Vice Presidents Nelson A. Rockefeller and Walter F. Mondale. The White House experience landed her a place in California Governor Jerry Brown's cabinet. She held the position of deputy secretary for the California department of business, transportation, and housing from 1977 until 1980. In 1980, Lynn Schenk became the first woman secretary of that department, serving for three years. After an unsuccessful campaign for San Diego County supervisor in 1984, she returned to private law practice. Schenk worked as the California co-chair for the presidential campaign of Michael Dukakis in 1988. From 1990 to 1993, she served as a commissioner and vice chair of the San Diego unified port district. In her role as commissioner she was responsible for overseeing San Diego Bay, where she spearheaded environmental protection programs.

Following California reapportionment in 1992, Schenk ran for a newly created U.S. House seat. The new district, which stretched along the coast from La Jolla to the Mexican border and encompassed downtown San Diego, retained some of retiring six-term Republican Representative Bill Lowery's constituency which had elected him for 12 years. Though the new district maintained its Republican majority, the new boundaries brought in more independent voters.[1] Schenk swept through the five-way Democratic primary with 53 percent

of the vote. She was one of 18 women among a record-breaking 35 female candidates to win a U.S. House primary in California.[2] She faced another woman in the general election: political novice and San Diego nurse Judy Jarvis. Despite her inexperience, Jarvis gained momentum with her upset victory in a crowded Republican primary; she took a 21 percent plurality against nine opponents.[3] Schenk was inspired by the sheer number of female candidates, "There's no question that, finally, being a woman [is] a positive rather than a negative in politics," she told the *Los Angeles Times*. "For decades, women had to be better just to get up to the starting line. But this year, the presumptions of confidence and effectiveness shifted to women."[4] The race between Jarvis and Schenk moved quickly into the spotlight as the two candidates battled to be the first woman to represent San Diego in Congress. Jarvis emphasized her role as a political outsider who was free from bureaucratic entanglements, arguing that Schenk saw Congress as "a position . . . for her resume."[5] Schenk pointed to her long record of public service, challenging her opponent to demonstrate a comparable record of commitment to the community. "[Jarvis] is trying to turn standing on the sidelines into a virtue," Schenk charged.[6] In her own defense, Schenk further emphasized her success as a women's rights activist as well as in her environmental pursuits as port commissioner. Schenk came out on top of the tight race with 51 percent to Jarvis's 43 percent. Two third-party candidates took an additional six percent.[7]

Upon her entrance in the 103rd Congress (1993–1995), Schenk's background in environmental protection won her seats on the Energy and Commerce and the Merchant Marine and Fisheries committees. Congresswoman Schenk focused much of her congressional career on balancing her interest in protecting the environment with tending to the business interests of her constituents. She supported strong enforcement of the Clean Air Act, pushed for greater pollution control, and supported establishing wildlife refuges in her district. However, she also supported business interests by encouraging development through tax incentives. She voted against the

North American Free Trade Agreement in an effort to maintain San Diego area jobs. In addition, she helped block part of President William J. Clinton's health care plan, which proposed creating an advisory council to regulate drug pricing and limit "price gouging" on prescription drugs. Many voters in Schenk's district, which boasted a growing biotechnical industry, opposed this policy.

In her bid for re-election, Schenk found herself among many nationwide incumbents in a close race to retain her seat. Most damaging to the Congresswoman's campaign was her vote in favor of President Clinton's five-year budget plan, which sought to lower the federal deficit by cutting spending and raising taxes for wealthy Americans. Schenk defended her vote as an act of solidarity with the Democratic President; however, many San Diego area residents were among those who saw increased taxes. The Clinton budget cost them an estimated $500 million dollars. Schenk's Republican opponent, former Imperial Beach mayor and San Diego County supervisor Brian Bilbray, capitalized on Schenk's unpopular position by running television ads highlighting her vote. "She came in on the Clinton tide and will go out with the Clinton tide," noted the challenger, using a metaphor familiar to oceanside San Diego residents.[8] Schenk spent much of the campaign on the defensive, attempting to distance herself from the President, pointing to her legislative achievements, and fighting a GOP tide that eventually produced a Republican majority for the first time in 40 years. Bilbray's similar strong stance on environmental issues diluted the incumbent's message. Schenk lost a close race by three percentage points, 49 to 46, with third party candidates splitting the remainder.[9]

Upon her departure from Washington, Lynn Schenk did not stray from the political arena. She eventually became the chief of staff to California Governor Gray Davis. In 1998, she made an unsuccessful bid for attorney general of California. After the campaign, she served as an educational advisor and on the board of directors for a California biotechnical company.

FOR FURTHER READING

Biographical Directory of the United States Congress, "Lynn Schenk," http://bioguide.congress.gov

MANUSCRIPT COLLECTIONS

University of Oklahoma (Norman, OK), The Julian P. Kanter Commercial Archive, Department of Communication. *Video reels:* four video reels. Includes four commercials used during Schenk's campaign for the 1984 county supervisor election in California, Democratic Party.

University of Southern California (Los Angeles, CA), Special Collections, Regional History Collection. *Papers:* ca. 1993–1999, 15 boxes. The papers of Lynn Schenk are currently unprocessed and may have restricted access.

NOTES

1   *Politics in America, 1994* (Washington, D.C.: Congressional Quarterly Inc., 1993): 244.
2   Judi Hasson, "Voters Debunk 'Myth' on Women," 4 June 1992, *USA Today*: 5A.
3   "California House: CA 49," 3 June 1992, *The Hotline*.
4   Barry M. Horstman, "San Diego County Elections; Women Flex Muscles in County Races," 4 June 1992, *Los Angeles Times*: B1.
5   Barry M. Horstman, "Style Eclipses Gender in 49th District," 11 October 1992, *Los Angeles Times*: B1.
6   Horstman, "Style Eclipses Gender in 49th District."
7   "Election Statistics, 1920 to Present," http://clerk.house.gov/members/electionInfo/index.html.
8   Bob Minzesheimer, "Challenger Rides Anti-Clinton Wave in California Race," 24 October 1994, *USA Today*: 9A.
9   "Election Statistics, 1920 to Present," http://clerk.house.gov/members/electionInfo/index.html.

Karen Shepherd

1940–

UNITED STATES REPRESENTATIVE ★ DEMOCRAT FROM UTAH
1993–1995

A successful businesswoman and Utah state legislator, Karen Shepherd won election to the U.S. House in 1992, the "Year of the Woman." Representing a competitive district with conservative leanings, Congresswoman Shepherd in her brief congressional career highlighted the promises and pitfalls of a period when power in the House was shifting from one political party to another.

Karen Shepherd was born in Silver City, New Mexico, on July 5, 1940. She grew up in several small towns in Utah before her family settled in Provo, where she attended high school. She graduated from the University of Utah with a B.A. in English in 1962 and, a year later, earned an M.A. in British literature from Brigham Young University (BYU). She also served as a staff assistant to Senator Frank E. Moss of Utah. From 1963 to 1975 she taught high school and collegiate English. She married Vincent Shepherd, and the couple lived in Cairo, Egypt, where she taught English and he wrote textbooks. After resettling in Utah, the couple raised two children, Heather and Dylan. Shepherd also managed a family-owned oil business. She served as the Salt Lake County director of social services and, in 1978, founded *Network Magazine*, which addressed women's issues. In 1988, she sold the magazine business and became director of development and community relations for the University of Utah's business school.

Karen Shepherd first ran for elective office in the fall of 1990, when she won a seat in the Utah state senate, where she served two years. When U.S. Representative Wayne Owens, a Democrat, announced he would not seek re-election to his Salt Lake City district, Shepherd won the party nomination to succeed the four-term incumbent.

Her platform supported abortion rights and a balanced budget amendment. She also envisioned an expanded role for the federal government in the areas of health care, education, and the environment. Shepherd developed a 10-point plan for improving children's lives that included measures to track down delinquent child support payers and to provide for full funding for Head Start programs.[1] In the general election, Shepherd faced Republican Enid Greene, an aide to Utah Governor Norman Bangerter. Greene was a fiscal and social conservative who opposed all of Shepherd's policy initiatives. The general election marked the first time in Utah history that the major parties pitted women candidates against one another. Shepherd narrowly edged out Greene with 50 percent of the vote to 47 percent, becoming only the second woman to represent the state in Congress.[2] It was a noteworthy win in a district that gave less than one-third of its vote to Democratic presidential candidate William J. Clinton (he received 25 percent statewide). From the outset, Shepherd's seat was politically vulnerable.

When Shepherd was sworn into Congress in January 1995, she received seats on the Natural Resources and the Public Works and Transportation committees. She voted for President Clinton's 1994 Crime Bill, the Brady Handgun Bill, requiring background checks and waiting periods for gun buyers, and the Clinton administration's 1993 budget package, which cut the budget and raised taxes. "It seems to me it's not perfect," Shepherd said of the proposed budget. "But the worst of all of the alternatives is not to pass it, and not move forward to health care, free trade and all of these other things we need to do."[3] The budget measure was especially unpopular in her district. With only a narrow margin of passage on the budget

bill, Shepherd's vote was especially important to Democratic House leaders, who chose her to help round up votes for the administration's anticipated health care plan. But she was barraged by phone calls and letters from unhappy constituents who opposed the 1.2 percent federal income tax increase and a hike in the federal gas tax contained in the budget. "Members feel isolated," she said at the time, summing up her situation and those of about a dozen other Democratic freshmen who were elected by slim majorities. "You have this sense when we go back to the districts of going to get beat up."[4]

Though a solid liberal vote, Shepherd also established herself as independent from the party leadership, becoming the first House Democrat to suggest that the President's and First Lady's Whitewater land deal be investigated by an independent prosecutor. "The public's concern with the President's business dealings has damaged his credibility and hampered his effectiveness," she wrote the U.S. Attorney General. She opposed congressional hearings, however.[5] Shepherd also co-chaired a panel of House freshmen for reform which suggested that gifts from lobbyists to lawmakers be banned and that Members be barred from chairing more than one committee. The House did not implement the majority of the recommendations, though her work as a reformer was hailed by one prominent political commentator as being in the tradition of progressive western politicians.[6]

In the 1994 general election, Shepherd again faced Enid Greene, who since had married and changed her surname to Waldholtz. In a campaign that centered on the federal tax increase and gun control, Shepherd promised to continue pushing for health care and welfare reform, as well as congressional reform. In one debate, she explained her support for gun control measures by noting, "We're awash in guns. I've talked to hundreds and hundreds of people and the people believe that if there are more and more guns out there, there is a better chance that someone out there holding a gun will shoot them."[7] But from the start—and based largely on her support for the 1993 Clinton budget and the 1994 assault weapons

ban—Shepherd was on the defensive. Running on the Republican "Contract With America," Waldholtz won handily in a three-way race with 46 percent of the vote to Shepherd's 36 percent; independent candidate Merrill Cook won 18 percent.[8]

After Congress, Shepherd was a Fellow at the Institute of Politics at Harvard's John F. Kennedy School of Government. In 1996, she was named executive director of the European Bank for Reconstruction Development, which steered loans to newly emergent democratic governments in Eastern Europe. Two years later, she chaired the East West Trade and Investment Forum of the American Chamber of Commerce. In 2000, Shepherd helped to found the Utah Women's Political Caucus, and she served as a member of the international delegation to monitor elections in the West Bank and Gaza.

FOR FURTHER READING

Biographical Directory of the United States Congress, "Karen Shepherd," http://bioguide.congress.gov

MANUSCRIPT COLLECTION

University of Utah (Salt Lake City, UT), Special Collections Department, J. Willard Marriott Library. *Papers:* 1992–1994, 10 linear feet. Congressional papers and correspondence, reflecting Shepherd's interests in congressional reform (five feet) and relating to the North American Free Trade Agreement, crime, welfare, theater missile defense, rocket motor programs, and some Utah issues, especially crime, welfare, and community development. Finding aid in repository and online. Restricted.

NOTES

1   *Politics in America, 1994* (Washington, D.C.: Congressional Quarterly Inc., 1993): 1548.
2   "Election Statistics, 1920 to Present," http://clerk.house.gov/members/ electionInfo/elections.html.
3   Kevin Merida, "For Some House Freshmen, Supporting Clinton Is a Balancing Act," 5 August 1993, *Washington Post*: A18.
4   Clifford Krauss, "Two Who Split on Clinton Budget Find Neither Won," 12 July 1993, *New York Times*: A15.
5   "Karen Shepherd," Associated Press Candidate Biographies, 1994.
6   Karen Foerstel, *Biographical Dictionary of Congressional Women* (Westport, CT: Greenwood Press, 1999): 248–249; E.J. Dionne, "A Winner Either Way," 11 October 1994, *Washington Post*: A17.
7   Tony Semerad, "Shepherd Vows She'll Keep Pushing Change if Re-Elected," 23 April 1994, *Salt Lake Tribune*: D3; Dan Harrie, "Shepherd, Waldholtz, Cook Come Out Firing on Gun-Control; Candidates Fire Salvos on Gun Control," 6 October 1994, *Salt Lake Tribune*: B1.
8   "Election Statistics, 1920 to Present," http://clerk.house.gov/members/ electionInfo/elections.html.

Karen L. Thurman

1951–

UNITED STATES REPRESENTATIVE ★ DEMOCRAT FROM FLORIDA

1993–2003

Karen L. Thurman, former teacher and Florida legislator, won election to Congress in 1992 and quickly came to focus on issues affecting seniors and military retirees in her northern Florida district. Reapportionment bookended her House career, providing her an opportunity to move into the national legislature but also making her vulnerable in an increasingly conservative district.

Karen Loveland was born on January 12, 1951, in Rapid City, South Dakota, daughter of Lee Searle Loveland and Donna Altfillisch Loveland. She received her A.A. degree from Santa Fe Community College in Stark, Florida, in 1970. In 1973, she earned a B.A. degree from the University of Florida in Gainesville, Florida. After graduation, she worked as a middle school math teacher. In 1973 Karen Loveland married John Patrick Thurman; the Thurmans raised two daughters, McLin and Liberty.

In the mid-1970s, Karen Thurman had her first experience with government and politics when she organized her students to protest the Dunnellon city council's proposal to close a public beach on the Withlacoochee River. After successfully opposing the closure, Thurman's students convinced her to run for the city council. She won her first election by five votes.[1] From 1974 to 1982 Karen Thurman served on the city council and, from 1979 to 1981, as mayor of Dunnellon. "I loved it from the beginning," she recalled. "It was wonderful getting to solve problems for people."[2] Her focus revolved around water usage and conservation. In 1982, Thurman was elected to the Florida state senate. Six years later, she became the first woman to chair the senate agriculture committee. She eventually chaired the committee on congressional reapportionment.

In 1992, following reapportionment of congressional seats, Thurman chose to run for Congress in a newly created U.S. House district that included the city of Gainesville and several counties on Florida's northern west coast. Thurman drew from her state senate seat constituency, which overlapped with a large portion of the new congressional district. In the Democratic primary, she rolled up 76 percent of the vote against Mario F. Rivera. In the three-way general election, she faced Republican Tom Hogan, a local prosecutor, whom she had defeated just two years earlier in a re-election campaign to the Florida senate, and independent candidate Cindy Munkittrick. Hogan ran on a platform that supported term limits, school vouchers, health maintenance organizations (HMOs), and tort reform to limit litigation for malpractice claims. Thurman highlighted her experience as a legislator and identified her central interest as health care reform. She also supported shrinking welfare entitlement programs, encouraging employers to offer flextime and parental leave to attend to family responsibilities, and women's reproductive rights. She energetically opposed the North American Free Trade Agreement (NAFTA), which she described as a threat to large agricultural areas of her district. "I think you stop promoting jobs going to other countries," Thurman said, when asked how she would revive a flagging national economy. NAFTA is "a devastating issue to Florida."[3] Thurman prevailed with 49 percent of the vote against Hogan's 43 percent; Munkittrick claimed seven percent of the vote.[4]

When she was sworn into the 103rd Congress (1993–1995), Representative Thurman had hoped to receive a seat on the powerful Ways and Means Committee but instead won assignments to the Agriculture Committee and the Government Operations

Committee (later named Government Reform and Oversight). In the 105th Congress (1997–1999), Thurman received a Ways and Means seat, which required that she relinquish her other committee posts.

Congresswoman Thurman was one of the important swing votes on the 1993 William J. Clinton administration budget, among a few dozen Democratic freshmen, moderates and others who had been in tight races, who were undecided when Congress began debating the bill. At one point, Ways and Means Committee Chairman Dan Rostenkowski of Illinois sidled up to Thurman to ask how she would vote on the measure. "This is not about you. This is not about the President. This is about the 600,000 people I represent," she replied. After requests and pleas from House leaders, fellow freshmen, and President Clinton, Thurman promised to support the plan. She explained to constituents that while it raised taxes, it also sought to reduce the deficit and encourage environmentally friendly energy sources and was better than a rival plan which would have hit seniors in her district with deep cuts in Medicare.[5]

Thurman also followed through on her promise to oppose NAFTA, organizing a Capitol Hill rally and working with fellow Democrats, including Majority Whip David Bonior of Michigan. She argued that the trade agreement would put local farmers, particularly the citrus and peanut growers who populated her district, at an extreme disadvantage against Mexican farmers. NAFTA passed the House in November 1993 by a margin of 234 to 200. "I don't know how many issues are out there that would bring people together at this kind of level," Thurman said. "It was an opportunity to . . . learn and to participate."[6] Thurman later voted against the General Agreement on Tariffs and Trade accord.

Thurman's middle-of-the-road vote reflected the composition of her district which, while majority Democratic, had conservative leanings. Thurman sided with the National Rifle Association in opposing two gun control bills put forward by the Clinton administration in her first term: the Brady Handgun Bill and the assault weapons ban (as well as the larger Clinton Crime Bill). She also

voted against lifting the ban on homosexuals in the military. Thurman joined with Florida freshman Republican John Mica to block a bill that would have given the Environmental Protection Agency Cabinet-level status. Though she ran as a pro-choice candidate and cosponsored the Freedom of Choice Act, Thurman also voted against a 1993 measure to provide federal funds for abortions, noting that she didn't "think government ought to get involved in the area of reproduction, and that includes financing." That position angered women's groups, though Thurman continued to walk a middle course on the issue, supporting a 1994 appeal from a group of lawmakers urging House leaders to include abortion and contraception coverage in a comprehensive health care bill.[7]

Nevertheless, in 1994, Thurman was one of 16 House freshmen targeted by the GOP in blistering radio advertisements for her vote in support of the 1993 Clinton budget. She faced Republican candidate "Big Daddy" Don Garlits, a former drag racer and a legend within the racing community but a campaigner who stumbled from one gaffe to the next. Garlits advocated "more medieval-style" prisons, declared the American Civil Liberties Union to be a "traitorous organization," suggested sending foreign refugees to Ellis Island to await transfer to Montana pending job openings, and advocated unfettered access to automatic weapons.[8] In a year when many Democrats succumbed to the GOP "Contract with America"—including many freshmen women Members —Thurman prevailed with 57 percent of the vote to Garlits's 43 percent. In her subsequent three re-election bids, she was not seriously challenged, winning more than 60 percent of the vote in each.[9]

Once re-elected to office, Thurman focused her efforts on meeting the needs of her district's large population of retirees and senior citizens: ensuring Social Security solvency and developing a comprehensive prescription drug program. Thurman voted to support reimportation of drugs from foreign countries to make them more affordable. She also supported legislation in the 106th Congress (1999–2001) that required pharmaceutical companies to provide seniors the same discount they awarded to sell

their products to HMOs and other large customers, a measure which could have saved 40 percent of the cost.[10] Veterans' issues received her attention, and she helped steer more than $350 million in funds into her state in the late 1990s, much of which benefited veterans by creating primary care clinics in areas where no Veterans' Administration hospital existed.[11] Her mission, she repeatedly told voters, was to curb deficit spending while protecting senior benefits. "I took that to heart," Thurman said. "I took some tough votes . . . and I am proud to have done it."[12] Thurman also supported most of the Clinton administration's lead on educational issues, backing nationalized testing standards and opposing private school vouchers. The House also passed a version of her bill to provide water-strapped Florida communities with $75 million to develop alternative water sources, including desalinized seawater.[13]

Over time, Thurman's district became increasingly conservative. In 2002, she faced a major redistricting challenge that carved out a heavily Democratic section of her district that included the University of Florida, and added more conservative areas with large retiree populations. Thurman also had to contend with a challenger who had name recognition: president *pro tempore* of the Florida senate Virginia "Ginny" Brown-Waite. With control of the House at a narrow six-seat GOP lead, the race was one of the more closely watched in the country. National GOP leaders made multiple campaign appearances with Brown-Waite; Thurman raised more than three times the money she had ever before poured into a race—$1.5 million to Brown-Waite's $800,000.[14] The heated campaign focused on federal aid and programs for seniors: Social Security, prescription drugs and Medicare, taxes, and veterans' services. Thurman touted her record on pushing issues important to seniors as a member of the influential Ways and Means Committee.[15] Brown-Waite prevailed, however, with a slim 3,500-vote margin, 48 percent to Thurman's 46 percent, with two other independent candidates splitting five percent of the vote. When Thurman's term expired in January 2003, she returned to Dunnellon.[16] Thurman later was elected chair of the Florida Democratic Party.

FOR FURTHER READING

Biographical Directory of the United States Congress, "Karen L. Thurman," http://bioguide.congress.gov

NOTES

1   Carrie Johnson, "Political Farewell Is Bittersweet," 29 December 2002, *St. Petersburg Times*: 1.

2   Johnson, "Political Farewell Is Bittersweet."

3   Collins Conner, "Three Candidates Offer a Choice of Solutions," 20 October 1992, *St. Petersburg Times*: 1; "The Race for U.S. House, District 5," 29 October 1992, *St. Petersburg Times*: 4X.

4   "Election Statistics, 1920 to Present," http://clerk.house.gov/members/electionInfo/elections.html.

5   David Dahl, "What Swayed Karen Thurman?" 28 May 1993, *St. Petersburg Times*: 3A.

6   Paul Kirby, "Congresswoman Thurman Pronounces First Year a Success," 17 December 1993, *States News Service*.

7   *Politics in America, 1996* (Washington, D.C.: Congressional Quarterly Inc., 1995): 287–288. See also, Johnson, "Political Farewell Is Bittersweet": 1.

8   William Booth, "High on Fuel, Low on Bull: Drag Racing Legend 'Big Daddy' Garlits Runs Full Bore for House Seat in Florida," 22 October 1994, *Washington Post*: A1.

9   "Election Statistics, 1920 to Present," http://clerk.house.gov/members/electionInfo/elections.html.

10 *Politics in America, 2002* (Washington, D.C.: Congressional Quarterly Inc., 2001): 218–219.

11 "Karen L. Thurman," Associated Press Candidate Biographies, 2000.

12 Jeffrey S. Solochek, "In Tight Race, Negativity Is Center Stage," 3 November 2002, *St. Petersburg Times*: 1.

13 *Politics in America, 2002*: 218–219.

14 Mitch Stacy, "Incumbent Thurman Vulnerable in Redrawn District," 22 October 2002, Associated Press.

15 Spring Hill, "Candidate's Husband Steals Signs," 12 October 2002, *Miami Herald*: B3; Jeffrey S. Solochek, "Brown-Waite Prevails," 6 November 2002, *St. Petersburg Times*: 1B.

16 Mike Wright, "Former U.S. Representative Shows Up in Candidate's Corner," 23 October 2004, *Citrus County Chronicle*, http://www.chronicleonline.com/articles/2004/10/24/news/news04.txt (accessed 24 October 2004).

Helen P. Chenoweth

1938–

UNITED STATES REPRESENTATIVE ★ REPUBLICAN FROM IDAHO

1995–2001

Elected during the "Republican Revolution" of 1994, Idaho Representative Helen P. Chenoweth[1] cast herself as a conservative populist and states' rights advocate by challenging everything from enhanced environmental regulations to affirmative action. Outspoken and, at times, controversial, "Congressman" Chenoweth, as she preferred to be called, focused on natural resource policy in western states.

Helen Palmer was born in Topeka, Kansas, on January 27, 1938, daughter of Dwight and Ardelle Palmer. After graduating from Grants Pass High School in Grants Pass, Oregon, she attended Whitworth College in Spokane, Washington, from 1955 until 1958. At Whitworth, Helen Palmer met and married Nick Chenoweth, and they raised two children, Margaret and Michael. The Chenoweths later divorced; Helen Chenoweth eventually married Wayne Hage. Several years after leaving college, Helen Chenoweth became self-employed as a medical and legal management consultant from 1964 to 1975. She managed a local medical center. She later entered politics, focusing on public affairs and policy. Her work as a lecturer at the University of Idaho School of Law and consultation experience landed her a position as the state executive director of the Idaho Republican Party, where she served from 1975 until 1977. From 1977 to 1978 she served as the chief of staff to Idaho Congressman Steve Symms. In 1978, Chenoweth and a business partner founded a lobbying group which handled issues related to natural resources, energy policy, environmental policy, government contracts, and political management.

In 1994 Chenoweth challenged two-term incumbent Democrat Larry LaRocco in an Idaho district that encompassed 19 counties along the state's western border,

including its northern panhandle. She campaigned with the promise that the state economy came above and before state wildlife and recreation. She vowed to fight the "War on the West"—the name she gave to federal policies in the 1990s which raised fees on commercial mining, logging, and grazing on federal property.[2] Her positions on sensitive environmental issues rankled activists. Chenoweth suggested that a state recreational area be used for metal mining, and later, in order to solve overpopulation of elk, proposed that a hunting season be opened in Yellowstone National Park.[3] During a radio debate, Chenoweth claimed that her anti-abortion position should not be a pivotal election issue since she viewed it as a matter to be decided in the individual states, not Congress. It "is a non-issue because *Roe vs. Wade* must be overturned in whole or part and the state must respond to the Supreme Court decision by altering the state code," Chenoweth said. "In Idaho, a woman has the legal right to have an abortion. That is already on the books. An alteration to that will come at the state, not the federal level." She also pledged herself to a three-term limit in Congress, a promise which she later fulfilled. LaRocco charged her with being a "stealth candidate" and evasive on critical issues because her positions were "extreme."[4] Nevertheless, Chenoweth prevailed by a 55-to-45 percent margin. She narrowly won re-election in 1996, surviving a challenge from Democrat Dan Williams with a 50-to-48 percent win, in which a third-party candidate contended. In her final re-election bid in 1998, Chenoweth again dispatched Williams with 55 percent of the vote.[5]

Once in Congress, it became apparent that Chenoweth was a radical even among her GOP freshman class of 73 revolutionaries. She insisted on being called "Congressman

Chenoweth," declared to the *New York Times* that affirmative action programs made white Anglo-Saxon men "an endangered species," and, after the federal government shutdown in late 1995, was one of just 15 Republicans who voted against reopening its operations (despite an appeal to vote for reopening from Speaker Newt Gingrich).[6] She was assigned to two committees as a freshman: Agriculture and Resources. In the 105th Congress (1997–1999), she added an assignment on Veterans' Affairs and, in the 106th Congress (1999–2001), also got a seat on Government Reform. In the 105th and 106th Congresses, Chenoweth chaired the Resources' Subcommittee on Forests and Forest Health.

True to her campaign promise, Chenoweth used her position on the Resources Committee to battle federal regulations over land use in Idaho. As a noted private property rights proponent, she took aim at the Endangered Species Act which, she argued, prevented property owners from fully utilizing their land. To curtail government interference in private life, she also advocated the dissolution of the Environmental Protection Agency and the Department of Energy (as well as the Education, Commerce, and Housing departments). "We want things to be the way they used to be," she told one interviewer.[7] In 1998, Chenoweth argued that national forest policy tilted too far in favor of conservation and, thus, jeopardized local economies like that in Idaho. "It baffles me why it is so trendy to oppose cutting trees," she added, vowing to fight a William J. Clinton administration plan to ban new logging access roads on federal land, "until hell freezes over, and then I will fight on the ice."[8]

Not surprisingly, Chenoweth became a lightening rod for environmentalists, holding events such as an "endangered salmon bake" in her district. At a 2000 conference at the University of Montana on western wildfires, a protester pelted Chenoweth in the head with a rotting salmon shouting "you are the greatest threat to the forest." Unruffled, Chenoweth brushed herself off, took to the podium, and quipped, "I would like to say that I find

it amusing that they used a salmon. I guess salmon must not be endangered anymore."[9]

Chenoweth consistently remained popular with her core constituents in Idaho—conservatives, states' rights advocates, and many of the states' citizen militia enclaves. An outspoken opponent of gun control, Chenoweth sought to rein in the power of law enforcement. Following the April 1995 bombing of the Murrah Federal Building in Oklahoma City, which killed 168 men, women, and children, Chenoweth condemned the bombers but not the militia groups to which they were linked. "While we can never condone this," she said, "we still must begin to look at the public policies that may be pushing people too far."[10] Inspired by a 1992 siege in Ruby Ridge, Idaho, in which Federal Bureau of Investigation agents shot and killed the wife and son of a federal fugitive, Chenoweth also introduced legislation in the House requiring federal authorities to secure state and local permission to conduct law enforcement operations in municipalities. Additionally, Representative Chenoweth called for the dissolution of the Bureau of Alcohol, Tobacco, and Firearms.

Helen Chenoweth honored the term limits pledge she made in her first House campaign by not seeking re-election in 2000. After she left Congress in January 2001, she returned to Boise and continued her work at her consulting firm.

FOR FURTHER READING

Biographical Directory of the United States Congress, "Helen Chenoweth-Hage," http://bioguide.congress.gov

"Helen Chenoweth," *In Profiles in Character: The Values That Made America* (Nashville: Thomas Nelson Publishers, 1996).

NOTES

1   This essay reflects Representative Chenoweth's name at the time of her first election and swearing-in. She subsequently hyphenated her name (Chenoweth-Hage) after her marriage to Wayne Hage.

2   Karen Foerstel, *Biographical Dictionary of Congressional Women* (Westport, CT: Greenwood Press, 1999): 53–54.

3   *Politics in America, 2000* (Washington, D.C.: Congressional Quarterly Inc., 1999): 414.

4   "LaRocco Hits Chenoweth on Abortion in New Radio Ads," 14 July 1994, *American Political Network*.

5   "Election Statistics, 1920 to Present," http://clerk.house.gov/members/electionInfo/elections.html.

6   Timothy Egan, "A New Populist: Idaho Freshman Embodies G.O.P.'s Hope and Fear in '96," 15 January 1996, *New York Times*: A1.

7   Eagan, "A New Populist."

8   *Politics in America, 2000*: 414.

9   "Something's Fishy: Protestor Pelts Congresswoman With Rotting Salmon," 17 September 2000, Associated Press.

10 Egan, "A New Populist"; Linda Killian, *The Freshmen: What Happened to the Republican Revolution?* (Boulder, CO: Westview Press, 1998): 18.

Karen McCarthy

1947–

UNITED STATES REPRESENTATIVE ★ DEMOCRAT FROM MISSOURI

1995–2005

An English teacher turned politician, Karen McCarthy became an influential Kansas state legislator before winning election as a U.S. Representative. Espousing a moderate political ideology, Congresswoman McCarthy focused on energy issues and the environment during her decade of service in the U.S. House of Representatives.

Karen McCarthy was born in Haverhill, Massachusetts, on March 18, 1947. As a teenager McCarthy moved to Kansas with her family. She graduated with a bachelor of science in English and biology from the University of Kansas in 1969. McCarthy became politically active in college after listening to Robert F. Kennedy make a speech on campus in 1968. "This was a man who spoke of peace and prosperity and empowerment for everyone," she recalled years later. "And that spoke to my heart. So I knew from that day forward I would work for him, and thus would be a Democrat."[1] In September 1969 she married civil rights attorney Arthur A. Benson II; they divorced in 1984. McCarthy taught English in public and private schools until 1976. She attended the University of Birmingham, England, in 1974 and received an M.A. in English from the University of Missouri, Kansas City, in 1976. In the fall of 1976, McCarthy won election to the Missouri house of representatives, a position she held until 1994. As a state representative, she chaired the ways and means committee for more than a decade. In 1984 McCarthy joined the Democratic platform committee and, in 1992, served as a delegate to the Democratic presidential convention. In 1994, she became the first woman president of the National Conference of State Legislators. During her tenure in the state house, she also worked as a financial analyst and consultant, earning an M.B.A. from

the University of Kansas in 1986.

In 1994, when incumbent Democratic Congressman Alan Wheat ran for the U.S. Senate, McCarthy entered the race for an open Kansas City-area House seat. In an 11-candidate Democratic primary, she won 41 percent of the vote. McCarthy faced a formidable opponent in the general election: Ron Freeman, an African-American Christian minister and former professional football player who ran on a platform that criticized unresponsive big government. McCarthy countered her opponent, arguing that "government does have a responsibility to see that each individual has opportunity. And sometimes people need boots in order to pull themselves up by those bootstraps. I see government's role as getting out of the way once that's accomplished."[2] While she supported a balanced budget amendment and a capital gains tax cut, McCarthy also advocated liberal social issues, favoring gun control and supporting abortion rights. In contrast to the GOP's "Contract with America," McCarthy offered her own "Contract with Jackson County Voters," a key constituency in her district. Her platform aimed at protecting Social Security and Medicare by opposing Republican initiatives for a flat tax rate. McCarthy defeated Freeman with 57 percent of the vote, despite a nationwide GOP surge, which put the Republican Party in the majority in the House of Representatives for the first time in 40 years. On her ability to overcome the rising GOP tide, McCarthy noted, "I think all politics is local and our message was . . . very clear about the value of my experience, my ability to get things done."[3] In her next four successful re-election campaigns, she was never seriously challenged, winning each with nearly 70 percent.[4]

After taking her seat in the 104th Congress

(1995–1997), McCarthy was assigned to three committees: Science, Small Business, and Transportation and Infrastructure. In the 105th Congress (1997–1999) she received a seat on the influential Commerce Committee (later renamed Energy and Commerce), which required her to give up her initial committee assignments. She served on Energy and Commerce for the remainder of her career. In the 108th Congress (2003–2005), she received an assignment to the newly created Select Committee on Homeland Security.

Throughout her House service, McCarthy identified herself as a "New Democrat," a moderate who supported some fiscally conservative policies such as the balanced budget, while opposing so-called unfunded mandates, which forced states to pay for federal regulations from their own budgets. Yet, she was a regular vote for such Democratic issues as a hike in the minimum wage, a patients' bill of rights, pro-choice initiatives, and gun control. "You can't make progress—if you are serious about making the world a better place—unless you can work at compromise and consensus building," McCarthy said. "You can't be an extreme anything and be successful. You must find that comfort zone in the middle."[5] One of her political role models was President Harry S. Truman, whose hometown, Independence, was in her district. She identified with the 33rd President because he "stood up for his beliefs and the idea that the buck stops here." She further noted, "I am a problem solver and I enjoy helping people solve problems."[6] True to her centrist ideology and pragmatic streak, McCarthy relished behind-the-scenes legislative work rather than appearing on the House Floor to join in sometimes sharp ideological debates.

McCarthy gained the legislative spotlight for her work on the environment, introduced from her Energy and Commerce Committee seat. Most notably, she attended the world summit on global warming in Kyoto, Japan, in 1997. The Kyoto Protocol, drafted by summit delegates, required nations to reduce carbon dioxide emissions to pre-1990 levels. McCarthy supported it, noting that the soy beans used to produce cleaner fuels were a major agricultural product in Missouri.[7] McCarthy promoted the use of these clean "biodiesel" fuels when she played an instrumental role in passing the Energy Conservation Reauthorization Act in 1998. She also played a major part in engineering a tax credit system in 1997 that was at the center of the "brown field" initiative, providing incentives for businesses which cleaned up polluted sites.

Kansas City's culture and history remained a priority for McCarthy throughout her five terms in the U.S. House. In her first term, she successfully teamed with local Kansas City politicians to create a bi-state cultural district that crossed the Kansas–Missouri border. The district levied a modest retail sales tax to support cultural events and to restore and maintain local historical landmarks. She led a call to renew the compact in 2000, also seeking federal grants to add to the tax revenue. In 2001, when major league baseball threatened to cut teams from the league to assuage their financial woes, McCarthy offered a resolution to share revenues between money-making teams and those losing revenue in smaller cities as an effort to save the Kansas City Royals franchise which was, at the time, unprofitable.[8]

McCarthy declined to run for re-election to the House for a sixth term, making her announcement in December 2003 following the revelation of alleged ethics violations and health issues. "I want to focus on balance in my life," she explained.[9]

FOR FURTHER READING

Biographical Directory of the United States Congress, "Karen McCarthy," http://bioguide.congress.gov

MANUSCRIPT COLLECTION

University of Oklahoma (Norman, OK), The Julian P. Kanter Political Commercial Archive, Department of Communication. *Video reels:* 1994, three video reels. Includes five commercials used during McCarthy's 1994 campaign for the U.S. Congress.

NOTES

1   Matt Campbell, "McCarthy Devoted to Public Service," 24 September 1994, *Kansas City Star*: C1.

2   Campbell, "McCarthy Devoted to Public Service."

3   Matt Campbell, "McCarthy Attributes Election Victory to Campaign Message," 10 November 1994, *Kansas City Star*: A19.

4   "Election Information, 1920 to Present," http://clerk.house.gov/members/electionInfo/index.html.

5   Campbell, "McCarthy Devoted to Public Service."

6   "Karen McCarthy," Associated Press Candidate Biographies, 1998.

7   *Politics in America, 2004* (Washington, D.C.: Congressional Quarterly Inc., 2003): 584–585; see also, "Karen McCarthy," Associated Press Candidate Biographies, 1998.

8   Kevin Murphy, "Baseball Must Cut Teams, Selig Tells Skeptical Lawyers," 7 December 2001, *The Kansas City Star*: A1; see the *Congressional Record*, House, 107th Cong., 1st sess. (20 December 2001): 10963.

9   Libby Quaid, "McCarthy Will Retire From Congress," 21 December 2003, Associated Press; Steve Kraske, "Congresswoman Considers Not Running for Re-Election," 6 December 2003, *Kansas City Star*: A1.

Lynn Nancy Rivers
1956–

UNITED STATES REPRESENTATIVE ★ DEMOCRAT FROM MICHIGAN
1995–2003

Lynn Nancy Rivers, entered politics as a "mom who got mad at the system."[1] As one of a handful of Democratic freshmen elected during the 1994 "Republican Revolution," Rivers championed the interests of her Michigan district, as well as lobbying regulations in Congress.

Lynn Rivers was born in Au Gres, Michigan, on December 19, 1956. Her father was a mailman, and her mother was a small business owner. The day after she graduated from Au Gres-Sims High School in 1975, she married Joe Rivers, who soon found work as a member of the United Autoworkers Union. The couple had two daughters, Brigitte and Jeanne; the Rivers later divorced. While working a series of low-paying jobs, Lynn Rivers put herself through college, graduating with a B.A. from the University of Michigan at Ann Arbor in 1987. In 1992, she earned her J.D. from Wayne State University in Detroit. While attending law school, Rivers served as a trustee of the Ann Arbor board of education, where she served from 1984 to 1992. In 1993, she was elected and served one term as a member of the Michigan state house of representatives.

When Ann Arbor Congressman William Ford, a Democrat, retired after the 103rd Congress (1993–1995), Lynn Rivers breezed through the Democratic primary in her bid to succeed the 15-term veteran and former chairman of the Post Office and Civil Service Committee and the Education and Labor Committee. In the general election she faced Republican John Schall, whose Harvard education and long service in the Ronald W. Reagan administration contrasted with Rivers's humble background.[2] Rivers ran on a platform identifying with Ann Arbor working-class voters as a former teenage mother

with an autoworker husband. "We went without health insurance when jobs didn't provide it. We were in the job market with not very salable skills. We had to get our education as adults and struggle through that," she noted, adding, "I think my experience has provided me with some real life understanding of the problems that are facing people."[3] Schall tried to paint Rivers as "a classic ultra-liberal," while emphasizing his more moderate political stance and goal to build business and high-tech jobs in the district.[4] In the late stages of the campaign, Rivers made a controversial disclosure, admitting her 20-year battle with bipolar depression. Though most politicians avoided discussing mental health problems for fear of drops in the polls, Rivers, who was on medication to control the disorder, accepted the risk. "It's very easy for Members of Congress to be advocates for mental-health treatment," she later admitted. "It's hard for Members of Congress to admit being consumers of mental-health treatment."[5] Voters were unfazed by Rivers's health problems. Despite a Republican sweep across the nation as well as GOP gains in traditionally Democratic Michigan, Rivers defeated Schall with 52 percent of the vote.[6] Congresswoman Rivers was re-elected to three succeeding Congresses, garnering between 57 and 64 percent of the vote.[7]

Rivers served as a freshman House Member in the 104th Congress (1995–1997), the first Congress in 40 years with a Republican majority. The change in party control was reflected in the fact that Rivers was one of just 13 Democrats in a new class of 73 Members. Her Democratic colleagues elected her as president of their class. Though she opposed partial-birth abortion, Rivers made it clear that the right to have an abortion was a

personal issue with her. "I look back at the difficulties we went through," she recalled of her years as a young mother. "I could never force that on somebody else."[8] The issue highlighted Rivers's toughness as a legislator and commanded the respect of her colleagues. In a 1995 debate on whether federal employees should have abortion coverage in their health plans, opponent Representative Henry Hyde of Illinois asked her to yield the floor. She quipped back, "I yield the gentleman the amount of time the gentleman yielded to me, which I think was about eight seconds."[9] Despite the tense debate, Hyde later observed, "She is smart and un-intimidated. [The debate] was spirited, but not mean-spirited."[10]

A member of the Science Committee for her entire career, Congresswoman Rivers also made her mark as a committed environmentalist. Among her more innovative pieces of legislation was a bill which required certain beverage bottles to carry a refund value of 10 cents. It further allowed states to cash in unclaimed refunds in order to fund pollution prevention and recycling programs.[11]

Rivers used her first term to highlight her adamant stance against accepting perks, gifts, and contributions from lobbyists. Rivers reasoned that "there's a familiarity that comes with a gift that makes people uncomfortable, a relationship between the lobbyist and the Member that Mr. and Mrs. Smith from the district would not have."[12] She suggested a "no-check zone" on the House Floor, preventing lobbyists from handing campaign checks to Members, as part of a Democratic campaign reform package in 1996.[13] She also came out against automatic pay raises for Members of Congress. Rivers sent her own pay raise back to the Treasury Department in April 1997. She also returned $600,000 from her office budget saved over her first three terms.[14] Rivers alluded to Edgar Allan Poe's "The Tell-Tale Heart," when discussing the controversial issue of campaign finance reform. No matter how hard the opposition fights it, "the heart of reform will keep on beating."[15]

Rivers was appointed to a prestigious position on the Budget Committee in her first term. She served on the committee's bipartisan Social Security Task Force in the 106th Congress (1999–2001) but soon concluded that the parties differed too widely to come to a consensus, charging that many of her colleagues on the task force were present merely to score points with voters.[16] She gave up the Budget Committee in the 107th Congress (2001–2003) in order to take a position on the Education and Workforce panel; the committee's jurisdiction covered two of Rivers's areas of personal interest. Citing her own experience of putting herself through school, she opposed a measure calling for interest on student loans to accrue at matriculation instead of at graduation. She chastised the bill's supporters, who had benefited from student loan assistance. "What hypocrisy," she declared, "I guess it is easy to pull up the ladder of success once you and your children are safely at the top."[17] Rivers also was a passionate protector of labor. Many of her constituents were autoworkers.[18] Rivers led several other Members from manufacturing districts in demanding investigations of the effect of the North American Free Trade Agreement, which opened domestic manufacturing trade restrictions between the United States and its North American neighbors. Rivers also fought a GOP proposal to allow companies to compensate employees who work overtime with extra time off rather than with extra pay. She cited employer pressure and discrimination against those who would choose pay over time off.

Well-respected in her party, Lynn Rivers was considered among the closest advisers to Minority Leader Richard Gephardt by the time she was elected to the 107th Congress (2001–2003).[19] Her favor with the leadership was not enough to carry her through a tough 2002 campaign, however, which pitted her against the dean of the House, Congressman John Dingell, Jr., when Michigan lost a congressional seat after the 2000 Census. Rivers declined to run in a newly reapportioned district, and instead chose to wage a Democratic primary battle against the 23-term incumbent, whose family had held a Michigan seat in Congress since 1933. Rivers began a fierce campaign, claiming that her opponent was too unfamiliar with the needs of her Ann Arbor constituents.[20] "Clout is a lovely thing, if you are using it for good," Representative

Rivers said.[21] She emphasized her humble roots and her frugal lifestyle, also noting that she could be counted on to represent her traditionally Democratic district with a solid liberal voting record. Dingell's favorable record on women's rights, including health care, equal pay, and other equity issues, appealed to women's groups and partly deprived Rivers of the support of one of her most powerful constituencies.[22] Michigan women and congressional colleagues were torn between the two candidates.[23] Dingell defeated Rivers with 59 percent of the vote. Afterwards Congresswoman Rivers returned to her Ann Arbor home. "I'm just going to have to wait and see what life serves up to me," she told supporters. "I've said repeatedly that you cannot have lived a life like mine without having an innate optimism and a belief that there are always second chances."[24]

FOR FURTHER READING

Biographical Directory of the United States Congress, "Lynn Nancy Rivers," http://bioguide.congress.gov

NOTES

1 *Politics in America, 2002* (Washington, D.C.: Congressional Quarterly Inc., 2001): 524.

2 David McHugh, "Candidates Offer a Clear Choice; She Persevered Against Adversity," 7 October 1994, *Detroit Free Press*: 1B.

3 McHugh, "Candidates Offer a Clear Choice; She Persevered Against Adversity."

4 Ibid.

5 Frank Rich, "The Last Taboo," 23 December 1997, *New York Times*: A19.

6 "8 Days Out, Roll Call's Guide to Races," 31 October 1994, *Roll Call.*

7 "Election Statistics, 1920 to Present," http://clerk.house.gov/members/electionInfo/elections.html.

8 McHugh, "Candidates Offer a Clear Choice; She Persevered Against Adversity."

9 *Congressional Record,* House, 105th Cong., 1st sess. (19 July 1955): 7194.

10 Doug Obey, "Rep. Rivers Runs Against GOP Tide," 26 July 1995, *The Hill.*

11 The measure, H.R. 845, was introduced early in the 107th Congress but never cleared the Science Committee; see *Congressional Record,* House, 107th Cong., 1st sess. (1 March 2001): 623.

12 Craig Karmin, "Chief Sponsor of Lobbying Gift Ban Legislation Defends Contribution Request to Lobbyists," 29 March 1995, *The Hill.*

13 Katherine Rizzo, "Democrats Turn Quiet When Asked About Handing Out Checks in the Capitol," 23 May 1996, Associated Press.

14 *Politics in America, 2002*: 525.

15 David E. Rosenbaum, "Capital Sketchbook; A Day of Debate and Forced Allusion," 15 September 1999, *New York Times*: A22.

16 *Politics in America, 2002*: 524.

17 Ibid.

18 McHugh, "Candidates Offer a Clear Choice; She Persevered Against Adversity."

19 Ethan Wallison, "Frustration Fuels Pelosi's Whip Bid; Women Aired Concerns During Gephardt Meeting," 14 October 1999, *Roll Call.*

20 Katharine Q. Seelye, "Dean of the House is Forced to Face Ex-Ally in Primary," 9 July 2002, *New York Times*: 16.

21 Seelye, "Dean of the House Is Forced to Face Ex-Ally in Primary."

22 Deb Price, "Dingell, Rivers Vie for Women," 7 April 2002, *The Detroit News*: 13A.

23 Price, "Dingell, Rivers Vie for Women."

24 Lauren W. Whittington, "Rivers Blames Auto Industry for Primary Defeat," 12 August 2002, *Roll Call*: 10.

Andrea Seastrand

1941–

UNITED STATES REPRESENTATIVE ★ REPUBLICAN FROM CALIFORNIA
1995–1997

A former state assemblywoman and GOP party member, Andrea Seastrand won election to Congress by riding the momentum of the Republican "Contract with America" in 1994. During her brief tenure, Representative Seastrand participated in the enactment of that agenda before losing re-election in a campaign that became a referendum on the Republican-controlled Congress.

Andrea Seastrand was born in Chicago, Illinois, on August 5, 1941. She graduated from DePaul University with a bachelor's degree in education in 1963. After college she moved to Salinas, California, and became an elementary school teacher. In 1965, she married Eric Seastrand, a stockbroker, and they raised two children: Kurt and Heidi. She left her teaching career to raise the children at home. Her husband, meanwhile, entered Republican politics and lost a 1978 bid for a U.S. House seat that encompassed portions of Los Angeles County and the cities of Burbank and Pasadena. In 1982 he was elected to the California assembly. During her husband's political career, Andrea Seastrand joined the California Federation of Republican Women and eventually served as its president. She also worked on the presidential campaigns of Barry Goldwater and Ronald Reagan. When Eric Seastrand died after a prolonged bout with cancer, Andrea Seastrand won election to the California assembly with 65 percent of the vote. As a member of the state legislature from 1990 to 1994, she served on the education committee and pushed for the creation of a commercial space port authority in California. Seastrand also served as one of three assistant Republican leaders, holding an organizational and managerial position with oversight of policy development.

In 1994, when California Republican Michael Huffington decided to forgo re-election to the House in order to run against incumbent U.S. Senator Dianne Feinstein, Seastrand entered the Republican primary to fill the vacant seat. The district, newly apportioned in the early 1990s, encompassed the cities of Santa Barbara, Santa Maria, and San Luis Obispo north of Los Angeles. In the GOP primary, Seastrand defeated Santa Barbara Supervisor Mike Stoker, 59 to 36 percent, running on the GOP "Contract with America." During the campaign, Seastrand declared, "I oppose higher taxes, period. Our national budget problems do not exist because we taxpayers send too little money to Washington, D.C. The problem is that politicians and special interest groups never run out of ways to spend our money."[1] As an advocate for smaller government and welfare reform, she maintained, "I believe our problems are generated in the federal government; it's a full-grown monster and we keep feeding it."[2] In the general election, Seastrand faced Walter Capps, a theology professor at the University of California at Santa Barbara and a political newcomer. Seastrand ran on a platform that opposed abortion, gun control, the provision of government aid and services to illegal immigrants, and extending certain rights and benefits, enjoyed by married couples, to homosexuals and domestic partners. In contrast, Capps supported these initiatives and he opposed the controversial Proposition 187 initiative, which would have banned education and welfare benefits to California's large illegal-immigrant community.[3] Seastrand carried the evenly divided district to defeat Capps, with a narrow 1,563-vote margin, 49.2 percent to 48.5 percent.

When Seastrand took her seat in the 104th Congress (1995–1997), she received assignments on the Science and the Transportation and Infrastructure committees. One of

her first actions in Congress was to cosponsor the Senior Citizens' Equity Act, an outgrowth of the "Contract with America," which proposed raising the Social Security earnings limit to $30,000, repealing a 1993 tax increase on retirees, and offering tax breaks to promote the purchase of private long-term care insurance. She described Democratic charges that GOP policies were detrimental to seniors as "absurd scare tactics."[4] During her term, Seastrand voted with the Republican majority on legislation to balance the budget, cut taxes, and dismantle the welfare system. In a symbolic move, Seastrand and other House freshmen ended the perk of daily free ice delivery to Members' offices, an expense-saving action which she portrayed as indicative of the GOP's commitment to shrink the size of the federal government.[5]

In her 1996 rematch against Capps, Seastrand embraced the notion that the campaign was a referendum on the accomplishments of the GOP Congress and the "Contract with America." Constituents were being asked to determine whether they were "to continue the philosophies of the 104th Congress, a new attitude of tightening the belt of Congress . . . or if we're going to go back to the 40 years of looking to the federal government as the source of all solutions."[6] Capps countered that "Seastrand got tricked. She went to Washington and listened to [Speaker Newt] Gingrich. She can't think independently. She does what he tells her to do. . . . I think she's a tragic figure." Seastrand bristled in reply, "to think that some 'man' in Washington was going to control my vote, that somehow I need a 'man' to give me marching orders" was insulting.[7] Capps benefited from discontent with the GOP agenda and incumbent President William J. Clinton's long coattails in the general election; Clinton carried California by 51 to 38 percent. Capps defeated Seastrand with a 10,000-vote margin, 48 percent to 44 percent.[8] When Capps died unexpectedly later that year, Seastrand ruled out running as the GOP candidate in the special election.

After Congress, Seastrand returned to California. In 1997, she became the founder and executive director of the California Space and Technology Alliance (CSTA). In April 2001, the CSTA became the California Space Authority, a group again headed by Seastrand that promoted the state's participation in commercial, civil, and national security space ventures.[9] Seastrand resides in Grover Beach, California.

FOR FURTHER READING

Biographical Directory of the United States Congress, "Andrea Seastrand," http://bioguide.congress.gov

MANUSCRIPT COLLECTION

University of Oklahoma (Norman, OK), The Julian P. Kanter Commercial Archive, Department of Communication. *Video reels:* 1994, three video reels. Includes nine commercials used during Seastrand's 1994 campaign for the U.S. Congress.

NOTES

1   "Andrea Seastrand," Associated Press Candidate Biographies, 1994.
2   "Profile, Andrea Seastrand," 27 June 1994, *California Journal Weekly*.
3   Bob Sipchen, "California Elections: 22nd Congressional District; Race Becomes Test of GOP's Ascension," 25 September 1996, *Los Angeles Times*: 3.
4   *Congressional Record*, House, 104th Cong., 1st sess. (27 January 1995): 200.
5   Karen Foerstel, *Biographical Dictionary of Congressional Women* (Westport, CT: Greenwood Press, 1999): 247–248.
6   Scott Lindlaw, "California Republican Campaigns on GOP's Agenda, But Not Gingrich's," 26 September 1996, Associated Press.
7   Dick Polman, "California Is Home to One of the Bitterest, Most Ideologically Polarized Congressional Contests," 24 October 1996, *Philadelphia Tribune*: A3; Matthew Rees, "By the Seastrand," 4 November 1996, *The Weekly Standard* 2 (no. 8): 17; see also, B. Drummond Ayers, Jr., "Gingrich Ally Under Siege at Home," 29 July 1996, *New York Times*: A10.
8   "Election Statistics, 1920 to Present," http://clerk.house.gov/members/electionInfo/elections.html.
9   See Seastrand's biographic profile on the California Space Authority's Web site, http://www.californiaspaceauthority.org/html/level-one/staff-bios/aseastrand.html (accessed 6 May 2005).

Linda Smith

1950–

UNITED STATES REPRESENTATIVE ★ REPUBLICAN FROM WASHINGTON
1995–1999

Casting herself as a populist politician, Linda Smith won election to two terms in Congress where she voted conservatively on social issues and repeatedly clashed with Republican leaders in her attempt to push gift bans, lobbying restrictions, and an overhaul of the campaign finance system. In 1998, Representative Smith chose to leave her House seat to challenge Senator Patty Murray for a seat in the U.S. Senate.

Linda Ann Simpson was born in LaJunta, Colorado, on July 16, 1950. She grew up in modest circumstances, and her biological father abandoned her and her mother, Delma Simpson. Her mother and stepfather eventually moved to Clark County in Washington state, where Linda was raised with four younger stepsiblings. Her stepfather worked as a mechanic and fruit picker to support the family. After her mother died, Linda often was left to run the household and worked part-time in an orchard and retirement home to make ends meet. "I felt like by 17, I had had more lives than most people," she recalled.[1] She graduated from Fort Vancouver High School in 1968 and married Vern Smith, a locomotive engineer, a few weeks shy of her 18th birthday. The couple raised two children, Sherri and Robert. Linda Smith worked as a district manager for seven tax preparation offices.

Smith considered herself a liberal Democrat until a large business tax hurt her enterprise. She then converted to conservative Republicanism. In 1983, she entered elective politics by defeating an appointed Democratic incumbent in a special election for a seat in the Washington state house of representatives. "I didn't have a clue what it would be like," Smith said. "All I knew was I wanted change. I didn't like what was happening. I certainly didn't understand the political system."[2] In 1986, Smith beat another

appointed Democrat to win election to the state senate—and swing it to GOP control. In the upper chamber, she successfully opposed the Children's Initiative, a tax hike earmarked for welfare programs and schools. She also carved out a reputation as a religious conservative who opposed gay rights and gay adoption laws. Unable to move campaign finance reform and tax relief through legislation, Smith sponsored two major ballot measures. In 1992, Initiative 134, which slashed campaign spending and amounts from big contributors, passed the Washington legislature. A year later, Initiative 601 passed, requiring voter approval for all tax increases. Smith considered the latter her greatest triumph.[3]

In September 1994, Smith made her first campaign for Congress, entering the race in early September for a southeastern Washington district that included the state capital, Olympia, and counties along the Pacific Ocean and, to the south, the Columbia River border with Oregon. Republican businessman Timothy Moyer initially challenged incumbent Democrat Jolene Unsoeld, but he dropped out in late August. Smith managed a write-in campaign with less than three weeks to go before the all-party primary—phoning 50,000 voters and mailing information to another 150,000 in an impressive grass-roots movement. She carried 29 percent of the vote (well ahead of the other GOP contenders), second behind the incumbent, Unsoeld, who carried just 40 percent. Smith became Washington's first candidate ever to win a congressional nomination as a write-in. In the general election Smith ran on her record as a ballot initiative specialist, and as an anti-abortion, tax reform, and campaign finance reform candidate. She had strong support from a network of followers drawn from the ranks of anti-environmentalists and the Christian right. In Unsoeld, she faced a leading Democratic feminist and

environmentalist. Unsoeld, a three-term incumbent, ran in opposition to gun control and to the North American Free Trade Agreement while trying to paint Smith as an extremist. But Smith's base, referred to sometimes as "Linda's Army," encompassed a variety of conservative-populists: anti-tax groups, government reformers, gun owners, and property rights advocates.[4] Unsoeld had been a GOP target for six years, since she had won the district narrowly in 1988. Against Smith, she was hurt by a third-party candidate, Caitlin Carlson, who siphoned off part of the gun-control vote. Smith prevailed with 52 percent to Unsoeld's 45 percent.[5]

When Smith took her seat in the 104th Congress (1995–1997), she received assignments on the Resources Committee and the Small Business Committee. She served in both capacities through the 105th Congress (1997–1999). During the 104th Congress she also chaired the Tax and Finance Subcommittee of the Small Business panel.

Upon arriving in Washington, D.C., Smith immediately set the tone for her tenure, telling a reporter, "This city is so awful. I can't wait to get back home."[6] She voted to support much of the "Contract with America" in an attempt to overhaul the scope and function of government. She was consistently rated one of the most conservative House Members in the 104th and 105th Congresses, voting against gun control and environmental legislation, perceiving the latter as a threat to property rights. She viewed homosexuality as a morally unfit "inclination" and also opposed using Medicaid to fund abortions for victims of rape and incest—telling *The New Republic* that "We don't kill children because the father is a jerk."[7]

But it was Smith's commitment to campaign finance reform which brought her national attention as a "rebel" among the GOP "revolutionaries" of 1994. It also brought her into open conflict with party leaders, whom she chastised for not carrying reforms far enough. During her first year in Congress, she insisted that House leaders had to overhaul the gifts-lobbying-campaign system to enact true reform. In a fall 1995 editorial piece in the *Washington Post,* she questioned how Congress could reform government without producing new laws to regulate itself: "You can't

perform surgery in a dirty operating room and with a team that hasn't scrubbed." Speaker Newt Gingrich of Georgia rebuked Smith for making her dissent public, eliciting a private letter from Smith to Gingrich (which also made its way into the public). "This institution, under your leadership, is truly on trial," she wrote.[8] After submitting her own plan for banning gifts and overhauling campaigns, she eventually backed the Shays–Meehan Campaign Finance Reform Bill. In an attempt to support that measure, Smith organized an unusual coalition of reform groups: the League of Women Voters, Ralph Nader's Public Citizen, and Common Cause. She also allied herself with Ross Perot, founder of United We Stand, and stressed her populist bona fides as she took on her party's leadership. "I am not Republican-hard core," she insisted. "I was not written in to come here and be part of this mess."[9] She seemed more comfortable with the reform mold. "I've always been a crusader," Smith said. "That's just been my nature from the time I was a little kid. I was going to change the world."[10] Appearing before the House Committee on Oversight, she declared, "A PAC ban is essential to stop the checkbook lobbying that goes on here."[11] As a result of her work, the 105th Congress adopted more stringent limits on gifts from lobbyists in November 1995.

In 1996, Smith faced Democrat Brian Baird, head of the department of psychology at Pacific Lutheran University, in the general election. Baird charged that Smith approved of slashing the Medicare budget and highlighted her support for the GOP "Contract with America." The Congresswoman stressed her independence: "Linda Smith is owned only by the people from the district."[12] On election night, Baird had racked up a 2,400-vote lead and was widely presumed to be the winner; however, a count of 40,000 absentee ballots gave Smith the election by 887 votes (50.2 percent to 49.8 percent).[13]

The razor-thin victory did little to deter Smith's attack on the institution and on GOP leaders. In January 1997, she voted against Gingrich as Speaker in favor of former Congressman Robert Walker of Pennsylvania. As a result, the leadership deprived her of her subcommittee chairmanship.

★ LINDA SMITH ★

She also was the only Republican to vote against an IRS reform bill in 1998, arguing that she could not support legislation which also slashed veterans' benefits by $10 billion. In addition, Smith rejected "most favored nation" trade relations with China because of that country's human rights violations, again parting company with the majority in her party.[14] Every year she was in office, from 1995 to 1998, Smith offered amendments to end tobacco subsidies, each time failing by a slender margin.

Several months into the 105th Congress Smith declared her intention to forgo a re-election bid to the House in favor of joining the 1998 Senate race against Democrat Patty Murray, then considered a vulnerable incumbent. Smith won the GOP nomination after an expensive contest against Seattle multimillionaire Chris Bayley, setting up just the third woman-versus-woman Senate race in U.S. history. Gender provided only a background issue, since both candidates were so distinctly split with Smith opposing nearly every issue that Murray embraced: affirmative action, tighter environmental restrictions, abortion rights, trade with China, and increased funding for the National Endowment for the Arts.[15] Combined, Murray and Smith spent more than $7 million, with Smith at a considerable disadvantage in the general election after emptying her coffers in the primary. Murray purchased large blocks of television time. She agreed to debate with Smith only once in a carefully choreographed campaign, leading to Smith's criticism that Democrats "hid" Murray from public view and the "people never got a campaign."[16] Murray won by the most lopsided margin of victory in a Washington Senate race since the days of Henry "Scoop" Jackson, taking 59 percent to Smith's 41 percent.

After Congress, Smith returned to Vancouver, Washington, where she started a nonprofit called Shared Hope International. Smith's group sought to buy women and children out of sex-slave status and end all forms of human trafficking. By early 2002, the organization operated 19 homes in India, Nepal, and Jamaica, accommodating up to 300 people.[17]

FOR FURTHER READING

Biographical Directory of the United States Congress, "Linda Smith," http://bioguide.congress.gov

"Linda Smith," in *Profiles in Character: The Values That Made America* (Nashville: Thomas Nelson Publishers, 1996).

NOTES

1   Gregg Zoroya, "A Rebel With Many Causes: Campaign Reform. A Ban on Gifts. Tightened Rules for Lobbyists. Conservative—Very Conservative—Rep. Linda Smith Is an Odd Amalgam of Energy and Extremism," 23 November 1995, *Los Angeles Times*: E1.
2   " Linda A. Smith," Associated Press Candidate Biographies, 1998.
3   *Almanac of American Politics, 1998* (Washington, D.C.: National Journal Inc., 1997): 1485–1487.
4   Eric Pryne, Jim Simon, and Robert T. Nelson, "Smith's Write-In Success Confounds Electoral Experts," 22 September 1994, *Seattle Times*: B1; Barbara A. Serrano, "Populist Opposites—Patty Murray: A Tightly Controlled Campaign—Linda Smith: Plays Up Image as Unapologetic Rebel," 25 October 1998, *Seattle Times*: A1.
5   "Election Statistics, 1920 to Present," http://clerk.house.gov/members/electionInfo/elections.html.
6   Robert T. Nelson, "U.S. House—Biggest Challenge to New Delegation: Coexistence," 9 November 1994, *Seattle Times*: B4.
7   Zoroya, "A Rebel With Many Causes."
8   Ibid.
9   Robert Novak, "Renegade From the Right; A Problem for Gingrich," 30 September 1995, *Buffalo News*: 3C.
10 "Linda A. Smith," Associated Press Candidate Biographies, 1998.
11 "Prepared Testimony of Congresswoman Linda Smith Before the House Committee on Oversight Hearing on Legislation Concerning the Role of Political Action Committees in Federal Elections," 2 November 1995, *Federal News Service*; see also, Christopher Hansen, "Smith Attacks Plan for Campaign Finance Reform Commission," 3 November 1995, *Seattle Post-Intelligencer*: A1.
12 *Almanac of American Politics, 1998*: 1485–1487.
13 "Election Statistics, 1920 to Present," http://clerk.house.gov/members/electionInfo/elections.html.
14 Serrano, "Populist Opposites."
15 See, for example, two articles by Sam Howe Verhovek: "Year of the Woman in Washington State: Women Will Go Head to Head in Race for a U.S. Senate Seat," 17 September 1998, *New York Times*: A14; quote from "Democrat or Republican, Woman Will Be Winner," 26 October 1998, *New York Times*: A18.
16 Gregg Harrington, "Q&A with Linda Smith: Where Was Patty Murray? Hiding, Says Linda Smith," 8 November 1998, *The Columbian*: A1.
17 David Ammons, "Linda Smith: Finding a New Crusade After Politics," 2 February 2002, Associated Press.

Enid Greene Waldholtz
1958–

UNITED STATES REPRESENTATIVE ★ REPUBLICAN FROM UTAH
1995–1997

Enid Greene Waldholtz,[1] a rising star in the Utah Republican Party, made her mark quickly in the U.S. House, earning a seat on the prestigious Rules Committee as a freshman and becoming only the second Member of Congress to become a mother while serving.

Enid Greene was born in San Rafael, California, on June 5, 1958, the middle child in a family of five siblings. Her father, Forrest Greene, was a San Francisco stockbroker who held a seat on the Pacific Stock Exchange for four decades. The family moved to Salt Lake City, Utah, and lived in an affluent neighborhood known as "the avenues." Enid Greene graduated *cum laude* from the University of Utah in 1980 and earned a J.D. from Brigham Young University in 1983. After school she worked as a litigator for a law firm. From 1990 to 1992, she served as deputy chief of staff to Utah Governor Norman Bangerter, leaving that position to make a competitive but unsuccessful run for a congressional district that encompassed Salt Lake City and its suburbs against Democrat Karen Shepherd. Greene lost by 51 to 47 percent. Greene then became a corporate counsel for a major high-technology company based in Provo, Utah. In August 1993, she married Republican consultant Joe Waldholtz in a ceremony presided over by Utah Governor Michael O. Leavitt. Meanwhile, Waldholtz, whom the Salt Lake media had dubbed the "Mormon Maggie Thatcher," was preparing to run again for the Salt Lake City seat in the U. S. House.[2]

In 1994, Waldholtz challenged the incumbent Karen Shepherd in the general election. She ran on a platform that mirrored much of the Republican "Contract with America": stressing her conservative and family values, supporting anti-abortion measures, and calling for wel-

fare reform and budget reductions. Joe Waldholtz joined the campaign as its treasurer. Enid Waldholtz trailed for much of the race, which also included an independent challenger, Merrill Cook. A late infusion of more than $1.5 million, which she claimed as personal and family money, helped her erase a polling deficit through huge direct-mailing efforts and large blocks of television advertising. On election day, in the most expensive House race in the nation, Enid Waldholtz handily defeated Shepherd by 46 to 34 percent of the vote; Cook finished with 18 percent.[3]

When Waldholtz took her seat in the 104th Congress (1995–1997), her notoriety in Utah and political contacts in the House (most notably Speaker Newt Gingrich) helped her gain a seat on the powerful Rules Committee, a virtually unheard of assignment for a freshman Member. By one estimate, she was the first Republican freshman since the 1920s to land an assignment on the committee which controlled the flow of legislation to the House Floor. She also made history in March 1995 after announcing that she was pregnant. Republicans threw her a surprise baby shower in the Speaker's office. In late August 1995, Waldholtz gave birth to a daughter named Elizabeth, becoming the first Republican Congresswoman to become a mother while serving in Congress; Democrat Yvonne Brathwaite Burke gave birth to a daughter, Autumn, in November 1973.[4]

True to her campaign platform, Waldholtz supported the "Contract with America." She took to the House Floor to oppose an amendment to an appropriations bill which would have prevented states from refusing to allocate Medicaid funding for abortions in cases of rape and incest. While she did not believe that women should

ENID WALDHOLTZ MADE HISTORY
IN MARCH 1995 AFTER
ANNOUNCING THAT SHE WAS
PREGNANT. REPUBLICANS THREW
HER A SURPRISE BABY SHOWER
IN THE SPEAKER'S OFFICE.
IN LATE AUGUST 1995, SHE GAVE
BIRTH TO A DAUGHTER
NAMED ELIZABETH.

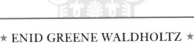
"be forced to base their decision on their ability to pay," Waldholtz believed that the "use of state funds should be left to the state governments."[5] She defended a constitutional amendment to prevent flag desecration; an outcome that she said had "no alternative" since the Supreme Court had overturned flag protection statutes as infringements of free speech.[6]

Just 10 months into her term, Congresswoman Waldholtz faced a political firestorm. In November 1995, Joe Waldholtz, under federal investigation for improperly filed campaign reports, disappeared for more than a week. Officials soon apprehended him, charging that he had embezzled millions from his father-in-law, Forrest Greene, about $2 million of which was funneled into Enid Waldholtz's 1994 campaign in the form of hundreds of faked donations.[7] Congresswoman Waldholtz held a five-hour press conference, apologizing to constituents and detailing how her husband had constructed the elaborate scheme without her knowledge.[8] The negative publicity, however, convinced her to forgo a re-election bid. She told the press that she had "made some terrible mistakes of misplaced trust, for which I take responsibility" but, she maintained, that she was "absolutely innocent of any intentional wrongdoing."[9] Representative Waldholtz filed for divorce and changed her name back to Greene. In June 1996, Joe Waldholtz pleaded guilty to bank fraud and falsifying campaign spending reports and was sentenced to two years in jail. The Justice Department cleared Enid Greene of any wrongdoing. Greene returned with her daughter to Salt Lake City where, in 1998, she joined a local law firm.

FOR FURTHER READING

Benson, Lee. *Blind Trust: The True Story of Enid Greene and Joe Waldholtz* (Salt Lake City, UT: Agreka Books, 1997).

Biographical Directory of the United States Congress, "Enid Greene Waldholtz," http://bioguide.congress.gov

NOTES

1   This essay reflects the Congresswoman's name at the time of her election and swearing-in. Midway through the 104th Congress, Waldholtz changed her name back to her maiden name, Greene.

2   James Brooke, "Congresswoman Faces Increasing Skepticism," 22 January 1996, *New York Times*: A10.

3   *Politics in America, 1996* (Washington, D.C.: Congressional Quarterly Inc., 1995): 1338; "Election Statistics, 1920 to Present," http://clerk.house.gov/members/electionInfo/elections.html.

4   Elaine Louie, "Chronicle," 2 September 1995, *Washington Post*: 22.

5   *Congressional Record*, House, 104th Cong., 1st sess. (4 August 1995): 1641.

6   *Congressional Record*, House, 104th Cong., 1st sess. (30 June 1995): 1388.

7   Ruth Marcus and Walter Pincus, "Enid Waldholtz: Savvy Politician or Duped Wife? Utah Congresswoman Faces Skepticism in Funding Probe," 26 November 1995, *Washington Post*: A1; Tamara Jones, "When Enid Met Joe ... After the Honeymoon and the Election, the Waldholtz's Moved Into a House of Cards," 18 November 1995, *Washington Post*: C1.

8   Tom Kenworthy, "Rep. Waldholtz Says Her Husband Duped Her; In 5-Hour Session, Utah Lawmaker Tells of Embezzlement, Fraud, Election Law Violations," 12 December 1995, *Washington Post*: A1; Walter Pincus and Ruth Marcus, "Waldholtz Campaign Illustrates Critical Role of Money," 24 December 1995, *Washington Post*: A6.

9   Walter Pincus and Ruth Marcus, "Rep. Waldholtz Won't Seek Reelection; Utah Republican Cites Investigation into Personal, 1994 Campaign Finance," 6 March 1996, *Washington Post*: A3.

Sheila Frahm

1945–

UNITED STATES SENATOR ★ REPUBLICAN FROM KANSAS
1996

An accomplished Kansas legislator, Sheila Frahm was appointed to the U.S. Senate to fill the vacancy created when Majority Leader Robert Dole resigned his seat to run for the presidency in 1996. Frahm, who had worked her way up from local politics to the Kansas lieutenant governorship, served just five months after failing to win renomination to fill the remaining two years of the unexpired term.

She was born Sheila Sloan in Colby, Kansas, on March 22, 1945. She received a B.S. degree from Fort Hays State University in 1967 and also attended the University of Texas at Austin. Sheila Sloan married Kenneth Frahm, and the couple had three daughters. Sheila Frahm embarked on a long career in public service with an emphasis on education. She chaired the Colby (Kansas) public schools board of education and the northwest Kansas educational service center board of education. In 1985, Frahm was appointed to the Kansas board of education. Re-elected in 1986, she became vice chair in 1987. She was elected to the Kansas state senate in 1988, serving from 1989 to 1994, and becoming the first woman to achieve the rank of Kansas senate majority leader. Frahm was elected the first woman lieutenant governor of Kansas in 1994 and was appointed the Kansas secretary of administration in 1995.[1]

On May 24, 1996, Kansas Governor Bill Graves appointed Frahm to the U.S. Senate as a Republican to fill the vacancy created by the resignation of Robert Dole, who had secured the GOP nomination for President during the spring primaries. Graves praised Frahm's "years of community and legislative experience." Frahm pledged "my heart and soul to the people of my beloved Kansas."[2] Senator Frahm was sworn in on June 1, 1996, and was

assigned to the Committee on Armed Services and the Committee on Banking, Housing, and Urban Affairs. The appointment made Kansas the second state to have two women serving simultaneously as U.S. Senators, as Frahm joined longtime Senator Nancy Kassebaum.

Frahm worked on a variety of legislation during her brief tenure, helping pass bills on workplace, health care, and immigration reforms. During her inaugural speech in the Senate, Frahm voiced her support for election finance reform but rejected a proposal to create a program to finance campaigns with federal funds. "Bad reform is not better than no reform," Frahm said on the Senate Floor. "I oppose federal financing of our elections, which would in effect turn our politicians into a new class of welfare dependents. I came here to reform welfare, not to expand it. I question why the Congress should seek to pass a bill that is almost certainly unconstitutional in many of its key reforms, and puts an unreasonable mandate of high costs on private business."[3] Shortly before the end of her term, Frahm managed to steer through the Senate a bill to designate national historic site status to Nicodemus, Kansas. Nicodemus, which was located in Frahm's former Kansas Senate district, was a settlement founded by African Americans in the 1870s as they moved west in pursuit of better livelihoods. By adding her bill to a larger omnibus parks bill, Frahm ensured historic status for the site, a move which historic preservationists believed would help them raise enough money to save it.[4] Frahm also embraced a pro-choice position on the abortion issue, which was a polarizing one within the Kansas Republican Party.

In the August 6 GOP primary, Frahm faced freshman Representative Sam Brownback, an anti-abortion conservative with a large network of pro-life supporters.

Frahm supported campaign finance reform but opposed federal financing of campaigns. "Bad reform is not better than no reform," Frahm said on the Senate Floor. "I oppose federal financing of our elections, which would in effect turn our politicians into a new class of welfare dependents."

Though she received the backing of Governor Graves and Senator Kassebaum, Frahm lost to Brownback by a wide margin.[5] Her term of service ended in the Senate on November 5, 1996. Frahm returned to Colby, Kansas, where she and her husband managed corn and wheat production in several nearby counties. In 2002, Frahm served as the executive director for the Kansas Association of Community College Trustees, which represented all 19 state community colleges.

FOR FURTHER READING

Biographical Directory of the United States Congress, "Sheila Frahm," http://bioguide.congress.gov

NOTES

1   *Congressional Record,* Senate 104th Cong., 2nd sess. (30 October 1996): 12275.

2   Dirk Johnson, "Moderate Chosen to Fill Dole's Seat," 25 May 1996, *New York Times*: A9.

3   *Congressional Record,* Senate, 104th Cong., 2nd sess. (28 June 1996): 7291.

4   *Congressional Record,* Senate, 104th Cong., 2nd sess. (21 October 1996): 12464.

5   "A Senate Primary Mirrors G.O.P. Split," 1 August 1996, *New York Times*: A16; "Abortion Foes Win Senate Primaries in 3 States," 7 August 1996, *New York Times*: A13.

Jean Carnahan

1933–

UNITED STATES SENATOR ★ DEMOCRAT FROM MISSOURI

2001–2002

Jean Carnahan, the former first lady of Missouri, was appointed to the United States Senate to fill the vacant seat from Missouri caused by the death of her husband of 46 years, Governor Mel E. Carnahan. Elected to Congress three weeks after his death in a plane crash, Mel Carnahan became the first U.S. Senator elected posthumously. Despite having never held public office, Jean Carnahan earned the distinction of being the first woman Senator from Missouri.

Jean Carpenter was born on December 20, 1933, in Washington D.C. The daughter of Reginald Carpenter, a plumber, and Alvina Carpenter, a hairdresser, Jean was just 15 when she met her future husband, Mel Carnahan, the son of Missouri Congressman Albert Carnahan. Both Mel and Jean attended Anacostia High School in Washington, D.C., where they sat next to each other in class.[1] In 1951, Jean became the first in her family to graduate from high school. Two years later, Mel and Jean married upon Mel's graduation from college. Jean soon followed suit, earning a B.A. in business and public administration from George Washington University in 1955. The couple went on to have four children: Roger, Russ, Robin, and Tom. In addition to her responsibilities as a homemaker and mother, Jean Carnahan was a public speaker and an author. She also played an active role in her husband's numerous political campaigns for state office, writing speeches and creating an extensive card-catalogued database of potential supporters and donors.[2] When Mel Carnahan became governor of Missouri in 1993, his wife flourished in her role as first lady. Interested in addressing the needs of children, Jean Carnahan helped to implement mandatory child immunization, organized projects to promote children's

increased exposure to culture and art, and cofounded Children in the Workplace to create childcare for working parents at their place of employment.[3]

During his second term as Missouri governor, Mel Carnahan decided to challenge Republican incumbent John Ashcroft for his seat in the U.S. Senate. On October 16, 2000, Carnahan, his son Roger, and a legislative aide perished when their private plane crashed en route to a campaign rally in New Madrid, a town about 150 miles south of St. Louis.[4] Despite the governor's death, his name remained on the ballot due to Missouri state law that prohibited any changes within a month of the election date.[5] Out of respect for his former opponent and his family, Ashcroft ceased his campaign efforts for 10 days after the tragedy. Political observers assumed Ashcroft would win by default; however, momentum shifted to the Democratic candidate in the days preceding the general election. "Don't let the fire go out," became the rallying cry for Missouri voters, who grew even more enthused about Carnahan's candidacy once his widow Jean made it known that she would accept an appointment to take his place in the Senate.[6] Still reeling from the death of her husband and son, Jean Carnahan recalled her reaction when Missouri's new governor, Roger Wilson, approached her with the prospect of serving in Congress. "I almost felt as if my world had come to an end," she said. "But I didn't want all the things that Mel stood for, that we had worked together for, I didn't want those things to die. I didn't want to feel like I was letting myself down or him down. And the people of Missouri wanted something to survive the plane crash, as well."[7]

In the November election Mel Carnahan posthumously defeated incumbent Senator John Ashcroft by 48,960

votes out of a total of about 2.4 million cast. Elated with the victory, Jean Carnahan vowed that "we will never let the fire go out"—a tribute to her late husband's political legacy.[8] Appointed for two years to the U.S. Senate to fill the vacancy, Jean Carnahan was sworn in on January 3, 2001, taking the Senate seat once held by Harry S. Truman.

In the Senate, Carnahan served on several committees: Armed Services; Small Business and Entrepreneurship; Governmental Affairs; Commerce, Science, and Transportation; and the Special Committee on Aging. Admitting that her jump to the Senate was overwhelming at times, Carnahan observed, "I've learned a lot. I'm not so lost anymore. But there's a lot I've still got to learn. Some issues I can't talk to you about yet because I don't know them yet. But I'm learning. I'm learning. And I'm enjoying myself."[9] During her first few months in Congress, Carnahan, viewed as a courageous widow, attracted attention from strangers and colleagues alike. She recollected that on one occasion, Senator Edward Kennedy of Massachusetts gave her a copy of John F. Kennedy's book *Profiles in Courage* with the inscription, "To Jean Carnahan, who has written some profiles in courage herself."[10]

Building on her experience as first lady of Missouri, Carnahan sought to continue the legislative interests she shared with her late husband, most especially with respect to furthering opportunities for children. The first legislation she introduced in the Senate was a measure to increase funding in public schools to help reduce class sizes, hire additional teachers, and build or renovate classrooms. In a speech on the Senate Floor, Carnahan called the education of children, "an issue that is close to my heart and one that is essential to our nation's future." She also explained that her desire to improve American schools derived in part from her husband's dedication to the issue and their shared belief that local schools should be given more flexibility on how to spend federal money to improve education.[11] In May 2001, Carnahan achieved an early legislative victory when her bill passed the Senate as an amendment to an education reform measure.[12] During her short tenure in

the Senate, Carnahan also worked to provide federal workers with greater access to child care services, another carryover from her time as Missouri's first lady.

As a Senator, Carnahan emphasized her moderate stance on the issues and desire to work with colleagues on both sides of the aisle. In 2001, she was one of 12 Democratic Senators to back President George W. Bush's tax cut. Although she voted in favor of the program, she later commented, "The bill passed by the Senate is far from ideal, however. In particular, I would have liked to have seen a greater portion of its benefits go to middle-income working class families."[13] Carnahan also worked to find common ground with fellow Missouri Senator Republican Christopher (Kit) Bond. Both supported a bill to provide assistance for farmers, and the two Senators worked to protect the jobs of more than 10,000 Trans World Airlines (TWA) employees in Missouri when the airline merged with American Airlines; on the latter issue, however, Carnahan received criticism from Republicans and some TWA officials for taking too much credit.[14]

A year after her appointment to the Senate, Carnahan announced her decision to run in the November 2002 special election to complete the six-year term. During her first year on the Hill, GOP leaders from Missouri avoided overt criticism of Carnahan, even when angered by actions such as her vote against John Ashcroft's appointment for U.S. Attorney General, a decision Carnahan classified "a vote of conscience."[15] Still wary of a potential backlash resulting from the perception of attacking a grieving widow, Republicans focused on Carnahan's lack of experience when she entered the senatorial election. The closely contested race between Carnahan and her Republican opponent, former U.S. Representative Jim Talent, attracted national attention from both parties. During the campaign, Carnahan attempted to distance herself from her husband's accident and instead highlighted her accomplishments in the Senate.[16] Ultimately defeated in a close race in which she earned 48 percent of the vote, Carnahan told her supporters after conceding to Talent, "Ours is a cause that has not been lessened by

defeat. Others will come to pick up the fallen torch."[17]

Since leaving Congress, Carnahan has remained active in Democratic politics, in particular promoting the candidacy of women. She also has devoted herself to her children's political futures. In 2004 her son Russ won election to the U.S. House of Representatives from a Missouri district.

FOR FURTHER READING

Biographical Directory of the United States Congress, "Jean Carnahan," http://bioguide.congress.gov

Carnahan, Jean. *Christmas at the Mansion: Its Memories and Menus* (Jefferson City, MO: MMPI, 1999).

———. *Don't Let the Fire Go Out!* (Columbia, MO: University of Missouri Press, 2004).

———. *If Walls Could Talk: The Story of Missouri's First Families* (Jefferson City, MO: MMPI, 1998).

MANUSCRIPT COLLECTION

University of Missouri (Columbia, MO). Western Historical Manuscript Collections. *Papers:* Senatorial papers.

NOTES

1   Jean Carnahan, *Don't Let the Fire Go Out!* (Columbia, MO: University of Missouri Press, 2004): 85, 88.
2   Lois Romano, "Late Governor's Name Holds Sway in Mo. Election; Senator Carnahan, Challenger Seek To Run on Own Records," 22 July 2002, *Washington Post*: A01.
3   "Official Biography of Senator Carnahan," http://carnahan.senate.gov/Bio.html (accessed 21 November 2001).
4   "Missouri Governor, 2 Others Reported Dead in Plane Crash," 17 October 2000, *New York Times*: A1.
5   James Dao, "Senate Candidate's Death Hurts Democrats' Chances," 18 October 2000, *New York Times*: A21.
6   Neil A. Lewis, "In Missouri, Campaign Flourishes After the Death of the Candidate," 31 October 2000, *New York Times*: A1.
7   Lizette Alvarez, "Senator-Elect Copes With Grief by Continuing a Legacy," 18 December 2000, *New York Times*: A12.
8   William M. Welch, "Widow Carries on Legacy, Dream," 9 November 2000, *USA Today*: 8A; "Governor's Widow Goes to the Senate," 6 December 2000, *New York Times*: A30.
9   Drummond Ayers, Jr., "Appointed to the Senate, Carnahan Rides High," 26 June 2001, *New York Times*: A17.
10 Carnahan, *Don't Let the Fire Go Out!*: 41; Alvarez, "Senator-Elect Copes With Grief by Continuing a Legacy."
11 Kevin Murphy, "Offering Her First Bill, Carnahan Proposes Money for Schools," 16 February 2001, *Kansas City Star*: A10; *Congressional Record*, Senate, 107th Cong., 1st sess. (15 February 2001): 1469.
12 "Carnahan School Amendment Approved," 17 May 2001, *Kansas City Star*: A6.
13 Kevin Murphy, "Carnahan Among Senators Backing Bush's Tax Proposal," 24 May 2001, *Kansas City Star*: A8.
14 Libby Quaid, "Missouri Senators Back New Farm Bill," 8 May 2002, Associated Press; Libby Quaid, "Spot Touts Carnahan's Support of Airline Merger," 12 July 2002, Associated Press.
15 Libby Quaid, "Carnahan Loses Seat of Late Husband in Missouri Senate Battle," 6 November 2002, Associated Press.
16 Romano, "Late Governor's Name Holds Sway in Mo. Election."
17 Kevin Murphy and David Goldstein, "Talent Wins Tight Race; Kansans Chose Sebelius, Missouri Contest Watched Closely," 6 November 2002, *Kansas City Star*: A1.

Denise Majette

1955–

UNITED STATES REPRESENTATIVE ★ DEMOCRAT FROM GEORGIA
2003–2005

After scoring an upset against a veteran incumbent in the Democratic primary for a congressional seat from Georgia, Denise Majette coasted to victory in the general election to earn a spot in the U.S. House of Representatives in the 108th Congress (2003–2005). As one of five new African-American Members elected in 2002, Majette described herself as "pro-choice, anti-death penalty, for protecting rights of workers and making sure that everyone has access on a level playing field."[1]

Denise L. Majette was born on May 18, 1955, in Brooklyn, New York, the daughter of Voyd Lee and Olivia Carolyn (Foster) Majette. She resided in New York until 1972, where one of her role models was Shirley Chisholm, the first black woman to serve in Congress. Majette attended Yale University, graduating with a B.A. in 1976. Majette's decision to attend law school after college resulted from her anguish over President John F. Kennedy's assassination in 1963. She later recalled, "I wanted to be able to use the law to effect social change and make things better for people who otherwise didn't have those opportunities."[2] After earning a J.D. in 1979 from Duke Law School, Majette began her professional career as a staff attorney at the Legal Aid Society in Winston-Salem, North Carolina, and later served as a clinical adjunct law professor at Wake Forest University. In 1983, Majette moved to Stone Mountain, Georgia, with her husband Rogers J. Mitchell, Jr., and their two sons, each from a former marriage, to accept a position as law clerk for Judge R. Keegan Federal at the superior court of DeKalb County. Over the next two decades, Majette served as law assistant to Judge Robert Benham of the Georgia court of appeals, special assistant attorney general for the state of Georgia, and partner in an Atlanta law

firm. In 1992, Majette became an administrative law judge for the Atlanta office of the Georgia state board of workers' compensation. On June 8, 1993, Georgia Governor Zell Miller appointed Majette as a judge on the state court of DeKalb County. During her nearly 10 years as a judge, she presided over a variety of court proceedings, including criminal trials, civil cases, and hearings.[3]

On February 5, 2002, Majette resigned from the bench, announcing her candidacy as a Democrat in the Georgia congressional district encompassing the suburban area east of Atlanta. Although she lacked the high public profile of the Democratic incumbent, five-term Representative Cynthia McKinney, Majette said that she decided to run for public office because she felt McKinney had become disconnected from the issues affecting DeKalb County. The race garnered national attention after McKinney implied that President George W. Bush deliberately ignored pre–September 11 intelligence reports suggesting an imminent terrorist attack and that the President's big business supporters profited in the wake of the attacks. Majette capitalized on the controversy which surrounded her opponent's remarks. She also received a strong endorsement from Zell Miller, by this point one of Georgia's two U.S. Senators. Middle-class voters flocked to Majette in the August 20, 2002, primary, joined by Republicans who took advantage of Georgia state law allowing voters to switch parties during primaries. Majette captured 58 percent of the vote. In the general election she easily defeated her Republican opponent, Cynthia Van Auken, gaining 77 percent of the vote.[4]

Upon being sworn in to the U.S. House of Representatives in January 2003, Majette reflected on the enormity of her upcoming responsibilities, observing, "I was just

OFFICE OF HISTORY AND PRESERVATION,
U.S. HOUSE OF REPRESENTATIVES

looking around the room and appreciating the kind of work the Congress will have to do and how that will impact the nation and the world."[5] Majette received assignments on the Budget, Education and Workforce, and Small Business committees and chaired the Task Force on Jobs and the Economy. She also assumed a leadership role in her brief tenure in Congress, as an Assistant Democratic Whip and as president of the freshman class of the House Democrats.

During her first year in Congress, Majette sponsored legislation to designate Arabia Mountain in southeast DeKalb County as a national heritage area, a classification that would increase tourism and make the metro Atlanta region eligible for millions of dollars of federal funding. Testifying before the House Resources Subcommittee on National Parks, Recreation, and Public Lands, Majette called the locale "a living history lesson," and she urged the preservation of the "area's unique heritage for future generations."[6] As a member of the Small Business Committee, she criticized President Bush's proposed fiscal year 2005 budget, citing concerns that the many female- and minority-owned small businesses in her district would suffer.

Majette fought to protect a variety of federally funded programs during her one term in the House. She believed that the Bush administration had failed to adequately fund education initiatives and was an outspoken critic of the President's record concerning domestic violence against women. On the latter, she declared that "it saddens me to think that millions of women continue to be abused each year, while this administration sits idly by, taking no initiative and, in some cases, decreasing resources available to battered women."[7] She also voted against overhauling Medicare, labeling the Republican-sponsored Medicare Prescription Drug and Modernization Act of 2003 as a "sham" that failed to include "adequate prescription drug coverage that our mothers and grandmothers absolutely deserve."[8] In 2003, she joined two of her Democratic colleagues, Chris Van Hollen of Maryland and John Tierney of Massachusetts, in proposing an amendment to increase spending for

Head Start. Majette argued for the additional funding because "the program doesn't just teach children to read." She went on to say, "It provides nutritional support, it makes sure that children are properly vaccinated at the appropriate time, that parents are also being supported and supportive of the efforts, that children are given the overall support they need. It's not just about teaching them their colors."[9]

On March 29, 2004, Majette surprised her House colleagues, and even some of her staff, when she announced her candidacy for the Georgia Senate seat being vacated by the retiring Zell Miller. Not wanting to miss out on the opportunity of running for an open Senate seat, Majette entered the race despite the absence of a statewide fundraising network and little name recognition outside the Atlanta area.[10] Forced into a runoff because she did not gain a majority in the Democratic primary, Majette utilized an effective grass-roots campaign to defeat millionaire businessman Cliff Oxford. Despite becoming the first African American to earn a nomination for the U.S. Senate from the state of Georgia, Majette lost in the general election when she received only 40 percent of the vote against three-term Republican Congressman Johnny Isakson.[11]

Majette expressed no regrets after her loss but instead reflected that "it was a leap of faith for me, another step in my spiritual journey."[12] In 2005, Majette began work as a judge in DeKalb County. A year later Majette sought the Democratic nomination for Georgia superintendent of schools, an elected position with oversight of the daily operations of the state's department of education.[13]

FOR FURTHER READING

Biographical Directory of the United States Congress, "Denise Majette," http://bioguide.congress.gov

NOTES

1   *Politics in America, 2004* (Washington, D.C.: Congressional Quarterly Inc., 2003): 277.

2   Jeffrey McMurray, "Majette Says Spiritual Calling Prompted Belated Senate Run," 16 June 2004, Associated Press.

3   "Who Is Denise Majette?" http://www.majetteforcongress.org (accessed 6 November 2002).

4   "New Member Profile: Denise Majette," 9 November 2002, *National Journal*; "Election Statistics, 1920 to Present," http://clerk.house.gov/ members/electionInfo/elections.html.

5   Melanie Eversley, "Enormity of Duty Awes Capitol Hill: Georgia's Freshmen Sworn in," 8 January 2003, *Atlanta Journal-Constitution*: 6A.

6   Donna Williams Lewis, "Majette Makes Appeal for Heritage Area; Designation Would Make as Much as $1 Million per Year Available," 25 September 2003, *Atlanta Journal-Constitution*: 1JA; Ben Smith, "Majette Coming Into Her Own in Congress," 1 May 2003, *Atlanta Journal-Constitution*: 2JA; Mae Gentry, "2004 The Year in Review; It Only Looked Like Politics Stood Alone in Reshaping the Country," 30 December 2004, *Atlanta Journal-Constitution*: 1JB.

7   *Congressional Record*, House, 108th Cong., 2nd sess. (22 June 2004): 4746; Brian Basinger, "Majette Defies Conventional Election Theories," 24 October 2004, *Florida Times-Union* (Jacksonville): A1.

8   *Congressional Record*, House, 108th Cong., 1st sess. (26 June 2003): 5956.

9   Melanie Eversley, "Majette Joins Head Start Fight; Bill Urges Federal Funding," 22 July 2003, *Atlanta Journal-Constitution*: 5A.

10 Lauren W. Whittington, "Majette Shaking Up Ga. Politics," 30 March 2004, *Roll Call*; Peter Savodnik and Michael Rochmes, "Majette Seeks Senate—Colleagues Stunned," 30 March 2004, *The Hill*: 1.

11 "Election Statistics, 1920 to Present," http://clerk.house.gov/members/ electionInfo/elections.html; Savodnik and Rochmes, "Majette Seeks Senate—Colleagues Stunned"; Dick Pettys, "Majette Looks for Funds, Foot Soldiers in U.S. Senate Battle," 20 October 2004, Associated Press.

12 Anna Varela, "Election 2004: Isakson's Romp Beats Expectations; 18-Point Margin Laid to Turnout, High Profile," 4 November 2004, *Atlanta Journal-Constitution*: 5C.

13 Corey Dade, "Majette Accepts Job as Part-Time Judge," 22 December 2004, *Atlanta Journal-Constitution*: 2D.

★ PART TWO ★

Current Women Members

★ INTRODUCTION TO ★
Current Members' Profiles

İN THE 90 YEARS SINCE ṘEPRESENTATIVE Jeannette Rankin of Montana became the first woman elected to Congress, a total of 229 women have served in the U.S. House of Representatives and Senate. Many themes central to the larger saga of American democracy resonate in the history of women in Congress: pioneering spirit, struggle, perseverance, gradual attainment of power, advancement through unity, and outstanding achievement.

The legacy of that dynamic history serves as prologue to the 84 women who now serve in the 109th Congress (2005–2007). The 67 Representatives, three Delegates, and 14 Senators constitute the largest group of women to serve in the history of the institution (15.5 percent of the total lawmakers in both chambers). In fact, they account for more than one-third of all the women who have ever served in Congress. All were sworn in to Congress after 1976; most first took office in the 1990s.

Part II of *Women in Congress* provides biographical profiles of these individuals in a format that echoes former Member entries—with information on precongressional careers, first House or Senate campaigns, committee and leadership positions, and legislative achievements. But because these are careers in progress, definitive accounts of current Members must await a later date. Current Members were given the opportunity to review their individual profiles prior to publication. In addition, Part II profiles differ in tone and style from, and they are half the length (750 words) of, most former Member entries. Part II profiles are also arranged alphabetically rather than chronologically, further distinguishing current Members from their predecessors. This section includes the 75 women who have served during two or more Congresses. The nine freshman Members elected to the 109th Congress—at the time of this writing—are covered separately in a résumé format in the book's first appendix.

Among the individuals covered in Part II is Senator Barbara Mikulski of Maryland—whose 29 years of congressional service make her the institution's longest-serving current woman. First elected to the U.S. House of Representatives in 1976, Mikulski served 10 years before winning election to the Senate in 1986— where she is that body's longest-serving currant woman. Also included in this section are Representatives Nancy Johnson of Connecticut and Marcy Kaptur of Ohio, both of whom were first elected in 1982 and are now the deans of House women. Women's ascent to leadership is a recent development. Part II also includes profiles on the highest-ranking House women in the history of either of their respective parties—Democratic Leader Nancy Pelosi of California and Republican Conference Chairwoman Deborah Pryce of Ohio.

As incumbent Members retire from public service, the editors of this volume hope that their profiles will be expanded to capture their full careers and fitted into the chronology of former Members. The publication of a companion, online version of *Women in Congress* will permit regular updates to the stories of these individuals' contributions to the rich history of women in Congress.

KEY TO MEMBER TITLES

★ SENATOR ★

★ REPRESENTATIVE ★

★ DELEGATE ★

Tammy Baldwin
1962–

UNITED STATES REPRESENTATIVE
DEMOCRAT FROM WISCONSIN
1999–

Image courtesy of the Member

TAMMY BALDWIN ACCOMPLISHED TWO "FIRSTS" when she was elected to the House from Wisconsin in 1998: She became the first woman to represent her state in Congress and the first nonincumbent openly gay candidate to run and win election to the federal legislature.[1]

Tammy Baldwin was born in Madison, Wisconsin, on February 11, 1962. She was raised there by her mother and maternal grandparents. Baldwin graduated from Smith College in 1984 and earned a J.D. from the University of Wisconsin Law School in 1989. From 1986 to 1994 Baldwin served on the Dane County, Wisconsin, board of supervisors. She also served briefly on the Madison city council, filling a vacancy in 1986. In addition, Baldwin maintained a private law practice from 1989 to 1992. At about the same time she joined the Dane County supervisors, Baldwin "came out" about her sexual orientation. "The fundamental lesson of the civil rights movement is that coming out—whether as an individual, part of a same-sex couple, or as a straight ally—is crucial," Baldwin once wrote.[2] In 1993, at 31 years old, she was elected to the Wisconsin legislature, where she served until 1999. During her first term, Baldwin chaired the committee on elections, constitutional law and corrections— becoming one of the first freshman lawmakers in Wisconsin history to head a standing committee.

In 1998, after Republican Congressman Scott Klug retired from the Wisconsin district that included the capital city of Madison, Baldwin won the seat in a close race against Republican Josephine Musser. In a well-financed campaign, she ran on a liberal platform that called for universal health care coverage, publicly financed childcare, and stronger environmental laws. Baldwin's victory was a grass-roots success, mobilizing so many voters (Madison, the district's biggest city, had a 62 percent turnout) that polls were forced to stay open until late in the night as city officials photocopied extra ballots. Baldwin claimed 52 percent of the vote to become the first woman from Wisconsin to serve in Congress. In 2000, she was re-elected by a slimmer margin, defeating Republican John Sharpless, a professor from the University of Wisconsin, by fewer than 9,000 votes—51 percent. In 2002 and 2004, Baldwin was elected by comfortable margins of 66 and 63 percent of the vote, respectively.[3]

In the 109th Congress (2005–2007), Baldwin was named to the House Energy and Commerce Committee and its Subcommittee on Healthcare, seats she had pursued tenaciously since her first term. Her driving motivation in politics is to pass legislation that will guarantee health care for all in America. She is working with conservative as well as liberal thinkers to craft proposals to meet this goal.

Previously, Baldwin served on the House Budget and Judiciary Committees. She also joined the Progressive Caucus, a group of liberal Democrats. Baldwin has been an advocate for health care reform and the preservation of Social Security and Medicare. On the Judiciary Committee she played a key role in the successful passage of the extension of the Violence Against Women Act in 2000. She earned a reputation as a supporter of a liberal policy agenda who, nevertheless, was a pragmatist. "I can't get legislation passed without Republicans," she once noted.[4] A strong supporter of civil rights legislation to promote social equality, Baldwin is one of the most ardent proponents of hate crime legislation, arguing that they "are different from other violent crimes because they seek to terrorize an entire community. This sort of domestic terrorism demands a strong federal response, because this country was founded on the premise that a person should be free to be who they are without fear of violence."[5]

Baldwin also has looked out for the interests of her largely rural and agrarian district. In 1999, she and other Members of the Wisconsin delegation fought to reverse a Depression-Era milk pricing system that paid farmers more money for their milk the farther they were from Eau Claire, Wisconsin. Strong farming interests in New England blocked the initiative, which won national attention. That same year, Baldwin also lobbied for an extension of Chapter 12 of the bankruptcy code to protect economically distressed farmers in the Midwest. "The family farm is the backbone of our rural economy in Wisconsin and all over this nation," Baldwin declared in a House Floor speech. "Without Chapter 12, if economic crisis hits a family farm, that family has no choice but to liquidate the land, equipment, crops and herd to pay off creditors, losing the farm, a supplier of food, and a way of life."[6]

FOR FURTHER READING

Biographical Directory of the U.S. Congress, "Tammy Baldwin," http://bioguide.congress.gov

MANUSCRIPT COLLECTION

Wisconsin Historical Society, Archives Division. *Papers*: 1981–1998, 1.4 cubic feet. Papers documenting Baldwin's early political career through her tenure in the Wisconsin state assembly. *Oral History*: In *Gay Madison: a History*, 0.1 cubic foot and 13 tape recordings. Oral histories conducted by Brian J. Bigler.

NOTES

1 "Tammy Baldwin Biography," http://tammybaldwin.house.gov/page.asp?pageffiaboutTammy (accessed 14 June 2002).

2 Tammy Baldwin, "Harvey Milk and Tammy Baldwin," 15 August 2000, *The Advocate*: 32.

3 "Election Statistics," http://clerk.house.gov/members/electionInfo/elections.html.

4 *Politics in America, 2002* (Washington, D.C.: Congressional Quarterly Inc., 2001): 1099.

5 *Congressional Record*, House, 106th Cong., 2nd sess. (7 June 2000): 3933.

6 *Congressional Record*, House, 106th Cong., 1st sess. (9 March 1999): 1033; see also *Politics in America, 2002*: 1100.

Shelley Berkley

1951–

UNITED STATES REPRESENTATIVE
DEMOCRAT FROM NEVADA
1999–

Image courtesy of the Member

SHELLEY BERKLEY, A FORMER NEVADA STATE LEGISLATOR with long ties to Las Vegas, won election as Representative in one of the nation's fastest-growing congressional districts. During her first terms in office, Congresswoman Berkley led the opposition to the federal government's plan to ship the nation's nuclear waste to a centralized site in Nevada.

She was born Rochelle Levine in New York City on January 20, 1951. Her parents moved the family to Las Vegas when she was 11. After graduating from Valley High School, she became the first member of her family to attend college, earning a B.A. from the University of Nevada–Las Vegas in 1972 and a J.D. from the University of San Diego Law School in 1976. She married and raised two sons, Max and Sam. In March 1999, she remarried, to Dr. Larry Lehrner, and gained two stepchildren, Stephanie and David. Berkley had wide experience in the private sector, including employment as vice president for government and legal affairs for a major Las Vegas resort. She also chaired the board of the Nevada Hotel and Motel Association. Berkley was elected to the Nevada state assembly in 1982 and served until 1985. She also was appointed to the board of regents of the university and community college system of Nevada in 1990 and then elected to a six-year term ending in 1998.

When Nevada Representative John Ensign relinquished his Las Vegas House seat in 1998 to run for the U.S. Senate, Berkley entered the open seat contest. Berkley narrowly defeated Republican Don Chairez and, in 2000, was re-elected by an eight-point margin over Republican Jon Porter, 52 to 44 percent. In subsequent elections, Berkley faced a unique challenge—trying to keep name recognition among a rapidly growing constituency (by 2001, Las Vegas was absorbing more than 6,000 new residents per month).[1] By 2004, she had secured her position in the Democratic-leaning district, convincingly defeating her GOP challenger by 35 percentage points.[2]

As a freshman in the 106th Congress (1999–2001), Berkley was assigned to three committees: Transportation and Infrastructure, Veterans' Affairs, and Small Business. During the 106th Congress, colleagues elected Berkley vice president of the Democratic freshman class. In the 107th Congress (2001–2003) she exchanged her Small Business assignment for a seat on the International Relations Committee, where she sits on the Middle East and Central Asia and Europe and Emerging Threats subcommittees. Berkley has served as a Regional Whip since the 107th Congress. In the 109th Congress (2005–2007), Berkley was appointed Ranking Member of the Subcommittee on Disability Assistance and Memorial Affairs on the Veterans' Affairs Committee.

Berkley, who bills herself as a moderate, joined the centrist New Democratic Coalition. Shortly after her election, she advocated expanding health care coverage to cover the costs associated with bone mass measurements, a procedure important for women susceptible to osteoporosis. In 2001, she sponsored a bill with Republican Patrick Toomey of Pennsylvania to curtail the power of Medicare administrators to cut off payments to health care providers, while also allowing those charged with improper billing to challenge such rulings.[3] Like many western state politicians from both parties, Berkley opposed additional gun control while supporting several gun safety measures.

As the Representative for the nation's fastest-growing congressional district, much of Berkley's focus was local—on water controls and "protecting my major industry" of gambling and entertainment.[4] Berkley has sought to increase federal funding for highways, other transportation projects, and school construction. Additionally, she advocates increased use of Nevada's federal lands for renewable energy development.

Berkley also emerged as a leader on the state's hot-button political issue: opposition to a federal plan to place radioactive nuclear waste from 42 states at Yucca Mountain, about 90 miles northwest of her Las Vegas district. Berkley led the Nevada delegation in laying out several arguments against the proposal: The geographically unstable mountain was prone to earthquakes; it sat atop an underground flood zone; trains transporting the waste were prone to accident or terrorist attacks; and the project was a "financial boon-doggle," costing much more than was appropriated.[5] "Nevada does not produce one ounce of nuclear waste," Berkley said in the spring of 2002 when the measure came to a vote. "Yet Nevada is being asked to carry the burdens of a problem it had no part in creating."[6] The House passed the measure 306–117. After it passed the Senate and was signed into law by President George W. Bush, Berkley vowed to fight the measure in the courts.

FOR FURTHER READING

Biographical Directory of the U.S. Congress, "Shelley Berkley," http://bioguide.congress.gov

NOTES

1 William Booth, "In Las Vegas Area Contest, All Bets on a Win Are Off; Ever-Changing Voter Population Means Names and Issues Don't Stick Easily," 23 October 2000, *Washington Post*: A13; see also, George F. Will, "In Vegas Politics, All Bets Are Off," 12 May 2002, *Washington Post*: B7; "Election Statistics, 1920 to Present," http://clerk.house. gov/members/electionInfo/ elections.html.

2 "Election Statistics, 1920 to Present," http://clerk.house.gov/members/ electionInfo/elections.html.

3 *Politics in America, 2004* (Washington, D.C.: Congressional Quarterly Inc., 2003): 621.

4 Edward Walsh, "Vote on House 'Managers' Draws Out Differences Among Freshmen," 7 January 1999, *Washington Post*: A8.

5 Matthew L. Wald, "House Panel Backs Nevada as Site to Bury Atomic Waste," 26 April 2002, *New York Times*: A26; *Congressional Record*, House, 107th Cong., 2nd sess. (8 May 2002): 2180.

6 Nick Anderson, "House Backs Nuclear Dump Site," 9 May 2002, *Los Angeles Times*: A13.

Judith Biggert

1937–

UNITED STATES REPRESENTATIVE
REPUBLICAN FROM ILLINOIS
1999–

Image courtesy of the Member

MODERATE ILLINOIS REPUBLICAN JUDY BIGGERT has emerged as one of the party's leading advocates for education reform and childcare programs. A former lawyer and state legislator, Representative Biggert is a regular face on C-SPAN as one of the few women Members who frequently presides over the House or chairs the Committee of the Whole.

Judith Borg was born in Chicago, Illinois, on August 15, 1937, the daughter of Alvin Andrew Borg and Marjorie Virginia (Mailler) Borg. She graduated from Stanford University in 1959 with a degree in international relations and earned a J.D. in 1963 from the Northwestern University Law School. After graduating from Northwestern, she clerked for the Honorable Luther M. Swygert in the U.S. Court of Appeals, 7th Circuit. She married Rody Biggert, and the couple raised four children: Courtney, Alison, Rody, and Adrienne. Judy Biggert operated a home-based private law practice specializing in real estate, estate planning, and probate law from 1975 to 1998. She became active in local politics, serving as school board president of Hinsdale Township High School District 86. She also chaired the Visiting Nurses Association of Chicago and served as president of the Junior League of Chicago. In 1992, Biggert won election to the Illinois house of representatives and served three consecutive terms (1993–1999), including two terms as assistant republican leader. In the state legislature, she passed strict anticrime laws, worked to balance the state budget without raising taxes, and sponsored tort reform legislation.

In 1998, Biggert ran for a congressional seat representing the southwest Chicago suburbs, vacated by retiring Republican Harris W. Fawell. Biggert topped a more conservative primary challenger, 45 to 40 percent. During the campaign, Biggert responded to remarks made by a high-ranking U.S. Senate Republican that were widely construed as being anti-gay. "It does bother me when people are discriminatory, and maybe that's because I've been discriminated against myself," she said. "What I will do is change their minds.... If I can't change them, then I will have to work with them."[1] She later remarked that women politicians "are held to an awfully high standard. We have to work three times as hard."[2] In the general election, Biggert defeated Democrat Susan W. Hynes, a business executive, with 61 percent of the vote.[3] In 2000 and 2002, Biggert was re-elected by wide margins against mortgage broker Thomas Mason. In the 2004 elections, she was returned to a fourth consecutive term, defeating educator Gloria Andersen by a 65 to 35 percent margin.[4]

In the 106th Congress (1999–2001), Biggert was appointed to three committees: Government Reform; Banking Financial Services; and Science. She later left Government Reform for assignments on the Education and Workforce Committee and the Committee on Standards of Official Conduct. In the 107th Congress (2001–2003), Biggert also co-chaired the Women's Caucus. In the 108th Congress (2003–2005), Biggert was appointed chair of the Energy Subcommittee of the Science Committee.

Biggert made her mark in the House as an advocate for education reform, child care for low income families, and expanded assistance for victims of domestic violence. In early 2001, Biggert introduced the McKinney–Vento Homeless Act of 2001, a bill which built upon 1980s legislation to extend educational opportunities to homeless children. According to Biggert's research, 45 percent of the approximately 1 million homeless children nationwide did not attend school on a regular basis. Her bill sought to ensure their enrollment and reduced bureaucratic red tape that might prevent children in homeless families from attending class. The bill also expanded federal funding to help states better track and aid these students. "Being without a home should not mean being without an education," Biggert said in a House Floor speech in 1999.[5] Much of her bill was passed by the House in the 1999 Students Results Act. When she submitted another version in 2001, the bill moved quickly through the Congress and was signed into law as part of the No Child Left Behind Act by President George W. Bush on September 20, 2001.

As chairman of the Energy Subcommittee, Biggert has emerged as a leading proponent of basic science research and development. She authored the Energy Research, Development, Demonstration, and Commercial Application Act of 2005, which later was incorporated into the Energy Policy Act of 2005, and was signed into law as P.L. 109-58. She cofounded and co-chairs, with physicist and New Jersey Democrat Russ Holt, the Congressional Research and Development Caucus.

Alarmed at studies showing that most young Americans lack the most basic understanding of economic and financial concepts, Biggert sponsored legislation that created the Office of Financial and Economic Literacy at the Department of the Treasury and secured federal funding for the Excellence in Economic Education (EEE) program. To raise awareness of the problem, she is the annual sponsor of the House resolution marking April as Financial Literacy Month, and she cofounded and co-chairs, with Democratic Representative Rubén Hinojosa of Texas, the Congressional Caucus on Financial and Economic Literacy.

FOR FURTHER READING

Biographical Directory of the U.S. Congress, "Judith Borg Biggert," http://bioguide.congress.gov

NOTES

1 William Grady, "Biggert Seeking Unity with GOP Foes; Candidacy of Hynes May Help Her Do That," 28 June 1998, *Chicago Tribune*: D1.

2 *Politics in America, 2002* (Washington, D.C.: Congressional Quarterly Inc., 2001): 331.

3 "Election Statistics, 1920 to Present," http://clerk.house.gov/members/electionInfo/elections.html.

4 "Election Statistics, 1920 to Present," http://clerk.house.gov/members/electionInfo/elections.html.

5 *Congressional Record*, House, 106th Cong., 1st sess. (21 September 1999): 8442; *Congressional Record*, House, 107th Cong., 1st sess. (14 February 2001): 191.

Marsha Blackburn

1952–

UNITED STATES REPRESENTATIVE
REPUBLICAN FROM TENNESSEE
2003–

Image courtesy of the Member

WITH ONLY FIVE YEARS' EXPERIENCE IN ELECTIVE POLITICS under her belt, Marsha Blackburn ran for the 108th Congress (2003–2005) to "effect a change for her family and fellow Tennesseans" through fiscal and social conservatism.[1] After arriving in Washington, D.C., Congresswoman Blackburn became a Republican Party star and won praise for her conservative voting record.

Marsha Blackburn was born on June 6, 1952, in Laurel, Mississippi. Her father was an oil industry salesman.[2] She graduated from Northeast Jones High School in Laurel, Mississippi, as an honors student and earned a bachelor of science degree at Mississippi State University in 1973. She married Chuck Blackburn in 1975, and the couple had two children, Mary and Chad. Marsha Blackburn worked as a businesswoman and owned her own marketing company. Heavily involved in Republican politics, she was elected chair of the Williamson County (Tennessee) Republican Party and served in that post from 1989 to 1991. In 1992, as a relative unknown, Blackburn challenged the Democratic incumbent U.S. Representative Bart Gordon. She ran on the issues of a balanced budget amendment and term limits, receiving 40 percent of the vote in a losing effort. From 1995 to 1997, she served as executive director of the Tennessee Film, Entertainment, and Music Commission. Determined to make a difference, Marsha Blackburn continued to run for elective office and was elected a Tennessee state senator in 1998, where she served for four years, eventually rising to the minority whip post. She gained state and national recognition as a leader in a statewide grass-roots campaign to defeat the proposed Tennessee state income tax.

In 2002, Blackburn ran for the congressional seat vacated when Tennessee Representative Ed Bryant campaigned for the U.S. Senate. In the Republican primary for the district including suburbs stretching from Memphis to Nashville, Blackburn faced three Memphis-area politicians: David Kustoff, Brent Taylor, and Mark Norris. Running on a platform that opposed the introduction of state income tax for Tennessee, Blackburn prevailed with 40 percent of the vote. The district had been a safe GOP seat since 1973 and, in the general election, Blackburn easily defeated Democrat Tom Barron with 70 percent of the vote. Pegged as one of the rising Republicans stars in the House, Blackburn was re-elected to the 109th Congress (2005–2007) without opposition.[3]

As a freshman Member of Congress, Blackburn was assigned to three committees: Judiciary, Education and Workforce, and Government Reform. She believed that her appointment on the Government Reform Committee would improve her knowledge of homeland security and benefit her district.[4] Blackburn served as vice chairman of the Government Reform Subcommittee on Government Efficiency and Financial Management, where she targeted waste, fraud, and abuse in federal government operations. Blackburn also was appointed to the Majority Whip's team in the 108th Congress and was mentioned as a potential Senate candidate to succeed Republican Senate Majority Leader Bill Frist, who announced his decision to retire from Congress in 2007.[5]

Upon taking office, Blackburn declared that she wanted to scale back the size of government. During the 108th Congress, she sponsored three bills to require across-the-board spending cuts in the federal budget. She supported the proposed tax relief measures advocated by President George W. Bush. Blackburn also voted along conservative lines for a number of social initiatives: school prayer, capital punishment, a constitutional amendment to protect marriage, and increased restrictions on abortion.[6] On the constitutional marriage amendment, Blackburn wanted to see marriage defined in conjunction with "faith, family, and freedom."[7] In the 109th Congress, Blackburn left her previous committee assignments to accept a seat on the prestigious Energy and Commerce Committee.

FOR FURTHER READING

Biographical Directory of the U.S. Congress, "Marsha Blackburn," http://bioguide.congress.gov

NOTES

1 "Marsha Blackburn," Associated Press Candidate Biographies, 2002.

2 "Members of Congress Remember Their Father," 12 June 2003, Scripps Howard News Service.

3 "Election Statistics, 1920 to Present," http://clerk.house.gov/members/electionInfo/index.html.

4 C. Richard Cotton, "Blackburn Chows Down With the Home Folks," 23 January 2003, *The Commercial Appeal*: NE1.

5 "Guide to Congress," 8 September, 2003, *Roll Call*.

6 "Guide to Congress."

7 Larry Bivins, "Several Tennessee Lawmakers Would Back Gay Marriage Ban," 26 February 2004, *The Tennessean*: 14A.

Mary Bono
1961–

UNITED STATES REPRESENTATIVE
REPUBLICAN FROM CALIFORNIA
1998–

Image courtesy of the Member

THOUGH SHE NEVER HELD ANY ELECTIVE OFFICE PRIOR to winning election to the House, and arrived amidst a presidential impeachment scandal, Mary Bono made the transition from the wife of a celebrity-turned-Member-of-Congress to a Representative in her own right.

Mary Whitaker was born in Cleveland, Ohio, on October 24, 1961, one of four children raised by Clay and Karen Whitaker. In 1984, she earned a B.F.A. in art history from the University of Southern California. In February 1986, she married the entertainer Sonny Bono and eventually raised two children with him, Chesare and Chianna. From 1988 to 1992, Mary Bono served as the first lady of Palm Springs, California, while her husband was mayor. In 1994, Sonny Bono was elected to the U.S. House as a Republican in a district encompassing the city of Palm Springs.

On January 5, 1998, Sonny Bono died in a skiing accident in South Lake Tahoe, California. Mary Bono entered and won the April 7 special election to fill her husband's seat by defeating Democratic candidate, actor Ralph Waite, with 65 percent of the vote. For the remainder of the 105th Congress (1997–1999), she served on the Judiciary and National Security committees. In November 1998, Bono again defeated Waite, this time with 60 percent of the vote, for the full term in the 106th Congress (1999–2001). In 2000, she compiled a similar re-election victory against Democrat Ron Oden.[1]

While initially filling some of her husband's committee assignments, Representative Bono eventually relinquished them as she developed her own legislative interests. In the 106th Congress, she held her Judiciary assignment and received a seat on both the Armed Services and Small Business committees. But in the 107th Congress (2001–2003), Bono gave up her other assignments to join the Energy and Commerce Committee and three of its subcommittees: Commerce, Trade, and Consumer Protection; Energy and Air Quality; and Environment and Hazardous Materials. In the 109th Congress (2005–2007), she was appointed to the Health Subcommittee.

Following the precedent set by many prior congressional widows, Bono's term in the 105th Congress was, in part, a memorial to her late husband.[2] She generally supported Sonny Bono's legislative positions as an advocate for decentralized government authority and greater local control, particularly in the field of education. A critic of the existing tax structure, she favored tax reform and a reduction in the size of the federal bureaucracy. She continued Sonny Bono's work to enact stricter environmental regulations to preserve the Salton Sea, a southern California lake, half of which lies in her district. In late 1998, Congresswoman Bono and other California Representatives convinced the House to fund an environmental study and begin the process of cleaning the Salton Sea. Mary Bono also directed through the House a copyright extension bill which had been introduced by her husband.

The biggest vote of Representative Bono's first term came with her assignment on the House Judiciary Committee, which had opened impeachment proceedings against President William J. Clinton. As the committee's most junior member, she began by often yielding her time for questions to other members. But by the end of the process she had largely won favorable reviews with her thoughtful examination of witnesses. Bono supported bringing an impeachment motion to the House Floor and, along with the Republican majority, later voted to impeach President Clinton.

Representative Bono also carved out her own legislative interests—different from her husband's. In 2000, she helped pass legislation establishing the Santa Rosa and San Jacinto National Monument in her district. She also cosponsored legislation to bar national forests from charging fees to recreational users. "To tax the great outdoors is offensive to the concept of the national forest system," Bono said.[3] On trade and labor, she disagreed with her husband, who supported "fast-track" legislation to ease trade restrictions, believing such a policy could hurt agricultural workers in her district. Representative Bono authored successful legislation requiring country-of-origin labeling for fresh fruits and vegetables.[4] She also differentiated herself from fellow Republicans on the contentious abortion issue. While supporting parental notification and opposing federal funding for abortions and partial-birth abortions, Bono said, "But in the end, it's between a woman, her family and her God. It's a moral decision, and she has to make it on her own. The federal government does not belong in it."[5]

After several terms in Congress, Representative Bono had established herself as an up-and-coming figure within the party, one who could appeal to the "soccer mom" demographic. Bono won re-election to the House in 2002, defeating Democrat Elle Kurpiewski with 65 percent of the vote. In 2004, Bono earned a fifth term in Congress by defeating Democrat Richard Meyer, 66 to 34 percent.[6]

FOR FURTHER READING

Biographical Directory of the U.S. Congress, "Mary Bono," http://bioguide.congress.gov

NOTES

1 "Election Statistics, 1920 to Present," http://clerk.house.gov/members/electionInfo/elections.html.

2 Lorraine Adams, "Keepers of the Flame," 1 November 1998, *Good Housekeeping* 227 (no. 5): 136; Jeanne Marie Laskas, "Oh, My God, We're Not Blond Anymore: The Transformation of Mary Bono," 1 July 1999, *Esquire* 132 (no. 1): 122.

3 *Politics in America, 2002* (Washington, D.C.: Congressional Quarterly Inc., 2001): 148–149.

4 "Official Biography of Mary Bono," http://www.house.gov/bono/bio.html (accessed 15 February 2005).

5 Frank Bruni, "The Widow's Run," 29 March 1998, *New York Times Magazine*: 34.

6 "Election Statistics, 1920 to Present," http://clerk.house.gov/members/electionInfo/elections.html.

Madeleine Z. Bordallo

1933–

DELEGATE
DEMOCRAT FROM GUAM
2003–

Image courtesy of the Member

A LIFETIME PUBLIC SERVANT FROM THE PACIFIC U.S. Territory of Guam, Delegate Madeleine Z. Bordallo won election in 2002 as the first woman to serve as Guam's Delegate to the U.S. House of Representatives. "I know how important it is to tell America about Guam," Bordallo said after being elected. "I would never retreat from what I feel is good for the people of Guam. It has always been my philosophy to fight for the will of the people." 1 Bordallo brings to Congress more than 40 years of public service experience in the executive and legislative branches of the government of Guam and numerous nongovernmental organizations.

While Delegate Bordallo has lived her entire adult life in Guam, she was born on May 31, 1933, in Graceville, Minnesota. In 1948, she moved to Guam with her parents, Chris and Evelyn Zeien, when the U.S. Navy hired her father as principal of Guam's only high school. Graduating from Guam's George Washington High School in 1951, she attended St. Mary's College in South Bend, Indiana, and graduated in 1953 with a degree in music and voice from St. Catherine's College in St. Paul, Minnesota. After returning to Guam that year, she married Ricardo J. "Ricky" Bordallo, a successful businessman from a family with a long political history in the territory.[2] They have a daughter, Deborah, and a granddaughter, Nicole.

Delegate Bordallo began her public career with local radio and television broadcaster KUAM in 1954. From 1959 until 1963, she produced a television program, "The Women's World," and narrated children's stories on the radio and on television. Her involvement in the community also has been extensive, with Bordallo founding the Guam Council of Women's Clubs, the Guam Symphony Society, *Y Inetnon Famalaoan* (Women for Service), and the Marianas Association for Persons with Disabilities. She also served as president of the Federation of Asian Women's Association and has taken a leadership role in dozens of other community organizations.

Bordallo was introduced to politics through her husband Ricky, who was a founding member of Guam's Democratic Party and served as Governor of Guam from 1975 to 1978 and 1983 to 1986. She first became Guam's Democratic National Committeewoman in 1964, a post she held for 40 years—the longest such service in the nation. As first lady of Guam, Bordallo was a strong advocate of promoting the indigenous Chamorro culture and the arts, both of which are lifelong passions. She entered elective politics herself when she became the first woman from the Democratic Party to win a seat in the Guam legislature, serving a total of five terms.[3] Following the death of her husband in 1990, she made an unsuccessful bid for governor, becoming the first woman in Guam's history to lead her party's ticket.[4] In 1994, she was elected to the first of two consecutive terms as Guam's first woman lieutenant governor. In this role, she championed the cause of island beautification as a way to enhance Guam's tourism-based economy.

In 2002, Bordallo was elected to the 108th Congress (2003–2005) as Guam's fourth Delegate to Congress, winning the open seat with 65 percent of the vote.[5] Delegate Bordallo was appointed to the Armed Services Committee, where she serves on the subcommittees on Readiness and Projection Forces. Bordallo has emphasized the importance of Guam's strategic location as the military considers force realignment in the region. She also serves on the Resources Committee, which has jurisdiction over territorial matters, with positions on the Subcommittees on Fisheries Conservation, Wildlife and Oceans and National Parks, Recreation and Public Lands. Bordallo also is a member of the Committee on Small Business and serves as Secretary of the Congressional Asian Pacific American Caucus.

Seven of Delegate Bordallo's bills were signed into law by the President during her first term. Some of her successful legislative initiatives in the 108th Congress included amending Guam's Organic Act to create an independent and unified judiciary, increasing federal assistance for the impact of immigration resulting from Compact Treaty obligations, and authorizing greater federal funding for the control and eradication of the invasive Brown Tree Snake. Bordallo's legislative efforts have benefited from the close relationships she has established with other territorial delegates, the Hawaiian delegation, and committee leadership on both sides of the aisle. She also has worked in a bipartisan approach with other elected officials from Guam to address federal issues that are important to the island. In 2004 and 2006, Delegate Bordallo ran unopposed for re-election.

FOR FURTHER READING

Biographical Directory of the U.S. Congress, "Madeleine Bordallo," http://bioguide.congress.gov

NOTES

1 "Highest Vote-Getters Look Ahead," 6 November 2002, Pacific Daily News: 5A.

2 "Bordallo for Congress," www.mzbforcongress.com/ aboutmadeleine/bio.shtml. (accessed 27 November 2002).

3 "Bordallo for Congress."

4 "Biodata of Madeleine Z. Bordallo" http://ns.gov.gu/webtax/ltgov_bio. html (accessed 27 November 2002).

5 Politics in America, 2004 (Washington, D.C.: Congressional Quarterly Inc., 2003): 1099.

Barbara Boxer

1940–

UNITED STATES REPRESENTATIVE, 1983–1993
UNITED STATES SENATOR, 1993–
DEMOCRAT FROM CALIFORNIA

Image courtesy of the Member

A FORCEFUL ADVOCATE FOR FAMILIES, CHILDREN, consumers, the environment, and her state of California, Barbara Boxer became a United States Senator in January 1993 after 10 years of service in the House of Representatives. In 2004, she received more than 6.9 million votes, the highest total for any Senate candidate ever.

Barbara Levy was born in Brooklyn, New York, on November 11, 1940, to Ira Levy and Sophie Silvershein Levy. She graduated with a B.A. from Brooklyn College in 1962 and married Stewart Boxer. The family relocated to northern California in 1965, where the Boxers raised two children: Doug and Nicole. From 1974 to 1976 Boxer worked for Congressman John Burton, who represented the California district encompassing Marin County. In 1976, she won election to the Marin County board of supervisors, serving as its first chairwoman.[1]

In 1982, John Burton decided to retire from the U.S. House and endorsed his protégée, Boxer. In the general election she defeated Republican Dennis McQuaid with 52 percent of the vote. Subsequent re-election campaigns provided no serious challenger, and Boxer remained in the House for four more terms. While serving in the House, Boxer was a member of the Committee on Merchant Marine and Fisheries, the Budget Committee, the Armed Services Committee, the Committee on Government Operations, and the Select Committee on Children, Youth, and Families.[2]

In 1992 Representative Boxer declared her candidacy for the U.S. Senate. She defeated Bruce Herschensohn, a conservative Los Angeles media commentator, by a margin of 48 to 43 percent. Her two subsequent re-elections to the Senate have seen her through with much more comfortable margins.[3]

As a U.S. Senator, Boxer is a strong proponent of medical research to find cures for diseases. Among the first in Congress to recognize health maintenance organization (HMO) abuses, she authored a Patients' Bill of Rights in 1997 and continues to fight for these protections and for affordable health care.

The Senate's leading defender of a woman's right to choose, Senator Boxer authored the Freedom of Choice Act of 2004 and helped lead the floor fight for passage of the Freedom of Access to Clinic Entrances Act. She also continues to take a prominent role in the efforts to prevent congressional opponents of abortion from weakening a woman's constitutional right to choose.

Senator Boxer has been recognized for her efforts to create a cleaner, healthier environment. She authored the amendment to the Safe Drinking Water Act to ensure that drinking water standards are set to protect children and other vulnerable populations. She has been a leader in the fight to remove arsenic from drinking water, to block oil drilling in the Alaska National Wildlife Refuge and along California's coast, and to revitalize the Superfund by making polluters pay to clean up the toxic waste they leave behind.

Senator Boxer has fought for policies that help women succeed at home and at work, from equal pay to family and medical leave. A leader in expanding quality after-school options for families, Boxer authored landmark legislation providing federal support for programs to increase student performance while decreasing juvenile delinquency and crime. Today, federal funding for after-school programs has risen dramatically from $750,000 in 1995 to almost $1 billion per year, covering about 1 million children each year. She is now pushing to reach 2.5 million children by 2007.

Senator Boxer joined colleagues to pass the 1994 Crime Bill, which banned assault weapons and established the Community Oriented Policing Services (COPS) program, helping local law enforcement reduce crime to its lowest rate in 25 years. Her bill to prevent the criminal use of personal information obtained through motor vehicle records was signed into law and upheld by the U.S. Supreme Court. She also authored the Violence Against Women Act (VAWA) while serving in the House and helped steer it through the Senate; it, too, is now law. She has authored the Violence Against Children Act, based on the successful VAWA.

In response to the September 11th attacks, Senator Boxer authored a bill to protect commercial airliners against attacks by shoulder-fired missiles, and she wrote the law allowing airline pilots with special training to carry guns in the cockpit. She wrote the law to ensure that air marshals would be on board high-risk flights, and she continues to press for implementation of this measure to make the skies as secure as they can be. She has also authored legislation on port security, rail security, and providing assistance to first responders.

Senator Boxer serves on the Senate Committees on Commerce, Foreign Relations, and Environment and Public Works, and is also the Democratic Chief Deputy Whip.

FOR FURTHER READING

Biographical Directory of the U.S. Congress, "Barbara Boxer," http://bioguide.congress.gov

Boxer, Barbara. Strangers in the Senate: Politics and the New Revolution of Women in America (New York, 1993).

Mikulski, Barbara, et al. Nine and Counting: The Women of the Senate (New York: William Morrow, 2000).

NOTES

1 Politics in America, 2002 (Washington, D.C.: Congressional Quarterly Inc., 2001): 65–66; "Official Biography of Barbara Boxer," http://boxer.senate.gov/about/index.cfm (accessed 16 December 2004).

2 Current Biography, 1994 (New York: H.W. Wilson and Company, 1994):63–66.

3 "Election Statistics, 1920 to Present," http://clerk.house.gov/members/electionInfo/elections.html.

Corrine Brown
1946–

UNITED STATES REPRESENTATIVE
DEMOCRAT FROM FLORIDA
1993–

Image courtesy of the Member

IN 1992, CORRINE BROWN BECAME ONE OF THE FIRST African Americans elected to the U.S. House from Florida since the close of the Reconstruction Era. During her House career, from her seats on the Transportation and Infrastructure and the Veterans' Affairs committees, Congresswoman Brown regularly brought federal programs into her Jacksonville district. She also earned a reputation as a tireless advocate of civil rights.[1]

Corrine Brown was born in Jacksonville, Florida, on November 11, 1946, and grew up in the city's Northside neighborhood, graduating from Stanton High School. As a single mother, she raised a daughter, Shantrel. She earned a bachelor of science degree at Florida Agriculture and Mechanical University in 1969 and an M.A. from the same institution in 1971. In 1972 Brown graduated with an Ed.S. degree from the University of Florida. She taught at the University of Florida and Edward Waters College before settling at Florida Community College in Jacksonville, where she taught and served as a guidance counselor from 1977 to 1992. Her close friend and political mentor, Gwen Cherry, was the first African-American woman elected to the Florida house of representatives. Cherry's death in a 1979 car crash prompted Brown toward elective politics. In 1980, she was a delegate for presidential candidate Senator Edward Kennedy at the Democratic National Convention. Two years later, Brown won a seat in the Florida legislature, where she served for a decade.

In 1992, reapportionment created a new district in northeastern Florida spanning the area from Jacksonville to Orlando. Brown won the Democratic nomination and ran a general election campaign that focused on improving the district's educational system, bringing more jobs to the area, and protecting Social Security and Medicare for the elderly. She won by 18 percentage points, making her one of three Florida candidates elected that year (including Alcee Hastings and Carrie Meek) who were the first African Americans to represent the state since Reconstruction. In her subsequent six elections, Brown won by comfortable margins. In 2004, she was elected to her seventh term without opposition in a district which still covered much of her original Jacksonville base.[2]

When Representative Brown took her seat in the 103rd Congress (1993–1995), she received assignments on the Government Operations Committee, the Veterans' Affairs Committee, and the Public Works and Transportation Committee (later named Transportation and Infrastructure). In the 104th Congress (1995–1997), she resigned from Government Operations. Brown also served as vice chair of the Congressional Black Caucus and as a member of the Women's Caucus.

Brown's primary focus is on improving the economy within her district, steering federal funds and projects into the north Florida region. She led the effort to construct an $86 million federal courthouse in Jacksonville, while using her influence on the Transportation and Infrastructure Committee to initiate Florida rail projects to meet the state's booming transportation needs. In 1998, Brown orchestrated a nearly 60 percent increase in funding for federal transportation programs in Florida.[3] While supporting reduction of the federal deficit by cutting welfare programs, Brown believed the system must be made "more advantageous for welfare recipients to get off welfare" by providing jobs and job training. "We must make sure that changes in the welfare system do not inadvertently hurt children," she added.[4] Brown also supported military defense spending, in part, reflecting the large military presence in her district, most notably the Jacksonville Naval Air Station. But Brown wanted more of the money to flow into personnel training, describing the military as a place where working-class Americans could find opportunities unavailable elsewhere. From her seat on the Veterans' Affairs Committee, Brown was particularly attentive to the needs of women veterans and health issues. After the 2000 elections, Brown was one of the most vocal advocates for voting reforms. To improve the voting process, especially in minority precincts, Representative Brown supported the Help America Vote Act of 2002, to streamline balloting procedures and provide money to modernize voting systems as a first step toward reform.[5]

Her interests have at times moved Brown's attention outside her district. In 1993, shortly after arriving on Capitol Hill, she began working behind the scenes to push the William J. Clinton administration to restore a democratic government in Haiti by installing deposed President Jean-Bertrand Aristide. She also urged U.S. officials to process the thousands of Haitians who arrived in the U.S. seeking political asylum.[6] Brown also has taken up the cause of Liberians, pushing to extend temporary visa status for thousands who came to America after a civil war in the African country during the early 1990s.

FOR FURTHER READING

Biographical Directory of the U.S. Congress, "Corrine Brown," http://bioguide.congress.gov

NOTES

1 Bruce I. Friedland, "Jacksonville's Pragmatic liberal U.S. Rep. Corrine Brown Passionately Pushes Her Causes and Delivers Bacon Back to City," 19 July 2000, *Florida Times-Union*: A1.

2 "Election Statistics, 1920 to Present," http://clerk.house.gov/members/electionInfo/elections.html.

3 *Politics in America, 2002* (Washington, D.C.: Congressional Quarterly Inc., 2001): 215–216.

4 "Candidates' Forum," 6 November 1994, *Orlando Sentinel*: G7.

5 Conference Report on H.R. 3295, Help America Vote Act of 2002, *Congressional Record*, House, 107th Cong., 2nd sess. (10 October 2002): 7836.

6 "Testimony of Congresswoman Corrine Brown," 13 June 1994, Judiciary Subcommittee on International Law, Immigration, and Refugees, Federal Document Clearing House Congressional Testimony.

Virginia "Ginny" Brown-Waite
1943–

UNITED STATES REPRESENTATIVE
REPUBLICAN FROM FLORIDA
2003–

Image courtesy of the Member

WITH NEARLY 30 YEARS' POLITICAL EXPERIENCE in two states, Ginny Brown-Waite approached her freshman term in the 108th Congress (2003–2005) with the goal of looking out for the interests of her Gulf Coast constituency that includes large numbers of retirees and veterans. Formerly the president *pro tempore* of the Florida senate, and a seasoned political aide in New York state, Brown-Waite pursued her legislative interests from her three influential committee assignments: Budget, Financial Services, and Veterans' Affairs.

Virginia Brown was born in Albany, New York, on October 5, 1943. She graduated from Albany's Vincentian High School in 1961 and was married that same year. In the next five years she had two daughters, Danene and Lorie (she would later adopt a third daughter, Jeannine). In the early 1970s, Brown took a job with New York state senator Walter Langley. She began a 17-year career in the state legislature, where she also worked for Long Island senator Owen Johnson. While working full time, Brown earned a bachelor of science in public administration from the University of New York at Albany in 1976 and was the first member of her family to earn a college degree.[1] She later earned her labor studies certificate from Cornell University.[2] Brown continued her education at Russell Sage College, in Troy, New York, where she earned her M.S. in public administration in 1984. After divorcing her first husband, Brown married Harvey Waite, a New York state trooper.

Brown-Waite's career in electoral politics began after the family relocated to Brooksville, Florida, along the Gulf Coast north of Tampa, following Harvey Waite's retirement. After finishing her duties in Albany, Brown-Waite began to care for her elderly mother. Her mother died a year later, and Brown-Waite became involved in local Florida politics, serving on the Hernando County board of commissioners from 1991 to 1993. In 1992, Brown-Waite won election to the Florida state senate by defeating a 24-year veteran state legislator. She served for three terms, chairing several committees: natural resources and conservation, health care, and criminal justice. She also was vice chair on the rules and calendar and fiscal policy committees. Brown-Waite became known for her work on welfare and health care reform and veterans' issues.[3] She climbed the GOP ranks and was named the majority whip in 1999 and served as president *pro tempore* of the Florida senate from 2001 until 2002. Meanwhile, she also worked as an adjunct professor at Springfield College's Tampa campus.

In 2002, redistricting favored Brown-Waite in the race for Florida's west central congressional seat in the U.S. House of Representatives. Formerly a solidly Democratic district, it had been redrawn and was evenly divided between Democrats and Republicans. Brown-Waite won the GOP primary in September 2002 and focused her energies in what she dubbed a "sleep-optional" campaign against the five-term incumbent, Democrat Karen Thurman. She depended on grass-roots volunteers for most of her campaigning, stating, "We knew it was going to be won on the ground, not the airwaves."[4] In a district populated by many retirees, Brown-Waite's platform focused on revamping Social Security, improving prescription drug benefits to seniors, and tax cuts as a catalyst for economic growth.[5] Brown-Waite prevailed over Thurman in a hard-fought campaign.[6]

Taking her seat as part of the Republican majority in the 108th Congress, Brown-Waite was appointed to the Financial Services Committee, serving on the Subcommittees on Capital Markets, Insurance and GSE's, Financial Institutions and Consumer Credit, and Oversight and Investigations. As she represented a large number of veterans in Florida's 5th District, she also gained an appointment to the Veterans' Affairs Committee, serving on the Subcommittees on Benefits and on Health. Brown-Waite also acted as the vice chair of the Congressional Caucus for Women's Issues. She remained loyal to her party and supported President George W. Bush, voting in favor of criminalizing partial-birth abortion, issuing private school vouchers in the District of Columbia, and supporting the President's tax cuts. She also cosponsored legislation which overhauled Medicare and created a prescription drug benefit. In 2004, Brown-Waite was elected to a second term, defeating Democrat Robert Whittel 66 to 34 percent.[7]

FOR FURTHER READING

Biographical Directory of the U.S. Congress, "Virginia Brown-Waite" http://bioguide.congress.gov

NOTES

1 Ginny Brown-Waite, "SGS '84: Newest Sage Graduate in College," *Sage Crossroads*, Winter 2003: 3. Available at www.sage.edu./TSC/news/pdfs/crossroads_winter2003.pdf (accessed 11 March 2004).

2 "Ginny Brown-Waite for U.S. Congress," available at www.brown-waiteforcongress.com/bio.htm (accessed 6 November 2002).

3 "Ginny Brown-Waite for U.S. Congress."

4 "How Brown-Waite Ousted Thurman," 7 November 2002, *St. Petersburg Times*: 1.

5 "Ginny Brown-Waite," 1 September 2002, *Lakeland Ledger*: S6; "Virginia 'Ginny' Brown-Waite," 8 September 2002, *Orlando Sentinel*: G6.

6 *Politics in America, 2004*: 228.

7 "Election Statistics, 1920 to Present," http://clerk.house.gov/members/electionInfo/elections.html.

Maria E. Cantwell
1958–

UNITED STATES REPRESENTATIVE, 1993–1995
UNITED STATES SENATOR, 2001–
DEMOCRAT FROM WASHINGTON

Image courtesy of the Member

MARIA CANTWELL HAS SERVED WASHINGTON STATE in both chambers of the U.S. Congress. In 1992, she won a House term during the "Year of the Woman" and, in 2000, was elected to the U.S. Senate when she unseated a three-term incumbent. A former high-tech company executive and state legislator, Senator Cantwell has focused on issues important to the Washington economy—aerospace, software, biotechnology, and agriculture.

Maria Cantwell was born in Indianapolis, Indiana, on October 13, 1958, the second of five children raised by Paul Cantwell, a city councilman and state legislator, and Rose Cantwell. She earned a B.A. in public administration from Miami University of Ohio in 1981, becoming the first in her family to receive a college degree.[1] In 1983, she moved to Washington state to direct Alan Cranston's presidential campaign in the northwest U.S. She also worked in public relations and, later, opened her own consulting company. At age 28, Maria Cantwell was elected to the Washington legislature, and she served as a representative from 1987 to 1993. She chaired the trade and economic development committee, working to draw biotech companies to Washington. Former state house speaker Joe King recalled Cantwell as "the best legislator I ever served with."[2]

When suburban Seattle Republican Representative John Miller announced his retirement in 1992, Cantwell declared her candidacy by invoking President John F. Kennedy's inaugural call to service.[3] The district—which included the northern suburbs of Seattle in King and Snohomish counties and extended across Puget Sound to take in Bainbridge Island and parts of Kitsap County north of Bremerton—was affluent and politically moderate.[4] Describing herself as a "pro-business Democrat," Cantwell ran on a platform that called for universal access to health care, proposed a 5 percent cut in federal discretionary spending, supported the presidential line-item veto, and backed the Brady Handgun Bill, which created a waiting period before buying a gun.[5] With 55 percent of the vote, Cantwell defeated a Republican state senator; it was the first time in more than 40 years that a Democrat won the district.

When Cantwell took her seat in the 103rd Congress (1993–1995), she received assignments on three committees: Foreign Affairs, Merchant Marine and Fisheries, and Public Works and Transportation. She specialized in high-technology issues.[6] In August 1994, Congresswoman Cantwell introduced the Electronic Freedom of Information Act, which built on the original FOIA bill to make government more accountable for storing digital information.[7] On trade issues, she supported the North American Free Trade Agreement. Cantwell also voted for the landmark Family and Medical Leave Act of 1993 and earned a reputation as an environmental advocate.

Cantwell left public office in 1995, after losing re-election during the "Republican Revolution" of 1994. For five years, she worked as a marketing executive for a growing Internet software company in Washington. She eventually served as the company's vice president of consumer products as it expanded by about 1,000 jobs.

In 2000, Cantwell challenged three-term incumbent Republican Senator Slade Gorton of Washington. In a narrow race not decided until after a December recount, Cantwell prevailed by a margin of 2,229 votes (one-tenth of one percent of all the votes cast). Hers was the last Senate seat still contested, and her win evenly split the chamber 50–50.[8] Upon taking office in the 107th Congress (2001–2003), Cantwell pledged to follow in the footsteps of the legendary Washington Senator Henry "Scoop" Jackson.[9] She received assignments on four committees: Energy and Natural Resources, Judiciary, Small Business, and Indian Affairs. In the 108th Congress (2003–2005), Cantwell left her Judiciary assignment to serve on the Commerce, Science, and Transportation Committee.

One of the first issues that Senator Cantwell took up in the Senate was campaign finance reform. "Until we craft a campaign system with a shorter, more intensive campaign period, funded with finite and equal resources available to candidates, we will not govern well," Cantwell said.[10] She supported the Bipartisan Campaign Reform Act, which became law in 2002. Cantwell's legislative priorities have centered on agricultural trade, high-technology business, and the environment. She has sought to open foreign markets to Washington's diverse agricultural products. She also has been a Senate leader in prohibiting energy price manipulations and empowering law officers and consumers against identity theft crimes. Senator Cantwell also wrote legislation to create the largest expansion of Mt. Rainier National Park in 70 years, passed a bill to establish the Lewis & Clark National Historic Park, and pushed for the creation of the Wild Sky Wilderness Act and has defended key provisions in the Marine Mammals Protection Act.[11]

FOR FURTHER READING

Biographical Directory of the U.S. Congress, "Maria Cantwell," http://bioguide.congress.gov

NOTES

1 *Politics in America, 2002* (Washington, D.C.: Congressional Quarterly Inc., 2001): 1062; *Almanac of American Politics, 2002* (Washington, D.C.: National Journal Inc., 2001): 1598–1599; Richard Jerome, Macon Morehouse, Mary Boone, "Up in a Down Market: Dot-com Dollars Depleted, Maria Cantwell Focuses on Her New Life in the Senate," 21 May 2001, *People*: 179.

2 "Official Biography of Maria Cantwell," http://cantwell.senate.gov/about/index.html (accessed 14 December 2004).

3 Marla Williams, "State Legislator Cantwell to Run for Miller's Seat," 11 February 1992, *Seattle Times*: D2.

4 *Politics in America, 1994* (Washington, D.C.: Congressional Quarterly Inc., 1993): 1611–1612.

5 Susan Gilmore, "Cantwell May Shatter Tradition in 1st District," 31 October 1992, *Seattle Times*: A12; Williams, "State Legislator Cantwell to Run for Miller's Seat."

6 *Politics in America, 1996* (Washington, D.C.: Congressional Quarterly Inc., 1995): 1398–1399.

7 *Congressional Record,* House, 103rd Cong., 2nd sess. (8 August 1994): 1676.

8 Ben White, "A Flush Candidate's Debt Worries; Sen. Cantwell Owes $3 Million, and Her Portfolio Is in the Tank," 15 March 2001, *Washington Post*: A12; for more on what companies each candidate "represented," see Chris Taylor, "One More Digital Divide; A Tech Millionaire Takes on 'Senator Microsoft,'" 30 October 2000, *Time*: 42.

9 *Congressional Record,* Senate, 107th Cong., 1st sess. (3 January 2001): 11.

10 *Congressional Record,* Senate, 107th Cong. 2nd sess. (27 March 2001): 2096.

11 "Official Biography of Maria Cantwell," http://cantwell.senate.gov/about/index.html.

Shelley Moore Capito
1953–

UNITED STATES REPRESENTATIVE
REPUBLICAN FROM WEST VIRGINIA
2001–

Image courtesy of the Member

SHELLEY MOORE CAPITO, DAUGHTER OF ONE OF West Virginia's most successful Republican politicians, made her own mark on state politics by running as a GOP candidate in a heavily Democratic district in 2000 and following her father into the U.S. House.

Shelley Moore was born in Glen Dale, West Virginia, on November 26, 1953, to Arch A. Moore, Jr., a Republican who served 12 years in the U.S. House of Representatives and another dozen as governor of West Virginia, and Shelley Riley Moore. Raised in West Virginia and Washington, D.C., she graduated with a B.S. in zoology from Duke University in 1975 and earned an M.Ed. from the University of Virginia in 1976. She married Charles Capito, Jr., and the couple raised three children: Charles, Moore, and Shelley. Shelley Moore Capito worked as a counselor at West Virginia State College and as the educational information center director for the West Virginia board of regents. In 1996, Capito was elected to the West Virginia house of delegates, where she served from 1997 to 2001. Her legislative career included service as minority chairperson of the health and human services committee, where she focused on areas of children's health and domestic violence.

In 2000, when incumbent West Virginia Representative Bob Wise retired from his congressional seat covering the central swath of the state, including the state capital, to run for governor, Capito challenged former Democratic state senator Jim Humphreys for the vacancy. At one point early in the race, she trailed Humphreys by more than 30 points–in addition to facing a heavy Democratic advantage in the number of registered voters.[1] Humphreys won the support of labor, including the United Mine Workers, but Capito closed the gap with a late infusion of national GOP support and her own extensive political network.

She benefited from family name recognition but insisted on her independence. "There's a whole myth out there my father is running my life and my campaign and it's not true. I am a 46-year-old woman. I have an independence of spirit."[2] She defeated Humphreys with 49 percent to 46 percent of the vote. In doing so, Capito became only the second woman ever elected from West Virginia and the first Republican Representative elected from the state since 1980. In 2002, Capito again faced Humphreys, prevailing with 60 percent of the vote. She won election to a third term in 2004 by defeating Democrat Erik Wells, 57 to 41 percent.[3]

When she took her seat in the 107th Congress (2001–2003), Capito received assignments on the Financial Services, the Small Business, and the Transportation and Infrastructure committees. She also served as a vice chairwoman of the Woman's Caucus.

During her first term, Capito hewed to a legislative agenda that focused on the constituents in her district. In the summer of 2002, as California energy woes and national energy policy were at the forefront of debate, Capito argued for a "smart plan" for energy, emphasizing coal and natural gas deposits in West Virginia. In a House speech, she said that "many of these resources have lain asleep, untapped, due partly to the effect of the overly restrictive regulations that have prevented the extraction, the production and the transportation of these sources of energy ... I think West Virginia's abundant resources can be used effectively, can be burned environmentally in a cleaner fashion; and it can give us, I think, a good baseline of the energy production that we so desperately need in this country."[4] She also cosponsored the reauthorization of the Appalachian Regional Development Act (ARC), first created in 1965, to boost economic and industrial development in rural Appalachia. "Whether it is building new roads, providing employee training or assisting local communities with flood damage, the ARC has proven itself to be a tremendous asset for West Virginia and the rest of the region," Capito said while urging her colleagues to reauthorize the bill in 2002.[5]

Her interest in health care and prescription drug legislation led Speaker J. Dennis Hastert of Illinois to appoint Congresswoman Capito vice co-chair of the House Prescription Drug Task Force. She expressed concern about prescription coverage for West Virginia's large senior population, more than a quarter of whom live below the poverty level. She pressed for catastrophic coverage for expensive drugs and especially called attention to the plight of older, widowed women with no source of income. Additionally, Capito, known for her energy and accessibility, fought hard to preserve West Virginia jobs.

FOR FURTHER READING

Biographical Directory of the U.S. Congress, "Shelley Moore Capito," http://bioguide.congress.gov

NOTES

1 Sandra Basu, "Shelley Moore Capito's Uphill Climb," May 2001, Campaigns & Elections: 22.

2 Lawrence Messina, "The Sins of Her Father: Arch Moore Casts Shadow in Daughter's Congressional Race," 1 November 2000, Charleston Gazette: 1C.

3 "Election Statistics, 1920 to Present," http://clerk.house.gov/members/ electionInfo/elections.html.

4 Congressional Record, House, 107th Cong., 1st sess. (20 June 2001): 3349.

5 Congressional Record, House, 107th Cong., 2nd sess. (26 February 2002):529.

Lois Capps
1938–

UNITED STATES REPRESENTATIVE
DEMOCRAT FROM CALIFORNIA
1998–

Image courtesy of the Member

WIFE AND POLITICAL CONFIDANTE OF A theology professor-turned-politician, Lois Capps won a special election to the U.S. House after the death of her husband, Walter Capps. In the subsequent Congresses in which she served, Capps carved out her own niche as an advocate for health care and environmental protection.

Lois Ragnhild Grimsrud was born in Ladysmith, Wisconsin, on January 10, 1938, to Jurgen and Solveig Grimsrud. Lois Grimsrud earned a B.S. degree in nursing from Pacific Lutheran University in 1959 and an M.A. in religion from Yale University in 1964. She received an M.A. in education from the University of California at Santa Barbara in 1990. Lois married Walter Holden Capps in 1960, and the couple raised three children: Lisa, Todd, and Laura. From 1960 to 1964, Lois Capps worked as a nursing instructor and head nurse at the Yale New Haven Hospital and also as a staff nurse in Hamden, Connecticut. When the family relocated to California, Capps worked as an elementary school nurse in Santa Barbara County, California, from 1968 to 1970 and from 1977 to 1996. She also taught part-time at the Santa Barbara City College from 1983 to 1995. In 1996, she worked on her husband's successful Democratic congressional campaign for a California U.S. House seat, which the GOP had held since World War II.

On October 28, 1997, Representative Walter Capps died suddenly of a heart attack, and in early 1998 Lois Capps announced her candidacy to fill the vacant seat encompassing California's central coast. Capps defeated Republican state assemblyman Tom Bordonaro in the March 9, 1998, special election, 53 to 45 percent.[1] On March 17, 1998, Capps was sworn in to the 105th Congress (1997–1999), where she received her husband's assignments on the International Relations and Science committees. She again faced Bordonaro in the general election for the 106th Congress (1999–2001) later that fall, winning with 55 percent of the vote. In the 106th Congress, she relinquished her two committee assignments to take a seat on the Commerce Committee, renamed the Energy and Commerce Committee in the 107th Congress (2001–2003). In the 108th Congress (2003–2005), Representative Capps secured a spot on the Budget Committee.

Capps draws on her health care background in her committee and subcommittee assignments and in many of the caucuses she chairs. She is a founder and co-chair of the House Nursing Caucus and the Democratic Vice Chair of the Congressional Caucus for Women's Issues. Capps also serves as co-chair of the Congressional Heart and Stroke Coalition, the House Cancer Caucus, the Congressional Biomedical Research Caucus, the Congressional School Health and Safety Caucus, the Congressional Hearing Health Caucus, and the House Democratic Task Force on Health.

Capps' experience in health care has made her a respected leader in Congress on issues of public health. In 2002 she passed the Nurse Reinvestment Act, legislation to address the national nursing shortage. Capps' legislation, the Domestic Violence Screening, Treatment and Prevention Act, focused on the health care aspects of domestic violence and was passed as part of the reauthorization of the Violence Against Women Act, which became law in 2006. Capps also passed legislation to curb underage drinking, improve mental health services, provide emergency defibrillators to local communities, bring CPR instruction to schools, and provide immediate Medicare coverage to patients suffering from Lou Gehrig's disease. In 2006 Capps introduced two bills, the HEART for Women Act and the Comprehensive Cancer Care Improvement Act, dedicated to improving public health and reflecting her commitment to patient advocacy.

Capps has also been at the forefront of environmental protection. Capps repeatedly led efforts to stop new oil and gas development off our coasts and on our public lands. The House repeatedly passed her amendments to continue the longstanding ban against new offshore oil and gas development. In 2005 Capps introduced the Los Padres National Forest Conservation Act (H.R. 3149), legislation to permanently ban new oil and gas development in the forest. Capps also led the effort to remove the harmful MTBE liability provision in the Energy Act of 2005, protecting consumers from shouldering the financial burden of cleaning up MTBE contamination in their water supplies. In 2006 she co-founded the National Marine Sanctuary Caucus.

In 2002, Representative Capps faced Republican businesswoman Beth Rogers in a newly apportioned California district and won election to a fourth term with her widest margin to date, 59 to 38 percent. Two years later, Capps earned a seat in the 109th Congress (2005–2007) when she defeated Republican Don Regan by a 63 to 34 percent margin.

FOR FURTHER READING

Biographical Directory of the U.S. Congress, "Lois Capps," http://bioguide.congress.gov

NOTES

1 Todd Purdum, "Democrat's Widow Wins California House Race," 12 March 1998, *New York Times*: A 12; "Election Statistics, 1920 to Present," http://clerk. house.gov/members/electionInfo/ elections.html. For a summary of Capps's legislative efforts related to health care, see *Politics in America, 2004* (Washington, D.C.: Congressional Quarterly, Inc., 2003): 110.

Julia May Carson
1938–

UNITED STATES REPRESENTATIVE
DEMOCRAT FROM INDIANA
1997–

Image courtesy of the Member

OVERCOMING POVERTY AND RACISM, Julia Carson served nearly two decades in the Indiana legislature and in Indianapolis administrative office before wining election to the U.S. House in 1996. Representative Carson, the first African American and woman to represent the Indiana state capital, has focused on issues affecting working-class Americans.

Julia May Porter was born in Louisville, Kentucky, on July 8, 1938. Her mother, Velma Porter, was single and moved to Indianapolis, Indiana, to find work as a domestic. Julia Porter grew up working a series of part-time jobs before her 1955 graduation from Crispus Attucks High School in Indianapolis. Shortly thereafter, she was married, raised two children, and subsequently divorced. She later studied at Martin University and Indiana University. In 1965 she was working as a secretary at a United Auto Workers local chapter when newly elected Indiana Congressman Andy Jacobs hired her as a caseworker and district aide. She worked for Jacobs until 1972, when he encouraged her to run for office in the Indiana legislature. From 1973 to 1977, Carson served in the state house of representatives before winning election to the Indiana senate. She served in the upper chamber until 1990, sitting on its finance committee and eventually holding the minority whip position. Throughout her state legislature service, Carson was employed as the human resources director at an engine company, a job she held from 1973 to 1996. In 1991, Carson won election as a Center Township Trustee. In that post, she administered welfare payments in central Indianapolis and was successful at erasing the agency's crippling debt—a $20 million deficit—leaving $7 million in the bank prior to winning a seat in Congress.

When Representative Jacobs retired in 1996, Carson won his endorsement and entered the Democratic primary for the open seat. The district encompassed the state capital of Indianapolis, a traditionally moderate political district that was 68 percent white and 30 percent black. In the Democratic primary she topped the former district party chair, with a margin of 49 to 31 percent. In the general election campaign against Republican Virginia Blackenbaker, who shared Carson's liberal support for abortion rights and opposition to the death penalty, Carson prevailed with 53 percent. In her subsequent four re-election campaigns, Carson has won by slightly larger margins in her competitive district. Reapportionment in 2001 added more than 100,000 constituents, many of them Republican. Nevertheless, Carson was re-elected in 2004 to her fifth consecutive term, defeating Republican Andrew Horning, 54 to 44 percent.[1]

Carson, who underwent heart surgery shortly after her election, was sworn in to office from her hospital bed on January 9, 1997. When Carson recuperated and claimed her seat in the 105th Congress (1997-1999) in March 1997, she received posts on two panels: the Banking and Financial Services Committee (later renamed Financial Services) and the Veterans' Affairs Committee. In the 108th Congress (2003-2005) she left Veterans' Affairs to accept assignment on the powerful Transportation and Infrastructure Committee. In the 108th Congress, she had risen to become the third-ranking member on Financial Services' Subcommittee on Housing and Community Opportunity.

Carson's legislative interests ranged from national issues affecting children and working Americans to local programs that affected her Indianapolis constituency. In the 108th Congress, she sponsored the largest Amtrak reauthorization bill in history. The National Defense Rail Act provided for the development of new rail lines including high-speed rail corridors. Amtrak's largest repair facility is located near Indianapolis. Carson also supported placing restrictions on the North American Free Trade Agreement, arguing that it has taken low-wage manufacturing jobs some of which are in her district.[2] Carson has also worked to bring about greater use of ethanol as a fuel to decrease pollution and U.S. dependence on foreign oil. She also co-chairs the Zoo Caucus.

From her seat on the Financial Services Committee, Carson has authored legislation to reform the debt consolidation industry. In order to increase the "financial literacy" of average Americans, she has helped create the Indiana Mortgage and Foreclosure Hotline to counsel homeowners and potential buyers on the mortgage process.[3] Carson supported measures to curb smoking among minorities and to promote child safety features on guns.[4] She also has been an advocate for moderating cuts to the welfare system, noting that a social safety net "can work if we are committed to weeding out excessiveness, abuse and apathy."[5] One of her crowning legislative achievements came during the 106th Congress (1999–2001), when Congresswoman Carson authored and introduced a bill, signed by President William J. Clinton, conferring the Congressional Gold Medal to civil rights activist Rosa Parks.[6]

FOR FURTHER READING

Biographical Directory of the U.S. Congress, "Julia May Carson," http://bioguide.congress.gov

NOTES

1 "Election Statistics, 1920 to Present," http://clerk.house.gov/members/electionInfo/elections.html.

2 Politics in America, 2004 (Washington, D.C.: Congressional Quarterly Inc., 2003): 373–374.

3 "Official Biography of Julia Carson," http://juliacarson.house.gov/display2.cfm?idffi778&typeffiNews (accessed 14 June 2002).

4 Karen Foerstel, Biographical Dictionary of Congressional Women: (Westport, CT: Praeger, 1999): 52.

5 "Julia Carson," Contemporary Black Biography 23 (Detroit: Gale Research, 1999).

6 For a history and full list of Congressional Gold Medal Recipients, see http://clerk.house.gov/histHigh/Congressional_History/goldMedal.html.

Donna M. Christensen
1945–

DELEGATE
DEMOCRAT FROM THE VIRGIN ISLANDS
1997–

Image courtesy of the Member

DELEGATE DONNA M. CHRISTENSEN WON ELECTION to the U.S. House of Representatives in 1997, the first woman to represent the U.S. Virgin Islands, a multi-island territory in the eastern Caribbean. The islands became part of the United States of America when they were purchased from Denmark in 1917. Since 1973, the territory has had nonvoting representation in the House of Representatives.[1] During her tenure, Christensen has focused on improving the social, political, and economic dynamic of the islands, especially as it relates to federal issues.

Donna Christensen was born on September 19, 1945, to the late chief judge of the Virgin Islands District Court, Almeric Christian, and Virginia Sterling Christian. She earned a B.S. from St. Mary's College at Notre Dame in 1966 and an M.D. from George Washington University School of Medicine in 1970. In addition to running an active family practice, Christensen also worked as a health administrator, rising to the position of assistant commissioner of health for the Virgin Islands.

Concurrently, she began her political career in 1980 as part of the Coalition to Appoint a Native Judge, which emphasized judicial appointments from within the community and later on as part of the Save Fountain Valley Coalition, which called for the protection of St. Croix's north side from overdevelopment. She served as Democratic National Committeewoman from 1984 to 1994 and vice chair of the Territorial Committee of the Democratic Party of the Virgin Islands and on the Platform Committee of the Democratic National Committee. From 1984 to 1986, she served as a member of the Virgin Islands board of education and was appointed to the Virgin Islands Status Commission from 1988 to 1992.

Christensen lost her first bid for Delegate to Congress in 1994, failing to secure the Democratic nomination. Two years later, she not only won the party's nomination, but also went on to defeat freshman Independent incumbent Victor Frazer after a three-way general election and a run-off election. In 1997, as a Member of the 105th Congress (1997–1999), she became the first female physician to serve in the House. Christensen has since won re-election to the House by at least 66 percent of the vote.[2]

As a Member of the House, she has served on the Resources Committee, which oversees the affairs of the offshore territories and where she is the Ranking Member of the Subcommittee on National Parks and Public Lands. She has also served on the Small Business Committee and, during the 108th Congress (2003–2005), gained a seat on the newly created Select Committee on Homeland Security, primarily because of her expertise in public health.

Christensen has focused on strengthening the Virgin Islands' economy and stabilizing its fiscal condition. Expanding traditional tax incentives that are central to the economy of the Virgin Islands and introducing legislation to encourage fiscal discipline have been the hallmarks of her tenure. She has also worked to expand business, housing, health, and educational opportunities in the territory.[3]

Delegate Christensen, a member of the Congressional Black Caucus, chairs the Health Briantrust and has been at the forefront of efforts to end health disparities, fight the HIV/AIDS threat both nationally and internationally, and extend health insurance coverage to as many Americans as possible.[4]

Delegate Christensen is married to Christian O. Christensen of St. Croix. She has two daughters from a previous marriage, Rabiah and Karida Green, and one granddaughter, Nia Hamilton.

FOR FURTHER READING

Biographical Directory of the U.S. Congress, "Donna Marie Christian Christensen," http://bioguide.congress.gov

NOTES

1 "America's Caribbean Paradise: History and Geography," http://www.house.gov/christian-christensen/vi_history.htm (accessed 29 December 2004).

2 "Election Statistics, 1920 to Present," http://clerk.house.gov/members/electionInfo/elections.html.

3 "Official Biography of Donna M. Christensen," http://www.house.gov/Christian-christensen/biography.htm (accessed 11 June 2003); *Politics in America, 2004* (Washington, D.C.: Congressional Quarterly Inc., 2003): 1130.

4 "Official Biography of Donna M. Christensen"; *Politics in America, 2004*: 1130.

Hillary Rodham Clinton
1947–

UNITED STATES SENATOR
DEMOCRAT FROM NEW YORK
2001–

Image courtesy of the Member

HILLARY RODHAM CLINTON WAS ELECTED to the United States Senate by the people of New York on November 7, 2000, after years of public service on behalf of children and families. She is the first First Lady of the United States to hold elective office.

Hillary Diane Rodham was born on October 26, 1947, in Chicago, Illinois, the oldest of three children of Hugh Ellsworth Rodham and Dorothy Howell Rodham. She attended Wellesley College, where she became a campus leader and was chosen by her classmates as the first student commencement speaker.[1] After earning a B.A. in political science in 1969, Hillary entered Yale Law School and finished her J.D. in 1973. Inspired by the work of Marian Wright Edelman, a Yale alumna and children's rights activist who later founded the Children's Defense Fund (CDF), Hillary worked for the CDF after graduation. In 1974, during the Watergate impeachment inquiry, she joined the staff of the House Judiciary Committee special counsel. Following her work with the committee, she accepted a teaching position at the University of Arkansas School of Law and, in 1975, married William J. "Bill" Clinton, whom she had met at Yale. They have a daughter, Chelsea.[2]

In 1977, President James Earl "Jimmy" Carter appointed Hillary to the board of Legal Services Corporation, an organization that disbursed federal money to legal aid bureaus nationally. She founded the Arkansas Advocates for Children and Families and, in 1978, was named to the CDF board (chairing it from 1986 to 1989). In 1992, she campaigned widely for her husband, who was elected U.S. President that November. For eight years, Hillary served as an active First Lady, working on health care reform, children's issues, and women's rights.

In 1999, when senior New York Senator Daniel Patrick Moynihan announced his retirement, Hillary joined the race to succeed him.[3] On November 7, 2000, she prevailed with 56 percent of the vote over New York Republican Representative Rick Lazio.[4]

Senator Clinton serves on three committees: Environment and Public Works; Health, Education, Labor, and Pensions; and the Senate Special Committee on Aging. She is the first New Yorker ever appointed to serve on the Senate Armed Services Committee. As the first woman to represent New York in the Senate, Hillary's efforts to master the chamber's legislative processes and her ability to work across the aisle have made her an effective and respected Member of the Senate.[5]

Senator Clinton's work has focused on building a better future for New York families, including greater opportunity through economic development; increased access to health care and education; energy independence through development of alternative fuel and energy resources; and security at home and abroad. She won support for legislation to clean up industrial pollution for economic development, to ensure the safety of children's medicine, and to repair and modernize schools. After the September 11, 2001, attacks, Senator Clinton worked tirelessly to enable New York to recover, including ensuring adequate federal funds for rebuilding. She also won passage of legislation improving communication for federal and local emergency first responders.[6] As a member of the Armed Services Committee, Senator Clinton led the bipartisan effort to extend health care benefits to members of the National Guard and Reserve.

FOR FURTHER READING

Biographical Directory of the U.S. Congress, "Hillary Rodham Clinton," http://bioguide.congress.gov

Clinton, Hillary Rodham. *It Takes a Village: And Other Lessons Children Teach Us* (New York: Simon & Schuster, 1996).

———. *Living History* (New York: Simon & Schuster, 2003).

NOTES

1 "Hillary Rodham Clinton" *Current Biography, 2002* (New York: H.W. Wilson and Company, 2002): 93–94.

2 *Current Biography, 2002*: 94–95; *Politics in America, 2002* (Washington, D.C.: Congressional Quarterly Inc., 2001): 671.

3 Adam Nagourney, "The Senate Campaign—the First Lady," 18 September 2000, *New York Times*: A1.

4 "Election Statistics, 1920 to Present," http://clerk.house.gov/members/electionInfo/elections.html; *Politics in America, 2002*: 671.

5 *Politics in America, 2002*: 671; *Almanac of American Politics, 2002* (Washington, D.C.: National Journal Inc.): 1047.

6 *Congressional Record*, Senate, 107th Cong., 1st sess. (3 December 2001): 12298; Frank Bruni, "Show Us the Money," 16 December 2001, *New York Times Magazine*: 60. See also John F. Harris, "Hillary's Big Adventure," 27 January 2002, *Washington Post Magazine*: W8; "Official Biography of Hillary Rodham Clinton," http://Clinton.senate.gov/about_hrc.html (accessed 14 December 2004).

Susan Margaret Collins
1952–

UNITED STATES SENATOR
REPUBLICAN FROM MAINE
1997–

Image courtesy of the Member

A LONG-TIME CONGRESSIONAL AIDE AND ADMINISTRATOR, Susan Collins won election to the Maine U.S. Senate seat once held by her political idol, Margaret Chase Smith. Senator Collins has developed a reputation as a fiscal conservative whose moderate views on health care, education, and election reform make her one of the chamber's most independent Members. In 2003, Senator Collins became one of just five women in Senate history to chair a full committee when she was named head of the Governmental Affairs Committee (later renamed Homeland Security and Government Affairs).

Susan Margaret Collins was born on December 7, 1952, in Caribou, Maine, one of six children raised by Don and Patricia Collins. After earning a B.A. in government from St. Lawrence University in 1975, Collins served as an aide to Maine Representative Bill Cohen; she followed him when Cohen won election to the U.S. Senate in 1978. In 1981, Collins became staff director of the Senate Governmental Affairs Committee's Subcommittee on Oversight of Government Management. Six years later Maine's Republican Governor John McKernan, Jr., appointed Collins commissioner of the state department of professional and financial regulation. From 1992 to 1993, Collins served as director of the New England Office of Small Business Administration. In 1994, Collins was the unsuccessful GOP candidate for governor of Maine. She later served as executive director of the Center for Family Business at Husson College.[1]

When her mentor William Cohen left the Senate to serve as President William J. Clinton's Secretary of Defense in 1996, Collins won the three-way Republican primary to succeed him. In the general election she faced former Maine Governor Joseph Brennan. Collins ran as a fiscal conservative who supported a balanced budget amendment, and proposed reducing estate taxes to help families keep small businesses intact from one generation to the next. At the polls, Collins prevailed with 49 percent of the vote.[2]

As a new Member of the 105th Congress (1997–1999), Senator Collins received assignments on three committees: Governmental Affairs, Labor and Human Resources (later renamed Health, Education, Labor and Pensions), and the Special Committee on Aging. On Governmental Affairs she became the first freshman to chair the Permanent Subcommittee on Investigations, focusing on consumer issues. In the 106th Congress (1999–2001), she was named to the Special Committee on the Year 2000 Technology Problems. In the 107th Congress (2001–2003), Collins left the Health, Education, Labor and Pensions Committee to serve on the Armed Services Committee in 2001. In 2003, Collins also received an assignment on the Joint Economic Committee.

Senator Collins has specialized in education and health care legislation, earning a reputation as an independent legislator. As a member of the Health, Education, Labor and Pensions Committee, Senator Collins co-authored the 1998 Higher Education Act which reauthorized federal education programs through 2003 and expanded government aid to college students. Collins added two amendments which allowed working students to earn more money before losing eligibility for federal tuition aid and increased aid for lower income students. Teaming up with Illinois Senator Richard Durbin, Collins wrote successful legislation which repealed a $50 billion tax break for tobacco companies. Collins also was an ardent supporter of campaign finance reform, supporting the McCain–Feingold measure from its inception.[3]

Perhaps her most notable accomplishment during her first term was to provide a compromise plan in late 1998 to end an impasse over how the impeachment trial of President Bill Clinton would proceed in the Senate. Collins suggested to then-Majority Leader Trent Lott of Mississippi that the Senate adopt "findings of fact" which detailed Clinton's misconduct, prior to the vote on the two articles of impeachment. Not convinced that the President had committed impeachable offenses, she nonetheless noted, "A lot of us are concerned about the message a straight acquittal would send to the White House and to the American people."[4] Though Collins helped craft the procedural settlement that laid the groundwork for the impeachment process, she and a small minority of Republicans eventually voted with Democrats to acquit Clinton on the two articles of impeachment.

In 2002, Collins won re-election with 59 percent of the vote against Democrat Chellie Pingree, the Maine state senate majority leader. When the 108th Congress (2003–2005) convened, Collins became chair of the Governmental Affairs Committee. From that post she co-authored and helped shepherd through the Senate an intelligence agency reform bill that incorporated many of the suggestions put forward by the *9/11 Commission Report* in 2004, which represents the most sweeping changes to the U.S. intelligence community in more than 50 years.

FOR FURTHER READING

Biographical Directory of the U.S. Congress, "Susan Margaret Collins," http://bioguide.congress.gov

Mikulski, Barbara, et al. *Nine and Counting: The Women of the Senate.* (New York: Morrow, 2000).

NOTES

1 *Politics in America, 2002* (Washington, D.C.: Congressional Quarterly Inc., 2001): 442–443; *Almanac of American Politics, 1998* (Washington, D.C.: National Journal Inc, 1997): 697–698.

2 "Election Statistics, 1920 to Present," http://clerk.house.gov/members/ electionInfo/elections.html.

3 *Politics in America, 2002*: 442–443; Michael Winerip, "Susan M. Collins: A Moderate's Moment," 20 July 1997, *New York Times Magazine*: 18.

4 Lorraine Adams, "A Freshman With an Endgame Idea; As Unassuming Advocate, Collins Hopes 'Findings of Fact' Will Send Message," 29 January 1999, *Washington Post*: A1.

Barbara L. Cubin
1946–

UNITED STATES REPRESENTATIVE
REPUBLICAN FROM WYOMING
1995–

Image courtesy of the Member

As the first woman to represent Wyoming in Congress, Barbara Cubin quickly established herself as a defender of western state interests in the House. Congresswoman Cubin also became one of the highest-ranking women in the GOP, serving as Secretary of the House Republican Conference and chairing the Committee on Resources' Subcommittee on Energy and Mineral Resources.

Barbara Sage was born in Salinas, California, on November 30, 1946, the daughter of Russell and Barbara Sage. She was raised in Casper, Wyoming, and graduated from Natrona County High School. In 1969, Sage earned a B.S. in chemistry from Creighton University in Omaha, Nebraska. She later took graduate courses in business administration at Casper College. She worked as a chemist, a substitute math and science teacher, and a social worker for the elderly and disabled. Barbara Sage married Frederick W. Cubin, a physician, and they raised two sons, William and Eric. From 1975 to 1994, while Barbara Cubin managed her husband's medical practice, she also was active in the local parent teacher association and as a shelter volunteer. In 1986 she won election to the Wyoming house of representatives, where she chaired the joint interim economic development subcommittee. Cubin also served as the Natrona County chairman for Craig Thomas during his successful bid for Wyoming's At-Large seat in the U.S. House of Representatives. In 1992, Cubin won a Wyoming senate seat, where she served on the revenue committee.

In 1994, when Representative Thomas campaigned for the U.S. Senate, Cubin won the five-way primary to succeed him in the At-Large House seat. In the general election, she ran on a pro-life platform and pledged to curb federal control of western lands. In a three-way race, Cubin prevailed with 53 percent of the vote, becoming the first woman to represent the "Equality State" in Congress. She has won her five re-election bids.[1]

When she claimed her seat in the 104th Congress (1995–1997) in January 1995, Representative Cubin received assignments on the Resources and Science committees. In the 105th Congress (1997–1999), she resigned the Science Committee assignment for a spot on the Commerce Committee (now Energy and Commerce). On the Resources Committee, Cubin chaired the Energy and Mineral Resources Subcommittee from the 105th Congress through the 108th Congress (2003–2005).

Cubin focused on western land, mineral, infrastructure, and transportation issues and earned a reputation as a tenacious fighter for western interests.[2] With the federal government owning half of Wyoming land, much of Cubin's legislative program was aimed at relaxing federal land use restrictions and bringing her state a higher profile in Washington. As a cofounder of the Congressional Mining Caucus, Cubin drew attention to the mining industry in her state, particularly coal and trona (a soda ash used in glass and baking soda) extraction. In the 106th Congress (1999–2001), she looked to nationalize a Wyoming pilot program allowing mining companies that worked on public lands to pay federal taxes in minerals rather than dollars. She also pushed for the placement of a federal meat inspector in Wyoming to encourage growth of meat packing plants in the state.[3] Cubin backed the George W. Bush administration's national energy policy in 2001. She advocated the development of alternative sources of energy, including coal, nuclear, hydroelectric, and wind.[4]

In October 1998, when a gay University of Wyoming student was brutally murdered—singled out for his sexual orientation—Cubin, whose sons also attended the school, led the chorus of indignation. "We cannot lie down, we cannot bury our heads, and we cannot sit on our hands," she said, cosponsoring a motion expressing the House's outrage over the incident.[5] Cubin also has spoken out about the importance of family values and stability. She has been a staunch opponent of abortion rights. She also has been an unwavering critic of gun control. In 2000, she was elected to the National Rifle Association's board of directors.[6]

Cubin rose into the GOP leadership quickly, serving in her early terms as a Deputy Majority Whip. In the 107th Congress, she was elected Secretary of the Republican Conference, the sixth-ranking GOP leadership position in the House. During the race, she called for regional balance and a western state perspective in leadership circles. "I believe the views of a Member from a Mountain West public lands state have too long been absent from the leadership table," she explained. "Achieving a better working relationship through issue education with Members who don't have to deal with an absent landlord is important to me and to the well-being of our conference."[7] Cubin also joined the Steering Committee, which parcels out committee assignments.

FOR FURTHER READING

Biographical Directory of the U.S. Congress, "Barbara L. Cubin," http://bioguide.congress.gov

NOTES

1 "Election Statistics, 1920 to Present," http://clerk.house.gov/members/electionInfo/elections.html.

2 Joel Achenbach, "See You in September: The GOP Freshmen Had a Giddy First Semester, but the Grading Gets Tougher When They Return," 14 August 1995, *Washington Post*: D1.

3 Charles Davant, "Away from Spotlight, Wyoming Congresswoman Prepares for Business," 8 January 1999, *States News Service*.

4 Chris George, "Cubin Favors Seeking New Energy Sources, Drilling in Arctic Lands," 15 August 2000, *Wyoming Tribune-Eagle*: A6.

5 "House Expresses Dismay at Murder of Gay Student in Wyoming," 16 October 1998, *Washington Post*: A24.

6 *Politics in America, 2002* (Washington, D.C.: Congressional Quarterly Inc., 2001): 1121–1122.

7 John Bresnahan, "Cubin Launches Leadership Bid; Wyo. Member Joins Conference Secretary Race,": 3 July 2000, *Roll Call*.

Jo Ann Davis
1950–

UNITED STATES REPRESENTATIVE
REPUBLICAN FROM VIRGINIA
2001–

Image courtesy of the Member

FROM HUMBLE ORIGINS, JO ANN DAVIS EMERGED as a successful businesswoman, state delegate, and U.S. Representative. Just four years after winning her first political office in the Virginia general assembly, Davis won election in an eastern Virginia district along the west shore of the Chesapeake Bay as the first Republican woman to represent her state in Congress. With seats on the Armed Services, International Relations, and Intelligence committees, where she serves as chairman of the Intelligence Subcommittee on Terrorism, Human Intelligence, Analysis and Counter-Intelligence, Davis has positioned herself as a strong advocate for the defense-related interests which dominate her district.

Jo Ann Davis was born in Rowan, North Carolina, on June 29, 1950. When she was nine years old, her family moved to Hampton, Virginia. Her upbringing—she recalls spending much of her childhood living in a trailer park—was modest. In 1968, she graduated from Kecoughtan High School in Hampton and later attended the Hampton Roads Business College. Afterwards she became an executive secretary at a Newport News real estate company.[1] She married Chuck Davis and they raised two children, Charlie and Chris, in Hampton Roads, Virginia. Jo Ann Davis earned a real estate license in 1984 and opened a property management company in 1988. She then established her own realty business in 1990. In 1997, one of her employees pulled her aside and said, "Jo Ann, come here. Have you ever thought about running for public office?" Davis replied that was a "crazy" idea.[2] She soon changed her mind, however, and ran a successful campaign that unseated a well–financed incumbent state delegate in 1996. She was re-elected with more than 70 percent of the vote. Davis served in the Virginia house of delegates from 1997 to 2001.

When nine-term U.S. Representative Herb Bateman of Virginia announced his retirement in September 2000 (he subsequently died before the general election), Davis entered the Republican primary with four other candidates. Utilizing an effective grass-roots campaign, she earned the Republican nomination. Davis, whose platform included a call to bolster defense and support for school choice and pro-life family values, easily won the general election in the heavily Republican district with 57 percent of the vote against a 30-year political veteran who was the former mayor of Fredricksburg, Virginia.[3] In the 107th Congress (2001–2003), Davis landed assignments on three committees: Armed Services, Government Reform, and International Relations. In 2004 she left her Government Reform post, where she had risen to chair the Civil Service and Agency Reform Subcommittee, to join the Permanent Select Committee on Intelligence.

From her post on the Armed Services Committee, Davis was attuned to the needs of her district, with naval and air force installations in the Hampton Roads area, the Quantico Marine Corps Base, and a group of smaller military and NASA installations scattered throughout the region. Once in office, she became a leading proponent for expanding the Navy fleet by nearly 60 ships, to 375. She supported a pay raise for military personnel and backed a veterans' benefits bill, the Veterans Opportunities Act of 2001. Davis introduced her own legislation, the Service-members' Group Life Insurance Adjustment Act, which sought to retroactively raise the family benefits for dependents of servicemen and servicewomen killed in the line of duty. The legislation passed the House in March 2002 and was signed into law several months later. She also led an effort to increase funding for a major overhaul of the aircraft carrier *Dwight D. Eisenhower* at the Newport News ship facilities.

Davis developed an environmental record that has won praise from both Democrats and Republicans. She was able to secure $48 million in federal funding to clean up and remove a portion of the "ghost fleet" of dilapidated decommissioned naval ships from a site on the James River near Newport News. Another one of Davis's environmental projects has been her longtime opposition to the growing trash importation industry in Virginia. She also opposed the construction of a Newport News water reservoir that would have flooded hundreds of acres of wetlands.[4] On the contentious issue of developing oil reserves in Alaska's north range, Davis voted with her party to allow exploratory drilling.

Davis has been a vocal supporter of the post–September 11th foreign policy of President George W. Bush, voting to authorize the war against Iraq and supporting the administration's defense budget increases. "To continue protecting the homeland and fighting the war on terror is certainly one of the greatest priorities for my district," Davis said.[5] Davis ran unopposed in her 2002 re-election campaign. Two years later, she won re-election to the 109th Congress (2005–2007) by defeating an independent candidate with 80 percent of the vote.[6]

FOR FURTHER READING

Biographical Directory of the U.S. Congress, "Jo Ann Davis," http://bioguide.congress.gov

NOTES

1 *Politics in America, 2004* (Washington, D.C.: Congressional Quarterly Inc., 2003): 1039.

2 Hugh Lessig, "Can Davis Make Her Mark in Politics?" 15 October 2000, *Norfolk Daily Press*: C1.

3 "Election Statistics, 1920 to Present," http://clerk.house.gov/members/electionInfo/elections.html.

4 Michelle Boorstein, "Entrenched Incumbent Faces Foe of Big Government," 10 October 2004, *Washington Post*: C5.

5 "Jo Ann Davis," 28 October 2004, *Washington Post*: Virginia Extra Section, T6.

6 "Election Statistics, 1920 to Present," http://clerk.house.gov/members/electionInfo/elections.html.

Susan A. Davis
1944–

UNITED STATES REPRESENTATIVE
DEMOCRAT FROM CALIFORNIA
2001–

Image courtesy of the Member

SUSAN DAVIS, A MOTHER AND GRANDMOTHER, served her San Diego community in the California legislature before upsetting an incumbent to win a seat in the U.S. House in 2000. "I'm probably one of the most apolitical people," Davis told the *San Diego Union-Tribune* during her first House election campaign. "I do this because I see it as a public service. When I can make some changes, even simple things, it's all worth it."[1]

Susan Carol Alpert was born in Cambridge, Massachusetts, on April 13, 1944, the younger of two daughters raised by Lithuanian immigrant parents. Her pediatrician father moved the family to Richmond, California, when she was young. She earned a B.A. in sociology from the University of California at Berkeley in 1965 and an M.A. in social work from the University of North Carolina at Chapel Hill in 1968. In college she met Steven Davis, a physician. They married, lived in Japan for two years, and settled in San Diego, where they raised two sons, Jeffery and Benjamin. Susan Davis worked as a community producer for a San Diego public television station. She also became politically active, serving as president of the local League of Women Voters. Davis was elected to the San Diego board of education in 1983, serving until 1992. For three years she also served as executive director of the Aaron Price Fellows Program, designed to teach multiethnic high school students leadership and citizenship skills. She won election to the California assembly and served from 1994 to 2000. Davis chaired the women's caucus and the government efficiency and economic development committee and also created and co-chaired a select committee on adolescence.[2]

In 2000, after being recruited by California Representative Nancy Pelosi, Davis launched a campaign to unseat three-term incumbent Republican Brian Bilbray in a competitive San Diego district in which Bilbray had won less than 50 percent in two of his prior campaigns. Davis was unopposed for the Democratic nomination and ran a highly effective door-to-door campaign. In a race that had about 10,000 votes siphoned off by Libertarian and Natural Law candidates, Davis defeated Bilbray by a four-point margin with 50 percent of the vote. In her subsequent two re-election campaigns, Davis won by comfortable margins over 65 percent in the reapportioned district which encompassed much of her previous suburban San Diego constituency.[3] In the 107th Congress (2001–2003) she was appointed to the Armed Services and Education and the Workforce committees. She served one term on the Veterans' Affairs Committee during the 108th Congress (2003–2005).

Davis introduced a number of bills in the U.S. House, based on her previous legislative experience. Two health care bills—the Women's Obstetrician and Gynecologist Medical Access Now Act (2001) and the Second Opinion Coverage Act (2002)—were directly influenced by patients' rights bills that Davis crafted in the California assembly. The former allowed women in health maintenance organizations (HMOs) to skip bureaucratic paperwork by visiting their OB-GYNs without first seeking a referral from their primary care physician. The Second Opinion Bill would require HMOs to pay for patients facing major medical treatments to get another opinion from a specialist inside or outside their plan. Another of her bills would provide more timely health care coverage for hospitalized veterans. In 2002, based on her experience with her father's late-life care needs, Davis authored the Long-Term Care Support and Incentive Act, which provided a tax credit and insurance deductions for seniors and their caregivers. "By encouraging people to plan ahead for the future and purchase long-term care insurance, we can ensure that seniors live dignified and independent lives," Davis said on the House Floor.[4]

Congresswoman Davis's legislative interests also extended to issues that directly affected Californians: environment, energy, and the military, with a major naval presence in her San Diego district. From her seat on the Armed Services Committee, she introduced the Military Pay Gap Act of 2002, to phase out pay inequities between the private sector and the military by 2013. Davis noted that men and women in the military "understand that a lifestyle of service entails a certain amount of sacrifice. In exchange for all their sacrifices, they have a simple request: that their nation make a commitment to them that parallels their commitment to the nation."[5] During the height of the California energy crisis in the summer of 2001, Davis introduced the Renewable Energy Act for Credit on Taxes, which provided for federal tax incentives further allowing homeowners to choose systems that were less reliant on fossil fuels and fossil fuel, generated electricity.

FOR FURTHER READING

Biographical Directory of the U.S. Congress, "Susan A. Davis," http://bioguide.congress.gov

NOTES

1 Dong-Phuong Nguyen, "Davis Left Suburban Comforts to Make a Difference for Others," 5 November 2000, San Diego Union-Tribune: B1; see also, Mark Murray, "The Newly Elected: California 49th House District: Susan Davis," 8 November 2000, http://nationaljournal.com/members/campaign/2000/profiles/Cali49.htm (accessed 26 November 2000).

2 Politics in America, 2004 (Washington, D.C.: Congressional Quarterly Inc., 2003): 157; Congressional Directory, 108th Cong., 1st sess. (Washington, D.C.: Government Printing Office, 2003).

3 "Election Statistics, 1920 to Present," http://clerk.house.gov/members/electionInfo/elections.html.

4 Congressional Record, House, 107th Cong., 2nd sess. (19 March 2002): 387; Congressional Record, House, 107th Cong., 2nd sess. (4 September 2002): 1490; Congressional Record, House, 107th Cong., 1st sess. (5 April 2001): 552.

5 Congressional Record, House, 107th Cong., 2nd sess. (21 June 2002): 1131.

Diana L. DeGette
1957–

UNITED STATES REPRESENTATIVE
DEMOCRAT FROM COLORADO
1997–

Congressional Pictorial Directory
109th Congress

IN 1997, FOURTH-GENERATION DENVER RESIDENT Diana DeGette succeeded Pat Schroeder, one of the most colorful and influential women's rights advocates in the House. As a freshman House Member, Representative DeGette earned a seat on the prestigious Energy and Commerce Committee, from which she has focused largely on health care issues. In her first five terms, DeGette has steadily climbed the ranks of Democratic Caucus leadership, being promoted from Floor Whip to Chief Deputy Whip for the 109th Congress (2005–2007).

Diana DeGette was born on a U.S. Air Force base in Tachikawa, Japan, on July 29, 1957, the oldest of five children. Her parents—her father was an architect and her mother a teacher—returned to their hometown of Denver soon thereafter. After graduating from Denver's South High School in 1975, DeGette earned a B.A. in political science and philosophy from Colorado College in 1979. She was awarded a J.D. from New York University in 1982. After graduation, DeGette served as a deputy state public defender in Colorado from 1982 to 1984 before going into private practice. In 1985, she married attorney Lino Lipinsky; the couple has two daughters, Raphaela and Francesca. In 1992, DeGette was elected to the Colorado house of representatives, serving from 1993 to 1996. After just one term she was appointed assistant minority leader.

DeGette entered the race for the open congressional seat vacated by Denver Representative Pat Schroeder, the dean of women in the House and a liberal icon, in 1995. With the endorsement of Schroeder and influential environmental and labor groups, DeGette easily defeated Denver councilman Tim Sandos in the Democratic primary.[1] In the general election, she faced Republican Joe Rogers, a lawyer who was the first African American to seek national office in Colorado. DeGette ran on a platform that included health care and education reform as well as environmental protection. She also regularly criticized the Republican efforts to slash core entitlement programs in the 104th Congress (1995–1997), arguing that the government must preserve programs such as Social Security, Medicare, Head Start, child nutrition, and prenatal care. DeGette cruised to a 57 to 40 percent win in the heavily Democratic district. In four re-election bids, DeGette has never seriously been challenged, winning between 66 and 73 percent of the vote.[2]

Representative DeGette has held a coveted seat on the Energy and Commerce Committee since her first term. In 2005, she was also named to the House Democratic Leadership as a Chief Deputy Whip after serving two years as Floor Whip and four years as a Regional Whip. On the Energy and Commerce Committee, DeGette serves on three subcommittees: Health; Oversight and Investigations; and Commerce, Trade, and Consumer Protection.

Even as a minority party member, Representative DeGette has shown an ability to work across the aisle to get legislation passed. DeGette focused on health care for children, introducing an amendment for "presumptive eligibility" for Medicaid for children from poor families, that allowed hospitals and doctors to start the application process for government aid. She also authored successful legislation that provided a higher priority for children on waiting lists for organ donations.

Using skills honed as a trial attorney in Colorado, DeGette played a leading role in a number of prominent committee hearings. These included the 2002 hearings into the corporate accountability scandals and the 2004 investigations into the safety of dietary supplements and the practice of prescribing antidepressants to children. In 2006, DeGette took a leadership role in the growing problem of child exploitation over the Internet.

As part of her work on health issues, DeGette emerged as one of the congressional leaders in the debate over embryonic stem cell research. In 2005 legislation to expand federal funding of embryonic stem cell research authored by DeGette passed the House with overwhelming bipartisan support despite strong opposition from President George W. Bush. DeGette's personal experience as the mother of a diabetic child factored into her work as the co-chair of the Congressional Diabetes Caucus, a group that seeks to educate Members on the disease and advance legislation on research and medical care.[3]

DeGette was a dependable vote for much of the Democratic Party's legislative agenda. She supported abortion rights and opposed the death penalty. In 2000, she supported permanent normal trade relations with China—a move welcomed by business but opposed by labor. DeGette also has focused on growth issues within her rapidly expanding Denver district. She sponsored a successful amendment to increase federal funding for the Environmental Protection Agency's Brownfields program which identifies and restores abandoned urban spaces. Since 1999, she has sponsored the Colorado Wilderness Act, a plan to protect 1.4 million acres of federal land on the western slope of the Colorado Rocky Mountains.

FOR FURTHER READING

Biographical Directory of the U.S. Congress, "Diana DeGette," http://bioguide.congress.gov

NOTES

1 Guy Kelly, "DeGette Easily Wins 1st District Over Sandos; Former State Representative Favored for Schroeder's Seat," 14 August 1996, *Denver Rocky Mountain News*: 5A.

2 "Election Statistics, 1920 to Present," http://clerk.house.gov/members/electionInfo/elections.html.

3 "It Doesn't DeGette Any Better; Congressional Representative Diana DeGette, Mother of Diabetic Child," *Diabetes Forecast* 52 (1 June 1999): 44.

Rosa DeLauro
1943–

UNITED STATES REPRESENTATIVE
DEMOCRAT FROM CONNECTICUT
1991–

Image courtesy of the Member

FROM HER WORKING-CLASS ROOTS, Rosa DeLauro worked as a political organizer, consultant, and aide before launching her own successful House career. With a seat on the powerful Appropriations and Budget committees and posts in the House Democratic leadership, Congresswoman DeLauro has become a leading advocate for working families and women's issues.

Rosa DeLauro was born in New Haven, Connecticut, on March 2, 1943, into a politically active family with roots in the Italian Wooster Square neighborhood of New Haven. Her parents, Ted, an insurance salesman, and Luisa DeLauro, a sweatshop seamstress, were New Haven aldermen. Luisa DeLauro was the city's longest-serving alderman, holding office from 1965 to 1998. Rosa DeLauro received a B.A. in history and political science from Marymount College in Tarrytown, New York, in 1964. She also attended the London School of Economics and earned an M.A. in international politics from Columbia University in 1966. DeLauro worked as a community organizer on urban renewal and initiatives to place minorities and women, and served as an executive assistant to the mayor of New Haven. DeLauro married Stanley Greenberg, an associate professor at Yale and, later, head of a national polling firm. She has three stepchildren—Anna, Kathryn, and Jonathan, and one grandchild, Rigby. From 1980 to 1986, DeLauro served as Connecticut Senator Christopher J. Dodd's chief of staff. She was executive director for "Countdown '87," a national campaign to stop U.S. military aid to the Nicaraguan Contras. From 1989 to 1990 she served as executive director for EMILY'S List, a political action group that supports pro-choice women candidates.[1]

In 1990, when four-term Democrat Bruce Morrison retired from the House, DeLauro ran for his vacant seat encompassing New Haven in the southern part of Connecticut. She easily won the Democratic nomination and, in the general election, emphasized her Italian working-class roots and support for middle class tax cuts and universal health care. Her platform called for economic and transportation initiatives, particularly effective in a state that already was suffering from a recession that would take on national dimensions in late 1991.[2] DeLauro won her first (and narrowest) election with 52 to 48 percent of the vote. In her subsequent seven re-election campaigns from 1992 to 2004, DeLauro was never seriously challenged, winning election to the 109th Congress (2005–2007) with 72 percent of the vote.[3]

When DeLauro was sworn in to the 102nd Congress (1991–1993) in January 1991, she received assignments on the Government Operations and Public Works and Transportation committees, as well as on the Select Committee on Aging. In the 103rd Congress (1993–1995), she gave up those posts to join the Appropriations Committee. She left Appropriations briefly to serve on the National Security Committee in the 104th Congress (1995–1997) but returned in the following term and has remained on Appropriations since. DeLauro joined the Budget Committee in the 108th Congress (2003–2005) and became the Ranking Member of the Appropriations Subcommittee on Agriculture in the 109th Congress.

In addition to her prominent committee assignments, DeLauro ranks among the Democratic leadership. In the mid-1990s, she served as Chief Deputy Whip. She twice lost races for the Democratic Caucus chair in 1998 and 2002, the latter by a single vote. In 1999, Democratic colleagues elected her to a newly created position—Assistant to the Democratic Leader. It made her one of the highest ranking Democratic women in the House. In 2002 and 2004, DeLauro was appointed co-chair of the House Democratic Steering Committee.

Representative DeLauro was described by one nationally syndicated columnist as a "hero for working families" for her work on labor and health issues. Inspired by her experience as a survivor of ovarian cancer, DeLauro authored legislation requiring health maintenance organizations (HMOs) to cover a 48-hour of hospital stay after mastectomies and secured research funding for cervical and ovarian cancer. She also has worked aggressively with a bipartisan group of legislators to lower the rising costs of prescription drugs. As a result of her efforts, the U.S. House passed legislation in the 108th Congress allowing the importation of drugs from countries like Canada. With rising instances of food safety and foodborne illness a concern for many Americans, DeLauro cofounded the Congressional Food Safety Caucus to explore remedies to secure the food supply. DeLauro supports an increase in the minimum wage and has authored legislation that would guarantee men and women equal pay for equal work. She led the effort in Congress to restrict the activities of corporate expatriates, U.S. corporations that avoid U.S. taxes by reincorporating offshore. DeLauro also has established numerous civic initiatives to improve children's lives, including the "Anti-Crime Youth Council," a program that sought to engage high school students on issues of violence, the "Kick Butts Connecticut" program, which recruits middle school students to act as antismoking counselors for elementary school children, and "Rosa's Readers," a program to interest first graders in reading outside the classroom.[4]

FOR FURTHER READING

Biographical Directory of the U.S. Congress, "Rosa L. DeLauro," http://bioguide.congress.gov/

NOTES

1 Current Biography, 2000 (New York: H.W. Wilson and Company, 2000): 145–147; Who's Who in American Politics, 1999 (New York: Bowker, 1999).

2 Current Biography, 2000: 145–147.

3 "Election Statistics, 1920 to Present," http://clerk.house.gov/members/electionInfo/elections.html.

4 "Official Biography of Rosa L. DeLauro" http://www.house/gov/delauro/biography.html; Politics in America, 2004 (Washington, D.C.: Congressional Quarterly Inc., 2003): 191–192; Almanac of American Politics, 2004 (Washington, D.C.: National Journal Inc., 2003): 347.

Elizabeth Dole

1936–

UNITED STATES SENATOR
REPUBLICAN FROM NORTH CAROLINA
2003–

Congressional Pictorial Directory
109th Congress

ELECTED IN 2002 AS THE FIRST WOMAN SENATOR FROM North Carolina, Elizabeth Dole has one of the most impressive public service careers of any American elected official. Her role as a Cabinet officer for two Presidents, her own bid for the Republican nomination for President in 2000, and her campaign work for her husband, former Senator Bob Dole, give Senator Elizabeth Dole a deep reserve of political experience to bring to her freshman term.

Mary Elizabeth Hanford was born on July 29, 1936, in Salisbury, North Carolina, to John Van Hanford, a flower wholesaler, and Mary Ella Cathey Hanford. In 1958, Hanford earned a B.A. from Duke University in political science. In the summer of 1959, she studied British history at Oxford University. Hanford subsequently moved to Boston and earned an M.A. from Harvard University in education and government in 1960. She completed a Harvard law degree in 1965, one of only 24 women in a class of 550.

After graduation, Elizabeth Hanford was drawn to the nation's capital, claiming "Washington was like a magnet."[1] In more than 30 years in the capital, she accumulated a formidable political résumé. Her first involvement in national politics was serving as the White House consumer affairs aide for President Richard Nixon. While serving as a consumer advocate for the Federal Trade Commission, Elizabeth Hanford met Kansas Senator Bob Dole, whom she married in 1975.[2] In 1981, President Ronald W. Reagan named her an assistant for the public liaison. From 1983 to 1987, Dole was the first woman to serve as Transportation Secretary.[3] Increased safety was her priority, promoting measures such as a third rear-brake light and airbags in all vehicles, as well as raising the drinking age to 21 years. In 1989, President George H.W. Bush named Dole as his Labor Secretary.

In 1991, Dole left her Cabinet position to become the president of the American Red Cross. During her first year at the helm of the nonprofit organization, she accepted no salary, and she improved the organization's financial health through corporate fundraising.[4] Elizabeth Dole also gained valuable political experience campaigning for her husband during his bids for Vice President in 1976 and for President in 1980, 1988, and 1996. She eventually sought the Republican nomination for President for herself and, before exiting the race in October 1999, was considered the first serious woman contender for the nomination in U.S. history.[5]

When longtime incumbent North Carolina Senator Jesse Helms announced his retirement in 2002, Elizabeth Dole decided to seek his seat in the U.S. Senate. Dole easily won the GOP primary, taking 80 percent of the vote against six opponents. She faced Democratic nominee Erskine Bowles in a hard-fought general election. She ran on a platform dubbed the "Dole Plan," which promoted new jobs in the economically depressed region. In a proposal inherited from Helms, both Dole and Bowles supported a tobacco buyout plan, that put money from the 15 percent tobacco tax towards paying producers more per pound. Dole's strength proved to be statewide, as she defeated Bowles with 53 percent of the total, garnering votes in both the coastal and the mountainous regions.[6] She received the highest percentage for any of the state's Senate candidates since 1978.

Upon her election, Senator Dole's long political service afforded her some important committee assignments. She serves on the Senate Armed Services Committee. Dole also sits on the Banking, Housing and Urban Affairs Committee—an important seat to her constituents, since Charlotte, North Carolina, continues to evolve as a financial hub. She also serves on the Select Committee on Aging. Her legislative agenda has reflected her background, particularly her humanitarian work. Nutrition and hunger are specific concerns, as Dole introduced a joint resolution recognizing hunger as a worldwide problem, provided legislation that expands eligibility for subsidized school lunches, and submitted a bill to provide tax benefits to trucking companies transporting food to distribution centers.[7] Her attention to her North Carolina constituents is reflected in the successful passage of the tobacco buyout program, accomplishing one of her biggest campaign promises. In the 109th Congress (2005–2007), Senator Dole serves as chairwoman of the National Republican Senatorial Committee.

FOR FURTHER READING

Biographical Directory of the U.S. Congress, "Elizabeth Hanford Dole," http://bioguide.congress.gov

Dole, Elizabeth, and Bob Dole. *Unlimited Partners: Our American Story.* (New York: Simon & Schuster, 1996).

NOTES

1 *Current Biography, 1983* (New York: H.W. Wilson and Company, 1983): 117.

2 *Current Biography, 1997* (New York: H.W. Wilson and Company, 1997): 146.

3 Quoted in *Current Biography, 1983*: 119.

4 *Current Biography, 1997*: 148.

5 *Politics in America, 2004* (Washington, D.C.: Congressional Quarterly Inc., 2003): 744–745

6 "Election Statistics, 1920 to Present," http://clerk.house.gov/members/ electionInfo/elections.html; John Morrill and Mark Johnson, "Dole Beats Bowles to Take Helms' Seat in the U.S. Senate," 6 November 2002, *Charlotte Observer*: 1.

7 These measures were introduced in the 108th Congress. See S. Con. Res. 114, S. 1549, and S. 2494.

Jo Ann Emerson
1950–

UNITED STATES REPRESENTATIVE
REPUBLICAN FROM MISSOURI
1996–

Image courtesy of the Member

THOUGH JO ANN EMERSON NEVER HELD ELECTIVE OFFICE prior to succeeding her late husband, Representative Bill Emerson, her upbringing, work experience, and marriage suited her to the task. Within a short period, Congresswoman Emerson established herself as one of the Republican Party's leading women. "I never sought this job. Fate put me here," she said. "So I want to take the skills that I have, whether it's coalition building or strategy or being able to solve problems, and put them to work. I'm very locally oriented. I want to get things done for the folks back home."[1]

Jo Ann Hermann was born in Bethesda, Maryland, on September 16, 1950, daughter of Ab Hermann, a former professional baseball player and executive director of the Republican National Committee, and Sylvia Hermann. She grew up near Washington and was initiated into politics at an early age. Hale Boggs, the Louisiana politician who eventually became House Majority Leader, was a neighbor and the families socialized often. Jo Ann Hermann earned a B.A. in political science from Ohio Wesleyan University in 1972 and pursued a career in public affairs as a lobbyist, first working for the National Restaurant Association. In 1975, she married lobbyist Bill Emerson of Missouri, and the couple raised five children. In 1980, Bill Emerson defeated an incumbent Democrat from a district representing the sprawling agricultural and mining region in rural southeast Missouri to win a seat in the U.S. House of Representatives. Jo Ann Emerson worked as deputy communications director for the National Republican Congressional Committee in the early 1980s. She later served as senior vice president of public affairs for the American Insurance Association.[2]

Shortly before his death from lung cancer in June 1996, Bill Emerson asked his wife to consider taking his seat, a request repeated by his staff and constituents.[3] Emerson agreed, and her first campaign reflected her husband's conservative philosophy and skills as a consensus builder. Her slogan was "Putting People First." She recalled that she had planned to make the seat "a living memorial to Bill."[4] For a role model, Emerson looked to Lindy Boggs, who served with distinction for nearly two decades after succeeding her husband in 1973 when he was killed in an airplane crash.[5] Two elections were scheduled for the same day that following November: a special election to fill the last two months of Bill Emerson's unexpired term and an election for the full term in the 105th Congress (1997–1999). Jo Ann Emerson received the Republican nomination for the unexpired term, but for the general election, she was unable to meet a filing deadline for the GOP primary won by Richard Kline. Emerson entered that contest as an Independent (later affiliating herself with the Republicans), winning the unexpired term with 63 percent and the full term with 51 percent. In each of her four re-election campaigns, Emerson has been returned to office without difficulty, capturing a high of 72 percent of the vote in 2002 and 2004.[6] In January 2000, Emerson married St. Louis labor lawyer Ron Gladney.

When Representative Emerson entered the 105th Congress in January 1997, she received assignments to three committees: Agriculture, Small Business, and Transportation and Infrastructure. In the 106th Congress (1999–2001), Emerson earned a seat on the prestigious Appropriations Committee which required her to give up her other assignments. She serves on three Appropriations subcommittees: Agriculture, Homeland Security, and Energy and Water Development.

In her early House career, Emerson's legislative interests were firmly local: improving Missouri's highways and securing federal funds for a bridge over the Mississippi River, as well as support for mining and timber interests, more student loan grants, and agricultural research. She also played a role in revitalizing the Rural Caucus in 2000, serving as one of its two co-chairs. Representing an agricultural district, Emerson has focused on trade issues. She has worked in bipartisan fashion with Democrats to prod U.S. officials to reopen trade with Cuba. In the spring of 2001, Emerson traveled to Havana, where she and a delegation of lawmakers opened a dialogue with Cuban leader Fidel Castro about expanding agricultural trade relations, to free the flow of American-grown rice and other commodities to the island nation.[7] Teaming up with Massachusetts Democrat Jim McGovern, Emerson has led efforts to fund international food aid for schoolchildren using U.S. commodities as part of the McGovern–Dole Food for Education program.[8]

FOR FURTHER READING

Biographical Directory of the U.S. Congress, "Jo Ann Emerson," http://bioguide.congress.gov

NOTES

1 Lloyd Grove, "The Congresswoman's House of Memories; Jo Ann Emerson, Following in Her Husband's Footsteps," 27 November 1996, *Washington Post*: B1.

2 *Politics in America, 2004*: (Washington, D.C.: Congressional Quarterly Inc., 2003): 590–591; *Congressional Directory*, 108th Cong. (Washington, D.C: Government Printing Office, 2003): 153.

3 Grove, "The Congresswoman's House of Memories; Jo Ann Emerson, Following in Her Husband's Footsteps."

4 Ibid.

5 Lorraine Adams, "Keepers of the Flame," 1 November 1998, *Good Housekeeping*.

6 "Election Statistics, 1920 to Present," http://clerk.house.gov/members/electionInfo/index.html.

7 Deirdre Shesgreen, "Emerson Says Cuba Visit Was Productive Despite Failure to Get Results," 17 April 2001, *St. Louis Post-Dispatch*: A4.

8 James Collins, "Rep. Emerson Suggests Strong Link Between Hunger, Terrorism; Feeding Children Abroad Is Good for U.S. Farmers, National Security, She Says," 5 July 2002, *St. Louis Post-Dispatch*: A5.

Anna Georges Eshoo
1942–

UNITED STATES REPRESENTATIVE
DEMOCRAT FROM CALIFORNIA
1993–

Image courtesy of the Member

ANNA ESHOO REPRESENTS THE 14TH CONGRESSIONAL DISTRICT which includes Silicon Valley, hub of the American high technology industry. Much of Eshoo's legislative focus has involved incorporating that technology into education, medicine, government, and Americans' everyday lives.

Anna Georges was born in New Britain, Connecticut, on December 13, 1942. Her mother, Alice Babaian Georges, was of Armenian descent; her father, Fred Georges, was of Assyrian descent. She earned an associate degree in English literature from Cañada College in Redwood City, California, in 1975, and an honorary degree from Menlo College. She also is a graduate of the Coro Foundation. She is the mother of two children, Karen and Paul. She served as a Democratic National Committeewoman from 1980 to 1992. From 1981 to 1982, Eshoo was chief of staff to Leo McCarthy, speaker of the California assembly. In 1982, she was elected to the board of supervisors of San Mateo County, serving for 10 years. She also was a member of the California National Commission on Presidential Nominations.

Eshoo was elected to Congress in 1992, when she won the U.S. House seat in California's 14th Congressional District. When Republican Tom Campbell retired from his seat to run for the U.S. Senate, Eshoo entered the Democratic primary and edged out two well-known Democrats, California Assemblyman Ted Lempert and San Mateo County Supervisor Tom Nolan. In the general election, Eshoo faced Republican Tom Huening, another San Mateo County supervisor. She ran on her experience of establishing a managed-care health plan in the county, environmental protection, and sound budgeting. Eshoo won a resounding 57 to 39 percent victory.[1] In subsequent campaigns, Eshoo has extended her margins of victory several points each year to 70 percent in 2004.[2]

When Eshoo entered the 103rd Congress (1993–1995) she received assignments on two committees: Merchant Marine and Fisheries; and Science, Space, and Technology. In the 104th Congress (1995–1997), she was elected to serve on the powerful Commerce Committee, later renamed Energy and Commerce. In 2003, she was appointed by Democratic Leader Nancy Pelosi of California to the House

Permanent Select Committee on Intelligence. She co-chairs the Congressional E-911 Caucus and the House Medical Technology Caucus, and serves as the Vice Chair of the 21st Century Health Care Caucus.

For more than a decade in Congress Representative Eshoo has defended consumers, promoted American competitiveness and innovation, fought for access to health care for families and children, and protected the environment. She has authored landmark legislation that created the use of electronic signatures, making legally binding digital documents possible and allowing online commerce to flourish; provided discounts to schools and libraries to increase public Internet access; secured funding for emergency call centers to obtain the necessary technology to locate mobile phone users when they call 911; promoted better labeling and testing of pharmaceuticals for children; exempted Federal Emergency Management Agency (FEMA) mitigation grants from income taxes, saving homeowners from being required to pay the government for vital damage prevention; ensured that low-income women who are diagnosed with breast and cervical cancer receive treatment; and required insurance companies to pay for reconstructive surgery for cancer patients.

Representative Eshoo has sponsored legislation aimed at "cleaning up the House" to restore the confidence of the American people in their government. She has co-sponsored numerous reform bills to require more transparency and accountability in lobbying, as well as a more fair and open legislative process. From her position on the House Permanent Select Committee on Intelligence, Eshoo has authored legislation to protect national security and civil liberties, as well as legislation to require that any surveillance or intelligence gathering be conducted in accordance with the law, requiring court warrants based upon probable cause. Her legislative efforts also have sought to reform the U.S. intelligence community, in part, by increasing human intelligence to better meet the security challenges of the 21st century.

In 2005, Rep. Eshoo led House Democrats in introducing "The Innovation Agenda-A Commitment to Competitiveness to Keep American #1." This comprehensive policy plan was developed in conjunction with leaders from the high technology, biotechnology, academic, and venture capital communities. The agenda calls for a national commitment to achieve U.S. energy independence in the next decade by developing legislation to increase investment in research and development to promote sustainable bio-fuels and hybrid technology. It also calls for the creation of the Advanced Research Projects Agency for Energy, a new laboratory within the Department of Energy to engage in high-risk, high-reward experimentation to yield discoveries of new sustainable energy sources. Education is a key element of the plan, with a national commitment to advance and enhance training and instruction in math and science.

FOR FURTHER READING

Biographical Directory of the U.S. Congress, "Anna Georges Eshoo," http://bioguide.congress.gov

NOTES

1 *Almanac of American Politics, 1994* (Washington, D.C.: National Journal Inc., 1993): 121–124; Bill Workman, "Democrat Favored in 14th District; GOP Candidate May Miss His Own Reform Session," 29 October 1992, *San Francisco Chronicle*: A21; "Election Statistics, 1920 to Present," http://clerk.house. gov/members/electionInfo/ elections.html.

2 "Election Statistics, 1920 to Present," http://clerk.house.gov/members/ electionInfo/elections.html.

Dianne Feinstein
1933–

UNITED STATES SENATOR
DEMOCRAT FROM CALIFORNIA
1992–

Image courtesy of the Member

DURING A PUBLIC CAREER SPANNING FOUR DECADES, Dianne Feinstein has merged her string of firsts as a woman politician with a reputation as an effective legislator whose political ideology is "govern from the center." As California's senior Senator, Feinstein holds key posts as the Ranking Member on the Judiciary Committee's Terrorism, Technology, and Homeland Security Subcommittee and the Appropriations Committee's Military Construction Subcommittee.

Dianne Emiel Goldman was born on June 22, 1933, in San Francisco, California, to Leon and Betty Rosenburg Goldman. She graduated with a B.S. from Stanford University in 1955. In 1960, California Governor Pat Brown appointed her to the state Women's Board of Terms and Parole, where she served until 1966.[1] In 1962, she married Bert Feinstein, who died of cancer in June 1978. Several years later, Feinstein married investment banker Richard Blum. Her daughter, Katherine Mariano, is now a superior court judge in California. During the 1970s, Feinstein's political star rose quickly. In 1969 she became the first woman elected to the San Francisco board of supervisors, serving from 1970 to 1978 and acting as board president for five of those years. The day she disclosed her intention to retire from the board, November 27, 1978, a supervisor assassinated Mayor George Moscone and Supervisor Harvey Milk. Feinstein discovered the crime scene and found Milk's body. She succeeded Moscone as the city's first woman mayor and, the next year, won election to the first of two four-year terms. Feinstein earned national prominence as a tough-on-crime, pro-business mayor with a moderately liberal social agenda. Compelled to leave by the city's two-term limit in 1988, she ran unsuccessfully for California governor in 1990 as the first woman on a major party ticket.

In 1992, Feinstein entered the special election for the U.S. Senate seat vacated by Republican Pete Wilson, who had won the governorship in 1990 and appointed an associate, John Seymour, to a two-year Senate term. Feinstein capitalized on the sentiment that women had been excluded from the political process. Her campaign paraphernalia proclaimed "Two percent is not enough," a reference to the fact that only two of the Senate's 100 Members were women. In the Democratic primary she handily defeated state controller Gray Davis and, in the general election, defeated

Seymour with 54 percent of the vote.[2] Feinstein took the oath of office on November 10, 1992, becoming the first woman to represent California in the U.S. Senate. Two years later, she won election to a full six-year term against Republican candidate Michael Huffington.

Senator Feinstein received assignments on the Appropriations, Rules and Administration, Select Intelligence, and Joint Printing committees. She also was one of a small group of women ever appointed to the Judiciary Committee. Most recently, she joined the Energy and Natural Resources Committee in 2001. When the Democrats controlled the Senate Chamber during the 107th Congress (2001–2003), Feinstein chaired the Appropriations Subcommittee on Military Construction and the Judiciary Committee's Subcommittee on Technology, Terrorism, and Government Information.

Senator Feinstein joined the moderate Senate New Democrats and the Centrist Coalition, becoming a strong proponent for issues such as women's reproductive rights, gay rights legislation, and gun control. One of her signal achievements was the passage of a ban on semi-automatic military weapons in 1994, the so-called Assault Weapons Ban. "I've lived a life that's been impacted by weapons," Senator Feinstein once wrote. "So this is not an esoteric, academic exercise for me."[3] Also concerned with environmental issues, Feinstein successfully steered the California Desert Protection Act through the Senate—an unprecedented measure which placed more than 7 million desert acres into the Joshua Tree and Death Valley National Parks, as well as the East Mojave National Preserve. In 2000, she also authored the Lake Tahoe Restoration Act, which authorized $300 million in federal money over 10 years to match California and Nevada conservation funds for the lake.[4]

Having lost her father and a husband to cancer, Senator Feinstein also has been a leader in the fight against the disease. She sponsored the Breast Cancer Research Stamp Act in the 1990s, raising more than $50 million for research. In 2002, she introduced the National Cancer Act, which proposed the modernization and restructuring of national cancer policy.[5] In the 108th Congress (2003–2005), Senator Feinstein teamed up with Senator Kay Bailey Hutchison of Texas to author legislation creating the national "Amber Alert" system for missing children. With Senator Jon Kyl of Arizona, Feinstein also won passage of the Victims of Violent Crimes Act, giving victims a core set of procedural rights under federal law and ensuring they have standing to assert their rights before a court. She sponsored the Combat Meth Act with Jim Talent of Missouri, which is now law, placing limits on the purchase of ingredients that can be used to manufacture methamphetamine. And she authored one of the first bills to help promote stem cell research, which offers hope to millions of people with catastrophic diseases. Feinstein won re-election to a second full term in 2000, defeating former U.S. Representative Tom Campbell with 56 percent of the vote.

FOR FURTHER READING

Biographical Directory of the U.S. Congress, "Dianne Feinstein," http://bioguide.congress.gov/

Mikuski, Barbara, et al. *Nine and Counting: The Women of the Senate* (New York: Morrow, 2000).

Morris, Celia. *Storming the Statehouse: Running for Governor With Ann Richards and Dianne Feinstein* (New York: Scribner's Sons, 1992).

Roberts, Jerry. *Dianne Feinstein: Never Let Them See You Cry* (San Francisco, CA: Harper Collins West, 1994).

MANUSCRIPT COLLECTION

University of Oklahoma (Norman, OK), The Julian P. Kanter Commercial Archive, Department of Communication. *Film and Video Reels*: 1971—1994, one film reel and 29 video reels. Includes 67 commercials used during Feinstein's campaigns for the 1971 mayoral election in San Francisco, the 1990 gubernatorial, and the 1992 and 1994 U.S. senatorial elections in California.

NOTES

1 *Current Biography, 1979* (New York: H.W. Wilson and Company, 1979): 130.

2 "Election Statistics, 1920 to Present," http://clerk.house.gov/members/electionInfo/elections.html.

3 Barbara Mikulski et al., *Nine and Counting* (New York: Morrow, 2000): 140.

4 "Official Biography of Dianne Feinstein," http://feinstein.senate.gov (accessed 12 December 2004).

5 *Politics in America 2002* (Washington, D.C.: Congressional Quarterly Inc., 2001): 64.

Kay Granger
1943–

UNITED STATES REPRESENTATIVE
REPUBLICAN FROM TEXAS
1997–

Image courtesy of the Member

KAY GRANGER, THE FORMER MAYOR OF FORT WORTH, won election in 1996 as the first Republican woman from Texas to serve in the U.S. House of Representatives. Congresswoman Granger quickly ascended the House leadership, serving as a Deputy Majority Whip and earning positions on the influential Appropriations Committee and the Select Homeland Security Committee. Her experience as a successful businesswoman and single mother of three children continues to influence her legislative work.

Kay Mullendore was born in Greenville, Texas, on January 18, 1943. Her parents divorced while she was a young teenager, leaving her mother, Alliene, to raise the family. "I was not self-made," she recalled years later. "I was made by my mother."[1] She earned a bachelor of science degree magna cum laude from Texas Wesleyan University in 1965 and considered a career in fashion design but followed her mother into teaching. She worked in the Birdville school district for nine years, teaching English literature and journalism. She married, raised three children, and later was divorced. To pay the mortgage and save for college tuition, Granger pursued a career as a life insurance agent. She opened a successful insurance agency, solidifying her ties to many key future constituents in the Fort Worth business community. From 1981 to 1989 she served as a member of the Fort Worth zoning commission. In 1989 she won election to the Fort Worth city council and, in 1991, was elected mayor, where she served until 1995. She brought an ambitious agenda to jump-start the Fort Worth economy that reeled from defense layoffs and a soaring per-capita crime rate. Granger's "Code: Blue" programs included citizen patrol initiatives that halved the rampant crime rate and joint public–private sector programs that drew major businesses to the city. Her resuscitation of Fort Worth's flagging economic fortunes drew national attention.

In 1996, when the incumbent Democratic Congressman for the Texas district encompassing Fort Worth decided to retire, Granger was the favorite to run for the seat. The mayoral post was nonpartisan, and both major parties enticed her to run under their banner. Running as a Republican in the November general election, Granger won by a 17 percent margin and, in her four subsequent re-election campaigns, has never been seriously challenged. As testimony to her popularity, Representative Granger is the first Republican in more than 100 years to represent the district which produced, among others, a former Democratic Speaker of the House. In 2004, Granger was elected in the newly reapportioned district, still covering Fort Worth, with 72 percent of the vote.[2]

When Congresswoman Granger was sworn into the 105th Congress (1997–1999) in January 1997, she was assigned immediately as a Deputy Whip and was named to an advisory board that consulted Speaker Newt Gingrich. She also received seats on three high-profile committees: Budget, House Oversight, and Transportation and Infrastructure. In 1997, she was appointed to the National Security Committee to fill the spot left vacant by the death of California Congressman Sonny Bono. In the 106th Congress (1999–2001) she resigned her previous posts to accept a seat on the powerful Appropriations Committee, where she currently serves on the Defense Subcommittee and the Labor, Health and Human Services, Education, and Related Agencies Subcommittee.[3] In the 108th Congress (2003–2005), Granger took on an additional assignment as a member of the newly created Select Homeland Security Committee.

Congresswoman Granger's personal experience shaped many of her initiatives. In 1997, Granger successfully introduced legislation for tax-free education savings. When Republicans introduced a "comp time" bill to permit businesses to either pay over-time or give time off to employees who worked extra hours, Granger, as a working mother, defended the measure by arguing it would give workers more flexibility to deal with family matters.[4] A strong advocate for a balanced budget, Granger participated in developing historic balanced budgets in the late 1990s as a Budget Committee member. She also has secured funding for defense projects centered in her district, particularly companies which have worked to develop the Joint Strike Fighter, the F-22 Raptor, and the V-22 Osprey.[5] In the 106th Congress she served as vice chair of the Women's Caucus, supporting abortion rights and pushing the caucus to broaden its agenda to include women's retirement security and fair workplace standards. She also was a member of an informal group called the Renewal Alliance, a coalition of about two dozen House and Senate Republicans who support public–private partnerships to meet social needs and problems. Her fiscal conservatism coincided with moderation on social issues, including her support for affirmative-action admissions in public universities.[6] She has authored a book about American values, *What's Right About America*. As co-chair of the Iraqi Women's Caucus, Granger was the congressional leader in assisting Iraqi women to gain equal rights and to attain leadership positions.

FOR FURTHER READING

Biographical Directory of the U.S. Congress, "Kay Granger," http://bioguide.congress.gov

NOTES

1 Jacquielynn Floyd, "Kay Granger: With Fort Worth in the Limelight, Its Mayor Basks in the Glow," 9 January 1994, *Dallas Morning News*: 1E; *Politics in America, 2002* (Washington, D.C.: Congressional Quarterly Inc., 2001): 979.

2 "Election Statistics, 1920 to Present," http://clerk.house.gov/members/electionInfo/elections.html.

3 Karen Foerstel, *Biographical Dictionary of Congressional Women* (Westport, CT: Praeger, 1999): 100–101.

4 Foerstel, *Biographical Dictionary of Congressional Women*: 101; *Politics in America, 2002*: 978.

5 "Official Biography of Kay Granger," http://kaygranger.house.gov/bio.asp (accessed 10 December 2004).

6 Foerstel, *Biographical Dictionary of Congressional Women*: 101; *Politics in America, 2002*: 978.

Jane F. Harman

1945–

UNITED STATES REPRESENTATIVE
DEMOCRAT FROM CALIFORNIA
1993–1999; 2001–

Image courtesy of the Member

JANE HARMAN WON ELECTION TO THE HOUSE of Representatives in 1992, the landmark "Year of the Woman." Harman has become a leading figure in Congress on defense issues as a member of the Select Committee on Intelligence and the Committee on Homeland Security. In 2001, after leaving Congress for a term in an unsuccessful run for California governor, Harman won re-election to her old seat, joining a handful of women to serve nonconsecutive terms in Congress.

Jane Margaret Lakes was born in New York City on June 28, 1945, to Adolph N. Lakes and Lucille Geier. Raised in Los Angeles, she graduated from University High School in 1962. After earning a B.A. in government from Smith College in 1966, she received a J.D. from Harvard Law School three years later.[1] She married Richard Frank and worked for two years at a Washington, D.C., law firm before joining the staff of California Senator John V. Tunney in 1972. In 1975 she was appointed chief counsel and staff director of the Senate Judiciary Committee's Subcommittee on Constitutional Rights. She served as deputy secretary to the Cabinet of President James Earl "Jimmy" Carter in 1977 and as a special counsel to the Department of Defense. In 1980 she divorced Richard Frank and later married Sidney Harman, the founder of a major audio electronics company. Over the next decade, Jane Harman worked as a corporate lawyer and as a director of her husband's multimillion dollar company. The Harmans have four children: Daniel, Justine, Brian, and Hilary.

In 1992, Harman first pursued elective office when she ran for a congressional seat in southern California. In the general election, she faced Republican Joan Milke Flores, a Los Angeles city councilwoman, and three minority party candidates. Harman employed a socially liberal but fiscally conservative message on her way to a 48 to 42 percent victory against Flores.

In Congress Harman served as a watch guard of the high-tech defense industry that resided in her district. From her seat on the influential Armed Services Committee (later renamed the National Security Committee) she kept the Los Angeles air force base off the list of post–Cold War closings. Despite a sharp decline in defense spending, Representative Harman steered lucrative military weapons and space defense projects into her district. Yet she also prodded the industry at home to retool for a peacetime economy. As a member of the Science Committee, with a seat on the Space and Aeronautics Subcommittee, Harman brought work to companies looking for nonmilitary projects. She said, "I have viewed it as a major part of my job to help my district transition from defense-dependence, which was a deadend strategy, to the robust diverse economy which it now enjoys."[2]

In 1994, running in one of the most evenly divided districts in the country, Harman nearly became a victim of the "Republican Revolution." She pulled out a thin 812-vote win against her Republican opponent, Susan Brooks. When Harman faced Brooks again in 1996, in an election that became a referendum on the Republican "Contract with America," she won by 19,000 votes. Subsequent races bore out the contention that neither party could dominate the competitive southern California district.[3]

Harman's record in Congress straddled the ideological middle ground that her district occupied. She cast her vote for President William J Clinton's 1993 budget, which increased spending and taxes, but by 1996, she advocated spending cuts, the balanced budget amendment, and the line-item veto. In 1995, Congresswoman Harman co-authored the Deficit Reduction Lockbox, requiring that spending cuts be applied to the deficit. She voted against the North American Free Trade Agreement but backed the General Agreement on Tariffs and Trade. Harman favored pro-choice measures and a partial ban on semiautomatic weapons but also supported the death penalty.

In 1998, Harman declined to run for a fourth consecutive term in the House to pursue the Democratic nomination for governor of California. She lost in the Democratic primary.[4] Harman reclaimed her House seat by narrowly defeating her congressional successor, Republican Steve Kuykendall, in the 2000 general election. In the 107th Congress (2001–2003), Harman received assignments on the powerful Energy and Commerce Committee and the Permanent Select Committee on Intelligence, a nod to her experience and continued influence. Shortly thereafter, she was promoted to Ranking Member of the Intelligence Committee. In the 2002 elections, she defeated GOP candidate Stuart Johnson with 61 percent of the vote. She won election to the 109th Congress (2005–2007) in 2004 by defeating Republican Paul Whitehead by a 62 to 34 percent margin.[5]

FOR FURTHER READING

Biographical Directory of the U.S. Congress, "Jane F. Harman," http://bioguide.congress.gov

MANUSCRIPT COLLECTION

Smith College (Northampton, Massachusetts), The Sophia Smith Collection. *Papers*: 1993–1998, 151 linear feet. Restricted access.

NOTES

1 *Politics in America, 2004* (Washington, D.C.: Congressional Quarterly, Inc., 2003): 136.

2 Paul Jacobs, "Defense Firms Were Key Donors to Harman Races; Gubernatorial Candidate Says She Backed Industry in Congress to Protect Jobs in South Bay," 11 May 1998, *Los Angeles Times*: A1.

3 "Election Statistics, 1920 to Present," http://clerk.house.gov/members/electionInfo/elections.html.

4 Cathleen Decker, "Showdown for Davis, Lungren: Voters Reject Millionaires Checchi and Harman in State's First Blanket Primary," 3 June 1998, *Los Angeles Times*: A1; Cathleen Decker and Mark Barabak, "Davis' 4th-1st Comeback 'Proved Pundits Wrong,'" 5 June 1998, *Los Angeles Times*: A1.

5 "Election Statistics, 1920 to Present," http://clerk.house.gov/members/electionInfo/elections.html.

Katherine Harris
1957–

UNITED STATES REPRESENTATIVE
REPUBLICAN FROM FLORIDA
2003–

Image courtesy of the Member

THE 2000 PRESIDENTIAL BALLOT RECOUNT IN FLORIDA thrust Katherine Harris into the national spotlight in her role as the state's chief election officer, but it also obscured her meteoric career and deep political roots. Having worked to bring business into Florida both as a state senator and as secretary of state, Harris won election to the House in 2002 and secured seats on the influential Financial Services, International Relations, and Homeland Security committees.

Katherine Harris was born on April 5, 1957, at the Key West Naval Base in Florida, to George Walter Harris, a banking executive, and Harriett Griffin Harris. Katherine Harris is the granddaughter of Ben Hill Griffin, Jr., a citrus magnate and Democratic state senator. She attended Bartow High School and graduated in 1979 from Agnes Scott College with a B.A. in history; she later earned an MPA from Harvard in 1996. After graduating from college, Harris worked as a marketing executive for a major computer corporation and then served as vice president of a Sarasota commercial real estate company. In 1996, she married Anders Ebbeson, a business executive, and they raised one child, Louise. Harris decided to enter politics in 1994 when she made a successful run for the Florida state senate. During her four years as a state legislator, she chaired the commerce and economic development committee. In 1998, Harris successfully ran for the Florida secretary of state post and was responsible primarily for handling corporate filings and implementing state election procedures. She used her office to attract international business, the arts, and historic preservation into the state. In 2000, she was named the Florida co-chair for the George W. Bush presidential campaign. Harris garnered national attention as Florida's top election official during the state's historic ballot recount which eventually decided the election in George W. Bush's favor by a slender margin. In 2002, she published a book about the experience, *Center of the Storm*.

In 2002, when five-term GOP Representative Dan Miller retired from Florida's west central gulf coast district seat encompassing much of Sarasota and Bradenton, Harris declared her candidacy. Harris had the advantage of a longtime connection to the area as a patron of the arts and civic philanthropist. She won the GOP primary by more than a 2–1 margin. Harris, who faced Democratic challenger Jan Schneider, ran on a general election platform that broadly supported the George W. Bush administration's war on terror, including increased defense spending. Harris backed tax cuts, school vouchers, and medical savings accounts. She also opposed U.S. funding for United Nations family planning programs.[1] In the general election she defeated Schneider by a margin of 55 percent to 45 percent.[2]

In the 108th Congress (2003–2005), Harris received committee assignments on Financial Services and International Relations. She had three subcommittee appointments for Financial Services: Capital Markets, Insurance and Government Sponsored Enterprises; Housing and Community Opportunity; and Domestic and International Monetary Policy, Trade and Technology. Harris also held two subcommittee assignments on the International Relations Committee. She served as vice chair of the Western Hemisphere Subcommittee and also held a seat on the Middle East and Central Asia Subcommittee. The leadership also tapped her for a seat on the Republican Policy Committee and made her an Assistant Whip. In the 109th Congress (2005–2007), she also received a seat on the Homeland Security Committee.

During the first year of her freshman term, Harris supported the overhaul of the Medicare program and the creation of a prescription drug benefit, as well as a measure to outlaw the partial-birth abortion procedure except in cases where it was used to save a woman's life. She sponsored the American Dream Downpayment Act, a program to help low-income families and individuals purchase their first home, which was signed into law by President Bush in December 2003. Key provisions of her "Carlie's Law" legislation, making any sexual crime or crime against children a crime of violence for the first time ever, can be found in the Children's Safety and Violent Crimes Act, which has passed the House. Harris voted for a $330 billion tax cut between 2003 and 2013 and backed a budget resolution that called for $1.3 trillion in tax cuts over 10 years. Also in line with her campaign promises, she supported a measure to create a pilot private school voucher program in Washington, D.C., that supporters hoped would become the basis for a national program.[3] In 2004, Harris won re-election, defeating Schneider by a similar margin, 55 to 45 percent.[4]

FOR FURTHER READING

Biographical Directory of the U.S. Congress, "Katherine Harris," http://bioguide.congress.gov

Harris, Katherine. *Center of the Storm: Practicing Principled Leadership in Times of Crisis* (Nashville, TN: WND Books, 2002).

NOTES

1 Manuel Riog-Franzia, "The Last Laugh: Florida's Katherine Harris Knows About Winning Elections. Just Count the Ballots," 19 October 2002, *Washington Post*: C1.

2 "Election Statistics, 1920 to Present," http://clerk.house.gov/members/ electionInfo/elections.html.

3 *Politics in America, 2004* (Washington, D.C.: Congressional Quarterly Inc., 2003): 243.

4 "Election Statistics, 1920 to Present," http://clerk.house.gov/members/ electionInfo/elections.html.

Melissa A. Hart
1962–

UNITED STATES REPRESENTATIVE
REPUBLICAN FROM PENNSYLVANIA
2001–

Image courtesy of the Member

SPURRED INTO POLITICS BY WHAT SHE PERCEIVED AS HIGH taxes and inefficient government, Melissa Hart entered elective politics at age 28, winning a seat in the Pennsylvania senate. After a decade in state politics, Hart was elected to the U.S. House in 2000—the first Republican woman to represent Pennsylvania in Congress. Representative Hart has focused on pro-life issues and reviving the economic prospects of her southwestern Pennsylvania district.

Melissa Ann Hart was born on April 4, 1962, in Pittsburgh, Pennsylvania, daughter of Donald Hart, a research chemist, and Albina Hart. After her father's sudden death, Hart and her two siblings worked their way through school to contribute to the family finances.[1] Hart graduated from North Allegheny High School and then majored in business and German, earning her bachelor's degree in 1984 from Washington and Jefferson College in Washington, Pennsylvania. She also joined the Young Republicans as an undergraduate. She completed her jurist doctorate at the University of Pittsburgh in 1987. For a while, she practiced as a lawyer in Pittsburgh. In 1990, at age 28, Hart won election to the Pennsylvania state senate. She told a local newspaper that her political career was spurred by a high property tax increase. "I had never thought of running for office until . . . I realized the money being taken from us wasn't being spent in an effective way," Hart said.[2] Despite hailing from an overwhelmingly Democratic district, she was re-elected twice by wide margins. During her tenure in the state legislature, she chaired the finance committee, helped implement $4 billion in state tax breaks, and served as vice chair of the urban affairs and housing committee. Phil English, Hart's chief of staff during her Pennsylvania senate career, later became a U.S. Representative.

Hart's ambition to serve in the U.S. Congress began in 2000, when four-term incumbent Democratic Representative Ronald Klink retired from his House seat to campaign for the U.S. Senate. Hart entered the race to succeed him. The district encompassed a large portion of southwestern Pennsylvania that included six counties. Though socially conservative, its history of union support usually kept it in the Democratic column. Hart's platform supported simplifying the tax code, ending married couples' tax penalties, and increasing economic development in western Pennsylvania, which had missed much of the 1990s high-technology boom. Hart also supported pro-life positions on the abortion debate. She ran unopposed in the GOP primary and won the general election against her Democratic challenger, a state representative, with 60 percent of the vote, becoming the first Republican elected in the district since 1976. In her subsequent two re-election campaigns, Hart won by similarly comfortable margins.[3]

After arriving at the start of the 107th Congress (2001–2003) in January 2001, Hart was appointed to the three prominent committees: Science, Judiciary, and Financial Services. In the 108th Congress (2003–2005), she was named the vice chair of the Judiciary Committee's Subcommittee on the Constitution.

Over the course of her career in the U.S. Congress, Representative Hart has achieved several significant legislative successes. In the 108th Congress, she authored the Unborn Victims of Violence/Laci and Conner's Law. The measure, which passed Congress and was signed into law by President George W. Bush, provided that in a federal crime of violence against a pregnant woman in which her unborn child is harmed, the perpetrator can be prosecuted for two crimes against two victims. Hart also has opposed the partial-birth abortion procedure and has introduced legislation that would withhold federal funding from universities that provide their students access to the morning-after birth control pill. Also during the 108th Congress, Hart inserted language into the final signed version of the CAN-SPAM Law requiring sexually explicit e-mails to be labeled so that parents can protect their children from Internet predators. Additionally, Hart introduced legislation to assist in the cleanup of old industrial sites ("brownfields") prevalent in her district and legislation reauthorizing the "Metals Initiative," which aims to make the domestic steel industry competitive.

Hart's principal legislative focus has been to boost the economy in her district. Along with other lawmakers from steel-producing districts, she has urged the Bush administration to impose quotas on imported steel. She also has backed legislation to help laid-off airline workers; Pittsburgh is a major airline hub. Hart also has offered legislation to provide business tax breaks to fund Army Corps of Engineers projects in her district and to expand the boundaries of metropolitan Pittsburgh to increase federal aid to the area.

In January of 2005, Hart won a seat on the House Ways and Means Committee. Serving on this powerful committee—with jurisdiction over taxes, Social Security, and Medicare—will allow Hart to work on the issues critical to Western Pennsylvanians and all Americans.

FOR FURTHER READING

Biographical Directory of the U.S. Congress, "Melissa A. Hart," http://bioguide.congress.gov

NOTES

1 *Politics in America, 2004* (Washington, D.C.: Congressional Quarterly Inc., 2003): 863.

2 *Politics in America, 2004*: 863.

3 "Election Statistics, 1920 to Present," http://clerk.house.gov/members/electionInfo/elections.html.

Stephanie Herseth
1970–

UNITED STATES REPRESENTATIVE
DEMOCRAT FROM SOUTH DAKOTA
2004–

Image courtesy of the Member

ON JUNE 1, 2004, STEPHANIE HERSETH BECAME THE FIRST woman from South Dakota elected to the U.S. House of Representatives. Hailing from one of the state's prominent political families, Congresswoman Herseth emerged on the national scene by winning a special election to the state's vacant At-Large seat. One of the newest women in Congress, Herseth was appointed to three committees important to her South Dakota constituents: Agriculture, Veterans' Affairs, and Resources.

Stephanie Herseth was born on December 3, 1970, to Lars and Joyce Herseth and was raised on her family's farm and ranch near Houghton, South Dakota. Her grandfather, Ralph Herseth, was once the state's governor; her grandmother, Lorna B. Herseth, was the secretary of state. Lars Herseth served in the South Dakota state legislature for 20 years and was a Democratic gubernatorial nominee. Stephanie Herseth graduated as a valedictorian from Groton High School in Groton, South Dakota. In 1993, she earned a B.A. from Georgetown University in Washington, D.C., graduating *summa cum laude* and Phi Beta Kappa with a degree in government. Four years later she earned her J.D. from Georgetown with honors and was a senior editor of the *Georgetown Law Review*. While in law school, Herseth worked for the South Dakota public utilities commission and the legal counsel for the elderly. After being admitted to the South Dakota bar, Herseth served as a faculty member of the Georgetown University Law Center and taught classes in the Czech Republic about the American system of government. Herseth later clerked for a U.S. District Court judge in Pierre, South Dakota, and for the U.S. Court of Appeals for the Fourth Circuit in Maryland. In 2003 and 2004, she served as the executive director of the South Dakota Farmers Union Foundation.

In 2002, when Republican John Thune decided to retire from South Dakota's sole U.S. House seat to run for the U.S. Senate, Herseth entered the race to succeed him.[1] She won the Democratic nomination, defeating three other challengers, with 59 percent of the vote. In the general election, she faced the state's popular four-term governor, Republican William J. Janklow. Herseth campaigned for fiscal responsibility, affordable health care for South Dakotans, expansion of ethanol and value-added agriculture, and tax credits for parents who need childcare. She also called for federal aid to improve the quality of life on South Dakota's Indian reservations. Herseth ultimately supported the George W. Bush administration's push for war against Iraq on the basis of Saddam Hussein's apparent development of weapons of mass destruction but cautioned early about the need for a strong coalition and warned that intervention in Iraq could sap resources from the nation's focus on terrorist threats. Janklow won, but Herseth made a close race of it—closing a double-digit gap in the pre-election opinion polls and eventually garnering 46 percent to the governor's 54 percent.

When Representative Janklow resigned his House seat on January 20, 2004, Herseth was an immediate favorite to run in the special election to fill the remainder of Janklow's term. She won the Democratic nomination and faced Republican Larry Diedrich, a farmer and former president of the American Soybean Association, in the special election. On June 1, 2004, Herseth won by a plurality of fewer than 3,000 votes out of nearly 260,000 cast, a 51 to 49 percent margin.[2] In November 2004, in a rematch against Deidrich, Herseth won by a 53 to 46 percent margin, polling more votes than any other candidate for statewide national office.[3]

On June 3, 2004, South Dakota's two Democratic Senators, Minority Leader Tom Daschle and Tim Johnson, escorted Herseth into the House Chamber to take the oath of office. Representative Herseth received assignments on several key committees. Her post on the House Agriculture Committee gave her a voice on issues important to South Dakota's primary industry—farming. Additionally, Herseth's seat on the Resources Committee allowed her to play a role in deciding matters of significance to her state, including Native American policy, forests, national parks, and wildlife. By the end of the 108th Congress (2003–2005), Congresswoman Herseth had introduced several measures, including a bill to amend the Social Security Act to preserve Social Security cost-of-living adjustments. As co-chair of the House Democratic Rural Working Group, Herseth is a leader for the needs of rural America, including the development of a strong renewable fuels industry.

FOR FURTHER READING

Biographical Directory of the U.S. Congress, "Stephanie Herseth," http://bioguide.congress.gov

NOTES

1 Peter Harriman, "Herseth Savors Return, Race for House," 22 September 2002, *Sioux Falls Argus Leader*: 1A.

2 Stephen Kinzer, "The Voters in South Dakota Send a Woman to Washington for the First Time," 3 June 2004, *New York Times*: 18; Joe Kafka, "Democrat Wins in South Dakota Special Election," 1 June 2004, Associated Press.

3 "Election Statistics, 1920 to Present," http://clerk.house.gov/members/electionInfo/index.html.

Darlene Kay Hooley
1939–

UNITED STATES REPRESENTATIVE
DEMOCRAT FROM OREGON
1997–

Image courtesy of the Member

A FORMER OREGON PUBLIC SCHOOLTEACHER, Darlene Hooley began a long climb in state politics in the 1970s, inspired initially by defective equipment at a local playground. Hooley served in city, county, and state government for 20 years before winning election to the U.S. House of Representatives in 1996. During her tenure in Congress, Representative Hooley has focused on identity theft and data security, education funding, affordable health care and prescription drug coverage, the National Guard, and veterans' health care.

Darlene Olson was born on April 4, 1939, in Williston, North Dakota, to Clarence Alvin Olson and Alyce Rogers Olson. When she was eight years old, her family moved to Salem, Oregon. Darlene Olson earned a B.S. in education from Oregon State University in 1961, and pursued postgraduate work at Oregon State University and Portland State University from 1963 until 1965. She also taught reading, music, and physical education in Oregon. Darlene Olson married John Hooley, a fellow teacher, and they raised two children, Chad and Erin, before they divorced in 1997. The lack of city response to playground equipment maintenance issues at a local public park, where her son had fallen off a swing onto the asphalt, convinced Hooley to enter politics. In 1976, she was the first woman elected to the West Linn city council. Four years later, she earned a spot in the state house of representatives, where she served until 1987. In the legislature, she chaired the environmental and energy committees where she helped pass energy conservation measures, recycling legislation, and a rewrite of land use planning laws. In her third term, she served on the Oregon house of representatives' ways and means committee, chairing its education subcommittee. She focused on establishing public kindergarten, passing pay equity laws, and reforming the state's welfare system. In 1987, she became the first woman member of the Clackamas County commission where she served until her election to Congress.[1]

In 1996, Hooley entered the race for an Oregon seat in the U.S. House of Representatives covering much of the northern Willamette Valley from West Linn in the north to the state capital, Salem, and the university town of Corvallis to the south. With backing from major women's political action committees such as EMILY's List, Hooley prevailed in the three-way Democratic primary with 51 percent of the vote. In the general election, she faced Republican Jim Bunn, a first-term incumbent. Her platform contrasted with the Republican "Contract with America" and was especially critical of Medicare cuts. Hooley defeated Bunn by a 52 to 45 percent margin in a race with two independent candidates. In her subsequent four re-election campaigns, Hooley has won by margins of between 53 and 57 percent of the vote.[2]

During the first year of the 105th Congress (1997–1999), Representative Hooley was elected Democratic freshman class president. She was then elected as Regional Representative to the Democratic Steering Committee in the 106th–107th Congresses (1999–2003). Hooley was appointed as Whip-at-Large (106th and 107th Congresses) and then Senior Whip. She received seats on the Banking and Financial Services Committee (later renamed Financial Services) and the Science Committee. In the 106th Congress, Hooley took leave from serving on the Science Committee to serve on the influential Budget Committee, but was termed out in the 109th Congress (2005–2007) and returned to the Science Committee as Ranking Member on the Research Subcommittee. In the 108th Congress (2003–2005), she added a third assignment by accepting a position on the Veterans' Affairs Committee.

On the Financial Services Committee, Hooley has become the leader of ID theft prevention efforts and for increased medical and financial privacy. In the 108th Congress, Hooley's consumer protection legislation providing all Americans the ability to see their credit reports from all three major credit bureaus annually at no cost was enacted.

Locally, Hooley has proven successful in securing public investments in Oregon's 5th District, including millions of dollars in county timber payments in lieu of taxes on federal lands for local schools and roads, federal funding for transportation, port and infrastructure needs, and agricultural research and bio-medical research funding.

In 2002, Representative Hooley voted against the authorization of the use of military force in Iraq. During the occupation of Iraq, she has been a vocal advocate for the proper training and equipping of troops serving overseas, and has worked to correct inequities between the active duty and National Guard. As the Ranking Member of the Veterans' Affairs Subcommittee on Oversight and Investigations, Hooley worked to improve the veterans' health care and increase funding for its medical centers.[3]

FOR FURTHER READING

Biographical Directory of the U.S. Congress, "Darlene Hooley," http://bioguide.congress.gov

NOTES

1 *Politics in America, 2004* (Washington, D.C.: Congressional Quarterly Inc., 2003): 847–848; *Almanac of American Politics, 2004* (Washington, D.C: National Journal Inc., 2003): 1344–1345; "Official Biography of Darlene Hooley," http://www.house.gov/hooley/biography.htm (accessed 24 November 2004).

2 "Election Information, 1920 to Present," Office of the Clerk, http://clerk.house.gov/members/electionInfo/index.html.

3 "Official Biography of Darlene Hooley," http://www.house.gov/hooley/biography.htm; *Politics in America, 2004*: 847–848.

Kathryn Ann "Kay" Bailey Hutchison
1943–

UNITED STATES SENATOR
REPUBLICAN FROM TEXAS
1993–

Image courtesy of the Member

AS THE FIRST WOMAN TO REPRESENT TEXAS in the U.S. Senate, Kay Bailey Hutchison has addressed issues ranging from transportation to family tax relief and defense. Having served in the Senate for more than a decade, Senator Hutchison chairs two powerful subcommittees: Appropriations' Military Construction Subcommittee and Commerce's Science and Space Subcommittee. In 2000, her GOP colleagues elected her Vice Chair of the Senate Republican Conference—making her the fifth-highest ranking member of the party leadership.

Kathryn Ann "Kay" Bailey was born in Galveston, Texas, on July 22, 1943, to Allan and Kathryn Bailey. She graduated from the University of Texas at Austin and, in 1967, earned an L.L.B. from the University of Texas School of Law. In 1969, when few law firms hired women, she began a career as a Houston television reporter covering state legislation.[1] She and Ray, her husband of 28 years, have two children, Bailey and Houston.[2] While a journalist, Hutchison was inspired after an interview with Anne Armstrong, co-chair of the Republican National Committee, to enter politics, first working as Armstrong's press secretary. In 1972, Hutchison was elected to the Texas state house of representatives. After two terms, she left the state legislature in 1976 to serve as vice chair of the National Transportation Safety Board. After three years in that post, Hutchison returned to Texas. In 1982, she made an unsuccessful bid for an open U.S. House seat representing portions of Dallas. She spent eight years in the private sector before winning election in 1990 as the Texas state treasurer. Two years later, Hutchison co-chaired the Republican National Convention.[3] As Texas treasurer, Hutchison increased returns on state investments to $1 billion annually, led a successful campaign against a state income tax, and helped cap the state debt.[4]

In January 1993, when Lloyd Bentsen of Texas resigned from the U.S. Senate to serve as Treasury Secretary, Democrat Bob Krueger was appointed to fill the vacancy until a special election was held on June 5, 1993. After topping a crowd of 24 candidates in an open primary, Hutchison prevailed against Krueger by a 29 percent margin and was sworn in to the U.S. Senate on June 14, 1993. In 1994, she was elected to a six-year term with 61 percent of the vote. She won her second full term in 2000 by a similar margin, with more than 4 million votes, the largest total of any Texas statewide official in history.[5] In the 108th Congress (2003–2005), Hutchison's committee assignments included: Appropriations; Commerce, Science, and Transportation; Rules and Administration; and Veterans' Affairs.

Senator Hutchison has served her entire career on the Commerce, Science, and Transportation Committee. She has used her role as the chairwoman of the Subcommittee on Surface Transportation and Merchant Marine to even the international playing field for American shippers as well as to deregulate and create greater accountability for Amtrak.[6] Following the September 11, 2001, terrorist attacks on the United States, she authored the airline security bill, which aimed at increasing cargo security on domestic flights while streamlining security checks for frequent travelers. In accordance with the North American Free Trade Agreement, Hutchison also supported opening the U.S. border to Mexican trucks only if they met the same safety standards as those in the United States.[7]

Senator Hutchison established herself as a fiscal conservative, supporting tax cuts, a constitutional balanced budget amendment, and cuts to government spending. Teaming with Democratic Senator Barbara Mikulski of Maryland, she co-authored the Homemaker IRA, which provided stay-at-home moms the same retirement tax credit as working women. In 2001, Hutchison was the Senate sponsor of legislation repealing the so-called marriage penalty tax, a provision which Congress incorporated into the 2001 tax overhaul package. In 2001, Senator Hutchison also wrote several provisions for the No Child Left Behind Act, including: helping recruit teachers who are retirees or midcareer professionals, giving parents regular updates on their children's school performance, and allowing local school districts to more easily offer single-sex education environments.[8] Hutchison worked with Senator Dianne Feinstein of California in the 108th Congress authoring legislation to create a national Amber Alert network to streamline the search for missing children.

A former member of the Armed Services Committee, Hutchison has advocated greater attention to Gulf War Syndrome victims and was a leading opponent of bombing Serbia and sending ground troops into Bosnia in 1995. From her position as chairwoman on the Appropriations Military Construction Subcommittee, she established a federal overseas basing commission to ensure the effectiveness of military installations abroad, and favored training troops at home instead of overseas because of space constraints.

FOR FURTHER READING

Biographical Directory of the U.S. Congress, "Kathryn Ann Bailey Hutchison," http://bioguide. congress.gov

Mikulski, Barbara, et al. *Nine and Counting: The Women of the Senate* (New York: Morrow, 2000).

NOTES

1 *Politics in America, 2004* (Washington, D.C.: Congressional Quarterly Inc., 2003): 950; Mikulski, Barbara, et al., *Nine and Counting* (New York: Morrow, 2000): 21–22.

2 "Official Biography of Kay Bailey Hutchison," http://hutchison.senate.gov/bio.htm (accessed 20 December 2004); *Politics in America, 1996* (Washington, D.C.: Congressional Quarterly Inc., 1995): 1248–1249; *Current Biography, 1997* (New York: H.W. Wilson and Company, 1997) :237–240.

3 *"Current Biography, 1997*:237–240.

4 "Official Biography of Kay Bailey Hutchison."

5 "Election Statistics, 1920 to Present," http://clerk.house.gov/ members/electionInfo/ elections.html.

6 Mikulski et al., *Nine and Counting*: 209.

7 *Politics in America, 2004*: 950–951.

8 "Official Biography of Kay Bailey Hutchison."

Sheila Jackson-Lee

1950–

UNITED STATES REPRESENTATIVE
DEMOCRAT FROM TEXAS
1995–

Image courtesy of the Member

SHEILA JACKSON-LEE WON ELECTION TO THE U.S. HOUSE of Representatives in 1994 in a Houston district once served by Barbara Jordan. From her seats on the Science, Judiciary, and Homeland Security committees, Congresswoman Jackson-Lee has focused on the needs of her district, which includes a large number of National Aeronautics and Space Administration (NASA) employees. She also has called attention to such national issues as health care reform and job training for working-class Americans.

Sheila Jackson was born in Jamaica, New York, on January 12, 1950. Her mother was a nurse, and her father was a hospital orderly. Jackson graduated from Jamaica High School and attended New York University. She transferred to Yale University and, in 1972, earned a B.A. in political science. Before receiving her J.D. from the University of Virginia in 1975, Sheila Jackson married Elwyn Cornelius Lee; they later raised two children, Erica and Jason. In 1977 and 1978, she worked as a staff counsel for the U.S. House Select Committee on Assassinations, which investigated the murders of Martin Luther King, Jr., and President John F. Kennedy. She left private law practice in 1987 to serve as an associate judge in the Houston municipal courts. Three years later, she won election to the first of two terms on the Houston city council.

In 1994, Jackson-Lee challenged three-term incumbent Craig Washington for the Democratic nomination to the Houston-area U.S. House seat. Her platform reflected broad agreement with the William J. Clinton administration agenda—including the President's plan for managed competition health care reform. Questioning her opponent's opposition to measures that would benefit the Houston economy, Jackson-Lee defeated Washington by a 63 to 37 percent margin in the Demo-cratic primary. She won handily with 73 percent of the vote in the general election against Republican Jerry Burley. In her subsequent five re-election bids, Jackson-Lee won by wide margins, capturing a high of 90 percent in 1998.[1] Jackson-Lee followed a succession of prestigious Representatives from her district. Created after the 1970 Census, Jackson-Lee's was the first Texas district in which the majority of the voters were African American or Hispanic. The congressional seat for the district was formerly held by Jackson-Lee's idol, intellectual powerhouse Barbara Jordan, for three terms and afterward by noted humanitarian Mickey Leland throughout the 1980s.

When Jackson-Lee took her seat in the 104th Congress (1995–1997), she received assignments on the Judiciary Committee and the Science Committee. By the 107th Congress (2003–2005), Jackson-Lee was the top-ranking Democrat on the Immigration and Claims Subcommittee of the Judiciary Committee. She served on both panels through the 108th Congress. Also, during the 108th Congress, Jackson-Lee was assigned to the newly created Select Homeland Security Committee. Her fellow freshmen elected her the 104th Congress Democratic freshman class president. Jackson-Lee also was appointed to the Democratic Steering and Policy Committee. In 1997, she was selected as a Whip for the Congressional Black Caucus.

In Congress, Jackson-Lee battled GOP initiatives to reduce welfare. In the 105th Congress (1997–1999) she pushed for legislation to protect child support and alimony payments from creditors. As a cofounder of the Congressional Children's Caucus, she also sponsored bills to create affordable childcare for working parents and to strengthen adoption laws. Jackson-Lee spearheaded two legislative efforts—one to reduce teenage smoking addiction and, the other, the "Date Rape Prevention Drug Act," aimed at curbing the availability of drugs used by rapists. She also was a strong defender of affirmative action programs, arguing that without such guidelines "institutions are left to favor the privileged as they did in the past."[2]

From her seat on the Science Committee, Jackson-Lee tended to the needs of her district, too, pushing in 1999 to restore appropriations in a funding bill for NASA. Several years earlier she voted to preserve funding for the construction of more B-2 bombers, whose components are assembled in her state. She supported the 1999 Commercial Space Transportation Competitiveness Act, extending provisions in a 1988 bill to grow the commercial space launch industry.[3] Jackson-Lee persuaded the Clinton administration to designate low-income neighborhoods in Houston as "empowerment zones," making them eligible for millions in federal grants, to promote business creation, job training, childcare facilities, and improved transportation.[3]

Jackson-Lee maintained that her advocacy on these issues was part of her job representing constituents. "You have an obligation to make sure that their concerns are heard, are answered," Jackson-Lee explained. "I need to make a difference. I don't have wealth to write a check. But maybe I can be a voice arguing consistently for change."[4]

FOR FURTHER READING

Biographical Directory of the U.S. Congress, "Sheila Jackson-Lee," http://bioguide.congress.gov

NOTES

1 "Election Statistics, 1920 to Present," http://clerk.house.gov/members/electionInfo/elections.html.

2 Congressional Record, House, 106th Cong., 1st sess. (4 October 1999): 9246.

3 Politics in America, 2002 (Washington, D.C.: Congressional Quarterly Inc., 2001): 990–991.

4 Politics in America, 2002: 990–991.

Eddie Bernice Johnson

1935–

UNITED STATES REPRESENTATIVE
DEMOCRAT FROM TEXAS
1993–

Image courtesy of the Member

A NURSE BY TRAINING, EDDIE BERNICE JOHNSON also was a political veteran decades before coming to Congress in the early 1990s. In 1972 Johnson became the first African American to hold a Dallas-area political office since the Reconstruction Era, after winning election to the state legislature. Elected to the House of Representatives in 1992, Johnson has attained a high-ranking seat on the Science Committee and has chaired the Congressional Black Caucus (CBC), stressing the need for minority inroads in the fields of science and technology.

Eddie Bernice Johnson was born in Waco, Texas, on December 3, 1935, daughter of Lee Edward Johnson and Lillie Mae (White) Johnson. She graduated from A.J. Moore High School in Waco, in 1952. In 1955, she received a nursing diploma from Holy Cross Central School of Nursing in South Bend, Indiana. Eddie Bernice Johnson married Lacey Kirk Johnson a year later. Before they divorced in 1970, the couple had one son, Kirk. Johnson graduated in 1967 with a B.S. from Texas Christian University in Fort Worth. She later became the chief psychiatric nurse of the Veterans' Administration hospital in Dallas. In 1976, Johnson earned an M.S. in public administration from Southern Methodist University in Dallas. Johnson has three grandchildren: Kirk, Jr., David, and James.

Eddie Bernice Johnson first became involved in elective politics at the state level. She was elected as a Democrat to the Texas state legislature in 1972, becoming the first African-American woman from the Dallas area ever to hold public office. As a member of the Texas legislature, she chaired the labor committee, becoming the first woman in Texas history to lead a major committee in the house. In 1977, President Jimmy Carter appointed her as a regional director for the Department of Health, Education, and Welfare, a post she held until 1981. After a six-year hiatus from politics, Johnson won election to the state senate, eventually serving as chair of the redistricting committee.

Following the Texas reapportionment of 1992, Johnson ran for the newly created U.S. House seat, which encompassed much of the Dallas and Irving area. She was elected as a Democrat with 72 percent of the vote. In 1996, court-ordered redistricting changed the boundaries of the Texas district, reducing the percentage of minority voters. Nevertheless, Johnson was re-elected with 55 percent of the vote. In her subsequent four re-election campaigns, Johnson won comfortably. In 2004, she won re-election to the 109th Congress (2005–2007) with 93 percent of the vote.[1]

Johnson has served on two committees since her House career began in January 1993: Transportation and Infrastructure (formerly called Public Works and Transportation) and Science (previously named Science, Space, and Technology). In the 108th Congress (2003–2005), Johnson was the Ranking Democrat on the Science Committee's Subcommittee on Research.

Representative Johnson's legislative interests have had both a local and a national focus. As a former nurse, Johnson has called attention to the problems facing the country's health care system and Medicare program. In 2002, she voted against a Republican-backed prescription drug plan. She also has been a proponent of a bill that called for increased federal funding for research into osteoporosis, a bone density deficiency. From her seat on the Science Committee, Congresswoman Johnson also has pushed for a program to encourage school children to study science and math. In the 109th Congress, Johnson serves as the Ranking Member on the Committee on Transportation and Infrastructure's Subcommittee on Water Resources and the Environment.

Johnson used her Transportation and Infrastructure Committee and Science Committee positions to look out for the economic interests of her district. Early in her career, Johnson supported the North American Free Trade Agreement, recognizing the fact that much of Dallas's business revolves around exports to Mexico. She later voted for normalizing trade relations with China, arguing that it would bring business to the Dallas–Fort Worth Area. In 1998, she received a post on the Aviation Subcommittee of Transportation and Infrastructure, an important position since her district covers part of the Dallas–Fort Worth International Airport. Johnson has helped bring federal money for transportation improvements and also has supported the production of B-2 stealth bombers, which are manufactured in her district.

During her House career, Johnson has been an active member of the CBC. As chair of the organization in the 107th Congress (2001–2003), she attempted to steer the CBC toward building coalitions with business groups in addition to its traditional reliance on labor and civil rights organizations. Representative Johnson also pushed the group to hold its first summit conferences on technology and energy.[2]

FOR FURTHER READING

Biographical Directory of the U.S. Congress, "Eddie Bernice Johnson," http://bioguide.congress.gov

NOTES

1 "Election Statistics, 1920 to Present," http://clerk.house.gov/members/electionInfo/elections.html.

2 *Politics in America, 2004* (Washington, D.C.: Congressional Quarterly Inc., 2003): 1008.

Nancy L. Johnson

1935–

UNITED STATES REPRESENTATIVE
REPUBLICAN FROM CONNECTICUT
1983–

Image courtesy of the Member

DURING HER TWO DECADES IN THE HOUSE, Nancy L. Johnson became the first Republican woman to gain a seat on the influential Ways and Means Committee; she has become the highest-ranking woman in the history of that panel.

Nancy Elizabeth Lee was born in Chicago, Illinois, on January 5, 1935, daughter of Noble W. Lee and Gertrude Smith Lee. She attended the Lab School at the University of Chicago, earned a B.A. from Radcliffe College in 1957, and went to the University of London Courtauld Institute from 1957 to 1958, where she studied art history. Nancy Lee married Theodore Johnson, an obstetrician, and they raised three daughters: Lindsey, Althea, and Caroline. They settled in New Britain, Connecticut, in the 1960s. At the urging of the local Republican committee, Nancy Johnson successfully ran for the Connecticut senate in 1976—the first Republican from solidly Democratic New Britain to achieve this feat in more than 30 years. She served in the state senate until 1983.

In 1982, Connecticut Representative Toby Moffet decided to run for the U.S. Senate. Johnson won the Republican nomination for Moffet's House seat and faced a fellow member of the Connecticut senate, Democrat William Curry, in the general election. She ran a campaign that reflected the fiscal conservatism of the Ronald W. Reagan administration but was moderately liberal on social issues. Both candidates, for instance, were pro-choice on the abortion issue, and both opposed constitutional amendments to allow school prayer.[1] Johnson won by a margin of about 7,000 votes—52 percent to Curry's 48 percent.[2]

During her first term in the House of Representatives, Congresswoman Johnson served on the Committee on Public Works and Transportation, the Veterans' Affairs Committee, and the Select Committee on Children, Youth, and Families. In her third term, Johnson joined the Budget Committee. In 1988, Johnson became the first Republican woman ever named to the powerful Ways and Means Committee, relinquishing all of her other committee assignments. Eventually she rose to chair three subcommittees on Ways and Means: Oversight (104th–105th Congresses,

1995–1999), Human Resources (106th Congress, 1999–2001), and Health (107th–108th Congresses, 2001–2005). During the 104th Congress, Johnson served as chair of the House Ethics Committee (officially known as the Committee on Standards of Official Conduct), one of just a handful of women in congressional history to chair a full committee.

Among her accomplishments serving in those capacities was her successful effort to shape and steer through the House the Taxpayer Bill of Rights II. On the Ways and Means Health Subcommittee, Johnson sponsored the legislation creating the State Children's Health Insurance Program and was a principal author of the bill adding prescription drug coverage, care for chronic illnesses, and other improvements to Medicare. Johnson's interests have ranged from the protection of industries and jobs in her district to federal policy for childcare and public health. She earned a reputation as an effective legislator and an important swing vote for both parties, voting with Republicans on fiscal policy and often crossing the aisle to vote with Democrats on social issues.

Johnson's legislative work also has focused on issues affecting working mothers and women generally. In 1997, she became co-chair of the Congressional Women's Caucus. She advocated a program whereby homemakers could contribute to an individual retirement account an amount similar to that contributed by their wage-earning spouse. Johnson repeatedly sought to moderate the GOP's welfare reform legislation by sponsoring a successful amendment that kept welfare recipients on the Medicaid rolls. She also fought to preserve welfare eligibility for mothers with children younger than 10 years of age, thus exempting them from the Republican-sponsored five-year cut-off limit.[3]

Completing her 20th year in Congress, Johnson emerged as the dean of women in the House (a distinction she shares with Marcy Kaptur of Ohio, also elected in 1982) and the dean of her Connecticut congressional delegation. In 2002, she was re-elected after one of Connecticut's House seats was removed due to reapportionment. In a race for the newly created Connecticut district seat against three-term Democratic incumbent James Maloney, Johnson prevailed by a margin of 54 to 43 percent of the vote. At the start of the 108th Congress she was the fourth-ranking Republican on Ways and Means. Johnson won re-election to a 12th term in 2004 with 60 percent of the vote, making her the longest-serving U.S. Representative in Connecticut history.[4]

FOR FURTHER READING

Biographical Directory of the U.S. Congress, "Nancy Lee Johnson," http://bioguide.congress.gov

NOTES

1 Matthew L. Wald, "Race in the Sixth District Is a Battle of Contrasts," 19 September 1982, *New York Times*: Section 11, 2.

2 "Election Statistics, 1920 to Present," http://clerk.house.gov/members/electionInfo/elections.html.

3 Karen Foerstel, *Biographical Dictionary of Congressional Women* (Westport, CT: Praeger, 1999): 136.

4 "Election Statistics 1920 to Present," http://clerk.house.gov/members/electionInfo/elections.html.

Stephanie Tubbs Jones
1949–

UNITED STATES REPRESENTATIVE
DEMOCRAT FROM OHIO
1999–

Image courtesy of the Member

STEPHANIE TUBBS JONES WON ELECTION TO THE U.S. HOUSE of Representatives in 1998, becoming the first African-American woman to represent Ohio in the U.S. Congress. Representative Jones, who holds a seat on the influential Ways and Means Committee, has focused on economic issues affecting her Cleveland-centered district: financial literacy, access to health care, retirement security, and education.

Stephanie Tubbs was born in Cleveland, Ohio, on September 10, 1949, the youngest of three daughters raised by Mary Tubbs, a factory worker, and Andrew Tubbs, an airline skycap. Raised in Cleveland's Glenville neighborhood, Stephanie Tubbs graduated from Collinwood High School, earning 10 different academic and athletic awards. At Case Western Reserve University, Tubbs founded the African-American Students Association and, in 1971, earned a B.A. in sociology with a minor in psychology. "All my life I had wanted to help others, and I had been active in helping others," she recalled. "I was always interested in service. In my day, the college watchword was relevant.... With a law degree, I thought I could bring about relevant change in the world."[1] She enrolled in the Case Western University Law School and graduated in 1974 with a J.D. Immediately after law school, she served as the assistant general counsel for the equal opportunity administrator, northeast Ohio regional sewer district. In 1976 Tubbs married Mervyn Jones, and they raised a son, Mervyn. Stephanie Tubbs Jones later worked as an assistant Cuyahoga County prosecutor and trial attorney for the Cleveland district equal employment opportunity commission. When Jones and several friends worked on a successful political campaign in 1979, the group pledged to select one among them and work to get that person into public office. Noting a lack of minority members on the bench, they chose Jones, who eventually won election as a judge on the Cleveland municipal court. Ohio Governor Richard Celeste appointed Jones to the Cuyahoga County court of common pleas, where she served from 1983 to 1991. She was the first African-American woman to hold that post in state history.

In 1992, she was appointed as the Cuyahoga County prosecutor, making her the state's first African-American prosecutor and the only black woman prosecutor in a major U.S. city. Jones won re-election twice.[2]

In 1998, when 30-year veteran U.S. Representative Louis Stokes retired from his Ohio district seat, Jones entered the Democratic primary to succeed him. She ran on the basis of her 17-year career in public office in the district and on her well-established political connection to constituents.[3] Capturing 51 percent of the vote in a field of five primary candidates, she later won 80 percent of the vote in the general election, becoming the first African-American woman to represent Ohio in the U.S. Congress. Jones faced no serious challenges in her three re-election bids, winning by 75 percent or more of the vote.[4] In 2004 she ran unopposed.[5]

When she took her seat in the 106th Congress (1999–2001), Jones received assignments on the Banking and Financial Services (later renamed Financial Services) and Small Business committees. In addition to serving on those two panels in the 107th Congress (2001–2003), she was appointed to the Standards of Official Conduct Committee. In the 108th Congress (2003–2005), Jones won a seat on the prestigious Ways and Means Committee, with jurisdiction over tax law.

Congresswoman Jones's district encompasses some of Cleveland's most affluent suburbs and parts of poor inner-city neighborhoods. Her seat on Financial Services helped her to secure funding for business, and to secure funding commitments for housing development. In the 108th Congress, Jones chaired the Congressional Black Caucus Housing Task Force, investigating allegations against subprime lenders, and introducing predatory lending legislation.[6] Her seat on Ways and Means has enabled her to focus legislative efforts on shoring up Social Security and Medicare, pension law, and long-term care.

Jones also has taken a legislative interest in children's issues, health, and education. She authored and successfully passed the Child Abuse Prevention and Enforcement Act of 1999 to increase training funds for child-protection workers through money generated from bail bonds, fines, and forfeited assets. In the 107th through the 109th Congresses (2001–2007), Congresswoman Jones introduced the Uterine Fibroids Research and Education Act, and also authored the Campus Fire Prevention Act to provide federal funds to outfit college housing with fire suppression equipment. In 2005, the Congresswoman introduced the Count Every Vote Act to improve electronic voting systems. Additionally, she authored legislation to clarify the legal status of cash balance pension plans. In the 109th Congress, she chaired the Congressional Black Caucus Retirement Security Task Force.

FOR FURTHER READING

Biographical Directory of the U.S. Congress, "Stephanie Tubbs Jones," http://bioguide.congress.gov

Fenno, Richard F. *Going Home: Black Representatives and Their Constituents* (Chicago: University of Chicago Press, 2003).

NOTES

1 Richard Fenno, *Going Home: Black Representatives and Their Constituents* (Chicago: University of Chicago Press, 2003): 193.

2 "Stephanie Tubbs Jones," *Contemporary Black Biography*, 2000, Vol. 24 (Detroit: Gale Research Inc., 2000).

3 Fenno, *Going Home*: 196–198; 201.

4 Ibid., 203.

5 "Election Statistics, 1920 to Present," http://clerk.house.gov/members/electionInfo/elections.html.

6 "Stephanie Tubbs Jones," *Politics in America, 2002* (Washington, D.C.: Congressional Quarterly Inc., 2001): 796–797.

Marcia C. "Marcy" Kaptur
1946–

UNITED STATES REPRESENTATIVE
DEMOCRAT FROM OHIO
1983–

Image courtesy of the Member

As the dean of Democratic women in the House, Marcy Kaptur has been a proponent of trade reform to enhance the economy of her coastal Ohio district and others like it. Kaptur was elected as the youngest woman to serve on the prestigious Appropriations Committee, where she is now the senior woman from either party. Her seat offers her a forum for speaking out on many issues from the economy, defense, and foreign affairs to energy independence. Further, Kaptur is a leading student of women's contributions to House history and she authored the original legislation to create a World War II Memorial on the National Mall.

Marcia Carolyn "Marcy" Kaptur was born on June 17, 1946, in Toledo, Ohio, to Stephen and Anastasia Kaptur. She and her brother, Stephen, were raised in that working-class town. Her Polish-American family owned and operated a corner market and her parents worked in auto factories. Kaptur graduated from St. Ursula Academy High School in 1964 and, in 1968, as a beneficiary of scholarships, received a B.A. in history with honors from the University of Wisconsin at Madison. She earned a master's degree in urban planning from the University of Michigan in 1974, and later conducted post graduate studies in new towns and development finance at Massachusetts Institute of Technology and the University of Manchester in England. From 1969 to 1975, Kaptur served as an urban planner on the Toledo-Lucas County plan commissions. For two years she directed planning for the National Center for Urban Ethnic Affairs. In 1977, Kaptur was appointed by the James Earl "Jimmy" Carter administration as the assistant director for urban affairs on the President's domestic policy staff. There, she acted as a liaison for 17 housing and neighborhood revitalization bills that passed Congress.[1]

Kaptur challenged Ohio Republican incumbent Ed Weber in 1982 for a seat in the U.S. House of Representatives and was elected as the first female to represent that district, just two years after Weber's own victory over 13-term incumbent Thomas Ashley. She is one of only 13 women to have defeated a male incumbent. The Ohio district, including Toledo, boasted a primarily blue-collar constituency to whom Kaptur appealed in her grassroots campaign. Arguing that the Toledo economy had plummeted during the first two years of the Ronald W. Reagan administration, Kaptur won with 58 percent of the vote in a race which captured national attention. In her subsequent 12 re-election campaigns, Kaptur won by two-to-one margins or better.[2]

During the 98th Congress (1983–1985), Kaptur received assignments on two committees: Banking, Finance, and Urban Affairs; and Veterans' Affairs. She left Veterans' Affairs for a seat on the Budget Committee in the 101st Congress (1989–1991). Later in that Congress, she resigned her previous assignments after securing a seat on the Appropriations Committee. In the 109th Congress (2005–2007), with 22 years' seniority, Kaptur became the first Democratic woman to be elected to the Subcommittee on Defense and continued to serve on the Subcommittee on Agriculture, Rural Development, FDA, and Related Agencies Appropriations.

From the start of her House career, Kaptur's greatest cause has been promoting trade practices more beneficial to her district and similar regions. In the 1970s and 1980s, Toledo began a decline in manufacturing and agricultural jobs, and in the iron and coal trade. Kaptur's Appropriations seat has given her a prominent perch from which to act as a leading opponent of all the major free trade initiatives of the 1990s and the early 2000s. In 1993, Kaptur was a critic of the North American Free Trade Agreement, arguing that it favored transnational corporate interests and would cost Ohio more than 100,000 jobs. She also opposed the 1994 law that established the World Trade Organization, the 2000 approval of permanent normal trade relations for China, and the 2002 legislation which granted the executive "fast track" authority to broker trade agreements that Congress could not amend.[3]

Representative Kaptur has steered millions of federal dollars into economic and community improvement projects in northern Ohio, including funding for the New Maumee River Crossing, the largest transportation project in state history. She also has been attuned to her constituents' agricultural interests. Ohio's two largest flower-producing counties are in Kaptur's district, as well as numerous greenhouse, vegetable, feed grain, animal, and sugar beet farmers.[4]

In 1996, Congresswoman Kaptur authored *Women of Congress: A Twentieth-Century Odyssey*, featuring biographical profiles of former Congresswomen.[5] Kaptur also has been a leader in bringing to the Capitol more art commemorating women and minorities. She is a recipient of the Ellis Island Award and is the only woman to have received the Veterans of Foreign Wars Americanism Award.

FOR FURTHER READING

Biographical Directory of the U.S. Congress, "Marcy Kaptur," http://bioguide.congress.gov

Kaptur, Marcy. *Women of Congress: A Twentieth-Century Odyssey*. (Washington, DC: Congressional Quarterly, 1996).

NOTES

1 "Official Biography of Marcy Kaptur," http://www.house.gov/ Kaptur/library/biography.aspx (accessed 12 September 2002).

2 "Election Statistics, 1920 to Present," http://clerk.house.gov/members/ electionInfo/elections.html.

3 "Rep. Marcy Kaptur," *CQ Weekly*, 28 December 2002: 49–50; *Almanac of American Politics, 2002* (Washington, D.C.: National Journal Inc., 2001): 1213–1214; *Politics in America, 2004* (Washington, D.C.: Congressional Quarterly Inc., 2003): 799–800.

4 "Rep. Marcy Kaptur."

5 Marcy Kaptur, *Women of Congress: A Twentieth-Century Odyssey* (Washington, D.C.: Congressional Quarterly, 1996): ix.

Sue W. Kelly
1936–

UNITED STATES REPRESENTATIVE
REPUBLICAN FROM NEW YORK
1995–

Image courtesy of the Member

A SMALL-BUSINESS OWNER, TEACHER, AND HEALTHCARE ADVOCATE, Sue Kelly won election to the House in 1994. As chair of a Financial Services subcommittee, she has investigated corporate scandals and terrorist financing. During her tenure in Congress, Representative Kelly also has been a leading proponent of women's health legislation.

Congresswoman Kelly was born in Lima, Ohio, on September 26, 1936. She graduated from Lima's Central High School in 1954 and earned a B.A. in botany and bacteriology from Denison University in Granville, Ohio, four years later. In 1960 she married Ed Kelly, settling in suburban New York, and they raised four children. Sue Kelly earned an M.A. in health advocacy from Sarah Lawrence College in Bronxville, New York, in 1985. Kelly first participated in elective politics by working on several campaigns; this experience included a position as adviser and campaign manager for New York Congressman Hamilton Fish, Sr., who represented the southern Hudson Valley, where Kelly lives.

When Fish announced his retirement, Kelly entered the race for the open House seat that spanned much of the lower Hudson Valley, from Poughkeepsie in the north to Westchester County in the south. The diverse district included computer corporations, dairy-based agriculture, and the army's U.S. Military Academy and had been represented by a Fish family member since the 1920s—one of the longer political dynasties in congressional history.[1] Kelly fended off a field of more-conservative candidates in the GOP primary and, in the general election, defeated Democrat Hamilton Fish, Jr., son of the retiring Congressman, by 14 percentage points in a race that included a third-party candidate, former U.S. Representative Joseph DioGuardi. In 1996, she won re-election with 42 percent of the vote, again in a three-way race, topping her closest competitor, Democrat Richard Klein, by seven percentage points.[2] In the subsequent four re-election campaigns, Kelly earned 60 percent of the vote or greater, aided by redistricting after the 2000 Census. In 2004, she won election to her sixth consecutive term by 67 percent of the vote.[3]

When she took her seat in the 104th Congress (1995–1997), Representative Kelly received assignments on three committees: Banking and Financial Services (later renamed Financial Services), Transportation and Infrastructure, and Small Business. She has remained on each panel throughout her House career. By the 107th Congress (2001–2003), she had risen to chair the Financial Services Subcommittee on Oversight and Investigations. She held that position in the 108th and 109th Congresses (2003–2007), by which time she also served as the third-ranking Member on the Small Business Committee.

From her seat on the Financial Services Subcommittee on Oversight and Investigations, Kelly has focused on corporate accountability and tracking terrorist financing. Her subcommittee conducted the first congressional hearings on the Enron and Global Crossing bankruptcies as well as the WorldCom accounting fraud. She contributed to and cosponsored the Sarbanes–Oxley Corporate Reform Bill, which aimed at stricter corporate accountability. In 2004, Kelly founded the Congressional Anti-Terrorist Financing Task Force, to better combat the financiers of terrorism and to examine federal programs already in place to break apart money laundering networks. She also has been an advocate of legislation to prevent identity theft and supported related provisions in the 2003 Fair and Accurate Credit Transactions Act.[4]

Congresswoman Kelly's seat on the Transportation and Infrastructure Committee has helped her steer federal dollars into her district for infrastructure projects and community organizations. She co-authored the Transportation Equity Act for the 21st Century (TEA–21) in 1998, which brought more than $11 billion to New York for transit and highway improvements. She has procured millions of dollars for Stewart International Airport, including funds to design and construct a new air traffic control tower. Kelly has sought to pass legislation to protect the environment in the Hudson Valley, including the Hudson River Habitat Restoration Act and a bill that set aside a large tract of land, the Sterling Forest, near Tuxedo, New York.

Kelly also has taken a legislative interest in women's health issues. A supporter of abortion rights, she has backed legislation for cancer research and the prevention of domestic violence. She was the chief House sponsor of the Women's Health and Cancer Rights Act of 1998, which requires health insurance companies to provide women reconstructive surgery after a mastectomy. In the 106th Congress (1999–2001), she served as the co-chair of the Congressional Caucus on Women's Issues.

FOR FURTHER READING

Biographical Directory of the U.S. Congress, "Sue W. Kelly," http://bioguide.congress.gov

NOTES

1 James Feron, "In the 19th, A Family Seat Vs. First Woman," 18 September 1994, *New York Times*: 13WC.

2 "Election Statistics, 1920 to Present," http://clerk.house.gov/members/electionInfo/elections.html.

3 *Politics in America, 2004* (Washington, D.C.: Congressional Quarterly Inc., 2003): 718.

4 "Official Biography of Sue Kelly," http://suekelly.house.gov/Biography.asp (accessed 2 December 2004).

Carolyn Cheeks Kilpatrick
1945–

UNITED STATES REPRESENTATIVE
DEMOCRAT FROM MICHIGAN
1997–

Image courtesy of the Member

A 20-YEAR VETERAN OF MICHIGAN STATE POLITICS, Carolyn Cheeks Kilpatrick won election to the U.S. House of Representatives in 1996. The first African-American woman to serve on a Michigan legislature appropriations panel, she joined the powerful House Appropriations Committee in only her second term. Representative Kilpatrick has focused on issues affecting working-class Americans, seeking federal dollars and programs to revitalize her south Detroit district.

Carolyn Jean Cheeks was born on June 25, 1945, in Detroit, Michigan, to Marvell Cheeks, Jr., and Willa Mae (Henry) Cheeks. Raised as a member of the Shrine of the Black Madonna of the Pan African Orthodox Christian Church, a politically active and powerful congregation in Detroit, she eventually served as its coordinator of political action.[1] She graduated from the High School of Commerce in Detroit and attended Ferris State University in Big Rapids, Michigan. Cheeks earned a bachelor of science degree in education from Western Michigan University in Kalamazoo in 1972 and an M.S. in education from the University of Michigan in Ann Arbor five years later. In 1968, Cheeks married Bernard Kilpatrick, and they raised two children, Ayanna and Kwame. The Kilpatricks later divorced. Early in her career, Kilpatrick worked as a teacher in the Detroit public schools. A protégé of longtime Detroit Mayor Coleman Young, she left teaching in 1978 to pursue a political career. That year Kilpatrick won election to the first of nine consecutive terms in the Michigan house of representatives, serving from 1979 to 1997. In the state house, Kilpatrick became the first African-American woman to serve on the appropriations committee. She also chaired the corrections budget for a decade and was the house Democratic whip—earning a reputation as a consensus builder.[2]

Kilpatrick sought election in 1996 to represent Michigan in the U.S. House. Among a large field of competitors in the Democratic party, including three-term incumbent Barbara-Rose Collins, Kilpatrick prevailed with a 19 percent margin of victory. The district, which covered the southern half of Detroit and several adjacent suburbs, was overwhelmingly Democratic; African Americans accounted for about 70 percent of the population. In the general election, Kilpatrick captured 88 percent of the vote. In her subsequent four re-election bids, she has won by similarly large margins, despite reapportionment in 2001. In 2004, Congresswoman Kilpatrick won election to her fifth term with 78 percent of the vote.[3]

When Congresswoman Kilpatrick took her seat in the 105th Congress (1997-1999), she received assignments on three committees: Banking and Financial Services and House Oversight and the Joint Committee on the Library of Congress. In the 106th Congress (1999-2001), Kilpatrick won a seat on the prestigious House Appropriations Committee which required her to leave her other committee assignments. She had two key Appropriations subcommittee assignments: Transportation and Foreign Operations. An active member and second vice chair of the Congressional Black Caucus (CBC), Representative Kilpatrick holds the distinction of being the first woman to chair the CBC's political action committee. Kilpatrick is also the first African-American Member of Congress to serve on the Air Force Academy Board, which oversees programs of the U.S. Air Force Academy.

Much of Kilpatrick's legislative work has centered on bringing federally funded projects into her district. From her seat on the Appropriations Committee, she has helped garner funding for Detroit-area projects for pre-college engineering, children's television programming, and enhanced rehabilitation services at the Detroit Medical Center.[4] She also supported a transportation bill that included $24 million for an intermodal freight terminal in her district that links rail, marine, and road delivery lines.[5] Kilpatrick's educational efforts brought the National Aeronautics and Space Administration (NASA) engineering and aeronautics program to Michigan for students ranging from kindergarten through 12th grade.

More broadly, Congresswoman Kilpatrick has focused on issues affecting working-class Americans. She has been an outspoken advocate for affordable health care for low-and middle-income families and for raising the minimum wage. Kilpatrick also proposed legislation to provide a $1,000 per month tax credit for medical doctors who practice in underserved areas. Representative Kilpatrick has sought to encourage corporate America and the federal government to invest more money in minority- and women-owned media outlets and advertising agencies. From her seat on the Foreign Operations Subcommittee of the Appropriations Committee, Kilpatrick has brought attention to health and economic woes in sub-Saharan Africa, securing funds for flood relief in Mozambique and South Africa and for funds for AIDS orphans in several countries.

Following in his mother's footsteps, Kwame Kilpatrick succeeded Representative Kilpatrick in the Michigan house of representatives. In 2005, he won election to a second consecutive term as mayor of Detroit.

FOR FURTHER READING

Biographical Directory of the U.S. Congress, "Carolyn Cheeks Kilpatrick," http://bioguide.congress.gov

NOTES

1 "Carolyn Cheeks Kilpatrick," Associated Press Candidate Biographies, 2000; "Carolyn Cheeks Kilpatrick," Contemporary Black Biography, Vol. 16 (Detroit: Gale Research Inc., 1997).

2 "Carolyn Cheeks Kilpatrick," Contemporary Black Biography; Hans Johnson and Peggie Rayhawk, The New Members of Congress Almanac: 105th U.S. Congress (Washington, D.C.: Almanac Publishing Inc., 1996): 58.

3 "Election Statistics, 1920 to Present," http://clerk.house.gov/members/electionInfo/elections.html.

4 Almanac of American Politics, 2002 (Washington, D.C.: National Journal Inc., 2001): 815.

5 Almanac of American Politics, 2002: 814.

Mary Landrieu
1955–

UNITED STATES SENATOR
DEMOCRAT FROM LOUISIANA
1997–

Congressional Pictorial Directory
109th Congress

MARY LANDRIEU HAS BEEN IMMERSED IN POLITICS her entire adult life, having come from a New Orleans family which her father once described as "up to its eyeballs in politics."[1] Her early career as a moderate in the Louisiana legislature and state treasury prepared her for the U.S. Senate, where she sought to be a bridge-builder in an increasingly divided chamber.

Mary Landrieu was born in Arlington, Virginia, on November 23, 1955, the oldest of nine children raised by Moon Landrieu, former Mayor of New Orleans, and Verna Landrieu. After graduating from Ursuline Academy in New Orleans, Mary Landrieu earned a degree in sociology from Louisiana State University in 1977. Two years later, at age 24, she won election to the Louisiana house of representatives, earning the distinction of being the youngest woman to serve in the state legislature. After eight years in the state house, Landrieu became Louisiana state treasurer, a position she held from 1988 to 1996. In 1988 she married Frank Snellings, and the couple adopted two children.

When Senator J. Bennett Johnston announced his retirement in 1996, Landrieu and GOP candidate Woody Jenkins joined the race to fill his seat. The campaign drew national attention when David Duke, a racial supremacist with ties to the Ku Klux Klan, also campaigned for the open seat. Landrieu ran as a moderate in the vein of former Louisiana Democratic Representative Lindy Boggs and embraced much of the William J. Clinton administration's agenda: welfare reform, a balanced budget, pro-death penalty, and pro-choice. When no candidate won the 50 percent required by Louisiana election law, the top vote getters, Landrieu and Jenkins, faced each other in a runoff.[2] Landrieu prevailed with a narrow margin of 50.17 percent of the vote, or about 5,800 votes out of 1.7 million cast.[3]

When she entered the 105th Congress (1997–1999), Senator Landrieu received assignments on three committees: Small Business; Energy and Natural Resources; and Agriculture, Nutrition, and Forestry. She resigned the Agriculture, Nutrition, and Forestry seat in the 106th Congress (1999–2001) for a post on Armed Services—becoming the first Democratic woman to serve on that panel, where she remained until 2002.[4] In the 107th Congress, Landrieu joined the Appropriations Committee. When the Democrats briefly controlled the Senate in the 107th Congress (2001–2003), she chaired two subcommittees: Appropriations' District of Columbia and Armed Services' Emerging Threats and Capabilities.

In the Senate, Landrieu maintained to her moderate politics, declaring herself a "New Democrat" centrist. "This isn't just about casting votes," she observed. "It's about shaping what comes before the Senate. Our goal is to convince colleagues to write legislation in ways that won't automatically set off alarms on the left or the right."[5] Her reputation was that of a dealmaker and consensus builder.

During her term on the Agriculture Committee, Senator Landrieu helped assemble a $6 billion farm bill that established significant drought relief for Louisiana farmers. She also cosponsored the Regulatory Fairness and Openness Act to provide farmers with effective pesticides while seeking to reduce reliance on toxic chemicals that threaten human health. In 1999, she advocated permanent federal funding for the Land and Water Conservation Fund, which benefited local parks and recreation areas in Louisiana. Her first major legislative victory was to secure hundreds of millions of dollars in offshore drilling revenue to be spent annually for 15 years on a host of environmental and conservation support programs.[6]

Two of Senator Landrieu's signal legislative achievements have been in the fields of defense and education. From her Armed Services seat, Landrieu forged a key compromise that ended a long impasse in the Senate over the National Missile Defense program. Landrieu's amendment to the legislation outlined a two-pronged approach to the program's development which included full deployment of the missile system and vigorous diplomatic negotiations with Russia and other nuclear powers to reduce standing nuclear arsenals. In 2001, working across party lines, Senator Landrieu also helped shepherd through the Senate the No Child Left Behind Act, one of the most sweeping educational reform packages in congressional history.[7] Her amendment targeted funding for school districts with the greatest number of poor students.

In 2002, during her first re-election campaign, Landrieu claimed 46 percent of the vote against nine candidates in the November general election. Louisiana state election law required her to face the runner-up, GOP challenger Suzanne Terrell, in a December runoff, which Senator Landrieu won with 52 percent of the vote.[8]

FOR FURTHER READING

Biographical Directory of the U.S. Congress, "Mary L. Landrieu," http://bioguide.congress.gov

Mikulski, Barbara, et al. *Nine and Counting: The Women of the Senate* (New York: Morrow, 2000).

MANUSCRIPT COLLECTION

University of Oklahoma (Norman, OK), The Julian P. Kanter Commercial Archive, Department of Communication. *Video reels*: 21 video reels. Includes 21 commercials used during Landrieu's unsuccessful 1995 campaign for governor of Louisiana.

NOTES

1 Thomas Fields-Meyer, Macon Morehouse, and Gabrielle Cosgriff, "Born to Run: Sen. Mary Landrieu of Louisiana Keeps Politics a Family Affair," 20 August 2001, *People*: 93.

2 *Politics in America, 1998* (Washington, D.C.: Congressional Quarterly Inc., 1997): 605–606; *Almanac of American Politics, 1998* (Washington, D.C.: National Journal Inc., 1997): 626–627.

3 "Election Statistics, 1920 to Present," http://clerk.house.gov/members/electionInfo/elections.html.

4 "Official Biography of Mary Landrieu" http://landrieu.senate.gov/about/bio.cfm (accessed 12 December 2004)

5 Barbara Mikulski et al., *Nine and Counting: The Women of the Senate* (New York: Morrow, 2000): 168; "Mary L. Landrieu," *Newsmakers 2002*, Issue 2 (Gale Group, 2002).

6 *Politics in America, 2004* (Washington, D.C.: Congressional Quarterly Inc., 2003): 431.

7 *Politics in America, 2004*: 431; "Official Biography of Mary Landrieu."

8 Mark Leibovich, "The Longest Race: Louisiana's Mary Landrieu Didn't Lose on Election Day. But She Didn't Win, Either," 26 November 2002, *Washington Post*: C1; Lee Hockstader, "Landrieu Aims to Avoid Making Louisiana History: A GOP Senator Would Be State's First," 14 November 2002, *Washington Post*: A3.

Barbara Lee

1946–

UNITED STATES REPRESENTATIVE
DEMOCRAT FROM CALIFORNIA
1998–

Image courtesy of the Member

A LONGTIME STATE LEGISLATOR AND AIDE TO Congressman Ron Dellums, Barbara Lee eventually succeeded her political mentor in the House, carrying on Oakland's and the East Bay area's tradition of progressive politics. As a member of the Financial Services and International Relations committees, Congresswoman Lee has promoted legislative programs to create better economic opportunities for working Americans and people of color, to stem the global HIV/AIDS pandemic, and to advocate for a foreign policy that balances the priorities of peace and security.

Barbara Lee was born in El Paso, Texas, on July 16, 1946.[1] In 1960, her family moved to the Los Angeles area, and Lee graduated from San Fernando High School in 1964. Lee married as a teenager, gave birth to two sons, Tony and Craig, and then divorced.[2] But she was determined, even as a single mother, to get a university education. Lee recalled that her family's support and "a safety net that existed in California that gave me access to higher education" changed her life.[3] In 1972, as the Black Student Union president at Mills College in Oakland, Lee arranged for Congresswoman Shirley Chisholm to speak on campus. Chisholm, Lee recalled, "convinced me that if I really wanted to make a significant impact, that I should get involved in politics."[4] After graduating with a B.A. in psychology in 1973, she earned an M.S.W. from the University of California, Berkeley, in 1975. Lee then joined the staff of Oakland Representative Ron Dellums, working in his office for 11 years, starting as an intern and eventually becoming his chief of staff. In 1990, Lee won election to the California assembly and then served in the state senate from 1997 to 1998.

When Congressman Dellums, a 14-term veteran, announced his retirement in late 1997, Lee emerged as his successor.[5] Politically, she followed in Dellums's footsteps, advocating military spending cuts in favor of economic opportunity and job training programs, more funding for education, and support for environmental protection.[6] Her California senate district covered much of the congressional district, so she enjoyed wide name recognition. In the April 8 special election, Lee prevailed with 67 percent of the vote.[7] In subsequent re-election campaigns she won lopsided majorities, capturing 80 percent of the vote or more.[8]

When Lee claimed her seat in the 105th Congress (1997–1999) on April 20, 1998, she received assignments on the Banking and Financial Services Committee (later renamed Financial Services) and the Science Committee. In the 106th Congress (1999–2001), she resigned the Science assignment and, in the 107th (2001–2003), secured a seat on the International Relations Committee, where she serves on the Subcommittee on Africa. In the 109th Congress (2005–2007), she served as Whip for the Congressional Black Caucus (CBC), as co-chair of the liberal Progressive Caucus, and as a senior Democratic Whip.

In the House, Representative Lee emerged as an advocate for the country's working poor and underprivileged. On her first day in Congress, Lee delivered a floor speech calling for improvements to the education system, universal health care, safeguards for Social Security, stronger environmental protection measures, and the importance of reproductive choice.[9] As a member of the Financial Services Committee, Lee sought to prohibit insurance companies from refusing to do business in geographic areas they deemed risky. Lee also criticized lenders for targeting poor Americans who often borrowed cash and then fell into a cycle of revolving debt.[10]

Lee also focused on the HIV/AIDS pandemic, which has afflicted the Bay Area and devastated sub-Saharan Africa. Lee secured $5 million to fund HIV/AIDS clinics in Alameda County. She co-authored the Global AIDS and Tuberculosis Relief Act of 2000, signed into law by President William J. Clinton, and the United States Leadership Against HIV/AIDS, Tuberculosis, and Malaria Act of 2003, and the Assistance for Orphans and Other Vulnerable Children in Developing Countries Act of 2005, both signed into law by President George W. Bush. In 2006, as chair of the CBC Global AIDS Task Force, Congresswoman Lee introduced legislation to reduce the vulnerability of women and girls to HIV infection in developing countries.[11]

Representative Lee has worked hard to balance the priorities of peace and security in U.S. foreign policy. In 1999, she opposed U.S. air strikes in Yugoslavia. Following the September 2001 terrorist attacks, she was the lone dissenting vote against a resolution authorizing broad authority to President Bush to use force in response. Lee cited a need for thoughtful consideration before taking military action.[12] She later offered an alternative amendment to the resolution authorizing the use of force in Iraq and introduced a resolution to repeal the doctrine of preemption.

FOR FURTHER READING

Biographical Directory of the U.S. Congress, "Barbara Lee," http://bioguide.congress.gov

NOTES

1 Karen Foerstel, *Biographical Dictionary of Congressional Women* (Westport, CT: Praeger, 1999): 156–157.

2 "Barbara Lee," 21 March 1994, *California Journal Weekly*.

3 Rick Del Vecchio, "Lee Wins Dellums' Congressional Seat," 8 April 1998, *San Francisco Chronicle*: A3.

4 "Barbara Lee."

5 Norah O'Donnell, "Dellums Redux Progressive Legacy Continues in the 9th," 6 April 1998, *Roll Call*; Venise Wagner, "Dellums Passes Torch to Long-Time Supporter; State Sen. Lee gets ringing endorsement; 27-Year Lawmaker's Departure May Bring Free-For-All to East Bay Politics," 11 December 1997, *San Francisco Examiner*: A9.

6 Foerstel, *Biographical Dictionary of Congressional Women*: 156–157.

7 "Dellums' Ex-Aide Wins House Seat," 8 April 1998, Associated Press.

8 "Election Statistics, 1920 to Present," http://clerk.house.gov/members/electionInfo/index.html.

9 "Official Biography of Barbara Lee," http://www.house.gov/lee/Biography.html (accessed 11 February 2003); *Congressional Record*, House, 105th Cong., 2nd sess. (21 April 1998): 2074.

10 *Politics in America, 2002* (Washington, D.C.: Congressional Quarterly Inc., 2001): 83–84.

11 "Barbara Lee," *Contemporary Black Biography*, Vol. 25 (Detroit: Gale Research, Inc., 2000); *Politics in America, 2002*: 83.

12 Peter Carlson, "The Solitary Vote of Barbara Lee; Congresswoman Against Use of Force," 19 September 2001, *Washington Post*: C1.

Blanche Lambert Lincoln
1960–

UNITED STATES REPRESENTATIVE, 1993–1997
UNITED STATES SENATOR, 1999–
DEMOCRAT FROM ARKANSAS

Image courtesy of the Member

AT AGE 38, FORMER TWO-TERM U.S. REPRESENTATIVE Blanche Lincoln of Arkansas became the youngest woman ever elected to the U.S. Senate. From her seats on the Agriculture and Finance committees, Senator Lincoln is a proponent for the farmers and rural families who reside in her state.

The youngest of four children, Blanche M. Lambert was born in Helena, Arkansas, on September 30, 1960, to Jordan Lambert, Jr., and Martha Kelly Lambert. The Lamberts were sixth-generation farmers of cotton, rice, wheat, and soybeans. In 1982, Lambert graduated with a B.S. in biology from Randolph-Macon Women's College, in Lynchburg, Virginia. In 1983, Lambert went to Washington, D.C., where she worked as a staff assistant for Arkansas Democratic Congressman Bill Alexander. From 1985 until 1991, she worked for lobbying firms as a researcher.

In 1992, Lambert challenged her old boss, Representative Alexander, for the Democratic nomination in his rural northeast Arkansas district, which included farmland along the Mississippi River as well as the city of Jonesboro.[1] She ran on a lean budget, traveling the sprawling district in a pick-up truck and using connections to local chapters of Business and Professional Women as a campaign base.[2] Lambert prevailed with 61 percent of the vote, carrying all but two of the district's 25 counties. In the general election, she defeated a Republican real estate developer with 70 percent of the vote.[3] In 1993, Blanche Lambert married Steve Lincoln, a pediatrician. In 1994, she was re-elected to a second term.

When Lincoln joined the 103rd Congress (1993–1995), she secured a seat on the influential Energy and Commerce Committee over the preference of the committee chairman, whom she soon impressed.[4] She also was assigned to the Agriculture Committee and was appointed to the coveted Democratic Steering and Policy Committee, the party leadership body that makes committee assignments. She advocated affordable health care coverage for farmers and the self-employed. On fiscal matters she was more conservative, voting for the Penny–Kasich plan to cut federal spending and, in her second term, approving a balanced-budget constitutional amendment. Lincoln also voted for the North American Free Trade Agreement in 1993 and the General Agreement on Trade and Tariffs in 1994. In January 1996, she announced her decision not to seek re-election in the House after learning she was pregnant with twins.[5] After the boys, Reece and Bennett, were born that summer, Lincoln served out the remainder of her term and returned to Arkansas.

When incumbent Senator Dale Bumpers announced his retirement in 1998, Lincoln won the Democratic nomination in a four-way primary to succeed him.[6] Her general election opponent was a tax reform and anti-abortion conservative from the Arkansas state senate. Lincoln, who supported women's reproductive choice, ran on her credentials as a mother and pledged to support women's and children's health issues in the Senate.[7] She prevailed with 55 percent of the vote. Her three committee assignments in the 106th Congress (1999-2001) included Energy and Natural Resources; Agriculture, Nutrition, and Forestry; and the Special Committee on Aging. In the 107th Congress (2001-2003), she left Energy and Natural Resources to join the Finance Committee (she was only the third woman in that panel's history) and the Select Committee on Ethics.

As a cofounder of the Senate New Democrat Coalition, Lincoln maintained her profile as a moderate in the Senate, voting for the 2001 tax cut but against other proposals of the George W. Bush administration, such as drilling for oil on Alaska's North Slope.[8] She focused on agricultural issues affecting Arkansas farmers, sponsoring legislation related to flooding and crop insurance. In the 106th Congress, she joined the World Trade Organization Caucus and tried to open Cuban markets to Arkansas rice farmers. In the 107th Congress she wrote a bill providing for tax credits to spur the development of biodiesel fuel made from soybeans. In December 2000, Lincoln successfully shepherded through the Senate the Delta Regional Authority, a centralized agency to foster economic development in the lower Mississippi Delta region.[9]

Senator Lincoln has stressed the importance of her maternal responsibilities, devising a work schedule where she forsakes the Capitol Hill reception circuit to be home each evening.[10] "The most important thing to me was to have a family," Lincoln said. "I always knew there would be filler. I just didn't know that my filler would be the Senate."[11] In 2000, she co-authored *Nine and Counting*, a book by and about the women of the Senate. In 2004, Lincoln was re-elected with 56 percent of the vote over a current Republican state senator.

FOR FURTHER READING

Biographical Directory of the U.S. Congress, "Blanche Lambert Lincoln," http://bioguide.congress.gov

Mikulski, Barbara, et al. *Nine and Counting: The Women of the Senate* (New York: Morrow, 2000).

MANUSCRIPT COLLECTION

Arkansas State University, Dean B. Ellis Library Archives and Special Collections. *Papers*: 1993–1997, 33 feet. Congressional papers and correspondence, including photographs, videotape, and sound recordings.

NOTES

1 Melinda Henneberger, "No Escaping Motherhood on the Campaign Trail," 13 June 1998, *New York Times*: A1; "Blanche Lambert Lincoln," Associated Press Candidate Biographies, 1996.

2 Joan I. Duffy, "Pressure Would Follow Lambert to Congress," 10 October 1992, *Memphis Commercial Appeal*: A1.

3 "Election Statistics, 1920 to Present," http://clerk.house.gov/members/electionInfo/elections.html.

4 *Politics in America, 1996* (Washington, D.C.: Congressional Quarterly Inc., 1995): 67.

5 Barbara Mikulski et al., *Nine and Counting: The Women of the Senate* (New York: Morrow, 2000): 92.

6 Bill Hewitt, Robin Reid, and Gabrielle Cosgriff, "The Long Shot: Freshman Sen. Blanche Lincoln, 41, of Arkansas Excels at the Nitty-Gritty of Politics—and Motherhood," 11 March 2002, *People*: 129.

7 "Blanche Lincoln," Associated Press Candidate Biographies, 2000; see also *Current Biography, 2002* (New York: H.W. Wilson and Company, 2002): 332–334.

8 *Almanac of American Politics, 2004* (Washington, D.C.: National Journal Inc., 2003): 132–134.

9 "Official Biography of Blanche Lincoln," http://lincoln.senate.gov/biography.htm (accessed 6 December 2004); *Congressional Record*, House, 103rd Cong., 2nd sess. (15 April 1994): 686.

10 *Almanac of American Politics, 2002* (Washington, D.C.: National Journal Inc., 2001): 127–129.

11 Hewitt, Reid, and Cosgriff, "The Long Shot."

Zoe Lofgren

1947–

UNITED STATES REPRESENTATIVE
DEMOCRAT FROM CALIFORNIA
1995–

Image courtesy of the Member

A FORMER HOUSE AIDE TO A JUDICIARY COMMITTEE MEMBER during the impeachment hearings of President Richard M. Nixon, Zoe Lofgren eventually sat on the same panel as a Member when it weighed articles of impeachment against President William J. Clinton. With a long background in south Bay Area politics, Lofgren's legislative focus includes high technology interests and legislation to protect mothers, children, and immigrants.

Zoe Lofgren was born on December 21, 1947, in San Mateo, California, to Milt Lofgren, a truck driver, and Mary Violet Lofgren, a Machinists Union secretary and school cafeteria cook. Lofgren attended Stanford University on a scholarship, graduating in 1970 with a B.A. in political science. She earned a J.D. from the Santa Clara University School of Law in 1975. From 1970 through 1978, Lofgren worked for U.S. Representative Don Edwards. She married John Collins and has two children. Lofgren was elected to the Santa Clara County board of supervisors where she served from 1981 to 1994.

In 1994, when Representative Edwards announced that he would not seek re-election, Lofgren entered the Democratic primary for his seat representing San Jose and the Silicon Valley. She centered her political platform on improving the lives of children through education, welfare, and healthcare reforms, while stressing her middle-class and maternal credentials. Her campaign made national headlines when, in April 1994, the state declined her request for her occupation to appear as "county supervisor/mother" on the primary ballot. She eked out a two-percentage point win in a heated primary and in the general election, Lofgren won handily with 66 percent.[1] In her subsequent five re-election bids, Lofgren faced no serious challenges winning by margins from 66 percent to 73 percent.[2]

When Lofgren took her seat in the 104th Congress (1995–1997) in January 1995, she received assignments on the Judiciary Committee and the Science Committee. In the 105th Congress (1997–1999), she also accepted a seat on the Committee on Standards of Official Conduct. Lofgren served on all three panels through the 107th Congress. In the 108th Congress (2003–2005) she left the Standards of Official Conduct Committee to take a seat on the newly created Select Homeland Security Committee and was also appointed to the Democratic Steering and Policy Committee. At the start of the 109th Congress (2005–2007), she took a seat on the Committee on House Administration, leaving the Science Committee. Lofgren is also a longtime member of the Democratic Committee on Organization, Study, and Review. Since 2003, Lofgren has served as the elected chair of the 33 Member California Democratic Congressional Delegation.

In Congress, Lofgren devotes much of her time to advocating for the high-tech industry, which employs many of her constituents. She is well-known in high tech policy circles for her co-sponsorship of the Safety and Freedom Through Encryption Act, her successful bipartisan effort to decontrol encryption technology and her sponsorship of the Public Domain Enhancement Act, which attempted to improve the nation's copyright laws. In 1997, Lofgren was a key supporter of "e-rate," providing Internet access to schools and libraries. In 2002, she introduced the Digital Choice in Freedom Act, which extended protection to buyers of copyrighted digital material while spurring technological innovation.[3] In the 109th Congress, she played a key role in the fight to protect net neutrality, introduced the BALANCE Act protecting consumer's rights to fair use, and helped to create the House Democrats' "Innovation Agenda."

Immigration law is another area of Lofgren's expertise. She has introduced several pieces of legislation relating to immigration, including a bill to provide automatic citizenship for Amerasian children, a bill to ease the adoption process for foreign children adopted by U.S. citizens, a bill to improve the way U.S. immigration services handle foreign children who arrive at the borders with no parent or guardian, and legislation to ease the visa process for foreign reporters who currently face many obstacles to enter temporarily into the United States.

Lofgren has emerged as a voice of opposition to much of the GOP-controlled House's welfare and social legislation. She supports women's reproductive rights, opposing the Unborn Victims of Violence Act of 2001 and introducing an amendment which imposed stiff penalties on persons who commit acts of violence against pregnant women.[4] In 2005, she introduced the successful Violence Against Women Reauthorization Act, which created new domestic violence funding provisions. On education matters, Lofgren opposed school vouchers and legislation that sought to deny public education to illegal immigrants.

FOR FURTHER READING

Biographical Directory of the U.S. Congress, "Zoe Lofgren," http://bioguide.congress.gov

NOTES

1 Mike Cassidy, "Lofgren Wins Easily for Congress," 9 November 1994, *San Jose Mercury News*: 10EL.

2 "Election Statistics, 1920 to Present," http://clerk.house.gov/members/electionInfo/index.html.

3 *Congressional Record*, House, 107th Cong., 2nd sess. (2 October 2002): 6932.

4 *Congressional Record*, House, 107th Cong., 1st sess. (24 April 2001):1594; *Politics in America, 2004* (Washington, D.C.: Congressional Quarterly Inc., 2003): 98–99.

Nita M. Lowey
1937–

UNITED STATES REPRESENTATIVE
DEMOCRAT FROM NEW YORK
1989–

Image courtesy of the Member

A FORMER NEW YORK STATE OFFICIAL WHO GOT HER START in politics working for Mario Cuomo, Nita Lowey won election to the U.S. House of Representatives in 1988, defeating the scion of a local political dynasty and a two-term incumbent. Representing sections of Westchester and Rockland counties, Representative Lowey holds an influential post on the Appropriations Committee and has been a passionate congressional advocate of women's issues.

Nita Sue Melnikoff was born in New York, New York, on July 5, 1937. She attended the New York public schools, graduating from the Bronx High School of Science in 1955. She earned a bachelor of science degree four years later from Mount Holyoke College in South Hadley, Massachusetts. Nita Melnikoff married attorney Stephen Lowey in 1961 and soon after left her advertising agency job to raise three children: Dana, Jacqueline, and Douglas. The family settled in Queens, New York, and Lowey became involved in community projects. In 1974, she joined the campaign of Mario Cuomo for lieutenant governor of New York. Cuomo lost, but was appointed secretary of state afterward. Impressed by Lowey's work, he hired her for a position in his department's antipoverty division. From 1975 to 1985 Lowey served as an assistant to the secretary of state for economic development and neighborhood preservation and as deputy director of the division of economic opportunity. Lowey then served two years as assistant secretary of state, from 1985 to 1987.

Lowey's first run for political office came in 1988 when she mounted an impressive campaign for the U.S. House seat, which represented much of affluent Westchester County outside of New York City. In the Democratic primary, Lowey defeated Hamilton Fish III, son of a sitting House Member and part of a long New York political dynasty. In the general election, she defeated a two-term Republican incumbent, Joseph DioGuardi, by three percent of the vote. Even after redistricting in the early 1990s changed her district's boundaries to encompass parts of Queens and the Bronx, Lowey defeated her opponents by large margins. In 2004, she won re-election to her ninth consecutive term by besting her Republican opponent with 70 percent of the vote.[1]

When Congresswoman Lowey was sworn into the 101st Congress (1989–1991) in January 1989, she received assignments on three committees: Education and Labor, Merchant Marine and Fisheries, and the House Select Committee on Narcotics Abuse and Control. In the 103rd Congress (1993–1995), she left all three of those panels to accept a seat on the powerful Appropriations Committee, where she rose to Ranking Member of the Subcommittee on Foreign Operations, Export Financing, and Related Programs. In the 108th Congress (2003–2005), Lowey also won a post on the newly created Select Homeland Security Committee. In the 107th Congress (2001–2003), Lowey became the first woman and the first New Yorker to head the Democratic Congressional Campaign Committee, where she set fundraising records.[2]

In Congress, Lowey has been a prominent proponent of women's health issues. She has been a vocal advocate for pro-choice initiatives and for continued funding for international family planning programs. In 1998, she successfully shepherded an amendment through the House that required federal health insurance plans to provide contraceptive coverage. A former co-chair of the Congressional Women's Caucus and the House Pro-Choice Caucus, Lowey also helped establish the Congressional Advisory Panel to the National Campaign to Prevent Teen Pregnancy to encourage sexual abstinence and responsibility among teens. Lowey has procured federal funding for domestic violence prevention programs, battered women's shelters, and screening programs for breast cancer and cervical cancer.[3]

From her position as the top Democrat on the Appropriations Subcommittee on Foreign Operations, Lowey has been one of the most determined congressional advocates for strong U.S. ties to Israel. She is the chief advocate for the annual U.S. aid package to the Jewish state; for instance, allocating $3 billion in military aid and economic assistance as part of the larger 1994 foreign aid bill.[4] More recently, Lowey has used her post to win increased funding for nation-building efforts in Afghanistan and for international programs for the prevention and treatment of HIV/AIDS.

Lowey's post on the Appropriations Committee has helped her look out for the interests of her district and New York state. After the 2001 terrorist attacks, Lowey was instrumental in securing $20 billion in federal funding for reconstruction and relief in New York City. She also has obtained federal funds to help local officials prepare for bioterrorist incidents and to provide local emergency workers with the latest communication and rescue equipment.[5]

FOR FURTHER READING

Biographical Directory of the U.S. Congress, "Nita M. Lowey," http://bioguide.congress.gov

NOTES

1 "Election Statistics, 1920 to Present," http://clerk.house.gov/members/electionInfo/index.html.

2 Miles A. Pomper, "Rep. Nita M. Lowey," 28 December 2002, *CQ Weekly*: 51.

3 "Official Biography of Nita Lowey," http://www.house.gov/lowey/aboutNita.htm (accessed 14 August 2002).

4 *Current Biography, 1997* (New York: H.W. Wilson and Company, 1997): 341; "Official Biography of Nita Lowey."

5 *Politics in America, 2004* (Washington, D.C.: Congressional Quarterly Inc., 2003): 716–717.

Carolyn Maloney
1948–

UNITED STATES REPRESENTATIVE
DEMOCRAT FROM NEW YORK
1993–

Image courtesy of the Member

FIRST ELECTED TO CONGRESS IN 1992, Carolyn Maloney represents a section of New York City once known as the "Silk Stocking District," which encompasses much of the East Side of Manhattan and parts of Queens. A leading advocate for women's issues both in America and abroad, Congresswoman Maloney also has championed homeland security programs in the wake of the 2001 terrorist attacks in New York City.

Carolyn Bosher was born on February 19, 1948, to R.G. and Christine Bosher in Greensboro, North Carolina. She earned a B.A. from Greensboro College, Greensboro, North Carolina, in 1968. In 1970, she traveled to New York City and decided to stay. She worked as a public school teacher and then as a community affairs coordinator for the New York board of education's welfare education program. Carolyn Bosher married Clifton Maloney, and the couple raised two daughters, Christina and Virginia.

Carolyn Maloney's political career began in 1977 when she became convinced she could effect more change in education through political processes. For five years in the New York assembly in Albany, she served as a legislative aide and analyst, and then as senior aide for the senate minority leader. In 1982, Maloney made her first bid for elective office, defeating an incumbent to win a seat on the New York city council. She served on the city council for a decade, implementing programs to eliminate waste and fraud in government and authoring the landmark New York City Campaign Finance Act.[1]

In 1992, Maloney challenged a seven-term incumbent, GOP Representative Bill Green, for a seat in the U.S. House. Maloney had two advantages. First, reapportionment after the 1990 Census redrew the "Silk Stocking" district's boundaries, bringing in more registered Democrats. Second, a large portion of the congressional district overlapped with Maloney's city council district, providing her with wide name recognition. She narrowly edged out Green, 50 to 48 percent. In her subsequent six re-election campaigns, however, she has won handily. In 2004, Maloney was re-elected to the 109th Congress (2005–2007) with 81 percent of the vote.[2]

In her first term, Maloney received assignments on two committees: Banking, Finance and Urban Affairs (now named Financial Services) and Government Operations (now Government Reform). She has remained on both committees throughout her House career and holds the Ranking Member post on the Financial Services Subcommittee on Domestic and International Monetary Policy, Trade, and Technology. In the 105th Congress (1997–1999), Maloney also earned a seat on the Joint Economic Committee, where she still serves.

Maloney's legislative interests ranged from national issues to local matters important to her constituents. Since the 2001 terrorist attacks in New York City, Maloney has focused on homeland security issues and economic recovery programs for Manhattan. She has commissioned several federal studies on the city's economic losses and has been persistent in her efforts to ensure that New York does in fact receive the $20 billion in recovery aid promised to the city by the George W. Bush administration. Maloney also has sought to enhance the resources of first responders, particularly in those places such as New York City that terrorists are most likely to target.[3]

From her seat on the Financial Services Committee, Representative Maloney also has helped pass legislation to modernize financial laws and to improve consumer protections. In the 106th Congress (1999–2001), she served as a conferee on the Gramm-Leach-Bliley Financial Modernization Bill. Maloney also was the lead Democrat on a bill to increase funding for the Securities and Exchange Commission, enhancing its regulatory function. In the 107th Congress (2001–2003), she authored legislation to reduce securities transaction fees by $14 billion over a 10-year period.

A great deal of Maloney's legislative work has dealt with issues affecting women. As past Democratic Chair of the Congressional Women's Caucus, Representative Maloney has been an advocate for women's equality in health care, reproductive rights, and pay. In 2002 and 2003, she coauthored a report showing that a 20 percent wage gap favoring men has persisted since the early 1980s. In every Congress since 1997, Representative Maloney has introduced the Equal Rights Amendment. A champion for efforts to end violence against women, in 2001, Maloney was the author of the original "Debbie Smith Act," legislation to end the backlog of unprocessed rape kits. This bill was signed into law as part of the "Justice for All Act." Maloney also was a leading cosponsor of the "End Demand for Sex Trafficking Act," which was included in comprehensive anti-trafficking legislation signed into law in 2006.[4] Since 2002, she has been a vocal proponent of restoring the contribution of the United States to the United Nations Population Fund for international family planning programs.

FOR FURTHER READING

Biographical Directory of the U.S. Congress, "Carolyn Maloney," http://bioguide.congress.gov

NOTES

1 *Current Biography*, 2001 (New York: H.W. Wilson and Company, 2001): 34–38.

2 "Election Statistics, 1920 to Present," http://clerk.house.gov/members/electionInfo/index.html.

3 "Official Biography of Carolyn Maloney," http://www.house.gov/maloney/bio.html (accessed 13 February 2003).

4 *Congressional Record*, House, 103rd Cong., 2nd sess. (28 June 1994): 5178.

Carolyn McCarthy
1944–

UNITED STATES REPRESENTATIVE
DEMOCRAT FROM NEW YORK
1997–

Image courtesy of the Member

PERSONAL TRAGEDY TRANSFORMED CAROLYN MCCARTHY from a career nurse to a national advocate for gun safety. Her activism brought the political influence that won her election to the House, where Congresswoman McCarthy continues to pursue gun-related legislation as well as health care and education reform.

Carolyn Cook was born in Brooklyn, New York, on January 5, 1944, to Thomas and Irene Cook. She graduated from Long Island's Mineola High School in 1962 and earned a nursing degree from the Glen Cove Nursing School two years later. In 1967, she married Dennis McCarthy, with whom she had one child, Kevin. For 30 years, Carolyn McCarthy worked as a licensed nurse in the intensive care unit of the Glen Cove Hospital. On the evening of December 7, 1993, a gunman opened fire on a commuter train bound from New York City to the Long Island suburbs. Her husband was one of six people killed in the attack. McCarthy's son, Kevin, was shot in the head, and 18 other commuters also were injured. The "Long Island Railroad Massacre" made national headlines and focused Americans' attention on the gun control debate. Carolyn McCarthy, with no previous experience in politics or public speaking, became a highly visible figure in the gun control movement. As she devoted much of her time to successfully nursing her son back to health, she also lobbied lawmakers in Washington on behalf of President William J. Clinton's 1994 Crime Bill and the Assault Weapons Ban.[1]

McCarthy decided to run for the New York House seat encompassing Nassau County, a New York Republican bastion, largely due to anger about then-Representative Dan Frisa's vote to repeal the Assault Weapons Ban. Discouraged from running in the GOP primary by the chairman of the Nassau County Republican Party, McCarthy, a registered Republican, opted to speak with Democrats regarding her congressional candidacy. Despite her inexperience, Minority Leader Richard Gephardt extended his party's support.[2]

During the 1996 general election, McCarthy and Frisa engaged in a nationally scrutinized battle. In spite of Frisa's assertion that his opponent was a one-issue candidate, McCarthy also campaigned on reforming the health care system, providing a basic guaranteed safety net for senior citizens, and environmental protection. Embracing many of the planks of the Clinton campaign, she favored fiscal responsibility and a balanced budget while also supporting a woman's right to choose.[3] McCarthy won election to the 105th Congress (1997–1999), resoundingly defeating Frisa by 57 to 41 percent of the vote. She had tapped into a cross-over vote composed of many Republican middle-class women who propelled her into office as the first woman ever to represent Long Island outside of the boroughs of Brooklyn and Queens. On election night, she wore two buttons: One read, "Failure is not an option," the other, "When women vote women win."[4] In subsequent elections, Republican Gregory R. Becker mounted challenges against McCarthy. McCarthy held off Becker's attack in 1998, capturing just 52 percent of the vote, enough to top Becker's 47 percent, which drew from conservative and right-to-life constituents. In 2000, McCarthy enjoyed a much more comfortable margin, with 61 percent to Becker's 39 percent. In 2002, she defeated GOP candidate Marilyn O'Grady, 56 percent to 43 percent. Two years later, she earned a seat in the 109th Congress (2005–2007) by capturing 63 percent of the vote.[5]

In the 105th Congress, Representative McCarthy was assigned to the Education and Workforce and the Small Business committees. In 1997, she attempted to add an amendment to a juvenile crime bill that would have required childproofing gun triggers. "It is a simple safety lock," McCarthy declared on the House Floor. Republicans and Democrats refused to adopt her measure, but McCarthy received enough national attention for the issue that the Clinton administration was able to win concessions from the major gun manufacturers to add the safety equipment. In 1999, in the wake of several school shooting massacres—the bloodiest of which was at Columbine High School in Colorado—McCarthy also pushed legislation to tighten background checks for gun purchasers, particularly at gun shows.

Congresswoman McCarthy won a seat on the powerful Budget Committee in the 107th Congress (2001–2003), trading in her assignment on the Small Business Committee. She largely voted with the Democrats, supporting their broad environmental, health care, and women's rights agenda. Several times, however, she voted with the Republican majority, supporting a constitutional amendment to forbid flag desecration as well as another to require a two-thirds congressional majority to raise taxes. She recently reversed her earlier vote to repeal the estate tax and has supported repealing the so-called "marriage penalty."[6]

FOR FURTHER READING

Biographical Directory of the U.S. Congress, "Carolyn McCarthy," http://bioguide.congress.gov

NOTES

1 Peter Marks, "From One Woman's Tragedy, the Making of an Advocate," 18 August 1994, *New York Times*: A1.

2 Marks, "From One Woman's Tragedy, the Making of an Advocate."

3 Ibid.

4 Dan Barry, "L.I. Widow's Story: Next Stop, Washington," 7 November 1996, *New York Times*: A1.

5 "Election Statistics, 1920 to Present," http://clerk.house.gov/members/electionInfo/index.html.

6 *Politics in America, 2002* (Washington, D.C.: Congressional Quarterly Inc., 2001): 676–677.

Betty McCollum

1954–

UNITED STATES REPRESENTATIVE
DEMOCRAT FROM MINNESOTA
2001–

Image courtesy of the Member

A FORMER TEACHER AND RETAIL SALES MANAGER, Betty McCollum entered public life as a city council member, later moving into state politics and eventually the U.S. House of Representatives. In 2001, McCollum became only the second woman elected to Congress from Minnesota since it became a state in 1858. Congresswoman McCollum has pursued legislative priorities focusing on education, global health, and human rights from her positions on both the Education and Workforce Committee and the International Relations Committee.

Betty Louise McCollum was born on July 12, 1954, in Minneapolis, Minnesota, and grew up in South St. Paul. She graduated with an associate's degree from Inver Hills Community College in 1980 and, in 1987, earned a B.A. in social studies with a minor in political science from the College of St. Catherine in St. Paul. She worked for 25 years in retail sales along with holding elective office and working as a substitute schoolteacher.

After her daughter, Katie, was seriously injured on a North St. Paul park slide that was not properly maintained, McCollum went to city hall to have the problem fixed. When problems persisted, she decided to take action and ran for city council. She finished in last place, but the experience inspired her to run again and she was elected in 1986. In 1992, McCollum challenged two incumbents in a reapportioned district and won a seat in the Minnesota house of representatives. Her legislative accomplishments included the passage of a school bus safety law and two state constitutional amendments. She compiled a strong environmental record, securing funding for an urban wetlands project and opposing a local utility's efforts to store nuclear waste by the Mississippi River. For six years, McCollum also served as assistant leader of the Democratic Farmer Labor Party Caucus.[1]

In 2000, when longtime U.S. Representative Bruce Vento announced his retirement due to illness, McCollum won the crowded Democratic Farmer Labor Party primary to succeed him in a district that included St. Paul and its surrounding suburbs. In the general election, McCollum championed a progressive agenda: protecting Social Security, creating a Medicare prescription drug benefit for senior citizens, providing increased federal funding for public schools and colleges, and environmental protection. She favored using federal budget surpluses to pay down debt rather than funding large tax breaks. McCollum prevailed in a three-way race with 48 percent of the vote. In her 2002 and 2004 re-election campaigns, McCollum won with 62 and 58 percent of the vote, respectively.[2]

In the 107th Congress (2001–2003), McCollum's committee assignments included the Education and the Workforce Committee and the Resources Committee. McCollum has become a leading advocate for children in public K-12 schools and a vocal opponent of the George W. Bush administration's No Child Left Behind Act, which imposed unfunded mandates on local taxpayers. With more than 20 colleges and universities in her district, McCollum has authored legislation to make higher education more affordable and accessible for students and families.

During the 108th Congress (2003–2005), McCollum brought a Minnesota perspective to U.S. foreign policy, taking a seat on the International Relations Committee. McCollum has been a consistent champion for human rights and increased U.S. support to fight the global HIV/AIDS pandemic. In 2003, the House unanimously agreed to a McCollum resolution condemning sentences of death by stoning, used by fundamentalist Islamic courts against women, as a gross violation of human rights. McCollum also emerged as a leader in Congress on behalf of AIDS orphans, authoring an amendment to direct 10 percent of the funding in the President's $15 billion HIV/AIDS initiative to AIDS orphans and vulnerable children. In 2005, McCollum cofounded the Global Health Caucus to focus on the challenges of HIV/AIDS and a possible Avian Flu pandemic.

With more than 35,000 Hmong and Lao Americans living in her district, McCollum successfully worked with the Bush administration to extend normal trade relations to Laos, ending nearly 30 years of economic isolation after the Vietnam War. The measure passed the House and Senate and was signed into law by President Bush in December 2004. McCollum also has tended to her district needs, working to secure federal funding for the Central Corridor light rail, the creation of a transit hub at St. Paul's Union Depot, and a $40 million renovation of the Warren E. Burger Federal Building.

In the 108th and 109th Congresses, McCollum served as a Regional Democratic Whip and also was appointed by Democratic Leader Nancy Pelosi of California to a seat on the Democratic Steering Committee.

FOR FURTHER READING

Biographical Directory of the U.S. Congress, "Betty McCollum," http://bioguide.congress.gov

NOTES

1 *Politics in America, 2002* (Washington, D.C.: Congressional Quarterly Inc., 2001): 543; "Betty McCollum," Associated Press Candidate Biographies, 2000.

2 "Election Statistics, 1920 to Present," http://clerk.house.gov/members/electionInfo/index.html.

Cynthia A. McKinney
1955–

UNITED STATES REPRESENTATIVE
DEMOCRAT FROM GEORGIA
1993–2003; 2005–

Image courtesy of the Member

CYNTHIA MCKINNEY WAS ELECTED TO THE U.S. HOUSE of Representatives in 1992, becoming the first African-American woman from Georgia to serve in Congress. With a résumé that included graduate work in international relations, Representative McKinney earned seats on the Armed Services and International Relations committees, where she was an influential voice on human rights and civil rights issues. Having lost her 2002 re-election bid, McKinney was returned to the House by voters in her DeKalb County-centered district in 2004, making her one of a handful of women to serve nonconsecutive terms.

Cynthia Ann McKinney was born on March 17, 1955, in Atlanta, Georgia, to Leola Christion McKinney, a nurse, and James Edward "Billy" McKinney, a police officer, civil rights activist, and longtime legislator in the Georgia house of representatives. During the civil rights movement of the 1960s, she and her father participated in demonstrations that inspired her to enter politics. McKinney graduated from St. Joseph High School and, in 1978, earned a B.A. in international relations from the University of Southern California. She later pursued graduate studies at the Fletcher School of Law and Diplomacy in Medford, Massachusetts. In 1984, she served as a diplomatic fellow at Spelman College in Atlanta. She then taught political science at Agnes Scott College in Decatur and at Clark Atlanta University. Cynthia McKinney married Coy Grandison, a Jamaican politician. The couple had a son, Coy, Jr., before divorcing in 1985. In 1988, spurred by her father, McKinney won election as an At-Large state representative in the Georgia legislature. The McKinneys became the first father–daughter combination to serve concurrently in the same state legislature.[1]

In 1992, when the Georgia legislature created three majority African-American districts, McKinney chose to run in one of them which encompassed much of DeKalb County east of Atlanta to Augusta and continued southward to the coastal city of Savannah. She won election to the 103rd Congress (1993–1995) with 73 percent of the vote against her Republican opponent. Despite court-ordered redistricting in 1994 (which placed McKinney in a newly created, majority-white district), she won her subsequent four re-election bids by comfortable margins of about 60 percent.[2]

When McKinney was sworn into the 103rd Congress, she received assignments on the Agriculture and Foreign Affairs (later named International Relations) committees. Over the next several Congresses she received membership on several other panels. In the 104th Congress (1995–1997), she won a seat on the Banking and Finance Committee, where she served two terms. In the 105th Congress (1997–1999), Representative McKinney was assigned to the National Security Committee (later renamed the Armed Services Committee).

In the House, Congresswoman McKinney was known for her unconventional attire—her trademark pair of gold tennis shoes—and a readiness to speak out on issues ranging from human rights abuses abroad to social inequities at home. As an advocate for poor and working-class Americans, McKinney opposed federal efforts to restrict abortions, particularly a long-standing bill known as the Hyde Amendment, which largely withheld federal funding of abortions through Medicaid. In one debate on the House Floor, McKinney described the amendment as "nothing but a discriminatory policy against poor women, who happen to be disproportionately black."[3]

On the International Relations Committee, where she eventually served as Ranking Member on the International Operations and Human Rights Subcommittee, McKinney tried to curb weapons sales to countries that violate human rights, sponsoring the Arms Transfers Code of Conduct, which passed the House in 1997, to prevent the sale of weapons to dictators. In 1999, she partnered with a Republican colleague to insert a similar provision into a State Department Reauthorization Bill. A year later, she voted against full trade relations with China, citing Beijing's poor human rights record. McKinney frequently challenged American foreign policy during this period: arguing against the 1999 bombing campaign in Kosovo, opposing U.S. sanctions against Iraq, and questioning much of Washington's Middle East policy. After the 2001 terrorist attacks, McKinney criticized the George W. Bush administration, implying that Washington officials did not do enough to prevent the devastating attacks in New York City and the nation's capital.[4]

In 2002, McKinney lost to challenger Denise Majette in a heated Democratic primary during her bid for re-election to a sixth term. Majette handily won the general election in November. Two years later, however, when the incumbent made a bid for an open Senate seat from Georgia, McKinney won the Democratic primary for the vacated seat and easily was elected to the 109th Congress (2005–2007) with 64 percent of the vote. McKinney won back her assignment on the Armed Services Committee and also received a seat on the Budget Committee.

FOR FURTHER READING

Biographical Directory of the U.S. Congress, "Cynthia Ann McKinney," http://bioguide.congress.gov

NOTES

1 *Current Biography, 1996* (New York: H.W. Wilson and Company, 1996): 352–353.

2 "Election Statistics, 1920 to Present," http://clerk.house.gov/members/electionInfo/elections.html; *Almanac of American Politics, 2002* (Washington, D.C.: National Journal Inc., 2002): 444.

3 *Politics in America, 2004* (Washington, D.C.: Congressional Quarterly Inc., 2003): 266–267; *Current Biography, 1996*: 353–354.

4 On McKinney's legislative interests relating to foreign affairs, see "Official Biography of Cynthia McKinney," http://www.house.gov/mckinney/bio.htm (accessed 23 July 2002); see also, *Politics in America, 2002*: 266.

Barbara Mikulski
1936–

UNITED STATES REPRESENTATIVE, 1977–1987
UNITED STATES SENATOR, 1987–
DEMOCRAT FROM MARYLAND

Image courtesy of the Member

CONSIDERED THE "GODMOTHER OF WOMEN IN POLITICS," Baltimore social activist, U.S. Representative, and U.S. Senator Barbara Mikulski is the longest-serving woman in Congress today. During her 29 years in Congress, Mikulski has brought the fighting instincts from her roots as a Baltimore social activist to a host of national issues ranging from women's health to care for veterans and the elderly to the stewardship of the environment. "Like most of the women I've known in politics," she said, "I got involved because I saw a community in need."[1]

Barbara Ann Mikulski was born on July 20, 1936, in Baltimore, Maryland, to William and Christine Mikulski. She graduated from Mount Saint Agnes College in Baltimore with a degree in social work in 1958, subsequently working as a caseworker for Associated Catholic Charities and Baltimore's department of social services. After earning an M.S.W. from the University of Maryland in 1965, she organized opposition to the construction of a highway in an East Baltimore historic district. The grass-roots campaign propelled Mikulski onto the city council of Baltimore, where she served from 1971 to 1976. During the 1972 presidential campaign she was a special adviser to the Democratic vice presidential candidate, R. Sargent Shriver. Afterward she chaired the Democratic Party's Commission on Delegate Selection and Party Structure.[2]

Mikulski already was known statewide when, in 1976, she campaigned for the Baltimore-based House seat vacated by Representative Paul Sarbanes. She won 75 percent of the vote in the heavily Democratic district and was never seriously challenged in her four House re-election campaigns, winning by margins of 74 percent or greater.[3]

Mikulski became the first woman to serve on the powerful Committee on Interstate and Foreign Commerce (now the Energy and Commerce Committee), a post she held for her entire House career. Mikulski's work on that panel earned her the reputation of being a strong consumer and environmental advocate.

She backed a bill which forced chemical companies to clean up toxic waste sites and supported a law requiring used-car dealers to disclose a vehicle's history.[4] Mikulski also served on the Merchant Marine and Fisheries Committee, an important position for her port city constituency. She became a voice for aid organizations. In the early 1980s, she obtained a "good guy" bonus, which allowed hospitals that legitimately cut costs to be spared cuts in Medicaid funding.[5] A lifelong advocate of women's rights, Mikulski also was a key founding member of the Congresswomen's Caucus in 1977.

In 1986, when Maryland's Senator Charles Mathias retired, Mikulski entered the race for his seat. She defeated her primary opponents, Maryland Governor Harry Hughes and House colleague Michael Barnes, with more votes than both her opponents' combined. Mikulski won with 61 percent of the vote in the general election. She was re-elected three times with large margins in 1992, 1998, and 2004, becoming the first Maryland politician to garner more than 1 million votes in 1992.[6] Mikulski received assignments on four committees: Appropriations, Labor and Human Resources (renamed Health, Education, Labor and Pensions), Small Business, and the Select Committee on Intelligence. In the 107th Congress (2001–2003), when Democrats briefly controlled the Chamber, Mikulski chaired the Labor Subcommittee on Aging and the Appropriations Subcommittee on the VA, HUD, and Independent Agencies. From 1994 to 2004, she served as Secretary of the Democratic Caucus, the third-highest-ranking position in the Democratic leadership.

The ability to sustain a legislative agenda ensured Senator Mikulski some major legislative triumphs, including the 1988 Spousal Impoverishment Act, which allowed a husband or wife to retain assets if Medicaid paid for the other spouse's nursing home costs. Mikulski also has been a leader in women's health issues, overseeing the creation of the Office of Research on Women's Health at the National Institutes of Health (NIH) in 1991 and helping to double NIH funding for women's medical research. Mikulski also backed the 2000 Breast and Cervical Cancer Prevention Act. She is a leading supporter of scientific inquiry and space exploration and has led the fight to fund major National Aeronautics and Space Administration (NASA) initiatives as well as the fight to double funding for the National Science Foundation. After the 2001 terrorist attacks, Senator Mikulski supported the creation of the Department of Homeland Security and increased the Federal Emergency Management Agency's fire grant program—providing equipment and protective gear to first responders—from $150 to $745 million annually.[7] A master of parliamentary procedure, Senator Mikulski also serves as a mentor to her women colleagues, who have tripled in number since the early 1990s.

FOR FURTHER READING

Biographical Directory of the U.S. Congress, "Barbara Ann Mikulski," http://bioguide.congress.gov

Mikulski, Barbara, et al. *Nine and Counting: The Women of the Senate* (New York: Morrow, 2000).

NOTES

1 Barbara Mikulski et al. *Nine and Counting* (New York: Morrow, 2000): 118.

2 *Current Biography, 1985* (New York: H.W. Wilson and Company, 1985): 292–295; "Democratic Reformer," 22 September 1973, *New York Times*: A15.

3 "Election Statistics, 1920 to Present," http://clerk.house.gov/members/electionInfo/elections.html.

4 *Politics in America, 1984* (Washington, D.C.: Congressional Quarterly Inc., 1983): 663–664.

5 *Politics in America, 1984*: 663.

6 "Election Statistics, 1920 to Present," http://clerk.house.gov/members/electionInfo/elections.html.

7 "Official Biography of Barbara Mikulski," http://mikulski.senate.gov/SenatorMikulski/biography.html (accessed 13 September 2002); *Politics in America, 2004* (Washington, D.C.: Congressional Quarterly Inc., 2003): 458–459.

Juanita Millender-McDonald

UNITED STATES REPRESENTATIVE

DEMOCRAT FROM CALIFORNIA

1996–

Image courtesy of the Member

JUANITA MILLENDER-MCDONALD IS KNOWN AS ONE OF THE FIVE most effective Members of the House of Representatives due to her ability to reach across the aisle and pass bipartisan legislation.[1] She has been dubbed a skilled legislator and creative leader whose relentless capacity to get the job done has produced many initiatives that were congressional firsts.

Millender-McDonald, the first Democratic Chair of the Congressional Caucus for Women's Issues to initiate a meeting with Justices Sandra Day O'Connor and Ruth Bader-Ginsberg to discuss relevant issues with women Members of the House; she was first to lead a delegation of women Members to the United Nations to speak on the plight of women globally and to draw attention to the issue of Human Trafficking and Sexual Exploitation among women and girls; she instituted the first National Teen Dating Violence Week to speak out against violence against teen girls; she was the first to bring a Central Intelligence Agency Director to the City of Watts to address the issue of drugs allegedly being dumped in the city; and first to lead a delegation of women to New York City to meet with Mayor Michael R. Bloomberg and the chairman of the New York Stock Exchange to develop strategies for increasing women's status in executive level management, financial portfolios, and investments.

She is the first African-American woman to hold the distinguished position of Ranking Member of the powerful Committee on House Administration, which oversees Federal Elections; the Library of Congress; Member Offices; the U.S. Capitol Police; the Capitol Fine Arts Board; the Smithsonian Institution; the National Zoo; and the Government Printing Office that produces the *Congressional Record*. She is a senior member of both the House Transportation and Infrastructure Committee and the Small Business Committee.

In recognition of women who served our county in uniform during wartime, Millender-McDonald initiated the first annual Memorial Day Tribute to Women in the Military at the Women's Memorial at Arlington National Cemetery. She has led the fight to secure millions of dollars for the maintenance of the memorial and another $50 million for counseling services for our returning men and women veterans serving in Iraq and Afghanistan. Additionally, she has spoken out against genocide in Cambodia, Darfur, and other regions of the world where human rights are in danger or ignored. She has also worked with former Secretary of State Madeleine Albright and Ambassador John Miller on human trafficking and women's rights issues globally.

Millender-McDonald has investigated widespread voting irregularities and voter disenfranchisement. She called for the first election reform field hearing held in recent congressional history in Ohio.

Congresswoman Millender-McDonald's effective focus on transportation issues has resulted in her becoming one of the most respected voices on the House Transportation and Infrastructure Committee, where she has secured billions of dollars for California. In the latter part of 2005, she led the fight to have the Pentagon reconsider its decision to halt production of the C-17 planes that are produced in California. Congresswoman Millender-McDonald led a delegation from her district for a meeting with the Secretary of the Air Force. The pressure she put on military officials has forced them to stall the closing of the C-17 manufacturing facility. Also in 2005, Congresswoman Millender-McDonald played a key role in the crafting and ultimate passage of the six-year Transportation Reauthorization Act (TEA-LU), the largest public works legislation in our nation's history.

Congresswoman Millender-McDonald is a life member of the National Association for the Advancement of Color People (NAACP) and Alpha Kappa Alpha Sorority, Inc. She serves on the board of directors of the Southern Christian Leadership Conference and the board of trustees of Second Baptist Church, Los Angeles. She is the founder and executive director of the League of African-American Women, an organization of more than 40 African-American women's groups, and the founder of the Young Advocates, a political leadership-training program for African Americans between the ages of 18 and 35.

Congresswoman Millender-McDonald earned a bachelor of science degree in business administration from the University of Redlands, a master's degree in educational administration from California State University-Los Angeles, and teaching and administration credentials from the California State University system. She is married to James McDonald, Jr., and they are the proud parents and grandparents of five adult children and five grandchildren.

FOR FURTHER READING

Biographical Directory of the U.S. Congress, "Juanita Millender-McDonald," http://bioguide.congress.gov

NOTES

1 John McCaslin, "Inside the Beltway: Top Producers," 13 April 2005, *Washington Times:* A9.

Candice Miller

1954–

UNITED STATES REPRESENTATIVE
REPUBLICAN FROM MICHIGAN
2003–

Image courtesy of the Member

ONE OF THE MOST POPULAR POLITICIANS IN HER HOME state of Michigan, Candice Miller rose through the ranks of local politics to become Michigan's first woman secretary of state. In 2002, Miller won election to the U.S. House, becoming the first Republican woman to represent Michigan in Congress in nearly 50 years. Representing Michigan's 10th District, she focused on national security and streamlining government in her first term.

Candice Snider was born on May 7, 1954, in St. Clair Shores, Michigan, daughter of Don and Jenny Snider. After graduating high school, she attended Macomb Community College from 1973 to 1974, before leaving school to sell boats at a family-owned marina on Michigan's Clinton River. Sailing boats, she noted, "was our livelihood but it was also our family sport and our family hobby."[1] A proposed tax rate increase on marinas got Miller involved in politics. She recalled that she became a "noisy activist."[2] She won election to the Harrison Township board of trustees in 1979. She was elected a Harrison Township supervisor the next year and served for 12 years. In 1984, she married Donald Miller, and the couple raised Candice's daughter, Wendy, from a previous marriage. Miller served as a local co-chair of the Ronald Reagan–George H.W. Bush presidential campaign in 1984. Two years later, she defeated four opponents to win the GOP nomination to the U.S. House of Representatives. She faced Democrat David Bonior, a five-term incumbent, and lost that race 66 percent to 34 percent. In 1992, Miller was elected to a term as the Macomb County treasurer in the suburban Detroit area by defeating a longtime incumbent to become the first Republican to win county-wide office in more than 40 years. Two years later, she challenged another longtime incumbent to win the first of two terms as Michigan secretary of state.[3] As secretary of state, Miller helped develop fraud-proof driver's licenses and instituted important election reforms which relied on technology, including putting more voter information on the Internet. In 1998, in her re-election bid, Miller set a state record for the most votes, outpolling even the popular incumbent Governor John Engler.[4]

In 2002, Miller made another bid for Congress in a newly reapportioned district which encompassed portions of Macomb County, Port Huron, and much of Michigan's "thumb." Representative Bonior, the incumbent, had decided to retire from the House to run for the Michigan governorship. Miller ran unopposed in the GOP primary and handily won the 2002 general election against Democratic candidate Macomb County Prosecutor Carl J. Marlinga, with a 63 to 36 percent margin.[5] Miller's victory helped Republicans capture a majority in the state's House delegation for the first time in decades. In 2004, she won re-election with 69 percent of the vote.

After being sworn into Congress, Miller received a plum assignment on the House Armed Services Committee, with seats on that panel's Readiness and Total Force subcommittees. In light of her background as Michigan's secretary of state, Miller also was appointed to the Government Reform Committee, with seats on three of its subcommittees, including Government Efficiency and Financial Management. In the 109th Congress (2005–2007), Miller also was assigned to the Committee on House Administration.

During her first term, Miller was a reliable vote for the Republican majority. She supported the overhaul of the Medicare program and the creation of a prescription drug benefit, voted for the creation of a private school voucher program in Washington, D.C., and favored the $330 billion tax cut over 10 years. Miller also voted to criminalize the partial-birth abortion procedure, except in instances when it may be used to save a woman's life. From her seat on Armed Services, the Michigan Congresswoman also was a supporter of the prosecution of the war in Iraq. In February 2004, Miller traveled with a congressional delegation to Libya for a meeting with Colonel Muammar Qaddafi. This delegation was the first group of U.S. officials to visit Libya in 38 years and marked Qaddafi's decision to shut down his country's nuclear weapons program and to open it to international inspectors. Miller later described those developments as "a pivotal moment in world history."[6] Miller also was attentive to the needs of her district, securing more than $6.5 million in federal dollars for local projects, including a hiking/biking trail and a communications system for the St. Clair County sheriff's department.

FOR FURTHER READING

Biographical Directory of the U.S. Congress, "Candice Miller," http://bioguide.congress.gov

NOTES

1 Heather Burns, "Port Huron-to-Mackinac Island Sailboat Race: Secretary of State Sails Into Elite Mackinac Club," 17 July 2001, *Port Huron Times Herald*: 1C.

2 *Politics in America, 2004* (Washington, D.C.: Congressional Quarterly, Inc, 2003): 524.

3 Christopher Cook, "Macomb Treasurer Wants Austin's Office," 24 February 1994, *Detroit Free Press*: 2B.

4 Peggy Walsh-Sarnecki, Dennis Niemiec, and Bill McGraw, "Miller Easily Wins Race for Congress; State Delegation to U.S. House to Be a GOP Majority for First Time in Decades," 6 November 2002, *Detroit Free Press*: 1.

5 "Election Statistics, 1920 to Present," http://clerk.house.gov/members/electionInfo/elections.html.

6 Dee-Ann Durbin, "Miller Says Meeting With Gaddafi Was 'Pivotal,'" 27 January 2004, Associated Press; Ruby Bailer, "Congresswoman to Go to Libya; Miller Part of 1st U.S. Delegations in 38 Years," 22 January 2004, *Detroit Free Press*: 2B.

Lisa Murkowski

1957–

UNITED STATES SENATOR
REPUBLICAN FROM ALASKA
2002–

Image courtesy of the Member

THE FIRST ALASKAN WOMAN TO HOLD NATIONAL OFFICE and the first Alaskan-born Senator to serve the state, Lisa Murkowski began her tenure in the United States Senate in 2002. Her father, newly elected Alaska Governor Frank Murkowski, appointed her to fill the Senate seat he had recently vacated. With years of experience in state and local politics, Lisa Murkowski quickly set to work on the economic and infrastructure projects important to her constituents, winning re-election to a full six-year term in the Senate in 2004.[1]

One of six siblings, Lisa Murkowski was born to Frank and Nancy Murkowski on May 22, 1957, in Ketchikan, Alaska. Frank Murkowski, a banker and former Alaska commissioner of economic development, first won election to the U.S. Senate in 1980, where he served for 22 years. He chaired the Veterans' Affairs Committee and the Committee on Energy and Natural Resources. Lisa Murkowski attended high school in Fairbanks, Alaska. She enrolled at Williamette University in Salem, Oregon, and went on to earn a BA in economics from Georgetown University in 1980. She then returned to Juneau, Alaska, to work as a legislative aide for the speaker of the Alaska house of representatives and became active in state Republican politics. In 1985, Murkowski graduated with a law degree from Willamette College of Law and returned to Alaska, where she met her husband.[2] In 1987, she married Verne Martell, a small business owner. They have two sons, Nicolas and Matthew, who were educated in the Anchorage public schools until they moved to Washington, D.C.

Before beginning her career in politics, Murkowski served as Anchorage District Court attorney and worked in an Alaska commercial law practice. Murkowski was active in local issues, serving on the Anchorage mayor's task force on the homeless, the Anchorage Equal Rights Commission, as well as serving as president of her sons' school PTA. In 1998, Murkowski was elected as a Republican to the Alaska house of representatives and subsequently won re-election to two additional terms. While serving in the state house, Murkowski sat on the Alaska Commission on Post Secondary Education and chaired both the labor and commerce and the military and veterans affairs committees. Her Republican peers in the state house selected her to be majority leader for the 2003–2004 session. During her time in the state legislature, Murkowski earned a reputation as a moderate willing to tackle tough issues.

In the 2002 elections, her father, Frank Murkowski, won the Alaskan governorship and formally resigned his Senate seat. On December 20, 2002, Governor Murkowski appointed Lisa Murkowski to the U.S. Senate, citing his desire to send an experienced legislator to Washington with values similar to his and who was young enough to accrue seniority that he, longtime Senator Ted Stevens, and veteran U.S. Representative Don Young had attained.[3]

In the Senate, Lisa Murkowski received assignments on several key committees, few more important to Alaskan interests than her post on the Energy and Natural Resources Committee, where she is chairman of the Subcommittee on Water and Power. In addition, she currently has assignments on three other committees: Foreign Relations, where she serves as the chairman of the Subcommittee on East Asian and Pacific Affairs; Environment and Public Works; and Indian Affairs. Within days of the start of her term, Senator Murkowski also was selected as one of the four freshmen (and the only woman) to serve as Deputy to the Majority Whip.[4]

During her first term, Senator Murkowski pursued a legislative program of economic growth, infrastructure, and improved social services in Alaska. The first bill she introduced was to expand the authorization and budget of the Denali Commission in an effort to build roads and transportation systems between Alaska's dispersed rural communities and natural resources. "You can't do any kind of economic development—development at all—if we don't have . . . the transportation access to it, so this is all about access," Murkowski said.[5] She also won passage of legislation to help relocate the Alaskan village of Newtok, which is threatened by river erosion. She also secured an Alaskan exception to federal Medicaid funding to help defray the much higher costs associated with health care delivery in Alaska. In 2004, energy legislation was passed that included a series of regulatory changes and financial incentives, offered by Senator Murkowski, that were critical for future construction of an Alaskan gas line to the Lower 48.[6]

In November 2004, Senator Murkowski defeated a popular former Democratic governor of Alaska to win a full six-year term in the U.S. Senate.

FOR FURTHER READING

Biographical Directory of the U.S. Congress, "Lisa Murkowski," http://bioguide.congress.gov

NOTES

1 *Politics in America, 2004* (Washington, D.C.: Congressional Quarterly Inc., 2003): 22–23.

2 Ben Pershing, "Filling Murkowski's Shoes Isn't Easy for Murkowski," 27 January 2003, *Roll Call:* 8.

3 Mike Chambers, "Alaska Gov. Appoints Daughter to Senate," 20 December 2002, Associated Press.

4 *Politics in America, 2004:* 22–23.

5 "Sen. Murkowski Offers Her First Bills," 6 February 2003, Associated Press.

6 "Murkowski 'Happy' With Transportation Bill," 20 February 2004, *The Frontrunner.*

Image courtesy of the Member

Patty Murray
1950–

UNITED STATES SENATOR
DEMOCRAT FROM WASHINGTON
1993 –

PATTY MURRAY NEVER PLANNED TO ENTER POLITICS, but today she is serving her third term in the U.S. Senate as a member of the Democratic leadership. From the classroom to the Congress, Patty Murray has been an effective advocate for Washington's working families and a national leader on port security, veterans issues, transportation, education, health care, and economic development. In 1992 she became the first Washington woman elected to the U.S. Senate. A parent, former preschool teacher and state legislator, Murray is known for her down-to-earth, determined style. She is the Ranking Democrat on the Appropriations Subcommittee on Transportation, Treasury, Judiciary, and H.U.D.; and the Ranking Member of the Employment, Safety, and Training Subcommittee. She serves in the Democratic leadership as the Assistant Floor Leader.[1]

Patty Johns was born in Bothell, Washington, on October 11, 1950, to David L. Johns and Beverly A. McLaughlin Johns. In June 1972, after graduating from Washington State University, she married Robert R. Murray. The Murrays raised two children, Randy and Sara. Senator Murray volunteered as a pre-school teacher at a parent-child cooperative education program in which her children were enrolled. In 1980, the Washington state legislature eliminated the program, and Murray launched a grassroots campaign to save it. During that fight, a male legislator dismissed her by saying, "You can't make a difference; you're just a mom in tennis shoes."[2] In response, Murray worked to build a grassroots coalition of 13,000 parents who saved the program. Murray was then elected to the Shoreline school board. In 1988, Murray won election to the Washington state senate where she served until 1992, working as the Democratic whip for her final two years.

In 1992, Murray saw that working families did not have a voice in the U.S. Senate, so she challenged Democratic incumbent Senator Brock Adams for the Democratic primary. Murray spoke on middle-class concerns. "Mom in tennis shoes" became a campaign theme. Adams announced his retirement before the primary, and Murray beat four other opponents.[3] In the general election, she beat five-term GOP Representative Rod Chandler with 54 percent of the vote. Murray's campaign focused on healthcare, improved schools, a woman's right to choose, and economic help for working families.[4]

Murray entered the 103rd Congress (1993–1995) and received assignments on three committees: Appropriations; Budget; and Banking, Housing, and Urban Affairs. In the 105th Congress (1997–1999) she dropped the third assignment for a spot on the Labor and Human Resources Committee (later renamed Health, Education, Labor, and Pensions). By the 108th Congress (2003–2005), Murray had become Ranking Member of the Subcommittee on Employment, Safety, and Training.

Murray has taken a special interest in veterans issues. Her father served in World War II, and during college Murray volunteered at the Veterans' Administration (VA) hospital in Seattle. She asked to serve on the Veterans' Affairs Committee, and became the first woman ever to serve on that committee. Murray has worked to save VA hospitals from being closed and to improve services for returning Guard and Reserve members. Murray earned a seat on the Senate Select Committee on Ethics during the 105th Congress. In the 107th Congress (2001–2003), while Democrats briefly controlled the chamber, Murray chaired the Transportation Subcommittee of Appropriations. She was the panel's Ranking Democrat in the 108th Congress and 109th Congress (2005–2007).

Senator Murray has focused on issues vital to her state. She has worked to improve transportation, agriculture, and trade. She has helped secure federal funding to clean up the Hanford nuclear facility and protected the Hanford Reach section of the Columbia River. Washington is the nation's most trade-dependent state, and Murray worked to open foreign markets to the state's many exports. Senator Murray has worked to improve security at the U.S. northern border. After the September 11, 2001, terrorist attacks, Murray worked to improve port security by increasing funding for the Coast Guard and developing legislation to improve cargo security.[5] In 1998, Murray led the Senate fight to hire 100,000 new teachers to reduce classroom overcrowding.[6] She worked to pass and reauthorize the Violence Against Women Act and is working to ban deadly asbestos. After a 1999 pipeline explosion killed three people in her state, Murray led a national effort that dramatically improved pipeline safety.

In 1998, Murray won re-election by defeating two-term U.S. Representative Linda Smith with 58 percent of the vote. By the 107th Congress, Murray was Washington State's senior Senator, and Democratic leaders chose her as the first woman to head the Democratic Senatorial Campaign Committee. In 2004, she won a third term, capturing 55 percent of the vote against Congressman George Nethercutt.[7]

FOR FURTHER READING

Biographical Directory of the U.S. Congress, "Patty Murray," http://www.bioguide.congress.gov

Mikulski, Barbara, et al. *Nine and Counting: The Women of the Senate* (New York: Morrow, 2000).

MANUSCRIPT COLLECTION

University of Oklahoma (Norman, OK), The Julian P. Kanter Commercial Archive, Department of Communication. *Video cassettes*: two video cassettes. Includes nine commercials used during Patty Murray's campaign.

NOTES

1 "Official Biography of Patty Murray," http://murray.senate.gov. (accessed 12 December 2004).

2 Timothy Egan, "Another Win by a Woman, This One 'Mom,'" 17 September 1992, *New York Times*: A16.

3 Barbara Mikulski et al., *Nine and Counting* (New York: Morrow, 2000): 45; Egan, "Another Win by a Woman, This One 'Mom.'"

4 "Election Statistics, 1920 to Present," http://clerk.house.gov/members/electionInfo/index.html.

5 *Politics in America, 2004* (Washington, D.C.: Congressional Quarterly Inc., 2003): 1063; "Official Biography of Patty Murray," http://murray.senate.gov.

6 Mikulski et al., *Nine and Counting*: 152.

7 "Election Statistics, 1920 to Present," http://clerk.house.gov/members/electionInfo/index.html.

Marilyn N. Musgrave
1949–

UNITED STATES REPRESENTATIVE
REPUBLICAN FROM COLORADO
2003–

Congressional Pictorial Directory
109th Congress

MARILYN MUSGRAVE JOINED THE 108TH CONGRESS (2003–2005) as the United States Representative from eastern Colorado. Her modest upbringing in a small rural community in Colorado helped to forge her core beliefs as a social and fiscal conservative.[1]

Marilyn Musgrave was born on January 27, 1949, in Greeley, Colorado. She attended Eaton High School and worked as a waitress and cleaned houses to earn money during her free time. She married Steve Musgrave while attending Colorado State University in 1968. After earning a B.A. in social studies, Musgrave taught school in Genoa, Colorado, before moving to Fort Morgan, where she and her husband started their own agricultural business, and then she devoted herself full-time to raising her children.[2] Once her children were in school, Musgrave became the "consummate volunteer," working for a variety of community organizations, including various Republican causes. Her active volunteer work laid the foundation for her future career in elective politics.[3]

Musgrave's political career began when she won a seat on the school board of Fort Morgan in 1990, a position that she held for four years. After completing the intensive Republican Leadership Program to prepare for a future in politics, Musgrave was elected to the Colorado state legislature in 1994. During her four-year tenure as a state representative, and her subsequent time in the Colorado state senate from 1999 through 2003, Musgrave supported a variety of conservative legislative initiatives, including tax cuts, free market solutions, the promotion of the sanctity of human life, support for traditional marriage, and the protection of Second Amendment rights.[4]

When Republican Representative Bob Schaffer retired from the House to fulfill his three-term limit pledge in 2002, Musgrave entered the race for the open congressional seat which covers most of eastern Colorado, swinging northward to Greeley on the northern edge of the Front Range of the Rocky Mountains. Musgrave won the August 13, 2002, Republican primary with two-thirds of the vote. Shortly after her victory, Musgrave outlined her political agenda: "I want to go to Washington to continue the conservative Reagan Republican agenda of lower taxes, limited government, a strong military, defense of our constitutional freedoms and protection of our pro-life, pro-family values."[5] In the general election, Musgrave defeated Democrat Stan Matsunaka, winning all 18 counties in the district, and continuing its 30-year tradition of sending Republicans to Congress. In 2004, running against Matsunaka again, Musgrave was re-elected.[6]

Musgrave serves on the Agriculture Committee, the Resources Committee, and the Education and the Workforce Committee. As a member of the Small Business Committee, Musgrave became chairman of the Subcommittee on Workforce, Empowerment, and Government Programs in her second term. Musgrave was elected by her peers to serve on the House Republican Steering Committee. She also is a leading member of the influential Republican Study Committee and is the Policy Chair of the Western Caucus.

As a Representative, Musgrave held true to her campaign promise to continue the conservative agenda. She opposed a Republican-sponsored measure to hike the federal gas tax, remaining firm in her conviction that "raising the gas tax is not only bad policy, it is bad politics."[7] Musgrave emerged on the national stage when she sponsored the Federal Marriage Amendment, which defined marriage as a union of one man and one woman.[8] On September 6, 2004, *Newsweek* magazine called Musgrave the rising star of Congress.

FOR FURTHER READING

Biographical Directory of the U.S. Congress, "Marilyn Musgrave," http://bioguide.congress.gov

NOTES

1 "Our Campaigns," http://www.ourcampaigns.com/cgi-bin/r.cgi/CandidateDetail.html?&CandidateIDffi2467. (accessed 30 March 2004).

2 "Our Campaigns."

3 M.E. Sprengelmeyer, "In the Spotlight for Better or Worse: Rep. Marilyn Musgrave," 27 November 2003, Scripps Howard News Service.

4 *Politics in America, 2004* (Washington, D.C.: Congressional Quarterly, Inc, 2003): 183.

5 "Our Campaigns."

6 *Almanac of American Politics, 2004* (Washington, D.C.: National Journal Inc., 2003): 319–321; "Election Statistics, 1920 to Present," http://clerk.house.gov/members/electionInfo/elections.html.

7 Bill McAllister and Mike Soraghan, "Beauprez, Musgrave Feted in D.C. as New Colorado House Members," 8 January 2003, *Denver Post*: A-6; Marilyn Musgrave, "Building More Roads Without Raising Taxes," 11 February 2004, *The Hill*: 22.

8 "Press Release: Musgrave Amendment Strengthens Marriage," http://wwwa.house.gov/musgrave/108th%20Web/pr_030522_federal_marriage_amendment.htm (accessed 2 April 2004).

Sue Myrick
1941–

UNITED STATES REPRESENTATIVE
REPUBLICAN FROM NORTH CAROLINA
1995–

Congressional Pictorial Directory
108th Congress

SUE MYRICK, AN ADVERTISING EXECUTIVE AND FORMER MAYOR of Charlotte, North Carolina, won election to the U.S. House of Representatives in 1994, during the "Republican Revolution." One of the leaders of the large GOP freshman class in the 104th Congress (1995–1997), Representative Myrick acted as a liaison between the leadership and a core group of conservatives and earned a powerful position on the Rules Committee. A fiscal and social conservative throughout her career, Myrick fought a personal battle with breast cancer that led her to become a chief proponent of legislation to combat the disease.

Suellen Wilkins was born in Tiffin, Ohio, on August 1, 1941. She graduated from Port Clinton High School in Port Clinton, Ohio, in 1959 and attended Heidelberg College for one year. She married and raised two children and was later divorced. Employed in a variety of jobs, she was an executive secretary for the Alliance, Ohio, mayor's office, an employee for the court of juvenile and domestic relations in Ohio, and a television personality in Harrisonburg, Virginia. In the early 1970s, she and her family relocated to Charlotte, where she switched careers, eventually running her own advertising companies. In 1977, she married William Edward "Ed" Myrick, who brought three children of his own to the marriage. Sue Myrick had no political ambitions before the early 1980s, when she and her husband had a dispute with the city council of Charlotte over a proposed property purchase. The experience convinced Myrick that government played a more immediate part in her life than she had previously believed.[1] In 1983, she won a seat on the city council as an at-large member, serving until 1985. She made an unsuccessful bid to become Charlotte's mayor in 1985 but, two years later, defeated the incumbent to become the city's first woman mayor. During her two terms as mayor from 1987 to 1991, Myrick made major transportation and infrastructure improvements to Charlotte, and enacted drug-and crime-fighting programs.

Myrick eventually turned her attention toward national office, making an unsuccessful bid for a U.S. Senate nomination in 1992. Two years later, when Republican Representative Alex McMillan announced his retirement from a North Carolina district seat covering a large part of Charlotte and Gastonia

FOR FURTHER READING

Biographical Directory of the U.S. Congress, "Sue Myrick," http://bioguide.congress.gov

NOTES

1 Noella Kertes, "Rep. Sue Myrick," 28 December 2002, *CQ Weekly*: 53–54.

2 "Election Statistics, 1920 to Present," http://clerk.house.gov/members/electionInfo/index.html.

3 Mildred Amer, *Women in the United States Congress: 1917–2004*, Congressional Research Service (CRS) Report for Congress (July 2004).

4 *Congressional Record*, House, 106th Cong., 2nd sess. (30 March 2000): 1624; *Politics in America, 2004* (Washington, D.C.: Congressional Quarterly Inc., 2003): 761.

in south-central North Carolina, Myrick entered the race to succeed him. Myrick prevailed in a five-way primary, and easily won the general election, with 65 percent of the vote. In her subsequent five re-election campaigns, Myrick boasted comfortable margins of 63 percent or more. In 2004, she was elected to the 109th Congress (2005–2007) with 70 percent of the vote.[2]

During her first term in the 104th Congress, Representative Myrick received assignments on three committees: Budget, Science, and Small Business.[3] She left those panels in the 105th Congress (1997–1999) to serve on the prestigious House Rules Committee, with oversight of all legislation headed for floor debate. Representative Myrick has chaired the Republican Study Committee, a group comprised of the chamber's most conservative Members. She also has worked as a member of the Republican Conference's Communications Working Group, drawing on her advertising experience to craft the GOP message.

From her seat on the Budget Committee and then on the Rules Committee, Congresswoman Myrick helped implement the "Contract with America," personally focusing on welfare reform. She also helped shape the 1997 budget which was the first balanced budget in nearly 30 years. Myrick still meets regularly with GOP leaders to discuss legislation and to express the resolve of fiscal conservatives.

Myrick's successful battle against breast cancer in the late 1990s reoriented her legislative focus toward initiatives that help fight the disease. She spearheaded through the House a measure to federally fund treatment for low-income women diagnosed with breast cancer or cervical cancer. She has also co-chaired the House Cancer Caucus since the 107th Congress (2001–2003).[4]

Representative Myrick has been attentive to her district's needs, particularly unemployment in sectors such as the state's ailing textile industry. Spurred by the disappearance of an 18-year-old college student from her district, Myrick focused on legislation to create a national clearinghouse for information on missing adults. Myrick's support of prayer in school and opposition to abortion reflects the conservative tilt of her district. She also has been a leading advocate in securing America's border and addressing North Carolina's immigration problems.

In the 109th Congress, Representative Myrick left her Rules Committee post to serve on the powerful Energy and Commerce Committee, where she focuses her time on issues such as cancer and brain disease.

Grace Napolitano
1936–

UNITED STATES REPRESENTATIVE
DEMOCRAT FROM CALIFORNIA
1999–

Congressional Pictorial Directory
109th Congress

GRACIELA FLORES NAPOLITANO ENTERED COMMUNITY POLITICS in the 1980s, built wide name recognition as a city mayor and California assembly-woman, and won election to the U.S. House in 1998. In Washington, Congresswoman Napolitano has focused on clean water, mental health, and transportation and on securing federal dollars for her district.

Graciela Flores was born in Brownsville, Texas, on December 4, 1936, daughter of Miguel Flores and Maria Alicia (Ledezma) Flores. After graduating from Brownsville High School in 1954, she married Federico Musquiz and had five children: Yolanda, Federico, Edward, Miguel, and Cynthia. The family moved to southern California, where she continued her education at Cerritos College. In 1982, several years after her first husband passed away, she married California restaurateur Frank Napolitano. The two live in the Los Angeles suburb of Norwalk, in the same home she has maintained for more than 40 years, and take great pride in their 14 grandchildren and one great-grandson.

Napolitano worked for 13 years for the California Department of Employment before moving to a major automobile manufacturing company, where she spent 22 years, moving from executive secretary to its transportation division. In 1974, Napolitano was appointed a commissioner on the International Friendship Commission, a sister city program in which Norwalk was paired with the Mexican town of Hermosillo. The program focused on cultural exchanges between children and some adults, and the experience pulled Napolitano into public service.[1]

In 1986, Napolitano was first elected to the city council of Norwalk by a 28-vote margin. Four years later, she won her second term by the largest margin in city history. In 1989, Napolitano's council colleagues elevated her to mayor. In 1992, she was elected to the California assembly, where she served until 1998. There she emerged as a leader on international trade, environmental protection, transportation, and immigration issues. Napolitano earned a reputation as a hard worker and a champion of small business, women, economic expansion, and job creation. She chaired the women's caucus and established the first new standing committee in a decade, the international trade committee, and served as vice chair of the Latino caucus.

In 1998, upon the retirement of Congressman Esteban Torres, Napolitano entered the primary race to succeed him. She used $200,000 of her retirement funds and drew from the political base of her assembly district that encompassed much of the largely Hispanic, middle-class Democratic congressional district. She won the primary by 619 votes and captured the general election with 67 percent of the vote. Napolitano has been re-elected three times by margins of 70 percent or higher and ran unopposed in 2004 in her newly reapportioned district stretching from East Los Angeles to Pomona.[2]

Napolitano has served on the Resources and Small Business committees since entering the House in January 1999. In the 107th Congress (2001–2003), she won an additional post on the International Relations Committee and also was elevated to Ranking Member of the Resources Committee's Water and Power Subcommittee in the 108th Congress (2003–2005). Napolitano has moved rapidly into the leadership of the Congressional Hispanic Caucus and was unanimously selected its chair for a two-year term during the 109th Congress (2005–2007).[3] She also serves as co-chair of the Congressional Mental Health Caucus. Prompted to take action by a report showing that Latina teenagers have the highest suicide rate of any ethnic or racial group in the country, she launched school-based adolescent mental health counseling programs in three middle schools and one high school in her district. Napolitano is focused on the effect of posttraumatic stress disorder on U.S. troops and on the problem of seniors who suffer from depression.

Constituent services top Napolitano's congressional agenda. "As far as passing legislation, that is not the main reason I went to Washington," Napolitano said. "I want to be able to open the doors like I have at the county and state level."[4] Her projects benefitted small businesses that reside in her district—for example, her effort to reform the practice of "contract bundling," which favors large corporations. Napolitano, who once owned an Italian restaurant, also has helped minority business owners obtain financial assistance to expand their businesses by working with the Small Business Administration.

In her role on the Resources Committee, Napolitano worked with then-Energy Secretary Bill Richardson to direct the cleanup in Utah of 10 million tons of spent uranium tailings that leached into the Colorado River, the source of water supplied daily to the states of Utah, Nevada, Arizona, and one-third of southern California. She also has teamed with regional Members of Congress to help secure $65 million in federal funds to continue the cleanup of key Superfund sites in Los Angeles-area aquifers. In 2004, Napolitano helped achieve congressional approval of CALFED, a $395 million program aimed at increasing the state's water supply and protecting its fragile ecosystems.

FOR FURTHER READING

Biographical Directory of the U.S. Congress, "Grace F. Napolitano," http://bioguide.congress.gov

Polanco, Richard G. and Grace Napolitano, *Making Immigration Policy Work in the United States*. (Sacramento, CA: California Latino Legislative Caucus, 1993).

NOTES

1 *Politics in America, 2002* (Washington, D.C.: Congressional Quarterly Inc., 2001): 129.

2 "Election Statistics, 1920 to Present," http://clerk.house.gov/members/electionInfo/elections.html.

3 "Napolitano Selected to Lead Congressional Hispanic Caucus," 18 November 2004, available at http://www.napolitano.house.gov/press_releases/pr111804.htm (accessed 29 December 2004).

4 Norah M. O'Donnell, "The Votes Are In: After Battling Torres, Napolitano Claims His Seat," 15 June 1998, *Roll Call*.

Anne Meagher Northup
1948–

UNITED STATES REPRESENTATIVE
REPUBLICAN FROM KENTUCKY
1997–

Image courtesy of the Member

A LOUISVILLE NATIVE AND 10-YEAR VETERAN of the Kentucky state legislature, Anne Northup won election to the House of Representatives in 1996, the first woman in more than 60 years to represent her state in Congress. As a freshman, Representative Northup gained a seat on the influential Appropriations Committee. Her chief legislative pursuits have centered on education issues, adoption practices in China, and the procurement of federal dollars for transportation projects and community programs in her Louisville district.

Anne Meagher was born in Louisville, Kentucky, on January 22, 1948, one of 10 children raised by James and Floy Gates (Terstegge) Meagher. In 1966, she graduated from Sacred Heart Academy of Louisville and, four years later, earned a B.A. in economics from Saint Mary's College in Indiana. In 1969, she married Robert "Woody" Northup. The couple settled in Louisville and raised six children: David, Katherine, Joshua, Kevin, Erin, and Mark. Anne Northup worked as a teacher and for a major automobile manufacturer. By the early 1980s, she began volunteering for election campaigns, including Ronald Reagan's two runs for President. Northup's first campaign for elective office was in a 1987 special election for a seat in the Kentucky legislature, representing a Louisville–Frankfort district in the state house of representatives. She won and was re-elected to four additional terms, serving from 1987 to 1996. In the number two tobacco state in the nation, she remained an outspoken critic of the crop and introduced legislation to curb the powerful tobacco industry. Northup focused primarily on business and transportation improvements as a member of the appropriations and revenue committee and the education and economic development committee.[1]

In 1996, Northup challenged one-term Democratic incumbent Mike Ward for his Louisville district seat in the U.S. House of Representatives. The district, which overlapped with portions of Northup's state legislature district, covered the larger Louisville and Jefferson County area, where registered Democrats outnumbered Republicans by a two-to-one margin. Tobacco, health care, shipping, and tourism accounted for much of the district's economy. Northup narrowly defeated Ward—by about 1,300 votes out of more than 225,000 cast—even though President Bill Clinton carried the district in his re-election campaign. In her next three re-election bids, Northup won by slightly larger margins in her competitive district. In 2004, however, she earned a fifth consecutive term by the largest margin of her career, 60 to 38 percent.[2]

When Northup first claimed her seat in the 105th Congress (1997–1999), Republican leaders identified her as a rising star in a vulnerable district and accordingly assigned her a seat on the powerful House Appropriations Committee. Representative Northup also sits on three of the panel's subcommittees: Labor, Health and Human Services, and Education; Transportation and Treasury; and VA, HUD, and Independent Agencies.

Northup has used her influential position on the Appropriations Committee to pursue two primary legislative interests: national education reform and steering federal dollars into local government and community projects in her Louisville district. In March 1998, Northup founded the Congressional Reading Caucus to raise awareness of the increasing numbers of illiterate school children. She also authored legislation that created the National Reading Panel to evaluate the effectiveness of federally funded reading programs. In 2002, the findings of that study were incorporated into the federal education law, which set standards goals.

Congresswoman Northup's Appropriations assignment also has allowed her to bring federal dollars into her district to support infrastructure improvements and community organizations. During her first four years in the House, she reportedly brought nearly $500 million into the district.[3] She has procured money for two new bridges over the Ohio River, grants for local medical research facilities, and money for service programs in local churches.[4] Northup, who has described herself as a fiscal conservative, is guided by a political philosophy that "supports policies that empower individuals and communities."[5] The federal government, she once told the Louisville *Courier-Journal*, should "partner" with communities rather expending billions through federal agencies in Washington.[6]

As a mother of two adopted children, Northup has taken an interest in fostering adoption programs between the United States and China, seeking to reduce bureaucratic obstacles in the process. A social conservative who opposes all abortion procedures, she has been tapped by Republican leaders as a regular spokesperson because of her pragmatism and her ability to effectively communicate GOP policy positions.

FOR FURTHER READING

Biographical Directory of the U.S. Congress, "Anne Meagher Northup," http://bioguide.congress.gov

NOTES

1 "Anne M. Northup," Associated Press Candidate Biographies, 2004.

2 "Election Statistics, 1920 to Present," http://clerk.house.gov/members/electionInfo/index.html/.

3 James Carroll, "Northup Balances Ties to District, Party," 30 October 2000, *Courier-Journal* (Louisville, KY): 1A.

4 *Politics in America, 2004* (Washington, D.C.: Congressional Quarterly Inc., 2003): 419.

5 "Official Biography of Anne M. Northup," http://northup.house.gov/bio.asp (accessed 20 February 2003).

6 Carroll, "Northup Balances Ties to District, Party."

Eleanor Holmes Norton
1937–

DELEGATE
DEMOCRAT FROM THE DISTRICT OF COLUMBIA
1991–

Congressional Pictorial Directory
109th Congress

A CIVIL RIGHTS AND CONSTITUTIONAL LAWYER and former chair of the
Equal Opportunity Employment Commission, Eleanor Holmes Norton carried
her lifelong commitments to Congress as the Delegate for the District of Columbia.
Since 1991, Norton has been a tireless advocate of D.C. statehood and congressional
voting rights, while successfully obtaining federal funds and legislation to improve
the city's economy and tax base. "I have been elected to Congress not to further
my own interests, but to bring resources and respect to the District of Columbia,"
she remarked. "The ethics of the bar require zealous representation. That's
how I understand my relationship to my folks."[1]

Eleanor Holmes was born in Washington, D.C., on June 13, 1937, the oldest
of three daughters of Coleman Holmes, a civil servant, and Vela Lynch Holmes,
a teacher. She attended Dunbar High School in Washington, D.C., and earned
a B.A. at Antioch College in Ohio in 1960. Norton earned an M.A. in American
studies in 1963 and a law degree in 1964, both from Yale University. While in
college and law school, she worked in the civil rights movement with the Student
Non-Violent Coordinating Committee and the Mississippi Freedom Democratic
Party. After graduating, she clerked for Federal Judge A. Leon Higginbotham
in Philadelphia. She then became assistant legal director of the American Civil
Liberties Union. In 1965, Eleanor Holmes married Edward Norton. The couple
raised two children, Katherine and John, before divorcing in 1993. In 1970, New
York Mayor John Lindsay appointed Eleanor Holmes Norton to chair the New
York City Commission on Human Rights.[2] In 1977, President James Earl "Jimmy"
Carter appointed her chair of the U.S. Equal Employment Opportunity
Commission, where she served until 1981. During the 1980s, she taught full-time
as a tenured professor at Georgetown University Law Center, where she still
teaches one course annually.

In 1990, Norton defeated five challengers in the Democratic primary for an
open seat as the District of Columbia's Delegate in the U.S. House. In the general
election, she won 62 percent of the vote in the heavily Democratic city. She faced
little or no opposition in her seven re-election bids.[3]

When Norton took her seat in the 102nd Congress (1991–1993) in January 1991, she chose three committees: District of Columbia, Post Office and Civil Service, and Public Works and Transportation (later renamed Transportation and Infrastructure). In the 103rd Congress (1993–1995), she was appointed to the Joint Committee on the Organization of Congress. For the first time in the city's history, she won a vote as Delegate on the House Floor in the Committee of the Whole through a new rule she requested. The federal courts ruled that the House could grant Delegates the right to vote in the House Floor committee by rule, as it had traditionally in other committees. This right was withdrawn in the 104th Congress (1995–1997) when Republicans assumed control. In 1995, the District of Columbia Committee was absorbed by Government Reform and Oversight (later renamed Government Reform), where, along with her seat on Transportation and Infrastructure, Norton served through the 108th Congress. She also won a seat on the newly created Select Homeland Security Committee. House rules limit Delegate participation in the legislative process. Delegates may introduce legislation, speak on the House Floor, vote in committee, and even head a committee, but they cannot vote on the House Floor. Norton is the only Member of Congress whose constituents have no congressional vote, although they pay federal income taxes and serve in the military.

In the fight to secure D.C. statehood and voting rights and to improve services and infrastructure, Norton was a vocal and articulate leader during the 1990s.[4] To grant the city statehood, she authored the New Columbia Admission Act, which went to an unsuccessful vote on the House Floor. She now sponsors the No Taxation Without Representation Act, a bill that has also been introduced in the Senate. She has made progress by partnering with the Republican chairman of the Government Reform Committee to secure bipartisan committee passage of a bill for a vote on the House Floor. In 1995, with the city in financial crisis, she joined with Republican leaders to create a financial control board to supervise city finances. Norton's bill to transfer some state costs to the federal government led to economic recovery in the late 1990s and the elimination of the control board. Stressing education and economic development, she has secured funds for residents to attend any public U.S. college, for a new Metro subway station, for special D.C. homebuyer and business tax credits, and for redevelopment of an entire area of southeast Washington. She successfully fought congressional initiatives to nullify local laws, including a repeal of the city's prohibition on handguns.[5]

FOR FURTHER READING

Biographical Directory of the U.S. Congress, "Eleanor Holmes Norton," http://bioguide.congress.gov

Lester, Joan Steinau, Eleanor Holmes Norton: Fire in My Soul (New York: Atria Books, 2003).

Marcovitz, Hal. Eleanor Holmes Norton (Philadelphia, PA: Chelsea House Publishers, 2003).

NOTES

1 Joan Steinau Lester, Eleanor Holmes Norton: Fire in My Soul (New York: Atria Books, 2003): 274–276.

2 "Eleanor Holmes Norton," Contemporary Black Biography, Vol. 7. (Detroit: Gale Research Inc., 1994).

3 "Election Statistics, 1920 to Present," http://clerk.house.gov/members/electionInfo/elections.html.

4 "Eleanor Holmes Norton," Contemporary Black Biography; Lester, Fire in My Soul: 286.

5 Almanac of American Politics, 2002 (Washington, D.C.: National Journal Inc., 2001): 358–359.

Nancy Pelosi
1940–

UNITED STATES REPRESENTATIVE
DEMOCRAT FROM CALIFORNIA
1987–

Image courtesy of the Member

WITH FAMILY ROOTS IN AND A DEEP COMMITMENT to the Democratic Party, Nancy Pelosi worked her way up the leadership ladder, eventually serving as House Minority Whip in 2001. On November 14, 2002, the Democratic Caucus elected Congresswoman Pelosi the House Minority Leader—the highest-ranking woman in the history of the U.S. Congress.

Nancy Patricia D'Alesandro was born in Baltimore, Maryland, on March 26, 1940, the daughter of Thomas D'Alesandro, Jr., a U.S. Representative from 1939 to 1947 and, later, three-time mayor of Baltimore. Nancy D'Alesandro graduated with an A.B. from Trinity College in 1962. She married Paul Pelosi, and they raised five children. After moving to San Francisco in 1969, Nancy Pelosi became active in California politics. In 1976, she helped orchestrate then-California Governor Jerry Brown's win in the 1976 presidential primary in Maryland. Starting in 1976, Pelosi served as a Democratic National Committeewoman (a post she held until 1996). She also worked as Philip Burton's campaign aide and became a close protégé of the San Francisco Congressman, who was dean of the state delegation. After his death, Burton was succeeded by his wife, Sala. From 1981 to 1983, Pelosi chaired the California Democratic Party.[1]

Shortly before Sala Burton's death in February of 1987, Burton endorsed Pelosi as her successor. With Pelosi's knowledge of the state party organization and the support of Burton's backers, she won a close race in the special primary and won easily in the runoff election of June 2, 1987. In nine re-election campaigns in her heavily Democratic San Francisco district, Pelosi received an average of more than 80 percent of the total vote.[2]

When Pelosi took her House seat in the 100th Congress (1987–1989) on June 9, 1987, she received assignments on two committees: Government Operations; and Banking, Finance, and Urban Affairs. In the 102nd Congress (1991–1993), Pelosi moved to two other assignments: Appropriations, where she remained through the 107th Congress (2001–2003), and the Committee on Standards of Official Conduct, where she served through the 104th Congress (1995–1997). She eventually rose to be the Ranking Democrat on the Appropriations Subcommittee on Foreign Operations. In 1995, she was given a seat on the House Select Intelligence Committee where, by the 107th Congress, she served as the Ranking Member. In the 108th Congress (2003–2005), she served as an ex-officio member of that panel.

As a Representative, Pelosi has focused attention on human rights issues abroad and health concerns in her San Francisco district. She has been an advocate for more research on and funding for HIV/AIDS. "AIDS," she noted in 1992, "is the paramount issue in my district."[3] Pelosi pushed for a federally funded needle exchange program to prevent the incidence of HIV infection among drug users. During a House Floor speech she declared, "Science, not politics, should lead on public health policy. The science is irrefutable. Needle exchange works and works well."[4] Pelosi also has been a consistent champion of human rights in China. To that end, she fought Presidents George H.W. Bush and William J. Clinton, who sought to extend China "most favored nation" trade status.

Pelosi rose steadily up the leadership ladder and earned a reputation as a master fundraiser for her strapped fellow Democrats. She served as a member of the formal Democratic Steering Committee and also held a vice chairmanship on the Democratic Study Group, an informal caucus of policy and reform-oriented liberals. In 1992 she was named to head the Democratic National Platform Committee. On October 10, 2001, Democratic colleagues chose Pelosi as the Democratic Whip, the number two party position in the House, when Michigan's David Bonior resigned the job to run for governor. When Pelosi assumed the post on January 15, 2002, she became the first woman ever to hold the position. As Minority Whip during the 2002 elections, she visited more than 90 congressional districts on behalf of Democratic candidates.[5]

Within a year, Pelosi topped her Whip milestone, when Democratic Leader Richard Gephardt relinquished his post. On November 14, 2002, the Democratic Caucus overwhelmingly chose Pelosi as Minority Leader, the highest position any woman has been elected to in Congress or in either of the two political parties. On her selection, Pelosi commented, "I didn't run as a woman. I ran as a seasoned politician and an experienced legislator. It just so happens that I am a woman and we have been waiting a long time for this."[6] In 2003, Pelosi became the first woman candidate for Speaker of the House. Over the past half-century, Democrats in the House were never more unified than they have been under Pelosi's leadership, voting together a record 88 percent of the time in 2005.[7]

FOR FURTHER READING

Biographical Directory of the U.S. Congress, "Nancy Pelosi," http://bioguide.congress.gov

NOTES

1 *Politics in America, 2004* (Washington, D.C.: Congressional Quarterly Inc., 2003): 82–83; *Who's Who in American Politics* (New York: Bowker, 1999).

2 "Election Statistics, 1920 to Present," http://clerk.house.gov/members/electionInfo/elections.html.

3 Glenn F. Bunting, "Pelosi's Prominence in Party on the Rise; Lawmaker: The San Francisco Congresswoman Will Deliver a Speech and Preside Over Proceedings to Adopt the Platform," 14 July 1992, *Los Angeles Times*: A6.

4 *Congressional Record*, House, 105th Cong., 2nd sess. (28 April 1998): 2445.

5 David Von Drehle and Hanna Rosin, "The Two Nancy Pelosis: New House Leader Stresses Her Political Skills," 14 November 2002, *Washington Post*: A1.

6 Edward Walsh, "House Democrats Take Pelosi to Be Their Leader," 15 November 2002, *Washington Post*: A11.

7 Martin Kody, "Party Unity: Learning to Stick Together," 9 January 2006, *CQ Weekly*: 92.

Image courtesy of the Member

Deborah D. Pryce
1951–

UNITED STATES REPRESENTATIVE
REPUBLICAN FROM OHIO
1993–

FIRST ELECTED TO THE HOUSE OF REPRESENTATIVES in 1992, Deborah Pryce rose through the ranks of leadership to become Republican Conference Chair a decade later, making her the highest-ranking Republican woman in House history. As a member of the Financial Services Committee and as a Deputy Whip, Congresswoman Pryce has drawn on her background as a former judge and prosecutor to act as a consensus builder in the House.[1] Her legislative interests range from consumer financial protection to pediatric cancer and adoption practices.

Deborah Denine Pryce was born in Warren, Ohio, on July 29, 1951. She graduated from Ohio State University in 1973 and received her J.D. from Capital University Law School three years later. From 1976 to 1978, Pryce served as an administrative law judge for the Ohio state department of insurance. She worked as a prosecutor and municipal attorney for the city attorney's office of Columbus from 1978 to 1985. Pryce served two terms as the presiding judge in the municipal court of Franklin County from 1985 to 1992. In 1990, she adopted her daughter, Caroline. After Caroline's death from cancer in 1999, Pryce founded Hope Street Kids, a nonprofit organization devoted to curing childhood cancer. In 2001, she adopted a daughter, Mia.

In 1992, when 13-term Republican Representative Chalmers Wylie retired from the House, Pryce ran unopposed in the GOP primary. In a hard-fought, three-way general election for the open seat in a district covering western Columbus and its outlying suburbs, Pryce prevailed with 44 percent of the vote. She has been successfully re-elected to the six succeeding Congresses, with comfortable margins. In 2004, she won re-election to her eighth term with 60 percent of the vote.[2]

From the beginning of her congressional service, Representative Pryce has occupied a leadership position. Elected Republican freshman-class president in 1993, Pryce also was named to the congressional Republican transition team in the following Congress, when Republicans gained control of the House for the first time in 40 years. Two years later in 1996, she was selected a Deputy Majority Whip for the Republican Party. In 1998, GOP colleagues elected Representative Pryce Secretary of the House Republican Conference, the body that oversees the organization of the party. Pryce ran unopposed for the Republican Conference Vice Chair spot in 2000, and in the race for Conference Chair for the 108th Congress (2003–2005) she defeated two opponents to become the highest-ranking woman in the Republican Party.

When Pryce first took her seat in the 103rd Congress (1993–1995), she received assignments on two committees: Banking, Finance, and Urban Affairs; and Government Operations. In the 104th Congress (1995–1997), Pryce left those assignments when she received a seat on the prestigious Rules Committee, with oversight of all legislation headed for floor debate. Aside from a brief stint on the Select Committee on Homeland Security in the 107th Congress (2001–2003), Pryce's committee focus was on the Rules panel. In the 107th and 108th Congresses, she chaired its Legislative and Budget Process Subcommittee. In the 109th Congress (2005–2007), she left the Rules Committee to accept a seat on the Financial Services Committee, where she is now the fourth-ranking Member. She chairs the Subcommittee on Domestic and International Monetary Policy, Trade, and Technology.

Congresswoman Pryce's legislation reflects her commitment to children and health care issues. She authored the Child Abuse Prevention and Enforcement Act in 1999, a law that boosted federal funding to investigate and prevent child abuse. As the mother of two adopted children, she has worked to ease transitional adoption practices for foster parents. Pryce also authored the Afghan Women and Children Relief Act of 2001, which authorized the President to provide health and education assistance to women and children living in Afghanistan through non-governmental organizations. In addition to the creation of her own pediatric cancer research foundation, Representative Pryce has been a leading advocate of increasing federal money for cancer research and expanding access to clinical trials for cancer patients. She authored the Patient Navigator, Outreach, and Chronic Disease Prevention Act of 2005, to help individuals in underserved communities overcome cultural, linguistic, and financial barriers to access the health system, which President George W. Bush signed into law.[3]

From both the Rules and Financial Services committees, Representative Pryce has authored key provisions of laws to modernize the nation's financial services industry and has sponsored legislation to protect consumers' personal and financial information. As chairman of the Financial Services Subcommittee on Domestic and International Monetary Policy, Trade, and Technology, Representative Pryce is leading efforts to overhaul the process by which foreign investments in the U.S. are reviewed by the federal government.[4]

FOR FURTHER READING

Biographical Directory of the U.S. Congress, "Deborah D. Pryce," http://bioguide.congress.gov

NOTES

1 Amy Borrus, "Is the Day of the Hothead Over?: The GOP Pols to Watch as Gingrich Moves to the Center," 8 September 1997, Business Week: 72.

2 "Election Statistics, 1920 to Present," http://clerk.house.gov/members/electionInfo/elections.html.

3 "Official Biography of Deborah Pryce," http://www.house.gov/pryce/biography.htm (accessed 18 July 2006); Politics in America, 2004 (Washington, D.C.: Congressional Quarterly Inc., 2003): 811–812.

4 Derek Willis, "Rep. Deborah Pryce," 28 December 2002, CQ Weekly: 58; "Deborah Pryce," Associated Press Candidate Biographies, 2004.

Ileana Ros-Lehtinen
1952–

UNITED STATES REPRESENTATIVE
REPUBLICAN FROM FLORIDA
1989–

Image courtesy of the Member

A CHILDHOOD REFUGEE FROM FIDEL CASTRO'S COMMUNIST REGIME, Ileana Ros-Lehtinen emerged as a powerful voice in her south Florida community and a major critic of the tyrannical regime. Her historic 1989 election to the House of Representatives made her the first Hispanic woman and the first Cuban American elected to the U.S. Congress.

Ileana Ros was born in Havana, Cuba, on July 15, 1952, and moved with her family to the United States shortly after Castro came to power in 1959. After completing public education in Miami-Dade, she earned an associate of arts degree from Miami-Dade Community College in 1972, a B.A. in higher education from Florida International University (FIU) in 1975, and an M.A. in educational leadership from FIU in 1987. In 2004, she received her doctorate in higher education from the University of Miami. She also founded a private elementary school, serving as its chief administrator. From 1982 to 1986, she served as a Republican in the Florida house of representatives (its first Hispanic woman) and, from 1986 to 1989, in the Florida senate. In the state legislature she met and married representative Dexter Lehtinen, who later went on to become the U.S. Attorney for the Southern District of Florida. The couple has two daughters, Amanda Michelle and Patricia Marie.

After the death of Congressman Claude Pepper on May 30, 1989, Ileana Ros-Lehtinen sought the Republican nomination for the vacant seat. With the backing of national GOP leaders, she won the August 29, 1989, special election. About 90 percent of the Cuban-American vote (which made up about 40 percent of the district) went to Ros-Lehtinen, who defeated her Democratic rival by a 52 to 48 percent margin. Her victory put the seat in Republican hands for the first time since its creation in 1962.

After Ros-Lehtinen took the oath of office on September 6, 1989, she was assigned to the International Relations and Government Reform committees, where she has served during her nine terms. Recently, Speaker J. Dennis Hastert of Illinois asked her to serve on the Budget Committee where she was the only Republican woman. In 1990 and 1992, Ros-Lehtinen comfortably won re-election by 60 and 64 percent, respectively.[1] From 1994 to 2000, she was re-elected without opposition. In 2002 and 2004, she won against Democratic candidates with 69 and 65 percent of the vote, respectively. Ros-Lehtinen has chaired several International Relations subcommittees: Africa, International Economic Policy and Trade, International Operations, and Human Rights. Currently, she chairs the Middle East and Central Asia subcommittee. She also served as vice chair of the Subcommittee on the Western Hemisphere. In the 109th Congress (2005–2007), she serves on the Government Reform Subcommittee for National Security, Emerging Threats, and International Relations.

Ros-Lehtinen's leadership in South Florida is well known and has included a number of initiatives providing revenue and jobs for the region, including projects that have shaped local infrastructure and transportation. She has worked tirelessly to bring more than $25 million in federal funds to revitalize the Miami River, helping to reinvigorate the river area in downtown Miami. She also has secured more than $40 million to dredge the Port of Miami so that it can serve bigger cruise and freight ships. Ros-Lehtinen has been a strong supporter of expanding Miami International Airport so it can continue to serve a growing south Florida community.

Congresswoman Ros-Lehtinen has brought more than $35 million in federal aid and appropriations into Monroe County since it was added to her district in 2002. That total includes more than $5 million for the Florida Keys Wastewater Quality Program to ensure that the waters of this marine sanctuary remain healthy—improving the quality of life for the residents and tourists. She also has been a strong champion of affordable housing, fighting to secure higher funding for Section 8, and Housing Opportunities for People With AIDS. Representative Ros-Lehtinen also is a strong supporter of the Everglades cleanup, one of the largest environmental projects in America.

As a Florida certified teacher, Ros-Lehtinen has been a strong supporter of educational reform. While in the Florida senate, she was instrumental in passing the Florida Pre-Paid Program. To this day she continues to speak about the importance of this program to south Florida schools and students.

On the international front, Congresswoman Ros-Lehtinen has been a leading advocate for the promotion of human rights in countries like Lebanon, Syria, Iran, Saudi Arabia, and China. She also steadfastly supports Israel's right to exist in peace and security as a democratic Jewish state.

FOR FURTHER READING

Biographical Directory of the U.S. Congress, "Ileana Ros-Lehtinen," http://bioguide.congress.gov

Fernández, Mayra. *Ileana Ros-Lehtinen, Legisladora* (Cleveland, OH: Modern Curriculum Press, 1994).

NOTES

1 "Election Statistics, 1920 to Present," http://clerk.house.gov/members/electionInfo/index.html.

Lucille Roybal-Allard
1941–

UNITED STATES REPRESENTATIVE
DEMOCRAT FROM CALIFORNIA
1993–

Image courtesy of the Member

FOLLOWING HER FAMILY'S TRADITION OF PUBLIC SERVICE, Lucille Roybal-Allard pioneered new political ground in 1992, becoming the first Mexican-American woman to be elected to the U.S. Congress. Running in a new congressional district, Roybal-Allard also was one of a handful of daughters to follow a father to Congress. Like her father, Edward Roybal, she serves on the Appropriations Committee and is a former chair of the Congressional Hispanic Caucus (the first Latina to hold both positions).

Born in Los Angeles, California, on June 12, 1941, Lucille Roybal is one of three children of Lucille Beserra and the late Edward Roybal. Lucille Roybal graduated from California State University in Los Angeles in 1965 with a B.A. in speech therapy. She worked in alcohol and drug treatment programs in Los Angeles as a public relations and fund-raising executive for the United Way and as the executive director of a national trade association for Hispanic certified public accountants in Washington, D.C. Lucille Roybal married Edward T. Allard III in 1981. They have four children: Ricardo, Lisa, Angela, and Guy Mark; and six grandchildren.

Edward Roybal served in the U.S. House of Representatives for 30 years—chairing the Congressional Hispanic Caucus (CHC) and rising to the rank of chair of the Appropriations Subcommittee of the Treasury-Postal Service-General Government. In 1987, Roybal-Allard followed her father into public office, winning a special election to fill a vacancy in the California state assembly, where she served until 1992. In the state legislature, Roybal-Allard was an advocate of women's rights and passed key legislation to protect victims of rape and domestic violence. She also was a proponent of environmental justice. She successfully led a campaign against the building of a commercial hazardous waste incinerator in her urban district. The battle led her to author several environmental bills that became law, including a measure requiring environmental impact reports. Roybal-Allard also worked on advancing Hispanic entrepreneurship and strived to enable the local communities to have economic and political control.[1]

Following the 1990 Census, a new congressional district was created, encompassing most of her assembly district. In 1992, Lucille Roybal-Allard ran for Congress in the new district, capitalizing both on family name recognition and on the legislative record she created in the state assembly. She easily won the primary, with 73 percent of the vote. In the general election, she defeated Republican Robert Guzman with 63 percent of the vote. Since her first campaign, Congresswoman Roybal-Allard has been re-elected to six additional Congresses with margins higher than 70 percent.[2]

When Roybal-Allard was sworn into the House in January 1993, she was assigned to two committees: Banking, Finance, and Urban Affairs (later renamed Banking and Financial Services); and Small Business. Starting in the 104th Congress (1995–1997), she took a post on the Budget Committee in exchange for her seat on the Small Business panel. In the 105th and 106th Congresses (1997–2001), Roybal-Allard served on the House Select Committee on U.S. National Security and Military/Commercial Concerns With the People's Republic of China. Roybal-Allard's reputation as a respected consensus builder won her the chairmanship of the California Democratic Congressional Delegation in 1997 and 1998. In assuming this position, she became the first woman to serve at the delegation's helm and the first Member to achieve this role through election rather than seniority.

Representing a district with one of the largest Hispanic populations in the nation (77.2 percent), Roybal-Allard followed in her father's footsteps in 1999 and 2000 when she became chair of the CHC. Under her leadership, the CHC played a major role in passing immigration reforms, increasing funding for Hispanic Serving Institutions and the partial restoration of food stamps, Social Security benefits, and Medicaid for legal immigrants.

Roybal-Allard relinquished all her prior committee assignments in 1999 for a seat on the prestigious Appropriations Committee, where she still sits. Roybal-Allard serves on two influential Appropriations subcommittees—Homeland Security; and Labor, Health and Human Services, and Education. From these panels, she oversees funding of the Department of Homeland Security, Citizenship and Immigration Services, Customs Service, Department of Labor, Department of Health and Human Services, and Department of Education. In the 108th Congress (2003–2005), Roybal-Allard also drew an assignment on the Committee on Standards of Official Conduct.

In Congress, Roybal-Allard concentrates on social and domestic legislation. Her legislative priorities include homeland security, reducing underage drinking, promoting maternal and child health, and making college affordable and accessible to all students, including immigrant youth. She also works to meet the needs of her constituents by bringing millions in federal dollars to her district for key priorities such as transportation, economic development, infrastructure, housing, public safety, health care, and education.

FOR FURTHER READING

Biographical Directory of the U.S. Congress, "Lucille Roybal-Allard," http://bioguide.congress.gov

MANUSCRIPT COLLECTION

California State Archives (Sacramento, CA). *Papers:* 1987–1990, approximately five cubic feet. Office files of Lucille Roybal-Allard from her tenure in the California state assembly. The files contain bill information, correspondence, invitations, and schedules.

NOTES

1 *Congressional Directory,* 108th Cong. (Washington, D.C.: Government Printing Office, 2003); *Politics in America, 2004* (Washington, D.C.: Congressional Quarterly Inc., 2003): 132–133; "Lucille Roybal-Allard," Associated Press Candidate Biographies, 2004.

2 "Election Statistics, 1920 to Present," http://clerk.house.gov/members/electionInfo/elections.html.

Linda T. Sánchez
1969–

UNITED STATES REPRESENTATIVE
DEMOCRAT FROM CALIFORNIA
2003–

Image courtesy of the Member

WHEN LINDA T. SÁNCHEZ[1] WON HER BID TO BECOME one of several United States Representatives from Los Angeles County on November 5, 2002, she not only earned a seat in Congress, she also made history: Linda and her older sibling Loretta, already on Capitol Hill, became the first sisters to serve together in Congress. Inextricably linked with her sister because of their similar careers, political agendas, and familial background, Linda Sánchez nonetheless has made clear her intention to shape her own identity in Congress: "I think we are both very qualified in different ways. I think I'm going to be able to make my mark in my way."[2] Sánchez has supported affordable health care, quality education, and increased opportunities for Latinos. She also has vowed to use her experience as an organized labor leader and her previous work with the National Organization for Women to advocate the rights of women and workers from her district.[3]

The daughter of Mexican immigrants Ignacio Sandoval Sanchez, a mechanic at a plastics and rubber plant, and Maria Socorro Macias Sanchez, an elementary school teacher, Linda Sánchez was born on January 28, 1969, in Orange, California. The second youngest of seven children in a traditional Latino family, Sánchez, as well as her parents, questioned the sometimes-strict cultural mores that encouraged boys to attend college and girls to marry and have children. Maria Sanchez, whose decision to attend night school to further her education made her a role model for her daughters, supported Linda's refusal to accept the status quo and suggested she work to change the inequalities in society.[4] Reflecting upon the importance of her family and parents in her life, Sánchez commented, "In every Latino family, there's a sense of 'We need to stick together.' It's us against the world." She went on to add, "But I think in our particular family, that's even stronger because our folks expected great things from us. They wanted us to take advantage of all the opportunities they never had."[5] Heeding the advice of her parents and the example set by her mother, Sánchez enrolled in the University of California at Berkeley while also working as a bilingual aide and an ESL teacher. After earning a B.A. in 1991, Sánchez graduated from UCLA Law School four years later.

Sánchez gained her first political experience working on campaigns while in high school and also participated heavily in her sister Loretta's campaign for the House against nine-term incumbent Robert Dornan in 1996. In 1998, she left her private practice as a civil rights attorney to become field director of her sister's re-election campaign. Following the election, she conducted national speaking engagements on the organization of effective grass-roots political campaigns and became the first Latina to head a countywide central labor council (Orange County Central Labor Council, AFL-CIO).[6]

Motivated by her desire to serve her community at a higher level, Linda Sánchez decided to run for the open seat in a newly created California district encompassing southeast Los Angeles County in 2002. The campaign for the congressional seat in the predominantly Democratic district that included a high percentage of Latino voters and a strong organized-labor movement received national attention. Sánchez joined a spirited race as one of three Latino candidates in a field of five contenders.[7] She won the Democratic primary on March 5, 2002, and went on to defeat Republican Tim Escobar and Libertarian Richard Newhouse in the general election, with 55 percent of the vote.[8] Shortly after her victory, Sánchez said: "I'm not here to take over the world. My passion is to get more women elected in politics. And if it's a Hispanic woman, it's even better."[9]

During her first term, Sánchez was named to the Judiciary, Government Reform, and Small Business committees and was a member of the Congressional Hispanic Caucus. As the only freshman Democrat to earn a seat on the Judiciary Committee during the 108th Congress (2003–2005), Sánchez remarked, "Having worked with laws in the courtroom, I've really seen how legislation impacts people."[10] Sánchez sponsored measures to improve school safety and to assist women, minorities, and veterans to establish small businesses. She also introduced legislation to raise the minimum wage and was a vocal supporter of immigration reform in the United States. At the start of her second term, Congresswoman Sánchez was named an Assistant Democratic Whip.

FOR FURTHER READING

Biographical Directory of the U.S. Congress, "Linda Sánchez," http://bioguide.congress.gov

NOTES

1 Linda Sánchez, unlike her sister Loretta, uses the diacritic in her surname.

2 Chelsea J. Carter, "L.A. Representative's Sibling Wins Primary; Sisters May Become First to Serve in House Together," 7 March 2002, *San Mateo County Times.*

3 *Politics in America, 2004* (Washington, D.C.: Congressional Quarterly Inc., 2003): 142.

4 "First Person Singular: Rep. Linda Sánchez (D-Calif.)," 25 April 2004, *Washington Post:* W09.

5 Roxanne Roberts, "House Mates: Loretta and Linda Sanchez Are Congress's First Sister Act," 12 December 2002, *Washington Post:* C1.

6 "Linda Sánchez for Congress," http://www.lindasanchez2002.com/about.shtml (accessed 6 November 2002); "New Members Guide: Linda Sánchez," 18 November 2002, *The Hill.*

7 Richard Marosoi, "Battle Shapes up in Latino District," 19 February 2002, *Washington Post:* 1.

8 "Election Statistics, 1920 to Present," http://clerk.house.gov/members/electionInfo/index.html.

9 Dena Bunis, "Congress Gets Its First Sister Act With Loretta and Linda Sanchez," 6 November 2002, *Orange County Register.*

10 *Politics in America, 2004:* 142.

Loretta Sanchez
1960–

UNITED STATES REPRESENTATIVE
DEMOCRAT FROM CALIFORNIA
1997–

Image courtesy of the Member

LORETTA SANCHEZ WON ELECTION TO THE U.S. HOUSE—her first political office—by defeating a longtime incumbent. During her tenure in the House, Congresswoman Sanchez has established herself as an advocate for economic development, a strong military, and education issues. In 2003, she also made history when her sister, Linda, won election to the House: The Sanchez sisters are the first pair of sisters to serve in Congress.

Loretta Sanchez was born in Lynwood, California, on January 7, 1960, the oldest daughter of Ignacio Sandoval Sanchez and Maria Socorro Macias Sanchez.[1] She graduated in 1982 with a B.S. in economics from Chapman University in Orange, California, and in 1984 she earned an MBA from American University in Washington, D.C. From 1984 to 1987, she worked as a special projects manager at the Orange County transportation authority. Sanchez then entered the private sector in the investment banking industry and, later, worked as a strategist at a leading consulting company. A registered Republican and fiscal conservative, she broke with the GOP in 1992, believing the party had marginalized immigrants and women.

In 1996, Sanchez declared her candidacy in the race for a California district encompassing central Orange County. During the campaign, she touted her business credentials, particularly her effort to secure funding from national companies to establish programs between local grade schools and state colleges in Orange County.[2] Despite her lack of political experience, she defeated three male contenders in the Democratic primary with 35 percent of the vote. In the general election she faced long-time incumbent Republican Bob Dornan, a controversial and outspoken conservative. Her platform included support for small- and medium-sized businesses, investment in high-tech research, and federal funding for school improvements. Sanchez appealed to the traditionally conservative district's voters with a tough-on-crime agenda; she also advocated a ban on assault weapons and the elimination of the gun show loophole. Sanchez prevailed with a 984-vote margin out of more than 100,000 cast, eking out a 47 to 46 percent win.[3] For more than a year, Sanchez had to contend with Dornan's challenge to her election. In February 1998, the House voted overwhelmingly to dismiss Dornan's complaint.[4] Later that year, she faced Dornan again in the general election, one of the most expensive races in the country. Sanchez prevailed with a 56 to 39 percent margin of victory. In her three subsequent re-election bids she won comfortably, garnering at least 60 percent of the vote.[5] Her clash with Dornan provided Sanchez with national exposure, making her one of the Democratic Party's primary congressional conduits for appealing to Latinos, women, and young voters.

When Congresswoman Sanchez took her seat in the House on January 7, 1997, she received assignments on the Education and Workforce Committee and the National Security Committee. In the 109th Congress (2005–2007), she serves as the ranking woman on the Armed Services Committee and as the second-ranking Democrat on the new Homeland Security Committee.

A former member of the United Food and Commercial Workers, with family roots in the union movement, Representative Sanchez is a congressional friend of organized labor despite her strong ties to business. She voted against "fast track" trade authority, which authorized the President to negotiate trade agreements without congressional approval, oversight, or amendment. Sanchez also broke with the William J. Clinton administration when she voted against granting China permanent normal trade relations. Sanchez has a mixed position on trade agreements, basing her approval of treaties on whether such agreements constitute "fair trade." Sanchez also is a congressional leader on global human rights issues.[6]

In line with her fiscally conservative principles, Sanchez joined the Democratic Blue Dog Caucus, advocated a major overhaul of the Internal Revenue Service, and supported budget deficit reductions. Nevertheless, she believed the federal government should play a role in improving local life, particularly in education. As a former pupil in the Head Start program, Sanchez vowed to make federally funded education programs available to low-income children. She also authored legislation to encourage tax-free bonds to spur funding of school construction. As a Representative, Sanchez also has enjoyed success steering federal money and projects into her district that have helped both the local and the state economy of California.

FOR FURTHER READING

Biographical Directory of the U.S. Congress, "Loretta Sanchez," http://bioguide.congress.gov

NOTES

1 *Politics in America, 2002* (Washington, D.C.: Congressional Quarterly Inc., 2001): 152–153.

2 "Loretta Sanchez," *New Members of Congress Almanac for the 105th Congress* (Washington, D.C.: Almanac Publishing Inc., 1996): 32.

3 "Election Statistics, 1920 to Present," http://clerk.house.gov/members/electionInfo/index.html.

4 "House Formally Dismisses Dornan Challenge to Sanchez," 13 February 1998, *Washington Post*: A6; Jodi Wilogren, "House Gives Sanchez Reason for Celebration: Task Force Drops Inquiry, Leaving Her With Incumbency, National Celebrity and Fund-Raising Prowess," 5 February 1998, *Los Angeles Times*: A1.

5 "Election Statistics, 1920 to Present," http://clerk.house.gov/members/electionInfo/elections.html.

6 *Politics in America, 2002:* 152–153.

Janice Schakowsky
1944–

UNITED STATES REPRESENTATIVE
DEMOCRAT FROM ILLINOIS
1999–

Image courtesy of the Member

As a former consumer rights activist and an Illinois legislator, Janice Schakowsky won the seat U.S. Representative Sidney Yates held for nearly half a century. An outspoken liberal, Congresswoman Schakowsky has focused on legislation concerning health care, childcare, and Social Security reform.

Janice Danoff was born in Chicago, Illinois, on May 26, 1944, to Irwin Danoff, a furniture salesman, and Tillie Cosnow Danoff, an elementary schoolteacher. She attended Sullivan High School in Chicago. In 1965, she graduated from the University of Illinois with a B.S. degree in elementary education and then worked for two years as a teacher. In February 1965, Janice Danoff married Harvey E. Schakowsky. The couple raised two children, but were divorced in 1980. (Later, Janice Schakowsky married Robert B. Creamer, a longtime Chicago political organizer who had one child, Lauren, from a previous marriage.) Schakowsky was a homemaker until, in 1969, she organized National Consumers United, a group that eventually succeeded in getting freshness dates placed on food products. From 1976 to 1985, Schakowsky worked as the program director for the Illinois Public Action Council, a consumer rights advocacy group whose work included preventing utilities from denying service to delinquent bill payers in the winter months.[1] Schakowsky then worked as the director of the Illinois State Council of Senior Citizens from 1985 to 1990. She left that post to make a successful campaign for the Illinois state general assembly, where she served until 1998, chaired the labor and commerce committee, and worked to create more day-care centers and pass tougher hate-crime laws.[2]

When 48-year House veteran Sidney Yates retired in 1998, Schakowsky entered the Democratic primary in the race to fill his seat representing a district north of Chicago. With funding from outside groups such as EMILY's List and intense grass-roots canvassing with 1,500 volunteers, she prevailed handily over a state senator and a hotel chain heir, emphasizing what she called "women's issues," such as health care, education, and food labeling. "People were interested in having a woman's voice in the House of Representatives," she declared after the primary.[3] In the general election Schakowsky continued to stress the theme of big government assistance to solve social problems, including equal rights for women, minorities and gays and national health care. In the heavily Democratic district that encompasses most of Chicago's lakefront, Schakowsky rolled past Republican candidate Herbert Sohn (her former physician) and a Libertarian candidate, compiling 75 percent of the vote. "I don't think I can be defined as too far left in a district like this," Schakowsky said.[4] She was easily re-elected in 2000 and 2002 with 76 percent and 70 percent of the vote, respectively.[5]

When Schakowsky took her seat in the 106th Congress (1999–2001), she received assignments on two committees: Banking and Financial Services (later renamed Financial Services) and Small Business. A few months later she was appointed to the Government Reform Committee and vacated her seat on Small Business. In the 107th Congress (2001–2003) Schakowsky became Ranking Member on the Government Reform Subcommittee on Government Efficiency, Financial Management and Intergovernmental Relations. She also served as vice chair of the House Democratic Caucus Special Committee on Election Reform and as a member of the Homeland Security Task Force.

In an era when government services were curtailed, Congresswoman Schakowsky advocated increasing federal aid to help abused children and women, developing a single-payer government health insurance system, and expanding accessible and affordable housing for persons with disabilities. She supported abortion rights and opposed the death penalty. Following a racially motivated July 4, 1999, shooting spree in her district, she authored a hate-crimes bill and redoubled her longtime advocacy of gun control. In the 107th Congress, she authored the Voting Rights Act of 2001, which guaranteed that no registered voters—including the homeless— may be turned away at the polls. She also wrote "First Things First," a bill which sought to freeze the 2001 tax break while the country addressed deepening economic problems and key national security issues.

Schakowsky quickly impressed House leaders and, in 2001, was named Chief Deputy Democratic Whip by Minority Leader Richard Gephardt. She proved an adept fundraiser, especially among women's issues groups. Schakowsky also emerged as a party spokesperson appearing on network political shows to articulate the Democratic Party's position on national issues ranging from tax reform to the congressional resolution for the use of force against Iraq in 2002. In 2004, Congresswoman Schakowsky was elected to her fourth consecutive term, with 76 percent of the vote.

FOR FURTHER READING

Biographical Directory of the U.S. Congress, "Janice D. Schakowsky," http://bioguide.congress.gov

NOTES

1 *Politics in America, 2002* (Washington, D.C.: Congressional Quarterly Inc., 2001): 526–528.

2 *Politics in America, 2002*: 526–528.

3 LeAnn Spencer, "Schakowsky Wins 3-Way Fight to Replace Yates," 18 March 1998, *Chicago Tribune*: N1.

4 "Janice D. Schakowsky," Associated Press Candidate Biographies, 2000.

5 "Election Statistics, 1920 to Present," http://clerk.house.gov/members/electionInfo/elections.html.

Louise M. Slaughter
1929–

UNITED STATES REPRESENTATIVE
DEMOCRAT FROM NEW YORK
1987–

Congressional Pictorial Directory
109th Congress

LOUISE SLAUGHTER, COMPLETING HER 10TH TERM as a U.S. Representative from western New York, serves as the Ranking Member on the House Rules Committee, the first woman to serve in this position. Slaughter, a microbiologist by training, is an expert on health and women's issues. "I have always said that the best training in the world for government is to be a woman, to be a mother," Slaughter once noted. "We learn that our budget has to stretch to the next paycheck... that every member of our family has to have food and clothing and an education."[1]

Louise McIntosh was born in Harlan County, Kentucky, on August 14, 1929. McIntosh earned a B.S. in microbiology from the University of Kentucky in 1951 and, two years later, an M.S. in public health. After graduation, she married Robert Slaughter. The couple eventually moved to Rochester, New York, and raised three daughters. Slaughter's political activism began in 1971 when she campaigned to save Hart's Woods in Rochester.[2] Although she was unsuccessful, the experience moved Slaughter toward a career in public service. She served as co-chair of the Monroe County Citizens for McGovern in 1972, joined the New York State Democratic Committee and, in 1976, was elected to the first of two terms in the Monroe County legislature. She later worked for Mario Cuomo, then-New York secretary of state. In 1982, Slaughter defeated a Republican incumbent to win a seat in the New York assembly, where she served until 1986.

Slaughter sought election to the U.S. House in 1986, running a grass-roots campaign to unseat conservative first-term incumbent Fred Eckert. She defeated Eckert with 51 percent of the vote. For a decade thereafter, Slaughter won re-election by comfortable but not large margins around Rochester, which had traditionally voted for moderate Republicans. In the late 1990s, she won by larger margins and, after reapportionment placed her in a newly redrawn district, which included much of her old district in the Rochester area, as well as new sections in Buffalo and Niagara Falls, she won by 25 points. In 2004, Slaughter was re-elected to her 10th consecutive term, with 72 percent of the vote.[3]

As the second-longest serving woman Democrat in the House, Representative Slaughter has worked on a half-dozen committees during her career, among them: Government Operations (later named Government Reform), Public Works and Transportation (later named Transportation and Infrastructure), Budget, the Select Committee on Aging, and the Select Committee on Homeland Security. She now serves on the powerful Rules Committee that oversees which legislation is debated on the House Floor. Appointed in 1989 to fill a vacancy on the committee caused by the death of Florida's Claude Pepper, Slaughter is the top-ranking Democrat on that panel. On the Rules Committee, she is a vocal proponent of women's reproductive rights and health.

During the early 1990s, she was responsible for securing the first $500 million dedicated by Congress to breast cancer research at the National Institutes of Health (NIH).[4] She was a leader in efforts to force the NIH to start including women in all clinical trials. She sponsored the first law directing the NIH to research the miscarriage drug diethylstilbestrol (DES), which had serious health consequences for some children exposed in utero. Slaughter also has authored legislation to improve research on women's environmental health, educate Americans about colorectal cancer, and reduce waste, fraud and abuse in the Medicare program.

Slaughter is acknowledged as the leading expert in Congress on genetic discrimination issues. For 10 years, Slaughter has introduced legislation to prohibit employers and insurers from discriminating against individuals based on genetic factors. This legislation has garnered more than 220 bipartisan cosponsors in the House and endorsements from dozens of health-related organizations. This bill has passed unanimously in the Senate twice.

Slaughter, who co-chaired the Congressional Women's Caucus in the 108th Congress (2003–2005), has been a leader on women's issues, ranging from family planning to reducing domestic violence. Slaughter was one of seven Congresswomen who marched on the Senate Democratic Caucus in 1991 to protest the Senate Judiciary Committee's treatment of Anita Hill during the Clarence Thomas Supreme Court confirmation hearings. She was an original author of the Violence Against Women Act (VAWA) in 1994, and she has been a cosponsor of subsequent VAWA reauthorization bills, including VAWA III which became law in 2006. She also has led the efforts to enhance the Pentagon's response to sexual assault against women serving in the U.S. armed forces.

Deeply concerned about the economic welfare of her district, Slaughter has steered millions of dollars into local building and transportation projects and has commissioned studies on the decline in local manufacturing jobs.

FOR FURTHER READING

Biographical Directory of the U.S. Congress, "Louise McIntosh Slaughter," http://bioguide. congress.gov

NOTES

1 Debbie Howlett, "For Some, A Great Notion: Parity-50% Female Congress Envisioned," 1 April 1992, *USA Today*: 5A.

2 *Politics in America, 2004* (Washington, D.C.: Congressional Quarterly Inc., 2003): 737.

3 "Election Statistics, 1920 to Present," http://clerk.house.gov/members/ electionInfo/elections.html.

4 "Official Biography of Louise Slaughter," http://www.slaughter.house.gov (accessed 17 November 2004).

Olympia Snowe

1947–

UNITED STATES REPRESENTATIVE, 1979–1995
UNITED STATES SENATOR, 1995–
REPUBLICAN FROM MAINE

Image courtesy of the Member

AS THE FIRST GREEK-AMERICAN WOMAN and one of the youngest women ever elected to Congress, Olympia Snowe has represented Maine for 27 years— 16 as a U.S. House Member and two terms as a U.S. Senator. A fitting representative for her politically independent Maine constituents, Snowe has balanced her Republican loyalties, personal convictions, and the needs of her rural state. In 2003, Senator Snowe was appointed chair of the Small Business Committee, becoming one of five women in history to head a standing Senate committee.

Olympia Jean Bouchles was born on February 21, 1947, in Augusta, Maine, daughter of George and Georgia Bouchles. Her parents both passed away before her 10th birthday, and Olympia Bouchles was raised by an aunt and uncle in Auburn, Maine. She earned a B.A. in political science from the University of Maine at Orono, and married state representative Peter Snowe in 1969. Four years later, Snowe died in a car accident. At the urging of the Maine Republican officials, Olympia Snowe ran successfully for her husband's vacant seat. She won a full term in 1974 and was elected to an open state senate seat in 1976.

In 1978, when Republican Congressman William Cohen vacated his U.S. House seat, Snowe entered the race to succeed him. The district, one of two in Maine, covered the rural northern two-thirds of the state. Snowe's principal opponent was Democrat Markham Gartley, Maine's secretary of state. With a moderate platform, Snowe prevailed with 51 percent of the vote to Gartley's 41 percent, for the first of eight consecutive terms in the House.[1]

When Representative Snowe took her seat in the 96th Congress (1979–1981), she received assignments on three committees: Government Operations, Small Business, and the Select Committee on Aging. Two years later she earned a seat on the Foreign Affairs Committee—where she remained for the balance of her House career. In the 98th Congress (1983–1985), after leaving her Small Business post, Snowe was assigned to the Joint Economic Committee, where she remained until her final House term, when she won a seat on the Budget Committee.

Representative Snowe's moderation and willingness to compromise won her bipartisan respect. Recognized as a loyal Republican (she was named a GOP deputy whip in 1984) she also demonstrated her independence.[2] From her position on the Small Business Committee, she favored trade protection, contrasting with the Reagan administration's free trade policies, in order to protect exporters in her district.[3] As a member of the Foreign Affairs Committee, Congresswoman Snowe supported a nuclear armaments freeze, aid for Nicaraguan rebels, and sanctions against South Africa to protest that nation's apartheid system.[4] Snowe served on the Congressional Caucus for Women's Issues for her entire House career, chairing it during the 98th Congress, fighting for the 1980 Economic Equity Act, and consistently supporting women's reproductive rights.[5] In 1989, Olympia Snowe married Maine Republican Governor John McKernan, Jr., a former House Member.

In 1994, when Democratic Senate Majority Leader George J. Mitchell of Maine announced his retirement, Snowe declared her candidacy for the open seat.[6] In the general election, she faced two-term Representative Thomas Andrews from southeastern Maine. Snowe's well-organized campaign and House experience helped her prevail with 60 percent of the vote. In 2000, she won re-election with 69 percent.[7]

Senator Snowe's initial committee assignments—Budget; Foreign Relations; Small Business; and Commerce, Science, and Transportation—reflected her House expertise. She later served on the Armed Services Committee and, in 2000, left the Budget Committee to join the powerful Finance Committee. In the 108th Congress (2003–2005), Snowe also joined the Select Intelligence Committee and, in addition to chairing Small Business, served as chair of the Commerce Committee's Subcommittee on Fisheries and Coast Guard.

Senator Snowe's Senate agenda has featured many of the legislative priorities she set as a Representative. Snowe sought funding for affordable health care, particularly for small businesses, as well as expanded drug coverage for seniors under Medicare. She remains a champion of women's issues, calling for easier access to contraceptives as well as better medical care for mastectomy patients. Senator Snowe also has been a proponent for a cleaner environment, advocating better gas mileage for sport utility vehicles and protections for Maine's fishing industry. She has fought to restore funding for a job training center and continued U.S. Navy presence in Kittery, Maine. From her position as co-chair of the Senate Centrist Coalition, a bipartisan group of consensus builders, she helped write an amendment to major campaign finance reforms convincing reluctant colleagues to support the legislation.[8]

FOR FURTHER READING

Biographical Directory of the U.S. Congress, "Olympia Jean Snowe," http://bioguide.congress.gov

Mikulski, Barbara, et al. *Nine and Counting: The Women of the Senate.* (New York: Morrow, 2000).

NOTES

1 "Election Statistics, 1920 to Present," http://clerk.house.gov/members/electionInfo/elections.html. *Current Biography, 1995* (New York: H.W. Wilson and Company, 1995): 543–544.

2 *Current Biography, 1995*: 545.

3 *Current Biography, 1995*: 546; John E. Yang, "House Upholds Reagan's Veto Of Trade Limits," 7 August 1986, *Wall Street Journal*: 5.

4 Douglas C. Waller, *Congress and the Nuclear Freeze* (University of Massachusetts Press: 1987): 116; *Current Biography, 1995*: 545; Rowland Evans and Robert Novak, "Arming Managua," 16 June 1986, *Washington Post*: A 11.

5 *Current Biography, 1995*: 545.

6 "Mitchell Leaving Bewilderment in His Wake," 7 March 1994, *USA Today*: 4A.

7 "Election Statistics, 1920 to Present," http://clerk.house.gov/members/electionInfo/elections.html.

8 Mary Agnes Cary, "Sen. Olympia J. Snowe," 28 December 2002, *CQ Weekly*: 35; *Politics in America, 2004* (Washington, D.C.: Congressional Quarterly Inc., 2003): 447–448; Thomas Fields-Meyer et al., "Survival Skills" 18 June 2001, *People*: 121.

Hilda L. Solis

1957–

UNITED STATES REPRESENTATIVE
DEMOCRAT FROM CALIFORNIA
2001–

Image courtesy of the Member

HILDA LUCIA SOLIS, AN ACCOMPLISHED LEGISLATOR in the California assembly, was elected to the U.S. House after defeating an 18-year incumbent in the primary. In Congress, Representative Solis has championed the interests of working families and women and has focused on legislation concerning health care and environmental protection.

Hilda Solis was born in Los Angeles, California, on October 20, 1957, the daughter of Raul and Juana Sequiera Solis, who raised seven children. In 1979, she earned a B.A. in political science from California State Polytechnic University, Pomona, and then worked in the White House Office of Hispanic Affairs during the James Earl "Jimmy" Carter administration. In 1981, she earned an M.A. in public administration from the University of Southern California. Later that year she worked as a management analyst in the civil rights division of the Equal Opportunity Program at the Office of Management and Budget. In June 1982, Solis married her husband, Sam, a small-business owner, and returned to southern California, where she became a field representative in the office of Assemblyman Art Torres. She also worked as the director of the California student opportunity and access program in Whittier from 1982 until 1992. In 1985, Solis was elected a trustee of Rio Hondo Community College, where she served for seven years, winning re-election in 1989. A year later, Solis won election to the California state assembly. From 1994 until 2001, she served as the first Latina elected to the state senate. In the upper chamber she chaired the industrial relations committee, where she led the fight to raise California's minimum wage standards in 1996. Her environmental justice legislation, the first in the nation to become law, earned her the distinction of a John F. Kennedy "Profiles in Courage" Award. She was the first woman to be so honored.[1]

Solis decided in 2000 to challenge a nine-term Democratic incumbent whose congressional district encompassed much of her state senate district in the San Gabriel Valley. Local labor unions and the state party switched their support to Solis. Portraying herself as an active progressive, she prevailed in the March 7 primary, 62 percent to 29 percent.[2] In the general election she faced no Republican challenger and captured 80 percent of the vote while three third-party candidates split the remainder. She has easily won re-election twice, earning a third term in the House with 85 percent of the vote in 2004.[3]

When Solis took her seat in the House in January 2001, she won assignments on the Education and Workforce Committee and the Resources Committee. Solis also was tapped as the 107th Congress (2001–2003) Democratic freshman class Whip. In the 108th Congress (2003–2005), she took a seat on the powerful Energy and Commerce Committee and became Ranking Member of the Environment and Hazardous Materials Subcommittee. She also was elected Chairwoman of the Congressional Hispanic Caucus' Task Force on Health and Democratic Vice Chair of the Congressional Caucus on Women's Issues. In the 109th Congress (2005–2007), she was re-elected Ranking Member of the Environment and Hazardous Materials Subcommittee and joined the Energy and Air Quality Subcommittee. She was also re-elected chairwoman of the Congressional Hispanic Caucus' Task Force on Health and was elected Democratic Chair of the Congressional Caucus on Women's Issues and chair of the Democratic Women's Working Group, the first Latina to hold such positions.

Solis continued to advance environmental justice when she was elected to Congress. In 2003, her San Gabriel River Watershed Study Act was signed into law. The bill authorized the Secretary of the Interior to conduct a special resources study of the San Gabriel River to investigate how the federal government can improve the area's recreational and environmental opportunities. In 2005, she authored an amendment to prevent human pesticide testing, which was later enacted into law. Solis also introduced a bill that would ease citizenship requirements for immigrants serving in the U.S. military and for immigrants serving as reservists, as well as provide immigration benefits to their family members. The immigration provisions from Solis's bill were included in a defense authorization bill measure signed into law in December 2003.

Solis also has been a longtime advocate for women's rights. She has been an outspoken leader in raising awareness about a spate of murders, dating to 1993, which have targeted nearly 400 women in the border town of Ciudad Juárez, Mexico. She authored a resolution to condemn the murders, to express sympathy to the families of the victims, and to urge the United States to increase its involvement in ending these human rights violations was passed by the House in the 109th Congress.

As chair of the Congressional Hispanic Caucus Health Task Force, she has traveled across the country educating policymakers, advocates, and community leaders about the health needs of the Latino community. In the 109th Congress, Solis was a lead co-author of the bicameral minority health bill titled the Healthcare Equality and Accountability Act.

FOR FURTHER READING

Biographical Directory of the U.S. Congress, "Hilda Solis," http://bioguide.congress.gov

NOTES

1 *Almanac of American Politics,* 2002 (Washington, D.C.: National Journal Inc., 2001): 241–242; and "Official Biography of Hilda Solis," http://www.house.gov/solis/bio.htm (accessed 21 November 2001).

2 Jean Merl and Antonio Olivo, "Solis Trounces Martinez in Bitter Race; Challenger Ousts 18-Year Veteran in a Fight That Split Latino Leadership," 8 March 2000, *Los Angeles Times*: A3.

3 "Election Statistics, 1920 to Present," http://clerk.house.gov/members/electionInfo/elections.html.

Deborah A. Stabenow

1950–

UNITED STATES REPRESENTATIVE, 1997–2001
UNITED STATES SENATOR, 2001–
DEMOCRAT FROM MICHIGAN

Image courtesy of the Member

DURING HER MANY YEARS OF PUBLIC SERVICE in the U.S. Senate, the U.S. House of Representatives, and the Michigan state legislature, Debbie Stabenow has earned a reputation as a hard-working leader focused on the issues directly impacting the daily lives of her constituents—issues like health care, education, and jobs. In 2000, she made history when she became the first woman to represent Michigan in the U.S. Senate. Four years later, her Democratic colleagues elected her Conference Secretary for the 109th Congress (2005–2007), the third-highest-ranking position in the party's Senate leadership.[1]

Deborah Ann Greer was born on April 29, 1950, in Gladwin, Michigan. She was raised in Clare, Michigan, graduated as valedictorian of her high school class, and attended Michigan State University, earning a bachelor's degree in 1972 and an M.S.W. in 1975. Greer married Dennis Stabenow; they raised two children and were divorced in 1990. Stabenow wed Tom Athans in 2003.

Debbie Stabenow worked in the Michigan public schools before being elected to the Ingham County board of commissioners in 1974 at the age of 24. She was the first woman and the youngest person ever to chair the board. In 1978, she was elected to the Michigan house of representatives, where she served until 1990. During that time Stabenow became the first woman to preside over the chamber. She was elected to the Michigan senate in 1990 and served four years. Stabenow's work as a state legislator helped reshape Michigan law and included a historic property tax cut, small business reforms, and nationally acclaimed legislation to protect children and families. Stabenow also wrote landmark laws addressing the issues of child support and the prevention of child abuse and neglect.

In 1996, Stabenow challenged a one-term incumbent, Republican Dick Chrysler, in central Michigan's Eighth U.S. Congressional District. She supported a balanced budget and led efforts to bring computers and the Internet to more schools and efforts for job expansion through the new technology-driven economy. She organized bus trips to Canada in search of cheaper prescription drugs and publicized the issue of high prescription costs. Stabenow won the election by a margin of 10 percentage points and, two years later, was re-elected with 57 percent of the vote.[2]

Once in Congress, Representative Stabenow earned a reputation as a moderate who worked with both Republicans and Democrats to get things done. "What I hear from people back home is, 'Forget the ideology. What are you doing to make government work in a way that helps my family every day?'" she said.[3] She was assigned to the Agriculture and Science committees.

In 1999, Stabenow announced her candidacy for one of Michigan's U.S. Senate seats. "It's about having the ability to get something done," Stabenow said of her desire to switch from the House to the Senate. "There are 435 people in the House. There are only 100 people in the Senate, and one person of either party can really get a lot done."[4] In a hard-fought campaign against one-term Republican incumbent Spencer Abraham, Stabenow prevailed in November 2000 with a margin of one percent of the vote.

Senator Stabenow's position as a moderate increased her influence when the Senate was split 50–50 at the start of the 107th Congress (2001–2003). She was assigned to four committees: Budget; Banking, Housing and Urban Affairs; Agriculture, Nutrition, and Forestry; and the Special Committee on Aging.

While in the Senate, Stabenow made health care her signature issue. Democrats chose her to co-chair their Senate Health Care Task Force. She authored and helped lead the passage of legislation in the U.S. Senate to reduce prescription drug prices by allowing states to negotiate lower prices and by providing citizens access to less expensive generic prescription drugs. She introduced legislation to permit the reimportation of prescription drugs sold in other countries for a fraction of the cost borne by American consumers.

On environmental matters, Stabenow authored a federal ban on drilling for oil and gas in the Great Lakes. She also mobilized thousands of citizens to stop the dumping of Canadian trash in Michigan and wrote successful legislation that required the inspection of Canadian trash trucks crossing Michigan's borders.[5] She led efforts to pass a $2 billion tax cut giving manufacturers incentives for job creation in the United States, rather than overseas and authored amendments to make it difficult for terrorists and drug dealers to launder the money that finances their criminal networks.

FOR FURTHER READING

Biographical Directory of the U.S. Congress, "Deborah Ann Stabenow," http://bioguide.gongress.gov

NOTES

1 Politics in America, 2002 (Washington, D.C.: Congressional Quarterly Inc., 2001): 500; "Official Biography of Debbie Stabenow," http://stabenow.senate.gov/biography.htm (accessed 14 December 2004).

2 "Election Statistics, 1920 to Present," http://clerk.house.gov/members/electionInfo/index.html.

3 Politics in America, 2002: 500.

4 Ruby L. Bailey, "Hunger Fed by Need to Get Things Done; Talk with Longtime Ally Leads to Bid for Senate Campaign Dynamo: Debbie Stabenow," 26 October 2000, Detroit Free Press: 1A.

5 Politics in America, 2004 (Washington, D.C.: Congressional Quarterly Inc., 2003): 504–505; "Official Biography of Debbie Stabenow."

Ellen O'Kane Tauscher
1951–

Image courtesy of the Member

UNITED STATES REPRESENTATIVE
DEMOCRAT FROM CALIFORNIA
1997–

A WOMAN PIONEER ON THE NEW YORK STOCK EXCHANGE, Ellen Tauscher used her Wall Street business experience and negotiating skills to become a prominent Democratic centrist in the U.S. House. Representing a suburban California district east of the Bay Area, Congresswoman Tauscher has developed an expertise in national security issues from her seat on the Armed Services Committee.

Ellen O'Kane was born in Newark, New Jersey, on November 15, 1951. The daughter of a grocery store owner, she earned a B.A. in early childhood education from Seton Hall University in 1974. In her mid-20s, she became one of the first women to hold a seat on the New York Stock Exchange, serving there from 1977 to 1979. During her 14-year Wall Street career she also served as an officer of the American Stock Exchange. In 1989, she married William Tauscher and raised a daughter, Katherine. The couple later divorced. In 1992, Ellen Tauscher founded a service for pre-employment screening of childcare providers. She later authored *The Child Care Source Book*. She also created the Tauscher Foundation, which donated $200,000 to California and Texas schools to buy computer equipment for elementary education. Tauscher received her first political experience serving as the state co-chair for Dianne Feinstein's successful 1992 and 1994 Senate campaigns.

In 1996, Tauscher challenged incumbent California Republican Bill Baker in a newly created delta district comprising bedroom communities that are the most conservative in the Bay Area. Tauscher ran on a platform of gun control, women's right to abortion, and increased spending on education, along with the reduction of wasteful fiscal spending. She narrowly won, with 49 percent to Baker's 47 percent, in a race with three minor-party candidates. "My message throughout this campaign was one of moderation and common sense," Tauscher declared afterwards. "I want to go back to Washington and stand in the middle . . . where most Americans stand."[1] In the next two elections, Tauscher won slightly more comfortable margins over GOP candidates, defeating Charles Ball 53 to 43 percent and Claude Hutchison 52 to 44 percent.[2]

When Tauscher took her seat in the 105th Congress (1997–1999), she received assignments on three committees: National Security (later renamed Armed Services), Science, and Transportation and Infrastructure. In the 106th Congress (1999–2001), Tauscher resigned her Science Committee seat to focus on her two other assignments.

Tauscher's committee assignments provided her a national platform from which she also was able to serve district needs. As a member of the Armed Services Committee, Tauscher outlined an activist role for America in the international arena. In the spring of 1999, when the William J. Clinton administration coordinated NATO air attacks against Serbia for its invasion of Kosovo and "ethnic cleansing" of the populace, Tauscher insisted that ground troops be sent.[3] In the 108th Congress (2003–2005), Tauscher played a vocal role in the Iraq War, calling for additional troops and equipment, and visiting the region four times. Her district is the only one which holds two national defense laboratories—Lawrence Livermore and Sandia/California. She secured nearly $200 million in funding for Livermore's "super laser" project. Tauscher also has a prominent role as the senior Democrat on the congressional panel overseeing the National Nuclear Security Administration, which manages the U.S. nuclear weapons program. From her seat on Transportation and Infrastructure, Tauscher steered federal funding to improve the Bay Area's badly strained transportation systems, including $33 million for projects in her district.

Tauscher was a vocal supporter of cutting taxes, especially the "marriage penalty" and the estate tax, and she voted to override President Clinton's 2000 veto of an estate tax repeal. She did not support Republican proposals in the 106th Congress to slash taxes by almost $800 billion and also opposed the 2001 tax cut proposed by the George W. Bush administration and passed by Congress.[4] Her alternative plan of tax cuts, "triggered" only after surplus money was confirmed, became the Democratic alternative to the $1.6 trillion cut proposed by the GOP.[5]

In 1998, *Time* magazine dubbed her moderate Democratic approach to politics "Tauscherism," a kind of middle-of-the road politics that blended fiscal conservatism with social liberalism.[6] "Tauscherism" also reflected the political realities of her suburban district which, until reapportionment in 2002, was more Republican than Democratic. When the lines were redrawn by the California legislature, Tauscher easily won election to a fourth term, with 75 percent of the vote against Libertarian candidate Sonia Harden. In 2004, Tauscher won re-election with 66 percent of the vote against Republican Jeff Ketelson.[7]

FOR FURTHER READING

Biographical Directory of the U.S. Congress, "Ellen O'Kane Tauscher," http://bioguide.congress.gov

Tauscher, Ellen O., with Kathleen Candy. *The Child Care Sourcebook* (New York: Macmillan, 1996).

NOTES

1 Barry Witt, "Race Seen as Bellwether of House Control; District 10 House Race: GOP-DEMO Bellwether," 16 October 1996, *San Jose Mercury News*: A1; John Wildermuth and Jim Doyle, "Tauscher Beats Baker in an Upset; Big Bay Area Surprise in Race for Congress," 7 November 1996, *San Francisco Chronicle*: A17; Erin Hallissy, "East Bay Congressman Focuses on Rival's Wealth; Ads Claim Challenger Is Trying to Buy Seat," 1 October 1996, *San Francisco Chronicle*: A1.

2 "Elections Statistics, 1920 to Present," http://clerk.house.gov/members/electionInfo/elections.html.

3 Christopher Heredia, "Tauscher to Urge Ground Troops on Congressional Visit to Balkans," 7 April 1999, *San Francisco Chronicle*: A22.

4 *Politics in America, 2002* (Washington, D.C.: Congressional Quarterly Inc., 2001): 85.

5 Marc Sandalow, "Ellen Tauscher: Movin' on Up," 1 March 2001, *California Journal*.

6 Peter Beinart, "Why the Center Can't Hold," 24 November 1997, *Time;* online at http://www.time.com/time/archive/preview/0,10987,1101971124-136899,00.html (accessed 7 December 2004); Mary Anne Ostrom, "Tauscher Typifies Demos' Visions," 31 March 1998, *Mercury News*: 1A.

7 "Election Statistics, 1920 to Present," http://clerk.house.gov/members/electionInfo/elections.html.

Nydia M. Velázquez
1953–

UNITED STATES REPRESENTATIVE
DEMOCRAT FROM NEW YORK
1993–

Image courtesy of the Member

THE *NEW YORK TIMES* DESCRIBED NYDIA VELÁZQUEZ, the first Puerto Rican woman to serve in Congress, as "an aggressive woman in a macho political world, operating outside any political machine. She was born and raised on the island and not shaped by the urban edge and political culture of the barrio."[1] First elected to the U.S. House in 1992, Representative Velázquez now serves as the Ranking Democratic Member of the Small Business Committee, using her position to advocate on behalf of small companies, particularly those owned by minorities and women. She is the first Hispanic woman in House history to serve as Ranking Member of a full committee.

Nydia Velázquez was born on March 28, 1953, to Don Benito Velázquez, a sugar-cane cutter, and Doña Serrano Velázquez, in Yabucoa, Puerto Rico. To support a family of nine children, her parents sold food to field workers and operated a small cinder block manufacturing business.[2] She inherited her father's inclination toward politics; he often delivered political speeches on behalf of workers' rights causes.[3] In 1972, she received her B.A. in political science from the University of Puerto Rico in Rio Piedras, becoming the first member of her family to receive a college diploma. Two years later, she moved to New York City and earned a master's degree on a scholarship at New York University. In 1976, Velázquez returned to Puerto Rico to teach at the University of Puerto Rico in Humacao. In 1981, she began a two-year stint as an adjunct professor at Hunter College in New York City, teaching Puerto Rican studies. Velázquez 's start in politics coincided with teaching in New York City. In 1983, she served as a special assistant for then-freshman Congressman Edolphus Towns of New York. A year later, she was appointed to fill a vacant seat on the New York city council, becoming the first Latina woman to serve on that panel. After she lost her re-election bid in 1986, Velázquez worked as the director of what became the Department of Puerto Rican Community Affairs in the United States.

In 1992, she sought a New York City U.S. House seat held by nine-term incumbent Democrat Stephen Solarz. The newly apportioned district encompassed the working-class parts of the Lower East Side in Manhattan, northern Brooklyn, and Queens. Velázquez mounted a grass-roots campaign for the Democratic primary, arguing that a Puerto Rican should represent the new district's Puerto Rican majority. She won the five-way primary over Solarz by five percent of the vote and, in the general election, won with 77 percent of the vote. Since 1992, Velázquez has been safely re-elected to six succeeding Congresses, usually by margins of 80 percent or more.[4]

Since arriving in Congress, Velázquez has served on two committees: Financial Services (formerly called Banking, Finance, and Urban Affairs) and Small Business. She serves on the Financial Services Subcommittee on Housing and Community Opportunity. In 1998, she became the Ranking Member on the Small Business Committee.

The Small Business Committee overseas federal programs and contracts that total more than $200 billion annually, and Velázquez has used her position as Ranking Member to cultivate greater federal support of small business and entrepreneurship in her district and nationally. She has sought to steer federal agencies toward contracting with small businesses, to help owners of small firms provide medical and retirement benefits to employees, and to make federal loan and grant programs more accessible to small firms. She has been critical of federal agencies for what she has described as their unsatisfactory efforts to do business with private companies, issuing an annual "report card" on such practices. In the 107th Congress (2001–2003), Velázquez called attention to the effects of the sweatshop industry on the working-class poor in her district. After the September 11, 2001, terrorist attacks, she introduced legislation that required the hiring of small businesses to help cleanup and reconstruct lower Manhattan.

Velázquez also has a keen interest on immigration matters and U.S. foreign policy in the Caribbean. Much of her district casework centers on immigration issues, as many of her constituents have family in the Dominican Republic, Haiti, and other Caribbean countries. She has worked for increased funding to reduce the immigration backlog at the Bureau of Citizenship and Immigration Services. Velázquez has consistently advocated ending practice bombing on the navy's test range at Vieques, an island just off the Puerto Rican coast, and advocated for liberating former Puerto Rican political prisoners. In 1994, she protested the William J. Clinton administration's policy of refusing Haitian refugees entrance into the United States.[5]

FOR FURTHER READING

Biographical Directory of the U.S. Congress, "Nydia Margarita Velázquez," http://bioguide. congress.gov

NOTES

1 Deborah Sontag, "Puerto Rican-Born Favorite Treated Like Outsider," 2 November 1992, *New York Times*: B1.

2 "Velázquez, Nydia Margarita," *Encyclopedia of World Biography*, 2nd ed., Vol. 17 (Detroit: Gale Research, 1998); *Politics in America, 2004* (Washington, D.C.: Congressional Quarterly Inc., 2003): 705.

3 Maria Newman, "From Puerto Rico to Congress, a Determined Path," 27 September 1992, *New York Times*: 33.

4 Newman, "From Puerto Rico to Congress, A Determined Path"; "Election Statistics, 1920 to Present," http://clerk.house.gov/ members/electionInfo/index.html.

5 "Nydia Velázquez," Associated Press Candidate Biographies, 2000; Douglas Jehl, "Clinton's Options on Haiti: Ever Harsher Choices Ahead," 6 May 1994, *New York Times*: A10.

Maxine Waters
1938–

UNITED STATES REPRESENTATIVE
DEMOCRAT FROM CALIFORNIA
1991–

Image courtesy of the Member

ON THE "MY HERO" WEBSITE, A YOUNG WOMAN NAMED MICHELLE describes U.S. Representative Maxine Waters as a "Community Hero" and adds, "[Waters] instills the belief that you can achieve whatever you wish as long as you really strive to do so."[1] In fact, over three decades, Congresswoman Waters has become one of the nation's most tenacious, unapologetic advocates for women, children, the poor, economic development, communities of color, and both human and civil rights.

Waters' passionate commitment to social and economic justice can be traced back to the struggles her family faced during her youth. Maxine Moore Carr was born in St. Louis, Missouri, on August 15, 1938, the fifth of 13 children in a family headed by a single mother. "I know all about welfare," she once recalled. "I remember the social workers peeking in the refrigerator and under the beds."[2] Although she has established a long list of significant achievements and is considered one of the most powerful women in American politics, she still carries with her the memories of starting work at age 13 in factories and segregated restaurants. Perhaps, it is her first-hand experience with those issues that has also made her one of the nation's most effective grassroots organizers.

Waters moved to California in 1961 and, in 1970, earned a B.A. in sociology from California State University at Los Angeles. During that time, she launched her career in public service with the Head Start program, where she eventually became an administrator coordinating the Parent Involvement Program. In 1976, Waters was elected to the California state assembly where she became the first woman in state history elected by her peers to the leadership post of minority whip. She eventually became chair of the Democratic caucus. As an assemblywoman, she successfully spearheaded efforts to start: the first statewide child abuse prevention training program in the country; the largest divestment of state pension funds from South Africa; landmark affirmative action legislation; and the prohibition of police strip searches for individuals charged with nonviolent misdemeanors.

In 1990, Waters was elected to fill the congressional seat vacated by the retiring U.S. Representative Augustus "Gus" Hawkins, the first African American to represent California in the national legislature. She captured 79 percent of the vote and has never been seriously challenged since, capturing similar percentages in her seven subsequent re-election campaigns.[3]

As a Member of Congress, Waters's legislative agenda has included: producing $10 billion under the Section 108 loan guarantee program for economic and infrastructure development in U.S. cities; successfully tripling funding for debt relief in poor nations; obtaining $50 million for the Youth Fair Chance Program; creating the "Center for Women Veterans"; and leading in the establishment of the Minority AIDS Initiative. Additionally, Waters has been a leader on global peace and international human right issues and remains actively involved in continued efforts to improve the plight of individuals oppressed in conflict-torn nations like Sudan, Haiti, and Liberia.

Waters's efforts have not gone unnoticed by her congressional colleagues. In 1997, she won the chair of the Congressional Black Caucus and later, her Democratic colleagues elected her to the post of Chief Deputy Minority Whip. She serves on the influential House Committee on the Judiciary and the Committee on Financial Services, on which she is the Ranking Member of the Subcommittee on Housing and Community Opportunity.

By the 109th Congress (2005–2007), Representative Waters was a leading woman member of the Democratic Party. She acquired that status, as an observer noted, by amplifying her record of advocacy at the local and state level to become "a community activist in Congress."[4] In 2005, Waters co-founded and was elected chair of the 72-member "Out of Iraq" Congressional Caucus. One of the largest caucuses in the House of Representatives, it was established to provide consistent pressure on the George W. Bush administration, to provide a voice in Congress for the individuals and organizations opposed to the Iraq War, and, ultimately, to end the war and reunite U.S. troops with their families as soon as possible.

One of the things which Waters prizes most is her family. She is married to Sidney Williams, the former U.S. Ambassador to the Commonwealth of the Bahamas. She is the mother of two adult children, Karen and Edward, and has two grandchildren.

FOR FURTHER READING

Biographical Directory of the U.S. Congress, "Maxine Waters," http://bioguide.congress.gov

Naden, Corinne J., and Rose Blue. *Heroes Don't Just Happen: Biographies of Overcoming Bias and Building Character in Politics* (Maywood, NJ: Peoples Pub. Group, 1997).

MANUSCRIPT COLLECTION

California State Archives (Sacramento, CA). *Papers:* 1979–1990, 30 cubic feet. In Maxine Waters's bill files.

Papers: In miscellaneous office files of Maxine Waters, 1978–1982, 11 cubic feet. Includes schedules and itineraries, ways and means committee records, budget conference, and elections and reapportionment committee working papers. Also includes judiciary committee correspondence on pending legislation.

Papers: In subject files of Assemblywoman Waters, 1977–1986, unknown amount of material. Includes documentation on the Commission on Status of Women. Restricted access.

NOTES

1 "Community Hero: Maxine Waters," http://myhero.com/myhero/hero.asp?hero=WATERS_TAFT_04 (accessed 21 July 2006).

2 *Almanac of American Politics, 2006,* (Washington, D.C.: National Journal Inc., 2005): 261.

3 "Election Statistics, 1920 to Present," http://clerk.house.gov/members/electionInfo/index.html.

4 John L. Mitchell, "Undeterred Waters Crusades for Answers," 4 March 1997, *Los Angeles Times:* A3.

Diane Edith Watson
1933–

UNITED STATES REPRESENTATIVE
DEMOCRAT FROM CALIFORNIA
2001–

Image courtesy of the Member

As an educator, state legislator, and former U.S ambassador, Diane Watson entered the U.S. House of Representatives as an unusually experienced freshman. From her seats on the Government Reform Committee and the International Relations Committee, Congresswoman Watson quickly established herself as a legislator whose interests ranged from welfare reform to foreign aid for African nations facing the HIV/AIDS crisis.

Diane Edith Watson was born on November 12, 1933, in Los Angeles, California, daughter of William Allen Louis Watson and Dorothy Elizabeth O'Neal Watson. She graduated with an A.A. from Los Angeles City College and a B.A. from the University of California, Los Angeles (UCLA) in 1956. Watson later earned an M.S. from California State University in 1967 and a Ph.D. in education administration from Claremont College in 1986. After graduating from UCLA, Watson worked as a teacher and school psychologist in the Los Angeles public schools. She was an associate professor at California State University from 1969 to 1971 and then worked in the California department of education and served on the Los Angeles unified school board. Watson won election as a state senator in 1978, an office she held for 20 years. She was the first African-American woman in the state senate and chaired the health and human services committee. In 1998, President William J. Clinton nominated her as U.S. Ambassador to the Federated States of Micronesia, a post she held for two years.

In December 2000, U.S. Representative Julian Dixon, who just had been re-elected to a 12th term in Congress from his central Los Angeles-Culver City district, died suddenly. In April 2001, Watson prevailed with a 33 percent plurality in the Democratic primary to choose a successor candidate, while her nearest competitor received 26 percent.[1] In the June 5, 2001, special election Watson carried the heavily Democratic Los Angeles district with 75 percent of the vote. In her two subsequent re-election bids, Watson won her district with more than 80 percent of the vote.[2]

When Watson was sworn into the U.S. House on June 7, 2001, she was assigned seats on the Government Reform Committee and the International Relations Committee. As a former ambassador, she took a keen interest in American foreign policy, particularly as it related to issues of racism and health in the developing world. In the summer of 2001, Watson attended the United Nations' Conference on Racism, Xenophobia, and Other Intolerance in Durbin, South Africa. She called on the United States to host its own conference on racism and reform to the educational, justice, and health care systems as possible avenues to make "reparations" for the practice of American slavery.[3] In early 2002, Watson took to the House Floor to support the Local Law Enforcement Hate Crimes Prevention Act, noting that incidents of violence against Arab Americans, which had risen since the 2001 terrorist attacks, were "the tip of a proverbial iceberg."[4]

Watson also called for the United States to expand aid to sub-Saharan African nations fighting an HIV/AIDs pandemic that in some countries had infected more than a quarter of the adult population. Aside from humanitarian considerations, she argued, the crisis had repercussions for regional stability and American national security because of the strain it placed on so many developing economies. The disease, she observed, "in the very near term, if not more is done, may challenge the very notion of law-based nation states." She also linked the chaos the disease could wreak on nation states with instability that favored terrorist actions. "Let us not forget that Al Qaeda terrorist leader Osama bin Laden has exploited the misery of another state where civil society has collapsed—Afghanistan—to serve as a base for his terror network," Watson said.[5]

During the 107th and 108th Congresses (2001–2005), Representative Watson established herself as an advocate for what she describes as "commonsense" welfare reform in California. Watson supported reauthorization of the Temporary Assistance for Needy Families program, which provides education, childcare, job training, and employment to welfare recipients by granting states federal funds to develop and manage their own welfare programs. Congresswoman Watson also has been an advocate for increasing funding to the Cal-Learn program to help teen mothers complete their educations and get jobs.[6] In addition, she introduced several bills, including legislation to develop state medical disaster response plans in the event of a biological or chemical weapons attack.[7] She also advocated passage of a fully funded medical prescription drug coverage plan for seniors.

FOR FURTHER READING

Biographical Directory of the U.S. Congress, "Diane Edith Watson," http://bioguide.congress.gov

Watson, Diane E., Ph.D. *1978–1998: Legislative History* (Sacramento, CA: California State Senate, 1999).

Watson, Diane E., and Beverly J. Rambo. *Your Career in Health Care* (New York: Gregg Division, McGraw-Hill, 1976).

MANUSCRIPT COLLECTION

California State Archives (Sacramento, CA). *Papers*: Correspondence and chronological files of state senator Diane Watson, 1978–1980, two cubic feet. Includes Sacramento and district chronological files, miscellaneous legislative counsel drafts; Jane Fonda and constituent problems correspondence; bill files, 1979–1982, four cubic feet; bill files, 1981–1986, 1.5 cubic feet; newsletter questionnaires of Diane Watson, 1987.

NOTES

1 "Diane Watson: Member of Congress, California 32, Democrat," July 2002, *Campaigns and Elections*: 18.

2 "Election Statistics, 1920 to Present," http://clerk.house.gov/members/ electionInfo/elections.html.

3 *Congressional Record*, House, 107th Cong., 1st sess. (6 September 2001): 5447.

4 *Congressional Record*, House, 107th Cong., 2nd sess. (7 February 2002): 219.

5 *Congressional Record*, House, 107th Cong., 1st sess. (29 November 2001): 572; *Congressional Record*, House, 107th Cong., 1st sess. (11 December 2001): 9089.

6 "Meet Congresswoman Diane Watson," http://www.house.gov/watson/meet _congresswoman.html (accessed 2 January 2005); *Congressional Record*, House, 107th Cong., 2nd sess. (17 April 2002): 384; *Congressional Record*, House, 107th Cong., 2nd sess. (8 May 2002): 2170.

7 *Politics in America 2002*: (Washington, D.C.: Congressional Quarterly Inc., 2001): 130–132.

Heather A. Wilson
1960–

UNITED STATES REPRESENTATIVE
REPUBLICAN FROM NEW MEXICO
1998–

Image courtesy of the Member

AN AIR FORCE ACADEMY GRADUATE, RHODES SCHOLAR, and former National Security Council staff member, Heather Wilson is the first woman veteran to serve in the U.S. Congress and only the second woman to represent New Mexico in Congress.

Heather A. Wilson was born on December 30, 1960, in Keene, New Hampshire. During her junior year in Keene High School, the U.S. Air Force Academy began admitting women. Wilson, who hoped to become a pilot, like her father and grandfather, entered the academy and graduated in 1982. She earned a Rhodes Scholarship to study at Oxford University where, by 1985, she earned a master's and a doctorate in international relations. Wilson served in the Air Force until 1989 when she joined the National Security Council staff as director for European Defense Policy and Arms Control. In 1991, she married lawyer Jay Hone, and the couple settled in New Mexico. They raised three children: Scott, Joshua, and Caitlin. Wilson then started a consulting firm and, from 1995 to 1998, served in the governor's cabinet as secretary of the New Mexico children, youth and families department.

When New Mexico's Albuquerque Congressman Steven H. Schiff declared he would not run for re-election in the fall of 1998 because of his battle with skin cancer, Wilson resigned her cabinet post and entered the Republican primary. She won the support of Schiff and U.S. Senator Pete V. Domenici, who lent her several trusted aides and called her "the most brilliantly qualified House candidate anywhere in the country."[1] But Schiff's death in March necessitated a June 23 special election. With Domenici's support, Wilson became the Republican candidate for the special election, propelling her to a sizable win in the June 2 primary for the fall election against conservative state senator William F. Davis. Three weeks later, Wilson won the special election (with 45 percent of the vote) in a three-way race against millionaire Democratic state senator Phillip J. Maloof and Green Party candidate Robert L. Anderson. She was sworn into office on June 25, 1998, making her the first woman since Georgia Lusk in 1946, and the first Republican woman ever, to represent New Mexico.[2]

The special election was but a preview for the fall election for the full two-year term. In both races, Wilson's slogan "fighting for our families" encompassed an agenda including better public schools, elimination of the marriage penalty, and an elimination of estate taxes. Both races were contentious and costly. For the June 23 special election Maloof spent $3.1 million and portrayed Wilson as an outsider. Leading up to the November 1998 general election, Maloof spent an additional $5 million to Wilson's $1.1 million, making it the most expensive House race in New Mexico's history. Wilson prevailed, with 48 percent of the vote. She won her 2000 re-election bid by a seven-point margin over her Democratic challenger. In 2002, she defeated Democrat Richard Romero with 55 percent to 45 percent of the vote. Two years later, she defeated Romero by a similar margin to earn a seat in the 109th Congress (2005–2007).[3]

Wilson took a seat on the powerful Armed Services Committee in the 107th Congress (2001–2003), thus offering her a prime vantage point from which to oversee personnel and infrastructure issues at two installations in her district: Kirtland Air Force Base and the Sandia National Lab. In the 109th Congress, Wilson moved to the House Permanent Select Committee on Intelligence, where she chairs the Subcommittee on Technical and Tactical Intelligence. Since the 105th Congress (1997–1999), Wilson also has served on the influential Committee on Energy and Commerce, including its subcommittees on Telecommunication, Energy and Air Quality, and Environment and Hazardous Materials.

Wilson's reputation in Congress has been that of a moderate Republican who is not reluctant to take positions independent of her party. She called for a simplification of the tax codes and became one of the GOP's point persons in the House to criticize the American bombing campaign in Kosovo. But on social issues, she has been more moderate than many of her GOP colleagues. She supported requiring federal workers' health plans to cover contraceptive coverage (although she opposes using public money to pay for abortions) and also voted down an amendment that would have banned adoptions by gay parents in the District of Columbia. She also opposed a plan by the Republican leadership to move management of the nuclear weapons program (largely based in New Mexico) from the Department of Energy to the Pentagon.[4] In 2006, Wilson led efforts to ensure congressional oversight of the President's terrorist surveillance program.

FOR FURTHER READING

Biographical Directory of the U.S. Congress, "Heather Wilson," http://bioguide.congress.gov

NOTES

1 John Mercurio, "GOP, Wilson Win in N.M.; Democrats Learn It's Not Easy Beating Green," 25 June 1998, Roll Call.

2 Rachel Smolkin, "Rep. Wilson Takes Office With a Little Help From 4-Year-Old Son," 26 June 1998, Albuquerque Tribune: A6.

3 "Election Statistics, 1920 to Present," http://clerk.house.gov/members/electionInfo/elections.html.

4 Politics in America 2002: (Washington, D.C.: Congressional Quarterly Inc., 2001): 660–661; Almanac of American Politics, 2002 (Washington, D.C.: National Journal Inc., 2001): 1023–1025.

Lynn C. Woolsey

1937–

Image courtesy of the Member

UNITED STATES REPRESENTATIVE

DEMOCRAT FROM CALIFORNIA

1993–

AS A WORKING SINGLE MOTHER, LYNN WOOLSEY spent several years receiving public assistance to help make ends meet while she raised three small children. "I know what it means to have a safety net when you need help getting back on your feet," Woolsey recalled. "I can go to Washington and say, 'I've been there.'"[1] Describing herself as the "first former welfare mom to serve in Congress," Representative Woolsey has focused on issues facing children and families since her first election to the House of Representatives in 1992.

Lynn Woolsey was born in Seattle, Washington, on November 3, 1937. She graduated from Lincoln High School in Seattle. She attended the University of Washington from 1955 to 1957, but left school to be married, settling in northern California in Marin County, just north of San Francisco. She had three children—Joseph, Ed, and Amy—before her husband left the family in the late 1960s. Following her divorce, Woolsey found a secretarial job at a local high-tech company, but was forced to accept welfare assistance for childcare and health care. She eventually became a human resources manager at her company and, in 1980, opened her own business. She remarried, and raised another child, Michael. Woolsey also returned to college and earned a bachelor of science degree from the University of San Francisco in 1980. Woolsey first entered elective politics in 1984, when she won a seat on the city council of Petaluma, in Sonoma County. She served on the city council until 1992, holding the post of vice mayor for the last year of her tenure.

In 1992, when five-term incumbent Representative Barbara Boxer decided to run for the U.S. Senate, Woolsey entered the race to succeed her. The district encompassed the two counties just north of the Golden Gate Bridge, Marin County and most of Sonoma County, one of the nation's most affluent areas. She won a crowded Democratic primary with 26 percent of the vote (to her nearest competitor's 19 percent). In the general election against her Republican opponent, a California assemblyman, Woolsey won with 65 percent of the vote. Re-elected in 1994 with 58 percent of the vote, Woolsey was returned to office in the next five elections by comfortable margins. In 2004, she was elected to the 109th Congress (2005–2007) with 72 percent of the vote.[2]

When Woolsey claimed her seat in the House in January 1993 at the start of the 103rd Congress (1993–1995), she received assignments on three committees: Budget, Government Operations, and Education and Labor (later renamed Education and the Workforce). In the 104th Congress (1995–1997), she left Government Operations, and in the 106th Congress (1999–2001) she was reassigned from the Budget Committee to the Science Committee. By the 108th Congress, she was the Ranking Member on the Education and Workforce Subcommittee on Education Reform.

From her seat on the Education and Workforce Committee, Woolsey has positioned herself as one of the foremost advocates of education issues in Congress. Drawing on her experience, she was a Democratic spokesperson during the mid-1990s welfare reform debates; and she was sharply critical of legislation that reduced the scope of many programs and placed lifetime limits on benefits. Representative Woolsey also has been a proponent of expanding childcare programs and supporting paid parental leave programs. In the 105th Congress (1997–1999), during the renewal of legislation on child nutrition, Woolsey inserted an amendment to expand school breakfast programs for all children and to make teenagers eligible for after-school snack programs. In the 106th Congress, she sponsored a measure that required the IRS to help enforce the payment of child support. In the 106th and 107th Congresses, she introduced her "Go, Girl" measure to encourage young girls to study science and math.[3] She now leads in an effort to bring U.S. troops home from Iraq.

Congresswoman Woolsey also has attended to her northern California constituents' range of needs—economic, medical, and environmental. She has delivered hundreds of millions of dollars to her district for a variety of capital-intensive projects: $9 million for a Petaluma River flood control project, $8.7 million for a major highway study and plan, and $52 million for a seismic retrofit of the Golden Gate Bridge.[4] During the 108th Congress (2003–2005), Woolsey worked to secure funding for breast cancer research, partly, to analyze the unusually high rate of the disease in Marin County. She is a proponent of export subsidies for wineries, which are a major Sonoma County industry. Representative Woolsey also has worked to expand the perimeter of the Point Reyes National Seashore, which is in her district.

FOR FURTHER READING

Biographical Directory of the U.S. Congress, "Lynn C. Woolsey," http://bioguide.congress.gov

NOTES

1 Jane Gross, "Running on Experience: On Welfare, Then Off It," 16 June 1992, *New York Times*: A16. See also, Carolyn Lochhead, "Ex-Welfare Mom Takes Congress to Task; Lawmaker Draws on Experience," 10 March 1994, *San Francisco Chronicle*: A4.

2 "Election Statistics, 1920 to Present," http://clerk.house.gov/members/electionInfo/elections.html.

3 *Politics in America, 2004* (Washington, D.C.: Congressional Quarterly Inc., 2003): 79; *Almanac of American Politics, 2002* (Washington, D.C.: National Journal Inc., 2001): 175.

4 Pamela J. Podger, "Woolsey Smokes Challenger in Primary," March 6, 2002, *San Francisco Chronicle*: A24.

First-Term Women Members of the 109th Congress (2005–2007)*

SOURCES

Biographical Directory of the United States Congress, 1774–2005 (Washington, D.C.: Government Printing Office, 2005); *New Member Pictorial Directory, 109th Congress* (Washington, D.C.: Government Printing Office, 2005); "Meet the New Members," 8 November 2004, *Roll Call;* Members' official U.S. House Web sites at http://www.house.gov.

* *Current through August 1, 2006*

Image courtesy of the Member

Melissa Bean

UNITED STATES REPRESENTATIVE
DEMOCRAT FROM ILLINOIS

CONGRESSIONAL COMMITTEES:
Financial Services
Small Business

BORN: Melissa Luburich, January 22, 1962, in Chicago, Illinois

FAMILY: Married to Alan Bean; two daughters, Victoria and Michelle

EDUCATION: Graduated from Maine East High School, Park Ridge, IL, 1979; A.A., Oakton Community College, 1982; B.A., Roosevelt University, Chicago, IL, 2002

MILITARY: N/A

POLITICAL CAREER: Unsuccessful candidate for election to the 108th Congress in 2002

PROFESSIONAL CAREER: President, sales consulting firm

PUBLICATIONS: N/A

Image courtesy of the Member

Thelma Drake

UNITED STATES REPRESENTATIVE

REPUBLICAN FROM VIRGINIA

CONGRESSIONAL COMMITTEES:
Armed Services
Education and the Workforce
Resources

BORN: November 20, 1949, in Elyria, Ohio

FAMILY: Married to Thomas "Ted" Drake;
two children, Lynn and J. Mark

EDUCATION: Graduated from Elyria High School,
Elyria, Ohio, 1967

MILITARY: N/A

POLITICAL CAREER: Member of the Virginia house
of delegates, 1996–2004

PROFESSIONAL CAREER: Realtor; business owner

PUBLICATIONS: N/A

Congressional Pictorial Directory
109th Congress

Virginia Foxx

UNITED STATES REPRESENTATIVE

REPUBLICAN FROM NORTH CAROLINA

CONGRESSIONAL COMMITTEES:
Agriculture
Education and the Workforce
Government Reform

BORN: Virginia Palmieri, 29 June 1943, in Bronx, New York

FAMILY: Married to Thomas Foxx; daughter, Theresa

EDUCATION: B.A., University of North Carolina,
Chapel Hill, North Carolina, 1968; M.A., University of
North Carolina, Chapel Hill, North Carolina, 1972;
Ed.D., University of North Carolina, Greensboro, North
Carolina, 1985

MILITARY: N/A

POLITICAL CAREER: Member of the Watauga
County, North Carolina, board of education, 1976–1988;
deputy secretary for management, North Carolina
department of administration, 1985–1987; member of the
North Carolina state senate, 1994–2004

PROFESSIONAL CAREER: Educator; education
administrator; business owner; former community college
president

PUBLICATIONS: N/A

Image courtesy of the Member

*Doris Okada Matsui**

UNITED STATES REPRESENTATIVE

DEMOCRAT FROM CALIFORNIA

CONGRESSIONAL COMMITTEES:
Rules
Science

BORN: Doris Okada, September 25, 1944, in Poston, Arizona (wartime internment camp); raised in Dinuba, California

FAMILY: Widow (wife of former Congressman Robert Matsui); son, Brian

EDUCATION: B.A., University of California at Berkeley, 1966

MILITARY: N/A

POLITICAL CAREER: N/A

PROFESSIONAL CAREER: White House staff (1992–1998); private advocate; president and board chair of Sacramento public television station KVIE

PUBLICATIONS: N/A

* Elected on March 8, 2005, to fill the vacancy caused by the death of U.S. Representative Robert Matsui

Image courtesy of the Member

Cathy McMorris

UNITED STATES REPRESENTATIVE

REPUBLICAN FROM WASHINGTON

CONGRESSIONAL COMMITTEES:
Armed Services
Education and the Workforce
Resources

BORN: Cathy Anne McMorris, May 22, 1969, in Salem, Oregon

FAMILY: Married to Brian Rodgers

EDUCATION: B.A., Pensacola Christian College, Pensacola, Florida, 1990; M.B.A., University of Washington, 2002

MILITARY: N/A

POLITICAL CAREER: Member of the Washington State house of representatives, 1994–2004, and minority leader 2002–2004

PROFESSIONAL CAREER: Family farm, public service

PUBLICATIONS: N/A

Image courtesy of the Member

Gwendolynne (Gwen) Moore

UNITED STATES REPRESENTATIVE
DEMOCRAT FROM WISCONSIN

CONGRESSIONAL COMMITTEES:
Financial Services
Small Business

BORN: Gwendolynne S. Moore, April 18, 1951, in
Racine, Wisconsin

FAMILY: Single; three children, Jessalyn, Adesolu,
and Sowande

EDUCATION: Graduated from Northern Division High
School; B.A., Marquette University, Milwaukee,
Wisconsin, 1978

MILITARY: N/A

POLITICAL CAREER: Member of the Wisconsin
assembly, 1989–1992; member of the Wisconsin state senate, 1993–2004

PROFESSIONAL CAREER: Housing and urban
development specialist; public official

PUBLICATIONS: N/A

Congressional Pictorial Directory
109th Congress

Jean Schmidt*

UNITED STATES REPRESENTATIVE
REPUBLICAN FROM OHIO

CONGRESSIONAL COMMITTEES:
Agriculture
Transportation and Infrastructure
Government Reform

BORN: Jeannette Hoffman, November 29, 1951, Miami
Township, Clermont County, Ohio

FAMILY: Married to Peter Schmidt; daughter, Emilie.

EDUCATION: B.A., political science, University of
Cincinnati, Cincinnati, Ohio, 1974

MILITARY: N/A

POLITICAL CAREER: Ohio state house of
representatives, 2000–2004; unsuccessful candidate for
Ohio state senate, 2004; trustee, Miami Township,
Clermont County, Ohio, 1989–2000

PROFESSIONAL CAREER: public servant

PUBLICATIONS: N/A

* Elected on August 2, 2005, to fill the vacancy caused by
the resignation of U.S. Representative Rob Portman

Congressional Pictorial Directory
109th Congress

Debbie Wasserman Schultz

UNITED STATES REPRESENTATIVE
DEMOCRAT FROM FLORIDA

CONGRESSIONAL COMMITTEES:
Financial Services
Judiciary

BORN: Born Debbie Wasserman, September 27, 1966,
in Forest Hills, New York

FAMILY: Married to Steve Schultz; three children, Jake,
Rebecca, and Shelby

EDUCATION: B.A., University of Florida, 1988; M.A.,
University of Florida, 1990

MILITARY: N/A

POLITICAL CAREER: Member of the Florida state
house of representatives, 1992–2000; Member of the
Florida state senate, 2000–2004

PROFESSIONAL CAREER: Public official

PUBLICATIONS: N/A

Image courtesy of the Member

Allyson Y. Schwartz

UNITED STATES REPRESENTATIVE
DEMOCRAT FROM PENNSYLVANIA

CONGRESSIONAL COMMITTEES:
Budget
Transportation and Infrastructure

BORN: Allyson Young, October 3, 1948, in Queens,
New York

FAMILY: Married to David Schwartz; two sons,
Daniel and Jordan

EDUCATION: Graduated from the Calhoun School,
New York, New York, 1966; B.A., Simmons College,
Boston, Massachusetts, 1970; M.S.W., Bryn Mawr
College, Bryn Mawr, Pennsylvania, 1972

MILITARY: N/A

POLITICAL CAREER: Member of the Pennsylvania
state senate, 1991–2004; unsuccessful candidate for
nomination for the United States Senate in 2000

PROFESSIONAL CAREER: Health care administrator;
public official

PUBLICATIONS: N/A

Women Representatives and Senators by Congress: 1917–2007

CONGRESS	HOUSE	SENATE
65th (1917–1919)	Jeannette Rankin (R-MT)	N/A
66th (1919–1921)	N/A	N/A
67th (1921–1923)	Winnifred Mason Huck (R-IL) Mae Ella Nolan (R-CA) Alice M. Robertson (R-OK)	Rebecca L. Felton (D-GA)
68th (1923–1925)	Mae Ella Nolan (R-CA)	N/A
69th (1925–1927)	Florence Prag Kahn (R-CA) Mary Teresa Norton (D-NJ) Edith Nourse Rogers (R-MA)	N/A
70th (1927–1929)	Florence Prag Kahn (R-CA) Katherine Gudger Langley (R-KY) Mary Teresa Norton (D-NJ) Pearl Peden Oldfield (D-AR) Edith Nourse Rogers (R-MA)	N/A
71st (1929–1931)	Florence Prag Kahn (R-CA) Katherine Gudger Langley (R-KY) Ruth Hanna McCormick (R-IL) Mary Teresa Norton (D-NJ) Pearl Peden Oldfield (D-AR) Ruth Bryan Owen (D-FL) Ruth Sears Baker Pratt (R-NY) Edith Nourse Rogers (R-MA) Effiegene Locke Wingo (D-AR)	N/A
72nd (1931–1933)	Willa McCord Blake Eslick (D-TN) Florence Prag Kahn (R-CA) Mary Teresa Norton (D-NJ) Ruth Bryan Owen (D-FL) Ruth Sears Baker Pratt (R-NY) Edith Nourse Rogers (R-MA) Effiegene Locke Wingo (D-AR)	Hattie Caraway (D-AR)
73rd (1933–1935)	Marian Williams Clarke (R-NY) Isabella Selmes Greenway (D-AZ) Virginia Ellis Jenckes (D-IN) Florence Prag Kahn (R-CA) Kathryn O'Loughlin McCarthy (D-KS) Mary Teresa Norton (D-NJ) Edith Nourse Rogers (R-MA)	Hattie Caraway (D-AR)

CONGRESS	HOUSE	SENATE
74th (1935–1937)	Isabella Selmes Greenway (D-AZ) Virginia Ellis Jenckes (D-IN) Florence Prag Kahn (R-CA) Mary Teresa Norton (D-NJ) Caroline Goodwin O'Day (D-NY) Edith Nourse Rogers (R-MA)	Hattie Caraway (D-AR) Rose McConnell Long (D-LA)
75th (1937–1939)	Elizabeth Hawley Gasque (D-SC) Nan Wood Honeyman (D-CA) Virginia Ellis Jenckes (D-IN) Mary Teresa Norton (D-NJ) Caroline Goodwin O'Day (D-NY) Edith Nourse Rogers (R-MA)	Hattie Caraway (D-AR) Dixie Bibbs Graves (D-AL) Gladys Pyle (R-SD)
76th (1939–1941)	Frances Payne Bolton (R-OH) Florence Reville Gibbs (D-GA) Clara Gooding McMillan (D-SC) Mary Teresa Norton (D-NJ) Caroline Goodwin O'Day (D-NY) Edith Nourse Rogers (R-MA) Margaret Chase Smith (R-ME) Jessie Sumner (R-IL)	Hattie Caraway (D-AR)
77th (1941–1943)	Veronica Grace Boland (D-PA) Frances Payne Bolton (R-OH) Katharine Edgar Byron (D-MD) Mary Teresa Norton (D-NJ) Caroline Goodwin O'Day (D-NY) Jeannette Rankin (R-MT) Edith Nourse Rogers (R-MA) Margaret Chase Smith (R-ME) Jessie Sumner (R-IL)	Hattie Caraway (D-AR)
78th (1943–1945)	Frances Payne Bolton (R-OH) Willa Lybrand Fulmer (D-SC) Clare Boothe Luce (R-CT) Mary Teresa Norton (D-NJ) Edith Nourse Rogers (R-MA) Margaret Chase Smith (R-ME) Winifred Claire Stanley (R-NY) Jessie Sumner (R-IL)	Hattie Caraway (D-AR)
79th (1945–1947)	Frances Payne Bolton (R-OH) Emily Taft Douglas (D-IL) Helen Gahagan Douglas (D-CA) Clare Boothe Luce (R-CT) Helen Douglas Mankin (D-GA) Mary Teresa Norton (D-NJ) Eliza Jane Pratt (D-NC) Edith Nourse Rogers (R-MA) Margaret Chase Smith (R-ME)	N/A

CONGRESS	HOUSE	SENATE
79th (1945–1947) *continued*	Jessie Sumner (R-IL) Chase Going Woodhouse (D-CT)	
80th (1947–1949)	Frances Payne Bolton (R-OH) Helen Gahagan Douglas (D-CA) Georgia Lee Lusk (D-NM) Mary Teresa Norton (D-NJ) Edith Nourse Rogers (R-MA) Margaret Chase Smith (R-ME) Katharine Price St. George (R-NY)	Vera Bushfield (R-SD)
81st (1949–1951)	Frances Payne Bolton (R-OH) Reva Beck Bosone (D-UT) Helen Gahagan Douglas (D-CA) Cecil Murray Harden (R-IN) Edna Flannery Kelly (D-NY) Mary Teresa Norton (D-NJ) Edith Nourse Rogers (R-MA) Katharine Price St. George (R-NY) Chase Going Woodhouse (D-CT)	Margaret Chase Smith (R-ME)
82nd (1951–1953)	Frances Payne Bolton (R-OH) Reva Beck Bosone (D-UT) Vera Daerr Buchanan (D-PA) Marguerite Stitt Church (R-IL) Cecil Murray Harden (R-IN) Maude Elizabeth Kee (D-WV) Edna Flannery Kelly (D-NY) Edith Nourse Rogers (R-MA) Katharine Price St. George (R-NY) Ruth Thompson (R-MI)	Margaret Chase Smith (R-ME)
83rd (1953–1955)	Frances Payne Bolton (R-OH) Vera Daerr Buchanan (D-PA) Marguerite Stitt Church (R-IL) Mary Elizabeth Pruett Farrington (R-HI) Cecil Murray Harden (R-IN) Maude Elizabeth Kee (D-WV) Edna Flannery Kelly (D-NY) Gracie Bowers Pfost (D-ID) Edith Nourse Rogers (R-MA) Katharine Price St. George (R-NY) Leonor Kretzer Sullivan (D-MO) Ruth Thompson (R-MI)	Hazel Abel (R-NE) Eva Bowring (R-NE) Margaret Chase Smith (R-ME)
84th (1955–1957)	Iris Faircloth Blitch (D-GA) Frances Payne Bolton (R-OH) Vera Daerr Buchanan (D-PA) Marguerite Stitt Church (R-IL) Mary Elizabeth Pruett Farrington (R-HI)	Margaret Chase Smith (R-ME)

CONGRESS	HOUSE	SENATE
84th (1955–1957) *continued*	Kathryn Elizabeth Granahan (D-PA)	
	Edith Starrett Green (D-OR)	
	Martha Wright Griffiths (D-MI)	
	Cecil Murray Harden (R-IN)	
	Maude Elizabeth Kee (D-WV)	
	Edna Flannery Kelly (D-NY)	
	Coya Gjesdal Knutson (D-MN)	
	Gracie Bowers Pfost (D-ID)	
	Edith Nourse Rogers (R-MA)	
	Katharine Price St. George (R-NY)	
	Leonor Kretzer Sullivan (D-MO)	
	Ruth Thompson (R-MI)	
85th (1957–1959)	Iris Faircloth Blitch (D-GA)	Margaret Chase Smith (R-ME)
	Frances Payne Bolton (R-OH)	
	Marguerite Stitt Church (R-IL)	
	Florence Price Dwyer (R-NJ)	
	Kathryn Elizabeth Granahan (D-PA)	
	Edith Starrett Green (D-OR)	
	Martha Wright Griffiths (D-MI)	
	Cecil Murray Harden (R-IN)	
	Maude Elizabeth Kee (D-WV)	
	Edna Flannery Kelly (D-NY)	
	Coya Gjesdal Knutson (D-MN)	
	Gracie Bowers Pfost (D-ID)	
	Edith Nourse Rogers (R-MA)	
	Katharine Price St. George (R-NY)	
	Leonor Kretzer Sullivan (D-MO)	
86th (1959–1961)	Iris Faircloth Blitch (D-GA)	Maurine Neuberger (D-OR)
	Frances Payne Bolton (R-OH)	Margaret Chase Smith (R-ME)
	Marguerite Stitt Church (R-IL)	
	Florence Price Dwyer (R-NJ)	
	Kathryn Elizabeth Granahan (D-PA)	
	Edith Starrett Green (D-OR)	
	Martha Wright Griffiths (D-MI)	
	Julia Butler Hansen (D-WA)	
	Maude Elizabeth Kee (D-WV)	
	Edna Flannery Kelly (D-NY)	
	Catherine Dean May (R-WA)	
	Gracie Bowers Pfost (D-ID)	
	Edith Nourse Rogers (R-MA)	
	Edna Oakes Simpson (R-IL)	
	Katharine Price St. George (R-NY)	
	Leonor Kretzer Sullivan (D-MO)	
	Jessica McCullough Weis (R-NY)	
87th (1961–1963)	Iris Faircloth Blitch (D-GA)	Maurine Neuberger (D-OR)
	Frances Payne Bolton (R-OH)	Margaret Chase Smith (R-ME)
	Marguerite Stitt Church (R-IL)	

CONGRESS	HOUSE	SENATE
87th (1961–1963) *continued*	Florence Price Dwyer (R-NJ) Kathryn Elizabeth Granahan (D-PA) Edith Starrett Green (D-OR) Martha Wright Griffiths (D-MI) Julia Butler Hansen (D-WA) Maude Elizabeth Kee (D-WV) Edna Flannery Kelly (D-NY) Catherine Dean May (R-WA) Catherine Dorris Norrell (D-AR) Gracie Bowers Pfost (D-ID) Louise Goff Reece (R-TN) Corinne Boyd Riley (D-SC) Katharine Price St. George (R-NY) Leonor Kretzer Sullivan (D-MO) Jessica McCullough Weis (R-NY)	
88th (1963–1965)	Irene Bailey Baker (R-TN) Frances Payne Bolton (R-OH) Florence Price Dwyer (R-NJ) Edith Starrett Green (D-OR) Martha Wright Griffiths (D-MI) Julia Butler Hansen (D-WA) Maude Elizabeth Kee (D-WV) Edna Flannery Kelly (D-NY) Catherine Dean May (R-WA) Charlotte Thompson Reid (R-IL) Katharine Price St. George (R-NY) Leonor Kretzer Sullivan (D-MO)	Maurine Neuberger (D-OR) Margaret Chase Smith (R-ME)
89th (1965–1967)	Frances Payne Bolton (R-OH) Florence Price Dwyer (R-NJ) Edith Starrett Green (D-OR) Martha Wright Griffiths (D-MI) Julia Butler Hansen (D-WA) Edna Flannery Kelly (D-NY) Catherine Dean May (R-WA) Patsy Takemoto Mink (D-HI) Charlotte Thompson Reid (R-IL) Leonor Kretzer Sullivan (D-MO) Lera Millard Thomas (D-TX)	Maurine Neuberger (D-OR) Margaret Chase Smith (R-ME)
90th (1967–1969)	Frances Payne Bolton (R-OH) Florence Price Dwyer (R-NJ) Edith Starrett Green (D-OR) Martha Wright Griffiths (D-MI) Julia Butler Hansen (D-WA) Margaret M. Heckler (R-MA) Edna Flannery Kelly (D-NY) Catherine Dean May (R-WA) Patsy Takemoto Mink (D-HI)	Margaret Chase Smith (R-ME)

CONGRESS	HOUSE	SENATE
90th (1967–1969) *continued*	Charlotte Thompson Reid (R-IL) Leonor Kretzer Sullivan (D-MO)	
91st (1969–1971)	Shirley Anita Chisholm (D-NY) Florence Price Dwyer (R-NJ) Edith Starrett Green (D-OR) Martha Wright Griffiths (D-MI) Julia Butler Hansen (D-WA) Margaret M. Heckler (R-MA) Catherine Dean May (R-WA) Patsy Takemoto Mink (D-HI) Charlotte Thompson Reid (R-IL) Leonor Kretzer Sullivan (D-MO)	Margaret Chase Smith (R-ME)
92nd (1971–1973)	Bella Savitzky Abzug (D-NY) Elizabeth Andrews (D-AL) Shirley Anita Chisholm (D-NY) Florence Price Dwyer (R-NJ) Ella Tambussi Grasso (D-CT) Edith Starrett Green (D-OR) Martha Wright Griffiths (D-MI) Julia Butler Hansen (D-WA) Margaret M. Heckler (R-MA) Louise Day Hicks (D-MA) Patsy Takemoto Mink (D-HI) Charlotte Thompson Reid (R-IL) Leonor Kretzer Sullivan (D-MO)	Elaine Edwards (D-LA) Margaret Chase Smith (R-ME)
93rd (1973–1975)	Bella Savitzky Abzug (D-NY) Corinne "Lindy" Boggs (D-LA) Yvonne Brathwaite Burke (D-CA) Shirley Anita Chisholm (D-NY) Cardiss Collins (D-IL) Ella Tambussi Grasso (D-CT) Edith Starrett Green (D-OR) Martha Wright Griffiths (D-MI) Julia Butler Hansen (D-WA) Margaret M. Heckler (R-MA) Marjorie Sewell Holt (R-MD) Elizabeth Holtzman (D-NY) Barbara Charline Jordan (D-TX) Patsy Takemoto Mink (D-HI) Patricia Scott Schroeder (D-CO) Leonor Kretzer Sullivan (D-MO)	N/A
94th (1975–1977)	Bella Savitzky Abzug (D-NY) Corinne "Lindy" Boggs (D-LA) Yvonne Brathwaite Burke (D-CA) Shirley Anita Chisholm (D-NY) Cardiss Collins (D-IL)	N/A

CONGRESS	HOUSE	SENATE
94th (1975–1977) *continued*	Millicent Hammond Fenwick (R-NJ)	
	Margaret M. Heckler (R-MA)	
	Marjorie Sewell Holt (R-MD)	
	Elizabeth Holtzman (D-NY)	
	Barbara Charline Jordan (D-TX)	
	Martha Elizabeth Keys (D-KS)	
	Marilyn Laird Lloyd (D-TN)	
	Helen Stevenson Meyner (D-NJ)	
	Patsy Takemoto Mink (D-HI)	
	Shirley Neil Pettis (R-CA)	
	Patricia Scott Schroeder (D-CO)	
	Virginia Dodd Smith (R-NE)	
	Gladys Noon Spellman (D-MD)	
	Leonor Kretzer Sullivan (D-MO)	
95th (1977–1979)	Corinne "Lindy" Boggs (D-LA)	Maryon Allen (D-AL)
	Yvonne Brathwaite Burke (D-CA)	Muriel Humphrey (D-MN)
	Shirley Anita Chisholm (D-NY)	Nancy Landon Kassebaum (R-KS)
	Cardiss Collins (D-IL)	
	Millicent Hammond Fenwick (R-NJ)	
	Margaret M. Heckler (R-MA)	
	Marjorie Sewell Holt (R-MD)	
	Elizabeth Holtzman (D-NY)	
	Barbara Charline Jordan (D-TX)	
	Martha Elizabeth Keys (D-KS)	
	Marilyn Laird Lloyd (D-TN)	
	Helen Stevenson Meyner (D-NJ)	
	Barbara Mikulski (D-MD)	
	Mary Rose Oakar (D-OH)	
	Shirley Pettis (R-CA)	
	Patricia Scott Schroeder (D-CO)	
	Virginia Dodd Smith (R-NE)	
	Gladys Noon Spellman (D-MD)	
96th (1979–1981)	Corinne "Lindy" Boggs (D-LA)	Paula Hawkins (R-FL)
	Marilyn Lloyd Bouquard (D-TN)	Nancy Landon Kassebaum (R-KS)
	Beverly Butcher Byron (D-MD)	
	Shirley Anita Chisholm (D-NY)	
	Cardiss Collins (D-IL)	
	Millicent Hammond Fenwick (R-NJ)	
	Geraldine Ann Ferraro (D-NY)	
	Margaret M. Heckler (R-MA)	
	Marjorie Sewell Holt (R-MD)	
	Elizabeth Holtzman (D-NY)	
	Barbara Mikulski (D-MD)	
	Mary Rose Oakar (D-OH)	
	Patricia Scott Schroeder (D-CO)	
	Virginia Dodd Smith (R-NE)	
	Olympia Jean Snowe (R-ME)	
	Gladys Noon Spellman (D-MD)	

CONGRESS	HOUSE	SENATE
97th (1981–1983)	Jean Spencer Ashbrook (R-OH) Corinne "Lindy" Boggs (D-LA) Marilyn Lloyd Bouquard (D-TN) Beverly Butcher Byron (D-MD) Shirley Anita Chisholm (D-NY) Cardiss Collins (D-IL) Millicent Hammond Fenwick (R-NJ) Geraldine Ann Ferraro (D-NY) Bobbi Fiedler (R-CA) Katie Hall (D-IN) Margaret M. Heckler (R-MA) Marjorie Sewell Holt (R-MD) Barbara Bailey Kennelly (D-CT) Lynn Morley Martin (R-IL) Barbara Mikulski (D-MD) Mary Rose Oakar (D-OH) Margaret Scafati Roukema (R-NJ) Claudine Schneider (R-RI) Patricia Scott Schroeder (D-CO) Virginia Dodd Smith (R-NE) Olympia Jean Snowe (R-ME)	Paula Hawkins (R-FL) Nancy Landon Kassebaum (R-KS)
98th (1983–1985)	Corinne "Lindy" Boggs (D-LA) Barbara Boxer (D-CA) Sala Burton (D-CA) Beverly Butcher Byron (D-MD) Cardiss Collins (D-IL) Geraldine Ann Ferraro (D-NY) Bobbi Fiedler (R-CA) Katie Hall (D-IN) Marjorie Sewell Holt (R-MD) Nancy Johnson (R-CT) Marcy Kaptur (D-OH) Barbara Bailey Kennelly (D-CT) Marilyn Lloyd (D-TN) Lynn Morley Martin (R-IL) Barbara Mikulski (D-MD) Mary Rose Oakar (D-OH) Margaret Scafati Roukema (R-NJ) Claudine Schneider (R-RI) Patricia Scott Schroeder (D-CO) Virginia Smith (R-NE) Olympia Jean Snowe (R-ME) Barbara Vucanovich (R-NV)	Paula Hawkins (R-FL) Nancy Landon Kassebaum (R-KS)
99th (1985–1987)	Helen Delich Bentley (R-MD) Corinne "Lindy" Boggs (D-LA) Barbara Boxer (D-CA) Sala Burton (D-CA)	Paula Hawkins (R-FL) Nancy Landon Kassebaum (R-KS)

99th (1985–1987) *continued*	Beverly Butcher Byron (D-MD) Cardiss Collins (D-IL) Bobbi Fiedler (R-CA) Marjorie Sewell Holt (R-MD) Nancy Johnson (R-CT) Marcy Kaptur (D-OH) Barbara Bailey Kennelly (D-CT) Marilyn Lloyd (D-TN) Catherine S. Long (D-LA) Lynn Morley Martin (R-IL) Jan Meyers (R-KS) Barbara Mikulski (D-MD) Mary Rose Oakar (D-OH) Margaret Scafati Roukema (R-NJ) Claudine Schneider (R-RI) Patricia Scott Schroeder (D-CO) Virginia Smith (R-NE) Olympia Jean Snowe (R-ME) Barbara Vucanovich (R-NV)	
100th (1987–1989)	Helen Delich Bentley (R-MD) Corinne "Lindy" Boggs (D-LA) Barbara Boxer (D-CA) Sala Burton (D-CA) Beverly Butcher Byron (D-MD) Cardiss Collins (D-IL) Nancy Johnson (R-CT) Marcy Kaptur (D-OH) Barbara Bailey Kennelly (D-CT) Marilyn Lloyd (D-TN) Lynn Morley Martin (R-IL) Jan Meyers (R-KS) Constance Morella (D-MD) Mary Rose Oakar (D-OH) Elizabeth Patterson (D-SC) Nancy Pelosi (D-CA) Margaret Scafati Roukema (R-NJ) Patricia Saiki (R-HI) Claudine Schneider (R-RI) Patricia Scott Schroeder (D-CO) Louise Slaughter (D-NY) Virginia Smith (R-NE) Olympia Jean Snowe (R-ME) Barbara Vucanovich (R-NV)	Nancy L. Kassebaum (R-KS) Barbara Ann Mikulski (D-MD)
101st (1989–1991)	Helen Delich Bentley (R-MD) Corinne "Lindy" Boggs (D-LA) Barbara Boxer (D-CA) Beverly Butcher Byron (D-MD) Cardiss Collins (D-IL)	Nancy L. Kassebaum (R-KS) Barbara Ann Mikulski (D-MD)

CONGRESS	HOUSE	SENATE
101st (1989–1991) *continued*	Nancy Johnson (R-CT) Marcy Kaptur (D-OH) Barbara Bailey Kennelly (D-CT) Marilyn Lloyd (D-TN) Jill Long (D-IN) Nita Lowey (D-NY) Lynn Morley Martin (R-IL) Jan Meyers (R-KS) Patsy Mink (D-HI) Susan Molinari (R-NY) Constance Morella (D-MD) Mary Rose Oakar (D-OH) Elizabeth Patterson (D-SC) Nancy Pelosi (D-CA) Ileana Ros-Lehtinen (R-FL) Margaret Scafati Roukema (R-NJ) Patricia Saiki (R-HI) Claudine Schneider (R-RI) Patricia Scott Schroeder (D-CO) Louise Slaughter (D-NY) Virginia Smith (R-NE) Olympia Jean Snowe (R-ME) Jolene Unsoeld (D-WA) Barbara Vucanovich (R-NV)	
102nd (1991–1993)	Helen Delich Bentley (R-MD) Barbara Boxer (D-CA) Beverly Butcher Byron (D-MD) Eva Clayton (D-NC) Barbara-Rose Collins (D-MI) Cardiss Collins (D-IL) Rosa L. DeLauro (D-CT) Joan Kelly Horn (D-MO) Nancy Johnson (R-CT) Marcy Kaptur (D-OH) Barbara Bailey Kennelly (D-CT) Marilyn Lloyd (D-TN) Jill Long (D-IN) Nita Lowey (D-NY) Jan Meyers (R-KS) Patsy Mink (D-HI) Susan Molinari (R-NY) Constance Morella (D-MD) Eleanor Holmes Norton (D-DC) Mary Rose Oakar (D-OH) Elizabeth Patterson (D-SC) Nancy Pelosi (D-CA) Ileana Ros-Lehtinen (R-FL) Margaret Scafati Roukema (R-NJ)	Jocelyn Burdick (D-ND) Dianne Feinstein (D-CA) Nancy L. Kassebaum (R-KS) Barbara Ann Mikulski (D-MD)

CONGRESS	HOUSE	SENATE
102nd (1991–1993) *continued*	Patricia Scott Schroeder (D-CO)	
	Louise Slaughter (D-NY)	
	Olympia Jean Snowe (R-ME)	
	Jolene Unsoeld (D-WA)	
	Barbara Vucanovich (R-NV)	
	Maxine Waters (D-CA)	
103rd (1993–1995)	Helen Delich Bentley (R-MD)	Barbara Boxer (D-CA)
	Corrine Brown (D-FL)	Dianne Feinstein (D-CA)
	Leslie Byrne (D-VA)	Kathryn Ann Bailey Hutchison (R-TX)
	Maria Cantwell (D-WA)	Nancy L. Kassebaum (R-KS)
	Eva Clayton (D-NC)	Barbara Ann Mikulski (D-MD)
	Barbara-Rose Collins (D-MI)	Carol Moseley-Braun (D-IL)
	Cardiss Collins (D-IL)	Patty Murray (D-WA)
	Pat Danner (D-MO)	
	Rosa L. DeLauro (D-CT)	
	Jennifer Dunn (R-WA)	
	Karan English (D-AZ)	
	Anna G. Eshoo (D-CA)	
	Tillie Fowler (R-FL)	
	Elizabeth Furse (D-OR)	
	Jane Harman (D-CA)	
	Eddie Bernice Johnson (D-TX)	
	Nancy Johnson (R-CT)	
	Marcy Kaptur (D-OH)	
	Barbara Bailey Kennelly (D-CT)	
	Blanche Lambert (D-AR)	
	Marilyn Lloyd (D-TN)	
	Jill Long (D-IN)	
	Nita Lowey (D-NY)	
	Carolyn B. Maloney (D-NY)	
	Marjorie Margolies-Mezvinsky (D-PA)	
	Cynthia McKinney (D-GA)	
	Carrie P. Meek (D-FL)	
	Jan Meyers (R-KS)	
	Patsy Mink (D-HI)	
	Susan Molinari (R-NY)	
	Constance Morella (D-MD)	
	Eleanor Holmes Norton (D-DC)	
	Nancy Pelosi (D-CA)	
	Deborah Pryce (R-OH)	
	Ileana Ros-Lehtinen (R-FL)	
	Margaret Scafati Roukema (R-NJ)	
	Lucille Roybal-Allard (D-CA)	
	Lynn Schenk (D-CA)	
	Patricia Scott Schroeder (D-CO)	
	Karen Shepherd (D-UT)	
	Louise Slaughter (D-NY)	

CONGRESS	HOUSE	SENATE
103rd (1993–1995) *continued*	Olympia Jean Snowe (R-ME)	
	Karen Thurman (D-FL)	
	Jolene Unsoeld (D-WA)	
	Nydia M. Velázquez (D-NY)	
	Barbara Vucanovich (R-NV)	
	Maxine Waters (D-CA)	
	Lynn Woolsey (D-CA)	
104th (1995–1997)	Corrine Brown (D-FL)	Barbara Boxer (D-CA)
	Helen Chenoweth (R-ID)	Dianne Feinstein (D-CA)
	Eva Clayton (D-NC)	Sheila Frahm (R-KS)
	Barbara-Rose Collins (D-MI)	Kathryn Ann Bailey Hutchison (R-TX)
	Cardiss Collins (D-IL)	Nancy L. Kassebaum (R-KS)
	Barbara Cubin (R-WY)	Barbara Ann Mikulski (D-MD)
	Pat Danner (D-MO)	Carol Moseley-Braun (D-IL)
	Rosa L. DeLauro (D-CT)	Patty Murray (D-WA)
	Jennifer Dunn (R-WA)	Olympia Jean Snowe (R-ME)
	Jo Ann Emerson (R-MO)	
	Anna G. Eshoo (D-CA)	
	Tillie Fowler (R-FL)	
	Elizabeth Furse (D-OR)	
	Jane Harman (D-CA)	
	Sheila Jackson-Lee (D-TX)	
	Eddie Bernice Johnson (D-TX)	
	Nancy Johnson (R-CT)	
	Marcy Kaptur (D-OH)	
	Sue Kelly (R-NY)	
	Barbara Bailey Kennelly (D-CT)	
	Blanche Lambert Lincoln (D-AR)	
	Zoe Lofgren (D-CA)	
	Nita Lowey (D-NY)	
	Carolyn B. Maloney (D-NY)	
	Karen McCarthy (D-KS)	
	Cynthia McKinney (D-GA)	
	Carrie P. Meek (D-FL)	
	Jan Meyers (R-KS)	
	Juanita Millender-McDonald (D-CA)	
	Patsy Mink (D-HI)	
	Susan Molinari (R-NY)	
	Constance Morella (D-MD)	
	Sue Myrick (R-NC)	
	Eleanor Holmes Norton (D-DC)	
	Nancy Pelosi (D-CA)	
	Deborah Pryce (R-OH)	
	Lynn Rivers (D-MI)	
	Ileana Ros-Lehtinen (R-FL)	
	Margaret Scafati Roukema (R-NJ)	
	Lucille Roybal-Allard (D-CA)	
	Patricia Scott Schroeder (D-CO)	

CONGRESS	HOUSE	SENATE
104th (1995–1997) *continued*	Andrea Seastrand (R-CA) Louise Slaughter (D-NY) Linda Smith (R-WA) Karen Thurman (D-FL) Nydia M. Velázquez (D-NY) Barbara Vucanovich (R-NV) Enid Greene Waldholtz (R-UT) Maxine Waters (D-CA) Lynn Woolsey (D-CA)	
105th (1997–1999)	Mary Bono (R-CA) Corrine Brown (D-FL) Lois Capps (D-CA) Julia Carson (D-IN) Helen Chenoweth (R-ID) Donna Christian-Green (D-VI) Eva Clayton (D-NC) Barbara Cubin (R-WY) Pat Danner (D-MO) Diana DeGette (D-CO) Rosa L. DeLauro (D-CT) Jennifer Dunn (R-WA) Jo Ann Emerson (R-MO) Anna G. Eshoo (D-CA) Tillie Fowler (R-FL) Elizabeth Furse (D-OR) Kay Granger (R-TX) Jane Harman (D-CA) Darlene Hooley (D-OR) Sheila Jackson-Lee (D-TX) Eddie Bernice Johnson (D-TX) Nancy Johnson (R-CT) Marcy Kaptur (D-OH) Sue Kelly (R-NY) Barbara Bailey Kennelly (D-CT) Carolyn Cheeks Kilpatrick (D-MI) Barbara Lee (D-CA) Zoe Lofgren (D-CA) Nita Lowey (D-NY) Carolyn B. Maloney (D-NY) Carolyn McCarthy (D-NY) Karen McCarthy (D-KS) Cynthia McKinney (D-GA) Carrie P. Meek (D-FL) Juanita Millender-McDonald (D-CA) Patsy Mink (D-HI) Susan Molinari (R-NY)	Barbara Boxer (D-CA) Susan Collins (R-ME) Dianne Feinstein (D-CA) Kathryn Ann Bailey Hutchison (R-TX) Mary Landrieu (D-LA) Barbara Ann Mikulski (D-MD) Carol Moseley-Braun (D-IL) Patty Murray (D-WA) Olympia Jean Snowe (R-ME)

CONGRESS	HOUSE	SENATE
105th (1997–1999) *continued*	Constance Morella (D-MD)	
	Sue Myrick (R-NC)	
	Anne M. Northup (R-KY)	
	Eleanor Holmes Norton (D-DC)	
	Nancy Pelosi (D-CA)	
	Deborah Pryce (R-OH)	
	Lynn Rivers (D-MI)	
	Ileana Ros-Lehtinen (R-FL)	
	Margaret Scafati Roukema (R-NJ)	
	Lucille Roybal-Allard (D-CA)	
	Loretta Sanchez (D-CA)	
	Louise Slaughter (D-NY)	
	Linda Smith (R-WA)	
	Deborah Stabenow (D-MI)	
	Ellen Tauscher (D-CA)	
	Karen Thurman (D-FL)	
	Nydia M. Velázquez (D-NY)	
	Maxine Waters (D-CA)	
	Heather Wilson (R-NM)	
	Lynn Woolsey (D-CA)	
106th (1999–2001)	Tammy Baldwin (D-WI)	Barbara Boxer (D-CA)
	Shelley Berkley (D-NV)	Susan Collins (R-ME)
	Judith Borg Biggert (R-IL)	Dianne Feinstein (D-CA)
	Mary Bono (R-CA)	Kathryn Ann Bailey Hutchison (R-TX)
	Corrine Brown (D-FL)	Mary Landrieu (D-LA)
	Lois Capps (D-CA)	Blanche Lambert Lincoln (D-AR)
	Julia Carson (D-IN)	Barbara Ann Mikulski (D-MD)
	Helen Chenoweth-Hage (R-ID)	Patty Murray (D-WA)
	Donna Christensen (D-VI)	Olympia Jean Snowe (R-ME)
	Eva Clayton (D-NC)	
	Barbara Cubin (R-WY)	
	Pat Danner (D-MO)	
	Diana DeGette (D-CO)	
	Rosa L. DeLauro (D-CT)	
	Jennifer Dunn (R-WA)	
	Jo Ann Emerson (R-MO)	
	Anna G. Eshoo (D-CA)	
	Tillie Fowler (R-FL)	
	Kay Granger (R-TX)	
	Darlene Hooley (D-OR)	
	Sheila Jackson-Lee (D-TX)	
	Eddie Bernice Johnson (D-TX)	
	Nancy Johnson (R-CT)	
	Stephanie Tubbs Jones (D-OH)	
	Marcy Kaptur (D-OH)	
	Sue Kelly (R-NY)	
	Carolyn Cheeks Kilpatrick (D-MI)	
	Barbara Lee (D-CA)	

CONGRESS	HOUSE	SENATE
106th (1999–2001) *continued*	Zoe Lofgren (D-CA)	
	Nita Lowey (D-NY)	
	Carolyn B. Maloney (D-NY)	
	Carolyn McCarthy (D-NY)	
	Karen McCarthy (D-KS)	
	Cynthia McKinney (D-GA)	
	Carrie P. Meek (D-FL)	
	Juanita Millender-McDonald (D-CA)	
	Patsy Mink (D-HI)	
	Constance Morella (D-MD)	
	Sue Myrick (R-NC)	
	Grace Napolitano (D-CA)	
	Anne M. Northup (R-KY)	
	Eleanor Holmes Norton (D-DC)	
	Nancy Pelosi (D-CA)	
	Deborah Pryce (R-OH)	
	Lynn Rivers (D-MI)	
	Ileana Ros-Lehtinen (R-FL)	
	Margaret Scafati Roukema (R-NJ)	
	Lucille Roybal-Allard (D-CA)	
	Loretta Sanchez (D-CA)	
	Janice Schakowsky (D-IL)	
	Louise Slaughter (D-NY)	
	Deborah Stabenow (D-MI)	
	Ellen Tauscher (D-CA)	
	Karen Thurman (D-FL)	
	Nydia M. Velázquez (D-NY)	
	Maxine Waters (D-CA)	
	Heather Wilson (R-NM)	
	Lynn Woolsey (D-CA)	
107th (2001–2003)	Tammy Baldwin (D-WI)	Barbara Boxer (D-CA)
	Shelley Berkley (D-NV)	Maria Cantwell (D-WA)
	Judith Borg Biggert (R-IL)	Jean Carnahan (D-MO)
	Mary Bono (R-CA)	Hillary Rodham Clinton (D-NY)
	Corrine Brown (D-FL)	Susan Collins (R-ME)
	Shelly Capito (R-WV)	Dianne Feinstein (D-CA)
	Lois Capps (D-CA)	Kathryn Ann Bailey Hutchison (R-TX)
	Julia Carson (D-IN)	Mary Landrieu (D-LA)
	Donna Christensen (D-VI)	Blanche Lambert Lincoln (D-AR)
	Eva Clayton (D-NC)	Barbara Ann Mikulski (D-MD)
	Barbara Cubin (R-WY)	Lisa Murkowski (R-AK)
	Jo Ann Davis (R-VA)	Patty Murray (D-WA)
	Susan Davis (D-CA)	Olympia Jean Snowe (R-ME)
	Diana DeGette (D-CO)	Deborah Stabenow (D-MI)
	Rosa L. DeLauro (D-CT)	
	Jennifer Dunn (R-WA)	
	Jo Ann Emerson (R-MO)	
	Anna G. Eshoo (D-CA)	

CONGRESS	HOUSE	SENATE
107th (2001–2003) *continued*	Kay Granger (R-TX)	
	Jane Harman (D-CA)	
	Melissa Hart (R-PA)	
	Darlene Hooley (D-OR)	
	Sheila Jackson-Lee (D-TX)	
	Eddie Bernice Johnson (D-TX)	
	Nancy Johnson (R-CT)	
	Stephanie Tubbs Jones (D-OH)	
	Marcy Kaptur (D-OH)	
	Sue Kelly (R-NY)	
	Carolyn Cheeks Kilpatrick (D-MI)	
	Barbara Lee (D-CA)	
	Zoe Lofgren (D-CA)	
	Nita Lowey (D-NY)	
	Carolyn B. Maloney (D-NY)	
	Carolyn McCarthy (D-NY)	
	Karen McCarthy (D-KS)	
	Betty McCollum (D-MN)	
	Cynthia McKinney (D-GA)	
	Carrie P. Meek (D-FL)	
	Juanita Millender-McDonald (D-CA)	
	Patsy Mink (D-HI)	
	Constance Morella (D-MD)	
	Sue Myrick (R-NC)	
	Grace Napolitano (D-CA)	
	Anne M. Northup (R-KY)	
	Eleanor Holmes Norton (D-DC)	
	Nancy Pelosi (D-CA)	
	Deborah Pryce (R-OH)	
	Lynn Rivers (D-MI)	
	Ileana Ros-Lehtinen (R-FL)	
	Margaret Scafati Roukema (R-NJ)	
	Lucille Roybal-Allard (D-CA)	
	Loretta Sanchez (D-CA)	
	Janice Schakowsky (D-IL)	
	Louise Slaughter (D-NY)	
	Hilda Solis (D-CA)	
	Ellen Tauscher (D-CA)	
	Karen Thurman (D-FL)	
	Nydia M. Velázquez (D-NY)	
	Maxine Waters (D-CA)	
	Diane Watson (D-CA)	
	Heather Wilson (R-NM)	
	Lynn Woolsey (D-CA)	
108th (2003–2005)	Tammy Baldwin (D-WI)	Barbara Boxer (D-CA)
	Shelley Berkley (D-NV)	Maria Cantwell (D-WA)
	Judith Borg Biggert (R-IL)	Hillary Rodham Clinton (D-NY)
	Marsha Blackburn (R-TN)	Susan Collins (R-ME)

CONGRESS	HOUSE	SENATE
108th (2003–2005) *continued*	Mary Bono (R-CA)	Elizabeth Dole (D-NC)
	Madeleine Bordallo (D-GU)	Dianne Feinstein (D-CA)
	Corrine Brown (D-FL)	Kathryn Ann Bailey Hutchison (R-TX)
	Virginia Brown-Waite (R-FL)	Mary Landrieu (D-LA)
	Shelly Capito (R-WV)	Blanche Lambert Lincoln (D-AR)
	Lois Capps (D-CA)	Barbara Ann Mikulski (D-MD)
	Julia Carson (D-IN)	Lisa Murkowski (R-AK)
	Donna Christensen (D-VI)	Patty Murray (D-WA)
	Barbara Cubin (R-WY)	Olympia Jean Snowe (R-ME)
	Jo Ann Davis (R-VA)	Deborah Stabenow (D-MI)
	Susan Davis (D-CA)	
	Diana DeGette (D-CO)	
	Rosa L. DeLauro (D-CT)	
	Jennifer Dunn (R-WA)	
	Jo Ann Emerson (R-MO)	
	Anna G. Eshoo (D-CA)	
	Kay Granger (R-TX)	
	Jane Harman (D-CA)	
	Katherine Harris (R-FL)	
	Melissa Hart (R-PA)	
	Stephanie Herseth (D-SD)	
	Darlene Hooley (D-OR)	
	Sheila Jackson-Lee (D-TX)	
	Eddie Bernice Johnson (D-TX)	
	Nancy Johnson (R-CT)	
	Stephanie Tubbs Jones (D-OH)	
	Marcy Kaptur (D-OH)	
	Sue Kelly (R-NY)	
	Carolyn Cheeks Kilpatrick (D-MI)	
	Barbara Lee (D-CA)	
	Zoe Lofgren (D-CA)	
	Nita Lowey (D-NY)	
	Denise Majette (D-GA)	
	Carolyn B. Maloney (D-NY)	
	Carolyn McCarthy (D-NY)	
	Karen McCarthy (D-KS)	
	Betty McCollum (D-MN)	
	Juanita Millender-McDonald (D-CA)	
	Candice Miller (R-MI)	
	Marilyn Musgrave (R-CO)	
	Sue Myrick (R-NC)	
	Grace Napolitano (D-CA)	
	Anne M. Northup (R-KY)	
	Eleanor Holmes Norton (D-DC)	
	Nancy Pelosi (D-CA)	
	Deborah Pryce (R-OH)	
	Ileana Ros-Lehtinen (R-FL)	
	Lucille Roybal-Allard (D-CA)	

CONGRESS	HOUSE	SENATE
108th (2003–2005) continued	Linda T. Sánchez (D-CA)	
	Loretta Sanchez (D-CA)	
	Janice Schakowsky (D-IL)	
	Louise Slaughter (D-NY)	
	Hilda Solis (D-CA)	
	Ellen Tauscher (D-CA)	
	Nydia M. Velázquez (D-NY)	
	Maxine Waters (D-CA)	
	Diane Watson (D-CA)	
	Heather Wilson (R-NM)	
	Lynn Woolsey (D-CA)	
109th (2005–2007)	Tammy Baldwin (D-WI)	Barbara Boxer (D-CA)
	Melissa Bean (D-IL)	Maria Cantwell (D-WA)
	Shelley Berkley (D-NV)	Hillary Rodham Clinton (D-NY)
	Judith Borg Biggert (R-IL)	Susan Collins (R-ME)
	Marsha Blackburn (R-TN)	Elizabeth Dole (D-NC)
	Mary Bono (R-CA)	Dianne Feinstein (D-CA)
	Madeleine Bordallo (D-GU)	Kathryn Ann Bailey Hutchison (R-TX)
	Corrine Brown (D-FL)	Mary Landrieu (D-LA)
	Virginia Brown-Waite (R-FL)	Blanche Lambert Lincoln (D-AR)
	Shelly Capito (R-WV)	Barbara Ann Mikulski (D-MD)
	Lois Capps (D-CA)	Lisa Murkowski (R-AK)
	Julia Carson (D-IN)	Patty Murray (D-WA)
	Donna Christensen (D-VI)	Olympia Jean Snowe (R-ME)
	Barbara Cubin (R-WY)	Deborah Stabenow (D-MI)
	Jo Ann Davis (R-VA)	
	Susan Davis (D-CA)	
	Diana DeGette (D-CO)	
	Rosa L. DeLauro (D-CT)	
	Thelma Drake (R-VA)	
	Jo Ann Emerson (R-MO)	
	Anna G. Eshoo (D-CA)	
	Virginia Foxx (R-NC)	
	Kay Granger (R-TX)	
	Jane Harman (D-CA)	
	Katherine Harris (R-FL)	
	Melissa Hart (R-PA)	
	Stephanie Herseth (D-SD)	
	Darlene Hooley (D-OR)	
	Sheila Jackson-Lee (D-TX)	
	Eddie Bernice Johnson (D-TX)	
	Nancy Johnson (R-CT)	
	Stephanie Tubbs Jones (D-OH)	
	Marcy Kaptur (D-OH)	
	Sue Kelly (R-NY)	
	Carolyn Cheeks Kilpatrick (D-MI)	
	Barbara Lee (D-CA)	
	Zoe Lofgren (D-CA)	

109th (2005–2007) *continued*

Nita Lowey (D-NY)
Carolyn B. Maloney (D-NY)
Doris Matsui (D-CA)
Carolyn McCarthy (D-NY)
Betty McCollum (D-MN)
Cynthia McKinney (D-GA)
Cathy McMorris (R-WA)
Juanita Millender-McDonald (D-CA)
Candice Miller (R-MI)
Gwen Moore (D-WI)
Marilyn Musgrave (R-CO)
Sue Myrick (R-NC)
Grace Napolitano (D-CA)
Anne M. Northup (R-KY)
Eleanor Holmes Norton (D-DC)
Nancy Pelosi (D-CA)
Deborah Pryce (R-OH)
Ileana Ros-Lehtinen (R-FL)
Lucille Roybal-Allard (D-CA)
Linda T. Sánchez (D-CA)
Loretta Sanchez (D-CA)
Janice Schakowsky (D-IL)
Jean Schmidt (R-OH)
Allyson Schwartz (D-PA)
Louise Slaughter (D-NY)
Hilda Solis (D-CA)
Ellen Tauscher (D-CA)
Nydia M. Velázquez (D-NY)
Debbie Wasserman Schultz (D-FL)
Maxine Waters (D-CA)
Diane Watson (D-CA)
Heather Wilson (R-NM)
Lynn Woolsey (D-CA)

Women Representatives and Senators by State and Territory

States are listed in descending order according to the number of women that each has sent to Congress.

STATE OR TERRITORY	MEMBER'S NAME[a] (IN CHRONOLOGICAL ORDER)	YEAR MEMBER TOOK OFFICE
California (30)	Mae Ella Nolan	1923
	Florence Kahn	1925
	Helen G. Douglas	1945
	Yvonne Burke	1973
	Shirley Pettis	1975
	Bobbi Fiedler	1981
	Barbara Boxer[b]	1983
	Sala Burton	1983
	Nancy Pelosi	1987
	Maxine Waters	1991
	Dianne Feinstein[c]	1992
	Anna Eshoo	1993
	Jane Harman	1993
	Lucille Roybal-Allard	1993
	Lynn Schenck	1993
	Lynn Woolsey	1993
	Zoe Lofgren	1995
	Andrea Seastrand	1995
	Juanita Millender-McDonald	1996
	Loretta Sanchez	1997
	Ellen Tauscher	1997
	Lois Capps	1998
	Mary Bono	1998
	Barbara Lee	1998
	Grace Napolitano	1999
	Susan Davis	2001
	Hilda Solis	2001
	Diane Watson	2001
	Linda Sánchez	2003
	Doris Matsui	2005
New York (19)	Ruth Pratt	1929
	Marian Clarke	1933
	Caroline O'Day	1935
	Winifred Stanley	1943
	Katharine St. George	1947
	Edna Kelly	1949
	Jessica Weis	1959
	Shirley Chisholm	1969
	Bella Abzug	1971
	Elizabeth Holtzman	1973
	Geraldine Ferraro	1977
	Louise Slaughter	1987
	Nita Lowey	1989
	Susan Molinari	1990
	Carolyn Maloney	1993
	Nydia Velazquez	1993
	Sue Kelly	1995
	Carolyn McCarthy	1997
	Hillary Clinton[c]	2001

STATE OR TERRITORY	MEMBER'S NAME[a] (IN CHRONOLOGICAL ORDER)	YEAR MEMBER TOOK OFFICE
Illinois (13)	Winnifred Huck	1922
	Ruth Hanna McCormick	1929
	Jessie Sumner	1939
	Emily Taft Douglas	1945
	Marguerite Church	1951
	Edna Oakes Simpson	1959
	Charlotte Reid	1963
	Cardiss Collins	1973
	Lynn Martin	1981
	Carol Moseley-Braun[c]	1993
	Judith Biggert	1999
	Janice Schakowsky	1999
	Melissa Bean	2005
Florida (10)	*Ruth Bryan Owen*	1929
	Paula Hawkins[c]	1981
	Ileana Ros-Lehtinen	1989
	Corrine Brown	1993
	Tillie Fowler	1993
	Carrie Meek	1993
	Karen Thurman	1993
	Virginia Brown-Waite	2003
	Katherine Harris	2003
	Debbie Wasserman Schultz	2005
Washington (8)	Catherine Dean May	1959
	Julia Butler Hansen	1960
	Jolene Unsoeld	1989
	Maria Cantwell	1993
	Jennifer Dunn	1993
	Patty Murray[c]	1993
	Linda Smith	1995
	Cathy Anne McMorris	2005
Maryland (7)	*Katharine Byron*	1941
	Marjorie Holt	1973
	Gladys Spellman	1975
	Barbara Mikulski[b]	1977
	Beverley Byron	1979
	Helen Delich Bentley	1985
	Constance Morella	1987
Michigan (7)	Ruth Thompson	1951
	Martha Griffiths	1955
	Barbara Rose-Collins	1991
	Lynn Rivers	1995
	Carolyn Kilpatrick	1997
	Debbie Stabenow[b]	1997
	Candice Miller	2003

STATE OR TERRITORY	MEMBER'S NAME[a] (IN CHRONOLOGICAL ORDER)	YEAR MEMBER TOOK OFFICE
Ohio (7)	Frances Payne Bolton	1940
	Mary Rose Oakar	1977
	Jean Ashbrook	1982
	Marcy Kaptur	1983
	Deborah Pryce	1993
	Stephanie Tubbs Jones	1999
	Jean Schmidt	2005
Connecticut (6)	Clare Boothe Luce	1943
	Chase Going Woodhouse	1945
	Ella Grasso	1971
	Barbara Kennelly	1982
	Nancy L. Johnson	1983
	Rosa DeLauro	1991
Georgia (6)	*Rebecca Latimer Felton*[c]	1922
	Florence Gibbs	1940
	Helen Douglas Mankin	1946
	Iris Faircloth Blitch	1955
	Cynthia McKinney	1993
	Denise Majette	2003
Missouri (6)	*Leonor Sullivan*	1953
	Joan Kelly Horn	1991
	Pat Danner	1993
	Karen McCarthy	1995
	Jo Ann Emerson	1996
	Jean Carnahan[c]	2001
Pennsylvania (6)	*Veronica Boland*	1942
	Vera Buchanan	1951
	Kathryn Granahan	1956
	Marjorie Margolies-Mezvinsky	1993
	Melissa Hart	2001
	Allyson Schwartz	2005
Texas (6)	*Lera Thomas*	1966
	Barbara Jordan	1973
	Eddie Bernice Johnson	1993
	Kay Bailey Hutchison[c]	1993
	Shelia Jackson-Lee	1995
	Kay Granger	1997
Arkansas (5)	*Pearl Oldfield*	1929
	Effiegene Wingo	1930
	Hattie Caraway[c]	1931
	Catherine Norrell	1961
	Blanche Lambert Lincoln[b]	1993
Indiana (5)	*Virginia Jenckes*	1933
	Cecil Harden	1949
	Katie Hall	1982
	Jill Long	1989
	Julia Carson	1997

STATE OR TERRITORY	MEMBER'S NAME[a] (IN CHRONOLOGICAL ORDER)	YEAR MEMBER TOOK OFFICE
Kansas (5)	*Kathryn O'Loughlin McCarthy*	1933
	Martha Keys	1975
	Nancy Landon Kassebaum[c]	1978
	Jan Meyers	1985
	Shelia Frahm[c]	1996
Louisiana (5)	*Rose McConnell Long[c]*	1936
	Elaine Edwards[c]	1972
	Corrine "Lindy" Boggs	1973
	Cathy Long	1985
	Mary Landrieu[c]	1997
New Jersey (5)	*Mary Teresa Norton*	1925
	Florence Dwyer	1957
	Millicent Fenwick	1975
	Helen Meyner	1975
	Margaret Roukema	1981
Oregon (5)	*Nan Wood Honeyman*	1937
	Edith Green	1955
	Maurine B. Neuberger[c]	1960
	Elizabeth Furse	1993
	Darlene Hooley	1997
South Carolina (5)	*Elizabeth Gasque*	1938
	Clara McMillan	1939
	Willa Fulmer	1944
	Corrine Boyd Riley	1962
	Elizabeth Patterson	1987
Tennessee (5)	*Willa Eslick*	1932
	Louise Reece	1961
	Irene Baker	1964
	Marilyn Lloyd	1975
	Marsha Blackburn	2003
North Carolina (5)	*Eliza Jane Pratt*	1946
	Eva Clayton	1992
	Sue Myrick	1995
	Elizabeth Dole[c]	2003
	Virginia Ann Foxx	2005
Alabama (3)	*Dixie Bibb Graves[c]*	1937
	Elizabeth Andrews	1972
	Maryon Allen[c]	1978
Colorado (3)	*Patricia Schroeder*	1973
	Diana DeGette	1997
	Marilyn Musgrave	2003
Hawaii (3)	Mary Elizabeth Farrington[d]	1954
	Patsy T. Mink	1965
	Patricia Saiki	1987
Maine (3)	Margaret Chase Smith[b]	1940
	Olympia J. Snowe[b]	1979
	Susan M. Collins[c]	1997

STATE OR TERRITORY	MEMBER'S NAME[a] (IN CHRONOLOGICAL ORDER)	YEAR MEMBER TOOK OFFICE
Massachusetts (3)	Edith Nourse Rogers	1925
	Margaret Heckler	1967
	Louise Day Hicks	1971
Minnesota (3)	*Coya Gjesdal Knutson*	1954
	Muriel Humphrey[c]	1978
	Betty McCollum	2001
Nebraska (3)	Eva Kelly Bowring[c]	1954
	Hazel Abel[c]	1954
	Virginia Smith	1975
South Dakota (3)	Gladys Pyle[c]	1938
	Vera Calahan Bushfield[c]	1948
	Stephanie Herseth	2004
Utah (3)	*Reva Bosone*	1949
	Karen Shepherd	1993
	Enid Greene Waldholtz	1995
Virginia (3)	*Leslie Byrne*	1993
	Jo Ann Davis	2001
	Thelma Drake	2005
Arizona (2)	*Isabella Greenway*	1933
	Karan English	1993
Idaho (2)	*Gracie Bowers Pfost*	1953
	Helen Chenoweth	1995
Kentucky (2)	Katherine G. Langley	1927
	Anne M. Northup	1997
New Mexico (2)	*Georgia Lee Lusk*	1947
	Heather Wilson	1998
Nevada (2)	Barbara Vucanovich	1983
	Shelley Berkley	1999
West Virginia (2)	*Maude Kee*	1951
	Shelley Moore Capito	2001
Wisconsin (2)	*Tammy Baldwin*	1999
	Gwen Moore	2005
Alaska (1)	Lisa Murkowski[c]	2002
District of Columbia (1)	*Eleanor Holmes Norton*[d]	1991
Guam (1)	*Madeleine Bordallo*[d]	2003
Montana (1)	Jeannette Rankin	1917
North Dakota (1)	*Jocelyn Burdick*[c]	1992
Oklahoma (1)	Alice Mary Robertson	1921
Rhode Island (1)	Claudine Schneider	1981
Virgin Islands (1)	*Donna M. Christensen*[d]	1997
Wyoming (1)	Barbara Cubin	1995

[a] Republicans are in roman type, Democrats are in *italics*.
[b] Denotes House and Senate service.
[c] Denotes Senate service.
[d] Denotes Delegate.

Note: Delaware, Iowa, Mississippi, New Hampshire, and Vermont have never elected or appointed a woman to Congress.

Women's Committee Assignments (Standing, Joint, Select) in the U.S. House and Senate, 1917–2006

House Standing Committee	TERM	CONGRESS		TERM	CONGRESS
ACCOUNTS [1881–1946]					
WINGO, EFFIEGENE LOCKE	1930–1933	71st–72nd			
AGRICULTURE [1881–present]					
FARRINGTON, MARY ELIZABETH	1954–1957	83rd–84th	McKINNEY, CYNTHIA	1993–1997	103rd–104th
KNUTSON, COYA GJESDAL	1955–1959	84th–85th	CHENOWETH, HELEN	1995–2001	104th–106th
MAY, CATHERINE DEAN	1959–1971	86th–91st	EMERSON, JO ANN	1997–1999	105th
HECKLER, MARGARET	1975–1981	94th–96th	STABENOW, DEBBIE	1997–2001	105th–106th
LONG, JILL	1989–1995	101st–103rd	MUSGRAVE, MARILYN	2003–	108th–109th
LINCOLN, BLANCHE LAMBERT	1993–1995	103rd	HERSETH, STEPHANIE	2004–	108th–109th
THURMAN, KAREN	1993–1997	103rd–104th	FOXX, VIRGINIA	2005–	109th
CLAYTON, EVA	1993–2003	103rd–107th			
APPROPRIATIONS [1881–present]					
KAHN, FLORENCE PRAG	1933–1937	73rd–74th	BENTLEY, HELEN DELICH	1993–1995	103rd
HANSEN, JULIA BUTLER	1963–1975	88th–93rd	DeLAURO, ROSA	1993–	103rd–109th
REID, CHARLOTTE THOMPSON	1967–1972	90th–92nd	LOWEY, NITA	1993–	103rd–109th
GREEN, EDITH	1973–1975	93rd	MEEK, CARRIE	1993–2003	103rd, 105th–107th
BURKE, YVONNE BRATHWAITE	1975–1979	94th–95th	NORTHUP, ANNE	1997–	105th–109th
SMITH, VIRGINIA	1977–1991	95th–101st	EMERSON, JO ANN	1999–	106th–109th
BOGGS, CORINNE	1977–1991	95th–101st	GRANGER, KAY	1999–	106th–109th
KAPTUR, MARCY	1989–	101st–109th	KILPATRICK, CAROLYN CHEEKS	1999–	106th–109th
VUCANOVICH, BARBARA	1991–1997	102nd–104th	ROYBAL-ALLARD, LUCILLE	1999–	106th–109th
PELOSI, NANCY	1991–2003	102nd–107th			
ARMED SERVICES [1946–1995; 1999–present]					
SMITH, MARGARET CHASE	1947–1949	80th	FOWLER, TILLIE	1993–1995; 1999–2001	103rd 106th
FARRINGTON, MARY ELIZABETH	1953–1957	83rd–84th	SANCHEZ, LORETTA	1999–	106th–109th
ST. GEORGE, KATHARINE PRICE	1957–1961	85th–86th	TAUSCHER, ELLEN	1999–	106th–109th
SCHROEDER, PATRICIA	1973–1995	93rd–103rd	McKINNEY, CYNTHIA	1999–2003; 2005–	106th–107th; 109th
HOLT, MARJORIE	1973–1987	93rd–99th	DAVIS, SUSAN	2001–	107th–109th
BYRON, BEVERLY BUTCHER	1979–1993	96th–102nd	DAVIS, JO ANN	2001–	107th–109th
LLOYD, MARILYN	1982–1995	97th–103rd	WILSON, HEATHER	2001–2005	107th–108th
MARTIN, LYNN	1985–1989	99th–100th	BORDALLO, MADELEINE	2003–	108th–109th
BOXER, BARBARA	1987–1989 1991–1993	100th 102nd	MILLER, CANDICE	2003–	108th–109th
FURSE, ELIZABETH	1993–1995	103rd	DRAKE, THELMA	2005–	109th
HARMAN, JANE	1993–1995	103rd	McMORRIS, CATHY	2005–	109th
BONO, MARY	1999–2001	106th			

BANKING AND CURRENCY
[1865–1975]

PRATT, RUTH SEARS BAKER	1929–1931	71st	SULLIVAN, LEONOR KRETZER	1955–1977	84th–94th
SUMNER, JESSIE	1939–1947	76th–79th	DWYER, FLORENCE PRICE	1959–1973	86th–92nd
WOODHOUSE, CHASE GOING	1945–1947	79th	HECKLER, MARGARET	1969–1975	91st–93rd
	1949–1951	81st			
BUCHANAN, VERA DAERR	1955–1955	84th	BOGGS, CORINNE	1973–1975	93rd
GRIFFITHS, MARTHA WRIGHT	1955–1963	84th–87th			

BANKING, CURRENCY, AND HOUSING [1975–1977]

BOGGS, CORINNE	1973–1976	93rd–94th	SPELLMAN, GLADYS NOON	1975–1977	94th
FENWICK, MILLICENT	1975–1977	94th	SULLIVAN, LEONOR KRETZER	1975–1977	94th

BANKING, FINANCE AND URBAN AFFAIRS [1977–1995]

FENWICK, MILLICENT	1977–1979	95th	SAIKI, PATRICIA	1987–1991	100th–101st
SPELLMAN, GLADYS NOON	1977–1981	95th–96th	WATERS, MAXINE	1991–1995	102nd–103r
OAKAR, MARY ROSE	1977–1993	95th–102nd	MALONEY, CAROLYN	1993–1995	103rd
ROUKEMA, MARGARET	1981–1995	97th–103rd	FURSE, ELIZABETH	1993–1995	103rd
KAPTUR, MARCY	1983–1991	98th–101st	PRYCE, DEBORAH	1993–1995	103rd
PATTERSON, ELIZABETH	1987–1993	100th–102nd	ROYBAL-ALLARD, LUCILLE	1993–1995	103rd
PELOSI, NANCY	1987–1991	100th–101st	VELÁZQUEZ, NYDIA	1993–1995	103rd

BANKING AND FINANCIAL SERVICES [1995–2001]

KELLY, SUE	1995–2001	104th–106th	CARSON, JULIA	1997–2001	105th–106th
MALONEY, CAROLYN	1995–2001	104th–106th	KILPATRICK, CAROLYN CHEEKS	1997–1999	105th
McKINNEY, CYNTHIA	1995–1999	104th–105th	LEE, BARBARA	1997–2001	105th–106th
VELÁZQUEZ, NYDIA	1995–2001	104th–106th	HOOLEY, DARLENE	1997–2001	105th–106th
WATERS, MAXINE	1995–2001	104th–106th	JONES, STEPHANIE TUBBS	1999–2001	106th
ROUKEMA, MARGARET	1995–2001	104th–106th	BIGGERT, JUDY	1999–2001	106th
ROYBAL-ALLARD, LUCILLE	1995–1999	104th–105th	SCHAKOWSKY, JANICE	1999–2001	106th

BUDGET [1974–present]

GRIFFITHS, MARTHA	1974–1974	93rd	MOLINARI, SUSAN	1995–1999	104th–105th
HOLTZMAN, ELIZABETH	1975–1981	94th–96th	MYRICK, SUE	1995–1997	104th
MINK, PATSY TAKEMOTO	1975–1977	94th	RIVERS, LYNN	1995–1999	104th–106th
	1993–1999	103rd–105th			
HOLT, MARJORIE	1976–1981	94th–96th	ROYBAL-ALLARD, LUCILLE	1995–1999	104th–105th
MARTIN, LYNN	1981–1987	97th–99th	CLAYTON, EVA	1997–2003	105th–107th
FIEDLER, BOBBI	1981–1987	97th–99th	GRANGER, KAY	1997–1999	105th
				2001–2003	107th
FERRARO, GERALDINE ANN	1983–1985	98th	BALDWIN, TAMMY	1999–2005	106th–108th
BOXER, BARBARA	1985–1991	99th–101st	HOOLEY, DARLENE	1999–2005	106th–108th
JOHNSON, NANCY	1987–1989	100th	McCARTHY, CAROLYN	2001–2003	107th
KAPTUR, MARCY	1989–1991	101st	MAJETTE, DENISE	2003–2005	108th
BENTLEY, HELEN DELICH	1989–1993	101st–102nd	DeLAURO, ROSA	2003–	108th–109th
SLAUGHTER, LOUISE	1991–1996	102nd–104th	BROWN-WAITE, GINNY	2003–2005	108th
KENNELLY, BARBARA BAILEY	1993–1995	103rd	CAPPS, LOIS	2003–	108th–109th
WOOLSEY, LYNN	1993–1995	103rd–105th	ROS-LEHTINEN, ILEANA	2005–	109th
SNOWE, OLYMPIA	1993–1995	103rd	McKINNEY, CYNTHIA	2005–	109th
MEEK, CARRIE	1995–1997	104th	SCHWARTZ, ALLYSON	2005–	109th

CENSUS [1901–1946]

	TERM	CONGRESS			TERM	CONGRESS
KAHN, FLORENCE PRAG	1925–1929	69th–70th				

CLAIMS [1794–1946]

	TERM	CONGRESS			TERM	CONGRESS
LANGLEY, KATHERINE GUDGER	1927–1931	70th–71st		MANKIN, HELEN DOUGLAS	1946–1947	79th
CLARKE, MARIAN WILLIAMS	1933–1935	73rd				

CIVIL SERVICE [1925–1946]

	TERM	CONGRESS			TERM	CONGRESS
ROGERS, EDITH NOURSE	1927–1943	70th–77th		BYRON, KATHARINE	1941–1943	77th
CLARKE, MARIAN WILLIAMS	1933–1935	73rd		STANLEY, WINIFRED	1943–1945	78th
JENCKES, VIRGINIA ELLIS	1933–1939	73rd–75th		MANKIN, HELEN DOUGLAS	1946–1947	79th

COINAGE, WEIGHTS, AND MEASURES [1881–1946]

	TERM	CONGRESS			TERM	CONGRESS
KAHN, FLORENCE PRAG	1925–1929	69th–70th		OLDFIELD, PEARL PEDEN	1929–1931	71st

COMMERCE [1995–2001]

	TERM	CONGRESS			TERM	CONGRESS
COLLINS, CARDISS	1995–1997	104th		LINCOLN, BLANCHE LAMBERT	1995–1997	104th
DeGETTE, DIANA	1997–2001	105th–106th		McCARTHY, KAREN	1997–2001	105th–106th
CUBIN, BARBARA	1997–2001	105th–106th		WILSON, HEATHER	1997–2001	105th–106th
ESHOO, ANNA	1995–2001	104th–106th		CAPPS, LOIS	1999–2001	106th
FURSE, ELIZABETH	1995–1997	104th–105th				

DISTRICT OF COLUMBIA [1808–1995]

	TERM	CONGRESS			TERM	CONGRESS
NORTON, MARY TERESA	1925–1939	69th–75th		MARTIN, LYNN	1987–1989	100th
JENCKES, VIRGINIA ELLIS	1933–1939	73rd–75th		MEYNER, HELEN STEVENSON	1975–1979	94th–95th
GRANAHAN, KATHRYN	1957–1959	85th		COLLINS, CARDISS	1977–1979	95th
WEIS, JESSICA McCULLOUGH	1959–1963	86th–87th		FENWICK, MILLICENT	1979–1981	96th
MAY, CATHERINE DEAN	1969	91st		HOLT, MARJORIE	1981–1985	97th–98th
GREEN, EDITH	1971–1973	92nd		NORTON, ELEANOR HOLMES	1991–1995	102nd–103rd

ECONOMIC AND EDUCATIONAL OPPORTUNITIES [1995–1997]

	TERM	CONGRESS			TERM	CONGRESS
MEYERS, JAN	1995–1997	104th		ROUKEMA, MARGARET	1995–1997	104th
MINK, PATSY TAKEMOTO	1995–1997	104th		WOOLSEY, LYNN	1995–1997	104th

EDUCATION [1883–1946]

	TERM	CONGRESS			TERM	CONGRESS
KAHN, FLORENCE PRAG	1925–1929	69th–70th		McCARTHY, KATHYRN O'LOUGHLIN	1933–1935	73rd
LANGLEY, KATHERINE GUDGER	1929–1931	71st		SMITH, MARGARET CHASE	1941–1943	77th
PRATT, RUTH SEARS BAKER	1931–1933	72nd		NORTON, MARY TERESA	1943–1947	78th–79th

EDUCATION AND LABOR [1947–1995]

	TERM	CONGRESS			TERM	CONGRESS
GREEN, EDITH	1955–1973	84th–92nd		FENWICK, MILLICENT	1981–1983	97th
HANSEN, JULIA BUTLER	1961–1963	87th		ROUKEMA, MARGARET	1981–1995	97th–103rd
MINK, PATSY TAKEMOTO	1965–1977	89th–94th		BURTON, SALA	1983–1985	98th
HICKS, LOUISE DAY	1971–1973	92nd		MINK, PATSY TAKEMOTO	1989–1995	101st–103rd
GRASSO, ELLA	1971–1975	92nd–93rd		UNSOELD, JOLENE	1989–1995	101st–103rd
CHISHOLM, SHIRLEY ANITA	1971–1977	92nd–94th		LOWEY, NITA	1989–1993	101st–102nd
REID, CHARLOTTE	1971–1973	92nd		MOLINARI, SUSAN	1991–1995	102nd–103rd
SMITH, VIRGINIA	1975–1977	94th		ENGLISH, KARAN	1993–1995	103rd
PETTIS, SHIRLEY	1977–1979	95th		WOOLSEY, LYNN	1993–1995	103rd

EDUCATION AND THE WORKFORCE [1997–present]

	TERM	CONGRESS		TERM	CONGRESS
McCARTHY, CAROLYN	1997–	105th–109th	BIGGERT, JUDY	2001–	107th–109th
MINK, PATSY TAKEMOTO	1997–2002	105th–107th	DAVIS, SUSAN	2001–	107th–109th
ROUKEMA, MARGARET	1997–2003	105th–107th	MAJETTE, DENISE	2003–2005	108th
SANCHEZ, LORETTA	1997–2003	105th–107th	MUSGRAVE, MARILYN	2003–	108th–109th
WOOLSEY, LYNN	1997–	105th–109th	BLACKBURN, MARSHA	2003–2005	108th
RIVERS, LYNN	2001–2003	107th	McMORRIS, CATHY	2005–	109th
SOLIS, HILDA	2001–2003	107th	FOXX, VIRGINIA	2005–	109th
McCOLLUM, BETTY	2001–	107th–109th	DRAKE, THELMA	2005–	109th

ELECTIONS NO. 2 [1895–1947]

	TERM	CONGRESS
MANKIN, HELEN DOUGLAS	1946–1947	79th

ELECTION OF THE PRESIDENT, VICE PRESIDENT, AND REPRESENTATIVES IN CONGRESS [1893–1946]

	TERM	CONGRESS		TERM	CONGRESS
McCARTHY, KATHRYN	1933	73rd	SMITH, MARGARET CHASE	1939–1941	76th
O'DAY, CAROLINE	1935–1943	74th–77th	McMILLAN, CLARA	1940–1941	76th
BOLTON, FRANCES PAYNE	1940–1943	76th–77th			

ENERGY AND COMMERCE [1981–1995; 2001–present]

	TERM	CONGRESS		TERM	CONGRESS
COLLINS, CARDISS	1981–1995	97th–103rd	ESHOO, ANNA	2001–	107th–109th
MIKULSKI, BARBARA ANN	1981–1987	97th–99th	BONO, MARY	2001–	107th–109th
SCHENK, LYNN	1993–1995	103rd	CAPPS, LOIS	2001–	107th–109th
LINCOLN, BLANCHE LAMBERT	1993–1995	103rd	WILSON, HEATHER	2001–	107th–109th
MARGOLIES-MEZVINSKY, M.	1993–1995	103rd	SCHAKOWSKY, JANICE	2003–	108th–109th
HARMAN, JANE	1997–1999	105th	SOLIS, HILDA	2003–	108th–109th
	2001–2003	107th			
DeGETTE, DIANA	2001–	107th–109th	MYRICK, SUE	2005–	109th
CUBIN, BARBARA	2001–	107th–109th	BLACKBURN, MARSHA	2005–	109th
McCARTHY, KAREN	2001–2005	107th–108th	BALDWIN, TAMMY	2005–	109th

ENROLLED BILLS [1876–1946]

	TERM	CONGRESS
NORTON, MARY TERESA	1943–1947	78th–79th

EXPENDITURES IN EXECUTIVE DEPARTMENTS [1927–1953]

	TERM	CONGRESS		TERM	CONGRESS
OLDFIELD, PEARL PEDEN	1929–1931	71st	CHURCH, MARGUERITE STITT	1951–1953	82nd
BOLTON, FRANCES PAYNE	1939–1943	76th–77th	HARDEN, CECIL MURRAY	1951–1953	82nd

EXPENDITURES IN THE DEPARTMENT OF COMMERCE [1913–1927]

	TERM	CONGRESS
HUCK, WINNIFRED MASON	1922–1923	67th

EXPENDITURES IN THE WAR DEPARTMENT [1816–1927]

	TERM	CONGRESS
KAHN, FLORENCE PRAG	1925–1927	69th

EXPENDITURES IN THE INTERIOR DEPARTMENT [1860–1927]

	TERM	CONGRESS
ROBERTSON, ALICE MARY	1921–1923	67th

EXPENDITURES IN THE NAVY DEPARTMENT [1816–1927]

	TERM	CONGRESS
ROGERS, EDITH NOURSE	1925–1927	69th

EXPENDITURES IN THE POST OFFICE DEPARTMENT [1816–1927]

	TERM	CONGRESS
NOLAN, MAE ELLA	1923–1925	67th–68th

FINANCIAL SERVICES [2001–present]

	TERM	CONGRESS		TERM	CONGRESS
ROUKEMA, MARGARET	2001–2003	107th	VELÁZQUEZ, NYDIA	2001–	107th–109th
SCHAKOWSKY, JANICE	2001–2003	107th	WATERS, MAXINE	2001–	107th–109th
JONES, STEPHANIE TUBBS	2001–2003	107th	BIGGERT, JUDY	2001–	107th–109th
CAPITO, SHELLEY MOORE	2001–2005	107th–108th	BROWN-WAITE, GINNY	2003–	108th–109th
CARSON, JULIA	2001–	107th–109th	HARRIS, KATHERINE	2003–	108th–109th
HART, MELISSA	2001–2005	107th–108th	McCARTHY, CAROLYN	2003–	108th–109th
HOOLEY, DARLENE	2001–	107th–109th	PRYCE, DEBORAH	2005–	109th
KELLY, SUE	2001–	107th–109th	BEAN, MELISSA	2005–	109th
LEE, BARBARA	2001–	107th–109th	WASSERMAN SCHULTZ, DEBBIE	2005–	109th
MALONEY, CAROLYN	2001–	107th–109th	MOORE, GWEN	2005–	109th

FLOOD CONTROL [1915–1946]

	TERM	CONGRESS
PRATT, ELIZA JANE	1946	79th

FOREIGN AFFAIRS [1881–1975; 1979–1995]

	TERM	CONGRESS		TERM	CONGRESS
OWEN, RUTH BRYAN	1929–1933	71st–72nd	MEYNER, HELEN STEVENSON	1974–1976	94th
WINGO, EFFIEGENE LOCKE	1931–1933	72nd	COLLINS, CARDISS	1979–1981	96th
ROGERS, EDITH NOURSE	1933–1947	73rd–79th	FENWICK, MILLICENT	1979–1983	96th–97th
BOLTON, FRANCES PAYNE	1941–1969	77th–90th	SNOWE, OLYMPIA	1981–1995	97th–103rd
DOUGLAS, EMILY TAFT	1945–1947	79th	MEYERS, JAN	1985–1995	99th–103rd
DOUGLAS, HELEN GAHAGAN	1945–1951	79th–81st	ROS-LEHTINEN, ILEANA	1989–1995	101st–103rd
KELLY, EDNA FLANNERY	1951–1969	82nd–90th	CANTWELL, MARIA	1993–1995	103rd
CHURCH, MARGUERITE STITT	1953–1963	83rd–87th	McKINNEY, CYNTHIA	1993–1995	103rd

GOVERNMENT REFORM AND OVERSIGHT [1999–2001]

	TERM	CONGRESS		TERM	CONGRESS
BIGGERT, JUDY	1999–2001	106th	MORELLA, CONSTANCE	1999–2001	106th
CHENOWETH, HELEN	1999–2001	106th	NORTON, ELEANOR HOLMES	1999–2001	106th
MALONEY, CAROLYN	1999–2001	106th	ROS-LEHTINEN, ILEANA	1999–2001	106th
MINK, PATSY TAKEMOTO	1999–2001	106th	SCHAKOWSKY, JANICE	1999–2001	106th

GOVERNMENT OPERATIONS
[1953–1995]

Name	Term	Congress	Name	Term	Congress
HARDEN, CECIL MURRAY	1953–1959	83rd–85th	KENNELLY, BARBARA BAILEY	1981–1983	97th
ST. GEORGE, KATHARINE PRICE	1953–1955	83rd	BOXER, BARBARA	1983–1987	98th–99th
				1989–1993	101st–102nd
CHURCH, MARGUERITE STITT	1953–1955	82nd–83rd	PELOSI, NANCY	1987–1991	100th–101st
GRIFFITHS, MARTHA WRIGHT	1955–1963	84th–87th	SLAUGHTER, LOUISE	1987–1991	100th–101st
DWYER, FLORENCE PRICE	1957–1973	85th–92nd	MINK, PATSY TAKEMOTO	1989–1993	101st–102nd
KEE, MAUDE ELIZABETH	1957–1963	85th–87th	ROS-LEHTINEN, ILEANA	1989–1995	101st–103rd
GRANAHAN, KATHRYN	1957–1963	85th–87th	DeLAURO, ROSA	1991–1993	102nd
WEIS, JESSICA McCULLOUGH	1959–1961	86th	MALONEY, CAROLYN	1993–1995	103rd
BAKER, IRENE BAILEY	1964–1965	88th	MARGOLIES-MEZVINSKY, M.	1993–1995	103rd
HECKLER, MARGARET	1967–1969	90th	BROWN, CORRINE	1993–1995	103rd
ABZUG, BELLA	1971–1977	92nd–94th	COLLINS, BARBARA-ROSE	1993–1995	103rd
REID, CHARLOTTE	1971–1973	92nd	PRYCE, DEBORAH	1993–1995	103rd
COLLINS, CARDISS	1973–1995	93rd–103rd	SCHENK, LYNN	1993–1995	103rd
JORDAN, BARBARA	1973–1979	93rd–95th	THURMAN, KAREN	1993–1995	103rd
SNOWE, OLYMPIA	1979–1981	96th	WOOLSEY, LYNN	1993–1995	103rd

GOVERNMENT REFORM
[2001–present]

Name	Term	Congress	Name	Term	Congress
MALONEY, CAROLYN	2001–	107th–109th	WATSON, DIANE	2001–	107th–109th
MINK, PATSY TAKEMOTO	2001–2002	107th	BLACKBURN, MARSHA	2003–2005	108th
MORELLA, CONSTANCE	2001–2003	107th	SÁNCHEZ, LINDA	2003–	108th–109th
NORTON, ELEANOR HOLMES	2001–	107th–109th	MILLER, CANDICE	2003–	108th–109th
ROS-LEHTINEN, ILEANA	2001–	107th–109th	HARRIS, KATHERINE	2005–	109th
SCHAKOWSKY, JANICE	2001–2003	107th	BROWN-WAITE, GINNY	2005–	109th
DAVIS, JO ANN	2001–2005	107th–108th	FOXX, VIRGINIA	2005–	109th

GOVERNMENT REFORM AND OVERSIGHT [1995–1999]

Name	Term	Congress	Name	Term	Congress
COLLINS, BARBARA-ROSE	1995–1997	104th	MALONEY, CAROLYN	1995–1999	104th–105th
SLAUGHTER, LOUISE	1995–1997	104th	MORELLA, CONSTANCE	1995–1999	104th–105th
THURMAN, KAREN	1995–1997	104th	NORTON, ELEANOR HOLMES	1995–1999	104th–105th
COLLINS, CARDISS	1995–1997	104th	ROS-LEHTINEN, ILEANA	1995–1999	104th–105th
MEEK, CARRIE	1995–1997	104th			

HOUSE ADMINISTRATION
[1947–1995; 1999–present]

Name	Term	Congress	Name	Term	Congress
NORTON, MARY TERESA	1947–1951	80th–81st	MARTIN, LYNN	1981–1983	97th–98th
KELLY, EDNA	1950–1951	81st–82nd	OAKAR, MARY ROSE	1983–1993	98th–102nd
WOODHOUSE, CHASE GOING	1949–1951	81st	VUCANOVICH, BARBARA	1983–1991	98th–101st
BOSONE, REVA BECK	1951–1953	82nd	DUNN, JENNIFER	1993–1995	103rd
SIMPSON, EDNA OAKES	1959–1961	86th	KENNELLY, BARBARA BAILEY	1993–1995	103rd
GREEN, EDITH	1957–1963	85th–87th	MILLENDER-McDONALD, JUANITA	2003–	108th–109th
HOLT, MARJORIE	1975–1977	94th	LOFGREN, ZOE	2005–	109th
BOGGS, CORINNE	1975–1977	94th	MILLER, CANDICE	2005–	109th

HOMELAND SECURITY
[2005–present]

Name	Term	Congress	Name	Term	Congress
LOFGREN, ZOE	2005–	109th	LOWEY, NITA	2005–	109th
JACKSON-LEE, SHELIA	2005–	109th	CHRISTENSEN, DONNA M.	2005–	109th
SANCHEZ, LORETTA	2005–	109th	NORTON, ELEANOR HOLMES	2005–	109th
HARMAN, JANE	2005–	109th			

IMMIGRATION AND NATURALIZATION [1893–1947]

	TERM	CONGRESS		TERM	CONGRESS
LANGLEY, KATHERINE GUDGER	1927–1931	70th–71st	O'DAY, CAROLINE	1935–1943	74th–77th

INDIAN AFFAIRS [1881–1947]

	TERM	CONGRESS		TERM	CONGRESS
ROBERTSON, ALICE MARY	1921–1923	67th	HONEYMAN, NAN WOOD	1937–1939	75th
ROGERS, EDITH NOURSE	1927–1929	70th	BOLTON, FRANCES PAYNE	1940–1943	76th–77th
GREENWAY, ISABELLA SELMES	1935–1937	74th			

INDUSTRIAL ARTS AND EXPOSITIONS [1903–1927]

	TERM	CONGRESS
ROGERS, EDITH NOURSE	1925–1927	69th

INSULAR AFFAIRS [1899–1946]

	TERM	CONGRESS		TERM	CONGRESS
WINGO, EFFIEGENE LOCKE	1930	71st	McMILLAN, CLARA	1936–1941	74th–77th
McCARTHY, KATHRYN	1933	73rd	RANKIN, JEANNETTE	1940–1942	77th
O'DAY, CAROLINE	1936–1943	75th–77th			

INTERIOR AND INSULAR AFFAIRS [1951–1993]

	TERM	CONGRESS		TERM	CONGRESS
BOSONE, REVA BECK	1951–1953	82nd	MINK, PATSY TAKEMOTO	1967–1977	90th–94th
FARRINGTON, MARY ELIZABETH	1953–1957	83rd–84th	BURKE, YVONNE BRATHWAITE	1973–1975	93rd
PFOST, GRACIE BOWERS	1953–1963	83rd–87th	SMITH, VIRGINIA	1975–1977	94th
GREEN, EDITH	1955–1959	84th–85th	PETTIS, SHIRLEY	1975–1977	94th
SIMPSON, EDNA OAKES	1959–1961	86th	BYRON, BEVERLY BUTCHER	1981–1993	97th–102nd
HANSEN, JULIA BUTLER	1961–1963	87th	BURTON, SALA	1983–1985	98th
KEE, MAUDE ELIZABETH	1963–1965	88th	BOXER, BARBARA	1983	98th
REID, CHARLOTTE THOMPSON	1963–1967	88th–89th	VUCANOVICH, BARBARA	1983–1993	98th–102nd

INTERNATIONAL RELATIONS [1975–1979; 1995–present]

	TERM	CONGRESS		TERM	CONGRESS
COLLINS, CARDISS	1975–1979	94th–95th	DANNER, PAT	1997–2001	105th–106th
MEYNER, HELEN STEVENSON	1977–1979	95th	DAVIS, JO ANN	2001–	107th–109th
PETTIS, SHIRLEY	1977–1979	95th	LEE, BARBARA	1999–	106th–109th
FENWICK, MILLICENT	1979–1981	96th	NAPOLITANO, GRACE	2001–	107th–109th
ROS-LEHTINEN, ILEANA	1995–	104th–109th	BERKLEY, SHELLEY	2001–	107th–109th
McKINNEY, CYNTHIA	1995–2003	104th–107th	WATSON, DIANE	2001–	107th–109th
MEYERS, JAN	1995–1997	104th	HARRIS, KATHERINE	2003–	108th–109th
CAPPS, LOIS	1997–1998	105th	McCOLLUM, BETTY	2003–	108th–109th

INVALID PENSIONS [1881–1946]

	TERM	CONGRESS		TERM	CONGRESS
LANGLEY, KATHERINE GUDGER	1927–1931	70th–71st	SMITH, MARGARET CHASE	1940–1943	76th–77th
CLARKE, MARIAN WILLIAMS	1933–1935	73rd			

INTERSTATE AND FOREIGN COMMERCE [1882–1981]

	TERM	CONGRESS
MIKULSKI, BARBARA ANN	1977–1981	95th–96th

IRRIGATION AND RECLAMATION [1925–1946]

	TERM	CONGRESS		TERM	CONGRESS
GREENWAY, ISABELLA SELMES	1934–1937	73rd–74th	HONEYMAN, NAN WOOD	1937–1939	75th

JUDICIARY [1881–present]

	TERM	CONGRESS		TERM	CONGRESS
THOMPSON, RUTH	1951–1957	82nd–84th	BONO, MARY	1997–2001	105th–106th
JORDAN, BARBARA	1973–1979	93rd–95th	WATERS, MAXINE	1997–	105th–109th
HOLTZMAN, ELIZABETH	1973–1981	93rd–96th	BALDWIN, TAMMY	1999–2005	106th–108th
SCHROEDER, PATRICIA	1981–1997	97th–104th	HART, MELISSA	2001–2005	107th–108th
SCHENK, LYNN	1993–1995	103rd	BLACKBURN, MARSHA	2003–2005	108th
JACKSON-LEE, SHEILA	1995–	104th–109th	SÁNCHEZ, LINDA	2003–	108th–109th
LOFGREN, ZOE	1995–	104th–109th			

LABOR [1883–1946]

	TERM	CONGRESS		TERM	CONGRESS
NOLAN, MAE ELLA	1923–1925	67th–68th	NORTON, MARY TERESA	1925–1947	69th–79th

LIBRARY [1806–1946]

	TERM	CONGRESS
PRATT, RUTH SEARS BAKER	1929–1933	71st–72nd

MEMORIALS [1929–1947]

	TERM	CONGRESS
NORTON, MARY TERESA	1929–1947	71st–79th

MERCHANT MARINE AND FISHERIES [1947–1995]

	TERM	CONGRESS		TERM	CONGRESS
BUCHANAN, VERA DAERR	1951–1952	82nd	SAIKI, PATRICIA	1987–1991	100th–101st
GREEN, EDITH	1963–1969	88th–90th	LOWEY, NITA	1989–1993	101st–102nd
SULLIVAN, LEONOR KRETZER	1953–1977	83rd–94th	UNSOELD, JOLENE	1989–1995	101st–103rd
THOMAS, LERA MILLARD	1966–1967	89th	ESHOO, ANNA	1993–1995	103rd
MIKULSKI, BARBARA ANN	1977–1987	95th–99th	CANTWELL, MARIA	1993–1995	103rd
ASHBROOK, JEAN	1982–1983	97th	FOWLER, TILLIE	1993–1995	103rd
SCHNEIDER, CLAUDINE	1981–1991	97th–101st	FURSE, ELIZABETH	1993–1995	103rd
BOXER, BARBARA	1983–1985	98th	LINCOLN, BLANCHE LAMBERT	1993–1995	103rd
BENTLEY, HELEN	1985–1993	99th–102nd	SCHENK, LYNN	1993–1995	103rd

MILITARY AFFAIRS [1822–1947]

	TERM	CONGRESS		TERM	CONGRESS
KAHN, FLORENCE PRAG	1929–1933	71st–72nd	LUCE, CLARE BOOTHE	1943–1947	78th–79th

MINES AND MINING [1865–1946]

	TERM	CONGRESS
JENCKES, VIRGINIA ELLIS	1933–1937	73rd–74th

NATIONAL SECURITY [1995–1999]

	TERM	CONGRESS		TERM	CONGRESS
DeLAURO, ROSA	1995–1997	104th	BONO, MARY	1997–1999	105th
HARMAN, JANE	1995–1999	104th–105th	McKINNEY, CYNTHIA	1997–1999	105th
FOWLER, TILLIE	1995–1999	104th–105th	SANCHEZ, LORETTA	1997–1999	105th
SCHROEDER, PATRICIA	1995–1997	104th	TAUSCHER, ELLEN	1997–1999	105th
GRANGER, KAY	1997–1999	105th			

NATURAL RESOURCES [1993–1995]

	TERM	CONGRESS		TERM	CONGRESS
ENGLISH, KARAN	1993–1995	103rd	SHEPHERD, KAREN	1993–1995	103rd
MINK, PATSY TAKEMOTO	1993–1995	103rd	VUCANOVICH, BARBARA	1993–1995	103rd

NAVAL AFFAIRS [1822–1947]

	TERM	CONGRESS		TERM	CONGRESS
McCORMICK, RUTH HANNA	1929–1931	71st	SMITH, MARGARET CHASE	1943–1947	78th–79th

OVERSIGHT [1995–1999]

	TERM	CONGRESS		TERM	CONGRESS
DUNN, JENNIFER	1995–1997	104th	KILPATRICK, CAROLYN CHEEKS	1997–1999	105th
GRANGER, KAY	1997–1999	105th			

PATENTS [1937–1947]

	TERM	CONGRESS		TERM	CONGRESS
McMILLAN, CLARA	1940–1941	76th	STANLEY, WINIFRED	1943–1945	78th

PENSIONS [1880–1947]

	TERM	CONGRESS
PRATT, ELIZA JANE	1945–1947	79th

POST OFFICE AND CIVIL SERVICE [1947–1995]

	TERM	CONGRESS		TERM	CONGRESS
ST. GEORGE, KATHARINE PRICE	1947–1957 1959–1965	80th–84th 86th–88th	FERRARO, GERALDINE ANN	1979–1983	96th–97th
HARDEN, CECIL MURRAY	1953–1959	83rd–85th	OAKAR, MARY ROSE	1979–1993	96th–102nd
PFOST, GRACIE BOWERS	1955–1959	84th–85th	HALL, KATIE	1983–1985	98th
GRANAHAN, KATHRYN	1957–1963	85th–87th	MORELLA, CONSTANCE	1987–1995	100th–103rd
NORRELL, CATHERINE DORRIS	1961–1963	87th	NORTON, ELEANOR HOLMES	1991–1995	102nd–103rd
ANDREWS, ELIZABETH	1972–1973	92nd	COLLINS, BARBARA-ROSE	1993–1995	102nd–103rd
SCHROEDER, PATRICIA	1973–1995	93rd–103rd	BYRNE, LESLIE	1993–1995	103rd
SPELLMAN, GLADYS NOON	1975–1981	94th–95th			

POST OFFICE AND POST ROADS [1808–1947]

	TERM	CONGRESS
SMITH, MARGARET CHASE	1941–1943	77th

PUBLIC BUILDINGS AND GROUNDS [1837–1947]

	TERM	CONGRESS		TERM	CONGRESS
OLDFIELD, PEARL PEDEN	1929–1931	71st	McCARTHY, KATHYRN O'LOUGHLIN	1933–1935	73rd
ESLICK, WILLA BLAKE	1932–1933	72nd	McMILLAN, CLARA	1940–1941	76th

PUBLIC LANDS [1805–1951]

	TERM	CONGRESS		TERM	CONGRESS
RANKIN, JEANNETTE	1917–1919	65th	RANKIN, JEANNETTE	1941–1943	77th
GREENWAY, ISABELLA SELMES	1934–1937	73rd–74th	BOSONE, REVA BECK	1949–1951	81st

PUBLIC WORKS [1947–1989]

	TERM	CONGRESS		TERM	CONGRESS
BUCHANAN, VERA DAERR	1951–1955	82nd–83rd	COLLINS, CARDISS	1973–1975	93rd
BLITCH, IRIS FAIRCLOTH	1955–1963	84th–87th	BURKE, YVONNE BRATHWAITE	1973–1975	93rd
PFOST, GRACIE BOWERS	1959–1963	86th–87th	LLOYD, MARILYN	1974–1976	94th
REECE, LOUISE GOFF	1961–1963	87th	BENTLEY, HELEN DELICH	1985–1988	99th–100th
REID, CHARLOTTE THOMPSON	1965–1967	89th	LONG, CATHERINE	1985–1986	99th
ABZUG, BELLA	1971–1977	92nd–94th			

PUBLIC WORKS AND TRANSPORTATION [1989–1995]

Name	TERM	CONGRESS	Name	TERM	CONGRESS
ABZUG, BELLA	1975–1977	94th	DeLAURO, ROSA	1991–1993	102nd
LLOYD, MARILYN	1975–1983	94th–97th	COLLINS, BARBARA-ROSE	1991–1995	102nd–103rd
FERRARO, GERALDINE ANN	1979–1985	96th–98th	HORN, JOAN KELLY	1991–1993	102nd
KENNELLY, BARBARA BAILEY	1981–1983	97th	DANNER, PAT	1993–1995	103rd
HALL, KATIE	1983–1985	98th	DUNN, JENNIFER	1993–1995	103rd
MARTIN, LYNN	1983–1985	98th	JOHNSON, EDDIE BERNICE	1993–1995	103rd
JOHNSON, NANCY	1983–1989	98th–100th	BROWN, CORRINE	1993–1995	103rd
SLAUGHTER, LOUISE	1987–1991	100th–101st	BYRNE, LESLIE	1993–1995	103rd
MOLINARI, SUSAN	1989–1995	101st–103rd	CANTWELL, MARIA	1993–1995	103rd
NORTON, ELEANOR HOLMES	1991–1995	102nd–103rd	SHEPHERD, KAREN	1993–1995	103rd
BENTLEY, HELEN	1985–1989	99th–100th			
	1991–1993	102nd			

REFORM IN THE CIVIL SERVICE [1893–1968]

Name	TERM	CONGRESS
HUCK, WINNIFRED MASON	1922–1923	67th

REVISION OF LAWS [1868–1946]

Name	TERM	CONGRESS	Name	TERM	CONGRESS
SMITH, MARGARET CHASE	1940–1941	76th	MANKIN, HELEN DOUGLAS	1946	79th

RESOURCES [1995–present]

Name	TERM	CONGRESS	Name	TERM	CONGRESS
CUBIN, BARBARA	1995–	104th–109th	McCOLLUM, BETTY	2001–	107th–109th
CHENOWETH, HELEN	1995–2001	104th–106th	BORDALLO, MADELEINE	2003–	108th–109th
CHRISTENSEN, DONNA M.	1997–	105th–109th	HERSETH, STEPHANIE	2004–	108th–109th
NAPOLITANO, GRACE	1999–	106th–109th	DRAKE, THELMA	2005–	109th
SMITH, LINDA	1995–1999	104th–105th	McMORRIS, CATHY	2005–	109th
SOLIS, HILDA	2001–2003	107th	MUSGRAVE, MARILYN	2005–	109th

RIVERS AND HARBORS [1883–1946]

Name	TERM	CONGRESS
HONEYMAN, NAN WOOD	1937–1939	75th

RULES [1880–present]

Name	TERM	CONGRESS	Name	TERM	CONGRESS
ST. GEORGE, KATHARINE PRICE	1961–1965	87th–88th	WALDHOLTZ, ENID GREENE	1995–1997	104th
CHISHOLM, SHIRLEY ANITA	1977–1983	95th–97th	PRYCE, DEBORAH	1995–2005	104th–108th
BURTON, SALA	1984–1987	98th–100th	MYRICK, SUE	1997–2005	105th–108th
MARTIN, LYNN	1989–1991	101st	CAPITO, SHELLEY MOORE	2005–	109th
SLAUGHTER, LOUISE	1989–1995	101st–103rd	MATSUI, DORIS	2005–	109th
	1997–	105th–109th			

SCIENCE [1995–present]

Name	TERM	CONGRESS	Name	TERM	CONGRESS
CUBIN, BARBARA	1995–1997	104th	SEASTRAND, ANDREA	1995–1997	104th
HARMAN, JANE	1995–1997	104th	CAPPS, LOIS	1997–1999	105th
JACKSON-LEE, SHEILA	1995–	104th–109th	HOOLEY, DARLENE	1997–1999	105th
				2005–	109th
JOHNSON, EDDIE BERNICE	1995–	104th–109th	LEE, BARBARA	1997–1999	105th
LOFGREN, ZOE	1995–2005	104th–108th	STABENOW, DEBBIE	1997–2001	105th–106th
McCARTHY, KAREN	1995–1997	104th	TAUSCHER, ELLEN	1997–1999	105th
MORELLA, CONSTANCE	1995–2003	104th–107th	BIGGERT, JUDY	1999–	106th–109th
MYRICK, SUE	1989–1997	104th	WOOLSEY, LYNN	1999–	106th–109th
RIVERS, LYNN	1995–2003	104th–107th	HART, MELISSA	2001–2005	107th–108th

SCIENCE AND ASTRONAUTICS [1958–1975]

	TERM	CONGRESS		TERM	CONGRESS
WEIS, JESSICA McCULLOUGH	1961–1963	87th	RILEY, CORINNE BOYD	1961–1963	87th

SCIENCE, SPACE AND TECHNOLOGY [1987–1995]

	TERM	CONGRESS		TERM	CONGRESS
LLOYD, MARILYN	1987–1995	100th–103rd	COLLINS, BARBARA	1991–1993	102nd
MORELLA, CONSTANCE	1987–1995	100th–103rd	ESHOO, ANNA	1993–1995	103rd
SCHNEIDER, CLAUDINE	1987–1991	100th–101st	HORN, JOAN KELLY	1991–1993	102nd
DUNN, JENNIFER	1993–1995	103rd	JOHNSON, EDDIE BERNICE	1993–1995	103rd
HARMAN, JANE	1993–1995	103rd			

SCIENCE AND TECHNOLOGY [1975–1987]

	TERM	CONGRESS		TERM	CONGRESS
LLOYD, MARILYN	1975–1987	94th–99th	HECKLER, MARGARET	1981–1983	97th
	1981–1983	97th			
SCHNEIDER, CLAUDINE	1981–1987	97th–99th	MEYERS, JAN	1985–1987	99th

SMALL BUSINESS [1974–present]

	TERM	CONGRESS		TERM	CONGRESS
FENWICK, MILLICENT	1975–1977	94th	KELLY, SUE	1995–	104th–109th
SNOWE, OLYMPIA	1979–1983	96th–97th	McCARTHY, CAROLYN	1997–2001	105th–106th
LONG, CATHERINE	1985–1987	99th	EMERSON, JO ANN	1997–1999	105th
MEYERS, JAN	1985–1997	99th–104th	BONO, MARY	1999–2001	106th
MOLINARI, SUSAN	1989–1991	101st	BERKLEY, SHELLEY	1999–2001	106th
ROYBAL-ALLARD, LUCILLE	1993–1995	103rd	CHRISTENSEN, DONNA M.	1999–	106th–109th
DANNER, PAT	1993–1995	103rd	JONES, STEPHANIE TUBBS	1999–2003	106th–107th
MARGOLIES-MEZVINSKY, M.	1993–1995	103rd	NAPOLITANO, GRACE	1999–2005	106th–108th
CLAYTON, EVA	1993–1997	103rd–104th	SCHAKOWSKY, JANICE	1999–2001	106th
VELÁZQUEZ, NYDIA	1993–2005	103rd–108th	CAPITO, SHELLEY MOORE	2001–2005	107th–108th
WATERS, MAXINE	1993–1997	103rd–104th	MUSGRAVE, MARILYN	2003–	108th–109th
MILLENDER-McDONALD, JUANITA	1995–	104th–109th	BORDALLO, MADELEINE	2003–	108th–109th
NORTON, ELEANOR HOLMES	1995–1997	104th	MAJETTE, DENISE	2003–2005	108th
SMITH, LINDA	1995–1999	104th–105th	SÁNCHEZ, LINDA	2003–	108th–109th
MYRICK, SUE	1995–1997	104th	BEAN, MELISSA	2005–	109th
McCARTHY, KAREN	1995–1997	104th	MOORE, GWEN	2005–	109th

STANDARDS OF OFFICIAL CONDUCT [1967–present]

	TERM	CONGRESS		TERM	CONGRESS
KELLY, EDNA FLANNERY	1967–1969	90th	LOFGREN, ZOE	1999–2003	106th–107th
REID, CHARLOTTE THOMPSON	1969–1972	91st–92nd	BIGGERT, JUDY	2001–	107th–109th
FENWICK, MILLICENT	1977–1979	95th	JONES, STEPHANIE TUBBS	2001–	107th–109th
PELOSI, NANCY	1991–1997	102nd–104th	ROYBAL-ALLARD, LUCILLE	2003–	108th–109th
JOHNSON, NANCY	1991–1997	102nd–104th	HART, MELISSA	2005–	109th

TERRITORIES [1825–1946]

	TERM	CONGRESS		TERM	CONGRESS
PRATT, ELIZA JANE	1946–1947	79th			

TRANSPORTATION AND INFRASTRUCTURE
[1995–present]

Name	TERM	CONGRESS	Name	TERM	CONGRESS
BROWN, CORRINE	1995–	104th–109th	MOLINARI, SUSAN	1995–1999	104th–105th
COLLINS, BARBARA-ROSE	1995–1997	104th	NORTON, ELEANOR HOLMES	1995–	104th–109th
DANNER, PAT	1995–2001	104th–106th	GRANGER, KAY	1997–1999	105th
FOWLER, TILLIE	1995–2001	104th–106th	EMERSON, JO ANN	1997–1999	105th
JOHNSON, EDDIE BERNICE	1995–	104th–109th	TAUSCHER, ELLEN	1997–	105th–109th
KELLY, SUE	1995–	104th–109th	BERKLEY, SHELLEY	1999–	106th–109th
SEASTRAND, ANDREA	1995–1997	104th	CAPITO, SHELLEY MOORE	2001–2005	107th–108th
McCARTHY, KAREN	1995–1997	104th	CARSON, JULIA	2003–	108th–109th
MILLENDER-McDONALD, JUANITA	1995–	104th–109th	SCHWARTZ, ALLYSON	2005–	109th

VETERANS' AFFAIRS
[1947–present]

Name	TERM	CONGRESS	Name	TERM	CONGRESS
LUSK, GEORGIA LEE	1947–1949	80th	KAPTUR, MARCY	1983–1989	98th–100th
ROGERS, EDITH NOURSE	1947–1961	80th–86th	PATTERSON, ELIZABETH	1987–1993	100th–102n
HARDEN, CECIL MURRAY	1949–1951	81st	LONG, JILL	1989–1995	101st–103rd
KEE, MAUDE ELIZABETH	1951–1965	82nd–88th	WATERS, MAXINE	1991–1997	102nd–104t
BUCHANAN, VERA DAERR	1951–1953	82nd	BROWN, CORRINE	1993–	103rd–109th
DWYER, FLORENCE PRICE	1957–1959	85th	CARSON, JULIA	1997–2003	105th–107th
HANSEN, JULIA BUTLER	1961–1963	87th	CHENOWETH, HELEN	1997–2001	105th–106th
HECKLER, MARGARET	1967–1983	90th–97th	BERKLEY, SHELLEY	1999–	106th–109th
CHISHOLM, SHIRLEY ANITA	1969–1971	91st–92nd	BROWN-WAITE, GINNY	2003–	108th–109th
HICKS, LOUISE DAY	1971–1973	92nd	DAVIS, SUSAN	2003–	108th–109th
GRASSO, ELLA	1971–1975	92nd–93rd	HOOLEY, DARLENE	2003–	108th–109th
JOHNSON, NANCY	1983–1987	98th–99th	HERSETH, STEPHANIE	2004–	108th–109th

WAR CLAIMS [1873–1946]

Name	TERM	CONGRESS	Name	TERM	CONGRESS
KAHN, FLORENCE PRAG	1927–1929	70th	BYRON, KATHARINE	1941–1943	77th
SMITH, MARGARET CHASE	1940–1941	76th			

WAYS AND MEANS [1795–present]

Name	TERM	CONGRESS	Name	TERM	CONGRESS
GRIFFITHS, MARTHA WRIGHT	1962–1975	87th–93rd	DUNN, JENNIFER	1995–	104th–109th
KEYS, MARTHA ELIZABETH	1975–1979	94th–95th	THURMAN, KAREN	1997–2003	105th–107th
KENNELLY, BARBARA BAILEY	1983–1999	98th–105th	JONES, STEPHANIE TUBBS	2003–	108th–109th
JOHNSON, NANCY	1989–	101st–109th	HART, MELISSA	2005–	109th

WOMEN'S SUFFRAGE
[1917–1927]

Name	TERM	CONGRESS	Name	TERM	CONGRESS
RANKIN, JEANNETTE	1917–1919	65th	NOLAN, MAE	1923–1925	68th
ROBERTSON, ALICE MARY	1921–1923	67th	ROGERS, EDITH NOURSE	1925–1927	69th
HUCK, WINNIFRED MASON	1922–1923	67th			

WORLD WAR VETERANS' LEGISLATION [1924–1947]

Name	TERM	CONGRESS	Name	TERM	CONGRESS
NORTON, MARY TERESA	1925–1933	69th–73rd	ESLICK, WILLA BLAKE	1932–1933	72nd
ROGERS, EDITH NOURSE	1925–1947	69th–79th	McCARTHY, KATHYRN O'LOUGHLIN	1933–1935	73rd

PERMANENT SELECT COMMITTEE ON INTELLIGENCE [1977–present]

	TERM	CONGRESS		TERM	CONGRESS
KENNELLY, BARBARA BAILEY	1987–1993	100th–102nd	WILSON, HEATHER	1999–2001	106th
				2005–	109th
PELOSI, NANCY	1993–	103rd–109th (108th–109th Ex-Officio)	ESHOO, ANNA	2003–	108th–109th
HARMAN, JANE	1997–1999	105th	DAVIS, JO ANN	2005–	109th
	2001–	107th–109th			

SELECT COMMITTEE ON AGING [1975–1993]

	TERM	CONGRESS		TERM	CONGRESS
BYRON, BEVERLY BUTCHER	1979–1993	96th–102nd	SCHNEIDER, CLAUDINE	1983–1991	98th–101st
LLOYD, MARILYN	1975–1993	94th–102nd	MEYERS, JAN	1985–1993	99th–102nd
MEYNER, HELEN	1977–1979	95th	BENTLEY, HELEN DELICH	1985–1993	99th–102nd
HOLT, MARJORIE	1979–1981	96th	MORELLA, CONSTANCE	1987–1993	100th–102nd
FERRARO, GERALDINE ANN	1979–1985	96th–98th	SAIKI, PATRICIA	1987–1991	100th–101st
HOLTZMAN, ELIZABETH	1979–1981	96th	SLAUGHTER, LOUISE	1987–1993	100th–102nd
SNOWE, OLYMPIA	1979–1993	96th–102nd	UNSOELD, JOLENE	1989–1993	101st–102nd
OAKAR, MARY ROSE	1977–1993	95th–102nd	DeLAURO, ROSA	1991–1993	102nd
FENWICK, MILLICENT	1981–1983	97th			

SELECT COMMITTEE ON ASSASSINATIONS [1976–1979]

	TERM	CONGRESS
BURKE, YVONNE BRATHWAITE	1976–1979	94th–95th

SELECT COMMITTEE ON CHILDREN, YOUTH, AND FAMILIES [1983–1993]

	TERM	CONGRESS		TERM	CONGRESS
JOHNSON, NANCY	1983–1989	98th–100th	BOGGS, CORINNE	1983–1991	98th–101st
SCHROEDER, PATRICIA	1983–1993	98th–102nd	BOXER, BARBARA	1983–1993	98th–102nd
MIKULSKI, BARBARA ANN	1983–1985	98th	COLLINS, BARBARA-ROSE	1991–1993	102nd
VUCANOVICH, BARBARA	1983–1991	98th–101st	HORN, JOAN KELLY	1991–1993	102nd

SELECT COMMITTEE ON COMMITTEES II [1979–1980]

	TERM	CONGRESS
SCHROEDER, PATRICIA	1979–1980	96th

SELECT COMMITTEE ON CRIME [1969–1973]

	TERM	CONGRESS
GRIFFITHS, MARTHA WRIGHT	1969–1971	91st

SELECT COMMITTEE ON CURRENT PORNOGRAPHIC MATERIALS [1952–1953]

	TERM	CONGRESS		TERM	CONGRESS
BOSONE, REVA BECK	1952	82nd	ST. GEORGE, KATHERINE	1952	82nd

SELECT COMMITTEE ON ETHICS [1977–1979]

	TERM	CONGRESS		TERM	CONGRESS
HECKLER, MARGARET	1977–1979	95th			

SELECT COMMITTEE ON HOMELAND SECURITY [2001–2005]

	TERM	CONGRESS		TERM	CONGRESS
CHRISTENSEN, DONNA M.	2003–2005	108th	LOWEY, NITA	2003–2005	108th
DUNN, JENNIFER	2003–2005	108th	McCARTHY, KAREN	2003–2005	108th
GRANGER, KAY	2003–2005	108th	NORTON, ELEANOR HOLMES	2003–2005	108th
HARMAN, JANE	2003–2005	108th	SANCHEZ, LORETTA	2003–2005	108th
JACKSON-LEE, SHEILA	2003–2005	108th	SLAUGHTER, LOUISE	2003–2005	108th
LOFGREN, ZOE	2003–2005	108th			

SELECT COMMITTEE ON THE HOUSE BEAUTY SHOP [1967–1977]

	TERM	CONGRESS		TERM	CONGRESS
GREEN, EDITH	1967–1975	90th–93rd	MEYNER, HELEN	1975–1977	94th
GRIFFITHS, MARTHA WRIGHT	1967–1974	90th–93rd	BURKE, YVONNE BRATHWAITE	1975–1977	94th
MAY, CATHERINE DEAN	1967–1971	90th–91st	SMITH, VIRGINIA	1975–1977	94th
HECKLER, MARGARET	1971–1975	92nd–93rd			

SELECT COMMITTEE ON HUNGER [1985–1993]

	TERM	CONGRESS		TERM	CONGRESS
BURTON, SALA	1984–1987	98th–100th	PATTERSON, ELIZABETH	1987–1993	100th–102nd
ROUKEMA, MARGARET	1983–1993	98th–102nd	LONG, JILL	1989–1993	101st–102nd

SELECT COMMITTEE ON MISSING PERSONS IN SOUTHEAST ASIA [1975–1977]

	TERM	CONGRESS			
SCHROEDER, PATRICIA	1975–1977	94th			

SELECT COMMITTEE ON NARCOTICS ABUSE AND CONTROL [1976–1993]

	TERM	CONGRESS		TERM	CONGRESS
COLLINS, CARDISS	1979–1993	96th–102nd	LOWEY, NITA	1989–1993	101st–102nd

SELECT COMMITTEE ON PAGES [1964–1965]

	TERM	CONGRESS			
GREEN, EDITH	1957–1959	85th			

SELECT COMMITTEE ON THE OUTER CONTINENTAL SHELF [1975–1980]

	TERM	CONGRESS			
MINK, PATSY	1975–1977	94th			

SELECT COMMITTEE ON POPULATION [1977–1979]

	TERM	CONGRESS			
CARDISS, COLLINS	1977–1979	95th			

	TERM	CONGRESS		TERM	CONGRESS
SELECT COMMITTEE ON STANDARDS OF OFFICIAL CONDUCT [1966]					
MAY, CATHERINE DEAN	1966	89th			
SELECT COMMITTEE ON THE HOUSE RECORDING STUDIO [1956–1987]					
BOGGS, CORINNE	1977–1987	95th–99th			

House Joint Committee	TERM	CONGRESS		TERM	CONGRESS
JOINT COMMITTEE ON ATOMIC ENERGY [1946–1977]					
MAY, CATHERINE DEAN	1969–1971	91st			
JOINT COMMITTEE ON BICENTENNIAL ARRANGEMENTS [1975–1976]					
BOGGS, CORINNE	1975–1976	94th			
JOINT COMMITTEE ON CONGRESSIONAL OPERATIONS [1970–1977]					
DUNN, JENNIFER	1993–1994	103rd			
JOINT COMMITTEE ON DEFENSE PRODUCTION [1950–1977]					
SULLIVAN, LEONOR KRETZER	1971–1977	91st–94th			
JOINT COMMITTEE ON DEFICIT REDUCTION [1985–1989]					
BOXER, BARBARA	1987	100th			
JOINT COMMITTEE ON THE ORGANIZATION OF CONGRESS [1993–1995]					
NORTON, ELEANOR HOLMES	1992–1995	102nd–103rd	DUNN, JENNIFER	1993–1995	103rd
JOINT COMMITTEE ON DISPOSITION OF EXECUTIVE PAPERS [1889–1946]					
NORTON, MARY	1947–1949	80th	GREEN, EDITH	1957–1959	85th

House Joint Committee	TERM	CONGRESS		TERM	CONGRESS
JOINT COMMITTEE ON IMMIGRATION AND NATIONALITY POLICY [1952–1970]					
THOMPSON, RUTH	1955–1957	84th			
JOINT COMMITTEE ON INAUGURAL CEREMONIES [Intermittent, 1948–present]					
PELOSI, NANCY	2004–2005	108th–109th			
JOINT ECONOMIC COMMITTEE [1957–present]					
GRIFFITHS, MARTHA WRIGHT	1961–1975	87th–93rd	FIEDLER, BOBBI	1985–1987	99th
HECKLER, MARGARET	1974–1983	94th–97th	MALONEY, CAROLYN	1997–2005	105th–108th
SNOWE, OLYMPIA	1983–1993	98th–102nd	DUNN, JENNIFER	2001–2005	107th–108th
HOLT, MARJORIE	1983–1985	98th			
JOINT COMMITTEE ON THE LIBRARY [1947–present]					
NORTON, MARY	1947–1951	80th–81st	KILPATRICK, CAROLYN CHEEKS	1997–1999	105th
VUCANOVICH, BARBARA	1983–1985	98th	MILLENDER-McDONALD, JUANITA	2003–2005	108th
OAKAR, MARY ROSE	1985–1991	99th–101st			
JOINT COMMITTEE ON PRINTING [1947–present]					
NORTON, MARY	1949–1951	81st	GRANGER, KAY	1997–1999	105th
MARTIN, LYNN	1981–1983	101st			
JOINT COMMITTEE TO STUDY BUDGET CONTROL [1972–1973]					
GRIFFITHS, MARTHA	1972–1973	92nd			

Senate Standing Committee	TERM	CONGRESS		TERM	CONGRESS
AERONAUTICAL AND SPACE SCIENCES [1955–1977]					
SMITH, MARGARET CHASE	1959–1973	86th–92nd			
AGRICULTURE AND FORESTRY [1883–1977]					
CARAWAY, HATTIE WYATT	1931–1945	72nd–78th	EDWARDS, ELAINE	1972	92nd
NEUBERGER, MAURINE	1961–1965	87th–88th			
AGRICULTURE, NUTRITION, AND FORESTRY [1977–present]					
ALLEN, MARYON PITTMAN	1978	95th	LINCOLN, BLANCHE LAMBERT	1999–	106th–109th
HAWKINS, PAULA	1981–1986	97th–99th	STABENOW, DEBBIE	2001–	107th–109th
LANDRIEU, MARY	1997–1999	105th	DOLE, ELIZABETH	2003–2005	108th

Senate Standing Committee	TERM	CONGRESS		TERM	CONGRESS
APPROPRIATIONS [1867–present]					
SMITH, MARGARET CHASE	1953–1973	83rd–92nd	HUTCHISON, KAY BAILEY	1997–	105th–109th
MIKULSKI, BARBARA ANN	1987–	100th–109th	LANDRIEU, MARY	2001–	107th–109th
FEINSTEIN, DIANNE	1993–1995	103rd	MURRAY, PATTY	1993–	103rd–109th
	2001–	106th–109th			
BOXER, BARBARA	1997–1999	105th			
ARMED SERVICES [1947–present]					
SMITH, MARGARET CHASE	1953–1973	83rd–92nd	CARNAHAN, JEAN	2001–2002	107th
FRAHM, SHEILA	1996	104th	COLLINS, SUSAN	2001–	107th–109th
SNOWE, OLYMPIA	1997–2001	105th–106th	CLINTON, HILLARY RODHAM	2003–	108th–109th
HUTCHISON, KAY BAILEY	1993–1997	103rd–104th	DOLE, ELIZABETH	2003–	108th–109th
LANDRIEU, MARY	1999–2003	106th–107th			
BANKING AND CURRENCY [1913–1971]					
NEUBERGER, MAURINE	1961–1967	87th–89th			
BANKING, HOUSING, AND URBAN AFFAIRS [1970–present]					
KASSEBAUM, NANCY LANDON	1979–1981	96th	BOXER, BARBARA	1993–2001	103rd–106th
	1989–1993	101st–102nd			
HAWKINS, PAULA	1983–1985	98th	DOLE, ELIZABETH	2003–	108th–109th
FRAHM, SHEILA	1996	104th	STABENOW, DEBBIE	2001–	107th–109th
BOXER, BARBARA	1993–1999	103rd–105th	MURRAY, PATTY	1993–1997	103rd–104th
MOSELEY-BRAUN, CAROL	1993–1999	103rd–105th			
BUDGET [1968–present]					
KASSEBAUM, NANCY LANDON	1979–1999	96th–100th	CLINTON, HILLARY RODHAM	2001–2003	107th
BOXER, BARBARA	1993–2001	103rd–106th	STABENOW, DEBBIE	2001–	107th–109th
SNOWE, OLYMPIA	1995–2005	104th–107th	MURRAY, PATTY	1993–	103rd–109th
CLAIMS [1815–1946]					
LONG, ROSE McCONNELL	1936–1937	74th	GRAVES, DIXIE BIBB	1937–1938	75th
COMMERCE [1825–1947 1961–1977]					
CARAWAY, HATTIE WYATT	1931–1945	72nd–78th	NEUBERGER, MAURINE	1965–1967	89th
COMMERCE, SCIENCE, AND TRANSPORTATION [1977–present]					
KASSEBAUM, NANCY LANDON	1979–1989	96th–100th	CARNAHAN, JEAN	2001–2002	107th
HUTCHISON, KAY BAILEY	1993–	103rd–109th	BOXER, BARBARA	2001–	107th–109th
SNOWE, OLYMPIA	1995–	104th–109th	CANTWELL, MARIA	2003–	108th–109th
DISTRICT OF COLUMBIA [1947–1977]					
SMITH, MARGARET CHASE	1949–1951	81st			

EDUCATION AND LABOR
[1869–1946]

	TERM	CONGRESS		TERM	CONGRES
GRAVES, DIXIE BIBB	1937–1938	75th			

ENERGY AND NATURAL RESOURCES [1977–present]

	TERM	CONGRESS		TERM	CONGRES
LANDRIEU, MARY	1997–	105th–109th	FEINSTEIN, DIANNE	2001–	107th–109th
LINCOLN, BLANCHE LAMBERT	1999–2001	106th	MURKOWSKI, LISA	2003–	108th–109th
CANTWELL, MARIA	2001–	107th–109th			

ENROLLED BILLS [1789–1946]

	TERM	CONGRESS		TERM	CONGRES
CARAWAY, HATTIE WYATT	1931–1945	72nd–78th			

ENVIRONMENT AND PUBLIC WORKS [1977–present]

	TERM	CONGRESS		TERM	CONGRES
KASSEBAUM, NANCY LANDON	1977–1983	95th–97th	HUTCHISON, KAY BAILEY	1999–2001	106th
MIKULSKI, BARBARA ANN	1987–1989	100th	CLINTON, HILLARY RODHAM	2001–	107th–109th
BURDICK, JOCELYN BIRCH	1992	102nd	MURKOWSKI, LISA	2003–	108th–109th
BOXER, BARBARA	1993–	103rd–109th			

EXPENDITURES IN EXECUTIVE DEPARTMENTS [1947–1952]

	TERM	CONGRESS		TERM	CONGRES
SMITH, MARGARET CHASE	1949–1953	81st–82nd			

FINANCE [1947–present]

	TERM	CONGRESS		TERM	CONGRES
MOSELEY-BRAUN, CAROL	1993–1999	104th–105th	SNOWE, OLYMPIA	2001–	107th–109th
LINCOLN, BLANCHE LAMBERT	2001–	107th–109th			

FOREIGN RELATIONS [1947–present]

	TERM	CONGRESS		TERM	CONGRES
HUMPHREY, MURIEL BUCK	1978	95th	FEINSTEIN, DIANNE	1995–1999	104th–105th
KASSEBAUM, NANCY LANDON	1977–1997	95th–104th	BOXER, BARBARA	1999–	106th–109th
SNOWE, OLYMPIA	1995–1997	104th	MURKOWSKI, LISA	2005–	109th

GOVERNMENTAL AFFAIRS [1977–present]

	TERM	CONGRESS		TERM	CONGRES
BOWRING, EVA KELLY	1954	83rd	CARNAHAN, JEAN	2001–2002	107th
HUMPHREY, MURIEL BUCK	1978	95th	COLLINS, SUSAN	1997–	105th–109th

GOVERNMENT OPERATIONS [1953–1993]

	TERM	CONGRESS		TERM	CONGRES
SMITH, MARGARET CHASE	1953–1959	83rd–85th			

HEALTH, EDUCATION, LABOR, AND PENSIONS [1999–present]

	TERM	CONGRESS		TERM	CONGRES
CLINTON, HILLARY RODHAM	2001–	107th–109th	MURRAY, PATTY	1999–	106th–109th
COLLINS, SUSAN	1999–2003	106th–107th	MIKULSKI, BARBARA ANN	1999–	106th–109th

HOMELAND SECURITY AND GOVERNMENTAL AFFAIRS [2005–present]

	TERM	CONGRESS		TERM	CONGRESS
COLLINS, SUSAN	2005–	109th			

IMMIGRATION [1899–1946]

LONG, ROSE McCONNELL	1936–1937	74th			

INDIAN AFFAIRS [1819–present]

KASSEBAUM, NANCY LANDON	1991–1997	102nd–104th	MURKOWSKI, LISA	2003–	108th–109th
CANTWELL, MARIA	2001–	107th–109th			

INTEROCEANIC CANAL [1912–1946]

LONG, ROSE McCONNELL	1936–1937	74th			

INTERSTATE AND FOREIGN COMMERCE [1947–1961]

BOWRING, EVA KELLY	1954	83rd	ABEL, HAZEL HEMPEL	1954	83rd

JUDICIARY [1815–present]

ALLEN, MARYON PITTMAN	1978	95th	FEINSTEIN, DIANNE	1993–	103rd–109th
MOSELEY-BRAUN, CAROL	1993–1995	103rd	CANTWELL, MARIA	2001–2003	107th

LABOR AND HUMAN RESOURCES [1979–1999]

HAWKINS, PAULA	1981–1983	97th	MURRAY, PATTY	1997–1999	105th
	1983–1987	98th–99th			
KASSEBAUM, NANCY LANDON	1989–1997	101st–104th	MIKULSKI, BARBARA ANN	1987–1999	100th–105th
COLLINS, SUSAN	1997–1999	105th			

LABOR AND PUBLIC WELFARE [1947–1977]

BOWRING, EVA KELLY	1954	83rd			

LIBRARY [1849–1947]

CARAWAY, HATTIE WYATT	1931–1945	72nd–78th			

MINES AND MINING [1865–1946]

GRAVES, DIXIE BIBB	1937–1938	75th			

POST OFFICE AND CIVIL SERVICE [1947–1977]

BOWRING, EVA KELLY	1954	83rd			

POST OFFICE AND POST ROADS [1816–1947]

LONG, ROSE McCONNELL	1936–1937	74th			

PUBLIC WORKS [1947–1977]

EDWARDS, ELAINE	1972	92nd			

Senate Standing Committee	TERM	CONGRESS		TERM	CONGRES
PUBLIC LANDS AND SURVEYS [1921–1946]					
LONG, ROSE McCONNELL	1936–1937	74th			
RULES AND ADMINISTRATION [1947–present]					
SMITH, MARGARET CHASE	1951–1953	82nd	FEINSTEIN, DIANNE	1993–	103rd–109th
KASSEBAUM, NANCY LANDON	1977–1983	95th–97th	HUTCHISON, KAY BAILEY	1997–	105th–109th
SMALL BUSINESS [1969–2001]					
MIKULSKI, BARBARA ANN	1987–1993	100th–102nd	SNOWE, OLYMPIA	1995–2001	104th–106th
HUTCHISON, KAY BAILEY	1993–1997	103rd–104th	LANDRIEU, MARY	1999–2001	105th–106th
MOSELEY-BRAUN, CAROL	1993–1995	103rd			
SMALL BUSINESS AND ENTREPRENEURSHIP [2001–present]					
CANTWELL, MARIA	2001–	107th–109th	SNOWE, OLYMPIA	2001–	107th–109th
CARNAHAN, JEAN	2001–2002	107th	LANDRIEU, MARY	2001–	107th–109th
VETERANS' AFFAIRS [1971–present]					
MURKOWSKI, LISA	2003–2005	108th	HUTCHISON, KAY BAILEY	2001–	107th–109th
MURRAY, PATTY	1997–	105th–109th			

Senate Joint Committee	TERM	CONGRESS		TERM	CONGRES
JOINT COMMITTEE ON ATOMIC ENERGY [1946–1977]					
KASSEBAUM, NANCY LANDON	1977–1979	95th			
JOINT COMMITTEE ON PRINTING [1846–present]					
ALLEN, MARYON PITTMAN	1978	95th	FEINSTEIN, DIANNE	1999–2005	106th–107th
JOINT COMMITTEE ON THE LIBRARY [1847–present]					
KASSEBAUM, NANCY LANDON	1977–1983	95th–97th	FEINSTEIN, DIANNE	1997–1999	105th
JOINT COMMITTEE ON THE ORGANIZATION OF CONGRESS [1993–1995]					
KASSEBAUM, NANCY LANDON	1993–1995	103rd			
JOINT ECONOMIC COMMITTEE [1957–present]					
HAWKINS, PAULA	1981–1983	97th			
COLLINS, SUSAN	2003–2005	108th			

Senate Select Committee	TERM	CONGRESS		TERM	CONGRESS
PERMANENT SELECT COMMITTEE ON ETHICS [1977–present]					
KASSEBAUM, NANCY LANDON	1985–1989	99th–100th	MIKULSKI, BARBARA ANN	1993–1999	103rd–104th
MURRAY, PATTY	1997–1999	105th	LINCOLN, BLANCHE LAMBERT	2001–2005	107th–108th
SELECT COMMITTEE ON INTELLIGENCE [1975–present]					
KASSEBAUM, NANCY LANDON	1977–1979	95th	FEINSTEIN, DIANNE	2001–	107th–109th
HUTCHISON, KAY BAILEY	1995–1997	104th	SNOWE, OLYMPIA	2003–	108th–109th
MIKULSKI, BARBARA ANN	2001–	107th–109th			

Senate Special Committee	TERM	CONGRESS		TERM	CONGRESS
SPECIAL COMMITTEE ON THE YEAR 2000 TECHNOLOGY PROBLEMS [1999–2001]					
COLLINS, SUSAN	1999–2001	106th			
SPECIAL COMMITTEE ON AGING [1961–present]					
NEUBERGER, MAURINE	1961–1962	87th	MOSELEY-BRAUN, CAROL	1997–1999	104th–105th
KASSEBAUM, NANCY LANDON	1979–1985 1989–1993	96th–98th 101st–102nd	LINCOLN, BLANCHE LAMBERT	1999–	106th–109th
HAWKINS, PAULA	1985–1985	99th	STABENOW, DEBBIE	2001–2005	107th–108th
BURDICK, JOCELYN	1992	102nd	CLINTON, HILLARY	2005–	109th
COLLINS, SUSAN	1997–	105th–109th	CANTWELL, MARIA	2005–	109th
DOLE, ELIZABETH	2003–	108th–109th			

Representatives and Senators Who Served Without Committee Assignments

BOLAND, VERONICA GRACE	Representative	None assigned 77th Congress
BUSHFIELD, VERA CAHALAN	Senator	None assigned 80th Congress
FELTON, REBECCA LATIMER	Senator	None assigned 67th Congress
FULMER, WILLA LYBRAND	Representative	None assigned 78th Congress
GASQUE, ELIZABETH HAWLEY	Representative	None assigned, never sworn in 76th Congress
GIBBS, FLORENCE REVILLE	Representative	None assigned 76th Congress
GREENWAY, ISABELLA SELMES	Representative	None assigned 73rd Congress
HALL, KATIE	Representative	None assigned 97th Congress
PYLE, GLADYS	Senator	None assigned, never sworn in 75th Congress

SOURCES

Amer, Mildred, *Women in the United States Congress: 1917–2004*
(Washington, D.C.: Congressional Research Service, 1 July 2004).

Canon, David T., Garrison Nelson, and Charles Stewart III,
Committees in the United States Congress: 1789–1946, four volumes
(Washington, D.C.: Congressional Quarterly Press, 2002).

Congressional Directory (1917–2005).

Nelson, Garrison, *Committees in the United States Congress: 1946–1992*, two volumes
(Washington, D.C.: Congressional Quarterly Press, 1994).

Women Who Have Chaired Congressional Committees, 1923 to 2007

Through the opening of the 109th Congress, 16 women have chaired congressional committees, including standing, joint, and select panels. This chronological list includes 11 Representatives and five Senators. Of them, only Representative Mary T. Norton (D-NJ, 1925–1951) chaired more than one standing committee (she chaired a total of four). Congresswoman Corinne "Lindy" Boggs (D-LA, 1973–1991) chaired two select House committees.

HOUSE OF REPRESENTATIVES

NAME	PARTY/STATE	COMMITTEE	CONGRESS/YEAR
Mae Ella Nolan	R-CA	Expenditures in the Post Office Department	67th–68th (1923–1925)
Mary T. Norton	D-NJ	District of Columbia	72nd–74th (1931–1933)
Mary T. Norton	D-NJ	Labor	75th–79th (1937–1947)
Caroline O'Day	D-NY	Election of the President, Vice President, and Representatives in Congress	75th–77th (1937–1943)
Mary T. Norton	D-NJ	Memorials	77th (1941–1943)
Edith Nourse Rogers	R-MA	Veterans' Affairs	80th, 83rd (1947–1949; 1953–1955)
Mary T. Norton	D-NJ	House Administration	81st (1949–1951)
Martha W. Griffiths	D-MI	House Beauty Shop (Select)	90th–93rd (1967–1973)
Leonor K. Sullivan	D-MO	Merchant Marine and Fisheries	93rd–94th (1973–1977)
Corinne "Lindy" Boggs	D-LA	Bicentennial Arrangements (Select)	94th (1975–1977)
Yvonne Brathwaite Burke	D-CA	House Beauty Shop (Select)	94th–95th (1975–1979)
Corinne "Lindy" Boggs	D-LA	Bicentennial of the U.S. House (Select)	99th–100th (1985–1989)
Patricia Schroeder	D-CO	Children, Youth, and Families (Select)	102nd (1991–1993)
Nancy L. Johnson	R-CT	Standards of Official Conduct	104th (1995–1997)
Jan Meyers	R-KS	Small Business	104th (1995–1997)

SENATE

NAME	PARTY/STATE	COMMITTEE	CONGRESS/YEAR
Hattie Wyatt Caraway	D-AR	Enrolled Bills	73rd–78th (1933–1945)
Nancy L. Kassebaum	R-KS	Labor and Human Resources	104th (1995–1997)
Dianne Feinstein	D-CA	Joint Committee on Printing	107th (2001–2003)
Susan M. Collins	R-ME	Governmental Affairs	108th–109th (2003–2007)
Olympia J. Snowe	R-ME	Small Business	108th–109th (2003–2007)

Women Chairs of Subcommittees of Standing Committees in the House and Senate
80th Congress Through the 109th Congress, 1947–2006[1]

WOMEN CHAIRS OF HOUSE SUBCOMMITTEES

CONGRESS	MEMBER	COMMITTEE	SUBCOMMITTEE
109th (2005–2007)	Judy Biggert (R-IL)	Science	Energy
	Nancy Johnson (R-CT)	Ways and Means	Health
	Sue Kelly (R-NY)	Financial Services	Oversight and Investigations
	Candice Miller (R-MI)	Government Reform	Regulatory Affairs
	Marilyn Musgrave (R-CO)	Small Business	Workforce, Empowerment and Government Programs
	Deborah Pryce (R-OH)	Financial Services	Services, Domestic and International Monetary Policy, Trade, and Technology
	Ileana Ros-Lehtinen (R-FL)	International Relations	The Middle East and Central Asia
108th (2003–2005)	Judy Biggert (R-IL)	Science	Energy
	Barbara Cubin (R-WY)	Resources	Energy and Mineral Resources
	Jo Ann Davis (R-VA)	Government Reform	Civil Service and Agency Organization
	Nancy Johnson (R-CT)	Ways and Means	Health
	Sue Kelly (R-NY)	Financial Services	Oversight and Investigations
	Deborah Pryce (R-OH)	Rules	Legislative and Budget Process
	Ileana Ros-Lehtinen (R-FL)	International Relations	The Middle East and Central Asia
107th (2001–2003)	Barbara Cubin (R-WY)	Resources	Energy and Mineral Resources
	Nancy Johnson (R-CT)	Ways and Means	Health
	Sue Kelly (R-NY)	Financial Services	Oversight and Investigations
	Constance Morella (R-MD)	Government Reform	District of Columbia
	Deborah Pryce (R-OH)	Rules	Legislative and Budget Process
	Ileana Ros-Lehtinen (R-FL)	International Relations	International Operations and Human Rights
	Marge Roukema (R-NJ)	Financial Services	Housing and Community Opportunity

1 Information on subcommittees prior to the Legislative Re-Organization Act of 1946 is not available in the published record. A complete analysis of the 1917–1947 period awaits a thorough study of committee minute books, which are deposited at the Center for Legislative Archives, National Archives and Records Administration (NARA). Not all committee records for this period are complete because the House and Senate did not have a formal process for transferring committee records to NARA until the Legislative Re-Organization Act of 1946 took effect.

CONGRESS	MEMBER	COMMITTEE	SUBCOMMITTEE
106th (1999–2001)	Barbara Cubin (R-WY)	Resources	Energy and Mineral Resources
	Helen Chenoweth (R-ID)	Resources	Forests and Forest Health
	Tillie Fowler (R-FL)	Transportation and Infrastructure	Oversight, Investigations, and Emergency Management
	Nancy Johnson (R-CT)	Ways and Means	Human Resources
	Sue Kelly (R-NY)	Small Business	Regulatory Reform and Paperwork Reduction
	Constance Morella (R-MD)	Science	Technology
	Ileana Ros-Lehtinen (R-FL)	International Relations	International Economic Policy and Trade
	Marge Roukema (R-NJ)	Banking and Financial Services	Financial Institutions and Consumer Credit
105th (1997–1999)	Barbara Cubin (R-WY)	Resources	Energy and Mineral Resources
	Helen Chenoweth (R-ID)	Resources	Forests and Forest Health
	Nancy Johnson (R-CT)	Ways and Means	Oversight
	Sue Kelly (R-NY)	Small Business	Regulatory Reform and Paperwork Reduction
	Susan Molinari (R-NY)	Transportation and Infrastructure	Railroads
	Constance Morella (R-MD)	Science	Technology
	Ileana Ros-Lehtinen (R-FL)	International Relations	International Economic Policy and Trade
	Marge Roukema (R-NJ)	Banking and Financial Services	Financial Institutions and Consumer Credit
104th (1995–1997)	Nancy Johnson (R-CT)	Ways and Means	Oversight
	Susan Molinari (R-NY)	Transportation and Infrastructure	Railroads
	Constance Morella (R-MD)	Science	Technology
	Ileana Ros-Lehtinen (R-FL)	International Relations	Africa
	Marge Roukema (R-NJ)	Banking and Financial Services	Financial Institutions and Consumer Credit
	Linda Smith (R-WA)	Small Business	Taxation and Finance
	Barbara Vucanovich (R-NV)	Appropriations	Military Construction

CONGRESS	MEMBER	COMMITTEE	SUBCOMMITTEE
103rd (1993–1995)	Barbara-Rose Collins (D-MI)	Post Office and Civil Service	Postal Operations and Services
	Cardiss Collins (D-IL)	Energy and Commerce	Commerce, Consumer Protection, and Competitiveness
	Marilyn Lloyd (D-TN)	Science, Space, and Technology	Energy
	Eleanor Holmes Norton (D-DC)	District of Columbia	Judiciary and Education
		Post Office and Civil Service	Compensation and Employee Benefits
	Patricia Schroeder (D-CO)	Armed Services	Research and Technology
102nd (1991–1993)	Barbara Boxer (D-CA)	Government Operations	Government Activities and Transportation
	Beverly Byron (D-MD)	Armed Services	Military Personnel and Compensation
	Cardiss Collins (D-IL)	Energy and Commerce	Commerce, Consumer Protection, and Competitiveness
	Barbara Kennelly (D-CT)	Perm. Select Committee on Intelligence	Legislation
	Marilyn Lloyd (D-TN)	Science, Space, and Technology	Energy
		Select Committee on Aging	Housing and Consumer Interests
	Mary Rose Oakar (D-OH)	Banking, Finance, and Urban Affairs	Int'l Development, Finance, Trade, and Monetary Policy
		House Administration	Personnel and Police
	Patricia Schroeder (D-CO)	Armed Services	Military Installations and Facilities
101st (1989–1991)	Beverly Byron (D-MD)	Armed Services	Military Personnel and Compensation
	Cardiss Collins (D-IL)	Government Operations	Government Activities and Transportation
	Marilyn Lloyd (D-TN)	Science, Space, and Technology	Energy Research and Development
	Mary Rose Oakar (D-OH)	Banking, Finance, and Urban Affairs	Economic Stabilization
		House Administration	Personnel and Police
	Patricia Schroeder (D-CO)	Armed Services	Military Installations and Facilities

CONGRESS	MEMBER	COMMITTEE	SUBCOMMITTEE
100th (1987–1989)	Beverly Byron (D-MD)	Armed Services	Military Personnel and Compensation
	Cardiss Collins (D-IL)	Government Operations	Government Activities and Transportation
	Marcy Kaptur (D-OH)	Veterans' Affairs	Housing and Memorial Affairs
	Marilyn Lloyd (D-TN)	Science, Space, and Technology	Energy Research and Development
	Mary Rose Oakar (D-OH)	Banking, Finance, and Urban Affairs	Economic Stabilization
		House Administration	Libraries and Memorials
	Patricia Schroeder (D-CO)	Post Office and Civil Service	Civil Service
99th (1985–1987)	Cardiss Collins (D-IL)	Government Operations	Government Activities and Transportation
	Marilyn Lloyd (D-TN)	Science and Technology	Energy Research and Production
	Barbara Mikulski (D-MD)	Merchant Marine and Fisheries	Oceanography
	Mary Rose Oakar (D-OH)	Post Office and Civil Service	Compensation and Employee Benefits
	Patricia Schroeder (D-CO)	Post Office and Civil Service	Civil Service
98th (1983–1985)	Cardiss Collins (D-IL)	Government Operations	Government Activities and Transportation
	Marilyn Lloyd (D-TN)	Science and Technology	Energy Research and Production
	Mary Rose Oakar (D-OH)	Post Office and Civil Service	Compensation and Employee Benefits
	Patricia Schroeder (D-CO)	Post Office and Civil Service	Civil Service
97th (1981–1983)	Cardiss Collins (D-IL)	Government Operations	Manpower and Housing
	Geraldine Ferraro (D-NY)	Post Office and Civil Service	Human Resources
	Marilyn Lloyd (D-TN)	Science and Technology	Energy Research and Production
	Mary Rose Oakar (D-OH)	Post Office and Civil Service	Compensation and Employee Benefits
	Patricia Schroeder (D-CO)	Post Office and Civil Service	Civil Service

CONGRESS	MEMBER	COMMITTEE	SUBCOMMITTEE
96th (1979–1981)	Cardiss Collins (D-IL)	Government Operations	Manpower and Housing
	Elizabeth Holtzman (D-NY)	Budget[2]	State and Local Governments
		Judiciary	Immigration, Refugees, and International Law
	Patricia Schroeder (D-CO)	Post Office and Civil Service	Civil Service
	Gladys Noon Spellman (D-MD)	Post Office and Civil Service	Compensation and Employee Benefits
95th (1977–1979)	Cardiss Collins (D-IL)	Government Operations	Manpower and Housing
	Elizabeth Holtzman (D-NY)	Budget[3]	State and Local Government
	Patricia Schroeder (D-CO)	Post Office and Civil Service	Employee Ethics and Utilization
	Gladys Noon Spellman (D-MD)	Post Office and Civil Service	Compensation and Employee Benefits
94th (1975–1977)	Bella Abzug (D-NY)	Government Operations	Government Information and Individual Rights
	Patsy Mink (D-HI)	Interior and Insular Affairs	Mines and Mining
	Patricia Schroeder (D-CO)	Post Office and Civil Service	Census and Printing
93rd (1973–1975)	Julia Butler Hansen (D-WA)	Appropriations	Interior
	Patsy Mink (D-HI)	Interior and Insular Affairs	Mines and Mining
	Leonor Sullivan (D-MO)	Banking and Currency	Consumer Affairs
92nd (1971–1973)	Edith Green (D-OR)	Education and Labor	Special Subcommittee on Education
	Julia Butler Hansen (D-WA)	Appropriations	Interior and Related Agencies
	Leonor Sullivan (D-MO)	Banking and Currency	Consumer Affairs
91st (1969–1971)	Edith Green (D-OR)	Education and Labor	Special Subcommittee on Education
	Julia Butler Hansen (D-WA)	Appropriations	Interior and Related Agencies
	Leonor Sullivan (D-MO)	Banking and Currency	Consumer Affairs
		Merchant Marine and Fisheries	Panama Canal

2 Listed as one of nine "subcommittees" of the Budget Committee; parenthetically referred to as a "task force."
3 Listed as one of eight "subcommittees" of the Budget Committee; parenthetically referred to as a "task force."

CONGRESS	MEMBER	COMMITTEE	SUBCOMMITTEE
90th (1967–1969)	Edith Green (D-OR)	Education and Labor	Special Subcommittee on Education
	Julia Butler Hansen (D-WA)	Appropriations	Interior and Related Agencies
	Edna Kelly (D-NY)	Foreign Affairs	Europe
	Leonor Sullivan (D-MO)	Banking and Currency	Consumer Affairs
		Merchant Marine and Fisheries	Panama Canal
89th (1965–1967)	Edith Green (D-OR)	Education and Labor	Special Subcommittee on Education
	Edna Kelly (D-NY)	Foreign Affairs	Europe
	Leonor Sullivan (D-MO)	Banking and Currency	Consumer Affairs
		Merchant Marine and Fisheries	Panama Canal
88th (1963–1965)	Edith Green (D-OR)	Education and Labor	Special Subcommittee on Education
	Maude Kee (D-WV)	Veterans' Affairs	Hospitals
	Edna Kelly (D-NY)	Foreign Affairs	Europe
	Leonor Sullivan (D-MO)	Banking and Currency	Consumer Affairs
		Merchant Marine and Fisheries	Panama Canal
87th (1961–1963)	Kathryn Granahan (D-PA)	Post Office and Civil Service	Postal Operations
	Edith Green (D-OR)	Education and Labor	Special Subcommittee on Education
	Maude Kee (D-WV)	Veterans' Affairs	Hospitals
	Edna Kelly (D-NY)	Foreign Affairs	Europe
	Gracie Pfost (D-ID)	Interior and Insular Affairs	Public Lands
	Leonor Sullivan (D-MO)	Merchant Marine and Fisheries	Panama Canal
86th (1959–1961)	Kathryn Granahan (D-PA)	Post Office and Civil Service	Postal Operations
	Maude Kee (D-WV)	Veterans' Affairs	Hospitals
	Edna Kelly (D-NY)	Foreign Affairs	Europe Spec. Subcom. Canada-US Inter-parliamentary Group
	Gracie Pfost (D-ID)	Interior and Insular Affairs	Public Lands
	Leonor Sullivan (D-MO)	Merchant Marine and Fisheries	Panama Canal

WOMEN CHAIRS OF HOUSE SUBCOMMITTEES

CONGRESS	MEMBER	COMMITTEE	SUBCOMMITTEE
85th (1957–1959)	Maude Kee (D-WV) Edna Kelly (D-NY) Gracie Pfost (D-ID) Leonor Sullivan (D-MO)	Veterans' Affairs Foreign Affairs Interior and Insular Affairs Merchant Marine and Fisheries	Administration Europe Public Lands Panama Canal
84th (1955–1957)	Maude Kee (D-WV) Edna Kelly (D-NY) Gracie Pfost (D-ID)	Veterans' Affairs Foreign Affairs Interior and Insular Affairs	Education and Training Europe Public Lands
83rd (1953–1955)	Frances Bolton (R-OH) Cecil Harden (R-IN) Elizabeth St. George (R-NY)	Foreign Affairs Government Operations Post Office	Near East and Africa Inter-Governmental Relations Postal Operations
82nd (1951–1953)	No women chaired subcommittees	N/A	N/A
81st (1949–1951)	No women chaired subcommittees	N/A	N/A

80th (1947–1949)	Frances P. Bolton (R-OH)
	
	Margaret Chase Smith (R-ME)
		Foreign Affairs
		
		Armed Services
			Africa and the
			  Mediterranean
			Hospitalization and
			  Health (Medical Corps)

WOMEN CHAIRS OF SENATE SUBCOMMITTEES

CONGRESS	MEMBER	COMMITTEE	SUBCOMMITTEE
109th (2005–2007)	Kay Bailey Hutchison (R-TX)	Appropriations	Military Construction and Veterans' Affairs
	Lisa Murkowski (R-AK)	Energy and Natural Resources	Water and Power
	Olympia Snowe (R-ME)	Commerce, Science, and Transportation	Oceans, Fisheries, and Coast Guard
108th (2003–2005)	Elizabeth Dole (R-NC)	Agriculture, Nutrition, and Forestry	Production and Price Competitiveness
	Kay Bailey Hutchison (R-TX)	Appropriations Commerce, Science, and Transportation	Military Construction Surface Transportation and Merchant Marine
	Lisa Murkowski (R-AK)	Energy and Natural Resources	Water and Power
	Olympia Snowe (R-ME)	Commerce, Science, and Transportation	Oceans, Fisheries, and Coast Guard
107th (2001–2003)[4]	Susan Collins (R-ME)	Governmental Affairs	Permanent Subcommittee on Investigations
	Kay Bailey Hutchison (R-TX)	Appropriations Commerce, Science, and Transportation	Military Construction Aviation
	Olympia Snowe (R-ME)	Commerce, Science, and Transportation Finance	Oceans and Fisheries Health Care
	Barbara Boxer (D-CA)	Environment and Public Works Foreign Relations	Superfund, Toxics, Risk, and Waste Management International Operations and Terrorism
	Dianne Feinstein (D-CA)	Appropriations Judiciary	Military Construction Technology, Terrorism, and Government Information
	Mary Landrieu (D-LA)	Appropriations Armed Services	District of Columbia Emerging Threats and Capabilities
	Blanche Lincoln (D-AR)	Agriculture, Nutrition, and Forestry	Forestry, Conservation, and Rural Revitalization
	Barbara Mikulski (D-MD)	Appropriations	VA, HUD, and Independent Agencies
	Patty Murray (D-WA)	Health, Education, Labor, and Pensions Labor and Human Resources Appropriations	Aging Aging Transportation

4 From January 3 to January 20, 2001, with the Senate divided evenly between the two parties, the Democrats held the majority due to the deciding vote of outgoing Democratic Vice President Al Gore. Senator Thomas A. Daschle served as Majority Leader at that time. Beginning on January 20, 2001, Republican Vice President Richard Cheney held the deciding vote, giving the majority to the Republicans. Senator Trent Lott resumed his position as Majority Leader on that date. On May 24, 2001, Senator James Jeffords of Vermont announced his switch from Republican to Independent status, effective June 6, 2001. Jeffords announced that he would caucus with the Democrats, giving the Democrats a one-seat advantage, changing control of the Senate from the Republicans back to the Democrats. Senator Thomas A. Daschle again became Majority Leader on June 6, 2001.

WOMEN CHAIRS OF SENATE SUBCOMMITTEES

CONGRESS	MEMBER	COMMITTEE	SUBCOMMITTEE
106th (1999–2001)	Susan Collins (R-ME)	Governmental Affairs	Permanent Subcommittee on Investigations
	Kay Bailey Hutchison (R-TX)	Appropriations Commerce, Science, and Transportation	District of Columbia Surface Transportation and Merchant Marine
	Olympia Snowe (R-ME)	Armed Services Commerce, Science, and Transportation Finance	Seapower Oceans and Fisheries Health Care
105th (1997–1999)	Susan Collins (R-ME)	Governmental Affairs	Permanent Subcommittee on Investigations
	Kay Bailey Hutchison (R-TX)	Commerce, Science, and Transportation	Surface Transportation and Merchant Marine
	Olympia Snowe (R-ME)	Commerce, Science, and Transportation	Oceans and Fisheries
104th (1995–1997)	Nancy Kassebaum (R-KS) Olympia Snowe (R-ME)	Foreign Relations Foreign Relations	African Affairs International Operations
103rd (1993–1995)	Barbara Mikulski (D-MD)	Appropriations Labor and Human Resources	VA, HUD, and Independent Agencies Aging
102nd (1991–1993)	Barbara Mikulski (D-MD)	Appropriations Small Business	VA, HUD, and Independent Agencies Export Expansion
101st (1989–1991)	Barbara Mikulski (D-MD)	Appropriations Small Business	HUD-Independent Agencies Export Expansion
100th (1987–1989)	No women chaired subcommittees	N/A	N/A
99th (1985–1987)	Paula Hawkins (R-FL) Nancy Kassebaum (R-KS)	Labor and Human Resources Commerce, Science, and Transportation Foreign Relations	Children, Family, Drugs, and Alcoholism Aviation African Affairs

WOMEN CHAIRS OF SENATE SUBCOMMITTEES

CONGRESS	MEMBER	COMMITTEE	SUBCOMMITTEE
98th (1983–1985)	Paula Hawkins (R-FL)	Agriculture, Nutrition, and Forestry	Agricultural Credit and Rural Electrification
	Nancy Kassebaum (R-KS)	Banking, Housing, and Urban Affairs Commerce, Science, and Transportation Foreign Relations	Consumer Affairs Aviation African Affairs
97th (1981–1983)	Paula Hawkins (R-FL)	Agriculture, Nutrition, and Forestry Labor and Human Resources	Agricultural Credit and Rural Electrification Investigations and General Oversight
	Nancy Kassebaum (R-KS)	Commerce, Science, and Transportation Foreign Relations	Aviation African Affairs
96th (1979–1981)	No women chaired subcommittees	N/A	N/A
95th (1977–1979)	No women chaired subcommittees	N/A	N/A
94th (1975–1977)	No women chaired subcommittees	N/A	N/A
93rd (1973–1975)	No women chaired subcommittees	N/A	N/A
92nd (1971–1973)	No women chaired subcommittees	N/A	N/A
91st (1969–1971)	No women chaired subcommittees	N/A	N/A
90th (1967–1969)	No women chaired subcommittees	N/A	N/A
89th (1965–1967)	No women chaired subcommittees	N/A	N/A

CONGRESS	MEMBER	COMMITTEE	SUBCOMMITTEE
88th (1963–1965)	No women chaired subcommittees	N/A	N/A
87th (1961–1963)	No women chaired subcommittees	N/A	N/A
86th (1959–1961)	No women chaired subcommittees	N/A	N/A
85th (1957–1959)	No women chaired subcommittees	N/A	N/A
84th (1955–1957)	No women chaired subcommittees	N/A	N/A
83rd (1953–1955)	Margaret Chase Smith (R-ME)	Armed Services Government Operations	Special Subcommittee Investigating Ammunition Shortages Reorganization
82nd (1951–1953)	No women chaired subcommittees	N/A	N/A
81st (1949–1951)[5]	Margaret Chase Smith (R-ME)	District of Columbia	Public Health, Education, and Recreation
80th (1947–1949)	No women chaired subcommittees	N/A	N/A

Note: Hattie Caraway (D-AR, 1931–1945), the first woman to chair a Senate subcommittee, headed an unspecified subcommittee of the Commerce Committee from 1935 to 1943. She is the only Senate woman who preceded Margaret Chase Smith as a subcommittee chair.

[5]According to records from the Senate Historical Office, Smith chaired the subcommittee even though the Democrats were in the majority.

SOURCES

• *United States Code Congressional and Administrative News* (formerly *U.S. Code Congressional Service*), 1947–1959.
• *Congressional Staff Directory*, 1959–1975.
• *Congressional Directory*, 1975 to present.

Women Elected to Party Leadership Positions, 1949–2006

Twenty-one women in congressional history have been elected by their peers into the Democratic and Republican Party leadership—16 in the House and five in the Senate. The first was Connecticut Representative Chase Going Woodhouse, who served a single term as Secretary of the Democratic Caucus in the 81st Congress (1949–1951). Illinois Representative Lynn Martin became the first Republican woman elected to a House leadership position when she won the vice chair post in the Republican Conference in the 99th–100th Congresses (1985–1989). The first woman elected to a Senate leadership position was Margaret Chase Smith of Maine, who chaired the Senate Republican Conference in the 90th–92nd Congresses (1967–1973). California Representative Nancy Pelosi is the highest-ranking woman in congressional history: A year after winning election as House Democratic Whip in the fall of 2001, Congresswoman Pelosi was elected the Democratic Leader.

HOUSE OF REPRESENTATIVES

CONGRESS	MEMBER	CAUCUS/CONFERENCE	POSITION
81st (1949–1951)	Chase Going Woodhouse (D-CT)	Democratic Caucus	Secretary
82nd (1951–1953)	N/A		
83rd (1953–1955)	Edna F. Kelly (D-NY)	Democratic Caucus	Secretary
84th (1955–1957)	Edna F. Kelly (D-NY)	Democratic Caucus	Secretary
85th (1957–1959)	N/A		
86th (1959–1961)	Leonor K. Sullivan (D-MO)	Democratic Caucus	Secretary
87th (1961–1963)	Leonor K. Sullivan (D-MO)	Democratic Caucus	Secretary
88th (1963–1965)	Edna F. Kelly (D-NY)[1]	Democratic Caucus	Secretary
	Leonor K. Sullivan (D-MO)	Democratic Caucus	Secretary
89th (1965–1967)	Leonor K. Sullivan (D-MO)	Democratic Caucus	Secretary
90th (1967–1969)	Leonor K. Sullivan (D-MO)	Democratic Caucus	Secretary
91st (1969–1971)	Leonor K. Sullivan (D-MO)	Democratic Caucus	Secretary
92nd (1971–1973)	Leonor K. Sullivan (D-MO)	Democratic Caucus	Secretary
93rd (1973–1975)	Leonor K. Sullivan (D-MO)	Democratic Caucus	Secretary
94th (1975–1977)	Patsy Mink (D-HI)	Democratic Caucus	Secretary
95th (1977–1979)	Shirley Chisholm (D-NY)	Democratic Caucus	Secretary
96th (1979–1981)	Shirley Chisholm (D-NY)	Democratic Caucus	Secretary
97th (1981–1983)	Geraldine Ferraro (D-NY)	Democratic Caucus	Secretary

1 Kelly and Sullivan shared the Secretary post during the 88th Congress, with Kelly serving in the second session.

CONGRESS	MEMBER	CAUCUS/CONFERENCE	POSITION
98th (1983–1985)	Geraldine Ferraro (D-NY)	Democratic Caucus	Secretary
99th (1985–1987)	Lynn Martin (R-IL)	Republican Conference	Vice Chair
	Mary Rose Oakar (D-OH)	Democratic Caucus	Secretary
100th (1987–1989)	Lynn Martin (R-IL)	Republican Conference	Vice Chair
	Mary Rose Oakar (D-OH)	Democratic Caucus	Secretary
101st (1989–1991)	N/A		
102nd (1991–1993)	N/A		
103rd (1993–1995)	N/A		
104th (1995–1997)	Jennifer Dunn (R-WA)	Republican Conference	Vice Chair
			Secretary
	Barbara Kennelly (D-CT)	Democratic Caucus	Vice Chair
	Susan Molinari (R-NY)	Republican Conference	Vice Chair
	Barbara Vucanovich (R-NV)	Republican Conference	Secretary
105th (1997–1999)	Barbara Kennelly (D-CT)	Democratic Caucus	Vice Chair
	Susan Molinari (R-NY)	Republican Conference	Vice Chair
106th (1999–2001)	Tillie Fowler (R-FL)	Republican Conference	Vice Chair
	Deborah Pryce (R-OH)	Republican Conference	Secretary
107th (2001–2003)	Barbara Cubin (R-WY)	Republican Conference	Secretary
	Nancy Pelosi (D-CA)	Democratic Caucus	Whip
	Deborah Pryce (R-OH)	Republican Conference	Vice Chair
108th (2003–2005)	Nancy Pelosi (D-CA)	Democratic Caucus	Leader
	Deborah Pryce (R-OH)	Republican Conference	Chair
109th (2005–2007)	Nancy Pelosi (D-CA)	Democratic Caucus	Leader
	Deborah Pryce (R-OH)	Republican Conference	Chair

CONGRESS	MEMBER	CAUCUS/CONFERENCE	POSITION
90th (1967–1969)	Margaret Chase Smith (R-ME)	Republican Conference	Chair
91st (1969–1971)	Margaret Chase Smith (R-ME)	Republican Conference	Chair
92nd (1971–1973)	Margaret Chase Smith (R-ME)	Republican Conference	Chair
93rd (1973–1975)	N/A		
94th (1975–1977)	N/A		
95th (1977–1979)	N/A		
96th (1979–1981)	N/A		

CONGRESS	MEMBER	CAUCUS/CONFERENCE	POSITION
97th (1981–1983)	N/A		
98th (1983–1985)	N/A		
99th (1985–1987)	N/A		
100th (1987–1989)	N/A		
101st (1989–1991)	N/A		
102nd (1991–1993)	N/A		
103rd (1993–1995)	N/A		
104th (1995–1997)	Barbara Mikulski (D-MD)	Democratic Caucus	Secretary
105th (1997–1999)	Barbara Mikulski (D-MD) Olympia Snowe (R-ME)	Democratic Caucus Republican Conference	Secretary Secretary
106th (1999–2001)	Barbara Mikulski (D-MD) Olympia Snowe (R-ME)	Democratic Caucus Republican Conference	Secretary Secretary
107th (2001–2003)	Kay Bailey Hutchison (R-TX) Barbara Mikulski (D-MD)	Republican Conference Democratic Caucus	Vice Chair Secretary
108th (2003–2005)	Kay Bailey Hutchison (R-TX) Barbara Mikulski (D-MD)	Republican Conference Democratic Caucus	Vice Chair Secretary
109th (2005–2007)	Kay Bailey Hutchison (R-TX) Deborah Stabenow (D-MI)	Republican Conference Democratic Caucus	Vice Chair Secretary

SOURCES

Mildred Amer, "Major Leadership Election Contests in the House of Representatives, 94th–108th Congresses,"
3 September 2003, Congressional Research Service (CRS) Report for Congress, Library of Congress, Washington, D.C.;
Mildred Amer, "Women in the United States Congress, 1917–2004," 1 July 2004, CRS Report for Congress, Library of Congress, Washington, D.C.; various editions of the *Congressional Directory*.

Women of Color in Congress, 1965–2006

Since Representative Patsy Mink of Hawaii won election to the U.S. House of Representatives in 1964, a total of 34 women of color have served in the U.S. Congress. Roughly three-quarters (26) of these women were elected after 1990. A total of 33 have served in the House; Carol Moseley Braun of Illinois served in the U.S. Senate (1993–1999). The first African-American woman to serve in Congress, Shirley Chisholm of New York, won election in 1968; 23 African-American women have followed her. The first Hispanic-American woman elected to Congress, Representative Ileana Ros-Lehtinen of Florida, entered the House in 1989; six other Hispanic-American women have followed her. In addition to Congresswoman Mink, two other Asian-Pacific-American women have served in Congress.

NAME[a]	PARTY/STATE	DATES OF SERVICE	ETHNICITY
Patsy Mink	D-HI	1965–1977; 1990–2002	Asian-Pacific American
Shirley Chisholm	D-NY	1969–1983	African American
Yvonne Burke	D-CA	1973–1979	African American
Barbara Jordan	D-TX	1973–1979	African American
Cardiss Collins	D-IL	1973–1997	African American
Katie Hall	D-IN	1982–1985	African American
Patricia Saiki	R-HI	1987–1991	Asian-Pacific American
Ileana Ros-Lehtinen	R-FL	1989–present	Hispanic American
Barbara-Rose Collins	D-MI	1991–1997	African American
Eleanor Holmes Norton	D-DC	1991–present	African American
Maxine Waters	D-CA	1991–present	African American
Carol Moseley Braun[b]	D-IL	1993–1999	African American
Corrine Brown	D-FL	1993–present	African American
Eva Clayton	D-NC	1993–2003	African American
Eddie Bernice Johnson	D-TX	1993–present	African American
Cynthia McKinney	D-GA	1993–2003; 2005–present	African American
Carrie Meek	D-FL	1993–2003	African American
Lucille Roybal-Allard	D-CA	1993–present	Hispanic American
Nydia Velázquez	D-NY	1993–present	Hispanic American
Shelia Jackson-Lee	D-TX	1995–present	African American
Juanita Millender-McDonald	D-CA	1995–present	African American
Julia Carson	D-IN	1997–present	African American
Donna M. Christensen	D-VI	1997–present	African American
Carolyn Cheeks Kilpatrick	D-MI	1997–present	African American
Barbara Lee	D-CA	1997–present	African American
Loretta Sanchez	D-CA	1997–present	Hispanic American
Stephanie Tubbs Jones	D-OH	1999–present	African American
Grace Napolitano	D-CA	1999–present	Hispanic American
Hilda Solis	D-CA	2001–present	Hispanic American
Diane Watson	D-CA	2001–present	African American
Denise Majette	D-GA	2003–2005	African American
Linda Sánchez	D-CA	2003–present	Hispanic American
Gwendolynne Moore	D-WI	2005–present	African American
Doris Matsui	D-CA	2005–present	Asian-Pacific American

a Listed in chronological order by dates of service.

b Denotes Senate service.

Marriage/Familial Connections of Women Representatives and Senators in Congress

Through the start of the 109th Congress in 2005, 46 women have succeeded their late husbands in Congress (38 in the House and eight in the Senate). Seven widows have represented California—more than any other state—including the first two in the House, Mae Ella Nolan (1923–1925) and Florence Prag Kahn (1925–1937). In 1931, Hattie Caraway of Arkansas became the first widow to succeed her late husband in the Senate. Seven other women have come to Congress with marriage connections, including two who were appointed to the Senate by their husbands. Five women married Members with whom they served in the same Congress (Ruth McCormick of Illinois, Martha Keys of Kansas, Nancy Kassebaum of Kansas, Olympia Snowe of Maine, and Susan Molinari of New York). One woman (Emily Douglas of Illinois) preceded her husband in Congress. Another (Marjorie Margolies-Mezvinsky) was elected from Pennsylvania after having married an Iowa Representative two decades earlier. Representatives Loretta Sanchez and Linda Sánchez of California are the first sisters to serve in Congress.

Other familial relationships include 12 women who followed their fathers into Congress, four of them directly succeeding their fathers. In addition, seven women have had sons who served in Congress; Frances Bolton was the only one to serve concurrently with her son, Oliver, and Maude Kee was the first to be succeeded directly by her son, John.

WIDOWS WHO DIRECTLY SUCCEEDED THEIR LATE HUSBANDS

CONGRESS TO WHICH WIDOW WAS FIRST ELECTED (DATE)	NAME (PARTY, STATE, FULL TERM OF SERVICE)	CHAMBER
67th (1921–1923)	Mae Ella Nolan (R-CA, 1923–1925)	House of Representatives
69th (1925–1927)	Florence Prag Kahn (R-CA, 1925–1937)	House of Representatives
	Edith Nourse Rogers (R-MA, 1925–1960)	House of Representatives
70th (1927–1929)	Pearl Oldfield (D-AR, 1929–1931)	House of Representatives
71st (1929–1931)	Effiegene Wingo (D-AR, 1930–1933)	House of Representatives
72nd (1931–1933)	Hattie Wyatt Caraway (D-AR, 1931–1945)	Senate
	Willa Eslick (D-TN, 1932–1933)	House of Representatives
73rd (1933–1935)	Marian Clarke (R-NY, 1933–1935)	House of Representatives
74th (1935–1937)	Rose McConnell Long (D-LA, 1936–1937)	Senate
75th (1937–1939)	Elizabeth Gasque (D-SC, 1938–1939)	House of Representatives
76th (1939–1941)	Frances Bolton (R-OH, 1940–1969)	House of Representatives
	Florence Gibbs (D-GA, 1940–1941)	House of Representatives
	Clara McMillan (D-SC, 1939–1941)	House of Representatives
	Margaret Chase Smith (R-ME, 1940–1973) [1]	House of Representatives
77th (1941–1943)	Veronica Boland (D-PA, 1942–1943)	House of Representatives
	Katharine Byron (D-MD, 1941–1943)	House of Representatives
78th (1943–1945)	Willa Fulmer (D-SC, 1944–1945)	House of Representatives
80th (1947–1949)	Vera Bushfield (R-SD, 1947–1948)	Senate

[1] Smith served in the House from 1940 to 1949 and then won election to the Senate, where she served from 1949 to 1973.

CONGRESS TO WHICH WIDOW WAS FIRST ELECTED (DATE)	NAME (PARTY, STATE, FULL TERM OF SERVICE)	CHAMBER
82nd (1951–1953)	Vera Buchanan (D-PA, 1951–1955)	House of Representatives
	Marguerite Church (R-IL, 1951–1963)	House of Representatives
	Maude Kee (D-WV, 1951–1965)	House of Representatives
83rd (1953–1955)	Mary Farrington (R-HI, 1954–1957)[2]	House of Representatives
84th (1955–1957)	Kathryn Granahan (D-PA, 1956–1963)	House of Representatives
86th (1959–1961)	Maurine Neuberger (D-OR, 1960–1967)[3]	Senate
	Edna Simpson (R-IL, 1959–1961)	House of Representatives
87th (1961–1963)	Catherine Norrell (D-AR, 1961–1963)	House of Representatives
	Louise Reece (R-TN, 1961–1963)	House of Representatives
	Corinne Riley (D-SC, 1962–1963)	House of Representatives
88th (1963–1965)	Irene Baker (R-TN, 1964–1965)	House of Representatives
89th (1965–1967)	Lera Thomas (D-TX, 1966–1967)	House of Representatives
92nd (1971–1973)	Elizabeth Andrews (D-AL, 1972–1973)	House of Representatives
93rd (1973–1975)	Corrine "Lindy" Boggs (D-LA, 1973–1991)	House of Representatives
	Cardiss Collins (D-IL, 1973–1997)	House of Representatives
94th (1975–1977)	Shirley Pettis (R-CA, 1975–1979)	House of Representatives
95th (1977–1979)	Maryon Allen (D-AL, 1978)	Senate
	Beverly Byron (D-MD, 1978–1993)	House of Representatives
	Muriel Humphrey (D-MN, 1978)	Senate
97th (1981–1983)	Jean Ashbrook (R-OH, 1982–1983)	House of Representatives
98th (1983–1985)	Sala Burton (D-CA, 1983–1987)	House of Representatives
99th (1985–1987)	Catherine Long (D-LA, 1985–1987)	House of Representatives
102nd (1991–1993)	Jocelyn Burdick (D-ND, 1992)	Senate
104th (1995–1997)	Jo Ann Emerson (R-MO, 1996–present)	House of Representatives
105th (1997–1999)	Mary Bono (R-CA, 1998–present)	House of Representatives
	Lois Capps (D-CA, 1998–present)	House of Representatives
107th (2001–2003)	Jean Carnahan (D-MO, 2001–2003)[4]	Senate
109th (2005–2007)	Doris Matsui (D-CA, 2005–present)	House of Representatives

2   Territorial delegate.

3   Neuberger was not immediately appointed to succeed her husband Richard Neuberger after he died in early 1960. However, she won the general election in November 1960 to serve the remainder of her husband's unexpired term in the 86th Congress and a full six-year term commencing on January 3, 1961.

4   Mel Carnahan was killed in a plane crash less than two weeks before the election for the Missouri Senate seat he was running for. His name remained on the ticket, and he posthumously defeated incumbent John Ashcroft by a narrow margin. Governor Roger Wilson appointed Jean Carnahan to her husband's vacant seat. Carnahan's re-election bid in a special election held in 2002 was unsuccessful.

WIVES WHO DIRECTLY SUCCEEDED HUSBANDS WHO WERE MEMBERS OF OR NOMINEES TO CONGRESS

DATES OF SERVICE	NAME	PARTY/STATE
1927–1931	Rep. Katherine Langley[5]	Republican/Kentucky
1963–1971	Rep. Charlotte Reid[6]	Republican/Illinois
1975–1995	Rep. Marilyn Lloyd[7]	Democrat/Tennessee

WIDOWS WHO FOLLOWED LATE HUSBANDS INTO CONGRESS WITHOUT DIRECTLY SUCCEEDING THEM

DATES OF SERVICE	NAME	PARTY/STATE
1929–1931	Rep. Ruth Hanna McCormick[8]	Republican/Illinois
1953–1977	Rep. Leonor Sullivan[9]	Democrat/Missouri

WIVES APPOINTED TO THE SENATE BY THEIR HUSBAND

DATES OF SERVICE	NAME	PARTY/STATE
1937	Senator Dixie Bibb Graves	Democrat/Alabama
1972	Senator Elaine S. Edwards	Democrat/Louisiana

WOMEN MEMBERS MARRIED TO OTHER MEMBERS OF CONGRESS

DATES OF SERVICE	NAME	PARTY/STATE
1929–1931	Rep. Ruth Hanna McCormick[10]	Republican/Illinois
1945–1947	Rep. Emily Taft Douglas[11]	Democrat/Illinois
1975–1979	Rep. Martha Keys[12]	Democrat/Kansas
1978–1997	Sen. Nancy Kassebaum[13]	Republican/Kansas
1979–1995 (House) 1995–present (Senate)	Rep. Sen. Olympia Snowe[14]	Republican/Maine
1990–1997	Rep. Susan Molinari[15]	Republican/New York
1993–1995	Rep. Marjorie Margolies-Mezvinsky[16]	Democrat/Pennsylvania

5   Her husband, John Wesley Langley, had won re-election to the House in 1924 for Kentucky's 10th District but was convicted of conspiring to transport and sell liquor in violation of the Volstead Act. He was placed in a federal penitentiary in Atlanta before his term expired. Katherine Langley ran successfully for his seat in 1926 and was re-elected in the 71st Congress in 1928.

6   The GOP nominee for Illinois' 15th District, Frank R. Reid, Jr., died in August 1962 while campaigning for the open seat. Republican officials convinced his widow, Charlotte Reid, to replace him on the ticket.

7   Just weeks after securing the Democratic nomination to challenge Republican incumbent Lamar Baker in Tennessee's 3rd District, Mort Lloyd was killed in a plane crash. Democratic leaders convinced his widow, Marilyn Lloyd, to replace him on the ticket.

8   Ruth Hanna McCormick won election in 1928 to one of Illinois' two At-Large House seats. Her husband, Joseph Medill McCormick, had served one term each in the House (1917–1919) and the Senate (1919–1925). He died days before his Senate term expired in February 1925.

9   John B. Sullivan died in January 1951, but Leonor Sullivan could not convince Missouri 3rd District Democrat leaders to give her the nomination for the special election. In November 1952, after redistricting merged her husband's old district with another, she defeated GOP incumbent Claude I. Bakewell, who had succeeded John Sullivan in the 82nd Congress.

10   (See note 8 above.) Ruth Hanna McCormick married Rep. Albert Simms, who had served one term in the House with her in the 71st Congress (1929–1931), in March 1932.

11   Married to Sen. Paul Douglas (D-IL, 1949–1967).

12   Married Rep. Andrew Jacobs (D-IN, 1965–1973, 1975–1997) in 1975 while both were serving in the House.

13   Married Sen. Howard Baker (R-TN, 1967–1985) in 1996 after he left office but while she still was in the Senate. They had served together six years.

14   Married Rep. John McKernan, Jr. (R-ME, 1983–1987) in 1989, after he had left the House and was serving as governor of Maine, but while Snowe was still in the House. They had served together four years.

15   Married Rep. Bill Paxon (R-NY, 1989–1999) in 1994 while both were serving in the House.

16   Preceded in the House by her husband, Rep. Ed Mezvinsky (D-IA, 1973–1977).

DAUGHTERS WHO DIRECTLY SUCCEEDED THEIR FATHERS IN CONGRESS

Rep. Winnifred Mason Huck (R-IL, 1922–1923) succeeded William E. Mason (R-IL, a Representative from 1887–1890; a Senator from 1897–1902; a Representative from 1917–1922).

Rep. Susan Molinari (R-NY, 1990–1998) succeeded Rep. Guy Molinari (R-NY, 1981–1990).

Rep. Lucille Roybal-Allard (D-CA, 1993–present) succeeded Rep. Edward R. Roybal (D-CA, 1963–1993).

Sen. Lisa Murkowski (R-AL, 2002–present) succeeded Sen. Frank Murkowski (R-AK, 1981–2002).

WOMEN MEMBERS OF CONGRESS WHOSE FATHERS PRECEDED THEM AS REPRESENTATIVES OR SENATORS

Rep. Katherine Gudger Langley (R-KY, 1927–1930) daughter of Rep. James Madison Gudger, Jr. (D-NC, 1903–1914).

Rep. Ruth Hanna McCormick (R-IL, 1929–1931) daughter of Sen. Marcus A. Hanna (R-OH, 1899–1904).

Rep. Ruth Bryan Owen (D-FL, 1929–1932) daughter of Rep. William Jennings Bryan (D-NE, 1891–1994).

Rep. Clare Boothe Luce (R-CT, 1943–1947), stepdaughter of Rep. Elmer Austin (R-CT, 1939–1941).

Rep. Louise Goff Reece (R-TN, 1961–1962) daughter of Sen. Guy D. Goff (R-WV, 1925–1930).

Rep. Elizabeth Patterson (D-SC, 1987–1992) daughter of Sen. Olin D. Johnston (D-SC, 1945–1966).

Rep. Nancy Pelosi (D-CA, 1987–present) daughter of Thomas D'Alesandro (D-MD, 1939–1947).

Rep. Shelly Moore Capito (R-WV, 2001–present) daughter of Rep. Arch Moore (R-WV, 1957–1968).

WOMEN MEMBERS WHOSE CHILDREN HAVE SERVED IN CONGRESS

Senator Rose McConnell Long (D-LA, 1936–1937), mother of Senator Russell Long (D-LA, 1948–1987).

Rep. Frances Bolton (R-OH, 1940–1969), mother of Rep. Oliver Bolton (R-OH, 1953–1957; 1963–1965). They were the only mother–son pair to serve simultaneously.

Rep. Katharine Byron (D-MD, 1941–1943), mother of Rep. Goodloe Byron (D-MD, 1971–1978).

Rep. Maude Kee (D-WV, 1951–1965), mother of Rep. James Kee (D-WV, 1965–1973). James Kee was the first son to directly succeed his mother in Congress.

Rep. Irene Baker (R-TN, 1964–1965), stepmother of Senator Howard Baker (R-TN, 1967–1985).

Rep. Carrie Meek (D-FL, 1993–2003), mother of Rep. Kendrick Meek (D-FL, 2003–present).

Sen. Jean Carnahan (D-MO, 2001–2002), mother of Rep. Russ Carnahan (D-MO, 2005–present).

WOMEN MEMBERS WHOSE SIBLINGS HAVE SERVED IN CONGRESS

Rep. Loretta Sanchez (D-CA, 1997–present), sister of Linda Sánchez (D-CA, 2003–present).

Index

Bold page numbers denote Member profiles
Italicized page numbers denote references to figure legends